ALSO BY SIMON HEFFER

Staring at God

Simon Heffer is a Professor at the University of Buckingham, where he teaches modern British History. Born in 1960, he read English at Cambridge University and subsequently took a PhD in history there. This is the third volume in a historical sequence that began with *High Minds: The Victorians and the Birth of Modern Britain* and continued with *The Age of Decadence: Britain from 1880 to 1914*. His other books include *Moral Desperado: A Life of Thomas Carlyle, Like the Roman: The Life of Enoch Powell, Power and Place: The Political Consequences of King Edward VII, Nor Shall My Sword: The Reinvention of England, Vaughan Williams, Strictly English, A Short History of Power* and *Simply English*. In a career of nearly 35 years in Fleet Street he was deputy editor of the *Daily Telegraph* and the *Spectator*, and now writes for the *Daily Telegraph* and the *Sunday Telegraph*.

Praise for *Staring at God*

'This colourful, character-driven political history of Britain in the First World War shows how the conflict changed our world . . . [A] gloriously rich and spirited history of Britain in the Great War . . . The sequel to his fine books on the Victorians and Edwardians, it focuses almost entirely on the home front, and especially on high politics . . . [It] might seem a daunting read. But it zips along . . . so many wonderful cultural and social details.'

Sunday Times

'Enlightening . . . Robust opinion, an eye for the telling detail and a _____ epic, ambi_____ e Year

'*Staring at God* is the first serious and really wide-ranging history of the Home Front during the Great War for decades. Scholarly, objective, and extremely well-written . . . The description of the effect of the war on ordinary Britons is filled with empathy, in particular for the women, on whom fell the burden of war work, single parenthood, and often widowhood.'

Daily Telegraph

'Magisterial . . . the third volume in his pioneering history of our country from the early Victorian age. This latest study has all the characteristics of the previous two, including exhaustive research, fresh insights, vast scope and caustic judgements. *Staring at God* is possibly the finest, most comprehensive analysis of the home front in the Great War ever produced . . . Heffer's grasp of political motivation and character ensures that his passages about the government crises are compelling reading.'

Literary Review

'Apart from the war itself, three great themes dominate these pages: Ireland, the role of women in British society, and what the author calls "the tenor of public life" . . . fascinating stuff . . . [*Staring at God*] successfully merges social, economic political and cultural history: more glorious still, see individuals as the principal agents of change . . . Serves to remind us that nowadays we really don't have it that bad.'

Spectator

'Every bit as good as its two predecessors . . . Heffer has an eye for the illuminating fact and quote . . . This book is not a military history of the period . . . but a political and personal one . . . I await volume four with eagerness.'

Daily Express

gift for bringing historical figure alive . . . An
nous book.

Daily Mail, books of th

Staring at God

Britain in the Great War

Simon Heffer

WINDMILL BOOKS

1 3 5 7 9 10 8 6 4 2

Windmill Books
20 Vauxhall Bridge Road
London SW1V 2SA

Windmill Books is part of the Penguin Random House group of companies
whose addresses can be found at global.penguinrandomhouse.com.

Penguin
Random House
UK

Copyright © Simon Heffer 2019

Simon Heffer has asserted his right to be identified as the author of this Work
in accordance with the Copyright, Designs and Patents Act 1988.

First published by Random House Books in 2019
First published in paperback by Windmill Books in 2020

www.penguin.co.uk

A CIP catalogue record for this book is available from the British Library.

ISBN 9781786090447

Typeset in 10.39/12.6 pt Dante MT by Jouve (UK), Milton Keynes
Printed and bound in Great Britain by Clays Ltd, Elcograf S.p.A.

MIX
Paper from
responsible sources
FSC
www.fsc.org   FSC® C018179

Penguin Random House is committed to a
sustainable future for our business, our readers
and our planet. This book is made from Forest
Stewardship Council® certified paper.

To Greville Howard

L'amitié, comme le vin, se bonifie avec le temps

This war has caught us at our worst . . . and now that shrapnel is killing an entire generation, we are left staring at God.

Margot Asquith, Diary, 26 October 1914

Kitchener, in creating an army, has created love. This is a great change in a country where only marriage was known before.

Report in a Spanish newspaper, sent to
Bertrand Russell by George Santayana, 5 May 1915

Someone will turn up. The war will disclose a genius.

Lord Northcliffe to Sir George Riddell, 5 June 1915

But this I would say, standing, as I do, in view of God and eternity. I realise that patriotism is not enough. I must have no bitterness or hatred towards anyone.

Edith Cavell to the Revd Stirling Gahan, Brussels, 11 October 1915

The direct descendant of Judas Iscariot.

Clementine Churchill, on Lloyd George,
letter to her husband, 30 December 1915

There seems to be something wrong with our bloody ships today, Chatfield.

Vice Admiral Sir David Beatty to Captain
Ernle Chatfield, Jutland, 31 May 1916

Believe me England is not rotten. It is a nation of lions led by asses and knaves. England is all right at heart. I have never lost faith in the people. But I have lost faith in *all* our leaders.

H. A. Gwynne, letter to Countess Bathurst, 15 January 1918

My Lords, is it not a terribly sad thing to think that we have practically made no progress during the last fifty years in acquiring the love and affection of the Irish people?

Reginald Brabazon, 12th Earl of Meath,
addressing the House of Lords, 12 March 1918

Every position must be held to the last man; there must be no retirement. With our backs to the wall, and believing in the justice of our cause, each one of us must fight on to the end.

Field Marshal Sir Douglas Haig, dispatch, 11 April 1918

One will have to look at long vistas again, instead of short ones, and one will at last fully recognise that the dead are not only dead for the duration of the war.

Lady Cynthia Asquith, Diary, 7 October 1918

CONTENTS

ACKNOWLEDGEMENTS

Extracts from the diary of His late Majesty King George V and from the papers of Lord Stamfordham are reproduced by gracious permission of Her Majesty the Queen.

A number of people generously provided assistance with access to archives, or supplied me with research materials, introductions and other information that was invaluable in writing this book. I should like to thank William Alden; Professor Chris Andrew; Professor Ian Beckett; Frank Bowles; the Rt Hon Sir Simon Burns; Dr Matthew Butler; Julie Crocker; His Honour Judge Edmunds QC; Professor Gerard DeGroot; Will Heaven; Laura Hobbs; the Revd Mark Jones; Professor Colin Lawson; Sam Lindley; Brigadier Allan Mallinson; Leo McKinstry; Iona McLaren; Annie Pinder; Lord Rayleigh; Andrew Riley; Hon William Strutt; Oliver Urquhart-Irvine; Mr and Mrs Tom Ward; and Melissa Whitworth. I am also grateful to members of staff in the Royal Archives at Windsor Castle; the Bodleian Library, Oxford; the British Library, London; the Cambridge University Library; Churchill College, Cambridge; the National Archives, Kew; and the Parliamentary Archives in the Palace of Westminster.

I was saved from various errors by Mary Chamberlain, who copyedited the book with a high degree of meticulousness and intelligence. The superlative design of the dust-wrapper is by Stephanie Heathcote. Sue Brealey once more undertook the proofreading with unusual skill and dedication, and I am immensely in her debt. The book was also proofread by Alison Rae, and it was indexed by Vicki Robinson.

My agent, Georgina Capel, supported me with her customary loyalty and commitment, as she has throughout the three volumes of this project, which was originally her idea. And I have been especially fortunate in having a publisher of the skill, patience and insight of Nigel Wilcockson, who once more has brought the highest standards of refinement and production to my manuscript, leaving it far more coherent than he found it. All errors that remain are mine alone.

My final and most important expression of gratitude is to my beloved wife, Diana, who has now lived for almost a decade with this attempt to retell and amplify recent British history, as have our sons, Fred and Johnnie Heffer. Some readers will assume I exaggerate in claiming that I could not have written this book, or either of its predecessors, without her unfailing and ungrudging support; other writers will know all too well that I do not.

Simon Heffer
Great Leighs
15 May 2019

INTRODUCTION

This is not a military history. It is the story of how the government and people of a great naval and mercantile power, shaped by the tenets of laissez-faire, broke with the traditions of their culture, liberties, doctrines and customs, and adapted to total war. It tells how, with speed and uncertainty, the British state suddenly mobilised in August 1914; how it created a vast army, restricted freedom of action and expression, and prevailed over a formidable enemy; and how the country emerged radically and irrevocably changed. It describes international events from the British perspective: how the government came to take Britain into a catastrophic war because a Yugoslavist nationalist murdered an Austrian archduke in distant Bosnia; the impact of the conflict on the nation and its people; and their difficult readjustment to peace after total war, in a new dispensation where women could vote, the Russian revolution had inspired the working class, and a coalition government of 'new men' had made promises it had little prospect of keeping.

This is the third of what is planned to be a four-volume account of Great Britain between 1838 and 1939, a transformative century surpassing even those after the Roman invasion, the Norman Conquest and the Reformation. The five years between the assassination of Archduke Franz Ferdinand in Sarajevo, on 28 June 1914, and the conclusion of the Versailles Treaty, on 28 June 1919, saw a metaphorical revolution in Britain to compare with the literal ones in parts of Europe and in Russia: though one was effectively accomplished in Ireland by the ballot box in December 1918.

In Britain, millions of men either volunteered for or were drafted into the Army, and their lives either cut short or overturned by it. Women were bereaved, enlisted, advanced and enfranchised, yet were still expected to hold together homes and families. In early 1917 it seemed for a time that the country might be starved into submission. Bombers attacked the south and east of England and ships bombarded towns on the east coast. Britain became hugely indebted and highly taxed; but above all the state ballooned, and exerted unprecedented control over the lives of the people. The war became an opportunity to inaugurate a welfare state, with plans hatched long before the Armistice for improved health care, housing and education. Britain also had to learn how to cope with and care for a legion of disabled ex-servicemen, and the widows and orphans of the dead. It did not always do so ideally.

Like the two preceding volumes, *High Minds: The Victorians and the Birth of Modern Britain*, which examined Britain from 1838 to 1880, and *The Age of Decadence: Britain from 1880 to 1914*, which took the story up to the eve of the European crisis, *Staring at God* seeks to be a social and cultural as well as a political history. But because of the desperate predicament the war created, and the consequent awareness that every man and woman, and many children, would have to contribute if Britain were to prevail, government and politicians imposed themselves unprecedentedly on the ordinary citizen. So this volume is, inevitably, concerned much more with politics and political intrigue than its predecessors, because of the central and dominant part the state came to play in the lives of individuals, and the direction of the nation and its vast war effort.

Staring at God also portrays a second conflict with which Britain had to deal as it fought Germany: that in Ireland. Soldiers, sailors and battles inevitably pass through its pages, but only insofar as they were a part of a strategy governed, ultimately, from Westminster and Whitehall; and for the effect their fates had on the people left behind. Numerous fine historians have told the story of the fighting, and of the detailed international background to the conflict. These were five tumultuous and tragic years in Great Britain and Ireland, whose details the horrific events on the Western Front and other theatres of war have long overshadowed. This book examines them freshly, and in detail; and charts a nation's transition from an almost arrogant certainty to a wounded insecurity.

SOUTH EASTERN & CHATHAM RAILWAY
Via DOVER and CALAIS, and via FOLKESTONE and BOULOGNE.

COOK'S
CONDUCTED TOURS

FRANCE
SWITZERLAND
GERMANY
THURINGIAN ALPS
THE RHINE
HOLLAND
BELGIUM
AUSTRIA
SALZKAMMERGUT
DOLOMITES
SCANDINAVIA
IRELAND
SCOTLAND

PROGRAMMES FREE FROM
THOS. COOK & SON
LUDGATE CIRCUS

DAVID ALLEN & SONS LTP

CHAPTER I

CONSEQUENCES

At 4 p.m. on Sunday, 28 June, 1914 the Foreign Office in London received a telegram announcing the murders of Archduke Franz Ferdinand of Austria–Hungary and his morganatic wife, the Duchess of Hohenberg. The royal couple – he the nephew of eighty-three-year-old Emperor Franz Josef and heir presumptive to his throne – had been killed while visiting Sarajevo, capital of Bosnia, a former Ottoman territory Austria had annexed with Herzegovina in 1908. The telegram was addressed to Sir Edward Grey, the foreign secretary, from J. Francis Jones, the vice consul in Sarajevo. 'According to news received here heir apparent [sic] and his consort assassinated this morning by means of an explosive nature.'[1] Two hours later Sir Maurice de Bunsen, Britain's ambassador to Vienna, confirmed the news, adding: 'From another source I hear that bomb was first thrown at their carriage on their way to town hall, several persons being injured, and later young Servian [Serbian] student shot them both with a revolver as they were returning to Konak.'[2] The news was transmitted immediately to the King and Queen, taking tea in the garden of Buckingham Palace on a hot afternoon. 'It will be a terrible shock to the dear old Emperor,' George V noted in his diary, 'and is most regrettable and sad.' The King consoled himself by marking up his new stamp catalogue.[3]

The next morning, as Britain learned of the murders from the press, Jones updated Grey. 'Local paper speaks of anarchist crime, but act was more likely that of Servian irredentists, preconcerted long ago.'[4] Grey, who had met Franz Ferdinand on his visit to England in 1913, sent 'sincere and respectful condolences' to Franz Josef on behalf of the government and himself. In a Europe of monarchies, an attack on one was seen as an attack on all: there was not the slightest sense that Britain would find itself against Austria on this question. The King declared a week of court mourning, and *The Times* reported that the Royal Family had been 'inexpressibly shocked'.[5] Grey wrote to Count Mensdorff, Austria's ambassador to London, that 'every feeling political and personal makes me sympathise with you.'[6] Grey and Mensdorff were close: theirs was one of several high-ranking friendships shattered in the unfolding tragedy. That afternoon the King himself went to the Austro-Hungarian embassy in Belgrave Square to express his regrets to Mensdorff.

Such sympathy was not, however, universal, and nor, where it was expressed, was it especially deeply felt. The Habsburgs had had a miserable passage in their history, of which this was but the latest episode. Franz Josef's brother, the Emperor Maximilian of Mexico, had been executed by the government that overthrew him in 1867; his son and heir, Rudolf, had been found dead in the imperial hunting lodge with his mistress in 1889, presumably (but not confirmed) as the result of a suicide pact, and after ructions with his father; his wife, Sisi, had been assassinated (their marriage had more or less broken down); and Franz Ferdinand, who became heir on Rudolf's death when his father renounced his right to the throne, was disliked by his uncle and most of his court. Few mourned him. In continental Europe, not just in the Dual Monarchy of Austria–Hungary, Franz Ferdinand was loathed. Such was the relief in Budapest at his death that Hungarian stocks rose 11 per cent.[7]

When the House of Commons met that Monday afternoon Herbert Henry Asquith, the prime minister, said he would move a motion in tribute to the murdered archduke; but the assassination was a low priority for him, and for the government he led. The cabinet was obsessed with trouble in Ireland over Home Rule.[8] By contrast, the event in far Sarajevo seemed to have no ramifications for the United Kingdom at all. Asquith's motion expressed 'the indignation and deep concern with which this House had learned of the assassination of His Imperial and Royal Highness the Archduke Francis Ferdinand' and asked the King to tell the Austrian emperor of the Commons's 'abhorrence of the crime and their profound sympathy'.[9]

Asquith praised the 'patient assiduity and devoted self-sacrifice in the pursuit of duty' of the aged and bereaved Franz Josef, who he said had attained 'the highest ideal of what . . . Kingship can be made to be' and was 'the heroic head of a mighty state'. He added: 'He and his people have always been our friends'.[10] Andrew Bonar Law, the Leader of the Opposition, concurred: 'The heart of the whole world is turned today in sorrow and in pity to the lonely and desolate figure of the aged Emperor.'[11]

Grey did not trouble himself by speculating on the possible consequences of the assassinations. Some of his staff, however, did. Experienced British diplomats were aware that the killings might provoke feeling in Germany, Austria's main ally, given the closeness of the two countries bound by a common language, history and culture, and shared international aims. On 30 June the first secretary at the British embassy in Berlin, Sir Horace Rumbold, wrote to Grey that the German Foreign Ministry had told Serbia it should 'spontaneously . . . offer to do all they could to help the Bosnian authorities' to give 'convincing proof that they dissociated themselves from the motives that had led to the perpetration of this dreadful crime.'[12] Sir Arthur Nicolson, the permanent under-secretary at the Foreign Office and its senior permanent official, wrote the same day to Sir George Buchanan, British ambassador at St Petersburg, that 'the tragedy which has recently occurred at Sarajevo will, I hope, not lead to any further complications; though it is already fairly evident that the Austrians are attributing the terrible events to Servian intrigues and machinations.'[13] But even Sir Arthur could see more silver linings than clouds, reflecting that the new heir, the Emperor's great-nephew Charles, would be more popular than his dead uncle 'though it may seem a little brutal to say so'. Proving his point, the Germans were not instantly bellicose and, indeed, seemed to be striving to avoid worsening tensions in central Europe. In Britain, life continued serenely: *The Times*, on 1 July, published advice on 'the servant problem', which it stated 'is one of the most serious problems of the present day.'[14] Other issues troubling the nation that summer were the nuisance of dogs in railway carriages, and the plague of noise caused by motor-horns.

Yet by 3 July Rumbold had sensed a shift in mood in Berlin – where the Prussian officer class that ran the army were strongly urging support of Austria, and alerted London about it. He told Grey that the murders had 'produced an impression almost amounting to consternation in Germany.'[15] Rumbold stressed that Franz Ferdinand had been an 'intimate friend' of the Kaiser, and that the German people felt 'universal sympathy' for Franz Josef. Some of the Berlin newspapers had 'pointed out that the aspirations of those working for a greater Servia constitute a danger to the peace of Europe.'[16] This, five days after the murders – but not received by Grey until three days later, as Rumbold communicated via the diplomatic bag rather than by telegraph – was the first time a British diplomat in the field had registered with London the potential for a conflict to drag in one European nation after another. He warned Grey of the 'anxious interest' with which Berlin was watching events, and said there was little doubt there that the plot to murder the royal couple had been hatched in Serbia.

The Serbs themselves were only too well aware of that. The British minister in Belgrade, Dayrell Crackanthorpe, said the city was in a state 'rather of stupefaction than of regret', but also of 'apprehension' lest reprisals be taken against Serbs outside Serbia and, indeed, Serbia itself.[17] He reported that both the Serbian government and press had denounced the murders, in the hope of placating Austria. However, Crackanthorpe had heard that when the Austrian chargé d'affaires called on the Serb foreign minister, to return his call of condolence, 'an interview of considerable violence' took place. By 4 July he was reporting Serb condemnation of 'the persecutions of the Serbs now daily taking place in Bosnia and Herzegovina', and how angry Belgrade was at the Viennese press's determination to blame the Serbian government.[18] According to Crackanthorpe, Serbia realised its vulnerability, and 'sincerely desires the establishment of good relations with the Dual Monarchy.'

The warning signs being transmitted to London about the potential for conflict became louder and more urgent as the days passed. However, they did not register strongly, partly because of the assumption that any continental conflict stemming from Austria punishing Serbia could not involve Britain. London, like other European capitals, had no doubt about the combustible relations between Austria and Serbia, but a week after the murders was making no effort to argue for calm. The delay, inevitably of hours and sometimes of days, between the dispatch of telegrams and their arrival at their destination would make managing the crisis all the more difficult as it unfolded, with the subject matter of some wires virtually ancient history by the time they were read – especially later in July, as the threat of mobilisations was raised.

British failure to comprehend the consequences of Sarajevo was partly because of the government's continuing preoccupation with Ireland. Both sides in the dispute over Home Rule – the mostly Protestant

Unionist minority, concentrated in the north-east of the island, who had bitterly resisted it, and the mostly Roman Catholic Nationalist majority, who wanted it – were squaring up for a civil war, illegally armed largely by German weapons manufacturers. Asquith's administration was in power solely because of support from Irish Nationalist MPs in the House of Commons, the most recent election – in December 1910 – having left the Liberal Party without an overall majority. The price the Irish exacted for that support was Home Rule; and the Liberals had obliged, even to the extent of forcing through a Parliament Act in 1911 that removed the right of veto from the House of Lords once a Bill had passed three times through the House of Commons. The Home Rule Bill had done just that, and the Unionist minority was determined, by use of force and insurrection if necessary, to prevent its being implemented. A further distraction in Britain was the death, after years of debilitation, of Joe Chamberlain, the great Liberal Unionist statesman who had split the Liberal Party over Home Rule in the 1880s and then sought to do some-thing similar to the Unionists over free trade; his memory was feted around the globe. As a mark of respect to him the Commons adjourned for the day on the afternoon of 6 July, oblivious to the growing turmoil in central Europe.

The French, similarly, had their own concerns, and were slow to appreciate the ramifications of Austrian anger at the assassination; on Wednesday 15 July the country's president, Raymond Poincaré, and his prime minister, René Viviani, departed from Dunkirk on a battleship from St Petersburg via the Baltic, for a three-day state visit from 20 July. They did not know that by the time they arrived there would be a mounting diplomatic crisis in which their great ally, and therefore they, would become deeply bound up. Indeed, the three days of summitry in St Petersburg would be dominated by discussion of the possibilities stemming from Sarajevo. But even Poincaré had his diversions; he was most concerned with the impending trial of Henriette Caillaux, wife of Joseph Caillaux, prime minister of France for seven months in 1911–12. Mme Caillaux had the previous March shot dead Gaston Calmette, the editor of *Le Figaro*, who she believed was about to publish highly dam-aging private letters about her husband. Poincaré was deeply implicated, for Caillaux claimed to have evidence of wrongdoing against him by the president, which he threatened to publish unless Poincaré used his influ-ence to secure Mme Caillaux's acquittal. She would be acquitted on

28 July. In Paris, the talk was of little else, just as in London it was mainly about Ireland.

Around Europe, the attention of most of the great powers was considerably more focused on the consequences of Sarajevo than it was in London, or indeed in Paris. When de Bunsen wrote on 2 July – received in London on the 6th – that the Viennese press was whipping up anti-Serbian feeling, he commented that Serbia was 'held responsible for having assisted to create the atmosphere in which the hideous crime of Sarajevo was hatched.'[19] He believed it was 'not unlikely' that 'great tension' would ensue between Austria–Hungary and Serbia. As he wrote, the two provinces of Bosnia and Herzegovina were put under martial law.

Yet beneath Austrian outrage at the assassinations there was the realisation that an opportunity had been created for them: the excuse they had sought since 1908 to bring Serbia to heel had now arisen. The dilemma their German allies had about this was of little concern to them, in the heat of their anger, any more than Austria itself had any idea what it would do with Serbia once, as expected, it had crushed the country in a short and violent war. (Indeed, Austria would soon rebuke its Hungarian brothers for suggesting an annexation and partition of Serbia.) The Germans, for their part, were well aware of the questionable reliability of their Austrian allies. Kurt Riezler, an adviser to Theobald von Bethmann Hollweg, the German Chancellor, noted that 'it's our old dilemma with every Austrian action in the Balkans. If we encourage them, they will say we pushed them into it. If we counsel against it, they will say we left them in the lurch. Then they will approach the western powers, whose arms are open, and we lose our last reasonable ally.'[20] Since 1907, and the Triple Entente between Britain, France and Russia, Germany had complained of encirclement; it was deeply fearful of isolation, which might result if Austria reached an understanding with France or Britain, so had to stand by its side during the crisis. Unhelpfully when it came to calming Austria down, the German ambassador to Vienna, Heinrich von Tschirschky, had told Berlin that a conciliatory policy by Austria to Serbia was pointless, a view not, at that stage, held by the Kaiser: nor by most Austrians.

The Germans were additionally rattled by a round of Anglo-Russian talks about naval matters in June 1914, which increased the paranoia of many in Berlin that the entente powers were plotting to carve Germany up. The Triple Entente was not on Britain's part a military alliance; and German foreign policy had been predicated on the belief that whatever the Russians and French might do, the British would not fight a war against Germany. As will be seen, Grey stuck to that view himself until Belgium was violated, thereby establishing a separate *casus belli* on which, as he and most of his colleagues saw it, Britain had to act.

Russia, the most internally unstable of the powers, also had immediate concerns that stemmed from existing considerations. Elements there wanted what a military journal had, at New Year 1914, termed 'the war of extermination against the Germans', for which it claimed Russia was arming itself.[21] Articles on this theme had continued to appear in the Russian press before Sarajevo, urging the country's French military allies to be ready. Germany was naturally rattled by such talk, particularly as, along with its Austrian allies, it was outnumbered by the Russians, and the Russian mobilisation procedures had been streamlined thanks to improved rail communications. Crucially, Russian rhetoric – designed to shore up the unsteady position of the Tsar – was beginning to persuade non-militant Germans that there was, after all, a considerable threat from the east that had to be taken seriously. Austria, too, had cause to fear Russia. For different reasons, both Russia and France had instinctive sympathy for the Serbs. To the Russians, they were fellow Slavs who had endured years of provocation from the Austro-Hungarian Empire. France was highly sympathetic to Serbia, aside from its alliance with Russia – the alliance of which Britain was also a part.

Although Grey, in London, failed at once to alert his cabinet colleagues or Parliament to these dangers, some of his officials, whether in London or abroad, did grasp the threat; though several of them, with long-standing mistrust of a Germany that had since 1870–71 been viewed as the Continent's main hegemonic power, did so all the more readily because of prejudice against it. British policy also took insufficiently into account the deep mutual suspicion between France and Germany – a Germany that had, since 1871, incorporated and tried to 'Germanify' the two French regions of Alsace and Lorraine. This not only made highly combustible any European question in which the two countries could engineer an interest; it also meant that any disagreement had the potential to go out of control very quickly, and that any estimate of the situation made by British diplomats was likely instinctively to weigh against Germany. The ruling belief in the Foreign Office was that France was a bulwark between Britain and Germany, and if relations deteriorated between the two continental powers there would be overwhelming pressure to shore up France – despite the non-military nature of the entente.

With events in Europe moving as fast as they were, Britain was slow to appreciate these threats to regional stability. Yet if certain aspects of the Anglo-French relationship were clear, the Anglo-Russian one retained elements of ambiguity. Edward VII had been instrumental not just in the *entente cordiale*, but in including Russia in 1907. Yet ministers knew that British public opinion widely reviled the Tsar as an autocrat, an oppressor and a tyrant; no reliance could be placed on widespread support for a war in which Britain and he were on the same side. Also, the idea of involvement in a continental war was one the British had resisted since Castlereagh's time, in the aftermath of the Napoleonic Wars: what mattered to Britain in the European context was the neutrality of the Low Countries, and freedom of the seas.

On 6 July de Bunsen telegraphed Grey to warn him that his Serb colleague in Vienna thought there was about to be systematic repression of Serbs in Austria–Hungary, and an attack on Serbia itself. Grey had already learned something similar from Prince Lichnowsky, the cultivated and popular German ambassador, who had called on him to express his government's satisfaction at recent naval cooperation between Britain and Germany. Lichnowsky told Grey that he 'knew for a fact' the Austrians would act: a key piece of information that ought to have shifted British perceptions of the urgency of the problem. Grey expressed shock that they might be about to seize Serb territory.[22] Austria was Germany's principal ally: both Grey and Lichnowsky knew that Berlin had great influence over Vienna but Grey struggled to grasp that where Vienna was determined to move, Berlin had at least to support and understand, and perhaps even follow. What no one in the Foreign Office knew then was that on 5 July Germany had given Austria–Hungary what Germans called '*carte blanche*', but what the English called a 'blank cheque', to deal with its enemies as it saw fit; there would, therefore, be little point in calling on Germany to demand its ally exercised restraint. Also, there were some in Austria who had been waiting for an opportunity to remove Russian influence from the Balkans and to replace it with their own: this could be it.

Lichnowsky discounted an occupation of part of Serbia, saying the

Austrians had no use for such territory: but acquainted Grey with German disquiet, which should have served as a further warning to him and to the British government. First, he asked Grey to understand Germany's predicament: that if it urged restraint on Austria at a time of national outrage, it 'would be accused of always holding them back and not supporting them'; whereas if it 'let events take their course there was the possibility of very serious trouble.'[23] This dilemma caused 'anxiety and pessimism' in Berlin, the chief pessimist being the Chancellor, Bethmann Hollweg; though it is not clear whether at that stage the Chancellor thought Britain might be part of that trouble. Lichnowsky pleaded with Grey that if Austria did attack Serbia, Britain might seek 'to mitigate feeling in Berlin,' that is to seek to persuade Berlin not to give too much encouragement to its ally: Lichnowsky dreaded the idea of Germany going to war. The dominoes were being lined up.

Lichnowsky disclosed that Berlin was convinced that Russia, which had recently greatly increased its military strength, had a 'very unfavourable' feeling towards Germany: this is the first hint Grey had that Germany feared an attack by Russia if it sided with Austria against Serbia, a Russian ally. Grey had previously given Lichnowsky assurances that no secret naval pact existed between Britain and Russia, nor a secret deal behind the Triple Entente between Britain, Russia and France – though there had been conversations with France since 1906 about military cooperation if either party were attacked: he reiterated them. A naval pact would, Lichnowsky said during their meeting, 'impair good feeling between England and Germany generally.' It had been the main aim of Lichnowsky's embassy to improve Anglo-German relations, and he appeared thus far to have succeeded. After this conversation Grey should have understood the possibilities of all the great European powers being embroiled in a conflict, and how the Germans felt it was Britain's responsibility to keep Russia calm. However, a lack of calm in Germany was as much of a problem: Lichnowsky said Austria and Serbia would come to blows at some point, and better to get the matter over and done with.

Britain's view of this was markedly different. After talking to Grey, Lichnowsky reported back to Berlin that Britain had no intention of leaving the Triple Entente, 'for she must preserve the balance of power and could not see France annihilated'. Then came the paradox, for Grey had also told Lichnowsky that 'we did not wish to see the groups of power drawn apart': Grey was anxious not just for Britain to maintain good relations with all the main powers in Europe, but also for those powers to have a serene relationship with each other. The diplomacy of ensuing days would represent an attempt to achieve what, in the light of events and reactions to them, would become this impossibility. Grey promised to use 'all the influence I could' to restrain Russia if Austria attacked Serbia 'and if clouds arose to prevent the storm from breaking.' His conversation with Lichnowsky – which he reported to Rumbold in Berlin at once – was valuable and informative.

Grey's apparent complacency in the face of the warning that the assassinations might have wider repercussions, however, may have been affected by the developing views of his permanent secretary. Nicolson, so initially alert to the potential for crisis, told de Bunsen on 6 July that he trusted 'the crime at Serajevo [sic] . . . will have no serious consequences, in any case outside of Austria–Hungary'.[24] Nicolson had been soothed by some of the Viennese press taking a more moderate line about making Serbia responsible for the crime of 'certain revolutionaries'. Sadly, the 'reasonable journals' in which this opinion appeared had little influence over the Austrian government or people. De Bunsen's next dispatch to Grey, describing the obsequies of Franz Ferdinand and his unfortunate wife, struck a rather different note, detailing the high level of police protection around the house of the Serb minister, protecting him from the mob. He said 'the entire Serb race' was a target, and special precautions were being taken to prevent the mob getting anywhere near the Russian embassy, in case of gratuitous provocation.[25] Extracts from Serbian newspapers commenting on the murders, reprinted in Viennese ones, 'unfortunately contain some expressions amounting almost to condonation, and even approval of the dastardly outrage.'

On 8 July Grey was sufficiently concerned by what his ambassador was reporting to him about the strengthening of Austrian feeling that he spoke 'quite unofficially' to Count Benckendorff, the Russian ambassador to London and the man most responsible for the Triple Entente, about the Austrian government's being driven by public opinion to attack Serbia.[26] Benckendorff expected Germany to restrain Austria; Grey told him of the tensions in Berlin about that, and the concern that Russia was planning an assault on Germany – a possibility Benckendorff repudiated. He could, however, understand a German cast of mind in which it would be argued that Germany should fight Russia now, before its military power increased, hoping to put Russia in its place; a view he refused to believe either the Kaiser or his ministers shared. Grey told him the Russians 'should do all in their power to reassure Germany, and convince her that no *coup* was being prepared against her.' Benckendorff agreed, and promised to write at once to Sasonov, the Russian foreign minister.

The next day Grey received a dispatch from de Bunsen that confirmed his fears. Sentiment was hardening in Vienna, from the top to the bottom of society. The French ambassador to Austria, Dumaine, had, de Bunsen said, 'repeatedly spoken to me during the past week of the dangers of the situation, which he fears may develop rapidly into complications from which war might easily arise.'[27] On 9 July Grey talked further with Lichnowsky, and told Rumbold that 'I would do my utmost to prevent the outbreak of war between the Great Powers.'[28] Grey accepted that Austria might retaliate against Serbia, but Lichnowsky hoped Berlin had succeeded in counselling restraint. Grey's fear was that Austria would react so strongly that St Petersburg would feel forced to send an ultimatum to Vienna because of outraged Slav feelings in Russia. In Vienna, the government debated how to respond to the assassination, and took its time: meanwhile, as *The Times* reported on 11 July by way of pointing out a cloud no bigger than a man's hand, 'the Vienna bourse has been during the last few days about as bad as could be.'[29]

Rumbold, on 11 July, confirmed to Grey Lichnowsky's view of caution in Berlin and a reluctance to see matters worsen; and Austria said it would stay its hand pending investigations in Sarajevo. An interlude of what appeared in the Foreign Office to be relative calm occurred. It was a delusion, as in Vienna particularly the mood was hardening. On 16 July de Bunsen telegraphed Grey: 'I gather that situation is regarded at the Ministry of Foreign Affairs in a serious light and that a kind of indictment is being prepared against the Servian government for alleged complicity in the conspiracy which led to assassination of the Archduke.'[30] He said Serbia would be told to clamp down on 'nationalist and anarchist propaganda'. The Austro-Hungarian government was 'in no mood to parley' with Belgrade, and failure to comply with the ultimatum it proposed to send would be met with force. Vienna had no intention of sending an ultimatum just yet: Poincaré and Viviani were still in St Petersburg: the ultimatum would not be released until the French were sailing for home and could not consult easily with the

Russians. It should now have been absolutely clear to Grey that Austria was prepared – in the interests of retaining its status as a great power – to use force, and all that would entail. What ought to have been more worrying still, de Bunsen reported that Germany was 'in complete agreement' with this proposal.[31]

The main concern for the Austrians was how the Russians would react to such an ultimatum. De Bunsen had asked the Austrian official who had told him of this development whether he imagined the Russians would stand idly by in such a circumstance, and was prepared to take a gamble on what he disclosed. 'My informant said that he presumed that Russia would not wish to protect racial assassins, but in any case Austria–Hungary would go ahead regardless of results,' he added. Austria firmly believed Russia would lose its position as a great power 'if she stood any further nonsense from Servia.' The Viennese press too believed Russia could not condone what it believed was regicide. Austria also feared that without strong measures it would lose its status as a great power. It was thanks partly to such presumptions and assumptions that war broke out: and it was confident it could get what it wanted from Serbia not least because, as de Bunsen had hinted, it held Germany's blank cheque.

Crackanthorpe told Grey the next afternoon that Belgrade was adopting a 'prudent and conciliatory' attitude towards Austria.[32] However, there were limits: censorship of the press, suppression of nationalist societies and the appointment of a commission of inquiry – all demands Austria was thought likely to make – 'could not be acceded to, since it would imply foreign intervention in domestic affairs and legislation.' Given all he now knew, Grey should have seen the warning signs and started to be more proactive: but he seemed trapped in inertia. Part of the problem was that he was a remote figure. He had, since the death of his wife in 1906, when he was just forty-two, been solitary; they had no children, and his friends lamented his failure to meet an ideal second wife. Moreover, Grey had always been secretive about aspects of foreign policy, not least about the way in which he had sought to maintain good relations with Germany without upsetting Britain's French entente partners; but now his cards were being played far too close to his chest. Like his chief, Asquith, in another context Grey had preferred to 'wait and see': it was an inertia that meant when he finally attempted to act as a mediator, it was too late, and British power could be used only as a player and not as an umpire. It is not clear that Grey had anyone outside his officials or his colleagues with whom he could discuss and debate what was happening. Had there been such a person, it is just possible he might have taken a more interventionist attitude, and caught the boat train to Berlin or Vienna for face-to-face meetings with his counterparts. Sadly, he would not be the last British political leader to fail to see the depth of a problem until too late, because of a reluctance to share details of it with his colleagues elsewhere in government, or a failure to ask the right questions. It would take sight of the ultimatum Austria would soon send Serbia to wake Grey up to the full potential for disaster that the assassinations had unleashed.

It did not require hindsight to be aware of the potential dangers, long before the ultimatum. Some with well-attuned political antennae began to realise the growing possibility of war. For example, James Keir Hardie, the British Labour leader, attending the annual congress of French socialists in Paris, was a proposer (with his French counterpart, Edouard Vaillant) of a motion to call a general strike among the working classes of any country involved in a war. The international socialist view was always against war, but delegates from parts of continental Europe brought with them to Paris a heightened awareness of the combustibility of the Austro-Serbian quarrel. The motion was carried, as a warning to governments of the possible consequences of fighting: though when the time came the working classes of all countries overwhelmingly supported the call to arms.

London watched anxiously as the Vienna bourse plunged. On 16 July *The Times* warned its readers that feelings in Vienna and Belgrade – where rumours had swirled, causing panic, about a plot by nationalists to blow up the Austro-Hungarian legation – were being inflamed by the 'reckless and provocative' language of the press 'in a campaign that may ultimately lead to disastrous results.' The paper urged Serbia to launch a full inquiry into the operations of nationalists and to report to the powers without delay, to help improve its standing in European opinion. It assumed Franz Josef and his 'sagacious' advisers perceived the peril to European peace if Austria were to respond with force: an assumption that soon would be tested to destruction.[33] The leader went down well in Berlin, however, being interpreted as an English warning to Serbia.

British preoccupations remained elsewhere, notably in Ireland, as the tension there grew. The public also enjoyed side dishes such as reports from the Royal Commission on Venereal Diseases, which caused great interest when taking evidence from the headmasters of Eton and Harrow: 'Hard exercise, hard work, wholesome society, and moderation in diet and drinking were of great use as safeguards against indulgence,' they agreed.[34] The great event of the summer in England was the review of the Fleet off Spithead. By 17 July most of it was in place, with the First Lord of the Admiralty, Winston Churchill, moored off Portsmouth in the Admiralty yacht *Enchantress*, busy entertaining senior officers to bibulous dinners. During those evenings the Fleet became 'a floating city of light'.[35] The King was arriving at the weekend to inspect his ships. One novelty would be seaplanes: Churchill had been zealous in establishing and building up the Navy's air capacity, with the Royal Naval Air Service instituted barely a month earlier. The sun shone and sightseers thronged the shore at Ryde and Portsmouth to watch the line of ships stretch across the Solent from Hampshire to the Isle of Wight. When, the following Monday, the procession passed the Royal Yacht it would be followed by a formation of seaplanes at 500 feet, alerted by a wireless signal. With the sea heavy with Dreadnoughts, the King and his people crowded on the coastline would witness the latest contributions modern technology could make to warfare. To almost everyone in Westminster and Whitehall – the exceptions were senior diplomats such as Sir Eyre Crowe, the assistant under-secretary, and Nicolson – there was no expectation that the Fleet would be needed in the foreseeable future. Crowe had been born in Leipzig, had a German mother and a German wife, spoke German as his first language but had also for years told Grey that Britain was too soft with the Germans. He would soon feel vindicated in his view.

II

In the third week of July the debate in Europe moved from whether there would be a conflict to whether it could be contained locally to Austria and Serbia or whether it would spread more widely. At lunchtime on 18 July Grey learned from Crackanthorpe that the Austrian minister to Belgrade was 'not personally in favour of pressing Servia too hard, since he is convinced that Servian Government are ready to take whatever measures can reasonably be demanded of them. He does not view the situation in a pessimistic light.'[36] This may have been merely soothing diplomatic reassurance – if so it was ill-founded – or it may have reflected a moment of caution by the Austrians, less sure than before that Russia would do nothing. Two hours later de Bunsen wrote that an article in the *Westminster Gazette* – which some in the Viennese press thought was an official organ of the British government – telling Serbia, effectively, that it would serve it right if the Austrians punished it severely, appeared to be Britain egging Austria on. This could not have been further from the truth, and de Bunsen told the Austrians so: it showed how febrile the atmosphere had become. In Vienna, *The Times* reported, it was believed – erroneously – that Serbia had called up 70,000 reservists 'and considerable movements of troops were taking place'.[37] Buchanan, that evening, reported from St Petersburg that the Russians felt 'great uneasiness' at Austria's behaviour, and wanted to avoid war at all costs: but an Austrian ultimatum to Serbia could not be ignored. The next day Crackanthorpe, from Belgrade, told Grey the Serbian foreign minister had said that 'Russia would not stand by and see Servia wantonly attacked'.[38] It was also that day that Austria finally decided to issue an ultimatum, having smoothed internal differences with Hungary about the strategy.

Mutual suspicions grew. On 20 July Grey received a letter from Rumbold retailing a conversation with Paul Cambon, the French ambassador to London, whose younger brother Jules was Paris's man in Berlin. Cambon had told Rumbold that 'matters as between France and Germany were by no means what they should be. The air would have to be cleared some time or other.'[39] France and Germany believed each was spying on the other, echoing suspicions Germany and Russia had about each other. 'The enormous masses of men at the command of Russia are a constant source of preoccupation,' Rumbold wrote of his German hosts. 'Speculation as to the events which might set those masses in motion against Germany seems to follow almost as a matter of course.'[40] In Vienna, *The Times* reported that morning, the *Reichspost* newspaper had asked: 'Do our statesmen not yet realise what the position is, and what they have to do?'[41] The Berlin press, *The Times* also reported, vociferously backed Vienna's demand for Serbia to clarify its position with Austria, and quoted one paper as expressing the hope that the discussion could remain 'localised'. It also reported the 'severe tension' and 'nervousness' because of the 'uncertainty' about Russia's attitude. Meanwhile Grey apologised to Buchanan for not having had the chance to consult colleagues about a proposal by the Russian foreign minister to improve

Anglo-Russian relations, promising to do so 'as soon as the parliamentary and Irish situation gives them time.'[42] He also urged Buchanan to use his influence to have Russia and Austria sit down and talk to each other if things became 'difficult'.[43]

That same day Lichnowsky, falling out of step with attitudes in Berlin and starting to fear a catastrophe, had told Grey that while he lacked definite news he was sure Austria was about to act, 'and he regarded the situation as very uncomfortable.'[44] The Germans, and to a lesser extent Grey, still expected Russia to act as a 'mediator' with Serbia, rather than crashing into a conflict on Serbia's side; that, too, was a fundamental miscalculation. Nevertheless, Grey was becoming extremely worried. He told Rumbold he 'hated the idea of a war between any of the Great Powers, and that any of them should be dragged into a war by Servia would be detestable.' Meanwhile a leading French newspaper, *Le Matin*, published full details of Russia's military strength, its mobilisation procedures, and the depth of its resources: the idea of a localised war in Europe was now being taken for granted, even though at the highest levels the belief remained firm that Austria would not make an unreasonable demand on Serbia. The Foreign Office either did not know of the enthusiastic advocacy that the Russian military leadership had for months been making for their 'war of extermination' with Germany, or chose not to take it seriously.

The Times reported on 21 July on an inside page – then there were only advertisements on the front – but given more prominence than usual for such a story, that the press campaign against Serbia in Vienna was 'increasing in intensity', the Vienna bourse had dived again, taking the Berlin stock market with it, and the belief was growing that the Austrians were going to use the crisis to 'settle' the Serbian question once and for all. 'In diplomatic circles,' the paper continued, 'the approaching crisis is considered grave. There is believed to be no ground for the assumption that Russia will withdraw support from Servia in case the Austro-Hungarian demands should be in any way derogatory to Servian independence or national dignity.'[45] This well-briefed story showed, twenty-three days after the assassination, how the crisis had entered a new order of magnitude.

Grey had further confirmation of this from, of all places, Rome, late on 22 July. The Italian foreign minister had told Sir Rennell Rodd, the British ambassador, that the Austrian communication to be made to

Serbia 'had been drafted in terms which must inevitably be unacceptable. He is convinced that a party in Austria are determined to take this
opportunity of crushing Servia.'[46] Earlier that day Grey had asked
Benckendorff to strive to ensure Russia opened communications with
Austria; but the Russian ambassador had told him this was a 'difficulty'
because 'at present there was nothing to go upon.'[47] Grey tried to persuade him that Russia could stop the escalation of trouble.

Grey also learned from his *Times* that morning that Count Berchtold,
the Austrian foreign minister, had gone to Ischl, where Franz Josef was
resting, for an audience during which (the Viennese press believed) a
decision would be taken about Serbia. Where *The Times* was misin-
formed, however, was in its assurance that the note Austria would send
'is in no way in the nature of an ultimatum.'[48] The Vienna bourse continued to plunge, and the press remained fervent for punitive action
against Serbia, leaving the government little room for manoeuvre. *The
Times*'s Berlin correspondent reported that although Germany was
desperate to preserve its neutrality, it was bound to support Austria
against attack from a third party, and that all eyes there were on Russia, where 'resentment' of Austria's attitude to Serbia was being voiced
in the newspapers.[49]

All the components of potential disaster were now present. *The Times*,
in a leading article, issued an alarm to the governing class to forget Ireland for a moment – the Speaker's Conference designed to solve the
problem of Ulster's rejecting Home Rule was in session – and examine
'a situation in European politics too serious to be ignored'.[50] It urged
the King of Serbia to see that justice was done to the assassins, whose
punishment 'is imperiously required by the first interests of society
and by the conscience of mankind.' But it told Austria to prove the conspiracy before punishing it: 'To obtain the moral support or the
acquiescence of others she must make it clear that she is not seeking to
gain political advantages under the cloak of legitimate self-defence.' It
urged moderation, and not submission to the views shouted by the Viennese and Budapest press; and advocated that sedition be treated not with
'severity' but with 'a judicious mixture of kindness and firmness.' However, the paper viewed the war that might otherwise break out as one
that could engulf the Balkans: there was still no sense, given German
protestations of peace, that it could spread westwards too.

The next day, 23 July, Buchanan telegraphed from St Petersburg that the Russian Foreign Ministry had instructed its ambassador at Vienna 'to concert with his French and German colleagues with a view to giving friendly counsels of moderation.'⁵¹ The French had briefed their ambassador similarly. However, later that morning Mensdorff gave Grey notice of the Austrian demand, promising him a copy the next morning. What most disturbed Grey, as he told de Bunsen, was that the demand *was* an ultimatum, with a time limit. 'I said that I regretted this very much,' Grey noted.⁵² He feared it would inflame Russian opinion and reduce the chance of a satisfactory reply from Serbia. Mensdorff blamed the Serbs for not having conducted a thorough inquiry into anarchist activity on its own territory. Grey noted: 'I could not help dwelling upon the awful consequences involved in the situation.'

He tried to articulate his fears, but in doing so still saw no possibility of British involvement. 'If as many as four Great Powers of Europe – let us say Austria, France, Russia and Germany – were engaged in war, it seemed to me that it must involve the expenditure of so vast a sum of money, and such interference with trade, that a war would be accompanied or followed by a complete collapse of European credit and industry.' Presciently, he added: 'This would mean a state of things worse than that of 1848' – the year of revolutions against the old order in Europe – 'and, irrespective of who were victors in the war, many things might be completely swept away.' Mensdorff said it would all depend on Russia: to a great extent, he was right.

The nature and tone of the Austrian memorandum, when it finally came, confirmed Grey's worst suspicions.

The note, in French, had ten points. The first was an order to suppress publication of material designed to excite hatred or contempt for the monarchy and territorial integrity of Austria–Hungary. The second called for the immediate dissolution of *Narodna Odbrana*, a militant nationalist group, and to confiscate their propaganda materials and those of similar groups. The third was to eliminate any other groups propagandising against Austria–Hungary. The fourth was to dismiss all military and state officials guilty of agitating against Austria–Hungary, and to inform Vienna of their names. The fifth was to agree to allow Austro-Hungarian agents to 'collaborate' with tackling subversion in Serbia.

The sixth was to hold a judicial inquiry into the activities of those behind the 28 June plot. The seventh was to arrest a specific senior officer in the Serbian army. The eighth was to take measures to prevent Serbian officials assisting in the illicit supply of arms and explosives to nationalists, and specifically to punish border officials who had allowed into Bosnia the explosives used in Sarajevo. The ninth demanded an official explanation of why Serbian officials had been allowed to express views hostile to Austria–Hungary. The tenth and final demand was that Vienna should be told immediately when the other nine points had been acted upon.[53] As the diplomatic traffic of succeeding days frequently said, acceptance of these points would effectively reduce Serbia to a vassal state. Crackanthorpe noted, in a telegram sent to London at 10.30 p.m. on 23 July, but not read until eight o'clock the next morning, that the demands delivered to the Serbian government were 'exceedingly harsh'.[54]

Serbia was given forty-eight hours to comply. Austrian officials warned de Bunsen that the note was 'stiff', but argued that nothing else would suffice.[55] The Under-Secretary of State in the Austrian Foreign Ministry told him that the 'complicity of Servian officials in crime was fully proved and that no government could remain in power here for a week that failed to call Servia seriously to account.' The French and Russian ambassadors had pleaded with Austria to tone the note down: they failed. Once Grey saw the note, at the same time it was rehearsed in detail in the London press, he registered an official protest about the forty-eight-hour time limit: and reflected later that 'the note seemed to me the most formidable document I have ever seen addressed by one State to another that was independent.'[56] Churchill called it 'the most insolent document of its kind ever devised'.[57] Grey told Mensdorff that the merits of the case were not Britain's concern: he was worried 'solely from the point of view of the peace of Europe,' which he now understood was on a knife-edge.[58] He went to a cabinet meeting at 3.15 where he outlined the European situation, which Asquith noted in his diary 'is about as bad as it can possibly be.'[59] The cabinet was told that if Russia decided to defend Serbia 'it is difficult both for Germany and France to refrain from lending a hand,' as Asquith noted. 'We are within measurable distance of a real Armageddon.'

Asquith's conception of Armageddon did not involve Britain. Apart from continuing the long-held policy of non-intervention in European conflicts, there was another practical reason why British involvement in any war seemed out of the question. The government had been told it would take the entire potential British Expeditionary Force – the number of soldiers earmarked by the Army reforms of 1908 to be dispatched to the Continent in the event of an emergency – to enforce Home Rule in Ireland; it could not mount a European campaign as well, so choices would have to be made.[60] However, this was the moment when Europe replaced Ireland as the main preoccupation of the cabinet or when, as Churchill memorably put it, 'the parishes of Fermanagh and Tyrone faded back into the mists and squalls of Ireland, and a strange light began immediately, but by perceptible gradations, to fall and grow upon the map of Europe.'[61] He already saw the danger to British security of a war between the continental powers, and was determined to persuade his colleagues of it. From then, according to the memoirs of Lord Beaverbrook, Churchill became 'the leader of the War party in the Cabinet.'[62]

That afternoon Grey received a telegram from Crackanthorpe relaying the plea of the 'anxious and dejected' Serbian prime minister to help moderate Austria's 'impossible' demands.[63] Within twenty minutes de Bunsen had wired from Vienna, reporting a conversation with the French ambassador there: the Frenchman had seen their Serbian colleague, who reported an 'active exchange' of telegrams between Belgrade and St Petersburg about the Serbian response. Almost immediately, Crackanthorpe telegraphed again to say the Serbian government had told him certain demands were 'quite unacceptable'.[64]

Later that evening de Bunsen reported that the ultimatum 'had given great satisfaction throughout Dual Monarchy, which felt its very existence was at stake'. The Austrian minister for foreign affairs, de Bunsen added, 'could not believe that any power could think of raising objections' to a note that Vienna's diplomatic community had agreed was 'curt and peremptory'. The ultimatum stimulated frenetic diplomatic activity across Europe. Grey saw Cambon and stressed it was only those powers without a direct interest in Serbia – Britain, France, Germany and Italy – that could moderate between Vienna and St Petersburg. Cambon said such moderation would have to wait until the Russians had expressed an opinion; but once Austria entered Serbia it would be too late, as pro-Slav opinion in Russia would force its government to act. Grey and Cambon agreed that German participation in this exercise was essential: and Grey, rather naively, believed that if Russia and Austria did prepare to fight, their advances could be stopped to allow mediation. Cambon countered that once Austria advanced on Serbia it would be too late to stop anything.

Grey asked Lichnowsky about the possibility of the combined powers mediating between Austria and Serbia. He was met by equivocation: Lichnowsky could not second-guess Berlin, where different interests – notably the army – were arguing for the ear of the Kaiser, and opinions on how to proceed seemed fluid. Grey told Lichnowsky that, given the stiffness of the Austrian note, there was no likelihood of his calming the Russians down. The silence from St Petersburg was also deeply troubling to Grey. Lichnowsky warned that if Serbia did not send 'a reply that was favourable on some points' Austria must be expected to move at once: he urged Grey to relay the message that Serbia had to buy time with Austria by being reasonable, to give others a chance to intervene.[65] Grey informed Berlin of this, and copied in Britain's other ambassadors among the great powers.

In the course of their meeting Lichnowsky clarified the German government's position to Grey. It was sure Serbia had engineered the Sarajevo attack, as part of a programme 'directed towards the detachment of the southern Slav provinces from the Austro-Hungarian Monarchy and their incorporation into the Servian Kingdom'.[66] This was, the Germans were also convinced, executed 'with at least the connivance of members of the Government and army.' Serbia had broken promises about its good conduct; and Germany believed Austria would no longer be a great power if it allowed Serbia to go unpunished. However Berlin, far from being bellicose, wanted the matter to remain a quarrel between Austria and Serbia: 'The Imperial Government desire urgently the localisation of the conflict,' its official response to the Austrian note said, 'because every interference of another Power would, owing to the different treaty obligations, be followed by incalculable consequences.' The next day *The Times* reported that the harsh tone of the note had been greeted with 'surprise' in Berlin, but the German government and most of the people supported the Dual Monarchy entirely 'because she cannot now go back.'[67]

The Foreign Office's first reaction was that the 'extreme nature' of Austria's demands and the time limit made it very difficult to contain the conflict to just Austria and Serbia. Crowe believed there was, as yet, insufficient evidence on which Austria could base its claim of Serbian control of the nationalists, and therefore that Germany's unequivocal support of those claims was dangerous. It was not until 8 p.m. on 24 July that Grey had the first evidence of Russia's position. Buchanan telegraphed to say that the Russian foreign minister's initial view was that the ultimatum 'meant war'.[68] Sasonov had seen Buchanan at the French embassy in St Petersburg: he and the French ambassador told him Russia and France had, before Poincaré's departure for Paris, agreed various points they wished to share with their British ally.

Buchanan relayed those points. The French and Russians agreed on the need to maintain peace and the balance of power; but felt the ultimatum was 'equivalent to an intervention in the internal affairs of Servia which the latter would be justified in regarding as an attack on her sovereignty and independence'; and there was a 'solemn affirmation of obligations imposed by the alliance of the two countries.' This introduced Sasonov's key point: 'the hope that His Majesty's Government would proclaim their solidarity with France and Russia.' He told Buchanan that Austria's conduct was 'immoral and provocative'. He believed Germany must have been complicit in the demands. Ominously, the French ambassador told Buchanan that France's support of Russia would not be confined to diplomacy.

Buchanan said he could not speak for his government, telling Grey he had said that 'I could personally hold out no hope that His Majesty's Government would make any declaration of solidarity that would entail engagement to support France and Russia by force of arms.' He had, he reported, added to Sasonov: 'We had no direct interests in Servia, and public opinion in England would never sanction a war on her behalf.' Sasonov, who said Britain could not stand apart on the general European question, dismissed this. He had thought a Russian mobilisation likely; but any decision to declare war on Austria, if it attacked Serbia, would be taken by a council of ministers under the Tsar the next day. The French ambassador told Buchanan what Cambon had told Grey: it was too late to intervene in Vienna, and Austria had either to attack or climb down.

The British ambassador continued to resist pressure from his fellow diplomats to pledge British support, but said he would urge Grey – and this was the crux of his telegram – to make the strongest representations to Berlin and Vienna about the dangers of attacking Serbia. He advised Grey to warn both powers that Russia would feel compelled to intervene, which would bring France into the field. If Germany followed, 'it would be difficult for England to remain neutral.'[69] Buchanan feared that if war broke out 'we would sooner or later be dragged into it', but also felt that if Britain did not make common cause quickly, war would be more likely. It was a perfect expression of the problem Britain faced. It might not have any interest in Serbia, but its allies did.

Crowe, on seeing Buchanan's note to Grey, observed it was manifestly too late to enlist the French to hold back Russia if Austria attacked Serbia. The internal dynamics of the Triple Entente were irrelevant. 'The point that matters,' he observed with acuity, 'is whether Germany is or is not absolutely determined to have this war now.'[70] The only way to make Germany hesitate was to create no doubt that she would 'find England by the side of France and Russia.' He suggested that a way to drive that message home was for the government to 'give orders to put our whole fleet on an immediate war footing' the moment Russia or Austria mobilised.

Crowe could see no merit in dithering: Britain had to know what to do 'in circumstances that may arise tomorrow.'[71] His logic was brutal:

Should the war come, and England stand aside, one of two things must happen:

(a) Either Germany and Austria win, crush France, and humiliate Russia. With the French fleet gone, Germany in occupation of the Channel, with the willing or unwilling cooperation of Holland and Belgium, what will be the position of a friendless England?

(b) Or France and Russia win. What would then be their attitude towards England? What about India and the Mediterranean?

Crowe disputed that war would be about Serbia. It would be 'between Germany aiming at a political dictatorship in Europe and the Powers who desire to retain individual freedom.' A show of willingness to use naval power might forestall this, so the effort had to be made. He advised an immediate decision to mobilise the Fleet in the event of any foreign mobilisation, with that decision notified at once to France and Russia.

Nicolson agreed Crowe's points merited 'serious consideration', and stressed the importance of not alienating Russia, who could make things difficult for Britain in the Mediterranean, the Middle East and India. Grey confirmed that Churchill had told him the Fleet could be mobilised within twenty-four hours, but Grey believed it was premature to alert either France or Russia to this. The Fleet had started to disperse after the review but was mostly in place, so getting it at the ready would be straightforward; and leaving the Fleet in a state of readiness was, Grey felt, 'entirely justified', given the diplomatic situation.[72]

Late on 24 July Grey telegraphed Crackanthorpe in Belgrade about his conversation with Lichnowsky, urging him to consult his French and Russian colleagues about a joint approach to the Serbian government 'to give a favourable reply on as many points as possible within the limit of time', and not to meet the Austrian demand with a blank negative.'[73] Grey then heard from Berlin that the French ambassador there had told Gottlieb von Jagow, the German foreign minister, that the Kaiser's government could not 'maintain [the] fiction' that the dispute between Austria and Serbia could be localised.[74] He had disputed that the Serbs would accept Austria's terms, saying if the King of Serbia ordered their acceptance he would probably be assassinated. Jagow had, though, conceded that the note was 'too stiff'. The French ambassador believed the Austrians were bluffing.

Austria then began to behave as though it *were* bluffing. After Grey had gone home Mensdorff rang the Foreign Office to ask whether he could see him at once. When Hugh Montgomery, the assistant clerk who took the call, could not find Grey, Mensdorff asked him to call at the embassy. He told Montgomery the Austrian note 'was not an ultimatum but a "*démarche* with a time limit"', and that if the Austrian demands were not complied with within the time limit his Government would break off diplomatic relations and commence military preparations (not operations).'[75] It seemed Austria had considered the consequences, and was blinking first. Grey wired the news to Buchanan, copying in Paris: 'It makes the immediate situation rather less acute,' he observed. That was not how matters appeared in Hungary. Britain's Consul General in Budapest, W. G. Max Müller, telegraphed that evening – his wire arrived just after midnight – to say the Hungarians did not expect Russian intervention, and were therefore putting it about that if a 'favourable reply is not received on Saturday [25 July], eight army corps will be mobilised on Sunday morning . . . monitors have already been sent to Lower Danube.'[76] The Hungarians' confidence about Russian intentions was misplaced. Early on 25 July the Russian government published a communiqué to say it was 'intently following' events between Austria and Serbia 'with respect to which Russia cannot remain indifferent.'[77]

The Times bluntly told the government to ignore the Irish conference – which had broken down – and concentrate on the 'grave crisis' in Europe.[78] Presumably to shock the government out of its inertia, it stated: 'We cannot share the confidence which is felt, or affected, in Berlin and Rome that a conflict between Austria–Hungary and Servia will be "localised" and that complications are improbable.' It added that 'the Wilhelmstrasse [the German Foreign Ministry and Chancellery], it is said, holds that Servia is "morally isolated". The news from St Petersburg is an ominous comment on such an assumption.' It condemned Austria's conduct as 'hardly . . . statesmanlike', and assumed the country wanted a fight: it also observed that the conflagration its aggression might provoke would place 'the very existence of the Monarchy at stake. No effort should be spared to save her and to save Europe from so grievous a mistake.'

Grey remained remarkably passive despite such exhortations: he neither sought instructions from his cabinet colleagues to engage in more active diplomacy, nor took any initiative of his own to talk directly to his counterparts in Vienna or Berlin. He learned that afternoon that the Austrian minister to Belgrade had been instructed to leave with his staff at 6 p.m. that evening if no satisfactory reply had been received. He now accepted that Austria and Russia would mobilise 'in very short time', and the only chance of peace was for the other great powers to ask Austria and Russia not to cross frontiers, and to try to talk some sense into the prospective belligerents.[79] He realised the cooperation of Germany would be 'essential'. Nonetheless he told Buchanan: 'I do not consider public opinion here would or ought to sanction our going to war in the Servian quarrel.'[80]

News from Belgrade for a moment seemed to suggest that, after all, there would be no cause to appeal to public opinion. That afternoon Crackanthorpe wired to Grey that he understood the Serbian reply 'will be drawn up in most conciliatory terms and will meet Austrian demands in as large measure as possible.'[81] The Serbs would agree to a mixed commission of inquiry 'provided that the appointment of the commission can be proved to be in accordance with international usage'. It agreed to dismiss and prosecute any officers whose guilt could be proved, and to suppress *Narodna Odbrana*. Crackanthorpe added: 'Opinion of Servian Government is that, unless Austrian Government desire war at any cost, they will accept full satisfaction offered in Servian reply.'[82]

Grey shared this sudden optimism: he told Lichnowsky so. He wanted to remind the German ambassador that 'it is difficult for anybody but an ally to suggest to the Austrian Government what view they should take of it.'[83] He hoped, if Crackanthorpe's understanding of the reply was correct, that Germany would exert its influence with the Austrians to persuade them to take a 'favourable view' of it. He reported this to Rumbold; he had tried to contact senior French officials to enlist their support, but Poincaré and his suite were en route from St Petersburg and incommunicado. Acting on a Russian initiative, Grey instructed de Bunsen to support his Russian counterpart's intervention in Vienna to plead for an extension of the time limit.

At 6 p.m. on 25 July, just as the ultimatum was expiring, Grey heard from Rumbold that Lichnowsky, as good as his word, had asked the German Foreign Office to request an extension. Rumbold also reported, however, that Berlin was pessimistic, believing Austria had decided 'to give the Servians a lesson, and that they meant to take military action.'[84] Serbia's reply conciliated Austria on almost every point, and those it did not wholly accept it accepted conditionally: but Austria was resolute. Britain had urged Serbia to conciliate Austria even though Austria could find no evidence for its assertions. 'The Serbian answer went further than we had ventured to hope in the way of submission,' Grey wrote years later. 'From that moment things went from bad to worse.'[85]

Rumbold had heard that Berchtold had told Russia's man in Vienna that Austria–Hungary had no intention of seizing Serbian territory; and, for what it was worth, the Germans believed this would soothe tempers in St Petersburg. The Germans had told Russia that the last thing they wanted was a general war, and they would back Grey's suggestion for a four-power solution or mediation, which the foreign secretary had made on 26 July. From Rumbold's report it is clear the German Foreign Ministry did not understand the depth of Russian feeling about an attack on their fellow Slavs: and for all their disappointment with their Austrian allies (Jagow 'confessed privately that as a diplomatic document [the] note left much to be desired'), the Germans seemed to think a conflagration could be avoided.[86] It was strongly Grey's belief that the only people it was worth Britain talking to, in the interests of stopping war, were the Germans.

Things were, as Grey soon learned, seen differently in Paris. A French newspaper had accused Germany of complicity in drawing up the note – something the Germans adamantly denied – and attacked

Germany and Austria for seeking to humiliate the Triple Entente, forcing this crisis when Britain was preoccupied with Ireland, Russia had
problems with workers' unrest, and the leadership of France was sailing
back from the Baltic. The Germans protested vociferously, but the damage was done in terms of French public opinion. Just after 9 p.m. Grey
heard that all preparations for 'instant mobilisation' had been completed in Vienna, and de Bunsen relayed an unconfirmed report that a
detachment of siege trains, loaded with howitzers, had left Vienna's
southern station.[87] In Britain, it would become widely believed – thanks
mainly to the press – that even if the Germans had not drawn up the
note, Austria's threatening behaviour was shaped by a sincere belief
that Germany would support them; and that the Germans had given
them reason for that conviction.

Grey claimed in his memoirs to have seen from this point that Britain's interests demanded it back France, if France had to fight alongside
Russia. 'I knew it to be very doubtful whether the Cabinet, Parliament,
and the country would take this view on the outbreak of war, and
through the whole of this week [before war was declared] I had in view
the probable contingency that we should not decide at the critical
moment to support France.'[88] He added that 'in that event I should have
to resign.' He also saw the imperative of giving no assurance to France
or Russia that Britain might decide not to fulfil. This would cause him
enormous strain over the following days. It happened to be Law's
position and was shared by the Unionists, partly because A. J. Balfour and
the Marquess of Lansdowne – not wishing to appear impotent as prime
minister and foreign secretary at the time – had always claimed that
Edward VII's policy to conclude the *entente cordiale* in 1903–04 was in fact
theirs. It was too late to back down now.[89]

At 10.30 p.m. on 25 July Grey heard that the Council of Ministers under
the Tsar in St Petersburg that morning had sanctioned the drafting of the
Imperial Ukase, calling up 1,100,000 men. Sasonov had assured Buchanan
that the mobilisation would not happen until forced on Russia; and
Buchanan had heard that 'France had placed itself unreservedly on Russia's side'.[90] He was being pressed about British support, but assured Grey
that he had done nothing more than suggest Britain would continue to
act as a potential moderator. This annoyed Sasonov, who replied that if
Britain did not pledge to fight with her two allies, 'rivers of blood would
flow and we would in the end be dragged into war.' Buchanan noted that

his French counterpart had said that his government 'would want to know at once whether our fleet was prepared to play [the] part assigned to it by Anglo-French Naval Convention. He could not believe that England would not stand by her two friends, who were acting as one in this matter.' France took unequivocally the Russian line that Austria sought a fight with Russia over influence in the Balkans, and that this was about the whole European balance of power, not just Serbia.

No sooner had Grey digested this than he received the unsurprising news, from Max Müller in Budapest, that the Serbian reply 'was not found satisfactory', the Austrian minister and his staff had left Belgrade, and Hungary had started to call up reservists. Rumbold told Grey that, from Berlin's point of view, whether the crisis remained 'local' would 'depend on whether, and, if so, to what extent, Russia and France think that they can reckon on active support of His Majesty's Government in the event of a general complication.'[91] It was now, effectively, up to the British to decide whether or not there would be a general war. Sir Francis Bertie, the veteran British ambassador to Paris, told the French foreign minister that no war could happen without public support; and he was sure there would be no such support in England for a war caused by Russia having 'picked a quarrel with Austria over Austro-Servian difficulty.'[92] At the time he made this comment he was echoing the foreign secretary's view, expressly not giving the French cause to believe Britain would join any military action they undertook with Russia: but that view was about to undergo a radical change.

Crackanthorpe told Grey at 11.30 p.m. that the Serbs had ordered a mobilisation. The first news Grey received the following morning, on 26 July, was from Vienna, where, de Bunsen told him, 'wildest enthusiasm' prevailed, and a special guard had been put on the Russian embassy.[93] Austria, too, called up its reserves and settled its mobilisation plan. The crisis now took on a new order of magnitude, in the context of which Grey's response was astonishing. Having had a brief audience of the King the previous day, at which he left the Sovereign with the impression that 'we were on the verge of a general European war', he went off to Itchen Abbas in Hampshire to go fishing.[94] In fact, even on the river he had no choice but to take a more active role. Acting on a suggestion of Nicolson, whom he had left in charge in London, he sent telegrams to his counterparts in Berlin, Paris and Rome to authorise their ambassadors to London to join him in a conference designed to 'prevent complications'.⁹⁵ Yet even Nicolson thought the idea had 'a very poor chance' of success, despite the suggestion thus far of German cooperation. He told Grey that Lichnowsky, with whom Nicolson had spent half an hour, 'was convinced we could stand aside and remain neutral – an unfortunate conviction', and one Nicolson had never shared.⁹⁶ Prince Henry of Prussia had been in London and had had breakfast that morning with the King, his cousin. The Prince assured the King that Russia faced revolution if it went to war, and so probably would not. Nicolson called this 'foolish procedure' a means to persuade Britain to 'remain quiet'. The King allegedly told Prince Henry that 'we shall try all we can to keep out of this and shall remain neutral', though the Prince, recognising Britain's ties with France, had doubts about how long neutrality might last.⁹⁷

That afternoon Lichnowsky wrote to Grey to say Berlin had learned of Russia calling up several classes of reserves. 'In this case,' he continued, 'we would have to follow as it would mean a mobilisation also against us.'⁹⁸ He urged Grey to use whatever influence he had in St Petersburg to prevent such a mobilisation; and reiterated Germany's willingness to accept Grey's four-power plan for mediation. Hoping to calm things down, Nicolson told Lichnowsky that although the Imperial Ukase had been drawn up it had not been issued. Rumbold wrote from Berlin on the afternoon of 26 July to say that although German public opinion remained firm behind Austria–Hungary, the consequences of a war were sinking in, and enthusiasm for that was waning. Lichnowsky, unknown to Grey, was pleading with his masters in Berlin to avoid war.

Crowe and Nicolson were dismayed that the German ambassador to Vienna had chosen to tell the Austrians that London hoped they would take a favourable view of the Serbian reply, rather than telling them straight to moderate their behaviour. Crowe found this lack of directness 'insidious' – he blamed Jagow, who he thought had privately 'egged on the Austrians' – and hoped Grey would protest about it. Rumbold told Grey that Berlin would go no further than associating itself with Britain's sentiments.⁹⁹ Germany – to the further exasperation of Grey's officials – clung to the belief that Russia would do nothing unless Austria started to annex territory. Meanwhile, Sasonov asserted that Britain should 'proclaim her solidarity with Russia and France' against Austria.¹⁰⁰ Asquith felt Austria was 'resolved upon a complete and final humiliation.'¹⁰¹ He now felt it was 'the most dangerous situation of the last forty years.'[102] How Britain might become involved in that situation, however, remained unclear: in Paris and indeed elsewhere Bertie's line on non-intervention still held.

Buchanan telegraphed Grey late on 26 July to implore him that in any statement he made in Parliament he would state it was Austria, not Russia, that was endangering the peace. 'Russia has done her very best,' he said, 'to induce Servia to accept all Austria's demands which do not conflict with her status as an independent state or with her existing laws.'[103] He reiterated St Petersburg's belief that the 'blow struck at Servia was . . . really aimed at Russia.' Buchanan warned Grey that it was believed Britain was really on Austria's side, and the Tsar had 'expressed great disappointment' about Britain's reluctance to be more belligerent.[104] Britain's position vis-à-vis Russia was now 'a very delicate one'. Minutes later a further wire arrived from Buchanan, saying the first signs of the mobilisation were evident in St Petersburg and Moscow. That night the Admiralty, under direct guidance from Churchill, gave orders to the First and Second Fleets not to disperse from their stations, where they remained after the Spithead review.

III

In London, at last, public men and, within another day or two, the general public had no choice but to turn their attention away from Ireland and focus, as the foreign secretary and his cabinet colleagues had had to, on the European crisis, given the realisation among the political class that Britain's own security might be affected – and, even, that Britain might have to become involved. Politicians, including ministers, had used speeches over the weekend of 24–26 July to share their views with the public. Sir John Simon, the Attorney General, had told Altrincham Liberals that Britain's only role, managed by the 'cool, calm hands of Sir Edward Grey', would be that of 'mediator'.[105] Grey's own under-secretary, Francis Dyke Acland, speaking in Sussex, confirmed that Britain's influence would be expended 'in the interests of peace'. Such views, however, did not coincide with what was actually happening.

In the succeeding days, as talk of war became concrete rather than abstract, Grey not only had to make progressively more and more urgent pleas to the chancelleries of Europe. He also found himself handicapped by having to pursue a course of action in the face of colleagues from different tribes in the Liberal tradition who disagreed with him, whether pacifists or bellicose politicians such as Churchill. The Liberal idealism of men such as Simon took no account of the realities of international treaties and obligations, and nor of what had been understood, for the preceding century, to be Britain's interests in Europe – something men such as Crowe grasped well. Once the Liberal Party did start to see the consequences of such things, divisions within it would open up. Liberals would be tortured again and again throughout the following four years, as Britain moved from being a Gladstonian nation of laissez-faire and individual freedom to one of total war, in which every man and woman became a commodity to be exploited by a government fighting for the salvation of the country and its empire. That, by the end of the war, the Liberal Party had fallen apart and haemorrhaged support was a phenomenon that could be traced back to these last days of peace. Indeed, it could be traced back to long before that, to the coalition of Whigs and radicals that made up the party, and to the rise in the 1890s and 1900s of the labour movement, to whose overtly socialistic ideals many radicals felt themselves deeply attracted. Like many socialists, Liberal radicals found the idea of supporting the Tsar of all the Russias in any type of conflict deeply inimical to their principles. Also, the nonconformists who made up an important section of the party had a distaste for imperialism, as did all but a minority of the most Whiggish grandees left in the party. Grey was one of those grandees: but he had been a Liberal long enough to remember the divides over the Second Boer War, when the leader, Sir Henry Campbell-Bannerman, had been deeply opposed, his own anti-war rhetoric exceeded in vehemence only by that of David Lloyd George, whose name as a front-rank politician was largely made by it.

Once the question of Britain's role in the crisis came before the cabinet it excited deep divisions reminiscent of that earlier conflict. Tribunes of the people and leaders of public opinion started to offer their views. On 27 July C. P. Scott, editor of the *Manchester Guardian* and a totemic figure in Liberal opinion, urged the government to keep out of any war.[106] Lloyd George, the Chancellor of the Exchequer, who like almost all his colleagues was still concentrating on threats of Irish and labour unrest, had a constituency in the party that was its radical, nonconformist wing, deeply opposed to wars. He told Scott there was 'no question of our taking part in any war in the first instance.'[107] Indeed, Lloyd

George – who had argued for months for defence cuts – had said in the Commons on 23 July: 'I cannot help thinking that civilisation, which is able to deal with disputes amongst individuals and small communities at home, and is able to regulate these by means of some sane and well-ordered arbitrament, should be able to extend its operations to the larger sphere of disputes amongst States.'[108]

Of Germany he said: 'Our relations are very much better than they were a few years ago. There is none of that snarling which we used to see . . . of those two great, I will not say rival nations, but two great Empires. The feeling is better altogether between them. They begin to realise they can co-operate for common ends, and that the points of co-operation are greater and more numerous and more important than the points of possible controversy.'[109] More remarkably, given Grey's and Crowe's views, Lloyd George told Scott that he 'knew of no Minister who would be in favour of it [war]' and doubted any officials supported the idea. However, he did suggest that if the Germans attacked French Channel ports and the French sowed the waters with mines, Britain might have a problem. The Chancellor also said he believed Austria wanted war to teach Serbia a lesson, but the Germans did not want to fight. At best, this was a deeply naive view. London had by now become aware of how virulently German newspapers were, to use Crowe's phrase, 'egging on' Austria–Hungary: and the Dual Monarchy felt duly egged on, and confident of German support. Nicolson and Crowe knew where Jagow's sympathies lay, and that Lichnowsky might have been misled, or not kept entirely in the picture, about thinking in Berlin, where opinion on a war was, as in London, divided.

The Monday-morning press on 27 July was suddenly swamped by the crisis, and public awareness of the threat to peace therefore rapidly spread outside the political class. Law saw Grey each afternoon for a private update on Privy Council terms: the Unionists, who included the keenest anti-Germans, had no desire to cause difficulties, unlike the non-interventionists and pacifists in Grey's party. Law had, however, warned him that the Unionists were not united over the idea of joining in a European conflict on the side of France and against Germany. That afternoon Grey answered a question from Law in the Commons about the situation: this was the first time Parliament had discussed the European situation since it had condoled with Franz Josef about Franz Ferdinand's murder four weeks earlier. He outlined the course the government had taken, repeating what he had privately said to various ambassadors: that so long as the quarrel remained localised Britain had no right to interfere, but if Russia became involved it would develop into 'a matter that concerned us all'.[110] He mentioned his four-power initiative, but said he awaited replies. Getting this out into the open reassured the press, and calmed public opinion. Grey said it was 'obvious' that if another great power were sucked into the Austrian–Serbian quarrel 'it can but end in the greatest catastrophe that has ever befallen the continent of Europe at one blow: no one can say what would be the limit of the issues that might be raised by such a conflict, the consequences of it, direct and indirect, would be incalculable.'[111] Thus informed, the Commons spent most of the day discussing Ireland: a catastrophe in Europe seemed less immediate.

Grey had raised the technical, but crucial, point that German violation of Belgian neutrality would create 'unanimous' support for war.[112] Britain, along with France and Germany, was a guarantor of Belgium's neutrality under a treaty of 1839; yet it was still concerns about upsetting the balance of power in Europe, rather than the possibility of any act that might draw Britain in, that remained Grey's overriding concern. Germany had fought France in 1870 without violating Belgium; he at this stage seemed to assume that history would repeat itself, even if the conflict was spread more widely across the Continent. Yet Grey was increasingly clear in his own mind that Britain, and British security, could be badly affected if the clout of the Central Powers increased as the result of a European conflict. He was coming to the view – shared by senior officials such as Crowe, with their ingrained distrust of Germany, and doubtless influenced by them – that the diplomatic alliance Britain had with France and Russia meant it could not stand by as a spectator in any war they fought together. He would soon acquaint his colleagues of that view, thereby inviting them to alter the dynamic of British policy on the question.

The cabinet met that day. Viscount Morley, the Lord President of the Council and a towering moral force in liberalism, noted in a private memorandum written shortly afterwards that Grey took 'a very important line'.[113] He spoke of the Buchanan telegram about Sasonov's hopes that Britain would declare solidarity with Russia and France, who were determined to fight Austria and Germany whether Britain joined in or not. According to Morley, Grey said 'in his own quiet way' that the time had come to choose between joining in with Britain's partners in the entente, or preserving neutrality: and if the cabinet chose neutrality, he could not discharge such a policy. 'The Cabinet seemed to heave a sort of sigh,' Morley recalled, 'and a moment or two of breathless silence fell upon us.'[114] It was unclear to Morley, who understood that the foreign secretary now regarded a diplomatic intervention as pointless and only the threat of an armed one as serviceable, whether the cabinet had a collective view. If Asquith's administration were to fall it would be 'from differences within, and not from the House of Commons.'[115]

Morley told a similar story to Lord Esher, Edward VII's former *consigliere*, the following January, though the date he assigned to these events cannot be right. 'On the 25th July, Grey came down to the Cabinet,' Esher recorded, 'and said that he thought that the time had come when the French should be told if we intended to support them; there was, he added, an alternative, which was that we should say plainly that we intended to observe a policy of neutrality; this, he said, was a policy which he personally did not feel qualified to conduct.'[116] Morley indicated that he would have to resign, and according to this account Lord Beauchamp, the First Commissioner of Works; Lewis Harcourt, the colonial secretary; Simon; and John Burns, President of the Board of Trade, nodded assent. Asquith, though, showed the facility of playing for time that would, in the end, undo him. 'Upon that, the Prime Minister said that no decision could be come to at that moment and adjourned the discussion.'

C. P. Scott, after seeing Lloyd George, had talked to Percy Illingworth, the Liberal chief whip, and made a prophetic remark: that if the Liberals took Britain into war 'there would be the end of the existing Liberal combination and the next advance would have to be based on Radicalism and Labour.'[117] After the cabinet had met, the Admiralty, War Office and Press Committee – set up in 1912 as the official channel of communication between the two departments and the press – met to inform Fleet Street that there might be substantial naval and military movements, and that secrecy would be essential. Sir George Riddell, chairman of the *News of the World*, told officials that 'the Press would publish nothing detrimental if asked to be silent.'[118]

That morning *The Times* reported 'scenes of great excitement' in Paris once news spread that diplomatic relations had been ruptured between Serbia and Austria–Hungary.[119] There was 'war fever in Vienna.'[120] In case British readers were slow on the uptake, its correspondent in Paris added that 'the imminent possibility of a general European conflagration has come as a bolt from the blue to the French'.[121] For the general public, the same was true in Britain. Awareness of a possible European war had grown in the preceding days, and the idea it might involve Britain would now unleash itself. The paper noted a widespread belief in France that the crisis was the result of a 'German plot', and that the Belgian minister of war was 'taking precautionary measures' by recalling soldiers on leave.

The Times in an editorial that day asked: 'Surely the EMPEROR FRANCIS JOSEPH, who has given the world so many proofs of his devotion to peace, is not going to jeopardise the safety of his Empire and the tranquillity of Europe because Servia has not at once acceded to the whole of the very humiliating contents of the Note?' Serbia had made 'unheard-of concessions for a sovereign state', and by rejecting them Austria was putting herself very much in the wrong.[122] However, the newspaper also raised the question of possible British involvement in the European war it saw as the inevitable consequence of Austria's pig-headedness: 'Should there arise in any quarter a desire to test our adhesion to the principles that inform our friendships and that thereby guarantee the balance of power in Europe, we shall be found no less ready and determined to vindicate them with the whole strength of the Empire, than we have been found ready whenever they have been tried in the past.'

Such talk not only alerted the public to the possibilities of a war involving Britain: it also sent the London stock exchange into a precipitate fall, mimicking continental bourses. Grey returned to his office that Monday morning to learn of an Austrian mobilisation. De Bunsen, in two dispatches sent at midnight on 26 July, told him mobilisation was expected to be complete by 31 July and that a concentration of troops would be on the Serbian border by 5 August. The Russian ambassador to Vienna told de Bunsen that his country now believed Austria–Hungary 'are determined on war, and that Russia cannot possibly remain indifferent.'[123] The Russians stepped up pressure on Britain but Buchanan held the line, despite Russian insistence that Germany would only act to call Austria off if Britain publicly allied itself with France and Russia.

Crowe spelled out to Grey that Austria was mobilising; Russia would follow; Germany would then follow too and, given that its own mobilisation would be directed largely at France, France would have to follow at once. Crowe believed Austria had determined on war from the start and at whatever cost. If he was right about that – and he was certain he was – 'it would be neither possible nor just and wise to make any move to restrain Russia from mobilising.'[124] Since restraining Russia from mobilising had been the core of Grey's policy, taking this advice from his German expert would require the cabinet to agree a profound change of approach. Grey had already reached that point. Once Austria and Russia had both mobilised, it was hard to see what would restrain them, or prevent Germany and France from following.

Crowe continued: 'This however means that within 24 hours His Majesty's Government will be faced with the question whether, in a quarrel so imposed by Austria on an unwilling France, Great Britain will stand idly aside, or take sides. The question is a momentous one'. Nicolson, advising Grey on the Serbian reply, said he felt it 'practically concedes all the Austrian demands, and it is difficult to see how Austria can honestly proceed to hostile operations when Servia has yielded so much.'[125] Most of its cavils were requests for clarification. Crowe thought the reply 'reasonable' and that 'if Austria demands absolute compliance with her ultimatum it can only mean she wants a war.' Thus Grey's two senior advisers both believed that if the Austrians proceeded against Serbia they would be so in the wrong that Russia would have to mobilise, and Britain would have to choose.

Nicolson was increasingly frustrated that Germany, while professing to want peace, would not use its weight to restrain Austria. France had asked the German ambassador to Paris to urge this on his government, a request met equivocally. Nicolson too grasped that Austria wanted to supplant Russian influence in the Balkans, hence its desire for a war. On the afternoon of 27 July this was confirmed by a telegram from de Bunsen, telling Grey: 'I believe that Austria–Hungary is fully determined on war with Servia, that she believes her position as a Great Power is at stake, that her note was drawn up so as to make war inevitable, and that she is unlikely to listen to proposals for mediation until punishment has been inflicted on Serbia.'[126] He thought the Germans could do nothing, and said he wrote from a country 'wild with joy' at the prospect of war. 'The outlook is bad,' Crowe noted when he read this. 'All now depends on what line Germany may be prepared to take.'[127]

That afternoon, following the foreign secretary's statement in the

Commons, Lichnowsky told him that Germany agreed to a four-power mediation between Austria and Russia, while reserving its right as an ally to help Austria if the latter were attacked. It seems Lichnowsky sincerely believed this to be his government's view; but whether Berlin had been entirely straight with an ambassador it regarded as excessively Anglophile is far from clear, and Lichnowsky may not have appreciated the force with which the German military high command was pressing for a fight with the country's rivals, to settle once and for all who ran Europe. Lichnowsky asked Grey, on behalf of the German government, to counsel restraint to Russia. Grey, whose charitable instincts were fading, told Lichnowsky the Serbs had gone further than could have been expected in placating Austria, which he felt was the result of Russian influence in Belgrade. 'It was really at Vienna that moderating influence was now required.'[128] Grey, hardening the line, also let the Russians know that the impression some of them had that Britain would 'stand aside in any event' was wrong, and countered by the decision not to disperse the Fleet: though Grey made it clear he was at this point promising no more than diplomatic action, despite this military readiness.

Diplomatic activity in Paris had almost closed down in Poincaré's absence abroad. Now, however, the president had cancelled visits to the kings of Norway and Denmark en route from St Petersburg and was steaming for home. The acting foreign minister in Paris had seen the German ambassador, Bertie told Grey, but he had put the ball firmly in Russia's court. Bertie said the French Foreign Ministry 'look upon this as a bad sign'.[129] Crowe thought the Germans were trying to drive a wedge between Russia and France; Nicolson felt Britain would best keep out of the French activity.

That evening Grey heard that Germany had shifted its position on the desirability of a four-power mediation, saying it would amount to a court of arbitration and could not, in Jagow's opinion, happen other than at the request of Austria and Russia. Jagow had confirmed that Germany would have to mobilise if Russia did in the north; it might not do so if it mobilised in the south. It all appeared too late: Mensdorff arrived at the Foreign Office to tell Grey that 'as an act of self-defence' Austria was preparing to use force against Serbia. It felt that, in doing so, it would 'serve a European interest', given what an 'element of general unrest' Serbia had been.[130]

Mensdorff said his government felt that 'they could count on our sympathy in a fight that was forced on them, and on our assistance in localising the fight, if necessary.' Grey replied that he could not understand the constructions the Austrians had put on the Serbian reply, and had discussed the matter with Lichnowsky; Mensdorff said the reply might seem satisfactory, but in refusing cooperation with Austrian officials and police it would allow further subversion. Grey expressed amazement that Austria seemed to think it could fight Serbia without bringing in Russia; and did not see how the consequences of such a conflict would be 'incalculable' – a word used by the German government in its expression of desire for peace. While not threatening British involvement, Grey told Mensdorff that the Fleet had not dispersed, as had been planned, because of the 'anxiety' the British government felt. He considered Serbia's reply 'the greatest humiliation . . . that I have ever seen a country undergo', and was disappointed that Austria had merely treated this prostration as 'unsatisfactory as a blank negative.'

Bertie wrote privately to Grey from Paris on 27 July, saying: 'I am sure that the French Government do not want to fight and they should be encouraged to put pressure on the Russian Government not to assume the absurd and obsolete attitude of Russia being the protectress of all Slav states whatever their conduct, for this will lead to war.'[131] He added that the Paris press was reporting, erroneously, that Germany had threatened France that unless other powers kept out of the quarrel 'they would have Germany to deal with and the prospect of a general European conflagration.'[132] Grey believed Germany's refusal to talk 'decided the fate of peace or war for Europe.'[133] In 1918 he told Gilbert Murray, Oxford Regius Professor of Greek, that 'the German veto on a Conference struck out of my hand the only effective instrument I could use for peace.'[134] Even after four years of reflection, it seems not to have occurred to him that more active diplomacy on his part – leaving London not for a trout stream but for some European chancelleries, to press on his counterparts the catastrophic possibilities of a Europe-wide conflict involving all its great powers, even if he could not threaten British involvement in it – might have been an even more effective instrument.

The first shots in that conflagration were fired on the night of 27/28 July. Grey learned on 28 July that the Hungarians had captured two Serbian merchant vessels, and two Serbian steamers had been fired on. On his own initiative, Crackanthorpe urged the 'greatest prudence and moderation' on the Serbian government. However, from this point onwards every step taken seems irrevocable. Grey learned from Buchanan that Sasonov had become more 'conciliatory', but shortly afterwards received a wire from de Bunsen reporting a meeting between the Russian ambassador to Vienna and the Austrian Under-Secretary of State for Foreign Affairs.[135] The ambassador had said a conflict would be 'impossible' to localise, as Russia had given way before on such matters and would not do so again.[136] The ambassador asked for talks: but the under-secretary referred to what he described as the 'skirmish' on the Danube in which Serbian boats were damaged, though he described the Serbs as the aggressors. However, the Austrians intimated that they would empower their ambassador in St Petersburg to have direct talks with Sasonov: something Crowe welcomed as 'the first ray of hope' and Grey as 'most satisfactory'.[137]

The hope was short-lived. Grey immediately heard from Benckendorff that Sasonov, in a frank discussion in St Petersburg with the Austrian ambassador, had stupidly told him Serbia could not hope to fulfil what it had promised: a gaffe that enraged Grey, who had told the Germans the opposite. The Russians claimed a mistranslation: but in so febrile an atmosphere, with rumours swirling around the press and the governments of all Europe's capitals, it was far from helpful. Benckendorff asked Grey for Britain to support Russia and France: Grey could give no such undertaking. That was consonant with public opinion; that day the Neutrality League – the idea of Norman Angell, a former Paris editor of the *Daily Mail* who would become a Labour MP and win the Nobel Peace Prize – published a manifesto, half a million copies of which circulated, contending that for Britain to support Russia would lead to Russia dominating Europe to the detriment of Germany, a nation 'racially allied to ourselves and with moral ideals largely resembling our own.'[138]

The French government agreed to the four-power intervention; but that same afternoon the Germans formally rejected it, following Sasonov's freelancing gaffe – though Berlin claimed they still wished to pursue peace. The chances of acting in concert appeared impossible; misunderstanding and mistrust became almost wilful. Grey telegraphed to Berlin that he would drop the four-power idea if there could instead be direct talks between St Petersburg and Vienna. Crowe suggested putting Germany on the spot and asking what, instead, it thought the powers should do; Nicolson advised making no fresh proposal, and allowing talks between Vienna and St Petersburg. Early that evening

Grey told Sir Edward Goschen, the ambassador in Berlin, that he would put Crowe's question direct to Jagow, depending on progress in any talks between Russia and Austria.

That afternoon Asquith had been asked in the Commons whether he had any new information. 'There are no new developments sufficiently definite to enable any further statement to be made,' he replied.[139] Asked by Lord Hugh Cecil whether hostilities had broken out, Asquith said: 'we have no definite information about that.' He told Venetia Stanley, his would-be *inamorata*, that one at least of his colleagues wanted war: 'Winston . . . is all for this way of escape from Irish troubles.'[140] A telegram reached Grey from Crackanthorpe at 6.45 p.m. to say Austria had declared war on Serbia. Acland, Grey's under-secretary, announced this almost immediately to the Commons. Meanwhile, detachments of soldiers were posted around naval bases on the English coast as an armed guard: the Fleet was almost entirely mobilised, but at anchor.

De Bunsen had warned Berchtold, Austria's foreign minister, of the potential consequences of a conflict. Diplomatic to the last, de Bunsen emphasised that whereas the Austrians had put their quarrel with Serbia first, Britain had put the peace of Europe first. At 11 p.m. Grey heard from Buchanan that Russia would mobilise the moment Austria moved against Serbia. Lichnowsky assured Grey that his government had contacted Berthold to urge him to talk to Sasonov, and breathlessly exclaimed: 'I begin to hope that it has once more been possible owing to Anglo-German collaboration to save the peace of Europe.'[141]

Grey's officials, however, were mired in pessimism. Nicolson wrote to Buchanan about Britain's response being regarded by Russia as a 'test of our friendship', and how the Russians failed to understand that a British government had to act with regard to public opinion: which certainly did not, at that stage, favour fighting in league with the Russians against the Germans.[142] He added that 'I think we have made it perfectly clear that in any case neither Germany nor Austria could possibly rely with any certainty upon our remaining neutral', and believed the clearest sign was the order not to disperse the Fleet. He told Buchanan how the press now understood that Britain could not stay out of the impending fight: and asked him to tell St Petersburg that 'there is no doubt whatsoever that were we drawn into this conflagration we should be on the side of our friends.' By that stage that was also the private view of the foreign secretary himself.

IV

Over the next few hours it became clear that Russia would not just act, but also expected the support of her entente partners. Buchanan wired from St Petersburg to say Sasonov had emphasised that the moment the Austrians crossed the Serbian border Russia would mobilise. 'I asked,' Buchanan continued, 'whether it would not be possible in last resort for Emperor Nicholas to address personal appeal to Emperor of Austria to restrict Austria's action within limits which Russia could accept. His Excellency replied to my question by repeating that only way to avert war was for His Majesty's Government to let it be clearly known that they would join France and Russia.'[143] Ironically, the German ambassador to St Petersburg had implored Buchanan to try to calm Sasonov down: Buchanan told his *confrère* that he might be better employed advising his colleague in Vienna to do something similar to the Austrians. Buchanan told the German that 'Russia was thoroughly in earnest, and that nothing would avert general war if Austria attacked Servia.'[144] That he did this suggests the German diplomatic service believed Russia was still not serious.

Soon there was no doubt: by the time Nicolson read Buchanan's dispatch on 29 July, word had reached London that Russia was mobilising in its southern regions. This seemed another dangerous, irrevocable step. In Berlin the previous afternoon Goschen had called, at the Chancellor's invitation, on Bethmann, who assured him Germany was doing all it could to get Russia and Austria to parley. He maintained that the quarrel between Austria and Serbia was none of Russia's business; and he, having heard also that Russia had mobilised fourteen army corps in the south, wondered how far he would get preaching moderation to Austria. 'This decision rested with Russia and Russia alone,' Goschen reported Bethmann as saying; he emphasised 'his desire to co-operate with England and his intention to do his utmost to maintain general peace.'[145] His final words to Goschen were: 'A war between the Great Powers must be avoided.'

Nicolson observed: 'There have certainly been no indications that Germany has exercised any moderating influence at Vienna. It is going rather far to put the responsibility on Russia, who has been willing to adopt any and every course likely to lead to peace. I suppose Germany wishes Russia to join with the other Powers in keeping the ring while

Austria strangles Servia.'[146] Grey recalled that on reading this dispatch 'I felt really angry with von Bethmann Hollweg and von Jagow.'[147] He thought Berlin had taken a casual view of Vienna's behaviour: 'The complacency with which they had let Austria launch the ultimatum on Serbia was deplorable.' He also believed Berlin had blocked the proposed conference, which he regarded as 'still worse'. He did not, of course, know about the 'blank cheque', which would have explained everything.

When formal word arrived from Vienna of the declaration of war, early on 29 July, Crowe and Nicolson advised Grey not to issue the usual declaration of neutrality. Nicolson observed: 'I ask myself what is the use of exchanging views at this juncture . . . I am of the opinion that the resources of diplomacy are, for the present, exhausted . . . Appeals either to Austria or Russia to alter their course would be futile and would lead to misunderstandings.' By lunchtime London had heard that shots were being fired in Belgrade; and Russia was mobilising, but had made a point of informing the German government of '*l'absence en Russie de toute intention agressive contre l'Allemagne.*'[148]

Matters had become sufficiently serious that the Americans offered their good offices. The King cancelled a trip to Goodwood, and it was reported that his plans to go to Cowes the following week, and to shoot grouse the week after, were on hold. A massive sell-off occurred on the stock exchange: it would close on 31 July and would not reopen until 4 January 1915. *The Times* declared that 'the peace of Europe would at first sight seem to hang by a thread.'[149] Although the Austrian ultimatum should have alerted the British people adequately to the growing dangers of conflict, it was only now that the question began to dominate the British press, drawing the public irresistibly in as the country contemplated the possibility not just of a war, but of a war in which Britain was not simply a spectator. The cabinet met before lunch and decided to put into force the precautionary measures outlined in the War Book, the manual – fortunately, updated only a month earlier – specifying the plan departments must implement during a national emergency. This included a call-up of the Territorial Army's Special Service Section for guard duties, a signal, to the public and to other powers, of the start of British mobilisation. That afternoon the General Officer Commanding at Aldershot, Sir Douglas Haig, like other GOCs, received a telegram from the War Office ordering him to adopt 'Precautionary Measures' prior to full mobilisation.[150]

A new consideration, which would prove fundamental, and which Law had already brought up with Grey, then arose. Sir Francis Villiers, the British minister in Brussels, telegraphed Grey late on 28 July to tell him that the Belgian government had discussed 'the various eventualities' that might arise 'and that they have determined to offer resistance to the utmost of their power should the integrity or neutrality of Belgium be assailed from any quarter.'[151] In 1870 Britain had told both parties in the Franco-Prussian War that it would not tolerate such a violation of sovereignty, and Gladstone's warning had been sufficient. Belgium did not at that stage expect that either France or Germany would breach its neutrality, but wanted to be prepared. There seemed no reason why history would not repeat itself.[152] Preparations were under way to mobilise 150,000 men.

Underpinning discussions Britain and France had had since 1906 about military cooperation had been the understanding that France would never invade Belgium; and if Germany did there would be a combined Anglo-French effort to expel it.[153] For a few more days yet, the entente powers continued to believe that the diplomatic conventions would be observed, in blissful ignorance of just how far German military thinking had changed since 1870–71. The construction of fortresses in eastern France, notably at Verdun, had forced Germany to come up with a different plan for attacking France from that used in the earlier war, when after countering a French attack they had entered through Lorraine. In accordance with the latest version of the plan drawn up in 1905–06 by Count Alfred von Schlieffen, Chief of the Imperial German Army General Staff, Germany now intended to attack France through Belgium.

The Schlieffen Plan entailed enormous risks for the Germans. First came the political calculation that Britain would not defend Belgian neutrality; second, a military one that France would have been defeated, with the Germans in Paris, by the time Britain could mobilise an expeditionary force to send to the Continent: firepower had increased exponentially since 1870–71 and Germany hoped it could blast its way to Paris (as it would in 1940). The War Office and the Foreign Office knew nothing about the Schlieffen Plan, but French intelligence, which as early as 1907 had had sight of German mobilisation plans, knew it was intended to devote most of Germany's military might in attacks to the west. That such a move was now a central part of German strategy should have emphasised to Britain and France just how hawkish their potential enemy now was. The strategy was also emblematic of divisions in Berlin between the Kaiser's aggressive military advisers and the more measured civilian ones, led by Bethmann Hollweg, who had only learned about the Schlieffen Plan in 1912.

On the afternoon of 29 July Lichnowsky visited Grey to assure him Bethmann was 'endeavouring to mediate between Vienna and St Petersburg, and he hopes with good success.'[154] Grey emphasised that the best possible solution would be an agreement directly between Russia and Austria; but told the German ambassador he understood the Austrians had rejected the Russian suggestion that their ambassador to St Petersburg should have such a discussion with Sasonov. He put the onus on Germany to sort this out, telling Lichnowsky that 'mediation was ready to come into operation by any method that Germany thought possible if only Germany would "press the button" in the interests of peace.'[155] Grey was pessimistic: he deduced it had become a question of the Kaiser's popularity, and for Germany to urge Austria to back down would risk his looking weak.

But Grey also realised that with France increasingly likely to be drawn into the conflict, Britain would soon have to decide whether or not it joined them in any fight, irrespective of what happened to Belgium. On 25 July he had attended a dinner given by Lord Haldane and his sister. Haldane was the Lord Chancellor who, as war secretary, had undertaken the Army reforms of 1908 that included the design of a British Expeditionary Force and the establishment of the Territorial Army. He and his sister had invited Grey, and Morley, to dinner with Albert Ballin, the Anglophile German shipping magnate. Haldane recalled that Grey and he told Ballin that the maintenance of good relations with Germany 'was dependent on Germany not attacking France.'[156] This shows how early on Grey had decided Britain should fight if France were attacked. Ballin, whose commercial interests would be imperilled if war broke out, was strongly against fighting; he committed suicide in 1918 on hearing of the Kaiser's abdication.

Poincaré returned to Paris on 29 July to find few signs among the public of desire for a war against Germany. Some saw it as an opportunity to recover Alsace and Lorraine, annexed by Germany after the Franco-Prussian War, but they were very much a minority. During the afternoon Grey saw Cambon and they agreed on the seriousness of the situation. Grey assured him he had just told Lichnowsky that Germany should not interpret the friendliness of Grey's dealings with him as a sign Britain would not go to war: Britain would do whatever British interests dictated. Grey recalled that these interviews were 'distressing' to both him and Cambon, mainly because Grey could not say to Cambon what he had intimated off the record to Lichnowsky, that Britain could not sit by and watch a German attack on France.[157] Grey stressed to Cambon, as he had to Lichnowsky, that if Germany and France entered the conflict that would change considerations for Britain. Cambon said he 'anticipated a demand from Germany that France would be neutral while Germany attacked Russia. This assurance France, of course, could not give; she was bound to help Russia if Russia was attacked.'[158] No such promise bound Britain.

That afternoon Asquith told the Commons – which listened in silence – that the situation was one of 'extreme gravity', and the government was doing all it could to prevent conflict.[159] Lloyd George, who knew very little about finance and trade, despite having been chancellor for six years, sought to calm anxieties by refusing to convene a meeting of bankers to address the financial uncertainties, saying nothing at present necessitated it. He quickly enlisted his friend Lord Reading, luckily on his long vacation as Lord Chief Justice, to advise him on these matters, in which Reading was an expert.

Meanwhile, the Paris correspondent of *The Times* reported that gold had 'disappeared' from circulation there, a warning to Britain of what might happen if the situation deteriorated further.[160] The Admiralty withdrew destroyers patrolling the Irish coast to prevent gun-running, and the First Fleet sailed from Portland into the Channel. Every movement of troops, or recall of a soldier from leave, fed the rumour mill. All government departments, and the Armed Forces, were put in a state of readiness for a 'precautionary period'. Asquith told Miss Stanley: 'Of course we want to keep out of it, but the worst thing we could do would be to announce to the world at the present moment that in *no circumstances* would we intervene.'[161]

That evening Goschen reported further discussions with Bethmann, mainly the Chancellor's protestations that he had urged his Austrian allies to confirm that their attack on Serbia was purely to enforce their ultimatum, not to exact territorial gains: but had had no reply from Vienna. Bethmann asked Goschen to impress upon Grey 'that he was sincerely doing all in his power to prevent danger of European complications.'¹⁶² Indeed, Bethmann felt he had gone so far that he implored Goschen to insist to Grey that his intervention be mentioned to no other power: Bethmann had not even told Lichnowsky. Bethmann and others were trying to restrain the bellicose instincts of the German army, which wanted to assert German might in Europe, and feared it might lose an opportunity to do so. Crowe, who noted a disclosure that the Kaiser and the Tsar had exchanged telegrams, dismissed Bethmann's views. Nicolson remarked that 'I do not think that Berlin quite understands that Russia cannot and will not stand quietly by while Austria administers a severe chastisement to Servia.'

Buchanan reported that his French colleague in St Petersburg had reassured the German ambassador that no military preparation France was making was against Germany: all France had done was recall officers on leave, as Germany had. Buchanan later confirmed the Russian mobilisation, reporting that Austria had refused the invitation of direct talks with Russia. Grey saw Mensdorff, but refused to discuss the merits of Austria's case against the Serbs, emphasising Britain's displeasure at events. For the moment, there was nothing Grey could do: he waited while Bethmann tried to broker some sort of discussion between Russia and Austria, which Lichnowsky had said was the plan.

Asquith found Grey after dinner on 29 July, in the Foreign Office talking with Haldane; and the three discussed the situation until one o'clock in the morning, looking for the 'miracle' that might avert war.¹⁶³ Haldane was noted for his intellect, based not least on his knowledge of German literature and philosophy; he was also alleged to have called Germany his spiritual home, but in fact had referred to that place as being a classroom at Göttingen, where he had studied; and he owned a dog named Kaiser. In the fevered times that were approaching, these interests would have consequences.

That night, as the three key figures in the British government shared their fears for the future, the Austrians shelled Belgrade. In Berlin, Bethmann sent for Goschen and made what the ambassador called a 'strong bid' for British neutrality.¹⁶⁴ The Chancellor recognised it was 'evident' that Britain would never allow France to be 'crushed', but 'such a result was not contemplated by Germany'. It would be 'to his great regret' that Germany's obligations to Austria might 'render a European conflagration inevitable', but Germany sought 'no territorial acquisitions at the expense of France,' although it did not commit itself to avoiding acquiring French colonies. Grey said that if Germany took France's colonies it would end France's status as a great power, and could not be tolerated; and that 'for us to make this bargain with Germany at the expense of France would be a disgrace from which the good name of this country would never recover.' That, of course, was now not the only issue: an attack on France such as Bethmann had hinted at would bring the Belgian question into play. 'The Chancellor also in effect asks us to bargain away whatever obligation or interest we have as regards the neutrality of Belgium. We could not entertain that bargain either.' Britain had to retain 'full freedom to act as circumstances may seem to us to require'; and, having consulted Asquith, he asked Goschen to relay to Berlin that the best way to maintain good relations between their two countries was to work together for European peace.

That telegram crossed with one from Goschen saying that the Germans had had no reply from Vienna; and Goschen reported that Jagow had 'begged' him 'to impress on you difficulty of position to Germany in view of Russian mobilisation and military measures which he hears are being taken in France'.[165] De Bunsen wired from Vienna a little later to say it was understood there that the Germans had spoken strongly to Austria about the dangers of their conduct sparking a European war; the problem was, de Bunsen added, that the German ambassador to Vienna was so deeply identified with anti-Serbian and anti-Russian sentiment that he could not be relied upon to do all he might to talk Austria out of its belligerence.

Bethmann promised to respect the neutrality of Holland: but was less categorical about Belgium. 'His excellency could not tell to what operations Germany might be forced by the action of France, but he could state that, provided that Belgium did not take sides against Germany, her integrity would be respected after the conclusion of the war.'[166] The implications of these remarks outraged London. Grey read the telegram with 'despair', because it seemed Bethmann was now resigned to war; and he should have seen he was offering Britain a dishonourable way out.[167] Goschen reported from Berlin that Bethmann had been visibly stunned by Grey's response to his suggestion of neutrality, and had asked for time to reflect upon it. Crowe noted that 'the only comment that need be made on these astounding proposals is that they reflect discredit on the statesman who makes them.' He realised that 'Germany practically admits the intention to violate Belgian neutrality but to endeavour to respect that of Holland (in order to safeguard German imports via the Rhine and Rotterdam). It is clear that Germany is practically determined to go to war, and that the one restraining influence so far has been the fear of England joining in the defence of France and Belgium.'[168]

The endgame, as Crowe realised, was now under way. In its editorial of 30 July, *The Times* said the government's efforts to limit the conflict represented 'a task which it may exceed all the wisdom of diplomacy to accomplish,' and warned again that, if necessary, Britain would fight and win – notably if Belgian neutrality were threatened.[169] This was not a view any minister was then keen to express in private, let alone in public, and it was the first time the prospect had been put before the public. *The Times* was exceptionally well briefed. The crisis was now greater than any in Britain since the Napoleonic Wars.

The Consul General in Hamburg reported that morning that along Germany's North Sea coast, forts were being manned and submarine defences installed, a sign Crowe and Nicolson interpreted as an expectation of Germany's having to fight Britain. Grey told Goschen: 'You must inform German Chancellor that his proposal that we should bind ourselves to neutrality on such terms cannot for a moment be entertained.'[170] Grey learned from Cambon that the German ambassador in Paris had told his Russian counterpart that if Russia did not stop making military preparations, Germany would mobilise. De Bunsen told Grey the same morning that Vienna had only just 'tardily realised' Russia was serious.[171]

Later, Goschen reported that the British military attaché in Berlin had been alerted to substantial German troop movements to the country's eastern and western borders and believed mobilisation was 'imminent'.[172] Consular staff from Hamburg and Dresden made similar reports, which Crowe regarded as 'ominous'.[173] Earlier, Grey had made a brief appearance in the Commons, to answer a question from Law. 'There is very little I can say,' he told the Leader of the Opposition, and repeated what most MPs had read in the papers, about the Austrians moving against Serbia, and Russia ordering a partial mobilisation. He assured Law the diplomatic community was keeping in touch, 'though it has not been possible for the powers to unite in joint diplomatic action as was proposed on Monday.'[174]

Law and Sir Edward Carson, leader of the Irish Unionists, invited

Asquith to see them. They told him that to maximise British influence for peace they and their followers would put into abeyance their differences with the government over the Bill that would amend the Home Rule Act. John Redmond, the Nationalist leader, whom Asquith saw afterwards, agreed that, provided the Act went on the statute book at once, he would agree to its not being operative until the Amending Bill became law. This was a relief to the prime minister, but was the only sign of light. He recorded in his diary: 'The City, which is in a terrible state of depression and paralysis, is for the time being all against English intervention. The prospect is very black.'[175]

Bertie wired Grey during the evening. Poincaré had told him the Germans had threatened to mobilise unless Russia stopped. He asked Bertie whether Britain would now promise to help France if conflict arose between her and Germany, for he felt such an announcement would cause Germany to 'modify her attitude'.[176] Bertie said that for the moment such an announcement would be 'difficult': Poincaré insisted that it would be in the interests of peace, and emphasised that France did not desire war. But he also felt that if war came Britain would be sucked in, and therefore should avert war by promising to fight with France now.

On 29 July the cabinet – recalling Gladstone's policy in 1870 – discussed the neutrality of Belgium for the first time, so the stakes were no longer in doubt: but, being still at that point theoretical, it was not deemed so important an issue as how to interpret the entente with France, which the French themselves were now adducing as a reason for Britain to support any military action they might feel minded to take in concert with the Russians. Crowe believed a British promise of solidarity would only encourage France and Russia to fight the Teutons. However, he also believed that if French and Russian participation occurred without any British encouragement, then Britain should stand by them as allies, and the decision to intervene should be immediate and unequivocal. Cambon was pressing Grey, reminding him that two years earlier they had agreed 'that, if the peace of Europe was seriously threatened, we would discuss what we were prepared to do.'[177] He was not seeking a commitment, but wished to discuss with Grey what Britain would do in certain eventualities, such as an attack on France by Germany. Grey said the cabinet was meeting the following morning, and would discuss this. Cambon stressed that France could not remain neutral in a war between Germany and Russia. Grey realised France needed to know how Britain

proposed to act in those circumstances: but, with the cabinet divided
and Britain under no obligation similar to France's understanding with
Russia under the terms of the Triple Entente, he could do nothing.

Bertie advised Grey that in Paris 'the feeling . . . is that peace between
the Powers depends on England . . . for Germany will not face the danger to her of her supplies by sea being cut off by the British Fleet at a time
when she could not get them from Russia and France and little from
Austria'.[178] He said the press, but not the people, were becoming bellicose; he criticised the French government for not urging Russia to pull
back, and agreed with London that a British show of support would
simply encourage the Russians. The Paris bourse was virtually closed
and the banks were refusing to issue coin in return for notes. Britain's
military attaché in Paris had discovered that all the necessary prelim-
inaries for a general mobilisation had been carried out.

By 31 July, a Friday, continental bourses had closed, and London
joined them. Despite Lloyd George's attempts to instil calm, panic pervaded the City, with business at a standstill. People had been 'flocking'
to the Bank of England the previous day 'to change notes for gold,' a discount house reported.[179] The Bank raised its discount rate from 4 per
cent to 8 per cent, to defend its supply of gold, and announced that it
'contemplated' an issue of £1 banknotes because of the hoarding of gold
sovereigns.[180] The next day the rate would reach 10 per cent. When customers demanded gold from clearing banks they were given notes and
told to take them to the Bank of England, resulting in hundreds queuing
around Threadneedle Street. This provoked Walter Cunliffe, the charm-
free governor of the Bank, to visit Lloyd George after lunch on 31 July to
complain about the joint-stock banks 'acting against and not with the
Bank of England' in encouraging people to deplete the gold reserves.
Cunliffe wanted the government to order the suspension of cash payments, but the Treasury refused: the Bank's reserves were down to £17
million, and it was agreed a loss of another £5 million would be the 'tip-
ping point'.[181]

That morning *The Times* declared that 'the instinct of self-preservation,
which is the strongest factor in national life . . . compels us . . . to be
ready to strike with all our force for our own safety and that of our
friends': it feared a German push to capture the Channel ports in France
and Belgium, 'which might then become German naval bases against
England.'[182] It said that even an occupation of Belgium and northern

France without control of the ports would threaten national security, and the enormous Army and Navy Britain would need to defend herself would crush the economy. However, the main travel agencies reported that their business was 'not much affected', and tours planned for the following week to France, Belgium, Germany, Italy and Switzerland were proceeding as planned.[183] The Neutrality League put up 10,000 posters around England and had 362 men on London's streets with sandwich boards: the feeling against war remained strong.[184]

The cabinet, now acutely alert to the possibility of a German infringement of Belgian sovereignty, following Goschen's report of his meeting with Bethmann and their exchange about British neutrality, met at 11 a.m. It discussed Belgium again, and agreed that everything hinged on whether its neutrality was respected. Morley noted how two factions – quite open, with no element of intrigue – were now operating for and against a military intervention. Grey had declared himself; Churchill was spoiling for a fight, whereas Harcourt was organising opinion in favour of neutrality. Asquith, in Morley's feline phrase, was 'seeing and waiting'.[185] Lloyd George had reported that financiers and industrialists to whom he had spoken were 'aghast' at the prospect of Britain joining a European conflict, because it would wreck London's place as the centre of the international system of credit.[186] When he eventually came out as pro-war, and Morley reminded him of this, he replied that he had never believed those sentiments, but had merely reported them. Morley also aired his fears about how things would be if Russia were to win such a war as a result of Britain fighting Germany. 'Will that be good for Western civilisation? I at least don't think so . . . Germany is unpopular in England, but Russia is more unpopular still.'[187] He added: 'Lloyd George told me after that he had never thought of all that.' By now Morley and John Burns had made common cause, with an unspoken understanding that neither would stay in a cabinet committed to war.

It was now, indeed, Russia that was making the running. Bethmann, so Goschen reported, had heard that Russia had effectively closed its frontier with Germany, and evacuated people and money into the interior. Crowe interpreted this as an attempt to blame Russia for any ensuing catastrophe, and Nicolson felt the Russians were simply taking sensible precautions. Cambon told Grey that Germany was mobilising unannounced: he believed Germany wanted France to announce its mobilisation first and thus appear the aggressor.

Grey told Lichnowsky that if Russia and France rejected any reasonable proposal that Germany could broker with Austria, Britain would wash its hands of the matter. Otherwise, he warned him that if France were drawn in so would Britain be. That afternoon the German embassy informed the Foreign Office that unless Russia withdrew its general mobilisation within twelve hours, 'Germany would be obliged to mobilise in her own defence.'[188] This would happen on both the Russian and French frontiers. Grey – in what he called 'a diplomatic step that contemplated the contingency of war' – asked the French and German governments separately whether each was prepared to respect Belgian neutrality, provided no other power violated it.[189] He also sought from Brussels confirmation that Belgium would 'to the utmost of her power maintain neutrality and desire and expect other Powers to observe and uphold it.'[190]

Until a treaty obligation was invoked, Britain's official position would not change. Grey said a refusal to observe neutrality would make it 'extremely difficult to restrain public feeling'.[191] Just as the Commons was rising that Friday, at 5 p.m. Asquith – who had just been to Buckingham Palace to brief the King and discuss a 'depressing' telegram the Sovereign had had from the Kaiser attacking the 'perfidy' of the Tsar – made a short statement to confirm that the Foreign Office had heard (from Germany, he emphasised, and not from Russia) 'that Russia has proclaimed a general mobilisation of her Army and Fleet, and that in consequence of this, martial law was to be proclaimed in Germany. We understand this to mean that mobilisation will follow in Germany.'[192] He declined to answer any questions until Monday: events would, however, move faster than he imagined.

Grey and his advisers now saw war approaching: the foreign secretary felt Germany had 'precipitated war'.[193] In fact, it was the Russian mobilisation that had made it impossible for Germany to stand aside: which may have been how Germany had wanted it. Bertie told Grey late on 31 July that The Times's correspondent in Paris had been summoned by the French Foreign Ministry and briefed on German troop movements, and how these exceeded anything France had done. The correspondent assumed France wanted British public opinion softened up before a British mobilisation. The French formally asked Grey what Britain's attitude would be if Germany mobilised. Bertie said the German ambassador to Paris was calling on the French foreign minister at 1 p.m. on Saturday 1 August to receive France's response, and had intimated he would require his passports.

Opinions hardened further in London with news that the Germans had appropriated French trains that were just over their frontier and had torn up lines going into France. Crowe felt Germany 'is throwing dust into our eyes for the purpose of delaying if not hindering . . . British preparations'; and Nicolson that 'Germany has been playing with us for the past few days.'[194]

Grey told Cambon it was 'quite wrong to suppose that we had left Germany under the impression that we would not intervene. I had refused overtures to promise that we should remain neutral.' But he admitted that the cabinet, when it had met earlier, had concluded it was still not in a position to make a pledge. 'The commercial and financial situation was exceedingly serious; there was danger of complete collapse that would involve us and everybody else in ruin.'[195] He warned Cambon that British neutrality might be the only means of preventing a Europe-wide collapse of credit, which is why that position was reserved. Grey, taking a line agreed with Asquith and the cabinet, stressed Parliament would have to be consulted, and public opinion gauged: and noted how 'the preservation of Belgian neutrality might be, I would not say a decisive, but an important factor, in determining our attitude.'[196] Cambon registered 'great disappointment', the greater when Grey still could not promise support for France if Germany attacked her. He asked Grey to resubmit his question to a meeting of the cabinet; Grey could only reply that the cabinet would meet again after further developments.

Asquith and Lloyd George managed that evening to reassure the directors of the Bank of England about the financial situation; and then Asquith dined with Edwin Montagu, under-secretary for India, and Grey: but after dinner Asquith heard from Berlin 'that the German Emperor's efforts for peace had been suddenly arrested and frustrated by the Tsar's decree for a complete Russian mobilisation.'[197] The Foreign Office had confirmation from the German embassy at midnight on 31 July that the Tsar had asked the Kaiser to mediate between Austria–Hungary and Russia. The Kaiser had immediately agreed and had spoken to Vienna, only to learn of the Russian mobilisation, 'whereupon the Emperor at once informed the Tsar that such action rendered his mediation illusory'.[198] The Kaiser asked Tsar Nicholas to stop his own mobilisation; the Tsar refused. The German mediation had continued nonetheless, and on the lines suggested by Grey, but the announcement of the mobilisation of the whole Russian army and fleet made any

constructive answer 'impossible'. That, according to the message from
the embassy, was why Germany had issued the twelve-hour ultimatum
to Russia, and had asked France where it stood.

Cambon sought, and received, an audience of the King just before
midnight on 31 July; but the King could act only on the advice of his ministers, and could say nothing to Cambon different from what Grey had
already told him. Asquith hailed a taxi and followed him to the Palace at
1.30 a.m., with a draft of a personal message from the King to the Tsar.
'The King was hauled out of his bed, and one of my strangest experiences was sitting with him, clad in a dressing-gown, while I read the
message and the proposed answer.'[199] London also learned that the Belgian army had mobilised, and railway communications between
Belgium and Germany had ceased. The question of the 1839 Treaty of
London, and its guarantees of Belgian neutrality, were becoming less
theoretical by the hour.

Bertie told Grey that the German embassy in Paris was packing up
and that the French government had reiterated its request to Britain on
where it stood should Germany attack. The French also answered Grey's
question about Belgian neutrality, which they promised to respect: no
reply came from Berlin until 3.30 a.m. on 1 August, in which Goschen
reported Jagow saying he must consult the Kaiser and Bethmann before
answering; Goschen asked him to do so quickly. Jagow responded that
Belgium had 'already committed certain acts which he could only
qualify as hostile', and cited an embargo on a grain shipment destined
for Germany as an act of provocation.[200] He then admitted it was
'unlikely' he could give an answer.

Grey, having been briefed by Cambon and Bertie, told Lichnowsky
that France proposed to observe Belgian neutrality. In the early hours
of 1 August the Foreign Office sent the personal message from the King
to the Tsar, urging him to talk to Austria again and halt his war preparations: the King said this was vital 'to secure the peace of the world'.[201]
The message was copied to Paris and shown to Poincaré, to reassure
him. In the early hours of 1 August the Foreign Office heard from Goschen that Jagow felt he could do nothing further until he heard from
Russia; and since he conceded the message Germany had sent Russia
was *de facto* an ultimatum, the chances of a constructive reply were
unpromising. Goschen reported that the demands to Russia had been
printed in the Berlin evening papers, 'and large crowds are parading the

streets singing patriotic songs.'[202] Britain's man in Brussels, Sir Francis Villiers, reported that not only would Belgium fight to defend its neutrality, it also expected other powers to support it. The Belgian foreign minister separately had a message delivered to the Foreign Office about the importance of the treaty of 1839; by that stage, such a reminder was unnecessary.

Nicolson had told Grey late on 31 July that it was 'essential' for Britain to give the order to mobilise.[203] 'It is useless,' he told the foreign secretary, 'to shut our eyes to the fact that possibly within the next twenty-four hours Germany will be moving across the French frontier'. He believed public opinion would rapidly shift in favour of France in those circumstances. Grey agreed, and said the matter would be considered the following morning: the cabinet had been summoned for 11 a.m. Crowe was even more incendiary, sending Grey a private memorandum that evening, which he invited Grey to disregard if he thought it 'worthless'.

'The theory that England cannot engage in a big war means her abdication as an independent state,' he began. 'She can be brought to her knees and made to obey the behests of any Power or group of Powers who *can* go to war, of whom there are several.'[204] He argued that such an attitude negated the point of an army and navy at an 'enormous annual cost'; the principle of force as a last resort on which British foreign policy stood would be exposed as 'an empty futility'; the balance of power could not be maintained by a state incapable of fighting. He warned Grey not to be deceived by 'commercial panic', the prelude to all conflict. He blamed the City panic on the behaviour of German financial houses, as part of that country's war preparations to destabilise others. Grey had, rightly in Crowe's view, dismissed the German proposal for Britain to remain neutral as 'dishonourable'. Refusing to fight for France would, however, be just that.

Crowe called the *entente cordiale* 'a moral bond', even if it was no treaty.[205] To repudiate it would cost Britain its name, and to endorse the idea that Britain could not go to war would be 'political suicide'. The French question was one of right or wrong first, political expediency second. 'I feel confident that our duty and our interest will be seen to lie in standing by France in her hour of need,' he concluded. The official collection of documents, which reproduces the memo in full, says it 'was written under the stress of intense emotion; he believed that decisions were being made which would hazard the whole future of the country and a policy was being considered which would irreparably destroy its reputation.'[206] Grey agreed with Crowe, but pending cabinet endorsement could not immediately act in accordance with the advice.

The Times echoed Crowe's line on 1 August, though praised the 'cool heads' in Germany trying 'to prevent the outbreak of a devastating war which will bring into collision Powers which have no good cause of quarrel, and are, on the contrary, knit together by many ties of interest.'[207] *The Times*'s editorials remained bellicose – its proprietor, Lord Northcliffe, had longed for a fight with Germany for years – and that morning it warned its readers that a war 'may even threaten our national existence'.[208] The King, receiving a constant stream of Foreign Office telegrams, decided there was practically 'no chance of peace'.[209] The government took further precautionary measures: not only were dockyards, magazines and other stores given garrisons, but guards were placed on strategic communications such as railway junctions, signal boxes, bridges and tunnels. Military and civilian dockyards and shipyards were guarded, and entry to Portsmouth, Devonport, Sheerness and other important naval areas restricted. Word arrived from Canada, Australia and New Zealand that those countries were ready to send expeditionary forces to Europe to defend the mother country. The imperial family meant any conflict would have a global aspect.

Grey had a political as well as a diplomatic problem. He warned Asquith before the cabinet that morning that if 'an out-and-out and uncompromising policy of non-intervention at all costs is adopted' he would resign.[210] As he recalled, 'outside the Cabinet I felt sure that the anti-war group were meeting, were arranging concerted action, if need be, to keep this country out of war or to resign if they failed in doing so.'[211] He knew the group included some of the most influential Liberals, 'sufficient in number to have broken up the Cabinet.' Hence he proceeded with the caution Crowe found so frustrating. Also, Grey made no attempt to change the minds of those who did not think like him: if war came, he wanted it prosecuted with unanimity: he didn't want anyone 'manoeuvred' into it. He knew the pledge to support France that he would have liked would not be forthcoming, and that it might bring the government down to try to procure it. He also sensed that while some wanted to take on Germany because of a hatred of Prussian militarism – perhaps he had Northcliffe in mind – most Britons wanted peace. Industry, he knew, especially did not want war, because trade was good. There was some pro-French feeling: few gave a damn about Serbia. Asquith resolved that if Grey went he would resign too. Yet he felt only Morley, and possibly Simon, would object to intervention if Belgium were invaded.

However, it would not come to that. In his memoirs, Grey said the mood of the 'anti-war group' in the cabinet changed by 1 August.[212] He attributed this to colleagues thinking about the consequences if war broke out; and, as they did, 'the more uneasy they became at the prospect of Britain sitting still and immoveable, while great events fraught with incalculable consequences were happening at her very doors.' The idea of the German fleet steaming down the Channel, bombarding France within sight of the English coast, was, he felt, what hardened opinion behind him. 'My recollection of those three days, August 1, 2 and 3, is of almost continuous cabinets and of immense strain,' he wrote in 1925.[213]

Disturbing news continued to flow in from the embassies around Europe. The German embassy in London repudiated the Tsar's claim that the mobilisation of Russian troops had no aggressive intent. The Germans saw it as 'a threat to our very existence' and 'a provocation . . . so strong that no German nor any foreigner would understand it if we failed to answer with strong measures.'[214] That afternoon Grey heard from Bertie that Poincaré had said a French mobilisation was 'necessary for self defence', but troops were being ordered not to go within 10 kilometres of the German frontier, to avoid accusations of provocation.[215] Then Grey heard from St Petersburg that the Austrians and Russians were willing to talk. He now placed his hopes on such talks buying some time, notifying all six main powers that London would host them.

V

On the morning of 1 August the cabinet, having met almost daily for the preceding week, discussed the crisis for two and a half hours – 'it is no exaggeration to say that Winston occupied at least half of the time,' Asquith told Miss Stanley.[216] It did so against the background of the rise in bank rate to 10 per cent, as the Bank of England reserves fell almost £6 million in the day to £11 million. Cunliffe obtained Lloyd George's permission to suspend the Bank Charter Act, which restricted the supply of new banknotes: but these were not measures Cunliffe wished to take unless necessary. It was the highest interest rate since 1866, when the bank of Overend, Gurney & Co. failed, but neglected to draw in gold deposits from abroad, deepening the crisis.

The cabinet discussion was mainly about Belgium, and Asquith thought the meeting ended in an 'amicable' atmosphere, though told Miss Stanley he felt a split was inevitable. That morning H. A. Gwynne, editor of the *Morning Post*, wrote to Sir William Tyrrell, Grey's private secretary, to assert that '80% are behind him', giving Grey 'enormous personal power' with which he should 'force his views on the Cabinet and the country.'[217] Grey was not yet ready to do that. The meeting was interrupted regularly by the arrival of dispatches, and after it Lloyd George convened a separate meeting at the Treasury with ministerial colleagues, senior bankers and financiers. The next day it was announced that the payment of certain bills of exchange had been suspended, and those with bank accounts were advised to pay bills by cheque to avoid shortages in the supply of ready money. It was decided that the banks, closed for the August bank holiday on Monday, would remain shut until Friday. *The Times* branded those hoarding gold against a serious crisis 'wicked'.[218]

The cabinet had decided it could not yet propose to send an expeditionary force to the Continent. Grey explained this to Cambon. Germany had agreed not to attack France if France remained neutral; and if it could not, 'it was because she was bound by an alliance to which we were not parties, and of which we did not know the terms. This did not mean that under no circumstances would we assist France, but it did mean that France must take her own decision at this moment without reckoning on an assistance that we were not now in a position to promise.'[219] Cambon could not bring himself to convey this message to his government. He had seen Nicolson and reminded him of the post-entente understanding that the French navy would lie in the Mediterranean, with the country's northern and western shores safeguarded by the Royal Navy. He now told Grey that 'the French coasts were undefended' and that 'the German fleet might come through the Straits any day and attack them.'

Grey, seeing Cambon's distress, told him such a move 'might alter public feeling here, and so might a violation of the neutrality of Belgium.' He told the ambassador to report that the cabinet was considering the Belgian problem, and he would ensure it discussed the naval contingency. Grey immediately consulted Asquith, stressing the urgency of the undertaking's being confirmed, or otherwise, within twenty-four hours. Cambon had argued that although Britain was under no treaty obligation to fight for France, long-term interests might force it to do so. By refusing to support France the entente would 'disappear', and, whoever won the war, Britain's position after it would be 'very uncomfortable'.[220]

Bertie wired that orders for the general mobilisation of the French army had been issued that afternoon at 3.40 p.m., because of a call-up of German reservists. The French had counted eight German army corps on the frontier with France, and expected an attack 'at any moment'.[221] Grey warned Lichnowsky that Germany's cavalier view of Belgian integrity would affect public opinion; prompting the ambassador to ask whether Britain would remain neutral if Germany promised not to violate Belgian neutrality. Grey refused to say that, but emphasised the terrible effect an invasion of Belgium would have on British feeling. Pressed on what conditions would allow Britain to promise neutrality, Grey could not say: the cabinet was too unpredictable.

That evening, Buchanan wired that the Germans had declared war on Russia, having had no reply to their ultimatum; and de Bunsen wired from Vienna that talks, and avoiding a wider European war, seemed unlikely. The cabinet met for a second time that day, at 6.30 p.m., after this news, and some who had been threatening resignation – notably Lloyd George, who was either activated by principle or saw a huge political opportunity for himself by going in the same direction as the wind was blowing – had reconsidered. Afterwards, Asquith called a meeting of the Army Council: and although at its first meeting the cabinet had refused Churchill permission to complete mobilisation of the Fleet, Asquith now gave the order. At 1.25 a.m. on 2 August Churchill also ordered the Naval Reserve to be mobilised.

At around that time Nicolson saw a telegram from Cambon saying German troops had violated France's border near Longwy, a claim later cast into doubt. He advised Grey that Germany had made herself the aggressor 'and in these circumstances there should be no hesitation as to our attitude.'[222] He counselled immediate mobilisation to ensure the British Expeditionary Force could be on its way quickly. 'Should we waver now we shall rue the day later,' he added. The French pressed Britain to signal its intentions; and later that morning Villiers reported that the Belgians had heard of German soldiers entering Luxembourg. The Luxembourgeois prime minister, Paul Eyschen, telegraphed Grey to remind him of the great powers' collective obligation under the Treaty of London of 1867, which had guaranteed Luxembourg's independence.

That weekend Law was in a house party on the Thames at Wargrave with other leading Unionists, including Carson, F. E. Smith and Sir Max Aitken, the Canadian adventurer and Unionist MP who was Law's closest confidant. The idea had been to discuss the Unionists' next steps on Ireland; but little was dealt with apart from the international crisis. Smith, a close friend of Churchill, relayed the news that the Liberals were split, causing Churchill to wonder about the possibilities of a coalition to prosecute a war if necessary. Smith believed Churchill spoke with Grey's support and the tacit agreement of Asquith, which was not the case. Law, wisely, distrusted Churchill and would treat only with Asquith. All Smith could do was send a message of general Unionist support for the government if it chose to declare war. 'All the Unionist leaders had been given to understand that everything was perfectly all right,' Leo Amery, a Unionist MP, recorded in his diary: so they had left town, and Amery and his colleague George Lloyd started a round-up.[223] Lloyd found Balfour, who was 'flabbergasted' at the news of how serious matters had become; Austen Chamberlain was at Westgate-on-Sea in Kent, and was wired to come back. Lord Lansdowne, Tory leader in the Lords, returned from Bowood, and in the early hours of 2 August convened a 'council of war' at his London house with Law and others, including General Henry Wilson, an intimate of Sir John French. Wilson would be a highly political soldier in the coming conflict.

Not everyone there was excited by the occasion: according to Blanche Lloyd, whose husband was one of the most passionate advocates of British entry into the war, 'the Duke of Devonshire sat on a sofa and slept.'[224] They agreed to support the government if war came. Churchill, whom Asquith described in his diary as 'very bellicose and demanding immediate mobilisation', had earlier visited Balfour to receive reassurances of Unionist support.[225] Law then wrote to Asquith: 'Lord Lansdowne and I feel it our duty to inform you that in our opinion . . . any hesitation in now supporting France and Russia would be fatal to the honour and future security of the United Kingdom, and we offer His

Majesty's Government the assurance of the united support of the Opposition in all measures required by England's intervention in the war.'[226] There was no mention of Belgium; it was France that mattered to the Unionists. Asquith received the letter at breakfast on 2 August, delivered by Lansdowne's chauffeur, but for the moment kept it to himself. He sent Law a secret reply saying the cabinet would ensure the protection of the French coast against the German fleet. Belgium, however, was a more important consideration. Any breach of Germany's treaty obligations in that regard would be taken very seriously. This may have been sophistry, given Asquith's sympathy with Grey's view about needing to support the French. Asquith did, however, make it clear that 'it is a British interest that France should not be crushed as a great power'; but then the only point in invading Belgium would have been for Germany to do that.[227] In 1918, when Leo Maxse, a highly partisan Tory journalist, wrote an article suggesting the letter (which he also claimed to have influenced) had been responsible for stopping the 'wavering' in the cabinet and forcing Asquith to take an 'active line', Asquith treated the suggestion with contempt. 'It was said,' he told his most trusted colleague Lord Crewe, who was Leader of the House of Lords and India secretary in 1914, 'that Aspasia's dog was the real author of the Peloponnesian War.'[228]

Britain was, by that Sunday morning, gripped by crisis: Northcliffe reflected it, both for ideological and commercial reasons, by publishing a special Sunday edition of *The Times*. It reported the German invasion of Luxembourg and fighting on the Russian frontier, and alleged that German troops had entered France. It chronicled events unfolding around the country, and the shifts in public feeling. Liners were returning to port in case the German navy captured them, derailing continental holidays after all. The Post Office telegraph service was being taken under government control. The King had decreed that Cowes Week be cancelled. There were fears about bringing in the harvest, and of continuing food imports (on which Britain relied), and reports of public figures warning against panic: a reliable way of whipping it up. The paper published maps of the theatre of war, and a detailed one of the area around Luxembourg. 'They should be preserved for reference,' it advised its readers.[229] *The Times* used its special edition to prepare public opinion. 'Above all, if war comes, must the people as a whole exercise calmness, patience, and self-restraint. In a great war we are bound to suffer many losses of men, of ships, and of material resources of all kinds. These losses must be borne without complaint and must be accepted without murmuring.'[230] It directed those who could not fight to 'sit still' and to resist hoarding gold or food, or sowing panic: as would be said in another conflict, 'keep calm and carry on.' Opinion was moving steadily towards war, if only to salvage national honour by defending France and Belgium.

Other Sunday newspapers warned the government of the 'shame' (the *Observer*) and of a 'Britain degraded' (the *Sunday Times*) if Britain allowed France to be crushed: but letters from readers showed opinion was divided.[231] The *News of the World* was equivocal; *Reynold's News* very strongly against a war. Blanche Lloyd recorded of her husband that while he was walking through London that morning to see Austen Chamberlain, 'on his way . . . to Carlton Gdns he saw a crowd of about 4000 cheering for France – and at every street corner people were reading newspapers and talking of nothing but war.'[232]

Asquith felt things were 'pretty black'.[233] His Sunday breakfast in Downing Street was shared by Lichnowsky. Asquith described him as '*emotionné*'; he had pleaded with the prime minister 'not to side with France'.[234] Asquith noted: 'He said that Germany, with her army cut in two between France and Russia, was far more likely to be crushed than France. He was very agitated, poor man, and wept.' Asquith emphasised that he did not want Britain to intervene, and it would not – provided Germany did not invade Belgium or send its fleet into the Channel, details he had failed to share with the ambassador before. Lichnowsky 'was bitter about the policy of his Government in not restraining Austria and seemed quite heart-broken.' Those responsible for the nation's spiritual welfare now took the opportunity to seek to influence proceedings. The Archbishops of Canterbury and York issued a special prayer for peace, said in churches across England that morning. The Primate, Randall Davidson, took a private service in Buckingham Palace for the Royal Family, and preached in Westminster Abbey in the afternoon. 'This thing which is now astir in Europe is not the work of God but of the Devil,' he told his congregation.'[235] Davidson had hoped governments had, since Waterloo, moved on from war to solve their quarrels: but apparently not. The only answer, he felt, was prayer.

The first cabinet meeting that Sunday, from 11 a.m. until 2 p.m., at last gave the French the reassurance Cambon had sought, but the agreement was reached with 'some difficulty', according to Asquith.[236] Grey admitted Britain was 'not bound by the same obligation of honour to France as bound France to Russia,' except (as he had told Cambon) if there was an action against France in the Channel or the North Sea.[237] He had read to his colleagues Law's letter, indicating Unionist support. Personally, he believed Britain had serious obligations to her neighbour – of honour, and because of France's assistance to Britain in the Mediterranean. However, not all of his colleagues were convinced. Some such as Morley still believed any such violation could be met by a diplomatic initiative from Britain, not force of arms. Burns said any authorisation of action in the North Sea or the Channel was 'neither more nor less than a challenge to Germany, tantamount to a declaration of war against her.'[238]

Burns, already provoked by the naval mobilisation, resigned immediately; but Asquith (who Morley felt 'took the blow a trifle too coolly') prevailed upon him to announce nothing until the cabinet met again at 6.30 that evening. Morley felt the moment for resignation had not yet arrived, and told Burns he thought he had made a mistake given that Germany would already be on Britain's doorstep in the event of such an intervention. 'I made just as much impression on John Burns as I had expected – that is, not the slightest.'[239]

Asquith and Grey were in complete agreement, which would be crucial to holding the tottering government and their party together. With the permission of the whole cabinet Grey told Lichnowsky that 'it would be hard to restrain English feeling on any violation of Belgian neutrality by either combatant.'[240] He then told Cambon: 'I am authorised to give an assurance that if the German fleet comes into the Channel or through the North Sea to undertake hostile operations against French coasts or shipping the British fleet will give all the protection in its power.'[241] He stressed this was not binding until the Germans attacked, but it represented a substantial shift in British policy. He also told Cambon that the cabinet was considering a statement to be made to Parliament the following day, 3 August, about Belgian neutrality, whose violation had far more direct consequences for Britain than did that of Luxembourg.

After the morning cabinet Lloyd George drove Morley to Beauchamp's house for lunch. 'Our talk was on the footing that we were all three for resignation', Morley recalled.[242] There were regrets that they had allowed Grey to reassure Cambon: Morley regretted not having pushed the point about having to commit an expeditionary force to what would be 'a vast and long-continued European war', a discussion he felt would have brought the government down. Morley was also concerned about the effect of a European war on resolving the Home Rule question, and in harming what Grey and Lichnowsky had painted as 'the blessed improvement in the relations of England and Germany during the last three or four years.'[243] For him, this was the pivot of the argument: but no one else seemed to see it that way. Samuel was also at Beauchamp's lunch, and went to see Asquith afterwards. To show how detached the prime minister was from the Chancellor of the Exchequer, and how much the survival of the government depended on the chancellor's not coming out against him, the main question Asquith asked was: 'What is Lloyd George going to do?'[244] Samuel, himself in two minds, felt unqualified to answer.

During the afternoon of 2 August the Foreign Office received a message from the Tsar to the King explaining the German declaration of war had come before he could agree to talks; he said he had found the declaration 'quite unexpected', as he had given 'most categorical assurances' to their cousin the Kaiser that no Russian troops would move while mediation negotiations continued. Buchanan urged support for Russia and touched the same nerve as the French: that whoever won a European war, Britain risked being friendless at the end and, if it refused to help Russia, with India being left vulnerable to attack by it.

With a state of war between Russia and Germany, with the Russians expecting to have war declared on them by Austria–Hungary, and with France on the verge, or so it seemed, of a German attack, Britain's room for manoeuvre was highly circumscribed. Grey, Nicolson and Crowe, representing the Foreign Office view, felt British honour depended on support for France; all now realised that a violation of Belgium was likely, however, to be the trigger. The Unionist Party openly advocated war, but Asquith believed three-quarters of Liberal MPs remained to be convinced, or were outright pacifists. That afternoon, a substantial anti-war demonstration organised by the trades unions and addressed by, among others, Keir Hardie gathered in Trafalgar Square. It met a counter-demonstration, which marched to Buckingham Palace and cheered loudly when the King appeared on a balcony to acknowledge it. At the 6.30 p.m. cabinet Burns resolved to go when Grey reported on his conversation with Cambon. Morley told Asquith he would go too, though Asquith implored him to sleep on it, which he agreed to do. For Morley, who spoke for Grey in the Lords and had seen all the diplomatic traffic, there had been no single trigger that had made him decide: it was, he recalled, 'the result of a whole train of circumstance and reflection'. He was seventy-five, and had had enough.

Matters were complicated by the Germans impeding telegraph traffic from Berlin: but when Goschen finally got through to Nicolson he warned him that not only were the Germans reluctant to answer Grey's enquiry about Belgian neutrality, but they were also cooking up stories about Belgian misbehaviour to provide a case for invading, starting with the supposed stoppage of the consignment of grain. At 7 p.m. on 2 August the Belgian government received an ultimatum from the Germans, offering an entente if Belgium would facilitate movements of German troops; the Belgian cabinet was meeting, and an answer was requested by 7 a.m. Belgium's answer was to reject the ultimatum absolutely; the French said they had five army corps ready to enter Belgium to fight the Germans, if Belgium wished. When he wrote to Venetia Stanley that evening Asquith emphasised that 'we have no obligation of any kind either to France or Russia to give them military or naval help', but added that 'it is against British interests that France should be wiped out as a Great Power.' This confirmed that he, at least, had made up his mind about what the security of Britain and its place in the world required the government to do.

VI

On Monday 3 August – a bank holiday – *The Times* wrote: 'The die is cast. The great European struggle which the nations have so long struggled to avert has begun.'[245] It added, presciently, that 'Europe is to be the scene of the most terrible war that she has witnessed since the fall of the Roman Empire.' It had no doubt where fault lay: 'The blame must fall plainly on Germany,' a fulfilment of Northcliffe's much-rehearsed prophecies. It argued that Germany could have called off Austria's dogs, a questionable assumption: and it took no account of Russia's precipitousness. Such assertions – made also in the *Daily Mail*, Northcliffe's other organ of opinion – defined the problem for most of the public, albeit somewhat inaccurately. But about Germany's breaches of faith and high-handed attitude towards Belgium and Luxembourg there could be little argument: Northcliffe had always said Germany was ruthless, and had been vindicated.

That morning Asquith's question about his chancellor was at last answered. After his breakfast, Morley had written to Asquith 'with heartfelt pain' to say that he could 'contribute nothing useful to your deliberations' and so had decided to go after that morning's cabinet meeting.[246] He told Lloyd George this before the meeting began, noting the chancellor seemed 'astonished'. What followed was confirmation of Lloyd George's *volte face*. He told him: 'But if you go, it will put us who don't go, in a great hole.' Germany's 'bullying' of Belgium was given as Lloyd George's reason for changing his mind, to which Morley said that 'war is not the only reply'. Morley was sure Churchill had talked Lloyd George round: he felt the chancellor had chosen 'the politics of adventure; and found in the German ultimatum to Belgium a sufficiently plausible excuse.' Esher, a gossip whose sources were superior to almost anyone else's, recorded in his diary that 'the Chancellor of the Exchequer, at first hostile to Germany, had been influenced to join the Peace Party of the Cabinet by the strong representations made to him by the Liberal Members of Parliament and by his supporters in the country.'[247] Esher did not record a reason for Lloyd George's final change of mind, which appears to have been a desire to be with the majority.

With the cabinet now moving towards a consensus, it became urgent to ensure that military preparations for a conflict were adequate. Asquith was also acting Secretary of State for War, having held the post as well as the premiership since Jack Seely's resignation over the Curragh incident in March.[248] So much had he concentrated on the overall picture that he was giving inadequate attention to preparing the Army for conflict. Henry Wilson had told Amery early on 2 August that there was 'absolutely nothing being done at the War Office.'[249] Haldane now took temporary charge of the War Office, and summoned the Army Council and ordered preparations for immediate mobilisation. He and General Sir John French, who would command the BEF, wanted six divisions to go to France at once: they were outvoted by other members of the council, who wanted to send four, with a fifth following shortly.

That left the question of who would be permanently appointed to the War Office, as Asquith could not possibly do that job as well as being prime minister. Grey believed the prime minister's first thought had been to send Haldane back to a job he had done from 1905 to 1912, and in which he had distinguished himself by implementing reforms of the Army. These had cut the size of the Army and made it more efficient, and had prepared it for a continental war. Grey had persuaded Haldane as early as 1907 that the most likely enemy the Army would have to fight would be Germany. Haldane had shared some of Asquith's burdens with him for the last four months, as the prime minister did not have the time to do the war secretary's job properly, so it would have been a natural move.

However, to many people the obvious candidate was one of those Army Council members who had voted for four divisions: Field Marshal Earl Kitchener of Khartoum, in London on leave from Egypt, where he was Consul General. He had many supporters. *The Times*, clearly well briefed, called the following morning for Kitchener to become war secretary for the duration, the cry led by its military correspondent, Lt Col. Charles à Court Repington, a crony of the Field Marshal, society ladies' man, philanderer and egomaniac. Churchill, egged on by Balfour, had suggested to Asquith that Kitchener should have the War Office. It was not a novel idea: Rosebery had advocated it after the Boer War. More recently, when Asquith had taken on the job, the mountebank, huckster and bankrupt Horatio Bottomley had suggested it in his magazine *John Bull*. Asquith tipped Haldane off that Kitchener would be appointed Secretary of State for War in the event of hostilities.

The cabinet met at 11.15 a.m., after the Privy Council meeting that had issued the proclamations. Asquith began by saying he had the resignations of four ministers – Beauchamp and Simon had joined Burns and Morley, whom he called 'the greatest source of the moral authority of the Government.'[250] Maurice Hankey, secretary of the Committee of Imperial Defence and a man whose name would be made by the war, recorded that Ramsay MacDonald, the leader of the Labour Party, had also been asked to join the government but, influenced in part by Morley, had refused.[251] Accepting that many Liberal MPs felt the same, Asquith said that if more ministers went he would have to offer his resignation to the King. He did not think any putative leader would handle the crisis better than he had; or that a coalition would work. Lloyd George spoke in his support and against further resignations, which calmed matters, and all four resigners promised to say nothing and to preserve national unity, for the moment.

Asquith had already had talks with Lansdowne and Law, and they had pledged support for the government if war was declared. Fighting with France, however, was still not an argument that would carry the cabinet to justify war: but defending Belgian neutrality was, and by the end of that meeting on 3 August the cabinet, with the exception of the resigners, was resolved that Britain would have to fight in that cause. Morley was deeply affected by breaking a relationship with Asquith of nearly thirty years: but could not reconcile with his conscience the cabinet decision to 'bind ourselves to Russia' by supporting France.[252] Over breakfast that day Grey persuaded Simon, whose ambition was legendary, and then Asquith persuaded Beauchamp, who had a genuine sense of duty, to go back. In his memoirs, Simon recalled 'the atmosphere of anxiety and distress into which many patriotic Liberals felt themselves plunged.'[253] For a time, he managed to surface.

At 12.30 p.m. Grey heard from the Consul General in Antwerp that Germans had crossed the Belgian border and occupied Tongres. Lichnowsky claimed that stories of Germans entering France were 'complete fabrications'.[254] The promise that the Royal Navy would defend the French coast had had an effect, since the Germans said there would be no attacks on that coast while Britain remained neutral. Now, that neutrality was becoming a German obsession. Later on 3 August Germany's London embassy sent the Foreign Office a list of alleged border violations by the French, pleading: 'Great Britain will no doubt recognise that Germany has done her utmost to preserve peace and the provocation of her enemies have [sic] forced her to take up the arms in order to maintain her existence.'[255]

Despite the bank holiday, Parliament met. There was an uneasy combination in the country of relaxation tempered by tension as the crisis loomed over people's lives. Day-trippers seeking trains found services cancelled, as rolling stock was diverted for troop movements and the government took over the railways. Instead of seaside excursions, many Londoners crowded into Whitehall and around Downing Street to witness the comings and goings. Hawkers sold huge quantities of little Union flags for the crowds to wave. Asquith noted how, as he went to and from the Commons, 'we are now always surrounded and escorted by cheering crowds of loafers and holiday-makers.'[256] London's museums reported attendances well down on 1913. The boat trains from Victoria were full, not of English travellers, but of Europeans returning to the Continent, 'their exceedingly grave expressions testifying to their anxiety,' as *The Times* reported.[257]

By Monday naval reservists swelled the crowds leaving Victoria; those whose excursions had been cancelled stood on the concourse and cheered the reservists. For many, however, nothing could dampen the holiday spirit: 60,000 went by train from London to Southend, for example, and others by steamer to there, Margate and Ramsgate.[258] Nearly 15,000 people filled the Oval to watch Surrey put up 472 for 5 against Nottinghamshire: Jack Hobbs made 226. But at the Canterbury cricket festival, where Kent also batted well, the Buffs' tent was almost empty, and tension hung over the ground. Elsewhere, the immediacy of a national emergency was palpable. British merchant ships were reported to be leaving German ports and heading for home or neutral berths. Experimental wireless stations were closed, and merchant shipping was banned from using wireless in British waters; the King issued a proclamation allowing the state to requisition merchant ships as troop transports. Another proclamation banned the export of goods that could be useful in war, from aeroplanes to pack animals, and explosive components to bandages and dressings.

The foreign secretary rose in a packed House of Commons just before 3 p.m. He had considered reading out Bethmann's request for British neutrality, and his response, but declined for fear it would cause 'indignation': Grey was determined a decision for war should be taken coolly, not in anger. He found Prussian militarism 'hateful', but his personal feelings were not enough.[259] His remarks, therefore, contained a calm assessment of developments up to that point, but he did not dilute the severity of the crisis: 'Events move so rapidly that it is exceedingly difficult to state with technical accuracy the actual state of affairs, but it is clear that the peace of Europe cannot be preserved. Russia and Germany, at any rate, have declared war upon each other.'[260]

The aim, he said, of the diplomatic activity of the preceding days had been to maintain peace: that approach had worked in the Balkan crisis of 1912, for the powers had united and, even though the Balkan League and the Turks had gone to war over Turkey's continued occupation of parts of mainland Europe, the great powers – led by France and Austria–Hungary – had agreed to keep out of the fight. However, diplomacy had not worked now. Grey blamed 'a disposition . . . to force things rapidly to an issue.'[261] He wanted the House to 'approach this crisis in which we are now, from the point of view of British interests, British honour, and British obligations, free from all passion as to why peace has not been preserved.' Unusually, he promised to publish the diplomatic correspondence, to prove Britain's good faith: when the book came out it proved a bestseller, was translated into several languages, and left the public in little doubt that the Foreign Office had sought, albeit ineffectually, to get the powers talking.

Grey said that until the preceding day Britain had promised nothing except diplomatic support to any party in the quarrel: he emphasised it would be for the Commons to decide whether to take further steps. He mentioned Britain's entente with France, and that the French had no desire to fight anyone over Serbia: but France's formal alliance with Russia forced them. Britain was not party to that alliance, and did not even know its terms; but he made public that any bombardment of France's Channel coast by a third party would not be a situation in which Britain could stand aside. 'I believe that would be the feeling of this country,' he added.[262]

He wished to regard Britain's predicament not in terms of sentiment, but of the national interest: and it was very much in British interests to keep the friendly French fleet in the Mediterranean, helping to keep open trade routes. He read out the statement he had made to Cambon to that effect. However, he said it was not a declaration of war, and nor did it entail aggressive action, but bound Britain to take such action should the contingency arise. Grey pointed out that the Germans undertaking not to attack the north French coast was not enough. 'There is the more serious consideration – becoming more serious every hour – there is the question of the neutrality of Belgium.'[263]

He explained Britain's obligations as guarantor of Belgian neutrality under the treaties of 1839 and 1870, citing Gladstone who, in 1870, had said how Britain's honour and interests rested on protecting Belgian neutrality, had that been necessary as a result of the Franco-Prussian War. He informed the House of his discussions with Paris and Berlin about the question; and disclosed that the King of the Belgians had just appealed to George V for a 'diplomatic intervention'.[264] Grey had made such an intervention: but circumstances seemed to have advanced beyond that. He confirmed Britain's 'great and vital interests' in maintaining Belgian independence, for Belgium's sake and for the sake of other small European countries that might be threatened by larger ones.

This was a moral as much as a strategic question, and again it was Gladstone who was brought to bear on the problems of August 1914. He had stated, in 1870: 'We have an interest in the independence of Belgium which is wider than that which we may have in the literal operation of the guarantee. It is found in the answer to the question whether under the circumstances of the case, this country, endowed as it is with influence and power, would quietly stand by and witness the perpetration of the direst crime that ever stained the pages of history, and thus become participators in the sin.'[265] For Grey and the government, those words described the present: to do nothing would allow what Gladstone had called 'the unmeasured aggrandisement' of another great power, and to encourage attacks on smaller countries. If France were beaten (though Grey said he was sure France would not be), that would leave Europe under German domination.[266]

Grey gave one notable hostage to fortune. Having made the case to support Belgium, he added that 'if we are engaged in war, we shall suffer but little more than we shall suffer even if we stand aside.' Like all others, he did not foresee the hecatombs of dead the Great War would build. His reasoning was that, even if Britain did not fight, foreign trade would stop, because there would be no customers; and that after the war it would have neither the wealth nor the moral authority to undo all the harm done during it. 'I am quite sure,' he said, 'that our moral position would be such as to have lost us all respect.'[267] Privately, he believed that if Britain did not fight, it would be 'isolated, discredited and hated'.[268]

He confirmed that no decision had yet been taken to send an expeditionary force, though confirmed the order to mobilise both the Fleet and the Army, the proclamation for which would be issued the following day. He refused to confirm unconditional neutrality on behalf of Britain, for the reasons he had outlined, and to avoid 'the most serious and grave economic consequences'.[269] He began his peroration: 'The most awful responsibility is resting upon the Government in deciding what to advise the House of Commons to do . . . We believe we shall have the support of the House at large in proceeding to whatever the consequences may be and whatever measures may be forced upon us by the development of facts or action taken by others.'[270] He added: 'I believe the country, so quickly has the situation been forced upon it, has not had time to realise the issue. It perhaps is still thinking of the quarrel between Austria and Servia, and not the complications of this matter which have grown out of the quarrel between Austria and Servia.' It was not merely the public who were at a loss, because of the speed of events. He admitted, apparently bewildered, that 'it is most difficult to describe what has actually happened.'[271] However: 'When the country realises what is at stake, what the real issues are . . . we shall be supported throughout, not only by the House of Commons, but by the determination, the resolution, the courage, and the endurance of the whole country.' Lord Hugh Cecil, a Tory not easily pleased, told a friend that 'Grey's speech was very wonderful – I think in the circumstances one may say the greatest speech delivered in our time . . . the greatest example of the art of persuasion that I have ever listened to.'[272]

Law was sure Grey, and the government, had done everything possible to preserve peace, and offered the 'unhesitating support' of the Opposition in whatever the government did for the 'honour and security' of the country.[273] John Redmond, leader of the Irish Nationalists, said that whatever might have happened before, at times of difficulty for Britain, because of the move towards Home Rule sympathies had changed in Ireland. 'The democracy of Ireland,' he said, 'will turn with the utmost anxiety and sympathy to this country in every trial and every danger that may overtake it.' He hoped that the two bodies of volunteers in Ireland threatening a civil war – the Unionist and the Nationalist – would join 'in comradeship' to defend 'our country.'[274]

Ramsay MacDonald spoke for Labour. He praised Grey's oratory, but said: 'He is wrong. I think the Government which he represents and for which he speaks is wrong. I think the verdict of history will be that they are wrong.' He did not believe Grey's point about honour, on which he blamed the conflicts in the Crimea and in South Africa. His party would support the defence of Belgium: but the war would not be confined to that. Given the labour movement's detestation of the Autocrat of all the Russias, he was reluctant to fight in a war that would shore up Russian power. He challenged Grey to describe the danger in which France found herself; Grey had been reluctant to do that, preferring to justify war by talking of the obligation to Belgium. He ended with a low blow, saying British neutrality was more consistent with 'the traditions of the party that are now in office.'[275] His speech divided Labour, and once war was declared undermined him so much that he resigned the leadership on 6 August: Arthur Henderson replaced him. The previous evening, MacDonald had told Sir George Riddell that 'in three months' time there will be bread riots and we shall come in.'[276]

Many MPs wanted to speak in the debate on Grey's statement: Asquith said the House would have the opportunity to discuss the crisis, but it would not be that day. This caused consternation, and the Speaker adjourned the sitting for two and a half hours, until seven o'clock, so discussions could take place between the parties, and so Grey could update himself on events. In the Foreign Office, Nicolson, informed by his private secretary that Grey had had 'a tremendous success', reflected that 'now the course is clear, but it will be a terrible business.'[277] As Grey spoke the Germans asked the Belgians whether they could occupy Liège 'peaceably', requiring an answer within twelve hours. The Belgians said their troops would fire on any Germans on their territory 'immediately', and believed German troops had already crossed the Meuse.[278] In reply to the French offer of five army corps, the Belgians said they were not, at that stage, appealing to their guarantors for help – though it reminded Germany that one guarantor of its independence had been the Kingdom of Prussia. This slowed down escalation of the conflict; and bought Britain a little more time.

However, that evening Villiers told Grey the Germans were claiming that the French intended to invade Germany through Belgium, so troops were being prepared to defend Belgium against French attack. The Germans promised to 'pay ready money for all necessaries of war and indemnify all losses caused in Belgium' and to evacuate Belgian territory on the conclusion of peace if Belgium would let them through. Germany threatened Belgium that if it adopted a 'hostile attitude', relations between them would be 'settled by arms'. The Belgians mocked Germany's interpretation of French intentions, and promised 'to repel by every means in her power' an attack by Germany.[279] At once, the German ambassador left Paris for Berlin: Germany had declared war on France. Haldane, having put through the mobilisation order, urged the sending of six infantry divisions.

In London that evening flag-waving crowds stretched down the Mall from Trafalgar Square to Buckingham Palace. They had done so the night before too, prompting Asquith to recall Walpole's remark that 'now they are ringing their bells; in a few weeks they'll be wringing their hands'.[280] The war fever was prompted by a sense of the country's standing up for justice and morality, in honouring the promise to defend Belgium; and helped by a complete lack of understanding of what modern war would actually mean. A nation reared on the imperial adventure stories of Rudyard Kipling and the Boy's Own Paper, not to mention the years of anti-German scaremongering of Northcliffe, was about to have the chance to make its own contribution to British glory, in the name of justice and decency, against what would quickly come to be called 'German frightfulness'.

'Every few minutes,' *The Times* reported, 'the singing of patriotic songs was punctuated with loud cries for the King.'[281] At 8.15, 9.00 and 9.45 p.m. the King and Queen appeared on the balcony to wave to the masses: 'the demonstration of patriotism and loyalty became almost ecstatic.' Grey had returned to the Commons at 7 p.m. and outlined the detail of the German note and the Belgian reply. He said the government was taking the significance of this into 'grave consideration'.[282] The King noted that Grey's speech had 'entirely changed public opinion'.[283]

A dissenting voice rose from his back benches. It was Philip Morrell, who unusually for a Liberal was a scion of a brewing family, from Oxford. Educated at Eton and Balliol, he was on the fringes of the Bloomsbury group through his wife Lady Ottoline, half-sister of the Duke of Portland. Theirs was an unconventional marriage: both had numerous affairs (Lady Ottoline's most notable conquest was Bertrand Russell) and Morrell fathered several illegitimate children. Lady Ottoline ran a salon of epic self-regard in Bedford Square: the Morrells were committed pacifists, and their country house at Garsington in Oxfordshire would become a refuge for various Bloomsbury conscientious objectors, including Lytton Strachey, Clive Bell and Duncan Grant. The speech her husband made that evening put him at the forefront of that movement.

Claiming to speak for many Liberals, Morrell did not doubt Grey had done his best for peace: but did doubt whether 'he has really made a sufficient attempt to make fair terms with Germany'.[284] This betrayed a deep misunderstanding – Germany had by bullying Belgium shown it was beyond an understanding of 'fair terms' – but did hint at Grey's initial inertia. As has been shown, Grey had for much of the preceding five weeks been passive, even though his officials (notably Nicolson) had spotted the potential for disaster almost from the moment of the Sarajevo assassinations. This was before shuttle diplomacy: but he could have reached Berlin in less than forty-eight hours, had he wished, and had face-to-face talks with Jagow that might, possibly, have altered history. However, given what in Berlin had come to be seen as the determination of the Prussian-dominated German army to have a war to assert national supremacy, efforts might have proved fruitless.

Morrell claimed the Germans had promised to respect Belgian integrity:

a heckler shouted 'at the end of the war!', which was the point.[285] He said he would concede Britain must act if Germany annexed or occupied Belgium: which, within days, it mostly had. Caricaturing Grey's reasoning, and ignoring his detailed exegesis on the treaties, Morrell claimed that 'we are asked to go to war because there may be a few German regiments in a corner of Belgian territory. I am not prepared to support a government which goes to war under those circumstances.' He believed 'fear and jealousy of German ambition', fostered by the press, were responsible. Certainly the press – especially those parts owned by Northcliffe – had long painted Germany as the natural enemy. But a study of the diplomatic background to the war makes it clear that such sentiments had nothing to do with Grey's reluctant decision to advocate war. Morrell made common cause with the socialists, saying Britain was being asked to fight 'as much to preserve the despotism of Russia as to interfere with German ambition.'[286] Although no admirer of Germany, he admired Russia even less: and he thought an 'honourable neutrality' would be possible, though did not detain the House by analysing how Belgium and France, for a start, would see it; and he steadfastly ignored the arrogance and aggression of the German note to Brussels.

Josiah Wedgwood, a Liberal MP from the Potteries and a descendant of the great potter himself, feared credit would run out, employment would dry up and people would starve, which would cause revolution. 'People are not the docile serfs they were a hundred years ago,' he proclaimed.[287] (Wedgwood was among the first to volunteer when war came. He was wounded in the Dardanelles, awarded the DSO, and ended up a colonel.) Lloyd George said the government was considering how to secure food supplies in the event of war, and promised further details the next day. He admitted he would also be forced to make a statement about the currency, and the circulation of banknotes. One backbencher taunted him about the contrast between his anti-war stance in the Boer War and his readiness to fight now. He kept his counsel.

Most MPs who spoke ignored the Austrian *ancien régime*'s determination to shore itself up against its internal critics by punishing Serbia, or of the German military leadership's determination to override men such as Bethmann, Jagow and Lichnowsky, and have a war. Hardie, for Labour, saw no problem with Belgian neutrality being restored after a war, and leaving the Germans to slug it out with the French if necessary. Arthur Ponsonby, a Liberal who later sat in a Labour cabinet, made a more measured, and therefore more telling, objection, though one whose assumptions were still questionable. Ponsonby had been at Eton and Balliol with Morrell, and a Page of Honour to Queen Victoria: his father-in-law was Sir Hubert Parry. He felt he was witnessing:

> the most tragic moment I have yet seen. We are on the eve of a great war, and I hate to see people embarking on it with a light heart. The war fever has already begun. I saw it last night when I walked through the streets. I saw bands of half-drunken youths waving flags, and I saw a group outside a great club in St. James's Street being encouraged by members of the club from the balcony. The war fever has begun, and that is what is called patriotism; I think we have plunged too quickly, and I think the Foreign Secretary's speech shows that what has been rankling all these years is a deep animosity against German ambitions. The balance of power is responsible for this—this mad desire to keep up an impossibility in Europe, to try and divide the two sections of Europe into an armed camp, glaring at one another with suspicion and hostility and hatred, and arming all the time, and bleeding the people to pay for the armaments.[288]

A decade after the war he published a book entitled *Falsehood in Wartime, Containing an Assortment of Lies Circulated Throughout the Nations During the Great War*, which led to his being credited with the phrase 'when war is declared, truth is the first casualty', though he may have been quoting an American senator, Hiram Johnson. His opposition to the war would not waver. He became a prominent member of the Union of Democratic Control, a leading anti-war movement in which he served with, among others, MacDonald and George Cadbury, the confectioner.

In defending Grey, Sir Arthur Markham, a coal-owner and Liberal MP for Mansfield, unwittingly took the pacifist line that this was about keeping Germany in its place, not about protecting Belgium, which was Grey's priority. 'No self-respecting country can admit the right of a great power in Europe to over-ride and beat down a small nationality,' he said.[289] He reflected the public mood in adding that 'this great Empire to which we belong has not been built up on the foundation of allowing close to our shores a great Power to be erected which might be a menace to the interests of the British people. If we falter this time, we falter, in my opinion, for the end of the British Empire, for the reason that no self-respecting people of the continent will ever believe that we, who have stood for liberty in the past, will stand for it again.'

A Liberal MP, Llewellyn Williams, blamed the press for creating enthusiasm for a war the public did not want, and accused Grey of trying to spread fear about German power, which another Liberal colleague felt could not possibly hold small countries in servitude in the way suggested. Robert Outhwaite, another Liberal, said that the Germans marching troops through Belgium to fight the French was but a 'technical' violation of neutrality and not a 'conquest'.[290] The House was reminded that it was despotic Russia that had, by mobilising, started the wider war, not the Germans. That, too, was an uncomfortable statement. As Joseph King, a Liberal MP, noted, the government was attacked (with one exception) from its own side, while Unionists remained silent. King asked: 'I want to know whether the policy on which we are embarking has the support of a united Cabinet. We hear rumours, both inside the House and outside, that there are divisions, and that even one Cabinet minister has resigned.'[291] Another shouted: 'That is a wicked suggestion!'

King, perfectly enunciating radical opinion on the matter, denounced the 'atrocious tyrannical government' of the Tsar and its 'cruelty' and 'injustice'.[292] Sir William Byles, another Liberal, asked whether Britain would fight France if it had marched into Belgium to attack the Germans. Eventually, after several hours of a stream of attacks on Grey, a Liberal – William Pringle, the MP for Lanarkshire – made a dignified speech about how the Liberal tradition required Britain to take 'the side of international morality against the forces of blood and iron.'[293] That was the cue, at last, for Balfour, the former Unionist prime minister, to plea for an end to what was an adjournment debate, and to await the opportunity Asquith had promised to discuss the policy properly, when he and Grey and others were in attendance – which they were not throughout the evening. The Unionists were keeping their powder dry.

VII

When Grey returned to the Foreign Office after his speech he received his friend and confidant J. A. Spender, editor of the *Westminster Gazette* and a devotee of the Liberal Party. A fortnight earlier, possibly at Grey's suggestion, and when very little was being spoken about the European crisis, Spender had written an article (widely circulated abroad) urging Serbia to see that Austria–Hungary had a point, and to do all it could to avoid 'warlike complications'.[294] Now all that was consigned to history: the mainstream of Liberal ministerial opinion was convinced Britain had to fight, and the achievement in securing this support was almost entirely Grey's. He wrote of his meeting with Spender: 'We were standing at a window of my room in the Foreign Office. It was getting dusk, and the lamps were being lit in the space below on which we were looking. My friend recalls that I remarked on this with the words: "The lamps are going out all over Europe; we shall not see them lit again in our life-time." '[295]

Why was Grey convinced the struggle would take so long? As an experienced diplomat – he had been foreign secretary for the best part of nine years – he understood the motivations of all the other parties involved. He knew how weak the Tsarist regime was, and how a victory over Germany on behalf of fellow Slavs would be seen as a perfect means to shore up the Romanov dynasty. He knew too how the Germans regarded Russia as an uncivilised country comprising masses of barbarians entirely inimical to European culture, and how vigorously they would fight to repel them, and to expand their own influence in Eastern Europe. He knew the determination with which Austria–Hungary would fight to quell its upstart Serbian neighbour, for the sake of its own security but also because, with an Emperor of almost eighty-four and nationalist groups within its continental empire agitating for change, like Russia it needed to impress its people with a show of strength. Best of all, Grey knew that France was steeled not to repeat the humiliation of 1870–71, which had led to the Prussians walking off with Alsace and Lorraine, and would fight to the last man if necessary. Then there were other nations who had obligations to or understandings with the various powers – Italy, Bulgaria, Romania and Turkey. Europe, as many diplomats and politicians knew, had been living in unease with itself since the Congress of Berlin in 1878; a reordering was sure to happen one day, and when it came it would be a titanic, and possibly cataclysmic, struggle. Grey knew that moment had now come, and the fact that he had been unable to prevent it – or to ensure a reordering by more peaceful means – nearly crushed him, and took an awful toll on his health.

At midnight on 3 August Asquith, who viewed things very much as Grey did but who would prove less adaptable to the demands of war, sat down in Downing Street and wrote to Morley 'after 30 years of close and most affectionate association' to say that 'to lose you in the stress of a great crisis is a calamity which I shudder to contemplate, and which (if it should become a reality) I shall never cease to deplore.'[296] Asquith begged him 'with all my heart, to think twice and thrice, and as many times more as arithmetic can number, before you take a step which impoverishes the Government and leaves me stranded and almost alone.'[297] Morley recalled that 'nothing short of mental anguish held me by the throat', but told Asquith his fundamental objection remained: 'To swear ourselves to France is to bind ourselves to Russia . . . I am more distressed in making this reply to your generous and moving appeal than I have ever been in writing any letter of all my life.'[298]

For most other ministers the German note to Belgium was the last straw. At 9.30 a.m. on 4 August, Grey asked Goschen to tell Berlin that 'His Majesty's Government are bound to protest against this violation of a treaty to which Germany is a party in common with themselves, and must request an assurance that the demand made upon Belgium will not be proceeded with, and that her neutrality will be respected by Germany.' Goschen was told to ask for 'an immediate reply.' No sooner had this gone than the German embassy in London sent the Foreign Office a note from Bethmann that read: 'Since France has, since 1st August, made repeated military attacks on Imperial territory, Germany is now in a state of war with France.'[299] The mobilisation order, calling up all reservists and inviting applications for service from officers on the retired list, was issued that afternoon. Shortly afterwards, the Admiralty announced that Admiral Sir John Jellicoe would command the Home Fleets. Asquith now had to install Kitchener rapidly, for matters were moving swiftly.

On the morning of 4 August Grey told Bertie he had advised the governments of Norway, the Netherlands and Belgium to resist any German attempt to pressurise them into departing from their neutrality. They would have Britain's support in doing so, and would join Russia and France in 'common action for the purpose of resisting use of force by Germany against them, and a guarantee to maintain their independence and integrity in future years.'[300] He ordered Bertie to ask the French government to make a similar offer. Once the Germans entered Belgium

and refused to leave, Britain would be at war with them. At 11.20 a.m.
Grey heard from Villiers that the Germans had told the Belgian foreign
minister that as his government had declined Germany's 'well-
intentioned' proposal they would 'deeply to their regret be compelled to
carry out, if necessary by force of arms, the measures considered indispensable in view of the French menaces.'[301] At noon Lichnowsky showed
the Foreign Office a wire from Jagow repeating a 'formal assurance' that
Germany would 'under no pretence whatever' annex Belgian territory.
'Please impress upon Sir E Grey,' Jagow had continued, 'that Germany's
army could not be exposed to French attack across Belgium, which was
planned according to absolutely unimpeachable information. Germany
had consequently to disregard Belgian neutrality, it being for her a question of life or death to prevent French advance.'[302]

At 2 p.m. Grey wired Goschen noting the German message to Belgium, and information he had received that Belgian territory 'had been
violated' at Gemmenich.[303] He asked him to tell the German government that Britain still awaited a reply to its question about Belgian
neutrality, and wanted it by 11 p.m. London time. 'If not, you are
instructed to ask for your passports and to say that His Majesty's Government feel bound to take all steps in their power to uphold the
neutrality of Belgium and the observance of a Treaty to which Germany
is as much a party as ourselves.'

Goschen saw Bethmann and Jagow that afternoon, and in a dispatch
that did not reach London until 13 August told Grey that they 'regretted'
being unable to give the answer he sought.[304] He found his interview
with Bethmann 'very painful'. 'He [Bethmann] could not but consider it
an intolerable thing that because they were taking the only course open
to them to save the Empire from disaster, England should fall upon them
just for the sake of the neutrality of Belgium. He looked upon England
as entirely responsible for what might now happen. I asked him whether
he could not understand that we were bound in honour to do our best
to preserve a neutrality which we had guaranteed. He said: "But at
what price!"' Later, Goschen told Grey that a 'very agitated' Bethmann
harangued him in English for twenty minutes, saying neutrality was a
word often disregarded in wartime, and that the British government
had acted 'just for a scrap of paper.'[305] The central aim of German policy, Jagow had told him, had been to secure better ties with Britain
and, through Britain, become closer to France. Now that was in ruins,

ostensibly because the British took treaties seriously and the Germans did not. Goschen protested vigorously at the attempt to blame Britain.

Asquith spoke to the Commons on the afternoon of 4 August, its numbers depleted by the absence of almost one hundred MPs, called up as reservists, and with John Burns's place empty on the Treasury Bench. The prime minister referred to three telegrams from the recent diplomatic traffic; the first was the appeal from the King of the Belgians, the second Villiers's wire confirming that the Germans, as a consequence of Belgium's determination to maintain her neutrality, would enter the country by force to attack France, and the third the Belgian legation's telegram announcing the violation of their border. 'We cannot regard this in any sense a satisfactory communication,' he continued. 'We have, in reply to it, repeated the request we made last week to the German government, that they should give us the same assurance in regard to Belgian neutrality as was given to us and to Belgium by France last week. We have asked that a reply to that request, and a satisfactory answer to the telegram of this morning . . . should be given before midnight.'[306]

Asquith believed the German claim that the French were plotting an invasion of Belgium to attack Germany to be 'a manifest and transparent lie'.[307] He told the House the King was calling up the Territorial Army because of the 'great emergency', and confirmed the protection of shipping to ensure food supplies. He went to the Bar of the House, bowed, walked to the Chair and handed the Speaker the proclamation of the mobilisation of the Army, signed in the King's own hand. With that, at 4.17 p.m., the Commons adjourned to await news from Germany. Asquith was deeply saddened by the prospect of war, and contrasted his feelings with those of the First Lord of the Admiralty: 'Winston, who has got on all his war-paint, is longing for a sea-fight in the early hours of the morning to result in the sinking of the *Goeben*.' Scott condemned Churchill for his 'light-hearted irresponsibility' and contrasted it with Grey's having 'burst into tears' at one of the cabinet's meetings, a scene relayed to him by Simon.[308] For Churchill, the war was the great romantic adventure he had always longed for; for him, it would not turn out quite as he had hoped, not least through his own inability to reconcile romance with reality. Ironically his friend Lloyd George, a last-minute convert to the idea of fighting, would, through keeping a level head and resorting to stealth and duplicity, end up turning the conflict hugely to his personal advantage.

Later that afternoon a German diplomat called at the Foreign Office to say it was 'absolutely untrue that a single German soldier had crossed the French frontier.'[309] Crowe noted that the French claimed to have shot some German officers on their territory. Villiers reported that the Germans had tried to force the surrender of Liège, but had been repulsed. Coincidentally, also at 4.17 p.m. – as the Commons was rising – the Foreign Office intercepted a telegram sent in English and *en clair* from Jagow to Lichnowsky (it had been intended for interception) justifying invading Belgium by saying 'we knew that France was ready for invasion' (of Belgium), and promising 'that as long as England will keep neutral our fleet would not attack the Northern Coast of France and that we would not touch the territorial integrity and the independence of Belgium.'[310] By around 5 p.m. most GOCs had received the single-word telegram from the War Office: 'Mobilise'.[311]

Grey told the American government that afternoon: 'There are two sets of people in Germany: people like the German Chancellor, Herr von Bethmann Hollweg, and the German Ambassador here, Prince Lichnowsky, who dealt with all these things as we dealt with them; on the other hand, there was the military party of force, who had no respect at all for these things.'[312] By 'these things' Grey meant treaty obligations, which he saw as 'the test of the progress of civilisation' and 'the foundation of all confidence between nations.' He explained that if Germany had come to dominate France the notional independence of Belgium, Holland, Denmark and possibly Norway and Sweden would be 'a fiction' with their harbours at Germany's disposal. This domination of Western Europe would, Grey argued, 'make our position quite impossible.' The American ambassador, Page, recalled Grey saying, as his eyes 'filled with tears': 'Thus the efforts of a lifetime go for nothing. I feel like a man who has wasted his life.'[313] Grey never understood why Morley and Burns resigned, but believed their decisions were based on 'deep and sincere convictions', not 'pusillanimity'.

That evening Grey sent a final note to Lichnowsky. He told him Goschen was coming home and added: 'I have the honour to inform your Excellency that in accordance with the terms of the notification made to the German Government today His Majesty's Government consider that a state of war exists between the two countries from today at eleven o'clock p.m. I have the honour to enclose passports for your Excellency, your Excellency's family and staff.'[314] He spent much of the evening in Downing Street with Asquith and other colleagues.

In Berlin Goschen, having observed the civilities, left his embassy with his staff in a fleet of taxis early on 6 August, returning home via a train to the Hook of Holland. He bore a curt message from the Kaiser to the King renouncing his appointments as a British admiral and field marshal. Because of hostile acts by Austria against France and Russia, war was declared on Austria at midnight on 12 August, and de Bunsen headed home on 14 August on a train to the Swiss frontier, after a day on which 'Countess Berchtold [the wife of the foreign minister] and other ladies of Vienna society called to take leave of Lady de Bunsen.'[315] Grey conveyed the news to Mensdorff, asking him to call on the morning of 13 August: 'I should like to see you to say good-bye, and to shake hands, and to assure you how much my personal friendship remains unaltered.'[316] The meeting was at Grey's house, to be 'quite private'. Mensdorff was 'deeply grieved' by the declaration of war but 'I highly appreciate and heartily reciprocate the friendly personal feelings expressed'.

The government asked doctors, motorcyclists, blacksmiths, lorry drivers, butchers, bakers and members of other trades to volunteer for the Army. Weddings were brought forward before officers rejoined their regiments. The masses sang and cheered outside Buckingham Palace. The Royal Family acknowledged them at 7, 9.30 and 11 p.m., as the ultimatum to Germany expired. The King held a Privy Council at Buckingham Palace at 10.45 p.m. with Beauchamp (who was about to become Lord President, succeeding Morley) and two courtiers to approve the proclamation of war on Germany. 'It is a terrible catastrophe,' the King wrote, 'but it is not our fault.'[317]

As Hankey walked through St James's Park he encountered 'crowds of excited folk . . . often with linked arms and singing patriotic songs'.[318] In his history of the conflict, Sir Hew Strachan has observed: 'Popular enthusiasm played no part in causing the First World War. And yet without a popular willingness to go to war the world war could not have taken place.'[319] That willingness was born of an inability to comprehend what modern warfare actually entailed, notably the ease of mechanised slaughter, and the fact that even then the Boer War was a distant memory to but a few.

A crowd gathered in Downing Street as 11 p.m. neared to hear whether the Germans had accepted Britain's ultimatum. In Whitehall, 'as the news of the declaration of war reached the street the crowd expressed its feelings with loud cheering. It left the precincts of Downing Street and gathered in front of the War Office, where patriotic demonstrations continued until an early hour'.[320] Nor was it just the masses who felt the war was right and just. Four days earlier Bertrand Russell, then a don at Trinity College, Cambridge, had started to collect signatures for a statement to be published in the *Manchester Guardian* expressing opposition to the war, telling Lady Ottoline Morrell that 'all think it folly and very unpopular'.[321] 'The day war was declared,' he recalled, 'almost all of them changed their minds.'[322]

A formal statement was issued from the Foreign Office at 12.15 a.m. on 5 August that because of the 'summary rejection' of the government's request to respect Belgian neutrality 'a state of war exists between Great Britain and Germany as from 11 p.m. on August 4.' As Big Ben had struck midnight, despite there being no formal confirmation that Britain was at war, 'a vast cheer burst out and echoed and re-echoed for nearly 20 minutes. The National Anthem was then sung with an emotion and solemnity which manifested the gravity and sense of responsibility with which the people regard the great issues before them.'[323]

CHAPTER 2

WAR

I

On the morning of 5 August 1914 newspapers carried advertisements for the Burberry officer's trench coat, a Boer War veteran that, in the new hostilities, could serve well all ranks from commander-in-chief to subaltern (non-commissioned officers and other ranks would have to settle for rubberised rain capes). Burberry's could also provide 'Active Service Kit' in four days. Another advertisement implored Territorial Army officers to buy, for a mere £275, Overland cars, which would withstand 'the roughest usage', take 'steepest hills in top gear' and do 20 to 24 miles to the gallon.[1] Within days the newspapers announced that 'Every Man accepted by his Country for Defence or Offence should take with him a Bottle of Dr J Collis Browne's Chlorodyne', available from all chemists at 2s 9d, and 'in Diarrhoea, Dysentery, Colic, and other Bowel Complaints it acts like a charm.'[2]

Webley & Scott, purveyors of service revolvers to the officer class, increased the price from 5 guineas to £10, outraging MPs. The firm claimed it had had to pay workers a 15 per cent bonus, and the price of steel had risen by 15 per cent. Stanley Baldwin would, observing the Parliament elected in 1918, talk of 'hard-faced men who look as if they had done very well out of the war,' some of the hardest-faced of whom had already served in what would become a wartime 'government of businessmen'.[3] In Britain's mercantile society that was inevitable: whatever else would distinguish it, the war would be the greatest sales opportunity in history. The customers were not always impressed. Major J. C. Ker-Fox, visiting the Army & Navy Stores on the first afternoon of the war, felt 'disgusted to see hundreds of people whom one cannot dignify by calling men and women, laying in tons of provisions.' Since Britain was fighting 'for our existence as a nation' the Major demanded that 'the Government ought to confiscate these private stores, and fine and imprison the selfish brutes who are hoarding them.'[4]

A huge trade was done in war maps, so the civilian population could follow events at the front. Northcliffe started a new periodical, *The Great War*, a weekly record of events. *The Times* printed its own weekly pictorial *History of the War*, and set up a telephone news service for subscribers so that, in the age before radio, they could receive information the moment it reached Printing House Square. However, at a guinea a week, and with restrictions on the capacity of the telephone system, it was for the very few. Such was the appetite for news that consumption of paper increased by 25 per cent in the first week of the war, and newsprint rose from a penny a pound to a penny three farthings: ten weeks' supply suddenly became six weeks'. Rationing was not contemplated, but the nation's excited thirst for news increased the possibility.

The fervent patriotism of the first day of the war was unavoidable. Grey, early that morning, had asked Villiers to tell his Belgian hosts that 'His Majesty's Government regard common action to resist Germany as being now in operation and justified by treaty of 1839.'[5] Britain was fighting to protect its honour, to keep its word to Belgium, to join (as a consequence) its friend France in resisting that country's crushing by Germany, and thus enhancing Britain's national security by keeping Germany from the English Channel. 'I discovered to my amazement,' Bertrand Russell recorded, 'that average men and women were delighted at the prospect of war.'[6] There was the odd dissenter: the Neutrality League, of which little would be heard again, advertised in the *Daily Citizen* that morning urging all Englishmen to 'DO YOUR DUTY' which was to oppose 'A WICKED and STUPID WAR'.[7] However, the line elsewhere was being firmly held. In *The Times* that morning Henry Newbolt – he of 'a breathless hush in the close tonight' – had published a poem entitled 'The Vigil', which began with the ejaculation:

> England! where the sacred flame
> Burns before the inmost shrine,
> Where the lips that love thy name
> Consecrate their hopes and thine . . .

and ended with the equally plangent:

Then let Memory tell thy heart,
'England! what thou wert, thou art!'
Gird thee with thine ancient might,
Forth! And God defend the Right![8]

It was a tone that Rupert Brooke, with a modicum of additional poetic talent, would take up, before the first winter of trench warfare extinguished it: but it was typical of the mood of August 1914. However, the next day, as reality arrived, *The Times* wrote: 'First and foremost – Keep your heads. Be calm. Go about your ordinary business quietly and soberly. Do not indulge in excitement or foolish demonstrations.'[9] A nation reared on British naval supremacy thought it knew what war to expect: some battles in which the German navy was obliterated, and the German army driven back into the Fatherland from both sides and its people starved into submission in a magnified repeat of the Boer War. Hostilities began with British morale high. When, on 13 August, Churchill ran out of petrol in Reading and went into a local club, the members cheered, 'and sang *Rule, Britannia*.'[10]

Sensing a commercial imperative the magazine *John Bull*, which had earlier demanded Serbia be wiped off the map, quickly became the most full-throated advocate of war. It emerged redesigned on 15 August, with John Bull in a sailor's cap with HMS *Victory* on it. A leading article, entitled 'The Dawn of England's Greatest Glory', exhorted every Englishman to 'gird on his armour'. It continued: 'It is not necessary to be a soldier, but it *is* necessary to be a MAN.'[11] Legends surrounded Horatio Bottomley, *John Bull*'s editor, mostly self-propagated, such as that his natural father had been Charles Bradlaugh, the Liberal MP who for six years refused to take the religious oath required to assume the seat he had won in the House of Commons, and to whom he bore a resemblance.[12] Born in Bethnal Green in 1860, Bottomley had spent part of his childhood in an orphanage, had launched a publishing company, been acquitted of fraud, made a fortune in gold-mining shares, been a philanderer and gambler, served as a Liberal MP and had had to leave the Commons in 1912 when being declared bankrupt.

John Bull would become the leading organ of jingoism and Hun-bashing; and Bottomley would lead an enormous recruitment drive, speaking at over 300 public meetings. Once he also acquired a column in the *Sunday Pictorial* in March 1915 he would become the leading demagogue of the age, loved by the masses but hated by intellectuals and the elite. Undetected by his adoring public, Bottomley's nefarious private conduct continued; his denouement would come after the war, in a less successful confrontation with the forces of law and order when he was convicted of fraud. Yet during the war his influence as one of the country's most self-advertising patriots was enormous. He told a friend, Henry Houston, that 'this war is going to be my opportunity', and until hubris fatally overtook him, he was right.[13]

Shopkeepers who showed the national sense of humour by displaying signs that read 'BUSINESS AS USUAL DURING ALTERATIONS TO THE MAP OF EUROPE' would, like everyone else, soon find that business as usual was over.[14] Farmers had an early awakening. The War Office requisitioned heavy horses, to the distress of the eastern counties – where agriculture was predominantly arable – because they were taken at harvest time. Asquith ordered this to stop, along with the drafting of horses needed to pull wagons of food and fuel. However, the government requisitioned all horse-boxes on the railways, and race meetings were liable to be cancelled. The Kent County Cricket Club committee said Canterbury Week would continue, but hoped the public would not suppose that 'they are indifferent to the grave crisis which affects the country'.[15] The county's slow left-arm bowler and England Test cricketer Colin Blythe took 6 for 107 in Sussex's innings: he would be killed at Passchendaele in November 1917. Surrey were ordered from the Oval for the duration, as it was required for military training. In the battle to maintain a semblance of normal life in abnormal circumstances, abnormality was already winning.

Men of all ages and ranks flocked to recruiting centres. For many working-class lads it was not merely the excitement of war that appealed, compared with the unskilled jobs many of them did; it was also the appeal of three meals a day, a solid pair of boots, new clothing and their own bed to sleep in. Such was the enthusiasm that a blind eye was turned to those obviously under age, and doctors (paid half a crown for each man passed fit) became used to taking an unduly positive view of the often undernourished and enfeebled human material before them. In some parts of Britain fit men of military age receiving charitable or parish assistance had it cut off, forcing them to enlist.[16]

The officer class were similarly enthusiastic. For some just out of school – such as Robert Graves – it meant a welcome break from university. For those whose life had seemed flat or disappointing, it promised adventure. Advertisements appeared in the better newspapers from old boys' associations of public schools offering to help to obtain commissions for their alumni. Those less privileged had more trouble: R. C. Sherriff, who was eighteen and had just left an excellent grammar school where he had been captain of games (and whose play *Journey's End* would in 1928 be hailed as one of the great representations of life at the front), was refused a commission because an adjutant told him: 'our instructions are that all applicants for commissions must be selected from the recognised public schools, and yours is not among them.'[17] He eventually secured one in the East Surreys. War would change the Army's class-ridden nature, with 'temporary gentlemen' joining the old officer class.

Others, more worldly or experienced, tempered their enthusiasm with a recognition of reality: the unspoken point was that a proportion would never return. At his farewell dinner on 10 August, before leaving for France, Colonel Jack Seely, Secretary of State for War until the Curragh incident, told Sir George Riddell that 'the mortality would be terrible.'[18] Bertrand Russell, who later claimed to have foreseen slaughter that most others had not, recalled that 'the prospect filled me with horror, but what filled me with even more horror was the fact that the anticipation of carnage was delightful to something like ninety per cent of the population. I had to revise my views on human nature.'[19]

Society cohered around the ideal of the young man doing his duty. When Sir Hubert Parry, as director of the Royal College of Music, welcomed students back for the new term in September 1914, he talked of those – including students such as Jack Moeran and Arthur Bliss, who would survive the war and become renowned composers, and teachers such as Ralph Vaughan Williams, whose music would for the rest of his life be coloured by his experience of war – who 'have been honourably inspired to go and chance the risks of military life.'[20] He added: 'We feel a thrill of regard for them. It gives a comfortable feeling of admiration for our fellow-countrymen when we see them moved by fine and honourable motives to face the awful conditions of modern warfare – to risk their lives, and sometimes even worse, for generous ideals.' How the bereaved public came to absorb the unprecedented loss of life, and no unrest resulted, remains one of the astonishing facets of the conflict.

Yet Parry hinted at the damage that would be done by the loss of so many young men – in this case of musical talent, but as would become apparent, of many other spheres of excellence too, as the country's future leaders, teachers, artists and scientists were slaughtered. 'Our pupils are made of different stuff from the pupils of ordinary schools. They are gifted in a rare and special way. Some of them are so gifted that their loss could hardly be made good. It would be a special loss to the community . . . The world cannot afford to throw away such lives as if they were of no more account than lives that give no special promise of a rare kind.' He asked what it would have meant had Wagner been killed in the Dresden disturbances of 1849, before *Tristan*, *Meistersinger*, the *Ring* or *Parsifal*; but also raised the paradox that 'the people who offer themselves to such risks are often of the very best quality, and very often such as the world can ill spare; while numbers of those who do not offer themselves are mere loafers and shirkers who would be no loss, and would even be better and happier for being forced to face the guns and learn what a gain some experience of a really strenuous life would be to them.' That theme permeated the months ahead. As more soldiers were needed, fewer enlisted willingly. Many who wished to were pressured by their families not to, or told by their employers there would be no job when or if they returned.

However, in the early days of the war, a spirit of adventure prevailed: youths borrowed motorbikes so they could offer their services as dispatch riders; some who did not join up tried to become war correspondents, a vocation hampered by France's refusal to allow such people on its soil. Older men abandoned retirement so younger ones could leave their office jobs and fight. Many volunteered as special constables once enrolment began on 17 August; within months a Volunteer Corps – later formalised as the National Volunteer Force for Home Defence – would absorb older men, along lines similar to the Home Guard in Hitler's war. Boy Scouts were enlisted in volunteer duties, such as guarding telephone lines, railway bridges and reservoirs, acting as messengers and, later, working on the land. Girl Guides assisted nurses, worked in hospitals, but also learned signalling.

Despite the harvest proving a problem for many landowners, and volunteers unsuitable for military service being asked to help, patriotic employers urged their staff to go: one, Lady Knox, of Sherborne St John's near Basingstoke, advertised for 'chauffeur, gardener and groom-gardener . . . to replace men who have joined the colours. No able-bodied

man who can handle a rifle need apply.'[21] The rich were exhorted to sacrifice personal comforts and encourage their staff to join up; many
followed Lady Knox's precedent. The Earl of Wemyss, with a large
establishment at Stanway in Gloucestershire, 'issued an abrupt ultimatum to all his employees servants etc – to join the Army or leave his
service,' noted Violet Asquith, the prime minister's daughter, who was
staying with the family.[22] Wemyss went to London, leaving his wife,
whom he had not consulted, to handle the resultant chaos.

The Duke of Sutherland provided his Scottish seat, Dunrobin Castle,
as a hospital and convalescent home for the wounded. He established a
committee of grandees to register houses for such purposes, and to
arrange their equipping. The figurehead was Princess Christian, Queen
Victoria's third daughter and the King's aunt. As well as Sutherland, the
committee included two other dukes, Marlborough and Portland: and
social titans such as Kitchener, Esher and Lord Charles Beresford. Within
ten days Sutherland had received two hundred and fifty offers of houses,
mainly near the south and east coasts, and including Glamis Castle (home
of the future Queen Elizabeth), Cowdray Park, Walmer Castle and the
North Hampshire Golf Club. The *directrice* of the Berkendael Medical
Institute in Brussels, Edith Cavell, appealed for funds for what she expected
to be the extensive treatment of British wounded in Brussels: Nurse Cavell
did not expect Brussels would soon be in German hands.

When the grouse season started – on the day on which four British
divisions left for France – Lord Knutsford wrote to *The Times* to urge the
birds be distributed 'and eaten instead of butcher's meat', with large
quantities put into cold storage; and that when the partridge and pheas-
ant seasons began the same should be done with them.[23] He urged
ground game – rabbits and hares – to be harvested too, saying that 'the
hospitals would be very grateful for some stags.' The call was widely
taken up, with the proviso that, once the season's game had been killed,
gamekeepers should join the colours. Grand society weddings meticu-
lously planned for the autumn were hurriedly brought forward, with
couples marrying in small private ceremonies before the groom left for
active service: many did not live to celebrate an anniversary.

The older well-to-do, and women of all ages, took a leading role in
raising funds and supplies for charities, notably hospitals. Queen Mary
(German by ancestry, but born and bred in London and a great-
granddaughter of George III, her family of Teck a morganatic branch of

the House of Württemberg) established a national Needlework Guild – whose council included Mrs Asquith, Lady Northcliffe and Lady Lansdowne – and commanded the presidents of local guilds to have their ladies boost collection and manufacture of garments for the troops. The Queen urged organisers to find paid work in clothes manufacture for jobless women, and clothes for indigent women and children whose breadwinner was away fighting. Almost the whole country was mobilised in some way. Beatrice Webb, who had longed for such a manifestation of solidarity, felt disturbed as a 'collectivist who is also a believer in love as the bond between races as well as between individuals.'[24]

The government encouraged local landowners, grandees and Members of Parliament to take the lead in encouraging men in their areas to enlist. Although the initial target for new soldiers was 100,000 men, Asquith announced directly after the Battle of Mons – the British Expeditionary Force's first engagement of the war – that there would be no limit: 'We want all the recruits we can get.'[25] There was an emphasis on volunteering; the government was adamant that, in keeping with the ethos of liberalism it sought to practise, it would not, and would not need to, introduce conscription: though the well-connected *Morning Post* surmised that that was because there was no organisation to cope with it. C. P. Scott, once more the voice of traditional liberalism, told his former colleague Leonard Hobhouse with regret that 'if the war goes on long no doubt some form of compulsory training will be proposed and whatever is proposed by the Government would, under existing conditions, be adopted.'[26] He was right, as in a further prediction that such a move would energise the labour movement and make it the ideal home for radicals. Scott, though, expressed the patriotism of many Liberals who had opposed the war when writing to a Manchester trades unionist who had wanted him to address a protest meeting: 'I am strongly of [the] opinion that the war ought not to have taken place and that we ought not to have become parties to it, but once in it the whole future of our nation is at stake and we have no choice but do the utmost we can to secure success.'[27] This contrasted with the general view of leftist intellectuals such as the members of the Bloomsbury group, who affected not to care less about the nation, and to see the war as a tiresome irrelevance. Of the many things that the war would destroy, liberalism would be chief among them.

Even though in August 1914 there was no question of conscription, the men enlisting and the massive new army they formed required careful overall management. If Grey was right, and Asquith had intended to leave Haldane at the War Office, he may have been swayed by public opinion not to do so: Haldane's misfortune in not being an intimate of Repington, *The Times*'s military correspondent, counted against him. 'He is not the best man available' was how the newspaper put it.[28] That man, it was widely felt, was Kitchener; and ironically, Haldane had told Asquith that 'in my opinion you should make Kitchener your War Minister. He commands a degree of public confidence which no-one else would bring to the post.'[29] The argument that he lacked parliamentary experience, *The Times* continued, 'may be instantly swept aside.' He had sat on the Viceroy's Council in India (no mention was made of intrigues and problems he had caused).[30] What was needed was not someone versed in the subtleties of debate, but who could direct forces in the field – the job of a commander-in-chief, not a cabinet minister, as the paper should have known.

Kitchener had told Asquith late on 4 August that he would serve his country in the War Office only in the post of Secretary of State: Asquith felt he had no choice, and began persuading his colleagues. Whether his qualities were sufficient to override his defects was less clear. Haldane later told Mrs Asquith that Kitchener was 'a man of great authority, and considerable ignorance'. He added: 'He will improve.'[31] Rudyard Kipling, who had met him in Cairo in 1913, felt he was 'a fatted pharaoh in spurs . . . garrulously intoxicated with power.'[32] Within a couple of months Mrs Asquith would write of Kitchener that 'telling the truth is not his strong point' and 'he is a man of good judgement and bad manners; a man brutal by nature and by pose; a man of no imagination but not without ideas . . . he has been the despair of the War Office ever since he succeeded Henry.'[33] However, she conceded that 'the British public and Tory party think him a god!' The country was indeed in raptures at his new post: Blanche Lloyd noted the appointment had 'the whole weight of public enthusiasm behind it.'[34]

And indeed for all Kitchener's faults – those of a career soldier used to giving orders, moved to a deliberative body as one of many equals – he had virtues too. He was a realist, who knew the war would not end quickly: an insight not then shared by Asquith or most of his colleagues, who saw it as a temporary difficulty. (Asquith confirmed as much when he told Venetia Stanley, his confidante and the woman he longed to have as his mistress, that Kitchener was 'an emergency man', until the war ended.[35] His job in Cairo was kept open for him.) The new Secretary of State, who understood the Germans' capabilities, shocked colleagues at his first cabinet meeting by warning that 'we must be prepared to put armies of millions into the field and to maintain them for several years.'[36] Had Kitchener not realised that a huge, more professional and better-trained army would be needed to win the war, with a massive supply of replacements after the BEF sustained heavy casualties, the outcome could have been disastrous for Britain. Yet one paradox of Kitchener's grip on his responsibilities was that although he realised the Army would need huge numbers of men, he had not grasped how much extra ordnance would be needed to keep them fighting. Munitions factories were put on twenty-four-hour working, and extra plant laid down as quickly as possible: but that would be nowhere near enough: what was actually required was the industrialisation of munitions production on a vast scale to cope with the mechanisation of war.

Kitchener's appointment distressed the radical wing of the Liberal Party, with Scott saying it signalled the end of a Liberal government, replaced by what 'to all intents and purposes [was] a coalition'.[37] Kitchener was a better administrator than an organiser. He did not know how to delegate. He had also lost the best staff officers from the War Office, as they were summoned to the front. He treated civil servants and ministerial colleagues as subordinates, acting as a field marshal unused to being questioned or criticised would. Until mid-September he attended cabinet in civilian clothes; then, as the situation became graver, he reverted to his field marshal's uniform.

With the surge of volunteering there came a growing demand for men to be allowed to serve with their friends and colleagues from civilian life. Some battalions were formed according to the men's role in peacetime, or shared backgrounds. The Lord Mayor of London formed a Stockbrokers' Battalion on 21 August, and on 11 September four Public Schools' Battalions were formed. Others brought together men from the same neighbourhoods or towns – the pals' battalions. On 29 August the Liverpool Pals were formed as part of King's (Liverpool) Regiment by the Earl of Derby. Known as 'The King of Lancashire', bosom friend of George V, chairman of the West Lancashire Territorial Association and a man who devoted himself to recruitment of the volunteer Army,

Derby annoyed the labour movement in his standard recruiting speech, which included this promise: 'When the war is over I intend, as far as I possibly can, to employ nobody except men who have taken their duty at the front. I go further than that, and say that, all things being equal, if two men come to me for a farm and one has been at the front there is no doubt who will get the farm.'[38] Many towns formed pals' battalions, their names carved on memorials across Britain and, metaphorically, in legend. The mayor of the town formed the Accrington Pals on 2 September, and within days the Bradford Pals and the Leeds Pals had been created. The Northumberland Fusiliers raised twelve pals' battalions, the Royal Fusiliers ten and the Middlesex, Manchester and Welch Regiments, and the Royal Irish Rifles, nine each.

So keen were men to serve with their neighbours that it caused great distress when volunteers from Essex were told that the Essex Regiment could not recruit because it was 'full'.[39] It was subsequently allowed to recruit 1,000 men, which it did within days, but was then told it could recruit no more: any men who tried to sign up in Essex would have to join a regiment with which they had no local connection, which deterred some. The War Office was implored to add extra battalions to county regiments, which it soon did: but it had been slow to recognise the emotional pull of fighting units linking their soldiers with their homes. Effective though the localisation of battalions may have been in aiding recruitment, the concentration of men in fighting units raised on a geographical basis would cut swaths through communities when their regiments were in particularly bloody battles, notably from the Somme onwards.

The large numbers flocking to join the colours even before the famous entreaty featuring the poster of Kitchener (published on 5 September) caused financial difficulties for many families. For those in the skilled working class and above, service would entail a financial sacrifice. Aware of this, the Prince of Wales – aged twenty and in the Grenadier Guards, but forbidden by Kitchener to fight lest he be taken prisoner – launched a relief fund on 6 August. It raised £1 million within the first week. The Queen made a special appeal to women; and Queen Alexandra headed an appeal for the Soldiers' and Sailors' Families Association, with which she had been closely identified during the Boer War: she enlisted lords lieutenant of counties, and the lord mayors and provosts of great cities, to act as local representatives. Within a week the appeals merged and issued a statement of intent in relieving all hardship, especially that caused by the death, capture or wounding of a serviceman. The public response was spontaneously generous: the King led with £5,000 but, as a mark of where financial clout now lay in Britain, George Coats, a Paisley cotton manufacturer, gave £50,000. In 1916 he was raised to the peerage as Lord Glentanar. By the end of March 1915 the appeal had raised £4,907,000, of which £1,960,000 had been disbursed.[40]

The question of how families shorn of a breadwinner would survive without charity troubled the government, and on 16 September the cabinet agreed to award a separation allowance, on a sliding scale from 12s 6d a week for a childless wife to 22s 6d a week for one with four or more children. 'Many of them will be better off than they ever were before,' Asquith claimed to Miss Stanley.[41] A widow's pension of 6s 6d was set for a childless woman whose husband was killed in action, with higher rates for those with children. Voluntary organisations sought to keep women occupied and remunerated – whether in making clothing for the troops, or training young women as nurses, though that was a calling for which the mores of the time deemed women from the middle and upper-middle classes best suited. University women were urged to become nurses, and one of their institutions, Bedford College in London, started to hold extensive training sessions for those interested.

The working class also closed ranks and looked after their own. Miners in many pits in Yorkshire donated 2d a week to a fund to help the wives and children of fellow miners who, as Territorials, had been called up. Engineering workers in Leeds, working longer hours for war production, agreed to put their overtime pay into a separate fund for such families. A *Times* correspondent, sent to Leeds to take the temperature, found that 'there is a real spirit of unselfishness abroad, and patriotism is showing its finer side.'[42] Dentists in the West Riding volunteered to check recruits without a fee; and Leeds's substantial Jewish colony promised to raise a volunteer corps.

Queen Mary was also instrumental in leading a drive to get women into work, to replace men and to boost family incomes. Many small businesses run by women were suffering from the war, and the Queen wanted to help sustain them. She sent her friend Lady Crewe to outline her wishes to the prime minister. Asquith had been the nation's leading anti-suffragist, and the Queen could have been forgiven for fearing he might have been slow to appreciate the industrial contribution women could make. He was happy for the National Relief Fund to adopt the scheme, which would prove a successful means of alleviating hardship for women and of boosting the economy. Mrs Pankhurst announced that the activities of her suffragettes would be suspended for the duration: her daughter Christabel proclaimed that 'Bismarck boasted that Germany is a male nation. We do not want male nations.'[43] Pursuing national unity, Reginald McKenna, the home secretary, announced on 10 August that the King would remit the sentences of all suffragette prisoners, who were to be released unconditionally. (Former strikers convicted of assault were also released, McKenna expressing the hope that both groups would help and not destabilise the country.)

However, a more subtle form of campaigning for women's rights would continue throughout the war, underpinned by the growing strategic and economic importance of women. Christabel Pankhurst's women's journal *Suffragette* was retitled *Britannia*. A Women's Emergency Corps was quickly founded by suffragette members of the Women's Social and Political Union, its aims being to train female doctors, nurses and motorcycle messengers. It evolved into the Women's Volunteer Reserve under the leadership of Lady Castlereagh, who in 1915 became Lady Londonderry on her husband's inheriting the marquisate. She also founded the Women's Legion, which trained 40,000 khaki-uniformed women volunteers to act as drivers, mechanics, farm workers and cooks; a number lost their lives during the war. Paul Rubens, a songwriter, published the song 'Your King and Your Country' within days of the war breaking out. It is better known by the words of its refrain, 'we don't want to lose you, but we think you ought to go', and was intended to be sung by women to their menfolk. The royalties from the sheet music were donated to Queen Mary's Work for Women Fund, and such was its enormous popularity that it raised nearly £500,000. It was also taken up by popular music-hall entertainers, such as Vesta Tilley, and sung by them with the express purpose of persuading men in the audience to go straight off to the recruiting office.

II

One of the United Kingdom's foremost cultural figures, George Bernard Shaw, took a less elated view of the war. His *Pygmalion*, starring Mrs Patrick Campbell as Eliza Doolittle and Sir Herbert Beerbohm Tree as

Professor Higgins, had been the theatrical success of the year after its London opening the previous April. However, Shaw's popularity crashed when he told an American interviewer in late September that soldiers on both sides should 'shoot their officers and go home'.[44] Having been in high demand to write journalism about the war, he found his telephone fell silent. By November he had revised his view; his pamphlet published in the *New Statesman* on 14 November, entitled *Common Sense about the War*, claimed to have 'stated the democratic case for it', by showing how the war could empower and enfranchise those further down in society and help them wrest control from the forces of capitalism.[45] This won him more abuse, and his role in shaping public discourse for the duration would be circumscribed. Even Christabel Pankhurst described him as 'beyond a joke'.[46] Others normally sympathetic to him, such as the equally polemical G. K. Chesterton, were appalled, and H. G. Wells, with whom he had scrapped before the war and whose own view of the struggle would in time become more Shavian, gleefully went for him, calling him 'an elderly adolescent'.[47]

Keir Hardie too radically challenged the climate of unity. He had opposed the war because he was by nature a pacifist, and because he perceived its most likely victims to be working men. He deplored an alliance with the Tsar, prime enemy of the labour movement. However, in his animosity he made claims about the conduct of the war that embarrassed and aggrieved even fellow Labour MPs, including one who with him represented Merthyr Tydfil, Edgar Jones. Jones recited Hardie's excesses in the Commons on 16 November: Hardie chose not to attend. He had seemed to belittle the suffering of Belgian women during the German invasion – suffering that outraged British sensibilities – by saying that 'the ravaging of women has always been an accompaniment of war'.[48] He had implied something similar was happening around Army camps 'at home', and claimed that letters from soldiers had been censored because they mentioned 'ghastly tales about the on-goings of our French Allies.'[49] Predictably, he imputed even worse crimes to Britain's Russian allies; more shocking, he said that atrocities such as the Germans were alleged to have committed were 'now happening in the towns and villages which are being recaptured by the Allies in France'.

Hardie had also claimed the Russians would dictate the terms of any peace; that the Belgians had committed atrocities in the Congo; he had 'sneered' at the loyalty of Indian troops; he had vilified as 'not to be trusted' General Botha, who was mobilising South Africa behind the Allied cause.[50] He had talked of the government having 'opened wide the gate of the lie factory in which tales of German atrocities are made to order', which he had called 'a sign that the Allies are not making headway.' Worst of all, he had compared the alleged military leadership of the Kaiser with Britain's own 'fireside-loving King.'[51] That last sneer especially upset His Majesty's loyal subjects in Merthyr Tydfil, hence the trouble to which Jones was going to distance himself from them.

At the opposite end of the social ladder Lady Ottoline Morrell, who ran a salon at 44 Bedford Square and had been, effectively, the Bloomsbury group before anyone had heard of it, flew the flag of pacifism with her husband Philip, the Liberal MP. By day Lady Ottoline did good works for destitute Germans and helped those upon whom British public opinion had turned. But on Thursday nights from November 1914 she gave soirées at number 44, to cheer up the *beau monde*, or at least those who did not regard the Morrells as 'pro-German' and felt able to attend. These included the cream of artistic life – the Clive Bells, Duncan Grant, Mark Gertler, Walter Sickert and Augustus John – and writers and thinkers such as Lytton Strachey, J. M. Keynes, Bertrand Russell and Arnold Bennett. 'Those who came often dressed themselves up in gay Persian, Turkish, and other oriental clothes, of which I had a store,' Lady Ottoline recalled, artlessly, in her memoirs.[52] While the British regular Army was being shattered on the Marne, Morrell would play the pianola ('a new toy'), Grant 'bounded about like a Russian ballet dancer', and Russell was 'a stiff little figure, jumping up and down like a child, with an expression of surprised delight on his face at finding himself doing such an ordinary human thing as dancing.' Sadly, the Thursday evenings ended in April 1915, when Lady Ottoline and her menagerie decamped to the Morrells' country house at Garsington, which would become a haven for pacifists and conscientious objectors in the era of conscription.

Such people were, however, in a minority: many who shared the artistic interests of the Morrells and their friends gave themselves entirely to the war effort. Lloyd George, himself a reluctant convert to war, now threw himself wholeheartedly into the fight, seizing initiatives in a way Asquith seemed incapable of doing. On 2 September, at Lloyd George's suggestion, Charles Masterman, Chancellor of the Duchy of Lancaster and former co-editor with Ford Madox Hueffer (later Ford) of the *English Review*, asked twenty-five 'eminent literary men' to Wellington House to form a secret Propaganda Bureau. They included Arnold Bennett, Chesterton, Arthur Conan Doyle, John Galsworthy, Hueffer, Thomas Hardy, Kipling, John Masefield, Newbolt, G. M. Trevelyan and Wells. Perhaps because of an oversight, one absentee was Robert Bridges, who that morning described the war as being, in his view, 'between Christ and the Devil', with the Germans taking their philosophical lead from Nietzsche.[53]

The operation at Wellington House – whose existence was not officially confirmed until 1935 – became a point of coordination for British propaganda to neutral countries. However, the government also grasped the broader benefits of the public reading its favourite writers extolling the virtues of Britain's fight. Masterman commissioned his literary friends to write pamphlets about the Hun's wickedness, such as *When Blood is Their Argument* by Ford, son of a German immigrant, a counterblast to Shaw's *Common Sense about the War*, which saw wrong on both sides and compounded his earlier offence in observing that as war broke out 'the ordinary war-conscious civilian went mad.'[54] Newbolt began writing adventure stories for boys to instil patriotic virtues, tramping the country giving a lecture entitled 'Poetry and Patriotism'. His audience at one point consisted of a small group 'mostly knitting'.[55]

Assisting ministers and men of letters in advocating war were dons in the faculty of Modern History at Oxford, who by 14 September had published a slim red hardback called *Why We Are at War: Great Britain's Case*. It noted European tensions since 1870, and described the perfidy of Germany's conduct during July 1914. It addressed constitutional philosophy: 'The war in which England is now engaged with Germany is fundamentally a war between two different principles – that of *raison d'état* and that of the rule of law.'[56] It evoked the old struggle between the Stuarts who had chosen to act above the law and Parliament that had fought to include the Crown within the law, and subject to its rule. At a more demotic level Ivor Novello, the songwriter, took up the message in 'Keep the Home Fires Burning'. According to legend, he wrote it because his mother was bored by 'It's a Long Way to Tipperary', and begged him to compose an alternative.[57] Its second verse includes:

> Overseas there came a pleading
> 'Help a nation in distress.'
> And we gave our glorious laddies –

Honour bade us do no less.
For no gallant son of freedom
To a tyrant's yoke should bend,
And a noble heart must answer
To the sacred call of 'Friend'.

Long before the dons of Oxford published their justification for the war, the government had established the line to be taken: Germany was the aggressor, and Britain had sought only to stop the conflict. Evidence of this was provided on 6 August, when the full diplomatic correspondence of the crisis was laid before the House, prior to an address by the prime minister. The only other such information had been published by the Germans on 4 August, and was incomplete, making no mention of the negotiations between Britain and Germany. It was a clever propaganda move, helping ensure no weakening of the general public resolve that Britain had been in the right. Asquith confirmed the price Germany had offered to keep Britain out of the fight: the nation breaking its word to Belgium, and disregarding its neutrality. 'Belgians are fighting and losing their lives,' he told the Commons. 'What would have been the position of Great Britain to-day, in the face of that spectacle, if we had assented to this infamous proposal?'[58] He could not have entertained such 'betrayal' and 'dishonour'.[59] He praised Grey for his attempts to maintain peace: and proclaimed that 'we are unsheathing our sword in a just cause', giving the definitive view of why war had been declared:

If I am asked what we are fighting for I reply in two sentences. In the first place, to fulfil a solemn international obligation, an obligation which, if it had been entered into between private persons in the ordinary concerns of life, would have been regarded as an obligation not only of law but of honour, which no self-respecting man could possibly have repudiated. I say, secondly, we are fighting to vindicate the principle which, in these days when force, material force, sometimes seems to be the dominant influence and factor in the development of mankind, we are fighting to vindicate the principle that small nationalities are not to be crushed, in defiance of international good faith, by the arbitrary will of a strong and over-mastering Power.[60]

III

The reduction of the causes of the war to a simple dualism of a virtuous Britain seeking to drive out of an oppressed nation an aggressive and duplicitous Germany had an inevitable, and swift, effect on how the public viewed Germans living in Britain, rendering them objects of suspicion. The natural desire to guard against German infiltration into British life quickly grew into anti-Germanism. After cabinet on 5 August – which resolved to ask Parliament for a vote of credit of £100 million to pay the initial expenses of the war, about which Asquith in a bipartisan spirit immediately consulted Law – the prime minister saw the King, whom he found 'a good deal relieved'; he told Miss Stanley the Monarch was 'becoming very anti-German'.[61] An Aliens Restriction Bill was introduced on the same day 'to remove or restrain the movements of undesirable aliens', in the words of Reginald McKenna, helping prevent espionage.[62] What would become MI5's Central Registry (staffed by women) denominated six classes of alien:

AA – Absolutely Anglicised or Absolutely Allied – undoubtedly friendly
A – Anglicised or Allied – friendly
AB – Anglo-Boche – doubtful, but probably friendly
BA – Boche-Anglo – doubtful, but probably hostile
B – Boche – hostile
BB – Bad Boche – undoubtedly hostile.[63]

The Bill dictated that the coming and going of such people would be rigidly controlled, as would their activities and places of residence. The law would punish those who helped aliens evade restrictions. Those thought hostile would be placed in internment camps – or as the government called them, 'concentration camps'.[64] Cases arose of wives and children of internees plunged into destitution: the local Boards of Guardians, who administered workhouses, were given grants to assist them.

The inevitable question was asked – by Joseph King, the Liberal MP – about Germans who had lived in Britain for years and who 'are much more British in sentiment than German': McKenna said they would be

unmolested, once they had registered, provided they did not live in prohibited areas, and gave the authorities no reason to believe they were
'secretly engaged in operations against this country'.[65] The Bill passed in
a few minutes: no one questioned its urgency. A few days later a Liberal
MP, Edmund Harvey, emphasised that 'it is very noteworthy that while
we are in a state of war there is no feeling of grudging or hostility against
the mass of the Germans. We have no sort of unfriendly feeling to them,
and we can show, in a time of crisis, friendliness and self-restraint to
these unhappy strangers in our midst.' That attitude would not prevail
much longer, eroded first by the press, and then by German excesses
against civilians. Within the first month 66,773 Germans, Austrians
and Hungarians registered, 37,457 of these in London and 949 in Ireland. By
1 November 17,283 enemy aliens had been interned.[66]

Signs of Germanness vanished from British life. Offices of German
steamship companies in London and elsewhere were shuttered. Shops
owned by Germans acquired British names; a chain of German delica-
tessens displayed notices proclaiming that 'the proprietor is a
naturalised British subject'. As an extra precaution another notice read:
'During war-time 25 per cent of the takings of all my shops will be given
to the British Red Cross Society.'[67] Newspapers published announcements by people who had changed their names, a trait the Royal Family
would adopt within three years. Felix Rosenheim, a Liverpool magistrate, became Mr Rose; two brothers from Holloway named Siegenberg
chose the aristocratic name of Curzon, and Alfred Schacht, a stock-
broker, transmuted into Alfred Dent.[68]

Matters were worse for those further down the social order. Areas
such as London's east end, with a high concentration of Germans, were
plastered with posters informing local residents of their obligations
under the Aliens Restriction Act. German shops had bricks put
through windows; a couple of Limehouse bakers and a grocer had their
premises wrecked, following rumours that German tradesmen were
poisoning the food they sold. Some tradesmen sold their businesses, at
very disadvantageous prices, and others retired. Some feared repatriation to Germany, which had become a foreign country to them. Many
Jews came under suspicion early in the war: the editor of the *Jewish
Chronicle* countered 'the ignorant assumption up and down the country
that every Jew is necessarily a German and is hence being made an
object of hatred as an enemy of this country . . . Jews are by their

tradition and, indeed, by absolute Jewish law, bound by loyalty to the country of which they are citizens.[69]

Parliament was asked on 7 August to pass a Defence of the Realm Bill, part of which would allow courts martial to try spies and saboteurs; this went through all stages in a matter of minutes. The new Act – universally known as DORA, whose powers would be increased six times – also made it illegal to undermine recruitment, the currency or allegiance to the Sovereign in a printed article, speech or conversation. It had unforeseen consequences: several painters were arrested for working out of doors, including Sir John Lavery and Augustus John, because it was feared they were drawing a landscape in order to pass information about it on to the Germans.[70] Legislation followed to punish anyone trading with the enemy, or giving commercial assistance. It was legislation far without normal British practice: it put the Army and Navy in charge of a field of civil law, with limited rights of appeal. However, for the first half of the war it impinged on relatively few. It was only in 1916, when conscription was enforced and public support for the war started to wane, and dissent rise, that the effects of DORA began to intrude seriously in ordinary lives.

Reports of German outrages fed loathing of the enemy: and by mid-September the offences extended to those against culture as well as against people. The Belgian university city of Louvain was reduced to ashes, provocative enough to more sensitive Britons: but the news on 21 September that Reims Cathedral was a smouldering shell seemed definitive proof of German barbarism. Frances Stevenson, Lloyd George's mistress and secretary, recorded that the destruction 'moved him more than anything else since the outbreak of the war.'[71] The Times called it a 'crowning atrocity' against something belonging not just to France, but to the 'whole world'; Germany had 'forsaken Christianity' and gone 'beyond the pale of civilisation.'[72]

The public's demand for harsh measures against Germans, Austrians and Hungarians in Britain was stoked up not least by the Northcliffe press, for which it had become a fetish. MO5(g), the forerunner of MI5, was highly active, intercepting cables and letters, which horrified McKenna when he was informed: such interference in communications was punishable by two years' imprisonment, he reminded MO5(g) officials, who talked him round. He was unaware that the department, founded in 1909, had done it before the war too. In mid-October a huge round-up of aliens took place in London's East End, and other major towns. Schweppes, the drinks firm, took large newspaper advertisements professing that they were Swiss, and asking for information that would allow them to bring a libel suit against whoever was spreading the rumour that they were German. On 21 October ninety aliens – mainly hotel staff and commercial travellers – were arrested in Newcastle and Gateshead; the next day one hundred hoteliers and businessmen in Sheffield were rounded up. *The Times* reported that 'it is estimated that there are between 700 and 800 enemy aliens in Birmingham. About 20 were arrested yesterday [22 October] and the process will be continued until the city has been cleared.'[73]

At Folkestone thirty-one aliens, mainly waiters, were run in, and within forty-eight hours the town was pronounced 'cleared' of military-age enemy aliens. On 22 October a thousand such aliens were arrested throughout Britain, and almost that number the next day. Those arrested in southern England – described by *The Times* as 'an army of waiters' – were held at a camp at Frith Hill in Surrey before being sent to the Isle of Man.[74] *Daily Mail* readers were urged to refuse service by German or Austrian waiters; and if one said he was Swiss, to 'ASK TO SEE HIS PASSPORT'.[75] As well as hitting the hotel and restaurant trade, the round-up hobbled Britain's dandies, since most of London's best trouser-makers were Germans, and tailoring firms were bereft after their arrest. Many had British wives, some of whom were thrown on the mercy of the parish. Other Germans were in the wrong place at the wrong time. On 26 October Northampton Town Council sacked its tramways manager, Mr Gottschalk, because he was born in Germany. The pill was sweetened by £300 compensation, but the fate of most of German origin, registered as aliens and law-abiding, was that if sacked no one would employ them, and they could not return 'home'. Naturalisation was dismissed: the notion of 'once a German, always a German' became common currency.

Anti-German feeling became worse as the enemy, repelled on the Marne, continued to advance elsewhere, nearing Calais in the northwest and only just held by the British in what would become known as the First Battle of Ypres. The King told Asquith on 23 October that he and the Queen had received 'heaps of letters' abusing them about their German cousins fighting against Britain: and, closer to home in every sense, about what one correspondent had termed 'the damned German spy', Prince Louis of Battenberg, the King's cousin, the First Sea Lord.[76] Asquith found the King 'a good deal agitated' about Prince Louis, and defensive of his cousins fighting on the other side: 'He told me rather naively,' Asquith relayed to Miss Stanley, 'that Cousin Albert is "not really fighting on the side of the Germans": he had only been "put in charge of a camp of English prisoners" near Berlin! – a nice distinction.' Asquith visited an internment camp at Deepcut on the Surrey/Hampshire border and realised what a cross section of society had been corralled there: 'They were a rotten looking lot – waiters, hairdressers & the scum of Whitechapel & the East End with a sprinkling of doctors, professors and educated men.'[77] On 27 October the government published a list of coastal areas where enemy aliens, even if registered and law-abiding, could not set foot, in case they observed movements of shipping. These included the entire counties of Norfolk, Suffolk, Sussex and Monmouthshire; most of coastal Scotland, and Orkney and Shetland; and almost every port in Britain with the exception of London. The next day the state, already struggling to billet, clothe and equip its new soldiers, ran out of accommodation for internees.

Prince Louis was not the only high-profile victim of anti-German feeling. Another casualty was the proprietor of Sanatogen, who being in Germany received no profits from his British subsidiary during the war. Also, the annuity of £3,000 a year paid to the last surviving grandchild of George III, the ninety-two-year-old Grand Duchess of Mecklenburg-Strelitz – born Princess Augusta of Cambridge to George III's seventh son, and beloved aunt of Queen Mary – was stopped, as the Grand Duchess (born at Kensington Palace, and married to her cousin the Grand Duke at Buckingham Palace) was holed up in Neustrelitz, in Pomerania. There was also Sir Edgar Speyer, who had been one of the great financiers behind London's underground railways in the 1890s and 1900s, and in their electrification. He had been rewarded with a baronetcy in 1906 and, more unusually, a privy counsellorship in 1909; his honours reflected his lavish donations to the Liberal Party. He had been born in New York in 1862 to German-Jewish parents, but then educated in Frankfurt. He was chairman of Speyer Brothers, his family's finance house, and a partner in its New York and Frankfurt branches. He took over the London branch in 1887, and in 1892 he took British citizenship. He and Leonora von Stosch, his violinist wife whom he married in 1902, were generous patrons of classical music, and Speyer counted Elgar, Richard Strauss and Debussy among his friends. Keen to enrich the cultural life of his adopted country, he also underwrote the promenade concerts at the Queen's Hall for thirteen seasons, from 1902 to 1914, as one of many acts of philanthropy, others of which included acting as treasurer to Scott's expedition to the Antarctic, being a founder of the Whitechapel Art Gallery and donating to numerous hospitals.

The day war broke out Speyer resigned from the Frankfurt bank; a month later he resigned his American partnership too, as British subjects were forbidden to do business with any firm still trading with Germany, as the New York bank was. However, this did not stop an onslaught against him. He had to remove his daughters from their schools and resign his positions on charitable boards. For months he lived with a police guard on his house. He had a property on the coast at Overstrand in Norfolk, from which it was rumoured – without any supporting evidence – that he signalled to the German fleet. In May 1915, in a torrent of anti-German feeling after the sinking of the *Lusitania*, he offered to resign from the Privy Council and forfeit his baronetcy. Asquith said the King refused to contemplate either, and added that he himself knew Speyer better than to think he was pro-German. However, Speyer resigned his chairmanship of the Underground Electric Railways Company of London; and when a campaign began to remove the privy counsellorship, he had had enough. He began to behave with what his friend Lord Reading called a 'studiously disrespectful' attitude, and took his wife and daughters to New York. He became increasingly hostile to Britain, so much so that in 1921 his and his family's naturalisations (and his privy counsellorship) were revoked .[78]

However, in October 1914 the Asquiths would still have the Speyers to dinner in Downing Street, even though some of their friends would shun them and others withdrew investments from Speyer's bank. It would not be the last time the prime minister would entertain them, though some who still felt able to attend would not discuss war-related topics in front of them. Unfortunately, Speyer's brother James, who ran the New York business, had proclaimed himself for Germany and had entertained the German ambassador to Washington.

Prince Louis, a naval officer and naturalised Briton since 1868, had to endure an assassination of his character led by the Northcliffe press. Churchill told Asquith that Prince Louis would have to go, not because of any wrongdoing or impropriety, but simply, like the man who ran the Northampton trams, because of his birth. Asquith concurred, and Churchill had 'a most delicate and painful interview' with the Prince, the more so since the Prince's nephew, Prince Maurice (Queen Victoria's youngest grandchild), had been killed at Ypres the previous day. Asquith noted that Prince Louis behaved 'with great dignity and public spirit' in resigning at once. Briefed by the First Lord, he wrote Churchill a short and dignified letter about how 'I have lately been driven to the painful conclusion that at this juncture my birth and parentage have the effect of impairing in some respects my usefulness on the Board of Admiralty.'[79] The King made the Prince a privy counsellor to show his faith in his loyalty and integrity: 'There is no more loyal man in the country.'[80] *The Times* – a Northcliffe paper that had not hounded him – called the campaign 'part of it honest if ill-timed, part of it monstrously unjust'.[81] Churchill said that 'no incident in my public life has caused me so much sorrow.'[82]

Hand in hand with anti-German feeling came the greatly increased fear, and prospect, of espionage. Since 5 August Scotland Yard detectives had been rounding up suspected spies, including one 'staying at a fashionable hotel in the vicinity of Hyde Park'.[83] It was reported that a dozen were arrested in London, out of twenty-one held that day, many near dockyards: and of four men remanded under the 1911 Official Secrets Act at Bow Street, three were German and the fourth a British subject of German origins. For days newspapers carried stories of arrests, and other spy scares, including rumours that the mayor of Deal had been arrested, as had an Australian with a camera 'acting very suspiciously' near the Windsor Castle waterworks. By mid-August the cells at Felixstowe police station were 'full of men arrested as spies.'[84] To cope with this epidemic MO5(g) more than doubled from seventeen people to forty by the end of 1914, and still could not manage its workload.[85] A year later it would have colonised a building in the Adelphi in London and found another 227 recruits, including wounded officers unfit for active service, but able to serve in an equally important way. Most of its office staff, however, were well-educated women, a pioneering example of the female contribution to the war effort.

The first spy executed in Britain in the war, Carl Hans Lody, was shot at dawn on 6 November. There had been no execution in the Tower of London since Lord Lovat's in 1747, after the Jacobite rebellion. Lody had been captured in Killarney on 2 October after a telegram he had sent to Sweden had been seen by MO5(g), who recognised the address as an enemy operation. Before fleeing to Ireland he had watched naval manoeuvres in the Firth of Forth. Letters to Berlin had been intercepted, packed with information about the Fleet, and signed, in a curious anachronism, 'Nazi'.[86] His trial, by a military court, during which he sat in the dock guarded by two soldiers with fixed bayonets, had been held in public (though the court was cleared when matters of national security were discussed) and reported almost verbatim in the quality press – the government wished to show the enemy how good its anti-spy defences were – though the sentence was delivered *in camera*. Lody denied nothing. MPs were angry that four days elapsed between his execution and its announcement: Sir William Bull, MP for Hammersmith, said: 'it is difficult to conceive the reason why the news that Lody had been shot should not have been immediately telegraphed over the Empire. There are a great many spies who never believed we should shoot anybody.'[87] There would be ten more such executions in the Tower.

Sir Stanley Buckmaster, the Solicitor General, had been drafted in to supervise the Press Bureau. He curtly reminded Bull not just of the need to protect the nation's security in ensuring information released was both accurate and of no use to the enemy, but that things could be much worse: 'We are,' he told them, 'the only institution that stands between the press and the untempered severity of martial law.'[88] Under DORA the press was subject to martial law: by printing only what the Press Bureau sanctioned, it had a cast-iron defence against any allegation that it had endangered national security. The public were not stupid, and contrasted reports of dead and wounded and the entrenched nature of the fighting with what was termed the 'deceptive optimism' of the newspapers. *The Times* argued, sharply, that 'the real responsibility for a one-sided impression of events rests with the Censorship.'[89] There could hardly have been clearer confirmation that what their customers were reading was far from the whole truth.

The public was ever more vigilant for spies, or other acts of treachery, following the Lody trial. It became known that the Duke of Cumberland and the Duke of Albany, both of whom had been born British subjects (and the latter of whom had been born in England), were now actively assisting enemies of the Crown. Cumberland, a great-grandson of George III, was a vocal supporter of the Kaiser; Albany, posthumous son of Queen Victoria's son Leopold, was commanding German troops. He had succeeded his uncle, her son Prince Alfred, as Duke of Saxe-Coburg and Gotha in 1900, aged sixteen, and had his education superintended by his cousin, the Kaiser. An MP, Swift MacNeill, asked Asquith whether both dukes were not guilty of treason; and whether they should not, in the first instance, have their British titles removed and be barred from the House of Lords. Asquith, conscious of the embarrassment this might cause the King, a cousin of both men, said it could wait until after the war. It would be revisited before then, however, in 1917, when the King decided to change his family name from the unappealing Saxe-Coburg-Gotha to the more homely Windsor.

Although the panic was overdone, security was appallingly lax. Lody had strolled into England off a boat at Newcastle, posing as an American tourist. Politicians, officers and their wives gossiped about troop movements, strategies and policies so loosely that anyone in London society could within a couple of days have picked up much that was going on. In Ireland, even though Nationalists had rallied to the Union flag, seditious anti-recruiting pamphlets abounded. The Earl of Meath told the Lords on 18 November that Ireland was awash with German money and German spies, and that 'Dublin at this moment is being swamped by literature which I should think came within the category of high treason.'[90]

As spy mania had, in the words of Basil Thomson, assistant commissioner of the Metropolitan Police, 'assumed a virulent epidemic form accompanied by delusions which defied treatment', it turned its wrath on the Germanophile Haldane, Asquith's closest political friend.[91] Unwilling to submit to such prejudice, he spoke in the Lords of the unfair treatment of some internees – such as a man, German by birth, who had two sons fighting for the King while he languished in a concentration camp. None of this did anything to allay the suspicions the Unionists and their friends in the press held about him, on account of what they believed to be his pro-German sympathies.

The Times renewed its attempt to smear Haldane, begun when it feared he, and not Kitchener, would be appointed to the War Office. It admitted Haldane was a 'faithful patriot', but had been 'long and honourably known for his warm predilections for Germany.' He was 'partially educated in that country, he has frequently spent his leisure there, his mind is coloured by his unremitting study of German literature and philosophy, he cherishes many close German friendships.' Having listed these disqualifications, the leader-writer deemed them 'innocuous enough': less so, it seemed, than his 'strenuous . . . efforts to promote Anglo-German friendship, and in pursuing this course he has unwittingly contributed to cloud British perception of the arrogant dominating aims of German national ambition.' The fact was that he had had the temerity to take a different approach to Germany from Northcliffe, provoking this tirade of prejudice and ignorance extreme even by the standards of *The Times* under his proprietorship. In the fevered mood, it hit home. Magnanimously, the paper advocated that he remain on the Woolsack. Lies about Haldane would circulate for months, enraging colleagues who knew the existence of the Territorial Army, many of whose members were about to be sent abroad, was his achievement. Nor was Northcliffe, who had inflamed sentiment by publishing a self-regarding pamphlet entitled *Scaremongerings* – which boasted about how right the *Daily Mail* had been to forecast German belligerence – the worst culprit. The main assault on the Lord Chancellor came from the ultra-Conservative *Morning Post*.

Haldane held his nerve and stuck to his principles. In a Lords debate on spies in November he emphasised that 'to arrest aliens wholesale, irrespective of their guilt or innocence, irrespective of whether or not they had wives or families dependent upon them, in such a way that you might be subjecting absolutely innocent people to the greatest hardship, was a policy as inhuman as it was inefficacious.'[92] Such reason and subtlety were lost on the public at the time, however, mainly because of the lead from elsewhere. Lord Curzon, a former viceroy and leading Unionist, mocked Haldane, saying that 'the noble and learned Viscount appeared to be more concerned with considering the degree of discomfort for aliens which might be caused in these operations, and which in my view is no matter for alarm or regret, and to bestow insufficient attention on the much greater necessity of the State.' Lord St Davids articulated the majority feeling: 'I do not want in the least to make any alien suffer unnecessarily. If you put aliens into concentration camps, I hold that they should be fed as well as our soldiers. I would not have any unnecessary hardship inflicted upon them. But the country must not run any unnecessary risk even if these aliens do suffer hardships. All countries in time of war have to be hard . . . His Majesty's Ministers should harden their hearts, and that on this particular matter they should adopt a much more drastic point of view.'[93] Even Haldane's Army reforms were used against him, as it was suggested that by cutting the regular Army and creating the Territorials he had weakened the military.

As autumn turned into winter, the public believed the east coast teemed with spies signalling to German ships, even though no case had been proven. Maurice Hankey, secretary of the Committee of Imperial Defence, noted that the countryside was full of flashing lights, usually from motor cars, or soldiers on night signalling manoeuvres.[94] The Earl of Crawford and Balcarres, in another spies debate on 25 November, asserted that 'the naturalised British subject of German birth is in many cases more dangerous than the alien enemy. I do not myself trust any man who has denationalized himself.'[95] MI5 records show that sixty-five German agents were convicted or imprisoned under the Aliens Restriction Act during the war; German archives suggest they sent one hundred and twenty agents to Britain.[96] Soon, German soldiers and sailors arrived as prisoners in camps in the countryside, providing another opportunity for the British to witness the character defects and shortcomings of the enemy. 'So far as one can judge,' a *Times* correspondent who had seen some at Frimley in Surrey reported, 'they are contented and at ease in their compound. The Teutonic character makes for resignation, not for cheerfulness in adversity, and probably the men's chief trouble is the monotony and the boredom of the camp life.'[97]

IV

In his survey of England from 1914 to 1945, A. J. P. Taylor noted: 'Until August 1914 a sensible, law-abiding Englishman could pass through life and hardly notice the existence of the state, beyond the post office and the policeman. He could live where he liked and as he liked. He had no official number or identity card. He could travel abroad or leave his country for ever without a passport or any sort of official permission. He could exchange his money for any other currency without restriction or limit. He could buy goods from any country in the world on the same terms as he bought goods at home.'[98] Now, suddenly – and despite the emphasis being placed on the British public giving up themselves, their time and their resources to the war effort – the state began to assert itself, not just by commandeering horse-boxes, railways and buses, but most of all in urging young, able-bodied men through a poster campaign and newspaper advertisements to join the services. These were the first steps towards the complete enlistment of the public in what would become total war.

Before war came Whitehall had, in fact, taken preparatory measures for such a mobilisation of the country. It had drawn up a document known as the War Book, outlining measures to be taken in an emergency, and the revised administrative procedures needed to cope with the growth of state power. They included the closure of military areas to aliens, banning trade with the enemy, and requisitioning merchant shipping. Its effects were immediate and, by the non-interventionist standards of the pre-war British state, far-reaching. For example, magistrates spent the first day of the war signing requisitions demanded by the War Book, not just for horses but for motor vehicles. In fact, its powers were rather limited. The true controlling power would come from the Defence of the Realm Act, and its subsequent amendments, which by 1918 would leave very few aspects of private life untouched.

The War Book had been the work of Maurice Hankey, a thirty-seven-year-old Royal Marines officer with a glittering career in intelligence, who had worked in Whitehall since 1902. As secretary of the Committee of Imperial Defence since 1912 he oversaw the implementation of these procedures. Hankey would be the central figure in running the war in Whitehall, and his power increased as the war progressed, not just because he ran key government committees, but also because he cultivated a role as intermediary between what became the two opposing factions in Whitehall: politicians and senior officers.

In his memoirs he noted that, in the early months, 'my main duty was to keep the Prime Minister personally in touch with all aspects of the war, and generally overlook the working of the Government machinery that had been brought into existence as a result of the pre-war work of the Committee of Imperial Defence.'[99] Asquith would come to rely on him almost entirely, though there were places to which even Hankey could not lead him. He was shocked when, on 4 December, his much-admired adviser suggested 'the immediate arrest of 25,000 German and Austrian subjects still at large in London', including, Asquith pointed out, 'thousands of Poles, Slovaks, Slovenes &c &c who hate their rulers worse than poison'.[100] Hankey feared these people were planning a massive campaign of sabotage: Asquith simply told him 'no'.

Hankey would later criticise how Asquith ran the war in its early months. He highlighted the absurdity that the cabinet had no secretariat to record decisions and ensure they were executed; and that conflicts arose between the War Committee that Asquith formed and the full cabinet. That Asquith would not see this showed why, for all his intellectual gifts, he failed to adapt from a peacetime prime minister to a wartime one, which made him politically vulnerable. His successor would install such a secretariat, with Hankey leading it.

Asquith was in other respects prepared for the war, though worn down by the battles of the last years of peace. He had chaired key meetings of the Committee of Imperial Defence since 1912 and understood exactly the plan being implemented. Hankey, working closely with him, described him as 'the kindliest, simplest and most human of men' with 'courage of a high order . . . I never knew him to falter or waver for a moment, in public or in private, in his determination to see the war through.'[101] To handle this stress Asquith poured out state secrets to Venetia Stanley, who, fortunately, kept them: he would write to her during cabinet meetings and sessions of the Council of War – a body of senior politicians and military men he had asked Haldane to assemble – and its successor, the War Council. He also maintained his habit of serious drinking, and – in the eyes of some colleagues the most inappropriate conduct of all – devoted as many of his evenings as possible to playing bridge.

War limited Asquith's meetings with Venetia Stanley in country houses at weekends, and drives round the park in London, such as they had taken before August 1914: while directing the war Asquith was pining for her, and (as he could not see her so often) writing her letters that now provide historians with a clear idea of what, in those first months of conflict, he was doing and thinking. On Saturday 22 August he was especially aggrieved to be unable to spend her twenty-seventh birthday with her. He had become emotionally dependent upon the escape from reality she provided: 'It is because I have got so used to one [letter] every morning (which I re-read at intervals through the day) that I was impatient yesterday and could not wait (as I ought to have done) for the second post.'[102] This obsession diluted his time with the war, Home Rule and Welsh disestablishment. Miss Stanley was well read, politically astute and intellectually energetic, and Asquith would seek her advice on key matters of policy.

She, however, was already finding his demands on her more than she could handle. Asquith did not know that one of his protégés and junior ministers, Edwin Montagu – memorably described by Duff Cooper as 'a man whose ugliness was obliterated by his charm' – was also pursuing her, and that she was coming round to the idea that Montagu might supply her with an escape route from Asquith's overwhelming attentions.[103] The prime minister was lucky that Miss Stanley was dis-creet: some of the secrets he shared with her, about troop movements especially, could have put scores of thousands of lives in danger, and possibly altered the course of the war. Asquith knew the risk and had complete faith in her confidentiality. It was as well that she repaid it.

Hankey was justified in criticising the cabinet's slow adaptation to the needs of war, though force of circumstances inevitably brought pro-found changes. On 6 August the Currency and Banknotes Bill passed through Parliament in a day, allowing the issue of Treasury notes for 10 shillings and £1 to prevent the public hoarding gold. These became known as 'Bradburys', Sir John Bradbury being the joint permanent sec-retary at the Treasury, who signed the notes. A Liberal MP, John Henderson, asked whether for reasons of 'dignity' the appearance of the new £1 note could not be improved, since it looked 'very much like a lot-tery ticket, or a ticket for a cloak-room.'[104] Lloyd George admitted that 'from an artistic point of view I cannot say that I am proud of this pro-duction, but it was the best we could do in the circumstances.'[105] The design would soon be revised. That day, once panic had subsided, bank rate fell from 10 to 6 per cent, calming the financial sector. The next morning the banks reopened, the first Treasury notes appeared in cir-culation, and bank rate was cut by another 1 per cent. The point of restricting the printing of notes had been to ensure sufficient gold was in reserve to pay out the sums in cash if necessary. Now the government was issuing its own notes, backed only by its reputation. Britain had gone off the Gold Standard.

In the House of Lords the Leader, the Marquess of Crewe, confirmed discussions his colleagues had had with representatives of the City and high finance, and assured peers that captains of industry and their work-ers had been consulted and would pull together. This did not stop several companies due to pay dividends announcing they would withhold them because of the crisis, a policy that outraged the well-to-do living on unearned income, and the government waiting to collect tax on the money. Businesses that feared trade would dry up sacked their staff. Despite this, there was industrial harmony unseen for years. Some minor disputes had been in progress – nothing widespread, but some among building workers in London and coal trimmers in Wales had potential to grow and cause great disruption – but were quickly concluded.

In military matters, while there remained no question of compulsion, the government initially wished to increase the size of the Army by 500,000 men, after the immediate recruitment of 100,000. There were 247,000 in the Army at the time, around half serving overseas, and another 145,000 on the Reserve. On 10 August the government advertised for 2,000 university men, or men 'of good general education' aged between seventeen and thirty, to take temporary commissions for the duration.[106] The next day advertisements appeared for 100,000 men aged between nineteen and thirty to serve for three years 'or until the war is concluded.'[107] General officers commanding were told that men in prison for minor offences could have their sentences remitted if they joined up. India, Asquith confirmed, had offered two divisions, and the 'self-governing Dominions, spontaneously and unasked', were sending troops: but the mother country had to lead.[108]

Asquith's sentiments were greatly approved: Balfour told Paul Cambon afterwards that his speech was 'the finest thing he had ever heard'.[109] Law endorsed the government's conduct and praised Asquith and Grey. His only advice was that industry and the means of supplying food should be on a war footing too. Other Members renewed pleas for the wives of volunteers to be looked after: within days, separation allowances were announced for them, and for motherless children. The money was agreed without a vote: the Commons had given its unanimous sanction to the war. The separation allowances had an unintended effect of exposing many bigamists, as both the legitimate and the illegitimate wife applied for them for the same man.[110]

Money was tight too because fears about shortages had inspired panic buying, which in turn had driven up prices, making it harder for the poor to feed their families. MPs urged the government to fix the price of bread, meat and other foodstuffs; and to order farmers to cultivate pasture, store cereals for government distribution and grow more the following season. The government resisted, but did not dismiss, such intervention in farmers' private business. On 6 August a cabinet committee recommended maximum prices for food, but was ignored: and the government announced it was taking over the running of flour mills. A trafficking operation had been set up in the east end of London by what a later war would call black marketeers, sending a small army of children into shops with money to buy as much food as they could so it could be sold on at inflated prices. The government protested, correctly, that there was no food shortage, except as such dealings created.

However, when stories circulated about 'the panic and greed of better-to-do people who have really disgraced themselves by placing long queues of motor-cars outside the stores and carrying off as much [*sic*] provisions as they could persuade stores to part with' – the words of Walter Runciman, president of the Board of Trade – the government had to act, even though Runciman maintained, on 8 August, that the panic was over.[111] To ensure the food supply the government would seek powers to requisition foodstuffs considered 'unreasonably withheld' from market, whether by traders or farmers: though he expected the inevitable rise in prices would attract more imports. It was also a thinly veiled warning that steps might be taken against hoarders. The government had to ensure adequate extra provisions were sent to small towns where territorial units were being assembled, to avoid the influx of soldiers buying up so much food that local residents went hungry. On 20 August the government took over the sugar trade, as two-thirds of the nation's supply had hitherto come from Germany and Austria-Hungary.

V

The mere declaration of war did not mean that the matters that had pre-occupied the government until the last week of July 1914 could be brushed aside. Ireland, in particular, could not be ignored. Asquith was depressed and bemused that it impeded his concentration on the war. Redmond, as leader of the Irish Nationalists, had lobbied Lloyd George about how a planned adjournment of Parliament must not prevent the Home Rule Bill from reaching the statute book, and on 5 August, after a meeting with an 'irreconcilable' Sir Edward Carson, leader of the Irish Unionists, he had told Asquith the same.[112] He said that if the government gave in to Carson – who was threatening that the Unionists would obstruct vital legislation – it would have 'disastrous' results in Ireland, and Asquith would lose 'the greatest opportunity that ever occurred in the history of Ireland to win the Irish people to loyalty to the Empire.' Asquith said the Bill would go on the statute book, but the short adjournment would proceed. By way of a Conservative response, Law and Lansdowne planned a press campaign to attack the government for undertaking Home Rule legislation when ninety MPs (mostly Unionists) had joined the colours and could not vote.

The Home Rule argument was potentially dangerous, but Asquith thought he had defused it by suggesting suspending the Act until an Amending Bill, excluding Ulster, could be passed. The cabinet was divided. Asquith confirmed on 10 August, as Parliament rose for a fortnight, that on its return the legislation would be dealt with. The recess would be used to try to reach an agreement, to ensure the Irish controversy did not plague Westminster and the country when there was an external enemy to fight: something Law, a main agitator against Home Rule, said would be 'a national calamity'.[113] Austen Chamberlain, another prominent Unionist, warned Lloyd George that party strife would have a 'disastrous effect on the City, on finance, and credit in all its branches' and 'would render a great financial crash certain.'[114] He, like most Conservatives, wanted nothing done until the end of hostilities, something the Irish regarded as tantamount to ignoring the will of the House of Commons. Redmond returned to England on 21 August and saw Asquith, who after a long discussion found the only option Redmond would accept was – as he had predicted – the Home Rule Act going on the statute book with an exclusion for six counties in Ulster, each of which would have three years to decide whether it stayed out for good. Redmond returned to Ireland, to be told by Augustine Birrell, the chief secretary, that the government would pursue the line he wanted – though there was uncertainty about how Unionists would react. At that stage, Asquith was not proposing to postpone implementation of the Home Rule Act.

To help formulate his party's response, Law took advice from A. V. Dicey, Britain's leading constitutional historian; though Dicey, in telling Law on 1 September that Asquith had made a pledge 'which ought never to have been given' in saying the Bill would go on the statute book, seemed oblivious to the passage of the 1911 Parliament Act (which he had also opposed), which said that once the Commons had passed a Bill three times it became law.[115] Recruiting from Protestant areas in Ireland was significant, thanks to Carson: but the National Volunteers – the pro-Home Rule forces assembled before August 1914 to oppose any illegal Unionist resistance to Home Rule in Ireland – awaited word from Redmond. Asquith wanted the Home Rule Act put on the statute book, accompanied by a one-clause Act postponing its implementation until the end of the war. The Archbishop of Canterbury, who had feared the end of the Welsh Disestablishment Bill, was placated by being assured it would have the same treatment. Any inclination Asquith might have had to soft-pedal with the Unionists was ended by the reversals the BEF suffered after its first engagement with the enemy at Mons in late August. The King, indeed, wrote to him once the news came from Mons to tell him to settle the Irish problem: but by that stage, shaken by events, Asquith needed no prompting.

Law learned of Asquith's plans 'with the deepest regret' on 11 September and accused him of bad faith.[116] The Liberals tried to cool the situation down, in the national interest. Churchill, on 13 September, wrote to Chamberlain: 'My dear Austen, I beseech you to realize what an act of recklessness and unwisdom it would be for us – either party – to start a quarrel with Irish nationalism here, in the colonies, and above all in America at this time of crisis.'[117] The government plan would merely create 'the sentimental satisfaction of having an inoperative bill on the Statute Book' until after the war and a general election; which he argued must be preferable to 'open Irish disloyalty' imperilling the British state. He promised that Ulstermen who had joined the Army would 'never' be the subject of coercion.

Chamberlain was implacable – he retorted that Ulster was being sacrificed because of 'blackmail' by the National Volunteers. Nevertheless, his party saw it had to end its opposition to the government, given the national emergency. On 14 September the Unionists met at the Carlton Club to discuss tactics: the party admitted defeat, and decided that Law and Law alone should speak in reply to Asquith when he notified the Commons of the move. Smith assured Carson that after the war the Unionists 'should revert to the most extreme fighting position.'[118] Lord Robert Cecil, to 'loud and prolonged cheers', told the meeting he no longer regarded members of the government as 'fit for the society of gentlemen,' but as 'cardsharpers'. Asquith, when notifying the Commons, took pains to disabuse his critics of the notion that he was exploiting 'the spirit of patriotism' at a time of 'supreme national emergency' to violate assurances previously given.[119] If no agreement on how to frame the Amending Bill to the Irish Bill could be reached, then there would need to be agreement on a moratorium for discussion of it.

He described a 'great patriotic uprising' in Ireland since war broke out: Irish Nationalists were joining Irish regiments to fight for King and country, and the last thing he wished to do was to poison this feeling by giving the Irish reason to accuse the British of betrayal, or to aggrieve Irish communities in America and the Empire. The Home Rule Bill – like that for Welsh disestablishment – would go on the statute book, but their operation would be suspended for twelve months or, if after a year the war continued, at a date fixed by Order in Council that would not go beyond the duration of the war. But he said the Amending Bill, to allow exclusions, would need to be reintroduced before the Home Rule Act came into force. Given the 'grave and unprecedented national emergency', Asquith felt this was the only means 'of acting fairly, reasonably and equitably'.[120]

Law and his party disagreed: he spoke of the feeling 'not so much of anger or of resentment as of sorrow' that came when he heard how the government 'took advantage of our patriotism to betray us.'[121] He said Asquith had broken his word in preparing to get the Royal Assent for the Irish Bill without having concluded the Amending Bill first, and – reverting to a partisanship not heard for six weeks – asked why the Opposition should believe the promise to have an Amending Bill before the Act was put into operation. Carson said that 'there has probably never been a grosser breach of promises and pledges in the history of Parliament.'[122] The Unionists wanted a complete moratorium – no enactment of the Bill, and no Amending Bill, but with an assurance that the provisions of the Parliament Act would still apply when it came to enact the Bill. They had thought the government was prepared to offer this, since the suggestions had been discussed the previous week: now they felt duped. Law complained that, but for the war, any attempt to do what Asquith planned would have caused an uprising in Ulster. Like Carson, Law felt the government now believed about Ulster that 'whatever injustice we inflict upon them, we can count upon them.'[123]

Law compared the breach of faith with that of Germany invading Belgium, and when he finished speaking led his party out of the chamber 'not as a protest, still less as a demonstration. We leave it because in my belief to have forced us to debate this subject at all under present circumstances is indecent, and we shall take no part in that indecency.'[124] The Suspensory Bill went through the Commons, and on the following day the Lords. 'The whole House rose and cheered wildly,' Asquith told Miss Stanley about the events in the lower House; it was 'a really historic moment.'[125] Law's speech questioning Asquith's *bona fides* caused the prime minister to observe that he 'never sank so low in his gutter as to-day'.[126] Redmond expressed the hope that by the time the Amending Bill was introduced Unionists and Nationalists would, in the pressing circumstances, have settled their differences. He would be disappointed.

The Government of Ireland Act and its accompanying Suspensory Act had the Royal Assent on 17 September, as did the Act disestablishing the Welsh Church. This was a historic moment for the British constitution. They were the first Bills the Speaker had certificated as meeting the conditions of the 1911 Parliament Act, and therefore could become law despite the Lords not having agreed. The King was displeased. 'I regret to say I had to give my assent to the Irish Home Rule and Welsh Disestablishment Bills . . . there must be an amending Bill for the former, the Govt have promised this.'[127] Redmond issued a 'manifesto' about the war once Asquith had had the Bill enacted, calling upon the Irish people to take their share in fighting for democracy, and for an Irish brigade to be sent to fight as part of the BEF, so the Irish could fight together and be officered by Irishmen. Telling his people that 'the democracy of Great Britain has finally and irrevocably decided to trust them and to give them back their national liberties', he urged the Irish to participate fully in 'a just war, provoked by the intolerable military despotism of Germany.'[128] Sinn Féiners, however, abhorred Redmond's pro-British sentiments, seeing Home Rule as the first and incomplete stage towards a republic: for the moment, they would be out of step with most Irish opinion. Unfortunately, the predominantly Protestant officer class of the Irish regiments, taking their lead from Kitchener, a militant Unionist, regarded former Nationalist Volunteers with disdain and distrust, which depressed recruiting.

VI

One criticism of the stewardship of the war during Asquith's administration was that it occasionally smacked of amateurism or complacency. An early example was that, once war was declared, the first meeting of the Council of War, whose priority was to decide how to deploy the BEF, found itself unable to proceed because it needed to hear the French military attaché; so the meeting was adjourned until the following morning. The first session of the council, chaired by Asquith, included Grey, Haldane and Churchill, as First Lord, and service chiefs. Sir John French, Sir Douglas Haig and Sir Ian Hamilton, newly appointed commander-in-chief of the Home Army, were present, as was Kitchener, who was not appointed to the War Office until after the meeting; and the doyen of the Army, Field Marshal Earl Roberts, a veteran of the

Indian Mutiny and the man credited with turning round Britain's fortunes in the Second Boer War. Roberts was almost eighty-two and would
die within weeks. This group would be formalised, but set a new constitutional precedent. Cabinet government was sidelined; the exigencies of
war relied upon swift decision-making. When the council at last got
under way, Haig agreed with Kitchener, stating that as Germany and
Britain were fighting for their existence it would be a war 'of several
years', requiring at once an army of a million men, 'and neither side
would acknowledge defeat after a short struggle.'[129]

Haldane and Balfour had discussed late into the night of 4/5 August
how large the BEF should be, and when it should go. Balfour thought
a swift, hard strike was in order. Haldane wanted to assemble a considerable home army first, and send it to attack the Germans when it could
do more damage: he did not know how fast the enemy was moving
through Belgium and into France. He believed any force sent early would
be 'trifling' compared with its opponents, and its destruction would be
catastrophic.[130] Balfour insisted 100,000 men 'could be sent at once without in any way entrenching upon the strength of the Home Defence'. He
noted that 'on the whole I was rather depressed by a certain wooliness of
thought and indecision of purpose,' something Unionists would decide
characterised the government's approach to the war.

Haldane soon changed his mind and thought the BEF should leave
quickly. The cabinet agreed that five, or possibly six, divisions could go
to France without denuding Britain of its home defences; the question
then was how rapidly they could be transported, and how it could be
done without alerting the Germans. It was also agreed to reinforce
Egypt with a division from India, and gratefully to accept offers of troops
from Canada, Australia and New Zealand. Finally it was decided to send
four divisions at once, a fifth when circumstances permitted, with the
sixth to follow later: it was estimated it would be twenty days before the
BEF was ready for action. An advance group arrived in Le Havre from
Southampton on 7 August: the bulk of the force travelled without incident to France between 12 and 17 August. Henry Wilson, then a major
general holding the post of sub-chief of staff, with typical cynicism,
described the discussions about this as 'an historic meeting of men,
mostly entirely ignorant of their subject.'[131] Wilson was a highly partisan
Unionist, with many friends high in the ranks of the Opposition; he was
also an inveterate intriguer, and ended the war a field marshal.

An advance party of the BEF arrived on the Continent on 7 August without, Asquith noted happily, any wind of it appearing in the newspapers. French, as commander-in-chief, was told what was expected of him: 'To support, and co-operate with, the French army against our common enemies. The peculiar task laid upon you is to assist (1) in preventing, or repelling, the invasion of French territory, and (2) in restoring the neutrality of Belgium.'[132] He was informed, in an interesting interpretation of recent events, that the justification for British involvement was not just 'the infringement of the neutrality of Belgium by Germany', but also 'in furtherance of the entente that exists between this country and France'. A future Chief of the Imperial General Staff, Sir William Robertson, noted that as Britain had 'no comprehensive war policy', no indication was given to French about what the means would be for him to discharge his task. He was ordered that, if called upon to advance without the support of the French army, he should consult London first. The reality was that reinforcements would not be trained for months, and Territorials now massing in England were under no obligation to serve abroad.

At the same Council of War Kitchener announced his plan to recruit at least another 100,000 men for overseas service: he would in fact recruit 2.5 million volunteers by March 1916. He made an early decision to retain at home some of the most experienced soldiers to train recruits: he was criticised for this, not least by Churchill, who later recognised it had been one of the smartest things Kitchener did, because of the high level to which men were trained. The Council of War's concentration on building a far bigger army would have surprised the general public, whose belief in British sea power was absolute, as was the conviction that Germany would eventually be starved into submission by the Royal Navy's command of the oceans. That belief was not entirely misplaced, but the timescale would be longer than even Kitchener had believed possible.

On 11 August French paid a farewell visit to Asquith. He told him the BEF would be in place within a fortnight, and that the forces of both sides were likely to be concentrated south of Luxembourg: this was a far cry from the imminent reality, of opposing armies dug in on a line of trenches from the Belgian coast to the Swiss border, with the British predominantly in the north. That evening Haig noted he had told the King, who had visited Aldershot, of his 'grave doubts' about French. In his diary, he went further. 'In my own heart, I know that French is quite unfit for this great command at a time of crisis in our Nation's history.'[133] Haig cited both lack of military knowledge and faults of temperament, but for the moment kept this assessment to himself and his Sovereign. By contrast, Asquith said of French to Miss Stanley that 'I am sure he is our best man.'[134] French would prove divisive: Sir James Edmonds, the war's official historian, branded him 'a vain, ignorant, vindictive old man with an unsavoury society backing.'[135] French certainly had his faults: a noted womaniser, he was lucky not to have wrecked his career in the early 1890s when an affair with the wife of a brother officer led to his being cited in the ensuing divorce case. He was reckless with money and almost went bankrupt in 1899, which would have necessitated his resigning his commission; and he had form as an intriguer, a hobby that would flourish during the war. He had distinguished himself as a commander in the Second Boer War, in which he ended up promoted to lieutenant general, but was nonetheless considered to have risen to the post of Chief of the Imperial General Staff more by patronage (he was a close confidant of Lord Esher) than by ability. Because of an error of judgement over the Curragh incident earlier in 1914 he had had to resign from that post. Haig had known him closely for twenty-five years and, despite all Haig's own faults of judgement, he was probably right about French's limitations, though not realising he shared some of them himself.

On 12 August, the day Britain declared war on Austria-Hungary, tempers were already beginning to fray in the supreme command. Asquith told Miss Stanley that 'Lord K has rather demoralised the War Office with his bull in the china shop manners and methods, and particularly his ignorance of and indifference to the Territorials.'[136] This was the yeomanry Haldane had set up and that Kitchener felt was useless. Asquith's response was to 'set Haldane on to him', which had calmed things down. However, these tensions between Whitehall and the Armed Forces were a portent of much unpleasantness to come.

On 25 August Kitchener struck a conciliatory note when he addressed the Lords for the first time not just as Secretary of State for War, but in his sixteen years as a peer. He explained his position did not 'in any way imply that I belong to any political party, for, as a soldier, I have no politics.'[137] This was not the view of many in Parliament and the press, who regarded him as a visceral Tory. However, it was true in this respect:

surrounded by colleagues for whom politics was a career, he would quickly become estranged from them because he lacked their motivation. He saw his duty as to save his country; some of them saw theirs as to preserve or advance their places. He compared himself with those he urged to enlist: his was a 'temporary' occupation and, like them, he had signed on for three years. That time limit, he explained, was because if the war should last so long, another wave of men would be ready to come and take their, and his, places. Such feelings did not enter the minds of many of his cabinet colleagues, who saw themselves first and foremost as professional politicians with careers to maintain.

Towns and villages across Britain saw columns of men marching through them most days, heading either for ports or training camps. Unbeknown to the British public, the BEF had reached France without a single loss of life. Ministers regarded this as a huge triumph because of the likelihood of the German navy attacking troopships. The movements had been reported in continental papers and the Germans must have been aware of them. London interpreted the failure to attack as proving the enemy's belief in the inferiority of their forces compared with the Royal Navy; or as Hankey surmised, the Germans' refusal to believe what they read in French newspapers unless they also read it in British ones.[138]

On 19 August Kitchener sent a fifth division to France. Two days later John Parr, a reconnaissance cyclist, aged perhaps fifteen, became the first Briton to die on the Western Front. The BEF reached Mons on 22 August and went almost immediately into battle. The first news of the fighting concentrated minds: the Germans had captured Liège on 16 August, and at dawn on 24 August Kitchener woke first Asquith and then Churchill with the news that Namur, supposedly a heavily fortified town on the Meuse, 45 miles east of Mons, had fallen. The forts built just thirty years earlier had been no match for German heavy artillery. French had told him he would be ordering a 'retirement' from the line the BEF held at Mons. Asquith was horrified, 'for we all assumed that Namur was safe, if not for a fortnight, at least for 2 or 3 days'.[139] French telegraphed for reinforcements of 10 per cent of his previous numbers, implying heavy losses. 'The casualty list has not yet come in,' Asquith told Miss Stanley, 'and one trembles to think what names it may contain.'

Kitchener warned Asquith that he was waiting to hear from French whether a sixth division should go almost immediately. In response to

this news that the BEF would need reinforcement – something Kitchener had leaked to Repington for the previous day's *Times* and which
caused his cabinet colleagues to rebuke him – it was decided to bring
two divisions of the Indian army to Egypt; by 28 August the BEF felt so
outnumbered they were told to continue to Marseille, where they were
disembarked. Kitchener had wanted the BEF at Amiens, held in reserve
in case the French were repelled: the French had wanted it at Maubeuge,
90 miles to the east, on the Belgian border due south of Mons, where it
would be in the fighting from the start. Mainly due to Wilson's
insistence – as French's sub-chief of staff – Kitchener had lost the argument: had he won it the BEF would not have been overrun at Mons and
might have been in a better position to resist the Germans. Kitchener's
relations with Wilson became poor.

The BEF sustained 1,600 casualties in the retreat from Mons: in the
four days from 20 to 23 August the French had suffered 140,000: not that
Asquith, or anyone in Britain, knew the extent of the debacle at the time.
Unaware of the facts, but briefed by Kitchener (who was livid with his
ally), Asquith thought the French had 'badly bungled' their plan of campaign, in contrast to the 'really gallant' Belgians.[140] French told London
his French allies were, as Asquith put it, 'stricken with hesitation and
something very like funk', and stopping the BEF – 'most anxious to take
the offensive' – from doing its job properly.[141]

Asquith knew most of the French were concentrated near their eastern frontier, and envisaged the Germans bypassing them and getting to
Lille, Dunkirk and the sea. The military situation confirmed Kitchener's
view, already outlined to his cabinet colleagues, of the need for an extra
600,000 or 700,000 men under arms by April 1915. Thus far, having asked
for 100,000 men he had got 120,000. 'He is not at all downcast,' Asquith
told Miss Stanley. 'Nor am I.'[142] But reliance on volunteers doing their
patriotic duty was not enough for Churchill. At a cabinet on 25 August,
he raised 'the necessity of compulsory service', something anathematical
to most Liberals.[143] According to Joseph Pease, the president of the Board
of Education, Churchill 'harangued' colleagues for half an hour. Although
such a step was unthinkable to most ministers, Kitchener agreed the
need might arise; but admitted he could not arm more men until April.
That should have alerted the cabinet to the poor rate of weapons production, about which, when a scandal broke on the matter in the spring of
1915, it would profess to be shocked.

The BEF's retreat from Mons and the French army's debacle there highlighted not only a need for more men, but also the certainty of a casualty rate unprecedented in the public's experience of conflicts involving Britain. General Sir John Cowans, the Quartermaster General, who lunched with the Asquiths on 24 August as the bad news was coming in, thought the BEF might have lost 6,000 men all told killed, wounded and taken prisoner, and observed, to Mrs Asquith's horror, 'if so, it's very good.'[144] When she asked how such losses could be regarded as 'good', he told her: 'The losses, my dear Mrs Asquith, will be tremendous in this war.'

The government then had to address the problem of how to convey the news of casualties to the public without wrecking morale, and without exposing the blunders that had caused the defeat. On the second day of hostilities Asquith went into the Council of War having just heard that the cruiser *Amphion*, which the previous day had sunk the *Königin Luise* after catching it laying mines off Harwich and Southwold, had itself been sunk by one of the mines. Seventeen officers, including the captain, and 143 men were saved: but the list of 148 petty officers and seamen who died that appeared five days later was the first of a stream over the next four years, and one of the shorter ones. Churchill told the Commons that the government was not 'alarmed or disconcerted': but that this method of warfare needed to be 'attentively considered by the nations of a civilised world'.[145]

Churchill also attacked the press for whipping up rumours. Newspapers had taken a self-denying ordinance in the national interest, but little was told to them anyway. In vain, war correspondents waited at home for an order to move, but after a month they learned they could not go (that would change the following spring). Some went unofficially, though risked arrest by the French authorities if caught. Churchill (a former war correspondent himself) claimed that because censorship restricted them from knowing what exactly was happening 'newspapers, in default of facts, are rather inclined to fill up their columns with gossip which reaches them from irresponsible quarters along the coast.'[146] His remarks would increase tensions with Fleet Street and make things uncomfortable for colleagues, and for himself.

A special edition of the *Daily Mail* on 8 August published a story about a great naval battle off Holland that a Unionist MP – the future home secretary, William Joynson-Hicks – said 'appears to be absolutely untrue in every detail': Joynson-Hicks urged the government 'to stop such infamous conduct'.[147] McKenna, as home secretary, confirmed that the story was fiction and urged the House to join him 'in an expression of condemnation in the strongest terms of the fabrication of false news'. He speculated this might have been 'wilfully done for the purpose of assisting the circulation of a newspaper.'

This could not continue, and so the Liberal government imposed the latest of the illiberal measures necessitated by the national emergency, and instituted a press bureau. It opened shop in a disused Admiralty building at Charing Cross, under the command of the First Lord's crony F. E. Smith, the Unionist MP, lawyer and rabble-rouser for Carson. Smith, one of the highest-paid barristers in England and with a lifestyle to match, was anxious that he would suffer financially: his friend Aitken guaranteed his bank account for an overdraft up to £7,000.[148] The bureau was staffed by naval and Army officers. At a time when the Navy was on battle stations but the BEF had yet to reach the front, McKenna trusted no newspaper would publish anything about naval activities that had not been approved by the bureau. The stricture would also extend to the Army's activities. To keep the people as informed as national security permitted, in the era before broadcasting, it was arranged to display press bureau bulletins at every post office, updated every Sunday. Like so much of importance during the war, the regulation of censorship developed *ad hoc*, rather than according to any great government plan. The Revd Andrew Clark, rector of Great Leighs in Essex, who kept an exhaustive diary of life throughout the war, called the bulletins 'extremely meagre'.[149] The squire of his village told him on 9 August that the BEF was being assembled – information gained from his son, a captain in the Coldstream Guards – so he at least was not entirely in the dark. In most towns and villages, since few had reliable information, rumours of varying degrees of absurdity abounded.

Ministers quickly realised the need to use propaganda to maintain morale and confuse the enemy, and the idea of a press bureau was central to this. Smith, a captain in the Territorials, was given the rank of colonel, and therefore discharged the function of heading it with military authority. However, he did not do so especially well, partly because of an occasionally rash temperament – especially after he had started on his formidable daily intake of alcohol – and partly because the bureau was understaffed. He soon ran into trouble. On 30 August a special

Sunday edition of *The Times* and another Northcliffe paper, the *Weekly Dispatch*, published unedifying and graphic accounts of the retreat from Mons from someone claiming to be in Amiens, with suggestions of an army overwhelmed, mildly chaotic and in headlong retreat and, above all, sustaining heavy casualties. H. A. Gwynne, editor of the *Morning Post*, told Lady Bathurst, his proprietrix, that he thought *The Times* had 'behaved abominably' in printing the reports.[150] 'It is no excuse for them that the censor passed it,' he added. 'Every Editor must be his own censor in these days when there is no law'. Gwynne was reluctant even to print casualty lists in case they sabotaged morale, and believed that 'the very existence of Northcliffe in a time like this is to my mind a great national danger'.[151] Before long Northcliffe would be described, without irony, as 'the most powerful man in the country'.[152]

The Commons held Smith to account on 31 August, after he had been attacked not just by MPs but by editors such as Gwynne, who had shown more restraint. Asquith upset Northcliffe by saying that although 'it is impossible too highly to commend the patriotic reticence of the press as a whole', this particular publication was 'a very regrettable exception.'[153] He said the public deserved better information, and would get it. *The Times* defended itself: the dispatch was 'from the pen of an experienced and trustworthy correspondent . . . not in the least likely to be deceived by idle rumours.'[154] The censor had seen it, and added 'embellishments'. The newspaper had come, 'not unnaturally, to the conclusion that it was the wish of the government that it should appear.'

It quickly became clear that Smith had souped the story up to encourage recruitment. The attack on his conduct was led by a Liberal MP, Sir Arthur Markham, who objected not only to his work but to the fact that Smith had appointed his brother Harold, also an MP, as secretary of the bureau. Markham had had complaints from newspaper editors that Smith *frère* 'acts more like one of the Kaiser's staff officers in his dealings with the press'.[155] He demanded the work of the censor be put under a member of the cabinet. Asquith said that, given the amount of work that had fallen on the shoulders of all his colleagues in taking through emergency legislation, he was loath to impose any more on them. Harry Lawson, a Liberal Unionist MP whose family owned *The Daily Telegraph*, made a point relevant to all accounts of war: that while the testimonies of individual soldiers may have been truthful and accurate, they only saw a small section of the action. It was the overall picture, obtained from his commanders by French and relayed to London, that was nearer the exact truth.

The censor defended himself: he had never sought the post, and its duties had been 'very arduous'.[156] He and his staff were learning on the job; and the latest amendment to DORA would punish those using information gained in areas of military sensitivity to cause 'alarm or disaffection', which would make editors think twice before publishing a damaging story.[157] He made a robust defence of his brother, his staff, and – being a good Tory – of the Northcliffe press. Esher noted laconically that 'FE Smith was remonstrated with for having allowed the publication of the telegram [the dispatch from Amiens], but he said that he thought it would do the country good. This was not Lord Kitchener's opinion.'[158]

Smith misled the House, saying that he should have written a covering note when he returned the censored story advising against publication. In fact, he did attach a covering note, but it said he was 'sorry' for having to censor 'this most able and interesting message', and urged the paper 'to use the parts of the article which I have passed to enforce the lesson – reinforcements and reinforcements at once.'[159] In September McKenna assumed responsibility for the bureau. Smith resigned as director a fortnight later, and tried and failed to go to France with his territorial regiment, the Oxfordshire Hussars. Then he was sent to Marseille to meet the Indian troops, charged with writing dispatches about their deeds and heroism that could be sent back to India. His remarkable war had, however, barely started.

The Times was unrepentant. If the story was accurate the censor was right to let it be published, and if it was not the censor made an error of judgement: 'In either event our hands are clean.'[160] Churchill was sent to rebuke Northcliffe, but Northcliffe told him that 'when it [the story] was not merely passed, but carefully edited, and accompanied by a definite appeal to publish it, there was no other possible conclusion except that this was the government's definite wish.'[161] Churchill berated him for the 'harm' done by allowing the publication of the story in *The Times*, and said: 'I do not think you can possibly shelter yourself behind the Press Bureau, although their mistake was obvious.' Northcliffe (who told Churchill that 'this is not a time for Englishmen to quarrel') stood his ground – the story had been 'not merely passed, but carefully edited, and accompanied by a definite appeal to publish it', so he had concluded it was the government's 'deliberate wish' to see it printed.[162] By now the news-papers, notably Northcliffe's *Daily Mail*, were thick with stories, and photographs, of German atrocities, which helped harden public opinion.

To allay press and public concerns about concealment, the govern-ment decided to send an official 'eye-witness', Major Ernest Swinton, to the front, to send back approved reports to the British press, a role he discharged until July 1915: he later became Chichele Professor of Military History at Oxford. Although his reporting was even-handed, the press found it inadequate, and stepped up their campaign to be allowed to send reporters. That would not happen until May 1915, and even then every-thing would be censored under DORA. In lieu of facts, the rumour factory stepped up its operations, its rumours condoned by the govern-ment if they increased admiration of Tommy Atkins and loathing of the Hun; if news such as that of the retreat from Mons was going to get out it had to be countered, and the government needed to take the offensive. Thus came stories such as the Angel of Mons, babies on bayonets, raped nuns, and a million Russian troops landing at Aberdeen for the Western Front, a collection of myths and lies containing occasional truths. Not everything was quite so sensational or so vaguely sourced. Asquith had spoken to a wounded soldier from Mons who claimed to have witnessed the Germans advancing behind a group of Belgian civilians being used as what a later generation would term 'human shields'. Another version had it that the civilians were schoolgirls.

The government's obsession with secrecy reflects how febrile public opinion was deemed to be, and why little was reported of the heavy casu-alties in the BEF around Ypres. Some regiments were left with only a handful of those officers and men who had been mobilised in early August. The 2nd Highland Light Infantry, for instance, had just thirty sol-diers left out of a thousand. Then a dreadnought, HMS *Audacious*, on gunnery exercise with the Grand Fleet, hit a German mine off County Donegal on 27 October, just as Prince Louis of Battenberg was preparing his resignation as First Sea Lord, and sank with, luckily, no loss of life. Jel-licoe asked that the loss of one of the Navy's most powerful ships be kept secret: Asquith and Churchill agreed, though rumours soon abounded, partly because the sinking had been witnessed by passengers on the RMS *Olympic*, sister ship of the *Titanic*, which had tried to tow *Audacious* into port. The British press, despite protests, published nothing until the Admir-alty announcement, three days after the Armistice, that the ship had gone down. A country used to a free flow of information found the restrictions on news hard to understand, especially where its broadcast could not assist the enemy. On 11 November, the morning of the King's Speech, HMS *Niger* had been sunk by a torpedo, and Fleet Street had known within hours: but it was not confirmed until after the next morning's newspapers had gone to bed, incomprehensible to a number of MPs who could see no benefit in delaying it by one day.

After the Dogger Bank action on 24 January 1915, when damage inflicted on Vice Admiral Sir David Beatty's flagship in an otherwise successful action was hushed up, Asquith complained to Miss Stanley that such secrecy was 'quite puerile . . . it is not the least likely to deceive the Germans, who no doubt know perfectly well that they hit and injured the *Lion*, and when the truth comes out people here will say with justice that they have been treated with lack of candour.'[163] The Admiralty admitted the damage to *Lion* in a terse communiqué three days later. However, it would be years before the realities of life and death on the Western Front came anywhere near a British newspaper's readers.

The military situation continued to deteriorate as the Germans headed towards Paris, crashing through the champagne towns of Reims and Épernay. Newspapers published maps showing the Germans crossing into France and, as a measure of how serious matters were, diagrams of the forts surrounding the capital, and news that Lille and Amiens were being evacuated. This avalanche of bad news was compounded on 2 September by the first casualty list from the Western Front, showing 188 officers and 4,939 men killed, wounded or missing.

Appropriately, a *Times* editorial calling upon the British to assert the superiority of their civilisation over the barbarous Hun shared a page with a poem by Laurence Binyon, a keeper in the printed books department of the British Museum. His reputation as a poet was sufficient that he had, in 1913, been considered for the laureateship that went, instead, to Bridges. Written in response to the first wave of heavy casualties, and entitled 'For the Fallen', it would enter the national consciousness, notably for its quatrain:

> They shall grow not old, as we that are left grow old.
> Age shall not weary them, nor the years condemn.
> At the going down of the sun and in the morning
> We will remember them.[164]

Asquith heard on 2 September that the Russians were being held back in East Prussia by the Germans: the expectation of the Tsar's army crushing all who came before it had proved as unrealistic as the impregnability of Belgian defences. This was the Battle of Tannenberg, and matters were even worse than London realised. Paul von Hindenburg's 8th Army destroyed the Russian 2nd Army, inflicting 30,000 dead and missing and 40,000 wounded, and taking 92,000 prisoners and around 500 heavy artillery pieces: it would then smash the 1st Army, rendering the Russians largely impotent for months. However, news soon arrived about the Austrian defeat at Lemberg, where the Russians inflicted 324,000 casualties and took 100,000 prisoners, breaking the back of the Austro-Hungarian army.

There was worse news from the Western Front. The weekly bulletin in post offices issued in the name of Sir John French on 6 September mentioned 15,000 dead, wounded or missing in the first actions of the war, and stated the BEF was now south of the Marne. Reims had fallen and Paris was in German sights. The government delayed the publication of lists until next of kin had been informed: but this release of news confirmed the cost of fighting, and caused a wave of concern about the superiority of the German army. On 8 September Asquith read a telegram from the British mission in Bucharest saying the Kaiser had told the King of Romania that 'the German troops in France will have crushed the Franco-British forces in 20 days . . . he will then leave 500,000 German troops in occupation of France and will "turn his attention" to Russia. *Qui vivra verra*.'[165] As Belgian refugees arrived in Paris at the end of August, some Parisians began a spontaneous evacuation further south, with the government heading for Bordeaux. Otherwise, as in 1870, the city prepared for a long siege, as the Germans headed towards them through northern France, and the BEF was not yet able to stand its ground. The French were expecting the Germans to head for the sea, and Boulogne had braced itself: and the British government knew that once the Germans were there, they were but a short step from England. Worries about supplies of guns and ammunition were exacerbated when the Belgians asked for, and received, 20 million rounds to defend Antwerp. Neither Kitchener nor anyone else had predicted constant trench warfare with frequent barrages, rather than big intermittent battles: therefore no one had foreseen the heavy rate of consumption of ammunition. By the spring, this would have grave military and political consequences.

The arrival of legions of wounded men, walking or on stretchers, became a familiar sight at London railway stations where trains arrived from the Channel ports. To help them, a flood of young women – around 47,000 – joined up as Voluntary Aid Detachments to assist the professional nurses of Queen Mary's Imperial Nursing Service, whose numbers rose from 700 to 13,600 by 1918.[166] On the afternoon following the publication of the first casualty lists, the King and Queen called unannounced on the wounded at a hospital near Buckingham Palace, the first of many such visits.

When an officer was killed the first his family knew would be a telegram from the War Office with the formula: 'Deeply regret to inform you that [name] was killed in action [date]. Lord Kitchener expresses his sympathy.' A few days later a telegram would arrive from the King and Queen: 'The King and Queen deeply regret the loss you and the Army have sustained by the death of your son in the service of his country. Their Majesties truly sympathise with you in your sorrow.' For NCOs and other ranks the notification was by letter, sometimes preceded by a letter from the dead man's platoon officer. It was a stark, bleak notification that would become familiar in hundreds of thousands of households, and of whose arrival families would live in dread. The decision was taken not to repatriate bodies, partly because many were so badly dismembered, irretrievably lost or unidentifiable. In a culture used to a ritual mourning process, having no body to bury was a dislocating experience.

Darker news from the front led to another burst of recruiting. Following an appeal by Esher, as president of the London County Territorials, more than 4,000 men joined up in London on 1 September alone; 1,488 men joined in Birmingham and 30,000 joined that day across the country; a similar number joined on 2 September.[167] The existing Territorials were in arduous training, or were deployed guarding docks, forts, railways and arsenals while the regular Army fought in France: the next wave, however, were signing up for service abroad. They would be required urgently, such would be the casualties inflicted on the Old Contemptibles – a nickname the pre-war regulars who had gone to fight bestowed on themselves in derision at a remark by the Kaiser that Britain was sending 'General French's contemptible little army' to fight the Germans.[168] Small towns teemed with men in khaki: and although discipline was good, the Young Men's Christian Association set up branches in 350 locations to help counsel the Territorials and to try to keep them free from the temptations of women and alcohol, through provision of 'cheap temperance drinks, table games, sing-songs and healthy amusement.'[169]

This influx of volunteers led to various practical problems. There were simply not enough old sweats to train recruits, who often had to spend weeks on drill or route marches to get fit before anyone was free to tell them how to engage the enemy, and use the weapons they would eventually receive. The War Office, to Kitchener's fury, agreed to pay men 3s a day to be sent home pending training and having barracks to live in: Asquith overruled Kitchener on the matter. Territorials and recruits were billeted on civilians near their training camps, requiring a huge effort to find, or create, spare rooms. The process was not voluntary, and those who refused to cooperate were subject to the full force of military discipline. The organisation to cope with such large numbers took some time to catch up. Major General Sir Ivor Herbert, MP for Monmouthshire Southern, blamed this in the Commons on 9 September on 'the want of reasonable forethought displayed by the War Office'.[170] He asserted that men who had enlisted for three years or the duration were being placed on the Reserve because Army depots were too congested, and this was almost certainly a breach of contract. Worse, when the government knew recruitment was essential, and the country was still dazed by Mons, recruits 'were sent back to their homes to tell the story of official incapacity and mismanagement.'[171]

Whether men were in camps or civilian billets, there were no adequate systems for ensuring they were paid; and an even greater insult was that those who had given up their jobs but been placed temporarily on the Reserve were being paid at the Reserve rate of just 6d a day. Those in camps found inadequate food and hardly any lavatory or washing provision. Some men not in camps had been forced to share hostels with tramps, and became verminous with lice: some preferred to sleep outside on the ground without a blanket because the blankets, too, were lice-infested. Herbert asked why men who wished to enlist could not simply be registered and sent home to continue their normal lives until the Army could cope with them. The War Office seemed to think a *levée en masse* of half a million men could be conducted by the old means 'of the recruiting sergeant at the corner of a street collecting corner boys and loafers. They have no idea of the men who have been coming forward, the finest type of working man in the country.'[172]

Jack Tennant, Asquith's brother-in-law, was under-secretary at the War Office and answered for Kitchener in the Commons. He did not gainsay Herbert, but suggested Monmouthshire had been unusually unlucky: which caused other MPs, with similar complaints from their constituencies, to heckle him. He conceded that 'those who have to deal with such numbers are only human.'[173] Those responsible at local level for processing volunteers and ensuring their proper training had proved unequal to their tasks, and it would be weeks before all ran smoothly. This placated no one, and Asquith spoke the next day about the scale of the problem. By the previous evening 439,000 men had joined Kitchener's army. The record for one day had been 3 September, when 33,204 enlisted: 2,151 in Manchester alone.[174] Territorial associations had been asked to help provision recruits, and generally had done so. Training centres were being established to ease the 'congestion'.[175] Asquith observed that county councils and municipal authorities owned many buildings and properties – schools, town halls and so on – that could have been used for the accommodation and training of recruits: his admonition was part of the process of waking up officialdom to the idea that this was total war, war on a scale never seen before in Britain even at the height of the Napoleonic threat a century earlier.

Asquith's and the government's main fear was that the public would see the inability of the state to handle its new fighting force, and men would stop volunteering just as the Old Contemptibles were being shattered. With an eye on the press gallery, he told MPs: 'Knowing, as we all do, the patriotic spirit which always—now, of course, with increased emphasis and enthusiasm—animates every class of the community, I am perfectly certain they will be ready to endure hardships and discomforts for the moment, if they are satisfied that their services are really required by the State, and that in due course of time they will be supplied with adequate provision for training and equipment.'[176] He confirmed that once the initial aim of 500,000 recruits had been met, the country would be looking for a further 500,000, to create an Army of more than 1.2 million. This required another vote of money, which the Commons gave within days.

Men who had flocked to the colours were left hanging around in civilian life while tales of heroism and sacrifice filled the newspapers, and this sometimes left them the innocent victims of domestic unpleasantness. Almost as soon as war broke out Vice Admiral Charles Cooper Penrose-Fitzgerald, a retired second-in-command of the China station, had formed the Order of the White Feather. The order encouraged women to give men of military age in civilian clothes a white feather – a traditional symbol branding a man as a shirker or a coward. The Vice Admiral had given thirty women in Folkestone a supply of these white feathers to distribute appropriately. Despite its vulgarity and unfairness, this direct shaming of men for a want of manliness was highly effective and caught on nationally, much to the chagrin of those who had enlisted but found themselves being impugned by their womenfolk (though many women found the movement appalling). MPs asked for a badge to be issued for men to wear in their buttonholes to show they had enlisted. Tennant promised to consider the idea. Public support for those who were obviously recruits was strong, but not always welcome: in late October Kitchener urged civilians not to show their appreciation by buying soldiers drinks in pubs, for their mission could be accomplished only 'if by hard work and strict sobriety they keep themselves thoroughly fit and healthy.' He urged that committees be formed in areas with heavy concentrations of soldiers to police and enforce this request: there is no evidence the public took any notice.

When Asquith went down to Aldershot on 13 September to inspect military preparations, with better news of the BEF driving the Germans back across the Marne and towards Reims, he found 'all the streets & byroads are swarming with K's new army – some in regulation khaki, but the vast majority loafing about in east end costumes: such a rabble as has been rarely seen.'[177] He saw for himself the legion of men awaiting training: and by then 213,000 men and 57,000 horses had been sent to France.[178] It would soon become apparent that the shortage of ammunition was matched by one of boots and uniforms. The head of procurement at the War Office was swiftly replaced.

The toll taken on those charged with prosecuting the war was enormous. Mrs Asquith noted on 2 September that Grey 'has nearly broken down', his colleagues were feeling the strain, but Churchill was, according to her husband, 'the one happy man . . . in his cabinet.'[179] Beatrice Webb felt that Grey, with whom she and her husband Sidney had dined on 28 August, was 'suffering . . . from an over-sensitive consciousness of personal responsibility' at failing to prevent war.[180] Matters were not quite so serene with Churchill as Mrs Asquith imagined, however. He was desperate for a naval offensive to drive the Germans out into the open, but his advisers were having none of it, causing him great anger. Military

men, including soldiers attached to the Admiralty, found that to give an
opinion with which he disagreed would ensure their not being consulted
again. 'I can't stand these fellows who oppose me,' he told one staff officer,
Lt Col. A. H. Ollivant.[181] It did not increase their respect for him.

VII

On 4 September Asquith made the first of four speeches in the constitu-
ent parts of the United Kingdom, at London's Guildhall, justifying the
declaration of war. Law and Balfour both spoke briefly in his support,
and the Archbishop of Canterbury lent his spiritual authority. Asquith's
programme (with speeches in Cardiff, Edinburgh and Dublin to follow)
was conceived so that, on going to Dublin, he might stop in North Wales
and see Miss Stanley, at her family's house at Penrhos on Anglesey.
Whatever the pretext, it gave him the chance to show his face throughout the kingdom in what The Times called his 'educational campaign'. At
the Guildhall he spoke of the war as 'a bloody arbitrament between might
and right'; and added that not to have fought – whether 'through timidity
or through perverted calculation, through self-interest, or through a paralysis of a sense of honour and duty' – would have left Britain 'false to our
word and faithless to our friends.'[182] Germany alone was responsible for
the 'illimitable sufferings which now confront the world'; he praised the
Empire for promising men and support, singling out India; evoked
the fight against Napoleon, quoting Pitt; and implored more men to volunteer. The speech was open to the public, and many more attended
than could fit in. At the end a recruiting sergeant patrolled outside.

Political differences continued to be buried. It was announced there
would be no contested by-elections for the duration (that would change
with the rise of Sinn Féin in Ireland); a party could nominate a successor
to its former MP. Labour, whose leaders had been so opposed to the war,
came out and proclaimed support for the decision to fight Germany, as
Europe was being threatened by a 'military despotism'. It asked that the
state should provide properly for the families of working-class men who
joined up. An even more formidable enemy of the government would
tour the country demanding the fight be taken ever more vigorously to
Germany: Christabel Pankhurst, in self-proclaimed exile in Paris since
early 1912 beyond the reach of the Metropolitan Police, announced she
would give her first speech on 8 September at the Royal Opera House.

Asquith delivered his second 'national' speech, this time in Edinburgh, on 19 September to 'alternations of deep silence & wild enthusiasm.'[183] The same day Lloyd George histrionically confirmed his new-found enthusiasm for war in a speech at the Queen's Hall in London. 'We have been too comfortable and too indulgent – many, perhaps, too selfish,' he said, 'and the stern hand of Fate has scourged us to an elevation where we can see the everlasting things that matter for a nation – the high peaks we had forgotten, of Honour, Duty, Patriotism, and, clad in glittering white, the great pinnacle of Sacrifice, pointing like a rugged finger to Heaven.'[184] The British had lived in 'a sheltered valley for generations.' As Gerard DeGroot has written, the message was to 'fight not for something new, but for something gloriously old.'[185]

By then, the sinking of three cruisers in a day by a U-boat in the North Sea had depressed morale even further, with submarine warfare seeming to threaten the supposed invincibility of the Royal Navy and the inevitability of victory. Hankey lunched in Downing Street as the news came out and noted that 'I do not remember any events in this part of the war which caused such an atmosphere of depression.' When *The Times* printed the names of the dead from HMS *Hogue* (48 killed), HMS *Cressy* (560) and HMS *Aboukir* (527) it took an entire page of small print to list them; and nearly half the following page was a list of the names of the dead of the BEF. The naval losses were regrettable, but the pre-war regular Army was being wiped out. William Inge, Dean of St Paul's Cathedral, who would later acquire the nickname of 'the gloomy dean' because of his incipient pessimism, warned a congregation at Temple Church on 4 October that the war would alter national character, since Britain would emerge from it 'to face bereavement, poverty, and the loss of that confident security in which we had wrapped ourselves for more than 100 years.'[186] However, he did expect a recovery of national self-respect, and hoped the crisis would put the political squabbles of recent years into perspective.

Asquith spoke next in Dublin, joined by Nationalists and Unionists. He endorsed Redmond's call for an Irish brigade – indeed, said he would like to see an Irish Army Corps. *The Times* reported that 'the immediate effects of Mr Asquith's recruiting appeal in Ireland have not been remarkable.'[187] The following week he was in Cardiff, following Lloyd George who had been in the city shortly beforehand launching a 50,000-strong Welsh Army Corps. By that stage – early October – Antwerp was under assault from the Germans, and the Belgians told London they would evacuate the city. Churchill left on a mission to the King of the Belgians and his ministers 'to try to infuse into their backbones the necessary quantity of starch.'[188] Churchill – who showed an immense reluctance to come home – succeeded in persuading them not to retreat to Ostend, but had to promise further British assistance although the BEF was already outnumbered and overstretched. He had, to the annoyance of his advisers but because he was determined to have a hand in fighting the war, raised a Royal Naval Division from men garrisoned to protect naval bases and some new recruits – they would be replaced by Indians – and suggested they be sent to Antwerp. Kitchener agreed.

What was not agreed to was Churchill's offer to resign from the Admiralty in order to command his new division, a suggestion Asquith noted raised a 'Homeric laugh' in the cabinet.[189] Asquith said he could not spare Churchill from the Admiralty, though Kitchener was prepared to make Churchill (who had served in South Africa, and was an officer in the Territorials) a lieutenant general if Asquith wanted him to go. When Churchill returned he berated Asquith for not having released him, saying the naval part of the war was effectively over, with British superiority assured, and there were greater battles to fight. 'His mouth waters at the sight & thought of K's new armies,' the prime minister told Miss Stanley.[190] Churchill could not believe these new 'glittering commands' would be entrusted to 'dug-out trash' with their 'obsolete' grasp of tactics. 'For about a quarter of an hour he poured forth a ceaseless cataract of invective and appeal, & I much regretted that there was no short-hand writer within hearing – as some of his unpremeditated phrases were quite priceless.'

The questionable nature of Churchill's judgement was highlighted again when Antwerp fell on 10 October, after a badly botched and ill-prepared operation. This was despite the efforts of the Naval Division, 1,400 of whose men the Dutch interned when they escaped to Holland. Almost another 1,000 were taken prisoner. They had a job landing at all, since the Admiralty had mined the sea as far as Ostend and, having promised to send a pilot ship to lead the forces in, forgot to do so. They had to be recalled and made a second attempt. Churchill lacked experts around him who would stand up to him: there was never the slightest chance his new division would be equal to the challenge. Asquith had a full account of the debacle from his son Arthur – known as 'Oc' – who had been there. What he heard led Asquith to conclude it had been a 'wicked folly': he felt that 'nothing can excuse Winston (who knew all the facts) from sending in the other two Naval Brigades.'[191] The first brigade had included 'seasoned Naval Reserve men'. The other two, however, were mainly 'a callow crowd of the rawest tiros [novices], most of whom had never fired off a rifle, while none of them had ever handled an entrenching tool.' He reported to Miss Stanley that the main officers in Oc's battalion had been 'R Brooke (the poet) Oc himself & one Dennis Brown [*sic*] (a pianist) who had respectively served 1 week, 3 days & 1 day. It was like sending sheep to the shambles,' he said, using a vernacular term for a slaughterhouse. Brooke and his friend W. Denis Browne (a composer) escaped to die in the Dardanelles: Oc survived. Asquith hoped Churchill (who blamed Kitchener) would learn from this, and expected him to hand over the Naval Division to the military authorities: the amateurism had been not only highly dangerous but also highly embarrassing. Asquith soon forgave Churchill, noting on 24 October that 'the lunatic who edits the *Morning Post* [H. A. Gwynne] writes me a long private letter this morning, urging the supersession of Winston by Jellicoe!'[192]

Interestingly, Gwynne's criticisms of Churchill were based on Antwerp, and similar to Asquith's: he had aired them in a sulphurous leader in the *Morning Post* on 13 October, and resolved to see Churchill (whom Tories such as Gwynne regarded as a turncoat) removed from office. Churchill was so incensed that he summoned Sir Stanley Buckmaster, the Solicitor General, now in charge of censorship, to ask whether action might be taken against Gwynne. Buckmaster told him his writ ran only so far as preventing the printing of sensitive military or naval information; it did not run to disciplining journalists who criticised ministers. Buckmaster did, however, write to Gwynne to suggest he might tone his attacks down; Gwynne would not. He was soon writing that 'Mr Churchill has gathered the whole power of the Admiralty into his own hands, and the Navy is governed no longer by a Board of experts, but by a brilliant and erratic amateur.'[193] Frances Stevenson recorded that Churchill had 'disgusted' Lloyd George by behaving 'in a rather swaggering way when over there, standing for photographers and cinematographers'.[194]

As if Churchill had not accumulated enough demerits because of his poor judgement, he now chose to court yet more controversy. When Prince Louis of Battenberg was forced out in October the First Lord, beleaguered after the fiasco of Antwerp, urgently needed an ally to replace him. That ally – to the bemusement of Whitehall and Westminster but the delight of the public – was a former First Sea Lord, Admiral of the Fleet Lord 'Jacky' Fisher. Though he had officially joined the retired list in January 1911, on his seventieth birthday, Fisher had been in and out of Churchill's office since the outbreak of war. The King, when Churchill told him of the appointment, felt 'great surprise', believing Fisher had 'created a state of unrest and bad feeling among the officers of the service' when previously in post.[195] According to Fisher, the King tried to dissuade Churchill by suggesting the job would kill Fisher: to which Churchill supposedly replied: 'Sir, I cannot imagine a more glorious death!'[196] He put other names to Churchill, all of which were swatted away. The King would not approve Fisher without consulting Asquith, whom he asked to stop the appointment. Asquith supported Churchill, who, he added, would resign if Fisher were not appointed. Lord Stamfordham, the King's crusty, loyal and powerful private secretary, present at the interview, said that 'from what Mr Churchill had said to the King on the previous day he would not be sorry to leave the Admiralty as its work was uncongenial to him: he wanted to go to the War & fight and be a soldier.'[197]

Fisher deserved some credit: from 1904 until 1910 he had ordered the scrapping of old ships and their replacement by modern ones. It was largely down to him that the Royal Navy was so well equipped. Asquith endorsed the appointment because he believed, wrongly, that Fisher would have a restraining influence on Churchill. The King, whose many reservations included his fear that Churchill and Fisher would fall out, eventually assented, but wrote that 'I do so with some reluctance and misgivings . . . I hope my fears may prove to be groundless.'[198] He added: 'I did all I could to prevent it, and told him [Churchill] that he [Fisher] was not trusted by the Navy, and they had no confidence in him, personally.'[199] However, Fisher was seventy-three, a loose cannon, and no great respecter of political authority. He had a lifelong disposition to seasickness; he was a superb dancer; he had been an intimate of Edward VII; and was intensely religious. He also had a sense of humour: his motto, when granted arms on being created a peer in 1909, was 'Fear God and Dread Nought'. However, he had an explosive and restless temperament: Fisher may have been close to the late King, but the reigning monarch disliked and distrusted him. George V came round, however, with Fisher telling Asquith that in a conversation to mark his appointment the King and he had got on 'like a house on fire'.[200]

Antwerp overshadowed the success the BEF and the French had had on the Marne in repelling the Germans beyond Reims, sparing Paris the fate of 1870–71. There would be no more great advances, as the Germans established a new brand of warfare. The first trenches had been dug on the Aisne in mid-September: a war of moving armies ended, as the entrenchments spread east and west. By October it was clear Kitchener had been right, and anyone who thought the war would be over by Christmas monumentally wrong. He warned Asquith that 'both in the West & the East the big opposing armies may in some months' time come to something like stalemate'.[201]

VIII

The first weeks of the war steadily proved it was not business as usual, whatever the propagandists said; and with the massive shift of men from business and industry to the Army, it could not possibly be. Other factors, too, brought the war close to home. The fear of successful, or even attempted, invasion instilled in the public for years through works of fiction was intense. Minefields were laid in the Straits of Dover and the mouths of the Tyne and the Humber as an additional precaution; seaplanes were stationed at Clacton and other points along the east coast to keep watch for approaching Germans. Kitchener expressed his concerns to Asquith about the vulnerability to invasion at a cabinet on 21 October.

However, it was the arrival on British shores of civilians from allied nations either invaded by Germans, or under threat of invasion, that brought home to the public the scale and the impact of the war. Refugees from Paris arrived in Folkestone and London, as they did from Belgium, 26,000 of whom came in the week after the fall of Antwerp. On 9 September Herbert Samuel, head of the Local Government Board (LGB), announced government support for Belgian refugees and appealed for public help. He recalled in his memoirs: 'The response was instantaneous and almost overwhelming. The LGB called for the formation of Local Reception Committees; at once no fewer than 2,500 sprang into existence all over Great Britain.'[202] Earl's Court and Alexandra Palace became distribution centres for refugees, and by late November had processed 45,000 people. As industry cried out for manpower after losing men to the services, those refugees unfit to enlist were urged to join the workforce.

Such was the concern about the possibility of an invasion that Herbert Samuel was put in charge of a new sub-committee that sought to draw lessons from the experiences of Belgian refugees about how best to manage the civilian population in the event of the Germans arriving. The committee recommended the cabinet rule that civilians should stay put, as moving them would impede the transit of defensive forces to engage the enemy, who – it was believed – would have their supplies cut off by the Royal Navy and run out of ammunition. Civilians should be told by proclamation, but only once an invasion had happened, 'to remain in their ordinary places of residence, not to drive livestock without orders from the military or the police, and not without orders to destroy food supplies, forage, bridges, rolling-stock, power stations, telegraphs, wireless stations, waterworks, sluices or locks, piers, jetties, boats or ferries.'[203]

The cabinet rejected telling civilians to stay in their homes, as ministers felt sure they would not, as panic took over. It was also decided to destroy such cattle as could not be moved and to burn supplies of grain. With Hankey's help, Balfour was put in charge of organising this plan, through meetings with Lords Lieutenant of all counties on the east coast of England and Scotland, to whom responsibility for activating it was delegated. It was also decided to brief the public, and not to wait until the immediate aftermath of an invasion to try to inform them. Posters were put up all over the counties affected, and there was no panic: some communities, without waiting for a government lead, had already made contingency plans.

Further unease at home was provoked by the use of Zeppelins on the Western Front, and reflected by the traffic in the London insurance market in early October from businesses and householders seeking cover against bombing raids. Police stations in the eastern counties and in London put up notices that lamps must be extinguished wherever possible. Most of the customers, predictably, were from London and the east of England, and it was good business. Private customers were charged 3s 4d, or 16.5 per cent, of their property's value; commercial ones 5s, or those on the east coast 7s 6d. This covered not just bomb damage, but also damage from 'riots or civil commotion'; but when it seemed no such civil commotion was likely, and customers sought insurance solely against bombing, a uniform rate was established of 2s per £1 of value, meaning a householder or business would need to pay a premium of

10 per cent of the value of the property each year to cover against these risks.[204] Trade was brisk.

At first, other changes to civilian life were gentle. The promenade concerts continued at the Queen's Hall in London, albeit with substitutions of patriotic music in the programme – Boyce's 'Hearts of Oak', the anthem of the Royal Navy, was included in the 15 August concert. People were told that the seaside was perfectly safe from German attacks, and although resorts started to empty, especially on the east coast, within a fortnight crowds began to return, as the weather became hotter and the trains were less committed to moving troops. At first, more race meetings were cancelled because of the difficulty in transporting horses, until in the second week of the war there was none at all. Trying to avert commercial catastrophe, the Jockey Club said on 13 August that, because of the number of livelihoods dependent on racing, fixtures should not be called off unless necessary: but in weeks of massive troop movements, they inevitably were. The sport soon resumed, and the St Leger was held in September and, after that, the autumn meeting at Newmarket. The King continued to enter horses in races, and therefore the sport felt it had official sanction to continue.

Although county cricket continued through August, amateur clubs cancelled their fixtures. The secretary of the Marylebone Cricket Club announced on 6 August that he felt 'no good purpose can be served at the present moment by cancelling matches unless the services of those engaged in cricket who have no military training can in any way be utilised in their country's service . . . Cricketers of England would be sure to respond to any definite call.'[205] F. H. Bacon, secretary of the Hampshire club, suggested a corps of professional cricketers be established: all his players agreed to serve. Nottinghamshire's ground, Trent Bridge, was commandeered for treatment of the wounded. Many prominent amateurs, notably Sir Archibald White, the Yorkshire captain, left for their regiments; but otherwise the professional game carried on throughout August, attracting small holiday crowds that shrank as the news from France became worse. Finally, after the retreat from Mons, a broadside on 27 August from Dr W. G. Grace – the most legendary cricketer alive – caused stumps to be drawn. He wrote to the *Sportsman*: 'I think the time has arrived that the county cricket season should be closed, for it is not fitting at a time like this that able-bodied men should be playing cricket by day and pleasure-seekers look on.'[206] Most clubs cancelled their remaining matches; MCC, to the apparent annoyance of its secretary, decided not to send a first-class-strength team to play at the Scarborough Festival in early September. There would be no county cricket in England again until 1919, by which time thirty-four of the two hundred and ten first-class players who appeared in 1914 would have died for their country.

Most other sports got the message: professional golfers decided to cancel all tournaments for the rest of the year, and the Rugby Union asked all its players to join up. Similarly, football clubs cancelled fixtures, putting grounds at the disposal of the War Office for training and recruiting. The Football Association promised that where matches were played, prominent local men would address players and spectators about the importance of enlisting. That was not enough. Frederick Charrington, the veteran temperance worker in London's east end, wrote to the King demanding he intervene to have football stopped altogether; and to Lord Kinnaird, president of the FA, demanding he resign given the FA's 'unpatriotic' decision to carry on playing professional matches: Kinnaird, in obvious discomfort, pleaded problems with contracts in ending the professional game.[207] On 6 September Arthur Conan Doyle directly appealed to footballers to join up, and the Middlesex Regiment formed a Footballers' Battalion for them; another was raised in Edinburgh as the 16th Royal Scots. Despite public criticism, the Football League played a full season in 1914–15: then both the League and the FA Cup were suspended until 1919.

The pressures on fit young men, whether paid to entertain or not, became ever stronger after the BEF's retreat. The 5 September edition of *London Opinion* was published with Alfred Leete's poster of Kitchener pointing his finger at the men of Britain and proclaiming: 'Your Country Needs You.' When the recruiting offices reopened on the Monday, two days later, almost 5,000 men enlisted in London. When court sessions resumed after the long vacation judges sent minor offenders to the recruiting office rather than to prison.

By early September, although the King himself had continued to patronise racing, voices demanded that the sport, too, be ended. Lord Robert Cecil led the call, saying that if football was stopping, so should racing. This was countered by a leading Newmarket trainer, George Lambton, saying that whereas football demanded big, fit men, racing demanded men usually so small that they would not be taken by the Army. This ignored the development of 'bantam battalions' that had specified a much lower height requirement for recruits; Lambton went too far in saying that the racing industry employed many men unfit for anything else, and who would be unemployed if meetings stopped. He also contended that horse-breeding would suffer if racing stopped, which would therefore affect the war effort. Racing at Epsom had been curtailed because of a military hospital's having taken over the course: but now, in the words of Charles Bright, a *Times* reader, the continuance of other racing stimulated 'a certain amount of disgust' because each meeting 'draws together probably as many undesirable loafers of military age as a League football match.'[208] Bright raised the question of class tensions, suggesting that those forced to forgo football would not understand why 'horse racing people' could have their fun. His newspaper agreed. 'Any attempt to hold the great popular racing festivals, such as Epsom, and above all Ascot, will make a deplorably bad impression upon our neighbours . . . can it be seemly to hold it [Ascot] when millions of men, including great numbers of our own people, will be at death-grips?'

The arguments, which continued through into the spring of 1915, fell largely on class lines, with Lord Rosebery, while claiming he wished to keep out of controversy, making the case for business as usual and claiming that the greatest Ascot Gold Cup in history had been run on 8 June 1815, ten days before Waterloo 'when Napoleon and Wellington were confronting each other to contend for the championship of the world.'[209] He agreed that the English thoroughbred would disappear if racing stopped, because 'no man can afford to keep bloodstock for the mere pleasure of looking at them in the stable.' However, J. Holland Rose, a fellow of Christ's College, Cambridge, asked why jockeys supposedly unfit for war service could not take horses and act as messengers at the front, 'benefiting their country and stimulating skulkers to join the Army. The spectacle of large race meetings and professional football matches is little short of a national disgrace.'[210] A survey of the 2,500 crowd at a meeting at Gatwick on 4 March 1915 found them mostly middle-aged, many female, and almost all those of military age in uniform: the war effort did not seem unduly compromised. *The Times* came under attack for condemning racing while continuing to report it. It pompously retorted: 'A great newspaper cannot possibly limit its survey to those occurrences of which it approves.'[211]

The following May, in the climate of harsh reality that followed the sinking of the *Lusitania*, and after months of debate, the government issued an instruction to the Jockey Club to end racing. There had been an outcry early that month when racegoers had impeded soldiers trying to return to the front, and wounded ones coming home, at Waterloo station. The Jockey Club promised to suppress the social side of race meetings, in keeping with their argument that the sport should continue to preserve the bloodstock industry. But public feeling was by then running so high that Runciman, president of the Board of Trade, issued the order, justified by 'the necessity for keeping the whole of our British railway system free from congestion at any time for the rapid and unimpeded transit of troops and munitions'; and free of what *The Times* called 'undesirable mobs'.[212]

The one exception was that racing could continue at Newmarket: the whole town was so dependent on the industry, leaders of the sport argued, that it would be devastated economically were racing closed down. Hardship on a more reduced scale was forecast for Epsom and Doncaster. Ireland was to be exempt, a further indication of how it did not share in Britain's war. A. W. Cox, who claimed to own 'one of the largest and most valuable studs in England', wrote to *The Times* to say he was glad to make a financial sacrifice for his country: but he now wanted the government's attention turned on 'a great number of useless hangers-on who owned no horses and only raced for betting and were quite capable of bearing arms for His Majesty.'[213] Cox trusted 'these loafers' would be put to serious work: a call that would resonate until conscription was introduced. Thus racing would continue sporadically until 4 May 1917. By that stage there was too little feed for the horses, its participants and most of its crowds were otherwise engaged, and those still attending were denounced as unpatriotic shirkers who wasted scarce rail capacity or petrol getting to meetings. By the same token, once racing was restricted the cry soon came for private motor cars to be banned for the duration, though that would be thwarted by the vehicles of volunteers being essential for war work.

The consequences of the BEF's fighting and the large number of casualties created not just more recruits but more recognition that normal life could not continue, because so many able-bodied men were required to fight. Also, the public were increasingly aware that ships and trawlers were hitting mines in the North Sea and sinking with increasing loss of life. The mood soured rapidly during that autumn. Her morale having slumped as the casualty lists lengthened, Mrs Asquith recorded in her diary on 26 October how 'this war has caught us at our worst'. She recalled the last months of peace – militant suffragettes, Ireland facing civil war, senior Army officers contemplating rebellion, London society divided and 'so flippant, callous, idle and blasphemous', politicians 'losing all sight of truth and courtesy', the Church without influence and culture itself 'grotesque' and 'invertebrate'.[214] She continued: 'All these things I have watched from far back, growing, growing: and now that shrapnel is killing an entire generation, we are left staring at God.'

CHAPTER 3

COALITION

I

The King opened a new session of Parliament on 11 November, the speech from the Throne dealing with one subject only: 'The prosecution to a victorious issue of the War on which we are engaged.'[1] Whatever might have been imagined three months earlier, with two entrenched armies in France and Flanders, and the expected naval war (and rapid British victory) nowhere in sight, it was now manifest the war would be long in duration. The King enunciated his speech 'with measured gravity', *The Times* noted, and 'its delivery made a deep impression.'[2] The Queen and many of the peeresses present were in black or purple, signifying mourning.

On 17 November Lloyd George introduced an emergency War Budget, designed to deal with a drawn-out conflict. It was preceded by notice that a new vote of credit, of £225 million, would be put before the Commons: as he said, the newspapers had all underestimated how much the war was costing, and until he announced the new Vote of Credit 'the public . . . had no idea as to the costliness of the undertaking.'[3] There were 2 million men under arms, and another million expected within a few months: and 'we are maintaining a huge Navy as well.'[4] The separation allowances were 'more liberal' than in any other country, and once the next million men had enlisted would cost £65 million a year. Before the war it was estimated public spending would be almost £207 million, and even that would have led to a shortfall of £11 million. The extra war expenditure for the year was predicted to be £328 million, so Britain was facing the most expensive year in its history: it had to find just under

£340 million from somewhere to fund itself. The Boer War had cost £211
million spread over four financial years: the first year of this war was
expected to cost at least £450 million.

It was 'out of the question' to raise the whole sum by taxation: but a
failure to 'tax and tax heavily' would depart from the policy adopted in
every war hitherto, and would undermine British financial soundness.[5]
Loans had paid for more than half of the Napoleonic and Crimean wars,
but the rest had come in taxes. In those lower-wage societies, Pitt and
Gladstone respectively had raised taxes proportionate to wealth that, if
copied by Lloyd George, would require no borrowing at all. It had not
just been that taxpayers – and Lloyd George pointed out that many
things were taxed to raise the money, not just income – had been aware
of their duty to their country; they had also been made aware of their
duty to posterity, in not saddling future generations with huge levels of
debt on which they had to pay interest.

For the present year he would need to find £16 million and the following £50 million just to cover the loss of revenue and the interest on the
loans; and perhaps as many as 2 million men who had been contributing
by direct or indirect taxes before war broke out would be abroad, and
not contributing, a year hence. To borrow to cover these costs would be
'cowardly finance in the extreme.'[6] His next justification for raising taxes
was that much of the additional state spending – possibly four-fifths –
would take place in Britain, giving a huge boost to industry. It was only
sensible to tax that windfall. He predicted a programme of reconstruction after the war: peace would bring with it severe economic problems,
a remarkably prescient assessment. Therefore, all the money that could
be raised by taxes should be thus raised.

He proposed to double income tax from 1s 3d to 2s 6d in the pound.
Beer was taxed very low, relative to its alcohol content, compared with
spirits; so he proposed to put a halfpenny on each half-pint of beer, which
researches had told him was the measure in which it was usually drunk.
'Every half-pint that a man drinks he will be contributing to the carrying-
on of the War,' he proclaimed, effectively making drinking patriotic. He
admitted that a heavy increase in spirit duties in 1909 had cost the Treasury money because it had driven down consumption and hit distillers
hard. He would not therefore be increasing those duties: but he would
be putting 3d on a pound of tea, which he expected to raise £3.2 million
in a year.

None of this came close to covering the additional expenditure – he estimated that after tax rises there would still be a 'deficiency' of £321 million – and so he announced a War Loan.[7] The government would issue a 3.5 per cent security, redeemable on 1 March 1928 or, on three months' notice, after 1 March 1925 if that happened to be a period of cheap money. In anticipation of such a loan, institutions and individuals had already offered £100 million, and prospectuses would be issued immediately for a total of £350 million. He justified the step by saying that 'it is a loan to help the country to fight the battle for its existence— to fight a battle which lends value to every other security which we have got. Victory means value, defeat means depreciation. It is an excellent investment, because the credit of Great Britain is still the best in the market, and after this War it will be a better investment than ever. There will be no more loose and malevolent talk about the decay and downfall of the British Empire.'[8] He called it an excellent way for those too old or ill to fight to make their contribution to the battle. In a largely non-partisan speech the shadow chancellor, Austen Chamberlain, endorsed his proposals, especially the loan. The next day the Commons began considering proper financial support for its servicemen, their families, their widows and a generous pension scheme for those whose wounds rendered them unfit for work.

However, for all Lloyd George's ingenuity, Britain's role as a great debtor nation had begun, and would survive him indefinitely. The country was handicapped by the fact that, because of the uncertain credit status of some of its allies, it was borrowing money (mainly from America) to lend on to them, but remained responsible for the debt. This would have dire economic consequences when Russia defaulted after the revolution and its unilateral peace treaty with the Central Powers. Also other nations – such as Romania that autumn – asked Britain to fund them as allies, having rejected offers from Germany. As Balfour told the War Council in December: 'if we were to become the treasurer and universal provider of a number of nations, we must maintain our economic position.'[9] With the war promising to last for years, the more men that enlisted, the more the economy was weakened by their leaving it, even with women replacing them. This tension would become explosive during 1915.

On 3 November the war reached the English mainland. A German naval raid – unreported at the censor's order – was launched on Great Yarmouth, the easternmost point of England. It seemed to support

Kitchener's thesis of Germany fighting an aggressive war against Britain itself and not just on the Continent, and the need for more ships in the southern North Sea. Shells were fired at the town but fell in the sea, serving to terrorise the inhabitants while providing cover for yet another German minelaying operation. However, this coincided with the news from the South Atlantic about the loss of ships at the Battle of Coronel, which caused some of the reinforcements destined for the east coast to be sent down there and led to the Battle of the Falkland Islands in December 1914 against the German East Asia Squadron, under Vice Admiral Graf von Spee. The German High Seas Fleet was not seen until Jutland in May 1916, and never came out again. Asquith, though, embarrassed by the attack on Great Yarmouth, was angry about Coronel. He told Miss Stanley that had Rear Admiral Sir Christopher Cradock, who commanded the 4th Squadron, not 'gone to the bottom' with HMS *Good Hope* 'he richly deserves to be court-martialled'.[10] This was a mightily unfair and ill-informed view: Cradock had engaged the enemy despite his own forces being hugely inferior, and had behaved with enormous gallantry; three days before he went down he had requested, and been denied, reinforcements.

A far worse German raid on Scarborough, Hartlepool and Whitby at dawn on 16 December provided another example of Churchill's volatility, and his failure to understand that his high-flown phrasemaking was not always appropriate. As with the Yarmouth raid it was cover for minelaying, but this time the shells did not all fall in the sea: there were (according to official figures at the time) 137 dead and 360 (later revised to 455) injured in the three towns after a bombardment lasting from just after 8 a.m. until 8.50 a.m.: Hankey later claimed there were 86 dead and 426 injured in Hartlepool alone.[11] There had been no programme to build shelters, and the War Office announced that evening that people in West Hartlepool had 'crowded in the streets, and approximately 22 were killed and 50 wounded' as a result.[12] It said there had, however, been 'an entire absence of panic' in all three towns, which ironically may have helped increase casualties as people chose not to hide away during the attack. Much housing was damaged, and three churches were struck in Hartlepool, as well as the gasworks. In Whitby the abbey ruins were damaged, and a church and hospital were hit in Scarborough, as was the Grand Hotel. Once order was restored, the mayor of Hartlepool issued a proclamation advising people to stay indoors.

The German ships were 10 to 12 miles offshore. The Royal Navy pursued them but, the official report claimed, lost them in the fog and failed to sink them. It seems the ships sent in pursuit were simply not fast enough. Under the 1907 Rules of War agreed at the Hague conference, Scarborough and Whitby were undefended towns, and the raids were therefore illegal. Churchill's gaffe was that he wrote a letter to the mayor of Scarborough that concluded: 'Whatever feats of arms the German navy may hereafter perform, the stigma of the baby-killers of Scarborough will brand its officers and men while sailors sail the seas.'[13] Mrs Asquith was outraged by his tone, 'because the one thing in war times that no one can stomach is rhetoric'. Her husband agreed, thinking the letter 'rather banal; a lot of cheapish rhetoric & an undertone of angry snarl.'

The public, however, seemed to side with Churchill, the raids provoking defiance and anger; and the press demanded to know why casualties had been so high. *The Times*, which had long called for a detailed programme of instruction to civilians of how to protect themselves, berated the government for 'dealing with the matter in piecemeal and furtive fashion.'[14] The authorities, acting under DORA, moved enemy aliens from the attacked towns 30 miles inland, allowing some back after the investigation of individual cases. Nevertheless, the vulnerability of the east coast was confirmed. On 21 December the Admiralty Pier at Dover was the apparent target of the first bombing from an aircraft over England, when two missiles were dropped from an aeroplane in the sea nearby; and on 29 December the first Zeppelin was sighted over the British coast.

Although the government thought a German invasion might be attempted to break the stalemate on the Continent, it had, illogically, done little to advance formal home defence beyond the earlier instructions to lords lieutenant of coastal counties. Counties adjoining coastal ones had received no guidelines, even though an enemy that had landed would almost certainly reach them. Under pressure in the Lords, Crewe, the Liberal leader in the Upper House, was forced to admit that the plans had been modified already, and might be modified further. However, he said it was not 'desirable' to issue instructions to every county, or for each to have a coordinator of home defence.[15] What he perceived as Crewe's complacency outraged Curzon. 'The poor people at Scarborough who went out into the streets at eight o'clock on the morning of December 16 had no time to go to the police and ask for the address of the chairman of the emergency committee,' he remarked.[16] He wanted the emergency instructions published for all to see and understand, not kept secret among a select group. He also criticised the lack of coordination of Volunteer Training Corps – bodies of men beyond military age designed to mobilise their energies – as rendering the corps 'useless' in the face of any emergency.[17] In Scarborough, the railway station had been besieged by people wanting to get away: Curzon feared a 'stampede' in the event of a serious attack, and rebuked the government for having made no contingency plans for transport.

On 19 January the Zeppelins returned, with lethal intent. From 8.20 p.m. bombs – thought to be from three airships sighted that afternoon off the Dutch coast – fell for ten minutes on Great Yarmouth. The municipal authorities turned off street lights immediately and, unlike in Scarborough and Hartlepool, people stayed indoors during the raid. Experimental blackouts were in force along the east coast. The airships went on to bomb Cromer, Sheringham and, at 11 p.m., King's Lynn. The bombing killed four people – a cobbler and an old lady in Lynn, a boy of fourteen and a twenty-six-year-old widow of a soldier in Yarmouth. A baby and an off-duty soldier were injured. With the country gripped by spy fever, word arose that a motor car with flashing lights had guided the airships. Further inquiry revealed the car in question belonged to the King's domestic chaplain, heading to the rectory at Sandringham: the Royal Family had returned to London that morning. The Zeppelins had not intended to target Cromer and Lynn: they had sought industrial plants on the Humber, but became lost in fog and jettisoned their bombs over the first urban areas they saw. The raid panicked the authorities along the coast: in London all special constables were called out and put on air-raid duties.

The reaction to the raid was one of predictable fury. 'The German Government and the German people alike have made it clear in a hundred ways to the whole world that they are ready to commit any outrage and do not propose to obey any of the laws of GOD or man,' proclaimed The Times.[18] 'They practise ruthless and inhuman destruction of the weak and helpless.' The paper expected that this brutality – which it claimed was 'such as the world has not witnessed for a thousand years' – would be renewed on a larger scale; but it said that Britain should not retaliate, but should concentrate on defeating the German army and winning the war. This manifestation of German 'beastliness' should have come as no

surprise: Wells had predicted it in his 1908 novel *The War in the Air*, showing how the home front and the military front would become one and
the same.

II

Yet for all the people's supposed commitment to the struggle, and the
attacks on the British coastline that reminded them of the war's immediacy and lethal potential, the industrial strife that had marked the years
before the war resumed. Miners in Yorkshire voted in January 1915 about
whether to strike in pursuit of an increase in the minimum wage. The
union wrote to colliery owners to ask whether they would support such
an idea; but before they could reply the industry's conciliation board was
convened, and the widespread belief was that the government would
intervene. The Yorkshire coalfield supplied power for textile mills working twenty-four hours a day to make uniforms. There was also a serious
shortage of labour, as around 20,000 Yorkshire colliers – a sixth of the
total – had enlisted. However, the owners said profitability had fallen,
and they could not afford to pay more.

The shortage of labour also disturbed farmers, who predicted problems of cultivation and harvest because of losing men for labour-intensive
work; and this came at the same time as a sudden rise in the cost of living. The price of food, having stabilised since August, was now rising
again, because of a shortage of imported wheat and the increased cost of
shipping and congestion at ports, again caused by a shortage of men.
Labour announced that when Parliament resumed on 2 February it
would demand full state control of the distribution and price of food,
ideas utterly abhorrent to the Liberal government, despite the compromises about state intervention made since August 1914. Shipowners,
attacked for profiteering, said they had not increased their charges, and
instead blamed foreign food producers for taking advantage of shortages
in Britain by raising prices. Even if the Liberals had had no ideological
objection to intervention, it would have been pointless. Sensing a larger
slice of the cake might be available, fish porters at Billingsgate also went
on strike.

The high price of food throughout the winter of 1914–15 also made the
public restless. In London, a 20-stone sack of flour that had cost 26s 6d a
year earlier was now 40s 6d.[19] Farmers were urged to grow more: but

that would bring no immediate relief, and the increasing shortage of labour caused by the enlistment of farm workers meant it would be hard to bring the 1915 harvest in. One possible solution was to grant exemptions under educational by-laws that existed in many rural districts to take boys as young as eleven out of school to work on the land: but this caused huge disquiet. Labour, and some Liberals, felt it was the continuation of a long campaign by farmers for more child labour, because it was cheap. As Hardie said on 25 February, the labour movement had campaigned for free and compulsory education for years, and many of its members had never been to school; they were loath to see this entitlement eroded, even by the war.[20] Hardie advocated the employment of women for certain farm jobs – a suggestion ahead of its time, which would quickly catch on – and also the nationalisation of the land and the formation of local workers' cooperatives – which would not. Sir Harry Verney, an agriculture minister, said farmers should make better use of labour exchanges, employing boys as a last, not a first, resort.

Problems of food supply worsened because Russia, instead of exporting wheat, now sought to buy on world markets, which had driven prices up. In early 1915 sugar (the average consumption of which was a pound and a half per person per week) went up from 2d a pound to 3½d, rice from 2d to 2½d, bread from 3½d to 4d a loaf: in all cases the increased price of freight was a factor, meaning that in remote parts of Scotland prices were even higher. A man earning 25s a week had spent 13s 9d on food before the war; now he spent 16s 6d, unless his family had cut down.[21] High-quality coal from Newcastle, sold in London before the war for 30s a ton, was now 34s. Even worse, the low-quality coal used by the poor, which had been 22s a ton, was now 32s, making life exceptionally difficult for them. The logistical problems of assembling a new army of seventy divisions – Kitchener's ultimate aim, whose creation would require a cultural revolution to establish a mentality of total war – were ceaseless, and for all Parliament's willingness to vote new loans, financial restraints remained. Nonetheless, further small increases in allowances for wives, children and widows were announced on 9 November, such as raising the widow's pension from 5s to 7s 6d a week: a move that caused outrage in a certain section of society. 'A Householder' – he was wise not to give his name – wrote to *The Times* to say that if wives and widows with children really were to be paid £1 a week 'we shall not be able to keep a single maidservant in my particular district. They will all be running after the men who are "worth a pound a week alive or dead." Numbers of young girls are already persuading men to marry them on the strength of these allowances."[22] He suggested allowances be paid only to women married before the war, or before enlistment.

The fundamental cause of the inflation, though, was the huge growth in the supply of money because of the issue of paper currency, not just in Britain, but around the world as a consequence of the disruption to commerce. Francis Acland, financial secretary to the Treasury, in response to requests to take some of the notes out of circulation, told the Commons on 22 February that 'there is no depreciation of the currency': which was rubbish.[23] Before the war there had been £28 million of high-denomination notes in circulation: by February 1915 there were £87 million, mostly 10s and £1 notes that had replaced half-sovereigns and sovereigns – which were either retained by banks, hoarded or had left the country. The overall supply of money had, however, increased, as the total sum of notes plus gold was above the pre-August 1914 level. Acland confirmed that any holder of a note could exchange it for gold at the Bank of England at will: had everyone done so, however, the economy would have collapsed, as the country would have been denuded of gold reserves.

Throughout the winter the government was never free from having to handle industrial unrest. Inexorably rising food prices continued to spur demands for higher wages – London dockers wanted an extra 2d an hour, but representatives of the owners refused to meet them until pressed by the Board of Trade – and there were threats of strikes. In February 1915 engineers on the Clyde walked out over pay, and other shipyards became restive. The government's committee on shipbuilding announced an award of 10 per cent for piece workers or 4s 6d a week for waged staff on government contracts: the unions had wanted 15 per cent and 6s, but accepted the lower figure as a compromise. However, the Clydeside workers, who wanted an extra 2d an hour because of the rise in food and coal prices, were not appeased. They renamed their strike committee the 'withdrawal from work' committee and ultimately agreed to return to work, but once there refused to do overtime and, when at their lathes, contrived to do as little as possible.[24] *The Times* quoted one operative as saying that while he was sorry if their action led to a shortage of ammunition, 'we regard our 2d an hour as much more important than ammunition for the Army.' Clydeside would vex the

government throughout the war: it became the base of the revolutionary Socialist Labour Party, who saw the war as an opportunity to kill
capitalism, and exploited it to that end. What they achieved for ordinary
workers rather than for their own ideological satisfaction is highly debatable. The newspaper's report said that was not the view of most men,
and the union urged a return to normal work, but such sentiments
inflamed public opinion.

Asquith was disturbed, when the industrial situation was discussed in
cabinet on 24 February, to note Churchill and Lloyd George trying to
outdo each other in suggested sanctions against unpatriotic workers,
including 'compulsory labour & martial law'.[25] With things going badly
in France, a collapse of industrial morale and social divisions were the last
things needed. However, because of censorship the true state of the war,
the shortage of ammunition and the huge dependence the Armed Forces
had on industrial production had been kept from the public, including
from striking workers who were almost certainly not aware of the damage they were doing. Such a world of make-believe was unsustainable.
The Times, constantly complaining about censorship, even suggested that
groups of workers be taken to the trenches to see things for themselves,
instead of 'squabbling over farthings'.[26] By early March there was a drift
back to normal work on the Clyde, mainly because money was running
short among strikers' families: but the unrest continued among London dockers and bootmakers in Northampton, in whose trade disruption
could cripple the fighting forces.

DORA gave the government power to seize a factory essential to the
war and to compel its owners and workers to carry on production; an
Amending Bill in March 1915 conferred the right to control plant not used
for war work, but which had that potential. It met little parliamentary
opposition. Understandably, Asquith was immensely reluctant to use
such a measure, and an early agreement in Northampton for a return to
work obviated the need. However, a strike then broke out on the North
Eastern Railway after a demand for a 20 per cent pay rise was refused;
and 2,000 Scottish steelworkers asked for a 25 per cent increase, while
4,000 blast furnacemen sought 50 per cent.

Lloyd George's indispensability to the government arose not because
of his knowledge of finance but because of the rapport he could establish
with the unions. Matters were so restive in the coal trade that the Miners' Federation of Great Britain called a conference to discuss its pay

demands, which turned into a three-day meeting at the Treasury, from 17 to 19 March, with the chancellor. However perilous the national situation, some workers were in no mood for sacrifice, and the rise in prices enriching many already well off gave them cause to take such a view. Nevertheless, the meeting ended with an agreement – known as the Treasury Agreement – by the unions (thirty-four of them) to accept arbitration instead of going on strike. There was a strict under-standing that new working practices would pertain for the duration of the war only. More controversially, the unions were promised a say in the management of the arms industry, and that profits would be restricted – which served the government's purpose, as the taxpayer was footing the bill.

In some respects society was changing more slowly than might have been imagined. There was still resistance to women doing men's jobs, hence the preference for schoolboys to be put on the land rather than direct the large number of unemployed women whose businesses had been hit by the war to do such work. Visitors from Canada and the United States – such as Mrs Alfred Watt, of Toronto University, who lectured the League of Honour in London on 4 March – spoke of the ubiquity of women in agriculture in North America, and how labour-saving devices for the home had been developed to allow them more time to work on the land. Yet the day she spoke it was reported that Leicestershire planned to issue permits for boys of eleven or twelve to abandon school and work on farms during the spring and summer. The Bishop of Oxford, writing to *The Times*, called such a policy 'a disas-trously reactionary measure': and, in a portentous observation, noted that the country clergy of his diocese had seen their soldier parishioners 'greatly improved by military service and better feeding' when home on leave, and wanting a better life than agricultural labour when and if they returned from the war. The boys of eleven would in all likelihood have to stay on the land for life: their older brothers, however, if they sur-vived, were minded to move on. The war was already expanding horizons for those lucky enough to be in the right place at the right time.

Civilians would soon have to become used to another privation: restrictions on the supply and availability of alcohol. On 15 March Kitch-ener had made a statement in the Lords about the Battle of Neuve Chapelle (which he called 'a marked success'), claiming the fighting had been confined to trench warfare because of the waterlogged ground:

either he did not grasp that mobile war was out of the question whatever the weather, or saw no reason to share that news with the wider world.[27] On munitions, he said orders of 'vast magnitude' had been placed with factories, and the 'great majority' of workers had 'loyally risen to the occasion'.[28] However, he reported manpower shortages and delays in producing plant; and 'instances where absence, irregular time-keeping, and slack work have led to a marked diminution in the output of our factories.'[29] He blamed 'the temptations of drink' and restrictive practices of unions, and warned the House that unless the supply of recruits for the Army and of munitions improved, the prosecution of the war 'will be very seriously hampered and delayed.' The shortage of munitions, especially, caused him 'very serious anxiety'. To incentivise workers he announced that the profits of their employers would be curtailed and a medal for loyal service would be issued at the end of the war.

Lloyd George, like Kitchener, believed drink was handicapping productivity in armaments factories: and that was what the government told the public, perhaps shifting some of the blame for the underperformance of the arms industry on to the shoulders of its inebriated workers, instead of concentrating it on the War Office, which needed to get a grip on this essential industry. Lloyd George's own constituency in the Liberal Party, being predominantly Nonconformist, was closely associated with the temperance movement: so taking a hard line on drink was personally helpful to him, and there were even this early in the war sufficient reports of drunken and absentee workers to provoke action.

The previous August, Parliament passed a law allowing local authorities to control the hours of public houses, something hitherto only possible if a riot was expected. In November 1914 a deputation, led by the Duchess of Marlborough, went to see McKenna, the home secretary, to demand the government 'take instant steps to deal with the lamentable increase of drinking among women.'[30] The grand ladies told the home secretary they believed – on what grounds it is unclear – that women who turned to drink did so in the mornings; so they asked him to ban the opening of public houses before noon. He told them he did not believe he could get parliamentary support for such a measure.

Although taxation had increased, the longer hours worked in arms factories, and in others concerned with war production such as textiles and machinery, meant a rise in disposable income. Much of this rise was spent on alcohol. The statistics did, however, prove that not only were women drinking more, they were doing so when the nation overall was drinking less, doubtless because so many men were now under military discipline and women were moving from the closely supervised and poorly paid world of domestic service into factories. At Bangor on 28 February the chancellor said that 'drink is doing more damage . . . than all the German submarines put together.'[31] The speech caused huge disquiet, not just among the drinks trade but among the public, who feared prohibition. The press was briefed that the speech was a warning rather than a threat; but Lloyd George intended to fulfil the long-held Liberal desire to bring the Tory-supporting brewing industry under control while claiming to do so for patriotic reasons. The question was how to do this without aggrieving drinkers, damaging the Treasury's revenues or intervening to an unacceptable level in private business. Mrs Asquith, who claimed hardly to drink at all, was 'violently hostile, and full of compassion for the drinkless workers, and of indignation against those who "would rob a poor man of his beer".'[32]

Lloyd George suggested to the King – to whom he had taken to referring, in private, as 'my little German friend' – that if he foreswore strong drink for the duration, and imposed that rule in all royal palaces, the nation would follow.[33] The King agreed: he was already being careful to make patriotic gestures whenever possible. In public he now wore only military or naval uniform; he had already toned down his social life, having given up eating out; and in the first days of the war, when the food panic was at its height, Buckingham Palace had announced that the Royal Family would eat only plain food for the duration. There were precedents for sacrifice. He told his diary, apparently enthusiastically: 'I am all for drastic measures & all alcohol being stopped during the war.'[34] Asquith, who had no intention of stopping drinking, was troubled. Claims that he was an alcoholic rely on a loose definition of the term: he certainly drank heavily, as did most men of his era and class, and he certainly drank more than was ideal for conducting great affairs of state.[35] He also increased his intake as the strain grew, and his colleagues occasionally detected a physical deterioration: Lord Crawford, joining the cabinet in the summer of 1916, noted that the sixty-four-year-old Asquith was 'somnolent – hands shaky and cheeks pendulous', and 'his eyes watery and his features kept moving about in nervous twitching fashion.'[36] Lloyd George told Asquith he could, of course, get a medical exemption. Churchill, also en route to such a state, said that if forced to abstain he too would consult his doctor. Lloyd George was thought to be teetotal, having signed a pledge when he was nineteen, and being heavily reliant on the support of Nonconformists. However, he drank throughout his life in moderation, and seems to have seen nothing hypocritical in urging the King to take the pledge too, while he, as one already pledged, systematically broke his promise not to drink.

The Chancellor of the Exchequer then put himself at the forefront of the nation's self-sacrificial spirit without doing too much self-sacrificing of his own. He made a speech in which he said: 'we are fighting Germany, Austria and Drink, and as far as I can see, the greatest of these three deadly foes is drink.'[37] The Temperance Department of the Wesleyan Methodist Church liked the quotation so much it produced a poster to plaster all over Britain proclaiming it. On 1 April a letter was published in the press announcing that the King, his family and his household would renounce drink from 6 April until the war ended. Kitchener announced he was following suit. Lloyd George and McKenna signed the pledge, and the Church of England issued an official call for 'restraint' in consumption. Elizabeth Asquith, the prime minister's daughter, observed of Kitchener that 'neither the retreat at [the] beginning of [the] War or [the Battle of] Neuve Chapelle affected his spirits as badly as 3 days on lemonade.'[38] Oc Asquith, en route to the Dardanelles with the Royal Naval Division, sent a telegram to his father that read: 'Reported spread of temperance alarms and amazes us. Stand fast.'[39]

The King, however, soon felt he had been wrong-footed because of the lack of other public figures actually abiding by his example, and was especially aggrieved that his other ministers were not following suit. He told Stamfordham to tell Lloyd George that the abstinence would be delayed – but Lloyd George told him it could not be. The Sovereign then complained to Mrs Asquith that he had never intended to give up drink unless the government passed 'drastic legislation on the subject'.[40] He was angry with Lloyd George about the way he had handled the temperance pledge, and the acrimony lingered. Over a year later, when knighting Lloyd George's former under-secretary Arthur Lee, the King told him he had 'persuaded him to give up alcohol during the War, as an example, but unfortunately the public did not respond and he felt he had been made a fool of.'[41] Most in public life ignored the pledge: the

King occasionally took alcohol for medicinal purposes, such as when he was thrown from his horse and injured while visiting troops later in 1915.

Lloyd George's desire for prohibition, which Asquith believed would lead to a general strike, among other things, therefore never extended far beyond the Monarch. He then looked for other means of controlling consumption, arguing that the government should buy all public houses, a suggestion by which the prime minister was 'entirely unconvinced'.[42] After that he tried but failed to secure agreement for sizeable tax increases on drink. He then wanted to nationalise the drinks trade, to control the production and distribution of alcohol, which would have cost the taxpayer £250 million. Asquith told Miss Stanley: 'I warned him to go very warily: a State monopoly in drink would I think be a most dangerous thing politically.'[43] However, Law wrote to Lloyd George on 7 April, having heard of the proposal, and said his brewer- and distiller-funded party would back it if such a measure were deemed 'necessary for the successful prosecution of the war'.[44]

Some steps to control drinking were taken nonetheless. An amendment to DORA in mid-May 1915 allowed the government to enforce special regulations for the sale of alcohol in any area deemed essential for the production or transport of materials of war. It established a Central Liquor Control Board – which, in the effect the board and the policies it enforced had in drastically reducing drunkenness, was regarded as perhaps the most effective act of bureaucracy imposed during the war. A bane of twentieth-century life, the licensing laws, had been born, and as well as enforcing them the board ordered the production of weaker beer, and limited off-sales.

That was not the end of the anti-drink campaign. Later in the spring, an attempt by Lloyd George to raise alcohol duties caused trouble for the government that Asquith, beleaguered on an increasing number of fronts by then, could have done without. The chancellor spoke to the Commons on 29 April about the government's policy on drink, and his 'perplexing and disagreeable' duty to implement it.[45] He claimed drink was third on the list of impediments to productivity, after restrictions on the mobility and availability of labour and the unions' restrictive practices. The other two had been dealt with, he claimed, thanks to DORA and his negotiations with workers' representatives. Drink alone remained. A report by an admiral said that in one shipyard there were 135 fitters of whom, one Monday, only 60 worked a full day. On the following four days only 90, 86, 77 and 103 turned up; of 7,155 man hours on what would have been normal peacetime shifts, only 5,664.5 had been worked. This was a loss of 30 per cent, and it was not peacetime: war demanded maximum effort.[46] Across the nation, 493 men in every 1,000 in private factories and yards were working under forty-five hours a week each, which was disastrous: and rises in wages, far from motivating the men, made matters worse, by supplying more money for drink and less need for overtime. On the other hand, in the Royal arsenals, according to Lloyd George, men were working up to eighty hours a week: there was no excuse.

He announced a quadrupling of the duties on wines, and surtax on strong beers. He proposed to double the spirit duty. Thanks to an increase in sparkling wine duty from 2s 6d to 15s a gallon, a bottle of good champagne would rise to £1 – the fact that this was not the *boisson du choix* of the Tyneside shipworker made the rise in beer prices seem less like class war. The 'four ale' – so called because it had long been 4d a quart – had risen to 6d a quart in the first War Budget and would now rise to 8d, a doubling in price in less than six months. Stronger beers, such as Guinness or Bass, would be even more expensive. A bottle of decent claret would rise from 2s 6d to 4s, and whisky from 4s 6d to 7s. More controversially, the government would close public houses or restrict sales of spirits and heavy beers in areas where their operation was 'prejudicial' to the output of local factories or to the well-being of locally stationed troops, though it would compensate those whose livelihoods were harmed.[47]

The *Daily Citizen*, a Labour-supporting paper, said the speech constituted 'the most sweeping indictment of the working classes that has ever been heard', with the British workman painted as a 'drunken sot . . . wilfully betraying his country into the hands of the enemy.'[48] *The Times* said the 'inevitable inference' was that the government 'in order to hide their own shortcomings were libelling the whole class of working men.'[49] The paper asserted that the casual labourer was most given to drink, not the skilled worker, and he could afford to drink to excess only when trade was good. But it understood the consequences could be terrible in wartime, and therefore endorsed heavy taxation of strong drink, and special restrictions on areas with a high concentration of key factories.

Lloyd George's measures did not simply outrage the tribunes of the working man; they were attacked not just by Unionists, who apart from their links with the brewing trade saw his proposed tax increases on wines as harming French exporters with whom Britain was allied, but by the Irish Nationalists, who saw a threat to the whiskey trade and Irish farmers. Redmond accused Lloyd George of proposing, 'in effect, to destroy root and branch a great Irish industry.'[50] He said he had failed to prove the 'necessity' of imposing the measures on Ireland. The Irish press was uniformly hostile, and forecast the closure of distilleries, breweries, and the provocation of unrest.

Justifying its drink taxation plans, the government issued a Treasury White Paper on 2 May entitled *Report and Statistics of Bad Time kept in Shipbuilding, Munitions, and Transport Areas*. It detailed drink-related delays in various shipyards on the Tyne and the Clyde, based on investigations made by senior naval officers. Although Unionists and their press supporters deemed some of what was in the report contentious, it did expose a restrictive practice in the shipyards that was causing such poor productivity. This was the 'black squad' system. The wages of a group of workers were paid to its leader. If he was indisposed – say by heavy drinking – the rest did not work. And the tradition was that the leader would take his men to a pub and divide the wages, and each bought a round of drinks. One squad the worse for drink was bad enough; if several squads were affected the losses could be enormous. A factory inspector remarked that earnings had risen, but the workers 'have not yet been educated to spend their wages wisely, and the money is largely wasted, for they have few interests and little to spend their wage on apart from alcohol.'[51] The report also contained pleas by officers superintending the production of ships to ensure pubs remained closed until 10 a.m., since men were having early drinking sessions before work: the captain superintendent of the Clyde district even advocated a ban on selling spirits.

The brewers, distillers and their political clients vowed to fight the taxes. There would have to be a vote in the Commons, and given the anger of the Irish it was far from clear the taxes would be approved. There were protests in Dublin, and claims that the taxation was contrary to the spirit of the inoperative Home Rule Act. With a third of champagne production coming to Britain, and export markets in Belgium and Russia lost, the potential effect of Lloyd George's super-tax was ruinous. Bordeaux was no less vociferous. The French Parliament made a formal complaint to France's Foreign Ministry and urged it to raise the matter with London. Australia complained too, fearing damage to South Australia's wine industry.

Jellicoe, the commander of the Grand Fleet, added his weight to the argument in favour of taxes, saying the Navy was in peril because of poor working practices. Having heard how men on the Clyde refused to work on Saturday and Wednesday afternoons, and often took the whole of Wednesday off, he said that 'my destroyer dockings and refits are delayed in every case by these labour difficulties, and they take twice as long as they need do.'[52] Jellicoe's words incensed Tyneside labourers, who blamed shipyard owners for not reallocating men from work on merchant vessels.

His support was to no avail. Such was the deluge of opprobrium that on 4 May, before a Budget with no further increase in taxes, Lloyd George arranged leaks to the press that the taxes would be scaled back. The rise in beer taxes would be delayed. The wine taxes, designed to prove it was not a class issue, would not be imposed. However, Lloyd George was as determined to impose the tax on spirits as the Irish were determined he should not. Yet after further talks with the drinks trade on 7 May all new duties were withdrawn (as Mrs Asquith had predicted to her husband they would be, even before they became public), but the sale of spirits under three years old – stronger and cheaper and therefore within the pockets of working men – was banned, all such spirits being compulsorily placed in bond. Government control of drinks outlets around munitions factories was, however, approved. It was reckoned that consumption halved by 1918, thanks mainly to the difficulty in obtaining alcohol.

III

Assisting productivity by restricting drinking was a useful measure, but far more effort would be required to bring essential industries up to necessary wartime output. As men left in large numbers for the Army, attention turned to how best women could contribute to the war: though this would require, in many instances, the breaking down of entrenched prejudices. Farmers still questioned the physical powers of women as agricultural labourers, and preferred to hire boys too young to fight. Ironically, the government itself was accused of putting obstacles in the way of civil servants who wanted to join up. It was obvious that women could be trained for many civil service jobs, though *The Times* reported that 'doubt is expressed as to whether it is practicable to substitute women for men to the extent which is said to be in contemplation.'[53] Despite the national emergency, departmental heads were still reluctant to open even the most junior jobs to women, apparently doubting their ability to be a basic male bureaucrat's intellectual equal. And although the government would soon lead the drive to have women employed in nationalised munitions factories, many privately owned arms businesses would take women only as a last resort. To encourage employers to see that a woman could be trained to do a skilled job that would enable a man to be released to fight, the government embarked on a campaign of what can only be described as re-education.

The Board of Trade had announced on 17 March that it wished women to volunteer for war work through labour exchanges, where registers of those available would be kept. The 1911 census had revealed 15,650,778 women in Britain aged between fifteen and fifty-four, only 5.5 million of whom were in work.[54] In the first eight days nearly 21,000 came forward, a third of them in London. By 16 April 47,000 had volunteered, with more than 8,000 seeking armaments work.[55] Many from the capital were described as 'middle class and well-to-do', a large number of whom expressed a wish to work in munitions.[56] Others offered to drive taxis or vans, or to replace men in government offices. Railway companies requested women employees, though not for engine-driving; and retailers sought women for shop work. Most skilled factory jobs were male preserves: the war started breaking those barriers down. The state did not compel private employers to take women: it did not need to, as businesses would soon be unable to function without them. Soon, women's organisations mounted recruitment drives among their members.

The Times, in an article written 'by a Woman Correspondent', conceded that 'there is an enormous number of capable women coming down from the universities employed . . . under the title of secretary for members of Parliament and other public men, who could fill such posts usually given to youths from Oxford or Cambridge with none of their experience or love of work.'[57] Working-class women were highly adaptable too. The 'male monopoly' of catering had decided to offer courses for women, and the 1911 census had discovered that there were four women bricklayers, so anything was possible. She also wrote that 'to suggest that the many gaps in the ranks of Parliamentarians should be

filled by women deputies would be perhaps hoisting the President of the
Board of Trade with his own petard. But the experiment, being a temporary one, would have its useful points.' The drafting of women into
the workforce, and their inestimable contribution to the war effort,
would make the final, unanswerable case for women's suffrage. In April
1915 an experiment in Glasgow to use women as tram conductors was
declared a success, and was soon emulated elsewhere; and agricultural
colleges began training women in light farm work. While not all women
might be suitable for manual labour (though Kitchener told Asquith he
had seen women loading ships in Zanzibar), a prime minister deeply
opposed to women's suffrage now began to realise there were jobs
women could do that would relieve men if not for the services, then for
jobs requiring physical strength.

But as well as being an untapped human resource, women were also
providing society with a challenge it would rather not have faced – the
lingering prudishness of the Victorians had yet to be eradicated – but
now had to: 'the large number of unmarried girls and women in this
country who are expecting to become mothers'.[58] The cabinet had discussed an aspect of this in January 1915. Randall Davidson, the Archbishop
of Canterbury, had signified his disapproval of unmarried women who
had lived with, and had children by, soldiers, being assisted at the same
rate as married ones. 'It appears that the Archbishop does not wish them
or their children to starve,' noted Frances Stevenson, who as Lloyd
George's mistress had an insight into such matters, 'but he does not wish
them to be openly treated as deserving of relief'.[59] Lloyd George, who
knew something about such relationships, argued for every woman living with a soldier as his wife to be treated equally, and won: which
prompted Davidson to tell the government it had dealt 'a death-blow to
the marriage tie, and [was] encouraging immorality.'

The Times was horrified by this social effect of the upheaval, fearing
that 'a great wave of emotional nonsense has been set in motion, and
much that is being said is subversive both of the principles of morality
and of the foundations of the State.' The consequences of this wave of
fornication could not, it seemed, be understated. The 'nonsense' was the
idea that the expected children were fathered by 'the men that fought at
the Marne and Mons.' This, the paper asserted, was true 'only in a very
few cases' and people were 'talking rubbish' about 'the children of our
dead heroes.' In the seclusion of his Essex parish the Revd Andrew Clark

recorded that 'very evil reports reach me of the immorality of young women in Chelmsford, Halstead and Terling, where soldiers have been quartered. The leading women at the Mothers' Meeting this afternoon affirmed that the illegitimacy of this year in all these three places will be shocking beyond not only record, but belief.'[60]

The Times continued: 'In the excitement created at the outbreak of the war many young girls lost their balance. It required such an abnormal situation to disclose how far the weakening of parental control, the decline of faith, the lowering of ideals, and the partial failure of the churches have sapped restraints.' The Establishment's view was not indulgent. 'These are cases for pity and help rather than condemnation, but we shall not solve the problem presented by foolishly excusing what has happened.' It asserted that the fighting forces 'responsible for the miserable position of these girls and women belong either to the Territorials or the new armies.' The overcrowding of towns through billeting was blamed, for the way in which it provided opportunities for liaisons. A War Babies' and Mothers' League was founded, and announced that by April 1915 it had already dealt with over 4,000 cases, handing out grants for food. It made a national appeal for money. The Bishop of Carlisle preached on the subject, and blamed a lack of discipline in the home; the Archdeacon of Surrey announced he would ask the forthcoming Synod to call attention to the need for 'well-managed maternity houses in which unmarried girls may be received for their confinements and may be taught the duty of self-control and purity of life'; better late than never.[61]

The legalistically minded worried about whether such children could be legitimised: but that would have an impact on inheritance law, and depended on knowing who the father was. State assistance for the affected women and children was unpopular, it being assumed a girl's parents would have thrown her out in such circumstances. 'We have already gone a long way in the direction of undermining the special recognition of the marriage tie, on which the whole structure of the State largely and in reality depends,' *The Times* continued. 'If every girl who is with child by some unknown male whom she says is a soldier is to be provided with a State allowance, we shall see an almost unthinkable upheaval in our social conditions. We shall be saying, in effect, that every future war is to be the signal for an outburst of indiscriminate licence for which the State will pay the cost.' It returned to the subject the next day, suggesting that if it could be proved a soldier had fathered a child out of wedlock, and he died, some allowance might be made for the child: but that while it might seem harsh that parents were under no obligation to support their adult daughters, and that employers had a perfect right to sack them, these harsh powers 'cannot be swept away for the benefit of the incontinent.'[62] Any legal changes, it argued, should be kept to a minimum.

The subject came up in Parliament, where it was given short shrift on the grounds that those airing it in the press were clearly suffering from a sex obsession. James Hope, a Unionist MP, asked: 'Is it not much more important, in order to deal properly with those writers on the subject in newspapers who are suffering from erotic hysteria to amend the law of lunacy?'[63] It amused Bertrand Russell to receive a letter from his mentor George Santayana, who had read about 'war babies' in a Spanish newspaper, which had written: 'Kitchener, in creating an army, has created love. This is a great change in a country where only marriage was known before.'[64]

The influx of women into essential jobs was, however, insufficient to meet the Army's requirements for men. Around 4,000 men a day were joining in early November, and the War Office dropped the regulation height to 5 foot 3 inches from 5 foot 6 to get more. Clothing and arms factories were working around the clock. But even 5 foot 3 was not short enough. Because of the chronic problem of undernourishment of the working classes it would be hard to find enough men without allowing even lower height and smaller chest measurements. The rules were relaxed, hence the formation of 'bantam battalions' whose soldiers were under 5 foot 3 and whose chest measurements were below 34 inches. Permission was initially given to four towns with large industrial populations to raise such battalions – Manchester, Leeds, Birkenhead and Bury. After protests, the scheme was extended to Glasgow and Edinburgh in February 1915. By late February some regiments were taking men as short as 5 foot 1.

Another drag on recruiting was that many reluctant to join were those whose families could not afford to live on the separation allowances for wives and children; and although numerous employers promised to keep jobs open for men after the war, others did not. Churchill lobbied Lloyd George about this, calling it a 'scandal': 'No soldier's wife shd be dependent on charity.'[65] Men feared either that they would return from the front and be unemployed, or be killed in action and leave their families destitute. The government also agreed to pay an allowance to unmarried men with a dependent relative, such as a mother or grandmother, to help them enlist. However, the trades unions asserted that a more generous system of allowances would obviate the need for desperate appeals for men.

Feelings ran high against 'shirkers': so much so that Derby suggested a badge be issued for men who had volunteered but been found unfit, as well as for those doing essential work or waiting to go into uniform. As the debate about compulsion grew, initiatives were used to persuade men to enlist: crowds (and teams) were still addressed at football matches; Harry Lauder – the King's favourite music-hall turn – took a band of pipers around Scotland, with War Office approval, to drum up 1,000 recruits. As a further inducement to enlist, many job advertisements specified they wanted only men unfit or too old for the forces.

IV

With the training of volunteers taking up to eight months before they were ready for service overseas, the military situation continued to deteriorate. The First Battle of Ypres was indecisive and Neuve Chapelle an embarrassment, when early gains could not be exploited for want of ammunition. The cabinet – few of whom had any military expertise – regarded Kitchener with awe when he took up his post, but this soon wore off as the rapid success they had expected him to deliver failed to materialise. Politicians had not prepared for the new, industrialised weaponry and the carnage it could cause, nor for the attritional nature of static warfare. On 25 October Lloyd George told Riddell – who was more than his tame press proprietor, being also landlord of his grace-and-favour house at Walton Heath in Surrey, an arrangement that would not pass today – that 'he [Kitchener] is a big man, but he does not understand English life; and whatever he may have done in the past, pays no attention to details and does not properly control his staff. He is just a big figurehead.'[66]

Three days later he berated Kitchener at cabinet about setting up Irish and Welsh battalions in the volunteer army, which he thought would enhance recruitment but which Kitchener regarded with suspicion. If Kitchener were to accept a Welsh corps the men should, he argued, not speak Welsh on parade or in their billets. It was not their first argument: a month earlier when Kitchener had complained about sending Nonconformist chaplains to the front, Lloyd George compared this unfavourably with Sikhs and Gurkhas, who could have religious men of their faiths with them. 'If you intend to send a Church of England Army to the front, say so!' Lloyd George proclaimed, 'but you cannot fight with half a nation.'[67] Kitchener backed down: but this time, he told Asquith that 'no purely Welsh regiment is to be trusted: they are (he says) always wild and insubordinate & ought to be stiffened by a strong infusion of English or Scotch.'[68] Lloyd George also attacked him for the War Office's dismal administration of the separation allowance, which was causing hardship; and, when Kitchener bridled at being rebuked, he reminded him he must take criticism like the rest. Kitchener was conscious of another, far graver, problem: on 29 October, the day after this row with Lloyd George, he told Asquith he believed both sides would soon run out of ammunition: he estimated that seven times as much ordnance was being used each day compared with any previous conflict.

Given the urgent need for men, Mrs Asquith took Kitchener's attitude to change and innovation as proving his 'stupidity and want of imagination'. She had asked him whether the recruiting post on Horse Guards Parade, visible from her bedroom window, should have a shelter built on it so men did not have to queue in the rain; and a military band playing next to it so that 'their womenfolk, often in passionate tears, should feel they were heroes.'[69] When Lloyd George failed to persuade Kitchener about the national battalions, he started to shake his fist at him and told him: 'You think you are a Dictator! You are only 1 of 18!' The Field Marshal allegedly replied: 'All right, if you think you can do things so much better than I can, come over and do my job', while pointing out of the window at the War Office. He conceded the point to Lloyd George, with a touch of resentment: they soon appeared to be on good terms again, though any affection on either part was almost certainly superficial and for the sake of form.

To give ministers – especially Asquith – more time to reflect, cabinet meetings had moved from daily to thrice weekly by early November. For the moment naval matters were a prime consideration. Kitchener argued that the Germans, stymied on continental Europe, would attempt an invasion. It was an argument advanced more in hope than fear: ministers and service chiefs were confident any attempt would end

in a debacle for the German navy, confirm supremacy of the seas, demor-
alise the enemy and be a significant step towards victory. One of Fisher's
first tasks, with the full approval of Admiral Sir John Jellicoe, commander of the Grand Fleet, was to bring battleships to the southern
North Sea and the English Channel to meet any invasion attempt. The
question of command of the seas was not, however, straightforward. As
well as effecting the sinking of *Audacious*, extensive German minelaying
had taken down several smaller ships and merchant vessels. Royal Navy
minesweepers cleared 'safe' channels in the North Sea, which friendly
shipping was warned to use and which the Navy patrolled; but U-boats
still picked off British ships in the Straits of Dover, such as the cruiser
HMS *Hermes* on 31 October.

The ability to fight successful land battles was, however, of constant
anxiety. Asquith's concerns about the situation on the Western Front
caused tensions with the Army, putting Kitchener, as a soldier and now a
politician, in an invidious position. Worse, there were tensions within
the Army too. French had heard that the government had lost confidence in him – which was untrue, even though he and Kitchener had
poor relations as brother senior officers. He sent his aide-de-camp, Freddie Guest – a Liberal MP and cousin of Churchill – back to London to
convey his displeasure, which Asquith strove to assuage by writing him
a long and laudatory letter. Unfortunately, the handling of the BEF had
been attacked in cabinet, and Kitchener had immediately offered to
replace French with General Sir Ian Hamilton, commanding the anti-
invasion force in southern England: so French was right to be concerned.
To make matters worse, the account Guest brought Asquith of conditions at the front was 'appalling'.[70] The newspapers were full of the short
obituaries of regular Army officers killed at the front, many well known
to those prosecuting the war in Westminster and Whitehall; under-
appreciated were the numbers of NCOs and men also being slaughtered.
Losses had so reduced the Army that 'a Corps now numbers little more
than a division', and reinforcements were taking too long to reach the
front. Hankey, in whom Asquith was coming to place enormous trust,
advised him the BEF needed a rest, which could happen only if it were
relieved by French troops – which seemed impossible.

In early November Asquith, intensely dependent on Venetia Stanley
as a form of psychiatric social worker and complaining to her, on 18
November, that 'I feel very solitary', sought to reorganise his own

management of the war.[71] To streamline decision-making he put his
Council of War on a more formal basis, and changed its name to the
War Council. Hitherto it had comprised whomever Asquith wanted –
whichever ministers or service chiefs happened to be around when he
needed to discuss developments. Now, under his leadership, it would
include Lloyd George, Grey, Churchill and Kitchener. The First Sea
Lord would accompany Churchill, and the Chief of the Imperial General
Staff would come with Kitchener. As a concession to the Opposition –
but also because Asquith valued his experience – Balfour was asked too.
Hankey acted as secretary.

The War Council was not a day-to-day decision-making body, which
was what was needed. Like the cabinet it usually met without an agenda,
much to Hankey's annoyance.[72] Its numbers swelled to thirteen by
March 1915, mainly because of Asquith's refusal to rebuff colleagues who
felt excluded; it often replicated discussions held in cabinet, but with – as
Edwin Montagu, who joined the cabinet in early February 1915 as Chancellor of the Duchy of Lancaster, put it – 'a different set of spectators'.
Montagu thought the council 'should be used by its political members to
get a frank opinion of the military experts.' He told Hankey that Asquith
should state this as its specific purpose.[73] Matters were becoming more
complicated, since Britain and France had declared war on Turkey on 5
November, because of the Ottomans' alliance with the Germans and a
Turkish attack on Russia's Black Sea coast. Troops were sent to Egypt,
including shiploads of men from Australia and New Zealand, as a potential force against the Turks in case they attacked the Suez Canal (in early
February they did, and it was a disaster for them). With the naval
encounters in the South Pacific and Atlantic, the war was taking on a
global aspect.

The stalemate between the British and German armies divided the
political class into Easterners and Westerners. The former, led by Lloyd
George and Churchill, who as well as being motivated by patriotism saw
an opportunity to hasten the war to its conclusion that would, coincidentally, benefit them, believed the attack should move to the east, and
be concentrated on Germany's allies in Austria–Hungary and the Ottoman Empire. The Westerners, led by Asquith and Kitchener and
including most Army top brass, believed the war could be won only on
the Western Front, and that to take troops from there for another theatre of war would simply allow the Germans to overrun the French,

especially if they could leave fighting on a second front to the Austrians or the Turks. Some ministers, notably Lloyd George, wanted Britain to send troops to defend Serbia; Asquith, fearing overstretch and realising how fragile things were in Flanders, resisted this. There was also the prospect of annexing Palestine from the Ottomans, making it a British protectorate and encouraging Jews to resettle there: Wells had suggested this in a letter in the *Daily Chronicle* the previous November, and Chaim Weizmann, leader of the British Zionists, had recruited Samuel, the first Jewish cabinet minister, to the cause. Ironically, British anti-Semites also embraced Zionism, as a means of removing Jews from British society.

There was a determination to help Russia in the Caucasus: but all such aid came at the expense of the battle in the west. On 7 October Asquith, who as a committed Westerner was just beginning disagreements with Lloyd George about strategy, noted that at a meeting of the Committee of Imperial Defence invasion was discussed but 'everybody agreed that nothing of the kind was likely to occur at present, which is just as well, as during the next fortnight we shall have fewer regular troops in the country than has ever happened before.'[74] By the time politicians went home for Christmas in 1914 the east–west debate, like the war, was becoming entrenched. Whether or not new fronts were opened, much more cannon fodder would be needed: the maximum recruiting age, originally thirty and then thirty-five, was raised to thirty-eight. The Army had by then ruled out an attempted German invasion, but feared isolated raids launched by anything up to 10,000 men. A home defence force was essential, but the government had no choice but to send more regular soldiers to France. Every military consideration had serious political ramifications, a problem that would stretch the capabilities of politicians for whom these were unprecedented circumstances. As the ensuing campaign in the Dardanelles would show, no strategy could work unless it was properly planned.

Churchill continued to trouble Asquith, who told him to concentrate on his own responsibilities as First Lord of the Admiralty. Perhaps therefore it was as well that he became more persistent about an eastern strategy after Britain declared war on Turkey on 5 November 1914. This, however, led to Churchill's suggesting what Asquith termed 'a heroic adventure against Gallipoli and the Dardanelles to wh I am altogether opposed.'[75] This was the revival of an idea of which Churchill had talked the previous August – even before Turkey was a formal enemy – about forcing the Dardanelles as a way to reach and occupy Constantinople. At the end of 1914 the plan took shape thanks to Hankey, who had concluded that it would be useful to open a second front; and it was endorsed by Lloyd George at a War Council meeting on 7 January 1915, at which he argued for the need 'to get at the enemy from some other direction.'[76] Churchill would persuade Vice Admiral Sir Sackville Carden, commander of the Eastern Mediterranean Squadron but a man of limited battle experience, to back the plan.

Churchill believed that once Turkey was attacked Balkan nations such as Bulgaria would rise against it, before attacking Austria–Hungary – a view Grey shared. Hankey also wanted the Army to take on the Turks; Churchill had already advocated a new naval campaign, but his idea was to raid Germany from the Baltic, a plan that had little traction, hence his adoption of Hankey's. He also, at least at first, had Fisher's support. If the Navy could break into the Baltic and take command of it, it would allow the Russians to land troops 90 miles from Berlin: but it would entail violating Denmark's neutrality en route, unless she could be prevailed upon to join the Allies. In early 1915 Churchill again pressed for the Baltic, even though by now the Admiralty was contemplating a landing in the Dardanelles, but the idea had no traction.

Even though he won support for his Dardanelles plan, Churchill continued to be a nuisance. He invented excuses for frequent visits to the Western Front, a distraction beginning greatly to irritate Kitchener, because he feared they were helping to feed friction between French and himself. He sought to visit Dunkirk in December, and Asquith told him explicitly he should not try to see French. Just before Christmas Asquith met French and Kitchener at Walmer Castle (which Lord Beauchamp, the Lord Warden of the Cinque Ports, had lent him for weekends), and French agreed with Asquith about the Churchill problem. Despite his 'affection and admiration' for the First Lord, French regarded his judgement as 'highly erratic'.[77] Churchill's excitability was of a piece with that of the heir to the Throne, and similarly irritating to the Secretary of State for War. Esher noted on 18 December: 'The King told me that when the Prince of Wales went to see Lord K, and pressed him to be allowed to go abroad, he said to Lord K, "I have plenty of brothers, what does it matter if I am killed!" and Lord K's reply was: "I don't mind your being killed, but I object to your being taken prisoner and you have no experience." '[78]

Nevertheless, Churchill understood earlier than most the unforeseen problems of trench warfare, not least in its shattering effect upon the armies fighting it. This did not justify his eastern strategy, but it helped explain the thinking behind it. Kitchener too was beginning to realise that what was happening on the Western Front was of a different order of magnitude to anything he had experienced – he told Grey: 'I don't know what is to be done. This isn't war.'[79] Hankey also thought like Churchill. In memoranda that they separately sent Asquith on 30 December they set out the murderous consequences of trench warfare, which makes it all the more alarming that they were ignored when planning the disastrous assault on the Somme eighteen months later.

The continuous line of trenches meant that traditional outflanking operations – the sort of thing Kitchener understood by 'war' – were impossible. And, as Asquith told Miss Stanley, 'the losses involved in the trench-jumping operations now going on on both sides are enormous and out of all proportion to the ground gained.'[80] So great were those losses that on 26 December the remnants of the BEF were reorganised into the 1st Army (under Haig) and 2nd Army (under General Sir Horace Smith-Dorrien). Hankey's answer to the challenges was to suggest the development of, effectively, tanks, but with 'petrol-throwing cata-pults' to crush barbed wire and protect men from machine-gun fire, which caused Asquith to observe that 'it will be strange if we are driven back to these Medieval practices.'[81] Churchill suggested something similar.

In a further memorandum, on the last day of 1914, Churchill accurately warned his colleagues: 'The war will be ended by the exhaustion of nations rather than the victories of armies.'[82] However, he still gave the impression of enjoying the war more than was tasteful. On 10 January 1915 he and his wife were among those staying at Walmer Castle with the Asquiths. In telling Mrs Asquith he had given up his ambition to be Viceroy of India – there was a vacancy – Churchill added: 'This is living history. Everything we are doing and saying is thrilling. It will be read by 1,000 generations – think of that! Why, I would not be out of this glorious, delicious war for anything the world could give me.'[83] Even Churchill sensed the adjective 'delicious' was indelicate, and implored Mrs Asquith not to repeat it.

Lloyd George spent Christmas fretting, drawing up a memorandum that he asked Asquith to circulate to colleagues. He joined the argument about opening a new front, in his case in Serbia and Syria. Beginning a strain of criticism that would run for two years and lead to Asquith's downfall, he demanded 'decisive measures to grip the situation.'[84] He attacked a lack of military leadership, and called for a series of War Council meetings – 'occasional meetings will end in nothing,' he said. 'A continuation of the present deadlock is full of danger.' Asquith had no excuse not to realise the chancellor was watching him. This attempt to influence great strategic questions would not be the last.

The new year began badly for Asquith. Percy Illingworth, the Liberal chief whip, upon whom he relied for his party management, died suddenly aged forty-five on 3 January, just two days after becoming a privy counsellor. The official version was that he had died of typhoid; the *on dit* was that his end came after eating a bad oyster. He had shown Asquith total loyalty and been a repository of innumerable confidences. The loss made Asquith even more dependent on Venetia Stanley, to whom he still wrote daily, and in ever more passionate terms: 'My darling . . . yours through life – always – everywhere' was a typical endearment, in the first of two letters on New Year's Day 1915.[85] Four days later he told her, in imploring her to write to him daily, that 'I think of you every hour, and your love is the *best* thing in my life'.[86] She had just started to train as a nurse, and Asquith's suffocating demands were the last thing she needed. It would have unhinged him to know that relations between her and her other admirer, Montagu, were heating up, but it was something with which he would soon have to deal.

While Lloyd George and Churchill were coming up with their respective strategies French was annoyed that the War Council rejected his request to open a new front between Ostend and Zeebrugge, to come in behind the Germans, because the plan required fifty-five battalions of men and incomprehensible amounts of artillery. As things stood, Kitchener told Asquith on 12 January that he had 1,750,000 men under arms, despite having been at war just five months and having sustained 80,000 casualties, numbers of men that, although insufficient for French's purposes, were nonetheless impressive from a standing start. French, despite all earlier reassurances, had convinced himself that, because of the stalemate he had achieved, once the first wave of Kitchener's army was trained – by April or May – he would be displaced and Kitchener would become supreme commander; something Kitchener had indeed been considering (though he later denied it) and which had leaked through to the Western Front.

Asquith and his colleagues may have disliked the stalemate, but they lacked the resources to change it; and Unionist criticism of the government was eroding public morale. It was in this context that the opening of a new front in the Dardanelles began to appeal to him. It also carried much weight with him that there was bipartisan support for an attack on the Turks. Balfour believed a successful blow 'would cut the Turkish army in two; it would put Constantinople under our control; it would give us the advantage of having the Russian wheat, and enable Russia to resume exports . . . it would open a passage to the Danube.'[87] The plan received the unanimous approval of the War Council on 15 January. Carden had planned the campaign: Churchill endorsed it at an Admiralty meeting on 12 January, and it was put to ministers the next day. Crucially – in the light of what followed – Churchill had consulted Carden, as a naval expert, about the plan's practicability before proceeding; Carden had replied that he did not consider the Dardanelles could be 'rushed' but 'they might be forced by extended operations with large number of ships.'[88] Fisher, on 3 January, had said to Churchill: 'THE ATTACK ON TURKEY HOLDS THE FIELD! – but ONLY if it's IMMEDIATE! However, it won't be!'[89]

It was at the War Council meeting on 15 January that approved the Dardanelles campaign when Haldane raised the question that would come to dominate the political debate in 1915: what would be called 'conscription' – his term was 'compulsion'. He took Kitchener's view that the war would be long, and it would be necessary continually to replenish the ranks of the wounded and fallen. The French had called up every adult man, and Germany had a huge army. Haldane's argument that 'by the common law of this country it is the duty of every subject of the realm to assist the Sovereign in repelling the invasion of its shores and in defence of the realm' was not universally accepted.[90] Haldane, a considerable lawyer, admitted this claim rested on no statute, but was 'inherent in our constitution'. The view was that compulsion was not yet necessary: but might become so and, if it did, it would be not just commensurate with but inherent in the idea of the state. Compulsion would require an Act of Parliament, but such an Act would be compatible with the constitution. *The Times*, normally no admirer of Haldane, pronounced there was an 'overwhelming' view that 'the Government should fight this war with the whole strength of the nation and every weapon at its disposal.'[91] It spoke for a group of prominent Unionists who, led by Curzon, were now volubly saying the government could not be allowed to proceed uncritically. 'We shall have to take steps for the purpose of defining our own attitude towards HMG,' Lansdowne told Law on 28 January. 'We can scarcely leave matters where they are.'[92] Curzon complained to Law that the alternatives were to muddle on or face a coalition; Law replied: 'I am reluctantly driven to the conclusion that the only proper course for us in the meantime is to continue along the lines on which we have acted since the war began.'[93]

At the Admiralty, relations between Churchill and Fisher were combusting after less than three months. Hankey – an old friend of Fisher – saw Asquith on 20 January to warn him that the First Sea Lord was in 'a very unhappy frame of mind': he liked Churchill personally but resented how the First Lord, who knew little about naval matters, overruled him, with his sixty years' experience.[94] Fisher thought few of the Navy's ships were in the right place, and that plans for where to move them were unsound. Fisher had written to Jellicoe the previous day to express concern that a Dardanelles operation would remove from the Grand Fleet ships 'urgently required at the decisive theatre at home.'[95] He had shared his fears with Hankey, who (despite his presence at the creation of the Dardanelles plan) passed them to Asquith. That same day Churchill admitted to Kitchener that 'until the bombardment of the Dardanelles forts has begun, we cannot tell how things will go.'[96]

'Tho' I think the old man is rather unbalanced, I fear there is some truth in what he says,' Asquith told Miss Stanley. Disagreements continued to multiply, with Fisher making plain to Asquith through the channel of Hankey his objection to the idea of the naval campaign in the Dardanelles. On 21 January Fisher elaborated on his misgivings in a letter to Jellicoe, telling him he believed the operation would impair the naval protection of Britain; and it would only work if supported by 200,000 troops, a view he believed Kitchener would share. Esher noted in his diary that Fisher 'finds Winston very brilliant, but too changeable; he has a different scheme every day.'[97] He deduced that Asquith was 'acting as arbitrator upon their differences.'

Churchill counted on Kitchener's support in the War Council, and on that of Balfour and Grey. Fisher, however, remained sceptical and when the War Council discussed the Dardanelles on 28 January the First Sea Lord – who had very nearly not attended at all because 'I am not in accord with the First Lord and do not think it would be seemly to say so before the Council' – first motioned to leave the room, until persuaded by Kitchener that duty dictated he should stay.[98] He then 'maintained an obstinate and ominous silence. He is always threatening to resign & writes an almost daily letter to Winston, expressing his desire to return to the cultivation of his "roses at Richmond",' Asquith said.[99] Churchill was livid about Fisher broadcasting the fact of their differences to Hankey, Asquith and Jellicoe, which suggested his Admiralty team was not coherent. He strove to confirm Fisher's backing, and when in 1916 the Dardanelles Commission questioned him about it, he claimed he would never have proceeded had Fisher not unequivocally promised his support. Asquith maintained that Fisher objected not because the plan was doomed to fail, but because (as he had told Asquith on the morning of 28 January, before the War Council met that afternoon) he preferred an assault on the Baltic.[100]

More worrying, Fisher – who knew he was outnumbered on the Dardanelles plan – claimed to Hankey that even Jellicoe, who was supremely level-headed, was now beginning to worry about some of Churchill's orders; and (like Hankey) was concerned about Fisher's reluctance to speak up against a First Lord whose judgement on naval dispositions seemed highly questionable, and who was increasingly unwilling to take advice. Unfortunately, Churchill's questionable judgement about the Dardanelles was matched by his failure to consider the worst outcome, and his expectations about how the drain of troops required to carry out his plan would increase Allied vulnerability in the west were wildly wrong. On 25 February he would tell the War Council that 'there is no reason to believe that Germany will be able to transfer to the West anything like 1,000,000 men at any time.'[101] In fact, German numbers increased from 1.5 million men on the Western Front in January 1915 to 2.35 million thirteen months later, at the start of the Battle of Verdun.

Important dispositions were taking place on the Western Front too, with the British Army taking over the extreme left flank from the sea eastwards, and the French concentrating on the eastern end of the line. Whether fairly or not, the British political and military leadership had been unimpressed with the performance of the French, and separating the two forces into two distinct sectors, after a negotiation between

French and his counterpart Marshal Joseph Joffre, made the British feel they could act without constant French interference, and regain some autonomy.

As Britain struggled in the early weeks of 1915 to define a new and more successful strategy, it also had to face a novel and even more direct challenge: the sinking of British merchant vessels by U-boats. On 21 January a ship bound from Leith to Rotterdam was sunk. It had not yet become official German policy: but in early February the Kaiser and his Chancellor announced that Britain would now suffer a blockade. The Germans proposed to challenge the supremacy of the Royal Navy with unrestricted submarine warfare. Neutrals were warned that any ships entering what the Germans decreed the 'war zone' around the British Isles would be liable to be sunk. However, the campaign was not quite what it seemed: the Germans, at that stage, had only twenty-two submarines, far too few to run an effective operation. The King was appalled at the attacks on unarmed ships: 'It is simply disgusting that Naval Officers could do such things,' he said.[102]

On 1 March Britain responded, an Order in Council announcing that 'the British and French governments will hold themselves free to detain and take into port ships carrying goods of presumed enemy destination, ownership or origin.'[103] The Germans had dug their own grave, because for the rest of the war they could trade with hardly anyone except their immediate neighbours, which by late 1916 would cause severe shortages. They were warned off the Straits of Dover after 10 April, when a net barrage caught a U-boat. Germany's willingness to adopt a policy that could threaten the lives of civilians turned opinion further against it, notably in America, and by the autumn American protests caused it to be suspended. The British blockade, however, continued.

Asquith announced on 8 February that the BEF had sustained 104,000 casualties – killed, wounded and missing – since reaching the Western Front.[104] The public, used to long casualty lists, received the news without surprise and with remarkable equanimity. Support for the troops remained unequivocal. When word arrived that British prisoners of war were freezing in German camps, a national campaign to make and send them warm clothing was started. The National Canine Defence League even ran a successful appeal for funds to pay the dog licences of recruits so their four-legged friends would not have to be put down if the 7s 6d annual fee was unaffordable. There was also an awareness that some soldiers were suffering from 'traumatic neurasthenia and cases of mental strain', and Tennant told the Commons on 4 February that a special Red Cross Military Hospital had been opened to treat such cases.[105]

The desire to pursue the enemy within, or those considered sympathetic to them, remained unwavering. Between 17 October 1914 – before which no records were kept – and 30 January 1915, 2,821 enemy aliens who had been detained had been released, their cases vetted by a branch of the War Office under a cabinet order of 11 November, 717 of them in January alone.[106] Nevertheless the search for scapegoats caused the campaign against Haldane to erupt again in early February, led by the Northcliffe press. Joseph King, the Liberal MP, raised it in the Commons on 8 February in a debate on the poor operation of press censorship. Introducing his defence of Haldane, King claimed the Press Bureau's work seemed 'guided by no clear principles, and has been calculated to cause suspicion and discontent.'[107] One example of this was that information denied to the British public about their soldiers was freely disseminated on the Continent. He remarked that everyone knew about the naval losses – casualties had been published – but the press had not been allowed to state what they were, leading to 'uneasiness, alarm, apprehension and even mystification as to the progress of the war'.[108] But another example of the bureau's incompetence was that one of its rules was not to allow attacks on ministers in case they damaged public confidence. King could not square this supposed principle with the 'extravagant and absurd' attacks on Haldane.

He accused his persecutors of 'terming him little better than a German agent'.[109] The attacks had caused many constituents to write to their MPs to ask whether there was any truth in them, and the stories were beginning to depress morale. King wondered what the point was of the Press Bureau if it allowed such things. Northcliffe's Times ignored the defence of the Lord Chancellor, preferring to attack 'a policy which laboriously conceals disaster and deadlock for fear of making the people nervous, which refuses to tell them of the doing of their soldiers even after an interval of months, which confuses and minimizes the casualty lists, which works by stealth even in issuing orders to the public for their conduct in case of a raid.'[110] Its suggestion was not to have a Press Bureau run by lawyers and amateurs, but instead to set up a new department.

V

The Royal Navy's bombardment of forts in the Dardanelles began on 19 February; the previous week Fisher had ordered thirty new ships, in expectation of battles ahead.[111] From the outset little went to plan. The straits were heavily mined and the Navy's minesweepers proved vulnerable and ineffective; the weather conditions were bad; the Turks were better armed than expected; and putting together troops for a subsequent land invasion proved difficult, because of Kitchener's caution at leaving the Western Front under-defended. Decisions that should have been taken by the War Council – a body that now met less and less frequently – were delegated to commanders in the field: so when General Sir Ian Hamilton arrived there in mid-March to command the military effort, it was left to him and his naval counterpart, Rear Admiral Sir John de Robeck, to decide when landings should take place. A naval attack on 18 March, just after Hamilton's arrival, had proved fruitless, with two battleships sunk; ten days earlier three ships had been destroyed after entering a minefield. 'The Admiralty have been very over-sanguine as to what they could do by ships alone,' Asquith told Miss Stanley, recording another black mark against Churchill.

French told Asquith that the trench warfare of mid-February had brought heavy casualties; but Kitchener remained convinced that the best-trained division still at home, the 29th, should stay there in case a sudden German breakthrough on the Russian front encouraged the enemy to send a big force west to try to smash the French lines. This caution led to trouble in the War Council on 6 March, when Asquith provoked Churchill by supporting Kitchener's plea not to send the 29th Division to the Dardanelles, where Churchill wanted them to reinforce the attack. The prime minister found the First Lord 'at his worst . . . noisy, rhetorical, tactless, & temperless – or – full'.[112] When the decision went against him his response was 'immense and unconcealed dudgeon'. Asquith believed the Dardanelles campaign was a risk worth taking. If it succeeded it would, he told Miss Stanley, mean 'occupying Constantinople & cutting Turkey in half, and arousing on our side the whole Balkan peninsula'.[113] The price of food and success in the Dardanelles were also inextricably linked, as Russian access to the Mediterranean would allow grain exports to resume: and the price of food was an increasing ministerial preoccupation. Ministers from Asquith downwards rubbished German propaganda claims that its navy was 'blockading' Britain. The prime minister stated that 'the German Fleet is not blockading, cannot blockade, and never will blockade our coasts.'[114] Yet it was undeniable that food prices were rising, and this left Asquith with a dilemma. A successful campaign in the Dardanelles would ease the pressure on food supplies, but it could be achieved only by taking the risk of sending troops against Kitchener's advice. In the following days it became clear that both the French and the Greeks were prepared to send substantial numbers of troops to the theatre, but the Russians – looking at Turkey with expansionist eyes, and contemplating incorporating Constantinople and the Dardanelles into their empire – strongly objected to Greek involvement.

Partly because of Asquith's having to deputise at the Foreign Office for Grey, who was ill, the War Council, after its meeting of 19 March, did not meet again until 14 May: another sign of how little Asquith grasped the gravity of events on the Western Front and the deterioration in the Dardanelles, and the active response they required. Hankey and Esher agreed that troops should have been ready once the bombardment began, not brought in afterwards, and there should have been no press announcements of the assault. All element of surprise had been lost. Hankey told Esher on 15 March: 'Now we have given the Turks time to assemble a vast force, to pour in field guns and howitzers, to entrench every landing place, and the operation has become a most formidable one.'[115]

At the 19 March meeting reports from the east, including news of the sinking of three ships and the disablement of two others, confirmed the deficiencies of the Dardanelles campaign. When Lloyd George asked whether 'any success had been achieved to counterbalance the losses' he was told by Sir Arthur Wilson, another former First Sea Lord whom Churchill had recalled from retirement, that 'so far as could be gathered . . . the forts had only been temporarily silenced.'[116] Churchill claimed it was too early to tell, but agreed to authorise de Robeck to continue operations 'if he thought fit'. Hankey noted: 'Lord F and I in the rather unenviable position of being able to say "I told you so".'[117] Churchill would devote enormous energy for decades to seek to escape responsibility for the failure in the Dardanelles, but facts were against him.

However, a new crisis now arose that would pose an even greater threat to the government's stability. Because he had no experience of the

trench warfare now prevalent on the Western Front, Kitchener instinctively felt French's demands for munitions were unreasonable and
exaggerated. He also disliked details of the munitions business being
revealed outside the War Office. Before the war the weapons industry
had been highly dependent on German technology, a ridiculously derelict situation given the widespread belief the next enemy would be
Germany.[118] It was only thanks to purchases of machine tools from Sweden, Switzerland and America that the industry could supply the Army
with sufficient engines, because the British were incapable of making
them quickly enough. The British chemical industry was also barely
existent – it had relied on German imports – and this not only meant a
shortage of proprietary medicines, but also of chemicals for ammunition
and aircraft fuselages. The other obstacle to higher production was the
unions, whose members had yet to adapt to practices unimaginable in
peacetime. The consequences of that period since the 1890s when the
spending rather than reinvestment of dividends had smothered innovation were now apparent.

Lloyd George had eased the restraints on arms expenditure and the
government had subsidised the expansion of armaments factories.
Asquith told the Commons on 1 March that by the end of the month the
war would have cost £362 million or, given that it would by then have run
for 240 days, an average of £1.5 million a day.[119] He said the present cost
was £1.7 million a day, and would rise to £1.9 million by the beginning of
1916. Nothing in the government's calculations was based on a swift end
to the war. However, Kitchener remained obstructive to any development in arms manufacture or supply that interfered with his control,
even though as early as 11 February French had had his chief of staff, Sir
William Robertson, warn Haig to be careful how many shells he was
using. Asquith wished to give Lloyd George control of a new Army Contracts Directorate to oversee munitions production, something Kitchener
would not countenance.

Directly after the Treasury Agreement of March 1915 Asquith, Lloyd
George, Churchill, Montagu – the new Chancellor of the Duchy of Lancaster and responsible for creating the administrative framework of how
the munitions industry would now work – and Balfour met to design a
new Munitions Committee, under Lloyd George, to control the process.
Kitchener threatened to resign: he felt the committee was entirely
unnecessary, because – in a move that confirms the grasp of political

cunning he had shown in seeing off Curzon in India – he had set up his own committee in the War Office. Asquith, however, faced him down: on 8 April he told Kitchener that Lloyd George would take charge of munitions, and the change was leaked to the press on 5 April. The new committee could not come soon enough: it was estimated that in the fortnight around the offensive at Neuve Chapelle, which lasted from 10 to 13 March, the British Army used as much ordnance as in the entire Second Boer War.[120]

VI

The journey towards a wartime coalition government was not accomplished overnight. It was first noted at Walmer Castle on 23 January 1915, when Lloyd George told his hosts, the Asquiths, that 'the opposition was longing for a coalition'.[121] Margot Asquith claimed she had heard this before; and Lloyd George, who privately viewed such an upheaval as an opportunity for self-advancement, said that, apart from Balfour, he could not think of any other Tory whose services would be useful. No love was lost between Lloyd George and Balfour, but the chancellor recognised the indispensability of the former Unionist leader to any possible coalition. Asquith felt that Balfour – who, in more than a decade of largely unsuccessful struggle to hold the Tory line since he had become prime minister in 1902, had perfected attitudes of languor and disinterest almost to Olympic levels – was 'the greatest fraud of our time'.[122] After six years in Downing Street, and having coped with an avalanche of adversity for most of that time, Asquith still saw no reason why he should need a coalition administration behind him to prosecute a successful war against Germany. His opponents, perhaps unsurprisingly, disagreed. Lansdowne told Law on 28 January that future relations should include 'the taking of the leaders of the Opposition into full confidence about all important matters connected with the conduct of the War.'[123]

Asquith's troubles with colleagues might have persuaded him of the desirability of choosing new ones. He remained wary of Lloyd George, who thus far was reasonably loyal to him, though that would not last much longer. Kitchener was autocratic; Haldane was under attack; Grey he thought 'tired out and hysterical'; and he told his wife that 'Winston is far the most disliked man in my cabinet by his colleagues . . . he is intolerable! Noisy, long-winded and full of perorations. We don't want suggestion, we want wisdom.'[124] Asquith had long decided Churchill was not so clever as Churchill thought he was: he told Miss Stanley on 11 August 1914 that the First Lord had spoken endlessly at cabinet, 'posing as an expert on strategy'.[125] Since she was a cousin of Churchill's wife, Asquith was possibly understating his feelings to avoid causing offence. With the debacle of Gallipoli to come – Asquith made the remarks to his wife in early March – the absence of support for Churchill meant he could not afford to fail.

Churchill made no secret of his belief in a coalition: Asquith had told Miss Stanley on 9 February: 'it is not easy to see what W's career is going to be here: he is to some extent blanketed by E Grey & Ll George, & has no personal following: he is always hankering after coalitions and odd re-groupings'.[126] Asquith was even minded to offer Churchill the viceroyalty of India, shortly to be vacant with the scheduled return home of Lord Hardinge of Penshurst, but doubted he would accept then, if ever. Churchill was an engine of ambition, and a coalition would provide him with new lands to conquer. One of his closest friends – F. E. Smith – was a leading Tory. However, what, surprisingly, Churchill did not grasp at the time was the level of hostility and distrust against him from almost everyone else in the party he had deserted in 1904 – though another exception was the leader he had deserted, Balfour, who had forgiven even if he had not forgotten. Many Liberals regarded Churchill as a Tory, justifiably: when he spoke of coalitions it was assumed it was to align himself with the likely next government, so colleagues distrusted him too.

From 10 March – the day Kitchener agreed to send the 29th Division to the Dardanelles – Asquith expanded his War Council to include Law and Lansdowne. The prime minister was unimpressed by them, telling Miss Stanley 'they did not contribute very much'. He would not, therefore, have been disappointed by Law's telling him on 15 March that while he and Lansdowne had 'enjoyed' the meeting, it would 'weaken their position in the Conservative Party' were they to attend again.[127] However, their joining Balfour on the War Council albeit temporarily proved how bipartisan the conduct of the war was becoming, and how bipartisan Asquith felt it needed to become. He asked Hankey to include them in the circulation of all the papers prepared for the War Council, but not to invite them to meetings. It was a long way from that, however, to formal coalition.

H. W. Massingham, editor of the *Nation*, told Mrs Asquith on 24 March that Churchill was intriguing to have Balfour replace Grey, to facilitate coalition. Asquith, appalled at the notion, thought Churchill 'a complex victim to B's superficial charm'; he sought Lloyd George's opinion, and the chancellor thought Massingham's information was 'substantially true'.[128] Asquith regretted Churchill's lack of a 'sense of proportion' and that he did not have 'a larger endowment of the instinct of loyalty.' Churchill's machinations could be seen only as undermining a senior cabinet colleague and also the authority of the prime minister himself. Asquith said of Churchill to Miss Stanley that 'I regard his future with many misgivings.' He continued: 'He will never get to the top in English politics, with all his wonderful gifts; to speak with the tongues of men & angels, and to spend laborious days & nights in administration, is no good, if a man does not inspire trust.' Grey was suffering from serious trouble with his eyesight. However, his taking off the first half of April 1915 to go fishing, when negotiations about bringing Italy into the war on the Allied side were at a delicate stage, was not designed to inspire confidence. Haldane normally took over the Foreign Office if Grey was absent, but because of the continuing criticism of him in the press as a pro-German, Asquith stepped in.

The other complication in Asquith's life, and one that would badly affect his general judgement, was his relationship with Venetia Stanley. There is no evidence to suggest this was physical: but his emotional dependence upon her grew constantly in the first nine months of the war. A letter of 16 March is signed off 'Your lover' after 'Good night my best beloved . . . my last thought tonight is of you, as will be my first thought in the morning, & my *best* thoughts all through the day.'[129] Two days later he ended with: 'I never loved or *needed* you more,' and promised not to consider moving Lloyd George to become a full-time munitions minister until he had consulted her. (It is interesting to observe the political power thus bestowed on one of the millions of women Asquith, as a resolute anti-suffragist, thought unfit to have the vote.) The pressure this put on her was becoming intolerable, and she was (still unbeknown to Asquith) increasing her intimacy with Montagu as a potential escape. Even if she decided to marry Montagu, the business of telling Asquith – who could not marry her himself, since a divorce from his wife was unthinkable – would be grim. When, on 19 March, she hinted she might have to go abroad as a nurse, he told her of 'the tragic

pall of black unrelieved midnight darkness' the prospect brought him.[130]
A month later, Mrs Asquith wrote to Montagu of her fears that she was
being supplanted by Venetia, and asked him to urge her to marry him.
He hardly needed encouragement.

For a man charged with the direction of the war, Asquith led a curious existence. He would sit in his club, the Athenæum, of an afternoon
and read a book when, by his own admission, he should have stayed in
Downing Street and read the memoranda piling up for him. It was, like
his obsession with Miss Stanley and the evenings spent playing bridge,
his way of coping with stress: but what those who saw him in an armchair reading a collection of modern English essayists on a Tuesday
afternoon, having had his hair cut, just after the British offensive at
Neuve Chapelle had been halted (with 7,000 British and 4,200 Indian casualties), must have thought can only be imagined.[131] Lloyd George told
Riddell: 'He lacks initiative and takes no steps to control or hold together
the public departments, each of which goes its own way without criticism. This is all very well in time of peace, but during a great war the
Prime Minister should direct and overlook the whole machine. No one
else has the authority.'[132]

Had the public known about the prime minister's *crise passionnelle* over
Miss Stanley, or of his afternoons reading *belles lettres* in the Athenæum,
or about his evenings of bridge, matters might quickly have become
unmanageable. It would have shocked the public had they also known of
his propensity to drink. On 12 April Gwynne told Lieutenant General
Henry Wilson, the principal liaison officer with the French and with
whom he regularly intrigued, that the prime minister 'has been letting
himself go very much of late and his example has been followed by his
wife, who was so drunk in a private house about ten days ago that she
was sick in the drawing room and on the stairs going away.'[133] Asquith was
a highly intelligent man and a gifted intellectual who could dispatch business rapidly and get quickly to the heart of a problem; he also had the
intellectual's gift of benefiting from periods of reflection, particularly
when faced with unprecedented problems such as war brings to a man
used only to the management of problems of peace – considerable though
those had been. Nor, unlike some of his colleagues, did he spend hours
each day on political intrigues. But his letters make it clear that he was
tired, distracted, and still had not quite grasped – as Kitchener and Lloyd
George had – the full implications, and different demands, of near-total

war. Gwynne's ungallant observation to Wilson suggests Mrs Asquith was suffering too.

In mid-March Lloyd George had C. P. Scott, the editor of the *Manchester Guardian* and the high priest of Liberal journalism, to breakfast and told him he thought the war 'would last another two years.'[134] The minimum terms the government would accept from the Germans was the surrender of Alsace and Lorraine, annexed from France in 1871, but that could not be sought until 'the Germans have been driven back to the Rhine': of which there was little immediate prospect. He told Scott that Poland had to be 'reclaimed' and that 'it was not a question of "crushing" Germany but of defeating her.' However, 'if we could produce 12 million shells a month instead of three the whole situation would be transformed.' Lloyd George told him he had visited France and seen the superior output of their munitions factories, and wanted something similar in Britain. 'The supreme need in this country was to organise the production on business lines and speed it up to the utmost . . . the difficulty was Kitchener.'[135]

Pressure increased on the government to mastermind a breakthrough as casualties rose and the public's attitude became more tense. Women in mourning became a routine sight in the streets, as did men in uniform on leave; and local newspapers featured rolls of honour with photographs of the often youthful dead, rolls that seemed to lengthen progressively. With no end in sight, the question of whether the direction of the war was in the right hands began to be more freely debated. Northcliffe's newspapers were not slow, after the problems of Neuve Chapelle and of the Dardanelles became apparent, to highlight them. In April 1915 Northcliffe told Riddell, his fellow press baron, that Asquith was 'indolent, weak, and apathetic' and thought 'LG may be the man.'[136] His sense of his own importance had yet to attain its full bloom. McKenna drew Asquith's attention to favourable comments in the Northcliffe press about Lloyd George, and suggested the two might be conspiring, perhaps with Churchill in tow. It was an idea ahead of its time – there was no plot – but it worried Asquith and his friends.

On 29 March Asquith confronted his chancellor with the rumours, and told Miss Stanley that 'I have never seen him more moved'.[137] Lloyd George thought McKenna was motivated by hatred of Churchill, and that the Tory press had been critical of Asquith because they believed Kitchener – who was really responsible for the ammunition shortages that were hampering the war – was a Tory and therefore should not be attacked. In Asquith's account, Lloyd George told him 'that he wd rather (1) break stones (2) dig potatoes (3) be hanged & quartered (those were metaphors used at different stages of his broken but impassioned harangue) than do an act, or say a word, or harbour a thought, that was disloyal to me . . . his eyes were wet with tears, and I am sure that, with all his Celtic capacity for impulsive & momentary fervour, he was quite sincere.'

That last observation, made to his closest confidante, reveals how unequal Asquith was to grasping Lloyd George's true character. He did not know it at the time, but Lloyd George was swift to tell his cronies about drift at the top of the administration, as he had Riddell. He also had a private life that made Asquith's *tendresse* for Miss Stanley seem childlike in its innocence, and in the spring of 1915 it was going through an especially baroque phase. He had started driving to his house at Walton Heath in Surrey whenever he could, claiming he could not sleep in London. The truth was that he was afraid of high explosive, and going there took him away from Zeppelin raids; and he would pick up Frances Stevenson, his mistress, on his way out of London, and take her with him. She was ill in March and April 1915; Lloyd George's biographer, John Grigg, speculates on whether she had had a miscarriage, or even an abortion: she noted at the time 'the idea of our love-child will have to go for the time being'.[138] According to Grigg, she told the daughter she eventually had with Lloyd George that she had had two abortions. Such a pregnancy, had it been known, would have ended the career, even in wartime, of the most indispensable minister.

Unlike Lloyd George, Asquith disliked the press, despite having one or two journalists (notably J. A. Spender, editor of the *Westminster Gazette* and a Balliol man like himself) close to him. However, he took seriously Massingham's interpretation of how fragile the cabinet was. (He did not realise it, but the fragility was clear also to Gwynne of the *Morning Post*, who was advising Law on the question.) Gwynne believed a coalition 'would weaken the Conservative party and break up the Liberal party', giving the Tories a short-term advantage only; he was convinced a coalition was unnecessary to the national interest.[139] Gwynne's preference would have been for a general election, or to let nature take its course without any help from the Tories. Asquith had to tread carefully with the press. Led by Northcliffe, proprietors were already angry with the government over censorship, and Asquith felt Fleet Street's claim that the public were being manipulated – or 'being unduly soothed and elated' – was entirely true.[140] He and several other ministers, and the censors, Buckmaster and Sir Frank Swettenham, met a deputation of proprietors and editors from all the London papers except *The Times* on 1 April. He said he was optimistic about ultimate victory; but repudiated any notion that the government was putting out entirely false statements of optimism.

An article about a plot against Asquith appeared in the *Daily Chronicle* on 30 March, and later that day he summoned Lloyd George and McKenna to clear the air (Churchill had been invited, but declined, feeling no need to defend himself). The chancellor accused McKenna of having put the *Chronicle*'s editor up to write the piece. McKenna denied it 'hotly' and blamed Balfour. Asquith ended a raging argument by saying he would resign at once if he thought any colleague had reservations about him. The three men agreed that Churchill was far too intimate with the former Unionist prime minister.[141] Asquith then had to broker a row between Kitchener and Lloyd George over the Munitions Committee. It was paradoxical that with matters of life and death being paramount, matters of vanity should absorb him so. Nevertheless, on the day he had to referee the McKenna–Lloyd George fight, he found time to write four letters to Venetia Stanley.

The next day a small group of Asquith, Churchill, Kitchener and Hankey met to approve the joint naval and military assault on the Dardanelles, de Robeck having signalled Churchill two days earlier to confirm that the naval one alone had failed. Lloyd George said afterwards that 'the calculations had gone hopelessly astray.'[142] Churchill had done much more of the planning than Fisher, whose enthusiasm for the plan ended by being non-existent, which is why so much blame for what happened would rest with him. A week earlier, on 6 April, Hankey had warned a meeting of ministers that landing troops would be difficult, but Churchill had brushed him aside – 'he anticipated no difficulties in effecting a landing,' the minutes record.[143] Putting men on the ground was now the only hope of salvaging the campaign.

The cabinet had been told the terrain was flat and the ships' guns could wipe out any Turkish soldiers trying to hold ground. It was nothing of the sort, and the Turks were easily able to dig themselves in. 'There are risks,' Asquith told Miss Stanley, 'but I am sure we are right to go through with it.'[144] He likened the chances of a favourable outcome, however, to 'so much depending upon whether the coin turns up Heads or Tails at the Dardanelles', which suggests an element of fatalism. Provided Britain and France could find the weaponry to do so, they were planning a joint offensive in early May to drive the Germans back to the Meuse. Asquith told Miss Stanley that if the coin landed the right way up in the Dardanelles, and the Allies' ammunition supplies improved in France, 'the war ought to be over in 3 months.' Few shared his optimism. When word reached England of the extent of casualties in the initial wave of landings, Gwynne, writing to Lady Bathurst, denounced the expedition as 'a mad Churchillian scheme.'[145]

The problems in the Dardanelles were symptomatic of the challenges now facing Asquith from every quarter, whether military or domestic. Miss Stanley's dilemma about her future was coming to a head. Montagu stayed with her and her family for the weekend of 16–18 April, and they appear to have decided to get married. Shortly after he had left Alderley to return to London, Miss Stanley wrote to him that 'this Sunday has made it very difficult to go on writing to the P.M. as tho' nothing had happened. Darling what am I to do?'[146] Asquith was, two days later, scheduled to make a big speech at Newcastle about the war, and she was reluctant to tell him before that. What must have cheered Montagu enormously was her *envoi*: 'Darling I *think* I love you, Venetia.' She did write to Asquith with a hint about the future – her letter to him is lost – about (and he quoted her) her 'potentiality of making me wretched', but he added that 'if you were to tell me tomorrow that you were going to be married, I hope I should have the strength not to utter a word of protest or dissuasion.'[147] She did not tell him she was going to marry – families had to be consulted – but she did say that *if* she did marry her feelings for Asquith would not change. He, however, required her undivided attention.

To add to Asquith's troubles the newspapers were, by early April, reporting the shell shortage as vividly as censorship would allow. Hankey, who had been to Ypres to meet senior officers, reported to Asquith about 'the universal demand for more shells'.[148] Two committees – one from the Commons under Lloyd George and including Montagu, Balfour and Arthur Henderson, the Labour leader; and a departmental one in the War Office, under Kitchener – were appointed to examine the problem and, in Asquith's words, 'to ensure the promptest and most efficient application of all the available productive resources of the country to the manufacture and supply of munitions of war to the Navy and Army.'[149] Kitchener's agreement to serve was interesting, given his intimation on 29 March that if such a committee were formed he would take it as a criticism and would resign. Asquith said the committee had full authority to order whatever measures were needed to improve the situation. In towns such as Leeds, Sheffield, Newcastle and Glasgow, where there were concentrations of armaments factories, local committees were formed of managers and union representatives to discuss how productivity might be improved. Obvious means were to import more labour from other industries not vital to the war, and to step up recruitment of women. A measure of urgency was that there were even calls for men trained as wheelwrights, blacksmiths or engineers but who were now in the police to be transferred to Woolwich Arsenal, the main explosives factory in Britain, and replaced by special constables. In London the City police announced that the chief commissioner had 'invited' all unmarried constables to enlist. No one of military age was being recruited to the force, and vacancies were being filled by pensioners. Nevertheless, Lloyd George was still at Kitchener's throat about the shell shortage: Asquith told Maurice Bonham Carter, his secretary and future son-in-law, on 16 April 'that LG really said some things that he would find it impossible to forgive had they been said to him.'[150]

It was not just shells but soldiers that were in short supply. The men who had answered Kitchener's call were still in training and few would get to France before June. The numbers enlisting were tailing off. On 13 April an embarrassing consequence of this was disclosed in the *Daily Mail*. Reproducing a map from *Le Matin*, it showed that while the French were defending 543½ miles of front the BEF had a mere 31¾, not much more than little occupied Belgium's 17½. The *Mail* called this 'an ignoble position' and blamed the government for its lack of foresight.[151] To free up yet more men for the Army, initiatives were taken to get those unsuitable for military service into essential jobs. On 1 April it was announced that a dockers' battalion would be formed in Liverpool, on the initiative of Derby and with the approval of Kitchener, to discharge government work in the port. It would be composed of men too old to fight, but who wanted to get into uniform. They would be under military discipline, so the threat of a strike paralysing a key port would be averted: if the Liverpool 'experiment', as it was termed, succeeded it would be repeated elsewhere.[152] However, to propitiate the union, no man would be taken unless he was a member, and any man who left the union would be discharged from the Army. The NCOs were all ex-union officials and veterans, one having been wounded at Ypres.

Recognising the challenges his administration faced, Asquith went to Newcastle on 20 April and made a speech to munitions workers there. He hoped his words would quieten the Tory press, damage Northcliffe's credibility, raise morale and highlight the importance of improved productivity. A Zeppelin raid there five days earlier – they had become routine on the east coast – appeared aimed at arms factories and shipbuilding workshops, so it was an appropriate moment for the prime minister to visit. The press smoothed the path for his arrival by retailing stories of alcoholic excess on Tyneside.

The Times said that while there were few complaints from munitions factories about the commitment of their workers, the same was not true in shipbuilding. 'The men who may need straight words from the Prime Minister are a section of the workmen employed on the lower reaches of the river,' it wrote.[53] The Admiralty were chasing ships that were on order: but 'some of the men, it is alleged, have so far refused to change their habits or increase their energy to meet the national emergency.' *The Times*'s reporter paid an afternoon visit to a yard and found 'the hammers were silent'. He added that 'a director told me that it seemed impossible to get the riveters to work more than 50 hours in the week.' There had been Sunday working, but it had been stopped because of the 'slacking' that followed on Mondays and Tuesdays. The clinching argument appeared to be that 'strong ale is drunk by these men – light beer is not popular in Newcastle – and while there may not be much actual drunkenness the employer with whom I spoke said he was convinced that the drinking indulged in at weekends lowered the efficiency of his men and made them indifferent to work on Monday.' The reporter added that after a four-day Easter holiday some departments had only 20 per cent of their men turning up for work on the Tuesday. Scarcity of labour meant such men could not be sacked; but if drink were proved to be the problem, the new government Armaments Committee had the powers to restrict its sale. Also, under recent amendments to DORA, the government could take over factories producing 'war material' and direct how the work was done. Within two months, those who missed work because of drunkenness were being prosecuted, though for breach of contract rather than under DORA, the first case being of four Tyne shipbuilders at Jarrow on 14 June.

Asquith went to Newcastle, with the country, thanks to the press, expecting him to tell the British working man to increase his productivity, work longer and harder, stop drinking and put his country before himself. As *The Times* put it on the morning of his visit, 'if our skilled workmen cannot be trusted to do their duty when they see it, like men, then the Germans are right about our national decadence and we do not deserve to win this war.'[154] Unlike the modern processes of drafting and redrafting by a team of advisers, this speech was given from notes scribbled by Asquith as he rode in the train to Newcastle, and then finished off in his hotel room. His audience was of munitions workers, most wearing the lapel badge that marked them as 'industrial soldiers'; the theme of his forty-minute speech was 'deliver the goods'. He flattered his audience for their key role in the war effort, and reiterated his case for entering the conflict. Problems with supply of munitions were because the 'best experts' had been unable to predict the 'unprecedented scale' on which ordnance would be expended.[155] He said the state would take over the employment contracts of many workers, and ensure they were put on the most important jobs; and that other engineering factories not currently producing munitions would be converted to do so.

However, his repudiation of press reports of an ammunition shortage by saying that 'there is not a word of truth in that statement' was highly ill-judged.[156] Kitchener had told Asquith that the shell shortage was rectified; this was based on a comment French had made to the war secretary about how he had enough ammunition for his next offensive, though French had been complaining to him since the end of October about shortages, something of which Kitchener had admitted he was aware.[157] It was an uncharacteristic act of clumsiness for Asquith to rubbish reports that there had been a shell shortage in previous offensives. Every soldier knew this was wrong, as did MPs and Asquith's own colleagues. Perhaps he was rattled by Miss Stanley's threat to withdraw: but it shows how little he had attended to the realities of the war and the requirements of leadership in his obsession with her, and his hours of retreat into bridge and his library.

Asquith did not confine his remarks to munitions and ships. He also had before him the latest coal production figures, which were alarming: an 11.9 per cent fall year on year in February and a 10.8 per cent fall in March, at a time when demand was rising. Around 20 per cent of miners had enlisted, but a third of them had been replaced by men from other industries. Therefore he singled out the miners in his speech – even though none was present – and having observed that munitions workers were putting in sixty-seven to sixty-nine hours a week, he issued an 'appeal to the miners who remain in the pits to rival the patriotism of their fellows who have gone, or are going, to the front, by regularity of attendance and, if possible, by increased output.' He reminded his audience that DORA gave the government powers in such matters, but was anxious to avoid 'compulsion'. The munitions workers cheered, but to miners it seemed a veiled threat. He added that coal-owners might have to limit their profits, and unions would have to end restrictive practices, in the national interest. Things would be back to normal after the war: but for now there had to be a 'mutuality of sacrifice'.

The Newcastle speech had a complicated background, its considerations rooted in lifting not just productivity but morale. Asquith understood the problems the war had created for working-class households. The cost of living for them, according to the Board of Trade, had risen by 20 per cent between July 1914 and March 1915. Although the opportunities for overtime had rocketed, and munitions workers were comparatively well paid, others felt the time had come for a serious pay rise to compensate for the erosion of their disposable income. The Miners' Federation of Great Britain led the way, demanding 12.5 per cent with immediate effect, reduced from an initial 20 per cent. The owners offered 10 per cent. However, Asquith travelled to Newcastle having heard that a substantial element on the executive of the MFGB was planning to advise all the country's million miners to resign on the same day. It was unlikely they would prevail, but the fact that such a move was being mooted constituted a desperate threat to the country. In defiance of the union's leaders, random strikes in pursuit of war bonuses would run throughout the spring and early summer in the West Midlands and South Wales, where a 15.5 per cent bonus was demanded.

Asquith bore the scars of the great industrial unrest before the war, which by late April 1915 seemed resurgent. He was aware of rising food prices, claims of profiteering and the adverse effect of such matters on morale. Therefore on 29 April he convened a meeting of miners' representatives and coal-owners over pay demands. A coal strike would have devastated Britain's fighting ability. The miners knew the opprobrium they would provoke if they walked out at such a time: even so, the South Wales Miners' Federation was calling for industrial action. Food prices had now risen to their highest point since the outbreak of war, and were predicted to rise further. A quartern loaf of bread, 5½d the previous August, was by late April 8½d. There was also widespread anger that Spillers, the milling company, had just posted profits of £368,000 compared with £89,000 a year earlier, taken as proof of profiteering while the workers made sacrifices. The prime minister agreed with the justice of the miners' case: but, recognising the variations from one coalfield to another, he refused to recommend a uniform pay rise across the country: instead, he said that if any regional discussions between the owners and the MFGB did not agree a rise in each area within a week, the government would impose one. This prompted a settlement.

The morning after the Newcastle speech Asquith went to Armstrong's arms factory outside the city, which had increased its payroll tenfold since August, from 1,300 to 13,000 operatives, and had colonised acres of adjoining fields in putting up new huts. The old anti-suffragist seemed surprised at how well the women in the factory worked on machines 'wh they learn if they at all clever to handle in 3 days, & if stupid in not more than a fortnight.'[158] However, the huts were unmanned for the want of skilled labour. He went having read that morning a deluge of criticism about his speech from the Northcliffe press, which branded it dishonest in his dismissal of reports of a shell shortage. *The Times* praised his appeal to patriotism, but added that it 'would have done more to encourage the nation at large, if he had displayed less anxiety to cover up the deficiencies of his Administration.'[159] It questioned Asquith's taste in seeking to establish his administration's 'infallibility' during such a 'solemn exhortation' and at 'a time so big with fate.'

The Times mocked his denial of under-equipment of troops and his claim that the government had addressed the munitions problem. It ridiculed Asquith's 'self-satisfaction'. If all was going so well, it asked, why the urgent appeal for better productivity? It questioned his credibility: it concluded he and his colleagues had made 'false calculations' and 'mistakes'. It stopped an inch short of demanding a cabinet reconstruction. The newspaper also noted that Asquith had not accused the men of Newcastle of being hampered by drink, which would not only have been provocative but also, coming from him, hypocritical.

Mrs Asquith recorded that *The Times*'s editor – Geoffrey Robinson, who in 1917 would for inheritance reasons change his name to Dawson, the name of his maternal aunt, and who would distinguish himself in the 1930s by being the main establishment cheerleader for appeasement of Hitler – was 'a real blackguard of the lowest kind.'[160] He 'has openly boasted that he will do for Henry. He wants a coalition Gov. – Ll G Prime Minister, Austen (Chamberlain) Home Office, B Law Foreign Office (or vice versa), H [Asquith] Ld Chancellor etc.' Dawson was an ex-member of the 'Kindergarten' of brilliant young diplomats assembled by the former proconsul Alfred, now Viscount, Milner, who had created the Union of South Africa; and was a fellow of All Souls. He was also, at this stage in his career, keen to show complete obedience to Northcliffe, with whom he would break after the war. While other papers were savaging her husband – the *Morning Post* 'who hates Winston first and Henry next has constantly abused us' – Mrs Asquith singled out *The Times* as 'extremely vindictive and underhand', and claimed no English paper 'has shown so little patriotism'. Because of its influential readership, its editorial line was of paramount significance when the only means of mass communicating news and opinion was through the printed word.

Newspapers of less prestige were by now writing about an intrigue against Asquith. The *Daily Chronicle* had been categorical about its existence, and Mrs Asquith believed the loose tongues of Lloyd George and Churchill, particularly with friends such as Balfour and Smith, caused much to end up in the Northcliffe press that would have been better left unsaid. Lloyd George believed McKenna was intriguing against him by telling tales to Asquith about the chancellor's loathing of McKenna. McKenna believed Lloyd George was intriguing against him, and trying to get him sacked from the Home Office. Both men were right about the other. Therefore Asquith had to referee a feud between his home secretary and his chancellor. From what Asquith said to his wife, Churchill was running out of rope – 'he will see FE Smith and discuss every cabinet secret with him', he told her – and he had reached the point where 'it is no good discussing things with Winston.'[161]

After he returned from Newcastle, and while the Commons was debating a backbench motion on whether the munitions industry should, in effect, be centrally controlled or nationalised to ensure it performed better, Asquith wrote to Miss Stanley about the 'worship and love' he felt for her: and although she had warned him it could not go on he still held out hope: 'I know that fate . . . has just cut me off from the chance of the best tho' it has given me, & please God will still give me, the richest plenitude of love and happiness that has fallen to the lot of any man of my time.'[162] He pleaded: 'Whatever you may be tempted to do, my own darlingest, don't "spoil the bread and spill the wine". *Don't* . . .' But he conceded that should she choose someone above him, it would signal he was simply not worthy, and he would rejoice in her happiness.

It was too late. That same day Miss Stanley was writing a letter – of which she later claimed to feel ashamed because of its lack of generosity towards Asquith – to Montagu about how she could once have moved on from Asquith and it would not have mattered: and now, 'I feel so ungrateful to him & yet at times I resent very bitterly that he should stand in the way.'[163] Asquith had told her that life would have nothing to offer him if they parted: 'How could he have been so cruel as to say that to me?' she asked Montagu.[164] In the following days she and Montagu tried to work out how to tell him they were marrying: 'I can't see the way out,' Montagu told her, 'but best beloved, we must find one . . . for we ought not to waste time.'[165]

Asquith continued to be savaged by what he called 'Northcliffe & his obscene crew' for the Newcastle speech.[166] With politicians largely silent in the interests of national unity, the press took over. *The Times* returned to kick him on 22 April, calling his speech 'short of courage and candour' after further reflection, and asserting that the initial enthusiasm for it would soon wear off and be replaced by 'disappointment'.[167] Singing its proprietor's tune, the paper continued that 'he said not one single word about the position in which the war stands, nor did he make the slightest attempt to warn the nation of the enormous magnitude of the task with which it is now confronted.' This was not entirely fair, for Asquith had stressed, without using the phrase 'total war', that this was a war that required everybody, whether at the front or not.

The main criticism of Asquith at this time – that he was insufficiently communicative to Parliament and to the nation about the progress of the war – was, however, justified. Chamberlain, a few days earlier, had accused him of putting blinkers on the nation: by which he meant the excessive censorship of details about the fighting, keeping the truth from the public and, perhaps, not making them realise how desperate the need for a stronger contribution from the workforce was. Derby used a recruiting meeting in Oldham on 22 April to call for accredited war cor-respondents, so that the public might learn the gravity of the situation and more men might see the importance of enlisting. A few days later he spoke at Manchester and said that Asquith's statements about munitions were 'absolutely and perfectly opposed to the facts. There is not a single man in the Army or, I believe, the War Office who would support that [Asquith's] view.'[168] The press lauded him for this, and others 'of high station' were urged to follow his example. Derby had worked tirelessly since the start of hostilities and was universally respected. Although a Tory, no one believed he criticised Asquith out of partisanship, but out of desperation. He did, however, apologise if anyone had interpreted his remarks as an accusation that Asquith had lied: he felt there had been a misunderstanding of what Asquith meant in his speech, an assertion that had quite the opposite effect from clearing the matter up.

The press had its own reasons for sympathising with the call to ease censorship, being sure that more graphic detail would sell more newspapers. *The Times* did not accuse Asquith of lying, but, returning for a second day to attack his Newcastle speech, it did say that his statements about munitions supply 'will not bear examination.'[169] It believed that the government had failed to take steps to increase output early enough, and it was right. Criticism of Asquith and his colleagues went far beyond Northcliffe. Supply problems at Neuve Chapelle had filtered back into London society from officers home on leave, and the shortcomings to which *The Times* referred were being widely discussed. Asquith, though, appeared less and less engaged, as his paranoia about his relationship with Miss Stanley grew. Late on 22 April he wrote his second letter of the day to her, pleading: 'I would rather know the worst – without disguise or delay . . . Do tell me – yes or no!'[170]

While Asquith fretted about this, Lloyd George used a Commons debate on the munitions industry to try to undo some of the damage of the Newcastle speech. The Army, he said, had quintupled in size since war broke out, and yet had been properly equipped with 'adequate ammunition' as part of 'one of the most magnificent pieces of organisation in our history.'[171] He praised Kitchener; he quoted an unnamed general who had told him the amount of heavy ammunition used had been 'the surprise of the war'. The chancellor believed the country should be 'proud'; and mentioned that a large proportion of German shells fired at the British had been duds, because of their inferior manufacture.[172] Between 2,500 and 3,000 firms had been subcontracted the work of making these munitions; and he claimed it had become apparent the previous December that things were moving too slowly. The response had been to use labour exchanges to find more men, but by March it had become obvious that not enough were prepared to move to unfamiliar districts to do this work. The more skilled they were, the less willing they were to move. Therefore, the government had amended DORA yet again to enable it to take over engineering factories and turn them entirely to arms production. Artillery munitions production was now nearly nineteen times more than the previous September. He praised the patriotism of the workers, and the cooperation of the unions.

These reassurances were inadequate for Northcliffe, recently back from the Western Front and talks with French and Joffre – the latter instrumental in removing some of the restrictions on war correspondents. At this stage he disliked Lloyd George nearly as much as he disliked Asquith – that would change, as it came to suit Northcliffe's ambition – not least over the chancellor's anti-drink policies. *The Times* described Lloyd George's intervention as having 'encouraged a revival of complacency.'[173] Given the mounting casualty lists in the papers – on some days there were 2,000 dead, missing and wounded – most would have regarded complacency as an unlikely state of mind. What Lloyd George had, it seemed, failed to get over – and the newspaper stated it baldly – was that 'the Germans stand at most points in the West where they did six months ago, that driving them out will be a costly and a deadly business, and that we are as far off as ever from the imperative task of the invasion of Germany.'

The last point was of huge interest and importance to Northcliffe, but was barely considered by anyone else, since the main war aim was to get Germany out of Belgium and France rather than conquer and subjugate the German people: as the leading article admitted. But the pungent criticism of the two leading men in the government was heading in only one direction: which was bringing some of Northcliffe's Unionist friends into government to improve the running of the war. In reply to Lloyd George's speech, Law – who for months had gone to lengths to ensure his party did not attack the government – expressed his 'anxious misgivings' about the distance between Lloyd George's version of events and what anyone who had talked to senior officers had heard since Neuve Chapelle. It exemplified an unease that Northcliffe, and other Unionists who wanted a coalition, could capitalise upon.

Asquith, however, was too preoccupied with his emotional turmoil to grasp these strategic considerations. Unknown to him, the last obstacle to a marriage between Montagu and Miss Stanley had been removed: she had agreed to convert to his faith of Judaism so he could fulfil a condition of receiving an inheritance of £10,000 a year under his father's will. However, she was due in Boulogne in the second week of May to nurse the wounded, and Asquith was preparing himself mentally for that separation. For him, it was not a minor matter, and would not have been even at the best of times: but problems were piling upon him, problems that his fierce intellect and enormous experience alone could not always solve. War presented him with a set of difficulties outside the scope of that experience, and that required a different sort of mentality and background to tackle: Lloyd George, notably, found them less of a challenge, not least because he was prepared to dissemble and act the showman in a way Asquith would not.

He saw Miss Stanley on 4 May and, after 'ruminating' as he walked back to Downing Street, wrote to her: 'I sometimes think that Northcliffe & his obscene crew may perhaps be right – that, whatever the rest of the world may say, I am, if not an imposter, at any rate a failure, & *au fond* a fool.'[174] She did not tell him of her impending marriage, and nor did she when Asquith took her for a drive the following afternoon and again two days later – these excursions had been a habit of theirs for three years. She was due to embark for Boulogne, but her health broke down – mainly because the tensions of her double life were making her feel 'ill and miserable' – and her departure was postponed. In his relief Asquith wrote to her on 10 May that 'you are everything to me', which cannot have helped her.[175]

VII

Paradoxically, the constant flow of bad news from both the Western and Eastern Fronts in the spring of 1915, and the lengthening casualty lists, stiffened the national resolve. The drain of men for the Dardanelles, and a setback at Ypres, were raising new questions about recruiting, and the question of the possibility of compulsion was no longer confined to the internal debates of the Unionist Party. As *The Times* observed on 6 May: 'the voluntary system has limits and we are rapidly approaching them.'[176] Thus far, because of a failure of planning, there had been more men than could be equipped: but now, if war production stepped up, there was likely to be more equipment than there were men. There was anger that public money was being spent on advertising campaigns to urge men to do their duty and volunteer, which The Times called 'a humiliating expedient for a self-respecting nation'. A system of compulsion was not yet imperative: but the government was urged to start planning for it in a way it had not planned for a huge supply of munitions until almost too late. To Asquith compulsion (which had operated in France from the moment war broke out) remained unthinkable; but not to Lloyd George, whose own brand of liberalism embraced statism in a way Asquith's never could.

Many vital trades and professions were being denuded of men, so the first step would be to train women, or co-opt the retired, to replace them. However, numerous businesses were not even trying. It was reported on 7 May that 20,000 men had been engaged by the Post Office since August, 11,000 of whom were eligible for the Army. Even Gwynne, who had been against compulsion, was by 11 May telling Milner that 'I am becoming more and more of opinion [sic] that conscription, so far from being distasteful to the people, at the present moment would be heartily welcomed.'[177] Sir Frederick Milner – no relation to the proconsul, but a former Unionist MP – evoked another reason for 'unpatriotic slackers' to be called up: once everyone was doing his 'duty' and the 'shilly-shallying had stopped the nation' would emerge from its ordeal 'purified'.[178] He was not alone in believing war was some sort of penance from which a morally renewed nation would arise.

Some on the Left – such as George Lansbury, editor of the Daily Herald and a future Labour leader, who would make his presence and his principles felt consistently throughout the war – felt nothing would be gained by further fighting; but his paper's attempt in May 1915 to rally support for peace among leftist intellectuals and trades unionists met resounding opposition. H. G. Wells and Arnold Bennett wanted nothing short of victory, the latter demanding huge indemnities from the Germans and 'a ceremonial passage of Belgian troops down Unter den Linden.'[179] Union leaders wanted a fight to the end; the only heads above the parapet were those of MacDonald, who suggested some frontier alterations, and Sidney Webb, who suggested a League of Nations. Bottomley used his Sunday Pictorial column to attack MacDonald for pacifism, demanding he be arraigned for treason. MacDonald had earlier called Bottomley 'a man of doubtful parentage who had lived all his life on the threshold of jail.'[180] Bottomley was a dangerous enemy, however; he obtained a copy of MacDonald's birth certificate and published it, proving that the Labour MP was illegitimate.

Then came an event that triggered a new and far more violent phase of anti-German feeling in Britain, with social consequences that Asquith's administration had to try to control. On 7 May 1915 the *Lusitania,* en route from New York to Liverpool, was sunk off the south of Ireland by *U-20,* which had claimed several merchant ships in the preceding days. There had been 1,959 passengers and crew on board; 1,201 died, including 128 Americans.[181] The German embassy in Washington had advertised in American papers warning US citizens not to travel on British ships, as they would be targeted once in British waters. The ship had carried 173 tons of ammunition, a point that was not made in the aftermath of its sinking, and of which the Germans were unaware. The Admiralty put out a statement that reports that the ship was 'armed' were 'wholly false', which was strictly true: it had no guns.[182]

The press perfectly articulated, and inevitably fed, the national torrent of outrage. *The Times* led the way, and assailed the Germans for this 'wholesale murder'.[183] The Germans had wilfully slaughtered civilians on a passenger ship: they had not targeted it because it was carrying ammunition, for they did not know. Otherwise, there would have been a different set of arguments, and quite possibly a political furore of a different dimension. Inevitably, the question was asked whether the Admiralty could have done more to protect the vessel in the light of German threats, a line of inquiry that could not have come at a worse moment for a government already accused of complacency. In the aftermath, *The Times* attacked Asquith's administration for 'a paralysing lack of prevision'.[184]

The matter of German 'frightfulness' was high in the nation's consciousness, because the government was about to publish a report by Viscount Bryce, a former ambassador to America and distinguished academic, on German atrocities in Belgium. The use of poison gas and the bombing raids on the east coast had already put Germany beyond the moral pale in the eyes of most Britons. The King himself wanted no quarter given to Germany. Esher saw him two days after the sinking and noted: 'I told the King that the Archbishop had spoken to me yesterday about the use of poisonous gases, and had expressed an almost violent hope that we should not retaliate. The King takes a diametrically opposite view, and rightly holds that the question is purely military, and that ethical considerations will not enter into it.'[185]

As news of the sinking was still being absorbed a Zeppelin dropped an estimated 100 bombs on Southend. London itself was now vulnerable to this aerial terror. But the *Lusitania* was the final straw. Scenes of injured and shaken crew members arriving at Liverpool from Queenstown, where survivors had been taken, sparked fury in the city. German-owned shops were wrecked, and a riot broke out in Everton that required fifty police to put it down. Further up the social ladder, it was announced that all enemy Knights of the Garter would be struck off and their banners removed from St George's Chapel at Windsor. Those affected included Kaisers Franz Josef and Wilhelm, the King of Württemberg, the German Crown Prince, Prince Henry of Prussia, and the Dukes of Saxe-Coburg and Gotha, and Cumberland. The King had not wanted to make a fuss about this, and insisted that the brass plates of the degraded knights remain on their stalls, to reflect the historical record. No such degradation in any order of chivalry had happened since 1814; and the press enthusiastically noted that in the case before that, in 1621, there had been a ceremony in which heralds in Westminster Hall hacked off the spurs of the extortionist Sir Francis Mitchell, cut his sword belt and broke his sword over his head before pronouncing him no longer a knight but a knave.

Press cartoons depicted the German as a grotesque monster in a *Pickelhaube*, the spiked helmet of the Prussian army. The *Daily Mail* published a picture of corpses of women and children from the disaster laid out in a mortuary at Queenstown. Anti-German meetings were held in the City of London, and a deputation from there went to the Commons. They met the Attorney General and demanded all Germans and Austrians be interned for the duration. The Royal Exchange decided to exclude all such nationals, even if naturalised, from its meetings. Germans were driven out of Smithfield market, and the police ordered German restaurants in the City not to open. On 11 May a mob attacked German shops in the east end of London, and sixty to seventy police and fifty Territorials struggled to contain it. A new recruiting poster, proclaiming the 'COLD-BLOODED MURDER!' of the *Lusitania* attack, said it had been designed to make Britons 'AFRAID OF THESE GERMAN BARBARIANS': to which the only answer could be to attend the nearest recruiting office and 'ENLIST TO-DAY'. Also on 11 May the cabinet discussed the implications of the sinking, worried that America would in consequence ban the export of munitions, 'wh wd be almost fatal,' Asquith admitted.[186]

However, the next morning Asquith himself was sunk. A letter arrived from Miss Stanley announcing her and Montagu's engagement. Unlike the conversational geniality of his other letters to her, his reply was stark:

> Most Loved –
> As you know well, this breaks my heart.
> I couldn't bear to come and see you.
> I can only pray God to bless you – and help me.
>   Yours.[187]

Her letter enraged and unhinged Asquith: enraged because he thought Montagu a preposterous choice (even though Asquith and he were socially close, and he was a cabinet colleague whose career owed everything to Asquith's patronage), not least because of the repudiation of Christianity Miss Stanley would have to make to marry him; and unhinged because he had been entirely emotionally dependent on her in handling the pressures of office, especially since war broke out. After seven years as prime minister, almost all of them distinguished by some major crisis or another even before the war, he was on the edge of exhaustion, prone to bouts of mild paranoia about the scheming of his colleagues, and finding the (for him) unprecedented circumstances of warfare management highly challenging. For his dream (and that was all it ever had been) of intimacy with Miss Stanley to be, as he saw it, exploded must have seemed like a gigantic physical assault upon him.

He managed to write a letter of congratulation to Montagu, with whom he had to continue to work; but immediately turned to Miss Stanley's sister, Sylvia Henley, and told her: 'I don't believe there are two living people who, each in their separate ways, are more devoted to me than she and Montagu: and it is the irony of fortune that they two should combine to deal a death-blow to me.'[188] He added that he felt 'sore and wounded'. Mrs Henley sent a 'sweet and understanding letter', and he replied saying: 'I must see you: I cannot say a word to anyone else, and you are wise and loving and know everything.'[189] She would to an extent assume her sister's place and become the emotional prop Asquith needed, and the recipient of frequent letters and over-lavish affections.

He could not conceal the blow from his wife, who noted with an understatement that was not her forte that 'H came into my bedroom much perturbed at his great friend's engagement.'[190] Raymond Asquith, in basic training for the Grenadier Guards in Richmond Park and cynically aware of his father's 'interested disapproval' of the match, declared himself in favour of it 'because for a woman any marriage is better than perpetual virginity, which after a certain age (not very distant in Venetia's case) becomes insufferably absurd'.[191] He thought she was 'well-advised' to 'make a marriage of convenience' because of her apparent incapability of 'conceiving a romantic passion for someone or other.' It was doubtless fortunate he did not share his views with his father. His sister Violet, echoing Duff Cooper, told her diary that 'M's physical repulsiveness to me is such that I wld lightly leap from the top story [sic] of Queen Anne's Mansions – or the Eiffel Tower itself to avoid the lightest contact – the thought of *any* erotic amenities with him is enough to freeze one's blood.'[192]

Events did not pause to allow Asquith to digest what fate had served him, which rendered him all the more incapable of dealing with them rationally, and made him intensely vulnerable to the political machinations of others. Bryce's report on German atrocities in Belgium – published the same day Asquith received Miss Stanley's letter – poured accelerant on the new surge of anti-German feeling. Bryce's commission had included academics and lawyers, and was endorsed by the neutral local commissioner of the American Red Cross. It was the government's first major anti-German propaganda exercise: Masterman had it translated into thirty languages, so its impact was maximised. It was based on depositions by 1,200 Belgian refugees and both British and Belgian soldiers.

However, the report's credibility was questioned. The witnesses were not on oath, many had no corroboration for their stories, or the stories were hearsay. The committee did not visit Belgium – much of which was occupied – and in most cases did not interview witnesses. Their statements disappeared after the war: some testimony, from babies on bayonets and the dismemberment of civilians to the widespread rape of Belgian women, may have been rubbish. This was unfortunate, because there was corroborated evidence of executions of civilians and the destruction of villages, whose impact would have been devastating enough to Germany's reputation without embroidering or resorting to fiction. However, it became a measure of patriotism to uphold and echo

Bryce's findings. With the imprimatur of the government, they were taken as gospel.

Nervous naturalised Germans wrote to newspapers distancing themselves from the barbarous behaviour of the Kaiser's forces. Rioting continued not just in Liverpool (where £40,000 worth of damage was done) and London, but also in Southend, angry after its bombing, where troops were called out. The rioting in London spread to Highgate, Camden Town, North Kensington, Fulham and Wandsworth. The attacks on shops were far from superficial. 'Not content with smashing doors and windows and looting the whole of the furniture and the contents of the shops, the interiors of the houses were in numerous instances greatly damaged,' *The Times* reported.[193] 'Staircases were hacked to pieces and walls and ceilings were knocked down.'

The police were too late to stop the wrecking and looting: those responsible drove cartloads of German possessions through the streets, having simply helped themselves. Magistrates, faced with defendants who claimed that their looting and pillaging had been a case of doing one's patriotic duty, fined and bound over most offenders: there was the rare prison sentence with hard labour, but little otherwise to deter the mob. An estimated £100,000 worth of damage was done in West Ham in three days. The national mood turned ugly; 'retaliation' was widely approved of, and those who found attacks on innocent and peaceable Teutons appalling – such as Mrs Asquith – were denounced as 'pro-German'.[194] A few condemned the inevitable attacks on entirely blameless people, and the fact that the attackers were, according to one outraged citizen who wrote to *The Times*, 'those who are too lazy or cowardly to enlist.'[195]

The public's appetite to hate the enemy was fed further by reports of the 'crucifixion' of a Canadian soldier at Ypres on 22–23 April. *The Times*'s correspondent claimed British headquarters staff had 'written depositions testifying to the fact of the discovery of the body'.[196] The corpse, of a sergeant, had been found pinned by its hands and feet to a wooden fence; 'he had been repeatedly stabbed with bayonets'. The report continued: 'I have not heard that any of our men actually saw the crime committed. There is room for supposition that the man was dead before he was pinned to the fence, and that the enemy in his insensate rage and hate of the English wreaked his vengeance on the lifeless body of his foe.' It added: 'That is the most charitable complexion that can be put upon the deed, ghastly though it is.'

With Asquith in a state of shock and able to engage in the required acts of leadership with even less concentration than usual, it was a terrible time for him to become the target of a campaign, mounted by Northcliffe, to force him to take a more muscular approach to the conduct of the war or to get out. Just as Miss Stanley dropped her bombshell, Northcliffe had his newspapers call for internment for non-naturalised Germans and Austrians without delay, to maintain public order and squash the spy menace ('the public are evidently in no mood to "wait and see",' *The Times* sneered). On 13 May Asquith – not needing to be told twice – announced that all enemy aliens would be deported or interned, other than in exceptional circumstances.[197] He would never, normally, have given such an indication that he was allowing Northcliffe, or any other press proprietor, to dictate government policy to him. Two months earlier, the government had resisted a Unionist call for a minister specifically responsible for dealing with the alien problem. Now, public opinion left it with no option but to take matters more seriously, not least to protect those at risk from vigilantes and thugs determined to make their alien status an excuse to attack them.

Asquith said that although 19,000 non-naturalised aliens had already been interned, 40,000 others – 24,000 men and 16,000 women – remained at large. He proposed that adult males should be interned 'for their own safety, and that of the community', and those over military age repatriated.[198] He conceded, however, that 'there will, no doubt, be many instances in which justice and humanity will require that they should be allowed to remain.' A quasi-judicial tribunal would decide such matters. As for naturalised aliens, he said, 'the *prima facie* presumption should be the other way.' Only in exceptional cases would naturalised subjects be interned, but the government reserved the right to do so. Law welcomed the proposals on behalf of the Opposition, as 'the only satisfactory way' to end the rioting; Asquith had consulted him the day before. It was a portent of how all business would soon be done.

By July 1916, however, 22,000 enemy aliens remained at large: 10,000 were women, many of them elderly, most of the rest married to British subjects with British subjects for children. The Austrian or German men still at large – 12,000 of them – were deemed 'friendly' because of their hatred of or opposition to Austria or Germany; such as Czechs, Poles, Slavs, Alsatians or Italians of Austrian citizenship; and around 1,500 of them were elderly and would be unlikely to survive an internment camp.[199] But even then, despite Asquith's pledges, 6,500 enemy alien men remained in society in mid-1916, exempted for reasons such as having British wives, or British children in the Armed Forces. Beyond that it was unquantifiable how many Germans or Austrians had anglicised their names to escape detection; or how many 'Swiss' waiters in London restaurants were really enemy aliens.

The commissioner of the Metropolitan Police announced a curfew for male enemy aliens, ordering them to confine themselves to home between 9 p.m. and 5 a.m. Even before that, numerous enemy aliens – mainly unmarried men – surrendered at police stations, causing existing internment camps to be expanded. As the climate became more febrile, rumours swirled around London that a huge fleet of Zeppelins and aeroplanes was about to bomb the city flat, before the advent of a German invasion, which would be assisted by the dropping of a new, fiendish device called the *Nebelbomb*, which when it exploded would create a fog over several square miles.[200] But every cloud had its silver lining: advertisements appeared for the 'Kyl-Fyre' fire extinguisher, a mere 5s 6d each, because 'the Fire Brigades cannot be in all parts at the same time.'[201]

Matters then became dramatically worse for Asquith. On 14 May *The Times* carried a report from Repington, its military correspondent, about the realities and consequences of the shell shortage – dismissed by Asquith at Newcastle – in impeding the Army.[202] A shortage of high explosive had prevented the Army from levelling to the ground the parapets on the German lines at Fromelles and Richebourg; trenches had been gained from the Germans, but could not be held, because the Army lacked the ammunition. There could, he argued, be no decisive victory at Ypres until the shortage was rectified. 'To break this hard crust we need more high explosive, more heavy howitzers, and more men,' he said.[203] He did not need to add that all these shortcomings were the government's responsibility, because the newspaper's editorial columns, following the proprietor's wishes, made a feast of it.

Kitchener – who had kept his distance from Repington since the cabinet had rebuked him over briefing the journalist – believed French had inspired the article, since the censor at the front had passed it, he maintained, on French's express instructions. He believed French had seen both Northcliffe and Repington, with the latter of whom he was long acquainted, and who had been at French's HQ in defiance of orders. Kitchener was right in his suspicions. Northcliffe had written to French

on 1 May to tell him that 'a short and very vigorous statement from you
to a private correspondent . . . would, I believe, render the Government's position impossible, and enable you to secure the publication of
that which would tell people here the truth.'[204] French had shown
Repington his correspondence with the War Office, and also sent it on
via his ADC and his secretary to Lloyd George, Balfour and Law. On 17
May Lloyd George, always keen to help the press, had a 'very useful'
discussion with Northcliffe at the latter's request, and invited Repington for a 'long talk'.[205] He gave Lloyd George a hastily written but
thorough paper on the situation; the political crisis by then in full swing
removed any need for Repington to do more. Kitchener banned Repington from the front, and he did not go again until the Somme. By then,
thanks to his article, the situation had been transformed. Repington's
position was hypocritical: he had called for censorship before war was
declared, until he saw it 'being used as a cloak to cover all political,
naval and military mistakes.'[206]

When the rumour of French's complicity was aired in Parliament, The
Times denied it, saying the censor in England had also passed the article,
albeit 'severely mutilated' by both him and his counterpart in France.[207]
Repington would observe in his memoirs that his earlier attempts to
allude to the shells shortage were 'censored as everything inconvenient
to the Government was censored during the war,' though he must have
realised how helpful it would have been to the enemy to have such information.[208] In an editorial, the newspaper wrote: 'British soldiers died in
vain on the Aubers Ridge on Sunday because more shells were needed.
The Government, who have so seriously failed to organise adequately
our national resources, must bear their share of the grave responsibility.
Even now they will not fully face the situation.'[209] The necessary policies
'should have been set in hand nine months ago.' There had been 51,000
casualties between 22 April and 9 May – a fact Repington saved for his
memoirs after the censor cut it out – which he attributed to a lack of shells
to take out the German guns.[210]

To prove the point, the paper sent a correspondent to Glasgow to
write about productivity on the Clyde. His report, published on 17 May,
was damning: 'men are working far below their capacity', he wrote, and
piece workers were engaged in 'the deliberate manipulation of work' to
drag it out far longer than necessary so they could demand more money.[211]
This was common in peacetime, but now the country suffered. Also,

union restrictions meant more efficient labour could not be brought in to man idle machines without provoking a strike.

On top of all this, the news from the Dardanelles was worse daily. Fisher tried to resign on 12 May but Asquith persuaded him to stay. There were 30,000 casualties already, 16,000 British Empire and 14,000 French; and the Germans had had such success on the Eastern Front against the Russians that they were able to move troops to reinforce the fight against Britain and France. Fisher sent Churchill a long memorandum advising caution and arguing against a naval attack after the failure of the land-ings, but was, according to Hankey, 'dissatisfied' by his 'slippery' reply.[212] On 14 May Kitchener told the War Council that 'we should never get through the Dardanelles' and that he had been 'misled by the Admiralty as to the number of men that would be required': Churchill had assured him there would be no 'siege'.[213]

Britain seemed on the defensive, its power weakening; the govern-ment and the prime minister had lost the initiative. Later that day the shadow cabinet discussed whether to call for a committee on the state of the nation, to meet in secret for 'free and frank' discussion.[214] It was felt to be too potentially disturbing to press for this: but Curzon and Lord Selborne insisted something had to be done to make the government adopt firmer measures, possibly including compulsory military or indus-trial service. Lansdowne and Law promised to make representations to Asquith; but events overtook them.

Fisher had threatened eight times in six months as First Sea Lord to resign because of disagreements with Churchill. His habitual indiscre-tion ensured everyone knew he opposed the Dardanelles expedition – 'the North Sea is the place where we can beat the German.'[215] However, he maintained to Mrs Asquith – while grabbing her by the waist and waltz-ing with her around a Downing Street office – that he had not expressed his opposition to anyone, but that Churchill had broadcast it to Smith and Balfour. 'The old boy is a fine dancer,' she noted.[216] It was also thought Fisher had been, albeit indirectly, the source of much of the inside information that underpinned Gwynne's increasingly savage attacks on Churchill in the Morning Post.

When, on 15 May, Churchill overrode Fisher on reinforcing the Navy in the Dardanelles, he resigned for the ninth and last time. Writing to Churchill, he said: 'I find it increasingly difficult to adjust myself to the increasingly daily requirements of the Dardanelles to meet yr views – As you truly said yesterday I am in the position of continually veto-ing your proposals – This is not fair to you besides being extremely distasteful to me.'[217] He told Lloyd George the campaign was 'bleeding the navy white', and the land operations were doing the same to the Army.[218] Once Asquith, who had not taken the resignation seriously when Lloyd George told him about it, received the letter containing it he immediately sent a message to Fisher that read: 'In the King's name I order you at once to return to your post.'[219] Bonham Carter was sent to look for him; and, Fisher having been found and brought to Downing Street, Asquith told him that 'he would cover himself in infamy and ridicule if he resigned now, at the moment we were in difficulties with our West line and in the Dardanelles: infamy for deserting the ship, and ridicule for not having resigned on the spot the day it was discussed in the War Council.' This ferocity stunned Fisher, who asked whether he could consult McKenna: Asquith hoped McKenna would talk him out of it, though he was aware that McKenna disliked Churchill far more even than Fisher did. The view of other senior Liberals, such as Lord Reading, the Lord Chief Justice, was that if Fisher did go, a coalition would become inevitable.

On 16 May, a Sunday, McKenna went to Asquith's Berkshire house, the Wharf near Sutton Courtenay, to tell him Fisher was adamant, citing his inability to work with Churchill for his decision. Churchill begged Fisher to reconsider, on the grounds of their friendship, the risk Churchill had taken in having him reappointed, and in order not to give the impression that the Admiralty was at war with itself. He argued that 'any rupture will be profoundly injurious to every public interest' – and, he might have added, to his career prospects.[220] Fisher was unmoved. Lady Lyttelton, wife of General Lyttelton and a friend of Fisher, told Riddell that 'one difficulty between Winston and Fisher was that the latter goes to bed at 9pm and rises at 4am, whereas Winston liked to do much of the naval consultation work between 10pm and 1am.'[221] Churchill wrote to Asquith the next morning to say he would happily leave the Admiralty, but would not serve unless in a military department; and if that was not possible he would rejoin the Army. His resignation was refused, so he set about finding Fisher's replacement.

The news leaked that Sunday evening. Law found an envelope, addressed to him in Fisher's handwriting, containing a cutting from the *Pall Mall Gazette* reporting that Fisher had had an audience of the King. Law deduced Fisher was resigning and went straight to see Lloyd George, with whom he was on better terms than with Asquith: Law later told Esher that 'he felt bound not to allow Fisher's resignation.'[222] He found Lloyd George with McKenna, who had returned to London and joined the chancellor at 11 Downing Street for a late-night smoke. Law asked straight questions and got straight answers: they concluded that Fisher's departure would trigger a crisis. Law said if matters were that bad in the Admiralty a coalition was essential. 'Of course we must have a coalition,' Lloyd George told him, 'for the alternative is impossible.'

The next morning, once Asquith returned from Berkshire, Lloyd George told him what had happened: and the two men 'not particularly at my instigation', as Lloyd George told Mrs Asquith, agreed that 'coalition was inevitable' if a destabilising row that would be a propaganda gift to the enemy were to be avoided.[223] Law sought confirmation that morning and was given it. He asked to see Asquith, and did so with Lloyd George. Law told Asquith he must either raise Fisher in the Commons, 'or we must have a National Government'.[224] Law – who according to Riddell had wanted Lloyd George to lead the government, but the chancellor refused to betray Asquith – noted that Asquith 'agreed to a coalition without a word.'[225] One can only conjecture whether Asquith's resolve and spirit were broken by the breach with Miss Stanley, and that Lloyd George spotted the vulnerability, without knowing its cause. Before going to bed that night Asquith told his daughter Violet that 'this has been the unhappiest week of my life': although she and her stepmother realised Asquith was in love with Miss Stanley, she only knew the half of it.[226]

A further symptom of Asquith's defeatism was how little he fought to protect one of his oldest friends, Haldane, whose dismissal from the Woolsack was another condition of forming the coalition, given Unionist assumptions of his pro-Germanism. J. C. C. Davidson, then a Colonial Office official but a future Conservative Party chairman, described Haldane's fate as 'a shameful triumph for the mob and for the gutter press, and the Tories gained no credit from it.'[227] Ironically, 17 May was also the day a dispatch arrived from Hamilton, commanding the Army in the Dardanelles, requesting reinforcements that might make a difference to the campaign. The new cabinet would not consider his request until 7 June, and the time that would elapse from his seeking troops to their arriving would be six weeks: and their arrival, thus, too late.[228]

Asquith wrote to his ministerial colleagues asking for their resignations so the government could be reconstructed on a 'broad and non-party basis'.[229] He admitted Fisher's departure had underpinned this decision, as had the 'more than plausible parliamentary case in regard to the alleged deficiency of high-explosive shells'. Esher told his diary that 'the cause . . . of the quarrel today is that Churchill is sending everything upon which he can lay his hands to the Dardanelles, and denuding the Grand Fleet and our Home Defences. He [Fisher] bitterly complains of Churchill's methods of corresponding with the admirals in the Mediterranean and his whole plan of concealment.'[230] Churchill's colleagues kept from him the fact that talks were under way with the Unionists; in his rather unreliable memoirs, Beaverbrook would assert that Churchill 'was treated shabbily.'[231]

Law specified that Churchill would have to leave the Admiralty; and he also told Asquith about the Unionists' deep antipathy to Kitchener, because of his secrecy and lack of collegiality as a cabinet colleague, and said that the Field Marshal had intimated he was keen to go. Asquith thought of giving the War Office to Lloyd George, making Law Chancellor of the Exchequer and Kitchener commander-in-chief, and said so to Balfour (his prospective First Lord, replacing Churchill, on account of his long service on the Committee of Imperial Defence). He had second thoughts, further delaying a decision; the economic liberal in Asquith could not countenance a tariff reformer such as Law at the Treasury.[232] The negotiations about the formation of a coalition saved both sides from embarrassment. Against Law's wishes, Unionist MPs had tabled a motion four days earlier on the shell shortage, due to be debated that evening. At the request of the government it was postponed, because no minister of sufficient seniority could be present.

While negotiations about the reconstruction continued, Northcliffe had *The Times* let rip. On 18 May the paper savaged Churchill – Fisher's resignation was common knowledge but remained unconfirmed – saying he had been 'assuming responsibilities and overriding his expert advisers to a degree which might at any time endanger the national safety.'[233] It continued: 'When a civilian Minister in charge of a fighting service persistently seeks to grasp power which should not pass into his unguided hands, and attempts to use that power in perilous ways, it is time for his colleagues in the Cabinet to take some definite action.' The final blow was the recommendation that Fisher should become First Lord, a serviceman running the Admiralty as one ran the War Office – 'which would undoubtedly command great public approval'.

The Unionists were not united about a coalition. Lord Robert Cecil and Carson led the objectors, some of whom found the idea of serving with Liberals distasteful, others of whom wanted a general election, however unpractical that might be in the midst of war. Law considered a party meeting to discuss the matter. Chamberlain advised him against, saying he should present the coalition as a *fait accompli*, explaining that Fisher's resignation left no other course. 'I loathe the very idea of our good fellows sitting with these double-dyed traitors,' Walter Long, a committed anti-Home Ruler and former chief secretary for Ireland, told Carson.[234] Long believed, as he said to Asquith, that 'we want to be led; we want to be governed.'[235] Carson and Cecil realised the traditional function of an Opposition was impossible in the circumstances. Later, on 18 May, the shadow cabinet gave Law unanimous approval for joining the government. It was also agreed Asquith should remain prime minister, despite his lack of 'push and drive', that Kitchener must stay at the War Office, and that Churchill had to go, as much for historic crimes against Toryism as for recent failures.[236] Fisher had urged Law to get Churchill out of the Admiralty because he was a 'REAL DANGER'.[237] This echoed what the King told the Queen during the crisis, which was that Churchill 'is the real danger'; he told his diary three days later that the First Lord had 'become impossible'.[238]

Law needed no persuasion: he had said the previous October that Churchill had 'an entirely unbalanced mind, which is a real danger at a time like this'.[239] The Tory press were unanimous: the *Morning Post* had accused Churchill of 'megalomania' and of being 'a danger . . . to the nation'.[240] Chamberlain, who became Secretary of State for India, argued that Alfred Milner should be included because of his 'brains, character, earnestness, courage, organizing power'; but because of Milner's record of fierce opposition both to the People's Budget of 1909 and to the Lords Reform of 1911, this was one ambition in which the Unionists failed. Milner had raised his head above the parapet during the war only to press for conscription, which also turned Liberals against him. Esher was sceptical about the changes: 'They may call the result by whatever name they like, but it will be in reality a Coalition, and a Coalition government has never yet succeeded in this country.'[241] There would be 'an inchoate Cabinet composed of jarring elements and of men whose training and mental equipment unfit them for carrying on a struggle with the Emperor and the German Great General Staff.' Esher deplored 'that

Milner's services should be lost to the State' and 'his gifts of character . . . obscured by clouds of factious and unfair criticism', for he felt Milner had the 'moral courage and tenacity' that were now needed.[242]

Lloyd George disguised his enthusiasm for the change by agreeing with Mrs Asquith, when they discussed it some days later, that to an extent they had been 'blackmailed' into it, but 'sooner or later it was bound to come.' Unwisely, given what the Asquiths thought of North-cliffe, Lloyd George said the press baron had been right to harry the government about the shell shortage. Mrs Asquith was livid, and told him: 'Northcliffe will run you against Henry.'[243] Lloyd George protested to her, as he said he had to Churchill, that 'wicked I may be, but I'm not a damned fool . . . Do you *really* think I don't know what Northcliffe is? Why, he'll turn on me and stab me in the back at any moment.' Mrs Asquith had spotted Lloyd George's susceptibility to flattery, and his readiness to hitch himself to any wagon that might further his ambition. Asquith never believed the coalition would run the war better than the Liberal government; but he did see it was inevitable, and knew how hard it was in politics to ignore momentum.

VIII

Most Britons first learned about the changes in the country's, and the war's, political direction in reports on 19 May that Opposition leaders had agreed to serve in a coalition government, details of which were awaited. The irreconcilable differences between Churchill and Fisher were stated as fact; as was the news that Churchill was 'packing up' his office.[244] Fisher had not been seen at the Admiralty for three days, but there was a widespread belief that he was, as Northcliffe hoped, biding his time until Churchill went and the call came. Fisher reappeared that morning to state the price of his return: the removal of Churchill, a replacement other than Balfour, and he as First Sea Lord to have such power that the First Lord would 'be reduced practically to the position of an under-secretary.'[245] He wanted status equivalent to Kitchener's, with 'absolutely untrammelled sole command of all the sea forces whatsoever.'[246] Hankey told him the idea was 'impossible', and Asquith was 'greatly incensed' by it. That was the end of Fisher. Asquith may also have been consonant with what Hankey wrote in his diary that evening, that Fisher was 'intriguing horribly with Northcliffe, the Unionist Party *et hoc genus omne*.'[247]

Esher's view was that 'the group controlled by Northcliffe and his press have been desirous all along to replace Asquith by Lloyd George; failing this, they wish to substitute Lloyd George for Lord K at the war office, and put Mr Balfour at the Admiralty.'[248]

According to Esher, at 1 p.m. on 19 May Asquith saw the King to explain the reconstruction, which he said was caused by disquiet over Fisher's resignation and Repington's report in *The Times*. He told the King that Fisher's demands 'showed signs of mental aberration.'[249] The King told Queen Mary: 'I am glad the Prime Minister is going to have a National Government. Only by that means can we get rid of Churchill from the Admiralty. He is intriguing also with French against K[itchener], he is the real danger.'[250] However, this conversation, according to the King's diary, seems not to have taken place until 22 May, when he returned to London after five days visiting shipyards, munitions factories and military bases in Scotland and the north: on 19 May he was in Newcastle.

Asquith made a statement to the Commons on the afternoon of 19 May. He had sat up until two o'clock that morning talking to his wife, and seeming 'very, very unhappy', before lunching with her and Sylvia Henley.[251] 'I cannot say more at the moment than that steps are in contemplation which involve the reconstruction of the Government on a broader, personal and political basis.'[252] He said nothing was settled other than that he would remain prime minister, and Grey would remain at the Foreign Office; and the policy of fighting the war against Germany would continue unchanged, 'with every possible energy and by means of every possible resource.' Any changes made would be for the purposes of the war, and not for any other reason. Given the eagerness among some Unionists to settle scores, not least with Churchill, that remark was disingenuous, to say the least. Law joined him in this mendacity, telling the House that 'the best method of finishing the war successfully' was the 'sole consideration', and that 'we shall leave out of our minds absolutely all considerations, political or otherwise, beyond the war.'[253] Long told Law that day that 'the view of the great majority [of Unionists] is that this Government are so unscrupulous, so dishonest, that it is almost impossible for two honest English gentlemen [Law and Lansdowne], however able they may be, to be even with them.'

Most of Asquith's MPs, few of whom had thought a coalition likely, were shocked and angry. The toll on him was enormous: his daughter-in-law Lady Cynthia Asquith, who lunched with him on 21 May in 'a tremendous atmosphere of tension and distress', noted that 'I have never before seen him look either tired, worried, busy, or preoccupied . . . but this time he looked really shattered with a sort of bruised look in his eyes'.[254] Lloyd George, due to visit industrial cities in the north to exhort the workers to higher production, but whose tour was cancelled, told Mrs Asquith the coalition was the result of the 'two Tories' in the Liberal cabinet, Churchill and Kitchener, an assertion that was only half-true and that helped him to conceal his own excitement and support for the idea.[255]

Liberal MPs gathered to express their outrage; but Asquith walked into the meeting, in a committee room, and spoke to them. He could not give his full reasons for having agreed to the coalition – he did not wish to expose disunity any further by going into details about the fight between Fisher and Churchill – but asked them to trust him. He also denied he had taken the step because of pressure from Northcliffe or any other press baron. He appealed to his colleagues' patriotism, and for them to believe he had done the right thing for the country: such was his popularity and their inherent trust in him that he won them round. His MPs, rebellious minutes earlier, cheered him. The next morning, however, *The Times* sought to take credit for the change: it reported that the main factor, since Asquith had declared the previous week in response to a question from an MP that there was no prospect of a coalition, had been its publication of Repington's dispatch and the outcry about the shell shortage. It added that the trouble at the Admiralty 'made it doubly plain that things could not go on as they were', and the coalition was 'the only patriotic way out of the difficulty.'[256] The unpatriotic alternative would have been an election, which would have crippled the conduct of the war for the duration of the campaign, and given a propaganda opportunity to the Germans.

As Mrs Asquith drove through London that evening she saw the words 'Are we to be governed by Northcliffe and Bottomley?' printed on posters.[257] Given what Northcliffe had set out to achieve, the posters asked a pertinent question.

On the afternoon of 18 May Churchill had gone to the Commons to make a statement about his new Admiralty Board; but was told no such thing could be announced because of the reconstruction, of which he heard for the first time. He was also told to expect to have to leave the Admiralty; and so, in his desperation to stay in the political front line, and at Lloyd George's suggestion, he said to Asquith that were he to be offered the Colonial Office he might see his way to staying in politics. However, he had made too many enemies; Lord Emmott, a former under-secretary at the Colonial Office, told Asquith bluntly that Churchill 'has neither the temperament nor manners to fit him for the post.'[258] Liberal MPs believed Churchill had brought down the administration not just by his mishandling of Fisher, but that his intrigue with French had led to Repington's revelations. On the evening of 19 May, having – it seems – belatedly acquired some self-knowledge, he told Violet Asquith: 'I'm finished.'[259]

A near-hysterical letter his wife sent Asquith on 20 May, before his fate was decided, did not help. Mrs Churchill (who was far from being a hysteric, so the nature of the cataclysm of her husband's dismissal was clearly awesome to them both) said the Admiralty would not recover from his dismissal, and that public confidence would be restored by it only in Germany. 'If you throw Winston overboard,' she wrote, 'you will be committing an act of weakness and your coalition government will not be as formidable a War machine as the present Government.'[260] Mrs Asquith thought the letter betrayed 'the soul of a servant' with its 'touch of blackmail and insolence, and the revelation of black ingratitude and want of affection'.[261] The Asquiths wondered whether the letter was her idea, or whether her husband had dictated it to her. Violet believed Churchill 'could not have perpetrated such a *bêtise*'.[262] It was not merely his long-perceived disloyalty to Asquith that caused disquiet with the prime minister and, more particularly, his wife, on whom he now leant heavily after Miss Stanley's departure from his life. Lloyd George, whom Churchill might have regarded as a loyal ally, had told Asquith a few days earlier that 'Winston . . . has not merely bad judgement, but he has none.'[263]

His overriding of Fisher about the Dardanelles counted enormously against him. His enthusiasm for war was also regarded as distasteful: Lloyd George told Mrs Asquith that 'he has no real imagination of the kind that counts.' He related to Frances Stevenson a story of Churchill losing his temper with him, accusing him of not caring 'whether I am trampled underfoot by my enemies' or for 'my personal reputation'.[264] Lloyd George allegedly told him tartly that he was right, because 'the only thing I care about now is that we win this war.' (That was not strictly true: Lloyd George wanted to win the war, certainly, but in a way that brought as much credit on him as possible.) When Riddell went to see Churchill on 20 May he found him 'very worn out and harassed' and proclaiming: 'I am the victim of a political intrigue. I am finished! . . . Finished in respect of all I care for – the waging of war; the defeat of the Germans.'[265] Churchill also wrote to Law begging to be retained in his job; but Law told him, curtly, that his end was 'inevitable'.[266]

'What a satire,' Mrs Asquith had noted during the deliberations, 'if the coming coalition Gov of which Winston has gassed so much should not contain him!'[267] When Churchill realised how isolated he was he started to act to save a vestige of a career. He told Asquith he would 'accept any office – the lowest if you like – that you care to offer me.'[268] That is what Asquith did, when they met on 22 May: 'I know you will ply a stout and labouring oar, whatever seat in the boat may be assigned to you,' his chief told him.[269] Churchill was, indeed, lucky Asquith managed to keep him at all, in the lowly post of Chancellor of the Duchy of Lancaster, without departmental duties. He burned with resentment, but Asquith – whom Churchill dismissed as 'terribly weak – supinely weak' – had no choice.[270]

Conscious that the public blamed him for the Dardanelles fiasco, Churchill's principal mission in life became to convince them otherwise. His main argument from even before his demotion was that Fisher had approved everything, and he had acted on advice from Carden and de Robeck. The argument would rest on whether Churchill had interfered in the minutiae of planning the expedition, which he adamantly claimed he had not. Eighteen months later Lloyd George would tell C. P. Scott that Churchill's problem was his 'egotism' – a subject about which Lloyd George himself knew a thing or two.[271] 'In the Dardanelles affair our failure was primarily due to his eagerness to do the whole thing off his own bat and his reluctance to wait for the co-operation of the land forces and thus to share the credit of success with Lord Kitchener.'

Lloyd George was quite right in that judgement; but his friend's misfortune in losing Fisher and forcing the government's reconstruction as a coalition would be his own great opportunity. The establishment of a Ministry of Munitions, under him, was the key element of the new government. Law, ideal for the job having worked as an iron merchant, wanted to lead the new ministry: but Lloyd George implored him, at

Asquith's behest, not to insist on the job. He accepted, instead, the role of Secretary of State for the Colonies, 'bitter at being given such a second-class post', according to his confidant, J. C. C. Davidson.[272] Law's entrance into government brought into public life his close friend, confidant and fellow Canadian Sir Max Aitken, later Lord Beaverbrook: Law was reluctant to make the slightest move without his counsel. Given Law's importance to the coalition he had a perfect right to Munitions. However, Lloyd George wanted the post because it furthered his ambition to direct the war and become prime minister; Asquith did not want Law to have it because he thought the Colonial Office was what his talents merited. That misjudgement was one of a series of crucial slips that ultimately cost Asquith his job.

Soldiers and civil servants in the War Office had overseen the production of arms; Lloyd George wanted to consign their practices to history, to work closely with business, and to use businessmen, who understood more about the rudiments of production. He described the Ministry of Munitions as having been 'from first to last a business-man organisation.'[273] The new minister immediately recruited such people – whom in March he had called 'men of push and go' – to handle negotiations with suppliers.[274] He succeeded in his new department through his ability to spot talent, and find men who could get things done, in this case transforming the rate of production of weapons of war. It was, as Wells put it, the end of conducting war as a 'gentleman amateur'.[275] Lloyd George, who as the term was understood was certainly not a gentleman and when it came to politics deployed the full, unscrupulous armoury of the professional – helped by the strong-arm support of DORA – gave a constant rhetorical lead, crossing the country in the weeks after his appointment explaining his plans, and enlisting the help of the working people. It was a new, more demotic, and more ruthless mode of government.

This may have helped efficiency, but it also played its part in creating the war profiteer, not least when some of those drafted in opened up negotiations on behalf of the government with firms from which they had been seconded, usually to the benefit of the latter. One notorious example, rumbled by Christopher Addison, the under-secretary, was a Colonel William Wright, a coal-owner who became Controller of Iron and Steel Production, and who was found seeking better terms for a business in which he had an interest, the Port Talbot Steel Company.[276]

Such men were, supposedly, civil servants: but after December 1916 some would become ministers. People took a cynical view of Lloyd George's network of friends; the Duke of Northumberland, on the Western Front the following winter visiting territorial units he had helped recruit, told Haig he thought that 'much of the money now spent on munitions is sticking to the hands of someone, or rather that Lloyd George's friends are drawing large salaries and doing very little in the way of turning out ammunition.'[277] Before long the words 'Lloyd George knew my father, / Father knew Lloyd George' became a soldiers' marching song. As well as moving the tectonic plates of government, the Welsh Wizard had become emblematic of a new, harsher form of politics, incomprehensible to the likes of Asquith but excusable in the name of national salvation.

The Shells Committee, formed the previous October and on which Lloyd George sat, had found that although Kitchener wanted seventy divisions in the field, the officer in charge of ordnance, Major General Sir Stanley von Donop, had ordered only enough ordnance for twenty-four, to be delivered in June 1915. Thanks to an initiative by Lloyd George the order was increased from 900 to 3,000 guns, to be delivered by the end of May. The committee had also persuaded the Ordnance Department to use suppliers not on its approved list. Despite the huge demand for munitions, Parliament learned on 8 June that the new ministry had an additional list of 300 firms who had offered to make ordnance, but had received no orders.[278]

This was the sort of institutional caution and sclerosis that, as well as the Germans, Britain was fighting, and Lloyd George had lobbied Asquith and his colleagues about the need to deal with it radically. He had von Donop in his sights, gladly absorbing tales from contractors that he had turned down their offers to make munitions. Unprecedented demands for ammunition had caught him, and other senior officers, by surprise. Nor had he the political means to deal with the restrictive practices of trades unions, and labour shortages. Lloyd George would strip powers from von Donop, but he would survive in post until late the following year; and Lloyd George, in keeping with the spirit of the times, would take the credit for the increased shell production von Donop had already instituted since war broke out, limited though that was. No one could question the munitions minister's energy; but he had never let principle stand in the way of anything he wanted, and the existentialist struggle gave him even less cause to do so.

Lloyd George wanted to remain chancellor too, but Asquith felt that if the new ministry were to respond to the crisis it would require the undivided attention of its minister. The ministry would have two main purposes. The first was to organise private industry to provide the most efficient service in the manufacture and supply of armaments. The second would be to take over the inspectorate of such factories from the War Office. A new network of munitions factories would be set up, starting in railway workshops. It meant a serious loss of responsibility for Kitchener and the War Office. A Bill was put through Parliament suspending the Act of Queen Anne to force ministers moving jobs to resign their seats and fight by-elections: Lloyd George, with more important things to do, would not have to endure such a distraction.

His hope of sidelining Kitchener (which Northcliffe shared, as did the Irish, who felt him unsympathetic to the National Volunteers) would not be granted. The war secretary had the support of rank-and-file Unionists – who had always believed, politically, he was one of them – if not of those of their leaders who had experienced working with him; and he remained a nationally inspiring figure who had raised a massive army from scratch. Lloyd George's criticism of him was simple: 'I blame K for not having, in spite of saying the war would last 3 years, got all the factories etc together from the very first.'[279] Also, that Asquith had no idea that French had asked Kitchener for more shells said much about the Field Marshal's methods.

In early June 1915 legislation settled the powers and responsibilities of the new department, the first ever to be termed a 'ministry' (before that all except the great offices of state had been 'boards'). Lloyd George saw central control of the industry as essential, but the powers he wanted to close the gulf between demand and supply were not all forthcoming until late 1915. He also recruited a small army of scientists – notably chemists – to develop explosives and to improve productivity. Almost immediately on his assuming office he formed a Liquor Traffic Control Board of a dozen men, mostly MPs and civil servants, but also including Neville Chamberlain, the Lord Mayor of Birmingham and half-brother of Austen, to ensure his best efforts to equip the Army were not sabotaged by drink.

Lloyd George's appointment was announced as 'temporary'. There was nothing temporary, however, about the system he sought to put in place. He ordered the construction of state-owned National Shell

Factories, National Projectile Factories (producing ammunition for heavy artillery) and National Filling Factories. Existing government arms factories at Enfield, Waltham Abbey and Woolwich were also expanded. Woolwich would be the centre of the industry. By 1918 it would cover 285 acres of land and contain nearly 150 miles of railway track. Its workforce rose from 15,559 in 1914 to 96,325 by 1917.[280]

The Munitions of War Act 1915 banned the resignations of workers without permission. This attracted fierce opposition from what had become known as 'Red Clydeside', whose main priority was to free workers to fight capitalism rather than direct their efforts against the Germans. The Clyde Workers Committee called the Act 'a method to furnish the employers with a machine which would shatter to its foundations the whole fabric of trade union liberties and customs.'[281] It determined to organise workers according to their station 'and maintain the class struggle until the overthrow of the wages system'. Winning the war was a lower priority. For other workers there was a different problem: their wages had now risen so much that they could afford to work three or four days a week and drink themselves insensible for the rest of the time.

The new ministry's approach to munitions manufacture would have far-reaching consequences, notably the enormous expansion of numbers of women in the workforce, in jobs that had been considered male preserves, as what were called 'munitionettes'. This required Lloyd George to talk round the trades unions: in many places local agreements existed to 'dilute' skilled labour by allowing unskilled and semi-skilled workers of both genders to do some of the jobs; in other areas it was forbidden. The new ministry also spurred the growth of what the later twentieth century would know as health-and-safety regulations, though these did not prevent three terrible explosions during the war: in factories at Faversham (115 dead, all men and boys as it was a Sunday, and no women were working) on 2 April 1916; Silvertown (73 dead) on 19 January 1917; and at Chilwell (134 dead) on 1 July 1918.

In the coalition negotiations Asquith managed to keep Unionists out of the main posts in the cabinet. His wife was surprised by his loyalty to Grey, whom she pronounced 'terribly egotistical' and 'useless' during the crisis.[282] Lloyd George, while effective, was in a different way unhelpful to Asquith through his love of intrigue and his capriciousness, but had a constituency in the party and the country so large that his retention was inevitable: he was the only man who could challenge

Asquith's authority, and Asquith knew that Lloyd George, however sceptical he was about him, was essential to his survival as prime minister. Law told Hankey in October 1920 that the Unionists had regarded entering the coalition 'as a stop-gap arrangement' because 'no-one expected it to last.'[283] It was also felt in Tory circles that a refusal to cooperate would have damaged them greatly, the argument Gwynne used to justify his and the *Morning Post*'s volte-face on the subject: the alternative, a general election, would, he told Lady Bathurst, 'be worse than letting the Germans get to Calais.'[284]

The greatest agony for Asquith was having, at Law's insistence, to sack Haldane, who took his removal with the stoicism to be expected of a philosopher. Asquith secured his appointment to the Order of Merit – for services to science and philosophy – as a consolation. To many, including himself and Mrs Asquith, this dismissal of a close and old friend gave every appearance of a caving-in to the press. Asquith insisted on the Attorney General, Buckmaster, replacing Haldane on the Woolsack. 'No-one knows,' Asquith told Samuel, 'how much I have suffered. Very gladly indeed would I have gone.'[285] In a meeting that included Lloyd George, Crewe, McKenna and Balfour, Asquith then pointed at McKenna and said to Law: 'I propose to keep my friend here where he is, he is indispensable to me. Have you anything to say?'[286] Law protested that McKenna was felt, as home secretary, to have been ineffectual about enemy aliens; Asquith asked McKenna whether he would like to move, but McKenna said he knew what he was doing and so might as well stay at the Home Office.

In fact, McKenna, a former banker, ended up as chancellor, succeeding Lloyd George. Asquith had intended to do the job as well as being prime minister, but met huge resistance from the Unionists, who said he could not devote himself full-time to the direction of the war if he held two cabinet posts. The Treasury, whose mandarins had disliked Lloyd George and never thought him up to the job, were delighted to have McKenna back: he had served as financial secretary in the Campbell-Bannerman administration. Simon, whose career had very nearly ended when trying to resign over the declaration of war, became home secretary, having declined the Woolsack: he was only forty-two and too young, he felt, to leave the Commons. Redmond, the Irish Nationalist leader, objecting to Carson's inclusion, declined to serve as a counterweight, maintaining the Nationalists' principle of non-participation in a

British government. Lansdowne, a Unionist as passionate as Carson, agreed to be joint leader of the Lords and minister without portfolio, even though it had been reported that his health was not equal to a cabinet place. The Nationalists promised to support the coalition so long as the Unionists did not impose their anti-Home Rule views on it. Asquith refused to allow any Unionists to serve in the Irish administration. These promises would be tested to destruction.

Arthur Henderson, as Labour leader, was invited, to make the new government truly representative of the country. Henderson was a Glaswegian iron-moulder and teetotaller who, despite having left school aged twelve, became president of the Board of Education. He was a devout Methodist and a sincere patriot, hugely popular among his colleagues and universally respected; he was the first Labour MP to become a cabinet minister, and would lose a son, killed in action, in 1916. Curzon came in as Lord Privy Seal – he would soon irritate Asquith through his tendency to go freelance, causing Asquith to tell Crewe that 'he would have to have his comb clipped before long'.[287] Selborne became minister of agriculture and Long president of the Local Government Board, thus, with Curzon, accommodating three other Unionists with considerable followings in the party.

Haldane remained philosophical about the attacks on him when writing his memoirs after the war. He recalled that he had made a visit to Berlin on government business in 1912 that his opponents later misrepresented, though all questions about what was discussed on it – mainly the railway to Baghdad and policy towards Portugal's African colonies – could have been cleared up by publication of papers by the Foreign Office, which it was reluctant to do. But beyond that, 'every kind of ridiculous legend about me was circulated. I had a German wife; I was an illegitimate brother of the Kaiser; I had been in secret correspondence with the German Government; I had been aware that they intended war and had withheld my knowledge of this from my colleagues; I had delayed the mobilisation as despatch of the Expeditionary Force.'[288] Nor was it just the Northcliffe press that persecuted him. 'On one day, in response to an appeal in the *Daily Express*, there arrived at the House of Lords no less than 2,600 letters of protest against my supposed disloyalty to the interests of the nation.'[289] Haldane admitted that he knew too much for his own good about Germany and the German character, but regretted that his fellow countrymen knew too little. He had offered his resignation to Asquith in the autumn of 1914, but Asquith had laughed it off. Haldane did not, but fumed that the Foreign Office's refusal to clarify pre-war negotiations left him needlessly vulnerable.

The insistence on Haldane's removal almost caused another casualty. Grey, who felt the matter 'intolerably unjust', told Asquith on 26 May that he had only not resigned because of the national interest.[290] But he reminded Asquith that allegations of Haldane's 'intriguing with Germany behind the back of his colleagues', of 'weakening the Army, more particularly by reducing the artillery', and of 'opposing or obstructing' the sending of the BEF to France were not merely rubbish, but the reverse of the truth. 'That, after this,' Grey continued, 'Haldane of all people should have been singled out for the special sort of attack that has been made upon him, and accused of lack of patriotism or public spirit, is an intolerable instance of gross ignorance, or malice, or of madness.'[291]

Grey had a private interview with Law to try to make him change his mind, but Law implied that his party had mandated him. A coalition was essential; it would not happen without the Unionists, and the Unionists would not tolerate Haldane. It remains one of the most shameful episodes in the Conservative Party's chequered history, made worse by the fact that Asquith – who told Grey the attacks 'are a disgraceful monument of the pettiest personal and political spite' – failed properly to explain himself to Haldane, and their relations were never the same again.[292] Haldane maintained a life of conspicuous public service, visiting the war zone whenever he could be useful, sitting as a judge, and doing heroic work to stimulate interest in the creation of new universities and opportunities for extramural students for after the war: and he would sit on the Woolsack again, as Lord Chancellor in the first Labour government in 1924.

IX

Kitchener had spoken in the Lords on 18 May, ostensibly to bring Parliament up to date on the war, which he did with the depressing admission that 'there has been no marked change or decisive action in the various theatres of war since I last addressed your Lordships on the military situation.'[293] Instead, there was confirmation of the struggle at Ypres, the extensive use of gas and significant casualties, especially among

Canadian troops, and 'necessarily slow' progress in the Dardanelles.[294]
Hours before Lloyd George's appointment relieved him of the worry,
he promised that poor productivity in arms factories was being
addressed – the King that day was visiting Clydeside to try to raise morale in the shipyards – and said that 'a very considerable improvement in
the output' had already occurred.[295] He announced that 300,000 more
men were needed for the Army. 'Those who are engaged in the production of war material of any kind should not leave their work,' he said. 'It
is to men who are not performing this duty I appeal'. The public agreed,
and had what The Times termed the 'thousands of youthful slackers'
increasingly in their sights.[296]

Within two days of Kitchener's speech in the Lords, advertisements in
the form of a facsimile letter from him appeared in newspapers, and new
recruiting posters were plastered over the nation's billboards and public
buildings. The upper age limit for recruits was raised to forty from
thirty-eight. However, the idea of voluntary appeals looked outdated.
The press were debating compulsion, and public opinion seemed increasingly to favour it. Although the demands for uncensored news – to bring
home the gravity of the situation, and the urgency of more men joining
up – continued, it may have been as well for morale that some veil was
drawn over the realities of war.

Having secured a coalition, though not one entirely to its liking, the
Daily Mail savaged Kitchener as a 'fighting general'. It attacked him for
neglecting the manufacture of high-explosive shells and instead sending
out shrapnel shells, which it said were 'useless' in trench warfare, not
least in their failure to destroy barbed wire.[297] These criticisms were
included in a leader written by Northcliffe himself. Lloyd George had
made the same point, privately, to Asquith two days earlier, and one can
only conjecture what input he might have had into the leader.[298] That
coverage went down exceptionally badly with the public; the Mail's circulation fell precipitately – from 1,227,000 copies a day in May to 1,070,000
copies a day in July – and many advertisers withdrew their custom.[299]
Most London clubs stopped taking it and copies were burned on the
Stock Exchange, the Baltic Exchange and in the streets. Esher noted in his
diary: 'This morning there appeared a virulent attack on Lord K in the
Daily Mail. It was engineered by a small knot of people who believe
themselves to be friends of Sir John [French].[300] He added that Cambon,
aware of how things were done in France, thought it 'mad' that the

censors had allowed publication of such an article. Repington, who at
that time took the Northcliffe shilling, observed after the war that 'all that
Northcliffe did by this particular attack was to get Lord K the Garter
and, by causing a revulsion of feeling in Lord K's favour, to confirm him
in his office.'[301]

The next day the *Daily News* blamed Northcliffe for the political crisis
and stated that getting him under control was the main task facing the
new government. However, Northcliffe was convinced he was right to
expose the shell shortage and the failings of the military leadership. He
believed he had acted patriotically, and was unconcerned by the effect on
his business. 'I did not care,' he later claimed, 'whether the circulation of
The Times dropped to one copy and that of the *Daily Mail* to two. I consulted no-one about it except my mother, and she agreed with it. I felt
that the war was becoming too big for Kitchener, and that public belief
in him, which was indispensable at the outset, was becoming an obstacle
to military progress. Therefore I did my best to shake things up.'[302] For a
time the *Mail* proclaimed itself as 'THE PAPER THAT REVEALED
THE SHELL TRAGEDY.'[303] When, within weeks, it was apparent that
Northcliffe had had a point, public enmity declined, circulations rose,
and his influence increased.

Northcliffe may have alienated some of his readers by his attack on
Kitchener, but Kitchener was, nevertheless, losing allies. Neither Law
nor Balfour trusted him. His colleagues persisted in the belief that he
was secretive about his failures, and was loath to take them into his confidence on matters that should have been subject to discussion under
collective responsibility. He once said about his relations with the cabinet that 'it is repugnant to me to have to reveal military secrets to
twenty-three gentlemen with whom I am barely acquainted.'[304] Churchill found himself similarly assailed. Having failed to remove the war
secretary, Northcliffe's *Times* now reported that rank-and-file Liberals
were 'raging' against Churchill, whose 'adventures' had brought the
government down.[305] The paper said his colleagues did not want him in
the new cabinet; but they had been disappointed, as Churchill clung
on. He himself was chastened and angry. He wrote to Hankey on 2
June to say, apparently without irony, that 'the lost opportunities of this
war from Antwerp to the Dardanelles are a tragic catalogue. Nowhere
has there been design or decision.'[306] He was unequivocal about his own
indispensability: 'Now it will be a hard and stern task to carry through

the Dardanelles: and without decision and design very terrible catastrophe may ensue.'

The one senior politician who seemed to have won the respect of the Northcliffe press was Lloyd George: and the effect Northcliffe's confidence in and support for the munitions minister had in propelling Lloyd George from one crucial job to another during 1915–16 cannot be overestimated. He admired Lloyd George's energy, and his already monstrous ego was fed by the minister of munitions's egregious flattery of him. It fed Northcliffe's sense of his own importance. In a talk with Riddell in May 1915 Northcliffe said he was a rich man and could, if he chose, spend all his time fishing, 'but I feel my responsibility to the nation. I feel that I must remain to guide and criticise.'[307] In A. J. P. Taylor's words, Northcliffe 'aspired to power instead of influence, and as a result forfeited both.'[308] Too many of Lloyd George's colleagues thought Northcliffe was simply doing his bidding, which was hugely damaging to a man who, with Asquith weakened, saw the ultimate prize moving into his grasp. He remained unhappy with Asquith's general approach to the war, but realised he would isolate himself if he resigned on so general a matter without the support of the Conservative Party. His close association with Law – which became closer by the day – would help him to find common ground with the other party, and that common ground would be the need for conscription.

Hankey, who was loyal to Asquith, saw how vulnerable he was, and urged him over lunch on 2 June 'strongly to insist in future on having all naval and military operations telegrams and letters, as well as the Foreign Office ones sent to him, so that he . . . would at least know all there was to know about the war.'[309] He saw how bad it was that no single person had a complete strategic overview of what was happening in the war, and knew the prime minister should be that man. Asquith agreed, and promised to appoint Hankey as liaison officer between himself, the Admiralty and the War Office. He also decided to issue a formal warning to the press 'against speaking of munitions, or strengths, dispositions, and movements of our fleets and armies, even in leading articles, without censorship.' Hankey noted that 'drastic action' would be taken against transgressors; and it was clear to him that Northcliffe's attack on Kitchener had only reinforced Asquith's determination to keep him.

It took several days for the coalition negotiations to be completed, and it was not clear until 24 May – Whit Monday – what the composition of the new administration would be. That bank holiday most of Britain basked in unbroken sunshine, and Lord Derby addressed an estimated 100,000 people at a recruitment rally on the sands at Blackpool. Among men not in uniform there was a self-consciousness if they were seen enjoying themselves: a *Times* correspondent said that a young man seen to be off to play tennis would be regarded as 'a double-dyed traitor' for not being at the front, and not behaving with more tact. It surmised that most who saw him would think he 'ought to be taken out and shot'.[310] Two or three times a week newspapers published casualty lists, often of hundreds of officers and thousands of men, and feelings were running high. A further pall was cast over the bank holiday by news of the Quintinshill rail disaster in Dumfriesshire, which happened just before 7 a.m. on 22 May. The death toll was believed to be 226 (some bodies were never recovered). It remains the worst railway disaster in British history, and was caused by a signalling failure on the main line outside Gretna Green, involving five trains. Half the occupants of a troop train – soldiers of the 1/7th Leith Battalion of the Royal Scots off to the Dardanelles – were killed.

The new cabinet first met on 27 May, in what Asquith told the King was an atmosphere of 'harmony and good will', but with elder statesmen already lining up to criticise it.[311] The Unionist Party had gathered at the Carlton Club the previous evening to express its support for the coalition, but there remained dissidents. Milner had written to *The Times* that morning to say that although it was full of talent it lacked leadership, signalling the start of the paper's eighteen-month campaign to remove Asquith. Milner's evidence was that the state had been forced to 'tout' for men in this time of extreme emergency, a sign the leadership had no idea how to prosecute the war.[312]

The cabinet's first discussion was about the Dardanelles, where matters were going exceptionally badly. A cabinet committee, under Asquith and including the deposed Churchill and leading Unionists, was set up to monitor the situation, and Hankey became its secretary. The War Council had wound up; but Hankey steered the Dardanelles Committee towards becoming a successor body, by inviting service chiefs from time to time. This lasted through the summer of 1915, as ministers debated whether to send reinforcements to the failing campaign. The following November it was renamed 'The War Committee'.[313] Its main shortcomings were that the Unionists found it hard to stop finding fault with

Liberal proposals; and its conclusions were not binding on the full cabinet, which slowed down the decision-making process. This was not the ideal mechanism for directing a great war.

Francis Hirst, the editor of the *Economist*, wrote to his former colleague C. P. Scott to ask: 'Will not this Coalition Government be weak and discredited from the start, without any common purpose or object? . . . Are not horror and disgust about the war prevailing everywhere? And is there not a reaction against the foul Northcliffe pogrom of people with German names . . . Why should all of us Britons be ruined because a little group of Liberal and Tory Imperialists has taken the idiotic resolution of destroying the German nation?'[314] That was too much even for the Liberal Scott, who told him the 'aggressive imperialism' of Germany had to be resisted. Even people such as him were coming round to the view that Britain had to 'remain armed and on something like the European scale. It is a dire and hateful necessity.'[315] Any idea of a general election to 'validate' the coalition was ruled out: the following month a Bill was introduced to prolong the life of the 1910 Parliament by another year. This too would be renewed, and no election would be held until after the Armistice.

On 15 June Asquith defended to the Commons his action in forming a coalition. 'I have a deep, an abiding and an ineffaceable sense of gratitude to the colleagues who, under the stress of new and unforeseen responsibility, for the best part of ten months, sustained with undeviating loyalty, and, in my judgement, with unexampled efficiency, the heaviest load which has ever fallen upon the shoulders of British statesmen . . . there is not one of them to whom I, as the head of the Government, and, I think, the nation at large, does not stand under a permanent debt of obligation. To part with them, or with any of them, has been the severest and most painful experience of my public life.'[316] He made clear his distaste for coalitions, citing that of Fox and North: and said the policy remained unchanged, 'to pursue this War at any cost to a victorious issue.'[317] He argued it was as well to show the parties were united in their determination to beat Germany, formalising the truce that had existed since August.

It was an anodyne version of the truth, but for all the subsequent criticism of him as lethargic, bloodless or – as his dismissive colleagues would often call him, 'judicial' in his approach to political questions – his peroration to this important speech was, to use an anachronism,

Churchillian, and reveals a conviction not always matched by action. 'We have for the moment one plain and paramount duty to perform: to bring to the service of the State the willing and organised help of every class in the community. There is a fit place, there is fit work for every man and every woman in the land, and, be it sooner or later—it will certainly come—when our cause has been vindicated, and when there is once more peace on earth, may it be recorded as the proudest page in the annals of this Nation that there is not a home nor a workshop over this United Kingdom that did not take its part in the common struggle, and earn its share in the common triumph.'[318]

His speech was emotionally draining, and when his wife visited him in his bedroom that evening he cried in her arms. 'I realised,' she wrote in her diary, 'how frightfully he is taken out of when he has to confess himself.'[319] She knew that was not the only reason: he was feeling battered by Liberal opposition to the coalition and 'is low about Venetia's marriage.'[320] Mrs Asquith was also more convinced than ever about Lloyd George's conspiring against her husband. Reading confided in her that he had warned the munitions minister to stop letting Northcliffe and his newspapers 'run' him. Mrs Asquith was convinced he was planning to break with the Liberals, 'not consciously to smash H, but he sees that after the war things will completely change, and the man who will be adored in England is the man who helps our poor devils in the trenches.' She detected a movement in the press to 'crush' Asquith and Kitchener, and was worried by Lloyd George's friendship with Riddell. Others warned the Asquiths that Lloyd George was 'a traitor and a cad': but it was up to the prime minister himself to take firm action to prevent his colleague from supplanting him.

He, meanwhile, had become obsessively devoted to Sylvia Henley. He told her that in a period of 'the chaos of munitions, and Dardanelles . . . and unfortunate gossip as to Lloyd George, fate of the coalition, leadership of party and government, the campaign in France . . . the future attitude of the United States, and about 199 other things – what (I say) emerges as *to me* the salient and dominant factor of the week? Can you guess? I know you don't need to guess. Of course, it is *You*.'[321] She did, however, give him one important piece of counsel on a point that had been noticed by, and brought him the disapproval of, colleagues: 'You gave me a great deal of good advice today, and I shall *never* write to you again from a Cabinet or War Council.'[322] He quickly pushed his luck too far, writing to her on 20 June about a 'cri de Coeur' she had made when she thought he was making an advance, causing Asquith to claim it had caused him 'a twinge of pain that you could ever have suspected that I shd be tempted to convert our wonderful relation of love and confidence into – what shall I call it? – an erotic adventure?'[323] She seemed embarrassed by his remarks, prompting him to promise never to mention the 'incident' again and telling her to 'burn the offending letter'.[324] The letters to 'my dearest and best' from 'your ever loving and entirely devoted' continued, but he was never as open with her as he had been with her sister. He also attempted in 1916 to forge an intimate friendship with Emily Strutt, daughter of Lord Rayleigh, a Nobel Prize-winning scientist, whom he had first met at her father's Essex house a decade earlier.[325] His intense loneliness had plagued him in the time of peace: in war it threatened to become unbearable.

X

On 31 May London suffered its first Zeppelin raid. Eight people were killed in Whitechapel and ten injured. The inquest into two of the deaths was told how the bodies of a married couple, killed in the blast, were found kneeling by their bed, as if in prayer. It was an ideal symbol of the victims of what the public now routinely termed the barbarism of the Germans. It took nearly three weeks for the government to issue standard advice on what to do in an air raid: which was not to go out in the street, and to keep supplies of sand and water upstairs to put out any fires, since the attacks were expected to happen at night. Downstairs, doors and windows were to be kept closed to prevent the intrusion of 'noxious gases'.[326]

Parliament, which had gone into recess early for Whitsun at the time of reconstruction of the government, did not sit again until 3 June. It passed the necessary legislation for setting up the Ministry of Munitions, stimulating opposition from a small number of pacifist MPs. Lloyd George was not present: he was in Manchester launching a new productivity drive, and Asquith had gone to France to see the commander-in-chief of the BEF, French. In Manchester Lloyd George made a speech that showed how the wind had changed, at least for him. The key passage was that 'when the house is on fire, questions of procedure, of precedence, of etiquette, of time, and division of labour, disappear. You cannot say that you are not liable to service at three o'clock in the morning if the fire is proceeding. You don't choose the hour; you cannot argue as to whose duty it is to carry the water bucket and whose duty it is to tip it into the crackling furnace. You must put the fire out.'[327] He reminded trades unionists who were blocking reform of working practices or use of female labour that men in the trenches could not stand down after working a prescribed number of hours, nor refuse to fight in a specified part of the line. But Lloyd George's other interesting observation, given what would happen over the ensuing eighteen months, was that 'party politics are gradually vanishing'. His remarks annoyed the Labour Party; but also many Liberals, as they smelt some sort of compulsion being introduced to industrial practices. But Lloyd George was right. As munitions minister he would inaugurate a programme of 218 national factories, financed by taxpayers' money, making all sorts of weapons and components essential to the war effort, as well as establishing control of the labour force and output of much of industry.[328]

He went on to Liverpool, to appeal again to unions to lift restrictive practices for the duration. He spoke, as in Manchester, of a situation of unprecedented gravity. The Germans had subjugated themselves entirely to winning the war. Now Britain had to do the same. This meant the unions making it easier to train unskilled men, and to have women in the workplace, as in France. But all had to work harder: 'There is no room for slackers,' he said to cheers. 'I don't want to get rid of the slackness. I only want to get rid of *their* slackness.'[329] More controversially, he made a further nod towards compulsion, civil and military. 'It ought to be established as a duty, as one of the essential duties of citizenship, that every man should put his whole strength into helping the country through, and I don't believe any section of the community would object to it if it were made into a legal right and duty expected of everyone.'

With the exodus of women into higher-paid jobs in industry causing a shortage of kitchen and parlour maids, and provoking more articles on the servant problem, some might have disagreed, unpatriotic though it would be to do so. Others in work of national importance refused to see the patriotic point; in early June the South Wales coalfields threatened to strike; colliery engine winders and stokers in the Black Country rejected a 10 per cent bonus as inadequate, even though their wages had doubled in two years; and 20,000 cotton workers in Rochdale were threatened with a lockout after their employers refused to pay a 10 per cent bonus for war contracts: all this on the same day, 9 June, when a further 50 officers and 2,100 men appeared on the casualty list from France. More than 50,000 men had died since August, and 53,000 were missing.[330]

On 10 June Lloyd George met seventy-five representatives from twenty-two unions in London and held private talks with them. That same day the first public meeting of the National Union of Women Workers was held in the capital, at which it was said that 'as a whole, the women have behaved well, but there were a number of young, giddy girls excited by the presence of so many men in khaki.'[331] The National Union wanted funds to set up clubs where girls could meet soldiers under supervision, and at which they could be taught 'greater self-control and greater modesty', and the men 'respect for women.' Of all the bursts of idealism since the outbreak of war, that was one of the more remarkable.

Lloyd George went to Bristol on 12 June to visit munitions factories, and to continue to plead for cooperation from the unions. He announced that Kitchener had been asked to return all skilled engineers to factories to make munitions. 'Britain means to make up for lost time,' he said.[332] At the moment of victory, 'the engineers will know with a thrill that the workshops of Britain have won a lasting triumph for the righteousness that exalteth a nation.' But he told the unions: 'There is only one way in which you can increase the labour supply, and that is by the suspension, during the war, of the regulation with regard to girls and unskilled labour helping the skilled.' The French had abandoned this luxury for the duration: he wanted Britain to do the same.

On 16 June, after four hours of talks, he had a signal success. He met representatives from forty-one unions who agreed that all union rules would be suspended in munitions workshops for the duration; that all workers in them would be placed under military discipline and made punishable for breaches of regulations; that work would be voluntary unless the unions failed to enlist the necessary workers; and that no private firm could engage a munitions worker without a certificate from his or her previous employer, to avoid 'desertion'. In return for these concessions, all war profits would be annexed by the state. The same day that Lloyd George exhorted the workers of Bristol, the Socialist National Defence Committee called for an end to 'the wasteful gamble and chaos of private enterprise' and wholesale nationalisations to maximise the war effort. It would not be long before the coalition pursued such a strategy, with government-owned munitions factories and state control of a railway network starved of maintenance and investment. Beatrice Webb noted that 'from all one hears Lloyd George is going the way of Chamberlain, exchanging the leadership of the Radicals for the leadership of an imperialist nationalist party . . . his present subservience to the Tories is pitiable; in politics the greatest enemies, once they get over their enmity, become the closest of conspirators.'[333]

At the Ministry of Munitions Addison, Lloyd George's junior minister, was charged with finding out how bad things were. His report, compiled with the head of the Statistics Department, was so alarming that Asquith banned its printing and circulation: those ministers who wished to read it, including even Lloyd George, were told to do so in Addison's office, which the report was not to leave. Although Kitchener wanted seventy divisions, the Army had enough small-calibre artillery – 18-pounders – for twenty-eight; enough 60-pounders for thirty-one; and enough howitzers for seventeen.[334] It would, at the then rate of supply, have taken until the 1920s to equip the army he wanted. There were enough rifles for thirty-three divisions, and between August 1914 and May 1915 only enough machine guns to equip twelve to a minimal standard. The War Office wanted 70,000 grenades a day delivered to France: the actual total was 2,500. The other difficulty was accommodating munitions workers near the new factories the government was proposing to build, or near existing ones that were being expanded. There was no manpower to build permanent structures: so an appeal was launched for donations to build temporary accommodation, under the auspices of the Young Men's Christian Association – prefabricated huts which workers could assemble themselves. Given the urgency of distracting the new industrial army from drink and the opposite sex, the YMCA was regarded as an ideal landlord.

To get production on course, between 19 and 26 June questionnaires were sent to 65,000 manufacturers to establish exactly what capacity was at the country's disposal. Once the answers were in, the ministry would put in its orders, monitored by local boards. Also in June, Lloyd George brokered an arrangement with the trades unions to set up a system of War Munitions Volunteers. These would be people who agreed, if required, to leave their present job and work for government contractors; full-page advertisements appeared in the press, and Lloyd George warned that if there was an inadequate response workers would have to be brought in by compulsion. In the first week 46,000 skilled workers volunteered, but it then slowed down dramatically: by November 107,000 had come forward, but because their existing employers could object, relatively few – about 10 per cent – were drafted.[335] The ministry set up its own National Factories, and extended the plant at existing ones, and many of these workers were transferred to those. While the working class transferred their skills into such factories, middle- and upper-middle-class women volunteered wherever they could. Two of Asquith's daughters-in-law – Katharine and Lady Cynthia – were typical, the former working in a canteen at Euston station, the latter spending some afternoons making respirators for the troops.

Although the report was suppressed, the dire situation soon became known, and Lloyd George – who told Henry Wilson, back from France to be knighted, that 'we are going to be beaten' – set about seeking more power to put things right.[336] On 1 July Sir Henry Dalziel – one of his cronies, a Liberal MP and newspaper proprietor – asked in the Commons for the Ministry of Munitions to take over von Donop's Ordnance Department. Mrs Asquith believed Northcliffe had planted the question so it could be reported in *The Times*, and that Lloyd George was complicit. Haldane broke his post-resignation silence to defend von Donop, causing Lloyd George to denounce Haldane's version of events: *The Times* gave a good show to the denunciation in its 8 July edition. Mrs Asquith was now systematically seeking to settle scores with those she held responsible for her husband's difficulties. When French returned from the front to brief the War Cabinet on 2 July she told him: 'If you had hated me and my man, you could not have done us a worse turn than you did by seeing swine like Northcliffe and Repington.'[337] She told him that if Kitchener had not reacted sufficiently to the shell problem, he should have written to Asquith direct: an unfortunate interpretation of the chain of command. She thought one of French's staff had briefed Repington, which was not the case: had she realised French himself had done it, he might not have left the room alive.

Meeting her husband off a train at Charing Cross in early June, Mrs Asquith was allowed on to the concourse of a station otherwise closed to the public while an ambulance train was unloaded. The sight of rows and rows of wounded and dying men laid out on stretchers on the ground, 'lying perfectly flat like so many corpses', stunned her.[338]

Such trains were mostly timed to arrive late at night or during the early hours, not least so the fleet of ambulances meeting them would avoid the public gaze. There could no longer be any doubt about the terrible scale and effect of the conflict. A few months before, in mid-January 1915, a correspondence in *The Times* settled a question vexing its readers: the struggle in which the nation was now engaged body and soul was to be known as 'the Great War'.[339]

CHAPTER 4

CONSCRIPTION

As the first anniversary of the outbreak of war approached, the conflict still had general public support, but the enthusiasm of August 1914 had long since passed. A sense of unease at the high level of deaths, and the reorientation of the country into a nation at war, began to be palpable. The Central Committee for National Patriotic Organisations urged MPs to address meetings in their constituencies on the anniversary. Kitchener hoped to turn a commemoration at St Paul's on 4 August into a recruitment rally, but the clergy dismissed the suggestion. The sense that young men were being sent off to die pointlessly, leaving families bereaved, was taking hold, and made the job of those charged with running the war increasingly difficult. Instead, a rally was arranged at the Guildhall on 9 July at which Kitchener pleaded for more recruits. 'In every man's life there is one supreme hour towards which all earlier experience moves and from which all future results may be reckoned,' he said. 'For every individual Briton, as well as for our national existence, that hour is now striking.'[1]

The government exerted such control over the public in the supply of information that it took time for many people, Kitchener's exhortations notwithstanding, to understand how bad things really were. Until 6 July anodyne newspaper headlines talked of one courageous battle after another in the Dardanelles: but that day General Sir Ian Hamilton's dispatch, dated 20 May and dealing with events until 4 May, was published, and began to show what a debacle the operation had been. The government had admitted on 31 May that 7,500 officers and men had been killed;

the public started to fear that the numbers would have risen substantially since. It was clear that the tremendous bravery of the troops, of which Hamilton made no secret, had been sacrificed to the incompetence of the planning that had led to a lack of coordination of the military and naval forces.

Soldiers wounded and on leave brought word back from Flanders, where the Second Battle of Ypres had been fought for five weeks from late April, of new horrors inflicted on them. The Germans used poison gas for the first time during the battle, a prime example of 'frightfulness' to rank with the sinking of the *Lusitania*. As the casualty lists were published it became clear that all parts of society had suffered: the summer commemoration events at Oxford were muted because 300 of the 8,000 alumni believed to be serving had been killed. Eton – some of whose boys were working five-hour shifts in a nearby munitions factory – decided to raise funds for ambulances, something the nation's lady mayoresses had been doing across Britain. It was estimated one officer in ten in the land forces thus far killed was an Old Etonian.[2] At an opposite extreme, 19,648 boys who had been through reformatories had served by late June 1915, almost 600 of whom had died: but three had won the Victoria Cross, twenty-five the Distinguished Conduct Medal and twenty were mentioned in dispatches. Perhaps most remarkably, eight of these former miscreants had been commissioned.[3] The casualties among officers for May 1915 alone were little short of those for the whole Second Boer War – 2,440 against 2,752. In February 1916 *The Times* published a list of forty-five heirs to peerages thus far killed; six of their deaths left peerages without an heir, including that of Lord Stamfordham, the King's private secretary.[4]

In his memoirs Bob Boothby, a fourteen-year-old Etonian when war broke out, recalled the cumulative effect the war had on his generation:

It is difficult to exaggerate the traumatic effect of the casualties in France upon the lives of boys who grew to maturity during the years between 1914 and 1918. Every Sunday the names of the fallen were read out in college chapel. As we saw all the heroes of our youth being killed, one by one, and not far away, our whole attitude towards life changed. 'Eat and drink and try to be merry, for tomorrow you will surely die,' became our motto. Neuve Chapelle,

Loos, the Somme and Passchendaele bit deep into our small souls. If early and bloody death was apparently an inevitable consequence of life, what was the point of it?[5]

The war was coming closer to home, increasing pressure for a decisive response. Despite the censorship of news from the Dardanelles, the sheer number of families who had been notified of deaths from that theatre of war ensured that various versions of the truth spread rapidly by word of mouth. Then on 7 September there were Zeppelin raids on south London, the capital's docklands and Cheshunt in Hertfordshire. The next day Zeppelins bombed London's Farringdon Road, killing twenty-two people and injuring eighty-six, the most damaging single bombing raid of the war; and attacked a benzole plant in Yorkshire. (In 1917, in a well-judged act of defiance, 61 Farringdon Road was rebuilt as the Zeppelin Building.) A further Zeppelin raid on London and the eastern counties on 13 October killed seventy-one and injured a hundred and twenty-eight. Complaints by politicians and the public about the lack of anti-aircraft protection were beyond the wit of the censor to stop, with the *Globe* newspaper organising a public meeting, chaired by Lord Willoughby de Broke, in London the day after the raids, and demanding reprisals. The Northcliffe press complained that it was unclear which minister was in charge of defending London – an astonishing indictment of Asquith's attention to detail – and it fell to Balfour, as First Lord of the Admiralty, to take that responsibility.

However, if the Germans hoped to break British resolve, another of their acts against a civilian in the autumn of 1915 would prove instrumental in hardening it more than ever. On 12 October the Germans shot Edith Cavell, the English matron of a training school for nurses in Brussels, for helping an estimated 200 British and French prisoners and Belgian civilians escape into Holland. France had shot two nurses in Paris during 1915 for assisting the escape of German prisoners; Miss Cavell had known the likely consequences of her actions, undertaken as part of the Brussels underground network. It was disclosed decades after her execution that she had also been gathering intelligence. She could have left Brussels in the autumn of 1914 when the Americans arranged for seventy Allied nurses to leave, but chose to stay. The Foreign Office had monitored her case since her arrest on 5 August, though had kept details out of the press. It had concluded it could do nothing to help. Her trial began on 7 October and she was condemned to death on the 11th.

The American ambassador to Berlin made the strongest representations, and the Spanish legation in Brussels tried to intervene; but diplomats were lied to about the intention to carry out the sentence. A promise to discuss the matter with the Americans before anything happened was broken. The civil governor, Baron von der Lancken, believed Miss Cavell should be reprieved, but he was subordinate to the military authorities. One of his colleagues, Count Harrach, expressed his regret that he did not have a few more Englishwomen to shoot. That was close to the view of the military governor, General von Sauberzweig, who ordered the sentence to be carried out. The Revd Stirling Gahan, an Anglican chaplain, was allowed to see Miss Cavell on the eve of her execution to give her Holy Communion. He found her 'perfectly calm and resigned.'[6] She said: 'I have no fear nor shrinking; I have seen death so often that it is not strange or fearful to me.' Her last words to him as he left were 'we shall meet again.' Word of her execution reached London via the American embassy on 14 October.

The Press Bureau released a bulletin for the newspapers on 16 October that reported the simple facts of what had happened, though mis-stated the date of her death as 13 October. One of Britain's most famous nurses, Mrs Bedford Fenwick, announced on behalf of the profession that Miss Cavell 'had died a glorious death'.[7] The outcry in England at this supreme example of German 'frightfulness', which went far beyond anything in the Bryce report in terms of its closeness to home, was deafening, a propaganda gift to a government constantly striving to maintain enthusiasm for the war by depicting the evil of the beastly Hun. The Bishop of London, Dr Arthur Winnington-Ingram – a serial and fervent Hun-basher who misunderstood what had happened and seemed not to know she had been nearly fifty years old – told a rally in Trafalgar Square that 'the cold-blooded murder of Miss Cavell, a poor English girl deliberately shot by the Germans for housing refugees, will run the sinking of the Lusitania close in the civilised world as the greatest crime in history.'[8]

Details of Miss Cavell's last hours, and the dignified way in which she met her death at dawn at a firing range on the edge of Brussels, added a golden aura to her sacrifice. She had also told Gahan: 'But this I would say, standing, as I do, in view of God and eternity. I realise that patriotism is not enough. I must have no bitterness or hatred towards anyone' – words engraved on her monument just north of Trafalgar Square, erected after the war, but for which plans began to be laid immediately.[9] Her last words, after saying she wanted her family to be told that she believed her soul was safe, were: 'I am glad that I die for my country.' It was a spectacular martyrdom; the Church of England would make the anniversary of her death a saint's feast day. A powerful legend was created that exemplified the wickedness Britain was fighting against. The international obloquy rattled the Kaiser sufficiently that he issued an order a few weeks later that no woman was to be executed without his permission.

The public outrage, too, was colossal; it inspired deeper loathing of the enemy, and impelled more men into uniform. Posters, books, pamphlets, penny dreadfuls, films, poems and almost every form of creative endeavour were applied to retelling the story of the German evil towards Nurse Cavell. Jocelyn Henry Speck, a clergyman from Bedford, wrote to *The Times* to announce that 'if ever a challenge rang out to the chivalry of our young men of military age not yet enlisted, it is surely to be heard in the dastardly execution of an Englishwoman at the hands of an enemy for whom self-respecting nations in future can have but one feeling, absolute abhorrence.'[10] The Revd Mr Speck continued that the Germans 'have murdered chivalry', and the 2 million young men it was believed had yet to answer the nation's call would join up at once 'if chivalry and manhood are not extinct in them.' He concluded: 'The call is a voice from the grave – the voice of Nurse Edith Cavell from that execution yard in Brussels. She being dead yet speaketh.'

Lansdowne gave the government's first reaction in the Lords on 20 October:

We have been during the last few months continually shocked by occurrences each more terrible and moving than its predecessor; but I doubt whether any incident has moved public opinion in this country more than the manner in which this poor lady was, I suppose I must say, 'executed' in cold blood not many hours ago. It is no doubt the case . . . that she may by her conduct have rendered herself liable to punishment—perhaps to severe punishment—for acts committed in violation of the kind of law which prevails when war is going on. But I have no hesitation in saying that she might at any rate have expected that measure of mercy which I believe in no civilised country would have been refused to one who was not only a woman, but

a very brave and devoted woman, and one who had given all her
efforts and energies to the mitigation of the sufferings of others.[11]

The Times waited until after Lansdowne's statement and the publication of correspondence between the Foreign Office, the Americans and
the Spanish before leading the Establishment's execration of the Germans. In its leading article of 22 October it mused whether the 'disciples
of Kultur' were capable of appreciating what Grey, in thanking the
Americans and Spanish for their exhaustive efforts, had called the 'horror and disgust' resonating around the civilised world at the story.[12]
'There is not in Europe, outside Germany and her Allies, a man who can
read it without the deepest emotions of pity and shame.' Miss Cavell
'had devoted her life to the noblest and most womanly work woman can
do,' the paper said. She had saved the lives of Germans, and this was how
her 'charity' had been requited. She had told the truth and her captors
had shown her no mercy. The Spanish and Americans who sought clemency had been told not even the Kaiser would intervene; yet he intervened
the moment the outcry erupted to reprieve two other women sentenced
by the same tribunal for similar offences. Noting Miss Cavell's last
words, the paper proclaimed: 'She did in very truth die for England, and
England will not lightly forget her death . . . By killing her they have
immeasurably deepened the stain of infamy that degrades them in the
eyes of the whole world. They could have done no deed better calculated
to serve the British cause.'

Unable to fathom the enormity of their act, the Germans then refused
an American request to have Miss Cavell's remains exhumed and handed
over to the British for burial. With neutral opinion already hardening
against Germany, The Times's view of the effectiveness of the action in
furthering the British cause was quickly proved entirely right: the American press, still nursing the grievance of the Lusitania, was ferocious. At
home, outpourings of incontinent rage from correspondents to newspapers confirmed the extent of the propaganda gift.

Stamfordham, on behalf of the King and Queen, wrote to Miss Cavell's
mother on 23 October to describe their Majesties' 'horror at the appalling
deed that has robbed you of your child. Men and women throughout the
civilised world, while sympathising with you, are moved with admiration and awe at her faith and courage in death.'[13] A memorial service
took place in St Paul's Cathedral on 29 October, where Queen Alexandra

led the mourners, and her son the King – who the previous day had fractured his pelvis when being thrown from his horse inspecting troops at the front, and his horse had rolled on him – and the Queen were represented; Asquith and several cabinet colleagues attended.[14] Seats set aside for the public were taken hours before the service began, and hawkers stood outside selling memorial postcards of the martyred heroine. Six hundred nurses attended, and the band of the Life Guards played Chopin's funeral march and the Dead March from *Saul*. The site of the Cavell statue was announced on the eve of the service; and cities from Melbourne to Toronto announced that they would commemorate her.

While Nurse Cavell's execution, and another wave of Zeppelin raids, unquestionably stiffened public resolve, the mood remained tense. A rumour circulated that 'the King and Queen have not regularly spent the night at Buckingham Palace, but slipt [sic] off to one of their London friends': it was entirely without foundation.[15]

II

By the time Miss Cavell became a symbol of martyrdom, Britain had also acquired a symbol of sacrifice. Word reached England at the start of the Gallipoli campaign that Rupert Brooke, whom Margot Asquith described as 'the beautiful young poet', had died of septicaemia on a French hospital ship near the Greek island of Skyros, with perfect timing, on the afternoon of St George's Day.[16] He was serving with her stepson Oc in the Royal Naval Division, and was in Egypt en route for the Dardanelles when a mosquito bite felled him. Brooke had been asked to join Sir Ian Hamilton's staff, but had refused, wishing to fight alongside the other men. Mrs Asquith had seen him, with Oc, just before embarkation: 'He put his hands on my shoulders and looked at me with his beautiful eyes and kissed me in Oc's little wooden tent at Blandford on 26th Feb 1915,' she recalled in her diary. The news had reached Downing Street by the evening, as the fleet in which Brooke had served was moving to its battle stations near Gallipoli: Asquith said: 'it has given me more pain than any loss in the war.'[17]

The Times, which wrongly reported Brooke as having died from sunstroke, carried an appreciation of him by 'WSC' – Churchill, the patron of the unit in which he had served. 'A voice had become audible, a note had been struck, more true, more thrilling, more able to do justice to the

nobility of our youth in arms engaged in this present war, than any other,'
the First Lord wrote.[18] 'Only the echoes and the memory remain; but
they will linger.' All the seeds of the myth are in this short article. 'He
expected to die; he was willing to die for the dear England whose beauty
and majesty he knew; and he advanced towards the brink in perfect
serenity, with absolute conviction of the rightness of his country's cause
and a heart devoid of hate for fellow-men.' One cannot doubt Churchill's
sincerity: but this was a propaganda opportunity of the highest calibre,
and he seized it. Others had already realised the potential to harness culture for the war effort: Brooke's death exemplified that potential.

He had told Mrs Asquith he expected to die, and embraced the prospect: that indeed was the theme of his five war sonnets, two of which
were published as he left England, and which accounted for much of his
posthumous fame when all were issued a month after his death in *1914
and Other Poems*. The war stimulated an outpouring of verse, most of it
execrable, with *The Times* publishing a poem almost daily during the
conflict, usually by reputable poets. Brooke's verse is far from execrable
and, as Wells noted, 'An early death in the great war was not an unmitigated misfortune.'[19]

The opening lines of the first sonnet are an ostentatious, but no doubt
sincere, death-wish:

> Now, God be thanked Who has matched us with His hour,
> And caught our Youth, and wakened us from sleeping
> With hand made sure, clear eye, and sharpened power,
> To turn, as swimmers into cleanness leaping . . .[20]

The sonnet ends proclaiming that 'the worst friend and enemy is but
Death.' The fifth and most celebrated of the poems seems to go further
and accept the likelihood of death. Its fame spread almost instantly,
supercharging the myth of Brooke even before he died, when on 4 April
William Inge, the Dean of St Paul's, read it from the pulpit:

> If I should die, think only this of me:
> That there's some corner of a foreign field
> That is for ever England. There shall be
> In that rich earth a richer dust concealed;
> A dust whom England bore, shaped, made aware,

Gave, once, her flowers to love, her ways to roam,
A body of England's, breathing English air,
Washed by the rivers, blest by suns of home.

And think, this heart, all evil shed away,
A pulse in the eternal mind, no less
Gives somewhere back the thoughts by England given;
Her sights and sounds; dreams happy as her day;
And laughter, learnt of friends; and gentleness,
In hearts at peace, under an English heaven.[21]

Ironically, what remained of this idealism would be blown away by the
failure at Gallipoli itself. Brooke's tone would rapidly pass out of fashion, as would the mostly vainglorious verse that *The Times* and other
periodicals published at this time, as the reality of mud, blood and rotting, mangled corpses impressed itself upon the men at the front.
Certainly, the glory of war was never the same again for Patrick Shaw-
Stewart, a fellow of All Souls, who served with Brooke and assisted at
his funeral amid a grove of wild olive trees on Skyros; and was so
deeply affected by the futility of his death that he seemed to lose the
will to survive his friends (he died on the Western Front in 1917). On
his way to the Dardanelles Shaw-Stuart had written the poem by
which he is remembered, 'Achilles in the Trench', and which finishes
with lines Brooke, perhaps with slightly fewer poetic gifts, must have
dreamt of writing:

I will go back this morning
From Imbros over the sea;
Stand in the trench, Achilles,
Flame-capped, and shout for me.[22]

Evoking the *Iliad*, Shaw-Stewart clings to the romance of war, to an
extent. He would not do so much longer. Two days after Brooke died,
the joint military operation at Gallipoli began.

The evolution of total war, with the civilian population increasingly
devoting itself to fighting, manufacturing or volunteering, had a profound effect on culture; and it would last well into the 1930s. It altered
the imagination; but it also inevitably interrupted, or re-routed, cultural

work in progress. Roger Fry had written to a friend in August 1914 that 'it is over with all our ideas.'[23] Given the new directions in which war would send creativity, Fry was right about that. The culture we associate with the Great War is often the culture produced by those who came through it and recorded it in the years afterwards. For example, Ford Madox Hueffer published his *Parade's End* tetralogy under his anglicised name of Ford Madox Ford between 1924 and 1928; Siegfried Sassoon, Edmund Blunden and Robert Graves would return, post-war, to their memories of the trenches; and so would composers such as Ralph Vaughan Williams and Arthur Bliss, whose music was heavily influenced by their experiences of war. Those experiences did not, with the odd exception, immediately translate into cultural output. However, some artists' reputations were inevitably based mainly on their work during the war, because they were dead by the Armistice: such as Wilfred Owen and, as a poet, Edward Thomas.

Culture in its broadest sense – notably music, art and literature – served two main purposes during the war. First, it maintained a sense of civilisation superior to the base values of the nation against which Britain was fighting, and thus had some utility in providing reasons to beat the Germans. Second, it provided relaxation and diversion for the public, as well as inspiration. Even when the Brooke idea of war had been utterly repudiated, the creative arts did not question the justice of the fight against the Germans. The cheaper sort of fiction – especially the weekly adventure stories for boys and young men – was soon dominated by tales of the war, and of heroic Tommies doing a beastly but necessary job. Cecil Mercer, a second lieutenant in the County of London Yeomanry, wrote weekly tales of derring-do until his regiment left for Egypt in March 1915; he survived and, as Dornford Yates, became one of the best-known writers of the inter-war years. From January 1915 Captain H. C. McNeile's stories of life at the front began to appear in the Northcliffe press. As serving officers were forbidden to publish under their own names, Northcliffe gave McNeile – a Royal Engineer – the sobriquet of 'Sapper'. McNeile knew his stuff: he had reached France with the BEF in November 1914, fought in the First and Second Battles of Ypres and on the Somme, and after participating in the great advance of September 1918 finished the war as a lieutenant colonel with a Military Cross and several mentions in dispatches: he had spent thirty-two months of the war in France, and said he started to write out of boredom. Well before the end of the conflict he was a household name, or nickname, his short story collection *The Lieutenant and Others* having sold 139,000 copies in less than two years. He later created Bulldog Drummond.

A cultural and recreational life continued, with concerts, the theatre, the cinema – mainly newsreels and American silent films – and new literary works. The theatre offered predominantly hack-written plays or musicals on patriotic themes, such as *England Expects* by Seymour Hicks, one of the more celebrated actors of the era (who would win a *croix de guerre* by taking his touring company to France to cheer up the troops) and Edward Knoblock. *England Expects* included the song 'We don't want to lose you, but we think you ought to go', and during the interval featured Horatio Bottomley, in front of a Union flag, orating about the wickedness of the Hun, and urging young men not in uniform to join up; at most performances some enlisted immediately.

For others, though, adaptation to the national mood proved difficult or impossible. Pre-war playwrights such as Galsworthy and Shaw wrote less than before, Shaw having continual trouble with the censor in wanting to make comments about the war and Ireland that were deemed unacceptable. Pinero passed out of fashion, his work representing, like Elgar's, an idea of an age that, after just months of war, was seen to have gone for ever. Elgar joined the special constabulary, but became so depressed by the war that he produced very little during it: incidental music to a play, *The Starlight Express*, and a ballet, *The Sanguine Fan*, were far from his most inspired works. *The Spirit of England*, settings of three poems by Binyon that when he began to write the work in 1915 were very much in keeping with the mood, already jarred when finished in 1917. In May 1916, in the first of a series of charity concerts for the Red Cross, its opening two movements were performed at the Queen's Hall, the first a setting of Binyon's 'For the Fallen', performed in the presence of the King and Queen. His creative drought was unfortunately timed, as patriotic impresarios were programming more and more British music in concerts. (Attempts to ban Wagner, Beethoven and Brahms failed dismally, proving that quality prevails in most marketplaces.) As the war neared its end Elgar's creativity suddenly had an Indian summer, culminating in the Cello Concerto of 1919: but it was a blossoming that died almost as soon as it had started, with the death of Lady Elgar in 1920.

The war years nevertheless produced notable enduring creative works. While working for the Red Cross in Egypt E. M. Forster was writing, but did not publish until 1924, *A Passage to India*. Despite working for the Ministry of Information, directing propaganda towards France, Arnold Bennett completed his *Clayhanger* trilogy with *These Twain* in 1916, then wrote two war-related novels, *The Pretty Lady* and *The Roll Call*, both published in 1918; a novel based on his wartime experiences in Whitehall, *Lord Raingo*, would not come out until 1926. His friend Wells also continued to produce novels despite later on being engaged in propaganda work, three of which dealt directly with the effects of war and urged hope: *Mr Britling Sees it Through, Joan and Peter* and *The Soul of a Bishop*. Hueffer, shortly before joining up in 1915, published *The Good Soldier*; Virginia Woolf, in exile at Richmond-on-Thames, published only *The Voyage Out* during the war, mostly written between 1910 and 1912: but it did launch her reputation as a novelist.

Painting was a rare art form – unlike musical composition, literary novel-writing, drama or architecture (the latter nearly non-existent because of manpower shortages), but like poetry – that did not greatly decline during the hostilities. London hosted numerous exhibitions throughout the war, albeit of more conventional art, and often depicting the conflict. The creative focus was increasingly war-related; at the Royal Academy Exhibition at the end of April, the most remarked-upon work was Richard Jack's magnificent *The Return to the Front*, which *The Times* described as 'a picture of Victoria Station crowded with khaki-clad warriors . . . [it] has about it something of the real thing.'[24] The newspaper hoped that 'Britain might thus become possessed of worthy memorials of the greatest epoch in the country's history, and a true Renaissance of Art might be brought about under the stress of a noble and all-pervading emotion.' Again, it was a means to assert moral superiority over the Hun.

Initially, war presented some artists with an opportunity to break with rules that they felt confined them, and go off in a wildly unpredictable direction. Indeed, this had begun towards the end of peace. Vorticism, a branch of modernism rooted in cubism and its geometric effects on design, but also applied metaphorically to the written word, had raised its head with the publication in June 1914 of the Vorticist magazine *Blast*, edited by Wyndham Lewis, who had trained at the Slade but had acquired most of his artistic influences in Paris. It rejected everything traditional about English art and culture. *Blast*'s second and final issue appeared in July 1915, following the opening on 10 June of the Vorticist exhibition at the Doré gallery in London.

Blast certainly influenced the radical changes in graphic design after the war and for some decades beyond: but its attempt to have art exceed life was rapidly and comprehensively challenged by life's ability to exceed art: nothing the Vorticists could do could shock so much as what was really happening in the war; and so even Vorticism found itself trumped and surpassed. In any case, most aesthetes had more on their mind in the summer of 1915 than a desire to explore and champion this self-conscious foray into cultural radicalism. Lewis himself became an artillery officer and, in December 1917, an official war artist.

Where innovation did thrive it often ignored the war altogether. In late September 1915 Methuen published Lawrence's *The Rainbow*. It upset reviewers, who were annoyed by its sexual content, especially by Ursula Brangwen's lesbian relationship with her teacher, Winifred, in whose arms Lawrence describes her as lying, 'her forehead against the beloved, maddening breast.'[25] Such talk interested the Director of Public Prosecutions, who had the police seize the publisher's entire stock of the book and charged Methuen under the 1857 Obscene Publications Act. On 13 November *The Rainbow* was banned, Methuen apologised and 1,011 copies were burnt. It would be more than a decade before it was again available in Britain. Two days later Lawrence sent the manuscript of the novel to Lady Ottoline Morrell: 'If you don't want it you can have it burnt, otherwise it might lie at Garsington till it is worth the selling. I don't want to see it any more.'[26] He thought about emigrating to Florida, but was denied the necessary official permission. Instead, he contented himself with going to his sister's in Derbyshire when not slumming it at Garsington and discussing human relations with Bertrand Russell, who was camping at Garsington while T. S. Eliot, a former pupil, and his wife stayed in his London flat. Lady Ottoline's reward for sheltering the Lawrences would be his parody of her as the ghastly Hermione Roddice in *Women in Love*, which he began to formulate that winter.

Gustav Holst, as a composer an artist in a very different medium, had been rejected for service because of poor health, and carried on teaching at St Paul's Girls' School and writing music. Some of this seems to ignore the war altogether: his *Nunc Dimittis* was first performed at Easter 1915. He remained the eclectic artist he had always been: his fascination with the Orient prompted his *Japanese Suite*, also written at the suggestion of

Michio Ito, a Japanese dancer then performing at the Coliseum in London. Japanese culture was very much in vogue; Holst sat in the dancer's dressing room one afternoon while he whistled Japanese folk tunes to him, and Holst noted them down. These works were written while he was composing *The Planets*, partly an exercise in bitonality, which took him the best part of two years, and the *Japanese Suite* became the first of Holst's works performed at a Promenade concert. Holst, once he had finished *The Planets* – which for another two years remained unperformed – embarked upon the *Hymn of Jesus*, and in 1916 began a Whitsuntide music festival in Thaxted in Essex, where he had rented a cottage since 1913, under the patronage of its socialist vicar, Conrad Noel. It would be ironic that later, because he needed the money, Holst – the least jingoistic or nationalistic of men – allowed the big tune from *Jupiter* in his *Planets* suite to be used for 'I Vow to thee my Country'.

Other than Holst, the only British composer of note whose rate of output seemed unaffected by war was Frank Bridge. He had a post-war reputation as an aggressive pacifist – he inspired his pupil Benjamin Britten to be a conscientious objector in Hitler's war – but for the duration wrote works inspired by the conflict, including one he dedicated to a little girl lost on the *Lusitania*; and another, magnificent setting of Brooke's third war sonnet, 'The Dead'. Bridge, like Holst, was not a rich man, and perceived the necessity of producing works that would be performed precisely because they caught the public mood. Cyril Rootham, the director of music at St John's College, Cambridge, set Binyon's 'For the Fallen' before Elgar did, and set it superbly. This resurgence of culture continued with five of Sir Hubert Parry's *Songs of Farewell* having their first performance at the Royal College of Music on 22 May 1916, a work *The Times*'s critic accurately described as 'one of the most impressive short choral works which have been written in recent years.'[27] What linked all these works was a tone of sorrow and regret rather than of patriotic celebration.

On 10 March 1916 Parry made the laconic entry in his diary: 'Wet and very cold. Wrote a tune for some words of Blake Bridges sent me.'[28] The words of Blake were his poem 'And did those feet in ancient time'. Bridges was Robert Bridges, the poet laureate. Sequestered with his piano in his house in Kensington Square, Parry wrote, on that bleak morning between breakfast and a luncheon engagement at the Royal College of Music, where he had been director since 1895, what we now call 'Jerusalem'. Of all the permanent cultural imprints left by the Great War, this work of a few hours, drawing on a lifetime of thought and skill as a composer, was through its combination of majesty, beauty and simplicity one of the most significant.

Bridges wanted Parry to set the words as a song for the Fight for Right movement, one of many patriotic groups set up since August 1914. Indeed, so many had been spawned (by love of country, but also out of spasms of Hun-hating) that a Central Committee for National Patriotic Organisations had been formed to coordinate their activities: Asquith was its president and Balfour and Rosebery vice presidents. The Central Committee's aims were to create 'such an abiding foundation of reasoned knowledge among all classes by emphasising the righteousness, the necessity and the life and death character of the struggle, as shall sustain the wills and sacrifices of the British people through the blackest days of weariness and discouragement.'[29]

Fight for Right was founded in August 1915 by Sir Francis Younghusband, an explorer and former army officer. Bryce, who had exposed the wickedness of the Hun in his report on the Belgian atrocities, became president. Among the vice presidents were Thomas Hardy, Elgar, Bridges and Parry himself. It drew heavily on cultural figures associated with Wellington House's efforts to promote Britain's cause. Another vice president was Gilbert Murray, a liberal intellectual who had agonised about supporting the war – his pamphlet *How Can War Ever Be Right?* had paraded his agonies in public. Other prominent supporters included Newbolt, for whom the distinction between poetry and propaganda had disappeared, and Mrs Fawcett, the suffragist leader.[30] Parry, a liberal of Murray's stamp and no rabid nationalist, became disenchanted with Fight for Right's direction, as it descended into rabid jingoism. He withdrew his immortal tune from the group's use, offering it instead to the women's suffrage movement; and when they had no further need of it, the song passed to a group whose attitude to the war was far more to Sir Hubert's taste, the Women's Institute.

If such men as Parry rejected what they felt to be the extremist tone of Fight for Right, they nevertheless remained determined to fight to the death to defeat Germany and her allies. So powerful a case had the government made to the public for Britain's declaration of war on Germany that there was very little opposition to it. Few would contemplate a negotiated settlement unless it compelled Germany to surrender all territorial gains made since August 1914. As late as 23 February 1916, when the military situation seemed hopelessly deadlocked, the House of Commons rejected the assertion of Snowden, the ardent Labour pacifist, that ordinary Germans desired peace. Asquith said his own terms had not changed since August 1914: the evacuation of Belgium and northern France, the security of France and Serbia, and the destruction of Prussian militarism. That the war would go on until those terms were met had the general agreement of Parliament and the public, though the debate about how best to wage it had hardly begun.

III

'Jerusalem's' appeal rests not least in how it articulates the patriotism, and love of an ideal of Christian England, that so many people felt during the war. The importance of sacrifice for a higher ideal had become a common value. Such an attitude helps explain why, although there was a fierce debate about the need for conscription, most people came to accept that it would be necessary if Britain were to prevail. While the public had a brief diversion from the war in following the trial of George Joseph Smith, the 'Brides in the Bath' murderer – sentenced to death on 1 July after the jury retired for just eighteen minutes – the government was, with little resistance, taking ever more control of their lives, far at odds from the liberalism practised during peacetime. It launched a massive campaign for thrift, in the hope that the public – rich and not-so-rich alike – would subscribe to the new issue of War Bonds to help finance the conflict. For the well-to-do, bonds came in multiples of £5, and the less well-off had vouchers for 5s a time. Children collected pennies, contributed to funds providing care for repatriated wounded soldiers. Money also flowed in from men in the trenches.

Democracy was a casualty of the war. The Elections and Registrations Act postponed local elections for a year, but was later renewed until 1919; and there would be many postponements of the general election due by December 1915. The government introduced geographically restricted areas where the state would for the duration control the supply and sale of alcohol: much of Bristol, Newhaven, north-west Kent and South Wales were affected, but also an area within a 6-mile radius of the centre of Southampton, a 10-mile radius of Barrow-in-Furness and Newcastle-upon-Tyne and much of the north-east. Liverpool and Merseyside were similarly restricted. Control of drink on the Clyde was delayed pending further consultations, because of the febrile atmosphere there. When the first restrictions were introduced – in Newhaven – drink could be sold for just four and a half hours a day on weekdays and four hours on Sundays.

As so often since the birth of a popular press, the public's mind was conditioned and influenced by the roar of newspaper editorials: the Northcliffe press in particular preached that sacrifice – whether of life, personal wealth or time – was essential for victory. Northcliffe's new campaign was for conscription, and the *Morning Post*, owned by Lady Bathurst, also took up the call. Northcliffe remained pungent about Asquith and Kitchener, telling Riddell the war would last 'for years' and he despaired of its current direction. He had a shred of optimism: 'Someone will turn up. The war will disclose a genius.'[31] The act of genius, or leadership, that he now thought indispensable was to fill the Army with every possible man the country could find.

Parts of the labour movement and a hard core of Liberals disagreed with Northcliffe's view about a commitment to what would come to be known as 'total war'. However, the tide was turning in favour of compulsion, and military conscription was not all that was being considered; Churchill used much of his first days out of the Admiralty to draw up a memorandum on national war service, by which workers could be requisitioned to do whatever the war effort required. Esher, who for a grandee of considerable grandeur was deeply conscious of public feeling, noted in his diary on 24 June: 'Last month, we lost 74,000 men when only fighting on a mile or so of front. What are our losses going to be when we make a really big attack?'[32] Clearly thinking along similar lines, the Independent Labour Party formally announced its opposition to conscription, indicating that an attempt to bring in compulsion would be actively resisted by organised labour. The ILP maintained that 'patriotic' men were serving their country in industry and should not be 'pressganged' into the Army. It claimed some workers were being forced out of their jobs by their employers and made to join up, turning the process into one of 'class oppression'.[33] A group of Liberal intellectuals was already massing against conscription: 'What right has the state to enslave men and ship them to unknown destinations to be slaughtered?' Hirst asked Scott.[34]

Fear of compulsion began to underpin industrial unrest, or the threat of it, even in jobs so essential to the nation's future that the chances of men being conscripted were minuscule – such as in the South Wales coalfield, which supplied coal to the Navy and to the munitions industry. The Miners' Federation of Great Britain insisted its members would not be brought under the industrial regulations the munitions minister had thrashed out with other trades, as central control would lessen the federation's power. Some of the most radical union officials – not usually found in the higher reaches of the MFGB, hence their relative conservatism – were influenced by the type of syndicalism that had predominated in France before the war, and which the most extreme socialists saw as a means of mobilising the unions for revolution. By early July it was believed a stoppage in the coalfields was imminent. Runciman, as president of the Board of Trade charged with preventing this, had been told by Asquith not to go to Cardiff to referee a fight between masters and men, because ministers were wasting too much time dealing with disputes. However, so nervous were coal-owners of falling foul of the government that they had placed the negotiations entirely in its hands. The South Wales dispute was settled by a narrow vote on 30 June, but nationally miners wanted an agreement for higher wages if they were to increase output; some South Wales miners did not return to work.

Riddell arranged for Runciman to meet the miners' leaders privately in London on 6 July, and a meeting of 2,000 miners' delegates from all over Britain was scheduled for the following day, before the agreement to hold it broke down. On 12 July South Wales rejected Runciman's latest proposals and threatened to strike from the 15th: they demanded a minimum wage of 5s 6d a day, whereas Runciman would promise only that all surfacemen earning less than 3s 4d a day would be raised to that rate. The government declared the strike illegal under the Munitions of War Act, and warned strikers they could be fined £5 a day. The MFGB recommended the men stay at work and persist in negotiations. Undeterred, Scottish miners demanded a 25 per cent increase.

Labour politicians were reluctant to support the miners; Snowden described the idea of striking with a war on as 'unthinkable'.[35] The great meeting of MFGB delegates was rescheduled for 21 July. Robert Smillie, the MFGB president, feared the government would use the Scottish unrest as an excuse to take an even heavier hand. In the event nearly 200,000 South Wales miners went out on strike, claiming the owners would stockpile coal and use it when the war ended to bring down its price and, therefore, miners' wages. A general munitions tribunal was established to consider offences under the Act, but stayed its hand while discussions continued behind the scenes: the miners, using Riddell as a conduit, asked him to convey their terms to Runciman. Many miners became agitated by how the action of the most militant was harming the reputation of all colliery workers: one South Wales agent said that 'we shall have the whole world against us, excepting Germany, Austria and Turkey.'[36]

The militants were listening to no one, least of all their supposed leaders, and this recklessness caused grave concern to the government. It was bad enough that this one important region had walked out; but ministers realised they could not give in, or there was a serious risk that the problem would become national. On 19 July Lloyd George, Runciman and Henderson went to Cardiff to meet the strikers. The newspapers highlighted reports of French disgust and German amusement at the miners' action. The ministers talked into the night with the miners' leaders: and then put out a statement confirming that 'no government responsible for a colossal war of this nature could possibly allow a continuance of a conflict between capital and labour to imperil the chances of victory.'[37]

A day of talks on 20 July resolved the strike, with a compromise offered by Lloyd George. He played the miners like the proverbial violin, congratulating 'my fellow countrymen' on their good sense when he spoke at Cardiff to mark the settlement.[38] He assiduously briefed the press to ensure the credit went entirely to him: it was reported that his tough talking to the miners about the catastrophe they could unleash made them see reason. He was said to have been hard-line with the owners too. In fact, the terms the miners accepted were those Runciman had offered three weeks earlier: the two variations were a promise of immunity for strikers, and an additional 10 per cent was found for the miners. The agreement would remain in force for six months after the war.

The other, and perhaps more important, factor in the settlement was how unpopular the syndicalist agitation was with rank-and-file miners, who had disliked being accused of treason. However, there would be many more disputes in vital industries, usually triggered by the belief that proprietors were reaping unfair profits because of the emergency, and their employees wanted a share. Increases in excess-profits taxes would answer that complaint, though never entirely. As soon as the strike was settled, the King left Windsor for a national tour of munitions factories: but by the end of August unrest had broken out again in the

Rhondda; and matters became so tense between coal-owners in the north-east and miners over an 11 per cent war bonus that Asquith had to convene a meeting in Downing Street between the two parties to find common ground. Meanwhile Lloyd George, the lustre taken off his reputation as a miracle-worker, was sent back to Cardiff with Runciman to try again. Unrest remained widespread in South Wales until September. Although Lloyd George had oversold the 'deal' earlier in the summer, he and Runciman continued to try to soothe the miners. A meeting on 31 August had suggested paying a bonus to a wider group of workers, something the owners found unacceptable; after a few more hours of negotiations they gave in and paid what was asked.

Amid the industrial discontent, the pressure on Asquith over conscription had been mounting since the spring: as long ago as 21 May *The Times* had published a letter from a Major Richardson in which he complained of the sight that met him when he had returned from active service after having seen 'the mangled mass of humanity after Ypres': 'I came across scores of lusty, able-bodied young men walking about in smug complacency, utterly callous and indifferent to the anguish of their brothers, so long as they got their war bonus.'[39]

Asquith was pressed in the Commons on 7 June about the need for a programme of 'compulsory military training for all healthy young men in Great Britain who are not required for other Government work'. Conscious of having to keep his party behind him, he denied there was such a requirement; which put him at odds with what Lloyd George had said in Manchester about the importance of everyone manning the pumps when a house was burning down. Asquith's questioner, Major Rowland Hunt, then asked: 'Is the Rt Hon gentleman aware that the people are tired of waiting for action to be taken to make those who will not volunteer do their share?'[40] Yet it was not just 'shirkers' who were at fault; bad central organisation, and tales of volunteers hanging around waiting to be properly trained, continued to deter men in some districts from enlisting. The MP for Mansfield, Sir Arthur Markham, told Asquith that when Britain needed all the coal it could get, 'there are many miners withdrawn from their work in Nottinghamshire, Yorkshire, and Derbyshire nine months ago who have not yet got rifles'.[41]

The same day, *The Times* had noted that the casualty list that morning – 80 officers and 5,500 men, bringing the total for the week to nearly 900 officers and 20,000 men killed, wounded or missing – was 'surely sufficient to take away the scales from the sleepiest eyes.'[42] Worse, 'these losses, it should be borne in mind, have not been suffered in a great action which would bring us appreciably nearer to the termination of the struggle. They represent the ordinary wastage of war as it is now being prosecuted'. The paper feared the toll had been so high because of inadequate supplies of munitions; another reason to ensure the 'mobil-isation' of the whole community, as Lloyd George had suggested. It was as well the public was becoming used to such appalling losses, because the logic of the argument was false: tactical mistakes by generals, rather than a lack of munitions, were exacting an ever greater toll. However, *The Times* did identify the inextricable link between compulsion and industrial conscription. The more men who were put under arms from vital industries, the more women or underage boys were needed to take their places.

On 5 July Asquith, Balfour, Kitchener and Crewe went to Calais to meet Joffre. Kitchener, in a private meeting with Joffre beforehand, had again committed Britain to put seventy divisions in the field. With the war at stalemate, much of the pre-war professional Army killed or wounded, and the first of Kitchener's army in the trenches and being killed, it was unlikely these divisions could be raised without conscrip-tion. Lloyd George, increasingly allied with the Tories, was breaking from his party's traditional position, irritating colleagues as a conse-quence. A Commons speech on 1 July in which he attacked von Donop annoyed Asquith, who sensed a conspiracy. He told Crewe, one of his most trusted colleagues, that 'Lloyd George's attitude . . . was quite inex-cusable. Some of our colleagues go so far as to think that the whole thing was a put-up job, to which he was party. He assured me yesterday morn-ing that this was not the case. Even so, his conduct was very bad.'[43] The relationship between prime minister and munitions minister was breaking down. Asquith's task would be made even harder by his wife, who became a figurehead of the anti-conscription campaign, to the annoy-ance of the Unionists.

Carson and Derby also spoke in the Commons that day, arguing that if the latest appeal for volunteers failed the government should bring in compulsory service. Derby was at odds with the War Office over two matters: he told Kitchener on 2 July that 'this new order which forces recruits for the Territorials to sign to say they are willing when enlisted to transfer to any other Regiment has simply murdered recruiting in this district.'[44] Three days later Derby complained that the erratic payment of separation allowances meant 'recruiting is dead as far as this part of the world is concerned.'[45] That informed his remarks on 9 July: 'They would come only when they are fetched,' he had told the War Office.

With opposition from a few Liberal and Labour MPs, the National Registration Bill went through the Commons, designed to compel all adult men and women between the ages of fifteen and sixty-five to declare themselves, their ages and occupations to the government, so the authorities could be aware of them for deployment on essential war work. Kitchener admitted that the register would be useful should such a measure be introduced. Mrs Pankhurst addressed a public meeting in London on 1 July about her visits to munitions factories in France, where women were heavily employed; she wanted the same in Britain. Again, registration would identify such women. She was supported by Clara Butt, the nation's leading contralto, who opened the meeting with a rendition of 'God Save the King' and whose reputation came to rest on her charitable public performances during in the war, and her legendary and inimitable 1911 recording of Elgar's 'Land of Hope and Glory'.

On 17 July Mrs Pankhurst led 30,000 women down Whitehall to the Ministry of Munitions, demanding the right to serve. Lloyd George received Mrs Pankhurst and a deputation, and she told him: 'The women in this procession today have taken part in it because they wished to demonstrate their desire to serve in any and every capacity in which they may be of use.'[46] She emphasised that where a woman was doing the same job as previously done by a man, she should be paid his rate; Lloyd George, delighted she should be singing his tune, assured her that women would not be exploited. He then went outside to Whitehall Gardens and addressed the rest of the demonstration, saying that while women could not expect equal pay while they were being trained and producing less than skilled workers, 'there should be a fixed minimum, and we should not utilize the services of women to get cheaper labour.'

These were impressive sentiments, but since the Munitions of War Act imposed the regulation of wages to prevent unions from strong-arming employers into paying them more, a whole new regulatory system would have to be devised, leading eventually to a new Act. He promised the unions that war work was for the duration, would end when the war ended, and no man need fear losing his job. The women seized the National Register, to be compiled four weeks later, as an opportunity to identify those who wished to serve. Inevitably, a woman heckled Lloyd George with 'what about the vote?' He replied: 'We will get her into the shell factory first.'[47] Lloyd George had no doubt about the importance of mobilising an army of women workers. In late June the War Office had asked for the arms to equip an army of seventy rather than fifty divisions; wishing to be ahead of demand, Lloyd George planned to increase output to a point where one hundred divisions could be armed. For once, his rhetoric lived up to reality. In the war's first year around 400,000 women had transferred to industry; in the second a further 1.25 million were recruited.

Soon 200,000 women were working in government departments, 500,000 took over clerical jobs, 250,000 were on the land and, most crucially, by the summer of 1916 there were 800,000 in engineering. Over 400,000 of them left domestic service.[48] More were training as doctors, and appeals were made for others to join them. Women also worked as temporary labour to give overworked munitions workers (some of whom routinely put in seventy to a hundred hours a week) a break; and females of all classes volunteered wherever possible. The sudden ubiquity of women workers where they had previously been absent brought the occasional difficulty; when a shopkeeper took a fancy to a fourteen-year-old messenger girl who delivered a parcel to his shop and kissed her several times – he claimed 'in a fatherly way' – the Bow Street magistrate fined him £3 with 10s costs. 'In these days, when girls were so much used in place of men, it was important that they should be protected against conduct of this sort,' the magistrate said.[49] On 16 June 1915 the Women's Institute (which had originated in Canada in 1897) was founded in Britain, its first meeting being held in Charlton, West Sussex, on 9 November: its main aim was to galvanise the gentle sex in the war effort and especially in the production of food.

Women seized opportunities to help the country: and not just working-class ones who saw the war effort as an escape from drudgery or domestic service. Among those enrolled at the Vickers factory in Erith in August 1915 were Lady Colebrooke and Lady Gertrude Crawford, who had both trained as master turners, and Lady Gatacre and Mrs England, Lord Loreburn's sister. Miss Vickers, daughter of the proprietor, was enlisting in the next batch of trainees; and Lady Scott, widow of the hero of the Antarctic, was working in the electrical department, 'where her deftness, acquired in her art as sculptor, allows her to do work requiring great delicacy of touch.'[50] Cynicism about what women might do was, however, rife: the Revd Andrew Clark, the rector of Great Leighs, heard from someone familiar with Woolwich Arsenal that 'they have never handled a tool and can do nothing' and 'they crack up within a week.'[51] Even those gentlewomen working in canteens attracted criticism, as men 'hate being served by young ladies, whom they are shy of', and preferred 'a motherly working woman.'

As fears grew of a smaller harvest than in 1914, there was a ridiculous struggle to persuade farmers to use the army of female volunteers who had offered to do agricultural work. Rider Haggard, who advocated training colleges to school women in the 'lighter branches' of agricultural work, voiced the prevailing view: 'I most earnestly trust that, save in very exceptional instances, no attempt will be made to use them for its heavier operations, with which Nature has not fitted them to cope. Even a Zulu woman could scarcely face a week's ploughing with heavy horses on heavy land, and to impose such tasks on English girls who are not bred to it must, in my opinion, lead to failure and often to the wrecking of their health.'[52]

Following the passage of the National Registration Act, compelling every adult to register on 15 August, 25 million forms were distributed. Each respondent had to cite his or her age, occupation, skills and marital status, to help the government deploy each worker to maximum effect. Some Liberal MPs felt it an unpalatable intrusion into the privacy of the public, and gave warning of the resistance that would be mobilised against conscription. A committee under Long deliberated on how to use this information. In October a Reserved Occupations Committee decided that 1.5 million of the 6 million men of military age were in jobs vital to the war effort.

The cabinet was divided roughly between Unionists and Liberals on compulsion, and the nature of cabinet decision-making – or lack of it – was a matter of increasing concern. Leo Amery had 'tea and a real heart to heart talk with Carson' on 21 July. 'He is very depressed about the hopelessness of the present system of governing by 22 gabblers round a table with an old procrastinator in the chair.'[53] A week later one of Asquith's own MPs and a former whip, Freddie Guest – Churchill's cousin and ADC to French – came to the Commons on leave and initiated an adjournment debate on conscription. Guest, who would become the ringleader of pro-conscription MPs, claimed he did not seek to embarrass the government, but felt it was time to give the issue a proper parliamentary 'ventilation'.[54] He proceeded subtly, reassuring the government that many lifelong opponents of conscription had changed their minds, and there would be substantial support for the policy. The question was now one of 'urgency', given that the Allies needed 'to win and to win quickly'.[55] He said the failure of more men to do their 'fair share' was corrosive of the morale of volunteers.[56] He also argued that skilled men had volunteered by claiming they were casual labourers, to the overall detriment of the war effort. He had numerous supporters in the House, such as Major Rowland Hunt, who said that his opponents' 'idea of individual liberty is liberty for a man to get somebody else to fight for him.'[57] Others stuck to the view that conscription was profoundly un-British, and appallingly Prussian. Yet the unpleasant realities of war were growing: between 9 August and 13 September there were frequent Zeppelin raids on the east coast, mainly on Kent, Essex, and on London, but as far north as Yorkshire and as far south as East Sussex, most of them inflicting deaths and injuries. The public avoided panic, but there was growing irritation that the bombers kept getting through. To stop them, more effort and sacrifice would be required.

Curzon, frustrated and under-employed since joining the cabinet in May, and an advocate of conscription since long before the war, wrote to Asquith in early August to warn him 'that before very long I – if no other – must bring up the question of compulsory service and seek a decision from the Cabinet'.[58] He added that his, and certain colleagues', positions might become 'intolerable' otherwise. Lansdowne, independently, wrote a similar letter. Asquith set up a cabinet committee on the question, but his handling of it showed why his coalition was doomed. He did not even consult Law, let alone put him on the committee. Law was outraged and complained to Asquith, who made matters worse by saying he had put Law's name on the list, but following a consultation with Curzon they had agreed to remove Law (and Simon) as they had heavy departmental responsibilities. Fed up with Asquith's disregard of him, Law flatly refused an invitation to serve that was issued when he complained about his treatment. The cabinet finally had a proper discussion about compulsion on 11 August, only for Asquith to adjourn it in mid-stream as 'it was already late for lunch.'[59]

Then Lloyd George brought up the inevitability of conscription at a meeting of the War Policy Committee on 18 August, just as the

Northcliffe press was opening a new front on compulsion: that morning *The Times* had run a leading article entitled 'The Case for National Service', in which it had argued that although Britain had industrial, commercial and financial obligations that drew on its manpower, 'the principle of universal liability to military service is the only rational basis upon which we can organise and co-ordinate, without waste and dissipation, our whole effort both military and economic.'⁶⁰ The King feared the issue might divide the country; he summoned Asquith, Balfour, Grey and Kitchener to Buckingham Palace to discuss it for two hours. Churchill wanted unlimited recruiting, which Grey called 'madness'.⁶¹ The foreign secretary pointed out a striking paradox: 'The Germans carefully exempt from military service the people necessary to carry on the life of the country: if they had not done so they would have had a break down by now. We on the other hand recruit without regard to the trades necessary to keep the country alive & even to supply military and naval needs.' The Northcliffe papers returned to the subject almost daily, and took Asquith's refusal to act on their advice as proof that 'there has been the same lack of forethought and leadership in the new cabinet as in the old.'⁶² Northcliffe's campaign ignored the fact that many of the fittest men of military age were engaged in work of national importance in mines, skilled engineering or munitions, and women could practically only replace them in the last of those. After a cabinet meeting in mid-August at which Curzon brought the matter up, Asquith, after listening to a debate on the question, observed that 'I have listened to a lot of very unsound talk,' which prompted Lloyd George to say, in sarcastic tones, 'then I suppose there is nothing for us to do but apologise.'⁶³

The question was now driving a wedge between the two leading men in the government, and splitting the Liberal Party. Balfour took Asquith's side, but whether he would defy Curzon and Smith, who had become Solicitor General in the coalition ministry, was doubtful. (For all Smith's enthusiasm for conscription, he had not enjoyed his time in uniform, and had been delighted to extricate himself from it as soon as possible.)

Asquith appeared increasingly isolated, and his wife realised the danger this put him in: or, rather, what she called 'this panic-stricken agitation for Conscription'.⁶⁴ There was an equally panic-stricken opposition to it: Derby, second only to Kitchener as a figurehead of the recruiting campaign and who from October would lend his name to the scheme to register men as willing to fight, believed that 'a lot of Trades Union people are dead against it and it might, though I do not say it would, end in a big general strike.[65] However, despite such warnings, Lloyd George told Riddell that he needed 120,000 skilled munitions workers back from the Army, and conscription of other men to replace them was the only means to achieve this.[66] Unfortunately for Asquith, the press and his colleagues were sympathetic to Lloyd George's case, and moving in favour of compulsion. On 16 August the *Daily Mail* called for conscription, and printed a form demanding that its readers cut it out, fill it in and post it to the government. Writing after the war, Churchill observed that the credit Northcliffe received for bringing down the Liberal government went to his head. 'Armed with the solemn prestige of *The Times* in one hand and the ubiquity of the *Daily Mail* in the other, he aspired to exercise a commanding influence upon events. The inherent instability . . . of the first Coalition Government offered favourable conditions for the advancement of these claims. The recurring crises on the subject of conscription presented numerous occasions for their assertion.[67]

In a private letter of 18 August about conscription, Gwynne, leading his own campaign in the *Morning Post*, told Asquith that 'the vast majority in this country are in favour of compulsory service being enforced at once; and I go further, and say that 95% of your Cabinet are in favour of it and that 85% of the House of Commons wish to see it carried now.'[68] By this time Gwynne was conspiring with Lloyd George and Sir Henry Wilson, seeking to bring Kitchener out against Asquith. On 24 August Kitchener, questioned by the War Policy Committee under Crewe, said he recognised that raising his seventy divisions would be impossible under voluntary means, and that he would ask for a Conscription Bill by the end of the year. Once Kitchener wanted conscription, its opponents were facing defeat. The prime minister was being cornered, and his concept of liberalism – attacked in the Northcliffe press as unserviceable in a national emergency – rendered obsolete.

IV

Although the German guns were devouring men, and those men had to be replaced, a balance needed to be struck in order to preserve those who had the skills essential to strategically vital industries. War production remained inadequate: Lloyd George told Scott on 3 September that Germany was producing 320,000 shells a week and Britain 30,000. He said

25,000 munitions workers had enlisted since May, further retarding output. Nonetheless, he told Scott that military compulsion was inevitable within three months, and he wanted it now: the only danger was introducing it too late, given the time it took to train men.[69] Such compulsion would, however, raise the issue of compelling those ineligible for call-up to work in munitions. Asquith remained opposed to military compulsion, but would go wherever the cabinet went: the cabinet was still divided, with Simon, McKenna, Runciman and Henderson the most strongly opposed. Henderson, however, believed that if the cabinet unanimously supported military conscription, and Kitchener recommended it, British working men would accept it.

Lloyd George said that, to keep organised labour happy, men would have to be recruited in drafts: 'If it were a question of calling up two million men at one time there might be danger, but not if they were called up only 30,000 or so at a time,' he told Scott. He suggested this might be done by ballot, but Scott advised him – and he agreed – that it would be better to call up unmarried men first, then men below a certain age. Local committees would have to ensure key industries were not being denuded of key workers, and no younger son from a family where his elder brothers had already enlisted should be forced to go.

This new turn to the conscription debate soured relations between Asquith and Lloyd George. The first the prime minister had heard of the munitions minister getting up a campaign for conscription was when Law told him about it. On the Unionist side Curzon – whom Simon described as 'the brazen pot among the earthen vessels' – remained the main agitator for conscription, not least as a means of presenting his credentials as the next leader of his party, who almost to a man echoed the public's widespread belief in the ubiquity of 'slackers'.[70] On 5 September Lloyd George asked Scott to Sunday lunch with him at Walton Heath, and told him that if he were defeated on compulsion – which he saw as 'practically our only chance of winning the war' – he would 'decline to be further responsible for the war', even though that would probably precipitate the fall of the government and the fracture of the Liberal Party.[71] Two days earlier Esher had written: 'The Government lacks courage and unity. Lloyd George, who might render such great service, is unfortunately a *Girondin* [a faction in the French revolution that campaigned to end the monarchy, and were themselves mostly executed] by temperament – a rhetorician of the first quality, but lacking in courage.

Robert Smillie [the president of the MFGB] and Ramsay MacDonald will one of these days have his head in a basket.'[72]

Lloyd George's tone allied him with the Unionists, who were becoming agitated by Asquith's style. Carson felt the cabinet useless – too many men, no agenda, and no way of ensuring that decisions, once taken, were acted upon. He asked Churchill whether there was any way of raising the question of a smaller, more decisive cabinet without it reflecting badly on Asquith, whose design the existing wartime body was: he said the cabinet should be 'vy small 5 or 6 sitting daily to consider the problems. Personally I look on all our Cabinet Meetings as useless & a waste of time & I earnestly wish I could humbly retire.'[73] Churchill agreed with him about the inefficiency with which the government was run.

Lloyd George now took his campaign for compulsion directly to the trades unions. On 9 September, two days after the Trades Union Congress at Bristol heavily passed resolutions against compulsion, he went to the city and addressed the TUC, seeking to confront some of the pre-war prejudices that threatened the drive for victory.[74] 'The German advance in Russia is a victory of German trade unionism,' he told them: now it was the turn of British trades unionists to rise to the challenge.[75] The state had set up sixteen arsenals and was building eleven more, but needed 80,000 skilled men and 200,000 unskilled ones to meet production targets. In case the workers thought the munitions industry was indecently enriching the owners of capital, Lloyd George said that 715 factories had become controlled establishments, which meant 95 per cent of their operatives were effectively working for businesses with profits regulated by the state. Union leaders, with a unanimous hatred of Prussian militarism, were generally cooperative: but too many of their members saw the war as an opportunity to advance the class struggle. Their stubbornness rendered 15 per cent of weapons-making capacity idle at night. By day, shop stewards told workers in several centres – he named Enfield, Woolwich and Coventry – to restrict their output. Woolwich had banned women from working at lathes.

He called for more skilled and unskilled workers of both sexes for munitions work, with trades unions abandoning remaining restrictive practices for the duration, a sacrifice comparable with their employers being heavily taxed on excess profits. He made a plea for skilled labour to help train unskilled. (However, away from the TUC – at the annual meeting of the British Association – it was reported there were many cases of fatigue caused by overwork in arms factories, leading either to accidents or low output.) Union leaders were delighted Lloyd George had exposed some of the practices of their members: he had sensibly stuck to the truth, and it would be easier for the leaders to bring the syndicalists into line. The munitions minister, posing as a man of working-class origins (which in truth he was not), also made a subtler point. 'After the war there will be things you can do, if you win the heart of the country, which you could not achieve in generations. The country will want a re-settlement and a reconstruction. It feels in its conscience that things are wrong, and it will want to do right. Don't put the country against organised labour.'[76] Mrs Webb, who was present and who reflected to an extent the feelings of the rank and file of the labour movement, felt the speech 'left a bad impression, it lacked sincerity: he told obvious little lies, and his tale of working-class slackness and drink was much resented . . . here and there men were boiling over with anger at his prevarications.' She also felt Lloyd George 'looked exactly like a conjuror'. When Ernest Bevin, attending his first TUC on behalf of the dockers, asked the minister 'whether he did not think that the workmen in the skilled trades would alter their regulations with more confidence if they were given a share in management,' he had an 'evasive' answer.[77]

Even if Mrs Webb accurately reflected some suspicions about Lloyd George, other speeches at the TUC showed massive support for the war – a resolution justifying it was passed by 600 votes to 7. The Congress also unanimously passed a resolution proposed by the Federation of Women Workers to demand equal pay for equal work: it recognised at last that there could be such a thing as equal work. A week later, in a further attempt to command confidence among the labouring classes, Lloyd George told engineering workers the war would not be used as an excuse to wreck their power; and drafted in Henderson, who had arranged the meeting, as chairman of a Labour Supply Committee within the Ministry of Munitions to see both sides played by the agreed rules while drafting in semi-skilled and unskilled workers of both sexes to jobs hitherto done only by skilled men. This was known as 'dilution', and greatly assisted the supply of labour.

The main pocket of resistance to dilution, and to the Munitions of War Act, was on 'Red Clydeside'. The Left in Glasgow had launched a two-pronged attack on the authorities. First, the previous May the Glasgow Women's Housing Association, led by Mary Barbour, Mary Laird and Helen Crawfurd, had started a rent strike over conditions and over-crowding in Govan. As well as refusing to pay rent increases the strikers led violent demonstrations against evictions. Rent strikes spread across the city into the slums and by October 15,000 tenants were refusing to pay rents (20,000 by November). Workers then took action in sympathy with them. Unions threatened factory strikes, and one broke out in September 1915 at the Fairfield Shipyards in protest over the Act. In October, when female 'dilutees' were sent, with the agreement of Henderson's committee, into the highly skilled machine-tool workshops of John Lang at Johnstone, engineering unions threatened to strike. Resistance to dilution became a cornerstone of Red Clydeside, whose cadre of revolutionaries saw the policy as a superb opportunity to build support by engaging in militancy, whatever the cost to the country. The dispute continued until December, when Lloyd George realised he had no choice but personally to intervene.

Just before Christmas Lloyd George went to Glasgow to meet workers' leaders and to try to reduce the revolutionary temperature. It was regarded as the only place in Britain where those opposing the war could rely upon a sympathetic hearing. He had a flavour of the mood when he met David Kirkwood, a prominent local union leader, who told him the Munitions Act had 'the taint of slavery about it'.[78] On the morning of Christmas Day Lloyd George addressed 3,000 trades unionists at the St Andrew's Hall. In a preposterous gaffe, he had not by then found the time to meet local union bosses – many of whom were moderates compared with their followers – and so they boycotted the meeting. As a result, it was filled with hard leftists and their followers. Girl munition workers in khaki adorned the platform, deemed a red rag to the anti-dilutionist bull. A band played 'See the Conquering Hero Comes' when Lloyd George entered the stage, only to be drowned out by 'The Red Flag' from the audience. Matters descended into absurdity when, his luxuriant hair falling down over his forehead, the minister was heckled with yells of 'get your hair cut'.[79]

It was unquestionably brave of Lloyd George to confront these men, and it won him grudging respect in the union movement. But his speech ended with his being shouted down, despite attempts by Henderson, who was with him on the platform, to calm the meeting. The men were outraged that he had made no attempt to address their grievances, but had instead concentrated on what many appeared to consider the secondary matter of defeating Germany. On his return he told Miss Stevenson that the Clydesiders were 'ripe for revolution' and 'completely out of hand'.[80] He was hardly exaggerating: one of Red Clydeside's main agitators, John MacLean, would be nominated by Lenin as the prospective head of a British Soviet government and, pending that, would be appointed Bolshevik consul in Glasgow: he was eventually imprisoned for sedition.

Lloyd George's rough ride was barely mentioned in the censored, official reports. However, a local workers' paper, *Forward*, printed full details, including the heckles that mocked the minister – such as, when he claimed that the job of a minister in wartime was an unenviable one, a man shouting out 'the money's good!'[81] *Forward* was immediately suppressed and its machinery confiscated, a move regretted by the government almost as it was made. William Anderson, the MP for Sheffield Attercliffe, asked a junior War Office minister once Parliament returned after the Christmas recess 'whether it has become an offence and a crime in this country to give a truthful account of the reception accorded by organised labour in Glasgow to the Minister of Munitions', and whether this was 'the first fruits of conscription'.[82] Lloyd George was warned that if such practices continued it would do nothing to stop labour unrest: angered, he told the Commons that 'My hon Friends did not give me any notice of this question being raised. If they had I should have supplied myself with a copy of the paper, and could have shown the House that this paper has been deliberately inciting the workers there not to carry out an Act of Parliament which has been passed by this House in order to promote the output of munitions.'[83]

A new Clyde Workers' Committee paper, *The Worker*, duplicated the suppressed report. It confirmed Lloyd George's view that the Clydeside agitation had to be suppressed before it got out of hand. The CWC then played into the government's hands, by printing an article in only its fourth edition entitled 'Should the Workers Arm?' Enough was enough. On 1 February 1916 the *Worker*'s editor, Tom Bell, and its printer, John MacLean, were arrested for sedition. Asquith had already announced that resistance to dilution was sabotaging the war effort, and would have to stop. Commissioners were sent in to enforce dilution. Arrests of strike leaders, including Willie Gallacher, president of the CWC, when industrial action began soon brought most of the workers into line. A separate commission, under Lynden Macassey, a barrister and King's Counsel,

examined the Clydeside problem factory by factory, and by the following
August had successfully placed 14,000 women dilutees there. By then six
more union leaders had been prosecuted and deported out of the Glasgow area; 1916 recorded the lowest number of disputes since 1907.

Opposition to female workers went far beyond Clydeside. There
were still reports of difficulties getting in the harvest because of farmers'
reluctance to have women working in the fields, as they did in France and
Germany. Elsewhere, however, prejudices slowly began to disappear. In
August Edith Smith of Grantham had become the first female police
officer with full powers of arrest; and women who had been working in
Glasgow as bus and tram conductors on a provisional basis since April
had their positions formalised on 20 October. By the following May
1,200 female conductors in the city outnumbered 400 men.[84] The Metropolitan Police lifted its objection to women working on London buses
and trams. On 30 September – the day of the funeral of the arch-pacifist
Keir Hardie, who died from pneumonia in a Glasgow nursing home –
union leaders met ministers and agreed to support new measures of
voluntary recruitment, to include a special Labour Recruiting Campaign. The government continued to press employers to allow men to
enlist and hold their jobs open for them; and on 23 October it was
announced that women in munitions factories doing the same work as
men would receive the same pay.

There was public sympathy for demands by railway workers for a substantial pay rise to compensate for the higher cost of living. (An increased
war bonus was agreed, after weeks of negotiation, on 16 October, but
once the railwaymen won it, the clerks threatened industrial action.)
Being a railwayman was a reserved occupation, and it was hard for workers to volunteer so their families could benefit from separation allowances.
An announcement that the 'triple alliance' between the miners, railwaymen and dockers had been renewed rattled the government. Leaders of
the unions said no coordinated action was contemplated, but reserved the
right to do so – which would, as in 1910–11, paralyse the country.

For its part, the government sought to remove provocations to organised labour. On 17 November legal action against rent strikers in Glasgow
was stopped. Thomas McKinnon Wood, the Scottish secretary, asked
the cabinet to agree to legislation that would freeze all rents at pre-war
levels. Just ten days later the Rents and Mortgage Interest Restriction Bill
was brought in, seeking to remove one of the great grievances behind

the unrest on Clydeside. Lloyd George asked Lord Balfour of Burleigh and Lynden Macassey to inquire into why Clydeside was so volatile; their report in December suggested that a failure to nip disputes in the bud before they got out of hand was the main problem, and that a full-time local arbitrator should be appointed.

On 25 November Charles Stanton, a miner's agent, won the Merthyr by-election, caused by Hardie's death, as an Independent Labour candidate opposed to the party's pacifist policies. This appeared to contradict assertions by some politicians that conscription, because it would mostly affect working men, would breed revolution and set class against class. It also temporarily silenced trades unionists and Labour MPs who had been advocating pacifism. Stanton's resignation from his job to fight his seat had been spectacular: in his letter to the executive of the Aberdare district – his employers – he told them that 'there is a pro-German section in your district that has made my life a hell for many months . . . I have always been loyal to my class without being a traitor to my country.'[85] Such evidence badly undermined Labour's denials that its movement harboured those seeking to exploit the war to overthrow the established order.

Yet unease was spreading among all classes. The war's stalemate, air raids, industrial unrest (although the mines were, with the exception of one rogue pit in the Rhondda, temporarily quiet, there was the threat of a widespread railway strike), the mounting cost of the war (on 15 September Asquith moved another vote of credit, this time for £250 million) and people realising food production was not being maximised, all contributed to falling morale. Shortages had caused rises in prices, hitting hard those on fixed incomes, and women on allowances. Asquith noted, though, that middle-class people whose businesses produced essential goods were doing increasingly well. A Food Production Committee was constituted under Milner, as it was realised the war could last beyond the 1916 harvest. Questions of manpower with which Milner had been concerned in his drive for conscription were highly relevant to questions of agricultural labour and food production.

On 21 September McKenna introduced the third Budget of the war. He raised income tax at the top rate to 3s 6d (17.5 per cent), lowered thresholds, levied an excess-profit tax of 50 per cent on all profits above a £100 increase on the previous accounting year. Only a fifth of national expenditure was being met from taxation. McKenna said borrowing could rise provided taxation covered interest repayments, and the sinking fund on the national debt. This rose from £625 million in 1914 to £7,809 million by the Armistice; but too much money chasing too few goods meant sterling was one third its value in 1919 as in 1914.[86] There were tariffs on luxury goods such as cars, many of which were imported, in the hope of freeing space on merchant ships for goods vital to the nation's survival.

These were not the only new privations. In late September Greater London was put under state controls for the sale and provision of alcohol. From 11 October it became illegal in the City, all of Middlesex, and parts of Essex, Hertfordshire, Kent and Surrey for someone to buy another an alcoholic drink, as it already was in many industrial centres around the country, except with a meal. The punishment was a £100 fine and six months' hard labour. Inevitably, what constituted a 'meal' became a matter of philosophical debate; equally inevitably, drunkenness declined. The government also ordered a crackdown on night clubs, where anecdotal reports had it that many young officers were succumbing to drink and drugs: the Army wanted all those in central London closed down forthwith, but the phenomenon took root and would flourish between the wars. A correspondent to *The Times* protested that such establishments were for the benefit of 'the prostitute, the harpy, the dissolute and the shirker.'[87] The profits and dividends of these businesses were 'based on corruption' and they were spreading westwards along the Thames. The London Council for the Promotion of Public Morality weighed in, in the person of its president, the Bishop of London, who described night clubs as 'the haunts and hunting grounds of sharks and loose women'.[88] As a further obstacle to creatures of the night, London instituted a blackout from 1 October, to thwart Zeppelin raids. As a result, numerous stores announced a 5 p.m. closure, because of the difficulties in getting around London in the dark. Nightclub patrons would have to take their chances.

V

Criticism of Asquith continued to grow, and throughout the autumn the Northcliffe press increased its attacks on him personally and his conduct of government, attacks about which Lloyd George showed no signs of protesting. Now that Asquith's political opponents saw his working methods at close hand, they linked his apparent lack of dynamism to lack of progress in the war. Backbiting would grow into full-blown intrigue. Disillusion was fast overcoming Lloyd George. He dined with Churchill and Curzon on 14 September, the latter telling him the Tories planned to demand conscription: the Commons, back that day after the recess, had debated the issue again. Asquith, who attended the brief debate and made it clear he deplored the fact that it had happened, said acidly that 'this is a matter which has not escaped the attention of His Majesty's Government. When the Government, without undue delay, with as much deliberation as the gravity of the subject demands, arrive at their conclusions, they will present them to the House, and they will become the subject of Parliamentary discussion.'[89] On 18 September Asquith told Hankey he 'has definitely made up his mind in favour of voluntary service and not compulsory service'.[90] Lloyd George told Miss Stevenson that 'he cannot possibly be a party any longer to the shameful mismanagement and slackness . . . things are simply being allowed to slide, and . . . it is time someone spoke out.'[91] For the moment, that would not be Lloyd George. Conscription and Lloyd George's unfulfilled threats to resign would be recurrent themes until late 1916.

The Battle of Loos, the largest British attack of 1915, started on 25 September. After a debate about 'frightfulness' and sinking to the enemy's level, Britain for the first time used poison gas. The outcome after a fortnight's fighting was around 60,000 British Empire casualties – more fuel for the fire of the conscription debate – against 26,000 German. The failure of the attack to gain ground was the beginning of the end for Sir John French. Most ministers had opposed a new attack on the Western Front as they believed it could only fail; but it was demanded by Kitchener, at Joffre's insistence, as a complement to an offensive by French troops. Lloyd George told Asquith that French's policy of highly optimistic attacks on an entrenched army – Haig had opposed Loos saying the ground was unfavourable – could not continue, or he would have to leave office. Lloyd George's friends – notably Churchill – were lobbying for him to replace Kitchener at the War Office, with Haig becoming military director (Kitchener was doing both jobs). The 1st Army commander was now much viewed as the coming man. Asquith bought time in the compulsion debate by setting up a committee under Lansdowne to consider how the new National Register might be used to find recruits.

Three days into Loos, Guest again asked Asquith in the Commons about conscription. Asquith said it was receiving the 'careful and anxious consideration of His Majesty's Government', but asked that all MPs, whatever their views, 'abstain from raising it here'.⁹² He felt it would do a 'disservice' to the Armed Forces and to the country if 'any suggestion go forth to the world that there is any division of opinion amongst us.' Guest ignored the plea, rising a few minutes later to deliver a speech in which he claimed that seventy divisions could not be put in the field by 1916 without conscription. Unless the government could guarantee 20,000 men a week being called up for the next year, it would have to concede his point. Unlike in France, where every possible man was under arms, the enemy occupied not a square inch of home soil, thereby cutting the incentive for Britons to volunteer: in that regard the war was out of sight and out of mind. As Asquith had predicted, opinion was divided. The main embarrassment came when it was recorded that much money and effort was being spent sending home underage boys whose real age had not been established until they saw an Army doctor at the front. Lansdowne reported there were an estimated 1,412,040 men available for recruitment in England and Wales.⁹³

By October the casualty lists, reflecting the losses at Loos, occupied pages of newsprint. What was termed 'a monster recruiting rally' under the banner of 'Wake up London!' was held in the capital on Saturday 3rd, with five columns of 1,200 men – regulars and Territorials – meeting in parks around the capital and marching 10 miles through separate areas of London, while senior officers and notables made speeches.⁹⁴ Bottomley was to have been the star turn, but he had sprained his ankle in a taxi-cab accident. Similar rallies were held in Glasgow, Birmingham and other major cities. On 5 October Derby, who had presided that Saturday at a rally in Bury, and who a week earlier had in a speech at Manchester called it 'degrading' that men such as him 'should have to go about the country begging and appealing for recruits to defend their wives and children', was appointed director general of recruiting by Asquith.⁹⁵ He had said the public would settle for a dictatorship to sort things out rather than the present government, and his appointment was depicted in the press as the last chance for voluntarism.

The cabinet had not been consulted about Derby's appointment. Lansdowne, Curzon, Chamberlain, Churchill and Smith attacked him for taking it: they were convinced they had had Asquith in a corner, and within a week he would have acquiesced to compulsion had Derby not bought him time by agreeing to serve. They urged Derby to withdraw, but he refused. Derby, who Haig would say bore the impression of the last man to have sat on him, had earlier told Kitchener he thought 'voluntary recruiting had practically come to an end, and that we must have compulsory service.' The Field Marshal had answered that 'he himself felt that compulsory service would be necessary, but he wished to put it off as far as possible.'[96] Kitchener's hope was to wear the Germans down, and 'then to have compulsory service as a final push.' He told the cabinet he needed 30,000 new men a week, and another 5,000, not necessarily of military age, to act as labourers; he had the immediate support of all the Unionists apart from Balfour. This would give him approximately 3 million men by the end of 1916.

Derby therefore conceived a scheme, with which Asquith had no choice but to go along, to summon every man of military age before a local committee to ascertain his willingness to serve and to attest that he would if required; and if he was unwilling, to hear his reasons why. Derby called for single men who had attested to be called up first. The Parliamentary Recruiting Committee and the recruiting committee of the TUC agreed this. Asquith fretted about the impact the scheme would have on his fellow Liberals: he told Pamela McKenna, wife of his closest ally, that his memo to the cabinet about it would 'rattle my scattered colleagues in their weekend retreats.'[97] Nonetheless, he sent Derby a letter agreeing that if the Derby Scheme – as it would be known – failed there would be no alternative but to bring in conscription. Derby admitted to Gwynne he was alert to the scheme's inadequacies, but political as much as military expediency demanded it be tried. Also, significantly, the scheme had Northcliffe's support, and that of his newspapers.

The process started at once and was scheduled to finish by the end of November. District recruiting officers received a government circular in early October telling them that 'as it is evidently the duty of every man who has not been starred [placed in a reserved occupation] to at once join the Army . . . you are to take whatever steps considered most effectual to induce such men to join the Army. In carrying out this, you will doubtless be assisted by the local authorities.'[98] The widespread complaint that men had not been 'fetched' – and therefore assumed the Army did not need them – was to be acted upon; recruiting officers, using the register, were to visit men in non-essential industries who had not been 'fetched', and seek to 'fetch' them. Those who refused to respond to being 'fetched' were to have their names taken for future reference. What remained of Liberal opinion was outraged, and the directive – though not the Derby Scheme itself – was withdrawn within days.

By now Asquith was becoming increasingly isolated. His closest associates, Grey and Crewe, wanted him to pull out of the Dardanelles. He was estranged from Lloyd George, and deeply suspicious of him, and the Tories were unimpressed by Asquith's leadership skills. The perception of disaster in the Dardanelles brought a point of no return in terms of Northcliffe's view of the Asquith administration, and thereafter the *Daily Mail* and *The Times*, with differing degrees of unpleasantness, proceeded to seek to harry him out of office. Northcliffe believed he would achieve this within three months. He believed by early 1916 a 'Committee of Safety', probably led by Carson, would be directing the nation's affairs with a single-mindedness that Asquith and his colleagues lacked.[99] To add to the climate of disunity, Lloyd George wanted troops sent to Serbia, under attack from the Central Powers, but was opposed by cabinet colleagues who thought more should go to Gallipoli.

The Times announced on 11 October that 'something is seriously amiss with the conduct of the war.'[100] It found the government guilty of 'mismanagement' and run by 'fumblers'. It demanded a smaller cabinet, that it might work more efficiently. The *Mail* too wanted a small war council, dominated by the military, to replace the cabinet in decision-making. Violet Asquith noted that 'loathing of Northcliffe is the strongest & most prevalent emotion' in her father's house.[101] It was a loathing that would increase after her marriage to Bonham Carter, her father's secretary, on 1 December 1915. The ostentation of the wedding, the finery of the guests and the opulence of the party afterwards (there was no 'reception', but many guests went to Downing Street for lavish refreshments) was seized on by some in the press as setting a bad example when the nation's resources should be devoted to pursuing victory; even Andrew Clark, the Essex clergyman, noted in his diary how the extravagance had annoyed his parishioners.

Discussion of compulsion dominated cabinet meetings, and imperilled the continuance of the administration. When Runciman left the meeting on 12 October he told Bonham Carter that 'we remain a united Cabinet for another 24 hours'.[102] Such was the desperation to find men for the Army that the basic educational test – of being able to read and write – had been scrapped in some recruiting centres for those trying to join up. It had also been decided that the practice of sending boys of seventeen back to their parents until they were old enough to join legally – eighteen – would be stopped, and the boys would continue to train: it was an effective drop in the recruitment age to seventeen. At the meeting on 15 October Lloyd George – who the previous day had told Scott there were now eight cabinet ministers who wanted compulsion – 'got very excited and lost both head and temper, not quite but very nearly.'[103] Unfortunately for Asquith, Kitchener had changed his mind, and agreed compulsion would be necessary: but even before the meeting Scott noted Lloyd George was speaking of Asquith 'with great bitterness.'[104]

Hankey explained that Kitchener's reluctance to have compulsion immediately was because trench warfare led to the slaughter of men who tried to take enemy trenches. Before calling more up for 'butchery', Kitchener wanted to see whether some means – such as the tank – could be developed to overcome the barbed wire and machine-gun posts that caused terrible carnage. By the time his fears were realised in their most horrific iteration – the 19,026 men who died on the first day of the Somme – he too would be dead, and in no position to protest. Never-theless, the war secretary had recognised the realities, and his decision added inestimable weight to the arguments of those demanding compulsion.

Once Asquith had learned of Kitchener's change of mind he appealed to him to tone down his support for compulsion, not least since those with whom he had thrown in his lot – notably Curzon and Lloyd George – were plotting to force his removal as Secretary of State for War. To Riddell, Lloyd George professed that 'The PM is a great man, but his methods are not suited to war.'[105] He believed that six Unionists and Churchill were prepared, with him, to leave the gov-ernment if no progress were made on conscription. Mrs Asquith was clear what was happening: having added Hankey to the list of people whom she bombarded with letters, she told him: 'It is clear as day that LlG, Curzon & Winston are going to try to wreck the Gov.'[106] However, the mass walk-out, which would have ended Asquith's administra-tion, did not occur. Tories who had threatened to resign if conscription were not brought in decided instead to see how the Derby Scheme progressed.

Despite the pressures on him, Asquith – whom Gwynne described as

'the most unpopular man in the country' – remained on the surface resolutely opposed to compulsion. He strongly believed in the idea of a
liberal society in which the state, even in a time of national emergency,
could not force people either into the Armed Forces or into a certain
branch of industry, even though the prospect of industrial conscription
did not disturb his party in the way that military compulsion did. He
believed the people were with him, and saw their rights as paramount –
and would fight to preserve them. He told his wife that 'you can't have
Conscription in this country without something very like revolution.'[107]
Yet the Liberal Party too was fracturing under the strain of this argument: Asquith told Bonham Carter and Hankey how 'Ll George is out to
break the Govt on conscription if he can.'[108] Churchill, although diminished, was fervently in favour; other Liberals, such as Grey and Crewe,
remained opposed, but their minds were open. And Asquith himself,
like Kitchener, slowly came to realise during the late autumn of 1915 that
he would have to give way, or risk the fall of the government. For him
the Derby Scheme was a means of buying time, not a solution to his
problems over military manpower.

The prime minister's health deteriorated; during a grim cabinet meeting on 18 October, when one minister after another predicted disaster,
he passed Lansdowne a note and left the room. Lansdowne announced
that Asquith 'had been obliged to retire as he was feeling unwell'.[109] That
night he slept badly, and in the early hours burst into his wife's bedroom
to say he thought he should resign. She calmed him down: but a doctor
was called, who ordered sleep and a reduction in his intake of food and
drink. A medical bulletin was issued saying that the prime minister was
suffering from 'gastro-intestinal catarrh' and required 'several days complete rest'.[110] After seven-and-a-half years in office – years tense and
difficult even before the war – he was starting to crack. Over lunch that
day Lloyd George told Repington – the two had become cronies – that 'a
large Cabinet is useless, and wants a small War Cabinet.'[111] He will have
understood the personal advantages of whistling a tune already popular
with the Northcliffe press.

The government then had to endure a high-profile resignation: Carson, the Attorney General, went on 19 October, ostensibly over the
government's failure to keep earlier promises about supporting Serbia
militarily. F. E. Smith, on a meteoric rise to the Woolsack, replaced him.
Carson's resignation had been rumoured for several days; and when it

happened the *Daily Mail* – he was close to Northcliffe – asserted he had gone because of his 'refusal to accept any policy of drift.'[112] The paper returned to the offensive. It accused the government, because of its implementation of censorship, of having 'deceived the democracy as to the course of the war.' It rubbished claims Britain would win a famous victory in the Dardanelles, or that the Russians had seen off the Germans on the Eastern Front; and Northcliffe had decided that if the truth were made public, there would be less trouble with recruitment. His other paper, *The Times*, saw Carson's departure as of huge significance, and the harbinger of problems ahead for a government with which Northcliffe felt intense disillusion.

Carson was indeed annoyed at how Asquith ran the war. His resignation embarrassed Law, his party leader, who should have made the running on this question; and Lloyd George, who shared these views. Both Law and Lloyd George could make the patriotic argument that it would have been wrong to desert the government at that stage, and cause a crisis; and that was their private reasoning. However, away from the public gaze, Lloyd George would bluster and threaten. On 26 October he told Scott that he would if necessary force a general election not technically on the conscription issue, but on manning the Army: the debate, he said, would be between getting the 30,000 men Kitchener wanted, and the 20,000 that anti-conscriptionists such as McKenna thought could be raised under the voluntary system. (In fact, as Asquith would stress, 30,000 men represented the maximum Kitchener felt the system could handle, not a minimum.)

Lloyd George's blustering made Asquith's job more and more difficult. The question was imminent whether the 1910 Parliament, due under the 1911 Parliament Act to expire in January 1916, could be extended: and Lloyd George said he would not allow it to be lengthened – he would resign and bring the government down – unless the conscription issue were settled. The munitions minister's own frame of mind was febrile: 90,000 workers on Clydeside, most of them in factories under his purview, were threatening to strike because three men, fined heavily for absenteeism in a trade subject to military discipline, had chosen to go to prison rather than pay.

But if that were not enough Lloyd George, backed up by Law, then threatened on 1 November to resign unless Kitchener was dismissed. Asquith ignored this latest ultimatum, and by the time he discussed the matter with his two colleagues their anger had died down. The next day Asquith announced the new War Committee that had evolved from the Dardanelles Committee, which, in his view and that of the cabinet, 'had outlived its usefulness'.[113] He would chair it: Balfour, Lloyd George and Grey were the other members. Lansdowne declined a place but chose to remain minister without portfolio. McKenna was originally excluded but demanded to be put on the committee to shore up Asquith, and Asquith, to Lloyd George's intense annoyance, relented. This brought about precisely the small executive body Carson had wanted, though its running alongside the cabinet would provide the conflicts Hankey had identified as so destructive to good decision-making.

It met for the first time on 5 November with Hankey as secretary. Although Curzon was aggrieved by his exclusion the main casualty of the arrangement was Churchill, who as Chancellor of the Duchy had at least, by remaining in cabinet and on the old Dardanelles Committee, had a chance to continue to influence war policy and, more to the point, defend himself as the situation in the Dardanelles became worse and worse. His elimination from the War Committee was the key for him on 29 October, when he first heard of the proposed change, to draft a letter of resignation, which was not sent. However, he continued to rage internally about his fate.

A far more important figure than Churchill was absent from the new committee as it began its deliberations: the Secretary of State for War. Kitchener remained distrusted by many of his colleagues, and his attempts to run the War Office as a one-man show were proving increasingly unpractical, both administratively and politically. His belated conversion to conscription did not erase memories of his culpability in the shells shortage of the previous spring. Hankey recorded that some of his colleagues 'hoped that he would never sit with them again in the position of War Secretary, for he had many critics'.[114] Asquith, well aware of Kitchener's faults as a statesman, decided to send him to the Dardanelles, mainly to placate Law and Balfour, and he ran the War Office during his absence. There were rumours that Kitchener might remain in the Near East as commander-in-chief of all forces outside Europe: but nothing came of that. Blanche Lloyd includes in her diary a story about Kitchener being blamed for not sending troops to Salonica to support the Serbs, as had been promised:

Joffre came to England and . . . thumped the table with his fist and demanded 'where is British honour?' Asquith, touched [to] the quick, turned to K and said 'This is all your fault. Why did you let us say we would do this if we couldn't?' Whereupon K resigned – but as his resignation was made to the Cabinet, and not to either the King or the Prime Minister (which is according to the book) our blameless premier was able to rise in his place in the House, white with passion at the accusation of being a liar, and reiterate that the War Minister neither had handed in, nor attempted to hand in, his resignation.[115]

When a newspaper, the *Globe*, tried to print the truth, it was suppressed.

'After the first meeting of the War Committee the usual process of rapid growth set in,' Hankey recalled, lamenting the inevitable mushrooming of what were supposed to be small, efficient, decision-making bodies.[116] Asquith had said the group would be no bigger than five, but within days Law and McKenna had joined too. It began by meeting every two or three days. Hankey kept minutes, and copies of the committee's conclusions were circulated to all members, of the cabinet, unless in some instances secrecy required the decisions to be passed on verbally. Sometimes, the whole cabinet would overrule the committee, and within six weeks it effectively ceased to function. George Lloyd, the Conservative MP and a future proconsul, told his wife – who recorded it in her diary – 'that he had been doing his utmost to persuade Lloyd George to come out of the Cabinet, and had on one occasion almost succeeded – only that Winston had come in and spoilt everything. His argument is that neither Carson, Bonar Law or LG are strong enough individually to make an alternative Govt to Asquith and Co – but that collectively they might do so.'[117]

Asquith was supposed to update the Commons on the progress of the war generally and on conscription on 18 October, but his illness – which Law thought a diplomatic one, though he conceded Asquith was sick with worry – prevented him. He went to the Wharf for a week to rest, and consider his options. On his return, however, he told Hankey he was minded, after Ypres and Loos, to move French from his command. He had been a marked man since July, when the King told Haig (whom he was investing with the Grand Cross of the Order of the Bath) of his dissatisfaction with the friction between French and Kitchener, and of his (accurate) belief that French had conspired with the press; the King, Haig wrote in his diary, 'had lost confidence in Field-Marshal French.'[118]

Three months later, on 24 October, Haig dined with the King, who was in France, and who sought Haig's opinion about French. This time Haig did not hold back, informing the King of French's 'conceit' and 'obstinacy' as manifested in the direction of the Battle of Loos. 'I therefore thought strongly, that, for the sake of the Empire, French ought to be removed.'[119] Haig had in fact detested French since the Curragh incident in March 1914, when officers with connections to Ulster, and stationed in Ireland, had been clumsily told to go on leave if they wished to avoid being ordered to confront Unionist rebels. Haig felt French had 'sacrificed the whole Army' by mishandling the political crisis with which he had been confronted.[120] Rumours soon reached French: Esher noted on 13 November that his close friend 'has been upset by rumours from London that the Government contemplate his removal.'[121]

Asquith's changing view of French was part of the prime minister's growing realisation, following that of several of his colleagues, that the general strategy for conduct of the war needed urgent revision. There was too much inertia: despite the furore of Carson's resignation over the issue, no decision had been taken about securing progress in south-eastern Europe, or indeed to continue that offensive at all. General Sir William Robertson, chief of staff of the BEF, made a point of telling Haig, when he visited him in France on 24 October, that it was vitally important no more British troops were sent to the Balkans, and urged him to write to 'some of my friends in Government' to that effect.[122] Robertson, known universally as 'Wullie', remains the only man in the British Army to occupy every rank from private to field marshal: and as might be expected from one who had made that journey in the class-ridden era before the Great War, he was formidable in his energy, intellect, abilities and character. He was the son of a postmaster from Lincolnshire, and formed strong views on the basis of vast experience and after much thought. His strong view of the war was that it would only be won in France and Flanders.

Recognising that French was a spent force, Asquith was at last clear that the question of who should command the BEF was now urgent. Esher was summoned from France, where he was a commissioner for the Red Cross and could gossip with his military friends, to see Asquith at the War Office on 23 November. This is his account of what followed:

'The government,' Asquith told him, 'have come to the conclusion that a change must be made in the Supreme Command on the Western Front.'[123] Esher asked whether the debacle at Loos had been the problem, and was told that was part of it. 'Sir John seemed of late to be unable to rise to the height which the situation demanded, and . . . he [Asquith] had asked me to come over in order that I might, as an old personal friend . . . return and break to Sir John the conclusions at which he had arrived . . . He suggested that in Sir John's own interest he should take the initiative, and tender his resignation on the ground of age and fatigue.'

Asquith said French would not be humiliated: he would receive a peerage, the offer of a Home Command and, after Esher had helpfully reminded him that French was not a rich man and might have expected a healthy grant of money had he led the BEF to victory, a promise by Asquith that such a grant would be made at the end of the war. Esher called this 'a very disagreeable task', and asked for time to consider whether he could do it. The next day, having checked that Asquith's views were final and unconditional how, he agreed to convey the news, and left the following morning. French, unaware of the King's lack of support for him, and of the part Haig had played in undermining him, was dumbstruck, and could not understand how he had merited the sack. Esher noted: 'There was nothing to be done except to give him time to calm down, and to point out all the obvious difficulties in fighting so intangible a thing as a Coalition government, and the hopelessness of such a contest.'[124] French was slow to take the initiative to resign, but soon understood what had happened: 'I was driven out of France by Asquith at the instigation of Haig.'[125]

Haig had argued with French against the Loos offensive, and the already reduced esteem in which he held his chief suffered as a result of the outcome; not least because French tried in his dispatches to put the blame on Haig. This was the moment when Haig's abilities as an office politician, learned a decade earlier in Whitehall, came to the fore. Using Esher as intermediary, he relayed his discontent about French to Asquith; and, more to the point, used an audience of the King to express his doubts. By less exalted means French's chief of staff, Robertson, made similar representations. The friendship between French and the man he had once called 'my dear, dear Douglas' was sunk by this act of personal disloyalty.[126] Haig, though, sincerely believed he was acting in the best interests of the Army and of the country; and may have felt he had done all he could for French, not least by having lent him £2,000 in 1899 to pay off debts that would, otherwise, have forced him to leave the Army.[127] The loan remained outstanding and Haig, a rich man, refused to embarrass French by demanding its repayment.

On 3 December Kitchener wrote to Asquith to recommend Haig be appointed to succeed French in command of the BEF; separately, Haig had recommended to Law that Robertson be made Chief of the Imperial General Staff, in succession to Sir Archibald Murray, who was deemed too subservient to Kitchener. Haig also wanted the General Staff moved from the War Office to Horse Guards to achieve both a physical and strategic separation from Kitchener. French was relieved of his command on 8 December, and Haig (whom Mrs Asquith considered 'a remarkably stupid man' though 'a very fine soldier') was offered his command.[128] French became commander-in-chief of Home Forces. The King would soon hint to Hankey that he felt largely responsible for Haig's appointment.[129] By 16 December, when French saw his old friend Repington to discuss his recall, he could give the impression that he was 'glad to be out of it, as during the last few months the Government had so pestered him with all kinds of worries, that he had not been able to attend properly to his work.'[130]

In a rebuke to Kitchener (who had egged French on to undertake the Loos offensive, but whose public standing was such that he could not be removed), the government agreed to Robertson's insistence that he alone, and not the Secretary of State for War, would determine strategy and answer to the War Committee, not the Army Council. With Haig in charge of the BEF, control of military matters had thus passed to two men who believed perhaps even more strongly than their predecessors that the war could only be won on the Western Front, and as new appointees without a record of failure had the authority to press the point on the politicians – notably Lloyd George – who disagreed with them. They were not natural allies. Despite his support for Robertson, Haig admitted he would have found it 'easier . . . to work with a gentleman'; however, their relationship would be conditioned by shared adversity rather than class empathy.[131] The newly empowered generals were fortunate that Asquith felt that once soldiers had been appointed to senior posts they should discharge their duties without interference. So long as he led the government this would cause no difficulties. Robertson now found himself with enormous power to direct the war.

Seeing he had been marginalised to the point where he was mainly a public totem and believing his functions were 'curtailed to the feeding and clothing of the Army', Kitchener asked to resign: but was told it was his duty to remain, Asquith being aware of the effect on public morale of letting him go.[132] He was also allowed to maintain direct access to the War Committee. Kitchener was not alone in feeling his nose had been put out of joint. On 11 November Churchill, seething since his exclusion from the War Committee almost a fortnight earlier, resigned from the government. He went with a tone of anger and defiance: 'I have a clear conscience which enables me to bear my responsibility for past events with composure,' he told Asquith. 'Time will vindicate my administration of the Admiralty, and assign me my due share in the vast series of preparations and operations which have secured us the complete command of the sea.'[133] The letter excluded a demand in an earlier draft, that the government should publish the details of how the decision to attack the Dardanelles was taken. Churchill's departure would facilitate a decision to evacuate the Dardanelles. 'I see no political future for him,' Mrs Asquith wrote, adding that Churchill was 'quite unprincipled'. He had an admirer in Scott, and the *Manchester Guardian* praised him for resigning: Scott told Mrs Churchill that 'we might want him at home again sooner than he expected.'[134] But Churchill, by then in France, would write to him on 19 December to say that 'I am determined not to return to the Government unless with proper executive power in war matters; and as this is not a likely condition to arise I intend to devote myself to my old profession and absorb myself in it.'[135] He felt Lloyd George had done him no favours, despite their long friendship, and his wife agreed: she wrote to her husband in France to advise him not to 'burn any boats' with Asquith, and to observe that Lloyd George, with whom she had had lunch the previous day, was 'the direct descendant of Judas Iscariot'.[136]

VI

To add to the government's problems the restructuring of the high command occurred in a context of heightened political tension, and did little immediately to improve matters. Hankey recalled that 'before October was over the existence of the Coalition Government was in jeopardy, and at one time a political crisis of the first order was threatened.'[137] He did not exaggerate, as it started to seem that almost everything was going wrong. Germany's beating back of the Russians caused deep concern, and Hankey noted that 'it seemed probable that the Turks would soon receive sufficient ammunition to shell us out of the Gallipoli Peninsula.' Losses continued to mount. On 28 October Asquith reported that there had been 493,294 killed, wounded or missing, of whom 365,046 were on the Western Front; 67,460 of those were confirmed as killed.[138] The conscription debate ran simultaneously with an argument mounted mainly by Liberals, including Asquith, that the British economic engine had to be maintained or there would be no resources to fight a war. Britain had to export or lose foreign exchange with which to buy essential food and materials from overseas, which (thanks to its sea power) gave it a long-term advantage over blockaded Germany.

Asquith's only Tory ally was Balfour, who had been among the first to point out the economic consequences of wider enlistment. However, his support was cancelled out by Lloyd George and Churchill, who wanted more recruitment. This uncertain approach by the government, and the confusion over national priorities, created problems in public perceptions. Many who were inclined to join up felt they would make mugs of themselves by doing so, when so many others refused. In May 1915 around 135,000 men had enlisted; by September the monthly total was 71,000. As Hankey put it, there was no 'equality of sacrifice' between those who had volunteered and died or been wounded, and those who had taken their jobs and were earning a comfortable living, out of danger.[139]

The National Register was now in place, an important step in allowing the government to see who was at its disposal, and how they might be deployed. Using the register, the authorities spoke to every man not in a skilled occupation essential to the war. As in an election campaign, the canvass was door to door, but officials were instructed to keep calling until they had seen the man face to face. He was invited to enlist: or to attest that he would enlist when the country's need for him was essential. 'Put before him plainly and politely the need of the country,' the canvassers were told. 'Do not bully or threaten.'[140] Those who refused to attest would be asked why, and the officials were urged to offer advice that might overcome their reasons, most of which were financial.

Under the Derby Scheme, unmarried men would be called up before married ones, and younger men would go before older ones in an age range from eighteen to forty. Every man of age and not already under arms or in a reserved occupation received a letter from Derby telling him that if he chose not to enlist he could expect the government would have no choice but to establish conscription; the system did not work perfectly for, as Derby himself admitted, one recipient was Kitchener. Finally, the King issued a message, printed in all newspapers on several days, about the 'grave moment' in which the country found itself. He called for more recruits. 'In ancient days the darkest moment has ever produced in men of our race the sternest resolve. I ask you, men of all classes, to come forward voluntarily and take your share in the fight.'[141] In Ireland, where recruiting was even less successful, Lord Wimborne, the Lord Lieutenant, made a similar appeal.

A correspondent to *The Times* observed that Derby should have sent his recruiters to Newmarket, for the Cambridgeshire meeting – one of the few still permitted – where they could have netted 'swarms of able-bodied slackers' who 'can hardly plead they are rendering useful service to the State by betting and gambling.'[142] Most men – though still, as it turned out, not enough – knew their duty. Cambridge University, where 1,100 men had matriculated in 1913, announced that fewer than 300 had done so in 1915: one college, Corpus Christi, welcomed just three new undergraduates.[143] In October 1915 the Derby Scheme brought 113,285 immediate recruits, rising to 121,793 in November. By 15 December 2,829,263 men of military age had joined since August 1914, against 2,182,178 of their peers who had not.[144]

On 2 November, nearly a month into the Derby Scheme, Asquith made an important pledge in the House of Commons: that married men who had attested under the scheme would not be held to their promise to enlist until unmarried men had joined – he hoped by 'voluntary effort, and if not by some other means.'[145] He made this promise at Derby's insistence, and as part of a speech reviewing the war for which Westminster had waited, to give the country a sense of direction after his fortnight's absence through illness. *The Times* was unimpressed: its leading article called the speech 'very largely a record of shortcomings and an acceptance of responsibility for them'; though it praised Asquith for his pledge to married men, believing it would assist Derby's campaign.[146] Northcliffe claimed the credit for the unmarried-men policy, using the *Mail* to trumpet that its campaign had won the day. *The Times* noted, however, that the prime minister had made no attempt to defend his direction of the war: his imminent announcement of the new War

Committee would have made such a defence irrelevant. Typical of the tone the newspaper of the Establishment was now taking against Asquith was its snide reminder, at the end of a leading article in which it noted Asquith's call for 'perspective, patience and courage', that 'we would remind him that there are three other qualities, of no less consequence, for which the nation looks in its rulers. They are called foresight, initiative and energy. They have been conspicuously lacking in the past . . .'

Asquith confirmed a total of 377,000 casualties and, without specifying the numbers of dead, said the rate of recovery from wounds meant the 'net permanent wastage' was 'on a much smaller scale'.[147] He spoke of the 'brilliantly conducted' Mesopotamia campaign that, like the Dardanelles, would soon be subject to an official inquiry. He admitted that the second of those campaigns was 'not so unchequered a chapter in the story of our operations in the Eastern theatre of war'. He admitted Fisher's reservations about the operation and that Kitchener had ruled out significant military support; but above all he admitted the War Council had taken the decision and the cabinet had approved it. Asquith said he took his 'full share' of responsibility. Without naming Churchill he defended him – 'I deprecate more than I can say the attempt to allocate the responsibility to one minister or another, or to suggest that in a matter of this kind some undefined personality, of great authority and overmastering will, controlled and directed the strategy of the operation.' It was technically, but not entirely, true. In his peroration, Asquith enlisted 'the imperishable story of the last hours of Edith Cavell' in his support. 'It has taught the bravest man among us the supreme lesson of courage.'[148]

The Derby Scheme quickly encountered difficulties. When Scott went to see Derby on 5 November to discuss whether an appeals board with large discretionary powers could be set up for his scheme, he found Derby 'hopelessly muddled and with no grasp whatever of the essential points . . . his committee were in despair.'[149] When Scott saw Asquith shortly afterwards and expressed reservations about Derby, the prime minister remarked that 'he had the best intentions, but unfortunately was short of brains.' Derby further proved his lack of grip over the widespread notion that unmarried men would be taken before married ones. In fact, there had to be a debate about what proportion of unmarried men would have to be called up before starting on the married ones, and whether to go back to unmarried ones once an identical proportion of marrieds had gone. Asquith told him to stop talking about numbers, not least because he himself was vague about what would constitute a success. He said that after 30 November 'a statement can then be made to Parl. showing the relative proportion of men enlisted & men who can serve, & if the nos. are adequate & it can be stated at the same time that sufficient young men had enlisted to ensure the postponement of the calling up of married men for some considerable time, the campaign can be called a success.'[150] He accepted that the Derby Scheme would not be completed by 30 November, but that that would be a suitable juncture at which to 'take stock'.[151]

To R. D. Blumenfeld, editor of the *Daily Express*, Derby admitted in early November that 'the numbers are decidedly better than they were but nothing like what I shall require to make it a success.'[152] By 20 November 270,000 men had attested, and Derby told Stamfordham he hoped to double that number within a fortnight. The slow response caused the scheme to remain open a fortnight longer than planned, into mid-December. Even the numbers attesting would have little impact given the casualties at Loos and, before that, Ypres. What was clear, though, was that hostility to conscription was not so widespread as its opponents had maintained. Recognising these things, Montagu tried to persuade Asquith to set the compulsion process in motion. He said that if it went on the statute book it would not need to be used, as more men would join voluntarily – unless, he told Mrs Asquith, the war went on another year.[153] She believed that the Unionists were using the question to force Asquith out and bring about a general election: she blamed Curzon as being 'out for mischief' on the matter – he had old scores to settle with Kitchener – and inevitably saw Northcliffe's guiding hand.[154] *The Times* went for Asquith after his Commons speech, which confirmed her suspicions.

The preliminary results of the Derby Scheme were shared with the cabinet on 14 December, though the figures were incomplete. Asquith told the King the results were not good, despite a surge in the last days of the scheme. Derby had warned the public of this: notably in a speech at the Stock Exchange on 24 November, when he said that 'men must come in very much larger numbers in the next three weeks if they are going to make the position of voluntary service absolutely unassailable.'[155] Few practical obstacles to recruiting remained: *The Times* reported that 'the medical examination to which recruits are subjected before attestation is, in some places at any rate, far from severe. The eyesight test has been suspended until men are called up and sent to their depots . . .' The 'indispensability' test had been deferred, so the argument about whether a man was in a reserved occupation could be deferred too. It was being said that the 'starring' of men – signifying that they were indispensable – had been 'too indiscriminate'.[156] Also, civil servants – starred or not – were told they should attest. Everyone who attested was offered a khaki armband to wear to signal his willingness to serve his country: armlets were also designed for men in reserved occupations, further marginalising those without one.

Asquith having recognised from its inception that the Derby Scheme had postponed rather than avoided the need to embrace compulsion, the moment had come when no further delay on the question could be contemplated. With Montagu not the only colleague to advise him to make arrangements, he had asked Curzon a month earlier to oversee the drafting of a Conscription Bill. He had done this with Leo Amery, a young MP who had entered the Commons as a Liberal Unionist in a by-election in 1911 and had worked as an intelligence officer. Now Curzon joined a committee on compulsion chaired by Long and including Smith, Crewe (who favoured conscription if the public would support it) and Simon, the only anti-conscriptionist. They awaited Derby's definitive report, published on 20 December. Asquith seemed seriously rattled by the row he knew would come with many in his own party. J. L. Garvin, editor of the *Observer*, writing to Churchill, told him that 'I think Asquith's confidence in being able to hold on is very considerably shaken.'[157] The public remained belligerent. When, a week before Christmas, Snowden tried to address a pacifist meeting in Blackburn, 'his speech was constantly interrupted by scenes of disorder.'[158] While holding such meetings was not illegal, those who facilitated and conducted them were warned that any consequent infringement of DORA would lead to their prosecution, and that police protection could not be guaranteed for those who expressed controversial views and started a disturbance. In this state of public opinion, the government proceeded to call up single men aged between nineteen and twenty-two who had attested.

On 21 December Asquith, unable any longer to conceal the difficulties with the Derby Scheme, moved a resolution in the Commons for another million men to join the forces. This was despite 2,466,719 having volunteered since the outbreak of war.[159] Separately, it was announced that all men not certified to be seriously diseased who had failed the medical examination for the Army would be asked to retake it. Asquith said he hoped every physically fit man not needed in a reserved occupation would volunteer. He asked that those who were fit and had not attested 'will even now seize the opportunity of following the example which has been so patriotically set to them by the great masses of the community.'[160] The resolution was passed without a vote. With the same lack of transparency that prevented him from revealing what he knew of the failings of the Derby Scheme, he also claimed French had relinquished his command of his own volition, and announced that the King had raised him to a viscountcy.

Asquith dreaded what would have to come next. He told Sylvia Henley on 22 December, after the cabinet discussion of the Derby report, that 'we seem to be on the brink of a precipice. The practical question is – shall I be able during the next ten days to devise and build a bridge?'[161] Derby's final report said that there were 5,011,441 men of military age; that 2,829,263 had either enlisted, attested or been rejected; and 2,182,178 had taken no action.[162] He believed most of the unattested were bachelors, and unless the unmarried were pressed into service there was only a weak case for married men to join. He promised to do all he could to get unmarried men into the Army before married ones: and so, over Christmas, it rested.

The second Christmas of the war illustrated how the conflict and the removal of men to the Army were beginning to change society, even without conscription. There were fewer reported cases of drunkenness, and many fewer people were fed in parish workhouses, a sign of the thoroughness of the recruitment campaign. However, the large number of those who still refused to be recruited left the government no choice but to proceed with compulsion, at least of unmarried men. Grey, Runciman, McKenna and Simon all claimed to be on the brink of resigning, Simon because he opposed conscription and the other three because they feared it would cause essential workers to be lost from mines, munitions and shipbuilding. Robertson, the new CIGS, stirred things further by telling the cabinet that a supply of 'not less than 130,000 men' a month was required if the war was to be fought adequately.

The cabinet met on 27 and 28 December, the two meetings interpreted by the press and broadcast to the country as 'the outward signs of a very grave political crisis'.[163] No decision was reached at the first meeting; Asquith told the King that 'much divergence of opinion was manifested.'[164] He warned the King that Runciman and McKenna 'said that they must consider their position'. His critics took this as a sign of his weakness, but he was desperately trying to stop the cabinet breaking up. Lloyd George sent a message to Asquith via Reading that if he came out in support of conscription he 'would stand by him through thick and thin' and that if a general election were precipitated by the crisis 'he would do all the dirty work up and down the country – speaking and the like and would work for him like a n–'.[165] However, if Asquith refused, Lloyd George would resign: the one consolation he offered was that he would never serve in a Tory government. No wonder Asquith told Mrs McKenna that the last week of 1915 was 'in the fullest sense of the word a Hellish week; one of the worst even in my storm-tossed annals.'[166]

Ministers waited for Asquith to raise the subject at the 27 December meeting, but he preferred to discuss other matters, and dragged on talk of everything apart from conscription. He then announced that as it was five o'clock there was no time to discuss compulsion. Curzon protested, accusing Asquith of having wasted time to avoid taking a decision; Lloyd George believed his behaviour was prompted by not knowing what answer to give to his ultimatum; however, fearing that four members of his cabinet would resign if he gave in to Lloyd George, Asquith was keen to avoid such a discussion. That evening Reading told Lloyd George that Asquith had been 'much touched by his promise of loyalty' and it had, after months of his trying to avoid the inevitable, swayed him in favour of compulsion, at least of unmarried men.[167]

At the second meeting Asquith at last started to address the question. He settled that unattested single men would be called up before attested married ones: Lloyd George and most of the Unionists had demanded enough men to fill seventy divisions. Asquith had not, however, squared everyone. Grey told Asquith on 29 December of his need to resign, in a letter which Asquith told him 'fills me with despair'.[168] He continued: 'If I am to be deserted in this time of stress by all my oldest and best friends, it is clear I must consider my own position.' He warned Grey his resignation 'would, of course, be universally interpreted as a German triumph.' Hard-line unionists such as George Lloyd had been losing patience with Grey, Lloyd having told his wife that 'Sir E Grey now says that he will have no hand in measures taken with a view to starving German women and children! . . . which explains why some people say that the War will end twelve months after Grey leaves the Foreign Office.'[169] Grey was not the only problem: McKenna refused to go above fifty-four divisions, which was far too small an army for what was required.

On 31 December, in the course of two more 'amicable though contentious' meetings, a majority in the cabinet decided on a degree of compulsion in calling up men of military age who had not attested and could give no good reason for exemption.[170] Single men and widowers without dependent children would go first. Runciman and McKenna felt able to stay because vital workers would not be called up; Grey came round. The King had told Asquith that 'he would stand by and support him, even if all his colleagues were to leave.'[171] The Sovereign noted, presumably on Asquith's information, that Runciman and McKenna wanted to go because Kitchener 'wants to maintain 70 divisions in the field & they say that our finances will only stand 50.'[172] Simon's resignation was announced in the press on 1 January 1916, after his failure to attend either of the two cabinet meetings on New Year's Eve. Aggrieved Liberals took the outcome as a triumph for Northcliffe, and saw Lloyd George increasingly as his creature. Judging by the letters columns of newspapers, and the lack of any widespread protest, the public applauded the decision, and were perplexed at the trouble caused in reaching it. On 2 January Scott told Balfour he had been 'honestly willing' to accept compulsion provided the voluntary system had first been tried and proved unfeasible; but despite the general view of the Derby Scheme, Scott argued that 'I do feel very strongly that compulsion is now being forced upon us without proof shown of its necessity, and I resent this the more deeply because it seems to me in the nature of a breach of faith'.[173] Scott feared it would divide Britain at a time when it badly needed unity, and would end up putting into uniform a 'negligible' number of men. Balfour replied that he thought Asquith had no choice.

Putting more men under arms was expensive. Robertson told Haig on 4 January that 'certain ministers are trying to render compulsion useless by making out that although we may have power to take the men we cannot pay for them, and that they cannot be spared from their trades . . . The arguments I advanced were that we need every man we can get, and that it is for the Government to say how many they can pay for and how many they can find.'[174] The old question of the most productive use of manpower was at the heart of the quarrel, and Asquith set up a special cabinet committee to investigate and discuss it. It met daily, sometimes twice daily, between 1 January and 2 February before finding a compromise about the use of manpower that prevented a cabinet split, the fall of the government and a possible general election. It was agreed the Army Council should aim to have sixty-two divisions in the field by late June with reserves for three months, and five divisions for home defence.

On 5 January the government gave the first official indication of the losses from Loos: 773 officers killed, 1,288 wounded and 317 missing; 10,345 other ranks killed, 38,095 wounded and 8,848 missing. Thus in a fourteen-day period from 25 September to 8 October the BEF had sustained almost 60,000 casualties.[175] Absurdly, until the summer of 1916 time-expired men from the regular Army were allowed to leave at the end of their agreed terms, and around 5,000 NCOs and other ranks did so each month until the legal power was introduced to prevent them.

Asquith introduced the Military Service Bill the same day, after publication of the Derby Scheme report. Around 275,000 had enlisted rather than simply attesting; and 343,000 single men and 487,000 married men said they were available. Asquith called the results 'wonderful and encouraging', but attestation was not the same as bringing men into the services. He confirmed Derby's figure that 651,000 single men of military age were unaccounted for: in other words, who had not attested.[176] In the last four days of the scheme – 10 to 13 December – 1,070,000 men had attested.[177] Yet Asquith said he still felt that 'no case has been made out for general compulsion' – in other words, for all men over eighteen and under forty to be called up whether single or not – and that the Bill could be supported by those who opposed conscription.[178] It was, he said, simply a Bill to enable him to keep the promise he had made the previous November, that no married man who came forward to enlist would be required to serve until unmarried ones had been called up. He said that not to have given the promise would have deterred married men from attesting. And he also claimed that even if Derby's figure of 651,000 turned out inaccurately high, the undoubtedly large numbers of unmarried men who could serve, and the promise he had given, now required action. Bachelors aged between twenty-three and twenty-six would be called up on 8 February. Two years later, Asquith made a comment on the issue of compulsion whose clarity retrospectively illuminated the workings of his mind at this point: 'the question of compulsion is not a question of principle but of expediency'.[179]

As so many married men had agreed to serve on the basis that unmarried men would be taken first, the unmarried had to be called up. Therefore, any single men with no grounds for exemption 'shall be deemed to have done what everyone agrees it is their duty to the State in times like these to do, and be treated as though they had attested or enlisted.'[180] All unattested men aged eighteen or over on 15 August 1915, who had not then reached the age of forty-one, and who were either unmarried or widowers without dependent children, would be regarded as having enlisted twenty-one days after the Bill received the Royal Assent. The exemptions, which other than those for men on work of national importance would be agreed by a tribunal, included those already rejected for service, those from families where their other siblings had already been killed and they alone were left, and clergymen of all denominations.

And he announced another exemption: 'A conscientious objection to the undertaking of military service.'[181] He reacted angrily to 'those expressions of dissent, and even of derision' that greeted this statement, pointing out that Pitt the Younger had introduced such legislation to protect liberty of conscience during the Napoleonic Wars: and that South Africa and Australia both had such laws in place for the present war, the wording of whose exemptions was emulated in the Military Service Bill. Many who objected to taking life would serve in other capacities, such as on minesweepers and in 'ancillary duties', where they exposed themselves to the same risks as combatants – for example, as medical orderlies – but were unarmed. The tribunals that would hear these and other exemptions would be based in each local registration district, and would effectively be a continuation of the committees set up to oversee the Derby Scheme; and at a regional level there would be an independent appeals tribunal. It would have a range of judgements to which it could come, though all those judged medically fit who professed a conscientious objection would be subject to military discipline.

Asquith said he deplored Simon's resignation 'more than I can express in words'.[182] Simon explained himself to the Commons as soon as Asquith sat down. He expressed the pain he felt at separating himself from a man to whom he owed so much, but said that 'the real issue is whether we are to begin an immense change in the fundamental structure of our society.'[183] He did not accuse Asquith of bad faith: but had thought the end of the voluntary principle would be abandoned only by general consent, which was wanting. He felt Asquith had been evasive in not specifying how many of his 651,000 men were able to serve and were avoiding doing so. Simon did not believe the total was sufficient to merit compulsion. The National Register included every man; thus many of those 651,000 were, he contended, medically unfit, or in the merchant marine, or clergy. On the basis of his constituency, Walthamstow, he argued that the numbers in the Derby report had been erroneously compiled, and should not have been used as the basis of a massive shift in policy.

Aside from creating division, Simon feared the Bill, if enacted, would lead to the wider application of conscription. The powers making it a crime under DORA to argue against compulsion were, he argued, unduly draconian. He blamed 'newspaper pressure', and pleaded with his fellow MPs: 'Do not tell the enemy without warrant that there are hundreds of thousands of free men in this country who refuse to fight for freedom. Do not pay Prussian militarism the compliment of imitating the most hateful of its institutions.'[184]

Jack Seely, the former war secretary, now a brigadier general on leave from Flanders, spoke as a former opponent of conscription who had changed his mind; and Redmond, while stating Irish opposition, said that as far as Britain was concerned conscription was a matter not of principle, as Simon had put it, but of necessity. Simon's argument attracted only hard-core pacifists and the Irish when the vote came: the government won by 403 to 105. Distressed by Simon's conduct, Asquith, his patron, told Curzon: 'I felt as if my son had struck me in the face in public.'[185]

Labour had to be propitiated; there were fears Henderson and two junior ministers would be mandated to resign, after a protest led by the National Union of Railwaymen. Despite the victory of Stanton, the anti-pacifist, in the Merthyr by-election, a congress of Labour delegates on 6 January expressed opposition to the new Bill by a factor of two to one, notwithstanding Henderson pleading with them to support the government, and despite his colleague John Hodge warning that the alternative was an election in which a Labour Party opposed to conscription would do badly and lose what influence it had. Henderson and two junior colleagues said they would have to resign from the government if their party persisted in this line. Asquith persuaded them to stay their hands, and met union leaders to assure them the tribunal system would prevent the law being abused, and that there would be no industrial conscription. This was deemed acceptable.

There were dangers even without an election, so febrile was the mood and so impatient were some – not just Unionists – becoming with Asquith's attitude. John Dillon, a leading Irish Nationalist MP, told Scott that 'the aim of the Tories would be, with Lloyd George's assistance, without an election to oust Asquith [who, when Scott saw him on 10 January, 'seemed a beaten man'] and put Bonar Law in his place.'[186] Carson would come back and he and Lloyd George, between whom there was a sinister alliance, would dominate the Government and Bonar Law would be wax in their hand.'[187] Dillon was right: Lloyd George would tell Miss Stevenson that Carson 'is a great man: he has courage, he has determination; he has judgment.'[188]

On 27 January 1916, the Military Service Act introduced conscription for unmarried men aged between eighteen and forty-one, from 2 March. At a conference in Bristol that day Labour voted against compulsion and the Act, but also voted against an agitation to repeal it. The Liberals too were damaged. Lloyd George felt he had acted according to his conscience, believing a bigger army was essential for victory. Some Liberals labelled him a traitor, betraying core Liberal values and throwing in his lot with the Tories. His Liberal colleagues were increasingly aware of his association with Northcliffe, for whom conscription was a victory, and deeply disliked it. Riddell told Miss Stevenson that 'if Lord N once gets a footing inside the Government, he will not rest until he is made Dictator . . . Lord N is unscrupulous, & a dangerous man.'[189]

The Military Service Act was, as Simon had correctly predicted, only the start. Despite this almost revolutionary measure, altering the whole balance between the state and the individual, recruitment remained far short of what was necessary. The government also had to consider the Navy's needs. The Admiralty was demanding more ships, which were being built more slowly because of the removal of much labour from the shipyards. The pressure for full conscription was unaffected by the Act, and Asquith continued to waver between two factions in the cabinet. Unattested married men would eventually have to be called up, and the arguments rehearsed all over again. Simon soon protested that the tribunals considering exemptions were conducted capriciously, and he was right. Auckland Geddes, a Lloyd George crony who became director of National Service in 1917, said that 'with, perhaps, more knowledge than most of the working of conscription in this country, I hold the fully matured opinion that, on balance, the imposition of military conscription added little if anything to the effective sum of our war effort.'[190] There were more soldiers than could be equipped, and the conscripts were less motivated than the volunteers. There were 748,587 new claims for exemptions from munitions workers and miners who hitherto could have volunteered, and who now found themselves called up.[191] There were only 48,000 enlistments of unattested single men in the first six months, roughly half the number who had come forward each month under the voluntary system.[192] Within weeks a poster campaign and a series of public appeals began, hoping to persuade married men who had not attested to come forward.

The new law created the conscientious objection movement, whose adherents would occupy much of the time of tribunals, which had the power to order non-combatant war work (such as on farms or in industry) or to imprison those who refused to fight. The tribunals were run largely by unsympathetic men, and many claims were rejected. Forty-one from the initial call-up who refused altogether were sent to France, where they could be shot for disobeying orders: but Asquith had them brought back after a month. By the end of the war 3,300 had agreed to join the Non-Combatant Corps, 2,400 did ambulance work at the front, and 3,964 joined working parties in Britain, engaging in tasks such as road-building. The 6,261 who refused to do any war work at all – 'absolutists' – were sent to prison, and despite Asquith's earlier intervention some were sent to France.[193]

Wells, commenting on the intellectual leap the country had had to make to accept conscription, called it 'a real turning about of the British mind, the close of a period of chaotic freedom almost unprecedented in the history of communities.'[194] But, setting a theme for the twentieth century with which he was intellectually at ease, he called it 'the rediscovery of the State as the necessary form into which the individual life must fit.'

VII

Kitchener had returned from the Near East on 30 November, despite Asquith's having given the impression that he would stay there. On 22 November, on advice from him telegraphed home, the War Committee agreed to recommend that the Gallipoli peninsula be evacuated. The final decision was left to the cabinet, which discussed it two days later. It postponed a ruling because of protests by Curzon, who circulated two memoranda, on 25 and 30 November, arguing against it. He was at odds with his leader, Law. Asquith asked Hankey, upon whose judgement he had come to rely, to set out his view. Hankey took Curzon's side, arguing that by relieving pressure on Constantinople Britain would make it easier for Turkey to attack Egypt or Mesopotamia, or even move against Russia in the Caucasus. This divided the cabinet still further. It was not until 7 December that it agreed on a partial evacuation, which happened on 20 December; a week later it was decided to remove all forces, which took place on 8 January 1916, both operations being conducted with relatively little loss of life. Although the aim of taking Constantinople had failed, Turkish losses were twice those of the British Empire troops. The consequent weakening of their army would eventually assist British progress in Palestine and Mesopotamia during the rest of the war. When it came to lowering morale in Turkey, destabilising and bringing about the fall of the Ottoman Empire and contributing to the capitulations of the autumn of 1918, the campaign paid some sort of dividend: but that should not detract from the reckless incompetence with which it was planned, and which rightly remained a blot on Churchill's reputation for the rest of his life.

Kitchener's relationship with Lloyd George had irretrievably broken down. They had argued over whether to evacuate Salonica – where troops had, on Lloyd George's suggestion, gone earlier in the year, opening a front against Austria and guaranteeing Bulgarian neutrality. The argument had ended with Lloyd George telling Kitchener that 'it seems you and the Germans want the same thing'.[195] Lloyd George told Miss Stevenson – who faithfully recorded every word in her diary – that he believed the War Office was systematically seeking to undermine the Ministry of Munitions. Whether or not this was true hardly matters: that Lloyd George, in the grip of his egotism and ambition, believed it to be true was all that did. On 12 December 1915 he asked Scott down to Walton Heath for lunch, and told him he did not just want Kitchener out of the War Office, but in the event of his defenestration would refuse to succeed him unless Kitchener had no other post from which he could disrupt what Lloyd George would want to do. His discontent went well beyond the Kitchener question: he also complained about the now institutional habit at cabinet meetings of failing to take decisions about how to deploy forces and prosecute the war more effectively: the main theme of his politics for the coming year. Lloyd George had convinced himself that he alone had the vision and the drive to put things right, but needed a free hand.

By now the munitions minister was umbilically close to the Northcliffe press. Perhaps awareness of this provoked Simon, on 30 November, having been attacked by those newspapers for the censorship policy he operated as home secretary, to make a marathon speech in the Commons attacking Northcliffe and his works. Mrs Churchill, writing to her husband, said the speech would 'have been very damaging had it not been made by a prig and a bore.'[196] However, Stamfordham congratulated Simon on the King's orders for having attacked 'the dangerous influence of the Northcliffe press'.[197] Inevitably, *The Times* went for Simon. 'If Ministers themselves would attack the Germans with half the energy they devote to *The Times* they would be a good deal nearer winning the war.'[198] In Simon's case, *The Times* and the *Mail* were just warming up.

Lloyd George's desire to aggrandise himself – and, by implication, belittle Kitchener as the minister previously responsible for munitions – was fed when he made a long-awaited statement about the supply of arms to the Commons on 20 December.[199] He told MPs that 'the German successes, such as they are, are entirely, or almost entirely, due to the mechanical preponderance which they achieved at the beginning of the War,' but that a level of mechanisation had been achieved by his ministry that had undone that advantage.[200] He admitted the shell shortage the previous spring; that the Germans had been turning out 250,000 shells a day, almost all of them high explosive, whereas Britain had made 2,500 high explosives a day and another 13,000 shrapnel shells. He was proud to have shipped in businessmen who had made huge sacrifices in salary to improve the manufacturing process, notably in securing raw materials such as metal and by forming an inspectorate to drive factories to higher productivity.

He added that the government had recognised the importance of the machine gun, and his ministry's first priority had been to increase enormously their output. Far larger numbers of rifles and trench mortars had also been produced; and he hoped better mechanisation would increase output and save taxpayers' money. He said Britain had more of the raw materials needed for the prosecution of the war and, so long as it retained command of the seas, would win it: 'The overwhelming superiority is still with us.'[201] The main difficulty, with the Army desperate for men,

was that the munitions industry required '80,000 skilled men, and from
200,000 to 300,000 unskilled men and women' for the new factories Lloyd
George was setting up.[202] He also, quite rightly, stamped upon one growing myth: 'I have heard rumours that we are over-doing it, over-ordering,
over-building, over-producing. Nothing could be more malevolent or
more mischievous.' To prove his point, he said: 'Take the last great
battle – that of Loos. You had a prodigious accumulation of ammunition. There is not a general who was in the battle who in giving his
report does not tell you that with three times the quantity of ammunition, especially in the heavier natures, they would have achieved
twenty times the result.'[203] He emphasised that it was better to take
risks with taxpayers' money than with soldiers' lives. If costs were too
high, then the best way to reduce them was to have improved
productivity.

The one caveat he expressed was the attitude of the unions, which raised
hackles on the Labour benches, where it was maintained (inaccurately)
that the unions had always since war broke out responded well to
demands the government had made upon them. It provoked from Lloyd
George perhaps the most memorable passage of any of his wartime
speeches, in which he complained about the failure to enforce the law on
dilution, under which men and women without experience in certain
trades were taught the skills essential to practise them, for the purpose
of war production. His speech was also read as a criticism of the way the
government of which he was so prominent a member was conducting
the war:

Unless the employer begins by putting on the lathes unskilled men
and women we cannot enforce that Act of Parliament. The first
step, therefore, is that the employer must challenge a decision upon
the matter. He is not doing so because of the trouble which a few
other firms have had. Let us do it. Victory depends upon it! Hundreds of thousands of precious lives depend upon it. It is a question
of whether you are going to bring this War victoriously to an end
in a year or whether it is going to linger on in bloodstained paths
for years. Labour has got the answer. The contract was entered into
with labour. We are carrying it out. It can be done. I wonder
whether it will not be too late? Ah! two fatal words of this War! Too
late in moving here. Too late in arriving there. Too late in coming

to this decision. Too late in starting with enterprises. Too late in preparing. In this War the footsteps of the Allied forces have been dogged by the mocking spectre of 'Too Late'; and unless we quicken our movements damnation will fall on the sacred cause for which so much gallant blood has flowed. I beg employers and workmen not to have 'Too Late' inscribed upon the portals of their workshops: that is my appeal.[204]

The Times's largely laudatory comment on the speech, reflecting Northcliffe's closeness to Lloyd George at that time, concluded with the observation that 'the way to be in time for the future is to recognise that you have always been too late in the past.'[205]

More trappings of normal life disappeared that winter. The government announced the closure of the British Museum, and most museums in the country, as an economy measure: the saving was estimated at £250,000 a year.[206] Although the government was highly reluctant to contemplate rationing, people were urged to eat less meat. Manchester became subject to the same restrictions on drinking hours and 'treating' – the buying of rounds – as London, Liverpool and other cities, despite local people having strongly campaigned to avoid them; not just to help factory output, but because of evidence that women were drinking heavily and neglecting their children. The government restricted the hops, malt and sugar available to brewers, forcing them to brew less, or lighter, beer. Private motorists were warned of serious petrol shortages, and told to restrict their driving. That at least would help lessen the numbers being mown down in the blackout, sometimes by hit-and-run drivers.

There were increasing demands for compulsory thrift, to channel some of Britons' higher earnings back to the government in the form of war loans. The Revd Andrew Clark described the outrage of his parishioners in Great Leighs 'where no-one has ever done anything else' than practise economy 'and where there is no increase of money received, since no-one has war-work . . . and no-one has any reserve either to give or invest.'[207] The public was warned to expect smaller newspapers, as shipping brought in food rather than pulp from Canada. More positively, resistance to women in the workforce seemed at last to have disappeared; the demand for them in munitions work became so high that a national appeal was launched to raise funds for the YWCA to provide

hostels, canteens and social facilities for them. Technological developments created jobs for women in which there was little or no exclusive
history of male dominance: notably in strategically important work in
wireless telegraphy.

Early in 1916 the government's strategic planning was shown to be
defective in another crucial respect. On the night of 31 January Zeppelins
bombed Suffolk and the East and West Midlands: fourteen were killed
in Tipton alone out of a total of seventy dead. The raids triggered a
spasm of public outrage over why the country's air defences remained so
poor that bombers could get so far into England. They arrived at 4.30
p.m., just before nightfall, and carried on more or less unmolested until
disappearing back over the North Sea at 5 a.m. The government had
issued the Royal Flying Corps with no orders of what to do in an air raid,
partly because of confusion between the War Office and the Admiralty
over who was responsible for directing the RFC. Just twenty-four aircraft were allocated to defend London, and only two for the rest of
England, hence the Zeppelins' free run. Lloyd George was concerned
about the ease with which Woolwich Arsenal might be bombed, and
implored his colleagues to improve the capital's air defences for that reason if for no other. It was decided to put French in charge of ensuring
London was defended, and the blackout was greatly extended.

Unfortunately, the same chronic indecisiveness that scarred the general conduct of government hampered resolution of this issue. The
cabinet argued for days about whether to set up a separate Air Ministry –
a suggestion of Curzon, who hoped to lead it – and, if so, whether it
would have an autonomy in military aviation comparable to the War
Office's for the Army. Northcliffe had the *Daily Mail* begin a campaign to
improve Britain's air defences, because of his belief – justified, as it
happened – that the Germans would soon be able to send squadrons of
aircraft to bomb England. He had also turned *The Times* on Asquith over
the War Committee's inadequacies, with too many decisions referred to
the cabinet – where Asquith's lack of direction helped ensure they were
not made.

The air defences question became so toxic that Asquith appointed a
cabinet committee under Derby to settle it: but after a month Derby
resigned, unable to secure cooperation between the Army and Navy air
services. Derby had sought Northcliffe's advice, and the press baron suggested he talk to businessmen and put a dynamic one in charge of

developing air defences: he may have had in mind his brother Lord Rothermere, who before the war was over would assume some related responsibilities. In his resignation letter Derby suggested Asquith create a combined air service. Asquith's response was to form an Air Board, under Curzon. This immediately caused the *Daily Mail* to run an editorial entitled: 'The Wrong Man. What Does Lord Curzon Know About Aircraft?'[208]

So angry was Northcliffe that, two months later, he made a rare speech in the Lords in a debate initiated by Lord Montagu of Beaulieu, who proposed the government set up 'a fully-fledged Air Ministry', a call seconded by Milner.[209] Northcliffe, careful not to criticise Curzon by name, said the ministry should have a board of inventions and give greater encouragement to manufacturers, to stimulate the high levels of production necessary for the long war he expected. He demanded the government train more pilots immediately, saying that 'I believe if we defer the training of large bodies of men until the autumn and winter we shall be lamentably short next year, when there will be a great need.'[210]

On 22 February the government's blockade policy, or lack of one, was also attacked in the Lords: too little, it was claimed, was being done to prevent supplies, particularly of food and raw materials, from reaching enemy countries. This was unfair: exports from America to Germany had fallen from £54 million in 1913 to £2.3 million in 1915.[211] The next target was Sweden, still trading extensively with the Germans, but pressure was also brought on Denmark, Norway and Holland. Peers considered the existence of any such trade absurd given the strength of the Royal Navy. The government was accused of hiding behind international law that had no relevance in a life-or-death struggle; and Lord Sydenham accused it of having allowed huge exports of cocoa to Holland that had been passed on to Germany to fortify troops in the German trenches. Admiral Lord Beresford complained that only an 'absolute blockade' would win the war, which, he said, would have finished by now had the policy been operated sooner.[212] That meant the Navy arresting ships on suspicion of carrying goods to the Central Powers and then taking the matter before a Prize Court. The cabinet was accused of not having taken a proper decision on this, as on other questions.

It further illustrated the government's propensity for muddle that Beresford was unclear who ran what passed for the existing blockade: the Foreign Office, the Board of Trade or the Contraband Committee.

Various Orders in Council had contradicted each other. The solution adopted was to declare anything entering Germany 'absolute contraband', and that all enemy property in neutral ships should be confiscated.[213] Lansdowne announced that a Ministry of Blockade would be established, under a cabinet minister – Lord Robert Cecil, appointed the next day. Its purpose was to blackmail neutral countries into not trading with Germany, threatening to starve them of supplies if they did, but offering to buy goods they would otherwise send there. This would be the policy that would help bring Germany to its knees in 1918.

Once the first round of the conscription battle had ended Lloyd George found himself isolated in the cabinet. His fellow Liberals did not trust him, and most Unionists did not like him. It stoked his disillusion. He told Scott on 18 February of his 'profound dissatisfaction with the whole conduct of the war' and said he was going off to Walton Heath 'to consider his whole position with a view to possibly resigning his place in the Cabinet.' He felt that he, Carson and Churchill 'would together make an effective opposition.'[214] His views about the war were, unbeknown to him, shared by the BEF's commander-in-chief. Haig complained the same day to Joffre that the British Army was '75,000 below strength in 39 divisions', with many soldiers inadequately trained and the transport to move them lacking.[215] To stave off the moment when married men would be called up, the government announced in late February that some attested married men would be moved to reserved occupations to replace single men, who would be sent to the front.

The Navy, too, had its problems. On 17 February Jellicoe attended the War Committee and told it the Grand Fleet needed light cruisers, destroyers and minesweepers, and that the recruitment drive was badly slowing down the rate at which ships were being built. Fisher, who since his resignation the previous May over his differences with Churchill about the Dardanelles had become chairman of the Navy's Board of Invention and Research, was asked to talk to the War Committee. When he did, he reiterated Jellicoe's views. Churchill picked up the point on 7 March – less than three months before the Battle of Jutland, the crucial encounter of the Great War between the Royal Navy and the Imperial German Navy – when the naval estimates were debated in the Commons.

On leave from the front but in civilian clothes, Churchill made one prescient observation, that the German High Seas Fleet was unlikely to be kept in port for the duration of the war. He warned that it had proved easier to recover from the munitions shortage than it would be to recover from a shortage of ships, which threatened British naval ascendancy. Nor could he understand, given the prevalence of air raids, why naval pilots had not bombed the Zeppelin sheds in Germany. He felt that this, and all the other problems in the Admiralty, was because of 'a lack of driving force and mental energy which cannot be allowed to continue . . . and can only be rectified in one way.'[216] That way was straightforward: 'I urge the First Lord of the Admiralty without delay to fortify himself, to vitalise and animate his Board of Admiralty by recalling Lord Fisher to his post as First Sea Lord.'

This was an astonishing volte-face. The previous July Churchill, steaming about his demotion, had berated Balfour about his having given Fisher a minor Admiralty appointment: 'This officer deserted his post in time of war. He was ordered by the Prime Minister to return to it in the King's name. He defied this order . . . for 14 days there was no First Sea Lord. During that period the German Fleet put to sea, and it was necessary to send the whole British Fleet to meet it. The decisive naval battle of the world might have taken place, while Fisher was refusing to do his duty, and engaged in creating a political crisis from which he hoped to obtain added power.'[217] It was a long road from there to where Churchill was eight months later: but just as sorting out the shells shortage had required someone as radical in approach as Lloyd George, and his 'men of push and go', so Churchill believed that only a force of nature such as Fisher, with his national prestige, could give the lead required to inspire the Board of Admiralty.

He was not alone in wishing to see Fisher brought back: his friend Scott had advocated it, and had tried – and failed – to persuade Law to embrace the subject. He had, though, also lobbied Northcliffe, whom he had seen at *The Times* on 18 February, and had found 'far from hostile' to the idea and indeed 'actively favourable', though it was clear to Scott that Northcliffe disliked Fisher.[218] Churchill had seen Fisher and they had agreed to let bygones be bygones; he had rehearsed his speech in front of Scott and Mrs Churchill, and it was only the latter who took exception to it. Asquith dined with the Churchills the night before the speech and Churchill informed him of what he intended to say. When he spoke, Fisher was in the gallery.

Balfour, who Scott, also in the gallery, had noted 'writhed visibly with irritation' during Churchill's performance, demolished him the next day.[219] He called the speech 'very unfortunate, both in form and substance'.[220] He denied that naval construction was behindhand, although he did admit that obtaining skilled shipwrights was a problem. He added: 'I will make no boast about the British Navy. I will not guarantee it against misfortune or accidents. But I say, in perfect confidence, that it is stronger in the face of any overt attack which it is likely to meet, that it is far stronger than it was at the beginning of the War, and is, I believe, stronger than it has ever been in its history.'[221] As for Fisher, Balfour observed there could not have been a single person who had listened to that part of Churchill's speech without 'profound stupefaction'.

He said Churchill had never concealed his view of Fisher, and crushed him with one of the better jokes in Parliament in the twentieth century: 'The great ancestor of my right hon Friend, the first Duke of Marlborough, was always supposed to be more cool, more collected, more master of himself, more clear in thought amid the din of battle than he was in the calmer occupations of peace, and perhaps my right hon Friend shares this hereditary peculiarity. I venture to suggest that that clearness of thought which we all desiderate is bought at a rather costly figure if it involves a European war in order to obtain it.'[222] Churchill was allowed to speak next, and said Balfour's case against him was 'crudely exaggerated': he failed to carry the House, not for the first or last time.[223]

Churchill, written off by many after the Dardanelles and far from popular, was widely attacked for his speech. The *Daily Mail*, reflecting Northcliffe's scepticism about him, savaged him. The prime minister told Scott that Churchill's speech had been 'a piece of the grossest effrontery' and 'impudent humbug'.[224] It cannot have improved Asquith's mood when Kitchener called on him to report that Churchill had asked to be relieved of his command 'in order to grapple with the political situation at home.'[225] As for Fisher, Asquith 'shouted' at Scott that for deserting his post the previous May 'he deserved to be shot, and in any other country he would have been shot.' Asquith sent for Churchill, who he also told Scott was 'a little mad', and reminded him that his father's political career had been ruined by an absurdly capricious act.[226] He advised Churchill not to persist in his demands; Churchill agreed, albeit with reluctance, his decision perhaps helped by the fact that Mrs Churchill had made the same point to him. He went back to France; but in his own mind this was only temporary, his return merely 'a question of preparation and of

The *Illustrated London News* imagines the diplomatic turmoil in the Foreign Office in July 1914: Sir Edward Grey is on the left, standing by the table; Count Benckendorff stands next to him; Paul Cambon is seated, engaging an unidentified man in conversation; opposite him, gripping his lapels, is Prince Lichnowsky; and the man sitting on the furthest right appears to be Sir Arthur Nicolson.

Henry and Margot Asquith just before the war, keeping up appearances.

Sir Edward Grey, later Viscount Grey of Fallodon, who saw the lamps going out all over Europe, painted by Sir James Guthrie.

Men queuing at the Whitehall recruiting office in London in the late summer of 1914: Mrs Asquith wanted a shelter built to protect them from the rain.

Viscount Haldane, whose mistake was to understand Germany, and Lord Kitchener, shortly to become a poster.

Sir John Jellicoe, who would command the Fleet and achieve a score-draw at Jutland.

To create a sense of the comforts of home at the front, the families of Tommies were urged to send them Oxo cubes.

Carl Hans Lody, the first German spy to be executed, in the dock at his trial in November 1914.

Ruins of the lifeboat station at Scarborough after being shelled by the German navy in December 1914: the raid provoked an outbreak of vulgarity from Churchill that distressed Mrs Asquith.

Bertrand Russell soaks up the sun at Garsington, Bloomsbury's country club.

Lady Ottoline Morrell, chatelaine of Garsington, with her daughter Julian.

A three-man tribunal questions a conscientious objector and his adviser, watched by family and friends.

Horatio Bottomley, recruiter, demagogue, jingoist, swindler and charlatan extraordinaire.

The Earl of Derby, bearing an impression of the last artist to paint him, in this case Sir William Orpen.

AN "OBJECT" LESSON

FATHER   BROTHER   MOTHER   SISTER   UNCLE   COUSIN

CONSCIENTIOUS OBJECTOR

Frank Holland

PLATE 9.   —By permission of John Bull

"This little pig stayed at home"

A cartoon from *John Bull* by Frank Holland – who also drew for the *Daily Mail* – depicting the popular attitude to conscientious objectors.

Sir George (later Lord) Riddell, proprietor of the *News of the World*, and crony-in-chief and landlord of Lloyd George.

Lord Northcliffe, founder of the *Daily Mail*, owner of *The Times*, megalomaniac and possibly the most powerful man in Britain until Lloyd George supplanted him.

A shop in London's east end advertises the nationality of its owners during the anti-German riots after the sinking of the *Lusitania* in May 1915.

Edith Cavell, whose execution became the ultimate example of German 'frightfulness'.

The British sense of humour as propaganda: another Boche headed for the corpse factory.

Below: The stark reality of the German U-boat war: a mass grave in Ireland of *Lusitania* victims.

Winston Churchill as First Lord of the Admiralty in his 'delicious' war.

David Lloyd George, the man who very nearly lost the war.

Maurice Hankey, the power behind two prime ministers – as he said himself.

Field Marshal Sir Douglas (later Earl) Haig, who committed suicide twenty-five years after his death.

opportunity.'²²⁷ He had not realised how much the old guard who ran the government disliked Fisher's publicity-seeking exhibitionism, perhaps because he shared the same traits. Asquith, possibly realising how little of a threat Churchill had become, told him that if in future he wished to be relieved of his command – he had been promoted to the rank of colonel and commanded the 6th Battalion of the Royal Scots Fusiliers – 'your relief will be arranged for, as soon as it can be effected without detriment to the Service.'²²⁸

The neutering of Churchill removed just one of the government's welter of problems. At a by-election in East Hertfordshire on 9 March a Unionist candidate with Liberal backing was defeated by an independent who campaigned for a strong air policy. The failure of an air ministry to materialise was yet another example of the dithering of the coalition. Lloyd George railed about this lassitude to Miss Stevenson on 11 March: 'Everyone tells the same tale – that the country is sick of the present Government & loathes & despises Asquith. And yet, now that there is no Opposition, it is very difficult to turn them out.'²²⁹ He went on: 'Bonar Law is limp and lifeless; Balfour can never make up his mind about anything. There *is* no one.' And Lloyd George himself could not force Asquith out as it would be attributed to 'personal motives', something of which he had an abundance.

VIII

Although Asquith had eventually admitted the need to start conscription, his position was increasingly precarious. The crisis had proved to Lloyd George and his supporters that the prime minister had failed to make the transition from a peacetime leader to a wartime one. Nor had the question of conscription of married men been settled, and opinion remained divided on that. Hankey feared there would be an attempt to 'stampede' the rest of the cabinet and Parliament into conceding compulsory military service for all men of military age the moment Asquith left, on 31 March, for Rome to persuade the Italians (who had the previous year declared war on Austria–Hungary) to enter the war against Germany.²³⁰ No such coup was attempted, and Italy did eventually declare war on Germany on 28 August. When Asquith returned he formed a cabinet committee of himself, Law, McKenna and Austen Chamberlain to try to reach a solution about general conscription.

By the late spring of 1916 there were calls for a massive government reconstruction; and the sequence of events begun by the formation of the coalition a year earlier, and which would culminate in Asquith's fall, accelerated. The Tory press – led by Gwynne's *Morning Post* – openly called for Asquith to be replaced by a more dynamic leader, a job for which Gwynne had earmarked Carson. He had been *de facto* Leader of the Opposition since leaving the government, and enjoyed support among Liberal as well as Tory MPs. He became chairman of the Unionist War Committee and called for immediate conscription for married men, which Robertson supported, on the grounds of ensuring equality of sacrifice. Asquith had his critics among senior officers too. General Sir Henry Wilson, in utter disregard of the constitutional proprieties, corresponded with Law trying to persuade him to bring Asquith down and form a government to prosecute the war properly. (Law warned Wilson not to meddle – he said if the government fell it would require a general election, which would divide the country.) Even the King was rattled about Asquith, to the extent where he asked Hankey 'very confidentially' about his suitability as prime minister. Hankey loyally said: 'he was the only man who could handle his team'. The King agreed, though spoke highly of Curzon, who had been overseeing shipping matters for the government, with his customary command and competence.[231]

Asquith's problems were stacking up further, however, as a familiar bugbear returned. Conscription had proved as contentious in practice as it had in principle. There was soon evidence that attested married men were organising in big cities around Britain to ensure none of them was called up until every unmarried man had been taken: the National Union of Attested Married Men held a rally in the Albert Hall on 31 March, at which a supposedly soothing statement by Derby about his loyalty to them was read out. It did not have the desired effect, being interrupted 'by bursts of ironical laughter and cries of derision'. Cheering broke out only when Derby confirmed he felt bound by honour to resign if the pledge he had given was broken.[232] He agreed to meet a deputation of them, and the government promised to reduce the number of reserved occupations.

In early April the pressure to extend conscription intensified, with Northcliffe taunting Asquith by running an editorial in the *Daily Mail* called 'Fiddling While Rome Burns'.[233] *The Times* had already assaulted the government on this issue, mocking Law for saying that he and his colleagues were still 'examining all the figures'.[234] It called the existing policy 'ill-drafted and cowardly' and observed that 'great wars are won by courage and action'. The Tory press was similarly critical of McKenna, even though he had earned widespread applause on 4 April for a Budget it was felt underpinned British financial stability, despite a deficit of £1,323 million. He increased income tax to 5s in the pound and the excess-profits tax was raised from 50 to 60 per cent. However, he was also the principal opponent of extending conscription, on the grounds that it would start to cause serious damage to the economy: something pro-conscriptionists actively disputed. Northcliffe, who had made several visits to France, was angered that the Army had men 'doing civilian and women's work', with the Pay Department 'packed with young men doing the clerical work of girls.'[235] He continued to blame all problems on the fact that a cabinet of twenty-three men ran the war, instead of a small group. This was not lost on Lloyd George.

Attested married men aged twenty-five to thirty-two were called up on 7 April. Asquith met a deputation of them: they demanded that either the government do a better job of calling up unmarried men, or release the married ones from their pledge to serve. Asquith admitted that a clause in the Military Service Act that said men from a reserved occupation could be made to do military service for two months had been 'abused': but he would soon be forced to recognise that with the mood becoming so restive, it amplified the case for total compulsion.[236] Opponents of conscription continued to mobilise against it. Supported by the likes of Russell, Lansbury and Snowden, Fenner Brockway, who would serve the Labour Party for much of the twentieth century, formed the No Conscription Fellowship. It held a rally in London on 8 April that Mrs Webb attended and noted was 'packed with 2,000 young men'.[237]

She observed the predominant type as being 'the intellectual pietist . . . saliently conscious of their own righteousness' and in whom she detected an unpleasant certainty. There were, too, 'professional rebels', who had alighted on the cause as a means, they hoped, to 'smash the Military Service Act'. But she also noted 'misguided youths who have been swept into the movement because 'conscientious objection' had served to excuse their refusal to enlist and possibly might have saved them from the terrors and discomforts of fighting – 'pasty-faced furtive boys, who looked dazed at the amount of heroism that was being expected from them.' She detected they were 'scared' by the unanimity with which it was decided 'to refuse alternative service': those who would not work behind the lines, or on farms, to help the war effort faced being put under military discipline and court-martialled. A failure to agree on tactics – whether to pursue martyrdom or take non-combatant roles – split the movement, and rendered it ineffectual.

A week later the Army Council formally advised Asquith to extend conscription. Robertson lunched with Repington afterwards, telling him that at the end of February the Army had recruited 250,000 men fewer than required, and of 195,000 men who had been due to appear under the Derby Scheme only 38,000 had come through, the rest either missing, unaccounted for or medically disqualified. Repington learned from Robertson that a quarter of the men who did appear were unfit for service.[238] A cabinet was called for 17 April, at which Lloyd George agreed to ask Robertson to back down, it having been agreed that to present the Germans with a show of government division would have been highly damaging. However, Lloyd George told Scott on 13 April 'of his strong and increasing dissatisfaction with the conduct of the war and his intention to bring matters to a head if a measure of general compulsory service were not adopted on the lines of the "equality of sacrifice" motion of which Carson had given notice for the following Wednesday [19 April] after the Prime Minister had made his promised statement on Tuesday as to the intentions of the Government based on the report of the cabinet Committee.'[239] Lloyd George, who was busy cultivating Carson, threatened to resign serially. Henry Wickham Steed, *The Times*'s foreign editor, quoted one of Lloyd George's friends as saying that 'he galloped gallantly towards the fence but, on reaching it, drew rein and looked round for a gate.'[240] Arthur Lee, a Unionist MP who worked under him at Munitions, told his wife of the main reason he would not resign: Carson had told Lee that 'if LG goes out, having practically no private means at all, he will drop from an income of £5,000 to the MP's £400 a year.'[241]

On 13 April Lloyd George, keeping the press on his side as ever, took Scott for tea with Riddell and Sir William Robertson Nicoll, editor and owner of the *British Weekly*, to discuss whether he should resign. He said that although conscription would be the reason, 'I should really resign as a protest against the general conduct of the war.'[242] He added that: 'There is no grip. Asquith and Balfour do not seem to realise the serious nature of the situation.'

The two press barons thought he should resign, if that would be the only way of effecting change. Scott kept quiet, but after the meeting warned Lloyd George that any resignation speech he might make should be 'extremely restrained and generous in tone.'[243] Lloyd George answered that he would make no speech, but simply send a carefully worded letter to Asquith outlining his reasons. He asked Scott to visit him at Walton Heath the following Sunday to go through the text of the letter with him: but, as Scott recalled, 'when I got there no letter of course had been written.'[244] After some dithering – which included Lloyd George falling asleep in the middle of his drafting the letter with Arthur Lee and his private secretary – a message arrived from Stamfordham, asking to see Lloyd George on behalf of the King. Law had told the Sovereign of the proposed resignation, and it was Stamfordham's job to urge him to change his mind. According to Scott, 'Stamfordham placed before him the obvious considerations of maintaining the Coalition, standing together in the face of the enemy etc, to all of which George replied that he would be most happy to act upon them "but for the oath I have taken to serve his Majesty faithfully" – a reply which appears to have considerably non-plussed the worthy Stamfordham, who is not, George says, a brilliant person.'

Lloyd George was not alone in scheming against Asquith. Churchill, who with other MPs at the front was ordered home to vote on Carson's motion, had been plotting his return to politics by letter with Lloyd George, Smith and Carson. On 12 April he sent his wife a letter for Asquith asking to be relieved of his command, and which she was to await the signal to deliver. He longed for Lloyd George to resign, so that with Carson they could form a proper Opposition. Yet since all the Unionists backed compulsory service, if Lloyd George resigned on that issue they would have no choice but to go too: so an interesting question would arise of what would be the government, and what the Opposition – a question that would end up being thrashed out the following December. Sensing the wind was changing, Churchill sent his wife the signal and was back in London on 11 May.

Negotiations over the extension of conscription continued, with a twice-postponed cabinet meeting eventually taking place late on Friday 14 April, its discussions then adjourned until 17 April at 4.30 p.m.; a meeting that began in the House of Commons and finished in Downing Street. It broke up at 6.15, but Lloyd George and other senior ministers stayed talking until 8 p.m. It was decided the cabinet committee on compulsory service would dissolve without reporting. A new committee – this time of Asquith, Lloyd George, Balfour, Crewe and Law – was formed to thrash the matter out. It was unable to agree, and Asquith twice had to tell the Commons he could not make the promised statement about the Bill. By this time Law, like Asquith, was having serious problems with his party, who admired the more robust stand Carson was taking. Law felt he was fighting for survival as leader of the Unionists.

By the end of 17 April Lloyd George, motivated in Scott's view too by his ministerial salary, had decided not to resign. His egotism also played a strong part. He told Miss Stevenson he was reluctant because a new minister 'would find lots of things not running quite smoothly, and some of the biggest factories not yet working. He would take all the credit himself for putting these things right.'[245] He felt that within six weeks he would have everything working, and he would get the credit, and so could hand over to a successor 'safely'. He said something similar to Scott.

The Unionist War Committee, with 125 members of both Houses present, met on 18 April under Carson's chairmanship and called for general conscription. The next day Asquith admitted the cabinet was split: he could not reconcile Henderson and Labour to the new policy of conscripting all adult men under forty-one.[246] Lloyd George told Stamfordham he thought Asquith feared strikes or possibly even revolution, threats he thought exaggerated. Churchill enlisted Fisher to try to persuade Lloyd George to resign; and Law told Lloyd George that if he resigned Law would too, which would probably have brought down the government and necessitated an election. The manoeuvring disgusted Scott: 'I left them closeted at the Munitions Office,' he recorded, 'glad to escape from this atmosphere of futile intrigue.'[247]

Meanwhile, the hitherto intransigent Henderson accepted a plan put to him by Robertson that compulsion should come only if 60,000 men did not join up in the first month of a new recruitment campaign, and 15,000 a week thereafter. The moment it fell below that, compulsion would be brought in by a parliamentary resolution. Lloyd George went along with this because he was convinced it would fail, and it was thus a question of waiting five or six weeks before the government had to accept conscription for all men was inevitable. Churchill, though, was disappointed: Miss Stevenson reported that he was 'very sick at the idea of the thing going through quietly.'[248] Asquith was buckling under the strain, and the efficiency with which he had conducted affairs in peace-time was now rather ragged. Therefore, senior colleagues suggested appointing a secretary to the cabinet to note its decisions and ensure they were carried out. At first it was thought this should be a minister, and Montagu suggested he was the ideal man. The idea's time would come, and when it did Hankey would be there to oblige.

The first parliamentary secret session of the war was held on 25 April, the second day of the Easter Rising in Ireland. The purpose of the secrecy was not to deny knowledge to the enemy but to conceal government rifts, while presenting the case for married men's conscription. North-cliffe's newspapers were furious at being unable to report this. Asquith – who over Easter had had Ottoline Morrell bending his ear about respecting conscientious objectors – proposed changes to the service regulations. Time-expired men would be made to serve until the end of the war; Territorials could be transferred to any unit where needed; men whose certificates of exemption had expired would be liable for immediate call-up; all youths would become liable to the Military Service Act the moment they reached eighteen; and (crucially) Parliament would be asked for powers to compel unattested men to serve if in any week the numbers joining up fell below 15,000.

The Commons rejected these proposals, thanks to Carson and his allies on the Unionist War Committee who wanted nothing short of total compulsion. Two days later they were reintroduced in the form of a Bill, which Asquith then had to withdraw, so heavily was it attacked; Carson demolished it point by point. The press was almost unanimous in attacking 'patchwork' recruitment. On 29 April the cabinet agreed to universal National Military Service. Although Asquith was personally opposed to this his confidence had been rocked by the tone of the secret session, and he went with the majority. The Bill, introduced on 3 May, was rushed through Parliament and became law on 25 May. As Asquith told the King, the cabinet 'agreed that the proposal to include Ireland in the Military Service Bill was impracticable and ought to be resisted' – initiating a controversy that would echo for the rest of the war.[249] Otherwise, the Bill would apply to every youth in the country thirty days after reaching his eighteenth birthday – giving him the opportunity to enlist voluntarily, if he desired that distinction. There would be a review of the cases of thousands of men exempted for medical reasons, so they could be called up for home duties and less arduous service than required overseas.

Asquith said the measure was 'urgently needed'; Hankey had noted the previous day, though, that he 'obviously hated the job.'[250]

At the Bill's second reading Lloyd George put the government's case, using the opportunity to deny that he had betrayed Liberal principles – something of which he was routinely accused by the Liberal press:

> Every great democracy which has been challenged, which has had its liberties menaced, has defended itself by resort to compulsion, from Greece downwards. Washington won independence for America by compulsory measures; they defended it in 1812 by compulsory measures. Lincoln was not merely a great democrat, but his career was in itself the greatest triumph that democracy has ever achieved in the sphere of Government. He proclaimed the principle of 'Government of the People, by the People, for the People', and he kept it alive by Conscription. In the French Revolution the French people defended their newly-obtained liberties against every effort of the Monarchists by compulsion and by conscriptionary levies. France is defending her country to-day by Conscription.[251]

Simon reiterated the arguments he had used when resigning: the Bill was contrary to the liberal principles for which Britain was fighting. Yet it passed by 328 votes to 36; the conscription debate, in parliamentary terms at least, was over. Derby told a Tory meeting in Lancashire after the Act passed that 'we ought to have had universal compulsion in the first week of the war.'[252] The day he gave the Bill the Royal Assent, the King issued a message to his people in which he expressed his 'recognition and appreciation of the splendid patriotism and self-sacrifice' many had shown by volunteering, and saluted in advance their 'additional sacrifice'.[253]

It was not only men who were being compelled to make a patriotic 'sacrifice'. The people who would pay the greatest price relatively for compulsion would be middle-class women. The allowances for the wives of soldiers from working-class occupations were regarded as generous; middle-class wives whose husbands had forfeited white-collar salaries were poorly compensated, and their standard of living plunged in a season of rising prices. The emphasis on volunteering would now shift to women, to become munitions workers, nurses or farm workers; within a month of the Somme offensive starting an urgent appeal was issued to them to volunteer for the Red Cross or as VADs, and to help at canteens set up to feed factory workers. A long list of remaining agricultural exemptions were removed as the Bill passed, forcing reluctant farmers to use female labour.

Numerous middle-class women were happy to work, and there was a high demand for them: but that raised problems of childcare. After May 1916 many such families moved to cheaper, smaller rented accommodation – few of them were freeholders or mortgagors. Women's groups and societies were organised to give mutual support. The government announced a system of grants, to a maximum of £104 a year, administered by local commissioners to help meet mortgage interest or rent payments, school fees, insurance premiums, and other middle-class outgoings. By the late summer of 1916 there were demands that 'educated' women be admitted to middle-grade clerkships in the civil service, liberating thousands of men who had received exemptions. Some women were doing heavy jobs that would have been unthinkable for their sex a few months earlier: *The Times* reported on 15 September that 'at a slag reduction works women have been set on for shovelling slag into a crusher. At an ironstone works 22 women have been substituted for men, chiefly at loading and unloading wagons . . . at several docks they are acting as pit prop carriers, and in several cases they are working as labourers in the building trade, though none are carrying hods.'[254]

Most obviously, the extension of conscription increased reliance on women in munitions factories and on the land. Concerns were raised about their health: night work for women had been banned in the textile industry in 1844 but had returned through necessity. Many women suffered from exhaustion because they undertook domestic duties by day too. The government was urged to enforce statutory rest periods for mothers with young children. The birth rate was falling because of the absence of so many young men; it was feared that the decline of women's health through overwork would depress it further.

Despite a patronising observation by Francis Dyke Acland, parliamentary secretary at the Ministry of Agriculture, that 'women workers cannot be regarded as a substitute for skilled men, they can only be regarded as supplementing male workers,' he conceded that women were perfectly capable of looking after livestock and poultry, and that 'many women are ploughing and doing it well, but that is, of course, exceptional.'[255] This attitude had echoes of the appointment the previous spring of a Miss Ruth Davis as town sergeant of Colchester, the previous incumbent having enlisted: it was reported that 'she will not have to carry the mace nor act as toastmaster.'[256] Acland announced a grant to the Women's National Land Service Corps to organise the training and placement of volunteers. Committees in each county undertook the organisation and registration of women, and 35,000 had registered by late May 1916. The Board of Trade also appointed a special committee, chaired by the Duchess of Beaufort and dominated by women, to deal with the welfare, and especially the housing, of women workers, to ensure they were not allocated unsuitable billets where moral danger might await them.

Acland told farmers that 'all who have tried women are pleased and swear by them . . . a few weeks' training makes all the difference.'[257] He added: 'The position is: "The women are here; we know they are useful— that is proved up to the hilt; you must try them. If you do not you are doing the Kaiser's work, not the King's." ' Even that, however, would not be enough: 250,000 to 300,000 of the 1,000,000 pre-war agricultural labourers had joined the forces. Therefore, Acland urged people not to take conventional holidays that summer, but to spend the time working on the land. Local committees would organise that too. There were calls for women to serve as Army cooks, and the War Office arranged for German prisoners of war to work on the land.

The government sent women to France to see how Frenchwomen organised and undertook farm work. County committees held recruiting drives: within a month 3,000 women had joined from 170 villages in Norfolk. Meriel Talbot, who would command the Women's Land Army, ran a panel of speakers to tour the country to recruit female workers. The Women's National Land Service Corps was formed to organise this labour, its first priority being to recruit those 'of the professional classes' as forewomen and to train others.[258] Gangs of university women spent their long vacations fruit-picking and harvesting. This was as well, because anger with the Irish over their reluctance to join the Army caused farmers in Lincolnshire and the Fens to boycott Irish potato pickers. A degree of organisation similar to that used to recruit Kitchener's army was finally being used to maximise women's contribution to the war.

Hankey's memoirs cited the official figures: 4,970,902 men served in the forces during the war: just over half – 2,532,684 – enlisted under the voluntary system, with 2,438,218 called up under compulsion.[259] No one would now escape the dragnet of the recruiting sergeants, including those who felt themselves too rarefied to engage in the somewhat vulgar collective activity of saving the country. In March the unmarried Lytton Strachey, a founder of the Bloomsbury group and limbering up to write his breakthrough work *Eminent Victorians*, had been ordered from internal exile with the Morrells at Garsington to attend a medical examination at White City. 'He told us,' Lady Ottoline recalled, 'that he had waited there from 11 to 3.30, reading Gardiner's *History of England*. He was then examined by an RAMC orderly. He undressed with three other young men, rough fellows, and then appeared naked before the Doctor. One of the young Doctors burst out laughing when he saw him, and no wonder, for he must have looked a very odd sight amongst the other strong sturdy fellows, he so tall and emaciated, with his long beard. They exempted him entirely.'[260] At a preliminary tribunal Strachey had been asked what he would do if he saw a German soldier trying to rape his sister, and he had replied: 'I should try and interpose my own body.'[261]

The alleged treatment of some conscientious objectors was far less amusing, and MPs started to raise questions about it. Sir William Byles asked for it to be confirmed whether Rendel Wyatt, a schoolmaster, Quaker and Cambridge graduate, had been 'arrested and imprisoned, and made to scrub floors and carry coal for fourteen or fifteen hours a day; whether he has since been given a month on bread and water and put in irons for refusing to drill; whether he is now in a dark cell with twelve others; and whether such treatment is in accordance with Regulations?'[262] He asked whether the War Office was aware that 'Oscar Gristwood Ricketts, a conscientious objector to military service, was arrested, charged at Brentford Police Court, fined two guineas, and handed over to the military authorities, and that in conveying him to Felixstowe they exposed him to the shame of being handcuffed in the public streets and railways; whether he is now in the Harwich circular redoubt, confined to a cell, and his only food dry biscuits and water; whether this young man has resigned a good post in a city bank and offered himself for any work of national importance that is consistent with his religious and moral convictions; and whether he proposes to take any action in the matter?'

Snowden claimed that conscientious objectors from Darwen in

Lancashire 'were taken to the military barracks at Preston and there subjected to the grossest ill-treatment, being forcibly stripped and marched round the barrack square practically undressed, and after being put in uniform one of them was taken into a room and, on the testimony of a person there, brutally kicked around the room until his groans could be heard outside'.[263] He said there were similar stories from all over the country, and demanded that such behaviour be stopped and the soldiers committing it punished. Tennant pleaded with colleagues not to demand inquiries into individual cases, because officials were so overworked; which prompted Snowden to ask: 'Are these men then to continue to be tortured because inquiry may involve a little trouble at the War Office?'[264] As other MPs turned on Tennant, he exclaimed: 'I am asking the House not to believe all this tittle-tattle.'[265]

Yet any conscientious objector who gave anything other than a religious reason for not wishing to fight was treated peremptorily. When Reginald Allen, chairman of the No Conscription Fellowship, told the City of London tribunal on 10 April that, 'as a socialist, he considered his life and his personality sacred', the military representative said the Act only recognised religious motivations. The chairman did at least offer Allen an exemption to do work of 'national importance'; Allen refused.[266] The argument continued over whether, as Samuel had put it, 'a moral objection is as good as a religious objection'. Some exemptions were easier to obtain than others: the Cambridge tribunal, supplied with expert evidence by John Maynard Keynes, agreed that Professor A. C. Pigou, head of the economics department at the university and identifier of the Pigou effect, a classical economic theory about how equilibrium is restored during a period of deflation, should be exempted. It is not recorded whether Keynes – who came violently to disagree with Pigou's theories – told the tribunal Pigou had used his private means to fund some of Keynes's research. Pigou volunteered as an ambulance driver during university vacations, and became renowned for his coolness under fire.

As conscientious objectors were shipped to France to serve in working parties behind the lines, and those who refused were jailed, more stories of their ill-treatment were raised in Parliament, to the embarrassment of a government still dominated by Liberals. The rough handling often began before they got into the Army's clutches: there were complaints about high-handed tribunals and men being mocked for their religion. The military representative on one tribunal asked a conscientious objector: 'Could he explain the text in Numbers "Shall your brethren go to war, and shall ye sit here?" '[267] The objector's wife was asked by the same man to comment on the text 'vengeance is mine', which she completed with 'saith the Lord.'

There was particular anger about the use of a punishment known as 'crucifixion' – Field Punishment No. 1, introduced nearly forty years earlier when flogging had been abolished – in which men were for long periods chained to a wall with their arms raised above their heads, causing many to faint. MPs were concerned that this ill-treatment was not being handed out just to the lower orders, but to men such as themselves. Philip Morrell proclaimed that 'when you have, as you have now, over 1,000 men of the highest character and the best education, many of them in good positions, all of them well known, who are willing to undergo arrest and become criminals rather than take part in a war which they say is against their conscience, the problem is a very serious one, and it is time that it should be dealt with in a serious spirit.'[268] At Cambridge in March 1916 seventy-two university men appeared before the local tribunal, which granted most of them exemption from combatant service only. One man said he 'would rather see England physically ruined than morally ruined, and therefore he could take no part in ejecting any foreign invader.'[269] George Sutherland, a maths and physics master at Harrow, appealed to his local tribunal not to be made to join the Royal Army Medical Corps, as he felt its main purpose was to put men back into the firing line as quickly as possible; and he could not himself take a life. 'You don't think murderers' lives should be taken by the state?' he was asked. 'No, the duty is to convert them,' he replied.

Even overage men who shared these views were subject to harassment: Bertrand Russell, aged forty-four, was invited to lecture on mathematics at Harvard in the autumn of 1916, but the government refused him a passport, claiming it would not be in the public interest to grant him one – fearing what he might say about the war and conscription once out of British jurisdiction, in a land where his words would be highly publicised. Then his college, Trinity, banned him from lecturing in Cambridge. Nor was it just distinguished public figures who were penalised. Government employees, from civil servants to postmen, who professed a conscientious objection were made to forfeit their pensions.

Russell worked almost full-time for the rest of the war in the anti-conscription cause. He claimed that as Asquith was about to leave for Dublin after the Easter Rising, he and several others went to see him – Russell and he were old friends through the Morrells – to demand that thirty-seven conscientious objectors who had been sentenced to death be reprieved. Russell recalled that 'it had been generally supposed, even by the Government, that conscientious objectors were not legally liable to the death penalty, but this turned out to be a mistake, and but for Asquith a number of them would have been shot.'[270] The men had been sent to France and, refusing to fight once there, were court-martialled. Haig also took the credit for reprieving them, but may have done so on Asquith's instructions. However urgent the need for soldiers, the propaganda effect of shooting thirty-seven non-combatant men in cold blood for refusing to fight would have been catastrophic.

Many who sought exemptions did so because their livelihoods would be threatened by service, or their employers sought it for them for the same reason: most such pleas were dismissed. A music-hall turn, Whit Cunliffe, won a four-month exemption because of his charity work, performing for wounded soldiers. Some who simply wanted to evade service, and could not prove a conscientious objection on religious grounds, went to extreme lengths to escape the draft. A carpenter was fined £10 in June 1918 for deliberately maiming himself to avoid service by sawing off two fingers; others posed as deaf and dumb, and one was recorded as dressing in women's clothing to avoid detection. However, with call-up papers occasionally being sent to babies, blind men and soldiers, many idlers and shirkers must have thought attempted evasion worth trying.[271]

Yet there was plenty of evidence that the caprice of the tribunals could also lead to leniency. Esher wrote to Asquith from his Scottish house, the Roman Camp at Callander in Perthshire, to say that in rural areas tribunals 'all proceed on the assumption that a man's first duty is to his business, whether it is that of a farmer or an employee in any trade that he mainly runs . . . This view is quite natural when it is realised that the Tribunals are composed of the applicants' neighbours, and the military representative is also a neighbour and possibly a friend.'[272] He told Asquith he had watched sixty cases, most of which led to deferrals. 'It is the line of least resistance for any committee.' Auckland Geddes, who would serve in the Lloyd George coalition, told Repington that 'there were vast numbers in the mines who were not working full time, and should either do so or come out and fight.'[273] Robertson gave Repington an 'extreme case' of a tribunal in an agricultural district that had exempted all but six out of two thousand men.

IX

At Bangor in North Wales on 6 May 1916 Lloyd George sought, if not to rebuild bridges with his fellow Liberals, then to justify himself: 'You must organise effort when a nation is in peril,' he told his audience. 'You cannot run a war as you would run a Sunday school treat, where one man voluntarily brings the buns, another supplies the tea, one brings the kettle, one looks after the boiling, another takes round the tea-cups, some contribute in cash, and a good many lounge about and just make the best of what is going. You cannot run a war like that.'[274] But if Asquith thought he had neutered his enemies by agreeing to compulsion he was wrong. On 3 May Gwynne, intriguing more violently than ever, wrote to Derby: 'For heaven's sake come out on Carson's side against Squiff. Don't mince matters . . . [with Asquith] we can't hope to win the war.'[275]

As so often since August 1914, military matters were not the government's only problem. Industrial action in munitions factories on the Clyde, political in inspiration rather than over pay or conditions, was so severe that on 28 March, when Lloyd George was in Paris, Miss Stevenson wired him to return urgently because the strikes 'are assuming alarming proportions, and no-one will take any responsibility for drastic action.'[276] The Clyde Workers Committee – previously known as the Clyde Labour Withdrawal Committee – had called strikes on what Addison said were 'trivial grounds'.[277] Agitation was manufactured over dilution, with self-appointed workers' representatives demanding the right to interview other workers without the permission of managers and during working hours. Under the DORA regulations, men who refused to work were 'deported' to other parts of Britain and kept under effective arrest, pending promises of good behaviour that would allow them to be returned to their homes and to factories. Carson argued that they were guilty of high treason and should be treated accordingly; and such was his influence that Addison promised to consider the matter.

The union to which the strikers belonged, the Amalgamated Society of Engineers, disowned them, declared the strike unconstitutional and denied them strike pay: that had immediately got 360 men back to work.

Arrests continued: agitators were told they could put their case before the Clyde Commissioners, appointed for that purpose. An uneasy truce was brokered, but the main influence on the strikers was the active resentment of most of their fellow Glaswegians, some of whom suggested Clydeside be put under martial law.

These were not the only trials. In the first six days of April there were nightly Zeppelin raids on England, and on 2 May the east coast would be bombed again. On 2 April 108 men were killed in a munitions factory explosion at Faversham. On 25 April German battle cruisers bombarded Lowestoft and Yarmouth. Losses at sea were rising: during April 140,000 tons of British shipping were lost, thirty-seven vessels being sunk by submarines and six more by mines. On 24 March a cross-Channel steamer from Folkestone to Dieppe, the *Sussex*, was torpedoed by the Germans with the loss of between fifty and eighty lives, one of them Enrique Granados, the renowned Spanish composer; injuries to American passengers inflamed opinion in the United States, forcing the Germans to promise there would be no repeat of the incident. The *Sussex*'s bow was blown off and it was towed stern first into Boulogne.

The vulnerability of shipping also raised the problem that would dominate British life for the rest of the war: a shortage of food. There had been a bad harvest in 1915, and submarine attacks meant imports (on which pre-war Britain, its agricultural industry in steep decline, had come to depend) slumped. Some goods became unobtainable, and queues outside grocers' shops commonplace, destabilising morale. Newspaper editors were called to Whitehall in late April and asked to show restraint in mentioning shipping losses and the consequent food shortages. Because Northcliffe – whose newspapers had come closer to prosecution under DORA for their perceived defeatism than he perhaps realised – despaired of politicians taking this or any other crisis in hand unless spurred on by the press, the *Daily Mail* discussed the problem openly on 4 May. Northcliffe told Wells that 'one strong man who would order the people to eat less would effect the desired result – or it might be achieved by a very rigorous campaign of publicity by speech and newspaper.'[278] The price of milk rose to 6d a quart; the press, scenting profiteering, advised consumers to shop around, and to patronise dairies selling it more cheaply.[279] Demands grew for the government to control the milk price, in the interests of child health; yet another measure offensive to Liberal sensitivities.

The government was forced, by the effect of the war on society, to respond to a debate about whether venereal diseases should be notifiable: men returning from France with one variety or other of such afflictions caused not just a predictable scandal among a civilian population yet to adjust from Victorian attitudes, but an epidemic among those who had been intimate with the returning heroes. A Royal Commission on Venereal Diseases was established, and it advised against making them notifiable, in case the problem was driven underground and became worse. Unfortunately, such measures would prove insufficient.

With fuel, like food, running short, the cabinet agreed in early May to introduce a measure discussed before the war, but dismissed as eccentric: the introduction of British Summer Time. Asquith was the only sceptic in the cabinet, but acquiesced, and a resolution in the Commons on 8 May was passed by one hundred and seventy votes to two, and the law was in place by 21 May. As well as providing this 'extra' hour of daylight – in high summer it would now become dark in London by 9.30 p.m. instead of 8.30 p.m., which was expected to save £2.5 million in lighting costs alone – Parliament decided to scrap the bank holidays at Whitsun and in early August for the duration. It began to appear as though there was no area of human existence in which the war would not force new accommodations, even including the hours of daylight.

POBLACHT NA H EIREANN.

THE PROVISIONAL GOVERNMENT

OF THE

IRISH REPUBLIC

TO THE PEOPLE OF IRELAND.

IRISHMEN AND IRISHWOMEN : In the name of God and of the dead generations from which she receives her old tradition of nationhood, Ireland, through us, summons her children to her flag and strikes for her freedom.

Having organised and trained her manhood through her secret revolutionary organisation, the Irish Republican Brotherhood, and through her open military organisations, the Irish Volunteers and the Irish Citizen Army, having patiently perfected her discipline, having resolutely waited for the right moment to reveal itself, she now seizes that moment, and, supported by her exiled children in America and by gallant allies in Europe, but relying in the first on her own strength, she strikes in full confidence of victory.

We declare the right of the people of Ireland to the ownership of Ireland, and to the unfettered control of Irish destinies, to be sovereign and indefeasible. The long usurpation of that right by a foreign people and government has not extinguished the right, nor can it ever be extinguished except by the destruction of the Irish people. In every generation the Irish people have asserted their right to national freedom and sovereignty : six times during the past three hundred years they have asserted it in arms. Standing on that fundamental right and again asserting it in arms in the face of the world, we hereby proclaim the Irish Republic as a Sovereign Independent State, and we pledge our lives and the lives of our comrades-in-arms to the cause of its freedom, of its welfare, and of its exaltation among the nations.

The Irish Republic is entitled to, and hereby claims, the allegiance of every Irishman and Irishwoman. The Republic guarantees religious and civil liberty, equal rights and equal opportunities to all its citizens, and declares its resolve to pursue the happiness and prosperity of the whole nation and of all its parts, cherishing all the children of the nation equally, and oblivious of the differences carefully fostered by an alien government, which have divided a minority from the majority in the past.

Until our arms have brought the opportune moment for the establishment of a permanent National Government, representative of the whole people of Ireland and elected by the suffrages of all her men and women, the Provisional Government, hereby constituted, will administer the civil and military affairs of the Republic in trust for the people.

We place the cause of the Irish Republic under the protection of the Most High God, Whose blessing we invoke upon our arms, and we pray that no one who serves that cause will dishonour it by cowardice, inhumanity, or rapine. In this supreme hour the Irish nation must, by its valour and discipline and by the readiness of its children to sacrifice themselves for the common good, prove itself worthy of the august destiny to which it is called.

Signed on Behalf of the Provisional Government,

THOMAS J. CLARKE,

SEAN Mac DIARMADA,   THOMAS MacDONAGH,
P. H. PEARSE,   EAMONN CEANNT,
JAMES CONNOLLY.   JOSEPH PLUNKETT.

CHAPTER 5

RISING

———————⇒⇐———————

I

As the conscription debate neared its end, news reached London of a significant military reverse far away from Flanders. There had been a military campaign in Mesopotamia since the autumn of 1914, and an attempt to take Baghdad in early 1916 led to defeat and disaster. Major General Charles Townshend, an egomaniac and womaniser who had routed 4,000 Turks the previous October, now found himself and his 20,000 Anglo-Indian troops surrounded by Ottoman forces at Kut-al-Amara, 100 miles south-east of Baghdad. A relief force under Sir Fenton Aylmer had been defeated at Shaikh Sa'ad in January. On 29 April Townshend surrendered after a siege of four months. An estimated 4,000 British wounded died because of a lack of hospital ships; 13,000 Allied troops were taken prisoner. The defeat had two consequences: it gave Asquith an excuse to move to the conscription of married men, and it necessitated a Mesopotamia commission which, like that already running on the Dardanelles, would allocate responsibility for the debacle. Chamberlain, as India secretary, technically oversaw the operation. Although he had demanded better medical facilities for the troops, conscious of the deaths in the Crimea sixty years earlier before Florence Nightingale's arrival, he would be forced to resign. There had been a shocking rate of attrition for which someone had to pay. After the Dardanelles, it was another serious setback for those who had advocated an eastern strategy: and the stalemate in the west showed no sign of being broken either.

It was at this stage of massive national self-doubt that a grave challenge arose far nearer to home. Asquith's attempts to paper over the cracks in Ireland by propitiating John Redmond soon after war broke out, and defying the Unionists to cause trouble in a time of national peril, seemed to have worked. However, republicans could not countenance Asquith and Redmond's deal. There was, by August 1914, a fundamental schism among those who wanted Ireland to govern itself. Constitutional Nationalists, led by Redmond, believed that by loyally fighting for Britain, with whom they would retain an association after Home Rule, the right to govern themselves would be granted out of gratitude. Republicans wanted no association with Britain. They saw Germany as the potential conqueror of their ancient enemy, and longed for a German victory: England's difficulty was once more Ireland's opportunity. It was the same mentality that sent Éamon de Valera, when Taoiseach, to the German embassy in Dublin in 1945 to offer his condolences on the death of Adolf Hitler.

How far the republicans would go to pursue their aims was clear from 13 September 1914, when Sir Roger Casement, a former consular official (for which services he had been knighted) and Ulster Protestant, met Franz von Papen, the Kaiser's military attaché to the United States, in Washington and asked for German support. What C. P. Scott, a convinced Home Ruler, called the 'treasonable' Irish press whipped up pro-German feeling from the start of the war; though the principal target was Redmond and the Nationalists, not the British government.[1] Nationalists believed German money was subsidising republican papers, notably the *Irish Volunteer*, given out free of charge. T. P. O'Connor, a leading Nationalist politician, told Scott that 'in the south and west the Sinn Féiners told the peasants that they were only asked to enlist in order that they might be conveniently killed off.'[2] On 9 September representatives of the Irish Republican Brotherhood (IRB) and James Connolly, the socialist leader of the Irish Citizen Army, met to evaluate the opportunity the war provided to strike at British rule. Connolly's aims were further reaching than most: he wanted to bring down capitalism itself.

On the eve of Asquith's speech in Dublin on 25 September 1914 that, like so many given by British politicians, made the mistake of seeing Irish considerations as very much secondary to the war effort, Eoin MacNeill, a former civil servant, and six other leading republicans issued a statement condemning Redmond for his pro-British attitude; it mentioned that but for his unavoidable absence abroad, Casement, by now a significant figure in the republican movement, would also have signed. Groups of volunteers, modelled on the British Army, had been drilling since the spring of 1914; but after the outbreak of war the movement split, with the Nationalist Volunteers following Redmond and in many cases joining the British Army, and a small minority identifying with the republican movement. They became known as the Irish Volunteers, and branches of Irish Volunteers were quickly established in areas where no volunteer group had previously existed. Each man was told to buy his uniform and rifle; women were encouraged to join and support the movement; MacNeill was appointed chief of staff.

The Irish Volunteers came to be known by their detractors as 'Sinn Féiners', even though the original Sinn Féin, moribund for several years, had subscribed to passive and not armed resistance and, according to the policy of Arthur Griffith, its leader, had sought a type of dual monarchy for Ireland and Britain. Within a month 13,000 men had joined; 8,000 were regularly drilling and the group was thought to have 1,400 rifles.[3] Bizarrely, there was no licensing system for firearms in Ireland, hence their proliferation and the inability of the authorities to control them. Although measures allowing the police to seize arms were effected under DORA in December 1914, the Irish Volunteers were allowed to grow permissively, as was the continued and largely unimpeded smuggling of arms into Ireland. The number of National Volunteers shrank after the split of August 1914, not least through some joining the British Army. That the movement became moribund and collapsed was an awful portent for Redmond, the Nationalists and their politics.

On 31 October *The Times* reported that Redmond's recruiting campaign had proved pitiful, with perhaps only 10,000 new recruits, most from Unionist areas of Dublin and Cork. It called the poor response 'of considerable ultimate and moral moment to the future of Anglo-Irish relations.'[4] By December, according to notes prepared by J. D. Irvine of the *Morning Post* for his editor Gywnne, 28,000 Ulstermen had joined Kitchener's army but there had been just 11,000 from Ireland's three other provinces. Fiercely anti-Redmond and anti-British propaganda circulated widely, especially in Dublin. Clan na Gael, American sister organisation of the Irish Republican Brotherhood, called Redmond a 'swindler' and accused him of 'a deliberate and wanton act of treachery to his own country in the interests of its only enemy.'[5] According to *The*

Times 'a small but venomous group of papers representing the Sinn Féin
movement and Larkinism [syndicalism named after James Larkin, the
Irish trades unionist] and the original anti-British spirit' were conducting 'a violent campaign against recruiting.'[6] These papers, *The Times*
continued, compared the act of joining Kitchener's army with that of
Judas, and insisted the fight was 'England's war'. There was even the
suggestion that Ireland should team up with India and Egypt to secure
advantageous terms when Britain was defeated. The claim that the English wanted Irish Volunteers to join up so the Germans could slaughter
them became widespread. The Volunteers should not join, republicans
argued: but every Irishman should join the Volunteers, and train for the
day when they overthrew the British. Irvine's report to Gwynne at
the *Morning Post*, much of which could not be printed for reasons of
censorship, confirmed *The Times*'s findings. Sinn Féin was conducting
'open pro-German and furious anti-British propaganda'.[7] Young men
who might otherwise enlist were being 'terrorised and threatened by
the extremists'.[8] He had witnessed fundraising at a meeting in Dublin
over which Redmond had presided 'to efficiently arm and equip the
National Volunteers of Dublin City', even though a proclamation had
just been issued forbidding the sales of rifles and ammunition. 'Subscrip-
tions amounting to £642 were raised on the spot.' It is not clear whether
Redmond's followers wanted the rifles to arm against republicans or
Unionists. Despite the United Kingdom's national emergency, many
Irish seemed to be arming themselves against another enemy.

Added to this febrile atmosphere was an assumption widely held
among the authorities that money pouring in from America for the
republican cause was from Germany, and that parts of Ireland teemed
with German spies. *The Times* felt the government's response was
entirely inadequate. It dismissed Augustine Birrell, the chief secretary,
as useless. While loyal British newspapers were rigorously censored,
Irish ones could 'preach treason, war on recruiting, and libel the British Army . . . with complete impunity.'[9] It suggested Kitchener should
call for the suppression of these newspapers, and for the law to be used
against those advocating treason. The loyal Ireland Redmond had
promised after the Home Rule Bill had not materialised, but rather
one that 'will suffer from a general alienation of sympathy when the
war is over.'

The economic hardships that had hit Britain were felt far more keenly in Ireland, and led to further discontent. Average pay was already low in Ireland: 78 per cent of workers lived on less than £1 a week, compared with 50 per cent in Scotland and 40 per cent in England.[10] That, and the postponement of Home Rule, made Redmond's life extremely difficult, and caused even moderate Irish people to look for an alternative that might prosecute their interests more actively. Redmond understood he was being tarred with complicity, which was why he refused Asquith's offer to serve in the cabinet in May 1915; but it did not work.

Despite their often-professed sympathy for the Belgians, it became clear that, to many, Irishmen joining the British Army was an act of betrayal. In January 1915 Casement was recorded making disloyal remarks, and his pension was withdrawn. The Royal Irish Constabulary (RIC) tore down posters plastered around Wexford that said: 'Take no notice of the police order to destroy your own property, and leave your home if a German army lands in Ireland. When the Germans come they will come as friends, and to put an end to English rule in Ireland. Therefore stay in your homes, and assist as far as possible the German troops.'[11] For a more prominent figure resistance took a form that was passive, but no less direct. In February 1915 Henry James asked William Butler Yeats to write a war poem. His response was pointed: 'I think it better that in times like these/A poet's mouth be silent, for in truth/We have no gift to set a statesman right;/He has had enough of meddling who can please/A young girl in the indolence of her youth/or an old man upon a winter's night.'[12]

After 16 March 1915, thanks to an amendment by Lord Parmoor, an independent peer strongly opposed to the war who would sit in the first Labour cabinets, anyone in the United Kingdom charged under DORA – such as those promulgating seditious literature – could demand trial by jury. This made it still harder to stop the circulation of such tracts or newspapers, given the reluctance of Irish juries to convict anyone for a political offence. The Irish Volunteers stepped up their propaganda activities: those whose job it was to monitor public feeling were well aware of the shift towards the republicans, and reported back to Dublin Castle. Birrell remained determined to avoid confrontation or provocation.

On 4 April 1915 – Easter Sunday – Redmond took the salute of 27,000 National Volunteers, as they marched past a crowd estimated at 100,000 in Dublin.[13] It was a delusional event: Nationalist support was ebbing, and at Westminster Carson's inclusion in the new coalition would boost his clout while diminishing Redmond's. Sir Matthew Nathan, Birrell's under-secretary and a former Army officer of distinction, noted that by the second half of 1915 the republicans were more confident, and seeking opportunities to trumpet their strength. At a banquet in Dublin on 2 July Redmond spoke, nonetheless, of his certainty that the Home Rule Act – which he called 'the greatest charter of liberty ever obtained for Ireland all through her history' – would be implemented the moment the war ended.[14] He attacked those who claimed the coalition would renege on the promise; though he admitted his 'distrust' for the government, demonstrated by his refusal to join it. He claimed Ireland's interests would be best served by an early victory – his underestimated rivals in the republican movement disagreed profoundly – and quoted official figures showing that of the 120,000 men to have enlisted, 71,000 were Roman Catholics and 49,000 Protestants.

On 1 August Patrick Pearse, a fanatical republican (and half-English) schoolmaster, orated at the graveside of Jeremiah O'Donovan Rossa, the eighty-three-year-old Fenian, IRB leader and advocate of the use of force against the British, who had tried him for treason in 1865. Tom Clarke, a prominent IRB man who had served fifteen years in English jails for terrorist acts in the 1880s, had cabled John Devoy, the leader of Clan na Gael, on hearing of Rossa's death in New York on 29 June, to 'send the body home at once'.[15] For three days before the funeral Rossa lay in state in Dublin's City Hall; and Dublin Castle, to prevent incidents, told plain-clothes policemen to keep their distance in Glasnevin Cemetery. Pearse's oration ended: 'They think that they have pacified Ireland. They think that they have purchased half of us and intimidated the other half. They think that they have foreseen everything, think that they have provided against everything; but, the fools, the fools, the fools! – They have left us our Fenian dead, and while Ireland holds these graves, Ireland unfree shall never be at peace.'[16] Pearse himself was thought to have a death wish (it would be granted, and for the cause he cherished), and Yeats accused him of having 'the vertigo of self-sacrifice', which made him rather a liability to others who wished to be driven by practicality and not romanticism.[17] Nevertheless, his words contained a fundamental truth.

Nathan observed, with mandarin understatement: 'I have an uncomfortable feeling that the nationalists are losing ground to the Sinn Féiners and that this demonstration is hastening the movement.'[18] Birrell did not even get that far; as he read a report of Rossa's funeral he remarked: 'I do not suppose anybody in the whole concourse cared anything for the old fellow, who never cared for anything at any time.'[19] It is a perfect illustration of his utter ignorance of a growing current of Irish feeling. During the autumn the Citizen Army, organised by Connolly in the trades union unrest of 1913 and pledged to achieve the 'emancipation' of the workers and an Irish republic, started to coordinate its activities with those of the Irish Volunteers.[20] The shocking housing conditions of the Dublin working class gave Connolly and his movement enormous scope for agitation and activism, and plenty of recruits. By this stage the Volunteers were believed to be 15,000 strong and to have 1,800 rifles and the same number of pistols and shotguns. The drilling of Volunteers continued; there were training classes for officers and in first aid. However, most leading Volunteers, led by MacNeill, still wanted to use violence only for self-defence; while other republicans resolved in September 1915, at a meeting convened by Clarke, that they would take up arms after a German invasion only if the Germans promised to secure an Irish republic.

For some republicans the idea of involving the Germans was more than rhetorical. Casement went to Germany and was joined there in late November 1915 by Joseph Plunkett, a poet, scholar and senior IRB man who had travelled via Spain, Italy and Switzerland. The two men tried to persuade the Germans to invade Ireland and join forces with a Volunteer uprising. They also asked that Irish prisoners of war be allowed to join an Irish brigade that would be part of the invasion force. Casement was convinced most Irish who had enlisted had done so to get a job and some prospects, not because of love for King George V. In the end he managed to interest a mere fifty-six men in the brigade. This highly risky mission bore little fruit beyond Germany putting out a statement on 20 November to say that if it ever invaded Ireland it would do all it could to advance Irish liberty. There would be no invasion, and Casement felt used. Asking himself why he had ever trusted the Germans he exploded: 'They are cads . . . That is why they are hated by the world and England will surely beat them.'[21]

When Casement failed to persuade Bethmann Hollweg, the German Chancellor, to meet him he should have realised the enormous improbability of the Germans opening a second front against the British in the Emerald Isle. The Royal Navy would probably have had an invasion force sunk before it had reached Heligoland, never mind Ireland. Yet Plunkett outlined a plan that entailed the Germans landing 12,000 men (and 40,000 rifles to arm the locals), but on the west coast, presumably after a tortuous journey around the Orkney Islands and down into the North Atlantic. This, thought Plunkett, would allow the Germans to set up a base camp in Limerick and from there occupy the country. The assumptions about the compliance of the Irish themselves (and not just those in Ulster, but what were then the many moderate Catholics with no desire to live under German favours) and the feasibility of German supply lines were breathtaking. Casement was more realistic, urging his comrades in Ireland to stop planning a rebellion when it became apparent the Germans had no intention of turning up for the party.

In late 1915 recruiting in Ireland for the British Army had plummeted to under 1,100 a week, despite Redmond's face adorning some recruitment posters. It would by February 1916 drop to 300 – even the higher figure was too little to maintain the desired two Irish divisions with adequate reserves. The disaffection in which Britain, in its supreme crisis, was held by Ireland was unrelenting, even before being exacerbated by the events of Easter 1916; and the low recruiting led to talk of conscription, causing immense disquiet. The Roman Catholic Church, which had begun the war by supporting Britain, was by mid-1915 becoming openly hostile. In July Cardinal Michael Logue, Archbishop of Armagh and Primate of All Ireland, attending an industrial exhibition in Dundalk, announced that 'the government that killed their Irish industries, and forced the people to emigrate, were looking out for men to fight for them, and the men were not there to be got.'[22] He was cheered. Logue would, however, after the Easter Rising rebuke priests who gave support to Sinn Féin. At the end of July Pope Benedict XV issued an encyclical demanding an end to the war because of its futility. Bishop Edward O'Dwyer of Limerick chose the first anniversary of the war on 4 August to write to Redmond and demand that, as a Catholic politician, he associate himself with the Pope's message. Redmond wished to be neither the tool of London nor, hoping Home Rule would embrace Ulster, of the Vatican, so replied blaming the Germans. It was not a distinguished performance.

On 14 September the Council of the Irish Volunteers debated whether to launch an immediate insurrection. The motion was defeated on the casting vote of MacNeill, signifying the potential threat many of his comrades thought the Volunteers posed to the government. Lord Midleton, a former India secretary and leader of the Irish Unionist Alliance, saw Birrell in November and urged him to disarm the Volunteers; Birrell refused, even though Dublin Castle was aware of the Volunteers' recruitment successes, aided not least by official inertia. By then intelligence sources believed republicans could launch an insurrection if Britain attempted to impose conscription in Ireland. Fearing they would be forced to join the British Army, many younger, unmarried men decided to emigrate to America. In November 1915, the Cunard and White Star lines barred 700 from boarding their ships in Liverpool, because the directors believed they should be enlisting. Redmond observed it was 'very cowardly' of them to try to leave.[23] This provoked Bishop O'Dwyer to savage him in a letter to provincial Irish papers – Dublin ones had censorship so strict that they could never have printed it – about the rights of ordinary Irish Catholic boys. It was printed on handbills and widely circulated; the power of the Church contributed greatly to the anti-authority climate.

However, some republicans did not need the provocation of conscription. A plan for a rising in Dublin had existed since May 1915. The IRB had had a three-man military committee discussing the feasibility and execution of such a rebellion: it comprised Pearse, Plunkett – who had devised the original plan – and Éamonn Ceannt, and later acquired Tom Clarke, who had long advocated violent revolution, and Seán Mac Diarmada, like many of his comrades an enthusiast for the Irish language, and born John MacDermott. On 26 December the IRB military council decided to launch a rebellion on Easter Sunday – 23 April – 1916. In January it co-opted Connolly and then, in early April, Thomas MacDonagh. Connolly had spent much of 1915 lecturing Volunteer units on street fighting; he convinced his comrades the British Army would not use artillery in Dublin, a dire misreading of another nation hardened by war and loss. The rebels' optimism about assuming the role of governing Ireland was also fed by a belief in wholehearted support from the populace inside Dublin and around the country, and the assumption of a quick capitulation by the Castle, neither of which was forthcoming.

On 8 January 1916 Midleton spoke in the Lords about widespread sedition and the potential for insurrection; Crewe dismissed his fears. Distressed, he asked to see Asquith, who met him on 26 January: having repeated his claims, Midleton was asked to send Asquith a memorandum detailing his information. Nothing happened, partly because a second meeting scheduled in March was cancelled as Asquith was ill. In February the debate on the King's Speech made no mention of Ireland: so the Independent Nationalist MP for Westmeath, Laurence Ginnell, moved an amendment demanding the Government of Ireland Act be implemented a month later. In Ireland, the Volunteers were becoming more daring; with many of Redmond's volunteers in the Army, they had the field to themselves; and Dublin Castle remained passive. There were only around 1,000 soldiers in Dublin; Birrell's forces were outnumbered.

On 4 March *The Times*'s Ireland correspondent detailed growing support for those who 'profess the doctrines of Sinn Féin' and who were doing all they could to hinder recruitment for the Army in Ireland.[24] The openness of the Volunteers' activities inspired young men to join. Republicans were active in Dublin, Wexford, Cork and Kerry. The *Times* report described Volunteers practising street-fighting and drilling while the authorities watched; it said that although such antics might amuse someone with Birrell's sense of humour, they might have a 'serious side'. This was complemented by the easy availability of subversive literature. 'It may become dangerous,' the writer concluded, 'unless the Irish government deals with it quickly and firmly'.

When Midleton warned Birrell that the Volunteers were drilling, the chief secretary replied: 'I laugh at the whole thing.'[25] Shortly afterwards Midleton warned Lord Wimborne, the Lord Lieutenant, and other officials, of the dangers of letting the Volunteers continue manoeuvres. No one would listen, although after a blatant incident in Dublin three Volunteer organisers were arrested and deported to Britain. Redmond, too, had received warnings of a rebellion starting in the spring or summer of 1916, its intention being to force the British to crush it, and then to discredit Redmond and his party for assisting the oppressors. As predictions went it was remarkably accurate.

The military council set the evening of Easter Sunday for mobilisation. A trial mobilisation was planned for St Patrick's Day, 17 March, when it could be passed off to the authorities as simply parades to celebrate Ireland's national day. 'The Dublin Brigade, practically fully armed, uniformed and equipped held that portion of Dame Street from City Hall to the Bank of Ireland for over an hour, during which no traffic was allowed to break the ranks of the Volunteers, Citizen Army and

Cumann na mBan [the women's republican organisation].'[26] Although not everyone in parades was armed, the authorities had no excuse to be surprised at the potential for trouble. An estimated one in three of the thousands of Volunteers who marched in St Patrick's Day parades was armed. Unnoticed on the mainland, and reported in just one Dublin newspaper, was a Sinn Féin manifesto, published on 28 March 1916. It said the organisation 'wish to warn the public that the general tendency of the Government's action [to threaten to seize Volunteer arms under DORA] is to force a highly dangerous situation'. It continued: 'The Government is well aware that the possession of arms is essential to the Volunteer organisation, and the Volunteers cannot submit to being disarmed either in numbers or detail without surrendering and abandoning the position they have held at all times since their first formation. The Volunteer organisation also cannot maintain its efficiency without organisers. The raiding for arms and attempted disarming of men, therefore, in the natural course of things can only be met by resistance and bloodshed.'[27] A meeting at Dublin's Mansion House to protest about the arrests and expulsions of the three organisers ended in a riot, with shots fired from a revolver only failing to wound or kill a policeman because they were stopped by his pocketbook, having pierced his greatcoat.

Recruitment meetings proliferated in early April, prompting Dublin Castle to consider, late in the day, whether it should try to disarm the Volunteers, for all their threats to kill anyone who tried. On 12 April Birrell minuted that the suggestion 'requires careful consideration'. Wimborne thought it 'a difficult point', wondering how the policy could be successfully carried out.[28] The RIC, which had asked the question, received no reply by Easter, though on 13 April two republicans were imprisoned for three months for illegally transporting guns and ammunition within the Dublin police district.

II

Casement had stayed, somewhat unhappily, in Germany, and was therefore no part of the planning of the Easter Rising. A fellow Irishman in Berlin, who was in contact with Dublin, informed him of the plan early in March. Although Casement had not been consulted, he realised this was his opportunity to take part in the creation of the Irish republic for

which he longed. The British authorities, ironically, had more knowledge of rebel activity than he did. From the outbreak of war to Easter
1916 the Admiralty intercepted thirty-two cables between the German
embassy in Washington and Berlin about assisting Irish rebels.[29] Casement was told a U-boat would take him to Ireland's west coast for a
rendezvous with rebels and with another – disguised – German ship
carrying arms, and he departed on 12 April. His U-boat broke down,
delaying his journey while he transferred to another.

Some of the intercepted cables revealed that a cargo ship, captured at
Kiel when war broke out and recommissioned into the German navy,
would bring in some arms; it was disguised as a Norwegian steamer, the
Aud. In March the Germans had offered to land 20,000 rifles and ten
machine guns in Tralee Bay via two or three fishing trawlers in the days
immediately before an uprising. In the end, just this one boat was sent.
It left Lübeck on 9 April and reached Tralee Bay on the 20th. The rebels
had no radio contact with the ship, so could not tell it not to arrive before
midnight on Easter Sunday, the 23rd: the rebels would not be ready to
receive the shipment until then. Therefore Karl Spindler, the *Aud*'s captain, was surprised when dropping anchor on the 20th that no pilot boat
met him. Nor was there Casement's U-boat: Spindler was poor at naviga-
tion and was 7 miles from the agreed rendezvous. On Good Friday, 21
April, the *Aud* conspicuously sailed up and down Tralee Bay looking for
a U-boat, or for some Volunteers to unload its cargo.

That morning the RIC arrested Casement on the Kerry coast after he
landed from the U-boat. He was taken to Tralee. The police did not
know who he was, but the collapsible boat in which he had landed suggested espionage. Once his identity was established he was taken to
London; on 15 May he was charged with treason under a statute of 1351.
Armed trawlers escorted Spindler, who never met his submarine, to
Queenstown, where he scuttled his ship and its cargo on 22 April.

There were tensions within the republican leadership. Pearse was
committed to an uprising; but MacNeill had always doubted the ration-
ale behind it and considered the argument for it to have been based on
wishful thinking about the relative strengths and abilities of the opposing forces. MacNeill conceded that defensive manoeuvres might be
necessary when he learned of a pamphlet, allegedly from Dublin Castle
but forged by other republicans, detailing 'plans' for a system of repression to forestall a rising. (It was based on genuine plans for dealing with

civil disobedience after the introduction of conscription, should that ever happen: there was no plan to implement it in April 1916.) However, when at midnight on 20 April Pearse told MacNeill that the Rising was happening the next day, and that the Volunteers were under IRB control, MacNeill and a small group loyal to him immediately sent an order to Volunteer branches across Ireland that 'orders of a special character issued by Commandant Pearse' were cancelled with immediate effect.[30] Branches were told to do nothing except on the order of the chief of staff – MacNeill – himself, with lieutenants sent from Dublin to spread the word; though the IRB kidnapped one, Bulmer Hobson, to prevent him fulfilling his mission.

The next morning MacNeill temporarily changed his mind again when Mac Diarmada, Pearse and MacDonagh visited him and announced that the German arms shipment had arrived. However, when he read of Casement's arrest he decided, again, that the action had to be cancelled. He then heard the arms had been scuttled, and that the Dublin Castle document was a forgery, and instructed Pearse to stop; but Pearse refused and said: 'it is no use trying to stop us.'[31] When MacNeill said he would send an order countermanding the mobilisation, Pearse told him it would not be obeyed. Nonetheless, MacNeill, at midnight on 22 April, sent an order cancelling the Rising. Driving through the night, his senior staff officers took the new order to branches outside Dublin, and Mac-Neill took a press notice – a modified and nuanced version of what was in the leaflets distributed to activists – to the *Sunday Independent*.

On the morning of Easter Sunday, 23 April, it was learned that 250 pounds of gelignite had been stolen from a quarry near Dublin. Alerted by the press notice, rather than by the theft of the explosives, officials met in the Castle. Birrell was spending Easter in London, reading an improving book on the Chevalier de Boufflers, an eighteenth-century French man of letters and colonial governor. Before his departure he had fretted with Nathan for days, as intelligence came in detailing the threat of a rising, about whether taking action would make matters worse. Wimborne and Nathan, holding the fort in Birrell's absence, decided Casement's arrest and the sinking of the *Aud* meant there would be no rising. Yet Wimborne, whom his friend Lady Cynthia Asquith – daughter-in-law of the prime minister – had recently described as 'a figure of fun, but rather a pathetic one', was less sure than Nathan that all would be calm, and wanted to show a firm hand. He demanded

Birrell be asked for permission to order the arrest of the leaders of the potential rebellion.[32] On Easter Monday morning, 24 April, Birrell finally agreed to have the men arrested, and to their being deported to England.

During Easter Sunday, copies of a proclamation of the republic were printed on the presses of a left-wing newspaper. To wrong-foot the authorities the Rising was postponed until noon on Easter Monday. The IRB's seven-man provisional government cancelled MacNeill's order to demobilise. This action was straightforward in Dublin, where communications were swift and much could be done by word of mouth; in the provinces it was complicated, and even in Dublin there was some confusion. Orders were being issued, countermanded and counter-countermanded; the command structure of the IRB was amateurish, and groups went without orders for hours on end, making both advances and coordination with other units nearly impossible. When the Rising eventually failed, MacNeill and his countermanding order were obvious targets of blame. In fact, as MacNeill knew, the plans for the Rising were entirely inadequate, and merely allowed the British Army to corner and kill men. However, many more rebels were alerted to come out and fight on Easter Day than appeared on the Monday, so MacNeill's final countermand had some effect, and almost certainly saved lives.

Pearse's Volunteers, and Connolly's Irish Citizen Army, supported by 200 women of Cumann na mBan, occupied strategic locations in Dublin on the morning of Easter Monday. These included the 4th Battalion of the Dublin Brigade, under Ceannt, taking the South Dublin Union – an enormous workhouse – and the 2nd Battalion, under MacDonagh, the Jacob's biscuit factory. A few were in the Citizen Army's green uniform, but most made do with what military-style clothing they could find – bandoliers, puttees and jodhpurs – and armed themselves with whatever came to hand, from rifles to pickaxes. With confusion rife, an estimated 700 people began the uprising, and it is thought their numbers rose to 1,500 in Dublin.[33] A so-called 'headquarters group' of around 150 marched from Liberty Hall in Beresford Place, long the meeting place of anti-British agitators, to Sackville Street – as O'Connell Street was still officially, but not colloquially, known – outside the General Post Office, a monumental Greek revival granite building of a century earlier, between 11.50 a.m. and noon. Connolly, who supposedly said, as he

started: 'we are going out to be slaughtered', led the group.[34] It says much
for the Castle's attitude that the police ignored the march as just another
exercise. The column, on Connolly's order, did a left wheel and entered
the GPO. Staff and customers were ordered out, though accounts suggest it took time for them to register that the rebels meant business. For
the next four days not only would the GPO be the headquarters of the
so-called provisional government, it would also be a point of refuge for
disconnected rebels fleeing from the British Army, inadvertently concentrating them in a position where their eventual defeat became
inevitable.

A Sinn Féin tricolour was hoisted on the GPO flagpole; and shortly
after noon Pearse went into Sackville/O'Connell Street and read the
proclamation of the republic (for whose drafting he was mainly responsible) to a bemused group of passers-by; although a contemporary account
from a reporter on the *Saturday Post* says a man resembling Clarke's
description proclaimed the republic from Nelson's Pillar at 1.30 p.m. Both
events may have happened.[35] The proclamation drew heavily on Irish
cultural roots, beginning with the summons: 'IRISHMEN AND IRISH-
WOMEN: In the name of God and of the dead generations from which
she receives her old tradition of nationhood, Ireland, through us, summons her children to her flag and strikes for her freedom.'[36]

Having proclaimed, too, that an army, supported by Americans
and from Europe, was ready to seize the moment and reveal itself, it
continued:

> We declare the right of the people of Ireland to the ownership of
> Ireland and to the unfettered control of Irish destinies, to be sover-
> eign and indefeasible. The long usurpation of that right by a foreign
> people and government has not extinguished the right, nor can it
> ever be extinguished except by the destruction of the Irish people.
> In every generation the Irish people have asserted their right to
> national freedom and sovereignty; six times during the past three
> hundred years they have asserted it in arms. Standing on that fun-
> damental right and again asserting it in arms in the face of the
> world, we hereby proclaim the Irish Republic as a Sovereign Inde-
> pendent State, and we pledge our lives and the lives of our comrades
> in arms to the cause of its freedom, of its welfare, and of its exalt-
> ation among the nations.

The proclamation claimed 'the allegiance of every Irishman and Irish-woman', in return for guaranteeing 'religious and civil liberty, equal rights and equal opportunities' and resolving 'to pursue the happiness and prosperity of the whole nation' while being 'oblivious of the differences carefully fostered by an alien government'. The IRB military council signed it: Clarke, Mac Diarmada, Pearse, Connolly, MacDonagh, Ceannt and Plunkett, all of whom placed their republic under the protection of 'the Most High God.' Many Dubliners, and Irish people in general, were unimpressed by what they deemed an extremist political act. The hint of German support contained in the proclamation's reference to Europe was distasteful even to many who were not Unionists. Those Dubliners not in Sackville Street or, later in the afternoon, around St Stephen's Green were slow to grasp that a rebellion was in progress: but by Tuesday morning, when the serious fighting started, central Dublin was effectively sealed off from the world.

Military strategists believe the reason the Rising began to falter so soon was the rebels' decision, having proclaimed the republic, not swiftly to occupy Dublin Castle and the fortress-like space of Trinity College. This may have been a calculated risk. They seemed to rule out particularly Protestant targets, such as Trinity, in case of appearing to embrace the sectarianism the proclamation had promised to avoid. A desire to preserve Dublin's heritage was later cited as a reason why the Bank of Ireland was not occupied; the last Irish parliament had met in the bank building. But some decisions about how to fight were simply incomprehensible, such as why the rebels chose to expose themselves to attack by gathering on St Stephen's Green rather than in one of the great buildings surrounding it. Their lack of numbers fatally undermined them and they had insufficient men adequately to garrison against a counter-attack the buildings they occupied. It was noted that a high proportion of those taking up defensive positions were barely more than schoolboys.

Lives were lost almost immediately. James O'Brien, an officer of the Dublin Metropolitan Police on guard at the Castle, was shot at around noon. A British sniper killed his murderer, Seán Connolly, a captain in the Citizens' Army and an Abbey Theatre actor, an hour later. Each was the first on either side to die. Soon afterwards rebels took the Castle's guardroom: but retreated, not knowing there were only another twenty-five soldiers there. One of the first Irish civilians killed was

F. W. Browning, a Dublin barrister who was also Ireland's most renowned cricketer: he had captained the Gentlemen of Ireland against Australia, and as an assiduous recruiter raised a footballers' company for the 6th Royal Dublin Fusiliers. He was on his way to report for duty and was targeted because he was wearing a khaki brassard bearing the royal cipher.

Significant failures of intelligence handicapped the rebels, as did absurd optimism. There is evidence that some leaders never stopped believing the Germans, like the 7th Cavalry, would appear: after he had surrendered, Mac Diarmada was heard to say: 'we were sure they would turn up.'[37] Nor did they receive support from their fellow Dubliners, few of whom then shared the revolutionary ethos of the provisional government. When they commandeered vehicles and carts for barricades they simply caused annoyance. The core problem with the plan was that there was no plan B. Asquith, facing an important debate in Parliament the following morning about the conscription crisis, heard the news late on 24 April, when he arrived at Downing Street from the Wharf. According to Hankey he observed: 'well, that's something', and went to bed.[38]

III

It is hardly surprising Asquith was untroubled. Apart from having bigger fish to fry, he had had no indication anything was amiss in Ireland. In the weeks before the Rising, Birrell had suggested to military commanders in Dublin that the Army should merely be seen going about its lawful business. For the next two or three days the story was of attempts by rebel battalions and smaller groupings in outer Dublin to secure positions too big or too vulnerable to hold, and to await the inevitable. The 3rd Battalion – which unlike other groupings refused to allow women to fight in it – made its headquarters in a bakery by the Grand Canal Street bridge around half an hour after the republic was proclaimed. De Valera, its commander, was a half-Spanish, half-Irish maths teacher of American birth who had risen through the ranks of the Volunteers. He had hoped to send his men out to occupy the port at Kingstown and stop British arms and reinforcements coming in by sea; but he lacked the men. The 2nd Battalion holed itself up in the Jacob's factory, waiting to be attacked: but they were not. The absence of a coherent plan, as MacNeill had warned, was palpable.

The General Officer Commanding in Ireland, Major General Lovick Friend – in his youth an occasional first-class cricketer of some distinction – had, despite warnings of a possible insurrection, like Birrell chosen to visit London for Easter. He returned the moment he heard of the Rising. On Easter Monday there was racing at Fairyhouse, and much of the officer class was there. There were very few soldiers left in the capital, something an intelligence operation superior to the rebels' would have discerned and exploited; when Pearse and his followers occupied the GPO only around 400 soldiers of the King were in Dublin, based in four separate barracks around the city.[39] The first instinct of their commanders was to secure the Castle.

Wimborne, as Lord Lieutenant, now became the focus of executive action *faute de mieux*. His position was mainly ceremonial; but he enjoyed the pomp and circumstance, and his wife was known as 'Queen Alice'. A former soldier, he had begun the war on the GOC's staff at the Curragh, and was now director of recruiting for the Army in Ireland. Still in his early forties, he was an aristocratic party hack, and a philanderer so celebrated that women were advised to avoid being alone with him. He landed the job not least because he was recommended to Asquith by Churchill, his cousin: hearing in November 1914 that the post would soon be filled, Churchill wrote to the prime minister 'to ask most earnestly that Ivor may not be overlooked . . . I am sure that the choice would be a right one.'[40]

Insofar as Wimborne was required to have a depth he was soon out of it. He was too lightweight, and lacked the political nous, to handle the situation sensitively. His main misjudgement was to act as though the entire population of Dublin had risen against the government, rather than just a loose band of rebels and fanatics who, but for the over-reaction that he initiated, would have attracted only the disdain of most of the population. He decided at once to declare martial law, on his own recognisance. Birrell, steeped in Liberal doctrine, was appalled at Wimborne's action, and urged Asquith not to extend martial law outside central Dublin. However, once the chief secretary was on the boat to Dublin, his credibility in tatters because of his complacency over the preceding months and years, the cabinet (despite some dissent from Lloyd George) put the whole country under martial law, which the King confirmed at a Privy Council on 26 April. This compounded an over-reaction that had not finished yet. Given that much of

Ireland had come to deplore the rebel action, this was pitiful public relations.

On the Tuesday morning, with Birrell still not in Dublin and Friend en route from Kingstown, Wimborne consulted Nathan, and sent a messenger to deliver by hand to the War Office in London a request for reinforcements. He reinforced himself, according to Cynthia Asquith, with draughts of brandy, which Lady Wimborne constantly refilled.[41] He asked for a brigade, and for two more to be held in reserve. On this occasion, at least, Wimborne had some sense on his side: after the shooting of police officers on Monday the commissioner had withdrawn them, leaving law and order in disarray; though some plain-clothes officers were deployed in an intelligence operation. Cynthia Asquith, briefed by Lord Basil Blackwood, who had been at the Castle, noted Wimborne 'was delighted to think he was at last really in the limelight and acquitting himself so well – flushed with importance and triumph.'[42] However, Wimborne's moment of fame would be brief. 'Altogether,' Lady Cynthia wrote, 'he seems to have behaved like the Emperor of Asses.' Certainly, Wimborne lacked both the literal and metaphorical authority to calm panic in others – such as the Dublin police – and to prevent the response to the actions of the rebels from getting out of hand. He had done nothing to cause the Rising, but the course he initiated in response to it would have grave consequences for the future relations of Britain and Ireland. On 28 April Wimborne sent Asquith his resignation. It was accepted, but not put into legal effect. Wimborne resigned not because he felt responsible – and indeed he was not – but because he wanted to give the government a clean slate from which to develop the future of Ireland.

By nightfall on Easter Monday a large contingent of rebels had set up camp on St Stephen's Green, notable among them Countess Markievicz, born Constance Gore-Booth in London forty-eight years earlier, the daughter of an Anglo-Irish baronet and landlord. While being drenched by rain during the night, the rebels failed to realise British troops had entered the Shelbourne Hotel, opposite, by the back door and set up a machine-gun post on the roof. At dawn on 25 April the British began to strafe the rebels, forcing them to flee to the College of Surgeons, where, predictably, they were besieged. An attempt by rebels from the Green to wreck nearby railway lines was aborted. Three volunteer battalions mobilised in the outer city, but again failed to secure strategic objectives, and soon went behind barricades to take a defensive rather than an offensive role in the campaign. Numbers remained considerably less than expected. From the moment the rebels went onto the defensive they were beaten; but because of a shortage of men (and women, for many were active in the fight) they had little choice but to retrench.

By Monday evening British reinforcements and artillery started to arrive from the Curragh, Athlone and Belfast. Brigadier General William Lowe, a cavalryman from the Curragh, took over command early on Tuesday morning and made a plan to restore order. More than 2,500 cavalry and infantry were in Dublin by then; there would be 16,000 by the end of the week: the British had stopped taking chances. The soldiers quickly cleared St Stephen's Green and City Hall. Lowe's plan was to establish a line in the centre of Dublin, including the station, the Castle and Trinity College, that would split the rebel forces on either side of the Liffey. This he did. Once properly trained, organised and commanded men were in place, and someone in charge with a grasp of strategy, it was but a matter of time before the rebels were defeated. Later on Tuesday morning a destroyer bearing Friend arrived at Kingstown. He could not improve on Lowe's plan, and left him in operational command.

Early the next day, 26 April, reinforcements, composed mainly of Sherwood Foresters who had never seen combat, landed at Kingstown. A disproportionate number were eighteen-year-old boys too young to be sent to France. Others came south from Belfast. Lowe's orders were to clear Dublin and its surroundings of rebels, with a machine gun at the head of each column of men; the column was not to advance beyond any building from which it had been fired upon, but to remove all resistance.

Asquith was now becoming anxious. A few weeks later, Esher heard from a friend on the General Staff that the following exchange had taken place:

Asquith: 'This rising is terrible. What are we to do?'
Robertson: 'Send every available man to Ireland.'
Asquith: 'Yes, but we might be invaded!'
Robertson: 'Well, there are a million Germans in France, a 'undred thousand in England won't make much difference.'[43]

The soldiers were reminded that the rebels were but a small proportion of the population, and were asked not to damage private property unless absolutely necessary; there was some sense that it would be wise not to alienate the public. However, much-fired-upon soldiers sought to find rebels wherever they could; from Tuesday until Friday afternoon the street fighting, though localised, was ferocious, and leaked into the suburbs, causing extensive damage. Some Dubliners showed little consideration for property, as systematic looting broke out in the luxury shops of Grafton Street.

On Wednesday the Crown forces brought four 18-pounder guns into central Dublin, and an armed yacht, HMS *Helga*, sailed up the Liffey. They launched a fusillade on Liberty Hall: its reduction to rubble made a symbolic point only as no rebels were inside. That morning Captain John Bowen-Colthurst, a Royal Irish Regiment regular officer, decided arbitrarily to shoot Francis Sheehy-Skeffington, a well-known Dublin writer, pacifist and school friend of James Joyce and Oliver St John Gogarty. Colthurst had arrested him the previous evening while Sheehy-Skeffington (who although imprisoned briefly in 1915 for making statements prejudicial to recruiting was a harmless crank who advocated Esperanto as the language of Ireland, feminism, vegetarianism and temperance as well as socialism) was touring Dublin trying to prevent looting.

British troops arrested Sheehy-Skeffington on the evening of Tuesday 25 April when they stopped a disorderly crowd of which he was an innocent part. He was detained at Portobello Barracks from which, at eleven that night, Colthurst took him as hostage on a raid of a tobacconist shop wrongly thought to belong to a leading rebel. As they proceeded Colthurst stopped two young men returning from a religious meeting, on the grounds that they were breaking the curfew. He then shot one of the men, a nineteen-year-old mechanic. Colthurst continued with the raid, leaving Sheehy-Skeffington at a nearby guardhouse, whose soldiers he ordered to shoot him if snipers attacked the raiding party. Colthurst told his hostage to start saying his prayers in case he was shot. When Sheehy-Skeffington refused, Colthurst started to say them for him.

He was not shot as a hostage, but taken back to Portobello Barracks. The next morning Colthurst announced to his junior officer that he intended to shoot Sheehy-Skeffington and two pro-British journalists who had been rounded up after curfew. The executions were carried out immediately by a firing squad. Colthurst's conduct was abominable but he was not of sound mind. He had been invalided home from the Western Front with suspected shell shock, and had spent all the night before ordering the executions reading the Bible and praying. The death of Colthurst's brother in action the previous year appeared to have unhinged him as much as religious mania. His comrades, not least Major Sir Francis Vane, his commanding officer, thought him mad. He admitted everything to Vane, who, unfortunately, was not in the barracks at the time. A fortnight later Colthurst said he had acted as he did because he believed (though on what basis it is impossible to know) that Sheehy-Skeffington and the two journalists were leaders of the Rising. He was court-martialled, found insane and sent to Broadmoor, an outcome that left the Nationalists outraged at what they considered a lenient sentence. The damage to Britain's reputation in Ireland that Colthurst's actions caused was unquantifiable.

As they marched towards the Mount Street bridge in Northumberland Road the reinforcements were attacked by Volunteers from de Valera's battalion, who fired from surrounding houses into their columns. They were held up for several hours until further reinforcements arrived, when the rebels were blown out with hand grenades. The Sherwood Foresters took 240 casualties. More soldiers arrived from Kingstown, and the cordon around central Dublin tightened.

In Britain, only the barest details of the Rising were made public, much to the anger of the press. Goading the government, *The Times* made the point after several days of official silence that – as American newspapers were saying – 'the silence of the authorities proves the revolt to be too serious for London to be frank.'[44] The authorities by then believed the revolt under control: the censorship was the usual extreme caution tempered with inexperience and incompetence; information until the end of the Rising was limited to official communiqués with the minimum of detail fed to the press. Most newspapers circumvented this by finding accounts of varying degrees of reliability from eyewitnesses.

On 27 April the Army Council appointed General Sir John 'Conky' Maxwell – the sobriquet referred to his considerable nose – as General Officer Commanding in Ireland, with immediate effect. The letter from the War Office to French, commander-in-chief Home Forces, announcing his appointment stated that:

His Majesty's Government desire that, in this capacity, Sir J Maxwell will take all such measures as may in his opinion be necessary for the prompt suppression of insurrection in Ireland, and be accorded a free hand in regard to the movement of all troops now in Ireland or which may be placed under his command hereafter and also in regard to such measure as may seem to him advisable under the Proclamation, dated 26th April, 1916, issued under the Defence of the Realm (Amendment) Act 1915. In regard to the question of administration, as also Military or Martial Law, Sir J Maxwell will correspond direct with the War Office, under the same system that obtains in peace time.[45]

Maxwell's main qualification was having no connection with Ireland; his other that he was available: which, given that Britain was in a life-or-death struggle, says something about his calibre. It was soon announced that he would be the military governor of Ireland, an appointment that suggested Asquith had decided to treat Ireland, effectively, as an enemy. If that was so, it created the idea of a British occupation among many Irish people to whom it had never previously occurred. It was something worse than alienation. By handing Ireland over to the Army to run, and to judge, Asquith began the process that would destroy the Irish Nationalism of Parnell and Redmond within two years, and deliver the country to Sinn Féin.

Early on 28 April Maxwell arrived to find much of central Dublin on fire. His principal aim was to end the fighting, but with the unconditional surrender of the rebels. The Crown forces continued to use artillery and grenades. By Wednesday the GPO was cut off; and at the Mendicity Institution the 1st Battalion, out of food and ammunition, decided to surrender. As other garrisons were encircled and the fires came nearer, it became clear that there could be only one ending. Inside the GPO morale was maintained by an unsubstantiated belief that Volunteers from outside Dublin would relieve it. Even if a relief column was on its way – and it was not – the British machine guns and artillery would have slaughtered it before it came anywhere near the GPO. Outside, by Thursday night Sackville/ O'Connell Street was burning almost from one end to the other. Connolly, fighting outside the building, was wounded in the leg by a ricochet and brought in during Thursday afternoon. Recognising the inevitable, Pearse ordered the women of Cumann na mBan out of the GPO on the Friday morning, much to their rage. Shells started to hit the building, and by the Friday afternoon it was burning. Late on the 28th Pearse led the evacuation of the GPO to a house nearby, at 16 Moore Street.

There had been skirmishes in the country around Dublin, but rebels there, as elsewhere in Ireland, relied on orders from the centre, and after Tuesday the centre struggled to get orders to them. MacNeill's counter-mand had in any case prevented a nationwide uprising. In some places Volunteers captured RIC officers and there was the odd shooting, but the country almost entirely failed to mobilise in support of Dublin. British troops dealt with substantial pockets of resistance near Galway, where British intelligence estimated there were 530 rebels, and at Enniscorthy in County Wexford, a small town where 600 Volunteers took control.

On 29 April Pearse realised he and his comrades were cornered. They were exhausted, out of food and with no medical supplies. The final straw was the sight of civilians being killed in the crossfire as the Army sought to finish the rebels off. He sent Elizabeth O'Farrell, a nurse, out under a white flag to broker a truce; and during it Pearse met Maxwell to discuss a surrender that would cause the leaders to be tried but the rank and file released. Maxwell, a soldier and not a politician, saw no cause to give quarter, and insisted on unconditional surrender. Notes from the meeting show that Maxwell said the rebels should 'throw themselves on our mercy': he felt the government would not be hard on the rank and file, provided the surrender was swift.[46] When the terms were put to the men in Moore Street some wanted to carry on fighting: but by the evening they all marched out to Sackville/O'Connell Street, under a white flag, and laid down their arms.

Early on the Sunday morning, Nurse O'Farrell took Pearse's written orders to the other battalions south of the Liffey. Eventually they sur-rendered; de Valera first demanded MacDonagh's counter-signature as he did not know Miss O'Farrell, then announced that he surrendered only because he was obeying an order from a superior. Whatever humili-ation the rebels felt, those who survived would treat what had happened as the beginning of the shift in Irish politics from using constitutional means to violent ones to secure their independence. Britain's conduct during and after the Rising began the Irish Nationalist community's abandonment of Redmond's ideas of an accommodation with London in a Home Rule state, and the wholesale pursuit of a republic. However, as they were marched into captivity some rebels recorded the howls of exe-cration from women outside Kilmainham Jail, the wives of soldiers who feared their separation allowances would be ended because of the rebel-lion and who wished to show their disapproval. As armed escorts marched them through the streets, before the execution of rebels turned public opinion, Dubliners howled abuse at them, and pelted some with rubbish. This reflected the fact that innocent people had been the largest group of casualties: the 256 civilians killed included 40 children, compared with 62 rebels, and of the 2,600 wounded most were civilians.[47] Wreckage around the GPO was extensive, as in other areas of central Dublin. Around 200 buildings were seriously damaged. The Army, with little or no experience of urban warfare, lost 106 men (including 17 officers) and sustained 334 wounded.[48]

A total of 3,430 men and 79 women thought to be part of the rebellion were arrested. Although an order was issued that a distinction be made between committed Nationalists, rank-and-file supporters of the Rising and 'dangerous' Sinn Féiners – that is, those either inciting violence or against whom there was evidence that could require a court martial – it was either not understood or was widely ignored. Prisoners were deported to English jails, often on cattle boats. By mid-May 1,600 were in England and Wales, held under DORA, on the dubious grounds that they were enemy aliens. Some were innocent of any involvement in the rebellion; this was usually realised within days, and 1,424 were freed without apology or compensation.

On 1 May the London press carried its most extensive reports yet of the Easter Rising: *The Times* published a lengthy description of the fighting by the editor of the *Irish Times*, who said the 'outbreak' had 'been directly induced by the criminal negligence and cowardice of the Irish Government.'[49] Beatrice Webb, digesting the coverage, called the Rising 'criminal lunacy ... playing into the hands of the reactionaries.'[50] Birrell – of whom a leading Nationalist landowner, Sir Horace Plunkett, said 'more than any other living man he fomented this rebellion' – resigned that day, and Nathan went shortly afterwards.[51] Asquith, when Birrell visited him to resign, was so stricken at the loss of his friend that he 'just stood at the window and wept.'[52] Birrell, believing Home Rule was inevitable given that an Act was on the statute book, was a liberal who rejected the heavy hand; and he had also tried to avoid unnecessary provocation in the last phase of British rule, thinking the Irish would soon be masters in their country.

Herbert Samuel, as home secretary, went to Ireland to take over temporarily until a new administration could be installed. He found Dublin 'a pitiful sight', with so many buildings in ruins.[53] Although the Rising had failed, the nature of the Irish question had changed. Used to having to deal with hard-line Unionists, the government now saw it would have to deal with hard-line republicans, their numbers swelling as aggressive actions by inexperienced and sometimes frightened boy soldiers continued to alienate normally pacific citizens. The reality would undermine the original perception that, so few were the rebels, the event could be taken as further proof of the loyalty felt to the Crown by the Irish.

IV

New measures were taken not so much to restore order as to emphasise who was in charge. On 2 May Maxwell told Kitchener he blamed the permissive regime in Dublin Castle for allowing the Rising, and said he trusted 'politicians will not interfere until I report normal conditions prevail.'[54] His way of achieving normality was to order house-to-house searches for rebels and illegal weapons, to arm the Dublin Metropolitan Police and to show 'no pity' to those who had been 'playing at rebellion for months past.' The country would be combed for Sinn Féiners who, if rebel sympathies could be proved, would be arrested whether they had taken part in the Rising or not. The intelligence services believed that had the Rising shown the slightest sign of succeeding a mass of people would have joined the rebels and sought to overthrow British rule. Within a couple of months 2,000 weapons were found, probably the tip of the iceberg: but the intrusion of troops into communities where there was little or no trouble bred anger and resentment, and continued despite loud warnings from John Dillon, Redmond's most senior colleague, of its effects.[55]

Dillon also wrote to Redmond on 30 April urging him to intercede with the government to prevent 'large scale' executions of rebels, a policy he said would represent 'extreme unwisdom' because 'the effect on public opinion might be disastrous in the extreme.'[56] Even he, though, seemed to accept that some ringleaders might be shot. Courts martial began at Richmond Barracks under Major General Charles Blackader on 2 May. They were held in secret and with the prisoners having no defence, which was later deemed illegal. Some of the Army officers conducting them had conflicts of interest as prescribed by the military manual. In the end, ninety were sentenced to death: Maxwell confirmed fifteen of these sentences and the executions happened from 3 to 12 May.

He said only ringleaders and cold-blooded murderers would be killed –
which Asquith had specified – but this was not inevitably so; de Valera
escaped because of his American birth. Patrick Pearse, Clarke and
MacDonagh – unquestionably ringleaders – were the first convicted of
'waging war against His Majesty the King, with the intention and for the
purpose of assisting the enemy.'[57] They were executed in Kilmainham
on the morning of 3 May, in the yard where those sentenced to hard
labour broke rocks.

Asquith told French he was surprised at the rapidity of the process and
'perturbed' by the executions: rather late in the day, having agreed to
the exercise of martial law, he observed that 'any wholesale punishment
by death might easily cause a revulsion of feeling in this country and lay
up a store of future trouble in Ireland.'[58] French, who like Maxwell
thought the rebels should get what was coming to them, nonetheless
told Maxwell to confirm that not all the Sinn Féiners would be shot,
though added ambiguously that he would not seek to interfere with
Maxwell's freedom of action. Thus supported by a senior officer, Maxwell carried on. All seven who had signed the proclamation were
executed. Connolly, unable to stand because of his leg wound, was shot
tied to a chair. Maxwell did, however, follow Asquith's wishes that no
woman – the prime minister specifically mentioned Countess Markievicz, who had kissed her revolver in the College of Surgeons before
handing it over to a British officer – should be executed before the case
was referred to him and to French. When an officer told her of her
reprieve, the Countess replied: 'I wish you had had the decency to kill
me.'[59] Four more men were shot on 4 May, and another on the 5th, and at
that point the lawyer in Asquith took over. He sent a warning to Maxwell to urge the military governor to proceed at a pace that suggested
nothing hasty had been done and that there had been adequate 'deliberation'. Above all, he wanted Maxwell to do nothing that might 'sow the
seeds of lasting trouble in Ireland'.[60]

However, it was already too late for that. Redmond, who had regarded
the rebels as criminals, praised the government's response to 'this insane
movement' that had 'tried to make Ireland the catspaw of Germany'; but
on 3 May, pressed by Dillon, he implored Asquith to stop the executions,
or risk making his position as leader of the constitutional Nationalists
impossible.[61] He argued, speciously, that they had committed treason
towards the liberty of Ireland, not against Britain. Asquith, maintaining

the line he had used to French and Maxwell, promised the executions would be limited, but some were necessary. Redmond warned him that Irish-American opinion was 'revolted by this sign of reversion to savage repression', something Asquith had to take seriously if, as he hoped, America were to enter the war. The executions had had a catastrophic effect on public opinion there, and myth-making was already well advanced. When more executions were reported, Redmond warned Asquith that if they continued he would feel forced to denounce them, and quite possibly to retire.

On 8 May, having failed to make Asquith order that no more death sentences be carried out, Redmond asked him in the Commons whether he was aware that the 'military executions' were causing 'rapidly increasing bitterness and exasperation amongst large sections of the population who have not the slightest sympathy with the insurrection', and whether he would put an immediate stop to them.[62] Although in private his reservations about the executions policy were mounting up, Asquith continued in public to defend Maxwell. He said the military governor had consulted the cabinet, and ministers had the 'greatest confidence' in his 'discretion'. He was sure Maxwell would sanction the extreme penalty sparingly, and only for 'responsible persons who were guilty in the first degree.'[63] Arthur Lynch, MP for West Clare, shouted out that Maxwell had ordered 'these shootings in cold blood'. Asquith refused to promise Ginnell that no more executions would take place until the Commons had discussed them. Ginnell accused him of 'murder'.[64] In Ireland, the industry of martyrdom was already well under way: publications were prepared listing the killed, the executed and the arrested, often with photographs. The continuance of the heavy hand spurred the creation of legends that would dog Anglo-Irish relations for decades.

Eventually, on 10 May, the day after Connolly and Mac Diarmada were shot, Asquith ordered an end to the executions. The press in London generally supported them: *The Times*, once they had finished, observed that 'a certain number . . . were absolutely necessary to teach the traitors who take German money that they cannot cover Dublin with blood and ashes without forfeiting their lives.'[65] It conceded that the public relations had been a disaster, in not explaining the reasons for each execution and not holding trials in public. The London newspapers, including *The Times* – which normally scrupulously avoided the vulgarity of photographs – published pictures of ruined buildings in

Sackville/O'Connell Street and other central Dublin locations; the gravity of the rebellion was evident, and British public opinion hardened against the rebels.

It is highly questionable, however, whether even if justice had been seen to be done the feelings of republican sympathisers would have been soothed, or the haemorrhage of Redmond's support staunched. The British government could never have responded to the use of force by rebels to concede Sinn Féin's demands to evacuate Ireland and allow complete independence. With a war on it was utterly inconceivable, not least because of proof of German complicity in Sinn Féin's campaign. But Redmond's fears about the response were soon justified. By 25 May Dillon was telling Scott that 'the executions had converted the Sinn Féin leaders from fools and mischief-makers, almost universally condemned, into martyrs for Ireland.'[66] He presciently told Scott that unless Asquith gave a measure of Home Rule immediately the Nationalists would break up, and Sinn Féin would control Irish politics.

V

On 3 May, hours after the first executions, Birrell made a resignation speech in the Commons, preceded by an attack by Ginnell on 'the shooting of innocent men by this Hunnish government'.[67] When, after interruptions by Ginnell, Birrell could speak, he admitted: 'I therefore, speaking for myself alone, say sorrowfully that I made an untrue estimate of this Sinn Féin movement – not indeed of its character or of the probable numbers of persons engaged in it or belonging to the association, nor of the localities where it is most to be found, nor of its frequent and obvious disloyalty, nor indeed of some of the dangers resulting from it.'[68] Ginnell would join Sinn Féin in 1917 and be imprisoned in 1918.

Some had told Birrell he should have suppressed the organisation:

I may have committed an error in not doing it; but I ask the House to consider what some of the consequences might have been, would have been, had that step been taken at that time. The unanimity of Ireland has, as I say, even yet been preserved. This is no Irish rebellion. I hope that, although put down, as it is being put down, as it must be put down, it will be so put down, with such success and with such courage, and yet at the same time humanity, displayed towards the dupes, the rank and file, led astray by their leaders, that this insurrection in Ireland will never, even in the minds and memories of that people, be associated with their past rebellions, or become an historical landmark in their history.[69]

On that, too, Birrell was wrong; and his next remark merely confirmed how badly he had misread the situation. Describing his departure from Dublin, he continued: 'When I viewed the smoking ruins of a great portion of Sackville Street, when I was surrounded by my own ruins in my own mind and thought, and all the hopes and aspirations and work I have done during the past nine years, one ray of comfort was graciously permitted to reach my heart, and that was that this was no Irish rebellion, that Irish soldiers are still earning for themselves glory in all the fields of war, that evidence is already forthcoming that over these ashes hands may be shaken and much may be done, that new bonds of union may be forged, and that there may be found new sources of strength and of prosperity for that country.'[70]

Asquith confirmed there would be an inquiry, and a debate: but said it would be 'most undesirable' for a debate in what was still the heat of the moment.[71] Redmond called what had happened 'a misery and a heart breaking', and pleaded: 'This outbreak, happily, seems to be over. It has been dealt with with firmness, which was not only right, but it was the duty of the Government to so deal with it. As the rebellion, or the outbreak, call it what you like, has been put down with firmness, I do beg the Government, and I speak from the very bottom of my heart and with all my earnestness, not to show undue hardship or severity to the great masses of those who are implicated, on whose shoulders there lies a guilt far different from that which lies upon the instigators and promoters of the outbreak.'[72] His calls for leniency were too late, and not entirely appreciated; Carson said that 'while I think that it is in the best interests of that country that this conspiracy of the Sinn Féiners, which has nothing to do with either of the political parties in Ireland, ought to be put down with courage and determination, and with an example which would prevent a revival, yet it would be a mistake to suppose that any true Irishman calls for vengeance.'[73]

The government reconsidered the viability of courts martial to try rebels. Irish Unionists, mainly from Ulster, wanted not merely an inquiry into the causes of the Rising, but a thorough examination of the credentials of all Irish public servants, to root out Sinn Féiners. The shock of events caused Carson and Redmond to seek a solution founded on the consent of their two parties. One possibility was for a Dominion prime minister to arbitrate: but they doubted they could bring their followers with them. On 10 May Scott lunched with Carson, who likened the effect of the events to 'a nail through his heart.'[74]

The Lords debated the Rising the same day. Lord Loreburn was a rare voice demanding the executions continue, though only for murderers. A far longer debate happened the next day in the Commons, on a resolution of Dillon 'that, in the interest of peace and good government in Ireland, it is vitally important that the Government should make immediately a full statement of their intentions as to the continuance of executions in that country carried out as a result of secret military trials, and as to the continuance of martial law, military rule, and the searches and wholesale arrests now going on in various districts of the country.'[75]

Dillon, prepared to attack the government in a way Redmond was not, spoke of the shock that an execution had taken place in Fermoy – the first outside Dublin. It seemed there was a 'roving commission' to carry out executions all over Ireland. He felt Asquith was not being kept properly informed: 'horrible rumours' were 'current in Dublin' and 'are doing untold and indescribable mischief, maddening the population of Dublin, who were your friends and loyal allies against this insurrection last week and who are rapidly becoming embittered by the stories afloat and these executions – I say the facts of this case disclose a most serious state of things.'[76] He continued: 'At this moment, I say, you are doing everything conceivable to madden the Irish people and to spread insurrection – perhaps not insurrection, because if you disarm the country there cannot be insurrection – but to spread disaffection and bitterness from one end of the country to the other.'[77]

He cited County Limerick, where there had been no uprising, but where the authorities were now doing house-to-house searches and arresting 'suspects'. The same was true in Clare and in his own county of Mayo. However, 'the primary object of my Motion is to put an absolute and a final stop to these executions. You are letting loose a river of blood, and, make no mistake about it, between two races who, after three hundred years of hatred and of strife, we had nearly succeeded in bringing together.'[78] Like Midleton, who had spoken in the Lords the previous day, Dillon believed nine-tenths of Ireland had remained loyal: and that was the position of strength the government, by letting martial law take its course, was now squandering.

His conclusion caused some unease, as had the rest of his speech.

> I do not come here to raise one word in defence of murder. If there be a case of cold-blooded murder, by all means try the man openly, before a court-martial if you like, but let the public know what the evidence is and prove that he is a murderer, and then do what you like with him. But it is not murderers who are being executed; it is insurgents who have fought a clean fight, a brave fight, however misguided, and it would be a damned good thing for you if your soldiers were able to put up as good a fight as did these men in Dublin – three thousand men against twenty thousand with machine-guns and artillery.[79]

Asquith was forced to admit ignorance of local circumstances. He reminded the House of the deaths of British soldiers and implored MPs: 'Do not let our sympathies be entirely monopolised by the unfortunate and misguided victims of this unhappy and criminal rebellion.'[80] He felt Dillon had lost a sense of proportion, and claimed the punishments had been 'necessary'. He promised any further courts martial for murder would not be held *in camera*, to allay public fears that justice was not being done.

Addressing doubt that some convictions had been unsound, he added: 'It is one of the most painful duties that can possibly be cast on any human being to be responsible for the death of another. I cannot – I tell the House fairly and frankly – reconcile it with my conscience or my judgment, believing as I do that the five other sentences were properly given and properly carried out, simply because we have reached this stage in point of time and numbers, that a differential or preferential treatment should be accorded to men equally or even more guilty.'[81] He agreed with Dillon that most rebels had fought 'very bravely' and with 'humanity': something he contrasted with the 'so-called civilised' enemy in France and Flanders.[82] He was also sure many who had taken part had not known what they were doing; and stressed that 'our desire is not only that they should be treated with clemency, but that every possible opportunity should be given to them – it is a very difficult task, and a task that requires a great deal of thinking out – in the future to redeem what, in their case, and not in that of those who led them, is a merely venial and pardonable error on their part.'

Asquith conceded Sheehy-Skeffington had been shot without cause, in circumstances everyone must 'deplore'; but did not believe the claims of Sheehy-Skeffington's widow that British soldiers had attacked and raided her house (they had). Asquith the lawyer demanded evidence; Asquith the Victorian, who found war in all its forms so alien, stated Maxwell would not be 'shielding officers and soldiers . . . guilty of ungentlemanly or inhuman conduct . . . It is the last thing the British Army would dream of.'[83] He would leave for Ireland that evening to meet civil and military authorities and to make arrangements for Ireland to be ruled under 'the general consent of Irishmen of all parties'.[84] He had not understood Dillon about the rise of Sinn Féin, the one Irish political movement that now had true momentum. Nationalists welcomed Asquith's conciliatory tones; but Nationalists were not the future.

Two cases gave Maxwell difficulty. He viewed MacNeill as a ringleader, but an absence of evidence led to his being given life imprisonment for spreading disaffection and impeding recruiting; he was sent to Dartmoor, but released the following year. The women were almost all released within a fortnight, leaving just eighteen in the women's section of Mountjoy. Soon five of those were released, and some were deported: only Countess Markievicz was court-martialled. Asquith stuck to his decision that she could not be shot, to Maxwell's chagrin: but this was just seven months after Edith Cavell, and would have reduced the British to German levels of barbarism. Like MacNeill, she had a life sentence from which she was swiftly released.

Asquith now lacked a chief secretary, and struggled to find anyone of stature to take the post. He had wanted Lloyd George to go but the minister of munitions declined, and Asquith was in no position to make him; the dynamic in their relationship was shifting and as self-confidence drained away from Asquith, it drained into Lloyd George. The usually faithful Montagu also declined; and he resisted Unionist pressure to appoint Long, which would have been highly provocative. He considered another Unionist, Lord Robert Cecil, running the crucial (and, as it would turn out, decisive) blockade policy; but Redmond vetoed him, and Asquith was not minded to disoblige Redmond.

Eventually, he chose to fill the vacuum himself and to go to Ireland to assess the situation. Shortly before he left, the Lords passed a vote of censure on the government's Irish policy. Asquith was away for a week. He went to Richmond Barracks to talk to some of the three or four hundred detainees, and, with his lawyer's instinct, reached the conclusion that many should not be there: hence the releases of so many of the prisoners rounded up in the immediate aftermath. He also ordered the detainees be given better food, which annoyed the soldiers guarding them who were on military rations. He told Samuel the day after his visit that, having spoken to 'many' detainees, 'in reply to my question whether they had anything to complain of in their treatment, they one and all answered in the negative, except one man who asked for a pillow.'[85] He encountered little hostility, which deluded him into thinking that, if treated well, the Irish would become cooperative.

He visited Cork and Belfast too, canvassing all shades of opinion, but making few public appearances and briefing the press minimally on his private talks. Maxwell told Asquith on his arrival that, apart from two already scheduled and announced, there need be no further executions. He told his wife that with the exception of the Sheehy-Skeffington case 'there have been fewer bad blunders than one might have expected with the soldiery for a whole week in exclusive charge.'[86] But he added: 'I am in despair for a Chief Secretary. If only Simon were available.'[87] He told Samuel that while he had been surprised by how well matters were, 'the giving in of arms, especially in Cork and some parts of the South, is not satisfactory.'[88] On his return he visited his Oxfordshire near-neighbours, the Morrells, at Garsington, and told Lady Ottoline that 'the poverty in Dublin was awful, and that this was the cause of much of the revolutionary feeling, more so he thought than the Sinn Féin movement, which he felt was more poetical than revolutionary.'[89] Despite his time in Ireland, and his normal perceptiveness and intelligence, Asquith underestimated the appeal of the republicans – though saw the necessity of implementing Home Rule as swiftly as possible.

On the eve of Asquith's departure for Dublin the Home Office announced the establishment of a Royal Commission into the causes of the Rising, chaired by Lord Hardinge of Penshurst. It held nine sessions, five in London and four in Dublin, and apart from when taking evidence about German sympathisers or police information, it met in public. Birrell was examined on 19 May, and did himself few favours, other than disclosing that a month before the Rising he had made an unsuccessful application to the War Office to send more soldiers to Dublin – something the War Office rapidly denied, albeit in a mealy-mouthed fashion. But Birrell's remoteness from the crisis seemed confirmed by his 'reading, at times in a somewhat rasping and dog-matic tone, and at others in his most detached mood, as though he were discussing something in another planet, a long type-written statement' in which he analysed Sinn Féin as having started as a literary move-ment. He also felt that Carson's entry into the coalition had signalled to the Irish that the prospects of Home Rule had gone.[90] Even if he was mistaken about that, he had nonetheless allowed the belief to shape his conduct of policy.

On most days that Parliament sat immediately after the Rising, Irish members raised stories of Army atrocities, some of which had grains of truth – some more than a grain – and others that were fabricated, not-ably to do with troops being marched into peaceful areas and making wholesale arrests. Ginnell was one of the most persistent questioners: and put on the record on 24 May details of one of the Rising's most dam-aging incidents. He asked the government about:

> the number and nature of the wounds which James Connolly when he surrendered was found to have sustained; whether the military authorities first decided that he should not be tried until his wounds were healed; whether on the surgeon reporting that Mr Connolly was dying of his wounds they tried him; whether, being too ill to walk to or stand for his execution, he had to be carried on a stretcher to the place of execution, propped up in a chair there, and shot in that condition; and if he will give the date and place of any prece-dent for the summary execution of a military prisoner dying of his wounds?[91]

Tennant, the under-secretary, could not answer. Ginnell alleged that Mac Diarmada had been left in his cell at night, including before his exe-cution, without a bed or a pillow, and had had to wrap a boot in one of his two thin blankets, to rest his head upon: and had been denied a priest. Tennant could not answer that either. The next day Asquith, whom Nationalist leaders had found stricken with indecision, made what Scott called a 'halting' Commons statement about the restoration of civil government in Ireland.[92] He said that 'martial law is continued as a precautionary measure. We hope that its disappearance will be speedy and complete.'[93] His only purpose in visiting Ireland had been to determine the truth. He had not, though, grasped the speed at which public opinion there was moving against Britain: he spoke of 'the strength and depth, and I might almost say I think without exaggeration the universality, of the feeling in Ireland that we have now a unique opportunity for a new departure for the settlement of outstanding problems, and for a joint and combined effort to obtain agreement as to the way in which the government of Ireland is for the future to be carried on.'[94]

He announced that Lloyd George, 'at the unanimous request of his colleagues', would mediate between Carson and Redmond or, rather, their supporters.[95] Although Lloyd George had not wished to be chief secretary, an *ad hoc* role such as this, acquired by acclaim, was just the sort of thing to appeal to his sense of himself, his vanity and his showmanship. Asquith pleaded with MPs to stop discussing Ireland, so damaging was the effect of rumours and so harmful were they to the chances of a settlement. Redmond called silence a 'severe test', but in the interests of unity said he would abide by it. Carson agreed, reminding the House there was also 'a War going on, in which your country is involved.'[96] Some Nationalists believed Asquith was afraid to confront Carson, and that Redmond was reluctant to persuade him to do so. Dillon, increasingly regarded as more influential than Redmond, was impressed that Asquith had visited Ireland, where he had 'run a real risk of his life'.[97] Unlike Lloyd George, who would retreat to Walton Heath for fear of air raids, physical courage was not a quality Asquith lacked.

VI

Gwynne saw Lloyd George on 30 May and told him that 'no Unionist, Irish or British, would accept Home Rule during the war.' The same day, Ginnell attacked Tennant again about Connolly's execution. Tennant hardly improved matters by saying Connolly had been wounded 'just above the instep' and, although he could not walk, there were no grounds to delay his execution. He accused Ginnell of 'inaccuracy and exaggeration'.[98] Two days later, when news from Jutland suggested a British naval defeat, Sinn Féin supporters marched through Cork in exultation. But in Ulster, a renewed prospect of Home Rule was regarded as a deep betrayal of Ulstermen at the front, who were not in Ireland to defend their interests. Worse, the slowness and secrecy with which the negotiation entrusted to Lloyd George proceeded, the more a society riven by rumour-mongering was destabilised. Lloyd George would routinely exceed his powers, starting with a letter to Carson on 29 May saying 'we must make it clear that at the end of the provisional period Ulster does not, whether she wills it or not, merge in the rest of Ireland.'[99] Carson took that to mean a promise to make Ulster's exclusion permanent: it is hard to see how else to interpret it, even though in August 1914, when the Home Rule Act was put into suspension, Asquith had been clear that any exclusion would be reviewed. Lloyd George had allowed himself to become over-mighty with arrogance, and with Asquith unable to rein him in any more, accidents such as this would happen.

Dillon warned Asquith on 1 June about how much and how quickly matters had changed in Ireland:

> Remember this: It is quite a common thing for one brother to be in this Sinn Féin movement and for all the other members of the family to be strong supporters of the hon and learned Member for Waterford [Redmond] . . . Families are divided, and I have come across several cases myself where one young man in a family has gone over to the Sinn Féin Volunteers much against the will of all the rest of the family . . . by holding these men in prison, and by other methods to which I will not allude, [you are] manufacturing Sinn Féiners, or, at all events, enemies of the Government, by the thousand.[100]

Similarly, T. P. O'Connor told Scott on 7 June that 'before the executions 99 per cent of nationalist Ireland was Redmondite; since the executions 99 per cent is Sinn Féin.'[101] That was an exaggeration: because Redmond and his party had supported the war, and the war had become increasingly unpopular in Ireland, the Nationalists' popularity was falling before the Rising. However, the executions and martial law would make it far harder to get the Nationalist community to accept the deal Carson and Redmond (to each of whom Lloyd George had told different things) were trying to sell. The press was briefed that Nationalist sentiment was the main obstacle.

For most Nationalists Home Rule had to be for the whole of Ireland, not just twenty-six counties: though O'Connor saw that a deal for all but

six Ulster counties would be one the rest of Ireland should accept, and
Redmond agreed. The press published details of Lloyd George's proposals on 12 June: the Home Rule Act would come into immediate operation;
but after an Amending Act it would apply only for the duration of the
war and briefly after it; all Irish MPs would sit at Westminster for that
period; six Ulster counties would be governed from London during
that period; an Imperial Conference including all Dominions would
convene after the war to discuss the future governance of the Empire,
including Ireland; after which a permanent settlement would be made.

Lloyd George told Riddell that Asquith had returned from Ireland
with 'no plan and he funked the task of endeavouring to make a settlement'.[102] However, it would become a moot point whether having no
plan, but intending after great consideration to devise one, was worse
than having a plan that risked being deemed unworkable. Carson was
happy with Lloyd George's idea, not just because of Ulster's exclusion,
but also because he saw no obligation to include the six counties in a
Home Rule state after the war. Law, while disliking Home Rule, saw its
inevitability. Lansdowne, though, refused to accept the scheme, having
told Long on 11 June that it was 'morally wrong and wrong politically' –
sentiments Long passed on to Lloyd George.[103] On 22 June eighty Unionist
MPs demanded 'insurance of sufficient protection for southern Unionists; guarantees that Home Rule would not endanger the war effort, and
the permanent exclusion of the designated counties.'[104] Redmond had to
struggle for the support of his grass roots, for the Catholic Church would
not forgive the Nationalists for the isolation they threatened to impose
on northern Catholics, which became an important factor in its growing
support for republicanism. Nonetheless, a meeting of Nationalists in
Ulster agreed by a majority of two to one on 23 June to accept exclusion
as suggested by Lloyd George.

The Earl of Selborne, the minister of agriculture, took exception to
the absence of cabinet consultation: he told Long that 'there can be no possible justification of the Prime Minister's conduct to us.'[105] He saw Lloyd
George acting as a plenipotentiary, formulating policy as he went along,
rather than as a representative. Two cabinet meetings took place on 24
June, with continued disagreement between a small number of hard-
core Unionists and Liberals, to such a degree that Lansdowne thought
the government would break up. He was, however, very much in a
minority: Law, Balfour and even Carson all favoured an immediate deal,

as did the Unionist press, apart from the *Morning Post*. The conversion of Balfour – 'Bloody Balfour' of the 1880s – to the cause of Home Rule shocked even some Unionist colleagues used to his taking the line of least resistance. Lloyd George told O'Connor that Balfour had fought for the plan to grant immediate Home Rule 'as if he had been a home ruler all his life.'[106] The Tory grandee had been convinced by what he had heard about the helpful effect on American opinion if Home Rule were granted. Asquith resorted to what would become a typical device in the last phase of his leadership, and appointed a cabinet subcommittee to discuss the problem. Lansdowne, for his part, feared he would have to resign. Also on 24 June a paper from Maxwell was circulated to the cabinet, warning ministers that although most rebel leaders were dead the cult of their memory was intense, and that 'the moment new leaders are found it will become dangerous . . . there is no doubt there is a great recrudescence of Sinn Féinism.'[107]

Selborne resigned on 25 June. He had not imagined Home Rule for twenty-six counties would be offered immediately; he believed that possibility had been put in abeyance in August 1914, and that the discussion would be resumed after the war. On that basis he had participated in the act of collective responsibility that led to Lloyd George's mission; but when he heard Lloyd George had intimated that implementation would be immediate, he not only told Asquith he was resigning, but emphasised to both sides in the negotiations that he dissented from the cabinet line. He claimed two days later in the Lords that he and those who thought like him had been duped. 'Mr Birrell never informed us that the condition of affairs in Ireland had grown worse, nor did private information reach us from other sources. Therefore we knew nothing about the drilling and manœuvring, and all those matters which were known to other people, and consequently the rebellion took us by surprise.'[108]

He added: 'Ireland is in a gravely disturbed condition, and in my judgment, to inaugurate a constitutional change of such magnitude during the war would be more perilous than any other course open to us.'[109] Yet on 26 June, as Casement's trial began in the High Court – he had eventually found lawyers to defend him after several turned the case down – the Nationalists of the rest of Ireland joined Ulster's in assenting to the proposals, just as a deputation of Unionists from the three excluded Ulster counties and the other three provinces met Asquith and Lloyd George and urged them to reflect that the proposed settlement would cause 'the

Sinn Féin movement themselves [to] usurp the power of government in Ireland.'[110]

The lack of transparency about what was actually being negotiated caused huge irritation. The cabinet's Unionists were especially annoyed by the secrecy around the negotiations, so when a meeting scheduled for 28 June to discuss Ireland was postponed until the following week, ostensibly so that Asquith could give further consideration to the situation and Law could consult more widely, frustration deepened. The failure of the cabinet to unite gave further ammunition to those who wanted the decision-making body for the war drastically reduced in size. On 29 June the Marquess of Salisbury, agitated by what Selborne had said in his resignation statement, demanded in the Lords that the government publish details of the proposals, and the report of Hardinge's inquiry. He was vexed that two versions of the proposals were in circulation – one leaked to the press, and another that Redmond had described to his colleagues on 12 June. The press had been told that the six mainly Protestant counties in Ulster could opt in or out of Home Rule as they pleased; Redmond, however, had said that any opt-out would merely be for the duration of the war. This was not Carson's interpretation: he believed the plan allowed permanent exclusion of the six Ulster counties.

Salisbury asked on what authority Lloyd George had made the proposals: because both sets suggested immediate implementation of the 1914 Act with some form of amendment, contrary to what Selborne said had been agreed in cabinet. He quoted Redmond saying that Lloyd George had acted 'on his own responsibility'.[111] Redmond, though, assumed these were government proposals: but were they, given what Selborne had said? Salisbury noted there had been no repression in Ireland since August 1914, and the rebellion had come 'like a thunderclap'.[112] He was outraged that a new form of Irish government should be contemplated while the report of the inquiry into the rebellion had still not been published – even though it was known to be complete – and when the country was still in such turmoil.

Salisbury asserted that:

> every day since that rebellion was suppressed things have grown worse there. We want to know – and, after all, the public has a right to know – how much worse they have grown. What is the state of

opinion in Ireland? We know that the few misguided men whom it was necessary to execute as leaders of the rebellion – extraordinarily few compared to the number of innocent persons on the other side who were shot – have excited an enormous amount of sympathy in Ireland. They have been styled martyrs, not merely by the ordinary people, but, I believe in more than one case, by the Roman Catholic hierarchy, men who have an enormous influence on public opinion in Ireland.[113]

Shrewdly, Salisbury remarked that in three-quarters of Ireland Sinn Féin now predominated, and its adherents were unhappy with the proposals 'whichever edition of them is correct', and had become 'enemies' of Britain; any elections to form a government for Ireland would return more members friendly to Germany than to Britain.

Crewe told Salisbury there was 'no public advantage' in disclosing the details he wished.[114] He skated over the question of Lloyd George's acting on his own initiative by claiming that whatever proposals were made they had been designed 'with and through' Carson and Redmond.[115] He promised Hardinge's report would be published, and that nothing would happen until Parliament had voted on it. Crewe refused to say how bad matters were in Connaught, Munster and Leinster: 'It has never been the custom to publish the confidential reports received from the Police authorities in different parts of Ireland, and I cannot imagine that any departure from that practice, which has proved in the past to be salutary, is likely to be engaged in now.'[116]

As the argument continued in the Lords the jury in the Casement trial, after retiring for eighty-three minutes, returned a verdict of guilty on the charge of treason. Before sentence, Casement delivered a long speech – having rejected a draft written for him by George Bernard Shaw – that argued the philosophy behind the idea of treason had changed greatly since the statute of 1351: he rejected the notion that 'that constitutional phantom, "the King", can still dig up from the dungeons and torture chambers of the Dark Ages a law that takes a man's life and limb for an exercise of conscience.'[117] He claimed this relic of 'the brutality of the 14th century' could not apply to Ireland; that he had been tried in a foreign court, not by a jury of his peers; and would accept only a verdict reached by Irishmen in an Irish court. And he remarked that Sir F. E. Smith, KC, MP, prosecuting him as Attorney General, had supported those in Ulster who opposed the policy of the government and of Parliament to the point of backing armed rebels, and yet had not been put on trial himself. 'The difference between us,' he said, 'was that the Unionist champions chose a path they felt would lead to the Wool-sack, while I went a road I knew must lead to the dock.'

Casement was more prescient than effective: Smith became Lord Chancellor in 1919. However, the Lord Chief Justice, Reading, presiding over the case, knew Casement had as a British subject broken the law as it applied to the whole United Kingdom. Sentencing Casement to be hanged, he announced that 'your crime was that of assisting the King's enemies, that is, the Empire of Germany, during this terrible war in which we are engaged.' *The Times* reported that 'the prisoner bowed and smiled, and then left the dock.' It was announced the next day that Case-ment's name had been removed from the Register of the Order of St Michael and St George, and his knighthood was forfeit.

On 10 July Asquith, having prevented Long resigning over the treat-ment of the Unionists, broke his silence and made a statement to the Commons. He still believed there was a unique opportunity for recon-ciliation and a new settlement after a process of 'give and take'.[118] He said Lloyd George had functioned as an 'intermediary' between the interested parties and had kept him informed at every stage. He had discovered that only one basis of an agreement was possible: the imple-mentation of the Government of Ireland Act as soon as Parliament had modified it to exclude six of the nine Ulster counties. This outcome would be widely supported, including by Law as leader of the Union-ists. Asquith indicated that appropriate measures would come before Parliament imminently.

He described the Selborne difficulty as a 'misunderstanding'.[119] He admitted that 'there are features in the proposed settlement which none of us, voluntarily, would have chosen; one or another of which, for dif-ferent reasons, all of us dislike.'[120] It had been thus at the Buckingham Palace Conference of July 1914: but common sacrifices made during the war meant, he believed, the two sides would compromise.[121] He spoke of the Irish divisions then fighting on the Somme, notably the Ulster Div-ision that had 'covered itself in undying fame', as having created a 'new bond' between Ireland and Britain.

He believed it would be 'in the highest degree inconvenient' to give any details of the Bill at that juncture, though said members of the Irish

House of Commons would be MPs sitting for Westminster seats; and the British government would appoint Appeal Court judges in Dublin. He also awaited proposals from Unionists outside Ulster. He imagined some sort of gentlemen's agreement between London and Dublin, that Ireland would do nothing to impede prosecution of the war, with DORA remaining in force there; and the proposed arrangement would endure until a year after the peace had been concluded or, if Parliament had not made a permanent arrangement by then, to be extended by Order in Council until it had. He wanted a united Ireland: but realised that could be achieved only by agreement with the excluded counties, not by force. He continued to misunderstand the role Sinn Féin now played in such calculations. He confirmed to Carson that an Act of Parliament would be required to include Ulster subsequently: the six counties would be struck from the 1914 Act, which Nationalists now accepted, having been assured it could be changed.

VII

Hardinge's report, delivered on 26 June, had come to several conclusions about Ireland that were embarrassing for the government, expressing barely concealed astonishment that the republicans' private army had been allowed to parade in Dublin and elsewhere unmolested before the Rising. 'It was owing to the activities of the leaders of the Sinn Féin movement that the forces of disloyalty gradually and steadily increased, and undermined the initial sentiment of patriotism,' Hardinge said.[122] It noted that the RIC – armed with carbines and thus a quasi-military force – was considerably under strength, having lost so many men to the Army. The Dublin Metropolitan Police were slightly below strength, but were unarmed, which was why when shooting broke out they were removed from the streets and the Army was sent in. The commission said the nature of arrangements in Ireland made the system 'almost unworkable in a crisis'.[123]

Birrell's regime came under withering attack, not least because it had done so little to halt sedition. As well as noting the comparatively free circulation of anti-British literature, Hardinge remarked how priests and schoolmasters, using the Irish language, had spread 'treason' among the young.[124] He believed a republican press campaign, branding any attempt to disarm the Volunteers as an English ruse to provoke 'bloodshed', had intimidated Dublin Castle.[125] 'The main cause of the rebellion,' Hardinge concluded, 'appears to be that lawlessness was allowed to grow up unchecked, and that Ireland for several years past has been administered on the principle that it was safer and more expedient to leave law in abeyance if collision with any faction of the Irish people could thereby be avoided.'[126] The report called this 'a negation of that cardinal rule of government . . . the enforcement of law and the preservation of order should always be independent of political expediency.'

The Royal Commission could not grasp why Dublin Castle had tolerated paramilitary activities by people 'under the control of men who were openly declaring their hostility to Your Majesty's Government and their readiness to welcome and assist Your Majesty's enemies.' It exonerated Wimborne, whose appointment in February 1915 post-dated Birrell's permissive policy; Wimborne was reappointed on 9 August. Birrell carried the can, along with Nathan, who was judged to have kept Birrell insufficiently informed, during the chief secretary's frequent and long absences from Dublin, about how febrile the situation had become, and 'the necessity for more active measures'.[127] The RIC and the Dublin Metropolitan Police, whose senior officers had demanded full reports from their subordinates and, having received them, passed them on to Dublin Castle, were exonerated. There had been no excuse for Birrell not to act. Dillon called the report 'scandalous . . . one-sided, full of misrepresentation.'[128] No Nationalist politician had been asked to give evidence.

The House of Lords debated the Hardinge report on 11 July, despite Asquith's plea not to do so lest it set back Lloyd George's attempt to broker a solution. The Earl of Ancaster dismissed Wimborne as 'ornamental' but demanded Birrell be held to account: 'It seems an extraordinary thing that the Minister who was in that responsibility and whose policy brought about this rebellion, with the loss of so many hundreds of lives, should go practically unscathed and practically without condemnation.'[129] Later, the Earl of Camperdown was yet more condemnatory: 'He is very much to be pitied for his misfortune in ever having been appointed to an office which he was by temperament and in every other way entirely unfitted to fill. He never tried to govern Ireland. Indeed, I do not believe he went there very much. His policy was influenced and dictated to a large extent by the Irish Members of Parliament, and he was deaf to the warnings which he received from every quarter'.[130]

Ancaster wanted a hard line to continue. 'While Britons have been sending their bravest and best to fight the battles of the country,' he said, 'the Government of the day have been openly allowing treachery and sedition to go broadspread throughout Ireland.'[131] He believed the government 'had sent repeated signals that bad behaviour would be tolerated.' The hard line was not gratuitous, he argued; it was because of the war, which meant Britain could not afford another front on which to fight. Ancaster said of ministers that 'when engaged in a great war they must not be guided by any false sentimentality or imaginary ideas or vague dreams, but must deal as practical statesmen with the circumstances as they are; and the first duty which the Government owe to the country is to see that those men who are traitors and who are working against us should have the power taken from their hands.'[132]

Wimborne, still then under the impression that his resignation would have legal effect any day, made matters worse by admitting that, in his view, the Rising could have been forestalled had there been more troops in Ireland, and had Dublin Castle acted more swiftly after Casement's arrest to understand the significance of his return, and to intern potential troublemakers. The system by which there was a Lord Lieutenant (with no power) and a chief secretary (with all of it) had been misunderstood and had functioned poorly. The divergence of aim between Ulster Protestants, who saw themselves as British, and the rest of Ireland who rejected rule from London, had made the country ungovernable. The shadow cast over the Asquith administration for the casual, almost amateur fashion in which it had run Ireland was considerable. It would contribute greatly to the momentum for change in the direction of the United Kingdom and of Britain's conduct of the war.

It was Lansdowne who dealt the killer blow. He demanded that until structural alterations were made to the Home Rule Act, to make Ulster permanently excluded, Ireland should be ruled by a variant of DORA that a Dublin parliament could not overturn. Thus it was southern Unionists – Lansdowne owned much of County Kerry – and not the Ulstermen who wrecked the plan to have the Government of Ireland Act effected as soon as possible, with Ulster's exclusion not permanent, but to be reviewed after the war. Nationalists were shocked and believed he could not stay in the cabinet; but he did. Asquith was horrified, telling Crewe that Lansdowne's speech 'has given the gravest offence to the Irish' and that 'it was with great difficulty' that he stopped Redmond asking him in the Commons whether what Lansdowne had said was now government policy.[133] Redmond told Asquith that a 'permanent and enduring' exclusion of Ulster was unacceptable, and that Lansdowne's allusion to such a change to the 1914 Act was 'totally uncalled for by the subject matter of the debate.' Nonetheless Lansdowne's remarks changed the climate and, just a day after Asquith's statement, the impression arose – accurately – that the new legislation would not be brought before Parliament just yet.

The Unionists in the government, led by Lansdowne and Long, also told Asquith they would not accept continued representation of a Home Rule Ireland in the Commons, and indicated their ministers would resign sooner than see Home Rule enacted on that basis. The prospect of breaking up the government, and its effects on the war effort, forced Asquith's and Lloyd George's hands. The Nationalists were adamant that they would not accept reduced representation at Westminster. The government was in a bind because Lloyd George had not obtained the prior consent of the cabinet before suggesting representation would remain as it was. Yet he was still talking tough. On 16 July he told Riddell a Bill would be brought in and would face a difficult passage because of attempts to amend it. 'However,' he added, 'I have pledged my word to the Irish, and if the pledge is not fulfilled, I shall have to resign. There are certain pledges which leave the person who makes them no alternative. This is one of them.'[134] Lloyd George's credibility would be a victim of his own braggadocio, and of Asquith's unnecessary timidity in the face of the Unionists – for the most influential of them supported Lloyd George's deal, and those who did not could have been let go. Long told Riddell that 'the PM is terribly lacking in decision, and it is strange that a man with such a great intellect should be so indecisive.'[135] Asquith shared these traits with Balfour; it was because of their high and analytical intelligence that they could see all sides of a problem and all consequences of any course of action: which made it far harder to decide which was the best.

Asquith said on 19 July that he hoped to introduce the Irish amending legislation the following week. The next day, however, Redmond was told that consideration had been postponed, and new proposals were being brought forward. He was also told he would not be consulted, at which point communications with him were cut off. He warned the government that further delay 'would be fatal'.[136] The Unionists were now driving the cabinet, unable to see how their intransigence was handing Ireland over to Sinn Féin. On 22 July Redmond learned that the new proposals were to exclude Ulster permanently and to end Irish representation at Westminster during the transitory period. This was presented as a *fait accompli*.

On 24 July Redmond forced Asquith to make a statement in the Commons on the draft Bill. Asquith said no Bill would be introduced without full agreement between all parties. Redmond sought to move a motion to discuss 'a definite matter of urgent public importance, namely, the rapidly growing unrest in Ireland and the deplorable effect on the Irish situation which must result from the fact that the Government do not propose to carry out in their entirety the terms proposed by them for the temporary settlement of the Irish difficulty, and which were submitted by us to our supporters and accepted by both Irish parties.'[137] Some MPs tried shouting him down – 'You will betray Belgium if you betray Ireland' – but he succeeded.

He recalled the previous two months' negotiations: how he had agreed to temporary exclusion because he hoped that, by the time the moment arrived to discuss a permanent arrangement, the excluded counties would see that Ireland could govern itself fairly and properly, and none would wish to stay outside the Home Rule state. The Nationalists viewed the retention of Irish members at Westminster as a safeguard of the 'temporary character' of the transitory arrangements.[138] Redmond had secured the support of his followers on the original proposals, and could not support a revised measure. He said the government 'have entered upon a course which is bound to increase Irish suspicion of the good faith of British statesmen, a course which is bound to inflame feeling in Ireland, and is bound to do serious mischief to those high Imperial interests which we are told necessitated the provisional settlement of this question.'[139] He added:

I cannot and I will not agree to new proposals which would mean an absolute and disgraceful breach of faith on my part towards my supporters in Ireland, and I warn the Government that if they introduce a Bill on the lines communicated to me my Friends and I will oppose it at every stage. Some tragic fatality seems to dog the footsteps of this Government in all their dealings with Ireland. Every step taken by them since the Coalition was formed, and especially since the unfortunate outbreak in Dublin, has been lamentable. They have disregarded every advice we tendered to them, and now in the end, having got us to induce our people to make a tremendous sacrifice and to agree to the temporary exclusion of six Ulster counties, they throw this agreement to the winds and they have taken the surest means to accentuate every possible danger and difficulty in the Irish situation.

Lloyd George made a poor response. He had become Secretary of State for War a fortnight earlier, and pleaded an inability to spend as much time as he would have liked on uniting Irish opinion. He claimed it had never been considered that the excluded counties would, at one point, be automatically included: which was not what the Nationalists had believed. But Lloyd George said specifically that 'Ulster could only be included . . . with its consent', and as part of a permanent settlement.[140] He believed that had been made clear; the Nationalists disagreed. Redmond told him it had been in the draft Bill; Lloyd George, resorting to weasel words perhaps sooner than he would have liked, pointed out that Bills went through stages of drafting. The government had changed the wording: but Lloyd George was determined to blame the Nationalists for any failure to proceed with the legislation rather than himself; he stressed that without a promise not to end Ulster's exclusion automatically, the Bill could not be introduced, because Unionists in the cabinet would not agree to it. He promised the government would not force the measure on the Irish. It was not a dignified performance; his earlier indication that he would resign rather than see the agreement wrecked evaporated.

Carson, despite having at first opposed an immediate grant of Home Rule, recognised hopes had been raised on both sides in Ireland to such an extent that it would be a 'calamity' if it were not to be implemented now; though it was his community that was safeguarded under the revised proposals, whereas the Nationalist aspiration of an Ireland united under Home Rule would be thwarted. He took a longer view: 'There is one thing: At the end of the War we will have had enough of fighting. We will have other great questions – reconstruction for the whole Empire, the reconstruction of the whole basis of society, financial difficulties so great that one does not like to ponder upon them, questions of trade so far reaching that one can hardly contemplate them. In the middle of all that we are to resume, forsooth, our old quarrels. I know that

many things I say do not please some of my own party, but I would
rather say them, because I know they are true.'[141] The problem for the
moment, however, was how the underhand behaviour of the government had destroyed trust. Dillon said: 'You have struck a deadly blow
at the whole future government of Ireland. How will you ever get the
Irish people to have confidence in the terms and the words of British
Ministers?'[142]

When Asquith wound up the debate – claiming to be mystified that
the Nationalists should have expected Ulster might be coerced – he
implored the Nationalists to change their minds; but they would not,
and a week later, on 31 July, it was announced there would be no Amending Bill. Dillon demanded an immediate statement about what, now,
were the government's intentions. He felt the Irish had been duped, in
that Lloyd George had pretended he spoke on behalf of a united cabinet,
when he did not. 'At every stage we were aware of the fact that Lord
Lansdowne had seen the terms and had not left the Cabinet or the Government on the terms, and that he allowed us to go and stake our
political life on the basis of these terms without sending us any word
of protest at all. I think that, according to our idea of honour and of
the obligations of Cabinet Ministers, Lord Lansdowne was bound by the
terms, and he was bound not to break up the settlement if it was agreed
to in Ireland.'[143]

Coercion cut both ways:

If we were to consent to leave the predominant counties of Ulster
free to shape their own fate, are we not to claim the same right for
the Nationalists of Ulster? If Belfast and Antrim are to be free to
come into a united Ireland or to remain out, are the same terms not
to be enjoyed by Tyrone, Fermanagh, and Derry City? How can you
apply this Bill in such a one-sided way? What about the overwhelming majority of the Irish people whom you have coerced for 116 years
to have to submit to a system of government which they detest,
and which the Prime Minister the other day, and even the Hardinge
Commission, spoke of as having hopelessly broken down?[144]

It had been replaced, Dillon said, by an 'unlimited military tyranny'.[145]

Asquith insisted he had never given anyone the impression that either
he or Lloyd George had been 'plenipotentiaries' or had purported to say

anything that bound their colleagues.[146] Asquith spoke the truth about himself: Lloyd George, however, had unquestionably over-reached himself. He announced the appointment of Henry Duke, a Unionist barrister and stranger to the Irish controversy, as chief secretary, signalling the end of martial law: Duke quickly promised an 'amicable settlement' to the 'grievances'.[147] His appointment was to be counterbalanced by the reinstatement of Wimborne, a Liberal Home Ruler, as Lord Lieutenant, but Law asked Asquith to postpone the announcement, which caused uproar among the Nationalists. Lloyd George could have threatened to resign to prevent Asquith caving in to the Unionists, but again did not, perhaps because of an admission to himself that he had handled the process badly. Redmond, who claimed Duke as one of his oldest friends, having been a fellow student at Gray's Inn, put it bluntly: 'The proposal simply to revive Dublin Castle at all is a very serious thing. But to revive it by setting up for all practical purposes a Unionist Executive in Ireland will most undoubtedly outrage still more the feelings of the Irish people. The right hon. Gentleman . . . has gone out of his way to point out that the position of Lord Lieutenant is a purely honorary one, a purely ornamental one, and that he has no power. The real governors of Ireland are the Chief Secretary and the Attorney General, and they are both to be Unionist.'[148]

Asquith, not least because of Lloyd George's mismanagement of his role, was at the mercy of the Unionists; and the decision to 'revive Dublin Castle', even though presented as a temporary measure, was another recruiting sergeant for Sinn Féin: the British press simply saw what Asquith had done as proving, in the words of a *Times* editorial, 'less and less cohesion, grip and driving power' in the administration.[149] Redmond spoke of the 150,000 Irishmen fighting and dying in France, and the tens of thousands of others of Irish descent fighting for Australian, New Zealand or Canadian regiments; but the spirit that had driven those men was disappearing among those at home.

One of Duke's first tasks was to devise a system of grants and loans to help rebuild parts of Dublin wrecked during the Rising, so businesses might reopen and staff be hired. This initiative also showed how the British Treasury could be brought to Ireland's aid when needed. Republicans were not impressed. Ironically, even some Nationalists – such as Sir Horace Plunkett, who would be prominent in the attempt to resolve the Irish problem in 1917–18 – had concluded by late July that even if the

Lloyd George plan were implemented, it would simply hand over Ireland to Sinn Féin; it was already too late.[150]

VIII

It is striking that Frances Stevenson, whose devotion to Lloyd George
was not in question, felt he damaged himself during the negotiations,
and should have resigned. The Irish took out their rage on him; those
who sought an amicable solution also felt he should have resigned when
Asquith capitulated. The Irish crisis showed typical aspects of both men's
characters: Asquith trying to do the right thing, but his lieutenant
exceeding his remit, proving increasingly incapable of behaving straight-
forwardly, and leaving a trail of destruction behind him. It would not be
the last time such a thing would happen. As is the wont of men in such
a situation, Lloyd George blamed everyone but himself. He felt the Irish
were being unreasonable. 'I don't think he has quite played the game,'
Miss Stevenson recorded in her diary, adding that she disagreed with
him and did not know what to say to him.[151] Within days she decided he
was right to stay: Riddell, at that stage Lloyd George's tamest press
baron, had told him that Asquith's closest associates, led by McKenna
and Montagu, were after him; and Miss Stevenson feared that if he went
he would be frozen out for good. In fact, to many who were not aware
of the intimate detail, the negotiations boosted Lloyd George's reputation, because of the impression he had given of being a man who could
handle a big problem with some degree of decisiveness. They marked
him as Asquith's natural successor, even though he had conducted them
so poorly: his usual negotiation weapons, of charm or bribery, were not
equal to so serious a challenge. The Nationalists were breaking into factions, and would never be effective again: in August the Irish trades
unions turned on them and expressed 'abhorrence' at the Nationalists'
endorsement of partition.[152] The Asquith coalition too was undermined,
though that, ironically, would benefit Lloyd George.

At 9 a.m. on 3 August Casement was hanged at Pentonville. He had
been received into the Roman Catholic Church before his execution.
Shortly afterwards, the government published a statement explaining
why his sentence had not been commuted, notably that he had made an
agreement with the Germans to raise an Irish regiment that would fight
against the British in Egypt. There had been many petitions to reprieve

him, not least from Scott, who on 5 July had asked Lloyd George whether such a move might be 'politically possible'.[153] Scott argued that Casement had suffered from poor mental and physical health – 'I think he is at least as much off his head as the religious fanatic who murdered Sheehy Skeffington and two other men and who – rightly I think – is not going to be hung [sic].' However, Sheehy-Skeffington's arbitrary killing and martyrdom did nothing to help Casement, who unlike Colthurst had been convicted of treason in the midst of the most brutal war in British history.

There remained a controversy over Smith, to whose own flirtation with treason Casement had alluded at his trial, prompting Smith, in an undignified gesture, to get up and walk out of court. He later refused permission, as Attorney General, for an appeal to the Lords. It was also a matter for concern that a diary had allegedly been discovered in Casement's papers proving not just his promiscuous homosexual activities, but also his unnatural interest in the genitals of underage boys; and that this fetish had been considered when deciding not to reprieve him. Asquith, in response to a plea for a reprieve from Lady Ottoline Morrell, told her Casement was 'a depraved and perverted man'.[154] Further evidence had also been found, however, of Casement's collusion with the Germans, far more damning than any lubricious sexual aberrations.

The law took its course despite worries about the effect on American opinion. *The Times*, while agreeing with verdict and sentence, accused the government of foul play in its management of the propaganda surrounding the case, and its crude attempts to have the press mention Casement's sexual practices: 'These issues should either have been raised in public and in a straightforward manner, or they should have been left severely alone.'[155] The government refused to allow the release of Casement's body for burial outside the prison. When it was eventually exhumed and handed over to the Irish in 1965, Casement received a state funeral in Dublin, attended by de Valera.

Many Volunteers sympathised with Sinn Féin for its Irish independent and republican ideals, but Sinn Féin had not intended the Rising. Effectively, the Volunteers took the movement over and turned a non-violent organisation into a military one. Count Plunkett, Joseph Plunkett's father and a former deportee who had been sacked from his job as a museum director, won a by-election in North Roscommon on 3 February 1917 as a Sinn Féin candidate. This was its first victory and a trigger for its relaunch. With some reluctance on Plunkett's part the movement decided not to take any seat it won in the Imperial Parliament. On 19 April 1917 the republican movement was reconstituted after a meeting called by Plunkett, the change formalised at an *Ard Fheis*, or party conference, on 25 October, when Sinn Féin became the formal umbrella organisation of the republican movement. It would, if necessary, pursue its objectives by violence. Plunkett's was the first of many by-election victories, and the next and most crucial stage in the disappearance of a constitutional alternative to Unionism.

SINGLE MEN

Hundreds of Thousands of married men have left their homes to fight for **KING & COUNTRY**

SHOW YOUR APPRECIATION

BY FOLLOWING THEIR NOBLE EXAMPLE

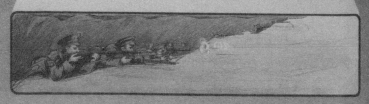

PUBLISHED BY THE PARLIAMENTARY RECRUITING COMMITTEE, LONDON. POSTER Nº 128.   PRINTED BY THE ABBEY PRESS, 24 & 26 ST. PETER ST. WESTMINSTER, S.W. W.9638. 51M./9/15.

CHAPTER 6

SLAUGHTER

———◆———

I

During February and March 1916 Edward 'Colonel' House, confidant of
Woodrow Wilson, the United States president, visited London and Berlin
to seek common ground for a peace initiative. He was greeted with cynicism, it being believed that Wilson, who faced re-election that November,
was hoping to acquire the reputation of a great peacemaker to boost his
standing. House, possibly taking German propaganda too literally, was
convinced the Allies faced an uphill battle. According to Hankey, he told
senior ministers that the German army and navy were 'stronger than we
calculate', that a new submarine was launched every three days and there
were plenty of German troops for another year's hard fighting.[1] This was
depressing news: the men directing Britain's war sensed that if the next
offensive, planned for the summer, failed, Britain would lack the men and
the money to fight at anything like that pitch again.

House's view was that it would serve Allied interests best to pursue a
diplomatic course. He told Grey that if the Allies told Wilson their peace
terms, he would ask Germany to a conference to discuss them. If Germany's terms were unreasonable, House said America would 'probably'
join the Allies.[2] The War Committee discussed the matter on 21 March,
and decided not to take a decision. Preparations for the summer offensive on the Western Front were already advanced, and it made no sense
to Asquith to dismiss the chance of triumph if it was there for the taking.
To make such a judgement the War Committee relied on Robertson's
advice about the prospects of victory. House returned to America in late
March to tell Wilson there was no likelihood of his good offices being

sought after just yet. A German overture three months later was rejected. Esher wrote to Asquith on 23 June, a week before the start of the Battle of the Somme, that 'an emissary has been employed by the Germans to sound the French, and to try and discover the terms upon which an armistice might be granted, with a view of subsequently discussing terms of peace. The answer that was given was that no proposition for an armistice would be considered unless it was accompanied by an offer to restore all French, British and Russian prisoners before hostilities were suspended. Nothing more was said.'[3] The French also wanted the German army withdrawn from French and Belgian soil before any discussion. Peace remained an illusion.

Asquith's confidence received a profound shock two months after the attempted House initiative. On 31 May, the day after the first drafts of conscripted married men went off to training, the German fleet came out and sought to engage the Royal Navy. The Battle of Jutland began that afternoon. It started badly for the Navy, with one ship after another going down, prompting Vice Admiral Sir David Beatty to remark to Ernle Chatfield, his flag captain, in one of the great *bons mots* of the war, 'there seems to be something wrong with our bloody ships today, Chatfield.'[4] Asquith was kept informed, though Hankey noted that late that night he 'was playing bridge as though nothing had happened'.[5] More news trickled in throughout 1 June. By the morning of the 2nd it was becoming 'worse and worse', not least because the first official news made no mention of German losses at all.[6] At 4 p.m., when Jellicoe's report reached Downing Street, it said that three British battle cruisers, three armoured cruisers and ten or twelve destroyers had gone down, heavier losses than it was believed the Germans had taken. Hankey called it 'the most bitter disappointment of this terribly disappointing war'; for if British sea power was that inadequate, Britain was nothing. Yet he did not believe the losses altered the effectiveness of the Navy's blockade of Germany, and he was right.

The next day's definitive reports brought better news. The Germans had lost one battleship against none for the Navy, one battle cruiser to the Navy's three, no cruisers against the Navy's three, but four light cruisers against none for the Navy, and five destroyers to a final Royal Navy total of eight losses. 'I do not think that they [the German High Seas Fleet] will venture out again,' Hankey noted, nor did they. It had also become clear, he added, what had gone wrong with 'our bloody

ships': 'defective arrangements for preventing the effect of a shell burst-
ing in the turret from reaching the magazine.' For his part, Fisher felt
Beatty had blundered by allowing the more lightly armed ships to
engage the Germans long before the more heavily armed ones arrived.
Even so, and despite the greater British losses and the U-boat menace,
Jellicoe had retained command of the North Sea.

When the Admiralty had received the news Balfour, as First Lord, had
'implored' Asquith to tell nobody, including the War Committee: so,
remarkably, it was not summoned.[7] Admiralty House was in such a
panic that Balfour enlisted Churchill, one of its sternest critics, to write
an officially briefed account of the battle to be issued to the press, in
which a more uplifting version of events was prepared. It was not until
the evening of Friday 2 June, two days after the battle had started, that
Lloyd George picked up a rumour about it. It gave him further ammunition against Asquith about how the government and the war were being
run. Once the news reached Northcliffe – with whom Riddell believed
Lloyd George was 'in daily contact' – his newspapers were merciless.[8]
The Times condemned Churchill's deployment as an act of 'weakness' by
the government.[9] However, the Germans had steamed back to safe harbours and the Royal Navy sailed the North Sea unimpeded. For Mrs
Asquith, such criticism confirmed her obsession about Northcliffe's
toxic influence, and her belief that he was orchestrating a coup against
her husband. St Loe Strachey, editor of the Spectator, who had become a
close confidant, told her the real difficulty with Northcliffe 'is the fact
that so many members of the Cabinet not only are unwilling to stand up
to him, but actually court him and ask him for his support.' Accusations
that Northcliffe was a 'public danger' were met with the question: 'Why
are Cabinet Ministers hand in glove with him?'[10]

With morale still shaken after the loss of so many ships at Jutland – and
with the adverse effect on the German navy still not entirely understood –
an even greater blow was struck against the morale of the country. Late
on 5 June the Admiralty learned that Kitchener and his staff had died
when HMS Hampshire, an armoured cruiser taking them from Scapa
Flow on a mission to Russia to discuss British financial and logistical support, hit a German mine east of the Orkneys. Hampshire sank in a force 9
gale; Kitchener had refused to wait for better weather so he could have
the destroyer escort Jellicoe offered him. Lloyd George should have been
aboard but had been detained in London dealing with Ireland. The

government realised this news required delicate management: partly because, as Beaverbrook put it years later, the mission was a 'disguised banishment' for the Field Marshal before his removal from Whitehall, but also because the public's love for him was undimmed.[11]

The effect on the national spirit was thus almost uniformly depressing: though Northcliffe, whose newspapers respected the public mood, supposedly said that 'Providence is on the side of the British Empire after all.'[12] Parliament was on its Whitsun recess, so it was not until 21 June that official tributes were paid; minsters poured cataracts of praise on a man they would have been glad to be rid of by any less terrible means. Esher, who had liked Kitchener, postponed his return from France. 'Another reason for not going to England,' he told Haig, 'is that I could not stand the whining over K from those who hated and depreciated him.'[13] 'His career has been cut short,' Asquith said, in the tones of the worst sort of canting clergyman, 'while still in the full tide of unexhausted powers and possibilities.'[14] The Army was ordered to observe seven days' mourning, with officers wearing crêpe armbands.

The public had no doubts about Kitchener's heroic qualities; the soldiery viewed his death as a serious blow; but the political class had come to see him as an obstacle. His death brought the silver lining of the chance to overhaul the running of the war. Hankey, who admired Kitchener because of his foresight and energy in August 1914, noted that as an 'autocrat' he had sat uncomfortably in cabinet.[15] He had trusted few of his colleagues to keep secrets on which lives depended, so did not share them. He had felt undermined since Robertson's appointment as CIGS, even though they had a good personal relationship. Kitchener told Derby just before he sailed that he knew his mission to Russia was about 'getting him out of the way' but 'he did not mean to leave without a struggle.'[16] He was under no illusions.

At breakfast on 6 June, before he had heard about Kitchener, Lloyd George – whom the Field Marshal disliked vigorously – told Scott that 'we are losing the war if indeed we have not already lost it.'[17] He attacked the Russians, who he said were now producing fewer shells each week than Britain did in a day: it had been confirmed that the army of British women munitions operatives were working an average of sixty-one and a half hours a week on the day shift or sixty hours on the night shift.[18] He dismissed the idea of a further offensive on the Western Front, claiming it was 'folly' to suppose, after Verdun – where the French had sustained 185,000 casualties thus far in heroically resisting a series of punishing German attacks since 21 February – that the BEF could break through German lines. He believed that 'our generals were largely incompetent.' Instead, he (like the French) wanted an assault on the Central Powers from Salonica, but in this was alone in the cabinet. Scott detected that Lloyd George's criticisms were more rhetorical than practical; Churchill, also at the breakfast, told him after their host had left that Lloyd George was 'still flapping about'.[19]

Later that day Scott saw Lloyd George again, and told him he should succeed Kitchener. Lloyd George was too conscious, however, of how little more than a figurehead Kitchener had been. He himself had siphoned off many of his powers as minister of munitions, and Robertson had taken many of the rest. Lloyd George would consider the job only were those powers restored. He distrusted Robertson, because he suspected him of lacking respect for the views of politicians and of conspiring with other generals, notably Haig, to get his own way; and he coveted his power to appoint officers to higher commands. He knew Asquith regarded him as 'indispensable', so was unlikely to strip him of this power in order to placate Lloyd George.[20] Robertson, however, was willing to work with the munitions minister: Churchill recounted that the CIGS had, speaking of the cabinet, described Lloyd George as 'the only live man in that set of bloody fools'.[21] Esher, who spent much of his life talking to generals, told Haig: 'I hope that Asquith will retain the WO himself, with a strong Under-Secretary. That would be the best scheme, and leave Robertson the freest hand, but I fear it is an unlikely solution.'[22]

Pushiness disgusted Asquith. He told Stamfordham: 'All this canvassing and wire-pulling about the succession, while poor K's body is still tossing about in the North Sea, seems to me to be in the highest degree indecent.'[23] Northcliffe wanted Milner, whose record as a proconsul in South Africa was but the most recent of his many executive achievements, and whose no-nonsense style of doing business commended him to the press baron. However, Northcliffe said through the leader columns of *The Times* that 'we cannot imagine any man of Lord Milner's strong character joining the Cabinet in these days without a very clear understanding about his powers' – and it doubted Asquith had the imagination to agree to such an understanding.[24] Inevitably, *The Times* advocated that, whoever became war secretary, he should answer to a small 'supreme War Council' rather than be hamstrung by the disputes of a full cabinet.[25] That argument would become persistent in the months ahead.

Sir Max Aitken, Law's fellow Canadian, chief confidant and crony and a Unionist MP who within months would become Lord Beaverbrook, was willingly being drawn more and more into the heart of political intriguing. He hosted a Sunday lunch at Cherkley, his house in Surrey, for Law and Lloyd George, to thrash out which of them should succeed Kitchener. It began badly, with Law accusing Lloyd George of being too much on the make. Lloyd George offered to back Law; but as the discussions continued into the afternoon it became apparent that Law would defer to Lloyd George, partly out of a natural lack of push and partly because he understood his rival's immense popular appeal, which the coalition needed to harness to its maximum benefit. He said he would see Asquith to recommend Lloyd George's appointment. The meeting took place the following morning, Whitsun bank holiday, at the Wharf, Asquith's weekend house in Oxfordshire. According to Beaverbrook the prime minister was playing bridge when Law arrived, and his visitor declined to wait for the hand to be completed; that, like all Beaverbrook's reminiscences, should be treated with caution. Asquith dismissed the idea of Lloyd George's succeeding Kitchener, but with enhanced powers, so briskly that it deepened Law's conviction that he was not taking his responsibilities entirely seriously. The prime minister then offered the job to Law, who said he was committed to Lloyd George. Once he understood Law's intentions Asquith, whose wife was now feeding his suspicions of Lloyd George's plans, was determined not to be rushed. As after the Curragh incident in 1914, he took over the War Office himself, without giving any indication of how permanent or temporary his tenure would be.

Nonetheless, by 12 June Lloyd George felt certain the job would be his. Although deeply personally ambitious, he also maintained – with some justice – that too many incompetent generals were in senior positions where they were harming the war effort and sacrificing the lives of innumerable men. He believed there was too much 'personal and professional favouritism' in the existing system of appointments, which he was confident could be eliminated if handed over to the Secretary of State.[26] Yet again, resignation was the alternative if Lloyd George was not content with what was offered him. To retrieve the powers of appointment given to Robertson an Order in Council would have to be revoked, which even Lloyd George accepted would not be easy: it would also have been a humiliation for Robertson, who might well not have swallowed it.

To the shock of Churchill and Scott, with whom he had this conversation, Lloyd George revealed that if pushed to resignation he had '5 very rich men – 3 Liberals and 2 Unionists – who were prepared to back him financially to an almost unlimited extent, to run elections and the usual party machinery.' Scott, whose worries about Lloyd George's ambition exceeding the national interest were stimulated by such talk, sought to calm him by saying he would dominate any administration, whoever was prime minister, after a 'reconstruction'.[27] On 15 June Esher recorded: 'I dined alone with Bonar Law this evening. He told me . . . he had been sent for by Asquith, who consulted him about the offer of the War Office to Lloyd George. He had agreed to this on the understanding that if Lloyd George refused he himself was to have the offer.'[28] However, Law felt that neither he nor Lloyd George could accept the post under the Kitchener–Robertson agreement. 'This seems to me very small and petty,' Esher wrote.

When Asquith admitted to his wife that Lloyd George 'had the best claim' to succeed Kitchener, she retorted that it was 'unthinkable' to have a 'sly, dishonourable, brilliant man' such as him at the War Office.[29] Mrs Asquith had shuddered when Isaacs told her over dinner that Lloyd George actively wanted the job. She had lobbied Lansdowne and Robertson, among others, to persuade Asquith not to make the appointment. In her diaries she recorded that 'the King was in despair when H told him of his intention'.[30] She was right: Lloyd George was disliked at court: Stamfordham advised the King on 17 June that the 'best solution is for PM to remain at War Office. Whole Army Council want this. Derby might be second in command.'[31] Their reservations notwithstanding, that day Asquith offered Lloyd George the job, though made it clear he would enjoy no more powers than Kitchener had had. For that reason Lloyd George turned it down, but on that question Asquith would stand firm; he would have the job on Asquith's terms, or not at all.

The press, led by Northcliffe's papers, demanded Lloyd George's appointment, even though Northcliffe had earlier privately advised him to refuse it as it would make it impossible to turn the government out and get rid of Asquith. Mrs Asquith's fear was that it would effectively put Northcliffe in the War Office, as she told Scott when she saw him by chance at Paddington station on 13 June. Lloyd George's proposed appointment caused her 'intense misery' and would be 'the greatest political blunder of Henry's lifetime'.[32] Of the Asquiths' circle only Montagu backed Lloyd George, though Mrs Asquith deduced that was because he feared the damage Lloyd George might do if passed over. It was almost as if there were no war.

The Unionists, too, had grave reservations about the job going to Lloyd George. Chamberlain, whom Asquith had consulted about the appointment on 29 June, expressed 'considerable apprehension', because of Lloyd George's history of 'intrigues'.[33] Also, his threats to resign unless he had his own way were now becoming fabular, a sense that intensified after his failure to fight for the post-Rising Home Rule proposals. Colonel David Davies, Lloyd George's parliamentary private secretary, claimed to have seen a memo sent to Asquith about the vacancy stating that Lloyd George's popularity with the public was such that it would be 'impossible not to appoint him'; but added that the job was 'far less important than it was thought to be by the public' and that 'LG would probably be engulfed by the machine, etc.'[34] So perhaps Asquith felt he was helping his colleague and rival to dig his own grave in offering him the job again.

Lloyd George did in the end take the War Office, without the powers removed from Kitchener, even though he protested to intimates such as Churchill that he had won concessions. Asquith appointed him on the condition that he was not to interfere with Robertson's authority; unfortunately, that proviso would lead to Lloyd George seeking to undermine the CIGS instead.

It may well have been his own sense – reinforced, as has been shown, by the opinion of Miss Stevenson – that he had handled the Irish situation poorly that forced him to accept the War Office job, despite not getting the powers from Robertson that he thought should go with the role. He may also have sensed that his intimates were beginning to realise his weaknesses, and his limited scope and willingness to throw his weight around because he so seldom seemed to have the courage of his convictions. Churchill complained to Scott after the change that Lloyd George, once his move created a vacancy at Munitions, 'had not lifted a finger to get him appointed Minister of Munitions'.[35] Churchill did not realise then (though within a few months he would) not only just how despised he was, but how it would have damaged Lloyd George's credibility even further to push him for a cabinet post.

It was not until 4 July that Asquith finally confirmed to Lloyd George that the War Office was his (though Bonham Carter, Asquith's son-in-law and private secretary, had told Hankey on 24 June), having seen off a last-minute attempt by generals to have him appoint Derby (who, to the King's relief, became under-secretary, and His Majesty's eyes and ears in the War Office). Haig found Derby 'a fine, honest Englishman. I wish we had more like him in the Government at this time of crisis.'[36] However, if Asquith thought the heat would be taken off him by appointing Lloyd George he was mistaken. Because some key ministers – Balfour, Grey and indeed Asquith himself – had deep reservations about Lloyd George, it seemed that in promoting him Asquith had undermined his own authority again.

Lloyd George not only had limited powers as war secretary; he would rely on cheerleaders in the press and the Army if he was to flourish. On 8 July Hankey noted that the first visitors to Lloyd George in his new office had been Northcliffe and Churchill, though the latter was simply soliciting support to exonerate him over the Dardanelles. As for Northcliffe, his deep belief in Haig's wisdom and in the 'success' of the Somme would ultimately estrange him from Lloyd George; though Lloyd George knew he needed Haig's support in his new post, however much he questioned his strategy.

Miss Stevenson's appointment as secretary to the new war secretary was widely publicised – it was good public relations to show a woman had such an important role – though Riddell, whose *News of the World* existed for such purposes, feared others would make hay with the accusation that she was more than an official. Given how widely known in political circles the relationship was, and since Riddell himself was effectively muckraker-in-chief, these fears were overstated. The other consequence of Kitchener's death, and his replacement by an MP, was that there was no Secretary of State left in the Lords, which was considered a constitutional requirement. Grey's eyesight was failing, and Asquith used this as a reason to ask him to continue in the office of foreign secretary as Viscount Grey of Fallodon. Grey was offered an earldom, but declined it to avoid confusion with his cousin Earl Grey of Howick, grandson of the 2nd earl who had piloted the Great Reform Bill.

II

Asquith's Commons support was haemorrhaging: conscription and economic *dirigisme* dismayed Liberals and radicals; the Irish were appalled at the handling of the Rising; and the Northcliffe press, especially but far from uniquely, echoed and fed these views. To make matters worse the prime minister was also losing the confidence of his high command. Haig, visiting on a Saturday morning in April to discuss the summer offensive, found him 'dressed for golf and evidently anxious to get away for his weekend.'[37] In peacetime, recreation had been important to Asquith, to refresh him and keep his considerable mind focused: he had not adjusted to the demands of war, and was exhausted by his eight years – conflict-filled years even before the war – in 10 Downing Street. When they did get to discuss official business, Haig found Asquith distracted and agitated, not least by the War Office's failure to carry out what Asquith had thought was government policy – to send newly trained soldiers to France rather than keep them at home. Yet Esher told Haig he thought Asquith would stay as prime minister 'because there was no-one else to replace him.'

The government was under constant pressure, mainly from Liberal MPs, about the treatment of conscientious objectors by soldiers into whose charge they were placed. Sir William Byles, as one of the Liberals' most ardent pacifists, once more led the charge, alleging that men who refused to obey orders given them by soldiers – on the grounds that they were not members of the Army themselves – were suffering 'punishments of great severity and brutality for conscience's sake'.[38] Such was the disquiet that Asquith was forced to make a Commons statement on 29 June to dispel the idea that the Army was out of control when dealing with these people.

He promised all cases in which conscientious objectors were threatened with punishment for refusing to obey orders would be referred to the War Office. By taking evidence from those who knew the accused it would be determined, first, whether the conscientious objection was genuine. If it was not, the man would remain under military control and would serve any sentence in a detention barracks. If the objection was deemed genuine, the men would be spared civil prison if they undertook to perform 'work of national importance' under civil control.[39] Asquith promised they would cease to be answerable to military discipline so long as they performed the tasks 'satisfactorily'. The home secretary appointed a committee to decide what that work should be, and under what conditions it should be carried out.

Asquith stressed 'that all men whose objections to active military service are founded on honest conviction ought to be and will be able to avail themselves of the exemption which Parliament has provided.'[40] However, the rest of the conscription programme would be imposed in a way that reflected the profound national emergency: 'It is necessary that men who put forward objections of this kind as a pretext and a cloak to cover their indifference in responding to the national call, and are therefore guilty of the double offence of cowardice and hypocrisy, should be treated as they ought to be treated, with the utmost rigour.'

Some MPs seized on that observation and made suggestions: Colonel Charles Yate, Tory MP for Melton, invited him to 'take steps to deprive these men, whom he has just described as cowards and hypocrites, of their civil rights in the future.' Admiral of the Fleet Sir Hedworth Meux, who had recently won a by-election in Portsmouth, asked 'if there is one single sentence in Holy Writ which justifies the cowards who will not defend their women and children?' As well as having masterminded the BEF's movement to France in August 1914, Meux had, on his own initiative, led a naval brigade to relieve Mafeking, and had the status of national hero.

There was another point of view. On 5 June a sideshow of cultural significance occurred at the Mansion House in London. It was the scene of Bertrand Russell's trial under the Defence of the Realm Act for having published a pamphlet against conscription and the operation of the tribunals, notably about the jailing of a conscientious objector who had refused to serve. Six men from the No Conscription Fellowship had been imprisoned with hard labour for distributing the pamphlet: and Russell had written to The Times on 17 May claiming authorship – 'if anyone is to be prosecuted I am the person responsible' – hence his court appearance.[41] The NCF committee was initially composed of men of military age; when they were imprisoned for refusing to serve, older sympathisers such as Russell had taken their places. The government relentlessly used DORA to suppress dissent: the previous month two Hertfordshire women had been given a choice between a £50 fine or jail (they chose jail) for distributing literature from the Church of England Peace Society, and copies of an appeal by the Pope to Europe's rulers to settle their differences peaceably. Watched by Lady Ottoline Morrell and Lytton Strachey, Russell was fined £100. The police raided the NCF offices in London that day, and took away 'large quantities of literature and propaganda leaflets.'[42] They would raid them again the following November, to the concern of Samuel, the home secretary, whom the police had not consulted.[43]

Russell appealed against his fine; his case was heard in late June, at the same time as the cases against Brockway and two others for a pamphlet they had issued called *Repeal the Act*. Derby ('a large, fat man, in tight khaki', according to Lady Ottoline's account of the event) was among those who gave evidence against them.[44] Russell lost his appeal and refused to pay the fine, so his books and furniture were confiscated and sold: a group of his smart friends, including Lady Ottoline, bought them back. Lady Ottoline's husband later described this as 'the first stage . . . in Mr Russell's pursuit by the Government.'[45] Brockway chose prison rather than pay a £100 fine.

During 1916 the Morrells' country house at Garsington became a haven for various of their Bloomsbury friends who had pleaded a conscientious objection. Through his friendship with Strachey and Keynes – both of whom had long been Garsington regulars – the first to arrive was Gerald Shove, like Keynes an economist at King's College, Cambridge, and a member of the Apostles. Ordered to do farm work, Shove asked Morrell to have him on the farm at Garsington, where he was supposed to look after the chickens. Lady Ottoline described how he went about his work 'very slothfully and doggedly and unwillingly'.[46] He also neglected his husbandry so badly that the birds laid fewer eggs and fell ill. Among others doing farm work – usually in theory rather than in practice – were Clive Bell, art critic and estranged husband of Virginia Woolf's sister Vanessa. Shove's wife, Fredegond, a poetess, and Lady Ottoline took swift exception to Bell and there was occasionally 'a scene'.[47] Asquith, on one of his visits (it was typical of his catholicity of mind that he should be happy to socialise with those determined to undermine his administration's vital policy on conscription), described Bell as 'that fat little yellow-haired bounder'.[48] Luckily for the Morrells, but unluckily for the Shoves, the refugees were put in a separate house on the estate, thus minimising Bell's impact on his hosts. Aldous Huxley moved in for the autumn of 1916, though his eyesight was so poor he was exempted even from clerical war work: his father deeply disapproved of his moving to Garsington, saying with some justification that it was full of 'cranks'.[49]

There were limits to Lady Ottoline's radicalism. 'Gerald Shove thought it necessary to try and organize a Union among the farm labourers,' she recalled. 'But the old hands merely shook their heads and thought they were well enough off as they were. It was hardly a suitable action for him to do, considering that he himself did the minimum of work and received good wages and a comfortable house.'[50] Shove, presumably, had noted the less comfortable conditions in which those who really were doing farm work had to live; his success in starting an anti-capitalist revolution was as successful as his poultry management. Not all the conscientious objectors made a point of being idle, like the Bloomsberries: one, a baker by trade whose pacifism was rooted in his devoutly religious views, went at five o'clock each morning to help at the village bakery before his day on the farm. Apart from him, the other Garsington refugees 'were naturally unpopular in the village', and in the autumn of 1916 a reporter arrived, intending 'to write an article exposing these "slackers" and "bogus" farm workers.' He was seen off by the threat of a libel action from Morrell, who spent much of his time giving evidence to tribunals for such as the Stracheys, Bunny Garnett and Duncan Grant, questionable conscientious objectors whose self-obsession was sufficient armour against any sense of shame that they were relying on millions of other men to keep German bayonets out of their bellies.

III

The decision to launch a great offensive on the Western Front in the spring or summer of 1916 had been taken on 28 December 1915, to allow a morale-boosting British initiative after the debacle in the Dardanelles. Among those directing the war there was no unanimity that it should happen: according to Hankey, 'Kitchener, in January, did not intend, if he could help it, that a great and prolonged offensive should be embarked upon.'[51] The then war secretary wanted 'attrition' to wear Germany down and grind it into submission. However, the remorseless German assault on the French at Verdun forced the issue: the fire of the German army would be drawn by an attack in the British sector. Thus, on 7 April, Asquith sanctioned Haig to implement what, on 1 July, became the Battle of the Somme. Kitchener informed Haig in person when the General visited London on 14 April.

Haig was a scion of the Scottish whisky firm; his father drank himself to death. He had spent three years at Oxford (he left without a degree, but with a reputation as an accomplished horseman) and passed out first from Sandhurst. He had joined the cavalry and served in India, the Sudan and South Africa, and entered the Staff College at his second attempt. Some of his biographers have blamed the Staff College's doctrinaire teaching for Haig's inability to think originally, and all that would entail when he ran the BEF. He spent three years in Whitehall from 1906 to 1909 on the General Staff, where he learned to be an office politician and, in the view of some of his peers, exerted a surprisingly strong influence over French, his senior by some years. Thinking along tramlines, he was hard for the subtle Asquith to fathom; always immaculate in turnout and with the quality of *capax imperii*, he was too smooth and sure of himself for Lloyd George, who disliked him but was beguiled by him. He distrusted politicians, yet saw the need for an impressive victory to get them off his back – and win the war.

Haig's planned attack has been seared into the British collective memory: days of preliminary bombardment to smash the German trenches, wire and machine-gun posts to smithereens: then an 'army of pursuit' marching through the wreckage, destroying enemy communications, putting it to flight and ending the stalemate of trench warfare.[52] Haig was so sure mobile warfare would resume that he urged Robertson to reopen recruiting for the cavalry.[53] Some military planners pinned their hopes on the development of the tank, which they predicted would change warfare and allow a breakthrough with less loss of life. However, the tank project, despite the enthusiastic support of Lloyd George, was nowhere near sufficiently advanced for these machines to join the required early offensive. They were first used on the Somme on 15 September, but to little effect. Around fifty were deployed in the first instance, but only thirty-two made it to the action; fourteen of those broke down and of the remaining eighteen only nine could go fast enough to keep up with the infantry. When it came it was another setback, and increased what had by then become severe tensions between Whitehall and the General Staff, who, it was felt, had used them in unsuitable conditions.

Robertson had consulted Haig in France on 25 May 1916 about

whether Britain should accede to a request from the French to attack in early July, to relieve pressure on Verdun. The alternative was waiting until mid-August, when more trained men would have been sent to France. Haig said unequivocally that support for the French had to come sooner rather than later. Joffre believed the latest feasible date was 1 July. Hankey recalled that critics were 'derisive' of Haig's plans to attack the entrenched German army on the Somme; but such derision as was voiced was, tragically, insufficient to prevent the offensive's execution.[54]

Lloyd George had cited Ypres, where a general 'had massed the men in the front trenches and the Germans simply slaughtered them with shell-fire without their being able to do anything.'[55] Early in June Churchill, like Lloyd George, had told Scott he was 'strongly opposed to our undertaking a great offensive.'[56] His reasons were that 'we could not get through the elaborately prepared German positions. We might create a salient; with good luck we might convert the salient into "a sleeve". But when we advanced up this "pipe" we should be met at the end by fresh positions and fresh troops and be attacked at the same time from both flanks.' He thought it would be far better to encourage the Germans to advance, and then entrap them.

Haig told Joffre an offensive would be ready from 15 June, and the initial plan was to launch it on the 29th; it was postponed by two days because of a better weather forecast. The bombardment designed to smash the German trench system began on 24 June; but despite its length and intensity, it used just 500 heavy guns, and much of the ordnance fired was shrapnel, not high explosive. On 28 June, reflecting concern at home, Esher wrote to Haig: 'You must, my dear Douglas, stimulate a little Press Propaganda *here*, while these great operations are in progress. Some intelligent young fellow should be turned on to telephone through . . . every night giving a resumé of operations . . . every two or three days a Liaison officer should bring down some rather extended little story, which can be deftly used here.'[57] Esher had a dim view of the domestic propaganda operation – 'no one knows where it is, or who has charge of it' – and warned Haig that 'it may at any moment be tainted by views that are not yours.'

On the evening of 30 June Haig noted that 'with God's help, I feel hopeful.' At 7.30 a.m. on the sunny morning of 1 July, the British offensive opened on the Somme. The pessimistic predictions based on Ypres were proved correct; history would repeat itself on a catastrophic scale. Haig's God was absent; and although when the battle ground to a halt four and a half months later the German war machine had suffered serious damage, it began with the bloodiest day in the history of the British Army. The effects changed the political course of the war. It finished without Haig having achieved his objectives, and, whatever damage it had inflicted upon the Germans – Ludendorff wrote that by the end of 1916 'the German Army had been fought to a standstill and was utterly worn out' – the British Army was badly crippled.[58]

The bombardment could be heard in Kent, on Hampstead Heath and as far away as villages in north Essex. 'All morning the Flanders (as it is supposed) guns have been booming forth, making the house quiver at times and shaking window sashes,' Andrew Clark recorded in his diary, from his parish between Braintree and Chelmsford. Bulletins announcing the offensive and claiming a British advance were put up in post offices later that Saturday. Monday's papers spoke of up to 3,000 enemy prisoners taken and the battlefield littered with German dead; they quoted *Boy's Own Paper* platitudes from official reports of British progress, without mention of British deaths. The public's initial impression was that the fighting was fierce, but the Germans were on the run. On 4 July a *Times* correspondent wrote that 'an exceptionally large proportion of our casualties are very slight wounds', but he did add that the infantry had sustained 'considerable losses' where the bombardment had not broken the barbed wire.[59] 'There can be no praise too high for the gallantry of our men,' he added. In fact, Haig's belief that the barbed wire outside the German trenches would have been shredded and the machine guns knocked out was wrong. The guns wiped out line after line of British soldiers.

Within a week the public realised the Battle of the Somme had entailed great loss of life. As some towns heard rumours of whole battalions being wiped out, local newspaper offices had soldiers' families turning up seeking further news. The rumours too often had substance: the Accrington Pals lost 585 men – 235 killed and 350 wounded – out of 700 who went 'over the top' on 1 July; around 2,250 of the Tyneside Scottish were killed, wounded or missing out of about 3,000; the 1st and 2nd Bradford Pals, around 2,000 men, suffered 1,770 casualties in the first hour of fighting. Newspapers could not print the details. Correspondents were confined by state censorship; they could mention British wounded, but that was as bad as it got. Philip Gibbs of the *Daily Chronicle* recorded: 'My dispatches tell the truth. There is not a word, I vow, of conscious false-hood in them . . . but they do not tell all the truth.'⁶⁰ Nor was it just the censor he was considering. 'I have had to spare the feelings of the men and women who have sons and husbands still fighting in France.' As the horrors multiplied, men on leave, or home wounded, censored them-selves for similar reasons, so the public were slow to understand how terrible matters were.

It is believed that on the first day alone 19,026 men were killed and another 38,200 wounded, roughly one-seventh of the total casualties in 140 days of the battle.⁶¹ Even beforehand politicians had been concerned about the effect of the number of casualties under Haig's command. Long had written to Law on 7 May: 'Have you noticed the steady and appalling increase in the death roll in France? Due no doubt in part to the increase in our front: but not wholly. I never believed that Sir D Haig was the right man to be C-in-C, and I told the PM so at the time.'⁶²

Haig himself, writing on 1 July, seemed clueless about how dreadful British losses had been. Early reports, he noted, seemed 'most satisfac-tory'.⁶³ A visit to a casualty clearing station the next day found the wounded in 'wonderful spirits'. Even though his staff had no idea of the total casualties – the Adjutant General's estimate of 40,000 by the second day was an underestimation of at least 20,000 – Haig remained remarkably sanguine. Forty thousand, he wrote, 'cannot be considered severe in view of the numbers engaged, and the length of front attacked.' He was habitually optimistic, used to boosting morale; either his subor-dinates joined in a collective delusion, or they simply could not compute, in the literal and metaphorical sense, the sheer scale of the disaster.

Esher, in France, gripped reality better than Haig. He wrote on 9 July that 'the total casualties in the first day were about 67,000 [men] and 3,000 officers. Laurence [Burgis, Esher's former secretary], who came from Hermaville to lunch at Amiens and tea here [Beauquesne, north of Ami-ens, where Esher was based], asked about casualties, and quoted the above figures. I said no-one here mentioned such things, and he might say that I told him that anyone who spoke of casualties would probably be *degommé*. This is the rock ahead in London, where there must be much gossip on this subject.'⁶⁴ Highly protective of Haig, Esher worried that if there was such talk in London people would ask: 'Whose fault is it?' It is no surprise that H. G. Wells would write in 1918 that 'the British army is at present commanded by oldish men who are manifestly of not more than mediocre intelligence, and who have no knowledge of this new sort of war that has arisen.'[65]

On 3 July – the day before Asquith confirmed his appointment – Lloyd George discussed the offensive with Hankey and Balfour. Hankey noted that it 'appears to have almost completely failed, with very heavy losses.'[66] There was no doubt in his mind why. 'To deliver a frontal attack on an entrenched force provided with every possible defensive organisation violates every military principle.' The tactics had been to send closely packed ranks of men towards the Germans, moving relatively slowly as each carried 66 pounds of kit, offering an easy target for the proliferating German machine guns. Lloyd George agreed with Hankey, and it would flavour his estimate of Haig for the rest of the war. Haig was too stubborn to change tactics, so the dead kept piling up. Robertson warned him on 7 July that his interests would be served by sending the CIGS 'a short letter which I could read to the War Committee' outlining the successes so far.[67] Some politicians were less convinced of this so-called success, taking events as an argument – which would continue until the Armistice – to seek a strategy other than defeating Germany on the Western Front. Churchill told Riddell the Somme was another example of the government's pitiful management of the war. 'They have engaged in the offensive on the West because they can justify the proceeding by saying we were compelled [by the French] to act as we did.'[68]

The bad news dripped through as the thousands of telegrams (for the families of officers) and letters (for those of NCOs and other ranks) went to the army of bereaved across the kingdom throughout July. On 7 July *The Times* published a list of forty officers killed on 1 July, and an account of the heroics of the Ulster Division – Carson's Ulster Volunteers of 1914 – that included the admission that 'the Ulster Division has lost very heavily'.[69] This was a rare mention of the effect of the battle on the British Army: the coverage was dominated by accounts of the drubbing Fritz was taking. There was then a separate list of some Ulster officers who had died.

Soon the lists lengthened, and there was room only to list those with commissions; either stunned or resolute, the public generally held its nerve. A Miss Llewellyn of Sheffield, a schoolgirl at the time, recalled: 'There were sheets and sheets in the paper of dead and wounded with photographs where they could get them of men. Of course everybody rushed to the paper every day to see if there was anyone they knew . . . There were numerous services in churches. It was a very, very sad time – practically everybody was in mourning. People were in deep black, the men if they couldn't wear black wore black armbands as a mark of respect.'[70] Over the next four months the ubiquity of death left no one in doubt of what the nation had suffered, even if the government remained deliberately vague about the calamitous losses. The Revd Andrew Clark would note on 30 October that a Chelmsford department store, J. G. Bond, 'said this forenoon that the mourning orders during the last three months had been overwhelming. They cannot get in materials fast enough to meet the demand.'[71]

By 14 July, two-thirds of a page of *The Times* was devoted to the names of a thousand other ranks who had been killed, and half a page of small print recorded casualties among officers. Censored news reports remained misleadingly upbeat. By the following week the lists of casualties from other ranks numbered around 2,000 names a day: they ran without comment on their scale, but no one could doubt that the great offensive had had a cost unprecedented in the conflict, or indeed in any other. On 31 July *The Times*'s casualty list included 580 officers and 5,770 men, covering two pages of the broadsheet in tiny print: during August there were lists of 4,000, 5,000 or 6,000 casualties a day.

Why were the public so resilient to this slaughter – to the hecatomb of sons, brothers, husbands and fathers who, suddenly, were never coming home? Part of the reason was that ever since the Marne in August 1914 the relentless roll of casualty lists had hardened nerves. Now, although the lists were on an unprecedented scale, people were at least used to seeing them. As early as May 1915 *The Times*, printing almost daily casualty lists from France and the Dardanelles, had warned its readers against losing a sense of perspective about the sheer numbers of dead through becoming inured to them.[72] The misleadingly optimistic tone of the heavily censored news also prevented morale from fracturing. However, even Gallipoli and the debacle at Loos had been inadequate preparation for the sheer scale of what was now, day by day, being reported from the Somme.

Countless letters from soldiers at the front testify to another reason why the public found it so hard to take in the scale of the horror on the Somme: that comparatively few were honest in their descriptions of what went on. Mail was censored, so there were limits on what could be put on paper. Even had there not been, it appears to have been the instinct of many soldiers to spare their families the details of what they had witnessed. Also, because most soldiers saw only a small section of the front, they were often themselves ignorant of how bad matters were over many sections of trenches and a number of miles: such awareness was confined to their senior officers. There was a reluctance – though this often declined over time – to talk too candidly to friends and family when home on leave, similarly to spare their sensibilities, but also because of an incipient doubt that those who had not been in the trenches could ever understand what it had been like: much of it was beyond the abilities of even the most articulate of soldiers to convey, as many of those who wrote about the war in the years after it were at pains to stress. There was also a contemporary culture of manliness, which many soldiers felt they had affirmed and endorsed by volunteering (and the army on the Somme, at the start of the battle, was entirely volunteers), and from which for their own morale and self-esteem they were reluctant to depart, especially with those closest to them, for fear of deepening their family's worries.

Perhaps, too, those who would die had prepared their families, as well as themselves. Stephen Hewett, an Oxford classicist, writing to his former tutor 'Sligger' Urquhart on 15 July 1916, a week before he was killed, said, as his regiment marched towards the line: 'We shall soon be earning either a big head-line or a place in the casualty-list.'[73] Writing to another friend the next day he observed that 'without disclosing any military secrets, I may say that we have arrived at a time when anyone who has outstanding debts of letters must settle up, and that at once.'[74] Four days before he died he told one of his sisters that 'if we have to suffer the heaviest losses, and even have a hard time for the rest of our lives, we should not consider ourselves unlucky . . . we have proved our own age equal in heroism and romance to any age in history'.[75] He wrote to another sister that if death came the action preceding it would be 'one moment of glory'.[76]

The idea of glory – or having no idea what modern war was like – unquestionably shielded many civilians from the truth, and thus kept them from protesting about the enormity of the tactical disaster the Somme represented. The Rupert Brooke school of poetry and its associated values of sacrifice and purification were now relics: soon, works by Siegfried Sassoon and others would convey with undiluted force a reality

Brooke could not have imagined. R. H. Tawney, who would after the war become a leading economic historian, used his convalescence from a wound that autumn to write two essays on his experiences on the Somme, including a description of the first day. Tawney perceived a barrier – he calls it a veil or 'the dividing chasm' – between those who had been at the front and those who had not; and was appalled by politicians who spoke about the country's fighting spirit without ever understanding what that fighting actually entailed, in either physical or psychological terms.[77]

To the public, helped by censored and self-censored accounts from the trenches, the war was still one of Brooke-style idealism, or of the 'duty', 'glory' and 'honour' on the pre-conscription recruitment posters. Mainly for commercial reasons, and also under government censorship, newspaper and magazine publishers produced daily papers and part-works that gave a heroic and rosy picture of the conflict. It was propaganda and not fact. Not until the scale of the slaughter became understood, later in 1916, did opinions start to change. It also helped Haig, and the cause of downplaying the scale of death for which he, through his tactical errors, had been responsible, that Northcliffe was devoted to him; a devotion Haig assiduously cultivated, and which kept the dogs of *The Times* and, more important for wider public perception, the *Daily Mail* off him.

The non-combatant public were not entirely ignorant of how life was on the Western Front. The war differed from earlier conflicts because of how photographs and moving pictures could now convey an impression to those at home of what was going on. Kitchener's attempt to ban photographers from the front had soon unravelled, and by 1916 images of destruction and desolation were familiar to readers of illustrated magazines and newspapers: however, even this further distanced the public from the realities, because the main condition under which photographers were permitted was that no British dead were depicted. What was presented was a sanitised picture of the war; and it was an inevitable step from allowing photography to allowing cinematography, and the government quickly realised the propaganda value of such an exercise. Two official cameramen with primitive, static cameras were sent to the front in the spring of 1916, and filed various items of newsreel footage. Masterman commissioned the film that would be entitled *The Battle of the Somme* as a morale-booster, and attached the cameramen to the 4th Army. For technical and censorship reasons no actual fighting was filmed – even had it been allowed and could the cameras have gone close enough, footage of men being mown down by machine guns would never have been permitted to be shown.

However, the crew was allowed to film the more distantly positioned artillery, soldiers marching up to the trenches and men in the trenches preparing to attack; and German prisoners of war and some German dead. The War Office wrote captions for the footage; and the film, more than seventy minutes long, was shown to an audience of officials, ministers, journalists and senior staff officers in London on 10 August. It opened at thirty-four theatres in London on 21 August, at which 'crowded audiences . . . were interested and thrilled to have the realities of war brought so vividly before them', though it was noted that 'women had sometimes to shut their eyes to escape for a moment from the tragedy of the toll of battle'.[78] It has no narrative but is a collection of scenes, almost all authentic; its appeal lay in giving the public a sight of the world of their soldiers, into which they were never otherwise admitted. Its audiences exceeded those for the films of the great star of the silent screen, Charlie Chaplin, who himself – being a Briton of military age – came under criticism for not having returned from Hollywood to do his bit. An estimated 20 million had seen the film by the end of September.

Lloyd George wrote a letter to be read out at the premiere (and shown on screen at all other performances) in which he described the film as 'an epic of self-sacrifice and gallantry'.[79] Men were exhorted to 'herald the deeds of our brave men to the ends of the earth'; and women, widowed in their thousands in the preceding weeks, and whose support for the war effort was even more vital if doubt, questioning and possibly even defeatism were to be avoided, were told that 'your hearts will beat, your voices will speak in honour and glory of the living and the dead.'[80] The part the film played in staying public disquiet in the immediate aftermath of the catastrophe of July 1916 is unquantifiable. It also raised £30,000 for military charities.

There was some distaste at the spectacle, sanitised though it was by the avoidance of the sight of British dead, being promoted as a form of entertainment; but the King too urged that people should see it, and its general impression was positive. There is one scene – shown constantly in documentaries about the war over the succeeding century, in which men go over the top and one is seen to slide back down the parapet, killed or wounded, and one or two others fall when out in no man's land.

The set piece was the only one to be entirely staged, and was filmed well away from the front: the prohibition of showing actual British death remained. Film, though, became an important cultural feature of the war after the success of *The Battle of the Somme*. From the following year news-reels, under the auspices of the War Office Cinematograph Department, appeared in cinemas twice weekly, and Charlie Chaplin and his friends had their films interspersed with two-minute 'shorts' urging the public to conserve food and fuel and buy war stocks.

Repington, writing after the war, said posterity would be amazed at how the public took such relentlessly heavy losses. He claimed that from the Marne onwards 'the heroines who suffered in the glorious deaths of those whom they loved set a notable example of fortitude, and it was thanks to their early example that public opinion subsequently remained so steady.'[81] Later in the war the public 'displayed unexampled courage in hundreds and thousands of stricken homes . . . nothing could exceed the steadiness with which they took good and evil news alike, or the ten-acity with which they set themselves to suffer anything rather than to lose the war.'[82] He was close to the truth. It was not merely that the public had grown to accept a massive toll of dead and wounded. Fear and detes-tation of the Germans was sufficient to drive people to endure such losses. Also, they were helped by a lingering deference to authority – though the Great War would do more than perhaps anything else to undermine that, when it was finally recognised how cack-handed author-ity had often been – and a strong sense of community.

In some parts of the kingdom that had endured enormous losses no amount of censorship could conceal the catastrophe, or prevent spon-taneous public demonstrations of loss and grief. The sheer number of bereaved families in Ulster made obvious what the censor would not admit; on the first day of the Somme the 36th (Ulster) Division sustained 4,900 casualties, including 79 officers and 1,777 other ranks killed. On 12 July, the anniversary of the Battle of the Boyne, there was a graphic demonstration of collective grief in Belfast. 'On the stroke of 12 all traffic came to a standstill, men raised their hats, ladies bowed their heads, the blinds in business and private houses were drawn, and flags were flown at half mast.'[83] The silence lasted five minutes: after which bells tolled. The scale of the losses further explained the resentment – not just in Ulster – caused by the refusal of so many in the other three provinces to enlist, and the demands they made for the government to extend conscription to Ireland. In the east end of London, as in other towns and cities that sustained heavy losses, makeshift shrines of photographs and flowers appeared in churches. In streets and in villages women stood outside looking for the arrival of the postman. At Rugby school the headmaster ended his practice of reading out the names of casualties among old boys because of the depression it caused among his charges, some of them shortly to start military training. The scale of the catastrophe Haig's strategy had caused was undisguisable.

The epic of death that the Somme caused drove many bereaved wives, mothers and fathers into the arms of spiritualists and mediums, most of whom appear to have been calculating charlatans, with a small minority genuinely believing they were talking to 'the other side'. Public interest was stimulated not just by the ubiquity of deaths for which most were completely unprepared, but also by some prominent figures – such as Sir Arthur Conan Doyle, creator of Sherlock Holmes – associating themselves with the psychical movement. Ironically, Haig's sister Henrietta was a convinced spiritualist, and she – and it seems to a limited extent he – believed during the war that the spirit of their brother George, dead since 1905, was guiding Haig.[84] Spiritualism was also helped by an almost biblical idea of the apocalypse being unleashed on the suggestible and grief-stricken, creating a climate in which anything, however unreal, was possible. After Captain Malcolm Leckie, Doyle's brother-in-law, had been killed at Mons in August 1914 – when an angelic host was said to have appeared above the trenches, but which existed only in fiction – Doyle, who had been interested in psychic phenomena since the 1880s and who in 1922 would proclaim the existence of fairies on the basis of a series of faked photographs, put his full heart and soul into the study.

Although Doyle would also lose a brother and son to the war, neither had died when in 1916 he professed to the public for the first time his belief in spiritualism. He would later claim that his son Kingsley came through to him after his death in 1918, to congratulate his father for spreading the 'Christ-like message' of spiritualism, as well as his old friend W. T. Stead (who had gone down with the *Titanic*) and Cecil Rhodes. He would tour Britain and America after the war, lecturing on spiritualism to audiences desperate to resume contact with lost sons, brothers, husbands and fathers.[85] Nor was Doyle, a qualified doctor, the only educated man drawn into the spiritualist obsession caused by the slaughter. Even more prominent was Sir Oliver Lodge, the physicist and pioneer of radio, who like Doyle had been investigating spiritualism since the 1880s. The two men were by 1916 old friends, having first met at Buckingham Palace in 1902 on the day they were knighted.

In 1909 Lodge – whose practical achievements also included developing the spark plug and the loudspeaker – had published *Survival of Man*, in which he argued that mediums had proved the existence of life after death. This would become of central importance to him when his youngest son, Raymond, was killed near Ypres in September 1915. Eight days after learning of his death Lady Lodge visited a Mrs Osborne, a celebrated medium, who by table-tilting relayed the message: 'tell father I have met some friends of his'.[86] In subsequent seances with Mrs Osborne and other mediums the Lodges built up a comforting picture of Raymond's life on 'the other side', in a place he called Summerland; but Lodge, who lacked Doyle's thirst for publicity and desire to evangelise on behalf of spiritualism, did not immediately publish details, fearing mockery.

When, in the darkest days of 1916, Lodge did publish his book, he received obloquy. Some were appalled that a man of his reputation should lend credence to the operations of charlatans; others pitied him; a few derided him or expressed outrage. One passage caused special opprobrium, in which Raymond said that men coming over to 'the other side' could, if they wanted, have cigars and whisky sodas. 'Don't think I'm stretching it when I tell you they can manufacture even that,' the spirit supposedly said. 'But when they have had one or two they don't seem to want it so much.'[87] Teetotallers and the anti-tobacco lobby joined many clergymen in denouncing the book, which was banned from at least one public library.

Wells took a more rational view of bereavement in what became the war's most popular novel, *Mr Britling Sees it Through*, published in September 1916 while the casualty list from the Somme was still lengthening. As in many of Wells's novels, the eponymous hero is a thinly disguised autobiographical construct: he lives in a gracious house in north Essex, is a sort of public intellectual, and a philanderer. Unlike Wells, he has a son who is killed at the front. Although he is in no doubt that Germany is to blame for the war, it causes him to question not just the conflict (a young German friend is killed and he grieves for his family, something not hitherto characterising the public mood in Britain) but also the nature of religion; and he begins to feel a community of grief brought by the war, united not merely in loss but by a wish to end the fighting: another unpopular sentiment at the time.

'And suddenly it was borne in upon his mind that he was not alone,' Wells writes of Britling.[88] 'There were thousands and tens of thousands of men and women like himself, desiring with all their hearts to say, as he desired to say, the reconciling word.' But then Wells, an atheist, continues: 'He was no longer lonely and wretched, no longer in the same world with despair. God was beside him and within him and about him.' Later, Wells has Britling write: 'Life falls into place only with God. Only with God. God, who fights through men against Blind Force and Night and Non-Existence; who is the end, who is the meaning.'[89] He is writing to the parents of his dead German friend and talks of 'our sons who have shown us God . . .' In a nation stunned by death, and the death of those with unfulfilled lives, it was no wonder Wells's account of an Englishman coming to terms with the consequences of the horror had such resonance.

IV

Politicians and generals took very different views of the slaughter. Although Riddell told Lloyd George, when they met on 16 July – on the basis of what evidence it is not clear – 'I think the nation is prepared for heavy losses,' Lloyd George confided in him that 'the casualties may shock the nation when they appreciate the small results.'[90] Three days later Lloyd George lunched with Repington and told him he 'did not see how we were going to win on the present lines.'[91] The Somme sowed within Lloyd George the seeds of utter conviction that such warfare should never be tried again. Churchill sent a memorandum to the cabinet via Smith on 1 August in which he deprecated the offensive, believing that in the first two days 40,000 men were either killed, had died of wounds or were so severely wounded that they could never fight again. He estimated at 150,000 the totals lost for good to the end of July, half the effective men of thirty divisions. The greatest advance for this huge loss was three miles, and the ground obtained 'utterly devoid of military significance'.[92] Having just been in the trenches for six months, Churchill knew what he was talking about; but even though his memorandum was designed to prevent the Army being used in such a way again it was the politician in him, rather than the soldier, that realised what effect the truth would have on the public if it knew. Hankey believed Lloyd George had had an input into the memo.

In France, Haig nevertheless continued to see the bright side of the hundreds of thousands of casualties – the British total on the Somme would be around 490,000: 'Proof given to the world that Allies are capable of making and maintaining a vigorous offensive and of driving the enemy's best troops from the strongest positions . . . Also impress on the world, England's strength and determination, and the fighting power of the British race,' he recorded in his diary.[93] Esher had noted two days earlier, on 27 July: 'Douglas is very calm and confident, and undisturbed by losses or criticism. We have lost about 150,000 men so far in this fight, but this is not more than the number upon which he calculated, and stated to the Cabinet, before the offensive commenced. He said he would require 200,000 drafts before the end of July.'[94] When apprised of Churchill's view, Haig observed that 'I also expect Winston's judgement is impaired from taking drugs.'[95]

Robertson told Haig on 29 July that the cabinet was unconvinced by what he had told them, given how casualties were 'mounting up': 'The powers that be are beginning to get a little uneasy . . . they will persist in asking whether I think a loss of say 300,000 men will lead to really great results . . .'[96] Since the battle began Haig had stopped maintaining the war would be won in 1916; but he believed the German army would be exhausted before the British was, and – fortunately out of earshot of the bereaved public – said July's losses were but '120,000 more than they would have been had we not attacked.'[97]

Haig would not wind the offensive down, which was what doubters in Whitehall were now starting to suggest he should. However, his response to Robertson was read to the War Committee on 5 August and, according to the CIGS, 'it pleased them very much indeed'. It would be circulated to the cabinet, not least to counter Churchill's memorandum in which he had criticised Haig's strategy.[98] Robertson was asked to send Haig a note minuting the government's 'full support' for his offensive.[99] Meanwhile, conscious of the mounting numbers of dead, Esher wrote to Hankey on 3 August to ask: 'Can you prevent people at home from fixing their eyes upon the Roll of Honour, and gluing their noses to the map?'[100]

Esher's parroting of the official line reflected his desire for opacity, not least as a means of protecting his friend Haig from criticism. When questions began to be asked in Parliament about the high casualties, the

government, and some backbenchers, responded by deploring such
enquiries, partly because of the information they might, if answered,
give to the enemy, but also because of the effect the confirmation of the
carnage might have on morale. Eventually, on 21 August, Henry Forster,
financial secretary to the War Office, told colleagues Asquith had agreed
that any MP might, 'privately and confidentially', be given the true figures; but even that level of disclosure was subject to considerations of
'military expediency'.[101] This remained the line for some time.

Such rigorous censorship symbolised how the state Asquith steered
was becoming more repressive and controlling, once the Rubicon of
complete conscription had been crossed. On 25 July the North of Scotland Special Military Area was declared, restricting access north of the
Great Glen. Sheppey, Newhaven, Harwich, Spurn Head and Dover
would all follow by late September: the police could demand to see
the credentials of anyone in those areas and arrest them if necessary. The
police also started to turn up at the remaining public entertainments,
locking the exits of theatres, music halls and sports grounds, questioning men of military age and demanding they produce certificates of
exemption. Such activities were cheered on by a press howling about
'shirkers, laggards and slackers', and found great sympathy among those
coming to terms with the Somme.[102] There was bitterness against the
Irish who, exempt from conscription, flocked from Ireland to take highly
paid work; it was often, however, as useful to the war effort as serving in
a trench.

One victim of this increasingly repressive spirit was Bertrand Russell.
Not content with banning him from going abroad, the government had
also banned him from lecturing in any prohibited area – those near garrisons or naval dockyards, or anywhere considered sensitive under
DORA – in case he engaged in subversive acts. Russell had planned a
series of public lectures once the governing body of Trinity College,
Cambridge had removed him from his lectureship, and had caused disquiet by giving speeches to munitions workers in South Wales, which
led to his being banned from that area. He reported to the War Office on
5 September for a meeting with General George Cockerill, who told him
that a sentence in his South Wales speech saying 'there was no good reason why this war should continue another day' was the root of the
problem.[103] 'He said that such a statement made to miners or munition
workers was calculated to diminish their ardour' and that Russell 'was

encouraging men to refuse to fight for their country.' Cockerill suggested that if Russell would return to teaching mathematics and stop
engaging in propaganda he could go where he wished; but Russell would
give no such undertaking. A philosophical debate ensued in which Cockerill, unsurprisingly, came off worse; but he insisted, nonetheless, that
Russell would be banned from delivering such talks anywhere if he persisted. H. W. Massingham, editor of the radical weekly the *Nation*, who
had publicly disagreed with Russell on several questions, wrote to *The
Times* arguing that the decision to control where Russell could go in Britain was a 'gross libel' and an act of 'persecution'.[104]

Charles Trevelyan, the Liberal MP for Elland and a former junior
minister who had resigned in opposition to the declaration of war, asked
whether instead of suppressing Russell's freedom of speech he might be
allowed to deliver his lectures, risking prosecution only if he broke the
law. Lloyd George responded that 'the Army Council has offered to
modify this Order so as to permit him to deliver the proposed lectures if
Mr Russell will give an honourable undertaking to abstain from using
them as a vehicle for propaganda that contravenes the Defence of the
Realm Regulations, but, as Mr Russell declines to give any such undertaking, no modification of the Order is thought desirable. Prevention is
better than prosecution.'[105] Asked to describe the specific threat, Lloyd
George said: 'We had information from a very reliable source that Mr
Bertrand Russell was about to engage in the delivery of a series of lectures which would interfere very seriously with the manning of the
Army.' He said it would be an 'unpardonable weakness' if the government allowed the lectures to be delivered, though was at a loss, in reply
to a question from one member, to say why the public interest would be
threatened by a lecture in Glasgow – near the heart of 'Red Clydeside' –
but not in Manchester.

Russell had said: 'My proposed course of lectures on "The world as it
can be made" is not intended to deal with the immediate issues raised by
the War; there will be nothing about the diplomacy preceding the War,
about conscientious objectors, about the kind of peace to be desired, or
even about the general ethics of war. On all these topics I have expressed
myself often already. My intention is to take the minds of my hearers off
the questions of the moment.'[106] He did not stick to his intentions in Cardiff, where he claimed he simply argued for peace negotiations to begin
swiftly. Charles Stanton, a Welsh MP, pointed out, 'at Cardiff he said

everything he could say in the way of traducing this country, his own nation. As far as words would carry him in betraying the nation, everything that man tried to do [*sic*]. I think it is disgraceful for anyone to get up in this House and champion his cause, merely because he is a man who is supposed to have great intellectuality, and a man whom the Americans would welcome. I do not know we have much to thank America for. The Americans have been none too friendly as regards our own country, and that Bertrand Russell should be welcome in America is no test of a true Britisher.'[107]

The government agreed. Russell found the designation of a restricted area covered all counties on the east and south coast, in case he chose to signal to enemy submarines, and most great centres of population. He did not deliver his lecture in Glasgow, but a local miners' leader read it out, in a meeting chaired by an ex-provost of the city. Morrell goaded the government about whether it would arrest the man who read out the lecture; if the government was determined to continue to hound Russell – though he protested there 'was not a word of truth' in the claims Lloyd George made about his lectures – Morrell had made his point about the stupidity of doing so.[108]

Russell was not the only victim of this determined clampdown on dissent. In the later months of 1916 the government turned the screw on individuals or organisations deemed pacifist or seeking to subvert the war effort. The targets included leftist political organisations such as the Independent Labour Party (which repudiated war as a capitalist conflict in which the workers of different nations had no quarrel with each other), but also the Union of Democratic Control (both of which counted Ramsay MacDonald as a member) and the National Council Against Conscription, some of whom had their premises raided. A book, *Two Short Plays* by Miles Malleson, the husband of Lady Constance – Russell's mistress – and a former officer, invalided out in 1915, caused special annoyance. Malleson was a west end actor of some renown, and prolific as a writer; he would later become beloved by cinemagoers as a character actor in films of the 1940s and 1950s, specialising in eccentric clergymen. Since his discharge he had become a committed pacifist, and the two plays – *D Company* and *Black 'Ell* – were both explicitly pacifist, the second featuring a decorated officer tired of killing. Copies were confiscated under DORA, and in the Commons both Byles and Morrell attacked the government for this. A military judgement and not an aesthetic one had caused the ban. Malleson also wrote two pacifist pamphlets, neither of which excited the attention of the authorities: which suggests an element of amateurishness on their part. The literary attitude to the war had changed since the days of Brooke: and in the hands of men such as Siegfried Sassoon it would become harsher and angrier still before the war ended. The difference was between those, such as Brooke, who wrote about the war before they had seen it, and those, such as Sassoon, who wrote about it after experiencing the reality.

As concerning to the liberal-minded was the habit of the police or Army 'round-up'. An instance of this came one September morning when police descended on Marylebone station in London. After questioning numerous men of military age they only found one who could not explain why he was not in uniform: he was 'Ernest Snowdon, of Harrow-road, Paddington, leather dealer and a conscientious objector, who had been granted exemption from combatant service.'[109] He should have reported for other duties, and having appeared in court later in the day and been fined £2 was handed over to a military escort. Others rounded up in other swoops included a professional boxer from Bermondsey arrested when in the ring; two hundred and fifteen men were detained after a football match in Hull, four of whom were found to be absent without leave from the Army; another forty-two were detained after a match between Reading and Queen's Park Rangers, and all found to have their papers in order – it was such events that caused anger and irritation. An actor in a revue company playing the Nottingham Empire was marched off by a military escort for having failed to report for service; as was a former lion tamer, starring in a drama at the Edmonton Empire. *The Times* protested at this attack on law-abiding men in the guise of finding 'shirkers', with the victims 'publicly branded with the degrading suspicion of being utterly unworthy of the name of citizens', and pointed out that 'the results of this high-handed action have been quite ludicrously small.'[110] The Army handed over the responsibility for these activities to the police, who quickly scaled them down.

V

The government may have managed, in the immediate aftermath, to keep from the public the scale of losses on the Somme. However, it could not conceal that the battle had made the demand for men even more desperate, to replace those killed or wounded. Therefore 500,000 civilians who had failed medical examinations were retested, the bar being set lower. Repington noted on 16 October that 1,000,000 men would be needed by September 1917 if units were to be kept at their existing strengths, and only 170,000 men remained to be called up under existing arrangements.[111] It was decided to review exemptions, with single men in munitions factories targeted for replacement by women. The War Office recruiting department set up a Substitution Bureau to ensure that any job that could be done by a woman was; and that men taken from businesses who were no longer fit for military service were substituted for men who were. It was stated that unless such efforts succeeded, men aged between forty-one and forty-five would have to be called up too.[112] Attested men of forty-one were, within days, told to report on 1 November: it caused such anger (because these men knew that many younger and fitter were still in civilian life) that the proposal was dropped. It was agreed, however, to 'comb out' all unskilled men in munitions work under the age of thirty and replace them with women or boys under eighteen.

There was also anger about the exemption for miners, as coal output was falling due to disputes; it was now 253,000,000 tons, compared with 287,000,000 in 1914, when demand was less.[113] Even Smillie, the leader of the Miners' Federation of Great Britain, admitted that if miners were exempted to dig coal and were not doing so, there could be little case for their exemption. The problem was worst in South Wales, where avoidable absenteeism during September 1916 rose from nearly 6 per cent to nearly 10 per cent, Monday being an especially bad day. The miners' response was to demand a rise in wages.[114] The dispute between the owners and the miners came to be seen as a private feud, but one that threatened grave national consequences, until the press began to urge the government to take coercive measures effectively to nationalise the Welsh coalfield.

A debate on 11 October on a new vote of credit turned more on the matter of manpower – a Manpower Distribution Board, chaired by Chamberlain, had been set up – and exposed an ugly obstinacy. Robert Houston, a Liverpool Tory MP, asked why troops from the African colonies were not being used: 'It is simply prejudice,' he said. 'They are fellow-subjects of ours. They enjoy all the privileges of the British flag and all the privileges of freedom, and they are fit to fight for freedom. If we were beaten now and crushed under the heel of the Germans, what would become of these coloured peoples?'[115] He quoted the Bishop of Pretoria as having said about his local black population: 'These fine races of men were in danger of being spoiled owing to the disgusting example often set them by white people . . . Our boys in German East Africa are being shot down by German trained blacks. Why don't we employ them also? The Prussian Guard would not stand up to a second Zulu charge.' He knew the reason was racism, and read a postcard – suitably censored – from an anonymous correspondent in response to a piece he had written in the *Daily Mail* a fortnight earlier suggesting the use of colonial troops. His correspondent had accused him of wanting 'to bring millions of negro soldiers to overrun Europe and to slaughter decent white people. You are nothing but a so-and-so and a so-and-so to make such a vile proposal.' For good measure, the writer suggested Houston should have his throat cut.

So desperate was the need for men that some – *The Times*, for example, in a leading article on 4 October – called for Irish conscription. This was foolhardy in the extreme. Six months after the Easter Rising, Ireland remained volatile and the Irish increasingly angry, and the Liberals in the government mostly felt that this was a means of making the overall situation worse, not better. Lloyd George believed such a move would be premature because the men would not be put to good use. He feared they would just be slaughtered, until strategy and tactics improved. Although he believed – somewhat naively – that when the time came conscription for Ireland could be 'properly handled', the Irish response, in its hostility, bore no resemblance to that. T. P. O'Connor, the veteran Nationalist MP, was 'violent and emphatic' against it, predicting 'bloodshed at every cottage door' – while conceding the idea was entirely logical.[116] Redmond made his first public speech since the Rising at Waterford on 5 October, and said he could not believe the government would be so 'insane' as to try to impose conscription on Ireland, where it would be 'resisted in every village'.[117] He countered the idea that recruitment had stopped since the Rising, quoting War Office figures that 61,000 men had enlisted since then; however, figures soon showed that there were 161,000 Irishmen of military age not engaged in agriculture or other reserved occupations who were available.[118] With an eye on Sinn Féin, he also took the opportunity to say that his party would never accept conscription, nor the permanent partition of Ireland. Carson pointed out that more men had joined up from Ulster than from the other three provinces combined.

In the Commons a fortnight later Redmond resumed his attack on the government, and argued that the administration in Ireland operated contrary to the ideals for which the British Army was fighting the Germans, and was responsible for the turbulent state of the country. He said this was 'a moment when the public interest can be served by plain speaking', and used the tones of a man who had realised that he, his party and moderate Nationalism were fighting for their lives.[119] He called the situation 'full of menace and danger' and on the verge of undoing forty years of work by the 'constitutional movement' in Ireland. He condemned the government for its handling of the Irish since August 1914, while also noting that 157,000 Irishmen – 95,000 Catholics and 62,000 Protestants – had joined the Army, and another 10,000 the Navy, the Catholics showing their goodwill after the arrival of the Home Rule Act on the statute book.[120] Around 30,000 Irish National Volunteers had joined up, but the snubbing by Britain of Ireland had, he said, resulted in many others being turned away, thwarting his desire to keep Ireland and its people in close step with Britain. The 'suspicion and distrust' these attitudes fostered had culminated, he said, in the events of the previous Easter.[121] Later in the debate Lloyd George disputed Redmond's figures: 157,000 men had offered their services, but 52,000 had been turned down on medical grounds, and the total proportion was far lower than the rest of the United Kingdom.[122] Lloyd George himself subsequently admitted this figure was erroneous too.

Inevitably, a debate about Irish conscription turned into a discussion of British conduct in Ireland since the Rising. Redmond estimated that at most 1,500 men had participated in the rebellion, yet all of Ireland had been 'scoured' for rebels, alienating the law-abiding population when thousands of innocent young men had been arrested. The implementation of Home Rule had been postponed again, martial law was still being imposed, and Unionist ministers were imposing it: and yet Irishmen were dying for the King of England on the Western Front. He believed the situation was salvageable if Home Rule were implemented quickly; but feared disaster if it were not, especially if an attempt were made to impose conscription on Ireland; and when new Irish volunteers were not being sent to Irish regiments, but to English and Scottish ones, much to their distaste.

In reply Henry Duke, Birrell's successor as chief secretary, adopted a conciliatory tone, but denied that government policy had assisted the rise of Sinn Féin. His and Redmond's divergent views proved theirs was no meeting of minds. Duke disputed the figure of 1,500 conspirators, claiming 3,000; and many sent to prison had had their sentences reduced. There were 560 men still interned: there was no sense trying all 560 for treason, but equally the government did not wish to let them loose to foment trouble in a divided country. He argued that martial law continued not for Britain's benefit, but for that of the ordinary, law-abiding Irish man and woman. He blamed Ireland, and not the government, for the failure to implement Home Rule that July: the people had failed to agree among themselves. That was a matter of interpretation, and not an especially reliable one. The upshot was that coercion would continue, and (whatever Duke thought) more Nationalists would cross to Sinn Féin, and hard-core republican ideals.

Also poisoning relations was the matter of 570 men locked up in an internment camp at Frongoch in Wales, reduced from 1,800 sent there after the Rising. The inmates slept in former malt stores, described as rat-infested, damp and unventilated, a description the government inevitably contested; it did not contest that, that October, 176 pounds of meat sent to feed them was declared unfit for human consumption.[123] An officer running the camp suggested the meat should be washed with vinegar to eliminate the smell. Although Samuel, responsible as home secretary, called the allegations about living conditions 'baseless', he also refused to let a deputation of MPs visit the camp to inspect it.[124] Many internees were intellectuals; the camp became known as the university of the revolution because of the classes organised for the less educated. Among the alumni would be Michael Collins, interned for having been aide-de-camp to Joseph Plunkett. Asquith denied that the Unionist ministers running the government of Ireland did so in an 'anti-home rule spirit'.[125] He did not even indicate a new plan for Home Rule: it was as if he were stuck in a swamp from which he could not move. Following the Somme, however, he had too much else to concern him. However, he was shrewd enough to decide that he would take the matter of conscripting Irishmen no further.

VI

The world had become very different. The streets were filled with men in khaki, either on leave or in uniforms bearing the extra piece of gold braid that signified they had been invalided home after a serious wound. In some parts of London, where houses had become nursing homes for the severely wounded, whistling for taxis was banned after 10 p.m. until dawn, to give the shattered heroes the rest they needed. Life was a struggle: although those doing war work were often paid far more than in peacetime because of high levels of overtime, their disposable income was hit by high taxation; and by late July 1916 food prices were estimated to be 65 per cent higher than two years earlier.[126] Clothing had increased in price by 55 per cent and that of coal had almost doubled.[127] The middle classes and those on fixed incomes were especially hard hit: the new army of industrial workers coped better, but still found that £1 was now needed to buy what 12s 6d would in July 1914, and that as a consequence meat was a luxury to be eaten once a week. A report in August 1916 said the working classes lived principally on a diet of 'tea, sugar, bread, margarine and vegetables' and bought scraps of ham ends and bacon rinds to flavour soups.[128]

Nor did civilian life inevitably protect one from the 'frightfulness' of the enemy. As the government tried to cope with the fallout from the Somme, it found itself under further attack from the press and the public after frequent Zeppelin raids on the eastern counties in early August inflamed criticism of the provision of air defences. It was a hot, dry spell, and many of their bombs were incendiaries dropped on open countryside. Farmers concluded this was an attempt to start fires to burn down fields of cereal crops awaiting harvest. To speed up that harvest, the Army Council had announced that 27,000 soldiers would be temporarily seconded to agricultural duties. Meanwhile, Chamberlain's Manpower Distribution Board was supposed to ensure the maximised use of labour, judging what was or was not a reserved occupation, and who else could claim exemptions.

The frequency of Zeppelin raids had increased again, with thirteen airships raiding on the night of 2–3 September, killing four civilians and injuring thirteen more. The raid stimulated one of the most morale-boosting acts of the war, however, when Lt William Leefe Robinson shot down a Zeppelin over Cuffley in Hertfordshire: his feat was witnessed by thousands on the ground who sang the national anthem as it came down. All sixteen on board were killed, and Leefe Robinson was awarded the Victoria Cross. Shot down and taken prisoner himself later in the war, he would die of Spanish flu. During September there were two even more damaging raids, with two Zeppelins being shot down on the 23rd, but this time forty civilians died as far apart as Nottinghamshire and Kent and one hundred and thirty were injured; two days later forty-three died and thirty-one were wounded in attacks on Lancashire, Yorkshire and Lincolnshire.[129] The government's anxiety about the raids forced the Press Bureau to restrict what could be published about them. Its justification was that 'the military damage has been slight, but at the same time, so long as the Germans think that the raids have great effect, they will be continued, and long accounts tend to produce the impression both in England and abroad that they are of greater importance than they are in reality.'[130]

The air defences eventually fought back. When twelve Zeppelins attacked London on the night of 23–24 September – an unprecedentedly heavy raid – an RFC pilot shot down one near Billericay in Essex, killing the crew of twenty-two. A little later, at 1.40 a.m., a crippled Zeppelin made a forced landing at Little Wigborough, on the Essex coast just south of Colchester. Although part exploded on landing, the nose and engines remained intact and the crew survived. A special constable who rushed to the scene told *The Times*: 'About halfway there I met about 20 men walking along towards me. They were mostly well-built young fellows, probably not much more than 20 years old. They wore a uniform not unlike that of a fireman, except that they wore no helmets.'[131] One, the commander, asked him 'in very good English' how far it was to the nearest town. He told him six miles, and they wished to walk there to surrender: but the constable took them to the village post office and rang for a military escort to be sent from Colchester.

The Zeppelin was cordoned off, and people came from miles around to stare at it, forced to keep their distance by soldiers with fixed bayonets; its frame was spread across two fields and a country lane, and the farmer who owned the field from which it could best be viewed charged admission by taking a collection for the Red Cross. 'It looks like a great monster with its back broken,' *The Times*'s man reported. Britain was getting its own back, but by this stage raids had accounted for 352 killed and 799 injured. That night Suffolk and Lincolnshire were also bombed, and the raid on London killed people in Streatham, Kennington and Brixton: the total casualties for that night alone were 40 dead and 135 wounded. Another 43 died on the south and east coasts two nights later. The censor allowed only vague references to the casualties, and no mention of the locations.

Such raids helped sustain the powerful sense of anti-German feeling that had grown since August 1914, and which the vicarious experience of the Somme had intensified. Earlier that year this sentiment had played itself out in an embarrassing sideshow. Three members of the extended Royal Family held allegiance to the enemy. They were the Duke of Cumberland and Teviotdale, a great-grandson of George III; and two grandsons of Queen Victoria, the Duke of Albany (who had inherited the title of Duke of Coburg and had thereby become a German prince) and Prince Albert of Schleswig-Holstein. Cumberland, who was seventy-one, was not fighting for anyone: he had left Hanover, of which he was still technically Crown Prince, in 1866 when Prussia annexed it, and fled to Austria, where he still lived and was a close friend of Franz Josef. He was also married to Queen Alexandra's sister, so was George V's uncle by marriage as well as his cousin by blood. He had not visited England for nearly forty years and had never taken his seat in the Lords. Prince Albert, son of Queen Victoria's daughter Helena, held no British titles, but had been born at Windsor. On the outbreak of war, aged forty-five, he had requested and received an exemption from the Kaiser from fighting against the British.

Albany, however, was a different matter. He was the King's first cousin (his father had been Prince Leopold, haemophiliac younger brother of Edward VII), and the Duke of Saxe-Coburg and Gotha. A posthumous child, he had been brought up as an English prince and educated at Eton until he was sixteen, when he inherited the German duchy. He then became a protégé of another cousin, the Kaiser, and was Germanified. In 1914 he had broken with his British family and joined a German infantry regiment: and although he had been invalided out with rheumatism in 1915, he continued to provide moral leadership for soldiers from his duchy, and made frequent visits to the front. Like Cumberland, he had had his name struck by George V from the roll of Garter knights in 1915.

Following a question in the Commons on 12 April the press – who had not noticed that an Irish MP, Swift MacNeill, had brought the matter up originally on 7 June 1915, to be swatted away by Asquith – whipped up a campaign against these men. It had short shrift from Stamfordham, who in a letter to Gwynne on 27 July blamed the 1772 Royal Marriages Act. 'So long as the Royal family have to go abroad for wives and husbands these complications are bound to arise in the event of a European War,' he said.[132] This was not strictly true: one of Queen Victoria's daughters, Princess Louise, had married the Duke of Argyll in 1871; and one of Edward VII's daughters, also Princess Louise, had married the Earl of Fife (raised to a dukedom two days after his marriage) in 1889, neither having to go further than Scotland to do so. It was the pursuit of rank, not the law, that had caused this problem.

Stamfordham acquitted Albany of outrageous behaviour because he was a German prince, and would have been a traitor to his adopted country had he not fought for the Kaiser. He told Gwynne that 'in my humble opinion the House of Commons seem to have lost all sense of proportion on this subject.' Gwynne assured Stamfordham that his only motivation for raising the issue was to prevent malevolent gossip about the King being unduly pro-German, in having taken no steps against his kinsmen. In an attempt to be helpful, on 2 August the *Morning Post* ran a concocted letter – written by Gwynne under a pseudonym – observing that an Act of Parliament could strike the three men from the succession, but since none was likely to succeed it would be a distraction when there were more important matters before Parliament. That very day the cabinet discussed it, and Asquith made an equivocal statement to the Commons. It would not go away and, along with other consequences of the King's German ancestry, would dog the Royal Family for months until decisive steps were taken.

VII

Once it became clear that the Battle of the Somme would not bring a rapid end to the war it was also apparent that, to avoid an election based on a badly out-of-date electoral register and with much of the electorate overseas, the life of the Parliament would need to be further extended. It was agreed to prolong it to 31 May 1917, six and a half years after the last election, in the hope that something approaching a satisfactory revised register could be drawn up, and a legitimate election held. This would not be easy, and Asquith set out to Parliament the complexities involved. Ideally, he had hoped to extend the vote to every soldier and sailor, which would mean some men under twenty-one would vote. But there would also be the problem about the constituency in which a man in France or Mesopotamia should vote. He said the military authorities opposed strongly a vote being held while men were on active service; and he also asked whether munitions workers, who 'have severed their old family ties and their old residential ties, and have gone into places hitherto unknown to them, and crowded there in enormous numbers', should not have their sacrifices recognised by enfranchisement, even if unqualified otherwise.[133]

And Asquith had an even more radical proposal to make about extending the franchise. He proceeded to make a historic statement, reaching a watershed in his political creed: it was an observation of such significance that it must be quoted in full:

And, further, the moment you begin a general enfranchisement on these lines of State service, you are brought face to face with another most formidable proposition: What are you to do with the women? I do not think I shall be suspected—my record in the matter is clear—that I have no special desire or predisposition to bring women within the pale of the franchise, but I have received a great many representations from those who are authorised to speak for them, and I am bound to say that they presented to me not only a reasonable, but, I think, from their point of view, an unanswerable case. They say they are perfectly content, if we do not change the qualification of the franchise, to abide by the existing state of things, but that if we are going to bring in a new class of electors, on whatever ground of State service, they point out—and we cannot possibly deny their claim—that during this War the women of this country have rendered as effective service in the prosecution of the War as any other class of the community. It is true they cannot fight, in the gross material sense of going out with rifles and so forth, but they fill our munition factories, they are doing the work which the men who are fighting had to perform before, they have taken their places, they are the servants of the State, and they have aided, in the most effective way, in the prosecution of the War.[134]

He had received a deputation of women's suffrage campaigners shortly before his statement, and it had made him that apparently unanswerable case.

However, even if Asquith was undergoing a remarkable conversion, he remained enough of a politician to see he was opening the proverbial can of worms, and that in the midst of war his ideal franchise reform would not be possible. He therefore offered a compromise. He said the register would be drawn up on the existing franchise: but after the war, the next register would need to take into account the contributions of unfranchised men and women. He planned that male munitions workers who had moved into lodgings and lost a property qualification to vote would have their right restored; but soldiers would be unable to cast a ballot unless they were at home on election day.

Asquith's change of mind on women's suffrage outraged one prospective voter, Lady Bathurst. In a letter to the newspaper she owned, the *Morning Post*, on 19 August, she denounced his change of heart as 'this final act of betrayal'.[135] She continued: 'I have seen much of women during the war and . . . I have seen nothing to make me alter my opinion that as a sex they are inferior to men, and are totally unfitted to take part in the government of this country.' Demanding government by 'real virile, strong men' (she gave Carson as an example), she set out her vision of the franchise. 'I should like every soldier and sailor who has fought in the Great War to have a vote for his lifetime, and later on to see the vote given only to males who have passed some test of education and usefulness to their country.' It was fortunate for Asquith that further discussion of franchise reform could be delayed until circumstances were more benign. It would prove less easy for him and the government to sidestep other controversies.

Throwing his weight around as war secretary, Lloyd George was doing little to endear himself to others. The ever-feline Esher, observing him at work at British headquarters in France on 17 September, delivered a damning judgement. 'The impressions left here by the PM, who remained three days on a visit, were excellent . . . Lloyd George made the *worst* impression and showed himself to be what he really is, a clever political adventurer seeking limelight. He came surrounded by satellites, Lord Reading, who lowers the dignity, authority and status of the great office he holds by dabbling in finance and politics, Murray of Elibank, whose reputation for honest dealing is more than doubtful, and lesser lights of equally questionable character.'[136] Reading was now Lord Chief Justice, and his presence was especially curious: but as Esher told Leo Maxse, it was 'the old Marconi Gang', the men whose political careers were almost ended in 1913 by dabbling in shares of a company run by Reading's brother Godfrey Isaacs.[137] Isaacs himself turned up too.

Esher had not finished with Lloyd George: 'He seemed to seek the camera, and the cheers of the soldiers. He was insolent and offhand. None of these things are [sic] surprising. You cannot make a silk purse out of a Welsh solicitor's ear.' This was not Tory venom: Esher was a Liberal. But it showed how much the old Establishment distrusted and disliked him, and why. When the time came for Lloyd George to assume the highest office, he would do so with a substantial segment of the political class believing he was at best shady, and at worst corrupt. In June 1916 Lord Salisbury had told his cousin Balfour, for example, that he considered Lloyd George 'a windbag and a liar'.[138] The war secretary's cause was not helped by the freedom with which he expressed his low opinion of British generalship, nor by his desperation to curry favour with the other ranks, who Northcliffe had said disliked him.

Lloyd George caused more offence on his return from France by giving, at Northcliffe's request, an interview to Roy W. Howard, president of the United Press of America. Esher, and many others, found it shocking. 'LG publishes an "interview" with an American journalist today,' he wrote on 29 September. 'The substance of what he says is sound enough, but the vulgarity with which he clothes his ideas, his common phraseology and braggadocio, make one blush for one's country. In their day Gladstone and Peel were accused of departing from the high standard of political manners which had been the glory of our public life. What would they say to this phenomenal little cad?'[139] Lloyd George's assertion in the interview that the Allies would fight the war 'to a knock out' caused most upset.[140] It was his way of signalling to President Wilson that his ambitions to arbitrate a peace, for which America would take credit, might not be realised. However, it was interpreted as Lloyd George meaning he wanted to destroy Germany as a great power, something he had privately claimed was impossible; but it also seemed he was keen to assert that Britain would prevail, and British morale would be elevated by victory: what Lloyd George called a 'natural demand for vengeance'.[141]

Referring to the group in France with the war secretary by the neologism 'the Marconigang', Esher ranted: 'He deliberately came out to France for a "joy ride" with his "pals" . . . He has allowed himself to be exploited by a set of adventurers, whose boldness increases with success; and under their suspicious flattery he is beginning to believe that a field-marshal's baton was hidden in his first dress-suit case. This illusion, if he does not promptly awake, may prove his undoing.' Northcliffe was immensely proud of his role in securing the interview. On 5 October he cited it to Aitken as proof of his apophthegm, 'the best propaganda, in my opinion, is newspaper.'[142]

Lloyd George had made a point of expressing his concern that casualties had been so heavy, which Haig could only take as an implicit criticism of himself. However, to the commander-in-chief the minister's gravest offence had been, on meeting General Ferdinand Foch, commander of the French army in the north, to question him pointedly about the relative performances of the French and British armies, and British generals, on the Western Front. Although Foch had been scrupulous in not talking down Haig, and had stressed that Kitchener's army lacked the experience of the French veterans, Lloyd George implied he was unimpressed with Haig's leadership. Haig noted: 'Unless I had been told of this conversation personally by Gen Foch, I would not have believed that a British minister could have been so ungentlemanly as to go to a foreigner and put such questions regarding his own subordinates.'[143] Haig must have led a sheltered life to acquire any notion that Lloyd George was a gentleman; and there was an element of hypocrisy attached to Haig's criticising the manners of others. He had episodes in his own conduct, such as in his replacement of French the previous year and what would, in early 1918, become the drama of the replacement of Robertson, that would call his own credentials in that respect into question.

Haig and Esher were far from alone in their criticism of Lloyd George. He had to use his speech on the vote of credit in October partly to justify himself as a loyal supporter of Asquith. The French had commented adversely on his self-advertising conduct while in their country, and British journalists sneered at him for inviting this rebuke. An attack by the *Manchester Guardian* caused him great embarrassment and, consequently, outrage, to the extent where he accused Scott of having had a journalist not in Paris make the story up. Scott rebuked him for the suggestion, saying the paper's man in Paris was 'honest, capable and well-informed.' The war secretary's public-relations drive had led to his being attacked by the *Morning Post* as well. In the vote-of-credit debate Charles Trevelyan, the pacifist Liberal MP who would later join Labour, put on the record a claim by *The Times* that casualties for the first three months of the Somme were 300,000, and 'cannot now be far short of half a million.' He said that while the 'sanguine Welsh temperament' might think the war could be finished in months, that it might not be was a terrible prospect, if losses were to continue at that rate.[144] That was why so many deplored the tone of Lloyd George's interview.

Also, he appeared to have made an enemy of Northcliffe. The press baron called at the War Office on 11 October – the Secretary of State, perhaps fortunately, was absent at the vote-of-credit debate – so he told J. T. Davies, Lloyd George's principal private secretary, that Robertson was so perplexed about political interference in his job that he could not sleep: and that Northcliffe would regard it as his 'duty' to expose this interference if it went on.[145] Esher picked up this intrigue, noting on 17 October: 'Last week Lloyd George, behind the back of Robertson, tried to get the Cabinet to agree to send Divisions from the French front to Salonika. Robertson went to the King and to Asquith, and threatened to resign if the S of S made incursions in to the Department of "Operations".'[146] McKenna, whose views on Lloyd George must come at a discount because of his vintage animus against him, had told Repington that Lloyd George wanted Robertson out because he 'really believed himself to be inspired and to have a divine mission, and would not let anyone else stand in his way.'[147] Repington told Northcliffe, who sent the message back to Robertson that his newspapers would support him, not least because Northcliffe agreed with Robertson's opposition to Lloyd George's Salonica ideas.

Miss Stevenson believed Northcliffe's threat to attack Lloyd George over interfering with Robertson was rooted in the fact that 'Northcliffe is furious because D does not take his advice.'[148] His views gave Lloyd George a grievance against Robertson, which would fester. Miss Stevenson also noted that 'as for Northcliffe, everyone says he has gone mad – suffering from a too swelled head.'[149] However, evidence kept coming of the intrigue which a mixture of crisis, mischief and poor judgement produce: Riddell saw Lloyd George on 16 October and told him: 'there is a conspiracy between Northcliffe and certain members of the Army in high offices to get rid of Ll.G', something of which there was already much circumstantial evidence, albeit from unreliable sources.[150] Also, it became noted that, for all Lloyd George's keenness to go to France, he spent most of his time there in Paris or well behind the lines and seldom went near the front: in contrast with his enthusiasm for visiting munitions workers in his previous job. His most authoritative biographer attributes this to 'his fear of high explosives' but above all to 'his squeamishness'.[151] It was fortunate the younger men he had spent the previous two years exhorting did not share these traits.

His relations with the Army were not helped by his deep disapproval of the continuing offensive: but by the end of October the armies in France were 80,000 men below strength, so practically he had a point.[152] Nor had he stopped trying to neutralise Robertson. He cooked up a plan to send him to Russia to report on the situation there. According to Esher, who heard of the plot, Robertson refused 'point blank' to go.[153] Lloyd George had felt it wise to inform the King of the plan, who had replied almost immediately: 'I will certainly not allow R to go to Russia. He is first of all much too valuable a man to run risks with like poor K . . . I will not hear of it.'[154] Riddell warned Lloyd George on 5 November that without 'substantial progress' in the next spring and summer campaigning season 'the nation will grow weary of pouring out blood, treasure and ships, and that there will be a danger of a strong peace party.'[155]

As Lloyd George schemed, Asquith laboured under a workload that would have overwhelmed a younger and even cleverer man. Since January 1916 the War Committee had met on average six times a month; but met fifteen times in November. Even then, according to Hankey, it could not 'keep abreast of its work'.[156] The struggle to keep the country functioning was growing: foreign exchange was running out, so more goods had to be produced at home rather than bought from abroad. This helped obviate the failure of Britain's shipyards to replace merchant shipping anything like so quickly as it was lost. At one of the War Committee's last meetings the prospect of industrial conscription for all men under sixty, and possibly for all women too, was discussed, and a subcommittee constituted to work out how this would happen.

Industrial conscription became an important topic because, throughout the autumn as the toll of casualties from the Somme mounted, the 'combing out' of unskilled men from reserved occupations for military service continued: not just from munitions factories, but also the railways. It created a demand for 800 to 1,000 women a week to replace them, and urgent appeals were made for them to volunteer; the railway unions had reluctantly conceded that women could do certain jobs in their industry. With Christmas coming, the Post Office asked for 7,000 women to volunteer to collect, sort and deliver the post. Nonetheless, the nation was starting to buckle. On 13 November Lansdowne circulated a paper to the cabinet saying the war was about to destroy civilisation, and arguing for a negotiated peace. He believed the death and destruction of the preceding year had been to little avail, and that to go on would mean that 'the war with its nameless horrors will have been needlessly prolonged, and the responsibility of those who needlessly prolong such a war is not less than that of those who needlessly provoke it.'[57] He noted that 1,100,000 casualties had already been acknowledged, with 15,000 officers dead and many others missing: 'We are slowly but surely killing off the best of the male population of these islands.'[58] In addition, the country was bankrupting itself and beggaring generations to come.

It was agreed the cabinet would consider his paper. Lloyd George's argument for a 'knock-out blow', made in his United Press interview and so antipathetic to the Americans, was, however, increasingly popular in the country, and most of his colleagues reluctantly agreed with the sentiment too. Lansdowne's Unionist colleagues adamantly rejected his paper, and the leading brass hats, led by Robertson, were contemptuous. Lansdowne was a wise and decent man, but was seventy-two, and his heyday had been in the years around the turn of the century. He, and those like him, such as Balfour at the Admiralty (as Jellicoe had recognised), were increasingly anachronistic, unsuited to all-out war and the rough-and-ready politics it necessitates; and the greatest example of this was Asquith. The much despised 'new men', with their coarser attitudes and more aggressive manners, were more suited to the fight. It was time for a changing of the guard.

As if to bring British policy failures even closer to home, on 28 November the first bombing of London by fixed-wing aircraft occurred, when six bombs fell near Victoria station. With perhaps unintentional irony, Hankey recalled that 'the atmosphere in the Government, as in London itself in that gloomy season, was becoming daily more sulphurous.' Revolution, as well as the whiff of high explosive, was in the air.

NATIONAL SERVICE
WOMEN'S LAND ARMY

"GOD SPEED THE PLOUGH
AND THE WOMAN WHO DRIVES IT"

APPLY FOR ENROLMENT FORMS AT YOUR NEAREST POST OFFICE OR
EMPLOYMENT EXCHANGE

CHAPTER 7

COUP

———◄►———

I

When, in the last weeks of 1916, Asquith's leadership of the nation finally came under irresistible pressure it was the culmination of a corrosive process that had its roots in the conscription debate, but which then branched out throughout 1916. He had been criticised for his administration's record in Ireland, and, after the mismanagement of the Rising, for failing to implement Home Rule there. The Navy's capabilities endured serious scrutiny after the indifferent performance at the Battle of Jutland. The debacle of the Somme saw criticism heaped upon the government within days of that battle starting, not least from its own MPs. And then, on 18 July, Asquith had come under further attack in the Commons for refusing to publish papers outlining the background to the Dardanelles fiasco. He had done this not least after reading a long memorandum on the matter from Hankey, who felt it was not in the public interest to publish. He thought the War Committee's deliberations should be as confidential as the cabinet's, and nothing should be published until the war was over. There was too much in the documents about Allied strategy and diplomacy that would help the enemy. Publication would, for example, reveal Churchill's plan to enter the Baltic and launch naval operations along Germany's northern coast. If the whole story could not be told – and Hankey argued that it could not – then best not to tell any of the story at all. Churchill still felt he was being blamed for the disaster, and believed publication would cast him not just in a better light, but in a light that would enable him to revive his political career. As it was, he told Riddell he would 'have to remain under a stigma until after the war.'¹ Asquith then faced demands to establish a select committee on the subject. His inclination was to resist, as hostilities were still in progress and such an inquiry would distract parts of the government better occupied pursuing victory. Also, it was not as if the news from the Somme – of which the public, at that time, was only beginning to have even the slightest conception – left the government in a position of strength.

Hankey supported Asquith by supplying precedents from the previous century where such a process had been refused. Not the least of Hankey's fears was that a select committee could bring down the government. Grey, like Hankey, thought the whole government should have resigned rather than give in to the demands for an inquiry. However, the War Committee took a different view; and on 20 July Asquith announced an inquiry to the Commons – though it would not be a parliamentary inquiry, but a commission, under Lord Cromer, a friend of Churchill's mother. It would meet in secret so it could consider all the evidence available. A second commission would meet to investigate the background to the humiliating British surrender at Kut-al-Amara. Asquith acceded to the demand because the last thing his administration needed at that stage was to be accused of mounting a cover-up of another of the war's most inglorious strategic decisions.

Hankey offered to write an extensive memorandum in which the government's case for initiating the Gallipoli expedition, and the way it was conducted, would be laid out. Asquith, who wanted as little to do with this morass as possible, readily agreed. Grey told Hankey on 4 August, while Hankey was preparing the memorandum, that he was 'very disgusted at the weakness of the Government in granting the Inquiry and threatening that, if people were taken away from their war work on account of it, he would resign in order to show the country it was preventing us from winning the war.'² Churchill would be allowed to attend only as a witness. Hankey set about finding all the available documents he could to support his case, and drawing up lists of other witnesses the commission should examine in order to ensure his side of the story was told.

The commission convened in mid-September. Hankey made the Government's case over two days on 19 and 27 September, though caused trouble in saying the commission could not see the minutes of meetings of the War Council. Eventually, the government agreed that Lord Cromer, the chairman of the commission, would be allowed to see the minutes to corroborate Hankey's story. Hankey did not make things difficult for Churchill, who was effectively the man in the dock: he said he had put both sides of the argument, and did not appear to have withheld vital information. He did stress, however, that the War Council had received the impression that Fisher was entirely supportive of the proposals. Hankey was pressed about the 28 January meeting at which Fisher had said nothing, and conceded that usually when a naval adviser kept quiet at such meetings his silence was deemed to indicate consent.

Churchill gave evidence on 28 September and 4 October, spending the first day delivering a long and detailed statement. He took full responsibility for everything that had happened under his rule at the Admiralty and specified that he had no complaint against any naval officer. 'I am,' he said, 'here to defend those by whose professional advice I was guided.'[3] He said the attack had been necessary to come to the aid of the Russians; and he implied that Kitchener's refusal to commit a substantial number of troops at the outset had caused problems. He denied ever having interfered in the planning process, which was the province of his naval experts and not of a politician; but said that the men who were now the Admiralty's two most senior advisers, Jackson, the First Sea Lord, and Rear Admiral Sir Henry Oliver, his chief of staff, had supported Carden's original plan to force a passage through the straits. Effectively, Churchill was challenging the commission to attack both of them. Asked whether he had pressed Jackson and Oliver to back Carden's plan, Churchill denied it. The War Council had at the outset unanimously backed the plan, and Fisher had not dissented, nor (at that stage, in mid-January 1915) made the case against Carden's plan. Churchill admitted his share of the collective responsibility of the War Council in making the later decision to land troops; however, in his mind the decision was mainly down to Kitchener and Asquith, taken when it was clear that a predominantly naval operation could not succeed.

He spoke for five and a half hours. Cromer, who would die the following February, was so exhausted he took to his bed. It was a week before the commissioners – a collection of parliamentarians, colonial politicians and military men – could question Churchill on his evidence. His main task was to persuade his questioners that Fisher had kept quiet during the early planning stages about his misgivings: which, for want of documentary evidence, it seems he did. Also, Churchill contended that his desire for troops to be landed was not to help the Navy get through, but to ensure their success in getting through could be exploited to the maximum. Landing soldiers once the naval push had failed was something he supported but had not originated. When Fisher gave evidence he did nothing to undermine Churchill; he said he had remained silent at the crucial moment on 28 January because the only other option was to resign, which he did not wish to do. However, when asked why no one on the War Council had asked his views, he answered: 'Why they all jolly well knew!'[4] In a letter to Cromer later Fisher emphasised about Churchill: 'Mr Churchill is quite correct. *I backed him up till I resigned.* I would do the same again. He had courage and imagination. *He was a war man.*'[5] The commission would drag on until 1919, to little effect, but Churchill's rehabilitation had slowly begun.

Asquith's credibility, by contrast, continued to erode throughout the late summer and autumn. Lloyd George asked Riddell on 30 July what would be the outcome of a general election on the issue of 'more vigorous prosecution of the war', with a new party led by Carson – whom Lloyd George described 'in eulogistic language' according to Riddell – arguing that case.[6] The main actors would be Lloyd George, Law and Chamberlain. Riddell feared the public's reaction, but Lloyd George asserted that 'I think the nation would prefer Carson to Asquith'; and stated he would be 'glad and proud' to serve under him.[7] Carson was now sixty-two. He had grown up in a family of Dublin Protestants, his father a successful architect and his mother the daughter of an old Ascendancy family. He had read law at Trinity College, Dublin, and by the 1880s had made a reputation as the greatest advocate in Ireland. His own country was too small a stage for him: he had been called to the English Bar in 1893 and had shot to fame defending the Marquess of Queensberry against Oscar Wilde's suit for criminal libel two years later.[8] In 1910 he had secured a victory for his client in the Archer-Shee case, when a boy expelled from Osborne Naval College for theft was exonerated – the case on which Terence Rattigan based his play *The Winslow Boy*.

His political career had begun in 1892 when he had been appointed Solicitor General for Ireland; he had been elected as Liberal Unionist MP for Dublin University, and had become Solicitor General for England in 1900, in Salisbury's administration. But this pillar of the legal establishment had spent the years immediately before the war masterminding the anti-Home Rule movement in Ulster, and coming close to organising sedition in the process. He had raised an armed volunteer movement

and had been the first of almost 450,000 signatories of the Ulster Coven-
ant, which pledged to resist Home Rule by all means necessary; and had
seemed prepared, just before the outbreak of war, to lead the UVF in a
civil war against the Nationalists.[9] Half statesman and half buccaneer,
his charismatic leadership qualities made him irresistible to those
charged with prosecuting the war.

Churchill, writing on 13 August to Seely, who was in France, said he
thought Asquith would survive the session but 'his position is however
not at all good. The Tories outside the Gvt despise him: the Irish have
lost faith in him & many of the Liberals are estranged or sore. There are
vy hostile forces at work in the Cabinet and at any time a collapse is possible.'[10] There was also the shadow of the first report of the Dardanelles
Commission, expectations of which added to the strain he was under in
the autumn of 1916.

One of Asquith's great defects as a prime minister, as Grey said of him,
was that he 'took no trouble to secure his own position or to add to his
personal reputation.'[11] He gave credit where it belonged and took responsibility for failures. He never, though, grasped the different tempo of war
and nor, despite the warnings of his wife and his friends, did he understand how senior colleagues could plot against him. Duff Cooper, then in
the Foreign Office and a member of the circle of Raymond Asquith, the
prime minister's eldest son, recalled him as 'a man of great dignity, some
what aloof and Olympian. He belonged to the Victorian age. He would
have thought it ill-bred to discuss current politics at the dinner-table or to
criticise other politicians.'[12] He also had a capacity to see all sides of any
argument, which could be regrettable in a time of emergency. In late
November 1916, writing to Haig to inform him of the political crisis, Robertson referred to a War Committee discussion on conscripting people for
industrial work. The plan was put to the full cabinet, some of whom
rejected it. Robertson wrote: 'The PM at once began to wobble and once
again the whole thing was thrown back into the talking pot. It is impossible to do business so long as each of 23 claims the right to "object" and to
"concur" in regard to war committee decisions.'[13]

Despite the lengths to which he had gone throughout his prime ministership, and even during the war, to make opportunities for recreation,
Asquith was exhausted. He was sixty-four, drinking heavily, and had
three sons on active service about whom he worried deeply. He exhibited none of the raucous dynamism that made people admire Lloyd

George and see him as a man of energy and determination, but remained the national leader whom Haig, with a sneer, had seen 'dressed for golf'. Law, Curzon and Balfour had all begun to lose faith in him. Then, Raymond, from whom he had grown somewhat apart, was killed on the Somme on 15 September, which proved a shattering blow.

The prime minister had made one of his many visits to the Western Front nine days before Raymond was killed, and had seen him in the village of Fricourt, recently recaptured from the Germans. Haig, with whom he dined, noted how heavily Asquith was drinking: 'The PM seemed to like our old brandy. He had a couple of glasses (big sherry glass size) before I left the table at 9.30, and apparently had several more before I saw him again. By that time his legs were unsteady, but his head was quite clear . . .'[14] On the evening of Sunday 17 September one of Asquith's secretaries rang the Wharf, where the Asquiths were spending the weekend, and told Mrs Asquith that Raymond had been shot dead two days earlier, having just led his men in an attack on the village of Lesboeufs: a letter from Haig had arrived at Downing Street with the news. When she conveyed it to her husband moments later he broke down. Instead of returning to London on the Monday for a cabinet meeting, Asquith went to spend time with his widowed daughter-in-law. Downing Street was inundated with messages of condolence, starting with one from the King and Queen.

II

Not only did Asquith still have to cope in his bereavement, but he also had increasingly to try to manage the economic impact of the war. On 11 October he had to ask Parliament for another £300 million, making a total of £1,350 million for the 1916–17 financial year thus far, and an extra £3,132 million since August 1914. In 113 days since he had previously asked for money the Navy, Army and munitions had cost £379 million, loans to allies and the Dominions had cost £157 million and miscellaneous items, including food and railways, £23 million. In describing the value the British taxpayer, and creditor, had had for all this money, Asquith put the brightest possible gloss on the Somme, claiming the Army had advanced 'some seven miles on a front of nine miles', that the RFC had obtained 'complete mastery in the air', and caused the Germans 'practically to abandon the attack on Verdun'.[15] British forces alone in the battle had taken 28,050 prisoners, 121 guns and 396 machine guns. Haig, he said, had told him how British forces had been 'equal to the test', and Asquith had accepted that, it seems, without cynicism. It was not, he said, 'a moment . . . for faint hearts, faltering purpose or wavering counsel.'[16]

Carson reminded MPs that Asquith, like some of them, had lost a son in the battle still raging: but for all the brave words, there was no disguising the reality. There had been 'considerable cost, and there is no use shutting our eyes to the fact, because it is a fact patent from day to day and patent to the whole world.'[17] A fight to the finish, he continued, would be 'a Herculean task'; he wanted undertakings about manpower. George Wardle, the MP for Stockport, speaking for Labour, said that 'the time perhaps never will come when the whole tale of the burden upon the hearts and lives of people can be told; but certainly whatever that burden may be, I believe that the cost, however great, must be borne because the cause for which that cost is borne is worthy both of this House and of the people for all time'.[18] In all the subsequent arguments about 'lions led by donkeys', it is worth recalling the support the party of the working class gave at the time to the direction of the Battle of the Somme; Wardle had made his reputation at that year's party conference, when a speech he made galvanised much of the party in support of the war. Conscious too of Asquith's personal strain, Wardle said he had just delivered 'what I think will rank as one of the most remarkable speeches that has ever been delivered in the history of this House'.[19]

The mounting sense of crisis increasingly coloured political action, and acted as a stimulant to those who in any case harboured teeming ambition. Lloyd George, the main offender, visited Asquith on 28 October to complain about the conduct of the war. Asquith told Hankey the war secretary had been 'very depressed about the war, very disappointed with the lack of imagination of the General Staff, and very disgusted at the heavy losses in the offensive on the Somme'.[20] Hankey agreed with Lloyd George's assessment, and told Asquith so. Three days later Lloyd George ranted at Hankey about the 'bloody and disastrous failure' on the Somme, and said he would resign sooner than be a party to a repetition. It would prove an ironic promise given the two calamitous offensives of 1917, both sanctioned by Lloyd George once in power.

The government tried to meet public concerns about the failed military strategies. In November 1916 an attempt was made to make the Admiralty more responsive to the needs of the Navy and the merchant

fleet: not by removing Balfour, but by replacing Jackson, the First Sea
Lord, with Jellicoe, who handed command of the Grand Fleet to Beatty.
However, at the War Office Lloyd George's relationship with Robertson
was steadily deteriorating. In October Lloyd George had complained to
Hankey about the 'lack of imagination' of the General Staff, and told
him he would not remain in office if for 1917 another 'bloody and disastrous failure' such as the Somme were contemplated.[21] Robertson knew
more about soldiering and strategy than Lloyd George, something the
Secretary of State would not accept; and he and Robertson disagreed
over Robertson's Western Front policy. Lloyd George saw the Somme
vindicating his view that a new front should be opened at Salonica.
His indiscreet remarks about some generals caused the upper ranks of
the Army to distrust him, and to complain to Robertson. To make
matters worse, Lloyd George also believed Robertson was in league
with McKenna, the chancellor and Lloyd George's sworn enemy, and
that McKenna was trying to have Lloyd George sent on a mission
abroad to get him out of the way, in the manner earlier, and fatally,
applied to Kitchener – and as Lloyd George had wanted to do with
Robertson.

Robertson had Asquith's complete support; and Hankey believed
even Lloyd George did not want to be rid of the CIGS, because there was
no obvious successor. Hankey refereed the fight between the two men,
which he feared would end in one of them resigning – 'Robertson's disappearance being a military disaster of the first magnitude and Lloyd
George's a political disaster which would smash the Government and
perhaps the alliance.'[22]

The war secretary's ambitions were by now widely known: Esher,
whose antennae were second to none, had discerned them long since.
He had written to Haig on 29 September about an attempt by the 'Marconigang' to take over the Liberal clubland newspaper, the *Westminster
Gazette*, edited by Asquith's close confidant J. A. Spender. When they
acquired a controlling shareholding, Spender successfully dug in his
heels. 'Lloyd George and his gang could not influence him to throw
over Asquith,' he told Haig. 'They bought *The Westminster Gazette*,
and threatened to dislodge him, but at the last moment they funked, and
contented themselves with putting Murray of Elibank as Chairman of
the Board of Direction.'[23] Murray's appointment only confirmed Esher's
view that Lloyd George's cronies were mobilising. 'There is no sort of

doubt that he and the Marconigang mean to take supreme power into their hands.'

Jellicoe, meanwhile, was so alarmed by the losses to shipping that on 30 October he bypassed Balfour, his political master as First Lord, and wrote direct to Asquith about the need to develop a means of dealing with U-boats. Convoys – the idea of grouping ships together as a protective phalanx – were discussed, but there were insufficient warships to protect merchant vessels, and by forcing convoys to move at the rate of the slowest ship there would be delays and congestion in ports. Jellicoe asked the War Committee, to which he was summoned on 2 November, to supply 3,000 guns to arm merchant vessels. Shipping losses, and their effect on the food supply, provided Lloyd George with another area of contention with Asquith. A poor potato harvest and commensurate rise in prices aggravated this. On 10 November Lloyd George asked at the War Committee that a 'shipping dictator and food dictator' be appointed to implement 'drastic measures' to secure and regulate the supply of food which, Miss Stevenson recorded, 'is getting serious'. Those close to Asquith rubbished the idea, as did Curzon, but having asked for his views to be minuted Lloyd George told his mistress that he 'can always point to it when they have failed to do anything and it is too late.'[24] The incident revealed much: Lloyd George's disillusion being such that he was not afraid to open another front on his enemies; his expectation of their failure; and his determination to protect his own reputation. Collective responsibility could not easily survive such an outlook, and it did not.

Unlike Asquith, Lloyd George grasped the necessities of total war – which, for patriotic reasons that were perhaps only secondary to his motivations, made his ambitions legitimate – and that traditional Liberal values had to be put aside. Others shared this understanding: such as the Glasgow MP George Barnes, who argued that the working class in particular was agitated about food prices and those speculating in food commodities – and the government was desperate to avoid working-class restiveness. 'The policy of *laissez faire* is no more good in regard to social economics than it is in regard to fighting the War,' Barnes said. 'It is as dead as Queen Anne, and the sooner [the president of the Board of Trade] recognises that fact and makes up his mind to step forward a good deal more boldly upon the lines of regulation and control, the better for all concerned.'[25] Barnes suggested the government nationalise Britain's entire wheat output, and all foreign imports, and fix the price.

However, his argument that the state should take ownership of agriculture and the food industry, rather as it had with munitions, was too radical to find favour.

Barnes nonetheless identified problems contributing to this national emergency that could only be solved by government intervention. He said that supplies of beef, bacon and milk were prey to speculators. Worse, there were stories that the well-to-do were behaving as though there were no war: 'The other day I read in a daily newspaper that it is still customary in the West End to supply dinners at £1 per head, and sometimes a good deal more than that; and I read, quite recently, that 2s 6d was paid for a peach and 2s for a pear. This is no time for that sort of extravagance, and where it is indulged in by the rich to that extent they are simply increasing the burden on the poor. I trust that will be kept in mind.'[26]

He said the price of sugar had risen by 120 per cent since August 1914 – in fact he understated the matter, as it had risen by 166 per cent – and asked how much this was due to the quantity of sweets eaten by the public, driving up the price of the commodity.[27] There were, however, Barnes said, wider problems with the food supply: not only were middlemen taking their cut, with farmers, millers, wholesalers and bakers all affecting the price of bread, but the demands on manpower meant that 112,000 acres farmed in 1914–15 lay fallow in 1915–16. The wheat crop of that latter year was estimated at only 88.5 per cent of the average of the preceding decade, a disaster in wartime.[28] Other MPs called for discharged soldiers to be called up to work on the land, and for men on the Reserve not yet in France to be drafted in too. However, Francis Acland, the parliamentary secretary to the War Office, had admitted to the Commons on 21 August that 27,000 soldiers had been provided for a two-week period in August 1916, but farmers had applied to use only 3,000, since many appeared unaware of the scheme. As so often, problems of administrative competence outweighed those of manpower: and MPs demanded to know why the government had not tackled these crucial difficulties.[29]

Such government control as existed was usually poorly thought through. For example, shops open late in the evening had been ordered, under DORA, to close earlier as autumn drew on, to conserve heating and lighting. However, because of people working shifts many small shops did much business after 7 p.m., and the effect of the new restrictions on their owners' livelihoods was severe. It was yet another blow to the small trader, already before the war suffering from the growth of larger retailers and chain stores, enterprises far better able to sustain restrictions on opening hours. One MP, Henry Chancellor, illustrated the difficulties faced by his Shoreditch constituents, reading out a letter from one:

> I have been a shopkeeper in the grocery and provision trade for twenty-four years, paying rates and taxes, and the best part of my trade is done in the evening after [the return of] the poor women who work in the City, mostly office cleaning, and [who] do not return till eight or ten o'clock at night, when they have to buy their food for supper, chiefly consisting of cheese, tinned meat, sausages, bread, butter, etc. If I have to close at seven I might just as well put the shutters up for good, while my neighbour who sells fried fish may keep open and therefore take my living away. I am a widow with one son, whom they are taking from me to join the Army, and I have no other means of getting my living.[30]

The government was implored to reconsider, or face the proprietors of such shops ending up en masse in the workhouse. It was also pointed out that essential workers, especially in munitions, would be unable to shop without missing shifts unless the restrictions were relaxed. Samuel, defending the order, cited recommendations from the Coal Supply Committee to conserve fuel; and he also listed trade bodies representing drapers, chemists, grocers, hairdressers, meat-traders, ironmongers and small traders that had, during a consultation process, endorsed the proposals. However, because of the force of opposition, he agreed to allow shops to open until 8 p.m. from Monday to Friday and 9 p.m. on Saturday.

As the food crisis began to trigger, at least in official circles, mild panic, many in the House of Commons began to consider the wider issue of centrally managed food control. On 15 November William Hewins, the Tory MP for Hereford and an academic economist, demanded the appointment of a food controller to 'diminish the risk of shortage and serious increase in prices in the event of war being prolonged'.[31] He launched a Commons debate on the subject, in which he said that there was 'considerable anxiety in the country' and a continued rise in prices was inevitable.[32] He blamed the coalition. 'Considering that we have under British control the largest area and the most fertile lands there are in the world, considering that you can grow everything in indefinitely large quantities that is required for the service of man in the British Empire, I say that the policy of the Government of this country in dealing with the question of food supplies is totally inexcusable. If you cannot do it with the British Empire at your back, then you cannot do it at all.'[33] The government had avoided any statement about food production in the Empire or at home, and questions of labour and transport that bore on the production and availability of food. It symbolised the dysfunction of the administration.

Hewins's aim was to smoke ministers out, but also to make them see that such a wide range of ministries was involved in the implementation of food policy that central coordination was crucial. Although he claimed that 'I am not making the slightest reflection on the Prime Minister or on any member of the Government', he had highlighted a critical failing of the administration just when its failures threatened to become fatal.[34] He argued that no business could survive without central direction: yet the government believed the food business could do just that.

Runciman, the president of the Board of Trade, reassured MPs that the government was taking measures to improve the food supply. He reported record harvests in Australia, Canada and America; but admitted shipping was not always available to bring the fruits of those harvests to Britain, something for which he partly blamed the French, for being so slow to turn round British ships in their ports. He claimed that, despite shortages of labour in shipyards, production would increase in 1917. Yet he also acknowledged serious problems. For example, Britain felt an obligation to supply food to its allies, which made the situation at home even more fraught: all the more remarkable, therefore, that it had not sought to improve matters sooner. Runciman admitted it was 'most difficult' when recruiting in rural areas to judge when to do any more would damage the food supply.[35] Also, high prices had not driven down consumption, so he admitted the government might be 'compelled' to control prices.[36] Sugar remained a problem: but there were also cases of potato profiteering, with prices rising after it became known that a Lincolnshire farmer had made £62-an-acre profit selling potatoes to the Army, thanks to incompetence by the War Office in procurement.

Runciman outlined a series of steps that he proposed to take to remedy these difficulties. He planned to order the pooling of skilled labour to ensure vessels were completed. Yet although labour could be directed to complete ships, the ships themselves could not be built without steel; and a shortage of skilled steelworkers had led to many blast furnaces going out. Runciman therefore promised these would be relighted, and skilled steelworkers brought back from the Army. He announced that no more full-time agricultural workers would be called up after 1 January; and no dairymen after 1 April, unless substituted for discharged men who had returned to the land. He also admitted that much agricultural machinery was in poor repair, and Britain lacked mechanics to fix it.

Runciman then conceded, on the government's behalf, that there would have to be a food controller, who would be appointed by an Order in Council under DORA. To have waited until the third year of the war to do this was a remarkable statement of ineptitude. He added that anyone wasting food – a story was current about gallons of milk being poured down a sewer because the farmer felt insulted by the contract price offered him – would be prosecuted. That farmer was not alone: one agricultural association advised its members to feed their milk to pigs if the contract price was unsatisfactory, though that at least benefited the food chain. He promised laws to punish anyone cornering the market in any foodstuff. There were no plans to fix maximum prices for foods, but there were some – such as milk – where the rise of prices would be controlled. It would be left to the food controller to assemble the evidence on matters such as buying up the wheat supply, and to recommend a policy. He admitted such measures were 'drastic' – though Carson felt they were not drastic enough, and Sir Alfred Mond, the Liberal MP for Swansea – and also an industrialist and plutocrat who would in 1926 create Imperial Chemical Industries – said, picking up the earlier theme of Barnes's proposals, the state should take over farms as it had taken over factories to make arms, and fix maximum prices for food as Lloyd George had for weapons.[37] The state had taken over pubs near munitions factories, and by putting in canteens had sought to make them more like working men's clubs.

Such policies were 'drastic' most of all in the effect they had on the non-interventionist idea of liberalism. Runciman concluded that:

> We have to abandon in some respects the old voluntary principle, to which I have long been wedded, and we may have to take steps in the way of State control which may cause a good deal of discomfort

and create some discontent in some quarters. But you can have no
State regulation which does not bear hardly on somebody. We have
the right to ask that all our people at home should be prepared to
put up with some hardship, which will be assessed and prescribed
and distributed as evenly as possible in order that those who are
giving far more for the country should be allowed to reach a glorious victory.[38]

The government would use Orders in Council to regulate the food
market in terms of price, availability, sale and distribution: but at this
stage, having taken such powers, it did not yet seek to devise and impose
regulations. This episode also showed how Lloyd George's influence
was growing: having dismissed his idea of appointing a 'food dictator',
within three days the cabinet had decided to do so.

In the short term, pressure on the government to intervene yet further
was somewhat mitigated by the attitude of the public, who became
fiercely censorious of extravagance and waste, which helped reinforce
the government's message; when the general manager of the Savoy hotel
published details of the 'gala dinner' at Christmas and on New Year's Eve,
at between a guinea and 25s a head (depending on the position of the
table), exclusive of wines, the outcry caused the offer to be withdrawn.[39]
The Board of Trade arranged a meeting with hoteliers and restaurateurs
to discuss 'economy menus', Runciman having 'made it plain that unless
the hotel proprietors took the necessary action on their own account the
Government would do it for them.'[40]

For all the government's attempts to ameliorate matters, the food
shortage added to the public's unease after the failure, and massive toll,
of the Somme offensive. That unease was stoked by newspapers, and not
just from the Northcliffe press. In late 1916 they depicted the government
as incompetent, lacking judgement, poorly led and incapable of taking
important decisions. The Dardanelles Commission had highlighted one
of its failures and further undermined its credibility. Some popular
papers demanded the drafting into the cabinet of Horatio Bottomley, a
national hero to many not just because of his recruiting efforts but also
because of highly remunerative 'lectures' he gave all over Britain to
packed and excited audiences. To colleagues, Asquith seemed to have
aged and, as Lord Crawford put it, was 'somnolent', and 'hopeless' at
managing his unwieldy cabinet.[41]

The political crisis of December 1916 therefore happened against a background of growing public unease, especially among the working class, about the war. Strikes became more frequent. In November 1916 a meeting held in Cardiff by critics of the war turned into a riot, when a mass of working men loyal to the war effort threw out hundreds of opponents. But even then the signs were that the working class, aware of the losses it had suffered through trench warfare, was moving from a position predominantly of loyalty to one of scepticism bordering upon dissent, and the labour movement could not easily or always control them.

III

On 9 November, just over a week before the Battle of the Somme ended, Lloyd George told Hankey: 'We are going to lose this war.'[42] Hankey replied that he had never believed Germany would be crushed by the offensive, but that there would be 'a draw in our favour'. The result of the Somme was, in the words of Hankey (who lost a brother there): 'the capture of large numbers of prisoners, and the occupation of some few square miles of shell-pocked mud'.[43] Two days later Lloyd George again told Hankey he could not stay in his post unless the strategy were changed, and added that if he resigned he would make no secret of why. Crucially, Law told him he too was dissatisfied with the conduct of the war, and that 'there is likely to be a break in the Unionist Party.'[44] Law had always backed Asquith, but Asquith, while loyal in return, had invariably kept Law at arm's length and, Law's friend J. C. C. Davidson felt, patronised him. Davidson knew Law was a 'misfit' among the grandees of the Liberal and Conservative parties with whom Asquith felt more comfortable, but felt Asquith's attitude was 'a fatal mistake, for I am sure that Bonar definitely wanted to help Asquith, and was rebuffed.'[45]

A lunch at Cherkley, Sir Max Aitken's country house, on 12 November, at which Law arrived to find Smith and Churchill ensconced, turned into a speech by Churchill about the iniquities of the government. This provoked Law to say: 'very well . . . we shall have a general election', which caused a deflated Churchill to protest that the suggestion was 'the most terribly immoral thing he had ever heard of.'[46] Churchill believed an election would put an Asquith-led coalition back in power with an increased majority, because it would have some Unionist support and there would be the absence of any coherent opposition, and that would be that. The next day, according to Frances Stevenson, Carson and Aitken saw Lloyd George, told him Law was about to resign, and asked him whether in that case, as the next most senior figure in the Liberal Party, 'he would be willing to form a ministry. He flatly declined.'[47] Talk of Law's resignation may have been exaggerated; Law was certainly aware of a restiveness in his party at Asquith's leadership, and (under pressure from Carson) had already told Asquith there would have to be changes. That, however, was not the same as being prepared to leave the coalition.

Beaverbrook – as Aitken would become the following year – tells it differently, saying Lloyd George summoned him and that his possibility of succeeding was not discussed: but Beaverbrook's memoirs, like Lloyd George's, are often unreliable to the point of fiction. Lloyd George's reasons for declining were that 'there is nothing but disaster ahead' and 'he would simply get blamed for losing the war.' Miss Stevenson told him it would be his patriotic duty to take over if Asquith went; but the Unionists would distrust him and the Liberals would dislike him for having effectively ousted his predecessor. She had an acute understanding of politics.

All the Liberals in the cabinet were fiercely loyal to Asquith, for despite his lack of energy they admired his political stance and his scrupulous loyalty to the party and its MPs. Also, the likely alternative to him was, in their view, worse. They had come to regard Lloyd George as a threat because of his obvious ambition, and as potentially disloyal because of the ease with each he had thrown aside his professed Liberal principles to advocate statism and centralisation. However, like Asquith, Liberal MPs had realised the strength of Lloyd George's following in the country and were unwilling to face him down. The reservations Liberal politicians had about him were shared by Haig, who had had extensive exposure to the war secretary since he succeeded Kitchener. The commander-in-chief told his wife: 'you will gather that I have no great opinion of LG *as a man or leader*.'[48] That opinion would get worse.

Meanwhile, Lloyd George was formulating other ideas: on 18 November, having breakfasted 'in a state of profound pessimism' with Aitken, because he felt Law was too much in thrall to Asquith, he confided in Miss Stevenson that 'he would like to resign & be made instead President of the War Committee.'[49] This is the first mention of a separate, small executive body running the war – as long envisaged by Carson – of which the prime minister would not be a member, but which would function separately under Lloyd George. He wanted to discuss this with Law, but Law, 'in a wobbly state of mind', had refused to see him; and had been open with an unsurprised Asquith about what was going on. There was little point Lloyd George discussing this with his fellow Liberals, as none would support him. All his backing came from Unionists, but their support for his plan required validation by their leader.

Helpfully for Lloyd George, Aitken, who was not only Law's closest political friend but had also behind the scenes taken control of the *Daily Express* for £17,500, believed the war could not be prosecuted properly while Asquith remained in charge. He would, in his view, act as Law and Lloyd George's go-between. Northcliffe, who misunderstood Aitken, had told him 'that he was out to destroy Ll.G', and wanted his help – 'I am going to get as many newspapers as possible to help me.' Aitken replied, allegedly, that he would be 'a traitor to his country' if he gave such help. It was the hardest proof yet of Northcliffe's status as an over-mighty subject. Given how things would turn out, his misreading of Lloyd George's guile and cunning also showed his defective judgement.

The press baron had started to turn against Lloyd George for the usual reasons that he turned against anyone – the war secretary's refusal to defer to his judgements and prejudices on all questions – and especially because of his awareness of Lloyd George's poor view, widely broadcast, of Northcliffe's friend Haig. He also believed Lloyd George was a braggart and lacked moral courage, having heard too often his threats to resign.

Thanks to Aitken, Law was now brought into a discussion about effecting profound change. In Aitken's room at the Hyde Park Hotel – where he lived – he, Law, Carson and Lloyd George met on 20 November to discuss an idea for a war committee of three that would not include Asquith. The Unionists shared Lloyd George's view about Asquith's lack of 'drive': notably his inability to wrap up a meeting, whether of a cabinet or a committee, decisively, by allowing talk to continue aimlessly; and the press, with or without Lloyd George's help, was maintaining a fusillade of criticism against the prime minister. But although Law liked the idea of a small war committee meeting frequently, he bridled at Lloyd George, whom he profoundly distrusted, having more power. According to Aitken, 'Law had formed the opinion that in matters of office and power Lloyd George was a self-seeker and a man who considered no interests except his own.'[50] Earlier that day he had told Aitken: 'I am not going to be drawn into anything like an intrigue against Asquith.'[51] Law's distrust increased when Lloyd George said he wanted Asquith excluded from the war committee. Law remained adamant about Asquith's inclusion. His loyalty to the prime minister would not make things easy for Lloyd George.

The next step for Lloyd George, having engaged to an extent with Law, was to get the key figure in the Whitehall bureaucracy onside. On 22 November Hankey took him to lunch at his club, where the war secretary disclosed that he wanted to 'secure a new War Committee – himself, Carson, Bonar Law and Henderson – the latter to conciliate Labour.'[52] Hankey told him he thought the idea, but not the cast list, sound. He, too, wanted to streamline decision-making to stop wasting time, but had a low opinion of the deliberative talents of Carson and Law. Lloyd George asked Hankey to dine with him, Law and Carson that evening to discuss it, but Hankey declined as it would appear disloyal to Asquith. It may or may not have occurred to him that Lloyd George's suggestion of leading this committee would invest sufficient power in him to make unfeasible his notion that Asquith could remain prime minister.

Law knew the war secretary was a supreme opportunist, but, according to J. C. C. (later Viscount) Davidson, his private secretary, 'came almost to be persuaded that Lloyd George was moved by rather high motives of patriotism'; yet at dinner that evening again expressed unease about excluding Asquith.[53] Carson was unenthusiastic about returning to office. Lloyd George, for his part, had convinced himself he could unify the country and win the war. Although his plan envisaged Asquith's remaining prime minister and running everything except the war, Lloyd George was now scabrous about him in private, telling Miss Stevenson that 'the PM is absolutely hopeless. He cannot make up his mind about anything, and seems to have lost all will-power.'[54]

Lloyd George's confidence was boosted when Addison (who thanks not least to the war secretary's patronage had succeeded him as minister of munitions the previous July) told him, not entirely accurately, that many Liberal MPs would support him as leader: and by the last week in November, partly because of Lloyd George's assiduous cultivation of colleagues and the press, the talk was of little else besides a need to change the leadership of the war effort, with the responsibility passing to the war secretary – 'with all his faults', as Churchill told Scott.[55] As Lloyd George neared his goal, Scott recorded that 'there is a rumour going about – I should hope quite unfounded – that Northcliffe has some information about this which he holds over George *in terrorem*.'[56] If true, he showed restraint on the matter – which Scott thought was the Marconi scandal, but could have been his near-bigamy with Miss Stevenson – then and thereafter.

Law, now on reflection realising the urgency of radical administrative change, told Hankey on 23 November he supported the plan for a small war committee. His backing for Lloyd George was the crucial development in the process of changing the administration: however, in keeping with his loyalty to the prime minister, Law envisaged Asquith would sit on the new committee. Hankey repeated to him what he had told Lloyd George. Law and Carson – who told Law he shared his reservations about Lloyd George – lunched with Lloyd George and Aitken on 25 November. Afterwards Law met Asquith to put the proposal – drafted by Aitken – that Law, Carson and Lloyd George should run the war under Asquith's ultimate authority: and said he would resign if Asquith disagreed. The prime minister wanted time to think, though told Law he feared this was not a final demand by Lloyd George, but a mere increment in a greater increase in his power. Even while Law and Asquith spoke, Lloyd George was having doubts about whether his plan could work, being convinced McKenna was poisoning Asquith against him: Miss Stevenson thought it would be best to get Asquith out entirely, for a clean break. 'I think D has doubts about it too,' she noted.[57] Carson, at Chequers for the weekend with Sir Arthur Lee, who worked under Lloyd George at Munitions, put the proposal bluntly: 'LG more and more "in command of the War" as a kind of Dictator, whilst retaining Asquith as nominal prime minister.'[58] Lee told Carson this was 'not very practicable'.

Asquith told Hankey he had received a joint proposal from Lloyd George and Law, and asked him for his view. Hankey's answer was the same as he had given the two principals behind the scheme. Asquith wrote to Law saying he took 'a less disparaging view than you do of the War Committee', which he admitted was unwieldy but was, he felt, doing a good job.[59] He spoke of difficulties in excluding valuable colleagues from so small a group; he thought that to include Carson, the government's most vociferous critic, would be 'a manifest sign of weakness and cowardice'; and to give Lloyd George such power would suggest he had engineered a means 'as soon as a fitting pretext could be found, of displacing me.' He did not see, therefore, how the plan could be effected without disobliging loyal colleagues and undermining his authority.

On 27 November, when Law received that letter, Asquith told Lloyd George he had rejected Law's ultimatum. The war secretary decided, yet again, to resign. Law then brokered a discussion between Asquith and Lloyd George, for Friday 1 December, so they could thrash out an accommodation. When, in a meeting on 30 November, Law told senior colleagues – including Lansdowne, Chamberlain, Curzon, Lord Robert Cecil, Long and Smith (Balfour was in bed with flu) – of the proposals he encountered tremendous hostility, mainly because of their dislike of Lloyd George. He did not even mention Carson, whom most of them disliked just as much. The plotting appalled Lansdowne, because he sincerely believed Asquith was the best option; he told Law after the meeting that the business 'left "a nasty taste in my mouth". I did not like your plan, and I am by no means convinced that the alternative is all that can be desired.'[60] He urged Law not to commit himself to Lloyd George 'until you have given us another opportunity of considering the situation', and said that 'we all of us owe it to Asquith to avoid any action which might be regarded by him as a concerted attempt to oust him from his position as leader.'

By the end of November there were clear signs that the government was fragmenting because of poor leadership, brought on by Asquith's loss of authority and his indecisiveness. The need for greater direction became widely accepted among politicians. Lord Robert Cecil, the minister of blockade – in a response to Lansdowne's paper about a negotiated peace – circulated his own views, declaring that the war had to be fought, but 'that to attempt to do so without drastic changes in our civil life would be to court disaster.'[61] Cecil's ideas were radical: he believed the owners of wealth now had to make sacrifices on the scale they urged on the working class, which meant paying themselves less and having many of their industries nationalised; and a civilian commitment to total war, guided by a small cabinet committee such as the one Lloyd George wanted to direct military matters, was now needed. Hankey pressed Asquith on 30 November to streamline and formalise the cabinet decision-making process, by working to an agreed agenda. However, when Lloyd

George realised that a discussion in the War Committee that day about
industrial conscription had happened without Runciman's knowledge –
the president of the Board of Trade was entirely against the idea – he
claimed he could take no more of such amateurishness.

Asquith conceded that some improvement in decision-making had
to be effected, and proposed to Lloyd George the establishment of a
'Civil Committee' under the war secretary's chairmanship to direct the
resources of the home front, while the War Committee ran military
matters. Lloyd George rejected the idea, because it would fail to give
him what he wanted and expected: control of the war. Therefore, on the
morning of 1 December, instead of having his heart-to-heart with
Asquith, he delivered to him, in the form of a memorandum, an ultimatum about the changes he expected – in which Asquith and the
cabinet would not have a veto on the committee's decisions. He had consulted Derby – his deputy in the War Office, and a key convert to the
idea of radical change – about the memorandum. Aitken had seen it too.
It proved Haig's point that Derby 'like the feather pillow bears the mark
of the last person who sat on him.'[62] Asquith promised to consider it.

Northcliffe, seemingly near the end of his tether, had seen Lloyd
George before his meeting with Asquith; but even before that he ('in
one of his ugliest moods,' according to Lady Lee) had telephoned Lee to
complain that 'I have wasted I don't know how many hours of my time
on LG already and it isn't worth it. He will never really do anything and
has not the courage to resign.'[63] That morning *The Times* carried a leading article entitled 'Weak Methods – and Weak Men'. It blamed poor
leadership for aggravating problems undermining the prosecution of
the war – manpower, food production and food control.[64] This was despite the government's having just acted decisively on another grave
problem, by taking control of the South Wales coalfield and leaving the
miners in disarray. 'The days mount into weeks without the slightest
sign of agreement or progress on a single point', the leader continued. 'Is
it surprising that the country is seething with dissatisfaction, and that
even the faithful friends of the coalition begin to trim their sails?' It categorised the nature of government as 'a series of debating societies' and
set out a superior alternative: a small war council in almost permanent
session. It did not call for Asquith's head.

One can only conjecture whether Northcliffe's mood stiffened the
war secretary before his meeting. Lloyd George had told Miss Stevenson

that Asquith was 'absolutely devoid of all principles except one – that of retaining his position as Prime Minister. He will sacrifice everything except No 10 Downing Street.'[65] She claimed in her diary that 'countless anxious letters from all parts of the country' were pouring in from a public 'pretty sick' of Asquith, and demanding Lloyd George take over. What was certainly true – as Lloyd George had told Haig over a lunch with him and Derby the previous week – was that the public were no longer, after the Somme, fooled by talk of great victories when scores of thousands of men died to capture a few miles of territory, and the mood was intensely bleak.

At their meeting, Lloyd George told Asquith that just three people should run the war: the Secretary of State for War, the First Lord and a minister without portfolio. They would have 'full power, subject to the Supreme Control of the Prime Minister, to direct all questions connected with the war.'[66] The prime minister would retain the 'discretion' to refer questions to the full cabinet, and the war committee could invite any minister, or any departmental official, to be questioned by it. As for Asquith's non-membership, Lloyd George cited precedents. Lord Liverpool, Gladstone and Salisbury had all kept their distance from day-to-day running of conflicts when prime minister. The comparison was scarcely an apt one; none of their wars, not even Liverpool's when Britain fought Napoleon, had made such demands on the manpower and resources of the nation as the one Asquith was fighting.

While Lloyd George reassured Asquith that he would continue to serve only under him, the two men had serious disagreements over personnel. Asquith wanted to retain Balfour, whom he had persuaded just a few days earlier to accept Jackson's replacement by Jellicoe by promising the First Lord that he would stay in his post. Lloyd George, however, saw Balfour as 'gaga, useless'.[67] By contrast, Asquith detested Carson, and did not want him back. Lloyd George knew how useful Carson could be to him; but he too would have a problem to overcome with Carson, namely his determination to extend conscription to Ireland. Asquith wrote to Lloyd George later that day, agreeing with many of his points, admitting that change was essential: but insisted the prime minister must chair the war committee and that a separate Committee for National Organisation should run domestic matters. His letter, in which he did not discuss personnel, ended with the (to Lloyd George) unacceptable statement that 'the Cabinet would in all cases have ultimate authority.'[68]

Law, who unlike Derby and Aitken had not been consulted about the memorandum, was shocked when he learned from Lloyd George immediately after the meeting with Asquith of the proposed reduction in Asquith's powers, to which Law had never agreed. Lloyd George claimed it would not harm the 'dignity' of the prime minister. However, he said he had insisted Asquith remove Balfour from the Admiralty. This was too much for Law, who said that 'not only could I take no part in any attempt to get rid of Mr Balfour from the Admiralty', but he would also refuse to succeed him – which appeared to be the plan – because of how honourably Balfour had behaved since Law succeeded him as Unionist leader.[69]

Despite Law's considerable misgivings he, Lloyd George and Aitken met again at the Hyde Park Hotel that evening. Law said if Asquith agreed to reconstitute the committee he would not feel it his place to dictate the membership, and neither should Lloyd George. Lloyd George agreed to give Law freedom of action; Law seemed prepared at that juncture to trust Asquith to streamline the committee and change personnel in a way that would improve the direction of the war. But the next morning, having received Asquith's letter, an angry Lloyd George sent a copy to Law, with a posturing covering letter that read simply: 'My dear Bonar, I enclose copy of PM's letter. The life of the Country depends on resolute action by you now. Yours ever, D Lloyd George.'[70] Law, who remained scrupulous in his desire not to act in any way to undermine Asquith's position as prime minister, now saw the necessity of calling a meeting of his Unionist cabinet colleagues to discuss the growing stand-off between Asquith and Lloyd George. He summoned them to his house the following morning. Lloyd George, who feared Law's colleagues would be against him, urged Derby to come to London to attend the meeting: but as Derby was not in the cabinet, and despite his clout in the party, Law felt unable to invite him.

Had Asquith hoped details of the crisis would stay confidential he would be disappointed: Aitken had decided to see the press was informed of the growing crisis. Using an American intermediary, he ensured a detailed account appeared in two newspapers (including his own) on Saturday 2 December. The reports named Lloyd George, Carson and Law as the nucleus of the new war committee; Mrs Asquith would describe the leaker as 'the greatest scoundrel of the lot' and a 'low Canadian blackguard'.[71] Northcliffe was monitoring the situation partly through Aitken. That morning he told him: 'Hope your man is not going to follow [Sir John] Simon into obscurity. It looks very like it today. We get some . . . abusive letters about his negative attitude, with much regret.'[72] Northcliffe's *Times* ran a leader attacking the government for the second successive day, only this time naming those it considered 'worn and weary men': Grey, Crewe, Lansdowne – none of whom would continue in office – but also Balfour, who would. Asquith's head was not demanded, doubtless because either Northcliffe or his editor thought that this might be so provocative as to be counterproductive. It branded the men it did name the ineffectual 'innermost circle' who, thanks to Asquith's misplaced loyalty, were mismanaging the country.[73] It observed there were men in the cabinet who were 'unworn', and could motivate change 'if they have the courage'. The challenge was issued.

IV

After lunch that Saturday Asquith left by car for Walmer Castle without having given an indication to colleagues of his next move. 'It was very typical of him that in the middle of this tremendous crisis he should go away for the weekend!' Hankey expostulated.[74] That day the *Morning Post* had run a leading article entitled 'The Need for a New Government', writing off Asquith but praising Lloyd George; the previous day it had warmed up with a leader entitled 'The survival of the unfittest'. In its second barrel, the paper lamented that 'nothing is to be hoped for as long as Mr Asquith remains prime minister.'[75] It also promised, or threatened, to publish frequent analyses of why Asquith had failed until, it seemed, he took the hint. Northcliffe, sensing the way the wind was blowing, suddenly turned up at the War Office, 'grovelling' according to Miss Stevenson, hoping to be friends with Lloyd George. Hankey believed that morning's stories had been 'obviously inspired by Ll George.'[76]

At Mrs Asquith's request Hankey saw Law, who told him about the party meeting he had called for the next day. By now, Law's reservations about Asquith's being excluded from the proposed war committee appeared to have been overcome by the prime minister's own acceptance of that condition in Lloyd George's memorandum. In the light of this development, Law told Hankey that if Asquith rejected the proposal to hand direction of the war over to Lloyd George, Law would resign and take his party with him, ending the coalition. He added that he wished to resign before Lloyd George, so as not to appear to be 'dragged at the heels' of the war secretary. Asquith had asked Reading, of whose closeness to Lloyd George he had been well aware since the Marconi scandal, to keep his friend under control; but when Hankey asked him to persuade Lloyd George to hold off resigning, Reading told him he had bought a stay of execution of just twenty-four hours.[77] Later on 2 December Asquith heard from Montagu, one of his closest colleagues and now the husband of Venetia Stanley, who told him that Lloyd George was adamant that the prime minister – whoever he might be – could not sit on the proposed war committee, because it would meet so often it would disrupt his other duties.

According to Miss Stevenson – whose chronology is not always accurate – Lloyd George had refused to see Asquith on the Saturday before he left for Kent because he felt he had reached a brick wall, and drafted his letter of resignation that afternoon.[78] Hankey realised it was vital to have Asquith on hand in Downing Street, and so sent Bonham Carter to Walmer to bring him back. Hankey and Reading discussed the absurdity of the quarrel: 'The obvious compromise is for the Prime Minister to retain the Presidency of the War Committee with Lloyd George as Chairman, and to give Lloyd George a fairly free run for his money.' But such a simple solution was beyond either man, close colleagues for the previous eleven years, who now had irreconcilable differences of personality and ambition as much as of policy. Asquith's point was simple: if he wasn't thought up to running the War Committee, then he wasn't up to being prime minister.

The Unionist meeting took place on the morning of Sunday 3 December, at Law's house. He went into it having been urged by Aitken to resign, and having been told Aitken would put the full force of the *Daily Express* behind Lloyd George because it was in the national interest to change the government. Aitken was never honest about his control of the *Express* at this time: as late as 1956 his private secretary told a professor at the University of Hawaii, researching the subject, that 'it was not until 1917 that he took over financial responsibility for the *Daily Express* and that he took no part in policy until 1 January 1919,' one of the many fictions also contained in his memoirs. His biographer, A. J. P. Taylor, tells the truth, saying the deal was completed on 2 December.[79] Aitken, anxious to elevate his less than central role, also claimed to have ensured an even more detailed version of events appeared in that morning's *Reynold's News*. This angered the Unionist ministers, who felt Lloyd George was trying to bounce them into unseating Asquith. Two potentially restraining influences from the old guard, Lansdowne and Balfour, were both absent, the former at his estate in Wiltshire and the latter still ill in bed in Carlton Gardens.

Law told his colleagues he would back Lloyd George's plan, and a resolution was passed (with only Lansdowne, consulted later, showing much reluctance) stating that:

> We share the view, expressed to the Prime Minister by Mr Bonar Law some time ago, that the Government cannot go on as it is.

> It is evident that a change must be made, and in our opinion the publicity given to the intentions of Mr Lloyd George makes reconstruction from within no longer possible. We therefore urge the Prime Minister to tender the resignation of the Government.

> If he feels unable to take this step, we authorise Mr Bonar Law to tender our resignation.[80]

Chamberlain argued that with Lloyd George in 'open rebellion' – he and his colleagues assumed the war secretary had dictated the article in *Reynolds News* – and Asquith apparently powerless against him, the Asquith administration was effectively over.[81] The question of who might succeed him, however, remained open.

By Sunday afternoon Bonham Carter had brought Asquith back from Walmer. He, Montagu and Reading – who had Lloyd George's interests very much at heart – persuaded Asquith to overcome his loathing of confrontation, to accept there was a serious crisis, and sort it out. Therefore, Lloyd George was summoned from Walton Heath to see him. Before he left Surrey Lloyd George shared his plans with Scott, who told him he thought the demand that Asquith should stop running the war was 'rather a tall order' and 'that he might well regard it as inconsistent with his position'.[82]

Law arrived at Downing Street before Lloyd George, to go into conclave with Asquith. He did not show – he claimed to have forgotten, rather than to have withheld it deliberately – the prime minister the exact wording of the resolution passed earlier that day. He did tell him

Unionist ministers would resign, not in support of Lloyd George but to force the issue of a reconstruction. All that remained to be decided was which Liberal prime minister the Unionists would agree to support, but Law seems not to have emphasised to Asquith how deep his colleagues' personal reservations were about Lloyd George, and how they might be happy to entertain Asquith as head of a different government. Asquith, though, interpreted the Unionists as asking him to resign, in order to see whether the King invited him back; rather than having him present the resignations of his colleagues and then remain in post himself to reassemble a new team.

Alarmed the Unionists might desert him, Asquith – who may not have understood what Law said – thus promised him a reconstruction, news of which on Law's advice was leaked to the press just before midnight on 3 December, and which appeared the next morning. When Lloyd George arrived at Downing Street that Sunday evening Asquith sent for Law. He told the two men there was agreement about the remit of the new war committee, with Lloyd George as chairman, but no agreement at that stage about other personnel. Asquith agreed to request the resignations of all ministers so he could reconstruct from scratch. Law told this to his colleagues that evening, and they in turn withdrew any call for Asquith to resign.

Lloyd George, even at this late stage, was making histrionic protestations of loyalty, saying that, as usual, McKenna was blackguarding him – 'he almost had tears in his eyes,' Asquith told his wife.[83] The same evening Curzon wrote to Lansdowne with an account of the meeting he had missed, describing Lloyd George as 'a merely destructive and disloyal force.'[84] Yet – and Curzon too could be disarmingly un-straight – he also told Lansdowne that 'we know that with him [Asquith] as Chairman either of the Cabinet or War Committee, it is absolutely impossible to win the war.'[85] Derby drafted but did not send a letter to Haig that same evening telling him what Lloyd George was up to and admitting: 'We can't go on as we are.'[86]

Lloyd George thought the matter settled: and at noon the next day, Monday 4 December, he sent for Hankey, who had spent his morning trying to calm down Mrs Asquith. Passing through ranks of journalists outside the War Office and in the Secretary of State's anteroom, Hankey found him reposing in an armchair by the fire. Hankey promised to work with him 'loyally and wholeheartedly'.[87] He asked Hankey to draft some 'rules' for the new war committee, to be circulated around the new cabinet. However, other forces had been at work since Sunday evening, and Montagu almost immediately told Hankey the deal was off. Two factors made Asquith change his mind. He felt he had bought Lloyd George off by letting him chair the war committee, and by promising that he would not necessarily attend every meeting. Mrs Asquith, however, thought this mad, and Asquith seems to have unduly discounted the reality of his power as prime minister while someone else controlled the most important policies. When he told his wife he would retain control of the war, and had told Lloyd George that, Mrs Asquith was deeply sceptical.

Most telling, however, was a leading article in that morning's *Times*. It, and a news story, had full details of the plan and the manoeuvrings of the weekend, suggesting a high degree of collusion with Lloyd George's camp: a supposition reinforced by its ultra-sympathetic approach to the idea that he should have more power. Elsewhere in the press it was portrayed as an unconditional surrender by Asquith, a smell of which also came from *The Times*'s coverage. The prime minister, his wife and his coterie detected Lloyd George's hand and were determined to put him in his place; they were especially angered by the accuracy of reports of private conversations between the two men. Asquith wrote to him that 'such productions' showed 'the infinite possibilities for misunderstanding and misrepresentation' of what they had discussed. 'Unless the impression is at once corrected that I am being relegated to the position of an irresponsible spectator of the War, I cannot go on.'[88]

Hankey described Lloyd George as 'totally innocent' of collusion, and said the war secretary had written to Asquith to say so – 'I cannot restrain, nor, I fear, influence Northcliffe.'[89] Asquith simply did not believe him.[90] Geoffrey Dawson (né Robinson), editor of *The Times*, later told Lloyd George he had written the leader on his own initiative, without any prompting from Northcliffe, because he disliked the sound of the new arrangement, details of which had been given to him by Carson (and also picked up during a Sunday at Cliveden from Waldorf Astor). However, Northcliffe, by this stage, because of his loathing of Asquith, intriguing in favour of Lloyd George, had visited him at the War Office at 7 p.m. on 3 December, so he may not have been blameless in the matter, though Aitken maintained that Dawson 'knew more than Northcliffe did.'[91] That Asquith could not bring himself to believe his war secretary was not intriguing against him with the hated Northcliffe meant their relationship was in ruins; even had he known what Dawson claimed to be the truth, the absence of trust made future cooperation impossible.

It did not help that Asquith relied on McKenna, whose hatred of Lloyd George was unbounded, for counsel in these troubled hours. McKenna, who had agreed with Runciman as long ago as August that the government had run its course, told him to face his rival down and construct a new administration, presumably without Lloyd George.[92] Asquith, in his letter that Monday morning, conceded he would not sit on the war committee, but insisted it would be subservient to him: 'The Prime Minister to have supreme and effective control of war policy. The Agenda of the War Committee will be submitted to him; its chairman will report to him daily; he can direct it to consider particular topics or proposals; and all its conclusions will be subject to his approval or veto. He can, of course, at his own discretion attend meetings of the Committee.'[93] Asquith's confidence should have been boosted when, during 4 December, Curzon, Chamberlain and Cecil visited him to announce that they, and Walter Long, the president of the Local Government Board, did not imply by their desire for a reconstruction that he should retire: 'They did not believe anybody else could form a Government, certainly not Mr Lloyd George,' Crewe noted afterwards.[94] Asquith took this to mean they would support him, and it made him bolder against Lloyd George. He was wrong. Long especially was far from sure Asquith should stay, since he shared Lloyd George's view on the conduct of the war.

At 4 p.m. on 4 December Asquith told MPs he had seen the King and had submitted the resignations of his colleagues; and the Sovereign had agreed to a reconstruction. The King (who told Asquith 'that I had the fullest confidence in him') had consulted Haldane on whether, if asked to dissolve Parliament – something the King wanted to avoid – he had the right to refuse.[95] Haldane said the King could only act on the advice of a responsible minister – his prime minister – and if he chose to reject that advice the prime minister would resign and he would have to choose another. The King seemed prepared to do this, Haldane (who regarded Lloyd George as 'really an illiterate with an unbalanced mind') having warned him not to enter into some sort of negotiation about who might end up as his prime minister.[96] Parliament was adjourned, and would not reassemble for any meaningful business until the 12th.

Stamfordham had seen Hankey that afternoon, and told him that he and the King regarded Lloyd George as a 'blackmailer.'[97] The King's private secretary was so alarmed by developments that he even asked Hankey whether he thought the King should take more of a role in government. Hankey, fortunately for the monarchy, strongly advised against this, however dire the circumstances.

On the evening of 4 December Law turned up to see Asquith, urging him to go through with the plan as agreed the previous evening, for the sake of stability, with Lloyd George controlling the war committee. Asquith would not budge, and Law stressed that if he did not he could not count on Unionist support. Asquith summoned Grey, McKenna, Runciman, Samuel and Lewis Harcourt, the former colonial secretary, to Downing Street to ask their advice. They agreed that Lloyd George's proposals 'would be an abdication of Asquith's position and be inconsistent with his responsibilities.'[98] They told Asquith he should resign, and put the onus on Lloyd George to form a government. Asquith told them he feared, in that case, a Lloyd George–Carson government, with Labour breaking away and breeding a sizeable pacifist movement. He then wrote his second letter of the day to Lloyd George; and, in respect of the war committee, told him: 'I have come decidedly to the conclusion that it is not possible that such a Committee could be made workable and effective without the Prime Minister as its Chairman.'[99] That chairmanship might be delegated sometimes to a subordinate, but if Asquith were to retain his authority as prime minister he would have to chair the war committee. He also insisted Balfour sit on it; and objected to Carson's participation.

Esher, predictably, was *au courant* with events, and even ahead of them. That day he wrote to Haig that 'in view of Lansdowne's Memorandum and of the reluctance of Asquith to give a decision on Man Power, Food, etc, I think Lloyd George was more than justified in resigning.'[100] That had not happened quite yet. Esher continued: 'It is hoped by his friends that he will become Prime Minister. It is realised that Asquith would lead an opposition, and that in less than two months LG would be beaten in the H of C, and we should have a general election.' Such expectation might explain why Esher, who despised Lloyd George, was so sanguine about his taking over. But he also realised that Asquith's methods were untenable: 'It may be the only method of extricating ourselves from an inertia that is going to lose the war.' He also saw how things would change. 'If LG does become Prime Minister, then his only chance of success is to govern for a time as Cromwell governed . . . It is no use to make a *coup d'état* unless you are ready with the whiff of grape-shot.' He grasped what made Asquith's rival different. 'The organizing of our resources is the objective of Lloyd Georgism.'

The next morning Lloyd George received Asquith's letter. 'Indignant', according to Scott, he said the whole affair 'was only another illustration of the indecision and vacillation on the part of the Prime Minister which had proved so ruinous in the conduct of the war'. This time he really did resign, in a hair-splitting letter to Asquith in which he (fairly) accused him of a history of delays and hesitations and (unfairly) said his 'supreme control of the war' would have been unaffected had he stuck to their initial agreement.[101] He showed Asquith's letter to Law, for whom it was a defining moment: 'I came definitely to the conclusion that I had no longer any choice, and that I must back Lloyd George in his further action.'[102] Conveniently, Lloyd George made no allusion to *The Times*'s leading article. Derby resigned too, while protesting – with more sincerity than his former master – his loyalty to Asquith: he would visit Downing Street shortly before Asquith went to Buckingham Palace to offer his resignation, to implore him to accommodate Lloyd George, but to no avail. Curzon, Chamberlain and Cecil visited again and told Asquith that, given he had altered the circumstances by rejecting Lloyd George's terms, the only option was for the whole government to resign. Cecil suggested that the 'finest and biggest thing' Asquith could do would be to offer to serve under Lloyd George, a suggestion Chamberlain noted was 'rejected with indignation and even with scorn.'[103] Chamberlain too was reluctant to serve, but Curzon and Cecil told him sharply that, if asked, it would be his duty to do so. Cecil followed up this verbal plea with a letter, arguing 'on national grounds' for Asquith to do this, but met with the same refusal.[104]

Asquith summoned his other Liberal colleagues, and Arthur Henderson, at 5 p.m. and read them his reply to Lloyd George, and Lloyd George's letter of resignation: they agreed with Asquith. Later in the meeting Carson brought a letter from Law withdrawing Unionist support, and Balfour, still ill, tendered his resignation; he told Asquith he thought 'a fair trial should be given to War Council à la George.'[105] This was a betrayal of Asquith by the Unionist to whom he was closest, and to whom he had shown conspicuous loyalty. Nearly a year later Mrs Asquith asked

Balfour's long-time friend the Earl of Wemyss: 'Has it ever struck you Arthur is jealous of Henry? It took me a *long* long time to even suspect such a thing.' Wemyss answered: 'Has it ever struck me?!! My dear, what do you take me for? Don't you know what Arthur is? Everyone has long known Arthur is jealous of Henry – very natural too.'[106]

Balfour's resignation made Asquith see the impossibility of carrying on, so at 7.30 p.m. he resigned too. Cynthia Asquith, dining with her father-in-law that evening, found him 'rubicund, serene, puffing a guinea cigar (a gift from Maud Cunard) and talking of going to Honolulu.'[107] His serenity may be explained by his conviction, which Lady Cynthia discerned, that even if Lloyd George were asked to form a government', it could not last long. Mrs Asquith 'looked ghastly ill – distraught', and Lady Cynthia retailed the gossip that the King was 'very terribly distressed' and had allegedly said: 'I shall resign if Asquith does.'[108] He offered Asquith the Garter, which he declined. In his diary that day the King recorded: 'I fear it will cause a panic in the city and in America and do harm to the Allies. It is a great blow to me and will I fear buck up the Germans.'[109]

The King saw Law late on 5 December and asked him whether he could form a government. Law said he doubted it, but would report in the morning. According to a note taken by Stamfordham, he told the Sovereign: 'The one essential thing is a reformed War Committee, which could meet daily, and if necessary twice a day; come to prompt decisions upon which equally prompt action must be taken. The present War Committee has become almost impotent.'[110] Law told the King he had asked Asquith to make this reform and been rebuffed; and that he was sure Lloyd George could form a government. In case Law was thinking of seeking a dissolution, the King, who deeply abhorred the idea of an election in wartime, said he would not grant one. Law urged him to reconsider, because he wished to retain the right to ask for a dissolution if his colleagues would not back Lloyd George. Law also told the King that Lloyd George believed the war had been 'mismanaged'.[111] Stamfordham noted: 'To this the King demurred and said that the politicians should leave the conduct of the War to experts.' He could not have made his view of Lloyd George clearer.

Thus Law left having not declined the job, but waiting to discuss with Asquith whether the Liberal leader would serve under him – which would change matters considerably. Law first saw Lloyd George, who, uncertain of his standing among Unionists but aware of his unpopularity among his former Liberal colleagues, said he thought a Law administration including Asquith might be the best option. Law went to Downing Street, where Asquith was dining with Crewe, and asked whether he would serve under him, or, if not, under Balfour (whom no one had yet consulted). Asquith refused and resumed his dinner.

The next morning Law, Lloyd George, Carson and Aitken met at Law's house, and decided to sound out Balfour, who knew how little regard Lloyd George had had for his work at the Admiralty. Lloyd George had made no secret to his co-conspirators of what he thought of Balfour, but recognised the enormous clout Balfour had in his party, and how impossible it would be to proceed without his approval. Balfour was asked to a conference the King had summoned that afternoon, to include also Asquith, Law, Lloyd George and Henderson, so the King could try to persuade them to work together in Britain's interest. The meeting was on Stamfordham's and Hankey's initiative, with Law's full support. Balfour, not merely an ex-prime minister but one who had served in cabinet office on and off for thirty years, was asked to arrive half an hour early. The King sought his opinion, and Balfour told him that 'the War Committee, as hitherto constituted, had proved an ineffective and unworkable body, and reform was necessary if the War was to be carried out successfully.'[112] He believed no government without Asquith would survive. When the full meeting started Henderson endorsed this. A new attempt was made to persuade Asquith to serve under Law, who said his Unionist colleagues would not serve under Asquith; but he refused to commit himself without consulting his colleagues. That was despite Balfour's urging him to do so, and pointing out that he, as an ex-prime minister, had happily served under Asquith. It was agreed that if Asquith decided to serve then Law would try to form a government; if not, the task would fall to Lloyd George.

The Liberals confirmed Asquith in his view. They felt it would be a Lloyd George government in all but name, with a problem of divided leadership. Lloyd George protested his own desire for a reconciliation with Asquith, but none was in sight. Asquith sent a note to Law in the early evening denying he had any 'personal feeling of *amour propre* in the matter' but that for him to serve would be 'an unworkable arrangement'.[113] Law answered: 'I greatly regret your decision'; and told the King at 7 p.m. he could not form a government. Asquith wrote to Mrs

McKenna that 'I have been through the Hell of a time for the best part of a month, and almost for the first time I begin to feel older. In the end there was nothing else to be done, tho' it is hateful to give even the semblance of a score to our blackguardly press.'[114] He knew he had chosen to be 'out in the cold'. To Sylvia Henley he wrote: 'This is a bit of a cataclysm, isn't it?'[115]

Thus on Law's advice the King asked Lloyd George, who had gone to the Palace with him, to form a government; he undertook to try. Those around him (including Miss Stevenson) genuinely believed he did not wish to be prime minister, but would have preferred Law to do it while he controlled the war – as he had wanted with Asquith. Law later stated that he thought he could have formed a government, but did not do so for two reasons. The first was: 'I was not at all sure that I was equal to such a position at such a time . . . Lloyd George was marked out in the public mind as the alternative to Asquith'.[116] The second was that while he felt he could rely on the Unionists to support Lloyd George, he did not feel he could rely on the Liberals to support him. Lady Lee declared Law was 'in a complete funk'.[117] Lloyd George told Miss Stevenson after seeing the King: 'I'm not at all sure I can do it. It is a very big task.'[118]

He and Law had been talking all day about possible appointments. With Carson they stayed at the War Office until after midnight, and agreed the next morning that Lloyd George should talk to the Labour Party about the possibility of their supporting him, because he wished, as Asquith had done, to include some Labour ministers so the government could be truly representative of the nation. This was essential, because with the exception of Addison, whose career had relied partly on his exceptional talents as a doctor and expert on poverty, but even more on the patronage of Lloyd George, no former Liberal ministers would serve under him. (Addison, in any case, joined the Labour Party in 1923, and served in Attlee's cabinet into his eighties.) Lloyd George's former Liberal colleagues otherwise believed he could not long survive in office, because the Liberal Party would go against him and with Asquith, who had no intention of relinquishing its leadership. They also believed Asquith would have more influence on events outside an administration that contained Lloyd George than within it; and as Asquith had shown great loyalty to his colleagues, they repaid it with distaste for Lloyd George and his methods, manner and naked ambition, and regarded him as having engaged in treachery.

None of his former colleagues was prepared to concede that Asquith's direction of the war had been unequal to the demands of the conflict. They remained loyal to him not simply because many had old ties to him, and owed their careers to him, but because they felt he genuinely had done the best possible job in the circumstances forced upon him. Also, they respected the way in which he had tried to uphold Liberal principles in a context that had become entirely anathematical to him; and, above all, they deplored Lloyd George. Yet, objectively, Asquith was not running the war well, and he was exhausted; and Lloyd George did have not just energy, but ideas, and the Unionists certainly felt that the break with the past that he represented was an essential one.

Aware of the delicacy of his position, Lloyd George saw Robinson, the editor of *The Times*, and asked him to tell Northcliffe not to make his task even more difficult by allowing his newspaper to assume 'too intimate a knowledge of his actions and intentions' and to resist 'too much vituperation.'[119] The *Mail* took little notice, bidding good riddance to what it called 'the Haldane Gang' – maintaining Northcliffe's fiction that the outgoing government had been a conspiracy of pro-Germans – and trumpeting the arrival of Lloyd George even before he had kissed hands with the King. None of this helped him in his task.

At Lloyd George's behest Derby tried to persuade the Earl of Rosebery, the former prime minister, to become Lord Privy Seal, which he thought would have added credibility to the ministry; but Rosebery refused, to the delight of the Unionists, who had received the suggestion 'unfavourably' because of Rosebery's capricious and often destructive conduct, as a former prime minister, towards other parties since 1895 when he lost office.[120] Rosebery mocked Derby's 'preposterous mission' to persuade him to join the ministry in a 'consultative capacity'.[121] 'There was not a word about policy. I was to give a blank cheque to a man whose policy I have disapproved of more often than most people. And whether consultative or not I should have to attend the House of Lords, which I have not entered for five and a half years and which I hope never to see again.'

Lloyd George faced a similarly uphill task in trying to persuade Samuel to remain home secretary. Samuel told him he had 'greatly disliked' the way the change of ministry had been made, and had found the press attacks on Asquith – which, like Asquith, he believed Lloyd George had inspired – 'intolerable'.[122] Lloyd George denied any involvement, blamed

Asquith for having changed his mind on Lloyd George's proposals, and asserted that he had 'foretold every disaster that had come upon us during the war' but had been ignored. Such a petulant, and barely honest, display hardened Samuel's resolve. Therefore Lloyd George had to rely heavily on the support of the Unionists – including Curzon and Chamberlain, who disliked Lloyd George's style and had had to be persuaded by Law – and the Labour Party, and a minority of backbench Liberals. In return Curzon, Cecil, Chamberlain and Long had Law extract a promise from Lloyd George 'that he had no intention of asking Mr W Churchill or Lord Northcliffe to join the Administration.'[123] Churchill, slow to understand that the Unionists would not tolerate his return to office, wormed the truth out of Aitken (according to the latter) at a dinner on 5 December with Smith and Lloyd George – after Lloyd George had left and, in a cowardly fashion, deputed it to Aitken to break the news – and was outraged. He sought to challenge the account in Beaverbrook's memoirs and was placated by a rewrite of the passage: it may or may not have happened, like much in those memoirs.[124] Cut off from most of the Liberal Party, unable to appoint two key figures who would have supported him, and heavily dependent on Unionists who disliked and distrusted him, Lloyd George would need to form a government without any of his long-term political allies. He could not have realised it, but his rift with Asquith had dug the grave of the Liberals as a party of government. It would be ninety-four years before its successor party had even a share of power in peacetime again, and then with similarly debilitating consequences for its future.

Lloyd George met Labour MPs on the morning of 7 December and, after some initial hostility, they backed him. He felt the early difficulty was because he had attacked Sidney Webb, who was not an MP but was present, and Snowden, who had been 'very unpleasant'.[125] Webb told his wife: 'Lloyd George was at his worst, evasive in his statement of policy and cynical in his offer of places in the government.'[126] At a private meeting after Lloyd George had left, the vote to accept office was carried by 18 votes to 12: Webb felt this 'a decision disastrous to the Labour party'.[127] The Northcliffe press, Aitken's *Express* and other newspapers were on board at once: *The Times* said that 'the burden is now set fairly and squarely on the right shoulders, and we believe that they are broad enough to bear it.'[128] Two days later the paper obediently ridiculed talk of a 'well-organised conspiracy.'[129] Davidson noted that Asquith 'had been outmanoeuvred in a field in which he had never operated or could bring himself to operate, namely political intrigue, mainly conducted through the columns of the less reputable newspapers.'[130]

The change was hugely popular with the public, who could hardly have cared less about the schoolboy antics around Westminster that had achieved it. In the period of gloom after the Somme, the end – or the hoped-for end – justified the means. *The Times* also claimed that 'the spirit of "pacifism" has been effectually exorcised, and the control of our whole war policy is to be vested in a small body of vigorous and resolute men.'[131] Yet it was the cultural change Lloyd George represented that was truly seismic, and Davidson's observation hints at it. Miss Stevenson captured a part of it in her diary of the day her *inamorato* became prime minister: 'It was very amusing to see them tonight when they came to see D and confer with him. They were actually kept waiting ten minutes or a quarter of an hour – all these great Tories – Curzon, Cecil and the rest, who a few years ago would not have shaken hands with him and who could find no words strong enough to express their bitterness and hatred – now waiting to be granted an audience of the little Welsh attorney!'[132]

Curzon had said: 'I would rather die than serve under Lloyd George.' When he became one of the key figures in the new administration, Asquith supposedly remarked: 'It is an almost unbelievable story.'[133] In that meeting, convened after Law had asked the Unionists present – Long and Chamberlain being the other two – on Lloyd George's behalf whether they would serve in the government, the putative prime minister claimed to have the support of 136 Liberals 'and believed that numbers would grow', according to a 'very secret' account written afterwards by Chamberlain.[134] It was confirmed to the Unionists that Churchill would not serve, and nor would Northcliffe, and that terms had been agreed with Labour. After this meeting Lloyd George realised he had sufficient support to return to the King and say he could form a government.

Although Asquith was not aristocratic he was a man of high education and learning, his personal probity so extreme that he often failed to see corruption, deceit or malevolence in others. He was by nature magnanimous, bore no grudges, and was not alert to offence or insult; there was much animosity in the process of bringing down his coalition, but others mostly exercised it, especially McKenna and Lloyd George. He had managed his party superbly through the vicissitudes that the six years of his peacetime premiership had thrown at him between 1908 and

1914. He was generally a good judge of character. His handicap was the classical education of the high Victorian period that he had enjoyed and that had provided his own social mobility from the middle to the upper-middle class: an education designed for a world of certainty, peace and a Whiggish idea of progress. It created not merely a world view, but a complacency and an attitude ill-equipped for total war. Just as the idea of liberalism had effectively died, one of its finest late practitioners would see his political career die with it. Hankey, writing half a lifetime later of the reasons why the first wartime coalition fell, said there were 'too many rancorous memories, too deep a distrust' between old adversaries for it ever to work: it was, he said, 'a coalition that never coalesced.'[135] Asquith's failure to find the wit or the resources to change gear when war broke out was not for want of trying; but the challenge to British power required a different sort of leader to meet it.

Lloyd George was that man. He has been described as the first working-class man to become prime minister; but his father had been a teacher, and although the uncle who brought him up was a shoemaker he was also a Baptist minister, so the young Lloyd George, destined from his schooldays to train as a solicitor, had a firm hold on middle-class life. His traits were of the man on the make, having lacked the refinement Asquith enjoyed from his minor public day school, Oxford and the Bar. He was schooled in deceit, exhibited in the Marconi scandal and his baroque private life; manipulative, as he had proved in his cultivation of Northcliffe and the almost as unlovely Riddell; rampantly ambitious; happy to challenge every institution from the monarchy downwards with as much insolence as necessary and irrespective of collateral damage. This could not have been further from Asquith's demeanour; but where Lloyd George would really change the climate was in the people he would bring into government, some of whose morals and manners were even less elevated than his. These were the precursors of Baldwin's 'hard-faced men'.[136] They helped win the war, but altered the tenor of public life in Britain for ever, and for the worse.

V

With the exception of Addison, Asquith's former cabinet colleagues stood by their decision not to serve: thus passed from office men such as Grey and McKenna, on the Liberal front bench in one capacity or another since 1905. Grey, relieved to be leaving the Foreign Office, stated after Asquith's death that 'Ll G was determined to oust Asquith and take his place.'[137] The lead that Asquith – said by Lord Burnham to be 'very bitter' – had given them was instrumental in splitting the party, and creating an Opposition.[138] Asquith retained the admiration of former Unionist colleagues as well as of Liberals: Cecil wrote to him that 'Lloyd George has many qualities, but he will never equal his predecessor in patience, in courtesy, or in that largeness of mind which despises the baser arts by which political success is attained.'[139] Asquith had never been in it for himself.

Late on 7 December, stranded from his party and with few friends, Lloyd George sent for Hankey to discuss what sort of administration he could assemble. Law was in and out of the room: Hankey found himself consulted so widely that he thought Lloyd George would offer him a cabinet place. The new prime minister told Hankey – with what degree of sincerity one can only conjecture – that he was 'the most miserable man on earth'.[140] He knew, though, that if he could not sustain an administration that would allow him to command a majority in the Commons, there would be no choice but to have a general election.

Hankey, concerned the government should suffer no rupture so great that the war could not be properly carried on, correctly assessed that, given how the new prime minister planned to run the government, he was creating something like a civil dictatorship, or what he called 'a dictatorship in commission'.[141] Lloyd George lacked the expertise to override his military and naval advisers; but that did not stop him conceiving strategic goals, and expecting the Armed Forces to achieve them. A. J. P. Taylor, an earlier historian of the period, called the events 'a revolution, British-style. The party magnates and whips had been defied. The backbenchers and the newspapers combined in a sort of unconscious plebiscite and made Lloyd George dictator for the duration of the war.'[142] Balfour said: 'If he wants to be a dictator, let him be. If he thinks that he can win the war, I'm all for his having a try.'[143]

The press, especially Northcliffe's but also Gwynne at the *Morning Post*, had played a considerable role in bringing down Asquith. On 8 December Asquith addressed a Liberal Party meeting at the Reform Club, singling out the leader in *The Times* on 4 December as the reason why he could not support an arrangement with Lloyd George. Had he served on those terms he would soon have been regarded as surplus to requirements, and the press would have urged his colleagues to get rid of him. Irrespective of what Northcliffe believed, Asquith told his colleagues that he and Grey had been targeted by 'a well-organised, carefully-engineered conspiracy'.[144] The party meeting showed overwhelming support for Asquith; Lloyd George would face stiff opposition, comprised entirely of those who until a few days earlier had been his colleagues.

It was ironic, given the press support he enjoyed, that when Lloyd George met Unionist ex-ministers, including Curzon and Austen Chamberlain, on the evening of 7 December, they discussed 'the desirability of taking further powers for the suppression of the kind of Press attacks which had done so much to discredit and finally to bring about the downfall of the late Administration.'[145] Lloyd George observed that 'restriction of the Press' would not be an ideal way to launch the new regime, but suggested enquiries be made about what the French government's policy on this question was. The next day he wrote to Gwynne to thank him for the 'brilliant help' the *Morning Post* was giving him.[146] Within a few weeks Gwynne was confiding in Lady Bathurst that 'I have no illusions about the little Welshman. He's cunning and sharp and quite unscrupulous but had good courage and means to win the war. Still, we must keep an eye on him.'[147] Hankey, visiting Lloyd George on 10 December, had their meeting interrupted when Lloyd George took a long call from Northcliffe, 'whom he seems to funk'.[148] The previous day, on Northcliffe's explicit instructions, the *Daily Mail* had run a front page jammed with photographs of effete-looking men in top hats and frock coats under the headline 'THE PASSING OF THE FAILURES': they were members of Asquith's cabinet, and the page exemplified the disrespect with which Northcliffe intended to treat any government that displeased him.[149]

Lloyd George announced his War Cabinet on 11 December. Law sat in it not as leader of his party or as Chancellor of the Exchequer (which post he also assumed), but as Leader of the Commons: a role that a prime minister in the Commons had always held. Lloyd George did not wish to be detained in Parliament, but to apply himself to winning the war, attending the Commons only when something of great significance had to be discussed. Law would represent him there. It upset the Commons, who expected a prime minister to attend if he was an MP; but Lloyd George was unrepentant. He knew he owed his place to Law, and handled him with respect and judiciousness: the two became friends. This entailed Law's turning a blind eye to some of his chief's excesses; but he knew that if he allowed his high sense of honour to take over and be applied to Lloyd George, he would bring the government down. As he said to Long, 'there is, I think, no alternative.'[150] That Law deputised so frequently for the prime minister meant Lloyd George had to consult him on everything, and they sometimes spoke for two hours a day. Lloyd George also knew too well the ease with which an aggrieved Law could bring him down. Law had unimpeachable integrity, something vital at the top of an administration led by Lloyd George.

The small War Cabinet (as it would be known) contained two peers of huge proconsular experience, Curzon and Milner. Curzon, who had seized the opportunity to serve without consulting any other Unionists, had great political experience too. He was fifty-seven, a man of significant intelligence, and one who had developed a capacity for duplicity and self-preservation in order to survive. The son of Lord Scarsdale of the palatial Kedleston Hall in Derbyshire, his grandeur was already so marked by the time he was at Oxford that a Balliol rhyme was made about him that began: 'My name is George Nathaniel Curzon/I am a most superior person.' He had become Viceroy of India in his thirties and did, by general consent, a superb job for which he was under-rewarded on his return home. He excited the jealousy of Balfour, which is why it took Curzon five years to acquire the earldom he thought, with much justification, was his by right. He divided opinion, but had, before some aggressive displays of partisanship in the tumultuous years before the war, always managed to have friends and enemies on both sides of politics. He had learned much of his deviousness from his experiences at the hands of Kitchener, when Kitchener was commander-in-chief of the Indian army during Curzon's viceroyalty. His political ambition, like his intellectual certainty and sense of his own significance, remained undimmed by age, hence his rapid acceptance of Lloyd George's offer to serve in his elite ministerial team.

Milner had never held ministerial office, though was considered Britain's most able administrator. His absence from the front rank of those conducting the war had been widely criticised. Both were adept at the dispatch of business, and Lloyd George used them to chair committees the War Cabinet set up to solve specific problems. He had told Riddell that Curzon was valuable because 'he has travelled a lot; he knows about the countries of the world. He has read a lot; he is full of knowledge which none of us possesses. He is useful in council. He is not a good executant and has no tact, but he is valuable for the reasons stated.'[151] Lloyd George also felt that 'Curzon's great defect is that he always feels that he is sitting on a golden throne, and must speak accordingly.'[152] He did not like him, but had he limited his choice of close colleagues to his friends he would have struggled. Curzon told the Lords that the new government was not for those willing to be led, but of those demanding to be driven.[153]

Of Milner, Lloyd George said: 'I think Milner and I stand very much for the same things. He is a poor man, and so am I. He does not represent the landed or capitalist classes any more than I do. He is keen on social reform, and so am I.'[154] Lloyd George's equation of himself socio-economically with Milner says much about his relationship with the truth: Milner's father had been a physician and his mother the daughter of a major general, and he had been to a public school followed by Balliol. Throughout 1916 Milner, Carson and Lloyd George had dined together frequently, so Milner's inclusion gave Lloyd George a colleague he knew he could trust and with whom he saw eye to eye. He might also have recognised that Milner was a deeply deliberative person, a quality he had in short supply and which was not pronounced in all War Cabinet ministers. Carson successfully argued for Milner's inclusion; but did not himself get a place because – according to Lloyd George – the new prime minister had to appease jealous Unionists who 'resented' the idea of his promotion.[155] In a conversation Lloyd George had with Stamfordham on 9 December there was an allusion to the King's strong desire for Carson to become First Lord of the Admiralty – which he did – and to be occupied by those duties rather than sitting on the War Cabinet, which he would attend regularly because of his office.

The final member was Arthur Henderson, leader of the Labour Party since the day after war broke out, because of Ramsay MacDonald's resignation. His presence completed what Hankey cynically called 'the façade of national unity'.[156] Henderson was fifty-three, the same age as Lloyd George, and his acceptance of office in the Asquith coalition had made him Labour's first cabinet minister. The son of a Glaswegian textile worker and a housemaid, he spent his youth in Newcastle-upon-Tyne, serving an apprenticeship in an iron foundry between the ages of twelve and seventeen. He was a devout Methodist and, on becoming unemployed in 1884, had spent some time as a preacher. His route to the Labour leadership had begun in 1892 when he became a paid union organiser for the Friendly Society of Founders. In 1903 he won a by-election as the candidate for the Labour Representation Committee, and when Keir Hardie resigned as Labour leader in 1908 Henderson replaced him for two years. His second leadership of the party began when he succeeded MacDonald. A man without side, guile or pretence, he was universally popular and known inside his party and beyond it as 'Uncle Arthur'. One of his three sons, a captain in the Middlesex Regiment, was killed in action in 1916; the other two fought and survived, and both ended up in the House of Lords.

Apart from Law, all these ministers were without portfolio, so they could focus entirely on the war. Lloyd George then appointed departmental ministers, with the rank of cabinet members, who could attend the War Cabinet only when invited to discussions concerning their briefs. Balfour succeeded Grey at the Foreign Office – which he agreed to do only because, as he told Lloyd George, 'you put a pistol to my head.'[157]

He had already told Law – who conveyed the offer from the new prime minister – that 'that is indeed putting a pistol to my head, but I at once say, yes.' Law felt his sense of duty was all that pushed Balfour to serve, and that otherwise he should have been happy to retire; that overlooks Balfour's keenness to stay at the centre of events and that, though sixty-eight, he had plenty of enthusiasm left for the game. Law felt that Balfour's intervention with the King had been crucial in enabling the new coalition, and that his serving had helped other Unionists take Lloyd George's shilling. Balfour argued that because almost every War Cabinet decision impinged upon foreign policy, he had the right to attend any meeting: and did. His appointment drove a wedge between Lloyd George and Northcliffe, but the prime minister knew the Unionists would not tolerate their former leader's omission. Carson, who went to the Admiralty, was also a frequent attender, as was Derby, who became Secretary of State for War.

Other Tories assumed high offices: Long, who initially refused to serve but came round once his co-conspirator Curzon did, became colonial secretary; Chamberlain took India. The change inevitably put many noses out of joint. Lloyd George was anxious, for practical and symbolic reasons, that Montagu, talented but also close to Asquith, should take charge of (civilian) National Service, since he had drawn up a plan to establish such a directorate: but he refused, despite a serious campaign by Hankey, but after a bombardment from Mrs Asquith questioning his loyalty. Also, Montagu told Lloyd George that to take so subordinate a position would cause it to 'be said that I have taken the only office I was offered', which would discredit him and the government.[158] Explaining Churchill's absence, Lloyd George maintained that 'they would not have Winston at any price. Had I insisted, the new ministry would have been wrecked.'[159] The Liberals assumed Northcliffe had chosen to stay out, the better to destroy the administration when it upset him. By contrast, Law agreed to serve despite no place being found for his main confidant, Aitken, whose disappointment was no secret.

For the first time, the cabinet worked according to an agenda, with papers circulated beforehand. The ubiquitous Hankey led its secretariat, servicing what (at Hankey's suggestion) were its almost daily meetings. After it first met on 9 December – to consider a lengthy memorandum by Hankey on war policy – a typed copy of the proceedings was sent to the King, breaking an immemorial tradition by which the prime minister wrote in his own hand a letter to the Sovereign outlining what had happened at each meeting: Lloyd George affected that he was simply too busy for such niceties. Stamfordham said he hoped that when there was cabinet business to report, as opposed to 'War Committee' business, the King would get a handwritten letter: but this never happened. Lloyd George went down with so heavy a cold that he missed the War Cabinet's first few meetings, which Law chaired.

Robertson saw the War Cabinet as the enemy; and Lloyd George had a similar view of him. 'He is awfully down on Robertson,' Hankey noted on 10 December, having motored down to lunch at Walton Heath.[160] Lloyd George was also disillusioned with Haig, believing Haig had 'bullied' Robertson, who had failed the country by not standing up to him.[161] Lloyd George had asked Robertson for a candid opinion about the chances of victory, to which the CIGS had given a blunt answer: 'I have no hesitation in saying that we can win if we will only do the right thing. If I thought otherwise I would tell you so.'[162] Robertson added that manpower at home was poorly organised and the railway system near the Western Front was a disaster – both matters Lloyd George would address rapidly – and that racism was stopping an effective deployment of 'coloured labour at home, and [we must] raise more coloured troops for use in suitable theatres abroad.'[163] He also said the French were dictating terms too much in the war, and the British had to be more forceful. That further exacerbated direct conflict with Lloyd George, who would never forget Haig's conduct of the Somme.

The prime minister may also have discerned that Haig thoroughly disliked him, believing – with absolute justification – that Lloyd George was not honest or honourable: theirs was a clash of moral and class codes. The Unionists – notably Curzon, Long, Cecil and Chamberlain – stressed to Lloyd George that Haig's retention was a *sine qua non* for them, as was Robertson's: so the best Lloyd George could do, faced with a military establishment with which he deeply disagreed and without a party machine behind him, was to rant about them to his trusties such as Hankey. On Boxing Day Hankey found Robertson 'in a very disgruntled state threatening to resign.'[164] But as Hankey noted, the War Cabinet may not have believed in Robertson's Western Front policy, but 'they will never find a soldier to carry out their "Salonica" policy.'

As well as the Unionists Lloyd George was obliged to pack into his administration in order for it to cohere, he drafted into what the *Daily Mail* called his 'Ministry of Action' those known as 'new men' and businessmen: Northcliffe himself was free with advice about who these dynamic individuals might be, such as urging on Lloyd George the impresario Alfred Butt, who ran twenty-two music halls: Butt would soon assist the food controller, Lord Devonport, the self-made grocery magnate who had shown his usefulness to Asquith when running the Port of London during the 1911 dock strike.[165] Many new men were cronies of Lloyd George, or had done him services; such as Leo Chiozza Money, an economic theorist who had done policy work for him and would in later life develop an unfortunate reputation for molesting young women in public; and the businessmen Lord Cowdray and Sir Alfred Mond. The new administration was not, however, designed to resemble parliamentary government, but to win the war.

Lansdowne, *eminence grise* of the Unionist Party and of the preceding cabinet, decided not to serve, bringing to an end almost fifty years in public life. He believed that 'the collapse of HM Government was catastrophic, and will puzzle the historians who have to account for it.'[166] The political world he had inhabited all his life was ending. He told the Duchess of Devonshire, his daughter: 'It makes me sad that we should be washing all this dirty linen at such a time, and I would have swallowed a good deal in order to avoid it, but the situation had got out of

hand.' He for one was glad to be shot of ministerial responsibility: 'I have
long wished to be released, but this is not the kind of last act to which I
looked forward for my poor play.'[167]

VI

Lloyd George realised the reputational damage the coup against Asquith
had caused him, and for years sought to repair it. 'Lloyd George told me,
often, that he never wanted to replace Asquith as Prime Minister,' Lord
Boothby recalled. 'What Lloyd George wanted was the direction of the
war, as Chairman of the War Committee of the cabinet.'[168] That remained
the official line. Boothby was also told – not just by Lloyd George but
also by Churchill – that Asquith's dilatoriness in that role was such that
he spent War Committee meetings writing to Venetia Stanley. That he
stopped doing that more than eighteen months before his fall shows the
nature of propaganda.

Some of Lloyd George's Unionist colleagues viewed his circle of
friends with disdain and even disgust; as, indeed, had some of his old
Liberal ones. One of the latter, Esher, noted the rise of Aitken, whose
baronetcy had been for services to Law, and who now received a peerage
for services to Lloyd George – not the least of which was prising Law
away from Asquith – and as a consolation for not becoming, as Lloyd
George had promised, president of the Board of Trade. 'They are a dirty
lot,' he confided in his diary on New Year's Day 1917. 'Max Aitken's peerage was given him because he paid £30,000 to get FE Smith out of a
scrape, and because he separated Bonar Law from Asquith . . . it is all
a sordid business.'[169] It was perhaps more sordid that Esher knew, given
Aitken's silent acquisition of a majority holding in the Daily Express:
something of which Lloyd George was almost certainly aware.

When the prime minister realised the outrage it could cause to propel
Aitken into so senior a post, he offered him an under-secretaryship at
Munitions instead, which he at once declined. Lloyd George wanted
Aitken's parliamentary seat for Sir Albert Stanley, a railway baron whom
he could make president of the board but who was not in the Commons. Thus, to create the vacancy, he offered Aitken a peerage. This
sparked an eruption of anger. Aitken was just thirty-seven and a junior
MP in Lancashire. Derby, patron of the powerful Unionist machine
there, told Law it would upset too many people if he were elevated. Law

agreed, and ordered Aitken not to accept the offer. Aitken agreed, but then Lloyd George talked Law round, ignoring the effect on Derby. However, neither had consulted the King, who regarded Aitken as entirely unsuitable. Stamfordham said the Sovereign was 'surprised and hurt' by the lack of consultation and 'does not consider that the public services rendered by Sir Max Aitken justify this further high distinction'.[170] Aitken himself was amused by the honour: lunching with Repington on 18 December, he joked that 'he was sure something was coming, for he had cut himself shaving in the morning and his blood had been blue.'[171]

Stamfordham ordered – an order quickly disregarded – that neither the prime minister nor any of his colleagues should ignore the Prerogative in future. It was left to Law to explain to Stamfordham that the offer had already been made, and the King, to his fury, was bounced into agreeing. The main casualty was Law's reputation, which appeared to have been sacrificed to give Lloyd George's chum a bauble. On 1 January Stamfordham sent a long memorandum on the subject of the King's being 'the fountain of Honour' and as such expected to approve all awards: it was an instruction of how to behave.[172] Manners were now in short supply, for the memorandum also noted that no reply had been received to the last letter of complaint about the failure to consult the Sovereign. It therefore ended with the comparatively threatening: 'His Majesty trusts that he may now receive an assurance that no offer of Honours or promise to recommend a grant of Honours shall be made by Ministers to any of His Majesty's subjects until his approval shall have been accorded either formally or informally.' Law had no interest in honours and rather despised those who did; as such he took an, at times, casual attitude to their grant: on 23 December the King was so cross he had promised Sir Hugh Graham, another Canadian press baron, a peerage that Stamfordham spelled out 'the recognised constitutional procedure: the Minister *advises*: the Sovereign *assents* – and the course adopted – but in this instance there was nether advice nor assent!'[173]

The Commons waited for Lloyd George to take it into his confidence: but when it assembled on 12 December, Law reported that the new prime minister was confined to bed with a chill, and proposed to adjourn the House for two more days. McKenna, from the Opposition front bench, said Asquith would be present when the time came, to engage in the debate: Asquith had said he regarded himself as a supporter of the new government, so there seemed no question of his becoming Leader of the Opposition. Law made the mistake of observing that there were no 'parties' in the war, which provoked William Pringle, a Liberal MP, to declare that 'we have had enough of that cant'.[174]

Lloyd George's succession marked a massive expansion of government and, in particular, an enormous growth in officials, with civil service numbers rising from 75,000 in 1914 to over 200,000 by 1919, though they would soon start to fall.[175] As new areas of civilian life required direction and control, so officials had to direct and control them, enforcing what would become a torrent of regulations. Realising he had lost his party but conscious that one day he would have to fight an election to retain his position, Lloyd George set up a 'policy unit' known as the Garden Suburb, because it was housed in corrugated-iron buildings in the gardens of 10 and 11 Downing Street. Into these huts he packed young intellectuals of his acquaintance and ordered them to have ideas to help win the war and, perhaps more significantly, improve the country after the peace.

Devonport was appointed food controller on 14 December. Lloyd George established a Ministry of Labour immediately on taking office. By Christmas he had established Ministries of Shipping, Food and Pensions, a key responsibility of the last being to ensure support for the many severely disabled men badly wounded or blinded in the war; and that efforts were made to rehabilitate them and train them for work, if possible. The Red Cross would be closely involved in the ministry's work. A Ministry of Reconstruction would follow in August 1917, of National Service in November, an Air Ministry in January 1918 (to prepare for the creation, that April, of the Royal Air Force) and a Ministry of Information – late in the day, given the government's long-term propaganda effort, in February 1918. This bureaucratic revolution was expensive: one of the first things the new government did was hold a vote of credit in the Commons for another £400 million.

The new order further suspended the constitutional practice dating from Queen Anne that an MP, on his appointment to most ministries (there were some designated exceptions), must resign his seat and fight a by-election to secure his constituents' approval. It was again temporarily dispensed with by an Act passed in a day on 15 December; it would not go permanently until 1919. The argument was that ministers who should be concentrating on securing victory, and available to the Commons to answer questions and explain policy, should not be in their constituencies seeking the favour of voters. Everything was subordinated to directing the war.

Concern grew in the succeeding months about the reduction in Parliament's perceived importance, as Lloyd George attended so rarely. It gave credence to the contention that the war provided an excuse to create a dictatorship that could evade proper accountability. In this the Liberal press thought it detected the hand of Northcliffe – who, as the *Daily News* would soon say, was seeking to fashion a 'mob dictatorship' and 'drive every self-respecting man out of public life.' It continued: 'The object is to destroy the authority and power of parliament . . . Lord Northcliffe . . . has no use for Parliament and is leading the mob against that institution. He is engaged in establishing government by the press.'[176] Northcliffe professed no desire to be in Downing Street, but otherwise his views were not far from what his opponents attributed to him.

As well as seeking to tighten the governance of the country, the new administration sought strategic change in the war. On 15 December Lloyd George, still stricken with a cold and sore throat, summoned Robertson and Haig to Downing Street. He wanted to move two divisions from France to Egypt, for an attack on the Ottomans at Jerusalem; and to move two hundred of Haig's heavy guns to Italy for the winter, returning them in the spring. Haig protested, explaining the preparation needed for the next summer's offensive, which would be undermined by losing so many men and so much materiel. Lloyd George 'could not believe that it was possible to beat the German Armies [on the Western Front] – at any rate, not next year.'[177] Further discussion was postponed until after the Christmas holidays, when, with the help of the French, Lloyd George would make his views about Robertson's and Haig's ideas abundantly clear. So far as he was concerned at this stage, another Somme-like offensive of the sort Haig seemed to have in mind was out of the question.

On 12 December, driven by food shortages at home, but also as part of an attempt to divide their opponents, the Central Powers made their first peace overtures, in notes sent to the neutral United States. The King warned Lloyd George that the overture required 'the utmost care and delicate handling'.[178] The press and public saw it as a sign of weakness, and of the success of the blockade, but also as an attempt to test what *The*

Times described as the 'cohesion' of the new government.[179] The War Cabinet considered the German note, and concluded – as did their allies – that it was, in Hankey's words, 'a boastful and vainglorious piece of propaganda.'[180] It was felt to be a ruse to buy time while enemy sea power was built up. The King, however, urged Lloyd George not to reject the note until it was clear what terms were being offered, not least to keep neutral countries – notably America, where President Wilson had just been re-elected and was seeking to broker a peace – from siding against Britain. Lloyd George put the matter before Parliament on 19 December, when he addressed it for the first time as prime minister.

His throat still sore, he made a speech laden with the tones of destiny:

> I appear before the House of Commons to-day, with the most terrible responsibility that can fall upon the shoulders of any living man, as the chief adviser of the Crown, in the most gigantic War in which the country has ever been engaged – a war upon the event of which its destiny depends. It is the greatest War ever waged. The burdens are the heaviest that have been cast upon this or any other country, and the issues which hang on to it are the gravest that have been attached to any conflict in which humanity has ever been involved. The responsibilities of the new Government have been suddenly accentuated by a declaration made by the German Chancellor, and I propose to deal with that at once.[181]

He, like the French and the Russians, believed the failure of the German note to spell out terms for peace helped prevent the War Cabinet from taking the overtures seriously. He said he saw his ministry's task as 'to complete and make even more effective the mobilisation of all our national resources' and that a 'speedy victory' would not happen.[182] He praised an Army with whose leadership he was about to enter a bitter conflict; he explained he had given the role of leading the Commons to Law 'because we came to the conclusion that it was more than any one man, whatever his energy or physical strength might be, could do to undertake both functions in the middle of a great war.'[183]

He explained he had chosen 'men of administrative and business capacity rather than men of Parliamentary experience, where we were unable to obtain both for the headship of a great Department.' He sought to ingratiate himself with his old clientele in the trades unions, promising 'a franker and fuller recognition of the partnership of Labour in the Government of this country. No Government that has ever been formed to rule this country has had such a share – such a number of men who all their lives have been associated with labour and with the labour organisations of this country. We realised that it is impossible to conduct war without getting the complete and unqualified support of Labour, and we were anxious to obtain their assistance and their counsel for the purpose of the conduct of the War.'[184] He had dispensed with the peace-time system of a cabinet of twenty-three men in the interests of quick decision-making. 'We are all perfectly certain,' he said, 'that the Allies have suffered disaster after disaster through tardiness of decision and action'.[185]

Asquith, who had finally decided to act as Leader of the Opposition, made no response, but when a moment later Lloyd George criticised the practice of no record being kept of cabinet meetings, he intervened to say that it is 'the inflexible unwritten rule of the Cabinet that no member shall take any note or record of the proceedings except the Prime Minister, and the Prime Minister does so for the purpose – and it is the only record of the proceedings kept – of sending his letter to the King.'[186] Lloyd George retorted that 'that is the real difference between the War Committee and the Cabinet', making the matter emblematic of his new order. The War Committee, of whose proceedings notes had been taken, and the War Cabinet were now the same thing.

Lloyd George addressed other pressing issues. 'The food problem,' he said, 'is undoubtedly serious and will be grave unless not merely the Government but the nation is prepared to grapple with it courageously without loss of time.'[187] The 1916 British harvest had been dismal; and because of poor weather only three-eighths of what should have been sown for 1917 was sown. The harvests in Canada and the United States had been poor; Russian grain was unavailable and there were transport problems with Australian foodstuffs. He asked 'the affluent' to refrain from over-consumption and, as the nation was 'fighting for its life', to 'play the game'.[188] He declared that 'every available square yard' had to be used to grow food.[189]

After describing what many of the nation's men had endured in the trenches – including an unprecedented admission about 'the horrors of the Somme' – he proclaimed:

You cannot have absolute equality of sacrifice. In a war that is impossible, but you can have equal readiness to sacrifice from all. There are hundreds of thousands who have given their lives, there are millions who have given up comfortable homes and exchanged them for a daily communion with death; multitudes have given up those whom they love best. Let the nation as a whole place its comforts, its luxuries, its indulgencies, its elegances on a national altar consecrated by such sacrifices as these men have made. Let us proclaim during the War a national Lent. The nation will be better and stronger for it, mentally and morally as well as physically. It will strengthen its fibre, it will ennoble its spirit. Without it we shall not get the full benefit of this struggle.

He detailed potential sacrifices. Law would seek to sequestrate the gains of profiteers, as in the munitions industry; and the government might have to compel every man not in the Army to engage in 'work of national importance'.[190] Men unfit or too old for military service would have to accept direction about where they worked for the duration, to discharge the same moral obligation that fit men were under. The War Cabinet had decided on 14 December to appoint a director of National Service, to whom a military and civil director would report. The former would take charge of recruiting, and hand over men to the War Office; the latter would work according to a schedule of industries in order of national priority, drawn up by the director of National Service.

Vital ones, such as agriculture, would have the first call on labour; less vital ones would have it rationed to them. He explained: 'Labour . . . from non-essential and rationed industries will be available to set free potential soldiers who are at present exempted from military service and to increase the available supply of labour for essential services. This labour will be invited to enrol at once and be registered as war workers on lines analogous to the existing munitions volunteers, with similar provisions as to rates of pay and separation allowance.'[191] All this was possible only because Henderson, in Lloyd George's absence in his sickbed, and his equally patriotic colleague John Hodge, a former puddler at an Ayrshire ironworks and the first man to be appointed minister of labour, had met and persuaded senior trades unionists to accept some sort of conscription for work. Humbert Wolfe, a civil servant closely involved with the establishment of the Labour Department of the Ministry of Munitions, reported that while the labour movement 'might be willing to be conscribed to die for an idea, they were not willing to live (as it might be put) for private profits.'[192]

Lloyd George said the system would be voluntary at first; but if there were insufficient volunteers he would not hesitate to return to Parliament and seek powers to conscript men for industry. 'The nation is fighting for its life,' he said, 'and it is entitled to the best services of all its sons.'[193] He had chosen Neville Chamberlain, Lord Mayor of Birmingham, son of Joe and half-brother of Austen, to be the first director of National Service, after Montagu had refused. It had been with 'very great difficulty' that Chamberlain had been persuaded to take the job, so dedicated had he been to maximising his city's contribution to the war. Now, he would be responsible for creating a 'large industrial army'. Lloyd George did not exaggerate Chamberlain's reluctance: his half-brother had told him it was his duty to do 'national work, *Imperial* work', rather than simply serve Birmingham, to which Neville had replied: 'I suppose I have no right to refuse.'[194] Neville had long nursed a poor opinion of Lloyd George, believing he had mismanaged some munitions disputes, encouraging workers elsewhere to cause trouble by making needless concessions. He took the job with few illusions, and quickly found it a task he lacked both the authority and the machinery to do properly. Montagu had been shrewd to refuse, for whoever would take the blame for a failure to create this new civilian army it would not be Lloyd George.

The new prime minister also mentioned Ireland, about which his conscience could hardly have been clear, and about which even now he could not be frank. 'I wish it were possible to remove the misunderstanding between Britain and Ireland which has for centuries been such a source of misery to the one and of embarrassment and weakness to the other. I wish that that misunderstanding could be removed. I tried once. I did not succeed.' An Irish MP told him to 'try again!' Lloyd George continued: 'The fault was not entirely on one side. I felt the whole time that we were moving in an atmosphere of nervous suspicion and distrust, pervasive, universal, of everything and everybody . . . It was a quagmire of distrust which clogged the footsteps and made progress impossible.'[195] Perhaps he was making excuses in advance for his impending failure to address the realities of Ireland.

Finally, he sought to justify himself in the guise of paying tribute to Asquith.

May I say, and I say it in all sincerity, that it is one of the deepest regrets of my life that I should part from the right hon Gentleman. Some of his friends know how I strove to avert it. For years I served under the right hon Gentleman, and I am proud to say so. I never had a kinder or more indulgent chief. If there were any faults of temper, they were entirely mine, and I have no doubt I must have been difficult at times. No man had greater admiration for his brilliant intellectual attainments, and no man was happier to serve under him. For eight years we differed as men of such different temperaments must necessarily differ, but we never had a personal quarrel.[196]

He claimed he had put country before party throughout the war 'because I realised from the moment the Prussian cannon hurled death at a peaceable and inoffensive little country, that a challenge had been sent to civilisation to decide an issue higher than party, deeper than party, wider than all parties – an issue upon the settlement of which will depend the fate of men in this world for generations, when existing parties will have fallen like dead leaves on the highway. Those issues are the issues that I want to keep in front of the nation, so that we shall not falter or faint in our resolve.'[197]

Asquith showed great magnanimity, congratulating his successor 'with all my heart.' He spoke from the Opposition front bench 'not because I claim in any sense to be the Leader of what is called an Opposition . . . I do not care for the moment by whom the Government of the country is conducted, although I am very glad to see a man of such ability as my right hon Friend in the place which he so worthily occupies – whatever experience I have gained, whatever it is worth, is at the disposal of the Government.'[198] That, too, was not entirely true, or Asquith would have been in the Lords, as Lord Chancellor. He said party differences were only 'in abeyance' and would one day 'revive'.[199] That was why he had stayed in the Commons.

He admitted that 'on the one hand it is to me a relief, and in some ways an unspeakable relief, to be released from a daily burden which has lately been carried under almost insupportable conditions, and, on the other hand, a matter for natural and deep regret that I should be compelled to leave unfinished a task at which I have so long and so strenuously worked.' He added that, under his rule, 'errors of judgment, defects of method, there may have been and there undoubtedly have been.' However, he continued: 'But that there has been slackness or lethargy, infirmity of purpose, above all want of thoroughness and want of whole-heartedness in our concentration upon our common task, not only on my behalf, but on behalf of my late colleagues, as well those who sit upon that bench as those who sit upon this, I emphatically deny. The full story cannot, of course, yet be told.'[200] He concluded: 'I am quite content, when all the facts come to be disclosed, to leave my Administration, and the part which I myself played in it, to the judgment of history.' Few noticed Asquith's contribution, it being overshadowed by the speech of his successor: which *The Times*, forsaking understatement, described as 'a great event in the history of the Empire and of mankind.'[201] Six months later, Mrs Asquith was still steaming: 'I've never got over his abominable treatment by our own men as well as Ll George,' she wrote on 28 May 1917, addressing posterity in her diary.[202] 'You may take it from me – we all know it was a put-up job! And I hope the whole country will know every detail of the most squalid political intrigue of my time or yours or anyone's!'

After consultation with the French on Boxing Day 1916, the Allies rejected the Central Powers' peace notes via the US ambassador in Paris. They told President Wilson they wanted the evacuation of all occupied territories, the restoration of their governments, the dissolution of the Austro-Hungarian Empire, reparations and guarantees of good behaviour: much as insisted upon at Versailles two years later. The fighting would, the Allies announced, continue until victory. Thus 1917 dawned with no end in sight. However, the man now running the British government had more power vested in him than anyone since the Protectorate; the country could not afford for him to fail.

LEND YOUR FIVE SHILLINGS TO YOUR COUNTRY AND

CRUSH THE GERMANS

CHAPTER 8

DICTATORSHIP

I

Barely had Lloyd George put his administration into place than a new German offensive, this time at sea, presented a critical threat to Britain. However, it also caused a sequence of events that helped the Allies win the war. President Woodrow Wilson of America had striven to keep his country neutral, not least because of anti-British feeling among Americans of German and Irish descent: but then Germany's renewal of unrestricted submarine warfare on 31 January 1917, with U-boats seeking to sink any ship approaching British waters, led to losses of American shipping that public opinion in the United States could no longer tolerate. The Germans resumed this policy despite the Chancellor, Bethmann Hollweg, and the Kaiser having agreed in 1916 that to do so would draw America into the conflict, which would lead to a 'war of exhaustion', the end of Germany as a great power and quite possibly the fall of the Hohenzollern dynasty.[1] They were more right than they knew. Wilson was left with no option politically but to bring America into the war and to try to defeat Germany. This radical change of circumstances in which the war was fought not only gave Britain a new major partner, but also transformed an international relationship.

The Germans realised they had had a lucky escape at Jutland and that another battle between the surface fleets would not necessarily end in a German victory. However, as victims of a blockade themselves they understood its effects, and sought to retaliate in kind. They were slowly losing the 'war of starvation', but believed poor harvests in 1916 in America, Argentina and Canada put Britain at serious risk of starvation too: which, because of British reliance on imported food, was correct. The growth in the U-boat fleet (from forty-one vessels in January 1916 to one hundred and three a year later) gave Germany an enormous advantage if it chose to use it, with, they wrongly believed, the possibility of making Britain sue for peace. As in August 1914, it was military men rather than politicians who forced the Kaiser's hand. Restricted submarine warfare had pertained in the North Sea since October 1916, using vessels based in Zeebrugge: now, unrestricted, it would move to the Atlantic, despite Bethmann's reservations.

Wilson broke off diplomatic relations with Germany on 2 February. Most American lines kept their ships in port, and New York's shipping activity almost ceased. As 60 per cent of America's exports went to Western Europe this badly hit the American economy and the New York stock exchange. Wilson still hoped that, in keeping with the tradition of American foreign policy, he could avoid declaring a war that meant an intervention in European politics. But once Arthur Zimmerman, the German foreign minister, admitted the veracity of the so-called Zimmerman telegram on 3 March – it was an offer to Mexico to restore territory lost to America in return for Mexican support of Germany – momentum to bring America into what Wilson called 'a war to end all wars' became unstoppable.

A Bill to allow the arming of merchant ships – which Wilson had initially resisted in case the Germans regarded it as a provocative act and declared war – was passed by the House of Representatives by 403 votes to 14 when the telegram's contents were disclosed. Throughout March 1917 America endured shipping losses, and the US navy decided to recruit 27,000 more men and build 260 more ships to 'chase' submarines. Eventually Wilson realised he had no choice. On 2 April he set out his reasons for entering the conflict, claiming his quarrel was with Germany's leaders for having started a war of aggression on the United States. Both Houses of Congress agreed to the declaration of war by large majorities, but without unanimity. America declared war on the German Empire on 6 April. In 1914 the German military elite neglected, in advocating the invasion of Belgium and the attack on France, to realise that the Schlieffen plan might fail; which was why, two and a half years later, their army was still bogged down on the Western Front. Now that elite would neglect to grasp the consequences of American participation in the war.

When Parliament resumed on 7 February 1917 Lloyd George, sticking to his view that he had more important things to do than sit in the Commons, was attacked for what William Pringle, the Liberal MP, called the 'studied disrespect' of the House that his absence from the debate on the Gracious Speech seemed to signify: Law spoke in his place, and Asquith replied from the Opposition front bench.[2] The prime minister's neglect of the House of Commons seemed to play up to the accusations that he was behaving like a dictator – or certainly like an executive president. Labour made a formal protest; another Liberal MP, Joseph King, complained: 'I wish to express my really profound surprise and disappointment. The House of Commons is not accustomed to this method of treatment, and in my opinion the sooner the Prime Minister finds time to attend to the business of the House of Commons the better the Government will get on with the war.'[3] Lloyd George did not need the Commons. He would, like most dictators, deal with the legislature only when essential. MPs deplored that he found time to make speeches on public platforms and to announce policies there before sharing them with colleagues.

Lloyd George believed the war could be fought as well with words as with weapons; and such was his determination to control the presentation of the government's activities that he absorbed the War Propaganda Bureau, run from Wellington House by Masterman – which he regarded as ineffective and which his friends in the press despised for being too low-key and gentle – into a Department of Information, based in the Foreign Office. John Buchan was brought back from a job in intelligence in France (where he had written speeches and communiqués for Haig) and made director of the new department on 9 February 1917; a year later Lord Beaverbrook, as Aitken had just become, would be made minister of information. (For the moment Beaverbrook was busy, with the cooperation of both Lloyd George and Law, compiling a semi-authorised account of the December coup – or, as Lloyd George ingratiatingly put it on 31 January, 'that interesting and memorable episode or series of episodes, in which you took such a determining part.')[4] Buchan had been Milner's private secretary in South Africa and a key member of his Kindergarten, and earlier in the war had worked for the Press Bureau. His fame resided in his work as an adventure novelist, which had made him a hero of schoolboys and in clubland, not least for his spy novel *The Thirty-Nine Steps*, published in 1915, and its sequel of the following year, *Greenmantle*. Buchan was the war's leading popular historian, for as well as turning out ripping yarns about white men he was also writing an instant history of the conflict, *Nelson's History of the Great War*, in twenty-four volumes. He understood the propaganda uses of the press and the cinema far better than Masterman: and saw the importance of directing information about the war to America.

Lloyd George engaged in business with an energy unknown in Whitehall, and radically differently from how Asquith had prosecuted the war. The War Cabinet met daily from Mondays to Fridays, sometimes at weekends and occasionally twice or three times a day. It spawned committees: and Lloyd George also summoned an Imperial Conference of prime ministers from the Empire, with Austen Chamberlain, as Secretary of State, representing India. In March 1917 this gave rise to an Imperial War Cabinet, just in time for America's entry to the war. It met several times in London that spring, involving the governments of the main imperial territories with the conduct of the war. It, too, bred bureaucracy. By the summer of 1917 there were over a hundred interdepartmental committees, putting a huge strain on the civil service.

Civil servants were not the only people to struggle under the weight of this new bureaucracy. Lloyd George, for all his organisational determination, could not cope with the consequent workflow. He soon gave up approving the agendas and minutes of War Cabinet meetings, leaving the task to Hankey, whose power increased accordingly. Much of what the War Cabinet discussed was highly secret and the minutes initially had limited circulation even among ministers. Those schooled in more traditional ways frequently expressed dislike of the new system, and of Lloyd George's methods: not everyone supported how he had gathered so much power to himself and to a chosen few, leaving out senior ministers who would normally have been closely consulted about the governance of the nation. In February Hankey recorded a talk with a 'disgruntled' Long, who called the system 'unworkable'.[5]

Another consequence of the Imperial Conference was that Lloyd George invited Jan Smuts to join the War Cabinet. Smuts, who attended on behalf of South Africa, was a lieutenant general in the British Army, despite having fought for the Boers in the Second Boer War. Lloyd George had been impressed by the originality of his ideas and felt it essential to retain his energies and insight. His contributions would be significant, not least his advocacy of establishing the Royal Air Force. It showed a breadth of mind on Lloyd George's part to accommodate him, because he was a fervent advocate of Haig's policy of attrition on the Western Front, a view that would be shaken after the Third Battle of Ypres in the late summer and autumn of 1917, and which the prime minister barely shared in the first place.

Considering his next step over Christmas 1916, Lloyd George still wanted to shift the Allied attack to the Italian front, concentrating on defence rather than offence in the west. By pressing an attack with Britain's Italian allies he believed the Central Powers would be forced to divert resources from the two existing fronts, rendering them vulnerable in those places. The two principal soldiers in His Majesty's Army, Robertson and Haig, profoundly disagreed. Despite the heavy losses on the Somme, they continued to believe that the war could only be won on the Western Front, and that Britain's military strength would be undermined there if troops were taken away to fight in Italy. Given how difficult it was proving to feed and equip the men sent there, Lloyd George had raised the Salonica campaign when the War Cabinet met on 9 December, and again after Christmas.[6] Despite so much resistance to his views, Lloyd George was determined to use his prerogative as the King's first minister to get his way, and not just on Salonica; getting his way, rather than allowing what he considered inferior strategists to get theirs, was why he had wanted the job. Had Asquith still been in charge a disloyal colleague might have leaked details of these problems to the newspapers. As it was, the public were almost entirely unaware of them, as the censor forbade mention of them in the press.

Still looking for alternatives to the western strategy, Lloyd George had in early January been to Rome to discuss with Allied leaders how to win the war; the conference achieved nothing. Then Haig, promoted to field marshal on 1 January, came to see him in London on 15 January with Robert Nivelle, the new French commander-in-chief, who at a turbulent time in French politics had replaced Joffre on 12 December. Lloyd George had met Nivelle in Rome and was impressed by him, and their meeting produced an outcome of unfortunate significance. In his admiration for Nivelle, Lloyd George abandoned what his colleagues thought to be his intense opposition to another offensive on the Western Front, to support one planned by Nivelle. So low was his regard for British generals by that stage of the war that he seemed to imagine anything a French one suggested must be a superior strategy. He would be proved disastrously wrong.

Haig, who wanted another western offensive, then brought Nivelle to London to present what he hoped would be a *fait accompli* to Lloyd George. However, the prime minister told Haig that that was no longer how things were done: any offensive would happen only if the War Cabinet sanctioned it.[7] Lloyd George left Haig in no doubt of his views, or indeed about his traits of character. In the process, he showed that he intended to discharge his high functions without tact or deployment of the mealy mouth. 'His general conclusions,' a seething Haig recorded, 'were that the French Army was better all round, and was able to gain success at less cost of life. That much of our losses on the Somme was [*sic*] wasted, and that the country would not stand any more of that sort of thing. That to win, we must attack a soft front, and we could not find that on the Western Front.'[8] Haig tried to counter, explaining Britain's duty to help relieve the pressure on the French at Verdun – something he wished the Army he commanded to do in accordance with an initiative he designed and led, and not one designed by the French army, for which he had mild contempt. Despite being in league with Nivelle, Haig sought to strip away the prime minister's illusions about the discipline of the French army – about which Haig would be proved right after several mutinies during the coming year.

When the opportunity came for him to argue his case, Nivelle was highly persuasive. A fluent Anglophone – his mother was English – he persuaded the War Cabinet to support a 'breakthrough' offensive, which he promised would not be like the Somme. He said that, if he was wrong, the offensive would be abandoned within days. Having heard Nivelle's proposals, the ministers had two more meetings, on the evening of 15 January and the next morning, to discuss its feasibility. The British Army would relieve the French along a large part of the front to allow the French to assault the Chemin-des-Dames, west of Reims, in what would become known as the Second Battle of the Aisne. Approval was eventually given: the first of 1917's military failures was set in train.

As Haig might have gathered from Lloyd George's unflattering remarks to him in January, the prime minister was also thinking ahead about improving military direction, contemplating a development that would come to fruition a year later: a unified Allied command that, reflecting his view about the superiority of French generals, might end up being led by a Frenchman. He signalled this to senior commanders at a meeting in Calais on 26 February, ostensibly called to discuss reservations Haig had now developed about the Nivelle plan having studied its logistics more closely, notably that the French railway system could not support the necessary troop and ammunition movements. Although, as Haig had seen, Lloyd George could be direct when it suited him, he often preferred to avoid direct confrontation, and resorted to more Machiavellian methods. With Lloyd George's connivance, and following his discussions with Aristide Briand, his French counterpart, Nivelle suggested a joint command from 1 March. He made it clear that he should lead it, having authority over the BEF, though with a senior British staff officer at his headquarters as a liaison officer. For all Lloyd George's cunning, this manipulative use of Nivelle would force the confrontation with Haig, and indeed Robertson, that he had been so keen to avoid.

The plan came as news to Robertson, who despite being CIGS had not been asked to a War Cabinet meeting two days earlier at which this had been settled. Derby had also been absent, and was furious, as war secretary, at not being consulted; Esher noted that 'Eddy Derby . . . complained bitterly of the ignorance in which he was kept. He was not told a word of the arrangements planned for the Calais conference.'[9] It was also kept from Haig. Lloyd George egged on Nivelle during his presentation of his plans 'to keep nothing back . . . as to his disagreements with Marshal Haig.'[10] This, according to Haig, surprised even Nivelle. Haig outlined his objections to parts of Nivelle's plan, notably the idea of attacking Vimy Ridge, because it would mean attacking into a pocket on the Hindenburg Line, the defensive line the Germans had built that winter towards the eastern end of the front, following their failure to break through at Verdun. Lloyd George asked the French to propose a system of command, so that he, Robertson and Haig could discuss it; this was done before dinner that evening, with a view to discussing it the following day. When Robertson and Haig had dined with the French – Lloyd George pleaded illness and did not join them – they were given the French plan. They went to discuss it with Lloyd George, who sprang on them the proposal that as the French would have the larger number of troops in the forthcoming offensive, the War Cabinet had decided the French commander-in-chief would command the British Army.

Haig said it would be 'madness', and that 'I did not believe our troops would fight under French leadership.'[11] It became a battle of wills, with the prime minister telling Haig that he and Robertson now had to carry out the decision of the War Cabinet. Robertson was equally outraged, the more so when Hankey told him and Haig that 'LG had not received full authority from the War Cabinet' for the proposals. 'We agreed we would rather be tried by Court Martial than betray the Army by agreeing to its being placed under the French. R[obertson] agreed that we must resign rather than be partners in this transaction.' Haig recorded: 'And so we went to bed, thoroughly disgusted with our Government and the Politicians.' The next morning the French generals apologised to Haig for the 'insult' Briand's paper – which they confirmed had been drawn up with the full cooperation of Lloyd George – had rendered to the British Army.

Haig, who had long thought Lloyd George 'cunning . . . shifty and unreliable' and for whom the episode confirmed his perfidy, enlisted the King in support. He wrote to him as the two-day conference ended, outlining Lloyd George's duplicity in leading him and Robertson to believe they had gone to a meeting about transport, only to be asked to rubber-stamp a temporary reorganisation of the command of the Army. He warned the King that he should be 'watchful, and prevent any steps being taken which will result in our Army being broken up and incorporated in French Corps.'[12] Haig also told him that Lloyd George claimed the French insisted upon the change, while the French said it was being done at the insistence of the British cabinet. This would not have raised the King's estimation of his prime minister. Haig ended by saying he would, of course, resign were it felt another general could do better – itself a slightly disingenuous point, since Haig knew that even if Lloyd George were to ignore the King's objection to such a course, he could not ignore the feelings of the Unionists. 'At this great crisis in our History,' Haig concluded with full pomp and circumstance, 'my sole object is to serve my King and Country wherever I can be of most use, and with full confidence I leave myself in Your Majesty's hands to decide what is best for me to do at this juncture.'[13]

Having thus lighted the blue touchpaper Haig awaited the reply, which came from Stamfordham on 5 March. The King's private secretary, who had already warned Derby to be 'extremely watchful' where Lloyd George was concerned, said Haig's letter had made 'anything but agreeable reading to His Majesty', not least because the King realised the plan had been kept from him too. Whether by chance or deliberately, the King did not receive minutes of the crucial War Cabinet meeting until 28 February, too late for him to object. The 'momentous change' proposed in the new arrangements would, Stamfordham stressed, have required 'further explanation' before the Sovereign's consent could be given. The King, who believed Haig's resignation would be 'disastrous', realised that Haig and Robertson had been ambushed. In his diary on 1 March the King noted after a 'long talk' with Robertson that Lloyd George 'makes things very difficult for him.'[14] Stamfordham assured Haig the King would do all he could to protect his interests. The Sovereign told his prime minister that 'no interference should occur in Haig's position'.[15] Derby described the plan as 'preposterous' and assured Haig he would have objected had he known of it. All had had an education in Lloyd George's methods.

The prime minister, according to Miss Stevenson, told the King that 'the most important thing seems to me that the lives of our gallant soldiers should not be squandered as they were last summer, but that they should be used to the best advantage.' He would not let Haig forget the Somme, and with some justice. Thanks to the diplomatic genius of Hankey and of General Sir Frederick Maurice, Director of Military Operations since 1915 and grandson of the Victorian divine Frederick Denison Maurice, a face-saving agreement was constructed, which gave Nivelle command for this operation, but allowed Haig a right of appeal to his own government if he felt Nivelle's plan threatened the safety of the British Army. When Nivelle wrote to Haig officially on 28 February to ask for details of the orders he was giving to his Army, Haig described it crustily as 'a type of letter which no gentleman could have drafted, and it also is one which certainly no C in C of this great British Army should receive without protest.'[16]

Most politicians would have learned from this, but not Lloyd George. Indeed, the distrust and hostility Haig and Robertson felt towards him after this attempt to sideline them only hardened his resolve – based more on prejudice than on efficacy, despite Haig's shortcomings having been exposed in the Somme catastrophe – to trammel the authority of his military top brass. The subsequent failure of the Nivelle offensive at least prevented him from insisting on the execution of another of his ideas, to attack Austria from Italy over the Alps: both, in Robertson's view, 'proved that he had no intention of being in any way guided by the advice of British military authorities unless it coincided with his own ideas.'[17]

Derby, who had a reputation as a pushover, having seen Lloyd George in action as prime minister, was now inspired not to allow him to ride roughshod over him. On 6 March he reminded the prime minister he had been promised, on his appointment, that he would be invited to attend all meetings affecting his office. But then 'on Saturday, the 24th February, a War Cabinet was held at which a momentous decision affecting the conduct of the war in France was reached, but to which no representative of the War Office was summoned. As this decision has already been acted upon, I see no use in arguing the merits of the matter, but I earnestly hope that steps will be taken which will prevent a recurrence of such procedure.'[18] It was typical of Lloyd George that, a week and a half later, he sent Derby a reply evading entirely the point he had raised. Ministers would simply have to get used to a less courteous, less consultative, more dictatorial style.

II

It was also Lloyd George's style to seek to apportion blame where it could do the least damage to him and, preferably, the maximum to his opponents: he was not above stabbing anyone in the back if it suited him. It was no surprise, therefore, that he took no steps in the spring of 1917 to prevent the Dardanelles Commission publishing an interim report, critical of a number of his former colleagues, but without publishing the evidence on which it was based: that, and a final report, would come after the war. Lloyd George allowed this because it presented a useful *post facto* justification for his coup against Asquith. The report showed a high level of dysfunction in the conduct of the war. It concluded that in the early months of the conflict the way in which ministers had taken important decisions had been 'clumsy and inefficient'; though Asquith, as one of the prime targets of criticism, could not understand why that observation had been made, for it fell outside the time span the inquiry had been supposed to examine; and no evidence was adduced for the conclusion.[19] However, it served to smear the reputation of the then prime minister. *The Times* said it proved that Churchill – whom Northcliffe despised – had been the 'prime mover', though it praised him for at least having been consistent 'when all the rest were vacillating'.[20] But it called this 'the consistency of a dangerous enthusiast, who sought expert advice only where he could be sure of moulding it to his own opinion'. It acclaimed his 'suppression' in the May 1915 reshuffle, a comment indicative of the hostility that would accompany attempts to restore him to office.

When Hankey saw an advance proof of the report in February 1917 he thought it 'a very unfair document and much too hard on Asquith, dwelling insufficiently on the difficulties of the times and the tiresome personalities whom Asquith had to handle.' Hankey believed it against the public interest to publish it. Balfour agreed; other colleagues, perhaps also feeling the need to justify the recent coup, dissented. However, the War Cabinet obtained Parliament's agreement to edit out what Hankey called 'some of the more dangerous passages'.[21] Asquith's own expectations, or fears, of the report added to the strain he was under in the autumn of 1916. He defended himself in a long Commons statement on 20 March, making it clear he was angered that the report had been published while the war was on, when far graver matters had to be settled. Publishing without the evidence carried 'a grave risk of injustice to individuals' and to the national interest.[22]

Asquith said that, having been confronted with problems on an unprecedented scale, he would be content to await 'the judgment of history' on his conduct. Nonetheless he questioned the depiction of Kitchener – who could not defend himself – in the report. 'Lord Kitchener by no means was the solitary and taciturn autocrat in the way he has been depicted . . . it is a complete mistake to suggest or to suppose that Lord Kitchener lived in isolation, and did not consult military opinion at the War Office and elsewhere during the conduct of this War. I am speaking of what is in my own knowledge, and I can absolutely deny that that was the case.'[23] He added: 'We were bound in military matters to defer to the judgment of the great soldier who had patriotically undertaken the duties of Secretary of State for War.'

Asquith was slow to anger, but this was an exception: 'Nothing in connection with this Report . . . has filled me with more indignation and disgust than that the publication of the criticisms made in it of Lord Kitchener's conduct and capacity should have been taken advantage of by those who only two years ago were in a posture of almost slavish adulation to belittle his character, and, so far as they can, to defile his memory.'[24] Kitchener, he said, had not taken the decision to support the Dardanelles campaign lightly; he had said there would not be sufficient available troops to make it a joint operation. Asquith disputed that the

War Council had inadequately assessed Kitchener's advice. 'Lord Kitch-ener may have been right or wrong, but no one can doubt that those are grave and weighty reasons, and it is perfectly monstrous to sug-gest that we, the civilian members of the War Council, in view of that veto – that temporary veto – from our great military authority, should have interfered to overrule him, and say, "You must send out the 29th Division, and send it at once." '[25] Had the War Council overruled Kitch-ener, he would have resigned, 'and that would have exposed us to the universal and just condemnation of our fellow citizens.'[26] For the new prime minister it was enormously convenient that a man so vigorously attacked in the report was dead.

Later, in the debate on the interim report, Churchill sought to justify the War Council's and his decisions. 'I am defending myself,' he said, 'but I am defending other interests besides my own. I am defending the Gov-ernment of which I was a member. I am defending the chief under whom I served, and who had acted on the advice which I had tendered. I am defending the authority and dignity of the Admiralty, because, believe me, you could do it no greater injury than to weaken the confidence of the officers and men of the Fleet in the orders they get from the Admiralty by favouring the impression that those orders had been made in a reckless, careless, amateur, and a haphazard way.'[27] If Lloyd George was using the report to bury Asquith, Churchill, commendably, refused to help him.

He conceded that Fisher had objected: but rejected the idea that he, Asquith and Kitchener – as ministers – had no right to discount that objection; and he referred to the bombardments in March 1915 when the loss of life in several days had been, he said, 'less than a battalion will lose on the Western Front in half an hour in their assembly trenches, or moving up to the attack . . . We must cultivate and observe a sense of proportion in these terrible matters. I may be accused of being reckless or sanguine, but I shall plead that if I am it is because the sense of propor-tion with which I have judged this War from the very beginning, is different in important respects from the accepted standard.'[28] He too was content to be judged when there had been time to reflect on the events of March and April 1915: 'When this matter is passed in final review before the tribunal of history, I have no fear where the sympathies of those who come after us will lie. Your Commission may condemn the men who tried to force the Dardanelles, but your children will keep their condemnation for all who did not rally to their aid.'[29]

The other side of Lloyd George's vindictiveness towards his opponents was his determination to surround himself with people who owed him total loyalty, having dispatched those who did not. He sometimes made some excellent choices, even if it meant breaking the mould of the usual characters from the landed and upper-middle classes who served their country in Whitehall and Westminster. His approach to the running of the Admiralty in the spring of 1917, when he became worried by food shortages and rising prices, was an object lesson in this.

In late April, urged on by Hankey and with Beatty's approval, he ordered Admiralty officials to introduce convoys, to try to prevent the destruction of so much merchant shipping: and losses were never again so great. Jellicoe, as First Sea Lord, had led opposition to the convoy system, but became a wholehearted convert. Nevertheless, Lloyd George relieved him of responsibility for overseeing naval and merchant marine shipbuilding, handing it over to Eric Geddes, elder brother of Auckland. Geddes became a Civilian Lord and Controller of the Admiralty, with a formal War Staff under him. It was not just another example of Lloyd George sending in a businessman where a politician had failed, but also an example of his management style in getting his chosen man in by inventing a new job with a new title, and which swallowed up all or much of the role of someone else: in this case Jellicoe.

Geddes epitomised the Lloyd George man of 'push and go' who would provide the dynamism for victory. After being expelled from his Edinburgh school in the early 1890s for ignoring his studies and preferring to play rugby, he had become, among other things, a lumberjack, before progressing to be deputy general manager of the North-Eastern Railway. Lloyd George brought him into the Ministry of Munitions soon after its formation in 1915 to oversee production first of machine guns and then of the filling of shells. When shell production had risen but the railway system in France proved unequal to the task of transporting them rapidly to the front, Lloyd George (who had just succeeded Kitchener) sent Geddes out (without Haig being properly consulted) in July 1916 to tackle the problem. He went in the rank of major general, despite having had no Army experience; and he went to the Admiralty as a vice-admiral on the same basis. Luckily, Geddes had got on well with Haig, and his ability to work 'amicably' with the Army was taken as a reason to send him to deal with shipping.[30] He did, though, become something of a figure of fun to many of his colleagues, not least through his almost Prussian enthusiasm for wearing any uniform to which he was entitled.

When Geddes joined the Admiralty to oversee shipbuilding he found the department badly run, echoing the Downing Street view that it was rife with maladministration. Even Northcliffe (whom Lloyd George would soon divert from mischief-making in London by appointing him head of a war mission to the United States) had turned on Carson, the First Lord, with an editorial in the *Daily Mail* on 2 May complaining about 'Too Much Civilian Control'.[31] A week later the paper called for food rationing, invoking the shade of Asquith in saying that a 'wait and see' food policy could have catastrophic results. Lloyd George realised Carson had few managerial gifts, and was too inclined to agree with admirals, notably Jellicoe, whom Lloyd George disdained. Milner, who had applied his considerable mind to the workings of the Admiralty, had also impressed on Lloyd George that he had to replace Carson. The prime minister did this, Hankey recorded, 'by the simple expedient of "booting" him up to the War Cabinet', where ministers had no portfolios.[32] Lloyd George then had to work out with whom to replace him, the post of First Lord having become even more sensitive than it already had been. The Army was now joining in the attack on the management of the Senior Service, using the difficulties there to distract attention from its own shortcomings.

Haig and Robertson agreed with Geddes and Milner's assessment of the Admiralty. Haig used the trouble to open a second front on the War Cabinet by protesting about the 'seriously inefficient state of the Admiralty': he caricatured this in his diary by writing that 'the First Lord (Carson) has recently married [to a woman thirty years his junior], is very tired, and leaves everything to a number of incompetent sailors!'[33] Geddes told Haig that Jellicoe was 'feeble to a degree and vacillating'. Lloyd George toyed with the idea (suggested by the War Cabinet secretary himself) of replacing Carson with Hankey but, as Hankey noted with his customarily monumental self-regard, he was 'practically irreplaceable' in his existing job. Even Robertson was considered, but said he would refuse because he could not face becoming a politician: his candidacy had been advanced by Haig, who had had differences of opinion with him over strategy – upsetting the prime minister's belief that Robertson was Haig's front man and apologist.

Therefore on 6 July – after a rough passage with Carson, whom he was afraid to disoblige – the prime minister offered the Admiralty to the ruthlessly efficient Geddes, who may have just been made a vice admiral but was not even a Member of Parliament. A by-election was arranged for him at Cambridge, which he fortunately won. His rise from railway executive to First Lord of the Admiralty within two years was emblematic of Lloyd George's business methods. He told Riddell he believed Geddes 'will double the output of mercantile shipping'.[34] The new First Lord and the prime minister agreed about Jellicoe: he lasted until Christmas Eve 1917 when he resigned as First Sea Lord, citing among other factors the unacceptable influence of Northcliffe on Lloyd George and naval matters. Geddes revolutionised the organisation of the Admiralty, forging the same direct relationship with shipyards that the War Office had with munitions factories; and Jellicoe's marginalisation and then removal ended what was left of the institutional resistance to the convoy system. By Christmas 1917 Britain's command of the seas, in peril from the submarine threat the previous spring, was now re-established.

There was a much older and more dangerous friend who commanded Lloyd George's attention once he had taken power, and that was Churchill. He remained widely despised in the Commons; but his thoughtful contributions to a secret session of the House on 10 May, about food rationing and conscription of labour, seemed to alter perceptions, and give Lloyd George a means of bringing him back inside the tent. Churchill argued that Allied strategy should be of defence and not attack until the Americans were fighting – which, as the troops required thorough training for trench warfare, would be some months yet. Guest, the chief whip (and Churchill's cousin), reported to Lloyd George that MPs considered Churchill's speech to have been 'a fine statesmanlike effort'.[35] The prime minister's appreciation of this performance helped repair a breach between them over his lack of a government post: a few days earlier Scott had recorded that Churchill's 'tone was rather bitter in speaking of Lloyd George whom he had evidently come to consider his destined antagonist'.[36]

In the succeeding weeks Lloyd George gave much thought to how Churchill – whom he had solemnly promised not to promote to the cabinet as a condition of Unionist support for his coalition – might be brought back. The prime minister's health, which had a habit of imploding whenever he was under stress, was poor. He worked long hours, and things were going badly. Even the indefatigable Hankey was felled by toothache. The War Cabinet became badly behind on its agenda, to the point where Hankey feared that the same sclerosis that had brought down the Asquith coalition would occur again. Northcliffe told Lloyd George he thought the government even more unpopular than its predecessor, though Miss Stevenson felt he made that observation because Lloyd George refused to consult him. The prime minister told her on 19 May he was considering a reshuffle. 'He says he wants someone in who will cheer him up and help and encourage him, and who will not be continually coming to him with a long face and telling him that everything is going wrong,' she noted.[37] The main depressive was Law, who was immovable. She added: 'I think D is thinking of getting Winston in in some capacity.' She knew they had talked about the prospect: and that Lloyd George 'knows his [Churchill's] limitations and realises he is eaten up with conceit.' Nevertheless, Lloyd George valued Churchill's spirit, resilience, energy, charisma, indefatigability and, despite his record of mistakes, his experience. The prime minister also craved support from the Liberal establishment, who despised him, and knew the only way to do that was to tempt Asquith back, thereby negating the reason why so many Liberals loathed him. He offered him the Woolsack, which he declined.

Some warmed to the idea of Churchill returning, but others were resolutely against it. 'To me he appears not as a statesman, but as a politician of keen intelligence, lacking in those puissant qualities that are essential in a man who is to conduct the business of our country through the coming year,' Esher told Haig on 30 May. 'I hope, therefore, that he remains outside the Government.'[38] Admiral Lord Beresford warned Law on 2 June that after Antwerp and Gallipoli, not to mention his orders to the Fleet during the 1914 Ulster crisis, he had 'the most violent feeling with regard to his ever being in office again.'[39] Beresford, to whom half-measures and understatement were unknown, said he was considering forming a committee to hold meetings all over the country denouncing Churchill if he were appointed; that he had 'papers and proofs' (of what he did not say) that he would make public; and that he had seen 'several Editors of important papers' who were prepared to unleash the dogs to help 'avoid this scandal and danger to the State.'

Curzon, who carried far heavier metal, also wrote to Law, on 4 June, to remind him he had only joined the War Cabinet 'on the distinct understanding that W Ch was not to be a member of the Govt.'[40] If Law told Lloyd George this it seems not to have troubled him. He asked Smuts to prepare Churchill for an offer of the Air Board instead of Munitions, which had been discussed, because Munitions was now routine whereas Air could become 'of decisive importance' in the war.[41] Smuts observed that 'in spite of the strong party opposition to this appointment, I think you will do the country a real service by appointing a man of his calibre to this department'. Sir George Younger, chairman of the Conservative Party, wrote directly to Lloyd George – he refused to bother Law as his son had just been killed in action – to warn him of the strain on Tory loyalty that would be caused by appointing Churchill to replace Lord Cowdray, who ran the Air Board under Derby. He felt Lloyd George failed to appreciate the difficulties that already existed in making Tories accept much of Lloyd George's programme: this might be the last straw.

Derby, who wished to retain Cowdray, had a frank exchange with Lloyd George about it. Derby was alarmed at the prospect of Churchill's interfering in the War Office, a predictable problem given how he had behaved while at the Admiralty and even in his last non-job as Chancellor of the Duchy. Curzon, having failed to make his point the first time, wrote to Lloyd George to make it again, warning him Churchill would be 'intensely unpopular' with the Army and Navy.[42] 'Is it worthwhile,' Curzon asked, 'to incur all these risks and to override some of those who are your most faithful colleagues & allies merely in order to silence a possible tribune of the people whom in my judgment the people will absolutely decline to follow?' Even Cowdray wrote to Lloyd George about the success the Air Board had had under him, not only in turning out more machines, but in turning out better ones than the Germans. One of his concerns was that 'Winston will see that he, and he alone, gets all the credit from the very brilliant achievements of the Air Services' if appointed.[43] He asked: 'Is it wise for you to have, as one of your Ministers, a dangerously ambitious man who will, I believe be able to point to achievements by the Air Services . . . that have largely revolutionised the war and being the means of bringing about the peace' because this would 'lead him to think that he was the most important man (in the eyes of the country) in the Government & therefore the proper man to make a bid for the Premiership.' The last remark shows that Cowdray at least understood his audience.

Lloyd George was sufficiently concerned that he asked Guest to enquire of Churchill whether he would return to the Duchy of Lancaster, if various duties were assigned to it. The answer was 'no'. All Churchill wanted was to 'help to beat the "Hun" ', either from the War Cabinet (which he said he would do without salary, a remarkable offer given how little disposable income he had), or in charge of any 'War Department'. Guest's 'utmost powers of persuasion' failed to make any difference – Churchill could not or would not grasp how profoundly rank-and-file Tories loathed him. The chief whip suggested the only course open to Lloyd George was to try to appeal to his Unionist colleagues to change their minds.[44]

Changing people's minds was, however, no longer the Lloyd George way. If the prime minister could not win consent, he would do as he wished, and dare colleagues to challenge him. On 17 July – the very day the King founded the House of Windsor – Churchill returned to government, as minister of munitions; Cowdray survived, for the moment, at the Air Board. Churchill was not allowed in the War Cabinet: that would have been too much for the Unionists, to a man furious at his return. Knowing how the land lay, it was a rare matter on which Lloyd George did not consult Law, who was presented with a *fait accompli*; in this instance, and recognising the depth of Unionist feeling against Churchill and, it seems, of his own discourtesy in bypassing Law, Lloyd George lacked the guts to tell Law himself, so sent Beaverbrook to do it. Law had again to face the choice of backing Lloyd George or bringing him down: he chose the former, and managed to quell the revolt in his own party. However, Long told him that 'the real effect has been to destroy all confidence in Ll G. It is widely held that for purposes of his own quite apart from the war he has deceived and jockeyed us.'[45] It seemed it was as much the prime minister's fear of how Churchill might destabilise the government if his exclusion continued as any friendship between the two men that had caused Lloyd George to bring him back.

Churchill replaced Addison, who was appointed the first minister of reconstruction. The ministry's creation showed the government's understanding that soldiers, or the widows and orphans of the fallen, could not be expected to endure the conditions the working class had tolerated in the era of the Great Unrest before 1914. No one was yet using the slogan 'Homes fit for heroes', but that was what was meant. However, until Germany was defeated little could be done except make plans: Addison's job would be as much overseeing social reconstruction – a fair deal for everyone with the support of an embryo welfare state – and its problems as physical and material rebuilding. In the course of shuffling his team Lloyd George made Montagu Secretary of State for India. He had been under-secretary in the India Office from 1910 to 1914, but it was his closeness to Asquith that mattered to Lloyd George, and gave the appointment a symbolic significance.

Montagu's return to office was a consequence of the report of the Mesopotamia Commission. The India Office had during the spring of 1916 handed over responsibility for the campaign in Mesopotamia (conducted largely by Indian army troops), but the Secretary of State, Austen Chamberlain, had had ultimate responsibility when Kut-el-Amara was besieged and for the failure to provide proper medical services for the men who fought there. Although Chamberlain's officials had largely kept him in ignorance of what was happening, the report included him in the list of those criticised either directly or by implication. He resigned, despite an attempt by Lloyd George to dissuade him. The respect accorded him by the public and colleagues for this principled act, ironically, won Chamberlain new status in the Unionist Party, and undermined F.E. Smith's *bon mot* that 'Austen always played the game and always lost it.'[46]

Geddes soon complained to Law that Churchill sought to interfere in Admiralty matters, and Law had Lloyd George tell Churchill to keep his nose out of other departments' affairs. Not even the War Cabinet's members were consulted about the changes, and senior ministers outside it – such as Derby – were appalled at the lack of collegiality. Derby offered his resignation over Churchill's appointment, but Lloyd George assured him he would not interfere in the War Office: so Derby withdrew it, though insisted that a 'great mistake' had been made.[47] Lloyd George, with his customary grace, blamed Law for not having kept Derby informed; Derby then discovered Law had not been consulted either.

Gwynne wrote to Esher on 19 July that 'I have never, since the war began, seen such indignation against a Government or man as is raging now against Lloyd George for the appointment of Winston.'[48] Asquith told Sylvia Henley that Smuts, with whom he had had lunch, 'thinks the present lot helpless and doomed, but is against forcing matters to a head.'[49] Beaverbrook called this the moment when 'Lloyd George's throne tottered. But it did not fall.'[50] Writing to Lady Bathurst, Gwynne noted that 'one of Winston's chief duties will be to deal with Labour, and if there is one man more unqualified, by his lack of tact, judgment and character, than Winston, I have yet to find him. It is an appalling disaster . . .'⁵¹ C. P. Scott and Robert Donald, editor of the *Daily Chronicle*, both wrote to Churchill to express congratulations; but by far the most sensible letter was from his aunt, Lady Wimborne, who ended with 'my advice is stick to munitions & don't try to run the Govt!'⁵²

Churchill realised how unfair he had been to Lloyd George for criticising him for not promoting him sooner: he had not grasped the scale of the opposition to him, and how much political capital Lloyd George had expended to recall him. Nor was his job straightforward. Riddell told him on 19 July that in the ministry 'most of the leading men are in a state of mutiny and that resignations are imminent.'⁵³ Nevertheless Churchill's time at Munitions was one of his most successful spells in government, though the infrastructure had been set up for him by Lloyd George and refined by Addison. He brought his customary vigour and commitment to the job, and his experience in that ministry had an unlikely effect on him; it convinced him that the productive effort of the munitions industry, superintended and controlled by the state, was 'the greatest argument for State Socialism ever produced.'⁵⁴ Although many in the political class deplored how it had been done, the reshuffle suggested a dynamism, and a determination to move on ministers, such as Carson, who had not proved suitable for their posts, that pleased even Esher. He wrote on 28 July to Murray of Elibank – one of Lloyd George's cronies-in-chief, so Esher's motives might be questioned – to proclaim that 'LG is the one vital asset left to us.'⁵⁵

Another man Lloyd George wished to keep close – and who, unlike Churchill, would almost defy him to do so – was Northcliffe. In Asquith's time ministers had become obsessed with the press; Lloyd George was especially sensitive to its influence, and realised Northcliffe was the man from whom he had most to fear. In time he would be cured of the awe in which he held the owner of *The Times* and the *Daily Mail*, but in the early months of his rule that stage had not yet been reached. Northcliffe was vexed about Britain's inability to get its message across to America before it entered the war, something he believed essential to get it to do so. Using his myriad intelligence sources across the Atlantic, he regularly informed Lloyd George how poor a fist Britain was making of presenting its case. It was not least following his advocacy that the new information department was formed. It was, it seems, no coincidence that on the evening of 25 February a German destroyer three miles off-shore shelled Northcliffe's country house at Broadstairs, killing a woman and her baby fifty yards away, wounding two others and causing shrapnel to rain down on the house. The Germans knew exactly how significant Northcliffe was in binding together British public opinion.

Once America entered the war Lloyd George swiftly appreciated that someone with good contacts there should head a mission to help integrate the two nations' approach to the war: there was no special relationship upon which to build. Balfour had undertaken a mission but was due home; there was talk of replacing him with Grey, but Lloyd George wanted to send a 'new man' and Northcliffe seemed to him an ideal choice. The two main purposes of the mission were to improve publicity about the war to a country that was careful to describe itself as an associate rather than an ally, and to improve business relations for supply reasons – and, third, Lloyd George was determined to get Northcliffe out of the way. Although it was a high-risk strategy, given the candidate's combustibility, megalomania and refusal to take instruction, Lloyd George offered him the post in April; but, for all his apparent thirst for power and influence, he initially refused it, perhaps realising the ulterior motive behind the suggestion. Balfour, when informed of the offer to Northcliffe, was horrified and expressed his deep opposition: something Lloyd George, typically, ignored and, even more typically, kept to himself. He resolved to try again.

On 24 May the War Cabinet discussed the unhelpful nature of articles in the Northcliffe press that Hankey recorded 'supply most valuable propaganda to the enemy'; yet Lloyd George proceeded nonetheless with his plan. Hankey, far from stupid, knew this 'is really a dodge to get rid of Northcliffe, of whom he [Lloyd George] is afraid.' Where Hankey was wrong was in his concluding observation that 'I am certain N will not accept it, even if he is asked.' Why Northcliffe changed his mind is a matter for conjecture; the second offer was of a slightly different nature, with no diplomatic responsibilities such as Balfour had discharged.

When the appointment was announced on 7 June it prompted predictable controversy, and little short of outrage in the Liberal Party. Lloyd George's few friends there had urged him to try to heal the wounds caused by Northcliffe's attacks on Asquith and his administration, and he had promised to do so: yet this was taken as a blind provocation. The prime minister admitted to Scott that 'it was essential to get rid of him.

He had become so "jumpy" as to be really a public danger'.[56] The absence
of detail – what Northcliffe was doing, whether he had been made a
member of the Diplomatic Service, and to whom he was accountable –
was raised in the Commons at questions to Sir George Cave, the home
secretary, who was unable to provide answers. What Northcliffe actually did was of little concern to Lloyd George compared with his being
away, for four months, doing it.

In mid-November Northcliffe returned from America where, contrary to expectations, he had improved Anglo-American relations. Lloyd
George, emboldened by his protégé's success, offered him the Air Ministry, a crucial appointment when the Royal Air Force was being
constructed. Northcliffe turned it down, his letter doing so being published, helpfully, in *The Times*. It included various damning criticisms of
the government. Lloyd George told Riddell that 'I did not see the letter
until I saw it in the newspapers.'[57] Having watched from afar for four
months Northcliffe had concluded that things were going badly in Britain, a view reinforced by a letter from Leo Maxse of the *National Review*
that he received on his return: 'Every kind of folly is being perpetrated
by the village idiots who misgovern this great country.'[58] He had told
Lloyd George privately that he thought he could be more useful in the
press, and that there were ministers towards whom he could not feel
loyalty.

It seemed the end of the road for the Northcliffe/Lloyd George relationship, the latter telling Riddell that Northcliffe was, after all,
'unreliable' and had 'no sense of loyalty and there is something of the cad
about him.' Nonetheless, and to the King's dismay, Northcliffe was
advanced to a viscountcy on 24 November for his work in America, just
as Lloyd George appointed his brother, Lord Rothermere, to the Air
Ministry. Northcliffe told Colonel House, to whom he had become close
while in Washington, that he did not wish to join 'so spineless a body'
and lose his right to criticise. House noted: 'It is common knowledge
that N treats LG as if he, the PM, was subordinate and speculation is rife
as to when the worm will turn.'[59] It was also House who recorded the
'denunciatory' way the King spoke of Northcliffe.[60]

If Northcliffe was offhand with Lloyd George, Lloyd George's conduct towards his colleagues was no better. Derby told Esher on 25
November that 'the last ten days are the worst I have ever been through',
though that was also because his son-in-law, Neil Primrose, Rosebery's

son, had been killed in Palestine. He claimed to like Lloyd George, but once more nearly resigned until the prime minister dissuaded him. Tensions about Robertson and Haig had been the issue between Lloyd George and Derby, and were far from ironed out.

Perhaps the most characteristic example of Lloyd George's manipulative and unscrupulous behaviour was his abuse of patronage and, as with the controversy over the Northcliffe viscountcy that would erupt in the autumn of 1917, his failure to consult the King properly on a matter the King, as the Fountain of honour, took exceptionally seriously. The 1917 New Year's honours list had mocked respectability, with too many featuring who had assisted in Lloyd George's rise. The list – delayed by the change of government – came out on 13 February, but Esher had a preview, and was horrified. The controversy over the Aitken baronetcy and peerage was also still fresh. However, perhaps because Lloyd George knew how bad his reputation was in some circles and had been keen to counter it, few blatant donors were rewarded. Yet enough of his supporters were favoured for Esher to describe the distribution of honours as 'an outrage' and to say that 'the jobbery is beyond belief'.[61] The Birthday list, due on 1 June, threatened to be worse. Stamfordham, whose job it was to vet the proposals and register concerns about the use of the prerogative, told Salisbury on 23 May that 'it is impossible to overstate the feelings of nausea with which the ever recurring consideration of honours fills yours very truly'.[62] Salisbury was one of forty eminent politicians who sent a petition to Lloyd George urging him to reform the honours system: they wanted reasons given for each award, to ensure the prerogative was used only for the irreproachable; that no honours had been given in return for money, or the expectation of money; and wanted an audit of party funds.

Lloyd George did not reply, but made his point in presiding over the longest honours list ever issued, which included a dozen peerages and two dozen baronetcies. Eventually, on 20 June, he agreed to meet Salisbury. He invited him to table a parliamentary question, and seemed willing to consider all the proposals Salisbury made about reforming the system and making it more transparent; but then the trail went cold. Salisbury and his friends put down a resolution in the Lords on 7 August, when Curzon, worthy of his hire, dismissed any notion of corruption: the petitioners were outnumbered and withdrew, but when the matter was debated again after the summer recess the resolution was passed and the government agreed to abide by it: compliance would, however, prove another matter.

The Times denounced the Birthday list, in a leader on 4 June. It noted that 'Mr Lloyd George . . . seems to have swallowed the system whole.'[63] Too many people had been rewarded for purely party services, and others in return for 'heavy disbursements'. A 'cynical traffic' had grown up: though the paper understood Lloyd George had no party machine or war chest behind him. Like Salisbury, it sought that an honest reason be stated for each award, and that party funds should be subject to proper audit. It returned to the fray after the Lords' debate, calling Curzon's arguments for doing nothing 'extraordinary', the scandal of honours sales 'notorious', and condemning 'the injury this furtive and illicit traffic does to the prestige of the Crown' and 'its contaminating influence upon the vendors, the purchasers and the brokers involved.'[64]

Esher, despite his devotion to the King, noted that 'The "Honours" list has been attacked in *The Times* with just criticism. It does not touch the Army, and showers distinctions upon all sorts of wretched people who have paid money for what they get. I fear the King's weakness in accepting such deplorable advice will do him harm.'[65] One can only presume the King did so because he had found the change of government destabilising enough six months earlier, without declaring war on his prime minister. The debate would flare up after the war, in lurid circumstances; and questions would be asked in both Houses of Parliament for the rest of the war about the liberality with which patronage was dispensed, and to whom. But the reformers' efforts were derailed by recipients of the lower ranks of the new Order of the British Empire, almost all blameless citizens rewarded for war work, complaining at the attempt by grandees to tar them with the brush of corruption. A period of silence was deemed wise, and the opportunity for condemnation of the distribution of higher honours would not take long to arise.

The new Order, and the more exclusive Order of the Companions of Honour, was proposed by Lloyd George to reward those who had done exemplary military or civilian service in the war. They were open to women as well as men: those awarded the equivalent of a knighthood or Knight Grand Cross of the Order would be known as Dames. Curzon, who relished such tasks, had been asked to report on the possibilities of the new Order, and had fretted over the place of women. 'It would probably be undesirable to give them the title of "Lady", because otherwise we might have "Mr Thomas Perkins ABE [Associate of the Order] and Lady Perkins, KCBE" – a fruitful source of domestic perturbation.[66] The overall effect was to democratise the system, which had previously been the province of an elite. As well as the five ranks there was, for the working class, the British Empire Medal, used to reward leadership and initiative. However, the great expansion of the system meant all the more patronage to be abused.

Lloyd George professed to Davidson, Baldwin's confidant, that giving honours for cash was 'a far cleaner method of filling the party chest' than methods used in America or by the Labour Party.[67] He continued: 'Here a man gives £40,000 to the Party and gets a baronetcy . . . the attachment of the brewers to the Conservative Party is the closest approach to political corruption in this country. The worst of it is you cannot defend it in public, but it keeps politics far cleaner than any other method of raising funds.' That was highly debatable: Lloyd George found the system serviceable because of the extent to which his conduct of policy relied on his using people, often ones who began with little regard for him or his methods.

Despite the preoccupations of the war, the Lords soon discussed, on a motion of Lord Loreburn, the taint on British politics caused by the prime minister making the King confer honours and dignities on men purely for giving substantial donations to party funds. Loreburn wanted the government to agree that a 'definite public statement' would be made of reasons for giving an honour to anyone outside the Royal Family, the Armed Forces or the permanent civil service.[68] He also asked that the prime minister be compelled to declare to the Sovereign that no money had changed hands before granting an honour. The Lords had made a similar, unanimous request in February 1914, and the Commons had chosen to ignore it. Loreburn raised the matter again because he believed the impropriety under discussion had recurred: but since all parties to such transactions conspired to keep them secret, he had no proof. One of his friends had been approached three times and told he could have a knighthood for £15,000 and a baronetcy for £25,000. When he refused to play, the price for the former was knocked down to £10,000. He was told he could upgrade to a baronetcy and the £10,000 he had already spent would count towards it.[69] He also believed the 'touts' who offered these baubles were on a commission. Most peers had heard similar stories.

Loreburn also disclosed that another friend – a former minister – had told him he had sold honours. He spoke of a man who wanted a baronetcy but who asked whether he could have one for giving £25,000 to a hospital the King was about to visit, rather than to a political party; he had been advised to donate to the party. 'Within a short time he came out as a baronet, and the hospital suffered in consequence.'[70] Loreburn invited former chief whips in the Commons – whose responsibilities had included acting as patronage secretary – to admit their part in this trade; none obliged. He said he knew a chief whip had to spend money on party organisation, and on propitiating the press; but was selling honours the way to raise those funds?

The Lords declined to pass Loreburn's motion, after Curzon suggested that to do so would scar the reputations of the four living prime ministers, namely Rosebery, Balfour, Asquith and Lloyd George: but agreed to an amended motion asking the prime minister to satisfy himself – rather than make a declaration to the King – that no money had changed hands. Lord Selborne, under parliamentary privilege, did choose to name names. Sir James Gildes, who ran a charity helping the families of servicemen, had been offered £25,000 and two sums of £10,000 for his charity if he would use any influence he had to secure a baronetcy or knighthood for the three men concerned. A Dr Millard, the medical officer of health for Leicester, asked a local political association to secure an honour for a friend. When asked what his friend would pay, he retreated. Friends of George Holman, several times mayor of Lewes, were told he deserved an honour, but would not get one unless money changed hands. When a friend of Sir George Kekewich, a Liberal MP in the 1906 Parliament and a former senior civil servant, wanted a knighthood at the time of the Licensing Bill before the war, Kekewich introduced him to a Liberal whip. He was told to withdraw his opposition to the Bill and pay £5,000. Agreeing to do both, he was knighted. Another who craved a baronetcy was told to pay £25,000: he said he would, but withdrew. After a period in British politics after the 1832 Reform Act that had been remarkably free of corruption, the old ways had returned.

III

Lloyd George's protracted absences from the Commons, and the Northcliffe press's useful habit of blaming the Asquith government for almost everything that went wrong in the opening months of its successor administration, helped the new prime minister to avoid confronting difficult issues directly and in public: notably the food shortage, the gravest problem to face the country in early 1917. Northcliffe, who perceptively told his staff the public did not realise that 'the British and German empires are involved in a starving match,' demanded rationing, and fed public unrest.[71] Sir Henry Newbolt, who when not writing patriotic doggerel was link man between the Admiralty and the War Cabinet, toured the country with a lecture entitled 'Patriotism, Pigs and Potatoes', in which he urged people to exercise self-restraint, grow vegetables and to conserve food waste to feed pigs.[72] It is easy to mock, but it was a deeply serious matter.

The winter was intensely cold, with snow lying for much of January and February and London recording its hardest frost since 1895. Coal was scarce because of a transport shortage, and too few strong men to deliver it. Petrol was denied for the few with private cars, unless they could prove their motoring was for the war effort. The hardships were piling up. Labour shortages had left large acreages of land unploughed. Cows were sold because there was no one to milk them; horses were idle because there was no one to work them. The Army's demand for skilled stockmen and other vital farm workers remained insatiable. Shortages were widespread: a few plutocrats were still guzzling five-course meals in West End hotels (and being publicly rebuked for it), but most people were hungry. Many public schools had days without meat, and, like the working class, schoolboys breakfasted on semi-edible bread, margarine and tea.[73] A Tonbridge boy, Walter Oakeshott – later headmaster of Winchester – recalled: 'We must have been hungrier than any generation at school ever was. We ate ravenously whatever we could, we cadged food shamelessly from the fortunate, we robbed orchards.'[74] Oakeshott's elders also suffered: by late February some of London's leading gentlemen's clubs – including Boodle's, Brooks's, the Travellers and White's – had reduced portions and established 'meatless days': other clubs followed suit.[75] Potatoes too had run out in parts of Scotland and the north-west by early February, and a month later were hardly obtainable in London. The London clubs, after another meeting of their secretaries at Brooks's on 26 March, agreed to stop serving potatoes at meals. Orders were made to hotels patronised by the better-off to serve smaller portions and have meatless and potato-less days.

By then there were hardly any fish at Billingsgate, and food shops in the capital had queues of shivering people outside from dawn onwards. Matters were so desperate that, to prevent their 'predations' on crops, it was agreed to allow the shooting of pheasants out of season.[76] Horse thefts rose, it being believed Belgian refugee butchers were turning the animals into joints of meat and sausages and passing them off as beef or pork. Despite an improvement in Britain's financial situation when America gave full backing to sterling, foreign exchange was short, and priority was given to using it to buy food rather than munitions: at one point it seemed Britain would not have the foreign exchange to buy Argentina's grain surplus, on which it had been depending, nor extra meat and dairy produce from America.

The King's Speech ignored food production, causing Leslie Scott, a Tory MP, to move a motion for the Commons to discuss it. Scott claimed the new government had done nothing to improve production, although the difficulties farmers faced were 'absolutely appalling', with concern about prices unsettling them greatly.[77] He also said talk of 1917 producing more food than 1916 was 'chimerical'. Ninety per cent of the labour Neville Chamberlain would shortly offer farmers through his National Service scheme would be untrained. Scott pleaded for experienced agricultural workers serving with yeomanry regiments and based in England to be released for farm work.

The government, nervous of public unrest, had put measures in place to try to alleviate the situation. Traders who sold regulated foods at above the controlled prices were prosecuted, notably greengrocers in breach of the Potato Order who claimed they could make no profit at the price dictated by the food controller. A greengrocer in Kentish Town was fined £5, with 5s costs, for refusing to sell potatoes to a woman unless she bought something else: it was his second offence. Nonetheless, it was clear even these measures were inadequate.

The crisis brought out Lloyd George's better qualities of energy and decisiveness. He delegated and intervened as necessary. He also showed a willingness to sack high officials who proved ineffective, and to take matters into his own hands – as with the enforcement of a convoy system to help secure food imports – where necessary. And he sought to balance the competing demands on manpower of fighting a war and feeding a nation. Such was his determination to get that equation right that he asked Rowland Prothero, president of the Board of Agriculture and a reflective man who had been a fellow of All Souls, to lead the task of increasing domestic food production.

Other than manpower shortages, the main factor inhibiting large-scale food production was the state of the land. The long pre-war agricultural depression, dating from the 1870s, had left a legacy of uncultivated and derelict land that required serious, coordinated work to ensure it could be drained and brought back into production. For example, cultivated land had fallen from 836,000 acres to 780,000 between 1875 and 1915 in one predominantly arable county – Norfolk – alone.[78] The county had 284,000 acres of grass, and for the 1918 harvest it would have to plough up 70,000 of these.[79] The Board of Agriculture introduced a Bill to make it easier to expand the amount of arable land. Prothero announced that an increase from 19 million to 27 million acres would secure enough food to make Britain free of the 'submarine menace'.[80] However, a quarter of a million extra men would have to cultivate it, and these were not available. Some modest increase in land to grow cereals and potatoes had happened since 1916 – 330,000 acres – and even uncooperative Ireland had cultivated another 700,000 acres, proving its men were useful to the war effort even if they were not fighting. The process was, however, slow: the board expected in the first year of the new programme to get only about 400,000 more acres of land into production.

Farmers in the east were directed to grow less mustard and use land for cereals instead; mustard was deemed not to be a 'patriotic' crop.[81] It was estimated that 10,000 extra acres of cereal could be grown as a result of this in Lincolnshire and the Isle of Ely alone. Despite the shortages, Prothero saw it would now be essential to offer a state guarantee of minimum prices of wheat and oats for years ahead. This would make it worthwhile for farmers to undertake the investment necessary to resume larger-scale arable farming.

He confirmed a minimum wage, of 25s a week: which MacDonald, on behalf of organised labour, dismissed as inadequate, being equivalent to only 16s before the war. Between 1914 and 1918 the cereal harvest rose from 1.706 million tons to 2.428 million. Britain never lost its reliance on food imports during the war, as it was forced to do after 1939; but from 1914 to 1918 net imports did fall from 16.7 million tons to 11.89 million.[82] Also, a serious advance in agricultural policy under Prothero's direction was the tripling of the use of sulphate of ammonia as a fertiliser, which hugely improved yields and moved British farming from traditionally organic to increasingly industrial.

Prothero needed serious support in his task, and Lloyd George sent for Arthur Lee, a Unionist MP and former professional soldier who had worked under him in Munitions and at the War Office. Lee had been disappointed and surprised not to have been chosen for the administration in December – apparently vetoed by Law – but Lloyd George now made him director general of food production. Beaverbrook claimed he had turned the job down 'on account of my bad health' (he would die forty-seven years later).[83] Prothero welcomed Lee and worked well with him in harness. Prothero had already announced that 260 tractors had been ordered from America and would be deployed by late March: they would be distributed over the country, the Transport Service would ensure they could be driven and maintained, and their work rate would improve production. Eventually, Lee ordered 10,000 tractors from Ford in Detroit (which were slow to arrive and not always ideal for British conditions), and instituted an intensive ploughing programme that ensured vast, long-uncultivated tracts of Britain were once more growing food. He pleaded with ploughmen to think the unthinkable, and to work on Sundays; and the minister of munitions asked in March for ploughmen working in munitions factories to return to their farms for six weeks to bring as much land under cultivation as possible. To general astonishment, many of the legion of women volunteers soon proved they could operate a plough and team of horses, too. Thanks to Lee's initiative, in 1917 an additional 4.9 million bushels of wheat, 5.1 million of barley and 36.7 million of oats were produced compared with 1916; and 42 million sacks of potatoes.[84] Milner, whose role before joining the War Cabinet had been to lead a committee on food production, saw the problem was addressed in detail at the highest level, including introducing legislation where necessary. For example, he brought in a Corn Production Bill to set minimum prices for cereals, tantamount to protectionism and therefore anathema to many Liberals. It also set minimum wages and gave landlords the right to evict inefficient tenant farmers.

In the short to medium term, though, these steps in themselves were not sufficient to cope with the huge challenges the country faced. That year's harvest was still several months away, and despite increased wheat imports, Britain was down to nine weeks' supply by mid-April, having fallen from fourteen weeks at the change of government the previous

December.[85] Food reserves would never be so low again during the war as in April 1917. Since Britain was so dependent on imported food, any gains in production were, during the U-boat war and beyond, cancelled out by the loss of food-carrying merchant ships. In the first six months of 1917 U-boats sank 2,136,126 tons of British shipping, 545,282 tons in April alone, representing 169 British ships: by comparison, in August 1916 Britain had lost just 43,254 tons. In those same six months only 631,000 tons of replacement shipping were produced in British shipyards.[86] It was estimated that food imports by March 1917 had fallen by a third compared with a year earlier. In the whole of 1917, despite the situation improving after April thanks to the adoption of the convoy system, 3,729,785 tons were lost.[87] Between February and June 85,000 tons of sugar went down, as in the whole of 1917 did 46,000 tons of meat.[88] The human toll was depressing: 6,408 members of the merchant marine.[89] The government allowed the press to print statistics of the shipping losses, which was either a commendable act of candour or a further means of urging the public to amend its eating habits.

To release shipping for essential food supplies the government restricted imports of commodities such as timber and paper: but sourcing more wood from home placed stresses on manpower. Newspapers shrank – The Times down from its usual sixteen pages sometimes to ten by April – there were restrictions on the use of paper for posters, and some magazines suspended publication. The Navy had to accept a slowdown in ship production, with five light cruisers stopped altogether, to allow the faster replacement of the merchant fleet. Sensibly, the production of anti-submarine craft was stepped up. It was decided to order forty merchant ships from America, but these would take time. Northcliffe, who prided himself on having intelligence sources in Germany, based on contacts made on frequent visits there before the war, believed even more lethal and stealthy U-boats were being developed, so things would get worse. He did not believe that Carson, whom he knew well and respected, was being entirely frank about the extent of the shipping losses and the effect on food supplies: he urged the government to introduce rationing immediately, an idea ministers abhorred because of its potential effect on morale. Carson did, in fact, warn Riddell on 10 March that Britain faced 'a serious shortage of food', with just three months' grain supply left and losses mounting.[90]

As soon as he became prime minister Lloyd George had brought in

Lord Devonport, proprietor of the grocery chain that evolved into International Stores, as food controller.[91] He endured a baptism of fire with the recommencement of unrestricted submarine warfare, and the consequent losses of essential food. He issued the first food control orders in mid-January, which included the state requisitioning land it considered inadequately cultivated – provided it could find the labour to do it: the Women's National Land Service Corps launched a new recruiting drive. The prices for cereals from the 1917 crop were set in advance, and Devonport issued recommendations for the weekly consumption per head of staple foods – four pounds of bread, two and a half pounds of meat and three-quarters of a pound of sugar.

Such state interference in the lives of the people prompted predictable opposition. A *Times* correspondent contended that the guidelines meant quantities 'are considerably less than those allowed to German prisoners and paupers in workhouses, neither of whom are presumably very actively employed?'[92] He continued: 'If so, will you or the Food Controller supply me with reasons to induce my household, who all work hard, to consume one-third less than they ever did before?' Conscientious objectors in Dartmoor were indeed getting over twice the recommended meat and bread allowances, and more generous quantities of other food. Their diet, and the already meagre one in the workhouses, was cut. (Within weeks, in response to complaints that Dartmoor was a place of undue leniency, a Home Office inspection took place. Discipline was made harsher and the warders – known as instructors – were given more power. Local people were especially hostile to the inmates; some wanted them kept permanently in chains, believing convicts who worked on the moor before the war were morally preferable and less prone to 'slackness'.)[93]

In response to complaints about the use of sugar and yeast, to conserve barley and maize and to save on transport, even beer output was restricted from late March, to 10 million barrels a year, compared with 26 million in the year to 31 March 1916. A reduction of 8 million barrels a day was the equivalent of freeing up thirty trains.[94] There was a rise in price of 1d a pint for light beer and more for heavier ale, and the non-beer-drinking classes were disobliged too: the amount of wines and spirits that could be taken out of bond was reduced by 50 per cent. The government instructed poulterers to rear hens for eggs and not to fatten them for the table; and for pigs to be fed on beechnuts, acorns and waste. By May 1917 retail prices were around 102 per cent higher than pre-war.

Much reliance was placed on public-spirited acts to improve the avail-ability of food. At Eton, boys cultivated one and a half acres during 1917 and produced 15 tons of potatoes, which they sold for £100, a profit of £45 19s 8d. The dividend went to a local hospital for convalescent soldiers.[95] On 2 May the King issued a proclamation urging better economy in the use of food, and to counsel the more careful feeding of horses, avoiding using oats or other grains that could provide human food; the proclam-ation was ordered to be read by clergy at Sunday services for four weeks. Strict rationing had been in force in royal palaces since February. Noth-ing like it had happened since George III, in the Napoleonic Wars, had in December 1800 issued a similar proclamation. Devonport had his depart-ment issue a recipe for what became known as 'War Cake', with the noble English tradition of afternoon tea branded a 'needless luxury', and with a threat to prohibit the opening of new tea-shops.[96] *The Times* took great pleasure in pointing out that even work at the Ministry of Food was daily interrupted by afternoon tea. However, the public chose not to listen, so in mid-April Devonport banned the manufacture of fancy cakes altogether.

Voluntarism and exhortations were not enough to prevent problems flooding into Devonport's office throughout the first half of 1917. Ques-tions were asked in Parliament, as the convoy system reduced shipping losses, about large quantities of food going off before it had been distrib-uted. In May and June the London County Council's sanitary inspectors condemned tons of bacon, because of a failure to work out the logistics of transport or cold storage; though the government alleged that much of the rotten meat had been unfit before reaching Britain. Shipments of Dan-ish bacon were taking ten days to get to London, and a further six to reach Portsmouth. This was precisely the sort of problem the food controller was supposed to prevent. Nor had the controller managed to stop profit-eering and speculation, a point about which the government, requiring the public's continued cooperation, remained highly conscious.

Fleet Street, led by Northcliffe, rounded on Devonport for his alleged inaction, demanding rationing and denouncing profiteers. Sadly for the food controller, some of his well-intentioned policies failed because they had not been properly thought out. On 22 March Devonport announced that it would become an offence punishable by imprisonment for any retailer to sell more than a fortnight's supply of sugar to any customer; and anyone with more than a fortnight's supply at home would be charged with hoarding, the police having right of entry to any house where this was suspected. However, many domestic jam-makers had stored sugar for that purpose, and there was outrage that they could be prosecuted: so the order had to be altered. As there was too little sugar to supply to fruit farmers for jam-making, a main purpose of growing fruit – which thanks to the tastes of the times was consumed in infinitely higher quantities in jam than in any other way – was negated. Cereals were then grown instead of strawberries. The chocolate supply was similarly blighted, and joined fancy cakes as something largely of memory. Also, the massive bureaucracy of the state, in its thirst for regulation, was often devoid of common sense and blind to how some of its directives conflicted with others, notably in the cultivation of fruit where the land could have been used for other foodstuffs.

Devonport's belief that people could be encouraged rather than compelled to control their food consumption was somewhat optimistic: as with the exhortations to join the Army before conscription, people nursed a strong sense of their self-interest, and resented state interference in their everyday lives. The government introduced a bread subsidy at a cost of £50 million a year, allowing the price of a quartern loaf to be pegged at 9d. However, the price was briefly increased in late March to a shilling for a four-pound loaf, in the hope of causing people to waste less. Yet the ministry was still forced to warn the public on 19 April that consumption of 'breadstuffs' continued to run at '50 per cent above present and prospective supplies.'[97] Devonport returned to the subject on 25 April, telling the Lords food would be a 'supremely decisive' factor in the war.[98] He wanted a one-pound cut in consumption, and said he was instituting the machinery to ration bread, sugar and anything else necessary if voluntary restraint was not applied. Still nothing changed.

Therefore on 29 May a letter, addressed to the head of the household, arrived in British homes signed by Devonport, imploring all families to cut their bread consumption, 'and so loyally bridge over the anxious days between now and the harvest.'[99] It continued: 'No true citizen, no patriotic man or woman will fail the country in this hour of need.' The sacrifice had become easier since March, when a new standard 'war loaf', including a high proportion of raw wheat, and potatoes, was inflicted on the public. It tasted unpleasant, so the measure had only limited success. Also, despite the anger caused by the order not to hoard sugar, on 5 April the government issued a blanket Food Hoarding Order, with powers to search any premises where it was suspected.

Devonport's initiatives were further brought into question by his failure to involve experts on nutrition in the decisions his department made. His existing recommendations for the weekly consumption per head of staple foods would have yielded only 1,200–1,300 calories a day, and would have required to be supplemented by other foodstuffs that were now in very short supply. Regulations were published in March to limit the consumption of food in catered premises such as hotels, restaurants, railway buffets and clubs, by restricting portions and having obligatory, rather than voluntary, days when meat or potatoes could not be served. The first compulsory meatless day in hotels and restaurants was on 17 April. The War Cabinet decided against seeking to impose one on private homes 'at present'.[100] The pressure on meat came from a request from the Army to commandeer a fifth of the imported supply of Argentinian beef for their food reserves in case the U-boat war starved fighting men. However, scientists pointed out that if meat consumption were to be cut, that would necessitate finding even more space in ships to import grain.

By the end of May Devonport had realised the need for overarching state control, rather than piecemeal reform, if he was to succeed in his task of feeding the nation. As he had told the Lords, he had drawn up plans for general food rationing during May (one of the leading civil servants to address himself to this problem, and to price controls, was William Beveridge), but they were not then executed. The constant nagging and doom-mongering had had some effect: the nation became peculiarly conscious of the use and availability of food, which was the intention. However, it was now widely accepted that exhortation was pointless, and rationing would be required: though the War Cabinet decided on 30 May, after yet another discussion, that such a policy 'was undesirable at present.'[101]

Lloyd George, in a rare Commons appearance on 10 May, had blithely admitted he had 'no real anxiety' about the food supply, which prompted someone to ask why the country had been led to believe in January that it might be starving by the summer. 'Because I wanted the people to cultivate!' he replied, which apparently provoked laughter, but was a further measure of his honesty.[102] Yet Riddell recorded on 2 June: 'I told Lloyd George that the sugar queues were causing grave discontent and that sugar distribution called for immediate reform. The working classes are angry that their wives and families should be compelled to undergo this trouble and indignity, while the wants of the rich are supplied much as they were before the war.'[103] Ministers could see that some changes to society would be permanent, but they wanted to manage the process and not impose what Riddell termed 'drastic changes in the social fabric', such as in Russia.[104] The Tsar had been deposed three months earlier, and two groups of revolutionaries were fighting for the future control of the country in a struggle in which the Bolsheviks, under Vladimir Lenin, would soon come out on top. Few in Britain, from the King downwards, were rash enough to discount the chances of a similar workers' uprising happening in Britain, should there be sufficient provocations.

With the ruthlessness for which he was now renowned, Lloyd George recognised that Devonport was out of his depth, and his resignation was received with relief on 30 May. Devonport had not endeared himself to his officials, and won the reputation of a procrastinator and a poor delegator. As a retailer himself, he was considered prone to avoid taking measures (notably rationing) that disobliged those in his trade. Doubts about his probity in this matter precipitated his resignation on the grounds, it was claimed, of ill-health. As with so many of Lloyd George's superannuated cronies, he collected a viscountcy on the way out.

His replacement, on 19 June, as food controller was Lord Rhondda, who had been president of the Local Government Board. Quarrels in the 1890s about Liberal organisation in Wales had caused him to fall out with Lloyd George, but the two eventually came to respect and admire each other when Lloyd George realised Rhondda was not a political rival. Unlike many of the prime minister's friends he was a man of some distinction, courage and genuine ability. He had survived the *Lusitania* and had, as David Alfred Thomas, been Liberal MP for Merthyr Tydfil. He had left Parliament in 1910, believing he would not obtain preferment; but Lloyd George recalled him with a peerage as one of his 'men of push and go', not least on seeing the success Thomas had made of his family's mining business in South Wales. A prominent opponent of war profiteering in the coal industry, he could be relied upon to oppose it in foodstuffs.[105] He was charged with managing shortages and keeping supplies moving while using the bread subsidy to keep its prices down, and seeking to impose a ceiling on the prices of other foodstuffs. Rhondda's terms verged on the draconian. He demanded the support of the War

Cabinet should he find it necessary 'to take over the whole food supplies of the Country, to reduce the price of the necessaries of life although it may involve an expense of many millions to the Exchequer, to utilise the Local Authorities for the purposes of food distribution, and to take strong measures to check profiteering.'[106] The government agreed. 'The man who seeks to profit by the necessities of his country at the time of our peril, when thousands are cheerfully making the supreme sacrifices in the cause of liberty, is nothing short of a blackmailer and must be treated as such,' Rhondda said as he took office.[107] He promised his 'first effort' would be to seek to lower prices.

On 6 August 1917 he announced new regulations for the control of the food supply, hoping not just to ensure all had enough to eat, but to help allay anger among the working classes. He proposed to enlist local authorities to ensure the system worked: 'Supplies must be conserved. Supplies must be shared equally by rich and poor, and prices must be kept down,' he told his colleagues in charge of local government, and the Scottish secretary.[108] He asked local authorities to set up food control committees to ensure economical use of food, acting on advice prepared by Rhondda's department. This might include communal kitchens, which would have the benefit of conserving fuel as well as regulating the supply of food. The committees were to oversee local distribution of sugar, bread and meat, and to ensure fixed prices were enforced. The alternative, Rhondda made clear, was the 'vexatious system of individual rationing.' There would be a new system of regulation for caterers and institutions, and a scheme for registered retailers to help stave off a black market.

Enforcement of price controls was rigid: in early September George Thompson, a seventy-four-year-old farmer from Spalding in Lincolnshire, was fined £5,500 – £100 on each count – and £250 costs after admitting fifty-five offences of selling potatoes at £15 a ton, £3 10s above the fixed price. The court was told he had disregarded the order 'to an enormous extent' and had made 'very large sums of money': estimated at £5,000 or so.[109] The defence described the 'resentment' felt among potato growers that those with the best produce, who could have sold it for £40 a ton, were being forced to sell at the same price as those producing inferior potatoes. That was deemed an irrelevance. Thompson's potato business was huge, and he was described as a 'pioneer' of potato farming; he was made an example of *pour encourager les autres*, particularly the small fry.

The huge fine did not put him out of business – which rather proved the point about his excess profits. Nor was it much of a deterrent: another Lincolnshire farmer was fined £200 for two counts of overcharging for potatoes, and the chairman of the bench announced that any further cases would be dealt with 'even more seriously' than the £100 per offence tariff.[110] Later in October a market gardener in Bedfordshire who pleaded guilty to thirty-seven counts of overcharging was fined £3,700, made to pay £200 costs, and sentenced to two months' imprisonment on each count: the thirty-seven custodial sentences, fortunately for him, to run concurrently.

Almost every sort of farmer and food retailer, no matter what the food-stuff concerned, deluged Rhondda's department with complaints about how the bureaucratic planning of the control of prices and production did not always coincide with reality, and the need to recoup investments made in the past. The government argued, with some justification, that farmers had done well in the first years of the war when prices rose, and should grin and bear the difficulties. That took no account of the many lean years farmers had had before the war, in an agricultural depression that had started in the mid-1870s, when many had run down their capital and businesses in order to survive. All Rhondda could do was appeal to their patriotism 'at this time of crisis, the gravest in the history of our nation.'[111] Such exhortation was not inevitably successful, but Rhondda tempered it with a warning that social unrest would explode if food prices did not fall: events in Russia were all too immediate. Landowners savaged Rhondda's policy – characterised by farmers as being 'to squeeze the producer to the last farthing' – and warned it would restrict supply.[112]

Throughout the autumn the avalanche of regulations continued: such as a ban on dealing in specified imported dried fruits, which became a state monopoly, and a Milk Order outlining a distribution plan and fixing a relatively high price – 7d a quart initially but rising to 8d from 1 November – to placate dairy farmers. The Ministry of Food issued a fort-nightly publication, the *Food Journal*, beginning in mid-September, in which Rhondda could take the public into his confidence about his plans. Writing on 12 September, he said that 'an urgent appeal is made to all classes to economise consumption' and that the 'unnecessary middleman' – the wholesaler – was, in respect of foodstuffs which the government now controlled, being eliminated, and with him went some of the scope for profiteering.[113] During September the ministry tightened control on the distribution and sale of sugar, potatoes, meat, bread, flour and cereals: and every time prices rose more agitation began among organised labour, with the miners still restless and, in September, representatives of shipyard workers demanding pay increases. Meat prices were fixed high, according to Prothero, to persuade farmers to move from the production of cattle to the production of cereals; nonetheless, in early October he had to plead with the country to eat less meat. Apparently, the price was not high enough.

The government also announced it wished to harvest the forthcoming crop of horse chestnuts. Though inedible, they could be processed and substituted for grain used in various industrial processes, notably in munitions manufacture, and the grain thus freed up used for feeding people. With manpower stretched – it was estimated that 5 million women were now working, 200,000 of them on the land, and the Women's Auxiliary Army Corps were seeking 10,000 recruits a month – it was decided that schoolchildren, used to collecting conkers, would be exhorted to harvest the nuts. Schools were urged to group together to supervise collections and arrange for them to be sent to the director of Propellant Supplies – yet another new branch of the bureaucracy. Landowners were also asked to collect chestnuts.

Rhondda's price ceilings started to limit food supplies. Farmers claimed they could not stay in business at the prices they were allowed to charge. By late November there was a butter shortage, because the prices fixed no longer made it economical for Dutch and Danish exporters to sell their goods to Britain. Rhondda's defence was that the price had almost doubled before his cap had been introduced; milk could not be imported, and it took much less to make cheese than it did to make butter, so the milk available should first be used to make cheese. He had, however, arranged imports of butter from Australia, New Zealand and Argentina. The government now bought and sold 85 per cent of food eaten by the public, with 2,000 food control committees around the country.

The scarcity of supplies prompted illegal hoarding, even though the harvest – in which many of the schoolboys of Britain participated, following an appeal the previous spring by Neville Chamberlain – had been good. Queues started to form at shops, a phenomenon hitherto rare in Britain. By interfering in the pricing of meat the government encouraged farmers to slaughter livestock before Christmas, causing a shortage of fresh meat in the new year; its availability had already been restricted by the turning of grazing land into arable land. Unrest followed, thanks to press stories that the moneyed classes – stigmatised as 'food hogs' – could still feast in expensive hotels and restaurants. There was certainly a class divide in the availability of food, and to an extent a geographical one. The government had since the spring of 1917 urged better-off families with gardens, or who could afford to rent allotments, to grow as much fruit and vegetables as possible, which further insulated them from hardship; and rural families were often better fed than urban ones, because of the availability of hare, rabbit and pigeon. The poorer families were, the harder it was to find decent food, and there were claims that the most impoverished were edging towards malnutrition and having to seek charitable help.

On 4 December Mrs Flora Drummond, the leading suffragette known as 'the General', led a deputation of housewives to Rhondda to demand rationing. They told him that 'some of them had to stand [in queues] for four, five or six hours for sugar and butter.'[114] They complained that luxury foods such as chocolate and fancy biscuits were still being produced when there were not enough basic foodstuffs to go round. Challenged by the deputation about the milk shortage, Rhondda said local food control committees had been ordered to ensure women and children had priority during distributions. However, he resisted rationing, even though London's meat wholesalers announced that 'we are mighty close to an emergency', and it was feared other big cities would run out before Christmas. It promised to be an unfestive season: it was almost impossible to buy spirits in London, and wine was twice the price of a year earlier.

The King and Queen, visiting Deptford on 11 December, had seen enormous queues and were distressed by 'the hardship experienced by the poor, while the richer portion of the community do not suffer in this respect.'[115] The King was worried that women in queues were losing pay by having to miss work, or being forced to neglect their children, and urged Lloyd George to act. There was also the sheer waste of time – time many women could have spent on the war effort. The King was agitated about the price of food, and lobbied Lloyd George about it throughout the winter of 1917–18: to him, it was an obvious trigger for revolution. Davies, the prime minister's secretary, on behalf of his master, promised the matter would have 'serious attention' and that Lloyd George would visit poorer areas the following week.[116] His solicitude had little effect: on 17 December it was reported that 3,000 people were queuing at a shop in south-east London for margarine; a third were unlucky.[117] A lack of tea had already harmed morale: so much so that the War Cabinet ordered the shipping controller to accommodate a request from Rhondda to supply more tonnage for tea imports.[118]

Fear of unrest spurred increasingly intense action, not all of it successful. The War Cabinet urged Rhondda, whose general dynamism was punctuated by an occasional remarkable lack of proactivity, to set up a nationwide network of 2,000 local committees to improve food distribution. On 18 December he upbraided the committees for not ensuring better distribution and thereby eliminating queuing, which he said 'must be stopped, and stopped immediately', but this had little or no short-term effect.[119] Rhondda's plea to his 2,000 local committees to improve distribution was also largely fruitless. And, for all his assiduousness, he seemed partly responsible for a shortage of butter: 3,000 tons had been imported in November and December 1917, compared with 30,000 tons in the same months of 1913. It was not because of shipping losses that butter was so scarce, but because Rhondda had fixed the price at £11 9s per hundredweight. This had stopped Dutch exports, because the butter cost £22 5s per hundredweight to produce.[120] Then a shortage of cereals renewed calls to ban the brewing of beer, something Lloyd George, understanding the country's difficult mood as it was, wisely dismissed.

Nor did Rhondda's pleas to the public to restrict their consumption of food, or for people to use their usual grocers and other retailers rather than touring looking for supplies, have much effect. The attempt to control food began to appear chaotic, which hardly boded well for formal rationing, given the bureaucratic complexity of the proposed scheme – not just with shoppers tied to certain shops, but with shops having their stock regulated according to the hours they were open for business; and goods distributed by a ticketing system. Hoarding was punished by heavy fines and imprisonment, but also provoked fears that officials would start raiding middle-class homes and inspecting their larders, and people would be denied the right to have any food other than that required for immediate consumption. As with so many other bureaucratic edicts, that against hoarding would require much explanation and refinement.

One notable success of Rhondda's first months in office was an expansion of factory canteens, whose existence helped regulate the supply of food. By the end of the war, one thousand industrial canteens were supplying a million cheap meals a day. However, as with much else that he did, these were not sufficient to solve such a widespread problem, and it was clear that an even more interventionist approach would be needed. Opening a communal kitchen in Silvertown, east London, on 3 January 1918, Rhondda conceded that compulsory rationing across the nation, and not just in urban areas, 'had to come'.[121] He warned the public that it would not eliminate queues, nor would it ensure 'absolutely fair' distribution. It was not fair as it was: despite the best efforts of the local food committee, 3,000 miners in Burnley went on strike in mid-January in protest at unequal food distribution, and demanded full rationing. Women protested in London suburbs when margarine ran out; 100,000 workers marched on a Saturday afternoon to Manchester town hall to demand better distribution.

It would not, indeed, be until Rhondda grasped the nettle of rationing that any degree of fairness would be introduced into regulating how the British were fed for the rest of the war. On 22 December 1917 the Ministry of Food issued a plan to ensure the more equal distribution of meat, margarine, tea and butter; on Christmas Eve local food committees had been authorised to implement rationing, using a system of customer registration, in areas where food was scarce. No sooner were butter and margarine on the ration than the combined amount per person per week was cut from 10 ounces to 8 ounces: but by the new year queues were shorter. On 31 December, with prices rising again (especially in urban areas) because of shortages, it was announced that sugar too would be rationed, with 8 ounces allocated per person per week, and the manufacture of ice cream was banned. Rationing of two other essential items – meat (16 ounces a week) and butter (4 ounces) – was brought in early in 1918 more to calm people down than because of shortages. In July 1918 jam, tea and lard were rationed, and by the end of the war bread too, at 7 pounds a week for a working man and 4 pounds for a working woman.

By February 1918 an estimated half a million people were regularly queuing for food, with the queues worst on Saturdays.[122] Lloyd George, still fearing a public revolt, wanted a food distributor appointed, because he saw the shortages as 'dangerous'.[123] Distribution failures caused most shortages, and were usually the fault of the government interfering in the pricing mechanism. Controls were vigorously enforced: there were

50,000 prosecutions in the following year, as rationing persisted beyond the Armistice, though the amounts were generous compared with what Germans were enduring and with what would be necessary during Hitler's war.[124] The new system meant the end of queues and arrested the decline of morale, though Lloyd George received reports from Wales in early January about unrest there, especially among munitions workers. Rhondda's proposed scheme was simplified to each customer registering with a retailer, and no retailer accepting more registrations than he could serve. Food was then distributed to shops in proportion to the numbers of their registered customers. The Labour Party and trades unions called for a universal scheme to ensure fair distribution of all foodstuffs.

Rhondda instituted one 'meatless day' per week – on which no meat could be sold – from 1 January. It was as well, because after his department had fixed its prices at new levels the previous week, cattle markets emptied as few farmers felt it wise to sell their cattle. Sheep and pigs could still be had, but the government announced it would fix their live price as well. Farmers then stopped sending this livestock, too, to market. By the end of the first week in January many London butchers were closed for want of merchandise, and by the second week closures had spread across Britain: most days became meatless days. Middle-class areas were as badly hit as working-class ones. The position was not rectified for some weeks, despite the King's ordering that cattle be sent from the royal farms at Windsor to the Slough market to set an example to other farmers. But in the second week of January 36.4 per cent less meat was sold at Smithfield than a year earlier, and queues and closures persisted around the country.[125]

In the end it was the attempt to rig the market, and not the institution of a meatless day, that reduced consumption. However, it created an impression of fairness, as there was supposedly an equality of sacrifice. On Friday 12 April, on a meatless day at the Savoy in London, diners could instead opt for *Homard Cardinal* at 12s (probably what a working-class family spent on food in a week) or, if not pushing the boat out, *Turbot poché, sauce Génoise* at 5s or *Omelette aux Pointes d'Asperges* at 3s. A *Punch* cartoon from February 1918 showed an elderly coroneted peer in morning dress looking in the window of a butcher's shop with a working man; each clutches his ration card. The worker says to the peer: 'What's your fancy mate? Mine's a couple of sausages?' His lordship replies: 'Well sir, I was wondering how much saddle of mutton I could get for fivepence.'[126]

Rhondda had inevitably attracted criticism for his management of the food supply, despite having had an almost impossible task and having inherited a poorly run control operation from Devonport. He sought to defend his policies – especially his price controls, which had angered producers – in the Lords on 27 February 1918, two days after meat rationing had been introduced in greater London. By this time fish prices had been fixed too. 'I took office in June last,' he said, 'when prices had been left to the free play of the laws of supply and demand, and when prices were soaring. They had continued steadily and heavily to rise for three years, although there was no shortage, until they were, in the case of imported foodstuffs, more than double the rate obtaining before the war.'[127] He outlined some of the historic price rises: from July 1914 to January 1916, flank of British beef had risen in price by 45 per cent; by July 1916 it was 80 per cent; and by July 1917 was up by 132.2 per cent. However, he claimed the price had fallen back, having risen by just 101 per cent to that time. Mutton in July 1917 was 142 per cent up on July 1914; that had been reduced to a mere 92 per cent by February 1918. Such evidence persuaded Rhondda to risk saying that these were 'two instances of the prices of British-produced food which have been brought under control.'[128] Bread was up by just 54 per cent, thanks to government subsidy. However, uncontrolled foodstuffs were surging in price: fish had risen 217 per cent before it was controlled; and eggs by 245 per cent since July 1914. Rhondda admitted the rise in prices had caused 'seething discontent': but controls had reduced that discontent and, therefore, increased Britain's chances of winning the war, by helping eliminate a major cause of industrial unrest.

He was determined to explain that the tenets of traditional liberalism simply could not obtain during a time of total war.

We are charged with offending against the laws of economics. Well, we are living in times of war. I think I explained pretty fully to your Lordships . . . [that] I intended to pursue the policy that we were going to set aside the law of supply and demand; and I gave your Lordships the reasons for that, one reason being that it was an established fundamental law of economics that a very slight shortage, below the requirements, of any article of prime necessity, leads, or may lead, to a several-fold advance in price. It was because of my knowledge of economics, and because of my knowledge that this law of supply and demand could not be allowed to operate in abnormal times such as these, that led me to take that definite line.[129]

So long as he remained food controller, he said, the restrictions would stay: in food as in so much else, the public had had to learn there could be no exceptions at such a time.

Cleverly, Rhondda soothed public opinion by producing statistics claiming to show the food shortage had improved rather than damaged the nation's health – as would also be the case after rationing in the Second World War. Even though the youngest and fittest men were abroad, the registrar general had announced that there had been fewer deaths in the three months to 30 September than in any other such period in the previous fifty years. Full employment and higher disposable incomes for the working class also helped. In ninety-six large towns the death rate had fallen from 13.5 per thousand in 1914 to 10.9 in the most recent period. Infant mortality had dropped from 128 per thousand to 91 at the same time.[130] In March, based on what he had learned about deficient maternity and child health provision, Rhondda sent the War Cabinet a memorandum on the groundwork for a Ministry of Health, a project it decided to pursue on 5 April.

In the late winter of 1917–18 dairy products, meat and game were all scarce, despite Rhondda's efforts. When word reached the Western Front, soldiers complained that the least the government could do while making them risk their lives for their country was to ensure their women and children were fed. The potentially disastrous effect of this on morale was quickly recognised, and distribution was steadily improved. Later in 1918 a similar feeling in the German army was a powerful reason for that country's capitulation, since almost every foodstuff there was severely rationed – by the late summer Germans were down to a quarter of an egg a week and an ounce of butter, fruit and cocoa were unobtainable and there was only ersatz tea and coffee. In London, as more merchant shipping came through and agricultural output improved, the queues disappeared. Rhondda worked himself literally to death in seeking to feed Britain: he was one of Lloyd George's more inspired ideas, and richly earned the viscountcy (with special remainder to his daughter, unusual in peerages not awarded for military service, who had survived the *Lusitania* with him) which he received a fortnight before his death on 3 July 1918, aged just sixty-two.

IV

Ensuring sufficient manpower for agriculture – and in essential wartime industries – remained a challenge for the duration of the war. A resolution passed just before Christmas by the 'triple alliance' of the miners, railwaymen and transport workers, to resist the import of 'coloured', Chinese and other foreign labour into the country, made matters worse.[31] Conscription further complicated the question. Lloyd George told Derby that shipping and agriculture now required such manpower, if Britain were not to starve, that 'we were down to bedrock and "must be content with the scrapings".' In military terms, he admitted after April 1917 that it was now a question of holding out until the Americans arrived. A Military Service (Review of Exceptions) Bill was introduced in late March, to ensure the re-examination of those earlier rejected on medical grounds, and to review serving Territorials previously judged unfit for overseas service. The medical profession was blamed for 'laxity' in its examinations of men who were keen to serve but forbidden to do so: it was believed there were as many as 100,000.[32] In April both Jellicoe and Robertson addressed a trades union conference about the urgency of more men coming forward, stressing the emergency in which Britain found itself.

Men in exempted occupations – such as eight Nottinghamshire miners – who refused to work were fined and sent to join the Army.[33] Being forcibly sent to the front for withdrawing labour was another weapon to suppress dissent, and for the duration the threat would be used against strikers. It had been announced in mid-March that another 20,000 miners would be urged to volunteer for the Army, and the 'combing out' of young, fit men in the mines proceeded, in the teeth of hostility from the MFGB. Then the government decided to re-examine not merely medically rejected men, but also those discharged from the Army because of the severity of their wounds. On 22 April a massed rally of discharged men was held in Trafalgar Square, some carrying a banner that read 'Comb them out of funk holes and discharged men will go again. Gott strafe the Cuthberts.'[34] The 'Cuthberts' were young, fit men in government employment exempted while the discharged were asked

to return to the front; they were named after a *Daily Mirror* cartoon character used to satirise 'shirkers'. One man's call-up papers had the order
written on them: 'Bring your artificial eye with you.' The men's temper
was not improved by some having been consigned to the workhouse on
their discharge.

Law claimed some men had escaped the trenches by 'fraud', and the
courts heard cases of bribery of doctors who had given obliging exemptions. Ireland was said to be full of English 'refugees' evading service.[135]
Some exemptions were simply bizarre, given the criterion of work of
national importance. The Essex tribunal in April 1917 granted, either temporarily or indefinitely, exemptions to a tobacconist, a licensed victualler,
a shorthand clerk, an auctioneer's assistant and a licensed hawker.[136] There
were cases of either the staff or families of local potentates – who themselves sat on the tribunals – being exempted, and despite the publicity
about ridiculous exemptions others arose – a toffee-maker in Maidstone,
a china merchant in Brighton and a tea-shop manager in Braintree.[137] To
compound problems, a shortage of women began to match that of men;
in April an appeal was launched for more VADs, to staunch a shortage of
nurses. Reports surfaced of the ill-treatment of young nurses, being used
as skivvies by senior colleagues rather than caring for wounded heroes,
which depressed recruitment.[138]

War Office incompetence in chasing up men had led to their avoiding
service on a technicality. Derby, who as war secretary found the weight
of new bureaucracy increasingly hard to deal with, was feeling less and
less supported by his cabinet colleagues, and his association with Lloyd
George, who did not rate him, was turning sour. On 29 April 1917 the
War Cabinet announced, with effect from 7 May, that fit men of military
age in munitions factories would no longer be exempted unless their
work was highly specialised. A schedule of such exemptions was drawn
up: and unless a man's work was included there could be no exemption.
Now that combing-out was under way in the mines, the other trade with
many fit young men in it was textile manufacture: it would be more
affected than any other by the new schedule.[139]

Neville Chamberlain, the newly appointed director of National Service, was ordered on 12 January 1917 to draw up a report on the problem
of too few men joining the Army, and on rationing the labour that was
left for other essential work. Lloyd George enlisted Addison, his bureau-
cratically competent munitions minister, to keep an eye on Chamberlain,

but Addison – who had a functionary's zeal and fervour when it came to building a state machine – felt the new National Service director second-rate, and was of little help to him.

Brigadier General Auckland Geddes, War Office director of recruiting since May 1916, was more helpful to Chamberlain, but both men encountered a civil service determined not to upset the trades unions. The growth of the state prompted the press to ask where the clerical and bureaucratic staff was coming from in the new offices along White-hall and the Embankment. Young men were being combed out of the civil service, and women were needed on the land or in factories. The loss of men from one area of public service had an enduring effect: because so many London postmen were serving, and their replacements did not know the geography, the great postal districts – such as EC, SW and W – were divided into smaller segments, giving birth to EC4, SW3 and W1.

The War Cabinet considered Chamberlain's report on 19 January at a meeting attended by twenty-seven non-members, representing the services and various departments. The report advocated abolishing all exemptions for the 280,000 fit men born between 1895 and 1898 – aged between eighteen and twenty-two. Theoretically, this would preserve older and more experienced and skilled workers for industry. Robertson had entirely endorsed Chamberlain's plan, which would nonetheless have meant taking 70,000 skilled men of twenty-two and under who had completed apprenticeships. Because of this potential loss of expertise the War Cabinet insisted the plan be hugely diluted by continuing exemptions for workers in munitions, metals, agriculture and shipbuilding. The rough rejection of his proposals angered Chamberlain. Robertson was also aggrieved: he had yet to grasp Lloyd George's reluctance to pour more men into the Western Front, to be slaughtered in ill-planned offensives. Chamberlain had also sought responsibility for the War Office Recruiting Department, but that was vetoed, further poisoning relations between him and Lloyd George.[140] However, the War Cabinet agreed that 30,000 farm workers should be called up, along with 20,000 miners and 50,000 semi-skilled and unskilled men.[141] It also decided to call up men the moment they were eighteen (hitherto it had been eighteen and seven months) and to send them overseas before the age of nineteen if trained and needed.

Chamberlain's report had also advocated asking all men aged between eighteen and sixty to volunteer to serve the country, and proposed to use labour exchanges and local authorities to help. He suggested they should be called 'the Industrial Army', which was rejected. The prime minister was happier with a terminology of National Service, which reflected that it was a national volunteering scheme, even if he did not want it unified with military recruiting; Chamberlain announced it in early February 1917. Henderson, removed from the day-to-day rough and tumble of herding his party together, had to defend the new Directorate of National Service – and the director, Chamberlain – in the Commons. In a refusal to comply with Lloyd George's dictatorial methods, MPs complained that this scheme to recruit civilian workers had been foisted upon Britain without parliamentary discussion about its potential expense and effect on industry.

Meetings to encourage volunteers were being held around the country, after a grand launch at Central Hall in Westminster; application forms to join the scheme were stocked at post offices. At the launch – flanked by Chamberlain, Henderson and Hodge, the minister of labour – Lloyd George emphasised that if the voluntary system failed, compulsion would follow. Chamberlain, alluding to the U-boat war, warned the public that 'Germany means to starve us out before she herself is starved out.'[142] A 'blow straight between the eyes' was required against the enemy, and 'national service can deal that blow.' To set the tone, the government ordered all state officials aged between eighteen and sixty to volunteer for National Service; which gave Chamberlain's department the chance to review all existing exemptions of public employees. Chamberlain stressed that no professional man who volunteered would be expected to do manual labour, but would be found something making better use of his abilities.

Lloyd George remained deeply concerned about the allocation of manpower and told Riddell on 11 February that he was about to have 'a big fight' with the Army over it. 'I have today determined to be quite firm,' he said. 'I will not have any more men taken from the farms, the collieries, the shipbuilding yards or the railways.'[143] The Army had demanded another 60,000 farm workers; Prothero said he could not release more than 30,000. That caused a row within the ministry, and on deeper enquiry he found he could only spare 6,000, even with the help of women volunteers. Lloyd George was by now no longer so blasé about conscripting the Irish, realising the anger it would provoke not just in Ireland – where men would, he feared, be had only 'at the point of a bayonet' – but in parts of the expatriate British Empire, and in America. In any case, most Irishmen of military age were working on the land and producing essential food. He recognised, therefore, that such extra numbers as were required would have to come from a population that had already been finely combed for recruits.

Prisoners of war – some 30,000 in due course – were now taken to work on the land. But their contribution was dwarfed by that of women. The Women's National Land Service Corps, begun as a voluntary society in February 1916 to channel women into agricultural work to release men for the front, had by the beginning of 1917 gathered 200,000 volunteers. Then in early 1917 the Board of Agriculture set up a women's branch that ultimately brought in 260,000 volunteers for farm work, far surpassing Prothero's target of 50,000 to 60,000 women (which he thought equivalent to 35,000 men).[144] Meanwhile, Meriel Talbot, director of the women's branch of the Board of Agriculture, set up a labour force of 12,000 mobile workers known as the Women's Land Army. Unlike the bigger army of women volunteers who lived where they worked, the Land Army women went wherever in the country they were most needed. After four weeks' training the women, many of them well-to-do and from urban areas, would be assigned to farm duties such as milking (for which they trained on dummy cows made of wood) and care of livestock, and paid 18s a week, rising to £1 after passing a proficiency test. This appeased women affronted that Chamberlain's scheme for a system of volunteering seemed restricted to men only (he said this was a misunderstanding). By March there were more women volunteers than the state could deploy, whereas the Army received just 140,000 of the 350,000 men it had requested for the first quarter.[145] Even though land girls had alleviated the demand for agricultural labour, releasing men for the services, the War Cabinet ordered the War Office to release 2,000 skilled ploughmen in October 1917 to ensure 1918's crop could be sown. The wet weather prolonged the harvest and delayed sowing; but 388,000 extra acres had been cultivated in 1917 compared with the previous year.[146]

Although the deployment of women in agriculture was a great success, other initiatives had mixed results. The manpower crisis worsened with every casualty list, and the measures the government discussed taking became more radical. Because of doubts about the practicalities, ministers had been dilatory in introducing the necessary legislation for Chamberlain's planned scheme of National Service in industry, and so Parliament had to wait to discuss it: that did not happen until 20 February, over two months after Chamberlain's appointment. The government had announced that, by enrolling in the scheme, every man from eighteen to sixty would place himself at the government's disposal, 'to go anywhere and do anything'.[147] William Anderson, a highly regarded Labour MP who would lose Sheffield Attercliffe at the 1918 election over his opposition to the war, and then die within weeks in the flu epidemic, feared an avalanche of applications from workers too valuable to be spared from their existing duties, and bureaucratic chaos processing their applications: he had a point. Also, very few men above military age and in work would volunteer for a scheme without having the slightest idea of where or in what trade they might end up, and without knowing the effect on their families.

There was public resistance to the notion that the government should direct the energies of working-class people in conscripting them for industry, yet not harness the skills and aptitudes of their social superiors. Anderson believed resources were being wasted because of the profligacy of the ruling class. 'Everybody will agree that it is wrong that men should be employed on, and that money should be spent upon pearls, jewellery of various kinds, golf courses, and so on,' he told the Commons on 15 February. 'I saw an advertisement in a high-class journal the other day offering strings of pearls at from £4,000 to £10,000, and that after two-and-a-half years of war. I am quite sure that nobody would object to the very strongest possible steps being taken to deal with that particular matter.'[148] Anderson wanted a scheme of redeployment from the least essential to the most essential work: but not compulsion. He feared the scheme was typical of Lloyd George having an apparently excellent idea, but no idea how to execute it: something even the pro-government press remarked upon.

Auckland Geddes, in a speech later in the year when the manpower problem remained severe, took up Anderson's theme. He emphasised that finding more men and women for 'work of national importance' meant some 'luxury trades' would effectively have to be closed down, with the Department of National Service reassigning those working for them.[149] 'At the very moment in a certain town, when we are looking for women to make aeroplanes, we have advertisements for girls to dress dolls and to fix wigs on dolls. Dolls versus aeroplanes, and the doll makers able to pay wages on the same scale as the aeroplane manufacturers. That is obvious misdirection of human effort.'

Anderson told the Commons that in 1916 two million women had applied to labour exchanges for work and only 800,000 had been placed.[150] Farmers remained reluctant to take them: and it was two and a half years before the Army realised it could use women as cooks, at home or behind the lines in France. Anderson voiced the widespread concern of further 'dislocation of home life' if more women were taken.[151] When the directorate was put on a statutory basis it was confirmed that this was for the purposes of males only: women were resources 'to whom a separate appeal and one of a different character will be made'.[152] Several such appeals would occur, notably when on 1 August 1917 the Women's Forestry Service was established, to help ensure felling of more trees for timber – needed for shoring up trenches in France – and their planting. Sourcing more timber at home liberated space on merchant ships for food. In February 1917 the commissioner of the Metropolitan Police agreed women could drive taxi-cabs: London's taxi-drivers, however, took a different view, and threatened to withdraw their labour if women appeared behind the wheel.

It was agreed that working-class men in the scheme would be compensated at the same rate as in their previous occupation; the government stressed that any professional man on a salary who volunteered would not be paid at his accustomed rate. As before, munitions workers, because of their special value and importance, would be treated differently. Farm workers could expect a minimum of 25s a week. The law constituting the directorate made it clear that no man would be taken out of his existing calling; but also that no volunteer would be allowed to work in a business not of national importance. The Army refused to cooperate with Chamberlain to get more skilled men back from the front to make munitions; and he felt deserted by Lloyd George, who made no effort to intervene to solve the problem. Northcliffe joined in and began to attack Chamberlain, who lacked the authority to resolve the matter. Northcliffe had a compulsion to search for weakness, and in Chamberlain he thought he had found it in the government whose creation he had done so much to effect.

Neville Chamberlain was one of the few brought into Lloyd George's orbit who would not accept the standard, obedient relationship the prime minister expected. His reputation now may be that of an appeaser and a weakling, or one who was unduly naive, but he was determined to show no such credentials to Lloyd George. They had had worsening relations from the moment of his appointment. Chamberlain had struggled to forge understandings with the other departments such as Labour, Munitions and the Board of Trade that were essential if he were to work effectively. He had failed properly to organise his department, and he and Lloyd George had had policy differences over exemptions. In late June the movement of a parliamentary secretary to another department without Chamberlain's being consulted had so outraged him that he wrote to Lloyd George to say that it 'seems to me an exhibition of discourtesy so extraordinary that I have difficulty in believing it to be unintentional.'[153] The prime minister, apologising, claimed it had been a misunderstanding. In fact the new parliamentary secretary, Cecil Beck, a rare Lloyd George Liberal, was already conspiring with the prime minister against the director.

Lloyd George encouraged Hodge, the minister of labour, who was hostile to Chamberlain and had stifled cooperation by labour exchanges with the national volunteer scheme, to present his views about how manpower policy should proceed. He asked Auckland Geddes, who had bolstered Chamberlain as director of recruiting, for a report too: Geddes recommended releasing men from exemptions by occupation rather than by age. This set him against Chamberlain, who reiterated his belief in cancelling all exemptions for younger men in his latest report to the War Cabinet on 13 July.[154] He said that 'unless the Government were prepared to reverse their present policy in regard to the younger classes of men, he did not see that there was much object in the continued existence of his Department.' Geddes said there were around 500,000 men of military age in the coal mines, and he wished to take a quota by ballot.

The War Cabinet decided in early August 1917 that a single director of National Service should control both military and industrial manpower, a job Chamberlain was deeply reluctant to take on. He had read briefings against his department in the press – which he now recognised as the traditional means of undermining someone – and prepared for his departure. With both Lloyd George and Northcliffe unimpressed by him his survival became improbable, and on Milner's advice he resigned. Auckland Geddes, a trained doctor and former professor of medicine who had imagined he was about to be put in charge of the Army's

medical service, replaced him: Chamberlain felt Geddes had been set up
to bounce him out of his job. The day before Chamberlain resigned
Lloyd George sent Geddes to meet him for an interview. Chamberlain
thought it was about Geddes occupying a subordinate position at
National Service; but Geddes learned from the prime minister's office
that Lloyd George had told Chamberlain that morning that if he didn't
feel he could do the job, Geddes could. Chamberlain never forgave Lloyd
George for this humiliation, and when the time came in 1922 it would
play a considerable part in his downfall and that of his coalition. Meanwhile, like trades unions squabbling over demarcation lines, a formal
agreement had to be drawn up between the Ministry of National Service
and the Ministry of Labour about which part of the bureaucracy would
do what. Bluntly, the latter would exist to help the former, and would be
subservient to it.[155]

At least Chamberlain was spared the struggles Geddes would have in
the months ahead, as men were fed to the guns at Passchendaele, and
others had to be found. The re-examination of the medically unfit
increased during the summer and autumn of 1917, with a large number
of fraudulent cases being discovered: men who, usually without (but
sometimes with) the complicity of the doctor, had been thought epilep-
tic or diabetic were the most frequent cases. It was believed 4,000 fit
men were deliberately evading military service in the London borough
of Stepney alone.[156] Later in the autumn Geddes announced a reform of
medical classification, assisting enlistment of those deemed unfit.

By contrast with the manpower scheme the management of the
nation's coal supplies worked reasonably smoothly. It was just as well:
industry, the trains and the electricity grid ran on it. In 1915 Asquith had
appointed a committee to monitor the coal industry, and by spring 1917
it had reported three times, on each with a greater degree of concern. By
1 September 1916 around 165,000 miners, or 14.8 per cent of the workforce, had enlisted; output had fallen to 253 million tons in 1915, 12.5
million less than in 1914. A coal controller had been appointed; more
than 15,000 men on home service had been recalled from the Army and
output had increased by 4 million tons. In December 1916 the government had assumed overall control of the South Wales coalfield: in
mid-March it became responsible for all mines in Great Britain, coordinating production and distribution. This was not nationalisation, but
a temporary measure during whose operation the government came to a

financial arrangement with the owners. Nonetheless, in unseasonably cold weather in April 1917 – the coldest April since 1839 – there were coal shortages in London, attributed to transport problems; the railways had had little investment during the war and were in appalling repair.[157] The new, more efficient organisation would take a while to bed in, but the controller would regulate output, terms and conditions of employment, distribution, price, export and consumption of coal.[158]

Production of munitions remained a crucial priority, but corners were too often cut in the attempt to raise output, sometimes catastrophically so. Munitions workers were routinely hauled before the courts and fined for falling asleep on duty, for 'failing to take all precautions against the occurrence of fire or explosion . . . and endangering the lives of thousands of hands', as a report in March 1917 recorded.[159] This report came in the aftermath of one of the gravest accidents of the war years. Just before 7 p.m. on 19 January 50 tons of TNT exploded at the factory at Silvertown, in the Essex docklands east of London, after a fire broke out. The government had taken over the site to purify TNT – a process more dangerous than its actual production – in September 1915, despite warnings from its owners that such a process was highly dangerous, and the factory was in a built-up and highly populated area. The warning was, if anything, understated. The plant was devastated; 900 nearby properties were wrecked or made unsalvageable; around 70,000 sustained some damage, usually from hot rubble dropping on them and starting fires; a gasometer in nearby Greenwich was hit, creating a huge fire. Silvertown's blaze could be seen 30 miles away, and straight after the explosion the whole London sky was illuminated 'like many golden sunsets in one'. The explosion was heard all over London and the eastern counties, and up to 100 miles away.[160] A seismologist found the earth had shaken in Radcliffe-on-Trent, 122 miles from the explosion.[161]

Miraculously, there were just seventy-three dead and four hundred injured, because many workers had gone home and most in surrounding houses were downstairs, as it was the upper storey that absorbed the blast. At least £2 million worth of damage was caused; the next day the site of the blast was 'a smouldering, steaming nothing'.[162] Few details were glossed over in press reports: all London knew what had happened. Efforts began to rehouse thousands of homeless, and a relief fund was established to ensure that those whose workplaces no longer existed had enough to live on. A government report – not published until the

1950s – attacked the casual attitude to safety at the plant. Most of the TNT had been outside in a goods yard, awaiting shipment, and its containers were inadequate to protect it from a blast starting elsewhere.

V

Despite the enormous demands of dealing with the day-to-day fighting of the war, Lloyd George hoped to show that the government was also thinking of the future. Asquith had formed a small reconstruction committee and, on 17 February, Lloyd George expanded it and altered its terms of reference. Montagu was executive vice chairman (under Lloyd George) and Vaughan Nash, Asquith's former private secretary, continued as secretary. Some MPs complemented a few of Lloyd George's 'Garden Suburb' lieutenants, such as Philip Kerr, the future Marquess of Lothian, as well as some Tory and Labour luminaries: among the latter was Beatrice Webb, who came to regard Montagu as a 'dead failure'.[163] It was suggested that both Shaw and Wells be invited to join, but Lloyd George – wary no doubt of the reputations for bloody-mindedness that preceded each man – struck their names off the list. The committee lasted until 17 July, when replaced by the Ministry of Reconstruction.

For purposes of morale it was vital to signal to the public that their rulers were giving consideration to how life after the war was going to be better. In the late winter of 1916–17 Robertson had observed that 'there are gradually accumulating in this country a great many wounded and crippled men who are not of a cheery disposition,' though voluntary organisations were assiduously setting up training schools to teach skills to them, and charities were supplying networks of hostels for them to live in.[164] The music hall and theatre played an important part in funding these hostels, through charity performances strongly supported by high society. Many factories were training the disabled for important work, making munitions and other goods vital to the war effort. However, the authorities remained slow in paying allowances to such men, leaving them and their families in serious hardship as a man's service pay and his wife's separation allowance were stopped on his discharge. With food being dear, this risked becoming a highly combustible problem. Moreover, the potentially sulphurous problem of these aggrieved ex-servicemen became worse still when mixed in with the agitations of pacifist leftists and trades unionists inspired by events in Russia.

Distracting though such matters were, however, Lloyd George's most fundamental responsibility remained the prosecution of the war: and from the moment he put his faith in Nivelle within weeks of moving into Downing Street, his judgement on how best to do that appeared highly questionable. In backing the Nivelle offensive, which had brought abject failure, Lloyd George had shown he was no better a judge of strategy than Asquith. Between 9 and 14 April 1917 the Battle of Arras caused 140,000 British casualties (including Edward Thomas, the poet, shot through the chest on the first day), against 85,000 German. Although the Canadians took Vimy Ridge, Haig and Robertson saw the failure of the offensive as proving Lloyd George's stupidity in putting the BEF, even temporarily, under French command. The French were highly sceptical about whether the offensive would work; Lloyd George's advocacy had been crucial; the political blame rested largely with him. It was a poor start to his stewardship of the British war effort. However, while the generals blamed him, he blamed them for supporting a Western Front offensive. The relationship would never detoxify.

Lloyd George continued to favour the 'Salonica' strategy, persisting in the view that attacking the Kaiser's more vulnerable allies would bring better results than constant attrition in France and Flanders. The rapid realisation that Russia, after the February revolution and the installation of the provisional government, could not hold its own militarily or in weapons production, caused Robertson and Haig to grasp that more German troops might reach the Western Front, which therefore could not be denuded of the troops to resist them.

The prime minister was, however, right in his belief that Britain's best hope lay in having Germany worn down by blockade before another great attack in the West. On 5 May 1917, after an Allied conference in Paris following the failure of the Nivelle offensive, a joint Anglo-French communiqué announced: 'It is no longer a question of aiming at breaking through the enemy's front and aiming at distant objectives. It is now a question of wearing down and exhausting the enemy's resistance and if and when this is achieved, to exploit it to the furthest possible extent.'[165] A sudden capitulation by the Germans was impossible: only attrition could defeat them.

Milner, on 7 June, argued that there was 'an urgent need of a fresh stocktaking of the whole war situation,' after events in Russia, and America's entry into the conflict.[166] He and others feared mutinies in the French army made France an unreliable ally. He identified a sense of 'drift', and felt a different initiative was needed. A possibility of this arose when the new Emperor of Austria–Hungary, Karl, who had succeeded his great-uncle Franz Josef in 1916, approached the French government via his cousin Prince Sixte of Bourbon for a separate peace in early April. Lloyd George, seeing a means of dividing the Central Powers, was enthusiastic: but the Italians, with an army in the field against Austria, were not interested, so the proposal failed. Robertson feared the prime minister nonetheless wanted to launch a new offensive in Italy, and warned Haig on 13 June to be on the alert against such a proposal. He told Haig 'there is trouble in the land just now' because 'the War Cabinet, under the influence of LG, have started . . . to review the whole policy and strategy of the war and to "get at facts".'[167] The War Cabinet was interviewing the relevant people, and his (and Robertson's) time would come 'and then the trouble would begin' because 'the railway people have been asked for figures regarding the rapid transfer of 12 divisions and 300 heavy guns to Italy! They will never go while I am CIGS,' Robertson declared.

Committed as they both were to a western campaign, he impressed upon Haig his need to avoid the habitual extreme optimism Robertson knew Lloyd George found so nauseating: 'Don't argue that you can finish the war this year, or that the German is already beaten.' He suggested Haig put forward his plan for the summer offensive and leave it to the War Cabinet to reject it – 'they dare not do that.' Unfortunately, when Haig came to London on 19 June, to argue for a new Flanders offensive, he forgot this useful advice. Flushed by the success of the Battle of Messines the previous week (in which, thanks to a superb mining operation by sappers, more than 10,000 Germans were reported missing, 7,200 of whom were taken prisoner), he outlined a new attack that, if successful, would take the Army to Ostend and the coast. He used a huge relief map of the terrain, in a presentation during which Lloyd George thought 'the critical faculties' of some of his colleagues 'were overwhelmed.'[168]

Haig felt each of his questioners seemed 'more pessimistic than the other'; he asserted that 'Germany was nearer her end than they seemed to think.'[169] He demanded more men and guns, and sidestepped Lloyd George's Italian ideas: despite serious competition, Haig was becoming his own worst enemy. That afternoon Smuts, trying to help, told him that Lloyd George 'was afraid that my plan would exhaust the British Army by the winter, and without gaining victory.' Haig made a point of hammering away at Robertson's caution: when the CIGS visited him in France before Haig's trip to London, Haig had told him that:

the German was now on his last legs and that there was only one sound plan to follow viz

Send to France every possible man
   „   „   „   „   possible aeroplane
   „   „   „   „   gun[170]

Robertson had visited Haig to warn him that if he tried any more great attacks without French support Britain would soon be without an army; but he returned believing Haig was right, and the part he played in convincing Lloyd George of this undermined his own career.

In the succeeding weeks Haig and Robertson pressed the War Cabinet to accept the plan. The politicians talked to Haig for days, though decided remarkably little. Haig colluded with Repington to have *The Times* demand more men be sent to France. Robertson was asked whether he believed the offensive would succeed; more cautious than Haig (to Haig's annoyance), he said it was the right course – though success would be more certain if Russia and France struck the Germans too. Lloyd George struggled to conquer his belief that his military advisers were clueless. He cannot have been reassured when, with disarming honesty, Haig conceded he expected 100,000 casualties a month, similar to the Somme.

Robertson outlined a further argument. 'I would recall the demoralizing effect upon troops which prolonged defensive tactics inevitably have; urge that, although the attacker might at first be the heavier loser, it was the defender who would certainly lose most in the long run, once his physical and moral powers began to break down; and that, as in the conduct of any business, civil no less than military, without offensive action, without initiative, success could never, in point of fact, be achieved.'[171] Ministers countered by talking of 'attrition' and 'the unintelligent application of brute force', arguments Robertson dismissed as 'fatuous'.

With the Austrians seeming to wish for a separate peace, Lloyd George became all the more determined to send men to north Italy, to attack Trieste and encourage an Austrian surrender. Curzon felt Flanders would be better for an attack than the Somme had been; Milner saw the value in getting the Germans off the Belgian coast; Haig claimed that by occupying more of that coast air raids on England would be reduced, a keen political consideration, given the raids by Gotha bombers that were now plaguing London and the east coast of England.

It was not until 18 July that Haig learned he could probably go ahead with what would be known as the Third Battle of Ypres: it took three more days for the prime minister to agree, which finally happened at what Robertson called 'a rough and tumble meeting' of the War Cabinet.[172] Given Lloyd George's fears of public outrage at the carnage, it was all the more astonishing he agreed to another such offensive; though perhaps not more astonishing than Haig, whom many already regarded as a butcher, apparently contemplating one with such equanimity. However, the War Cabinet (on Jellicoe's advice) also feared the shortage of shipping would starve Britain into submission and, as Haig put it, 'it would be impossible for Great Britain to continue the war in 1918.' And it was that, as much as anything, that caused Lloyd George to agree to Haig's plan. The decision was taken 'with reluctance and misgiving', though Lloyd George was conscious Haig had been right about the Nivelle offensive.[173] Haig was told another Somme would not be allowed: if the offensive failed, it would be stopped quickly. He warned the politicians it might take several weeks, with commensurate casualties, before the Army attained its main objective, the Passchendaele ridge.

On 31 July the Third Battle of Ypres began. The torrential rain that would turn it into a sea of mud arrived that evening. It quickly became a disaster, fought in the wettest August for decades. It achieved a mere four-mile advance, a huge loss of men and an even larger proportionate loss of officers. Although it unquestionably harmed the morale of a German army so short of supplies that its men only received the full bread ration when in the front line, it harmed British morale too. The great offensive was reported with heavy censorship, but one did not have to read between the lines too carefully to discern how little progress was being made. To make matters worse, *The Times* commented on the lack of information from the Western Front, and it was clear the public were uneasy because of the lack of news about progress. Whether because of the shortage of newsprint or in order not to exacerbate despair, the paper of record now usually printed daily lists of casualties only among officers instead of pages of NCOs and other ranks, though these returned during September.

The slaughter at Ypres was less shocking than that of the Somme, because it was less novel: the flood of letters and telegrams to the bereaved nonetheless depressed morale. As on the Somme, it took even ministers a while to grasp the sheer scale of British losses on the Western Front. The huge and rapid expansion of the state meant the War Cabinet was in almost permanent session, so that for ministers to keep track of how the war was being fought, and to hold the generals to account, became an increasingly tall order. By 2 August the War Cabinet had held 200 meetings in 235 days. Smuts told Riddell that 'drastic revision of the organisation' was necessary.[174] 'There is no sufficient delegation and Ministers have no time to think out the really great problems of the war. At the end of the week the mind is in a haze owing to the number and complexity of the problems which have arisen.' Indeed, one reason the debacle in Flanders was allowed to continue was because the politicians were so preoccupied that they failed properly to engage with it. Hankey would later tell Riddell that 'ministers are so overwhelmed with work that they cannot follow the naval and military operations in detail from day to day.'[175] Matters were not helped by Haig's disingenuousness and his decision to press ahead in the face of the evidence of the failure of the new offensive, even though he had undertaken to call it off immediately in such an event. Senior soldiers may privately have regarded Lloyd George as dishonest, but it is hard to know what to make of a report Haig sent to the War Cabinet on 4 August, the third anniversary of the outbreak of the war and the fifth day of the Ypres offensive, in which he proclaimed the results thus far were 'most satisfactory'.[176]

Along with the continuing food problems the news depressed morale, as did recurring, and blatant, daylight air raids. On 12 August, a Sunday afternoon, Gothas attacked Southend-on-Sea, packed with day trippers and holidaymakers: thirty-two people were killed and forty-three injured. They also attempted to bomb Clacton and Margate, whence the RFC drove them out to sea before they could do more than superficial damage. In Southend the police had had a few minutes' warning: it was not enough to warn the public in the streets. The jury in the inquest on the deaths called the raid 'inexcusable' as there was nothing of military interest anywhere near Southend.[177] It also registered dismay at the inadequacy of the warnings. Soon, there were demands to build shelters, or at least for churches and buildings with crypts or cellars to open them up during raids so people could take cover. On the night of 3–4 September there were military casualties nearer home: a raid targeting the naval establishment at Chatham on the Medway killed 152 people, including 130 naval recruits sleeping in their barracks.

This happened almost a fortnight into the horror of Passchendaele, as the casualty lists were beginning to inform the public about the enormity of the strategic blunder. One of the many astounding features of this bloodbath was that its architect, Haig, survived in his job. Passchendaele was, to Lloyd George, when he eventually discovered the truth about what had happened (for Haig had starved even Robertson of information), the final proof of Haig's inadequacy. The prime minister realised he was twice bitten – by Nivelle and now by Haig – which increased his determination to improve strategic military decision-making and the quality of advice. Since this advice was usually channelled through Robertson, Lloyd George chose to focus his wrath on him, even though Haig had been the driving force behind the offensive. A week into the Third Battle of Ypres, and by now utterly convinced that his generals were wrong and their strategy a disaster, Lloyd George reopened his demand for a strengthened Italian front. He was supported, to Robertson's dismay, by Foch; who, in London for a combined conference, also proposed setting up an Allied Staff in Paris, an idea Robertson and Haig had hoped was dead and buried after the Nivelle offensive. 'I can see Lloyd George in the future wanting to agree to some such organisation,' Robertson told Haig on 9 August, 'so as to put the matter in French hands and to take it out of mine.'[178] Robertson indicated he would not go without a fight. 'However we shall see all about this,' he told Haig.[179] For Lloyd George, an Italian campaign was a means of diverting troops from Haig's efforts to slaughter them.

Exasperated by the politicians, Robertson complained about their inadequacies to Haig: 'Milner is a tired, dyspeptic old man. Curzon a gas-bag. Bonar Law equals Bonar Law. Smuts has good instinct but lacks knowledge. On the whole he is best, but they help one very little.'[180] He told General Sir Launcelot Kiggell, Haig's chief of staff, that the prime minister was 'an under-bred swine.'[181]

On 29 August Lloyd George, on a semi-holiday in a Sussex as battered by wind and rain as Passchendaele, ordered Robertson down to see him to discuss what to do next. He argued for an Italian offensive. Robertson strongly disagreed. He claimed the Germans were on their knees and short of reserves, and a victory in Flanders was inevitable – according to

Haig. Later, Robertson wrote to Gwynne (whom Haig regarded as 'very self-satisfied and highly conceited'), criticising the press for having built up expectations to an unreasonable level, and warned him 'there *must* be a row one day I fear.'[182] He outlined what he perceived to be the problem with the prime minister: 'Each day brings a proposal more wild than its predecessor, regardless of time & space . . . *interference is constant.*'

The French continued to support Lloyd George's idea of reinforcing Italy, with Foch offering to send 100 guns, subject to British approval, which he came to London to seek on 3 September: but the Italians themselves were on the defensive, and in no position to lead a joint attack on Austria. Haig joined the meeting with Foch and insisted the Western Front could not possibly lose one hundred guns. Law vacillated, but Smuts, still then a Western Front man, and Carson took Haig's side. Haig agreed to a private entreaty from Lloyd George to try to find fifty guns. The prime minister confided in him that he was distressed by the collapse of the French government of Alexandre Ribot, which had just fallen after a series of crises including the mutinies in the French army; and he said that 'Russia could be of no further help to the Allies in the War.'[183] Churchill told Haig on 13 September that he too supported concentrating efforts for 1918 against the enemy in France and Flanders, but 'admitted that Lloyd George and he were doubtful about being able to beat the Germans on the Western front.'[184] The next day Smith and Carson assured Haig they would urge Lloyd George to stick to a Western Front strategy.

In despair and unwell, and increasingly vexed by news from Russia about the growing anarchy there, Lloyd George went to his home in Wales for a rest. When Hankey visited him at Criccieth on 14 September he found him 'despondent' and 'disgusted at the narrowness of the General Staff, and the inability of his colleagues to see eye to eye with him and their fear of overruling the General Staff.'[185] With an Italian excursion ruled out, his attention turned to Turkey, an idea for which he had the support of Milner, who also came to Criccieth for consultations; but nothing would come of that idea.

Although he had his partisans in the second tier of ministers, Haig was exhausting the patience of most of the War Cabinet; after Milner's implicit disavowal of him, Law then wrote to Lloyd George on 18 September to say he had told Robertson the previous day 'that I had lost absolutely all hope of anything coming of Haig's offensive and, though he did not say so in so many words, I understood he took the same view . . . it is evident that the time must soon come when we will have to decide whether or not this offensive is to be allowed to go on.'[186] After a conversation with Riddell, who like Milner had also been asked to Criccieth, the newspaper proprietor believed that 'he has evidently decided to press for a cessation of the Western offensive. He has said on many occasions that he was opposed to it and has prophesied its failure.'[187] Milner, again, entirely supported this view. A confrontation was, in Riddell's and Hankey's view, brewing between Lloyd George and the generals.

When word reached Criccieth that Haig and Asquith had met for talks, it prompted Lloyd George and his friends to conclude that the Field Marshal was expecting an onslaught from his political masters, and had enlisted Asquith to support him. Nevertheless the Flanders offensive carried on until it petered out, with great loss of life on both sides, in early November: the figures are highly disputed, but a consensus view is that each side had over a quarter of a million casualties. Lloyd George realised that to end it sooner would have forced the resignations of Robertson and Haig, for which he was not then ready. However, at the War Cabinet he found another way of provoking them, by stepping up demands for Turkey to be taken on and forced out of the war.

In a long talk on 15 October with Hankey, Lloyd George said he saw no chance of the war ending before 1919, when he felt the Allies would at last have the resources for a devastating attack. But he was contemplating seeking formation of what became known as the Supreme War Council, a coordinating body of all Allies. His view would be reinforced by a general with an axe to grind, critical of the Flanders offensive and who shared his belief that a regular conference of British, French, Russian and Italian leaders could give the war better and more varied direction. Sir Henry Wilson, at that stage commander-in-chief of Eastern Command and based in London, was driving the idea, which bore signs of his personality as an intriguer. Some Allied generals had long discussed this possibility: Lloyd George embraced the notion to counter his generals' obsession with the Western Front.

Determined, irrespective of the proprieties, to seek alternative advice, Lloyd George had the War Cabinet summon Wilson and French as well as Robertson to give their views on the question on 10 October. Robertson was incensed at his two fellow generals being asked, believing it was a vote of no confidence in him: that evening he offered Derby his resignation. Derby refused it and consulted colleagues: Curzon told him to tell Robertson that Lloyd George had merely been consulting widely, and wisely, before taking a big decision, as Asquith had been wont to do. However, Robertson was conveniently on hand to be blamed for the failure of the latest offensive, and Lloyd George's old yearning for a unified command not run by his CIGS was becoming unstoppable.

The day before the War Cabinet meeting Robertson told Haig: 'He is out for my blood very much these days.'[188] He correctly realised that Lloyd George would no longer suffer what he deemed poor military advice in silence, and that anything that did not advocate Allied unity of command constituted such poor advice. He also told Haig: 'Milner, Carson, Curzon, Cecil, Balfour have each in turn expressly spoken to me separately about his intolerable conduct during the last week or two and have said they are behind us.'[189] He hoped matters would come to a head because 'I am sick of this damned life.' Wilson dined with Lloyd George on 17 October and noted that 'it became very clear to me to-night that Lloyd George means to get Robertson out, and means to curb the powers of the C in C in the field.'[190] This was exactly what Wilson had wanted and advised.

However, the prime minister had to proceed with caution. More than just Robertson's *amour propre* was at stake: Curzon stressed to Hankey that if Robertson were forced out all leading Tories, except possibly Law, would leave the government, which would inevitably be brought down. Law was of little use at that moment; the second of his three sons had been killed in Palestine in April, a heavy blow then compounded by the loss of his eldest, an RFC pilot, in France in late September; while loyal to Lloyd George, he was for weeks *hors de combat* in political terms. Hankey impressed on Lloyd George the need to tread carefully, and he 'took the hint very quickly.'[191] Eric Geddes also intervened, apparently decisively, telling Robertson the War Cabinet's consulting widely was no reason to resign. Robertson stayed, but the drama continued. Wilson and French were asked to state their views about a Supreme War Council in writing; and Robertson demanded to see their reports. Both men recommended a central staff of generals in Paris as part of an Allied council, and independent of national general staffs; both argued against a Flanders offensive in 1918, which was Robertson's policy. French heavily criticised other policies of Robertson and Haig. Lloyd George and Hankey had seen these reports, and realised that were Robertson to read them he would resign again.

Lloyd George asked French to rephrase parts of his report before Robertson saw it. French agreed solely because he did not wish to be accused of personal bitterness against Robertson; but declined the prime minister's suggestion to say something positive about Haig. Lloyd George and Robertson had a conciliatory talk on 26 October, which included Lloyd George promising to see whether the Supreme War Council could be situated in London. Nonetheless, the failure of the Flanders offensive, and the huge loss of life, increased Lloyd George's determination to effect change. In self-exculpatory mood, the prime minister told Hankey on 18 October – two days after sending Haig a congratulatory telegram on behalf of the War Cabinet for the 'achievements' of the Army at Ypres – that 'no-one would have voted for that offensive had they not been considerably influenced by his [Haig's] optimism.'[192] Yet Haig, whose main mistake had been to believe he could make the decisive strike of the war without French direction and before American troops arrived to take a share in the glory, would not be the scapegoat when Lloyd George realised the direction of the Army could not continue as it was.

News then came of Italy's disastrous defeat, by what Haig had asserted was the demoralised German army and the Austro-Hungarian army, at Caporetto, allowing the Central Powers to advance 100 miles in a fortnight. Half the Italian army had either been killed, or had surrendered, or been wounded, or simply run away after Caporetto, provoking decades of jokes about Italy's martial prowess. Lloyd George took the opportunity to call an Allied conference in London, setting in motion his plan for a permanent grouping.[193] The Supreme War Council's first meeting took place at Rapallo on 7 November, where it agreed to investigate assistance for Italy. On his way there Lloyd George stopped at Paris, and consulted Haig about setting up the Supreme War Council. Haig insisted it was unworkable. 'The PM then said that the two Governments had decided to form it,' Haig noted. 'So I said, there is no need saying any more then!'[194] The two men had a stand-off about Italy: Haig urged Lloyd George not to take troops from his command to send there; the prime minister countered that he would decide that when he saw how bad things were. In the end, five divisions were sent to Italy.

The prime minister berated Haig about attacks on himself in the press that he believed were 'evidently inspired by the Military.' Haig had recently had the editors of the *Morning Post*, the *Westminster Gazette* and the *Daily News* out to France, so may not have been entirely innocent.

Lloyd George accused him of having briefed Asquith's friend J. A. Spender, the *Gazette*'s editor, about prime ministerial interference in military tactics. Haig denied it and promised to write to Spender – at which Lloyd George, presumably because he had no evidence for this somewhat paranoid assertion, begged him not to. Haig wrote that 'his position as PM is shaky and [he] means to try to vindicate his conduct of the war in the eye of the public and try and put the people against the soldiers. In fact, to pose as the saviour of his country, who has been hampered by bad advice given by the General Staff!' The clash of egos was almost as terrible as that of the Allies and the Central Powers.

With Lloyd George's plan for the Supreme War Council now accepted, the new body agreed to meet monthly, its members kept daily informed by their military representatives, of whom Britain's was Wilson and France's Foch. Contrary to Lloyd George's promises to Robertson, it would meet at Versailles. Hankey, whose opinions had become oracular to the prime minister, had long disliked Wilson for his conspiratorial and self-serving behaviour; but – and this would be crucial to Wilson's progress – Hankey had recently modified his opinion, and told Lloyd George so. This inflicted collateral damage on Robertson, who was unequal to the politics that was now taking place. Esher wrote of him on 10 November: 'He was not the Wully of a month ago, but rather a pathetic shadow.'[195] He added something of which Robertson was already well aware: 'It is placing himself in a false position, if, now that he is no longer the sole military adviser of the Government, he remains CIGS.' Amery, appointed liaison man between the secretariat of the War Cabinet and the new Council, noted: 'Looking back over the best part of a year at the Cabinet, I cannot recollect Robertson on a single occasion indicating what he thought the enemy was really likely to do or what we might do ourselves, beyond expressing the general hope that we were going to obtain our objectives in the West.'[196]

On his way home Lloyd George stopped in Paris again on 12 November to speak on the dangers of Allied disunity, and to give the public his reasons for setting up the Supreme War Council. There was a further chance for Esher to discuss Robertson with him; Lloyd George disclosed that he thought Robertson, too, was using the press against him. 'He would have no objection if Wully spoke his mind, however vigorously, but he added, "Robertson gives a grunt and then sends for Gwynne and Leo Maxse."'[197]

The prime minister included in his speech a snide remark about the alleged victories on the Western Front, and how the 'appalling casualty list' made him wish 'it had not been necessary to win so many.'[198] This had the presumably unintended effect of sowing divisions within the government in London. Derby was so alarmed at the tone of the speech and the aspersions cast on the Army that he wrote to Haig to 'express my entire confidence in you and your men.'[199] Haig believed political expediency motivated Lloyd George and 'would like to make the soldiers the scapegoat in the hope of remaining in power for a little time longer.'[200] He feared that 'with such a dishonest fellow as prime minister' victory would be impossible. Haig and Lloyd George deserved each other.

As befitted a man accused of being a dictator, Lloyd George had driven this crucial policy without consulting Parliament. Nor had he consulted President Wilson. He finally reported to the Commons on 14 November when reading out the terms of agreement between the British, French and Italian governments to have a Supreme War Council, stressing its advisory and not executive function. He had also heard from Colonel House, Wilson's man in London, that House would recommend Wilson to appoint a military representative to the new Council. Robertson remained deeply hostile. Hankey learned from Asquith, who asked him to lunch on 15 November, that Robertson had consulted him, and Hankey concluded Robertson was 'intriguing like the deuce.'[201] A long Commons debate on the 19th revealed deep parliamentary opposition to diluting British power through the Supreme War Council. Nonetheless the plan was followed through, and the Council – by this time with unequivocal US support – met at Versailles on 30 November, under the presidency of Georges Clemenceau, the former doctor and journalist who, at seventy-six, had just become prime minister of France for the second time and its minister of war. Hankey wrote Lloyd George's opening speech for the first main session the following day.

Having secured this long-desired aim, Lloyd George continued to tinker with the machinery of government to try to deliver the victory. His next target – sensibly – was to combine the aviation capabilities of the Army and Navy into an air force. The idea had, in fact, been Smuts's, but Churchill championed it with gusto. This annoyed Unionist ministers, who recalled recent assurances that Churchill would not interfere in war policy. The munitions minister stepped outside his department and, summoned to the War Cabinet on 24 August, argued for the formation of an Air Ministry to merge the RFC and the Royal Naval Air Service and to control the new force, as the Admiralty and the War Office did for the Navy and Army. An Air Force Bill went through Parliament that autumn and the Air Ministry was formed on 2 January 1918; the Royal Air Force came into being on 1 April that year.

If that boded well for the future, so too did the successful deployment, on 20 November 1917 in a minor offensive at Cambrai, of tanks that for the first time preceded the infantry into battle, destroying the German wire and allowing the overrunning of enemy lines: but the men who might have created a permanent breach in the line were on their way to Italy. Typically, Lloyd George held the 'failure' to capitalise on Cambrai against Haig and Robertson. Despite promises made to Haig, attacks on the leadership of the Army in what Haig called 'the LG press' continued through the autumn, even though Milner claimed to have warned Lloyd George to call his dogs off.[202] Haig characterised the policy as one 'of undermining the confidence which troops now feel in their leaders and [to] eventually destroy the efficiency of the Army as a fighting force.' With the transfer of resources to the Italian front, Haig told all who would listen that any further attacks in France and Flanders would be impossible: which was what Lloyd George intended.

However, while this squabbling went on in Whitehall, Germany appeared to be losing its self-confidence. On 19 September news had reached London via Sir Arthur Hardinge, the British ambassador in Madrid, that the Germans were again talking about peace negotiations, which the Vatican had been trying to broker since the spring. Germany's new foreign minister, Richard von Kühlmann, had been deputed to see whether the restoration of Belgium, on the condition that Germany had a free hand in Russia so it could expand to the east, and the return of colonies seized in 1914, would be a basis for talks. Lloyd George had gone to Boulogne to meet Paul Painlevé, a professor of mathematics at the Sorbonne who days earlier had become French prime minister when Ribot had lost the support of Painlevé's socialists, and would himself last only four months. No immediate decision had been reached. The Americans preferred to divide the German people, trying to persuade them they were ill-served by the quasi-autocracy that ruled them, and would benefit from overthrowing them and negotiating peace with fellow democrats. On 6 October, following a meeting between Balfour and representatives of other friendly countries, a message was sent to the Germans via Madrid asking for more details. There was no reply. On 9 October Kühlmann told the Reichstag there was no question of concessions in Alsace or Lorraine; and no mention was made of evacuating Belgium, so the discussions ended. Then news arrived from Germany of a naval mutiny in early October, and of plunging civilian morale caused by shortages of food and fuel, and despair of a military breakthrough. The Allies might have had their setbacks and disasters, but their enemy was manifestly far from invulnerable.

ARE <u>YOU</u> HELPING THE GERMANS?

You are helping the Germans

When you use a Motor Car for pleasure.

When you buy extravagant clothes.

When you employ more servants than you need.

When you waste coal, electric light or gas.

When you eat and drink more than is necessary to your health and efficiency.

SET THE RIGHT EXAMPLE, free labour for more useful purposes, save money and lend it to the Nation and so

HELP YOUR COUNTRY

CHAPTER 9

ATTRITION

I

The case for continuing the war was reinforced by a constant flow of morale-boosting – and circulation-boosting – newspaper stories designed to remind readers not only why the war was being fought, but to amplify the dangers of seeking to come to any kind of accommodation with a nation as barbarous as Germany. On 17 April 1917, for example, Northcliffe's *Daily Mail* and *Times* printed stories about a German 'corpse factory' near Koblenz in the Rhineland, where dead soldiers' bodies were said to have been taken to be boiled down and turned into glycerine for weapons, food for pigs or even margarine. The story, which had been picked up from an underground Belgian newspaper, was completely false and probably based on a mistranslation of the word *Kadaververwertungsanstalt,* which refers to boiled-down animals, not boiled-down (human) cadavers. (Helpfully, a number of German scholars wrote to *The Times* pointing this out, though they couldn't prove it was the case in this instance.) Nonetheless, John Buchan's Department of Information, some of whose staff moonlighted as 'special correspondents' on newspapers, so helping to ease the blurring between fact and fiction, published a four-page pamphlet about it, and Cecil, answering questions in the Commons, refused to rubbish the stories, not least because Robertson had told the War Cabinet it was true.[1] The Germans inevitably denied that they were perpetrating such an outrage; within days even the French were dismissing the story as a misunderstanding, though the Northcliffe press continued to publish earnest accounts of the boiling down of humans – usually based on stories from Tommies who had taken German prisoners – and letters from correspondents who were themselves boiling at this predictable example of the savagery of the Hun. If such stories showed the desperation the authorities felt by this time in maintaining morale, they also displayed the credulousness of the public: such German atrocities seemed to them entirely plausible.

As such matters were exposed they helped feed a mood of cynicism about the war that grew throughout 1917, as ever greater levels of sacrifice were countered by more stalemate and bloodshed. The feeling was shared by politicians and the public, and, of most concern to the authorities that were seeking to direct the war effort, began to be expressed by combatants too, against a background of sporadic, and futile, peace initiatives. Even before the 1917 summer offensive opened the more cerebral soldiers who had witnessed the realities of the Western Front were reaching the end of their tether. One was Siegfried Sassoon, who having won the Military Cross on the Somme had been on convalescent leave, and had come under the influence of the Morrells and Bertrand Russell. Returning to his battalion, encamped near Liverpool, he wrote a letter entitled *Finished with the War: A Soldier's Declaration*, and sent it to his commanding officer. One of the Morrells' friends, John Middleton Murry – who would become the second husband of Katherine Mansfield, the New Zealand writer of short stories – had helped draft it, though Murry was not a conscientious objector, having been declared unfit for military service. It was printed and distributed by Francis Meynell, a pacifist active on the Labour left who was business manager of George Lansbury's *Daily Herald*. Meynell had pleaded a conscientious objection in 1916 and was ordered, but refused, to do war work. Imprisoned in January 1917, he went on hunger strike. He was discharged from the Army after a fortnight, on the grounds that he would be unlikely to become an efficient soldier; but more likely because he had convinced the authorities of his determination to die rather than fight, and was too ill to survive forced feeding.

The statement began by Sassoon defining his letter 'as an act of wilful defiance of military authority', provoked by his belief that the war was being 'deliberately prolonged by those who have the power to end it.'[2] He said he believed he was speaking for other soldiers; and he thought a war of 'defence and liberation' on which he had embarked had become one of 'aggression and conquest'. Having seen so much slaughter, he felt he could 'no longer be a party to prolonging those sufferings for ends I believe to be evil and unjust.' He blamed politicians for sacrificing men, and attacked ministers for the 'deception' they were practising upon soldiers. It was only 'callous complacence' that allowed the war to continue, and which prevented those at home from abhorring 'the continuance of agonies which they do not share, and which they have not sufficient imagination to realise.' The statement was sent to the press, its publication coinciding with that of the most scandalous novel of the year, Alec Waugh's *The Loom of Youth*. Although mainly attacked for its mild depiction of schoolboy homoeroticism, it caused if anything even more offence for its mockery of the social conditioning undertaken by the public schools, tens of thousands of whose chivalrous products were already rotting in graves in France and Flanders and countless others of whom, such as Sassoon, had been mentally or physically damaged in the service of King and country.

Sassoon's letter was read into the parliamentary record on 30 July; but the row he hoped to provoke (and which, egged on by Lady Ottoline and others, he had been encouraged to believe would make waves) did not happen, which prompted him to throw the ribbon of his MC into the Mersey. Robert Graves, who served with him, called him a 'silly old thing'. Graves added that his brother officers in the Royal Welch Fusiliers agreed with Sassoon but felt what he had done was 'not quite a gentlemanly course to take.'[3] Rather than court-martial him, and following interventions from Eddie Marsh, Churchill's former private secretary and Rupert Brooke's literary executor, and Graves, the War Office instead treated Sassoon as a psychiatric case. He was sent to Craiglockhart Hospital in Edinburgh, to be treated for neurasthenia, or shell shock, by the leading expert in the study, W. H. R. Rivers. It was there, on 17 August 1917, that he met Wilfred Owen, whom he influenced as a poet and with whom he became friends. Sassoon gave Owen a critique of his most celebrated (and then unpublished) poem, 'Anthem for Doomed Youth'; and after the war would do much to promote Owen's work and establish his reputation as possibly the greatest of all the British war poets, Owen having been killed in action seven days before the Armistice. Sassoon returned to the Western Front in 1918, having spent much of his time in Craiglockhart writing poetry: Rivers, an officer in the Royal Army Medical Corps who realised his role was to restore the men he treated to a mental state in which they could return to the front, feared his psychological discussions with Sassoon were turning him into a pacifist. Whether Sassoon himself was a pacifist is a moot point. Unlike some Craiglockhart alumni – notably Max Plowman, whose memoir *A Subaltern on the Somme* would appear in 1928, who was dismissed from the Army when he refused to return to the trenches – Sassoon did go back to fight. But then Plowman, although a volunteer, had had ethical qualms about joining up in 1914, whereas it is clear from Sassoon's writings that he felt a moral commitment to stay in the fight with his comrades.

Pacifism was becoming ever more rife in the labour movement, and presented a difficult challenge for Arthur Henderson as Labour's man in the War Cabinet. MacDonald, in a Commons debate on 12 February about financing the war, gave the impression that he spoke for the whole Labour Party when saying the government should conscript money from the rich just as it had conscripted men for the war. He correctly predicted that debt would be the main problem facing the country once hostilities ceased; but the case for a negotiated peace, not debt, was his main point. The new German submarine policy meant 'killing became murder', and the Germans had indicated that 'all humanitarian considerations must be put upon the scrap-heap': in his view, the only sort of war that would be prosecuted now would be one of utter barbarism.[4] He wanted 'a peace by consent of the people that have hitherto been at war'.[5] He believed the Germans were beaten in the west, and the fight now was in Eastern Europe: a view he shared with the prime minister. But he sought an alternative to fighting: 'If negotiations can do it, it should be done that way—and by negotiations I do not suggest that the Foreign Secretary should address a Note to Berlin, but I mean simply that diplomacy should use the opportunities which it now has got and that it should keep on defining its position, expounding its position, removing misunderstandings . . . our Foreign Office should show the same activity which our Army in the field is showing.'[6] In a fight to the finish, he predicted, America would crush Europe economically, using its enormous resources to maintain and expand its foothold in markets it had entered during the war. But he added: 'To me, "finish" is the securing of the maximum political result from the minimum military effort, although that minimum may be a very big one. If the House does not do that, if we simply gamble the future of Europe and throw away the prospect and the guarantees of the future of Europe, in view of the position in which we are now, do not let us delude ourselves that we are fighting the last of the wars, because we are only fighting one of many which are still to come.'[7]

This incensed MacDonald's colleagues. George Wardle, who became leader of the parliamentary Labour Party when Henderson moved to the War Cabinet, denounced him in the Commons two days later, saying that whomever he spoke for, it was not Labour. He called his speech 'amazing', and not approvingly.[8] The most recent Labour conference, in January, had 'inflexibly resolved to fight until victory was achieved,' supporting Henderson's motion saying so by 1,850,000 to 300,000.[9] Wardle said: 'Negotiations, definitions, expounding positions, will not remove the misunderstandings which have arisen in this War. A nation guilty, as Germany was in this War, of an unprovoked attack upon Belgium, a nation guilty of Zeppelin outrages and of murder on the high seas, is not going to be deflected from its purpose by explanations and by expounding positions. Was such a futile policy as that ever proposed in this House?'[10] Wardle stressed there would be a price to pay if the Allies withdrew from the war at this stage: 'But what about the danger if Constantinople is allowed to remain in the hands of Germany, for it is practically in the hands of Germany now? What, if we leave this War unfinished, without a military victory, and we leave Germany in possession of Middle Europe, with a straight run from Berlin to Bagdad, and with the East in her possession? I think we shall have sown the seeds of future wars there with a vengeance, indeed—a vengeance which not only our children but our children's children will have to pay for.'[11]

His was a bravura description of the patriotic impulse that still, in the third year of war and after appalling losses, fired millions of Britons to continue making sacrifices, and eloquently expressed why so many Britons still wished to wage war on Germany:

We did not go into this War willingly. We did not seek it. It was forced upon us, and to talk about making peace until Germany has given up the war aims with which she set out seems to me an impossible position for anyone who loves his country to take up. To me fighting to a finish and victory do not mean the same thing as they seem to mean to the hon Member. They mean to me much more. They mean the defeat of the war aims of Germany. They mean the destruction of the vilest plot that ever disgraced humanity. They mean chastisement for crimes which will remain for ever an indelible stain on the page of history. They mean, first, a military victory, and then a reasonable and a settled peace.[12]

He dismissed MacDonald's assertion that this should be the 'last war'. 'We cannot rule the future. We can fight as far as we can to make this the last war, but it does not rest with us to say that it shall be the last war. We can only take care that in the settlement, as far as possible, we shall do our part to remove the causes of future war; but if it is necessary in order to do this to talk Germany into peace, I for one refuse to accept such a statement. Germany cannot be talked into peace . . . the hon Member's speech had no relation at all to the facts as they now stand.' Labour's fissures, of which this episode was a salutary example, suited Lloyd George very well.

However, within months, the prime minister felt it necessary to counter growing cynicism by reiterating the case for war. In Glasgow on 29 June 1917 he gave an idealistic view of Britain's war aims. Serbia and Belgium needed their independence restored and their people compensated; the Turks had to surrender Mesopotamia and Armenia; Prussian military power was to be destroyed and the German government democratised. The British would negotiate only with a German leadership radically unlike the one that started the war: and victory was assured. However, he deluded himself on one key point. Playing to the gallery in a socialist heartland, he predicted a resurgent Russia 'more formidable than ever, because in Russia in future the whole of her power will be cast on the side of liberty and democracy and not of autocracy.'[13] A little later, at Dundee, he stuck to his theme, seeking to raise morale by saying the government would punish food profiteers – official figures would show in July that food prices had risen by 104 per cent since before the war. He claimed, rashly in view of the food situation, 'there are no privations in this country. There are in Germany, and there are in Austria, and they are still fighting.'[14] The British had deep reserves to use up before seeing any danger of defeat.

Henderson's ability to rein in MacDonald and the pacifist wing of his party was handicapped by his being absent for much of the summer of 1917 on a mission to Russia, to make contacts with the Russian provisional government, under Alexander Kerensky, that had displaced the Tsar, with the aim of persuading Kerensky to keep Russia in the fight against Germany. He then went to an international socialist meeting in

Paris. There, he participated in a discussion about whether to attend a pacifist conference in Stockholm, called by leftists from neutral countries in Scandinavia and Holland, at which socialists from enemy nations would be present. Suspicions about Henderson's commitment to the war were further deepened by the fact that he had gone with MacDonald, who was to most of the British public the incarnation of pacifism, at a time when Britain was fighting for its life. On 1 August, having returned to England, Henderson was excluded, to his outrage, from a War Cabinet meeting that discussed whether he should be allowed to go to Stockholm. He forced himself into the room and told his colleagues their behaviour was an insult to him and to the working class. The minutes stated that 'no slight had been intended.'[15] His colleagues' fear was that the socialists in Stockholm – which would include Russians, keen to get out of the war – would seek a negotiated peace that would not deliver the decisive victory to which Lloyd George and his colleagues were committed.

That evening there was a vigorous debate in the Commons about why so senior a minister should have gone abroad on non-ministerial business with a notorious pacifist. Lloyd George urged MPs not to rush to judgement. Anxious to retain the support of organised labour, he had no desire to see Henderson, its political leader, humiliated. Henderson had a poor reception when he tried to explain himself. He pointed out that he remained secretary of the Labour Party and had duties to discharge in that capacity. However, that remark was met with 'ironical cheers'.[16] Public feeling was that the conference would give British leftists a measure of communication with citizens of an enemy country – Germany – which would be illegal; although any Germans they met in Stockholm would have no power to change anything. Lloyd George hoped Henderson would think better of it.

In the event, Henderson did not. On 10 August the Labour conference voted by more than three to one to be represented at Stockholm. Henderson had failed to argue to his members that they should not attend – the view of the War Cabinet and all Allied governments – but in any case Henderson had by this point decided to resign. Lloyd George, however, was so angry that he dismissed him, writing him 'an extremely trenchant but not too grammatical letter' that Curzon had to edit and 'soften' before the War Cabinet agreed to its dispatch; but Henderson had in any case decided to resign.[17] Lloyd George claimed

Henderson's ministerial colleagues had been 'taken completely by surprise' by his speech, and told the errant Labour leader so in his response to his resignation.[18]

The mood of rage is detectable in the War Cabinet minutes for 10 August, which contain the note: 'The Secretary was instructed not to summon Mr Henderson to future meetings of the War Cabinet, nor to circulate War Cabinet documents to him.'[19] *The Times* credited Henderson with being an 'honest patriot' undone by 'stupid conceit', which was harsh: he had a duty to his country, but also, pursuing that duty, to maintain his party's cohesion.[20] George Barnes, Labour MP for the Gorbals and since the previous December minister for pensions, replaced him. Ironically the Stockholm conference was, in Mrs Webb's words, 'a fiasco', thanks to a lack of unanimity about the future conduct of the war, posturing Russian revolutionaries and in-fighting within delegations.[21] But pacifism was growing in Britain just when the maximum war effort was vital: Henderson, in the Commons on 13 August, emphasised that had he resigned before his party conference the pacifist vote would have been even higher.

Henderson's experience in Russia convinced him that a constitutional and democratic socialist alternative to Bolshevism had to be established; though ironically this would entail his leading the Labour Party in a more hard-line direction, and create even greater scope for conflict with a wartime government dominated by Tories. This change of tone necessitated a new structure and constitution for the party, about which Henderson had his first meeting with TUC representatives in September 1917. Out of office, he worked almost full-time on the party's plan for the future, aware that the large number of working men, and women, who would be on the electoral register after the Franchise Bill passed – an increase from around 8 million eligible voters to 16.3 million – would put new demands on the party, and provide new opportunities. He told Scott of the *Manchester Guardian* that Labour might put up as many as 500 candidates at the next election, though once the Bill was on the statute book he revised down the estimate, in a speech at West Bromwich on 9 February 1918, to between 300 and 400.[22] His energy, decency and competence were a loss to Lloyd George.

The Labour Party's new constitution, in which Sidney Webb, the leading Fabian, played a major role as draftsman, included a section that, seventy-five years later, would represent a red-in-tooth-and-claw past

John Redmond, leader of the Irish Nationalists, whose warnings went unheeded.

Sir Roger Casement, who blundered his way to the gallows.

Éamon de Valera, the face of fanaticism and of Ireland's future.

British soldiers man a barricade in Dublin during the Easter Rising.

Andrew Bonar Law, who passed the keys of
Downing Street from Asquith to Lloyd George.

Earl (later Marquess) Curzon of Kedleston, the
grandest of Tory grandees.

Arthur Henderson, Labour leader and patriot.

Viscount Milner, Kindergarten manager turned
cabinet minister.

General (later Field Marshal) Sir William Robertson, adversary of Lloyd George.

Lord Stamfordham, a courtier of the old school, and his master, King George V.

Major-General Sir Frederick Maurice, who believed prime ministers should tell the truth.

H. A. L. Fisher, intellectual dynast dedicated to building a better post-war world.

A 'clippie' on a London bus in the summer of 1918.

Top left: A game of two halves: the munitionettes' football XI 1917–18 from the AEC factory at Beckton, Essex.

Mary S. Allen, a former prominent suffragette thrice imprisoned, inspects women police officers.

Below: Three college girls pull their weight on a flax farm in Somerset.

Children pushed into the front line of the Glasgow rent strike, 1915.

Right: A handbill encouraging attendance at a celebration of the Russian revolution, 1917.

Below: Miners further the war effort by going on strike in South Wales in 1915.

Great Labour, Socialist *and* Democratic Convention
to hail the Russian Revolution
and to Organise *the* British Democracy
To follow Russia

May 23rd, 1917.

To Trades Councils, Trade Unions, Local Labour Parties, Socialist Parties, Women's Organisations, and Democratic Bodies.

DEAR COMRADES,

The Conference to which we recently invited you is already assured of a **great success.**

It will be one of the greatest Democratic Gatherings ever held in this country. It will be historic. It will begin a new era of democratic power in Great Britain. It will begin to do for this country what the Russian Revolution has accomplished in Russia.

There is little time for preparation. Action must be taken immediately by every Branch and Society desiring to be represented. It seems not unlikely, owing to the rush of applications for delegates' tickets that the Committee may be unable to give facilities for those who delay till the last moment.

The Conference will be held in the **ALBERT HALL, LEEDS,** on SUNDAY, **JUNE 3rd,** commencing at 10.30 a.m.

We now send you the Resolutions which are to be discussed. Owing to the shortness of time for the preparation for the Conference the proceedings will not be subject to the rigid rules which usually govern Labour and Socialist Congresses. It will be a Democratic Conference to establish Democracy in Great Britain.

Russia has called to us to follow her. You must not refuse to answer that appeal.

Send in your application for Delegates' Cards at once. You are entitled to send one delegate however small your membership may be, but an additional delegate for each 5,000 of your membership above the first 5,000, or part of 5,000.

Applications, accompanied by a fee of 2s. 6d. for each delegate, must be sent to one of the Secretaries as under:

ALBERT INKPIN, Chandos Hall, 21a Maiden Lane, Strand, London, W.C.2
FRANCIS JOHNSON, St. Bride's House, Salisbury Square, London, E.C.4

In the confident hope that your Society will join in this great event,

On behalf of the United Socialist Council,

We remain,

Yours fraternally,

H. ALEXANDER	GEO. LANSBURY
CHAS. G. AMMON	J. RAMSAY MACDONALD
W. C. ANDERSON	TOM QUELCH
C. DESPARD	ROBERT SMILLIE
E. C. FAIRCHILD	PHILIP SNOWDEN
J. FINEBERG	ROBERT WILLIAMS
F. W. JOWETT	

Lord Rhondda, who survived the *Lusitania* to become 'food dictator' in 1917.

Top right: A woman worker selling tickets at a National Kitchen.

Right: The menu for a dinner of 74 Squadron of the Royal Flying Corps before it returned to action, March 1918.

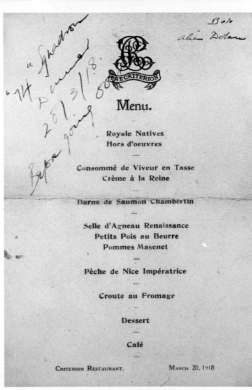

Above: C. R. W. Nevinson's uncensored depiction of a food queue, 1918.

Left: An advertisement that appeared in the *Sketch* on 30 October 1918, at the height of the influenza epidemic.

Ravages of Influenza spreading everywhere Safeguard Yourself by Using Milton

One of the great advantages of MILTON, and one peculiar to itself, is that although it is so wonderfully efficient in destroying germs, bacteria, and offensive smells, it is so absolutely innocuous that it can be applied without the slightest risk for personal use.

For instance, there is nothing equal to MILTON for preventing and relieving influenza.

MILTON

in proportion of half a teaspoonful to a glass of tepid water, used three times a day (snuffed up the nose or used with an ordinary spray and also as a gargle) will be found to work like a charm.

Get a 1/3 or 2/6 bottle of MILTON from your dealer to-day. It contains a booklet of fifty-nine practical household recipes. Nos. 1 to 12 give full directions for the relief and prevention of Autumn and winter ailments—such as Influenza, Chilblains, Catarrh.

Don't Sneeze
Milton will stop it.
Use it every day.

MILTON is priceless as a gargle for a sore throat and as a mouth wash & dentifrice

1/3 and 2/6 bottles
To be obtained from all Dealers.

Milton Manufacturing Co., Ltd., 129, Bunhill Row, London, E.C., and 64, Wellington St., Glasgow.

A food ration book from the last days of the war.

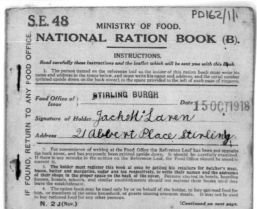

Servicemen and VADs rejoice on Armistice Day, 11 November 1918.

Unforgotten: Nurse Cavell's cortège passes the Palace of Westminster as crowds throng the streets,
May 1919.

that had to be disavowed: the so-called Clause IV. It seems to have been Webb's work, and the uncompromising language of his draft showed that the Liberal Party could not, without abandoning its own deep-seated principles, match his vision of socialism. Webb had long pressed the Fabian view that the middle class (of which he was a member), like the working class, had a vested interest in pursuing the socialist ideal, and reflected this by his reference to the desire 'to secure for the producers by hand or brain the full fruits of their industry, and the most equitable distribution thereof that may be possible, upon the basis of the Common Ownership of the Means of Production and the best obtainable system of popular administration and control of each industry or service.'[23] Not only did this begin to separate the Liberal Party from working people, but it also announced that Labour aspired to be more than a party of manual workers, extending its ideas of radical socialism to those who did not earn their living by physical labour: something of which *The Times* remarked: 'the eventual consequences will be far-reaching.'[24] The newspaper cast doubt, though, on the willingness of those who profited by their brains to join the Labour Party, not least because of the difficulties of dividing up the spoils of their talent.

Most of Labour's new ideas – and the constitution settled in the winter of 1917–18 – were rooted in the pacifist movement, and dependent on the doctrine of the Union of Democratic Control, formed in 1914 in the Morrells' house in Bedford Square by Labour pacifists such as MacDonald. Among the Liberal intellectuals sympathetic to the UDC was Bertrand Russell, another prominent pacifist. He had shown little inclination to be silenced on the issue since his brush with the law the previous year. His high-minded approach to any question caused him to disdain some of his *confrères*, who he thought spent more time squabbling about which of them should lead the pacifist movement than about how actually to achieve its aims. 'Nevertheless, they were all there was to work with, and I did my best to think well of them.'[25] The paradox of Russell's pacifism had been his feeling in 1914 that 'for several weeks I felt that if I should happen to meet Asquith or Grey I should be unable to refrain from murder.'[26]

He claimed to have felt 'tortured by patriotism' and to have longed for Germany's defeat: 'Love of England is very nearly the strongest emotion I possess, and in appearing to set it aside at such a moment, I was making a very difficult renunciation.' He had disregarded his love of country and acted upon a compulsion to protest because 'the massacre of the young wrung my heart.'[27] He had organised a branch of the UDC at Trinity College, Cambridge, where dons and undergraduates had shown an interest in the ideas: nonetheless, he admitted feeling surprised when, having said in a speech: 'it is all nonsense to pretend the Germans are wicked', the whole room applauded him.[28] For Russell, Cambridge in the early phase of the war was a comforting escape from reality. His mentor George Santayana consoled him, not least because 'he had not enough respect for the human race to care whether it destroyed itself or not.'

That, though, had been before the *Lusitania*, after which Russell began to be shunned. On Lady Ottoline's advice, he overcame his despair by visiting destitute Germans, in the months before they were all interned. Another of her circle, D. H. Lawrence, befriended Russell only to question his supposed pacifism: 'Your basic desire is the maximum of desire of war, you really are the super-war-spirit . . . as a woman said to me, who had been to one of your meetings: "It seemed to me so strange with his face looking so evil, to be talking about peace and love. He can't have *meant* what he said." '[29] Russell, in turn, thought Lawrence a fascist after conversations they had about the lectures Russell was preparing, which subsequently appeared as *Principles of Social Reconstruction*. 'Gradually I discovered that he had no real wish to make the world better, but only to indulge in eloquent soliloquy about how bad it was.'[30]

Russell would have been impressed to know that in July 1917 the War Office director of recruiting had told his superiors that the system of recruitment since the Military Service Act was 'thoroughly bad', not least because of the arbitrary operation of tribunals that heard appeals from men who did not wish to fight. 'The injustices that were being perpetrated daily', Robertson recorded, 'were, in his opinion, undermining the morale of the nation and fanning the embers of pacifism.'[31] He cited an example: 'In Wales eleven Tribunals had recently refused to continue their duties on the ground that elderly married men were being taken while young men were left in civil life.'[32]

The impact of men such as Russell and the growing prominence of UDC ideas restored MacDonald's influence, as did his making of common cause with Henderson. Henderson was adamant there would be no more coalitions for Labour, but that the new party would be a broad church, another nail in the coffin of the Liberal Party as a party of government. By 1917 the UDC had 300 affiliated organisations, and a membership of over 750,000, and the potential for civil unrest and even revolution which the organisation represented was of increasing concern to the authorities.[33] Although not wholly pacifist, it had been given an extra edge of militancy by conscription, and it called for more transparency in the making of foreign policy. And pacifism grew in spite of – indeed, perhaps because of – its suppression.

II

Towards the end of 1917 there was one final flurry of proposals for a negotiated peace. On 8 November Lenin, whose armed followers had toppled the provisional government in Russia the previous day, called for an armistice with the Central Powers. The Bolsheviks then signed an armistice with the Germans on 2 December. This geopolitical shift helped prompt Lansdowne, now a year into his retirement, to write to *The Times* about his plans for peace – wishing to make public essentially the same argument about negotiation that he had put to his cabinet colleagues in the last days of the Asquith administration. However, the paper refused to publish the letter. Geoffrey Dawson (as Robinson was now known, having changed his surname to secure an inheritance), the editor, feared it would destabilise the first meeting of the Supreme War Council in Paris. Also, anyone writing, printing or distributing leaflets calling for peace talks was liable to arrest, a heavy fine and possibly a prison sentence, with heavier censorship regulations and even harsher punishments introduced in November 1917. Attempts to hold peace meetings – especially in London's east end, where one of the main proponents was Lansbury – were routinely thwarted by bands of discharged and wounded soldiers, and irate women.

Lansdowne wanted Balfour to read his letter, to ensure nothing in it was felt damaging to the Foreign Office or his old colleague; and a few days earlier he had sent Balfour a nine-page memorandum about the need for a negotiated peace and moderate war aims that would appeal to rational people on both sides. However, Balfour – who had tactfully told Lansdowne that 'I don't know that this is a very suitable time for discussing peace matters' – was leaving for Paris, for the conference, and had no time to read the letter: so asked Lansdowne to show it to Lord Hardinge, the permanent secretary, instead.[34] Hardinge was an enormously experienced diplomat – he had been the main facilitator behind Edward VII's initiative on the *entente cordiale* in 1903, which had made his reputation, and had returned in 1916 from six years as Viceroy of India. 'He observed that it was "statesmanlike" and would "do good",' Lansdowne recalled.[35] Lansdowne then saw Lord Burnham, owner of *The Daily Telegraph*, in the Lords and asked whether his newspaper would take the letter instead; and Burnham agreed, even though he dissented from Lansdowne's argument, because he assumed it was not entirely adrift from Foreign Office thinking.

The letter quoted ministers on the apparent impossibility of a 'lasting peace', and reiterated some of the arguments of Lansdowne's cabinet memorandum.[36] He said a war aim of beating the Germans was 'not an end in itself.' He quoted Asquith in saying that the Allies sought, beyond the defeat of the Central Powers, 'reparation and security', though he felt no reparation could 'undo the grievous wrong which has been done to humanity.' That prophetic note, had it been recognised at Versailles, might have spared the world even more horror; for, as Lansdowne continued: 'Just as this war has been more dreadful than any war in history, so we may be sure would the next war be more dreadful than this. The prostitution of science for purposes of pure destruction is not likely to stop short.'[37] He called for an international arbitration arrangement to avoid 'the repetition of such an outrage as that of 1914.'

Lansdowne claimed some of the initial war aims, such as a 'wholesale rearrangement of the map of South-Eastern Europe', had 'probably become unobtainable', though reparation for Belgium remained 'in the front rank'.[38] His principal concern was for the war to be ended before it provoked 'a world-wide catastrophe'; but this would happen only if both sides realised it had already lasted too long. He said he believed many Germans, Austrians and Turks felt that way, because of their grave economic difficulties; and quoted Eric Geddes, who had spoken of their 'constant efforts' to initiate peace talks. He wanted an official promise that the Allies did not desire Germany's 'annihilation' as a great power, that they did not seek to impose a type of government upon them that they did not wish for themselves, that they did not wish to ostracise Germany internationally, that 'freedom of the seas' was up for discussion, and that Britain would support arbitration for future international disputes. He felt this would encourage a peace party in Germany. He claimed authority for these promises could be found in recent ministerial speeches, and the Americans had raised freedom of the seas – to

Britain's outrage. If these points could be adopted, in 1918 'a lasting and honourable peace' could be obtained.[39]

Northcliffe, in Paris when Lansdowne offered his letter, said that had he known about it he would have published it with a 'stinging leader'.[40] Having missed that opportunity, he had The Times attack Lansdowne in a fashion even Lloyd George thought 'in bad taste'; and had the Mail write that 'if Lord Lansdowne raises the white flag he is alone in his surrender.'[41] (The first Lloyd George knew of the letter was when he read about it in the newspapers.) The Morning Post called the letter 'a stab in the back'.[42] The Times's broadside included the questionable assertion that the paper had declined the letter because 'we believed it to reflect no responsible phase of British opinion.'[43] It dismissed Lansdowne as an old man – he was seventy-two – who had held no serious office since 1905. It called his quotations from statesmen 'reckless' and 'hardly honest'. Its main fear was that Britain's allies and its enemies would recall that Lansdowne had been foreign secretary and, therefore, merited being taken seriously.

Law also attacked his fellow Tory and the Telegraph for having published it: which angered Burnham, given Hardinge's approval of the text, a factor in his agreeing to publish it. Law had no idea Hardinge had approved the letter, and implored Burnham not to tell Lloyd George 'as this would only occasion trouble'; and 'begged' Burnham not to publish a paragraph confirming the sequence of events, to protect the Telegraph's reputation.[44] After an intervention by Riddell, Burnham backed down. Milner, however, agreed with Lansdowne, and so did many leader-writers in the provincial press, the tone of whose newspapers was usually designed to address the sentiment of their readers. Asquith – who, by chance, had Lansdowne to lunch in Cavendish Square on the day of publication – told his wife: 'it's an excellent letter, extremely sensible and will make a great clatter and hullabaloo . . . I am glad he has written it.'[45] Asquith's adherents – Grey, Haldane and Esher – also warmly endorsed Lansdowne, as did MacDonald and Henderson.

Esher observed: 'Lansdowne has written an interesting letter to The Daily Telegraph, drawing attention to much the same point made by Robertson two nights ago, when he was dining with us at GHQ,' he noted.[46] 'There is no "appreciating" by the FO of your peace objectives, and no co-ordinated "after war" policy.' When Northcliffe attacked Lansdowne in the French press, Esher noted that 'Northcliffe's "interview" in the Matin, in which he says that Lansdowne's utterances are those of a man stupid and senile, who has lost his self-control, has caused widespread disgust.'[47]

Lansdowne told his daughter, the Duchess of Devonshire, that 'I have been snowed under with letters from all manner of folk – a few hostile, but mostly in complete sympathy with me.'[48] It was thought Cecil had put Lansdowne up to it, and Earl Percy, the King's ADC, told Gwynne it was 'aimed at Lloyd George whom Lansdowne has never forgiven for kicking him out.' However, Lansdowne had left office voluntarily, without help from the Welsh Wizard's boot. The letter went down badly in America, and Lloyd George claimed it almost wrecked the Paris conference, because no one believed Lansdowne could have acted without government approval. Within weeks, Lansdowne would tell his daughter that his one regret was that 'I should have added a good deal of padding as to my abhorrence of anything which could be called a German Peace.'[49] He failed to recognise a fundamental contradiction in his argument: that, if the Central Powers were under such economic strain, it only required an additional effort to break them altogether – which, eventually, was what happened.

The official government line was that Lansdowne 'spoke only for himself.'[50] It added, entirely wrongly, that he had consulted no member of the government about it. Balfour washed his hands of it, a shameful act not just by an old friend of Lansdowne, but by one who professed high standards of honesty and integrity. Lansdowne, who was genuinely honourable, never embarrassed Balfour by telling the truth. Law distanced himself from Lansdowne, who endured a torrent of obloquy from Unionists and felt he suffered an 'official excommunication' from his party.[51] His reputation took years to recover. But whatever the politicians said about Lansdowne, and however right or wrong he was, both Lloyd George and President Wilson would make public statements of war aims within weeks.

The Labour Party too continued to diverge from the orthodox line on the war. At a special conference in December 1917 in Westminster it adopted, jointly with the TUC, a Memorandum on War Aims heavily influenced by the views of the Union of Democratic Control. It supported the idea of a League of Nations, which was also the government's view, but condemned secret diplomacy and imperialism. It was in an attempt to stave off the acceptance of UDC views among the unions, and demonstrate that Britain was not seeking an unreasonable path to peace, that Lloyd George made a politically crucial speech on 5 January 1918 to union leaders at Caxton Hall in London. Speaking against this background of continuing dissent, he stressed that the Allies were 'not fighting a war of aggression against the German people', but were pursuing justice for the small nations of Europe – Belgium, Serbia and Montenegro – and for the restitution of Alsace-Lorraine to France as well as the liberation of occupied France, Italy and Romania.[52] He also argued for an independent Poland, reparations to countries damaged by German aggression, recognition of aspirations of nationalities within the Austro-Hungarian Empire, and for an international order in which the 'sanctity of treaties' was respected.

He made the speech to the unions, not to Parliament, because with the shock of events in Russia still reverberating, he was desperate to keep working people on side. His words were almost universally applauded, although Scott turned the *Manchester Guardian*'s leader column on him for having refused to endorse the Bolsheviks, whom Scott thought rather wonderful. Scott also voiced a fear, on what evidence it is not clear, that Lloyd George was planning a peace deal with Germany to carve up territory for them in the east to compensate for losses in the west. The War Cabinet had discussed its aims – drawn up by Smuts, Philip Kerr and Cecil – over the previous week. Its purpose was to bolster morale and remind the public why Britain was fighting. A subsidiary purpose was to show how far the reasonable demands of the Allies were from any unreasonable proposal for peace from the Germans. The same weekend as Lloyd George spoke, a national meeting of shop stewards called for Russian peace proposals to be accepted, while engineers on the Clyde recommended strikes to force the government to negotiate a peace. Three days later President Wilson echoed Lloyd George by announcing his fourteen points for a settlement, though these were more limited in some ways than Lloyd George's. The aims having been set out, all that remained was to win the war and implement them.

Although those advocating peace remained a minority, the authorities were sufficiently concerned that they kept a constant eye on them. The National Anti-Conscription Fellowship was neutered. By spring 1917 over 3,000 conscientious objectors were in prison, and in total 5,000 would be locked up. On their release they could look forward to being banned from voting for five years, under the new Franchise Act.[53] Simultaneously, chief constables sent the Home Office reports on pacifist activity, and kept local military commanders apprised of industrial unrest; and Basil Thomson, who oversaw criminal investigations at Scotland Yard, began to collect information on pacifist or potentially revolutionary groups and sent it to the War Cabinet. The War Cabinet urged a government statement about these seditious activities that could become the basis of a propaganda campaign.

The police regularly raided premises thought to be producing literature aimed at undermining the war effort by promoting a negotiated peace. In November 1917 they turned over the National Council for Civil Liberties, where such seditious writings as Mill's *On Liberty* and reprints of an article by Wells in the *Daily News*, and passed by the censor, were confiscated. It seemed as though it was now an offence to defend civil and industrial liberties; a sentiment increased by raids on the London offices of the Indian Home Rule movement, which seemed aimed at suppressing legitimate dissent. Newsprint was scarce, and left-wing groups found it harder to broadcast their message: the right-wing press had increased its prices, and Northcliffe at least once helped the *Express* stay in business by selling Beaverbrook enough paper to tide him over. Nonetheless, the Left's heightened activity fed official paranoia, which the events in Russia during 1917 fed exponentially.

In August 1917 a National War Aims Committee, funded by the various political parties but from November that year by the Treasury, was formed to counter pacifist propaganda. It took over the work of the Central Committee for National Patriotic Organisations and used their network of branches. The NWAC invited respected politicians to make speeches about what Britain was fighting for: though it seemed its concerns were not so much about maintaining the war effort as seeing that there were no nasty surprises once peace came. It produced short propaganda films for cinemas. Between September 1917 and the Armistice it held almost nine hundred meetings, including rallies, and made aerial drops of leaflets.

III

Official fears about pacifism were motivated by more than just a terror of simple defeatism. Because those on the left of the Labour Party were both pacifist and sympathetic to the Bolsheviks, there was a growing fear that a refusal to fight would also prove to be the progenitor of revolution, that the abandonment of war against the Germans would allow the Left to concentrate on fomenting a class war within Britain. Frances Stevenson, perhaps echoing Lloyd George, felt the unrest was 'sinister' and 'simply being engineered by German agents and Pacifists who are trying to corrupt the workers.'[54]

Such anxieties came to the fore when news arrived that the Tsar had abdicated on his own part and on behalf of his son, the Tsarevich, who was seriously ill, on 15 March. This created a diplomatic problem for Britain, and a personal one for the King. On the one hand the Sovereign – who noted in his diary that night: 'I am in despair' – was the Tsar's cousin, and had always enjoyed close ties with him. On the other, the Tsar was immensely unpopular among the working class, who saw him as a tyrant.[55] Therefore, both the Monarch and his ministers proceeded with caution. On 19 March the King sent, via the military attaché in Petrograd, a telegram that said: 'my thoughts are constantly with you and I shall always remain your true and devoted friend as you know I have been in the past.'[56] On 22 March Lloyd George convened a meeting in Downing Street with Law, Lord Hardinge – the permanent under-secretary at the Foreign Office – and Stamfordham to discuss how to handle a request from the Russian provisional government to grant the Tsar and his family asylum, even though many of the King's loyal sub-jects abominated the ex-autocrat. The initial decision, conveyed via Buchanan, still in post in Petrograd, was that such a request would be granted, though it would be specified that the request came from the provisional government and not from Britain. Stamfordham empha-sised, however, that the King would have to be consulted before anything happened. When Lloyd George casually suggested the King could make one of his houses available to the Tsar, Stamfordham 'reminded the Prime Minister that the King had got no houses except Balmoral, which would certainly not be a suitable residence at this time of year.'[57]

Esher, watching the left wing in France in the spring of 1917, warned both Lloyd George and Stamfordham that the effects of the Russian revolution were spreading through Europe as those of the French had in 1789. Such fears became incipient, and provide the essential background to the decision, weeks later, not to allow the Tsar and his family to settle in Britain. The King was worried – or at least Stamfordham was, and persuaded the King of the correctness of his view – that organised labour in Britain might object. On 31 March George Lansbury, a future Labour leader, presided over a rally in the Albert Hall to celebrate the fall of the Tsar, an innocuous event made less so by the censor's decision to forbid newspapers from running any story about it. It was in this climate, and amidst other calls for a wave of republicanism – including one by Wells in *The Times* that the newspaper said proved how 'clever men can sometimes write very foolishly' – that the King wrote to Balfour to ask whether he would consult Lloyd George further on the question: this despite the 'strong personal friendship' the King felt for his cousin.[58] He was less enamoured of the Tsarina, whose behaviour he deemed a cause of Russia's upheavals, and whom he especially did not want close by.

The King hoped that Switzerland or Denmark might offer asylum instead. However, Balfour told him on 2 April that following discussions by the War Cabinet an invitation had been sent for the Romanovs to settle in Britain, and could not be un-sent. Concerns were nevertheless expressed about how the ex-imperial lifestyle would be sustained in British exile; Buchanan was told to ask the Russian government to send funds if they sent the Romanovs, as the Royal family lacked the resources to sustain them, and asking the taxpayer to do so was unthinkable. Nor was it just organised labour that was agitated: a friend of the King, Sir Harry Verney, a Liberal MP who had served under Asquith as an agriculture minister, wrote to Stamfordham on 21 March to warn that if the Romanovs arrived they would be 'surrounded by a vast system of intrigue and espionage' and would bring a huge entourage of hangerson.[59] Buchanan's effectiveness as ambassador, and the role he was trying to play in calming matters down and keeping Russia in the war, would be ruined. Verney's main fear, however, was that 'our King's position might become extremely awkward' and he suggested: 'Would a palace at Venice or Corfu be quite unsuitable?' In later life Verney was twice convicted of indecent assaults on underage boys, so would become well versed in extreme awkwardness.

The press discussed the possibility of a grant of asylum, and the King started to receive letters of abuse about it. He, and Stamfordham, became so concerned that on 6 April Stamfordham wrote twice in a day to Balfour about the unsuitability of the Romanovs coming to England, and of the 'very unfair position' the King had been placed in by the discussion that was taking place 'not only in Clubs but by working men'.[60] The second letter said that, having realised the strength of public opposition, the government had to withdraw the earlier invitation. This weight of lobbying forced Balfour to tell Lloyd George he thought the King had been placed in 'an awkward position'.[61]

The Royal Household was sufficiently alarmed to keep copies of *Justice*, edited and written by Henry Hyndman, a veteran of the socialist agitation of the 1880s, whose 5 April number was headlined 'The Need for a British Republic', an article Stamfordham cited in his second letter.[62] The popular press ran lurid articles about the Tsarina's relations with Rasputin: those who did not vilify the Romanovs mocked them. On 10 April Stamfordham visited Lloyd George 'to impress upon him the King's strong opinion that the Emperor and Empress of Russia should not come to this country'.[63] He told the prime minister that 'even if the Government publicly stated that they took the responsibility for Their Imperial Majesties coming, the People would reply that this was done to screen the King.'[64] Lloyd George 'admitted that evidently the situation was more serious than he was aware.'[65] The matter came before the War Cabinet, who on 13 April learned that 'there was a strong feeling hostile to the Czar in certain working-class circles' and that if the Tsar came to Britain 'these tendencies might be stimulated and accentuated.'[66] With Russia an ally, the cabinet agreed a grant of asylum might strain relations. It was decided the south of France would be best for the Romanovs. A telegram expressing these sentiments was sent to Buchanan, seeking his opinion: he was told not to communicate on the question with the Russians.

Cecil wired Buchanan on 23 April saying that 'we are sounding French as to whether they would receive ex-Emperor and Empress. In the meantime you should not hold out any hopes that they can be received in England during the war.'[67] That was that. Lloyd George, to appease the King, but conscious of the need to keep the new Russian government as an ally, managed to get France to offer asylum, but by then the moderates who could have secured the Romanovs' safe departure from Russia had lost influence. In any case, it was widely believed the Tsar would refuse to leave even had the means been provided. On 27 April Cecil answered a question in the Commons about the Romanovs, saying the government had taken 'no initiative'; and there it rested.[68] Word came in July that for their safety the Romanovs would be moved to Siberia.[69] After a further year of increasingly harsh treatment, during the night of 16–17 July 1918 Nicholas II and his family were murdered in the cellar of a house in Ekaterinburg.

When he heard the news the King was horrified. A month of Court mourning for 'dear Nicky' was declared, at the prompting of the King's uncle, the Duke of Connaught; 'dear Nicky, who I fear was shot last month by the Bolshevists, we can get no details . . . it is a foul murder, I was devoted to Nicky, who was the kindest of men, a thorough gentleman'.[70] Yet the King had consciously thrown up a chance to prevent it, to keep the revolutionary ethos at bay in Britain, and to ensure the stability of his own throne at a time of deep public discontent. It was not until well after his death that the role he and Stamfordham (who predeceased him by five years) played in the end of the Romanovs was disclosed, with Lloyd George, who knew everything, omitting on instructions from Hankey any reference to it from his memoirs.

Despite the provocation of welcoming the Tsar and his family to Britain being avoided, a lively debate about republicanism in Britain continued throughout the summer of 1917, not least as a result of Wells's intervention, with various pamphlets circulated. It petered out long before the Armistice but, until it did, the Royal Family remained anxious for their future. The King's notoriously dim mother, Queen Alexandra, to whom he was devoted – he called her 'motherdear' – may partly have influenced his views. The Queen Mother told Mrs Asquith, who visited her in early July, that 'I suppose all thrones will vanish now'.[71] She added for good measure: 'That horrid little man Ll G behaved so abominably to your husband – but your Henry will come again . . . but I must say nothing!!'

During the succeeding months, as Stamfordham remained on high alert about anti-monarchist feeling, further steps were taken to shore up the popularity of George V and his family. Lloyd George urged the King to visit industrial centres and praised him heartily when he did. In a memorandum, his private secretary recorded that 'we must endeavour to induce the thinking working classes, Socialist and others, to regard the Crown, not as a mere figurehead and as an institution which, as they put it, "don't count", but as a living power for good, with receptive faculties welcoming information affecting the interests and social well-being of all classes, and ready, not only to sympathise with those questions, but anxious to further their solution'.[72] He hoped the King could show these qualities in his conversations with working men.

The King's anxieties after his cousin's enforced abdication were not helped by his sensitivity to his German heritage, and to the fact that his House bore a German name. He came to fear this was a provocation to his people at a time when they were already potentially volatile. By early May 1917 he was contemplating changing the name, and began a consultation process in deep secrecy, among senior privy counsellors and his uncle Arthur, the Duke of Connaught, a close confidant. A Bill had already been published, on 8 March, to deprive the King's German kinsmen – the Dukes of Albany (a descendant of Queen Victoria) and Cumberland (descended from George III) – of their British titles, for having supported the Kaiser. Acquiring a new family name was a natural next step.

The Duke of Connaught suggested Tudor-Stewart; but Asquith deplored Tudor with 'its recollections of Henry VIII and Bloody Mary' and observed that one Stewart was beheaded and another driven from the Throne.[73] Rosebery too felt the names had unfortunate associations and wanted 'Fitzroy'.[74] Stamfordham, having read that Edward III had been known as Edward of Windsor, suggested that; this hit the target, despite objections from Sir Alfred Scott-Gatty, Garter King of Arms. 'I feel it my duty to point out,' he told Stamfordham on 25 June, 'that the surname "Windsor" is the family name of Lord Plymouth and other families both gentle and in humble circumstances' (the 'in humble circumstances' replaces 'tradesmen' in the original draft).[75] Garter liked 'Plantagenet' as it was 'as far as I know extinct'. Stamfordham felt it was 'grand' but, echoing a point of Asquith, 'too theatrical'.[76]

So Windsor it was, and Stamfordham bested Garter by pointing out that Plymouth's surname was Windsor-Clive. The King confirmed it to Stamfordham on 15 June; it was agreed that Queen Victoria – dead for sixteen years – would be regarded as having founded the new dynasty, so all her descendants then living, unless married females, would bear the new name. On 17 July the Privy Council, attended by several Dominion prime ministers, the Archbishop of Canterbury, Lloyd George and Rosebery, approved a Royal Proclamation that 'Our House and Family shall be styled and known as the House and Family of Windsor', and relinquishing all German titles and honours.[77] The Kaiser, hearing the news, is reputed to have said how he looked forward to attending a performance of *The Merry Wives of Saxe-Coburg-Gotha*.[78]

The King also told the Council that 'May & I had decided some time ago that our children would be allowed to marry into British families', which would have a profound effect on the succession.[79] This followed a campaign, led by the *Daily Mail*, demanding that never again should a

British prince marry a German bride. He did not understate matters when he told his diary: 'It was quite a historical occasion.' It was indeed: so much so that Asquith was livid that the Palace forgot to notify him of the meeting so he could attend.[80] German relations of the King living in England, such as his brothers-in-law the Duke of Teck and Prince Alexander of Teck, relinquished their German titles, becoming the Marquess of Cambridge and the Earl of Athlone, despite Asquith's having advised that the public might take a creation of several such peers badly (they did not): it was understood that they would not engage in party politics in the Lords, any more than Royal dukes did. Rosebery congratulated Stamfordham for having 'christened a dynasty . . . it is really something to be historically proud of. I admire and envy you.'[81] A year later the King would tell Franklin Delano Roosevelt, the assistant secretary of the navy in President Wilson's administration, that 'I have a number of relations in Germany, but I can tell you frankly that in all my life I have never seen a German gentleman.'[82]

IV

The monarchy may have felt that it had seen off incipient republicanism by a change of name, but the government remained acutely alive to the broader threats of radicalism in wartime. In particular, as Kerensky's interim administration in Russia succumbed to a Bolshevik coup, worries grew that the Russian example was attracting imitators among workers in Britain. In May 1917, therefore, Lloyd George appointed a commission to inquire into mounting industrial unrest. Having lived through the problems of 1910–1912 he had seen the damage wrought by widespread action during peacetime; to risk a repeat during an all-out war would be fatal.

Military leaders were similarly concerned. Derby told Haig after a dinner with Robertson and Lloyd George on 25 May that 'there is no doubt that the Russian revolution has created an unrest that is revolutionary and dangerous. The House of Commons too is in a very nasty mood.'[83] Esher had already gauged Derby's unrest, when the war secretary had visited France a week earlier and had dined with him. 'Derby arrived late last night,' he wrote in his diary on 19 May. 'He is excited and pessimistic over affairs in England. The food supplies, man power, and strikes worry him. The spectre of revolution stands behind his chair.'[84] Henderson visited Russia in May and advised Lloyd George that Britain recognise the new Russian administration. The prime minister agreed, but was forced to change his mind to appease the French.

A hardening of a radical mood in some areas triggered the wave of industrial unrest in the spring of 1917 that the country could ill afford. It suited the government to blame this on food shortages: workers often believed their employers were making a fortune out of the war, despite heavy taxation on high incomes, while they were forced to pay high prices for food, a large proportion of their weekly expenditure. Lloyd George invited a deputation of miners to see him to reassure them personally about food supplies. He was by then searching for a more sympathetic figure than Devonport to be food controller, or at least someone who would inspire the confidence of working people. He considered appointing a leader of the cooperative wholesale movement; but offered Devonport's job to Robert Smillie of the MFGB, a vocal anti-conscription man, hoping it would shut Smillie up; but he declined, causing Lloyd George to appoint Rhondda.

But morale remained low because of the failure to achieve a break-through in the war. Pacifists especially felt justified when the usual mild triumphalism of the heavily censored press about the Battle of Arras – Britain's share of the Nivelle offensive, which opened on 9 April – soon turned to a grim, familiar reality when stalemate reimposed itself. Elsewhere on the left, radicals in the union movement were agitating, constantly on the alert for the erosion of the privileges of their skilled members. Engineering workers started to fear their pay was falling behind inflation. Isolated strikes began in Lancashire from mid-March, over women at a Rochdale factory being asked to do skilled work for which no dilution had been negotiated. The firm sacked men who objected, which was illegal; but the Ministry of Munitions dreaded a confrontation with owners as well as workers. Lloyd George warned colleagues on 6 April that 'he had received indications from several sources of a very considerable and highly-organised labour movement with seditious tendencies' in major industrial centres.[85] He conceded some workers had 'genuine and legitimate grievances', and were ripe for exploitation by 'violent anarchists'.

Within days unrest broke out amongst members of the Amalgamated Society of Engineers, over the abolition of the Trade Card Scheme. The Manpower Board had instituted this in November 1916 to allow union leaders to give cards of exemption from enlistment to some members, but it had been discontinued when the combing-out of the munitions industry was ordered. Engineers in Barrow went on strike over the cutting-down of a bonus system, and the government gave them an ultimatum to return to work within twenty-four hours or face arrest; the ballot to return succeeded by only 1,623 to 1,200 even then.[86] The King, on his prime minister's advice, sent exhortations to workers in Barrow coupled with expressions of confidence that they would do everything they could to play their part in the war effort; and in early May he and the Queen undertook a week-long tour of shipyards, mills and munitions factories in the north-west.

By 3 May 60,000 men were striking in Lancashire, and engineering workers elsewhere followed them until within a week 200,000 were out. The strikes were unofficial: on 11 May the government issued a warning notice urging 'all loyal citizens to resume work immediately', adding that 'all persons who incite to any stoppage of work on munitions are guilty of an offence under the Defence of the Realm Regulations, the penalty for which is penal servitude for life or such less punishment as may be awarded.'[87] Despite the need to win the war, and draconian penalties for industrial action, in 1917 a total of 5.6 million days would be lost to strikes.[88]

Lloyd George put Addison in charge of negotiations. He had the good fortune of having the strikers' official leaders behind him, since they believed that extremists who disdained them even more than their employers were behind the unrest. There was hostility among the wider public to the strikers, who were regarded as betraying the country, and by 15 May some were drifting back to work. Despite having delegated matters to Addison, Lloyd George intervened, deciding on 17 May to prosecute the unofficial strike leaders. Seven were arrested and sent to Brixton the next day, and charged under DORA. Shop stewards led the strikes locally, twenty-two of whom the government eventually ordered to be arrested.

Within government circles opinions were divided on how to handle the strikers. The prime minister was determined to divide the working class against the militants; but Sir James Stevenson, director of area organisation at the Ministry of Munitions and former joint managing director of the Johnnie Walker whisky distillery, sought to tone down Lloyd George's aggression towards the workers. Stevenson said many saw a conspiracy between the government and the owners of capital, with the latter exploiting the war to use cheap labour that it hoped to retain, at the expense of better-paid skilled operatives, when peace came. Negotiations continued, with the government dropping the trade card scheme and agreeing to release the seven men from jail if they gave an earnest of good behaviour. Despite Lloyd George's bellicosity the government had no choice but to concede almost all the strikers' demands. However Smith, the Attorney General, threatened that the full might of the law would be brought down on the men if they stopped work again. The strike was settled on 19 May.

Although Addison had been instrumental in reaching an agreement with the engineering workers' leader, Robert Brownlie, Lloyd George's manipulation of it threatened to destabilise the situation again. When the concordat was published by Downing Street it removed all mention of Addison, saying Lloyd George had settled the problem: which was untrue. Addison, who was completely loyal to Lloyd George and had done just what he had been asked, was livid. 'God knows,' he wrote in his diary, 'that I of all men have never been backward in giving LG all the credit I could and that he deserves, and I hate the idea of trying to advertise myself, but this business discredits the whole ministry as well as myself.'[89] William Sutherland, Lloyd George's press officer, who would distinguish himself as one of the leading hawkers of honours, removed Addison's name. The prime minister, who badly needed Addison's competence as well as his loyalty, professed outrage at this distortion of the truth. However, it showed how those around Lloyd George – whom detractors branded his political parasites – did business on his behalf, usually following direction from the top. Such was Addison's clout that he forced Lloyd George to make an explanatory statement in the Commons on 21 May in which he confirmed the credit was his subordinate's.

The Leeds Convention of socialists, on 3 June, gave further evidence of the militant feelings of some in the working class. It was held, against a backdrop of industrial unrest in the city at the time, 'to hail the Russian revolution and to organise the British democracy to follow Russia', and called for workers and soldiers' soviets in Britain.[90] MacDonald proposed the resolution praising Russia, and the thousand or so delegates came not just from the Labour Party, the unions and the Union of Democratic Control, but also the women's movement and the Plebs League, a Marxist–syndicalist 'educational' organisation that sought to radicalise working people. The socialists had trouble finding a venue, as after 'patriotic pressure' the Leeds Albert Hall refused to accommodate them; the meeting went ahead at the Coliseum when the city council, also under 'pressure', decided it would be wrong to suppress freedom of speech.

Organised labour, angry at industrial compulsion, resolved at a meeting in late June of the Triple Alliance of miners, railwaymen and transport workers that 'the conscription of wealth should have preceded the conscription of human life', and demanded that a register of wealth and property be established 'to prepare for a real equality of national sacrifice.'[91] It was further proof of the popularity of Bolshevik ideas. James O'Grady, an Independent Labour MP and president of the General Federation of Trade Unions, announced that despite legal restrictions on strikes there had been one hundred and twenty-three in the previous twelve months, and 'he had never known a time when the relations between the Government Departments and organised labour had been so bad as now.'[92]

Shortly after these events, in July, a shortage of beer caused discontent in a number of large towns, and in towns with big munitions factories. London, Birmingham, Leeds, Sheffield, Newcastle and Barrow-in-Furness were among those affected. There were calls for a 50 per cent increase in production, to 15 million barrels a year; and, inevitably, accusations that the price of beer had risen to a shilling a quart in some country districts during the hay harvest, with profiteering by brewers and publicans. The government acknowledged 'difficulties' (blamed on distribution) in rural areas.[93]

Fearing a breakdown of civil order, the government announced that in the next quarter the food controller would permit an increase of one-third in beer production; and the priority would be to distribute this to areas with substantial tracts of arable land to harvest, and to areas with munitions factories. The catch was that the strength of the beer would be reduced. This upset the Irish, whose stout and porter could not be brewed at such a low gravity: it was added to the lengthening list of grievances. Later in the summer, in the cause of cheering up the working man, the government pegged the price of beer – including an officially approved new 'Government Ale' – at 5d a pint, while specifying that the lighter beer popular in the eastern counties should sell at no more than 4d a pint. The government further increased, by a third, the quantity of beer that could be brewed until the end of September, men being thirstier in the summer, and those bringing in the harvest having to be catered for. The brewers, accused of profiteering, cut the price of mild and porter: they wished to escape blame for any rioting.

For the first time, the Home Office became active in the monitoring and suppression of dissent, when Sir George Cave, the home secretary, decided to take more precautions against revolution. He established an informal security committee with representatives of the Armed Forces, the police and several interested government departments to review intelligence; and from April 1917 Scotland Yard had a section of its Criminal Investigation Department operating routine surveillance of the organised working class, of areas where defeatism was thought rife. Lists of 'dangerous, suspicious persons' were drawn up.[94] When later in the year the National War Aims Committee was established, the Home Office would work closely with it and with the British National Workers' League, comprised of 'patriotic' socialists and a counterweight to the Union of Democratic Control. The policy was ruthless, but effective.

Unrest among the working classes was further fed by poor and unrepaired housing, threats of food rationing and rises in prices. Yet sporadic strikes, usually provoked by specific local complaints, continued to vex the government into the autumn of 1917. Railwaymen, for example, complained about working conditions – they sought an eight-hour day, which would have cost the government £10 million a year in overtime – and the engineers' union made similar demands, which threatened munitions factories. The government used DORA to ban them from striking, offering to provide a conciliation service to mediate between management and men instead.[95] Afraid the railways might be compromised, the government ordered a review of canals, with a view to using them to shift goods. Railway workers then demanded another 10s a week. The War Cabinet authorised the Railway Executive to give members of the National Union of Railwaymen an extra 5s a week. The NUR refused the offer. It was raised to 6s, and accepted; and the government braced itself for other unions to put in claims.[96]

Apart from such local difficulties there was, nonetheless, evidence of the rise of a more deep-seated radicalism. A series of articles in *The Times* in September contended that 'behind the meaningless and stupid term 'labour unrest' lies a conscious revolutionary movement which aims at the complete overthrow of the existing economic and social order, not in some uncertain future, but here and now.'[97] The newspaper argued that workers in areas such as Clydeside had long regarded the real conflict as between the ruling elites of the combatant countries, and irrelevant to the international brotherhood of the working class. The growth of revolutionary ideas in Russia, inspired by the theories of Marx, helped promote hitherto continental ideas – collectivism, syndicalism and anarchism – among British workers. *The Times* felt that those workers were unwitting tools of arch-manipulators in the revolutionary movement, and the public were ignorant of the plot to wreck capitalism. 'The upshot is that obscure revolutionaries have the Government and the nation by the throat and mean to strangle them,' it wrote in a leading article that reflected on the others it had published on the subject. It believed Britain would rise up against them 'when it realises the danger.'

Wage rises for munitions workers took the average pay to £3 15s a week for skilled workers and £2 3s for unskilled. Nevertheless there was a week-long strike in Coventry in late November over union recognition, and the failure of employers to agree to union procedures: no amount of public outrage at its effect on the war effort made any difference. Inevitably, the government had to impose a settlement, which was as simple as offering discussions about the role of shop stewards.

Precisely because the demand for labour remained inexorable the union movement was in a position to demand more money, however unpatriotic that was. By late 1917 around 10,000 workshops were making munitions of war, 5,000 of them controlled by the Ministry of Munitions, including 150 national factories. The building of workers' housing absorbed almost the entire construction trade, with 1,500 new homes in greater London alone. Any non-essential building costing more than £500 now required a licence. On the land, prisoners of war worked throughout 1917 and, without them, the nation might have gone hungry. With shipping losses reduced but still running at twice the rate of new tonnage, the Army had to release 200,000 men to work in shipyards. This could not have come at a worse time: the end of the fighting between the revolutionary regime in Russia and the Central Powers allowed a movement of German men and guns from the Eastern to the Western Front, where British troops were already under strength. Demand for steel, and the coal to make it, rose, but there was a shortage of miners: there had been sporadic strikes of colliers over pay and the condition of their machinery in South Wales during the summer, with at times 12,000 men idle. It was feared coal for households would run out during the winter.

In late September the miners demanded an extra 10s a week, on top of a request for a 25 per cent pay rise, which alone would have cost between £25 million and £30 million a year, and would mean their pay would have risen 65 per cent in three years. Guy Calthrop, the coal controller, told the War Cabinet that 'the men were out of hand', but conceded that since 1914 the cost of living had risen by 83 per cent.[98] He doubted munitions factories could function for more than ten days without continuing supplies of coal, and most had no space for stockpiles. The War Cabinet realised it had to make concessions, 'while recognising that the demand by the miners was unreasonable and deeply to be deplored'. The public deplored the consequential rise of 2s 6d a ton in the price of coal. The granting of such concessions was, however, the means with which a government in desperate straits dealt with the legacy of industrial unrest that had poisoned British life before 1914.

V

Having resolved to pursue the war to its end, the government found itself struggling to cope not just with labour relations and supplies, but with ever-mounting costs. By the spring of 1917, and despite the levying of higher taxation, the financial situation was dire. In 1913 the state had spent 8.1 per cent of the nation's gross domestic product; in 1917 it would spend 38.7 per cent of it.[99] And although many incomes had risen because of overtime, Treasury figures had shown it took a sovereign to buy in March 1916 what in March 1914 had cost 15s.[100] On 3 April Law told the cabinet that Britain's gold reserves were down to $219 million, and the war was costing $75 million a week: within three weeks the country would run out of money. The previous December the rate of loss of reserves had been $5 million a day, or $35 million a week, so the problem was increasing.[101] The national debt in April had been £4 billion – compared with £651 million before the war – and was rising by £135 million a month. By July it was rising by £180 million a month; the interest alone was costing £110 million a year.[102] The fighting was but one expense: welfare services were increased, especially for soldiers' dependents, and hostels were provided for war workers. The public voiced concern about the availability of treatment for soldiers discharged because of wounds or disabilities, which would require more expenditure.[103] Also, the dependents of such men, and of the dead, had to be looked after. Government figures in March 1917 showed 518,741 of these reliant on the largesse of the Ministry of Pensions, created to administer this proto-welfare state.[104] There were 140,275 disabled men; 62,796 widows; 128,294 children of widows and 157,544 children of disabled men; and 29,832 other dependents. In addition, around 125,000 widows had not yet reached the pensionable stage, and another 130,000 men were either medically unfit for work after their war service or still in hospital with their injuries being assessed.

By 1917–18 Britain also had loans of £1,333.2 million outstanding to its allies, and £194.5 million to the Empire. The national debt rocketed by over 1,000 per cent, from £706 million in 1914 to £7,481 million by the Armistice: only around 22.1 per cent of the cost of the war was met by taxation.[105] During the war the numbers paying income tax more than trebled from 1.1 million to 3.5 million, and revenues almost equal to those from income tax were raised by the excess profits duty, introduced by McKenna in 1915 to placate trades unionists who feared employers were going to become unduly rich. Law would eventually raise income tax to 30 per cent and the excess profits duty to 80 per cent.

The cost of war continued to rise inexorably. In April 1917 it was £6.25 million a day; by July it was £7.75 million. The difference, over a year, between prediction and reality was equivalent to the country's total revenues. Law had claimed an excess profits tax should raise an extra £7 million a day; but had been forced to rein in tobacco and entertainment taxes, so it would raise at most £4 million a day. A deputation of working men visited him, complaining that high tobacco taxation would bring unrest because of its regressive nature: it hit those on lower incomes harder than the middle class.

The average rate of income tax in 1914 was 1s in the pound; now it was 5s, and 8s 3d (or 41.5 per cent) for those paying super tax, causing qualms about improving production and investment if it continued to rise.[106] The excess profits duty raised £29 million in the first year of the war, but £125 million in the second. The government maintained it could outlast Germany; some MPs were not so sure, or worried that Britain faced ruin. Luckily, the inclination of many wage-earners to donate to charities that helped servicemen and their families or to buy War Bonds eased pressure on the Treasury. Indeed by 1917 the National War Bonds, bearing a 4 or 5 per cent rate of interest and redeemable after five to ten years, had become the main means of raising money. The money supply doubled during the war. When peace came and lenders redeemed their bonds, Britain avoided the hyperinflation that wrecked the German economy. This was because so much of its debt was held by overseas investors, and the liquidity did not go back into the domestic economy. Also, unlike the Germans, the British paid considerably higher taxes throughout the war. Nonetheless the government would have to borrow to repay its debts, and this would store up problems for later in the 1920s and 1930s.

The Commons debated public spending on 6 July, as much to complain about the new, apparently unaccountable style of government as to warn ministers about out-of-control expenditure. A motion, signed by MPs of all parties, demanded a select committee to scrutinise spending decisions. Colonel Godfrey Collins, its proposer, said: 'the supreme object of the House of Commons is to control expenditure. But the necessary knowledge is deliberately withheld, and without knowledge control cannot be effective.'[107] In another swipe at Lloyd George's *modus operandi*, Collins observed that 'the Government use the Press daily for their purposes, and the increasing use of the Press by the Government has diminished the power of this House. The House of Commons is not properly informed about finance. The Government ask for supplies of money and refuse supplies of information.'

Collins claimed Law could not act as chancellor properly while being Leader of the House in Lloyd George's almost permanent absence. The financial secretary to the Treasury – Stanley Baldwin, in his first government job – was also hardly ever in the House, because he was in the Treasury doing Law's job. 'If the Government refused the appointment of this Committee the public will say it is a deliberate attempt to shield their actions from criticism. To-day there are 3,000,000 Income Tax payers, and every citizen is feeling the financial effect of this War. I challenge the moral right of the Government to impose taxation if they withhold control and knowledge of expenditure from this House.'[108] He blamed the bureaucracy, notably for having put functionaries with no experience of the working man in control over him.

The creation of vast new government responsibilities, as central to Lloyd George's plan to give an impression of dynamism as to the necessities of prosecuting the war, had dramatically driven up public spending. Collins complained that 'everywhere men are crying out against bureaucracy and the multiplication of unnecessary Departments. The evils of borrowing and inflation are apparent to all. What we are now proposing every business man recognises as essential for the successful prosecution of his own business.' Other speakers commended nineteenth-century finance ministers, notably Gladstone, in cutting expenditure after the Crimean and other wars. Law said he could not cut expenditure during a war, but had to counter talk of mortgaging Britain's future to fund the enormous state payroll. One MP alleged there were 8,000 'clerks, porters and others' in the Ministry of Munitions alone.[109] The authorisation of extra expenditure rested with the War Cabinet, or even just Lloyd George himself. Law promised a select committee, though was vague on its terms of reference.

It was scarcely surprising, given all the pressures, hardships and sense of bereavement that prevailed in Britain, that a spirit of privation and gloom pertained at the start of 1917, and lasted throughout the year. The gloom, to start with, was literal as well as figurative: for days after Christmas 1916 fog paralysed London. Food and fuel were in ever shorter supply, with temperance campaigners agitating to have the government ban brewing to save sugar, which was especially scarce. Railway companies announced reductions in services and station closures, with journeys slowing down and fares rising by around 50 per cent, with a view to deterring civilians from travelling: a forerunner of the 'Is Your Journey Really Necessary?' posters from the next war. Regulation was seen as the answer to any difficulty, but ignored fundamental causes. Where it was brought in – be it price controls, rent controls or intervention in essential industries – it caused or aggravated long-term problems of supply.

The last vestiges of pre-war life were being eradicated. All racing was finally cancelled after the Newmarket Spring Meeting of 1917: train travel for civilians was too difficult, motoring almost impossible, and those attending race meetings were stigmatised as loafers, shirkers and unpatriotic. However, a powerful lobby from breeders forced the War Cabinet to decree on 4 July that the sport could be resumed, and forty days' racing were allowed 'in view of the national importance of horse-breeding' provided they were mostly at Newmarket or at other courses where the horses would not travel far from their stables, and not more than 1,200 horses were in training – to conserve feed.[110] Other animal enthusiasts were less favoured: even dog shows were banned, under DORA.[111]

Repington, observing British life *de haut en bas*, noted in July 1917 the effect of the conflict on his upper-middle-class world. 'The only visible signs of war are that the men now wear usually short coats and black ties in the evenings, that dinners are shorter, and that servants are fewer and less good. There is a want of taxis and of petrol, and sugar in some places is rather scarce.' He did not feel there had been too bad an effect on his social inferiors. 'The working classes are well paid, and food is abundant if dear. There is the minimum of privation, and no general and real suffering from the war' – an astonishing assertion, but a sign of how easy it was as a well-to-do Englishman in 1914–18 to carry on partying.[112]

'The greatest sufferers,' he believed, 'are the middle classes, especially the humble gentlewomen, with fixed incomes, and those who have lost husbands or sons.' There was a degree of truth in this. Although the traditional officer class took a disproportionately high number of casualties in the fighting, the richest had tended to live off unearned income and continued to do so, albeit more highly taxed. The middle classes had no such cushion of capital and a station in life to keep up for which no separation allowance would compensate, if their breadwinner was in the services; and if he were killed there was often terrible hardship, an awareness of which caused the formation of various charities to support the widows and orphans of 'temporary gentlemen'. The well-to-do also endured a magnification of the old 'servant problem', in that there was hardly any spare labour to undertake tasks for them. Even Repington, as he explained in his usual lofty tone, suffered when trying to have repairs done on his house; his builder said that 'he has eleven men instead of the forty he had before the war, and that they are all old and not venturesome on high ladders. Their wages are one-third up, and the price of materials is awful.'[113]

Inevitably, the privations were harshest for the working class, and particularly for those whose lives had been uprooted by the need to move to another part of the country to work in the war effort. For example, the Ministry of Munitions' determination to improve iron ore production to help speed up the replacement of shipping required thousands of workers to be moved to iron-producing areas. However, there were huge shortages of housing in such places in which to billet the immigrant workers. Since August 1914 civilians had been used to having soldiers and workers billeted on them, but it had been done on a voluntary basis and among people glad to earn extra money for letting a spare room. Now the problem seemed insoluble without a massive construction programme of temporary hostels: Barrow-in-Furness had had its population trebled, and the influx of women workers was causing special problems. Those with spare rooms, alert to the laws of supply and demand, were putting up rents above what workers – especially the more lowly paid women – could afford. The population of Carlisle had increased by 20,000 and there were no more lodgings.

In an attempt to grapple with the problem, local welfare committees had been set up to ensure workers could be absorbed successfully into their new locations; and a Central Billeting Board had local representatives organise accommodation, settle complaints and allocate rooms. However, matters had reached the point that when all those willing to take lodgers had been exhausted, so those with spare rooms who had not offered them would now be compelled to do so under yet more new provisions of DORA. All occupiers would be forced to disclose what accommodation they had. Addison, as minister of munitions, aware of this infringement of individual rights, promised that 'I myself believe, however, that in very few instances will it be necessary to exercise any compulsory powers or extreme measures.'[114]

Nonetheless, there were widespread objections, with MPs accusing the government of lacking foresight in setting up factories without planning to house those who would work in them. Addison protested that a programme of hostel building was unfeasible; there were not men to build them nor the materials. James Hogge – an Edinburgh MP who would become government chief whip after the 1918 election – protested about the sort of people who might be about to be imposed upon his and other MPs' constituents: 'I have heard that on certain days in the week you cannot get along certain roads . . . on account of the drunken people in the way. That may or may not be true, but if it is true, they are the people who are to be compulsorily billeted on ladies who knit socks and mufflers.'[115] Realising it had to act, the Ministry of Munitions announced an initiative to build 500 permanent and 500 semi-permanent houses at Barrow-in-Furness for workers, many of whom had been living in glorified barracks.

A regime of compliance and inspection was proposed to ensure the billets were up to standard, which incensed Hogge. He feared an 'inquisition into the home life of respectable women whose sons and husbands, many of them, are serving across the water at the front.'[116] He asked

Addison to envisage the consequences of introducing compulsion. 'Surely he must see that the woman who has to provide that accommodation must have more protection. Take some of the Scottish villages. Those women have given up their men for the Army, and frequently there is nobody left at home but the woman and her girls. Can my right hon Friend contemplate with equanimity a defenceless woman and her daughter in a Scottish village in which munition workers have settled being saddled with the rough type of men engaged in munition works?'[117] Another criticism was that it was not compulsory billeting, but better wages, that were required: young women were paid on average 23s a week, and with the rise in the cost of living since 1914 that severely limited the range of accommodation they could afford.

Snowden, who had just been elected chairman of the Independent Labour Party at a conference that (to the government's alarm) had cheered the overthrow of the Tsar and celebrated pacifism, pointed out the main danger of young women being moved into such overcrowded conditions: 'Immorality.'[118] He was 'appalled' when he considered the consequences of the government's policy. More to the point, 'no interference with individual liberty . . . has been more outrageous than this which is proposed.' John Henderson, Liberal MP for West Aberdeenshire, said that 'no Bill has been introduced into this House which has had such an evil aspect as this one.'[119] He added: 'I also dread this eternal appointment of salaried officials and local committees', and feared the numbers working for the state were 'getting enormous and beyond all control and knowledge': the old Britain in which the state barely touched, let alone interfered in, individual lives was being buried.[120] The billeting of soldiers had been helped by their being subject to military discipline; munitions workers were not. The Bill had its second reading, thanks to the large government majority, but there was no concealing the unease among backbenchers.

VI

To add to the public's woes the threat to life and property from air raids grew throughout the year, despite an important advance in 1916 from a dramatic improvement to London's anti-aircraft defences. Zeppelin raids on the city had stopped in September that year, and the RFC became highly effective at shooting down enemy planes. As a result, defences had been reduced in early 1917, when it seemed the Germans would not return. Yet on 25 April 1917 a daylight bombing raid on Folkestone killed ninety-five people. In the following days German destroyers sporadically shelled the Kent coast, notably Ramsgate, inflicting few casualties but destroying various properties. Soon, demands were made in and out of Parliament for the entire civilian population of towns on the east and south-east coasts to be evacuated, which would have made the already dire accommodation problem effectively unmanageable. The government quite sensibly refused to consider any such thing, claiming it was improving both the nation's air defences and the air-raid warning system. To boost morale the government had also ordered the bombing of occupied towns on the European coast, such as Zeebrugge.

As the threat from the air increased, the government was urged to appoint a minister for the air defences, the War Office's existing control of the RFC being deemed untenable because, although there was an Air Board, no minister was answerable to Parliament. The War Cabinet also considered 'the possible spread of epidemics by dropping germs from the air'.[121] It had long expected the Germans to try such a tactic on the British public as part of a 'campaign of frightfulness'; experts thought germ warfare would be ineffective, unless the water supply were directly infected with typhoid or cholera. It was felt 'improbable' this could be done from the air, but the government asked its scientists to consider possible retaliation if it was.

Churchill, showing welcome proactivity, realised how vulnerable his munitions factories were to air raids, and instigated a programme of building dugouts and shelters lined with sandbags to protect workers. This, as he admitted, was only copying practice in many privately owned factories. Although constructing the shelters would affect productivity – the workers themselves would dig them – he argued it would result in higher output as workers would not retreat home during a raid. Churchill wanted to take this principle further, and urged the War Cabinet to sanction a network of shelters in residential areas near such factories. The cheap housing in which working-class communities tended to live was deemed especially vulnerable to collapse if bombed; and the government accepted that, whether bombed or not, the national housing stock would require a huge public subsidy after the war to be raised to an acceptable standard, and local authorities had been invited to submit applications for help.[122]

However, in believing they had tamed German air power, the British authorities had not reckoned on the Gotha fixed-wing bomber, which flew from bases in Belgium and, flying as it did largely over water, was until it reached its target largely free of molestation by British anti-aircraft guns. Flying at 10,500 feet and heavily armed with machine guns, the Gothas killed seventy-one and injured a hundred and ninety-two people in and around Folkestone on 25 May in a daylight raid, having aborted an attack on London because of thick cloud. At the inquest the following week the jury condemned 'in the strongest possible manner the negligence of the local and military authorities for not having made arrangements whereby the public could be warned.'[123]

The first such raid on the capital, on the morning of 13 June, left a hundred and sixty-two dead and four hundred and thirty-two injured, mainly around Liverpool Street Station: eighteen children died at Upper North Street school in the East India Dock Road, with a little girl being dug from the rubble three days later, alive. A fifth of the casualties were children. The King went to the scene of the raid and drove slowly through the streets, being cheered by survivors; he then visited the injured in hospital. A Zeppelin was destroyed the next day (just as a privately owned TNT factory blew up at Ashton-under-Lyne, killing forty-three and injuring a hundred and twenty others. The government offered to pay for the funerals). There was inevitable criticism of the slow response of the air defences – there had, William Joynson-Hicks, the Tory MP, alleged in Parliament on 14 June, been forty-five minutes between the Gothas being spotted and bombs being dropped. When planes were spotted, warnings were telegraphed ahead and the police were sent out to order people under cover. There had been a failure to warn institutions, notably schools and hospitals. Joynson-Hicks also demanded retaliatory raids on German towns.

That evening a meeting of London citizens convened and passed a resolution demanding reprisals, and their example was followed around the country. The public urged MPs to hold a debate in Parliament; the government refused, relying instead on raising morale by improving warnings and defences. Air resources were limited, and the War Cabinet decided they were better used defending rather than attacking. It also ruled that to bomb German towns within range of the RFC was a suggestion 'in reality one of "frightfulness".'[124]

The Germans fed, however, on British inactivity in tackling the

Gothas. On 7 July there were two hundred and fifty more casualties, including fifty-seven dead, in a daylight raid on London by twenty-two bombers. A clamour built about poor air-raid warnings, not least because the bombers had been spotted over the east coast. The government admitted a reluctance to issue warnings because the home defence had had three false alarms the previous week; had all been acted upon the loss of productivity would have been damaging. *The Times* detected 'widespread indignation', provoked by a sense that Britain was being humiliated, but also by a growing fear that air power might decide the war, and the country seemed unequal to the challenge.[125] The War Cabinet authorised Cave to initiate a system of warnings 'when the course followed by the raiders left practically no doubt as to their destination or objective.'[126] The RFC attacked the Gothas over the Essex coast as they returned home, and one was reportedly shot down. A small riot broke out in London's east end, wrecking property owned by, or thought to be owned by, Germans: twenty-four people were arrested.

The War Cabinet was propelled into mild panic as the press expressed its outrage at such raids being allowed to happen, and the public demanded retaliation. The London Air Defence Area was created and, despite objections from Haig, the War Cabinet ordered back two RFC squadrons from the Western Front to protect London. Lloyd George blamed the shortage of planes on Asquith's 'vacillation', a convenient excuse with some truth in it – Asquith had failed to take a grip on the Air Board – but not one the new prime minister could use for much longer.[127] In the short term the new plan worked; in August three raids on London failed, and the Germans switched to trying to bomb by night. It had long been established that the anti-aircraft guns around London lacked the range to shoot anything down, so fighter planes were essential for the job.

Robertson was summoned to a special War Cabinet meeting after the raid. He found ministers in a near-hysterical panic about the raids and, through the prism of what he knew of the infinitely greater carnage at the front, told Haig, 'one would have thought that the world was coming to an end.'[128] French, as home commander-in-chief, was present, and complained about the inadequacy of the forces at his disposal to defend England. Robertson privately agreed, saying the defenders of the country were mainly 'oddments' – men unfit for active service abroad, or too young by law to serve there. He added that 'our anti-aircraft artillery was apparently of no use, and our airmen arrived in driblets and were powerless, but succeeded in getting one machine down. The fact is we have not enough machines to meet our requirements.'

On 9 July the Commons held a secret session about air defences. According to the official report issued by the Speaker, Lloyd George said that 'complete protection in the air could never be secured.'[129] He felt one of the main reasons the Germans were bombing England was to force the withdrawal of aeroplanes from France to defend the homeland: a strategy the War Cabinet was determined to avoid. Instead, Lloyd George promised that aircraft production, which had increased in the preceding six months, would continue to do so: he was confident that French would soon have enough planes to defend London adequately. A week later a system of sirens was tested in the City of London, but most people indoors could not hear them: cannon fire, flares, police firing blanks from pistols in the streets and boats on the river sounding their whistles were also tried. The search for the perfect system culminated with what the government called 'sound bombs', three maroons fired at fifteen-second intervals, while police put up notices in the street ordering people to 'take cover'.[130] Lloyd George assured the Commons that Royal Navy bombers were regularly attacking German aerodromes in Belgium, and dropping a heavier tonnage of bombs on them than the Gothas were on London.

A series of six raids on London occurred between 24 September and 1 October, which included new aeroplanes known as 'Giants' that could fly at 19,000 feet and drop 1,000-kilogram bombs: these were beyond the range of not just guns but searchlights and, more to the point, fighter aircraft.[131] There was a debate about sounding warnings for night-time raids in case half-asleep civilians rushed into the streets and became even more vulnerable to the bombs. A tactic that would be familiar in Hitler's war was introduced, with tens of thousands of Londoners spontaneously taking refuge in the Underground. Maroons were fired to signal an imminent raid; unfortunately, some mistook these for anti-aircraft guns and panicked, thinking the raid had started; the government was asked to use sirens as a warning instead, but said these were harder than maroons to hear above the traffic.

The prime minister's own reaction to the raids was less than stalwart. He was about to pursue successful libel actions against several news organisations that had accused him of retreating to his house at Walton

Heath during raids: which he had, because of his fear of explosions. He claimed he was suing not because of the personal attack on him, but because of the fear it might sow among the public, prompting them to think raids were more dangerous than they actually were. The raids were also continuing to fuel demands for retaliation. On 2 October Lloyd George toured bombed areas, and met protestors calling for reprisals. He was heard to say to some of them: 'we shall do that.'[132]

Later that month the King and Queen toured the east end, inspecting air-raid shelters. Some east enders sent a telegram to the King asking that he command the War Office to receive a deputation to deliver their demand for reprisals: he passed the telegram to the prime minister, and Stamfordham took the precaution of telling the press he had done so. Mayors of several London boroughs added to the clamour, as did the mayor of Ramsgate, whose town was used for target practice by bombers coming down the Thames estuary. The government briefed that the delay in reprisals was not because of an unwillingness to share in German 'beastliness', but because there was not the air power to do it without exposing the Western Front: but such power was being increased. It was also reported that although German civilians were not being attacked, the aerodromes of the planes bombing London were. Within a fortnight RFC planes were bombing factories in Saarbrücken. In early November Ben Tillett, the veteran dockers' leader, easily beat a government candidate in a by-election at Salford, on a manifesto including a demand for 'air raid reprisals on a large scale', as well as for better pay for servicemen and their dependents. It was a fair reflection of public disillusion with the government. The War Cabinet implored Lord Montagu of Beaulieu to withdraw a question to Curzon on air-raid precautions, as 'he would be unable to answer it without revealing valuable information to the enemy', but in fact so that 'deficiencies' should not be publicly exposed.[133]

Air raids continued on the capital, Kent and the eastern counties throughout the winter of 1917–18. Gwynne, reflecting the general feeling that too little was being done to protect the British people against murderous attack, told Lady Bathurst on 15 January 1918: 'Believe me England is not rotten. It is a nation of lions led by asses and knaves. England is all right at heart. I have never lost faith in the people. But I have lost faith in *all* our leaders.'[134] Some leaders, political and military, would not have disagreed. On the night of 28 January the Germans bombed Ramsgate; a hundred and sixteen houses sustained damage, but there were no casualties. A shelter in a basement in Odham's printing works in Covent Garden took a direct hit, killing thirty-eight people and wounding sixty-five; the raid killed sixty-seven and injured another hundred and sixty-six, including women and children trampled to death in a stampede at Bishopsgate station. The War Cabinet decided to release the figures, as failure to do so might, in the climate then existing, lead to wild and demoralising rumours.[135] General Hugh Trenchard, managing the creation of the RAF, was promised planes to bomb Germany into submission; he never got them.

VII

The displacements caused by war, with people being uprooted and communities shifting, had other malign effects on behaviour and on society, and these became apparent before 1917. From early 1916 cocaine, a drug then still available over the counter to persons known to the chemist, or introduced by someone the chemist did know, caused an epidemic of addiction, though the expense of the substance tended to confine the problem to the better-off. A substantial black market had grown up in the drug for the benefit of those not well connected to an obliging chemist. 'I am informed,' Samuel told the Commons on 22 June 1916, 'that there has been increased use of cocaine among certain classes.'[136] It was widely believed it had become the drug of choice since the suppression of opium, which had happened under the 1908 Pharmacy Act; the government banned its sale to members of the Armed Forces and considered restricting it to the public. So-called 'pick-me-ups' containing ether or cocaine were widely available in shops in London's more fashionable districts, and their use was thought to encourage a craving for pure cocaine. Suppliers and traffickers came before the courts almost daily, and most received harsh prison sentences; there were also concerns that Germany was flooding Britain with the drug through its agents, to undermine the health and morale of soldiers on leave. A high proportion of those convicted were foreigners, notably Russians. As a public panic developed, the government decided on 28 July 1916 to ban by Royal Proclamation the importation of cocaine and opium, except under licence.

Soldiers in France had often become used to frequenting brothels, not so much for recreation as to help cope with alleviating the trauma of war; and demand for the services of prostitutes rocketed even in cities such as London, where prostitution had long been a problem. This helped fuel an epidemic of venereal disease, which gratuitously added to the casualties sustained by the Army. Questions were asked in the Commons from early in 1917 about the leniency of penalties imposed on those keeping 'disorderly houses'.[137] Cave promised on 13 February to give extra powers to magistrates to deal with brothels, and that new legislation would be introduced. The maximum fine for a repeat offender keeping a brothel was £40, which Cave described as 'a mere flea bite'. He increased it to £500 or a year in prison for a third and subsequent offence; the maximum penalty for soliciting would be a month in prison. Most radically, he proposed to make it a criminal offence for someone knowingly carrying a venereal disease to have sexual intercourse with anyone else; and proposed to extend the 1889 Indecent Advertisements Act 'not only to all advertisements relating to this disease, but to advertisements of means for procuring miscarriage or abortion, or suggesting that premises can be used for immoral purposes. We are also increasing the penalties, which seem to be too light. The penalties are increased to £100 and six months' imprisonment, instead of 40s and one month's imprisonment, and £5 and three months' imprisonment respectively.'[138] The purpose of banning advertisements for VD cures was to try to ensure that quack medicines – which included almost all so-called cures – were not taken as a substitute for genuine treatment.

The war did not invent VD, a sufficient scourge in peacetime Britain that a Royal Commission on prevention and the better organisation of treatment had been established in 1913; but war had made the situation far worse. The Royal Commission wanted sex education to alert young people to the dangers; a conference of headmistresses of girls' schools in July 1916 agreed the duty lay with parents 'to give their daughters necessary moral instruction in the matter', although a woman doctor who was present warned them that 'her experience of middle and upper class parents was that they were unwilling and unable to deal with these things' and parents from the lower orders 'had not the gift of expression.'[139] Self-appointed experts toured Britain lecturing on the dangers of VD. Mrs Bessie Ward, from the Council of Civil Liberties, in January 1917 addressed a meeting of the Women's Co-operative Guild in Richmond-on-Thames, organised by Virginia Woolf. Mrs Ward spoke on conscription – a subject familiar to the Bloomsbury set, most of whose eligible members strove to avoid it – which inevitably caused her to talk about the dangers of VD to unwary young soldiers. After the meeting a regular member, a Mrs Langston, expressed her outrage at Mrs Ward's remarks; she felt only a childless woman could have made such a speech and said, before bursting into tears, 'for we mothers try to forget what our sons have to go through.'[140] Mrs Woolf's biographer describes her as 'unrepentant', and to have regarded the poor woman's outburst as 'nonsense'; Bloomsbury's callous detachment from the realities that its members did so much to avoid encountering was seldom displayed so vividly.

By 1917 politicians believed Britain was in the grip of a VD epidemic. Despite a determination to discuss the matter as little as possible, the public too were increasingly aware of the problem. Cave's Criminal Law Amendment Bill made it an offence punishable by up to two years' imprisonment (with or without hard labour) for a person with a venereal disease to solicit another person for sexual intercourse, or to commit the act. Once this came before Parliament it became harder to contain public concern. A hospital in London specialising in VD, the Lock, had recorded 23,974 cases in 1913, but by 1916 there were 36,500 of them.[141] The diseases affected infant mortality and child health, and a doctor who gave evidence to the commission said the effect on the nation generally was perhaps worse than tuberculosis. The higher incidence of the disease also helped drive up the divorce rate, and with it demands for liberalisation of the divorce law.

In the Army, 43 men in every 1,000 were suffering, or a total of a 107,000 men in an army of around 5 million, a disaster when every man counted.[142] Sir Arthur Conan Doyle was so alarmed that he demanded all 'notorious prostitutes and brothel-keepers' should be interned until six months after the war; to others this smacked of the Victorian Contagious Diseases Act (which had left women in the vicinity of naval dockyards and military barracks liable to arrest and medical inspection), and the idea was deeply resisted.[143] London was viewed as the centre of depravity, with the area around Waterloo Road regarded as 'an open sewer' where prostitutes solicited soldiers on leave, whose wallets they would routinely rifle after business was done.[144] Even more horrific to contemporary sensibilities were reports that boys were 'touting' for business on behalf of the prostitutes in the 'open sewer'. The problem was compounded by a number of 'amateur' women supplementing the already swollen ranks of the professionals.[145] After a story in *The Times* highlighted the problem, patrols of military police went to the district to arrest soldiers for breaches of military discipline; and the local police rounded up women talking to servicemen and charged them with 'interfering with soldiers'.[146]

For civilians, the Local Government Board had asked a hundred and forty-five local councils to provide treatment plans; ninety-nine had done so by late April 1917 and sixty-one were already approved, serving a population of three million.[147] The ratio of sufferers was roughly two or three men for every woman; to stop quacks making things worse the Bill made it an offence punishable by a fine of £100 or six months in prison to treat VD if unqualified. A publicity campaign would advertise the new centres, ending the culture of pretending the diseases did not exist. In the war until April 1917 there had been 27,000 cases of syphilis, 7,000 of gonorrhea and 6,000 of other syphilis-related diseases. Guest, the coalition chief whip, said women waited at railway stations for soldiers returning from leave to lure them to brothels, and advocated better supervision of men at home on leave. He also believed VD should be made notifiable, a view shared by many of his colleagues, with sufferers who refused treatment subject to arrest and detention while they were treated. In March 1918 he had his wish, when an amendment to DORA – Regulation 40D – made it an offence for a woman with any venereal disease to have sexual intercourse with a member of the Armed Forces. Some constabularies caused outrage by allowing the press to publish the names of woman charged with having sexual intercourse with a soldier while infected, but keeping the soldier's name secret. Nor did it occur to the zealots that a woman could be charged for infecting her husband, even if he had infected her in the first place but had subsequently been cured.

Rates of illegitimacy rose from 3.94 per cent in 1907 to 5.54 per cent in 1917; but the death rate among such children was said to be twice as high as among legitimate ones.[148] There remained a severe social prohibition on sex outside marriage, a huge stigma on illegitimacy and single motherhood, and abortion was illegal. However, the latter phase of the Great War saw the first tentative steps towards a more permissive attitude regarding sex. Marie Stopes, a thirty-seven-year-old palaeobotanist at University College, London, who had at the age of twenty-three become the youngest doctor of science in the country, was trying to find a publisher for her book *Married Love*, which advocated more widespread knowledge and use of contraception, and which would be published in March 1918.

Dr Stopes, a committed eugenicist, was passionately opposed to abortion, not least because of the dangerous and sometimes lethal conditions in which it was carried out; which caused her to write the book. Eventually, a philanthropist (whom she subsequently married) had to pay to have it published because no commercial publisher would touch it. When it ran to five editions in its first year, its patron rapidly recovered his investment. Marriage rates yo-yoed during the war: in 1913, in England and Wales, 286,583 marriages took place; in 1915 there were 360,885; in 1917, 258,885; in 1919, 369,411. There was hardly any increase in divorce, which did not take off until during and after the Second World War.

Some took the idea of married love too literally. In 1912, 2.75 per cent of cases heard at the Central Criminal Court concerned alleged bigamous marriages. By 1918 it was 20.2 per cent; whether this was confined to soldiers, whose absences from home were easily explained, or became a wider problem is not clear. That bigamy prosecutions fell after the war suggests it was the former.[149] The *palme d'or* went in June 1918 to Tom Wilkinson (alias Williams), a thirty-eight-year-old sapper. He was sentenced to seven years' penal servitude at Kent Assizes for bigamy, having already been given an identical sentence at Derby Assizes for another bigamy. 'It was proved he had gone through ceremonies of marriage with five women,' *The Times* reported, 'and that at the time of his arrest he was making arrangements to marry three other young women.'[150] Something of a pluralist, he had also deserted from three different regiments.

Women were often working long hours in factories or on the land, compounding the sense of parental detachment in children with absent fathers. With so many men in the services the traditional family unit came under intense pressure. There was a marked rise in juvenile delinquency as boys, and a few girls, went out of control; this was the opposite of the rate of adult crime. With so many men in the services, crime began to fall so much that by March 1916 eleven prisons had been mothballed and several others partially closed. By 1918 there were only 1,393 men on average each day in convict prisons – the harshest institutions – compared with 2,704 in 1913, and 7,335 in local prisons compared with 14,352 five years earlier.[151] Those too young to serve their country, however, kept the crime rate up.

On 3 February 1916 *The Times* reported several cases of the manifestation of what it called 'the bad boy'. In London, a magistrate at the

Guildhall had ordered the ringleaders of a gang known as 'the Black Hand' to be birched for breaking windows and theft.[152] The previous day a record number of cases for one day – fifty-five – had been listed at the Tower Bridge children's court, and other London magistrates reported a similar workload. The incidence of boys stealing valuables, robbing people in darkened streets where police (as opposed to 'specials') were scarce, and even stealing parcels from Post Office vans was causing concern. There was no shortage of adults willing to act as Fagins and recruit young criminals to steal goods for them to sell on; but the more enterprising young criminals became Fagins themselves. In February 1916 Kingston magistrates sent a twelve-year-old boy, William MacQuerney, who had already been birched for stealing from an offertory box, to a reformatory for breaking into a tennis club and stealing the club silver, with a gang of other boys whom he had taught to steal.

Contemporary society deemed fathers absent fighting for King and country to be the root of the problem: as *The Times*'s correspondent put it, 'the unruly boy who roams the streets and is open to all their temptations is not very amenable to a mother's discipline.' Nor were many older brothers there to set an example. In the spring of 1916 the commissioner of the Metropolitan Police, reflecting on a 50 per cent increase in juvenile crime over the previous year, blamed 'the absence of parental control. In numerous cases the father is away on service and the mother has obtained employment in a munitions factory or on work of some other description, with the result that no adult is left in charge of the children.'[153] The temptation to go off the rails without fear of paternal wrath and discipline had, for some, proved irresistible. A more humane view was taken by Lord Lytton, chairman of the State Children's Association, who said: 'the war spirit has produced in them a desire for adventure which in many cases can only be gratified through acts of lawlessness.'[154] However, with fathers unable to dole out the necessary thrashings, the state assumed the responsibility instead. The matter was raised in the Commons on 4 May 1916, and Samuel, the home secretary, said that 'it is generally believed that one of the causes is to be found in the character of some of the films shown in cinematograph theatres.'[155] Films showing burglaries were especially condemned.

He sent a letter to justices and chief constables on the subject. When the final figures were collated it showed that whereas in 1915 there had been 43,981 cases before the juvenile courts, there were 47,362 in 1916.

The scale of offending became relentlessly worse: in 1917 the total was 53,300, by which time there had been well-publicised outbreaks of gang crime in Glasgow and Manchester.[156] Larceny and malicious damage were the two most popular crimes. The problem was compounded by police numbers, which were also down because of men volunteering for the Army. Many of those left were inevitably older, less fit and less adept at catching young criminals. By October 1916 the magistrates of Liverpool, alarmed at the steep rise in juvenile crime, implored the government to extend the age up to which youths could be birched on a magistrate's order from fourteen to sixteen, and to allow more severe sentences. They also wanted the power to fine parents.[157] However, in addition they called for the greater provision of cadet corps and Scout troops to divert youthful energies; and for more youth clubs to occupy them of an evening.

On 23 October 1916 Samuel convened a conference at the Home Office to discuss the problem, including several MPs, the chief inspector of reformatory and industrial schools and the head of the Children's Department at the Home Office. He admitted a 30 per cent increase in juvenile crime in the last year for which figures were available; in the Metropolitan district offences had risen from 1,708 in 1914 to 2,713 in 1915 for boys and from 76 to 130 for girls.[158] Matters had become so serious that the King and Queen had expressed 'grave concern' at this rise in delin-quency, and Samuel had been asked 'to convey His Majesty's hope that adequate measures might be taken to deal with the evil.' He ran through familiar reasons: the war having encouraged a spirit of adventure among boys; darkened streets since the blackout; absent fathers; and the cinema creating a 'spirit of lawlessness'.

Exhortations for the Boy Scouts or Boys' Brigade to organise these youths were qualified by the fact that 70 per cent of men who ran such groups were on active service. Sir Robert Baden-Powell, who was pres-ent, said the problem was being addressed in the Scout movement by women and the boys themselves taking over the leadership; he wanted more active recruitment of 'hooligan' boys so they could be tamed, and felt schoolmasters should introduce boys to such groups. In December 1916 the Home Office devised a plan for a national Juvenile Organisa-tions Committee, which would coordinate the efforts of clubs for boys and girls to occupy the young in constructive ways. In January 1917 the Board of Education announced grants to local authorities to set up 'play centres where children from public elementary schools can be amused and profitably occupied after school hours.'[159]

Meanwhile, matters had become still worse. In November 1916 three children, a brother and sister aged ten and a boy of nine, were convicted of safe-breaking. On the day of their conviction yet another conference was held to discuss the epidemic of delinquency, with the secularisation of society now being brought into the frame as a cause, and demands for the extension of birching as a punishment: though the Earl of Sandwich, who chaired the meeting, said he had been birched at school and it had made him 'a most tremendous hero'.[160] A full moral panic exploded: in December 1916 the Bishop of Birmingham, presiding over a conference in London of the National Council of Public Morals, said 'the moral conditions prevailing now are very serious. Every kind of looseness of life, almost, was encouraged by the war conditions.'[161] Thousands of young people had come to work in munitions factories in his diocese and 'every temptation was put before them'. A clergyman from Lambeth said although 2,000 brothels had closed in his area in the twenty years before the war, there was now more prostitution than ever, 'and the streets were full of girls of 15 and 16 who were throwing themselves at the feet of soldiers and sailors.'

By February 1917 a Tory MP, Colonel Charles Yate, asked Samuel's successor, Cave, whether, 'considering the increase in juvenile crime, and that there is now said to be no place of detention to which young criminals can be sent owing to all such places being full, he will take into consideration the opinions expressed by county magistrates and the chairmen of county education committees regarding the necessity for the application of the birch rod and issue instructions accordingly?'[162] Cave refused, but did say 'considerable additions' had been made to the capacity of reformatory and industrial schools. He hardly needed to issue instructions: in 1917 in England and Wales 5,210 male juveniles, up from 2,415 in 1914, received a sentence of corporal punishment.[163] The stipendiary magistrate at Old Street magistrates' court in London disclosed that 'it is quite common now for parents, especially mothers, to charge their own children with larceny – a rare thing a few years ago. Had the father been at home the boy would have been thrashed, but now he is away the mother has no alternative but to go to the police.'[164]

Some MPs believed that even that was not enough, and wanted such sentences substituted for short prison sentences that youths would serve in adult jails. There was a shortage of probation officers because of men serving in the Army, though it was suggested as an ideal occupation for soldiers too badly wounded to return to the front. Yet for all the lack of discipline these youths had, they also possessed an unprecedented value. Boys aged between fourteen and eighteen – having left school but too young to join the Army – were snapped up by businesses and, given the shortage of male labour, could earn sums undreamt of before the war for lads their age. If they went wrong it was not because of economic deprivation. And the male of the species was not alone in offending: the number of girls sent to borstal in 1917 was one hundred and nine, compared with forty-nine in 1913.[165] It was notable that in two English cities – Leicester and Bradford – where social work was actively used with young children, offences remained the same in the former and decreased in the latter. The use of youth clubs and other organisations from early 1917 coincided with a fall in the total number of offences, which suggested that punitive measures alone were not the answer.

VIII

By the end of 1917 the almost unrelieved gloom was pierced by small shafts of light, in the form of people thinking ahead for the challenges of peace that, however distant, it was still believed must surely come. The government had the previous summer set up a Commission on Industrial Unrest to investigate the causes of unhappiness among the working class in South Wales: in an enlightened approach it blamed 'the monotonous housing, in valleys hemmed in by high mountains', and the absence of 'dignified municipal buildings . . . the scarcity of recreation grounds and of land suitable for gardens and allotments; and the general isolation of the coalfield from the large centres of population.'[166] There was 'an absence of social solidarity' in the region that encouraged political activity and, with it, militancy and hatred of capitalism, and a suggestion that the government might start 'combing out' men from the pits to join the Army was potentially the last straw.[167]

The commissioners urged radical measures after the war to prevent matters worsening: not just better housing and working conditions, but compulsory union membership, with one union per industry, better education, and job security based on no worker being dismissed without the agreement of his colleagues as well as of his employers. It envisaged tax reform to reduce duties on working-class entertainments, and the confiscation of 'excess profits'. Lloyd George dealt with another recurring demand of the labour movement, for the universal application of the national health insurance that applied to around 12 million workers, when he met a deputation led by J. H. Thomas, general secretary of the NUR, on 11 October. Thomas asked Lloyd George to set up a Ministry of Health, mainly to safeguard the well-being of overworked women. Lloyd George countered that the existing insurance system was being exploited by some women and required better supervision: Thomas admitted there were 'isolated cases of malingering' but claimed most women pulled their weight.[168] The prime minister said that until the war was won the money required for a health ministry and improved insurance coverage was devoted to the pursuit of victory. However, he promised a health ministry as a means of repairing 'the ravages of war' once the conflict ended; the War Cabinet had discussed this, and agreed on its necessity the previous spring, having endorsed a memorandum drawn up by Lord Rhondda that began with the statement: 'Public opinion is now keenly aroused on the existing deficiency and inefficiency of our public medical services . . . there is a widespread insistent demand for improvement.'[169]

With a view to calming industrial relations for the long term – and accepting that a large measure of state intervention in the private sector should continue after the war – the government established a committee under the chairmanship of J. H. Whitley, Deputy Speaker of the House of Commons, to design a new framework for the relationship between masters and men. He devised formal consultative bodies in which both sides would meet regularly to discuss grievances, and could seek arbitration if there was no agreement. The annual meeting of the TUC in September welcomed this, not least because of the input the bodies would give workers. Employers found them preferable to the variant of workers' control in revolutionary Russia. When they began in 1919 they were known as Whitley Councils, and they still survive in the public sector.

It was recognised, too, that Britain's housing stock would require an overhaul after the war. The Garden City Societies, largely moribund since 1914, held conferences to discuss how they would expand such settlements once the building trade resumed normal service. The Ministry of Reconstruction began to draw up plans for the numbers of houses required – estimated at 300,000 by the end of 1918 – and to obtain the supplies necessary for such a huge construction programme, not just of the housing, but of the infrastructure to support it: and to control the prices of those materials, to make the programme feasible.

Plans also began to be made to ensure the welfare of discharged and disabled soldiers. Lloyd George made George Barnes, the minister of pensions, responsible for the care of these men once they left military hospitals. Institutions were established for their rehabilitation, where psychological therapy as well as physiotherapy could be applied. The Red Cross and the Order of St John played a significant part in rehabilitative work, and Sir Arthur Pearson, founder of the *Daily Express* (who had begun to go blind a decade earlier), established a new charity – which became known as St Dunstan's – to support blinded ex-servicemen. The government knew it would be judged by its treatment of those disabled in defence of their country. Pearson had a revolutionary aim for St Dunstan's: that it would train blind men to work rather than simply offer them charitable support. Other charities would take the same approach to men with different disabilities.

Arguably, however, it was the improvement in the status of women that suggested the most significant social change for the future. The role and importance of working-class women had been transformed because of the almost insatiable need for their service. There was a glimmer of light further up the professional ladder for women's opportunities, too. The Bar Council, for example, debated a report to admit women to the Bar. *The Times* backed the idea, arguing there was no reason why if a woman could be a journalist or a doctor she could not be a barrister. However, it contended that 'the bulk of womankind are less well-equipped by nature than a corresponding number of men with the logical qualities of mind and the great physical strength demanded by the highest work of the legal profession.'[170] It was ironic that men of the highest intelligence should have been among the slowest to recognise the relentlessness of the momentum, and the unanswerable nature of the case, for the empowerment of women, though the first would not be called to the Bar until 1922.

By 1917 only a fool or a bigot could fail to appreciate the reliance of the war effort on women, and the inevitability, therefore, of extending civil rights to them in the way some of them had demanded since the 1860s. In late March 1917 the Commons voted to prolong its life again, to

30 November 1917, almost seven years after it was first elected. Even if an election were held then, it would be on a register compiled according to qualifications for the suffrage in 1913, and with millions of men displaced because of military service or war work; but the general recognition that women had to have the vote before any election could be held rendered the register doubly useless. As Asquith, who supported the prolongation, argued, any election on such a register would be regarded as lacking 'representative authority'.[171] He had been instrumental, the previous October, in setting up a Speaker's Conference to discuss franchise reforms; Lloyd George wanted the process to continue, and twenty-six meetings had been held. The conference proposed thirty-seven resolutions, with thirty-four passed unanimously. They included, effectively, universal manhood suffrage: anyone with a roof over his head (owned or rented) or with a business could vote. Those with a business address had a second vote, as did university graduates; but no man would be allowed to cast more than two votes. To avoid corruption election expenses would be restricted, and a redistribution of seats would ensure each MP represented around 70,000 people.

The most far-reaching proposal, though, was that women should have the vote. Asquith, having advertised his conversion to the cause of female suffrage the previous autumn, outlined how it might happen: they would not have the vote at twenty-one like men, but at thirty or thirty-five; and it would be confined to those who occupied a house, owned land with an annual value of £5 or who had a husband on the electoral register. Some women had felt the age barrier should be for older women rather than younger ones, as the younger had played the bigger part in the war and therefore deserved the vote more.

Asquith explained the reasons for his conversion:

My opposition to woman suffrage has always been based, and based solely, on considerations of public expediency. I think that some years ago I ventured to use the expression, 'Let the women work out their own salvation.' Well, Sir, they have worked it out during this War. How could we have carried on the War without them? Short of actually bearing arms in the field, there is hardly a service which has contributed, or is contributing, to the maintenance of our cause in which women have not been at least as active and as efficient as men, and wherever we turn we see them doing,

with zeal and success, and without any detriment to the preroga-
tives of their sex, work which three years ago would have been
regarded as falling exclusively within the province of men. This is
not a merely sentimental argument, though it appeals to our feelings as well as our judgment.[172]

He also foresaw a new post-war order, during the 'reconstruction' of the
country; and in that new order it would be 'impossible' not to let
women's voices be 'directly heard'.[173] Another consideration made it possible to extend the franchise; the suspension by Mrs Pankhurst of the
militant suffragette campaign in 1914 meant the decision to enfranchise
women could not be seen as a response to violence. Because of the imprac-
ticability of drawing up a new register, the hope was that no election
would take place until after the war. Lloyd George said there could not
be an election on the old register 'because by taking the old register you
would be excluding the men that had made the new Britain possible.'[174] An
MP shouted out 'and women!' and the prime minister corrected himself: 'men and women'.

Lloyd George was alert to what the 'new order' would entail. 'When
we come to settle the conditions of labour with hundreds of thousands,
running now into millions, of women in work in which they were never
engaged before,' he said, 'when we come to recast the whole of our
industrial system, are we going to fling them out without giving them a
voice in determining the conditions? All I can say is it is an outrage, it is
ungrateful, unjust, inequitable. I do not believe that the people of this
country will do it.'[175] The government had decided to leave to a free vote
of the Commons whether women should be enfranchised, but he said he
had no doubt what the outcome would be – and that the reforms could
be settled 'without the bitterness of political controversy.'[176]

On 29 March he received a deputation of women suffragists at Downing Street, led by Mrs Fawcett, but including other titans of the pre-war
movement such as Mrs Pankhurst and Mrs Despard.[177] He stated that
'from the moment the legislature started to interfere in the home, to
interfere with the health of the people, with the education of their children and their upbringing . . . it was inconceivable that half the
population, and especially that half of the population which was most
concerned with the home and with the health and upbringing of children, should have absolutely no voice at all with what was to be done.'[178]

The war would ensure 'that women must be admitted to a complete partnership in the government of the nation,' and a Franchise Bill would be drafted at once. Nonetheless, there were still dissenters in the Commons, with one MP demanding a referendum.

An attempt at proportional representation was defeated in the Lords, and the government had no appetite to force the issue. On the same day as the Commons debate, as if to reinforce the point, the Women's Army Auxiliary Corps was founded. There was still anger that Lloyd George attended the Commons so rarely, and the other members of his War Cabinet hardly more often. Swift MacNeill, an Irish MP, complained that 'all these proceedings may tend to make a Colossus of the Prime Minister, but certainly they most surely tend to make pigmies of the House of Commons and of popular rights and liberties.'[179] There was also a school of thought that, despite the difficulties of compiling a new register in wartime, the government was deliberately not doing so to prolong its life. However, the Franchise Bill had its third reading in the Commons on 18 April by 203 votes to 42; many of the opponents were Irish, and seeking to punish the government for failing to end rule from Dublin Castle.

During June the Franchise Bill went into committee in the Commons. All men would have the vote at twenty-one; women would, supposedly on the advice of a Speaker's Conference, need to wait until thirty. Some members of the conference, however, denied they had agreed such a limit. It was argued that women took longer to form a fixed view of politics and therefore needed more time to mature – a view with which by no means all MPs agreed, with some arguing about the obvious intellectual superiority of women graduates aged under thirty compared with men of the same age who lacked their educational advantages. As Lord Hugh Cecil, a strong supporter of an equal franchise, argued: 'Can there be a more foolish, a more unsound, and a more unstable condition than the condition of age? It is not merely illogical; it has no rational bearing on the problem at all. You might as well give votes to women who have red hair and make hair-dyeing a corrupt practice. It is not commonsense.'[180]

But another consideration was that Parliament was prepared to give women the vote; it was not prepared to give them the whip hand. On pre-war figures, it was estimated that if women received the vote on the same basis as men there would be 12 million of them compared with

10 million men in the electorate: the disparity was partly because of the birth rate, partly because of women's greater longevity. The numbers of men killed in the war had made the imbalance even greater.[181] However, to enfranchise the number of women some MPs would accept – 7 million – the age would have had to be forty.

Once the Commons had agreed to the principle of women's suffrage – which it did overwhelmingly, by a majority of 330 with just 55 MPs against – the most vocal advocates of an equal voting age were found among the opponents. They argued that it was neither rational nor logical to restrict the age, as their principal objection was one of gender: having lost that argument, they could see no point quibbling about an age barrier. They remained in a minority; on 6 February 1918 the Representation of the People Act finally enfranchised women over thirty, the restriction pertaining until 1928 when women were granted the vote at twenty-one. It removed the property qualifications for men over twenty-one and confined elections to one day. In 1914 only two-thirds of men had had the vote: now every man would have it, Parliament recognising how the working class, of both genders, had kept Britain afloat in the worst crisis since the Napoleonic Wars.

IX

If in 1917 two of the great difficulties that faced the Asquith administration immediately before the war had been brought to some kind of resolution – the incipient industrial unrest (thanks to a willingness to bribe workers with pay rises), and the call for women's suffrage – the third and perhaps most destabilising, Ireland, remained an unwelcome distraction, diverting time, effort and resources from the fight against Germany. Henry Duke, the chief secretary for Ireland, attended the War Cabinet on 19 February 1917 and requested authority to deport from Ireland thirty-one men previously imprisoned after the Rising, because 'a situation of some danger' now prevailed there.[182] It was granted, but Duke was told not to arrest Laurence Ginnell, a Nationalist MP, the newly elected Count George Plunkett or a priest, Father Michael O'Flanagan, accused of 'promoting sedition'. On 7 March T. P. O'Connor, in the Commons since 1880, pleaded 'for a united and genuine effort to settle the Irish question.'[183] He was keen to avoid controversy because he realised, as most Irish did, the creeping annihilation of the Nationalist vote by

Sinn Féin. The question was playing badly around the world, not just in America, but in Canada and Australia. But as the Unionists and Nationalists still could not settle a way forward – and Unionists continued to claim there were 200,000 fit men of military age in Ireland who had failed to volunteer, and that half the 100,000 who had joined were from Ulster – the government rejected immediate constitutional change.

In the 7 March debate Lloyd George affirmed that the Irish question should be settled, 'not merely for the sake of Ireland, but for the sake of the Empire.'[184] All he lacked was the means. Britain had offered 'centuries of ruthless and often brutal injustice' and 'of insolence and of insult [that] have driven hatred of British rule into the very marrow of the Irish race.'[185] This had created 'the greatest blot' on Britain's international reputation: although he described the land, educational and economic reforms in Ireland since the 1880s that had transformed it for the better. Yet 'after all this great record of beneficent legislation, in spite of the fact that Ireland is more materially prosperous than she has ever been, there remains the one invincible fact to-day that she is no more reconciled to British rule than she was in the days of Cromwell. It proves that the grievance is not a material one. It is something which has to do with the pride and self-respect of the people.'[186] At the same time he acknowledged that 'the other fact is that in the north-eastern portion of Ireland you have a population as hostile to Irish rule as the rest of Ireland is to British rule, yea, and as ready to rebel against this as the rest of Ireland is against British rule.'

As a result, 'to place them under national rule against their will would be as glaring an outrage on the principles of liberty and self-government as the denial of self-government would be for the rest of Ireland. It would be a stupid way of attempting to redress the past in Ireland by repeating in Ulster the fatal error of Irish misgovernment, to reproduce the condition of the past in a corner of Ireland, whilst you are redressing the past in the rest of Ireland. It would be government against the will of the people.'[187] For the avoidance of doubt, he asserted that the British would not tolerate their Ulster brethren being forcibly governed by those they considered unlike them: and the government would not make them. In this, he said, his policy maintained that announced by Asquith in September 1914, when assuring Ulster that Britain would not repay the loyalty of its people in the war by handing them over to rule from Dublin.

The problem thus remained intractable. 'Are Irish Members prepared to leave out the six counties until they are ready to come in? No. If not, are they ready to wait for Home Rule until the six counties are willing to be included? No. If neither of these, are they prepared to coerce Ulster? The answer is, No.'[188] He was afraid the only alternative was the permanent division of Ireland; whereas if the Irish accepted the right of the six counties to make their own decision, it might be that within a few years they would come in. He believed if Ulster were coerced the results would be divisive and would undermine the Home Rule state. He urged the Irish to convene a conference, and talk to each other; but said the other twenty-six counties could have Home Rule now if they would let Ulster take its time. MPs heckled him about the Roman Catholic enclave in West Belfast, and the large Nationalist communities in Fermanagh and Tyrone; that was not a degree of detail into which Lloyd George was prepared to go. Nor would he discuss how the instability of Ireland was in part caused by its economic problems.

Asquith suggested an Imperial Conference to arbitrate on the question: it provoked Lloyd George's interest. Redmond, however, attacked the prime minister for offering Home Rule to just twenty-six counties: striking a low blow, he said the policy was one of 'wait and see'.[189] He dismissed the idea of yet more talks: 'I take leave to tell him that after my experience of the last negotiations that I will enter into no more negotiations.' He thought the Germans would 'chuckle with delight' when they read the reports of the debate.[190] He warned Lloyd George what would happen unless matters changed. 'That great issue is whether Ireland will still rely, as she has been doing for so many years, upon constitutional action to obtain her national rights, or whether she will go back to the methods and ideas of revolution.'[191]

Redmond was deeply pessimistic.

If the constitutional movement disappears, I beg the Prime Minister to take note that he will find himself face to face with a revolutionary movement, and he will find it impossible to preserve—there is no good in him thinking he can do it—any of the forms even of constitutionalism. He will have to govern Ireland by the naked sword. I cannot picture to myself a condition of things in which the right hon Gentleman, with his record behind him, would be an instrument to carry out a government of that kind in Ireland. But that is what he must come to if he persists in taking a course which plays right into the hands of the revolutionists and weakens and tends to destroy the constitutional party.[192]

There was no point constantly appealing to the Nationalists to give ground; it was time to make that appeal to Carson and his supporters, to let the Home Rule Act apply to all of Ireland, and to let the Ulster people see they had nothing to fear. Otherwise, a Sinn Féin government, and all that entailed, was the likely outcome.

Redmond then led his party out of the House rather than continue to participate in a 'useless, futile and humiliating debate.'[193] Given that the Irish had voted against the government in most divisions since December 1916, it made little odds that they absented themselves now. The next day they issued a statement saying that if Lloyd George stuck to his views it would 'involve the denial of self-government to Ireland for ever.'[194] The party said it could 'never assent' to giving an effective veto to Ulster. They accused Lloyd George of lying about never having changed his mind on the coercion of Ulster, given his support for the Home Rule process in 1912–14; and said he had spoken only of a 'temporary war arrangement' for Ulster's exclusion during the failed negotiations of 1916. The constitutional movement could be saved, but was 'hampered by a British Government which plays into the hands of the Irish pro-German revolutionary party with a stupid perversity worthy of the worst reactionaries of Petrograd.' It was barely an exaggeration. More alarming, the Nationalists drew attention to the support of the Australian Senate for Home Rule, implying they would seek to divide the Empire over the question.

The question pervaded not merely imperial policy, but the most important areas of foreign policy. President Wilson, knowing the ubiquity of Americans with Home Rule sympathies or Irish roots, was pressing Lloyd George to act; and the prime minister was sure there would have been more recruits from Australia had the matter been settled fairly. But he could not escape the domestic political question: if the government granted full Home Rule, it could count on Irish Nationalist votes in the Commons. That would stop them teaming up with the Asquithian Liberals and defeating the government on an Irish question, of which there was a high possibility. Lloyd George dreaded such a defeat, because he feared Asquith would form a government without an election – there being no up-to-date register upon which to hold one. That might explain why, a few weeks later, when he discovered that Lord Reading, one of his closest cronies, would be staying with Asquith for the weekend, Lloyd George asked Reading to invite Asquith to join the government in 'almost any post . . . except that of head of the Government.'[195] Asquith replied that he would continue to support the government if it prosecuted the war 'in the proper spirit', but that 'under no conditions would I serve in a Government of which Lloyd George was the head. I had learned by long and close association to mistrust him profoundly. I knew him to be incapable of loyalty and lasting gratitude.'[196] Reading persisted, and to shut him up Asquith said: 'I could not associate myself with what he called "the counsel" of any Government unless I had supreme and ultimate authority.' Asquith sent Crewe notes of the discussions marked 'secret' that he said 'show at any rate in what direction the wind is blowing.'[197]

Typically, what really vexed Lloyd George about Asquith and his friends returning to power was that 'they will take the credit for all the measures I have taken for the prosecution of the war.'[198] For all his protestations, the good of the country always came second to his *amour propre*. Yet Ireland got under his skin: he told Miss Stevenson he had been a 'coward' not to resign when Asquith backed down on Home Rule the previous July.[199] He asked Carson to moderate his opposition 'for the sake of the Empire'. He secretly put pressure on him by asking Wilson to write to him to emphasise American concerns, and Lord Bryce, the ex-ambassador to Washington, also wrote to him. Carson was certainly reluctant to dismiss their pleas out of hand, and Lloyd George offered Redmond the twenty-six/six deal of the previous year again: however, Redmond refused, since Sinn Féin was winning every by-election and threatening to wipe his party out. On 16 April the War Cabinet discussed Ireland at length, starting by agreeing that the 1914 Act was 'in certain respects, out of date'.[200] It also agreed that 'the permanent partition of Ireland has no friends', but that an attempt to impose Home Rule on Ulster would end in failure. It appointed a committee of three under Curzon to draw up a Bill to amend the Act, but also not to force it through if the Irish objected: which meant the impasse remained.

Attempts throughout the spring of 1917 to find a settlement failed, because of the steady haemorrhage of Nationalist supporters to Sinn Féin, especially among younger men. The Russian revolution was interpreted by some optimists as 'the peaceful triumph of democracy' that could promote a peaceful settlement in Ireland.²⁰¹ The feeling did not last: as in Russia, a more extreme outcome quickly evolved. Lloyd George was sufficiently concerned by mid-May to consult his predecessor about how to proceed. Stamfordham received a letter from a member of the public asking the King to take an active role in soothing Ireland: he was told that 'Loyalty to the Throne, in my humble opinion, must be inspired by the Throne itself, and not be the result of organisation or propaganda.'²⁰² Dillon, who had grasped the new, post-Rising reality, told Scott on 15 May that if Sinn Féin found a capable leader 'they would wipe the floor with us'.²⁰³

The next day Lloyd George proposed to Redmond and to the Unionists that a Bill be introduced to grant Home Rule immediately to all but six counties in Ulster, whose exclusion Parliament would reconsider after five years. The hope was that Nationalists, and not Sinn Féin, would rule Ireland, and that Ulster Unionists would soon see that the rest of their island was governed in a way sufficiently acceptable to them to end exclusion. It was also suggested a Council of Ireland be established to deal with questions affecting the whole country, to be composed of Ulster MPs and an equal number from Dublin: it could decide to end exclusion before five years were up if it wished. The government also admitted the proposed financial settlement for Ireland under the 1914 Act was inadequate. Were this idea rejected, Lloyd George said he would establish an Irish Convention, composed of representatives of all parties, to consider the future.

Northcliffe, like Asquith, had suggested the matter could be handed to a tribunal of the Dominion prime ministers, gathered in London for the Imperial Conference; but that was dismissed as unpractical. Redmond rejected partition immediately – he told Lloyd George his colleagues believed it would 'find no support in Ireland'.²⁰⁴ However, he was much taken with the convention idea, not least because he had recently suggested it to Crewe, who had passed the idea to Downing Street: Redmond knew the constitutions of various Dominions had been agreed solely by those who lived in them, so it might work in Ireland. Southern Unionists, led by Midleton, reluctantly agreed, while stating their belief that 'Imperial government under the Union' was the only solution.²⁰⁵

Lloyd George told the Commons on 11 June that the chairmen of Irish county and county borough councils would be invited to form the convention. They would be joined by two representatives of smaller communities in Ireland from each of the four provinces; by leaders of the Roman Catholic, Protestant and Presbyterian churches; by businessmen; and those of the trades unions. Political parties would be asked to send members, including separate representation for southern Unionists, though the prime minister was vexed that Sinn Féin had refused in advance to take part unless independence for all of Ireland could be discussed: the terms of reference were to settle 'a Constitution for the future government of Ireland, within the Empire', which was unacceptable to republicans.[206] Sinn Féin also wanted the convention to be chosen by universal suffrage and for interned rebels to be treated as prisoners of war, none of which the government would brook. Lloyd George pledged to reserve five places for them in case they changed their minds. The government would also nominate fifteen leading Irishmen to ensure every shade of non-political opinion was heard: and the total number would be one hundred and one.

He hoped the Irishmen would agree on a chairman but, if not, the government would nominate one. He still seemed unable to grasp that a huge swathe of Irish opinion now supported Sinn Féin. Indeed, one reason Lloyd George was so little concerned whether Sinn Féin sat in the convention or not was that he believed the movement would survive just a few months, before returning to the margins of Irish political discourse. Yet during May and June around seventy Sinn Féin clubs were formed across Ireland, ostensibly to help elect Sinn Féiners to local government posts, but as an embryonic political machine for a general election.

On the day Parliament heard Lloyd George's proposals it also heard tributes to Major William Redmond, younger brother of the Nationalist leader, who had enlisted at the age of fifty-three and been killed at Messines Ridge in Belgium. His death, after his determination to join up over age and to be in the thick of the fighting, had massive resonance in Britain, exemplifying the sacrifice that Home Rulers were prepared to make fighting 'side by side in the trenches' for what Carson called 'the common cause of liberty'. Sinn Féin held such men in contempt, and would see that recognition of their gallantry was suppressed in Ireland for decades.[207]

On 15 June Bonar Law announced that as an 'earnest' of British goodwill – and in order not to prejudice the convention – all prisoners still being held after the Rising would be released. This happened two days later. Law professed that 'the Government are inspired by a sanguine hope that their action will be welcomed in a spirit of magnanimity, and that the Convention will enter upon its arduous undertaking in circumstances that will constitute a good augury for the reconciliation which is the desire of all parties in every part of the United Kingdom and the Empire.'[208] Ginnell, the Nationalist MP who had become a voice of Sinn Féin in the Commons, warned Law that 'the majority of the Irish people repudiat[e] the proposed Convention as being unrepresentative, composed of persons whom no section of the Irish people would now elect, held under martial law and the suppression of public opinion and of the right of public meeting, precluded from entertaining the only form of settlement now acceptable, denied power to give effect to any decision, restricted by the reference to a prearranged decision so detested by the Irish people that no power is now strong enough to enforce it upon them'.[209] He believed that 'a Convention thus restricted to pro-English purposes would be a betrayal of the principles and sacrifices of 1916 which have made a settlement urgent', and wanted 'a free Convention elected by adult suffrage . . . or the idea of a Convention abandoned'.

The prisoners returned to Dublin to a welcome of unprecedented jubilation, proving republicanism was no longer a minority sport. The released leaders, such as de Valera, started to contest by-elections: he won in East Clare, whose electorate he said embodied 'the ideas of the men of Easter Week' and whose victory 'set up a lasting monument to the dead.'[210] In keeping with the doctrine of republicanism, he did not sit in the Imperial Parliament. As prisoners returned to their communities the Volunteer movement, heading for coalition in Sinn Féin with other separatist groups, revived and became more powerful than ever, with Volunteers out canvassing for de Valera showing the extent to which they were part of the political process.

The convention assembled on 26 July in Trinity College, Dublin, where it met over the next nine months, often picketed by Sinn Féin demonstrators. The government asked the chief secretary to act as a provisional chairman, because of a failure to agree on one. Sir Horace Plunkett, an agricultural reformer from the old Ascendancy who believed in Home Rule, soon assumed the post. He lacked the confidence of Midleton and the other southern Unionists, not because of his views but because of his perceived abilities as a chairman. The government warned Sinn Féin that no civil unrest, riot or sedition would be tolerated.

The convention temporarily calmed the question down; even more usefully for Lloyd George, it bought goodwill with the Americans early in the new alliance, and with the Dominions. However, despite long discussions, nothing else was achieved except buying some time. Another reason the convention was doomed was that the ten members representing southern Unionism, led by Midleton, and the twenty-one from Ulster simply could not agree: as Midleton noted, 'co-operation between ten men who were bent on finding a solution of this age-long problem and twenty-one men who were determined to frustrate any settlement for Ireland as a whole was soon found to be hopeless.'[211] In October 1917 the convention visited Cork for a special session and saw the reality of feelings in a rebel stronghold. 'On landing,' Midleton recalled, 'a number of roughs began to hustle Redmond, who had to be rescued by his colleagues.'[212] The next day, after an official lunch, 'the police had to spirit Redmond away by a side door directly after his speech.'

Reports of deliberations of the convention were illegal under DORA, leaving the nation mystified about progress despite the anodyne reports released after each session. The Irish might, however, have taken some consolation from a change of policy in another branch of Britain's imperial relations, when Montagu went to the India Office and instituted a far-reaching reform. On 15 August, thirty years almost to the day before Indian independence, and in recognition of the services India had performed during the war, Montagu announced that 'the policy of His Majesty's Government is that of the increasing association of Indians in every branch of the administration, and the gradual development of self-governing institutions, with a view to progressive realisation of responsible government in India under the aegis of the British Crown.'[213] This would lead in 1918 to a report outlining the Montagu–Chelmsford reforms (named after himself and the viceroy, Lord Chelmsford) that acknowledged the need for India to evolve into a dominion such as Australia or Canada. Most of its proposals would be embodied in the 1919 Government of India Act, which began a process of self-government albeit only at lower levels. It was an early step in the dismantling of the British Empire, and a crucial one – and one perhaps insufficiently noticed by those working for a measure of autonomy in Ireland.

In mid-November Duke told the War Cabinet he feared the talks
might break down over the Ulster Unionists' refusal to accept proposals
made by the rest of Ireland. Nationalist predictions that their support
would collapse in favour of Sinn Féin were coming true. Éamon de
Valera, who had become its leader, was described by Viscount Chaplin (who had served in Salisbury's cabinet) in a Lords debate as touring
the country making 'plain, deliberate, and cold-blooded incitements
to rebellion . . . at meetings, one after the other all over the country, in
studied terms.'[214] He said de Valera's speeches 'point to three things
in particular. One is the complete separation of Ireland from England,
another is secession, and the third is the sovereign independence of
that country. That is the policy of the Sinn Fein party as laid down
by the leader of that party himself, who at present is allowed to go
unmolested about the country preaching these seditious doctrines
whenever and wherever it pleases him to do so.'[215] De Valera's victory
in the East Clare by-election, caused by William Redmond's death, was
by a majority of more than two to one. Ever since the rebels had been
released there had been sporadic outbreaks of rioting, notably in and
around Cork. Duke believed Sinn Féin was developing a policy of violence; and that the end of emigration to America since 1914 had left
many frustrated young men in Ireland who were rich pickings for the
republicans.[216]

The government continued to provide the republican movement with
martyrs. Thomas Ashe, president of the supreme council of the Irish
Republican Brotherhood, was arrested in July under DORA for making
a seditious speech. He died after forced feeding in Mountjoy prison on 25
September; he had gone on hunger strike in protest at being treated as a
criminal and not a political prisoner. His body was taken to lie in state in
City Hall, and thousands filed past it. The funeral was stage-managed
for maximum effect: a procession from Dublin city centre to Glasnevin
cemetery, the volley over the grave, and Michael Collins saying simply:
'Nothing additional remains to be said. The volley we have just heard is
the only speech which it is proper to make above the grave of a dead
Fenian.'[217] The authorities 'agreed that it would have been quite impossible for the Executive to have interfered with any popular demonstration
connected with the funeral without provoking the bitterest antagonism
and serious disorder', the War Cabinet learned.[218]

Ashe had been a devout Roman Catholic, and a bishop attended his funeral, confirming where the power of the Church was being placed. Days after this show of organisational strength the *Ard Fheis*, or party conference, was held where the political wing, Sinn Féin, united with the Volunteers. The movement claimed 1,200 branches: the notion that it was a passing phenomenon was manifestly wrong. By acclamation, de Valera became leader of the united movement. His support of Eoin Mac-Neill in the executive elections sealed his readmission to republicanism's top table. Dillon pleaded with the War Cabinet to allow 'special rules' for the treatment of Sinn Féin prisoners, to avoid another rebellion.[219] The War Cabinet told Duke to exercise 'discretion'.[220] With around forty men on hunger strike, it was decided to change the rules; the government harboured the delusion that 'if the Convention proved successful the Sinn Féin movement would collapse like a pack of cards.'

De Valera had been freed from Lewes jail in July 1917 under the amnesty. He urged the arming, and training, of an army to achieve the movement's stated aims. Such talk made a mockery of the convention. Following his victory in East Clare, Sinn Féin was now winning every by-election outside Ulster. Chaplin, and many like him, felt Duke should end the routine incitement in which de Valera engaged; the government, aware of the damage caused by the heavy hand post-Rising, moved with caution: though Duke's use of DORA to silence men such as Ashe was highly ill-advised.

A meeting addressed by de Valera in Waterford was allowed to go ahead; and in Dublin, when thirty-seven men were charged with illegal drilling, they refused to accept the jurisdiction of the court and were fined £10 each and discharged. Many in de Valera's audiences were boys of fourteen or fifteen, who three or four years later would fight in a civil war. In response to Chaplin's complaints, and those of other peers, Curzon asked whether they would prefer 'wholesale repression'; the government, who already had 50,000 soldiers tied down in Ireland rather than on the Western Front, had few options. Worse, a general disarming of Ulster Volunteers to show the government was being even-handed was thwarted when it threatened to cause strikes in the north's munitions factories.

Food shortages in parts of Ireland, notably County Cork, in the winter of 1917–18, further helped Sinn Féin mobilise as a political force: they highlighted not just the incompetence of the government but also laid it open to accusations of selfishness in exporting food to England while

Irish people did without. Sinn Féin talked about the danger of 'famine' whenever possible. It also rattled the government by threatening an unofficial plebiscite about independence. The movement's high profile in the food crisis also helped create more Sinn Féin clubs, which would assist the party's success at the 1918 general election. It soon claimed a membership of 250,000; all that remained to be settled was whether it would pursue its aims by political, or paramilitary, means. De Valera justified Ireland's non-participation in the war by saying it was not being fought for the benefit of other small nations, such as Belgium or Serbia, but to secure the dominance of great powers such as Britain and France. A rumour of a new rising in November proved groundless; occasionally, Sinn Féiners were arrested for illegal drilling, but there was little appetite to provoke the movement by mass arrests. What did concern the government was that the Roman Catholic clergy, increasingly critical of the British government since the Rising, now seemed to be reaching militancy, especially among its younger members.

The organised Left in Scotland was watching developments in Ireland closely. On 23 October Lloyd George received a deputation of trades unionists, the majority from Clydeside, some of whom wanted Scotland granted Home Rule after the war. He parried this by saying it would require the creation of an English Parliament, so mighty that it would rival the Imperial one, leaving Scotland overshadowed. For the moment, the Scottish demands died down; the problem of Ireland was carried into 1918, where it would take on an even graver dimension.

WOMEN ARE WORKING DAY & NIGHT TO WIN THE WAR

£25,000 IMMEDIATELY NEEDED FOR THE

WOMEN'S WAR TIME FUND

TO PROVIDE REST·ROOMS CANTEENS & HOSTELS

LORD SYDENHAM
HON TREASURER

YOUNG WOMEN'S
CHRISTIAN ASSOCIATION

26 GEORGE STREET
HANOVER SQUARE. W.

CHAPTER 10

ESCAPE

By December 1917, even allowing for the imminent arrival of American troops in France, the Army was desperately short of men. Every possible source of new recruits was examined. So desperate were matters that on 26 November the War Cabinet discussed, but rejected, the notion of con-scription in Ireland. The hard-line policy on conscientious objectors continued: some were being repeatedly sent to prison. There were 1,300 in jail by late 1917, around two-thirds for at least the second time; 419 were serving a second term, 489 a third, 34 a fourth and 4 a fifth. It had become usual for these men to have the worst conditions – appalling food and, often, solitary confinement. One, James Brightmore from Manches-ter, was confined in a camp at Cleethorpes; and when he refused to obey orders was made to spend eleven days in a hole ten feet deep in which he was soon up to his ankles in water. Soaked and in a state of collapse, he was eventually found by a visiting officer from the General Staff. The punishment was ended, and the officer who had ordered it, a Major Grimshaw of the Manchester Regiment, was made to retire.[1] Grimshaw denied everything.

The next month there was a further incident at Cleethorpes, where a conscientious objector who told an NCO he could not, as a Christian, obey military orders, was made to walk around with his full kitbag tied around his neck, almost strangling him. Angered by reports of genuine Christian objectors being, effectively, persecuted, Hensley Henson, the Dean of Durham, who supported the war, wrote to *The Times* complain-ing of the lack of 'that respect for the individual conscience which the religion of Christ requires'; and adding that the nation would rejoice if sincere Christian men imprisoned because of their consciences were released.[2] Henson also regretted 'the unfortunate exemption of ministers of religion from military service', which he said 'weighs heavily on those upon whom it was imposed and by whom it was neither demanded nor desired.' He believed if Christians who wanted to fight were allowed to do so, Christians who did not could be excused jail.

Some tribunals were incompetent; and a blind eye was often turned to their idiocy, more so as the desperate need for men increased. Ministers refused to interfere when complaints were made about decisions taken by local tribunals to refuse to grant exemptions. As a result, men who would have been quite happy to do war work, such as in agriculture, were put in defiance of the law. A number of those refused exemptions were practising Quakers whose objection to military service was long attested: many tribunal decisions bore no relation to the facts they had heard. When a man came out of prison he was immediately put under military rather than civilian law, which meant he was considered to be a soldier and in conflict with authority again for refusing to serve; he was court-martialled and sent back to prison. Some went on hunger strike and were force-fed. There was little public sympathy for pacifists: mobs, including a high proportion of women, often broke up meetings at which conscientious objection was encouraged, with wounded soldiers and men on leave joining in. An incident in Hackney in July 1917, involving an insurgency of between two and three hundred anti-pacifists, included a wounded man making a speech about the impossibility of peace while 'Germany uncrushed' existed, and renditions of 'Rule, Britannia' and 'God Save the King'.[3]

In early May Bertrand Russell at last obtained martyrdom, being jailed for six months in the second division – that is, with common criminals. He had written an article in January in the *Tribunal*, the newspaper of the No Conscription Fellowship of which he had been editor, advancing his belief (for which there were no grounds whatsoever) that American troops would be used to intimidate British strikers, 'an occupation to which they are accustomed when at home'.[4] He was convicted on 9 February but appealed against his sentence: and when that failed was sent to Brixton. On his conviction the Bow Street magistrate, Sir John Dickinson, condemned Russell's language as 'mischievous'. He had no doubt Russell had sought to prejudice Britain's relations with

America, and described his offence as 'deplorable' – and Russell as clever enough to know better.

Thanks to an intervention by Balfour he was made a first division prisoner, meaning books and food could be sent in. His brother, Earl Russell, had been there fifteen years earlier for bigamy, and when visiting Bertrand was delighted to renew old friendships with the warders. In an era when most books still had uncut pages, Lady Ottoline Morrell would smuggle in letters from herself and from his present mistress, Lady Constance Malleson, tucked into the bound proceedings of the London Mathematical Society. The highlight of Russell's spell in Brixton was his reading of *Eminent Victorians* by his friend Lytton Strachey, published that spring, the progenitor of the post-war world's assault on Victorian values, the radicalisation of the post-war mind and its commitment to revisionism. Once when reading it 'I laughed out so loud that the warder came round to stop me, saying that I must remember that prison was a place of punishment'.[5]

This was hardly the case for Russell. 'I found prison in many ways quite agreeable,' he wrote: but then he was not forced to mix with common criminals. 'I had no engagements, no difficult decisions to make, no fear of callers, no interruptions to my work.' He wrote his *Introduction to Mathematical Philosophy*, and found such prisoners as he did meet 'in no way morally inferior to the rest of the population, though they were on the whole slightly below the usual level of intelligence, as was shown by their having been caught.' He found German prisoners with whom he could discuss Kant; and could write to his mistress in French, claiming to the authorities that they were passages copied out of a French book he was reading. 'I suspect the Governor did not know French,' he recorded, 'but would not confess ignorance.'[6]

It was not surprising that the authorities pursued with such vigour those trying to undermine conscription and the duty to fight for King and country. The Army on the Western Front, where an attack was most likely to come, was particularly under strength. Hankey worked out it was 720,000 men short, and home defence, which was recruiting eighteen-year-old boys, was 120,000 under.[7] Haig told the Army Council on 24 November that he feared the infantry alone would be 250,000 men short by the end of March 1918.[8] The formation on 29 November of the Women's Royal Naval Service ensured there were more men for fighting duties at sea – Wrens (as they quickly came to be known) worked not just as cooks and in secretarial functions, but as telegraphists and electricians – but this was of little help to the Army.

At the War Cabinet on 6 December Derby read out a warning from Haig that if no steps were taken to produce more men the infantry divisions in France 'would be 40 per cent below their present establishments by the 31st March 1918.'[9] A reduction in size of each division, cutting the number of its battalions from twelve to nine, was discussed: the War Cabinet finally agreed to this in January 1918. Robertson had already acquainted Lloyd George with the full reality of the military situation. As so often when confronted with difficulties, Lloyd George became ill and took to his bed, though not before berating his CIGS with examples of Haig's groundless optimism and other exaggerations. The prime minister told Derby he wanted Haig out, prompting Derby to advise him of the unwisdom of so doing.

The Navy, however, would undergo a change of leadership. Jellicoe was dismissed as First Sea Lord. It was tactlessly handled: Geddes sent Jellicoe a letter shortly before he went home on Christmas Eve 1917 saying he was being relieved of his duties. Sir Rosslyn Wemyss, an old shipmate and friend of the King, a veteran of both the Dardanelles campaign and the final evacuation, and since October deputy First Sea Lord, replaced him. Inevitable ever since Geddes had taken over the Admiralty, it was an unattractive end to a distinguished, if unimaginative, career. There was more high-ranking bloodshed to come. Milner told General Sir Henry Wilson on 30 December that 'Lloyd George is so angry with Robertson that he proposes to kick him out and put [Wilson] in.' With fake magnanimity, Wilson replied that 'I am opposed to this, though all in favour of Lloyd George giving me more power at Versailles, and reducing Robertson from the position of a master to that of a servant.'[10]

Robertson knew too well how the prime minister was keen to shift responsibility for strategic mistakes on to everyone but himself. He told Haig on 8 December that the War Cabinet 'are at last scared as regards manpower', Lloyd George – as Robertson reported to Haig – choosing to blame the Army Council (which had regularly warned them about the shortage of soldiers) for having 'misled' them.[11] Robertson cited this manipulation of the facts as 'proof of the impossibility of honestly working with such a man.' This was the first manifestation of a dishonesty over troop numbers that would dog Lloyd George for the rest of the war (and his historical reputation thereafter), and put the Allies at risk of defeat. There were more men in the Army on home defence than remotely necessary – as Churchill pointed out at the 6 December meeting – but Lloyd George would not send them to the front because he feared Haig would find a way of slaughtering them to no obvious Allied advantage. The prime minister did this even though Haig had predicted that thirty German divisions would come from the Eastern Front now Russia was leaving the war – though by 6 December only six had arrived. Derby wrote to Haig, with Lloyd George's endorsement, to urge him to ensure the better safety and security of his troops, perhaps by building better concrete pillboxes, such as those the Germans had.

It was also apparent that American assistance, which was mainly discussed in terms of the numbers of men it promised to bring into the fight against Germany, was a double-edged sword, because of how it would shape American power. Over Sunday lunch at Walton Heath on 9 December Riddell warned Lloyd George of a grim year ahead: more shipping losses, a slump in foreign trade, and a £3 billion increase in debt. But, perhaps more ominously, he added: 'Naturally, the Americans desire to make America the first nation in the world. At the end of 1918 they will hold all the gold in the world; they will have a huge mercantile fleet . . . they will have opened new markets all over the world, markets which they have been developing while we have been fighting. They resent our command of the seas . . . [they] will endeavour to clip our naval wings. Wilson is cool and crafty. We shall have to watch that in our efforts to annihilate the Germans we do not annihilate ourselves.'[12]

Riddell's worries were consistent with a growing sense of pessimism and frustration. The hitherto ebullient Haig was no longer talking of the next offensive, but had realised that on the Western Front only a defensive war was now feasible. The miracle of defeating Germany might have to await the arrival of the Americans, with fresh men or fresh thinking, or rely on a catastrophic error by the enemy. Northcliffe, who when leaving for America the previous year had ordered the *Daily Mail* in his absence always to take the side of the Army, was so appalled by the failure to consolidate gains at Cambrai that he turned his newspapers' fire on the General Staff, notably Robertson. On 12 December *The Times* had called for an inquiry to find those responsible for the failures after Cambrai, though Northcliffe maintained a regard for Haig, believing he had been let down by poor subordinates. Auckland Geddes, the minister of National Service, lamented on 14 January that 'no dramatic stroke less than a divine miracle would simultaneously solve all the problems which are loosely called one problem and labelled manpower.'[13] He proposed repealing legislation providing certificates of exemption from military service on occupational grounds, and had long advocated abolishing exemptions for boys of eighteen.

The government adjusted its priorities from week to week: if there was suddenly spare capacity in the shipyards, men no longer needed there could go to the front. Geddes claimed recruiting was going well: but the modern Army needed men adept at engineering, electrics and the science of explosives, and they could only be obtained from reserved occupations. He believed up to 450,000 potential recruits of military age in non-essential trades and war industries could be combed out and replaced, where necessary, by older men or women not yet in the workforce. The maintenance of morale no longer allowed those who had been seriously wounded, or older men realistically past the age for military service, to be sent back to fight, or to stop the leave of those at the front, while young, fit men enjoyed high wages and immunity from German shells and bullets.

In an apparent echo of the prime minister's disdain for Haig, Geddes announced to the Commons in early January 1918: 'The Government has gone most carefully into this question of casualties. While seeking not to hamper the action of our Commanders in the field by judging their actions by the casualty returns alone, it is determined that carelessness with regard to human life and thoughtlessness with regard to casualties shall be stamped out wherever it appears.'[14] It showed the public, at least, what the government thought of the Somme and Passchendaele; and may have been a calculated move by Geddes to prove to a restless population that had endured such misery that the government understood their feelings.

However, he had also to ensure he did not provoke resignations by senior commanders. 'I do not wish to be misunderstood. We are accusing no admiral or general of recklessness or of disregard for human life. The Government is laying down a perfectly plain, general principle which I am abundantly clear ought at all times, and more especially at this time, while we await the coming of America, to guide the Government in its supervision over the action of the Commanders whom it has appointed.' He reaffirmed that the government still believed it would do more harm than good to introduce conscription to Ireland. A million men had been granted exemptions; and Geddes did not rule out the possibility that some had been obtained corruptly.

The debate on the proposed law to remove automatic exemptions by trade allowed one of the government's most consistent critics, William Pringle, an Asquithian Liberal, to deride the coalition for having taken thirteen months to address the manpower problem. He taunted the Treasury Bench with the observation: 'We know that the situation of this country and the Alliance has never been worse than it is to-day. The Minister of Munitions said only a day or two ago that the British Empire was now hanging in the balance. That is a very serious situation.'[15] He claimed there was now such an oversupply of shells that piles were 'rusting' in France.[16] A measure of desperation was shown when James Macpherson, under-secretary at the War Office, admitted on 17 January that 'the question of the employment of coloured men in the fighting line has received, and is now receiving, the most careful consideration. Every possible use is being made of their services in the various theatres of war.'[17] Elements in the Army and politics had long resisted the idea of black men serving with white ones. The next day Lloyd George spoke to another group of trades unionists, their cooperation essential for the success of Geddes's scheme, with an even starker message than before. 'My own conviction is this: the people must either go on, or go under.'[18]

While politicians and soldiers squabbled about what to do next, British military intelligence was becoming aware that, with the war against Russia over, the Germans meant to use all their resources to drive Britain and France under. The German army (which put boys of eighteen in the line whereas the British Army, officially at least, waited until they were nineteen) was redeploying what the government estimated to be at least 950,000, and possibly as many as 1,600,000, men from the Eastern Front thanks to the Russian 'secession' from the Allies.[19] Even *The Times* wrote about German troops now 'swarming westwards'. For the first time since 1914 it seemed as though the German army might be in a position to go back on the offensive. That was precisely the plan. Exactly a year before the Armistice, on 11 November 1917, Erich Ludendorff, the German Quartermaster General, chaired a meeting of senior officers at Mons to discuss strategy. It decided that 'we must strike the English'.[20] The reasoning was straightforward. On the home front matters were, as the British public was constantly (and truthfully) being told, worse in Germany than in Britain. The blockade had created huge food and fuel shortages, and other necessities, such as clothing, were in short supply. Allied manufacturing of armaments now outstripped Germany's, thanks to Lloyd George's effective mobilisation of the munitions industry in 1915–16. The withdrawal of Russia from the conflict meant that resources on the Eastern Front could be transferred without disadvantage to the west. And above all, the Americans, after extensive training and superbly equipped, were coming. For the Germans it was, essentially, now or never. The target would be the BEF on the Western Front.

Churchill wrote bluntly to Lloyd George on 19 January 1918: 'I don't think we are doing enough for our army. Really I must make that point to you. We are not raising its strength as we ought. We ought to fill it up at once to full strength.'[21] He was right – perhaps more right than he knew – but Lloyd George had not taken him into his confidence about his fear of letting Haig loose with huge amounts of manpower. Indeed, the prime minister saw things rather differently. In early 1918, with the Russians out, the Italian army wrecked, the French hobbled by poor morale and the BEF lacking men, he had expected the war to last into 1919. Depressed by his military advisers and their repeated failure, Lloyd George sought to shake up the Army's command and find new ideas and new means of victory. He had tried to clip Robertson's wings by setting up the Supreme War Council, but then told Scott on 19 December 1917 that he intended to replace Robertson with Sir Henry Wilson.[22] Wilson and Lloyd George understood each other, sharing the view that French generals were better than British ones. Wilson's rampant ambition made him pliant where his master was concerned. His presence on the Supreme War Council meant there would be a higher chance it would offer advice that the prime minister felt happy to accept. Wilson's addiction to political intrigue had handicapped him until he met an admirer in Lloyd George, who perhaps saw in him a kindred spirit. Esher wrote of him at this time: 'Henry Wilson . . . is one of the cleverest fellows we have; unfortunately, he dabbled in politics and, like so many Irishmen, is fond of the shillelagh. This has done him harm, which, perhaps is irremediable, and, if so, the Army and the nation are both heavy losers.'[23]

Over breakfast on 28 December 1917 Lloyd George told Scott: 'The generals are absolutely callous as to the gigantic casualties and order men to certain death like cattle to the slaughter. Again and again splendid men have been ordered to do perfectly impossible things, such as to advance against uncut wire and enfilading machine-gun fire.'[24] It outraged him that when everyone in the chain of command relayed upwards the impossibility of such tasks, GHQ decreed: 'Tell them to obey orders.' That was why Lloyd George wanted Robertson and Haig's powers restricted. The CIGS was his first target, even though Derby had told Lloyd George that if Robertson went he would resign as Secretary of State for War. Haig learned of the plans for Robertson on New Year's Day 1918, when seeing Derby in London.

Haig, as usual, harmed his own cause, by casting doubt on the likelihood of a German offensive when talking to Derby before his return to France; and therefore undermining his appeal for more manpower. He believed the Germans would in time move thirty-two divisions westwards, but felt a widespread attack would be too costly; he spoke from experience. Haig's political stupidity in expressing his feelings so openly dismayed Robertson, who was arguing day and night for more troops to be sent; although Haig was right that if the Germans tried and failed they would be finished – hence his belief that they would not. Haig seems to have started to tone down his demands for more men in an attempt to conceal the full extent of the damage the disastrous 1917 offensive had done to the Army, which would have been clear at once had he told Derby what he really needed; he had earlier claimed 116,000 men were necessary to replace those losses.[25] Derby – who shared Robertson's goals – was also angry at Haig's blunder, and told Robertson to advise him, in future, to think before opening his mouth. 'You do not understand these people as well as I do,' Robertson told him, referring to the politicians and their ability – especially Lloyd George's – to twist anything to serve their purposes. Haig and Derby lunched with Lloyd George on 9 January, and Derby bet the prime minister 100 cigars to 100 cigarettes that the war would be over before 1919; Haig agreed, shrewdly, 'because of the internal state of Germany'.[26]

It was not only Robertson among senior military advisers whom Lloyd George and, by extension, the War Cabinet sought to disregard. When General Maurice reported on 11 January that signs of a German offensive were increasing, he noted: 'Cabinet don't believe in this offensive and think Germans really mean to attack Italy and perhaps Salonika.'[27] A shortage of men was causing the British Army to wind up 120 battalions, just as the Germans were moving troops from the Eastern Front. Amery reported that Lloyd George 'cannot get it out of his head that Haig and Co are almost indifferent to casualties and are really clamouring about the danger of the situation in order to have men enough to try another bloody attack as soon as the Germans show signs of not attacking themselves.'[28] The British were dancing to the tune played from Versailles, where the view was that the Western Front was so stable that troops would be better deployed in the Middle East. By 26 January Maurice was recording: 'relations between LG and WR rapidly becoming impossible.'[29] This might also have been because the prime minister started to sense that in some regards Robertson might have been right: intelligence that there were 600,000–700,000 more Germans on the Western Front than previously thought had, according to Amery, 'upset LG's basis on which his plans are built.'[30] Indeed, on 7 February 1918, at a meeting of the War Cabinet, Major General Sir George Mac-Donogh, director of military intelligence, announced that 'since October last thirty German divisions in all had been transferred to the Western front' and the enemy could move 'twenty-seven more'.[31]

II

By the late winter of 1918 the state's control over civilian life was ever more absolute. Throwing away food still fit for human consumption was criminalised. Those with any land were encouraged to grow food and to keep pigs, but were warned not to feed them on anything that might be eaten by humans. A national debate broke out on how to feed them, which *The Times* earnestly termed 'the pig question': 'No-one who has the slightest knowledge of the pig can deny that he possesses many admirable qualities', the paper observed, one of which being that he would happily gorge himself on 'refuse materials'.[32] Inevitably, the government oversaw the manufacture and distribution of special 'cake' for pigs, comprised of the by-products of palm kernel and coconuts, instituting a government pig-feeding scheme. The next step was the urging of groups of rural householders to form pig clubs, and rear herds collectively.

Prosecutions for breaking food regulations, notably for selling at the wrong price or wasting food, became ubiquitous, with middle-class householders particularly liable for prosecution for hoarding. Some astonishing war chests were found: a John Robertson, of Burstow in Surrey, was convicted on 9 March of having 95 pounds of sugar, 161 pounds of flour, 55 pounds of rice, 42 pounds of treacle, 45 pounds of biscuits, 9 pounds of margarine, 33 pounds of tea, 100 pounds of oatmeal, 41 pints of soup and 234 Oxo cubes.[33] His household comprised his wife, an adult daughter, a ten-year-old son and two servants, with two other sons away at school, though he alleged that members of his extended family were staying at the time. He was fined £50 with 32 guineas costs, and all food beyond four weeks' supply was confiscated. Companies and wholesalers, too, were frequently victims of the regulations, not because of their wilful disobedience of them but because they were sometimes so complicated to interpret. Offenders included Lipton's the tea merchants, who operated by appointment to Their Majesties.

The meat rationing scheme imposed on the Home Counties on 25 February – photographs of Their Majesties' ration cards appeared in the press to illustrate the equality of sacrifice underpinning the war effort – was made national on 7 April: it should have happened on 25 March, but the bureaucracy was not ready, not least in computing the extent of supplementary rations for men on heavy manual work. Offal, too, was rationed, and it was urged that people eat more game – snipe, plover, rabbit, hare and the ubiquitous wood pigeon. It took butchers ages with each customer to check the ration card; but by mid-March the worst was over. The hope of making Britain self-sufficient in bread was abandoned too: and J. R. Clynes, who succeeded Rhondda as food controller on his death on 3 July, warned the War Cabinet that a lack of feed threatened livestock production, and the availability of working horses. And although on 30 April the exemption for agricultural workers aged eighteen to twenty-three, granted during the food crisis of 1917, was felt able to be lifted, and a recruitment target of 30,000 set, this move proved unrealistically optimistic. A plan to plough up yet more disused arable land was abandoned because of manpower shortages, despite the best efforts of the Women's Land Army. Partly as a result, widespread food rationing was introduced in July.

It was not only scarcity of food that affected the public. In late March, because of a shortage of coal and electricity, shopkeepers were banned from illuminating their windows, and restaurants and theatres were ordered to close earlier. The London Underground also closed early and ran few Sunday trains; and railway services, already heavily curtailed, were pared down even further, with many branch lines closing on Sundays. Tobacco wholesalers were warned that if they did not improve distribution the state would do it for them, and tobacconists were reminded that selling their products other than at the regulated price was a summary offence. Manpower shortages had widespread effects. So few men were available that trial by jury was restricted in civil cases; and the upper age for jury service was raised from sixty to sixty-five. Most buildings, public or private, had not been maintained since before the war. Paint was peeling and drabness ubiquitous. By the late winter of 1918 Britain and the British were down-at-heel and subdued. Clothing and fabrics were scarce, with mills devoted to producing miles of khaki instead of materials for suits and dresses. And it was not just life that was being compromised; the British Undertakers' Association warned the public of a scarcity of coffins, because of the lack of elm timber. Elm was in fact plentiful: but the government's distribution system was useless. Rather than mend it, the government suggested papier-mâché coffins.

Fuel shortages led to the rationing of gas and electricity supplies; restaurants had to stop serving food at 9.30 p.m. and all places of entertainment had to close by 10.30 p.m. to save fuel. The government opened National Kitchens to help provide takeaway meals of soup, stews and puddings for those without fuel with which to cook. Bank holidays were still suspended and going on holiday was deemed unpatriotic. Train services were often disrupted because of the difficulty in maintaining the lines, and fares had increased substantially.

Despite all the privations, stresses and fears of the last phase of the war – or perhaps because of them – creativity continued, as did some sort of life of the mind and a search for recreational and intellectual refreshment. War had not suffocated art, but as it became more intense produced lasting artistic works. A cultural life, of a sort, continued, and provided new inspiration: though much of what the war inspired would not come to fruition until the years after it. H. G. Wells, prolific during the war as before it, published *The Soul of a Bishop*, describing a spiritual crisis allegorical of a nation questioning its faith after severe loss and privation; less profound, but more controversial, was Alec Waugh's *The Loom of Youth*. Poetry made more of a lasting impact. T. S. Eliot published *Prufrock and Other Observations*, a slim volume including 'The Love Song of J. Alfred Prufrock', first published in a magazine in 1915. The pamphlet was an early modernist statement, the main poem using a stream of consciousness and extensive allusion. *The Times Literary Supplement* was contemptuous; of its contents it wrote: 'They have no relation to poetry.'[34] Robert Graves's first volume of verse, *Fairies and Fusiliers*, celebrated his friendship with Siegfried Sassoon, whose own poems, *The Old Huntsman*, with a dedication to Thomas Hardy, also appeared in 1917. Ivor Gurney, who had trained as a composer at the Royal College of Music, published his volume of poetry *Severn and Somme* in November 1917: Gurney had shown signs of manic depression before the war, and being wounded and gassed while the poems were being written and published intensified his mental problems. He had written songs in the trenches, and resumed studies under Vaughan Williams after the war, writing several minor works: but his mental illness became so intense that he spent much of his life – he died in 1937 – in asylums. Edward Thomas's *Poems* was published shortly after his death at Arras: Gurney set nineteen to music.

There was a social side to music, in terms of its public performances and presentation of new works, that suggested a continuing sense of civilisation in a time of profound bleakness. At a concert in the Queen's Hall on 22 October 1917 *Lady Audley's Suite*, a work for string quartet, had its premiere and a rapturous critical reception: 'The most promising new work we have heard from an Englishman for some time.'[35] It was remarkable in more ways than one. Its composer, Herbert Howells, had been rejected for military service for medical reasons: he had been diagnosed with Graves' disease – an illness of the thyroid – and given six months to live. There was one possible cure – radium treatment, discovered the previous decade by the Curies. Howells, whose father was a bankrupt Gloucestershire shopkeeper, could not afford it. His teacher at the Royal College of Music, Sir Hubert Parry, could, and told Howells he would pay for it. Howells lived into his ninety-first year, and became perhaps the greatest composer of English church music in modern times, dying in 1983.

Frank Bridge had written chamber music and a few orchestral works throughout the war; compared with his pre-war output the music is subdued and reflective, and some directly linked to the war. In 1915 he had been acclaimed for his *Lament*, in memory of a nine-year-old girl drowned on the *Lusitania*; in 1916 he wrote a choral work *For God and King and Right*. In 1917 his music became more escapist, his *Four Characteristic Pieces* including movements called 'Water Nymphs' and 'Fragrance', followed by *Three Pastorals* and a suite, *Fairy Tales*. In 1918 Bridge majestically set Brooke's sonnet 'Blow out, you bugles', ironic given his later reputation for pacifism.

Bridge at least managed to keep composing throughout the war, helped by not seeing active service. Parry, weighed down with teaching and administration as director of the Royal College of Music, and by charity work, produced a handful of masterpieces – 'Jerusalem' (as he did not call it), his choral ode 'The Chivalry of the Sea', his *Songs of Farewell* and some organ chorales. Sir Edward Elgar wrote mostly songs during the war, and some incidental music and short orchestral works; his great creative impulse, which until the war had produced large-scale works, had declined. Elgar's sadness at the passing of the world in which he had flourished would be heard in four works begun in 1918: his Violin Sonata, String Quartet, Piano Quintet and, most renowned of all, his Cello Concerto, the last considerable work he completed.

One young conductor – Adrian Boult, exempted from active service because of his health (he would live until shortly before his ninety-fourth birthday) – directed the London Symphony Orchestra in a series of concerts of British music from early 1918 onwards. Boult had served as an orderly in a reserve battalion until 1916, but was then transferred to the War Office as a translator because of his proficiency in French, German and Italian. His concerts included only the second performance of Vaughan Williams's *London Symphony*, premiered just before the outbreak of war, Parry's *Symphonic Variations* and works by Butterworth, killed on the Somme: but one especially would pass into legend.

Throughout the war Gustav von Holst (the von, of Swedish origin, was dropped early in the conflict) had applied for various types of non-combatant service, but even then had been dismissed as medically unfit. At last he secured the post of director of music for the YMCA, which was arranging orchestral and other musical entertainments for soldiers in Europe: and Holst would take up the post in Salonica in early October 1918. His friends knew that between late 1914 and early 1916 he had written his orchestral suite *The Planets*, but it remained unperformed. One of his patrons, Henry Balfour Gardiner, decided to mark Holst's departure by paying for a private performance before he left, on 29 September in the Queen's Hall in London.

Holst enlisted his friend Boult to conduct the first performance. Holst taught music at St Paul's Girls' School in Brook Green in west London, and its choir was enlisted to act as the chorus in the last movement, 'Neptune'. Despite the innovations of Elgar, Vaughan Williams and even, in his Fifth Symphony of 1912, Holst's teacher Parry, the work was like nothing heard before in the English orchestral canon: though Holst's friend Edward Dent said it sounded 'much less modern' than he had expected from his study of the score.[36] Some first performances of great musical works have gone down in legend for their dreadfulness, but not *The Planets*, one of several that reveals Holst as a genius to compare with any of his European contemporaries, such as Strauss or Stravinsky or Ravel. It is one of the towering works of the English musical renaissance. The invited audience was overwhelmed; an impresario immediately recruited Boult to give the first public performance in the ensuing season.

A week after his pupil's triumph, having fallen victim to the flu epidemic to which his already weak heart was not equal, Sir Hubert Parry died at his house in Rustington, Sussex: but he had trained the composers – Vaughan Williams, Herbert Howells, Arthur Bliss, Jack Moeran, John Ireland as well as Holst – who would ensure this growing part of British cultural life would continue and flourish after his death, and after the war whose end was by that stage, at last, in sight.

The general run of privations among those for whom high culture was no consolation provoked occasional acts of resistance. The MFGB voted by 248,000 to 219,000 against the combing-out of 50,000 men from their industry. The next day the Amalgamated Society of Engineers fought Auckland Geddes to prevent younger members being combed out to fight, though most dissent vanished when the expected German offensive materialised. Eric Geddes told Parliament that it seemed Britain did not realise how short of merchant shipping it was; monthly output in the last quarter of 1917 had averaged 140,000 tons, but in January 1918 it was just 58,000 tons.[37] The timing was unfortunate, because his statement coincided with a visit in early March by the Prince of Wales, who had become popular during the war, to factories on the Clyde, where he congratulated workers on their contribution to victory and exhorted them to continued effort, not least because production of shipping remained inadequate.

Geddes blamed the management and workers in equal measure. His target of 3 million tons a year – 250,000 a month – seemed unobtainable given the then rate of production. His achievement was to unite shipbuilders and their unionised workers, who jointly put out a statement condemning him for asserting that they did not understand the gravity of the situation. They blamed the government for breaking a promise by Lloyd George, made the previous November, that conditions for shipyard workers – certainly in terms of food rations for heavy labourers – would be improved. They also claimed that government direction of labour – towards warships and away from merchant vessels – was the root of the problem, and production would rise without the interference between masters and men.

A wave of strikes afflicted production early that summer, as union membership once more rose steeply (it would increase by 19 per cent over the year) and despite pay rises for munitions and agricultural workers. The booming aircraft industry was a hotbed of unrest. By late May 40,000 miners in South Wales were on strike over the refusal of management to recognise a workers' committee, and the coal controller was called in. All demands were met, though many miners did not go straight back to work. Then in June the MFGB demanded another 9s a week for its members. The government capitulated, fearing the effect a coal strike would have on overall production. From 23 to 26 July engineering workers in Coventry and Birmingham walked out because of talk of conscripting them, the strike ending only when the government threatened to call up its leaders and put them under military discipline. For all the bluster, the government was sufficiently agitated that Lloyd George asked for hourly reports. The total of strikes in all industries, at 1,165, was over 400 up on 1917, and the highest since 1913.[38]

The unrest in the coalfields, which lasted all through 1918, was of particular concern because it affected so many areas of life, from powering the Royal Navy to domestic heating and electricity, the essential production of iron and steel, and transportation of troops, people and goods by steam-powered railways. In 1913 the mines had produced 287.4 million tons of coal; by 1918 it was down to 222.7 million. The quality of the coal also fell. It wasn't just strikes that were to blame for the shortage of coal, even though in the first eleven months of 1918 there were 134 disputes in the mines, costing 1,081,000 days' labour.[39] The combing-out of coal miners was having a serious effect on productivity, too. Before the war 1.16 million men had worked in the coalfields; 289,000 had joined the services, and the government had decided to call up 50,000 unmarried colliers despite the wishes of the Miners' Federation. A further 25,000 miners were called up after March 1918, further reducing output. Churchill warned the War Cabinet that if the war continued into 1919 this would inevitably lead to a fall in the production of shells. Ministers had to balance their efforts between ensuring the country could hold up against the Germans and keeping morale high.

With these massive manpower problems, women continued to be co-opted into the war effort with ever greater rapidity. As they reached working age they were absorbed into the National Service scheme; at eighteen they could join the Women's Army Auxiliary Corps or the Women's Royal Naval Service and many, sensing an excitement similar to that felt by young men who had joined Kitchener's army in 1914, did. In March 1918 the WAACs advertised for 3,000 women clerks, 1,700 to serve in France. The young of both genders were being warned with increasing ferocity about venereal disease, which despite hospitals offering treatment free of charge continued at epidemic proportions. Advertisements about the scourge became ever more graphic, with horror stories of babies being born blind through syphilis. This being no time for prudishness, the King – but not the Queen – visited a VD treatment centre in London's Rochester Row in February 1918, and issued a statement afterwards on the importance of the work done there.

Across society, there could be no let-up in the sacrifices. On 22 April Law introduced what became the last wartime Budget, what he described as 'a financial statement on a scale far exceeding any that has ever been known at any time or in any country'.[40] The war was now costing £7 million a day; but even had it ended the cost of running the country would be greatly higher than pre-war.[41] Expenditure in 1914 had been £173 million; Law said that, excluding war expenditure, spending in 1918 would be £270 million, largely because of the rise in the cost of pensions, but also to keep promises about an expanded state education system that was being proposed.[42] The national debt had, he said, risen to £7,980 million, and part of that was because of money advanced to Russia that was not being repaid, after the revolution: though Law refused to concede it was a bad debt. Revenue would fall short of expenditure by £110 million in 1918–19, which Law proposed to cover by raising taxes. He gave a measure of how things had changed since 1914: 'This addition to taxation which I propose this year is something well over 60 per cent of the total tax revenue in the last year before the War.'[43] Even so, only 26.3 per cent of the cost of the war was met by taxation; the rest was debt.

Even in putting up taxes, Law was struggling. He could not raise the excess profits duty, because the Treasury had realised any rise was likely to cut the total amount raised, by discouraging additional production.

So he had to be ingenious. One such measure was ending the penny post on letters, which had lasted for seventy-eight years since the introduction of the postage stamp in 1840. Letters would now cost three-halfpence. The stamp duty payable on cheques would rise from a penny to twopence, which would bring in an extra £1 million a year. Income tax would rise from 5s to 6s in the pound, which was projected to raise another £41.4 million a year; but would only apply to incomes above £500 a year.[44] The super-tax would rise from 3s 6d in the pound to 4s 6d, and would start at incomes of £2,500 a year rather than £3,000. Someone earning £5,000 a year – the prime minister's salary – would pay an effective rate of 7s 2d in the pound, or 36 per cent; anyone making £20,000 a year would pay 9s 5d in the pound, or 47 per cent.

The public believed farmers were making huge profits, and Law proposed to send the Inland Revenue after them; it was estimated that 90 per cent of farmers kept no accounts. That was expected to raise £5.3 million a year. He said he would more than double the duty on spirits to bring in £11.15 million; and to double the duty on beer, bringing in £15.7 million. Because the food controller fixed the price of beer, the full tax rise could not be passed on to the consumer; but the public also believed the brewers were profiteering. Law was taking a huge risk, given the brewers' support for the Tory Party. The rise in tobacco taxes was smaller, from 6s 5d to 8s 2d per pound weight; and their controlled price meant that, as with beer, some of the cost would be borne by the producer. Although imports were severely restricted, the government agreed to allow as much tobacco into the country as the consumer desired because, as Law explained, the rate of tax was so high that importing tobacco was 'almost importing money'.[45] The increased taxation would raise £8 million a year; and a new sugar tax £13.2 million.

Law proposed a new tax that played to newspaper reports of the rich avoiding sacrifices that everyone else had to make. His proposed luxury tax, which he had considered the previous year, would be levied in three ways: on luxury items, such as jewellery; on items perceived as luxuries because of their high price; and on luxury establishments, such as hotels and restaurants. He proposed to levy this at 2d in the shilling, or 16.5 per cent. It was, he said, a higher rate than the comparable tax in France, which raised £24 million a year: he aimed to raise even more. There would now be very few pies of which the state would not get a slice. However, the public, or at least those in work, were still bringing in high real incomes.

The labour movement renewed calls for the 'conscription of wealth', which the government parried by further issues of War Bonds, imploring those with reservoirs of cash to fund the ever-more expensive fight. The second week of March was deemed 'Business Men's Week', when the King led an appeal to plutocrats to subscribe £100 million within seven days. A Liverpool shipping line, Frederick Leyland & Company, led the way by subscribing £2 million; an act not entirely philanthropic, given the competitive rate of interest of 5 per cent. Within four days the required amount was reached, and the total raised was almost £139 million.

III

The press, whose clout had grown enormously during the war because of the public's thirst for information, became more and more strident about what it perceived to be the shortcomings over the direction of the fight. Robertson – as Chief of the Imperial General Staff – became the obvious target of increased attacks by the Northcliffe papers during January 1918. Northcliffe might have thought he was doing Lloyd George a favour; Repington, *The Times*'s military correspondent, believed his proprietor had 'tied himself to LG's chariot wheels.'[46] On 21 January the *Mail* accused Robertson of following 'the strategy of the stone age'; in ensuing days the paper accused the General Staff of making scapegoats of politicians for their failures, and rubbished arguments about manpower shortages.[47] Far from these attacks helping Lloyd George, they actually presented him with two problems. If he sacked Robertson it would seem he was doing Northcliffe's bidding; and there was a danger that, as with the assault on Kitchener in 1915, it would encourage support for Robertson, and make him unsackable. Unionist MPs were angry and their War Committee demanded the government condemn Northcliffe: Lloyd George asked Northcliffe to call his dogs off, and told Stamfordham he 'could have taken him out and shot him'.[48]

Dawson, Repington's editor, had been cutting passages from his articles that he felt would annoy either the government or Northcliffe. Dawson – whose reputation would be destroyed by his support for appeasement twenty years later – chose to indulge his proprietor by rewriting Repington to match the line taken in the paper's leaders, an interesting example of modifying facts to suit opinion. Dawson's conduct outraged Repington, who felt he could no longer work for Northcliffe, and so resigned from *The Times* on 16 January 1918. In his resignation letter he said his proprietor had taken 'a subservient and apologetic attitude' to Lloyd George while showing 'neglect of the vital interests of the Army.'[49] The final straw was a *Times* leader misrepresenting what would happen to some 420,000 men combed out of reserved occupations. Repington had been told they would go to the Navy and the nascent Royal Air Force and be used just to 'maintain' the Army, but the leader said they would all go to the trenches. 'This was too much for me,' the Colonel wrote. 'I should deserve to be hanged as a Boche agent if I remained with these imbeciles any longer.'[50] He gave Dawson a preview of his letter of resignation, adding for good measure that the leader had been 'mendacious'. *The Times* published an equally mendacious statement giving its version of the resignation, Northcliffe being rattled by Repington's celebrity and his assertion that the paper's 'intrigue' against Haig and Robertson had forced him out – 'for that inference there is not the very slightest foundation in fact.'[51]

Some – notably Strachey, editor of the *Spectator*, believed Northcliffe's attack on the Army was another sign of megalomania, and a possible belief that he could supplant Lloyd George as prime minister. Repington, meanwhile, consoled himself in Paris, seeing Esher and doing some useful personal public relations. 'Repington came to Paris in a furious mood,' Esher noted. 'He has been scurvily treated by Northcliffe.'[52] A senior officer had told Repington the Germans had 165 divisions in the west: just as Lloyd George, who knew the real figure was 175, proposed to send more soldiers to Palestine, with the War Cabinet continuing to ignore warnings about German troop movements. With an estimated 201,000 fit men at home that the government refused to send abroad, the next row was brewing.[53]

The prime minister's own western strategy consisted of not launching any more attacks there, following the debacles of the previous two years. Whether he believed Palestine was a satisfactory alternative strategy, or simply felt he needed to have an alternative plan to pursue in order to avoid pouring men into the Western Front, it is impossible categorically to say: he was not always straight even with Miss Stevenson, let alone in his own memoirs. He was, however, unquestionably sincere in wishing to avoid further wholesale slaughter, whatever his motives.

All was not well in the government. Carson resigned on 21 January – to the prime minister's 'deepest and most unfeigned regret' – when the

War Cabinet discussed extending conscription to Ireland, introducing Home Rule as a quid pro quo.[54] Since he had nominally overseen propaganda, and the department of which John Buchan was director, Carson's departure left an important job to be filled. On his resignation Buchan told Northcliffe there should be a minister accountable to Parliament to drive the work of the department. He had Northcliffe in mind, not realising that such an appointment would make the potential for rifts in the government even worse, given the toxicity many ministers felt was attached to Northcliffe. The question did not arise because Lloyd George, recalling his obligations to Law, sent for Beaverbrook; in any case, Northcliffe claimed he would not compromise his newspapers' independence by joining the government. Beaverbrook was shrewd enough to persuade Northcliffe to oversee foreign propaganda, though not as a minister. He was based at the British War Mission in Crewe House (put at the nation's disposal by the Liberal politician) and would report to the prime minister, to whom he gave an assurance of loyalty. Beaverbrook was cynical: 'I expect to lose my life in a deadly scrap with Northcliffe which is sure to come sooner or later,' he told Riddell.[55] Buchan became director of Intelligence; Arnold Bennett took charge (unpaid) of propaganda in France, his experiences providing material for one of his better late novels, *Lord Raingo*.

Beaverbrook became Chancellor of the Duchy of Lancaster several days after agreeing to reorganise what would now be called the Ministry of Information: the delay was needed to secure the King's agreement, which required Lloyd George to plead that he only sought to enlist 'in the King's service all the best brains and energies of the nation'.[56] The King assented, saying he did not know Beaverbrook 'personally' and therefore had based his low estimate of him on what he had read in the newspapers.[57] He may have heard the view of his uncle, the Duke of Connaught, who had been governor-general of Canada and was alleged to have said that 'no decent man would need Beaverbrook.'[58]

Scott told Lloyd George that he, like the King, thought the appointment of Beaverbrook and Northcliffe unwise. The prime minister defended the latter by saying 'it was necessary to find occupation for his abounding energies if they were not to run into mischief.'[59] The controversy rumbled on, as the old order failed to comprehend the vulgar, corrupt and entirely improper way that Lloyd George chose to run his administration. In a debate in the House of Lords that he instigated on

6 March, to discuss what he considered to be the highly unsuitable appointment of Beaverbrook and Northcliffe, Lord Ribblesdale, subject of perhaps the finest Edwardian swagger portrait, complained about the two press barons, deploring how their methods 'largely controlled and animated' the government with which they were now connected.[60]

Even before this debate the corrosive effects of a tripartite battle between politicians, generals and the press were already apparent. Lord Beresford, a retired admiral, savaged the press in the Lords on 12 February, for attacks on senior officers; he said any serviceman would know how destructive these were to morale in the Army and the Fleet, because they undermined confidence in military leadership. He believed DORA should be used to punish those publishing such material. 'I warn the Government and the Prime Minister that there is a great deal of unrest in the country, and that there is a great deal worse in the trenches and in the Fleet, because of the power that the Press has to make or to unmake officers in the Services.'[61] That was before Northcliffe's appointment.

Austen Chamberlain, about whom there had been rumours of a return to office, attacked the culture of government using the press to undermine public servants, a view Asquith shared. Chamberlain reflected a disquiet that ministers, and particularly Lloyd George, were too close to Fleet Street, and a smell of corruption was abroad. He said the slurs of Northcliffe and others 'are not only deplorable in themselves, but they are cowardly, and the men who make them are not only acting in a way in which a patriotic citizen would not act in war-time, they are acting in a way in which gentlemen do not act at any time.'[62] He accused Lloyd George of dereliction in protecting Robertson against attacks; but added that no attack on government policy should be traceable back to a senior officer, an allusion to the free flow of criticism between Haig and Robertson about how the prime minister ran the government's affairs.

Chamberlain also had a more specific complaint:

The functions of the Press are not the functions of the Government, and the functions of the Government are not the functions of the Press, and it is not possible, without misconception and misunderstanding, that they should be combined in the same person. What is the function of the Government? Three great newspaper owners are members of, or are intimately associated with, the Administration. Their papers are found from time to time to contain matters which the Government repudiates with energy; and I, for one, say at once, with truth and with sincerity, you will never persuade the public that a member of the Government or a person connected with the Administration can conduct a campaign in his newspaper contrary to the policy of the Government of the day.[63]

He said Lloyd George had caused 'suspicion and distrust' by including the proprietors in the government:

I tell my right hon Friend what everyone is saying in the Lobbies, outside the House, where men meet, but what I think it is now time for someone to say publicly and as a responsible man in this House. You cannot escape misconception, you cannot escape trouble of this kind as long as you try to combine in the same person the functions of a director of a Press which asserts its independence and a member of a Government who owes loyalty to the Government. You cannot do the two things.[64]

He added:

You would not allow a colleague not the owner of a newspaper to go down and make speeches contrary to the policy of His Majesty's Government or to attack men who are serving His Majesty's Government. You cannot allow them, instead of making speeches, to write articles or to permit articles to be written in their newspapers. My right hon Friend and his Government will never stand clear in the estimation of the public, and will never have the authority which they ought to have, and which I desire them to have, until they make things quite clear, open, and plain to all the world and sever this connection with the newspapers.

Several serving officers added their condemnations to Chamberlain's. Colonel Sir Harry Verney attacked the 'discreditable and dangerous alliance with the Northcliffe Press' that the government had fostered, and said it 'looked like a dirty business'.[65] Major Walter Guinness spoke of the 'extraordinary indignation' felt by soldiers in France for which 'the Government . . . have only themselves to blame.' Colonel Claude Lowther asserted that newspapers run by Northcliffe, Rothermere and

Beaverbrook would be loyal to the government that both men now served: an interesting assumption. Colonel Martin Archer-Shee referred to a claim by Beaverbrook about the Second Battle of Ypres, that British troops had 'deserted' the Canadians there, and thundered: 'I say that to make a man capable of making a statement like that, which I venture to say was a gross libel on our troops, and absolutely inaccurate, Director of Propaganda in this country, on top of having been smothered with honours before, is to my mind also a matter which does not inspire one with trust in the Government.'[66]

Chamberlain was consistent: three weeks later, at a dinner at Carson's house, he announced to the assembly (including Milner and Amery, who recorded it in his diary) that it had been an act of 'infamy' to promote Beaverbrook and Northcliffe and 'if he and Carson liked to combine in a resolution on the subject, the Government would collapse.'[67] Milner warned him 'he was barking up the wrong tree.' No such challenge was issued. Beaverbrook took issue with him privately, but Chamberlain fought back: the 'connection between the Govt and the Press . . . destroys the independence of the Press and involves the Govt in responsibility for all the opinions expressed in the Press.'[68] But he also feared an attempt to 'nobble' the press by ministerial appointments and to facilitate 'subterranean intrigue . . . against servants of the Crown and public men.'

The same day the Unionist War Committee, led by Salisbury, passed a resolution demanding the government stop recruiting newspaper proprietors unless those men relinquished control of their businesses. This sufficiently worried Lloyd George that he addressed the committee and, in the privacy of the meeting, conceded that the characters of some he had promoted were not ideal. But he added: 'In these times we must not be squeamish. For dirty work give me the dirty man.'[69] Chamberlain felt that 'Lloyd George bamboozles the House too easily and they don't make him sweat for his offences as they should.'[70] Chamberlain's critique, both in the Commons and around society, of Lloyd George's methods had rattled the prime minister. It was highly accurate and carried great weight, coming from a man of uncontested probity; and Chamberlain had great clout in the Unionist Party, on whose support Lloyd George relied to stay in office. Before he addressed the Unionist committee, the prime minister had an hour's private talk with Chamberlain, in which he said 'he had laid it down that any Minister must absolutely dissociate himself from control of a newspaper while in office, and that Rothermere and Beaverbrook had been appointed 'on their merits'. Eventually, on 11 March, he made a public statement to that effect in the Commons. Rather pathetically, he told Chamberlain he had stated 'the other side of the case' to the press because soldiers had 'intrigued' against him. In the House, he absolutely denied that either he, or any official in his name, had 'inspired paragraphs attacking admirals and generals'. He was heard in silence, apart from a cry of 'what about Northcliffe?'[71]

Later that day the House held a long debate on government relations with the press, introduced by Chamberlain, who said he had taken Lloyd George at his word. Others had not, such as Spencer Hughes, a journalist and the Liberal MP for Stockport, and one of the most popular men in the Commons. 'We know that the Northcliffe Press conducted a campaign of insult and slander against the right hon Gentleman the Member for East Fife (Mr Asquith),' Hughes recalled. 'That was a proceeding on the part of these papers which I regarded not only as deplorable, but as detestable. I have sometimes wished, when I read those criticisms of public men, that we could have the man who wrote the article produced, and put by the side of the man he assailed. Let us judge which of the two has rendered the country and the Empire the greater service.'[72] Hughes then quoted an unnamed editor on the state of the contemporary British press:

> We have never hesitated to stand up for the light when we felt that public opinion was with us. We have always protested against the wrong when we saw it to be unpopular. We have stated the truth when we happened to know the facts, and have never hesitated to resort to fiction when we have been convinced of its superior validity. We have never employed the lumberings and tedious methods of demonstration when we felt we could rely on the credulity of our readers, and we have never asked for gratitude when we have found self-satisfaction the surer road to happiness.

He continued: 'A good many papers are run on those lines to-day. I cannot think it is right that the fate of any public man—statesman or sailor or soldier—should be left in the hands of papers so conducted, nor can I think it right, indeed it is scarcely credible, that the policy of such papers should control or influence in any degree the policy of any Administration which is worthy the name of Government.'[73]

Other members raged about the wickedness of the Northcliffe press: the 'vendettas' against Kitchener, Robertson and Jellicoe were aired, followed by the grudges Northcliffe held against other countries, ordering his editors at different times to write nothing positive about the French, then about the Germans.[74] Inevitably, the faked stories about German corpse factories were mentioned. John McKean, an Irish Nationalist, gave Northcliffe credit for having pioneered aviation, and for ensuring the *Daily Mail* was not a servile organ; but for most MPs the opportunity to attack him was long overdue. Another Nationalist, Arthur Lynch, summed up the widespread feeling: 'I do not think that this Government is strong enough even against unjust pressure of the Northcliffe press. The Northcliffe press is their mother and their father, the Government has been nursed, fostered and spoon-fed and brought up to its doubtful maturity by the Northcliffe press. What the Northcliffe press has made it can unmake, and to-day the Government dare not have an opinion contrary to the Northcliffe press.'[75]

Pringle openly accused the prime minister of having fed the press, especially Northcliffe's, with stories disobliging to his rivals while climbing to the prime ministership. When Lloyd George spoke – he regarded the matter as of such personal importance that he paid one of his increasingly rare visits to the Commons – he ignored such accusations but defended Beaverbrook, his new minister. 'Since the appointment I have seen men who have come to me, and criticised this appointment. I have said to them, "Would you mind giving me the name of anyone who would do it better?" I have never had an answer up to the present.'[76]

Northcliffe in fact did his job well. He was constantly hampered by a series of respiratory illnesses in the spring of 1918, but worked hard to flood Germany with propaganda about its responsibility for the war, and the probability of its defeat. He enlisted Wells to help. At a meeting on 31 May it was agreed the threat of eventual starvation through blockade should be matched by the promise of the prosperity of peace, overseen by a League of Nations – one of Wells's pet ideas, given his commitment to world government. The matter was referred up to Balfour, and was stuck for weeks in the Foreign Office machine; though even existing propaganda leaflets were held back for want of planes from which to drop them over enemy lines. Wells soon became disillusioned, and Northcliffe struggled to rein him in, promising to take up the organisational failures with Beaverbrook.

Censorship, to which the press fell victim, continued to irritate. In March 1918 one of the official war artists, Christopher Nevinson, tried to show his painting *Paths of Glory* at an enormously successful exhibition of war art in the Leicester Galleries in London; it showed two dead Tommies lying in a blasted landscape. He was told that under DORA he could not depict dead British soldiers, so he put a diagonal piece of brown paper across the painting covering them up, with the word CENSORED emblazoned on it. This also caused trouble, because that word was allowed to be used only by official sanction. Later in the year a painting of two dead Germans in a trench, by Sir William Orpen, created no difficulties precisely because the corpses were German. Although the war had arrested the Vorticist movement early on, since 1914 painters had put their skill at the nation's disposal. Wellington House commissioned war artists including Nevinson, John Lavery, Paul Nash and Eric Kennington to visit the front and paint it.[77] The results were not explicit, and often romanticised: they were, after all, part of the propaganda effort, hence Nevinson's difficulty when he crossed the line into realism. The depiction of acts of heroism, in paintings or in the various periodicals describing the war that the public lapped up, was highly popular. Illustrations by those such as Bert Thomas – best remembered for his cheeky, pipe-smoking Tommy saying 'Arf a "mo", Kaiser!' as he lit up, featured in magazines and on a rich variety of posters for recruitment and national savings.

One key case of censorship reached the courts. Having walked out of *The Times*, Repington moved to the *Morning Post*, where he would become, with Gwynne's support, a one-man campaign against his ex-proprietor's ideas on military strategy. He told St Loe Strachey that he considered Lloyd George and Northcliffe 'a curse to the country' and, ironically like the prime minister, thought the Army Council should have the latter taken out and shot.[78] Repington's first article in his new paper, on 24 January, discussed the 'procrastination and cowardice of the Cabinet'. It had not been through the censor, and prompted Lloyd George to demand his prosecution, until his colleagues talked him out of it.[79] On 11 February Repington wrote about the Versailles meeting and how under-resourced the BEF was, given a possible German attack. This time the War Cabinet decided to prosecute, Lloyd George feeling especially vindictive towards anyone who dared illuminate his failures.

He had wanted Repington and Gwynne tried for treason, until his law officers convinced him such a prosecution would fail, and make the Germans think Repington had a point. Repington had imparted nothing of value to the enemy, whose newspapers had given more extensive reports of the Versailles meeting than he had been able to do. Nonetheless two Scotland Yard officers arrived at his Hampstead mansion (whose substantial mortgage had propelled Repington into his new post, as his creditors were circling) the following afternoon to question him, and the next day he was summonsed to appear in court. For the 'technical offence' of printing his piece without passing it through the censor the paper was fined £100, and Repington the same amount. This disappointed Lady Bathurst, the *Morning Post*'s proprietrix, who had wished to show solidarity with her employees to the extent where she said she hoped she would be locked up with them.[80] The court case, which brought to Bow Street the largest crowd since the arraignment of Dr Crippen – 'there came to look on a great number of friends and many ladies,' Repington noted – greatly increased his celebrity and authority, precisely what Lloyd George did not need.[81] The Colonel stepped up the vitriolic tone of his articles, much to the prime minister's rage, and would soon have even more scope to do so.

Later in the summer of 1918 a new anti-alien campaign, led by the Northcliffe press, convulsed Britain: the target was naturalised Germans, Austrians and Hungarians who had escaped the great round-up of 1914–15. The campaign was bred by a fear, common that summer, that the war might be lost: it reflected not least a determination to get retaliation in against the Germans before they dictated terms. Northcliffe's newspapers sent correspondents to major cities to whip up, and report, anti-alien feeling. On 30 July 8,000 people filled the Albert Hall, and unanimously passed a resolution demanding immediate internment of all people of 'enemy blood', irrespective of gender, rank or naturalisation.[82] Beresford, who made the keynote speech and who supported the Northcliffe press when it suited him, blamed alien influence for the wave of strikes, what he considered the weakness of the blockade, and various other difficulties for which he could adduce no evidence. Assisting Northcliffe was Noel Pemberton Billing, an independent MP, former officer in the Royal Naval Air Service and an early advocate of the RAF, but also a man who had learned much of what little he knew from Horatio Bottomley.

In 1916 Billing had founded a *John Bull* soundalike periodical called the

Imperialist (later renamed the *Vigilante*), which he had filled with his conspiracy theories, almost all of which involved networks of Jews and homosexuals. He believed the Germans had a list of 47,000 British 'perverts', supposedly including the Asquiths and, inevitably, Haldane, whom they were blackmailing to undertake espionage.[83] In the summer of 1918 he was victor in a notorious libel trial, brought by Maud Allan, an actress, whom he had in a charmingly headlined *Vigilante* article, 'The Cult of the Clitoris', accused of lesbianism (which was true) – or as it was reported, of her having 'associated herself with persons addicted to unnatural practices' – and of conspiring with the Germans (which was not), and being one of that legion of 47,000 perverts.[84] Among those who gave evidence for Billing was Lord Alfred Douglas; Miss Allan – 'lewd, unchaste, immoral' – had made her name as a scantily dressed Salome. The Lord Chamberlain's censor had banned Wilde's play for public performance; Miss Allan had appeared in a private subscription performance.

The case led Curzon, at a meeting of the War Cabinet, to demand press censorship in the case because 'opportunity was being taken to attack every section of society, and the social effect must inevitably be bad'.[85] Sir George Cave, the home secretary, said the judge, Mr Justice Darling, had asked the press not to publish certain parts of the evidence; but had said he could not hold the trial *in camera* because of the 'suspicion and talk which would have arisen outside court' if he had. Billing's eventual victory, won not least by his persistent attacks on the judge, but also by the jury accepting his contention that anyone who acted in *Salome* was manifestly degenerate, was the signal for Northcliffe to take up his allegations, and to demand further round-ups of aliens and their prohibition from coastal areas. There were allegations of people who were really Germans owning banks and businesses, and an 'Intern Them All' campaign.

Northcliffe ordered both his national newspapers to stay on the attack throughout July. He had decided the government would not pursue a proper aliens policy because of Milner's membership of it, and urged the editor of *The Times* to demand a statement about Milner's ancestry. Milner had been born in the Grand Duchy of Hesse in 1854, to British parents, but his father's mother had been Prussian. Several hard-right MPs espoused the cause, asking numerous questions about the alien 'problem'. Frederick Leverton Harris, a junior minister in the Department of Blockade, was harried because his wife had visited an internment camp to see a family friend, Baron Leopold von Plessen. When Cecil, his senior minister, heard a rumour that Law had advised Harris to resign, he wrote to Law that 'if he does I resign too – I had rather sweep a crossing than be a member of a ministry at the mercy of Pemberton Billing and his crew.'[86] Law rowed back; Harris stayed, but chose not to fight the next election. Churchill was furious because some expert scientists at Munitions were of German origin, forcing the War Cabinet to agree that a ban it imposed on aliens working for government departments should be variable 'for definite reasons of national importance.'[87] It was pointed out that many of the soldiers arriving in Britain with the American forces had German parents, or had been born in Germany.

To seek to calm the hysteria, now led not least by local government worthies, Lloyd George formed an Alien Committee. It demanded the internment of all male aliens aged eighteen years and over, the repatriation of all females (or their internment, if repatriation was not feasible), the review of all naturalisations of enemy aliens since 1 January 1914, the removal from public office of anyone with German origins, the banning of aliens from prohibited areas and the closure of all German businesses. The War Cabinet decided that 'no person not a natural-born British subject should be permitted to change his name without a licence, this rule to be made retrospective for the period of the war.'[88] Cave acted on most of the recommendations, though not the removal of aliens from public office, which might have included Milner. An Aliens Investigation Committee, chaired by a High Court judge, examined the circumstances of 6,000 Germans and 18,000 other enemy aliens. The *Mail* attacked the committee for only getting round to questioning 300 of them. The National Party organised rallies to demand mass internments, and to institute local Committees of Public Safety: the party, founded the previous year, organised a 'monster petition' of 1.25 million signatures, on a roll two miles long. A shift of fortunes in France would silence the hysteria.

Beaverbrook, Northcliffe's master at the Ministry of Information, fed up with the Foreign Office blocking his initiatives, put in his resignation on 24 June. Balfour held his ground, saying there could not be two ministers making foreign policy, which is what Beaverbrook, through the messages he wished to insert in propaganda to enemy countries, seemed determined to do. It was, as with Neville Chamberlain's appointment, an example of how Lloyd George's determination to overhaul government caused conflicts, and required him to intervene to solve them – which he lacked time to do. After days of wrangling the government agreed to resume 'bombing' Germans with propaganda leaflets, and Beaverbrook rescinded his resignation. However, complications meant the leaflet drops from aircraft (as opposed to balloons) did not resume until the last days of the war, three months later.

IV

The Supreme War Council met at Versailles on 30 January 1918. It was occupied largely by a discussion about manpower shortages, and the possibility of reducing divisions considerably in size. Lloyd George, who believed he had produced plenty of men for his campaign in the Holy Land – what Repington called his 'insane plan of winning the war by fighting Turks' – asked for the evidence of these shrinking numbers.[89] He and Robertson fell out further when the latter challenged him over the security of the Western Front during the meeting: Lloyd George later berated the CIGS for disagreeing with him in front of foreigners – 'having given his advice in London, it was not necessary for him to have it repeated here.'[90] To be fair to Lloyd George, Robertson seems, in his frustration with the prime minister, to have forgotten a basic truth about the chain of command, which partly explains the prime minister's determination to sideline him, however bad his methods of doing so. Yet Robertson believed in the essential sovereignty of his position as CIGS, and that the British Army should not be in any way under French control or influence: and never diverted from the belief that the war could be won only on the Western Front, with the Germans driven out of territory they illegally occupied.

The press was ordered not to report the Supreme War Council's deliberations, the details of which were also shaped by French resentment at Britain never, in France's view, having pulled its weight on the Western Front. The reason given for the censorship was that the details would help the enemy, but Maurice believed it was 'really to prevent discussion which would be harmful to the government.'[91] The key political point, however, was an agreement between Lloyd George and Clemenceau to give executive powers to the Supreme War Council, allowing it to move British and French troops to wherever on the Western Front seemed most vulnerable. That, for the moment, was kept strictly secret, but rumours soon spread.

Robertson, with support from the King and Asquith that he ought to have realised compromised him even further with Lloyd George, refused to work with the Council, which he correctly saw had been set up as an alternative source of military advice. Lloyd George, on 22 January, had met Stamfordham and made no secret of his dissatisfaction with the Army's leadership. Who would take responsibility for deploying a strategic reserve of thirty divisions, to be formed jointly with the French, had become the main *casus belli*. It was intended that Sir Henry Wilson, as the man in Versailles, would have that power, overriding Robertson, Haig and the Army Council if he chose. Edward Spears, the main liaison officer between the British and French armies, regarded Wilson 'as a man in whom laziness first, then ambition, had destroyed all the military virtues with which he had been endowed.'[92] He also had 'a very arresting personality and a fascinating ugliness of which he was quite proud, boasting that somebody having addressed a postcard to the ugliest man in London it had come straight to him.'[93]

Robertson had told Lloyd George that the CIGS had to retain that power, 'because he was the only person directly responsible to the Army Council and the Government for the British Army.'[94] He would not contemplate any other arrangement, 'because it would involve the handing over of executive power to a committee which would not be responsible for the consequences of its actions.' Robertson expressly felt that his job was not just to give advice; it was to ensure the welfare of the soldiers of the Army of which he was head, and to stop anything that might imperil that welfare. Executive authority had to be accompanied by responsibility: so any Anglo-French strategic reserve would have to be administered jointly by Robertson and Foch. An American and Italian representative would sit on the committee, even though hardly any American soldiers were in Europe, and Italians were deployed only on the Italian front. So there were those on the Supreme War Council with no soldiers in the field who would influence the movement of British and French troops without having to face the consequences.

The Army Council closed ranks against political interference and unanimously endorsed Robertson's view. The idea behind the Versailles plan 'struck at the root of every elementary principle of command'; and the council sent the War Cabinet a memorandum saying so.[95] Lloyd

George had been heavily influenced on this point by Milner, who had supplied the intellectual justification for this change. However, Milner had failed to see, or had ignored, the probability that the military mind would not easily accept a bureaucratic, or technocratic, intervention such as this in its way of doing business. On 9 February, having consulted Derby to try to prevent him resigning, Lloyd George decided to solve the Robertson problem by making him British Permanent Military Representative at Versailles, swapping jobs with Wilson. Haig had told Lloyd George he would not accept Wilson giving orders from Versailles, but was not consulted about the move. Lloyd George told Robertson he would remain a member of the Army Council; he would have equality of status with Foch and with him share responsibility for deploying the strategic reserve; and (in a gesture that said more about Lloyd George than it did about Robertson) would receive a £1,000 annual salary increase, and a house in Paris free of charge. This would create, effectively, a dual command, with Wilson as CIGS, and the two men competing for Lloyd George's ear.

Robertson, who received a formal memorandum from Derby setting out his proposed role on 11 February, declined the job, as his integrity demanded; though Haig urged him to take it because he would, if he became the man at Versailles, essentially be 'Generalissimo'. Although he could not contemplate working with Wilson in that capacity, continuing what would effectively have been his existing relationship with Robertson presented him with no problems.[96] Derby also urged Robertson to stay: 'if I had thought this was derogatory to you I should not have assented'.[97] But Robertson told Lloyd George that to accept it would mean 'he would be accepting a principle which both he and the Army Council had condemned.' Having failed to persuade Robertson not to resign, Haig asked the King to intervene, as 'in the first place it was necessary for all soldiers to work together at this time, and secondly, Robertson might save us from defeat by opposing Lloyd George's desire to send troops to the East against the Turks.'[98] The King never acted in any matter that might require him to criticise his prime minister without consulting Stamfordham; and Haig found the private secretary 'slow in understanding the present situation', a failure perhaps on Haig's part to appreciate that Stamfordham felt this was a fight the King did not need to have and, indeed, constitutionally could not have. If he opposed this executive act by Lloyd George and Lloyd George stuck to his guns he would have no choice but to resign, causing massive destabilisation and undermining all the King's previous efforts to appear to be at one with his people and their elected representatives.

However, on 13 February Stamfordham did express the King's 'surprise' – for which read 'outrage' – that he had not heard of this plan until the preceding day.[99] Lloyd George was certainly angry at the lengths to which Robertson and his comrades had gone to try to thwart him, but as so often when dealing with matters in which the King took a close interest he had made the situation worse by either a lack of courtesy or deliberate concealment of the facts. Stamfordham told Lloyd George 'that the King strongly deprecated the idea of Robertson being removed from the office of CIGS, that his loss in that capacity would be an incalculable one to the Army, would be resented in the country, rejoiced in by the enemy.' Lloyd George told Stamfordham he entirely disagreed; if the King had heard of Robertson being so highly regarded then the opinions must have been fabricated. 'He did not share His Majesty's extremely favourable opinion of Sir William Robertson'; and if that was fighting talk, it paled against what followed – that if the King insisted on Robertson's staying 'the Government could not carry on and His Majesty must find other ministers.'[100] Seeing he was beaten, Stamfordham backed down. He found, also, that Derby (who usually followed the line of least resistance, and had no desire to referee a fight between Lloyd George and Robertson) was so fed up with the CIGS being 'unreasonable' that he simply wanted to resign as war secretary. The King wrote in his diary: 'I am much worried as the PM is trying to get rid of Robertson, if he doesn't look out his Govt will fall, it is in deep water now.'[101]

In the event, Robertson did not resign as CIGS, but was suspended from his post, having been asked by Stamfordham in the name of the King to make the proposed system work. Derby – effectively subordinated to Robertson in not being allowed to communicate with the commander-in-chief without the CIGS's permission – was asked to offer General Sir Herbert Plumer, commanding the Expeditionary Force in Italy, Robertson's job: but did so in terms that, according to Hankey, encouraged Plumer to refuse. Hankey redrafted the offer before it was sent, but Plumer declined anyway, expressing support for Robertson. 'In conversations which took place during the next two days Lord Derby showed that he was now desirous I should remain CIGS,' Robertson recalled, 'and on February 13 he handed me a copy of a note which he had addressed to the Prime Minister proposing that this should be done.'[102] Wilson was to stay at Versailles. So Lloyd George was left in the damaging position of having had two of the most senior generals turn down the job of CIGS because they objected to how the Supreme War Council would operate.

On hearing that Robertson had dug in his heels, Milner – who having shaped Lloyd George's thinking on the Supreme War Council was not willing to see Robertson frustrate it – told Hankey via William Ormsby-Gore, his parliamentary private secretary, that if Robertson did not resign, he would. On 12 February, in remarks on the King's Speech, Asquith attacked Lloyd George over the management of the war, and especially on this aspect of it. Well aware – because both soldiers were briefing him – about what was going on beyond the public gaze, he marked out his territory by asserting that, for all the setbacks of the preceding months, 'nothing . . . has in the least shaken the confidence of the nation and of the Empire in the two great soldiers, Sir Douglas Haig, our Commander-in-Chief, and Sir William Robertson, the head of our General Staff at home.' He elaborated: 'For more than two years, and amidst all those vicissitudes of fortune which during that time have befallen the Allied cause, they have proved over and over again their possession in a pre-eminent degree of the qualities of foresight, tenacity, patience, and unperturbed resolve, which go furthest to win and to retain the trust and loyal devotion of British troops. I am echoing the voice, not only of the House, but of the whole country, when I say that we owe them unstinted gratitude and unwavering confidence.'[103]

Asquith's other, related, concern was that Lloyd George was breaking a promise made when announcing the Supreme War Council, that it would have no executive function; for rumours of what had really happened at Versailles a fortnight earlier were now rife. This brought him back to Haig and Robertson:

The Commander-in-Chief and the Chief of Staff cannot serve two masters. The Chief of Staff can serve only one, and that one ought to be his own Government. Similarly, the Commander-in-Chief ought to get his orders through the Chief of Staff, and through the Chief of Staff alone. I should be very sorry to think that that which seems to me, until I am convinced of the contrary, a sound, practical maxim of carrying on the War, and which was recognised in the original constitution and definition of the functions of this Council, has been abandoned or seriously modified.'[104]

Asquith taunted Lloyd George about rumours of changes at the top of the Army, and hoped he would get a 'plain and definite answer'.[105] In a practised *de haut en bas* tone, and exercising mockery with which many of his colleagues were unfamiliar, he continued: 'I rule out as absolutely irrelevant in matters of this kind the wretched personal rivalries, intrigues, and squabbles, if such there be, of which we read. They are beneath notice, and I cannot believe—and until I have overwhelming evidence to the contrary I will not believe—that considerations of that kind can influence the action either of politicians or of military men.' He knew that was exactly what was happening, and that the national interest was not being put first.

As so often on important occasions, the prime minister was run-down and ill with a cold, and the government looked incompetent and ill at ease. He tried to accuse Asquith of discourtesy for not having given him notice of his questions. He told what was at best a half-truth about Haig and Robertson's acceptance of the Versailles system: 'Complete unanimity was reached,' he claimed.[106] 'There was not a division of opinion on any resolution that was come to.' He prevaricated about the Supreme War Council, alleging that he might disclose important information to the enemy were he to give Asquith the detailed answer he wanted; Asquith challenged him on this, and disputed it hotly. Asquith's supporters heckled and interrupted Lloyd George, and the more they did, the shiftier he appeared. His means of running the war were not commensurate with being held accountable by Parliament and abiding by its traditions of honour.

He blustered that those from the four Allied nations who took part in the Versailles conference had agreed not to speak publicly about its conclusions; he accused his predecessor of seeking to discuss 'military decisions', which Asquith protested was not what he wanted at all. At this, Lloyd George lost his temper: 'When you are conducting a war, there are questions which a Government must decide. The House of Commons, if it is not satisfied, has in my judgment but one way of dealing with the situation; it can change that Government.'[107] There then followed the key lie. George Lambert, an Asquith loyalist, interrupted and asked: 'Did Sir Douglas Haig and Sir William Robertson approve those decisions?' And Lloyd George answered: 'Certainly; they were present there, and all those representatives approved.' More of Asquith's friends taunted him, about how rumours concerning the disregard in which Haig and Robertson were held were being sown by Downing Street, and how the leading mischief-maker, Northcliffe, was acting with impunity. Lloyd George denounced this 'unmitigated falsehood' and claimed to have been 'fighting hard against these paragraphs appearing in the press.'[108] He did not convince. MacDonald proclaimed that 'the House must have been very deeply impressed with the failure of the Prime Minister's speech this afternoon,' and no one gainsaid him.[109]

Lloyd George saw Robertson again, and the General told him he would accept reduced powers if he stayed as CIGS. Lloyd George, unwilling to be seen as Northcliffe's poodle, still felt he could not sack him. Hankey told the prime minister of Milner's restiveness; he asked the cabinet secretary to calm him down. Milner said he would accept Robertson's continuation in post provided he loyally executed policies agreed at Versailles, and that it was made public that he had turned down the job there. However, on 14 February Robertson again declined either to stay in his post or to go to Versailles. He attended the War Cabinet by invitation and said that as it seemed reluctant to accept his advice, it should sack him as its Supreme Military Adviser; but if it did not, he wondered whether it would be 'wise or fair' to retain him to run a system 'which he regarded as dangerous and unworkable'.[110] Fearing the implosion of his administration, Lloyd George sent Balfour and Derby to talk Robertson round; though Balfour, despite Hankey's briefing him about what he was to say, had the wrong end of the stick and never properly made the offer. Derby was so annoyed at Robertson's treatment that he was minded to resign; Haig urged him not to, for he feared Northcliffe would succeed him if he did.

The King, always loyal to Haig and Robertson, made his feelings known. Lloyd George, who usually managed to pretend to be courteous when dealing with royalty, told Stamfordham irascibly that the Monarch 'was encouraging mutiny by taking up the cause of those officers . . . whom the Government has decided to get rid of.'[111] Stamfordham, shaken by this direct assault, assured Lloyd George the King had no such intention. Robertson – one of those officers – wrote to Lloyd George on 16 February to outline how his 'conscience' would not allow him to do as the prime minister wished.[112] He warned Lloyd George that 'the method you have decided to adopt must prove unworkable and dangerous.' Nevertheless, the War Cabinet was then told, the same day, that a statement would be issued announcing Robertson's resignation, and his replacement by Wilson; Lloyd George had made up his mind to act in a dictatorial fashion. The King was appalled: 'I don't trust him,' he wrote of Wilson.[113] Curzon, who was absent, was feared to be contemplating resignation, and Hankey was ordered to contact him by special messenger.

Robertson claimed the official statement told two falsehoods. It said he had refused to stay with reduced powers, which he had not, and that he had resigned, which he also had not. Nor did it give his reasons for refusing to go to Versailles, namely that he believed the system to be unworkable. At one point Lloyd George had asked him, a senior general of two years' standing, to become deputy at Versailles to Wilson, whom he outranked: this slight was not mentioned.

Lloyd George bracketed Haig with Robertson, but having forced out the latter had no plan to get rid of the former, even though he had considered various generals as suitable to succeed him. The South African general and War Cabinet member Jan Smuts, who was Lloyd George's favourite soldier and who as an outsider could keep historical ideas about personality out of his judgements, advised Lloyd George to keep Haig as, he felt, there was no one better. The prime minister's next encounter with Haig can hardly have convinced him that this judgement was correct. On the evening of 16 February Haig arrived in London, determined to see Lloyd George, and straight from a meeting of Army commanders in France where he had learned of the greatly increased strength of the German forces and 'that we must be prepared to meet a very severe attack at any moment now.'[114] Such a contradiction of the wild view he had expressed in early January can have done nothing to enhance his credibility in Downing Street – even though this time he would be proved right. Derby met him at Victoria station and told him Wilson had replaced Robertson. Haig can have been under no illusion that Robertson had been forced out; first thing the next morning – a Sunday – Robertson saw Haig and told him he felt Derby had not been 'quite straight'.[115] Nevertheless, he seemed determined to accept the official version of events and to make no fuss about it, perhaps in case a protest led to his own dismissal by a trigger-happy prime minister.

Derby then took Haig to Lloyd George's house at Walton Heath, which Haig thought 'reminds me of summer lodgings at the seaside'. Lloyd George was resting when they arrived. Once he appeared, Haig stressed he had never approved any of the arrangements they were discussing, but would implement them loyally now they were cabinet policy. Lloyd George left the room temporarily, which gave Derby the opportunity to tell Haig that the Field Marshal had stated his position 'quite clearly', and that the war secretary at least was in no doubt about Haig's objections to the new system. Derby then promised Haig that if the prime minister 'made any mis-statement regarding me [Haig] in the House of Commons on this subject, he was prepared to get up in the House of Lords and deny it flatly.' Unity of Allied command might have been established, but that was all.

Haig was asked to see Wilson and discuss who should assume Wilson's vacated post at Versailles. It went to Sir Henry Rawlinson, with which Haig was happy. Derby felt compromised by the events of which he had just had a mainly spectating part. He saw Haig that evening and again said he was thinking of resigning, a view he had also expressed to the King, who had agreed that resignation was the best course. Derby duly prepared to carry out his threat. Haig urged him to stay for the good of the Army; Law also pressed Derby to stay, and Hankey deterred Long (angry at Robertson's treatment) from resigning as colonial secretary. Had they gone just as Beaverbrook was entering the government, and as Northcliffe was being given an official post, the unrest caused by Robertson's departure could have fatally undermined the government. However, by 17 February Haig's personal narrative had become that his main concern was not Robertson but 'only whether I was satisfied with the proposed arrangement for giving me orders.'[116] Rawlinson was content that, as he was a member of the Army Council, any instructions he gave to Haig would constitute 'lawful commands'.[117] If Robertson had relied on Haig as reinforcement in the political game, he would have been disappointed; Haig, when it came to deciding whether to put his own job on the line to save Robertson's, was found wanting. But then, apart from not being a gentleman, Robertson had committed the ultimate crime of being bested by Lloyd George.

The next morning, as Derby (having vacillated) decided not to leave the government, Robertson 'read in the morning papers that he had resigned.'[118] Asquith demanded an explanation, but Law said Lloyd George could not attend the Commons because of 'a very severe chill'; he hoped to come the following day.[119] Law took pains to see Haig that morning, to tell him what Lloyd George proposed Law should say about Haig in a statement he had asked him to read out in Parliament that afternoon: that Haig found the new arrangements 'a workable scheme'.[120] Haig was not having that. 'I said that was not my opinion because I thought it a bad scheme and unsound since it set up two authorities who would give me orders, i.e., dual control.' He noted: 'He must not say that I thought the scheme was workable but that I will do my best to work under it.' Law understood Haig's point, and did not misrepresent him. David-son, Law's secretary, told Hankey to phrase the statement as Haig had suggested.[121]

The statement also announced that Robertson had accepted com-mand of the Eastern Division, which prompted James Hogge, one of Asquith's partisans, to ask why he had not been offered command of the Boy Scouts. The next day Lloyd George made his promised statement. What he did not say – but what Hankey wrote in his memoirs – was that the only remarkable thing was how Robertson had lasted so long. Hankey felt he was 'the embodiment of much which the Prime Minis-ter had come into office to get rid of.'[122] The General had survived because he enjoyed great popularity among servicemen and politicians. It was only now that Lloyd George finally felt sufficiently authoritative to dispose of a CIGS with whom he disagreed profoundly on matters of strategy. Robertson had the last laugh: 'The Executive Committee completely broke down as soon as put to a practical test, and on March 26 it was replaced by a generalissimo, General Foch, who retained that post until the end of the war.'[123] Robertson would be shabbily treated by Lloyd George after his departure: the peerage he might have expected was never forthcoming, and he was paid a war bonus small compared with that of other senior generals. So much of his assessment of strategy would be justified by the events of the last months of the war that it must have irked Lloyd George even to think about it: his own grasp of strategy, as seen from his concern with side-shows, was dismal.

Having dealt with Robertson but feeling unable to be rid of Haig, Lloyd George decided instead to starve him of troops, so he could not launch another offensive; but this also meant that Lloyd George had to take responsibility for starving the Western Front of sufficient men to defend it, a point that seems barely to have occurred to him any more than the real reason for the shortage of troops occurred to Haig. Wilson, as the new CIGS, shared (wilfully or otherwise) Lloyd George's blindness to the dangers now facing the Allies on the Western Front. When on 4 March Maurice told Wilson he expected an attack by the Germans around Cambrai, Wilson disagreed. Whether this was because he genuinely believed it, or knew of Lloyd George's views and wished to avoid a confrontation with him, one can only conjecture – though Lloyd George had a month earlier sent Smuts and Hankey to the Western Front to inspect the state of readiness against such an attack. The new command system was not perfect, partly because Haig was determined to be his own man: in March Lloyd George learned that he and Pétain had been engaging in freelance policy-making about the deployment of troops between the Western Front and Italy.

Throughout late February more intelligence reached the War Office about German divisions moving to the line. Yet as Maurice recorded on the 28th, 'ministers still disinclined to believe in attack on Western front.'[124] By the middle of March questions were being asked in the Commons about the shift in the war caused by German armies 'massing' in the west: yet the government affected to ignore the problem.[125] Maurice told them an offensive would be ready by 15 March and would probably take place around Cambrai. The weather was exceptionally dry for the spring, which only added to the chance of an attack. Four days later Maurice told Wilson he was 'certain' the attack would come; Wilson told him that there was no point the Germans trying to attack through the devastated area of the Somme.[126] On 12 March Wilson amplified this advice to the War Cabinet, saying there was no certainty of an attack. 'The Germans are not piling up divisions in the West for fun,' Maurice noted.[127] Yet Haig, summoned to London on 14 March, noted with the zeal of a convert how Lloyd George and Law 'did their best to get me to say that the Germans would not attack.'[128] Haig then had another example of Lloyd George's pathological dishonesty. 'The PM remarked that I had "given my opinion that the Germans would only attack against small portions of our front." I said that I had never said that.'

Haig emphasised that if he were a German general, drunk on the success of closing down the Eastern Front, he would attack. He told the coalition leaders that 'we must be prepared to meet *a very strong attack indeed on a 50 mile front, and for this drafts are urgently required.*' Even without such an assault, he feared he would be 100,000 men short by June.[129] Lloyd George ignored him, agreeing only not to ask for any of Haig's divisions to be withdrawn to form a general reserve, a suggestion from Versailles. Not every minister was complacent: Churchill realised the Western Front was dangerously under-defended and started to urge Lloyd George to send Haig more troops from those being massed in England. The prime minister's continued refusal, coupled with a War Office decision to keep a reserve of 120,000 at home – a decision assisted by Haig's often-expressed belief that his Army could resist easily for eighteen days any attack thrown at it – would bring Britain within inches of losing the war.

At 4.43 a.m. on 21 March 1918 the German offensive began, just in front of Cambrai as Maurice had predicted, at the junction of French and British armies where the German high command had deemed the front was weakest, and in fog. The enemy deployed seventy-six divisions against twenty-six divisions of British infantry and three of cavalry: eight more were in reserve. The Americans had not yet reached the front in sufficient numbers to make a difference, and were not deployed. There were enormous British casualties on the first day, when the Germans advanced four and a half miles, taking almost as much ground as the Allies had in the entire Battle of the Somme: over 7,000 killed and 10,000 wounded, but also 21,000 taken prisoner. The Germans suffered heavy losses too, with nearly 11,000 killed and 29,000 wounded, but only 300 taken prisoner.[130] Repington noted that 'only the valour of the British soldier can atone for the follies of the War Cabinet.'[131] Wilson, having been proved wrong to rubbish the idea of such an attack, told the War Cabinet on the morning it began that it was possibly 'nothing more than a big raid'.[132] When Maurice had told him it was under way he simply could not believe it. His biographer, Major General Sir Charles Callwell, tactfully observes that it must have taken some time for the 'extreme gravity' of events in France to permeate through to London.[133]

On the contrary, bad news having travelled fast, Law was asked in the Commons that afternoon what the government thought was happening. His reply entirely misrepresented events in Whitehall in the preceding weeks. While admitting that details, at that stage, were few, he added: 'I do feel justified in saying that, as it has not come as a surprise, and as those responsible for our Forces have foreseen and have throughout believed that, if such an attack came, we should be well able to meet it, nothing that has happened gives us in this country any cause whatever for additional anxiety.'[134]

Within days the Germans had gone 40 miles, albeit into an empty space on the desolate Somme battlefield: they occupied little of strategic value. British soldiers trained only for trenches were hopeless in open country, but the ensuing retreat saved many lives. It was not only Maurice who had correctly identified where the attack would come. According to Hankey, many senior Allied officers had expected it there: he had travelled to the front with Smuts in early February, and had talked to plenty of them. 'It is one of the decisive moments of the world's history,' he noted in his diary, 'but I think our fellows will hold them up.'[135] It became clear quickly that 'our fellows' would do nothing of the sort. Such was the scale of the retreat that by 23 March Hankey was talking of a 'debacle'; and that afternoon Colonel Walter Kirke of the General Staff, flown in specially from the Western Front, told the War Cabinet there had been perhaps 40,000 British casualties, and the loss of 600 guns including 100 heavy ones.[136] Perhaps most depressing was his remark that the trenches abandoned at the start of the Battle of the Somme were now being made ready for the Army to retreat into.

The War Cabinet discussed removing men from Italy and Palestine, and sending in an Indian division, to bolster the front. It decided, as 'the emergency had arisen', to send the 50,000 eighteen- and nineteen-year-olds committed to home defence to France to reinforce the Army, even though it left the British Isles vulnerable. Astonishingly, given what Intelligence had said for weeks about the build-up of enemy forces, there were also 88,000 men home on leave who would be sent back as fast as they could be moved – about 8,000 men a day. For Wilson, disbelief that the debacle was happening gave way to disbelief at its extent.

In an astonishing spasm of hypocrisy – for he was more to blame than his arrogant and often blinkered commander-in-chief – Lloyd George was furious with Haig, who 'had made no preparation for the attack, notwithstanding that he was warned that it would probably take place exactly as it did.'[137] He believed, however, that Wilson had foreseen it, something entirely contradicted by the evidence. Lloyd George felt his Versailles plan had not been acted upon, with the French bringing up reserves too late. Wilson continued to dupe him, and the War Cabinet, saying on 23 March that he thought the opposing forces 'might be reckoned as approximately equal', even though Maurice reported that there were in fact 191 German divisions against 165 Allied ones, a German superiority of 117,600 in effective rifle strength.[138] No wonder it was Lloyd George of whom Clemenceau said, after the war, that he was 'the greatest liar he had ever met.'[139] Wells, completing his novel *Joan and Peter*, observed in this moment of national despair that 'no Nelson had arisen to save the country, no Wellington; no Nelson or Wellington could have arisen; the country had not even found an alternative to Mr Lloyd George.'[140]

The War Cabinet was 'in a panic and talking of arrangements for falling back on Channel ports and evacuating our troops to England.'[141] Wilson, with reckless understatement, called it 'an anxious day' and admitted that although the French had promised reinforcements these would take three days to arrive.[142] Sir Philip Sassoon, Haig's aide-de-camp, felt he knew exactly where the fault lay. He wrote to Esher on 23 March: 'The situation is a very simple one. The enemy has got the men and we haven't. For two years Sir DH has been warning our friends at home of the critical condition of our manpower; but they have preferred to talk about Aleppo & indulge in mythical dreams about the Americans.'[143] However, Haig – whose own publicity had it that he had worn down the German army in 1916 and 1917 – had never imagined that, unlike the BEF, it could roll his troops over and advance as it had.

The news was markedly worse the next day: even Haig, to that point bullish about the fighting spirit of his men despite their having to retreat, sent a message to Whitehall conceding that 'the situation is serious.'[144] 'They have broken through,' Lloyd George told Riddell, 'and the question is what there is behind to stop them.'[145] Churchill, threatened with losing 25,000 munitions workers with military experience, and Wilson demanded Lloyd George authorise a mass conscription of men over age and in other reserved occupations. The northern part of the front was holding but the retreat in the southern sector was becoming a rout. On 25 March, when *The Times*'s first leader proclaimed 'a grave situation' and called for even greater sacrifices, the War Cabinet began to discuss extending compulsion to Ireland – a measure of the extreme desperation this sudden collapse had caused – and changing the age limits to seventeen and a half at the bottom and fifty at the top.[146] Conscripting men previously medically discharged as unfit for service was also considered. It conceded that 'expert opinion' was 'divided' on 'the probable fighting value of conscripted Irishmen.'[147] Duke, at a War Cabinet meeting on

27 March convened specifically to discuss Irish conscription, argued that the gesture would be pointless: and would unite all shades of Catholic opinion against Britain. It would concentrate 'many dangerous men' in Irish fighting units.[148] He was ignored. The government was more concerned that while it scraped the barrel in Britain, non-conscription in Ireland would cause outrage.

It was also agreed that men aged nineteen and twenty could be released from munitions factories to fight, and by July 120,000 had been: but Churchill fought, successfully, against releasing any more. The Germans were now rampaging across the Somme battlefield, despite its being the most difficult territory to overrun, full of craters and other obstacles. Hankey concluded that they could only be doing so well because the British were exhausted. There was a further drive to get women into the war effort – particularly, as summer approached, on the land. On 2 May an appeal was made for 50,000 'girls' for farm work. Those who responded were assured they would be properly billeted and have 'at least' a shilling a day in their pockets once all had been found: but even their numbers were running low.[149]

Lloyd George, although ostensibly calm and resolute, feared 'disaster'; but not everything was going Germany's way, and Churchill sought to stiffen him. 'Even if the land war collapsed the sea, the air, & the United States will give us the means of victory. But now is the time to risk everything.'[150] Furthermore, despite the Allies being driven into retreat, the main strategic objective of the attack – to separate the British and French armies – did not succeed. There was also a tremendous success in arms production: in each of the three months after the German advance Woolwich Arsenal produced 48 million small-arms rounds, which entailed some of its employees working 100 hours a week.[151] By this stage 3.4 million people, three-quarters of a million of whom were women, were working in munitions. The system for manufacturing arms and ammunition was now so efficient that supply easily met demand, and made a key contribution to the eventual turning of the tide on the Western Front.

Even an appalling civilian tragedy could not undermine this superlative work. On 1 July 1918 eight tons of TNT blew up at the National Shell Filling Factory at Chilwell in Nottinghamshire, the most productive such factory in Britain. It made 19 million shells between 1915 and the Armistice. The explosion killed 134 people; only 32 could be identified, because of bodies being blown to pieces. Another 250 were injured. The blast was heard 30 miles away, and was the worst ever disaster in Britain caused by an explosion. It was three days before an official announcement was made, and the censor heavily restricted press coverage. Churchill, as the responsible minister, sent a telegram praising the morale of the factory workers; the managing director of the plant replied that their only concern was to maintain the war effort. Work resumed the next day. Lord Chetwynd, who had founded and designed the factory after the shell shortage in 1915, claimed the explosion was the work of saboteurs. It seems more likely it was caused by failure to observe safety procedures while working with an inherently unstable substance on a hot day, as the factory strove to beat its own production records.

Further evidence of this new industrial superiority came from closer to home. On 19 May London witnessed its biggest air raid of the war: forty-three German bombers attempted it but thirteen either crashed or were shot down. However, it would also turn out to be its last. Because of shortages of materials the planes had been poorly constructed, and were more liable to be destroyed. The raid claimed forty-nine lives with one hundred and seventy-seven people injured, and several villages in Kent and Essex were bombed. From then on, the deteriorating German position demanded the use of the aircraft on the Western Front. This, too, was down to greater efficiency in manufacturing aircraft in Britain for the RAF. In 1914 just 245 planes had been manufactured; in 1918 the total was 32,018, more than twice the 1917 figure.[152] The air superiority this conferred on the Allies became another crucial factor in reversing the German advance. Also, at a meeting of the Imperial War Cabinet in London in June, Lloyd George highlighted the far smaller shipping losses, the superior anti-submarine campaign of the Royal Navy and internal strife caused by food shortages in Germany and Austria: there were reasons for optimism.

French, still settling scores with Haig, offered his political masters another analysis when invited to the War Cabinet on 26 March. He said Haig was 'no judge of men, had surrounded himself with stupid people and bad commanders . . . Haig had badly let down the Army in shattering it in the hopeless Flanders offensive.'[153] Haig, writing on 26 March, indicated that he believed the Germans had twenty-five divisions in reserve; such an assertion, uttered at a time when the Germans had made the war mobile again, only confirmed the desperate need to find more men. This was great even though the French were now pouring men into the sector against the Germans, thus slowing them down – not least because the enemy were, for the first time since September 1914, within 75 miles of Paris, which huge guns were now bombarding even from that distance.

V

The main damage that French did at the War Cabinet's 26 March meeting, however, was idiotically to advise ministers that conscription could be applied to Ireland with relative ease, with only a few more troops required there 'to maintain order'.[154] This contrasted greatly with the Irish view. W. B. Yeats wrote to Haldane in April, 'because you are a man of letters, and we, therefore, may speak the same language.'[155] He continued: 'I have met nobody in close contact with the people who believes that conscription can be imposed without the killing of men, and perhaps of women . . . there is in this country an extravagance of emotion which few Englishmen, accustomed to more objective habits of thought, can understand. There is something oriental in the people, and it is impossible to say how great a tragedy may lie before us.' Yeats called the apparent frame of mind of the British government 'strangely trivial', its policies based on having canvassed opinion from those who knew the Irish least. He feared that if the determination to make Irishmen die for England continued, 'all the work of my lifetime . . . to clarify and sweeten the popular mind, will be destroyed and Ireland, for another hundred years, will live in the sterility of her bitterness.' Nor was it just the Irish who felt that. Duke was deeply opposed to conscription, and indeed Lloyd George had until recently agreed with him. He had told Riddell in February 1917 that Irish conscription would recruit just 160,000 men, but only 'at the point of a bayonet' and many would claim a conscientious objection.[156] As with the majority of Lloyd George's opinions, this would prove fluid.

Desperate to find more conscripts, the War Cabinet took counsel about Ireland beyond French's. It should have been alerted by the view of Brigadier General Sir Joseph Byrne, head of the Royal Irish Constabulary, that to proceed with the Bill would be 'a mistake'; and by the 'grave doubts' harboured by Duke, who observed at the War Cabinet on 27 March that 'we might almost as well recruit Germans'.[157] General Sir

Bryan Mahon, the General Officer Commanding, Ireland, said conscription could be enforced, 'but with the *greatest* difficulty.' Mahon said extra troops would be required not just to implement compulsion, but to impose martial law, which would be required to control an enraged Ireland after the law was imposed. Oddly, none of the senior officers asked how any man forced to join the British Army would be made to accept military discipline or to fight, since an attempt to force them at the point of a rifle would presumably end in mutiny. French, naively, believed the men drilling for Sinn Féin could be turned into fine British soldiers if only they could be removed from the poisonous influence of their leaders.

Lloyd George had earlier rationalised the government's failure to conscript Irishmen, arguing that many of them were producing food or working in factories, which was often as vital. Now, however, he dismissed half-measures, not because of the gravity of the situation in France, but because imposing conscription was essential if the Tories were to embrace Home Rule: something Sir Horace Plunkett thought 'madness'.[158] In a full-dress panic after the initial success of the German offensive, the prime minister seemed under some sort of delusion; when the cabinet considered the Irish Convention report on 6 April, which was supposed to provide a pathway to a settlement in Ireland, he glossed over the fact that the sizeable minority who opposed its findings were all Unionists, and that the report came to no new conclusions beyond the Nationalist majority wanting Home Rule. He told his colleagues that even Sinn Féin (who had ignored the proceedings) would have accepted the report, had it given Ireland fiscal autonomy. An equal state of delusion was driving him to demand Irish conscription, against which the convention, in a rare show of unanimity, also warned the government.

The Tories would not see why, when every available man in Britain was being called up, the Irish were not: but that was a wilful disregard of political reality. They were shocked by talk of an immediate announcement of Home Rule to sweeten the conscription pill: in that regard they had not moved on from the summer of 1916, when they had effectively exercised a veto that had only encouraged the success of Sinn Féin. Friends of Lloyd George, notably Scott, had warned him against such a move: 'It is no part of statesmanship and must destroy all hope of a conciliatory policy in Ireland,' Scott wrote to him on 7 April. It would, not least, sabotage all hope of the Irish Convention achieving anything.

Events continued to conspire against a happy outcome: Redmond, the leader and personification of constitutional Nationalism, had died after a long period of poor health on 6 March. He had been paid extravagant tribute in London, where a funeral service was held at the Brompton Oratory, but in Dublin the obsequies were, according to Midleton, 'perfunctory'. Dillon succeeded him as Nationalist leader; but the party was evaporating as Sinn Féin grew stronger, despite faltering in some spring by-elections. As Midleton said of Redmond, 'his death was used to quash his policy.'[159] The old, constitutional Irish Nationalism was effectively buried with Redmond.

The convention report, with its unanimous opposition to conscription, was made public on 8 April. Lloyd George nonetheless announced that policy the next day; it was the latest in a series of blunders in relation to Ireland since Asquith's handing over of Irish rule to General Maxwell. It came the day after intelligence that de Valera would welcome conscription so Sinn Féin 'could undertake systematic and violent opposition to its enforcement.'[160] The government would, though, deny the existence of a quid pro quo in order to avoid exposing the split in the cabinet, or suggesting conscription was not important in itself; but on 11 April the War Cabinet ordered the immediate drafting of a Home Rule Bill.[161]

Lloyd George shared his intentions on Irish conscription in a debate on manpower in the Commons: 'When an emergency has arisen, which makes it necessary to put men of fifty and boys of eighteen into the Army in the fight for liberty and independence . . . I am perfectly certain it is not possible to justify any longer the exclusion of Ireland.'[162] Dillon shouted: 'You will not get any men from Ireland by compulsion – not a man.' The prime minister read out a declaration made by the Nationalists in 1914 that they were prepared to support 'a war for the defence of the sacred rights and liberties of small nations, and the respect and enlargement of the great principle of nationality.'[163] Alfred Byrne, an Irish Nationalist, observed pointedly: 'We have had a revolution since then.'

Dillon said he would have supported conscription had Ireland been allowed to decide her own fate. What had begun as a war to defend small nationalities had become, to the Irish, a war in which they felt the need to defend their own nationality against the English. Lloyd George could not admit that the mishandling of the Rising and its aftermath, in which he had played such a central part, had gravely limited his room for

manoeuvre. When he said Irish conscription would be introduced by
Order in Council 'as soon as arrangements are complete', William O'Brien,
the veteran Nationalist MP for Cork, called out: 'That is a declaration of
war against Ireland.'[164] His colleague Michael Flavin added: 'And against
Irishmen all over the world.' Lloyd George then announced that 'we
intend to invite Parliament to pass a measure for self-government in Ireland,' but Byrne told him: 'You can keep it.' The prime minister said each
of the proposals would have to be judged on its merits as they were not
conjoined; he ignored the (correct) claim that a non-sectarian subcommittee of the convention had unanimously opposed conscription in
Ireland. Hankey, watching from the gallery, felt it a poor speech, not least
because of Lloyd George's weak grasp of detail. 'It was not the trumpet
call of a leader to the nation, which the moment demands.'[165] He noticed
how much Lloyd George – who had become fifty-five the previous
January – had aged in the previous year: 'His hair has turned almost
white,' he recorded.

Asquith (who, Hankey thought, did 'much better') wished to reserve
his opinion on Lloyd George's suggestions. But he feared that 'never, in
my judgment, since the War broke out, has this country been face to face
with anything like so grave a situation as that which at this moment
confronts us.'[166] Lloyd George had refused to disclose casualties; Asquith
said he did not doubt it would be 'the most serious casualty list in the
whole of this war', given what he assumed were the numbers of guns
and prisoners taken in the massive advance. He asked Lloyd George to
think carefully about calling up middle-aged men, many of whom were
struggling to run businesses denuded of younger men by the earlier call-
up, and whose livelihoods might disappear if they went to fight, even if
they survived. He did not talk about Ireland; but others in the debate
did, and the mood turned ugly as Unionists and Irish Nationalists
insulted each other about Ireland's loyalty to the Crown and to civilised
values, or lack of it. Dillon, in one of the more reasonable contributions,
asked of Lloyd George: 'Whom should he consult before he came to this
decision? Have the War Cabinet consulted one single Irish representative? If so, let him name the man. Is that his idea of liberty, that he is to
apply Conscription to Ireland, and the War Cabinet are to decide on that
question, without consulting one solitary representative of the people of
Ireland? That is worse than Prussianism.'[167]

The views of the convention had, he emphasised, been completely ignored; and he said that in forty years in public life he had never known so serious a situation in Ireland as it now faced. He railed at Lloyd George: 'You take a decision which plunges Ireland into bloodshed and confusion, and opens up a new war front, in addition to the Eastern and Western Fronts. You do that with a light heart, without consulting one solitary representative of Ireland or without reading the Report of your own Convention . . . I hope that for the sake of the country, and for the sake of this Empire, that [sic] the methods of the War Cabinet are somewhat different, in dealing with the War, from their methods in dealing with Ireland.'[168] Dillon was furious that instead of a separate measure imposing conscription on Ireland, it had been 'sneaked' into an English Bill embodying other policies.

Yet perhaps the most scathing criticism came from Captain Daniel Sheehan, Nationalist MP for mid-Cork.

> The one thing above all others which he is succeeding in doing is in uniting all Nationalist opinion in Ireland in resistance against this proposal. I speak myself with some feeling in this matter as one who, with his family, have humbly borne our part in this War, because we believed the principle for which the Allied side were fighting was righteous and just. Conscription cannot apply to me. Every grown-up member of my family has served. I have lost one son, another has been wounded, a third is at this moment in hospital in France, a brother-in-law has been killed, a nephew-in-law is a prisoner in Germany, and a brother of mine is serving in the Irish Guards. Therefore, I am able to speak with some earnestness and solemnity when I tell the right hon Gentleman the Prime Minister that he is heading, absolutely heading, for disaster if he attempts to apply Conscription to Ireland. There is not an Irishman worthy of his salt who will not resist it, and I say that any service we give in this War for this cause will be voluntarily given – it will flow from conscience and never from compulsion.[169]

He was sure that the proposal would hinder, and not help, prosecution of the war: 'It would take him three Army Corps in Ireland to get one Army Corps out of it.'[170] Sheehan argued, from experience, that recruiting had been killed in Ireland because of the insistence that Irish regiments should have mostly English officers, who lacked sympathy with the soldiers. 'Why, I remember myself, when we were training with the 9th Munster Battalion, which was raised by myself almost to a man, that the adjutant, an English officer, who was a mere insurance clerk in London before the War, declared, because four cadets were sent to our battalion from the 7th Leinsters, "Four more bloody Irishmen coming to your regiment!" '[171] He concluded:

> All the sacrifices which we have made in the past will, by your blundering methods, by your incapacity to understand the country, be rendered nugatory and vain, and you are going to render them more futile than ever. Those of us who have lost our boys believed in the War, and we believed that Ireland deserved better treatment than you are meting out to us in this matter, that we deserved consideration for our national demands . . . I will stoutly resist any attempt to impose Conscription upon my fellow countrymen. Give us national self-government. Give us equal treatment with the treatment you give to your Dominions. We demand that at the very least. Give us these things and we will do the rest, for the Irish instinct never failed to respond to generous treatment.

Sinn Féin did not want equal treatment: they wanted Irish sovereignty. They would not accept conscription because they denied the authority of Britain over Ireland. It would be apparent by the end of the year that Irish Nationalism, in its constitutional form, was dead.

When Asquith spoke in the 9 April debate he demanded unity, to present to the public, the Allies and the world 'an unbroken front'.[172] This could be accomplished, he said, only by avoiding the 'terrible shortsightedness' of 'imposing upon Ireland a measure which, as we know, rightly or wrongly, is obnoxious to a very large number of the Irish people.'[173] This pushed Lloyd George further into a corner. Law asserted that men likely to be called up from Ireland would 'make a difference of military strength'. He suggested over 120,000, when asked to quantify it.[174] However, a sign that the government was having second thoughts came with the admission that Irish conscription would not be automatic, but would wait to be enforced by Order in Council, an idea Duke had put to Lloyd George on 5 April. Law, heckled too, proclaimed: 'we are not going to alter on this matter'. 'Neither are we,' cried an Irishman.[175] Repington thought Lloyd George had 'misled' Parliament and the public, and added:

'I expect that history will find the detachment of over a million men on these futile Eastern campaigns inexcusable.'[176]

On 17 April Plunkett noted: 'For 8 months I struggled to unite my countrymen so that they could inaugurate self-government by a big Irish part in the war. The Government in as many days have successfully united them in a determination not to fight England's battles.'[177] The Bill was enacted the next day; there was no sign of Home Rule. Lloyd George had asked Long to draft a Bill acceptable to all sides, a tall order given that the convention was divided forty-four to twenty-nine over its report, and that the feelings of Britain's new American allies had to be satisfied too. To complicate matters, Long had become a federalist – believing that Irish Home Rule should begin the federalising of the United Kingdom.[178] A large minority of MPs agreed, as did Austen Chamberlain, but most of the cabinet profoundly disagreed, not least because of England's disproportionate size in any federation. Lloyd George thought the notion too radical and insufficiently considered, and it was dropped.

French remained trigger-happy in his desire to enforce the Act, though admitted it 'would not be easy'. General Sir Nevil Macready, the Adjutant General, suggested court-martialling any Irishmen who refused to serve: a grip on reality seems to have been lost. The War Cabinet trod with more caution. The RIC were less sure of success, and Duke maintained that a call-up was simply impossible to organise, and would lead to martial law throughout the whole of Ireland.[179] The Catholic Church became increasingly vocal in opposition to conscription, telling men not to cooperate. It was feared they would ask Catholic RIC officers not to help enforce the Act; they already appeared to have the support of much of the legal profession outside Ulster. There were rumours of a general strike being about to paralyse Ireland; and fears that food supplies from Ireland, on which Britain depended, could be cut off. 'Hatred of England,' Plunkett noted on 1 May, was now 'the all-pervading passion' among the Irish.

This sentiment presented a massive problem even without an attempt to force Irishmen to fight for the King. In February Sir Horace Plunkett, chairman of the convention, had been to London and asked Riddell, as a conduit to Lloyd George, to tell him that 'an early settlement of the Irish question is absolutely essential' because under the 'superficial appearance of being quiet and contented' Ireland concealed 'a seething mass of rebellion which may break out at any moment.'[180] The Ulstermen were 'intractable and unyielding', and Plunkett felt that while the convention rather than the government should settle the question, so that those who designed the settlement had the responsibility of executing it, some coercion would be necessary. Plunkett had noted in his diary on 11 January that 'Carson is supreme in cabinet', which Duke had hinted to him was the main obstacle to progress.[181] On his February visit Plunkett told Law that Ulster's attitude was 'indefensible' and that 'the Gov't must intervene. A democratic settlement must be forced.'[182]

Having consigned the fate of Ireland to the convention, Lloyd George had been free to occupy himself shaping the Versailles system and disposing of Robertson, which had diverted his attention from the question. The relentless advance of Sinn Féin brought widespread disturbances, with men in prison on hunger strike and, as they were not being force-fed, in appalling health. Lloyd George wrote to Plunkett suggesting fiscal incentives that could be given to a Home Rule state, and picked up on suggestions by the convention for ruling Ulster by a committee within an Irish parliament that could opt Ulster out of measures it disliked. However, Ulster's representatives would not end their opposition to one Irish parliament.

During February 1918 there had been incidents of Sinn Féiners seizing farms and livestock and declaring them the property of the Irish republic, cutting telegraph wires and ambushing the police. *The Times* reported on 25 February that 'it is the bare truth to say that the King's writ has ceased to run in the counties of Clare, Sligo, Roscommon and Mayo, something of which the War Cabinet had been made aware in the preceding days.'[183] The War Cabinet considered interning Sinn Féin activists, but Cave, the home secretary, and Smith, the Attorney General, said that as the likely internees were British subjects it would be hard to prove they had committed 'hostile association'; therefore internment would be legally questionable.[184] Lawlessness in the west of Ireland made it impossible for the convention to appear credible and its decisions workable.

The Lords debated Ireland on 12 March. Salisbury mocked the assertions Curzon had made four months earlier, and which had shown a grotesque unrealism about where Ireland was moving: 'The noble Earl said, speaking of Mr de Valera's speeches, "They are not dangerous to public order, and the extreme Sinn Fein Party is in a minority that becomes smaller instead of larger from day to day". He added: "There is no general prevalence of crime in Ireland. There is no policy of violence in the proceedings of the Sinn Fein party." I wonder whether my noble friend reflects with satisfaction upon those assurances which he gave your Lordships in November of last year.'[185]

Salisbury described an Ireland out of control: masses of young men in uniform brandishing revolvers and tricolour flags on the streets; a rebel army openly drilling; the police at bay; cattle rustling; rebels raiding houses in the search for arms; even an instance of an American flag being torn down and destroyed because of America's alliance with Britain. The worst trouble was in the south and west, in counties such as Kerry, Galway, Tipperary, Limerick and Clare. He was furious that Duke had operated a policy of such weakness, which included hunger strikers being released rather than allowed to die in jail to avoid the manufacture of more martyrs. He argued that no confrontation had been allowed because the government did not wish to sour the atmosphere in which the convention was held. Salisbury felt the government was betraying the law-abiding people of Ireland by its weakness; but in truth they were betrayed, and left to their fate, in April and May 1916. His conclusion applied to a world that no longer existed: 'I urge the Government to exercise that strength which is entrusted to them—that strength to see that law and order are maintained. It has been said that force is no remedy, and, no doubt, force is no remedy against injustice and against maladministration; but force is a remedy against disorder. Indeed, the essential foundation of all government is strength.'[186] The Earl of Meath, who agreed with Salisbury, put a different dimension on the problem: 'My Lords, is it not a terribly sad thing to think that we have practically made no progress during the last fifty years in acquiring the love and affection of the Irish people?'[187] The government could only have changed the course of events in Ireland by blood-soaked coercion, and even that would probably have failed. Most Irish people had, after the mismanagement of the Rising, simply abandoned any faith in constitutional Nationalism.

This loss of faith was particularly the case because any imposition of law and order in Ireland had to be undertaken by the Army. Sinn Féin had instituted a boycott of the RIC that was supposed to leave its officers as social outcasts, but which often veered into violence and intimidation, as in the Land War of the 1880s when the tactic was developed.[188] It had neutered the police. In North Tipperary it was reported, for example, that the RIC 'are practically always confined to their barracks fearing an attack.'[189] In West Cork the attacks were so bad that outposts of the RIC were closed and the force concentrated in more substantial buildings where they could better defend themselves: thus tracts of the country began to be unpoliced. This was a great help to Sinn Féin, as it raided private houses looking for arms.

The prime minister summoned Scott to Walton Heath on 21 April for Sunday lunch and told him 'he was determined to put conscription through in Ireland. He knew there would be trouble – rioting, bloodshed, but it was better to face all that and get it over.'[190] He said there would be no repeat of the drawn-out executions after the Easter Rising: if anyone had to be shot, he would be put up against a wall and shot on the spot, a lesson learned, he said, from the Paris Commune. He dismissed Scott's objection that an army larger than the one that would be recruited would be needed to hold Ireland down while conscription was undertaken. Scott described this attitude as 'entirely reckless'.[191] To Riddell, with whom he was used to a complete and undiplomatic frankness that he did not exert with Scott, Lloyd George admitted over dinner that evening that 'we are in for a big fight with the Irish', and stated his certainty that Sinn Féin was in league with the Germans.[192] 'If Home Rule is granted and the Irish are not prepared to play their part in the defence of the Empire, we must show them that we mean to govern.' Duke had told him the Irish trades unions were mobilising; a one-day general strike on 23 April was widely observed, a portent of the chaos that would ensue if conscription were enforced. De Valera had succeeded in persuading the Catholic Church to have priests read out a statement in every parish on 21 April asserting that conscription was an 'oppressive and inhuman law' to impose upon the Irish, who had 'the right to resist by every means that are consonant with the law of God'. Cardinal Logue, the Archbishop of Armagh, told de Valera: 'When I talk about passive resistance, I don't mean we are to lie down and let people walk over us.'[193]

Duke was exasperated and, imploring Lloyd George not to enforce the policy, offered his resignation, which was accepted on 5 May. Edward Shortt, a Liberal barrister, whose solution – not adopted – was to encourage the Irish to join the French army, replaced him.[194] Wimborne, the Lord Lieutenant, also resigned, as in 1916; but this time for good. The job was offered to Midleton, who turned it down when Lloyd George declined his terms – that conscription had to happen separately from

Home Rule, to avoid annoying Nationalists and Ulster Unionists at the same time and making Ireland ungovernable. Lloyd George told Midleton, with some hyperbole, that these were terms 'which no previous viceroy had ever been accorded'.[195] The job was then offered to French, who agreed with Midleton but felt it his duty as a soldier to accept. He had the great advantages of his passionate belief in conscription and of being an Irishman from an old Roscommon family, albeit born in Kent: but Plunkett dismissed him as 'very unintellectual & not very intelligent.'[196] To provide Ireland, at that time, with what was effectively a military governor was yet another public relations disaster by the supposedly sure-footed Lloyd George. Haldane, a close friend of French, wrote to him to assert the impossibility of imposing conscription, and warned him: 'Remember that coercion has never succeeded and never will succeed in Ireland.'[197] Midleton, visiting French shortly after he took up his post and after the new Lord Lieutenant – or Viceroy, as he preferred to be known – had survived an assassination attempt, noted that 'the conditions under which he had taken office made his task quite impossible.'[198]

Having discussed the issue with the prime minister, Scott thought he knew what drove the policy. He told Dillon:

> You have to bear in mind (i) his love of and exaggerated belief in the value of force; (ii) his eagerness for more men – conscription would at least give him four or five Divisions from Ulster; (iii) his conviction that only by imposing conscription can he carry his Government for Home Rule; (iv) his belief that the Home Rule movement in Ireland has developed, or is developing, into a definitely Separatist movement, and that the question of the control of the Imperial Parliament of the armed forces of the Crown (which includes the raising as well as the use of them) is the touchstone of this.[199]

None of this prevented Scott writing in a leader on 11 May that Lloyd George was on the verge of doing 'some very evil work' and would destroy every advance made in Ireland since Gladstone's day.[200]

French, acting as a quasi-military viceroy, aggravated matters by arresting around 150 prominent Sinn Féin activists on the night of 16–17 May, on the grounds of collaboration with the Germans. The ringleaders, including de Valera, were deported to England. Days passed, with the promised 'evidence' of collusion failing to appear; eventually an account of the enemy's role in the Easter Rising was published, which hardly justified arrests in May 1918. There was, however, a statement by de Valera, in January 1918, that 'so long as Germany is the enemy of England, and England the enemy of Ireland, so long will Ireland be the friend of Germany.'[201] The statement asserted that it had been planned for the Germans to land arms in Ireland, and that documents had been found on de Valera describing 'in great detail' the constitution of his rebel army: and it was claimed there had been activity by U-boats off the west of Ireland that were not seeking to sink merchant shipping.

With the government under increasing pressure to explain its heavy-handed approach, Curzon was eventually brought in to stoke up the rhetoric. In June he told the Lords that Sinn Féin had planned to commit 'treason'.[202] There had been well-documented cases of Sinn Féiners stealing weapons – breaking into houses where guns were kept, attacking policemen for their rifles or sidearms, and stealing explosives from quarries – but this pointed to a further attempt at an uprising, not to a German plot. Yet when asked whether the government intended to put the deportees on trial, Curzon said that that would reveal to the enemy the means by which they and their conspiracy had been discovered. They were interned: evidence beyond assertion remained largely non-existent. As with conscription – the imposition of which would have been even more explosive – the government knew that to start trying Sinn Féiners for treason would be lethally provocative. The aim of the arrests seems to have been to discredit Sinn Féin; it only achieved further strife, but by then it was too late to dampen the rise of republicanism.

French had managed to arrest some of the more moderate members of the movement. This allowed Michael Collins (a member of Sinn Féin's executive, a veteran of the Rising and the Frongoch internment camp, and a London-trained lawyer) and Cathal Brugha (second-in-command of the South Dublin Union during the Rising) to use their freedom to expand their influence in the organisation; they both escaped the authorities' clutches. Lloyd George charged Chamberlain to manage the Irish question. With Sinn Féin still winning by-elections, it was not easy.

The prime minister, as so often, was longer on words than on action, and had to back down from his threats once he saw not just the size of the opposition, but realised he would be opening up another front in the war. Rather than conscription, a version of the Derby scheme was introduced in Ireland on 15 May, enabling men to attest their willingness to serve. Dillon led his party out of the Commons for three months in disgust at the passage of the Act. The Order in Council required to trigger Irish conscription was never issued. Esher admitted: 'I am worried about this Home Rule business. It is a difficult moment in which to set about re-casting a Constitution. The worst of LG is that he does not prepare alternatives – a Torres Vedras. His agility has served him too well.'[203] A committee chaired by Long on Home Rule reported on 19 June to the War Cabinet, but was unable to improve on the compromises suggested in the summer of 1914. The War Cabinet agreed to drop the matter; no conscription, and no Home Rule. French was given little direction on what to do, except to hold the line: which, until the general election six months later, he did. Meanwhile, as the Marquess of Londonderry said in the Lords on 20 June, 'it is the British Government who have permitted Sinn Féin.'[204]

Shortt, addressing the Commons on 25 June, put a brave face on the convention's achievements, claiming the time would come when its findings would be acted upon. He explained that conscription and a Home Rule measure had been put aside because of two significant events: what he called the 'German plot' in Ireland, in which an enemy agent had allegedly been captured off the coast of Clare; and the transformation of Sinn Féin from 'a harmless literary society' to one run by 'extremists and the physical force men'.[205] The latter had happened long before the convention met, though the decision after the Rising to label the rebels 'Sinn Féin', even though that 'literary society' had not taken part in the rebellion, perhaps confused matters. It hardly mattered what those opposing the Crown called themselves; their movement had grown relentlessly for over two years, and the government deluded itself if it thought the militancy was of recent birth.

Sinn Féin had allegedly circulated propaganda in Ireland encouraging people to support the Germans. Shortt gave examples: ' "Take no notice of the Police Order to destroy your own property, and to leave your homes if a German Army should land in Ireland." "When the Germans come they will come as friends, and to put an end to English rule in Ireland. Therefore stay in your homes, and assist the German troops as far as you can." "Any stores, hay, corn or forage taken by the Germans will be paid for by them." ' He continued: 'Somebody in Ireland wrote these out, somebody in Ireland pasted them up, somebody in

Ireland is responsible for scattering this sort of thing about Ireland. What can be their object?'[206] He claimed to have evidence that one of the interned leaders had pointed to the German advance and indicated that the time was near when an 'opportunity' would arise again; and in the meantime the Irish could make it impossible for England to govern their country. Another Sinn Féiner had said: 'So long as England is our enemy it is our duty to assist her enemies, and the best way we can assist the enemies of England is by organising, arming and drilling our Irish Volunteers, and by giving England the knock-out blow at the earliest opportunity.'

The problem was not just propaganda. 'From the time her big offensive began in the spring . . . we found that Germany was in touch with Ireland and not only were messages going into Ireland from German sources, but messages were coming out of Ireland to German sources. These two facts were clear. Our sources of information were able to warn us that an agent from Germany would be landed, as landed he was on the 12th April on the West Coast of Ireland.'[207] Two German submarines, filled with arms, were said to be en route to Ireland; a rising was planned for late May; and the intelligence said the Germans might try to land men too. The Irish conspirators were, Shortt said with shock, men released following their involvement with the 1916 Rising; he seemed especially amazed that they 'had proved absolutely irreconcilable and absolutely untouched by the generosity shown to them.'[208] Having been humiliated in 1916, the authorities now had no choice but to arrest potential rebels. As Curzon had said earlier, when telling the Lords to forget about Home Rule for the moment, more detailed evidence could have been given were it not for the fact that it would harm the Armed Forces: at least that was the excuse.

Shortt claimed that evidence of the timing of a rising had been gleaned from a correspondence between de Valera – 'the acknowledged leader of these extremist people in Ireland' – and a comrade.[209] A Tory MP called out to ask whether the writer of the letter had been shot, and Shortt – one lesson of 1916 having been learned – said he hoped no one would have to be executed again. The proclamations that French had issued to try to enlist Irishmen voluntarily had been designed to avoid conscription and therefore remove one provocation for a rebellion. But the misapprehensions, wilful or otherwise, about Ireland persisted: Shortt felt that the problems were limited to '200 or 300 extremists,' something the dramatic rise in support for Sinn Féin in by-elections should have been sufficient to convince him was nonsense.

His statement was taken as proof that conscription would not be enforced; and Lloyd George, who was present, struggled to deny it. Carson, referring to remarks Curzon had made about the Catholic Church's opposition to conscription, accused the government of 'crawling upon your knees' to the hierarchy of that Church, who acted as though there were a 'religious war.'[210] Curzon, who had said the Catholic clergy 'advised their flocks, under penalties of eternal damnation, to resist conscription to the uttermost', found himself set upon by the Roman Catholic Church in England, and *The Times* dismissed his statement as one of 'crude hopelessness'.[211] He defended himself, publishing a statement laced with quotations from clergymen about the divine opprobrium awaiting those who colluded with the English oppressor.

The Irish Nationalist, John McKean, the only member of his party to attend the debate, enlightened Shortt about what had happened:

At the beginning of the War the people of Ireland were as enthusiastically in favour of the Allies as the people of Great Britain. A change took place. It was the mistaken, the criminal, policy of the Government after the rebellion of 1916 that changed the whole state of feeling in Ireland. If the people of Ireland are not now taking what is called their right share in the fight for self-determination, for liberty and for civilisation, you have only got to blame the British Government, which never does the right thing in Ireland even by chance. By these wicked executions the whole face of the situation in Ireland was changed with regard to the conduct of the War.[212]

Lloyd George intervened to ask for some indulgence rather than the unrelieved criticism the government was receiving 'due to the conditions under which we have to administer affairs.'[213] He claimed considerations solely of 'equity and fair play' had lain behind the decision to legislate for conscription; that if Britons of fifty were being called up, so should young, fit Irishmen be. However, that the process awaited an Order in Council showed, he said, that the government recognised the need to treat Ireland differently from England. He finally admitted a link between the attempt to grant Home Rule and the desire for conscription. 'You cannot force through in the middle of a war a measure which is regarded as highly contentious by powerful bodies of opinion in this country. You cannot do it.'[214] This applied as much to conscription in Ireland, however, as it did to Home Rule being accepted in Britain. He had wished to give a measure of Home Rule to twenty-six counties, with a framework of regular meetings on all-Ireland questions with the other six to maintain some measure of Irish unity. However, now it was known that some leading the separatist movement were in league with the Germans, he felt he could not possibly sanction such a course.

The prime minister called the association of the Catholic Church with the alleged plot 'one of the most fatal mistakes that they have ever committed.'[215] It had shattered the hard-won trust of those Unionists prepared to concede Home Rule, who now once more feared domination by a Catholic state and the loss of the religious freedoms of Unionists stranded in the twenty-six counties. However, he confirmed that the only recruiting in Ireland for the foreseeable future would be on a voluntary basis. Asquith asked, again, for Dominion prime ministers, in London for the Imperial War Cabinet, to be asked to solve the Irish question; but was ignored. So was a call from Morrell for the interned Sinn Féin prisoners (who were denied visitors) either to be put on trial, or released.

The landing of an agent, to which Shortt referred, at least showed the government had learned something from its handling of the Rising. A former professional soldier, Lance Corporal Joseph Patrick Dowling of the Connaught Rangers, had been captured during the retreat from Mons in September 1914, and recruited into Casement's Irish Brigade. On 12 April he had landed in a rubber dinghy from a U-boat off the coast of County Clare. British intelligence had cracked the German codes and knew Dowling was coming; he was eventually arrested on the way to Galway, brought to London, held in the Tower and court-martialled in early August on three charges of cooperation with the enemy. He was sentenced to death by firing squad but the King immediately commuted the sentence to life imprisonment, on ministerial advice. He was released in 1924.

On 3 July, after sporadic rioting that had included shooting dead an RIC man in Tralee, French proclaimed Sinn Féin and the Irish Volunteers 'dangerous organisations', banning all meetings without a government permit. Arms and ammunition were frequently seized. Duke's softly-softly approach was finished; and French had Byrne, whom he regarded as ineffectual, removed from running the RIC. In other respects the government continued giving gratuitous offence to the Irish. When in mid-July Mrs

Hanna Sheehy-Skeffington, widow of the man murdered by a mad officer
in 1916, returned to Liverpool with her nine-year-old son from America,
she was banned from going across the Irish Sea to her own country; Lon-
don justified this ban because the government in Dublin viewed her
presence in Ireland as 'injurious'.[216] To aggravate the question the officer,
Colthurst, had been released from Broadmoor the previous January; but
Mrs Sheehy-Skeffington had yet to receive a penny in compensation.
Eventually, the government decided the reason for keeping her out of
Ireland was that 'she has been engaged in anti-British propaganda in the
United States'.[217] After a short spell in Holloway she was, at least, moved
to a hotel.

In late July the Irish Nationalists, diminished after losing by-elections
to Sinn Féin, returned to the Commons after a three-month boycott.
They hoped to use their presence to bolster their credibility and win
back the mass of support lost to the republicans, given that a general
election was expected within months. Dillon accused the government of
moving to totalitarianism; it had, he said, instituted

a system of universal coercion which is wantonly provocative to
Ireland, and in many of its details utterly unnecessary. I give one
point only, a small matter but of vital importance to us, because it
touches this whole question of the breach of faith. They have in
Ireland martial law in full force, a military dictator and the Defence
of the Realm Act in a more severe form than in this country. I cannot conceive any Government, no matter how great the danger
may be, which could hold that it was not sufficiently covered by
these powers. But not content with these powers they have revived
the odious and detestable perpetual coercion Act of 1887, quite
unnecessarily, and simply therefore for the purpose of wanton
insult and provocation, and they have done that in spite of the fact
that all the Liberal Ministers of the late Government of 1906 are
pledged solemnly never to use that Act again, and that this House,
as well as my memory carries me, repealed that Act by a large
majority, and the final repeal was only prevented by the House of
Lords, and without a shadow of an excuse or reason they have
revived it in spite of all the great powers they had. That, in my
opinion, proves that one of the purposes of the Government is to
flout and outrage the Irish people.[218]

He said the government had thrown 'the Irish people into the hands
of the revolutionary party' by failing properly to consult the Nationalists about conscription.[219] The Irish people believed no military
necessity had caused the policy, but it had been used as an excuse to
abandon Home Rule. He ridiculed the idea of a German plot: and
noted that the pronouncements of Sir Horace Plunkett, which had
once had oracular status in England, were now not printed in the English press, thanks to his having denied knowledge of the alleged plot
too. Dillon knew there had been a plot in 1916: he refused to believe
there had been one in 1918, though it had suited the government to
claim otherwise.

He was speaking days after confirmation of the murder of the Tsar
and his family by another brand of revolutionaries. 'What are you going
to do about Ireland when you have turned her over altogether to Sinn
Fein as you are now doing your best to do?' he asked. Prophetically, he
continued: 'You are up against a problem which will try British statesmen more than they have ever been tried before. And look at the
language that is being used by you with regard to other nationalities and
think of the effect which it has on Ireland. Some men in discussing the
Irish problem talk about it as if nothing had happened during the last
four years, as if there had never been a war, as if there had never been a
Russian Revolution, as if none of the mighty changes that we have witnessed had taken place.'[220]

Britain supported not just the idea of Belgian sovereignty, but also
that of restoring Poland to the map and the concept of Czechoslovakia.
But, he asked, 'What about Ireland, who is more ancient than any of
them, and whose struggle for nationality has been unquestionably
more persistent than that either of the Czecho-Slovaks or even of the
Poles?'[221] The Irish wanted to catch this wave of European emancipation but were told the Ulster question prevented them. Dillon, however,
contended that in its blithe support of the Czechoslovaks, Britain
ignored the protests of what a later generation would know as the
Sudeten Germans, who did not wish to be ruled by Czechs. The double
standard was obvious, but it would turn out to be an unfortunate
comparison.

The time and energy spent on the question of Irish conscription did
little good to the war effort, and the campaign of exhortation to help
recruitment in Ireland was largely fruitless. British propaganda had it

that this would provide 50,000 men by August: in fact, by the Armistice, it had produced 9,000, though even that number was remarkable given the state of Irish opinion.

VI

With Ireland unpromising as a source of manpower, and the Germans still heading towards Paris, other means of saving Western Europe became necessary. On 29 March, Good Friday, the War Cabinet resolved to ask President Wilson to send 100,000 men a month for the following three months to fight in British brigades, for it was impossible to maintain the Army's strength otherwise. Wilson quickly agreed, offering to send 120,000 men for four months rather than just three. Later that day it seemed the tide might be turning: the Germans had sustained heavy losses and had been stopped outside Amiens. Following a conference with the French and General Pershing, the American commander, at Beauvais on 3 April the British confirmed Foch as commander-in-chief of the Allied Armies on the Western Front. Haig was content, though he had the right of appeal to his own government about any decision with which he disagreed. According to him, Lloyd George, who was present, 'looked as if he had been thoroughly frightened, and he seemed still in a funk . . . he appears to me to be a thorough impostor.'[222]

Haig feared Lloyd George was looking for a military scapegoat. He believed the prime minister was expecting to be attacked in the Commons following the Army's retreat, and 'for not tackling the manpower problem before, also for personally ordering Divisions to the east at a critical time against the advice of his military adviser, viz, the CIGS.'[223] Lloyd George indeed turned on Sir Hubert Gough, who had commanded the routed 5th Army, but Haig defended him for having done the best he could in difficult circumstances.[224] Haig had already told Gough he wanted him out of the front line so that he could prepare a new line of defence along the Somme. On 28 March therefore he handed over command of what was left of his army to Rawlinson. This was not enough for Lloyd George, who wanted Gough sacked altogether. Haig said Gough should not be dismissed without a hearing, and told Lloyd George that if he wanted Gough punished, he would have to send Haig an order to that effect. Haig branded Lloyd George a 'cur', a view reinforced the next day when he received a telegram from Derby saying 'it is quite clear to me that his troops have lost confidence in Gough' and that he should be relieved of his command.[225]

Haig had no choice but to obey, but disagreed with Gough's treatment so vehemently that he wrote to Derby saying that he would place his resignation in the Secretary of State's hands, if that was the government's wish: he knew full well it was not and so Gough, like Haig's other senior comrade Robertson, bit the dust. With his customary bluster, and to justify his own excessive treatment of an officer who had done his best in adverse circumstances that the prime minister's own policies had done so much to create, Lloyd George even hinted in the Commons on 9 April that Gough could well be court-martialled. There was no depth to which he would not sink to cover up or distract attention from his own misjudgements.

The Army was not Lloyd George's only problem. Sir Hugh Trenchard, who had commanded the RFC in France, became Chief of the Air Staff at the formation of the RAF on 1 April, after he had masterminded the merger of the RFC with the Royal Naval Air Service. However, he resigned almost immediately because of severe differences with Rothermere, the air minister, for whom he had not wanted to work but to whom he was accountable. The minister constantly interfered in decisions about the allocation of service manpower, despite having a small fraction of Trenchard's knowledge and expertise. Rothermere had also made it clear during an interview with Trenchard the previous November that he and his brother, Northcliffe, would campaign against Robertson and Haig, to whom Trenchard was personally loyal. In the three months as Chief of the Air Staff that Trenchard had to prepare for the birth of the RAF he and Rothermere disagreed on almost everything, with Rothermere routinely disregarding his advice. The War Cabinet accepted Trenchard's resignation on 10 April and asked him to resume command of the RAF in France: he refused because of the outrageous slight it would have represented to his colleague Major General John Salmond, whom he would displace. Esher, hearing of these absurdities, noted that 'there literally is no Government in this country.'[226]

The King, as had been seen over the dismissal of Robertson, hated political interference in his Armed Forces and thought Trenchard's departure 'a great misfortune'. He summoned him to Buckingham Palace; and Trenchard did not hold back.[227] After the meeting he wrote to Lloyd George to explain himself, and his letter was shown to the War Cabinet.

Rothermere dug his own grave by circulating a vicious response; with questions about his judgement and competence raised by more than just Trenchard, he resigned on 25 April. Trenchard took command of a long-range bombing force in France. The King – who, as with so much else during Lloyd George's rule, was not consulted – was outraged by Trenchard's treatment and by the evidence it gave of his prime minister's disregard for him. Rothermere went quietly, having been promised promotion to a viscountcy. When, in April 1919, the time came to pay the debt, Stamfordham told Law (who asked the King to approve it) that the Sovereign (again unconsulted) did so 'with much reluctance'.[228]

Over the Easter recess Auckland Geddes was charged with drawing up a Bill to solve the military manpower problem. It reflected the desperation of the political class, and an existential threat to the British polity, that had arisen since the 21 March offensive. Military age would be lowered to seventeen and raised to fifty-five – subsequently lowered to fifty when it became clear the military use of men so old, except as doctors, was limited. Tribunals would be scrapped, with medical fitness and occupation being the only criteria for whether a man could serve; and not just the Irish – on French's advice – but also residents of the Isle of Man and the Channel Islands would be called up. Fears of invasion, dormant since the early weeks of the war, flared up again. Hankey told Esher that 'the Admiralty are well prepared for the *worst* that can happen, and have been considering for days and planning what they will do, if the Channel ports are threatened, or seized by the enemy.'[229]

Conscious that many men of military age were to be found in civilian life, the police reintroduced round-ups, handing over suspects to the Army to question. One Saturday evening in June twenty such men were detained at a cinema in Finsbury Park.[230] A comb-out continued in agriculture, in heavy industry and even in Whitehall. A system of summer camps for schoolboys was instituted to replace the 30,000 adult men combed out from farms, so the harvest could be brought in. Three thousand young women from universities and teacher training colleges, who also lived under canvas, brought in the flax harvest in Somerset and in the fens around Peterborough.

Lloyd George addressed the Commons on 9 April, following the Easter recess, and a day after Repington had written in the *Morning Post*: 'Why have the reiterated demands of the Army for men remained unanswered? Who but Mr Lloyd George is responsible for the failure to supply the Army's needs? I think we shall have to be more ruthless towards Ministers who have failed the country and that our easy toler-ance of incompetence is a public danger.'[231] This was also the debate in which Lloyd George set out his plans for Irish conscription, so it was no wonder that when Hankey lunched with him beforehand he found him 'rather depressed and nervous and ill at ease.'[232]

In proposing new measures to help win the war he told MPs that 'they will involve, I regret, extreme sacrifices on the part of large classes of the population, and nothing would justify them but the most extreme neces-sity, and the fact that we are fighting for all that is essential and most sacred in the national life.'[233] Anxious to acquit the government of blame for the recent reverses, he stated: 'Notwithstanding the heavy casualties in 1917, the Army in France was considerably stronger on the 1st January, 1918, than on the 1st January, 1917.' Similarly – conscious of how he had prevented reinforcement of the British sector of the Western Front – he protested there 'was no proof that the full weight of the attack would fall on us,' and this had made it 'exceedingly difficult' for the generals to decide where to deploy their troops.[234]

He explained the necessity of cancelling soldiers' leave, and because of the 'emergency' the need to send boys of eighteen and a half, after just four months' training, to France, instead of waiting until they were nineteen. But the country had to train more soldiers: 100,000 medically fit men were being taken from the munitions industry; 50,000 had already been taken from the mines, and another 50,000 would be called. All men in the civil service under twenty-five who passed the medical would have to serve. Confirming the rise in the maximum military age, he said: 'There are a good many services in the Army which do not require the very best physical material, and it would be very helpful to get men of this age to fill those services, in order to release younger and fitter men to enter into the fighting line.'[235] Similarly, they could replace younger men in home defence who could be sent to France.

By the time the Military Service Bill had its second reading the next day the government had modified some of the proposals. Men aged between forty-two and fifty would mostly not be called up, because many were skilled workers in industries of national importance; though Law, when he spoke (Lloyd George resumed his absence from the Com-mons, despite the importance of the measure), admitted the effect on trade and production would be serious. With the exception of doctors, who were desperately needed, men between fifty and fifty-five would, Cave said, be called up only 'in some very great national emergency'; which some MPs thought had already arisen.[236] Clergymen and other ministers of religion would be required to serve, but could choose between combatant and non-combatant units. MPs would be given the choice of serving or staying in the Commons: it having been deemed by the government that their constituents had elected them to do 'work of national importance'.[237]

VII

It seemed in early April that the Germans had run out of steam: it was later learned that this was because of a breakdown in the loyalties between men and their officers, and because of supply shortages attributable to the Royal Navy's blockade that largely prevented the import of goods to Germany by sea. The difficult terrain of the old Somme battlefield was also partly responsible. Thus the Germans looked for new points at which to attack; though the capture of Armentières on 10 April, as the Commons debated the second reading of the Military Service Bill, raised new fears that they might reach, and take, the Channel ports. The French were still reluctant to pour troops into that sector to hold up the advance, even though before long Paris would be in the Germans' sights. The next day Haig, master of optimism, issued an order whose words have passed into the British cultural memory, and that at last dripped with realism: 'Every position must be held to the last man; there must be no retirement. With our backs to the wall, and believing in the justice of our cause, each one of us must fight on to the end.'[238] It was enough to ensure the Military Service Bill was passed, despite Irish outrage.

Others sought to apportion blame for Britain's predicament. For Gwynne, who had done so much to get Asquith out, Lloyd George was the culprit: 'He has lied to everybody, including the House of Commons and now, with the enemy battering at our gates, he still wants to play his dirty little political games,' he told Lady Bathurst on 16 April.[239] 'I don't believe he is sincere, even in his desire to conscript Ireland. He has played fast and loose with England and will bring her to the dust . . . whoever succeeds him must be better. He has surrounded himself with the rotters of finance and the newspaper world. There is neither good nor conscience nor any sense of right in him – only low political cunning.'

The dishonesty of Lloyd George's statement that the British Army was stronger in France in January 1918 than a year earlier horrified Maurice. It also caused outrage in France when word reached the trenches, where the men driven back by the German offensive knew they were outnumbered and that they had not, as Lloyd George had implied, been beaten by a smaller army. More to the point, soldiers such as Maurice knew the Army was outnumbered solely because the War Cabinet had refused reinforcements when warned of the likelihood of an attack. Lying was not solely Lloyd George's prerogative. Maurice recorded on 9 April that 'Curzon made a number of absolutely untrue statements in the House of Lords' about manpower: whether he knew they were untrue was another matter.[240]

On 17 April it was announced that Derby had been offered, and had accepted, the post of ambassador and minister plenipotentiary on a special mission to France. The King, 'not only surprised, but hurt', according to Stamfordham, at not being consulted, even though he had just had a long talk about the cabinet with Lloyd George, was unhappy with the move. He argued against removing Lord Bertie, an experienced diplomat trusted by the French, and a good friend of Clemenceau, at a sensitive time, to replace him with a novice: but he also sensed one of his closest friends was being demoted, and that he would lose the counsel of one he trusted implicitly in the cabinet.[241]

Lloyd George had flirted with the idea of becoming war secretary, but appointed Milner after objections from the King. The small reconstruction allowed Austen Chamberlain's appointment to the War Cabinet, without portfolio. This induced mockery from the Northcliffe press, which regarded him as an 'ineffective mediocrity'; Northcliffe had noted the impact Chamberlain's attack on the press had had on the public.[242] Others saw the appointment as calming Unionist tensions after the Robertson affair, and as proof that Lloyd George could, when he chose, defy Northcliffe. Chamberlain was under no illusions about Lloyd George, but found the prospect of a change of government 'unthinkable' and told the prime minister: 'The crisis is so grave that those of us who support the Government must do so ungrudgingly and give whatever help you require of us.'[243]

It was in this state of crisis that Lloyd George's statement on 9 April about the greater size of the Army compared with 1917 came back to bite him. Sir Godfrey Baring, a Liberal MP, asked in the Commons whether the numbers included labour battalions and other non-combatant units; a War Office under-secretary told him the fighting strength was greater year on year; but that was not true. Colonel Kirke of the War Office had sent figures to the under-secretary, Ian Macpherson, that were wrong because they inadvertently included soldiers on the Italian front. Nor was this the only error. Maurice read in *The Times* on 24 April that Law had said, in the Commons the previous day, that British and French commanders had earlier agreed to extend the British front, taking over a French sector, without the government disregarding advice from Haig and Robertson. Maurice knew that was untrue too, and it had badly over-stretched the BEF: as did Haig, who complained to Milner about the same report.[244]

As Spears put it: 'He [Maurice] took this answer to be a clear proof of the Government's determination to avoid any shadow of responsibility for the present near disaster.'[245] Maurice did not believe Law knew he was inaccurate, but whoever had prepared the answer for him had done so to ensure the government escaped blame. On 30 April he wrote to Wilson, as CIGS, to tell him the statements about manpower had had a seriously destabilising effect on morale among those on active service, who knew of the severe reduction in battalions since 1 January; and said another statement to correct this misunderstanding would be advisable. He received no reply.

On 7 May, the government having refused to correct the record, Maurice wrote to the *Morning Post*, *The Times*, *The Daily Telegraph*, the *Daily Chronicle* and the *Daily News* to say Lloyd George and Law had lied to the Commons about the strength of the Army in France. He had told his son and eldest daughter that 'you know for some time past that the Government has not been telling the truth about the War. The object is to show that they did everything possible and that the blame rests with the Generals. This is absolutely untrue, and I am one of the few people who know the facts.'[246] He knew he was breaching military discipline, but believed this was a rare occasion 'when duty as a citizen comes before duty as a soldier'.

Haig, hearing the news in France, was unimpressed. He thought Maurice's actions 'a grave mistake' because 'no-one can be both a soldier and a politician at the same time. We soldiers have to do our duty and

keep silent, trusting to Ministers to protect us.'[247] This was shocking hypocrisy: Haig had seldom kept silent when confronted by Lloyd George's
dishonesty, running either to Robertson when he was CIGS, or to his
friend in Buckingham Palace. One must assume Haig was embarrassed
to have let this grotesque lie pass unchallenged himself, for what it said
about his moral courage and leadership. Amery noted that 'there is no
doubt that Maurice has been got hold of by Repington', which Maurice
had not.[248] Lloyd George's initial view, from which he would not be
shaken, was that a political conspiracy was directed at him to bring him
down and replace him with Asquith, and he would fight ruthlessly to
defend himself.

All the papers except the *Telegraph* printed the letter. It said Law's
statement on 23 April had given 'a totally misleading impression' of discussions at Versailles about extending the British front; 'the latest in a
series of misstatements which have been made recently in the House of
Commons by the present Government.'[249] He talked about Lloyd
George's untruths on 9 April, adding that he had taken 'the very grave
step' of writing the letter because 'the statements quoted above are
known by a large number of soldiers to be incorrect, and this knowledge
is breeding such distrust of the Government as can only end in impairing the splendid *moral* [sic] of our troops at a time when everything
possible should be done to raise it.'[250] He demanded a parliamentary
investigation into his assertions.

Maurice was a straight-as-a-die soldier of the old school. Spears, who
worked under him and who was by this time head of the British Military
Mission to Paris, described him as 'the soul of military honour' and one
who 'suffered acutely from the tactics of the politicians and their too
subtle methods.'[251] Spears observed that 'Lloyd George in particular he
came to distrust profoundly', and that Maurice 'ruined his career in
the Army . . . by defying the all-powerful Prime Minister and telling the
nation the truth that was being withheld from it.' Spears, a highly intellectual soldier, observed Lloyd George closely, and dismissed his grasp
of strategy as 'amateurish' and of military matters as 'ignorant'. Robertson had regarded Lloyd George's views as 'silly, too silly to argue about.'[252]
Spears saw that the generals 'failed to realise the supreme importance of
carrying with them the political leader of the nation.'[253] The generals had
written him off after his attempt to put the BEF under French command
before the Nivelle offensive.

Many years after the war and after Lloyd George's death, Spears wrote that his claim to be 'the man who won the war' was a 'fallacy': 'Because he refused to heed the warnings of his military advisers in the spring of 1918, he brought us nearer to defeat than at any other period in the war.'[254] He blamed the heavy British casualties of the first four weeks of the German offensive – 70,000 higher than the fourteen weeks of Passchendaele – directly on the prime minister's 'strategic conceptions'. In a memorandum written after his retirement, Maurice said that on the eve of the battle on 21 March 1918 the infantry was 100,000 men weaker than on 1 January 1917; in all there had been a reduction not of 120 battalions as expected, but 140, and two cavalry divisions had been broken up; and he contradicted the claims that soldiers had been brought back from Salonica to reinforce the Western Front. The figure Lloyd George touted had been inflated thanks to the presence at the front of 300,000 unarmed labourers and Chinese coolies, whom he included.

Asquith, to whom Maurice had sent a copy of his letter on the eve of publication – but whom he had not consulted, to avoid his having to take responsibility for it – questioned Law about the letter in the Commons. Maurice had told Asquith that 'I have been guided solely by what I hold to be the public interest,' and Asquith did not doubt it.[255] Law said a Court of Honour, comprising two senior judges, would inquire and report as swiftly as possible. Asquith sought a debate on the subject, and Law agreed – after the judges had reported. The inquiry would be held in private and those questioned would not be on oath. This prompted Admiral of the Fleet Sir Hedworth Meux to announce that the Army and Navy were 'sick to death of the way things are going on in the House of Commons.'[256] Asquith pressed for the debate before the court sat, and Law, sensing an ugly mood rising, agreed.

Hankey called the episode 'a veritable bombshell'.[257] The meeting of the War Cabinet on 8 May discussed it, and Lloyd George, thanks to extensive research by Hankey, outlined the defence he would make; he asserted that his main problem was not that he lied, but that defending himself thoroughly was impossible because of not wishing to disclose information of use to the enemy. The War Cabinet worried that Haig had felt 'under an obligation' – in other words, pressured by the government – to take over more of the front.[258] Hankey did find that the Army's rifle strength had decreased by 100,548; almost exactly as

Maurice had said: he found the only way to defend Lloyd George was to engage in hair-splitting nonsense about whether 'rifle strength [is] the only criterion of fighting strength'.[259]

The Commons debate the next day, 9 May, was the only time the official Opposition divided the House against the government during the war. Repington had briefed Asquith the previous evening, calling unannounced at Cavendish Square before dinner and, so Asquith told his wife, 'vibrant with indignation'.[260] Repington claimed to have up-to-date figures proving Lloyd George was wrong. Asquith called for a select committee to investigate Maurice's claims. He denied he was attempting effectively a vote of censure on the government. Asquith thought the government would have accepted his request without demur; that assumption was partly because he thought Maurice's accusations would so concern ministers that they would want them properly scrutinised without delay. After all, said Asquith, 'It was a letter written by a general who must have known when he wrote it that he was committing a serious breach of King's Regulations, and that he was really putting in jeopardy the whole of his military future. He, therefore, presumably, would not have taken a course so obviously fraught with possible and even probable disaster to his own prospects unless he was writing under a grave sense of responsibility and of public duty.'[261]

Asquith knew Lloyd George too well, and how with him all had not always been what it had seemed. He sensed with some disgust the change of tone and manners that accompanied Lloyd George's administration. He did not want to believe what some of the consequences of this might have been. He upheld the old values, values the 'new men' felt dispensable. 'I say most emphatically,' he intoned, 'that in this House we are accustomed to accept—we are bound to accept—statements made by Ministers of the Crown upon their authority as accurate and true, unless and until the contrary be proved, and I hope we shall always uphold that well-founded Parliamentary tradition.'[262] He believed much hinged on the probity of ministers: 'In the interests of the Government, in the interests of the Army, in the interests of the State, in the interests of the Allies, in the supreme interest of all, namely, the unhampered prosecution of the War itself, it is our duty to set up a tribunal of inquiry which, from its constitution and from its powers, will be able to give to Parliament and to the country a prompt, a decisive, and an authoritative judgment.'[263]

Law provoked cries of 'Shame!' for mocking Asquith's assertion that a select committee would consider the question without prejudice. Asquith rounded on him, the 'custodian and trustee' of the 'great traditions' of the Commons as Law was, being the Leader of the House. 'Is it right, or is it even decent, to suggest that you cannot get five men in this House not so steeped in party prejudices that, upon a pure issue of fact, they cannot be trusted to give a true decision?'

Lloyd George, who spoke next, had set Hankey to work for a couple of days to provide all the information needed to rebut Maurice in a speech: knowing it would bring the government down if he failed, he had rehearsed it the previous evening to senior colleagues, including Milner, Chamberlain and Hankey, who suggested numerous changes. The prime minister made the obvious point that Maurice had never questioned the statement when still working in the War Office. He claimed to have had almost daily contact with Maurice, and had considered him a friend (whether Maurice agreed is highly debatable: Lloyd George was raising, cynically, the spectre of betrayal). He made his own counter-accusation:

> Was it not his business to come to me—especially if he thought that this was so important that it justified a great general in breaking the King's Regulations and setting an example of indiscipline—was it not his business, first of all, to come to the Cabinet, or, at any rate, to come to the Minister whom he impugned, and say to him, 'You made a mistake in the House of Commons on a most important question of fact'? He might have put it quite nicely. He could have said, 'I dare say you were misled, but you can put it right.' Never a word was said to me! Never a syllable until I saw it in the newspapers! I say that I have been treated unfairly.[264]

This display of wounded *amour propre* was brilliantly manipulative.

He and his colleagues had decided against a select committee because it 'was not the best tribunal for investigating facts when passions were aroused.'[265] Judges, on the other hand, were 'accustomed to examine facts', which was what was required. However, Lloyd George was determined to lend the judges a helping hand. 'The figures that I gave,' he said, 'were taken from the official records of the War Office, for which I sent before I made the statement. If they were incorrect, General

Maurice was as responsible as anyone else. But they were not inaccurate. I have made inquiries since.'[266] There was some hair-splitting: 'Does anyone mean to tell me that they are not part of the "fighting strength" of the Army? Take the men who, when the British Army retreated, and had to abandon trenches which took months to prepare, and who had to improvise defences under shell fire to relieve the Infantry—are those men no part of the fighting strength of the Army? When you have not got them, you have to take Infantry out, and set them to that work.'[267]

Lloyd George produced the document from Maurice's office that contained the figures. When George Lambert, an Asquithian Liberal, asked whether it was initialled, Lloyd George said it was – by Maurice's deputy. He expressed outrage at the ensuing laughter. 'I do not suggest that he was the man who worked out these figures, but he was responsible for the document issued.'[268] He added, maintaining his wounded tone: 'If there was anything wrong in these figures, I got them from official sources, for which General Maurice himself is responsible, and I think he might have said that in his letter when he was impugning the honour of Ministers.' In fact, the office responsible was the Adjutant General's, but by this stage Lloyd George had transcended fact.

After explaining why the British line had been extended, and on whose authority, Lloyd George made two final points: that Maurice's intervention had undermined Army discipline and that, whatever Asquith maintained, his motion was a vote of censure. He deplored this, at a time when the Germans were still attacking and, he claimed, 'preparing perhaps the biggest blow of the War'.[269] His speech was designed to allow Unionists and his Liberal supporters to support him; it was not designed to prove he was a man of probity. Pringle, who spoke next, accused him of appealing to the emotions of the House, 'an appeal which no man is able to make with greater skill and greater irrelevance than himself.'[270] Lord Hugh Cecil observed that his speech had been an excellent attack on Maurice, but no defence of the government. Given its majority, though, no defence was necessary; the motion was defeated by 293 votes to 106.

Asquith was universally deemed to have made a pitiful speech – not least because, declining to prejudge a select committee, he had avoided going in for the kill with Lloyd George. Haig, who to his wife had slightly altered his tune, told her: 'Poor Maurice! How terrible to see the House of Commons so easily taken in by a clap-trap speech by Lloyd George.

The House is really losing its reputation as an assembly of common-sense Britishers.' Hankey was sufficiently embarrassed by the truth to suppress it from his memoirs over forty years later; what he actually recorded in his diary about Lloyd George's speech was: 'I felt all the time that it was not the speech of a man who tells "the truth; the whole truth; and nothing but the truth".'[271] Hankey knew Lloyd George had seen the Adjutant General's revised figures and chosen to ignore them. Esher noted that 'the danger now is that LG and his Entourage may get "swelled heads". The triumph was easy, but in politics the wind veers in a moment.'[272] The press, which knew barely half the story, jumped on the bandwagon to execrate Maurice and praise the government: *The Times* called the outcome 'nothing less than annihilating' to Lloyd George's critics, and accused Maurice of being a 'pawn' in a 'spiteful intrigue' against Wilson by partisans of Robertson.[273]

That Asquith could have cast such aspersions on his successor and former colleague as to demand an inquiry into his probity spelt the end of the Liberal Party. The Unionists supported Lloyd George in the Maurice debate not because his arguments were convincing, but because of their tribal dislike of Asquith. Northcliffe rallied the press to support the prime minister too, without troubling to analyse the facts. It was perhaps the greatest service the press baron afforded Lloyd George, for never did he come closer to being toppled until 1922. Hankey believed Asquith did not hit harder because he feared he could bring down the government, a tricky prospect at that stage of the war.

Maurice admitted he had been 'prepared for the abuse which was heaped upon me in a certain section of the press', but not for 'the methods pursued by the Government to defeat my request for an enquiry.'[274] These included denying him access to official papers that would have substantiated his claims, and asserting – entirely falsely – that he had been in the Commons on 9 April and had heard Lloyd George's statement, yet said nothing: this was a story spread by Sutherland, Lloyd George's private secretary and press officer, who lied about a conversation he had on the subject with a lobby correspondent.[275]

Maurice also believed Lloyd George had prejudiced his case by claiming – again dishonestly – that Maurice had made no representations to him or anyone else before leaving office; that he had not been at Versailles at the crucial meeting; and that Lloyd George's claim on 9 April had been based on information supplied by Maurice or his department.

On Versailles, Maurice had seen verbatim transcripts, so knew exactly what had happened. Aficionados of the Marconi scandal of 1912–13 will detect Lloyd George's unscrupulous *modus operandi*.[276]

The prime minister's determination to include non-combatants in the numbers of soldiers went against all conventional practice; but that, too, was typical. Nor could Maurice recall ever being asked to supply, or supplying, the figures to which Lloyd George referred on 9 April. Most disingenuous of all, Lloyd George had been told of Kirke's error on 8 May (presumably after the War Cabinet meeting, for it is not mentioned in its minutes) – and the number of troops in Italy wrongly included amounted to 86,000 – but chose not to mention it the next day, and instead deliberately used the wrong figure again. This shocked officials, who knew the truth; Kirke, indeed, offered to resign. It apparently also upset Milner, who was aware of the fact, and whom Lloyd George proceeded to isolate and marginalise. No correction to the record was made.

Maurice knew there was no road back: the Army Council placed him on the retired list on 11 May, after he told them he knowingly breached discipline as 'a matter of conscience', and his retirement was announced on 13 May.[277] The next day it was revealed that he had become military correspondent of the *Daily Chronicle*. He would serve there for five months until a proxy of Lloyd George, funded by money from the sale of honours, bought the newspaper and turned it into a mouthpiece for the prime minister. Maurice then moved to the *Daily News*. Out of spite he was retired not on the half-pay of a major general – £750 a year – but on that of a major, £225 a year. That appalled the Army Council, and the following October it was increased to the correct amount.

Maurice would continue to badger Lloyd George to tell the truth for years after the war, with no success, and to the embarrassment of Lloyd George's former colleagues, notably Balfour, who knew Maurice had been done a serious wrong. Lloyd George would, in 1936, attack Maurice in his memoirs, one of many passages that underlines that work's unreliability and reinforces Lloyd George's posthumous reputation as a consummate liar. Even Frances Stevenson, in her diary, admitted to the existence of the document sent to him setting out the true figures before his speech on 9 May, and says it was burned; Sir Joseph 'JT' Davies, a key member of Lloyd George's secretariat, told her as he put it in the fire that 'only you & I, Frances, know of the existence of this paper.'[278]

VIII

As summer approached, Britain continued to experience food shortages. Meat distribution broke down because of inadequate cold storage, with substandard food barely fit for human consumption reaching wholesalers. Dairy farmers protested about the price of milk, and claimed that some would be put out of business. On 15 July new ration books were issued for butter, margarine, lard, meat and sugar, though the size of rations had increased since the scheme was initiated, and some offal and meat products were off the ration. The next day Leo Amery noted that the cabinet secretariat were told to start making plans 'for carrying on the war if France and Italy were out' – what decades later he called 'a 1940–43 situation'.[279]

Despite the government's continual references to the grave national emergency, industrial action remained rife. A strike of aircraft manufacturers in London was caused by a management refusal to recognise a system of shop stewards; an agreement was reached allowing for recognition, but not until obloquy had been directed at the ministry for allowing the strike in the first place: the assumption was, with the country in peril, that workers should have their demands met before serious damage was done. Then there was an outbreak of industrial action in munitions factories, beginning in Coventry, despite strong pressure from leaders of the Amalgamated Society of Engineers for its members to return to work. The strike was over the rationing out of skilled labour among munitions firms, and was overtly political, motivated by what Churchill (in a draft press statement that was never issued) called the 'undercurrent of Pacifism, Defeatism and Bolshevism' that held that if production of arms stopped then so too would the war.[280] By 24 July 12,000 skilled men were out in Coventry, defying the ASE executive; it was reported that 100,000 men in Birmingham walked out the next day (the figure was then revised down to 15,000, which was damaging enough). As they did, representatives of, it was claimed, 300,000 men met in Leeds, and called a general strike for the following week.

On 26 July the government put out a statement in Lloyd George's name, but written by Churchill, that if the strikers did not return to work on 29 July they would be drafted into the Army under the Military Service Acts, for they were trying to force the government 'to change the national policy essential to the prosecution of the war'; the threat to bring charges against anyone who incited a man to leave his job had already been made.[281] *The Times* claimed it was 'no ordinary labour dispute, but a plain challenge to the State.'[282] The public, more set on victory than ever after the spring crisis, strongly supported the government's threat; which, with the intervention of local union leaders to urge their members to see reason, rapidly brought a return to work.

In 1914 there had been 9,500,000 men under the age of forty-three, and 6,100,000 of those had been recruited into the forces or into 'National Service' in work of national importance. All others were of a 'very low' physical standard; the nation had effectively run out of recruits, with 500,000, mainly boys and older men, taken since 1 January, putting a massive strain on essential industries.[283] Women, aware of their importance to the war effort and their consequent industrial muscle, started to strike for equal pay and conditions. In mid-August conductresses on London buses and trams walked out after a weekly 5s war bonus was paid to men doing the same job, but not to them. It was argued that the women were mostly receiving separation allowances and therefore did not need the bonus. Such was the chaos their strike caused that the government sent in Sir George Askwith, Asquith's industrial fixer from the Great Unrest, to sort matters out.[284] The management decided to pay the women the 5s bonus too. A strike of Yorkshire miners over pay and conditions was quickly settled, because the government already feared shortages for the coming winter, and was urging people to get in supplies of logs instead: the War Cabinet learned on 16 August that there was 'a very serious position', with production down by around 40,000,000 tons a year, not just because of 'combing out', but because of the arrival in Britain in the summer of 1918 of the Spanish influenza epidemic.[285] Sir Albert Stanley, president of the Board of Trade, asked for 42,000 men, in fitness categories A and B1, to be returned to the mines by 30 September.

Even more alarming, on 30 August a Metropolitan Police strike over pay came 'like a bolt from the blue', according to Hankey.[286] The home secretary, the commissioner of the metropolis and the permanent under-secretary at the Home Office were all on holiday; and that morning London was denuded of its constabulary. The officers, who had given a few hours' notice of their walk-out, had no official union – an unofficial one, the National Union of Police and Prison Officers, had been founded before the war but was technically illegal – but were associated with the Workers Union, whose secretary, Charles Duncan, a Labour MP, advised them not to strike. He admitted to Lloyd George – who had just returned from Criccieth where he had been brainstorming about a possible election, and summoned him to Downing Street – that the police had 'behaved badly'.[287] The union wanted a war bonus of 12s a week increased to £1, as well as recognition of the union and reinstatement of an officer dismissed for being a union organiser. By late on 30 August 12,000 men were thought to be on strike, with only the plain-clothes Criminal Investigation Department and special constables (whom a procession of striking policemen booed as 'scabs' and 'blacklegs') defending the citizens of London.[288] After an intervention by Smuts, 600 guardsmen were sent to stand outside key public buildings. Lloyd George ordered Duncan to see the police leaders, charging him to tell them that their grievances would be fully discussed on the condition that they return to work.

Hankey's solution was a drastic one of sweeping away local forces and establishing a national police, in which existing officers would be allowed to serve if they resumed duties at once; and in the meantime to have the Army police London. He did, however, believe the complaints about pay were legitimate. At an hour-long meeting on 31 August Lloyd George quickly agreed to pay them a second bonus in eight months' time, and sacked Sir Edward Henry, the commissioner of the metropolis – even though the Home Office had allowed the grievances to multiply – with the consolation of a baronetcy. His replacement, Sir Nevil Macready, the former Adjutant General of the Army, calmed matters and embarked on reforms, including the recruitment of women officers. A month later workers on the Great Western Railway stopped the trains between South Wales and London: the government declared the strike illegal, and the threat of six battalions of soldiers moving in to restore order helped the strike evaporate. This was not so much a return of pre-war class conflicts as a recognition by organised labour of the extent to which the country depended on its goodwill, and its preparation to have its voice heard in a new era of near-universal adult suffrage.

Any form of industrial action was grave, because Britain still faced shortages for the coming winter: not just of coal – which caused the government to order the dimming of lights in public buildings – but of foodstuffs, despite the food controller's efforts. Jam would be rationed

from 3 November; milk was subject to a new and supposedly improved
distribution system; potatoes were increasingly used to make bread; the
price of fish was cut to persuade people to eat it instead of meat; the price
of apples rocketed to 3s a pound. However, compared with Germany,
Britain was a land of plenty. When a particular food was cheap people
tended to eat it; when what had traditionally been cheap cuts of meat
became expensive they ceased to represent value, and people went elsewhere. That fish were more plentiful showed the success the Navy had
had in protecting the fishing fleet, providing an alternative to increasingly expensive, and unavailable, meat. It that sense, central direction
succeeded in avoiding yet another crisis.

It was a huge advantage to Britain to keep its people fed throughout
the war. In Germany, by contrast, the successful blockade had by the
autumn of 1918 led to a collapse in food supplies, driving down living
and nutritional standards, especially for those in urban areas. Fuel and
clothes were also in short supply. In large centres of population the fall
in morale became infectious. This in turn spread to men at the front,
who started to surrender rather than fight. These were the soldiers
whom Allied and American forces (by the Armistice there were 2 million Americans on the Western Front) were now encountering, and
consequently the entire complexion of the war changed.

Although the enemy advance had slowed down, the drastic measures
taken to recruit as many men as possible convinced pacifists that any
further fighting was pointless. Morrell and Snowden, two of the most
consistent opponents of the war, called in the Commons on 20 June for a
negotiated peace. Morrell had little hope of success. 'I can well understand that at a time like this, when the Germans are thundering almost
at the gates at Paris and the Austrians are approaching Venice, or are not
very far from it, and the situation, as the Prime Minister said, is a grave
and menacing one, there are many people in this House who will think
that no word with regard to peace ought to be uttered.'[289] He claimed that
'never before, I believe, was the desire for peace so deep, so widespread,
so passionate, as it is to-day, I am not saying in the minds of the governing classes, but in the minds of the people in all the warring countries of
Europe.'[290]

He reiterated the gravity of the casualty figures. In the week ended 9
June, he said, 700 British soldiers had been killed every day; and over the
week 30,000 men had been wounded or gone missing. In five months

from the beginning of January to the beginning of June 71,000 men had been killed, and more than half the period was before the great enemy advance. The wounded and missing amounted to 300,000. He believed the German figures were even worse, which was why the German public demanded an end to the war. In Austria, he said, there were riots and stop-the-war meetings. But what mattered was happening closer to home. 'I was speaking,' he said, 'the other day to an old man who had lost several sons in the War, and he said to me, in tones which I shall not easily forget, "It is not war; it is murder!" That is the feeling which is growing in this country.'[291]

Morrell asserted that even Germany's government could not afford to ignore public opinion: in that he was more right than he knew. He asked for the 'weapon of diplomacy' to be deployed, for that reason.[292] But – reflecting on the several occasions during 1917 when the Commons had discussed a negotiated peace – he said phrases such as 'knock-out blow' made diplomacy even harder. He doubted the Prussian army – as he called it – could be destroyed and, even if it was, he was sure Prussian militarism could not. Snowden berated Lloyd George for never attending the House when this subject was debated – he usually left it to Balfour, as on this occasion – and upbraided the government for not using Russia's exit from the war to reopen the question. Balfour accused his opponents of trying to divide the Allies and encourage the Germans to believe they were near victory; he said the Allies sought the kind of peace that would prevent such an outrage as the violation of Belgium from happening again, and that secured the future of liberty. That, however, did not seem to be a German desire.

He stressed that the government would never reject a serious peace offer, but asked: 'Have the German Government ever openly and plainly said, in any document, or in any speech, that Belgium is to be given up, that Belgium is to be restored, that Belgium is to be placed in a position of absolute economic as well as political independence? I know of no such statement.'[293] National honour would not allow Britain to concede this point. He talked of a future in which a 'League of Nations' would offer true security and peace. However, he concluded: 'We shall never get that peace, and we shall never deserve to get that peace, if we listen to the counsel given to us by the hon Gentleman who has just sat down, if we fail to look facts in the face, if we fail to see what German ambitions really mean, what German statesmen are really driving at, and what it is they are determined to have.'[294] He carried the House with him: Germany's utter refusal to discuss the return of any territory it had occupied remained the great obstacle.

However, even as Morrell spoke it was becoming clear that the tide on the Western Front had turned. On 18 July the French army started to drive back the Germans from Champagne, and Allied troops soon retook the bulge in the line conquered since March. The news, together with the absence of air raids, helped revive morale that, for reasons beyond the military reverses of the preceding four months, had dipped badly, leaving many people in an unprecedented attitude of stunned compliance. The German people were now feeling the full psychological impact of the war, and they would not prove equal to it.

EVERY TANK

PRODUCED·IN·THESE·WORKS

WILL SAVE BRITISH LIVES

CHAPTER II

ARMISTICE

I

On Sunday 4 August 1918 the fourth anniversary of the declaration of war, religious and secular events were held around Britain to mark what the press called 'Remembrance Day'. The King and Queen led the solemnities, attending a service at St Margaret's, Westminster, conducted by the Archbishop of Canterbury, who in his sermon warned the nation against 'slackness' and 'lack of grip'.[1] The Bishop of London led a service for 20,000 people in Hyde Park that afternoon, and Marble Arch served as a shrine for people to lay flowers 'in memory of those who have fallen'. At all gatherings a resolution was read out proclaiming that those attending were 'silently paying tribute to the Empire's sons who have fallen in the fight for freedom on the scattered battlefields of the world-war'.[2] It also called for recognition of the sacrifice of those still fighting, and especially of prisoners of war, and of those engaged in vital war work in munitions factories and elsewhere 'for the preservation of civilisation'.

Three days later Lloyd George reviewed the war in the Commons. He began in a way that suggested either a highly defective memory, or that he was so used to lying that it had become second nature to do it even in Parliament, and even when his lies or misrepresentations could be easily exposed. 'We had a compact with France,' he told the Commons, 'that if she were wantonly attacked, the United Kingdom would go to her support.'[3] This was a travesty, and bore no resemblance to the events of August 1914; a couple of MPs expressed their surprise. But then the point of his speech was not to give an accurate picture of the war; it was to boast about how the system he had implemented the previous winter, with Foch becoming 'generalissimo', had helped arrest the German advance: and had he been allowed to implement it sooner one factor in that advance would have been removed. This outraged the Asquithians; some inevitably knew that had Lloyd George not starved the Western Front of troops in order to disoblige Haig, the advance might have been far less of a problem, and the great national panic of the previous spring might have been avoided. He bragged that the government had sent a huge new force rapidly to repel the German advance.

Herbert Samuel followed him, and set about correcting his bizarre version of history. 'I think the Prime Minister, if he reviews the facts, will find that his memory has deceived him as to that,' he said about France. 'Our hands were entirely free.'[4] He quoted exactly what Grey had said on 3 August 1914, all of which was a matter of undisputed record. Samuel was not seeking to expose Lloyd George's dishonesty or incompetent grasp of fact, though he incidentally did; he acted to avoid a damaging misunderstanding among the public. 'It is essential that the country should not think there was anything in the nature of a secret treaty or any private compact which obliged us at the beginning of August, 1914, to enter this War. It was our sense of duty, our obligation under the treaty that safeguarded the independence of Belgium, and our sense of duty to safeguard the reign of public law and the freedom of Europe against the wanton aggression of the moment, and that alone, and no specific contract with the French Government which required us at that time to enter this War.'[5]

Samuel reminded Lloyd George of his boast the previous November that the unified command had been devised to ensure there would be an effective response to any attack. He made him squirm: 'While we rejoice that it was possible to send from this country 268,000 men at such short notice,' he said, 'and while we cordially congratulate the Government and the War Office on the rapidity with which they were thrown across the Channel at the crucial moment, the House will feel that if those large forces had been available on the spot and had already been dispatched in anticipation of a blow being struck, the battle might have taken a different course.'[6] Lloyd George tried to claim the troops were drafts kept in reserve for such a moment; Samuel reminded him that he had sat on a War Office subcommittee in 1917–18 that had repeatedly warned the government about the folly of keeping large numbers of troops at home. It was not surprising Lloyd George had steered so far from the truth; what was astonishing was that he thought no one would notice.

Later in the debate Lloyd George rose again to admit that perhaps the word 'compact' was wrong. 'In my judgment it was an obligation of honour,' he said, a different matter altogether.[7] No one lacked the tact to remind him how close he had come to not supporting the war before the attack on Belgium, and when the 'obligation of honour' was all there was to it. However, Samuel did point out that Grey had specifically said, in his Commons speech on 3 August 1914, that there was no obligation of honour. However Lloyd George tried to twist the truth, the truth would out. Asquith, who was not present, read what Samuel had said and wrote to congratulate him on having corrected Lloyd George's 'monstrous and most mischievous misrepresentations of our 'understanding' with France.'[8] In case anyone still wondered about the true nature and character of Lloyd George, this speech gave a helpful preview of the tone and methods he would deploy when seeking a mandate from the country later in the year.

The next day came the real turning point on the Western Front: the Battle of Amiens launched the German army on a retreat that would continue until the Armistice. Ludendorff, the German commander, called 8 August 'the Black Day of the German Army'. They were soon driven back 7 miles towards the Hindenburg Line, which prompted the obedient Wilson to write to Haig and advise him the War Cabinet would be upset if he incurred heavy losses attacking the Hindenburg Line unless he did so successfully. Haig was appalled. 'The Cabinet are ready to meddle and interfere in my plans in an underhand way, but do not dare openly to say that they mean to take the responsibility for any failure though ready to take credit for every success,' he told his diary. 'The object of this telegram is, no doubt, to save the Prime Minister in case of any failure.'[9] In his memoirs Lloyd George denied knowledge of Wilson's telegram.

On that first day of the Allied assault 400 guns and 22,000 prisoners were taken.[10] After Amiens Haig was secure in his post: a fortnight earlier Lloyd George had summoned the Earl of Cavan, a lieutenant general commanding the Army in Italy, to London to 'vet' him as a possible replacement. Hankey, who noted the visit in his diary, persuaded Lloyd George to stick with Haig.[11] As the papers reported the continuing advance, and the public realised the Germans were on the run and the war had become truly mobile in the Allies' favour, the mood at home changed to one of excitement and expectation for the first time in four years. When MacDonald tried to address an Independent Labour Party meeting on Plumstead Common in south London on 31 August he was shouted down, mainly but not exclusively by discharged and disabled soldiers, and a small riot ensued.

Haig went to London on 10 September to explain to Milner how radically the situation at the front had changed since 8 August, so the cabinet could be better informed before it made decisions. In four weeks 77,000 prisoners had been taken, and 800 guns. The German prisoners were in a revolutionary frame of mind, refusing to obey their officers or NCOs, and had given intelligence officers good reason to believe discipline was breaking down in the whole Army among those still fighting. Haig told Milner 'it was the beginning of the end,' though his history of optimism may have caused Milner to question his assertion.[12] Haig asked him to send all home troops to France at once to finish the Germans off; he refused to plan for troop numbers up to the middle of 1919, arguing that with the right action the war would have ended by then.

The story of the ensuing weeks was of a German army exhausted by months of attack, its morale sinking, and no match for the superior manpower or equipment of the Allied armies as it was driven back into Belgium. American troops were now pouring into France: by the time of the Armistice there were 6,432,000 Allied and American soldiers on the Western Front and only 3,527,000 against them.[13] The Austrians wished to sue for peace, the political situation in the Habsburg lands being even worse than in the Hohenzollern. The Allied and American armies had better supply lines, more food, more horses, better output of ammunition, better intelligence and better air power. Low morale in the German and Austro-Hungarian armies was betrayed by an increasing number of desertions and surrenders throughout September and October. In a typical moment of dramatic pessimism, Northcliffe may have said in September that 'none of us will live to see the end of this war'.[14] However, the fact was that even as he spoke the fighting men of the Central Powers were contemplating giving up.

The end result was made more certain when Germany suddenly began to find itself without allies. The Turkish front was imploding, with Allied victories in Palestine and at Salonica, and on 27 September a note from Bulgaria arrived asking for an armistice. Terms were offered, and accepted, on 30 September. On 3 October Wilhelm II's new more liberal government, under Prince Max of Baden, recognised the impossibility of defeating the forces now ranged against the Central Powers; and in an attempt at divide and rule, sued for peace with President Wilson. America had never been one of the Allies; to preserve independence of action, it had only been 'associated' with them, so could have separate war aims and make a separate peace if it wished. It was this separation that the Germans chose to exploit and, for the moment, the Americans seemed happy to contemplate a divergence of their war aims from those of the European Allies. Austria too asked Wilson for an armistice on 4 October, and made the request unconditional on 27 October.

France and Britain would join in discussions with Wilson, though they had reservations about some of his fourteen points, which he had set out the previous January as America's war aims. These had been largely drawn up by Colonel House, as Wilson's main foreign policy adviser. Most were easy for Britain to accept. These included a commitment to democracy, free trade, a league of nations, and to the making of public rather than private understandings in diplomatic dealings. Britain was also happy with the demand for the evacuation of occupied territory – notably Belgium – and its restoration to its own people, which had been integral to British war aims since August 1914. And, despite its determination to retain its own empire, Britain could endorse Wilson's belief in self-determination for the peoples of the Austro-Hungarian Empire. There was, however, anxiety about Wilson's demand for freedom of the seas, because this would affect Britain's conduct of imperial policy and the Royal Navy's ability to police the overseas possessions. This was of little consequence to Americans, who saw no need to preserve the British Empire. Were Britain to subscribe to such a principle it would seriously restrict its ability to mount precisely the sort of blockade that had undone Germany. Nor did Wilson's proposals for the Middle East take into account British interests there, such as the fate of non-Turkish peoples in the former Ottoman Empire. Wilson wanted them to be guaranteed 'autonomous development' and for the Dardanelles to be left permanently open for free passage of ships; ideals that would not inevitably suit British needs in the area. Nor had Wilson covered reparations, and Britain was keen on Germany being made to pay an economic price for the consequences of its aggression.

By early October morale was collapsing among the civilian population of Germany, putting extreme pressure on the Kaiser and his political
advisers, and necessitating the approach to Wilson. Food, fuel and clothing shortages had been bad enough: but in early October the 'Spanish'
influenza epidemic, which was relentlessly attacking much of Europe
and the rest of the world, reached Berlin, and started to kill an undernourished and exhausted population. At a conference of the Supreme
War Council, meeting in Paris on 6 October, officials began work on
terms for a German armistice, suspecting the German government's
plea for peace was not another empty gesture and that the country's
capitulation could be imminent. President Wilson was reluctant to convey a view to his representatives in Paris about what he made of the
separate requests by Germany and Austria; his main concern was acceptance by the enemy of the fourteen points.

He did, however, emphasise to the Central Powers that he could not
recommend an end to hostilities to the Allies while the armies of those
powers were on Allied soil. What was also clear, even as early as 8 October, was that those with forces ranged against the Germans all had
different ideas about what might be required to end hostilities, beyond
British reservations about some of the fourteen points. President Wilson, to general annoyance but especially that of Lloyd George, had
replied to the petitions for an armistice without consulting the Allies,
and it was not until 9 October that his reply was shared with them.
The Allies had their own conditions they wished to impose besides the
evacuation of occupied territory. The French – whose views were
expressed by Foch – sought conditions from Germany that Hankey, who
was at the meeting, termed 'too extreme' and 'humiliating'.[15]

When the Germans replied to Wilson on 12 October, seeking to
negotiate the process of evacuation from all the territories they had
invaded, the British interpreted that as the Germans playing for time
in which to regroup. Lloyd George, after consultation with Law, Balfour, Churchill and service chiefs, sent a telegram to Wilson urging
him to 'disillusion' the Germans about the conditions of an armistice,
and to consult his allies about them.[16] Wilson still did not consult them,
but his next note to the Germans took account of Lloyd George's telegram, making it clear Germany would have to respect the military
supremacy of the US and Allied armies in organising its evacuation of
occupied territory: there would need to be an end to submarine

warfare and to the retreating German army's wanton destruction of all in its path.

Haig was summoned to Downing Street on 19 October to give his views on the state of the German army, and on what terms should be offered if the Germans sought an armistice. He believed the Germans remained disciplined enough to defend their country, even if driven out of France and Belgium; they would not accept unconditional surrender. He remarked that the French army seemed to have decided the war was over, and the Americans, lacking an experienced officer class, were insufficiently trained and organised to be of much use. As for terms, he suggested the immediate evacuation of Belgium and occupied France; Alsace and Lorraine to be surrendered and occupied by the Allied army; and the return of French and Belgian rolling stock and of civilians to those areas. Lloyd George asked Haig what he thought the consequences would be of offering terms so stiff that Germany carried on fighting; Haig replied that the Allies should offer only what they were prepared to hold themselves to: 'We should set our faces against the French entering Germany to pay off old scores,' something for which he felt the British would not wish to fight.

He emphasised in a telegram to the Germans that the only acceptable armistice would be one that 'would leave the Allied and Associated Powers in a position to enforce the arrangements made, and to make the renewal of hostilities on the part of Germany impossible.'[17] The president also stressed that there would be no negotiations, but rather a demand for surrender, until Germany removed the Hohenzollerns and became a republic. Germany accepted Wilson's terms the next day, and it was left to his military advisers to draw up the exact details of how those terms would be enforced. Wilson communicated none of this to the Allies officially until 23 October.

Pending German acceptance of Wilson's proposals and Allied agreement to them, the fighting continued, with Allied and American troops now routinely prevailing. Meanwhile, throughout October British troops were conquering Syria and Mesopotamia as Ottoman forces were routed. However, Haig and Sir Henry Wilson remained cautiously pessimistic – Haig perhaps realising the harm he had done himself in the past by claims of success. They warned Lloyd George in late October that the German retreat was orderly rather than disorganised; that their army was not actually shattered; and that when attacked they hit back hard. Wilson could see no reason why Germany should surrender, and Haig pointed out that the numbers of guns captured had fallen. However, the soldiers did not understand the fast-changing political situation in Germany, and the collapse of civilian and service morale there, which had prompted acceptance of President Wilson's terms. The loss of allies such as Bulgaria and Turkey had not helped. Exhausted and short of supplies, the German army on the Western Front could at best hold the ground it had: its commanders did not expect breakthroughs.

Between 28 October and 4 November there were ten meetings of the Supreme War Council in Paris to settle the terms Germany would be offered. The Allied and Associated Powers discussed the fourteen points at the Quai d'Orsay – the French Foreign Ministry – on 29 October. Lloyd George arrived with an instruction from the War Cabinet not to concede freedom of the seas. Clemenceau supported Lloyd George: House, Wilson's representative and (in Hankey's view) the author of the point about freedom of the seas, threatened that if it were not accepted America might have to conclude a separate peace with Germany. In that case, Lloyd George and Clemenceau concurred, the Allied Powers would carry on fighting. Lloyd George told House that Britain was not a military nation, but a naval one, and its power was its Fleet: and it would not give up its right to use its Fleet as it saw fit. The next day that reservation, and another about the need for Germany to compensate civilians whose property their aggression had damaged, was communicated to Wilson. America did not conclude a separate peace, and on 3 November Wilson said he 'sympathetically' recognised the Allied concerns, and the question of blockade.[18]

Before that meeting on 29 October Lloyd George had told Haig how he wanted to maintain a strong Army for a year after the peace, while letting classes of key workers return to civilian life – notably miners. 'He evidently feels that we may have to face both internal troubles, as well as difficulties with some of our present Allies.'[19] Meanwhile, the Central Powers continued to implode. On 28 October Czechoslovakia and Poland declared their own governments. On 29 October the German High Seas Fleet mutinied. On 30 October the Ottoman Empire brokered its armistice with the Allies, and Austria requested an armistice with Italy. Kaiser Karl of Austria–Hungary saw his empire crumbling and his peoples longing for an end to the war: the Dual Monarchy was consigned to history. The Austrian fleet was handed to the Jugo-Slav National

Council. On 3 November Austria and Hungary concluded armistices with the Allies.

Ludendorff, as German Quartermaster General, had been deeply unhappy with his country's agreement to Wilson's terms. To start with he was reluctant to swallow them, and then proceeded to decide that they were completely unacceptable. He then thought he had convinced himself, at the end of October, that Germany should fight on. A month earlier he had believed the war was lost. However, he quickly realised, and told his government, that German forces could not defend central Europe. In the event of holding the Western Front (which was extremely unlikely, as soldiers were continuing to surrender in their thousands as the Allies advanced, with 18,000 capitulating in the first week of November) the Reich would be under assault from the south and east.[20] It was becoming clear to the German political class that their people would not tolerate another winter of war that left them hungry and without fuel; their soldiers saw the great offensive had been beaten back and, unlike the Allies who had hundreds of thousands of Americans ready to pour into France, they had no more resources to plumb. Order started to break down in German cities, with workers' soviets being formed, and revolts in cities as far apart as Hamburg and Munich. Once this happened, it became clear to all but the most blinkered Germans that defeat was unavoidable.

At the 1 November meeting of the Supreme War Council the proposed terms for an armistice, which Lloyd George had with other Allied leaders and plenipotentiaries earlier approved, were read out. Haig thought them 'very stiff': the Germans to withdraw 40 kilometres east of the Rhine, surrendering 5,000 guns and much rolling stock as well as evacuating territory.[21] Political and military leaders in Britain were against a 'humiliating' peace being inflicted on Germany, Milner and Derby describing the prospect as 'against the best interests of the British Empire.'[22] However, for some, what was being proposed was not enough: Northcliffe, who spoke for a considerable proportion of the public, called for unconditional surrender via The Times. Just before the Armistice, after a series of increasingly short-tempered meetings with Lloyd George in which Northcliffe warned him against lenient treatment of Germany, repeated his demands to know who was being considered for the government, and possibly asked for a place on the delegation at the forthcoming peace conference, the prime minister supposedly told him to 'go to Hades'.[23]

II

As the tide turned on the Western Front, speculation began that Lloyd George would call a general election 'in the late autumn': those around the prime minister fed the speculation, on his orders.[24] He told Riddell in August that he was 'strongly in favour of an appeal to the country in November' because, with the tide by then having turned, he thought it would favour him, and he could deny any such advantage by saying it had, in any case, been almost eight years since the last election, and this was the earliest opportunity to have one.[25] It gave the political class something to talk about during the recess; and the imminence of a new register that had 'completely changed the electoral map and revolutionised the machinery of elections' made an early election irresistible, whether or not the war still raged.[26] Yet when the subject was first discussed, it was believed the war might continue for another year or two.

There was, objectively, an overwhelming case for an election, as the Parliament was three years past its normal span, having had five Acts of Parliament passed at different times to extend its duration by a few more months. Half the House of Commons had not been returned at the December 1910 poll, but in by-elections since, most of them uncontested and therefore unreflective of democracy. Moreover, not only was there a huge new electorate that 'enfranchised new classes like the soldiers of 19 years of age and a new sex in women', but on 23 October the Commons debated a resolution put down by Samuel that a Bill should be passed to allow women to become Members of Parliament too; two hundred and seventy-four MPs, including the once implacable Asquith, supported it, with only twenty-five against, despite calls for a new House of Commons to make the decision. As Samuel put it, 'you cannot say that 6,000,000 women shall be voters, but that not one shall ever be a legislator. By our deliberate action in passing the Representation of the People Bill we have given up the old narrow doctrine that woman's sphere was the home and nothing but the home.'[27] However, Admiral Meux observed that 'I do not think this House is a fit and proper place for any respectable woman to sit in . . . what about all-night sittings, sitting up till two or three in the morning? "Who goes home?" It will be a question of "Who will take me home?" '[28]

In late August, as another early sign of the government's electioneering mood, it was announced that a film recounting the life of Lloyd George would be released to cinemas in November, which further fuelled election speculation. On 12 September he opened what was effectively his campaign with a speech at Manchester, where he received the freedom of the city of his birth. He did not mention an election: but expressed hopes of the future, beginning with the certainty of victory – 'the Germans have no America.'[29] He expressed the aspiration of a League of Nations. He also mentioned reconstruction, better transport and better use of Britain's 'human material'; and stressed improved health care – perhaps his most celebrated remark was that 'we cannot maintain an A1 Empire with a C3 population', and his claim that a doctor had told him an extra million men could have been under arms 'if the health of the country had been properly looked after.' He had formulated these views earlier, knowing that a promise of change had to be paramount. In August, discussing the future with Riddell, he had mentioned 'disquieting' statistics given him by Auckland Geddes that showed 'the physique of the people of this country is far from what it should be, particularly in the agricultural districts where the inhabitants should be the strongest.' He continued: 'This is due to low wages, malnutrition and bad housing. It will have to be put right after the war.'[30]

He had planned a tour of northern cities: but he keeled over on the evening of his Manchester speech and was diagnosed with Spanish flu. A bedroom was made for him in the city's Town Hall, with the trams diverted from the side of the building in which he was resting to give him peace and quiet. One of Manchester's leading specialists attended him; he recovered and returned to London, still enfeebled, on 21 September.

He started to sound out colleagues about who could be in a government of all the talents, to reconstruct Britain after the war. He was even, at that stage, prepared to include Northcliffe, though was warned by friends that he would be impossible to work with. Beaverbrook, in his unreliable memoir *Men and Power*, claimed that during the anxious months before Amiens Northcliffe had enlisted him and Reading to advocate to Lloyd George that he should become Lord President of the Council, and assist Lloyd George in saving the country. There is no other evidence for this; and such stories detract from the fact that Northcliffe was doing a superb job in his propaganda work, the shattered morale of the German army being further undermined by the leaflet drops that, in the last phase of the war, were again under way. Even before aircraft were used balloons dropped 7,820,367 leaflets between June and August, causing an alarmed Hindenburg to warn his troops of the Allied war on 'the German spirit'.[31]

For all Northcliffe's achievements, and Lloyd George's readiness to consider him for a cabinet post, the prime minister realised he could not be trusted. But then neither could Lloyd George: one of Northcliffe's great gripes was that he thought Lloyd George had promised to call an election the moment the new register was in force: but did not. Northcliffe then demanded to know, through Riddell, the names of those whom Lloyd George was considering including in a new cabinet, as he would not use his papers to support an administration including men from what he called 'the Old Gang' – the Asquith coalition. This was too much for Lloyd George, who sent back word that he would 'give no undertaking as to the constitution of the Government and would not dream of doing such a thing.'[32] As nothing would possess him to take Northcliffe into his confidence in that way, or seek his approval for what he might or might not do, he realised the support of his newspapers – vital given that Lloyd George effectively had no party – could be withdrawn. Since the prime minister was determined to have an election the moment circumstances permitted, he needed another means of press support.

He had for months known the nature of British politics was about to change. At a dinner at Haldane's house in the spring he had told his host and Sidney and Beatrice Webb, who were also present, that 'the future would lie between two new parties, with the old Liberal Party split between them.'[33] The plans for the election of December 1918 – a contest between supporters of the existing coalition and the remnants of other parties – were drawn up long before it was clear it would be a postwar election, but rather in expectation that the main issue would be whether the war was fought to a finish or an attempt was made at a negotiated peace. Lloyd George was determined to secure the former, many Asquithian Liberals (though probably not Asquith himself) the latter.[34] Guest, the chief whip, had as early as July 1918 been drawing up lists of MPs who deserved government support.[35]

The prime minister had been keen since early in 1917 to have a friendly businessman buy the *Daily Chronicle*, whose circulation was 800,000 a day and which therefore had serious reach. It also, as already noted, had General Maurice as its military correspondent; so another motivation for Lloyd George to have a friend to buy it was to force Maurice out, and stop him writing disobliging articles about the conduct of the war. It was for sale for £1.1 million, with profits of roughly £200,000 a year (though £130,000 of that went in excess profits duty). The friendly businessman was Sir Henry Dalziel, the Liberal MP and owner of *Reynolds News* and the *Pall Mall Gazette*, who, helpfully, had been advanced to a baronetcy the previous January. Riddell, part of the conspiracy to buy the *Chronicle*, had noted in early September that there was 'some difficulty' in arranging the finance.[36] It would soon be made public what the nature of the difficulties were.

On 1 October the deal was done. 'LG to have full control of the editorial policy through Sir H Dalziel, who will in effect be his agent,' Riddell noted. 'The experiment will be interesting.'[37] The propriety of a prime minister using other people's money – and money from a highly questionable source at that – effectively to own a newspaper seems never to have struck him, but then the morality of Lloyd George's cronies was rarely superior to his. It was soon common parlance that money from the sale of honours had funded the purchase. Beaverbrook, highly improperly for a minister, had been closely involved in the conspiracy, which caused so much concern that it was discussed in the Commons on 15 October. 'If the springs of public information come into the hands of a few groups or of one group, you really have a travesty of genuine democratic conditions,' William Pringle, the Lanarkshire MP and a strong supporter of Asquith, said.[38] He claimed entirely accurately that the *Daily Chronicle* was 'really under the control of the government'.[39]

The Asquithians knew that few voices in the press would speak for them, come the election, magnifying what Dalziel had achieved for Lloyd George. Pringle wanted the government to hold an inquiry into the sale of the paper: but there was more chance of it giving Belgium to the Germans. He put on the record reasons why there would not be such an inquiry. The government had honoured two earlier prospective purchasers, Lords Leverhulme, the soap and detergent magnate, and Colwyn, thus getting them out of the way; and Guest, as chief whip, had also had a hand in those negotiations, so several distinguished politicians stood to be damaged by such an inquiry. Pringle challenged those present who knew the truth – Dalziel and Guest – to correct any error of detail. They remained silent.

He continued by disclosing that an accountant had been asked to value the business, which he did at £900,000, less than the owners wanted; and this figure had been conveyed to Guest. 'After this report was received it turned out that Lord Leverhulme was not the real person involved,' Pringle continued, 'but that behind the rays of Sunlight soap there was the interesting and significant figure of Lord Beaverbrook. That was at a time when Lord Beaverbrook was Minister of Information. It is a matter which, I think, concerns this House that the Minister of Information, a member of the Government and a responsible Minister, should have been negotiating for the purchase of a newspaper at a time when he was advertising himself as having divested himself of all control in another newspaper which he had previously owned.'[40]

However, Pringle disclosed that Beaverbrook had backed out: the price was too high, and if the government wanted the *Chronicle*, party funds would have to pay for it. Beaverbrook had agreed that had he bought the paper he would have supported Lloyd George for a further five years: a promise he had been unprepared to make on behalf of the *Daily Express*. A further complication had been that the *Chronicle*'s proprietor, Frank Lloyd, had refused to sell it to a Tory. Learning this, Guest had tried to persuade Lloyd that Beaverbrook – whose entrée into British politics had been through Law, whose Conservative politics he shared entirely – was not in fact a Tory, even though he had been a Tory MP. Guest was not one of the ghastly 'new men' who had risen partly by sharp practice and duplicity, and should have known better: he was the younger brother of Wimborne, and Churchill's cousin, and had won the DSO before being invalided out of the Army. Soiling his hands in this way gravely demeaned him.

Dalziel spoke in the debate, mainly, he claimed, because any further silence would have been misinterpreted. He denied that, having acquired the *Chronicle*, he had sought to 'muzzle its independence', though the content of the paper had rapidly suggested otherwise.[41] He claimed it had been sold because of the previous owner's ill health, and that he had bought it largely to prevent a group of Tories coming in and taking it over: an unlikely story given the refusal to sell to Beaverbrook. He denied knowing anything about Beaverbrook's approach or, indeed, Leverhulme's. He denied, too, that he was subservient to anyone, or that he had been guilty of impropriety – 'my public life is an open book'.[42] Lloyd George would mark his public service with a peerage in 1921.

 This deal exemplified how far Lloyd George, sundered from mainstream Liberals and party funds, would go to acquire new means of influence, and new rich friends. Maurice was forced to resign, as was Robert Donald, the editor who had appointed him, even though Lloyd George had given him a part-time job under Beaverbrook earlier that year as director of propaganda to neutral countries, and Scott had regarded him as 'a kind of scout for Lloyd George'.[43] Donald's decision to hire Maurice appears to have signed his own death warrant; he made it quite clear through his newspaper that he no longer trusted Lloyd George, and so Lloyd George showed he did not trust him. The torrent of criticism the *Chronicle* had poured on the government about manpower shortages and Irish policy became, like criticism of war policy, a thing of the past. The *Chronicle* would be slavishly loyal when the election came. On 4 November Beaverbrook resigned to have an operation on his throat, infected by a bad tooth, and the Ministry of Information wound down: his successor, Lord Downham, served two months before it was abolished.

 Although Northcliffe's influence was manifestly on the wane, with Lloyd George now preparing to assert himself as the man who had won the war and far less troubled than before about the conceit of a newspaper proprietor, others remained apprehensive of Northcliffe's power. On 7 November, in a debate on the Ministry of Information, Carson attacked Northcliffe, aware that he had been trying to get Lloyd George to make him a formal delegate to the peace conference. 'I am quite alive to the fact,' he said,

> that it is almost high treason to say a word against Lord Northcliffe. I know his power and that he does not hesitate to exercise it to try to drive anybody out of any office or a public position if they incur his royal displeasure. But as at my time of life neither office nor its emoluments nor anything connected with Governments, or indeed public life, makes the slightest difference, and the only thing I care about is really the interests of decent administration, I venture to incur even the possibility of the odium of this great trust owner, who monopolises in his own person so great a part of the Press of this country, and has always for himself a ready-made claque to flatter him and to run any policies for him that he thinks best in his own interests.[44]

Carson spoke for a political class sick and tired of Northcliffe's imagining he had some sort of mandate; he was determined to show the
press baron that he could not behave in that way without criticism. The
last straw had been an attack in the Northcliffe press on Milner, which Carson not only considered unfair but which he thought 'indecent', given
Northcliffe's official propaganda work.[45] Milner, at Versailles, had given
an interview to which Northcliffe objected, and a leading article had
quoted a telegram from someone in France claiming the interview
had done 'great damage' there. Carson believed Northcliffe himself had
sent the wire. 'I think it is really time to put an end to this kind of thing,'
he added, saying the 'best elements' of the public 'resent' such conduct.
For those in any doubt, Carson said: 'Everybody knows who has been in
public life or in public office that the moment Lord Northcliffe's displeasure is incurred, from that moment onwards a kind of man-hunt
commences until he drives anybody whom he looks upon as an adversary out of office.'

His peroration was ferocious: the reasons for these

attacks from an official of the Government upon Lord Milner
[were] to drive him out of his office . . . In order that Lord Northcliffe may get it or may get into the War Cabinet, so that he may be
present at the Peace Conference, whenever it comes. The whole
thing is a disgrace to public life in England and a disgrace of journalism. I know perfectly well how difficult it is to ever criticise the
Press. I know perfectly well the reward you reap for it. Thank God,
I never cared what they said about me. I have never cared, but I do
hope that Members of this House, whether they agree with Lord
Milner or whether they agree with any other Minister, will see
that, at all events, at a crisis like this fair-play, fair criticism, honest
dealing, and decent life are necessary.[46]

The furthest Stanley Baldwin, the spokesman in the debate for the
government that had availed itself of Northcliffe's services, would go to
defend its propagandist was to say that with the war ending the ministry
for which he had worked was 'not only moribund, but *in articulo mortis*
and . . . defunct.'[47]

Meanwhile, Lloyd George continued to lay his plans for an early election. As soon as the German position began to crumble those close to

the prime minister entered discussions with supporters of Asquith about their possible place in a new coalition, after the election. On 26 September Murray of Elibank, the former Liberal chief whip, acted as go-between to offer Asquith the Woolsack again, with two cabinet jobs for his followers – Runciman and Samuel were suggested – and six junior jobs too, in return for supporting the coalition and agreeing to an immediate election. Asquith refused.

Not all of Lloyd George's usual supporters were happy to hear rumours that a poll was being rushed forward. Scott turned the fire of the *Manchester Guardian* on the man who would call it, his friend Lloyd George. 'Such a Government, so elected,' he wrote on 1 November, 'would have no real authority for the future. It would have selected a moment when the country was, as it were, disarmed and all political parties but its own at a disadvantage and in disarray, in order to seize power.'[48] That was remarkably acute. The next day Lloyd George wrote officially to Law to put the proposal to him, and he accepted. On 5 November the King, at one with the *Manchester Guardian*, reluctantly agreed to dissolve Parliament, 'being against it before' a long discussion with his prime minister, and Law and Lloyd George began to debate tactics.[49]

III

To its credit, and thanks to the dynamism and high-mindedness of a few ministers, the coalition had begun to seek to shape the world after the war long before the conflict entered its decisive phases. The reform of the franchise was the first and most obvious example; but it was also accepted that there was an acute need to rebuild Britain – not because of war damage, of which there was relatively little, but because of the shattering of families and the need to replace decaying and substandard pre-war infrastructure. It would be enough of a problem to deal with demobilisation and to place back in civilian life all those returning from combat when hostilities ended: but there needed to be better preparation of the nation's human resources if Britain were to have a prosperous and successful future. So the rebuilding would have to be of society as well as of physical structures.

In developing the nation's human capital, education would be the key. Even in the depths of the war, in the first days of the Somme, the Lords had discussed planning for this, aware of the enormous shortcomings the existing system had, and the waste of talent it perpetuated. Haldane had introduced a motion on 12 July 1916 'to call attention to the training of the nation and to the necessity of preparing for the future'.[50] He understood perhaps better than anyone how superior the education systems in some of Britain's competitor nations, notably Germany and America, were. German working-class children left school at fourteen rather than thirteen; and most went into training or apprenticeship for four years, rather than drifting into the unskilled labouring that was the lot of all too many working-class British boys. Middle-class children stayed at school for between two and four more years, and then some went to university. The main weakness in the British system, as Haldane admitted, was that it was almost impossible for working-class children to get to a university. In that respect at least Britain was ahead of Germany, since a small number of scholarships and bursaries were available; but it was not good enough.

The scale of the problem was immense. In England in 1916 there had been 2,750,000 boys and girls aged twelve to sixteen. Around 1,100,000 left school at thirteen. Slightly more left at fourteen. Only 250,000 attended proper secondary schools, often for just a year or two. Of the 5,850,000 younger people aged between sixteen and twenty-five, only 93,000 attended full-time courses, most of short duration. Haldane had pointed out the massive advantage to nations that took education and training seriously.[51] He had said: 'We have to do our utmost to prepare the future generation, to prepare it intellectually, morally, and physically, to endure the strain which it will have to face . . . other nations have been coming up and devoting themselves with an assiduity and a science which are in excess in some respects of our own; and it is from that excess of assiduity on their part that the danger to us arises. We must see to it that we are not caught unprepared in the struggle. The reforms which are necessary are reforms which will involve the direction of energy.'[52]

Haldane's ideas and vision had a profound effect on H. A. L. Fisher, president of the Board of Education and, before that, vice chancellor of the University of Sheffield. He was a high-minded Liberal intellectual, imbued with Arnoldian ideals of sweetness and light, but also impeccably connected to Britain's intellectual aristocracy. The son of H. W. Fisher, the historian, he was a first cousin of Virginia Woolf; his sister Adeline was married to Ralph Vaughan Williams; and another sister married first the eminent legal historian F. W. Maitland and then Sir Francis Darwin, botanist son of the naturalist.

Fisher wanted to abolish the half-time system, under which children in industrial areas such as Lancashire and Yorkshire could work provided they spent a certain number of hours in education. He wanted children under fourteen to concentrate entirely on academic work; something to which the trades unions put up enormous resistance, and which brought complaints from agriculture, under severe pressure because of manpower shortages. He was also determined to create county education committees with the vision to expand the reach and content of the education system. His first great initiative had been to persuade Parliament in March 1918 to raise the school-leaving age to fourteen. He proceeded on the basis that it was all very well for Britain to win the war, as by September 1918 it appeared it would; but capitalising on victory would require a revolution in attitudes.

While stressing the importance of training minds by teaching the humanities, he specifically wanted more scientific training and education, and a receptiveness to new ideas: he also wondered 'how many Watts's, Kelvins, and Darwins have been lost in the vast mass of untrained talent which the children of the working classes afford. Our greatest mistake in this country has been in concentrating upon the education and training of the well-to-do . . . for the child of the workman what provision is there unless he has a very exceptional and keen father? Why, none whatever . . . 90 per cent of our population have not that education which is required if we are to make the best use of our available talent.'[53] Haldane had wanted the planning to start in 1916, but it had taken Fisher until 1918 to finish laying the ground for Haldane's vision of 'continuation schools' that working-class children might attend after the age of thirteen, and more provision of university places.[54]

On 13 March 1918 Fisher outlined some of his vision. 'There was a time when every elementary school teacher was expected to know every subject contained in the curriculum equally well or equally badly. There was a time when schools were subject to payment by results, when the results seldom went beyond a mechanical efficiency in the three Rs. We have got beyond that stage. Our teachers are encouraged to specialise, our curriculum is wider and more varied, we no longer rely upon the mechanical test of payment by results.'[55] It was estimated that more than a million disabled children were denied a proper education; Fisher's aim was not just to have the state provide opportunities for them, but also to seek to improve public health so there might be fewer to begin with; and for healthy children there would be a strong emphasis on physical education. He was also anxious to make parents take a closer interest in their children's education, and to support a school's efforts to extend learning opportunities.

Fisher did not hold back. 'The object of the Bill is to provide the greatest possible number of outlets for talent of all description. We are proposing in the Bill to make it an obligation, resting upon the local, education authority, to provide secondary education for all those pupils who are fit to receive it.' This would be accomplished by 'the provision of central schools, of higher elementary schools, of junior technical schools, and of junior commercial schools.' That was not all. 'The fact that we are, in addition, proposing a scheme of compulsory part-time education for the whole adolescent population between fourteen and sixteen, subject to certain exceptions, is not incompatible with the operation of the scheme for the selection and development of special talent.'[56] He said that, eventually, the cost of raising the school leaving age and of providing this additional education would be under £10 million a year, to be met jointly from taxes and local rates; about a day and a half's expenditure on the war. He also proposed increased teachers' salaries and central funding for schools, wanted local authorities empowered to provide nursery schools, and the creation of a pension scheme for secondary and technical school teachers.

The new policy was informed by Fisher's belief that the adolescent mind was highly susceptible to influence – as the relentlessly rising juvenile crime figures proved – and in education the young would be exposed to more good than bad influences. If someone went into work at fourteen, 'continuation classes' of around eight hours a week until the age of sixteen or eighteen would continue to instil some learning beyond the school leaving age. 'When it is proposed in the Bill to give to these children of poorer parents some measure of the moral guidance and direction which are universally claimed for the children of richer homes, I confidently claim that I shall have behind me the whole moral sense of the community.'[57]

Fisher was no utilitarian, but believed in education for the purposes of edification and development of character. He ended, though, on a practical note:

I ask then whether the education which is given to the great mass of our citizens is adequate to the new, serious, and enduring liabilities which the development of this great world war creates for our Empire, or to the new civic burdens which we are imposing upon millions of new voters? I say it is not adequate. Any competent judge of facts in this country must agree with me. I believe it is our duty, here and now, to improve it, and I hold that if we allow our vision to be blurred by a catalogue of passing inconveniences we shall not only lose a golden occasion but fail in our great trust to posterity.[58]

There was also a recognition that Britain was entering into a new era of stiff competition with other nations, and that a better-educated workforce was economically essential. The Liberal MP Francis Acland said in the debate on the second reading: 'Industries that do not want workers with a broader outlook, a better trained character and an increased power of applying their brains, not only to the particular industry concerned but to the ordinary problems of citizenship, are not industries that we shall be able to encourage or even to keep in this country. Undoubtedly there are difficult times coming. We simply cannot afford to let our industries lack the better mental equipment which all those engaged in them will obtain if the main provisions of this Bill are carried out.'[59]

Fisher's Bill was regarded as the first step in a programme of extending educational opportunities to those without the means to pay for them. There were predictable objections. Unionists protested that it could result in the over-education of many young people, who would find insufficient vacancies for those with their accomplishments. It was neither understood nor countenanced that the expansion of the educated population would create the prosperity that created higher-calibre work opportunities. Some MPs complained about the cost, not least because Fisher and his supporters intended his reforms to lead to more people going to university, and not merely the children of the privileged classes. Acland said: 'We want surely such a development of our scholarship system, including maintenance grants in the later years, as shall make us drop altogether the expression "educational ladder" out of our vocabulary, so that we may speak instead of the educational highway.'[60] He also outlined the aspirations beyond the Bill: 'We want the bringing of our private schools for all classes, the rich as well as those less well off, under the effective supervision of the Board of Education. We want a simplification of our system of examinations. We want great changes and developments in the methods in which we teach certain subjects, particularly science and modern languages.'

As well as Unionist MPs' concerns about the cost, many working-class people worried about the cost of their children's delaying their entry to the workforce – as they had about every education reform since 1870. This was partly why the legislation for Fisher's plans, which affected 95 per cent of children of school age and which the War Cabinet had sanctioned in February 1917, had taken so long to get through Parliament. Yet, as Fisher knew, the working class were also, paradoxically, the great advocates of the measure, because they were also aware of the chance it would give their children to lead better lives, in better jobs, than their parents, and to escape the drudgery of domestic service or unskilled labour: he categorised his Bill as a measure to guarantee the rights of young people.

However, there was also a constitutional consideration militating against the Bill. Fisher's opponents believed the Bill was too radical to be passed in the eighth year of a Parliament, and required the specific mandate of a general election; to some, such as Basil Peto, a Unionist MP, 'it constitutes a very large advance towards the Socialist theory that children belong to the State, and that the men and women, who are citizens of the State, are to be regarded as mere breeding machines.'[61] The measure came into effect before the new school year began in September, the same month as Wells published his novel *Joan and Peter*, which was devoted to exploring the rule of teachers with 'no ideas about education at all' in pre-war Britain.[62] By now the country was acutely aware of how under-skilled it had been at the start of the war, and how deficiencies in general education had retarded the war effort. Indeed, some of Fisher's critics argued that he had not been ambitious enough, and they were right. But he had taken an essential first step to opening up educational opportunity to everyone.

Further help for children, even before they went to school, came in the form of the Maternity and Child Welfare Act 1918, which allowed local government to set up committees to oversee the welfare of mothers and their offspring, funding coming partly from central government and partly from local rates. Ever since the National Insurance legislation of 1911, women in work had had health insurance, but those who did not work were denied it. These welfare committees were an important development in preventive medicine, and sought to improve the health of those who had recently given birth and to reduce the already falling levels of infant mortality and sickness.

The other major social issue the government promised to address – and, as with mentioning health and education reforms, it was with an eye to an imminent election campaign – was housing. William Hayes Fisher, the president of the Local Government Board (and no relation to the education reformer), told the Commons a fortnight before the Armistice what the government would do about housing. 'A very large policy of reconstruction' was promised, since he argued there was no point in pursuing policies such as improved child welfare or the elimination of tuberculosis if people had only insanitary, unventilated housing to return to, with no access to sunshine.[63] Like ministers before him since the 1870s, Fisher intoned that 'new houses must be built, old houses must be reconstructed and repaired, and slums must gradually be swept away.' There would, he promised, be extensive legislation in the next Parliament.[64] He raised the question of council housing, promising that councils could take out eighty-year loans to fund it. Town and district councils already had the power to provide housing for the working classes, but this would be extended to county councils.

The lack of manpower to build houses during the war had compounded the problem that in the most populous areas of Britain construction had fallen during the five years before 1914. Ironically, and because of the muscle of the Irish Nationalists, the only part of the kingdom to have had an extensive housing programme before the war had been Ireland. Shortages were so bad elsewhere in the United Kingdom that newspaper advertisements appeared offering rewards for information leading to finding housing in certain large cities. MPs dreaded the return of millions of soldiers to these inadequate conditions; there were calls for a million new houses at least, with every county providing its own assessment of its needs.

A survey in Scotland, whose population was roughly an eighth of England's, showed that 121,000 houses were needed there alone.[65] Some MPs suggested that instead of local authorities competing for loans to fund these, the government should grant them the money in recognition of the special circumstances. Only after that should developments be funded privately. There was also a call for more rural housing, to fit with the government's policy of persuading returning soldiers to work on the land. However, there were still no promises of capital from the Treasury to fund a building programme, and no compulsion on or incentives for councils to launch one. Many Liberals disliked the idea of state intervention; but as Runciman put it: 'For my own part, I do not like State action—I think it has been most inefficient and very expensive, but the need is so great at the present time that I place the necessity for houses in the very forefront; and I regard the means by which they are to be obtained as of somewhat secondary importance.'[66]

Colonel Josiah Wedgwood, a stricter Liberal than Runciman, rounded on Fisher's proposals: 'We have before us a Bill to-day which embodies within a very small scope two very important principles. The first is that the State should undertake the building trade of this country, and the second is that it should undertake that building trade on unsound, uneconomic lines.'[67] Wedgwood feared that building houses at 'charity rents' would wreck the business of every private landlord and undermine private enterprise; and lead to 'jobbery' and corruption on local councils as people sought a cheap house rather than one with a market rent. He also feared the creation of an army of housing inspectors to check the satisfactory progress of this new state authority, and the massive expansion of an unproductive state payroll. He in turn was savaged by Lord Henry Cavendish-Bentinck, son of the Duke of Portland: 'While we have been squabbling in this House before the War and laying down our Early Victorian economics, as the hon Member has just done, vested interests have been driving the people into a corner and depriving their children of any kind of playgrounds except the gutter, the alley and the court, and have been killing off their children by the thousands.'[68]

IV

Although it was clear from the late summer of 1918 that Britain was heading towards peace, the political class were far from convinced that the transition would be easy, or that the expectations of the public after four years of extreme hardship and sacrifice would be easy to maintain. The urgency with which housing, for example, was being addressed was not merely to keep faith with the fighting man on his return; it was to avoid giving the working classes any excuse to participate in Bolshevik-style activities that had not only transformed Russia, but were threatening to engulf Germany. Memories lingered of Lansbury's Albert Hall meeting the previous March, to welcome the Russian revolution, the first great public manifestation of support for revolutionary ideals, and at which a packed assembly had sung 'The Red Flag'. Lansbury had referred to how the Russian army had refused to shoot protestors, and had said: 'We can understand that when the working classes of all nations refuse to shoot down the working classes of other countries, Government won't be able to make wars any more. This war would end tomorrow if the troops on all sides march out into No Man's Land and refused to fight any longer.'[69]

The next Labour conference, at Leeds in May, called for the establishment of 'Workers' and Soldiers' Councils', like the soviets that now ran western Russia: Snowden was one of the main advocates. A motion was passed to set up the councils, but in the absence of any serious organisation nothing happened. Another conference in late June called for the truce with other parties to end, and for Labour MPs to withdraw from the government in preparation for an election. Henderson held the line, confirming that proper political warfare would break out once an election was called, not before. By then Labour already had 301 potential candidates, and announced that it expected to field another 100. A surprise visitor to the conference was Kerensky, the deposed socialist prime minister of Russia; all but a few hard-line Bolshevists gave him a rapturous welcome. In September, the TUC voted by a majority of 3 million to continue to cooperate with the Labour Party: a minority wanted a trades union labour party that would have been further left than Labour. The vote ensured a coherent labour movement, an essential underpinning of the party's march to power. The government was thereafter keenly alert to professions of Bolshevism: Sylvia Pankhurst, whose main political aims for women appeared now to have been achieved, was arrested under DORA after a speech in Derbyshire in which she advocated hard-line socialism.

As the Allies' position became stronger so, paradoxically, did the industrial climate deteriorate at home. A cotton spinners' strike was quickly settled, but a railway strike over demands for higher wages began in South Wales in late September and spread to London and elsewhere in the country. Sensing they had the whip hand, the railwaymen refused to negotiate with the government if the government insisted on negotiating with elected officials: the militants had their own representatives. The government said it would send in the Army to run essential trains – and at once 3,000 men of the London Rifle Brigade went to Newport, a centre of the trouble, and to the Great Eastern Railway's main depot at Stratford in east London. Even the labour movement disowned the strikers: the British Workers' League called them 'Bolshevist and anarchical'.[70] J. R. Clynes, the most influential Labour MP in the government, also attacked them, for holding up food and munitions supplies while fellow working men died in the pursuit of victory. Because there were no trains to move coal 100,000 colliers were idle in South Wales, where two-thirds of the Navy's and the merchant fleet's steam coal was mined. The government told striking railwaymen they would be conscripted; that threat, coupled with the arrival of armed troops, stimulated a return to work. However, it was then the turn of the South Wales miners to ask for a shorter day, and to threaten to strike otherwise. The War Cabinet offered to reduce the hours within six months of peace, which restored calm.[71]

At the same time, it threatened conscription to striking shipwrights on the Clyde, who sought a minimum wage of £5 a week and had been told by their union leaders to return to work. While the government reserved the right to prosecute the ringleaders under DORA, it felt the creation of martyrs in such a volatile area would be counter-productive. Conscription of men who refused to work was another matter. On the morning of 28 September a Royal Proclamation was posted around Clydeside that concluded: 'It is now necessary for the Government to declare that all shipyard workers wilfully absent from their work on or after Tuesday, the 1st October, will have voluntarily placed themselves outside the special protection afforded them.'[72] For the avoidance of doubt, the proclamation ended with the promise that such men would be called to the colours by age group, mirroring the threat at Coventry two months earlier. If that was the stick, the carrot was the suggestion that a Whitley Council would be constituted to settle shipwrights' wages. A ballot held after the proclamation defeated the appeal to return to work by 1,025 votes to 1,014. Since a two-thirds majority was needed to continue the strike, the men were back in time for the Tuesday deadline, with the understanding that a Whitley-style committee would hear their grievances. However, around sixty men under twenty-five who did not return to work received their call-up papers.

Nature, too, then provided an even greater example of adversity. The first signs of what would become a devastating influenza epidemic became apparent in the British Isles in June 1918, even though it was high summer. There had been outbreaks in several parts of Ireland that same month, and it spread to the mainland. It was already known as 'Spanish flu' because it was said to have spread through Spain a few weeks earlier; its origins were more likely in a holding camp for American troops in Kansas, where it had struck in March. The necessary mass movement of people during wartime and undernourishment because of food shortages and high prices exacerbated the problem. After Belfast had reported an epidemic, Letchworth, Cardiff and Huddersfield were among the first mainland towns to announce one; Hitchin Rural Council, which covered Letchworth, urged people 'to avoid picture palaces and other crowded places.'[73]

By the first week of July London was affected, notably in the textile factories of the east end, where up to 20 per cent of workers fell ill. The symptoms were violent headaches, renal pains and a rapid rise in temperature to 103 or 104 degrees Fahrenheit. Indoor workers were peculiarly vulnerable; outdoor ones seemed 'practically immune'.[74] Outbreaks were then recorded as far apart as Surrey, the Midlands and Tyneside, with collieries in the last two regions badly depleted; high absenteeism badly affected industrial efficiency across the economy. In early July the first deaths were reported, from Dublin and London. Then the munitions industry in and around Birmingham began to be afflicted; and throughout Manchester, and then London, elementary schools closed, mainly because of sick teachers.[75] London's Central Telegraph Office, a crucial communications hub, had 700 people off sick on one day in July.[76] Shortly before the summer holidays all the schools in Huddersfield were closed down, and in some places undertakers ran out of coffins. Ammoniated quinine was administered to victims but had no effect. Those proposing quack remedies and others of less doubtful but still uncertain provenance – such as taking cocoa three times a day – had a field day. Newspapers were filled with suggestions for precautions, such as eating porridge, forcing oneself to sneeze first thing in the morning and last thing at night, and to take brisk walks and get plenty of fresh air. Writing from the Garrick Club, a celebrated repository of clinical excellence, a Mr Harry Furniss proclaimed that the only known cure was 'to take snuff, which arrests and slays the insidious bacillus with great effect'.

In October the epidemic entered a second and more deadly phase.

When Sir Hubert Parry, the composer, succumbed on 7 October he was one of eighty people to die in London that week.[77] The new epidemic quickly took hold, with outbreaks in Liverpool, Dublin and Middlesbrough by mid-October. The death rate in Southampton rose from fourteen per thousand to forty-four; in Glasgow it rose from twelve per thousand to forty-one, with five hundred and ten deaths in the third week of October.[78] Half the deaths in Hornsey in the four weeks to 21 October were from flu; schools closed across north London, which was especially badly hit, because of sick children and teachers.[79] In Ilford, where 11,000 children were sent home from schools and long queues formed outside doctors' surgeries, undertakers complained they could not cope, and in neighbouring East Ham children under fourteen were banned from public places of amusement. In Leytonstone, nearby, so many were felled by the flu that families gave the local doctor keys to let himself in and out of their houses. Elementary schools in Brighton were ordered to be closed for a month. When the Local Government Board, three weeks into the new wave of the epidemic, issued advice on how to avoid the disease, *The Times* remarked that 'it would have been better to lock the stable door before the escape of the horse . . . the need for a Ministry of Health to protect the public in matters of this kind has never received a more forcible illustration.'[80]

On 28 October the government admitted that the mortality rate had risen enormously, though Hayes Fisher, who had the cabinet responsibility for dealing with the problem as president of the Local Government Board, said matters were not yet so bad as in Paris or Vienna: even so, an estimated 4,000 people died in a week. The transport of troops was thought to aggravate the problem, with Fisher saying the deaths were caused largely by flu victims contracting secondary infections that had been passed on by a highly mobile population. In Sunderland, it was reported that queues of funeral cortèges had to be managed around the city's cemeteries and churches.[81] Death could come swiftly, and people were seen dropping from the disease in the streets. Inflaming an already delicate situation, it was reported at the end of the month that 111 'political' prisoners in Belfast jail were afflicted. Worse still, given the shortage of men for the forces, was the report that at the RAF camp at Blandford in Dorset, where the average daily complement was 15,000 men, there had been 252 cases of flu in five weeks, 198 of which had required hospitalisation and 59 of which had resulted in death.[82]

The Medical Research Council spent an increasing amount of its resources on seeking how to prevent the spread of the flu; but because of the work it was doing on the treatment of wounds, it could not devote anything like the necessary effort to the epidemic. The Local Government Board, operating on a skeleton staff of a medical officer, four assistant medical officers and twenty health inspectors to cover the whole of England and Wales, oversaw the production of posters, leaflets and press announcements to warn the public of the best ways of preventing infection: though the only certain way was to lock oneself indoors and avoid contact with anyone else. Schools were closed and the public was warned to avoid crowded spaces such as cinemas; and in them the time between performances was greatly increased, to allow for a complete change of air inside the building. The uncertain response to the epidemic was, as *The Times* and many others had predicted, a factor that would soon result in the creation of a Ministry of Health.

V

The flu epidemic, unprecedented in living memory and reaping its own holocaust, provided an unexpected context for the dawning realisation that Germany was near being driven to surrender; and contributed to a strange sense of ambivalence about it. Lady Cynthia Asquith, whose husband would survive the war but two of whose brothers, a brother-in-law and several close friends would not, wrote on 7 October: 'I am beginning to rub my eyes at the prospect of peace. I think it will require more courage than anything that has gone before. It isn't until one leaves off spinning round that one realises how giddy one is. One will have to look at long vistas again, instead of short ones, and one will at last fully recognise that the dead are not only dead for the duration of the war.'[83] In her diary on 4 November Mrs Webb asserted that 'there is little or no elation among the general body of citizens about the coming peace': she felt this was because Britain shared her earnest apprehension at the prospect of a dislocated society, an overbearing government and huge public debt.[84] However, these were things she and the political class felt far more keenly than did the masses, whose displays of joy awaited the declaration of peace. She herself took no pleasure in it. 'Great Britain and France are themselves exhausted, living on their own vitals, whilst they smash German civilisation. For whose benefit?'

But even among the victors the realisation of an approaching peace could be salutary.

The following day Lloyd George told the Commons details of the armistice with Austria–Hungary, including a complete evacuation of all remaining foreign territory occupied by forces of the Dual Monarchy and the surrender of its navy. The capitulation of Austria–Hungary exposed Germany on its southern and eastern borders, and its own end was now but a matter of time. On 8 November, a Friday, the Allies and Americans outlined terms for an armistice with Germany and gave the Germans until Monday – 11 November – to decide whether to accept. The victorious powers offered terms that reflected the matters on which they agreed, so based largely but not entirely on the fourteen points, and (a particular concern of the French) allowing discussion of reparations. A Bavarian republic had already been declared in Munich the previous evening. Prince Max of Baden, the German Chancellor, resigned. The German army withdrew support from the Kaiser; the next day he abdicated and fled to the Netherlands, and the Crown Prince renounced his claims to the throne. The dynasty of Frederick the Great had lost power for ever.

On Sunday 10 November crowds thronged the Mall (which was littered with captured German guns) and the front of Buckingham Palace in expectation of an announcement of peace, much as they had four years earlier in expectation of a declaration of war. The King and Queen went for a drive around London and were cheered wherever they went; the King, about to undertake the umpteenth morale-boosting tour of munitions works, cancelled it to be in London at the crucial moment. The government issued details, the evening before the Armistice, of what would happen to munitions workers and soldiers. All overtime would be stopped, and anyone wishing to leave and return to civilian employment could do so forthwith. Most factories would go on half-time work and some workers would be discharged; they would be given rail warrants to return home, and special unemployment pay until they could be found work. It took just a few days for displaced workers to realise that the benefits offered were inadequate: on 19 November 6,000 women, mainly from Woolwich Arsenal, marched on Whitehall demanding more generous support. For the services, 'pivotal men' – those essential for reconstruction – would be released at once. This, too, satisfied few of those anxious to come home.

A cabinet meeting that evening discussed the imminent collapse of Germany into Bolshevism unless an armistice were agreed in time to leave the authorities in Germany some chance of regrouping: thus the decision was taken. 'Our real danger now is not the Boches but bolshevism,' Henry Wilson noted in his diary.[85] At 2 a.m. on 11 November Foch met German delegates in a railway carriage in the Forest of Compiègne: at 5 a.m. the Armistice was agreed, to come into force at 11 a.m. Private George Edwin Ellison of the 5th Royal Irish Lancers was the last man to die, killed on a patrol at Mons at 9.30: he was a veteran of Mons in 1914, as well as of Yprcs, Armentières, Loos and Cambrai. His grave adjoins that of the first man to die, John Parr.

The cabinet met at 9.30 a.m. and decided bells would be rung at 11 a.m.; it then delegated to officials the start of work on demobilisation. Amery got off his number 24 bus in Whitehall and reached Downing Street as a crowd ran into the street ahead of him 'and was in time to see LG at his doorstep telling them (being then about five minutes to eleven) that the war was over at eleven o'clock . . . [they] started singing "God Save the King", a performance politically though not musically quite satisfactory.'[86] A maroon – the usual way of announcing an air raid – went off in London at 11 a.m. to mark the end of the war, and sirens and church bells sounded and rang all over Britain. It was a cheerless, dull, wet day, and Arnold Bennett, in his office at the Ministry of Information, noted his pleasure when the rain fell heavily, 'an excellent thing to damp hysteria and Bolshevism.'[87] Even Mrs Webb had to admit London was 'a pandemonium of noise and revelry'.[88] Yet, as always, she was peering ahead: 'How soon will the tide of revolution catch up the tide of victory?'

Crowds again congregated outside Buckingham Palace, and several times during the day the King and Queen – who noted in her diary that it was 'the greatest day in the world's history' – came on to a balcony to acknowledge wild cheering that persisted for hours.[89] There was singing and much waving of flags, and cries of 'We want King George'; King George frequently obliged.[90] The cheering reached a climax at lunchtime, when the band of the Brigade of Guards paraded playing a triumphal march before going through the card from 'Land of Hope and Glory' to 'Tipperary'. Newbolt told his wife that 'I can hear as I write the cheers rolling along Fleet Street and the Strand. The sound of the guns over London this morning was thrilling . . .'[91] Duff Cooper, in a taxi from

Liverpool Street as he returned to London after a shooting weekend, noted that 'amid the dancing, the cheering, the waving of flags, I could think only of my friends who were dead.'[92] Mrs Asquith recorded how for days 'my heart has been so heavy at the raging chaos, famine and huge volcanic upset of all Europe'.[93] To the King, it was 'a wonderful day, the greatest in the history of this country': yet there was a note of old-world sentimentality when, noting in his diary his cousin's abdication, he observed that 'William arrived in Holland yesterday.'[94] In the afternoon, despite the rain, he and the Queen drove in an open carriage through cheering crowds down the Strand to Mansion House, then home via Piccadilly. While Lloyd George basked in victory, the King sent Asquith a telegram thanking him for his 'wise counsel and calm resolve' in earlier times; Mrs Asquith transcribed it in her diary with the note: 'this is well worth a little ridicule'.

In the high streets across Britain, as soon as the news was telegraphed to post offices, men and women massed in the streets and cheered, flags were raised and work came to a standstill. Those schools not already closed because of the flu epidemic declared half-holidays. The Revd Andrew Clark, in his Essex parish, heard that 'Braintree was wild with excitement' and in his village 'the cottagers were very excited.'[95] The ringing of bells, which in some places lasted all day, became infectious as word travelled from village to village in the countryside: it would be another three and a half years before the advent of broadcasting, with the inception of the BBC. Flags were hung out of windows and on the fronts of pubs. Esher, in Perthshire, recorded in his diary: 'I was on the moor with Kenneth McLeod, who had a few minutes before shot a woodcock. We heard the village bells, and knew that the Armistice had been signed . . . A few men, no better and no worse than the mass of their Countrymen, will be glorified for all time. The real glory rests upon the thousands of young and nameless dead.'[96] In Dublin, supposedly a seat of pro-German sentiment, Plunkett (using a term from celebrations during the Boer War when a siege was lifted) witnessed 'Mafficking . . . in which Sinn Féiners caught the infection.'[97]

Russell, recently released from Brixton, was in the Tottenham Court Road at 11 a.m.: 'Within two minutes everybody in all the shops and offices had come into the street. They commandeered the buses, and made them go where they liked.'[98] A bonfire burned in Trafalgar Square, causing serious damage to the plinth of Nelson's Column. Munitions workers left their factories and danced in the streets, their appearance made distinctive by the yellow staining of their skin from picric acid. Virginia Woolf, with self-conscious preciousness, noted the guns going off and observed: 'A siren hooted on the river. They are hooting still. A few people ran to look out of windows. The rooks wheeled round and wore for a moment the symbolic look of creatures performing some ceremony, partly of thanksgiving, partly of valediction over the grave . . . so far neither bells nor flags, but the wailing of sirens and intermittent guns.'[99]

A sign that normality was being restored was that from 1 p.m. Big Ben, silent for the duration, began to strike the hours again: the government announced that because of the complexity of the mechanism, it would be two or three weeks before the Westminster chimes were heard again too. Lloyd George formally announced the Armistice in the Commons that afternoon. The Germans were to evacuate all the invaded territories in the west – not just Belgium, but Luxembourg and Alsace-Lorraine – within fourteen days, to be replaced by Allied forces, which would take prisoner any Germans still in the territories. Within those fourteen days all nationals from those territories being held in Germany would be repatriated. Allied prisoners of war were to be returned too: the fate of German ones would be decided at the peace conference. Large amounts of machinery and weaponry were to be surrendered, and the Germans were ordered to destroy nothing in their retreat, and to hand over railways, coal and rolling stock to the formerly occupied territories. Much of the German navy and auxiliary fleet was to be handed over too, and all its submarines.

The duration of the Armistice was set for thirty-six days, subject to renewal; and the arrangement could be cancelled by any of the contracting parties at forty-eight hours' notice. But Germany was leaderless, starving, humiliated, exhausted, and in no state to carry on the fight. After the prime minister's statement the Commons and Lords adjourned and went across to St Margaret's, Westminster for an impromptu thanksgiving service. Lloyd George and Asquith walked to St Margaret's together, discussing, with an appropriate lack of controversy, their respective daughters. For the next five days the King and Queen drove round different areas of London – mainly the poorer parts – in an open car, the King saluting and taking the salute of his people.

Many who had fought, or had been bereaved, thought only of what

came to be called 'the unreturning army', and found celebration harder
to manage. It was hardest on the legion of widows, orphans and parents
who had lost sons, many of whom faced financial hardship as well as an
emotional vacuum. There was scarcely less pain for the men who survived. Robert Graves, in a camp in Wales, went out for a long walk
'cursing and sobbing, and thinking of the dead.'[100] His friend Sassoon, in
Oxford recovering from a wound, came to London for the evening 'and
found masses of people in streets and congested Tubes, all waving flags
and making fools of themselves – an outburst of mob patriotism. It was
a wretched wet night, and very mild. It is a loathsome ending to the
loathsome tragedy of the last four years.'[101] In Shrewsbury, the mother of
his friend and protégé Wilfred Owen received the War Office telegram
informing her that her son had been killed in action while crossing the
Sambre–Oise canal exactly a week before. As Owen had written in his
poem 'Dulce et Decorum Est', finished the previous March but which
would not be published until 1920: 'My friend, you would not tell with
such high zest/To children ardent for some desperate glory,/The old
Lie; Dulce et Decorum est/Pro patria mori.'

A. J. P. Taylor, in his account of Armistice night, wrote: 'Total strangers copulated in doorways and on the pavements. They were asserting
the triumph of life over death.'[102] The authorities became concerned
about the partying, which lasted several nights, notably the habit of
lighting bonfires in the streets. However, the War Cabinet minutes
report that at 10.30 p.m. on 12 November Eric Geddes had visited 'some
of the principal centres affected' and found 'the temper and the conduct of crowds were everywhere good. There was very little drunkenness,
and few excesses were committed at that hour. Of those few, Australians
were prominent participants.'[103] The London that celebrated was still
being ravaged by flu. Between 27 October and 2 November there were
2,200 deaths from it in the capital alone. Altogether, 150,000 died in England. Hankey, exhausted after a spell in Paris with Lloyd George settling
the Armistice terms, went down with the flu on 6 November, though
his wife (who like the rest of their household had the virus too) 'threw
open the windows for a minute' at 11 a.m. on 11 November 'that I might
hear the joy bells' pealing for the Armistice.[104]

In his private diary Hankey congratulated himself extensively and
without restraint on all he had done to win the war: 'I initiated and forced
through all our preparations for war . . . the War Cabinet itself is

my design and my conception; and my creation . . . I have been the confidant and consultant first of one great Prime Minister and then of another . . . I have steered the great ship of state round one dangerous headland after another into a port of serenity.' He managed a modicum of self-effacement in his memoirs: 'The war was won primarily by a tremendous combined system of co-ordination and goodwill, which focused all the efforts of the Allies on the supreme task of defeating the enemy, but which only reached its zenith in the last year of the war.'[105] So far as it went, and with a discount for Hankey's obsessive self-regard, that was true: but the exhalations of relief in November 1918 ought also to have recognised the good fortune of the Americans eventually reaching the Western Front, the Germans over-reaching in the spring offensive, and the long-term success of the blockade. Tommy Atkins's massive sacrifices had kept the Germans at bay, but British sea power had played the decisive part in winning the war.

While strangers copulated in doorways Lloyd George, Churchill, Smith and Henry Wilson dined in Downing Street. The election was the main topic; Churchill, indeed, had been badgering Lloyd George about his role in a new administration, fearing that with the war won the Tories might not agree to his joining the cabinet – which Churchill assumed would be reconstituted on 'Gladstonian' lines.[106] However, another, not unrelated, issue was discussed. 'LG wants to shoot the Kaiser,' Wilson recorded in his diary. 'FE agrees. Winston does not.'[107] Walking back to his house in Eaton Place after dinner, Wilson encountered 'an elderly, well-dressed woman, a pathetic figure in deep mourning, alone and sobbing her heart out.' The General asked whether he could help her, but she answered: 'Thank you, no. I am crying, but I am happy, for now I know that all my three sons who have been killed in the war have not died in vain.'

Churchill was realistic about what a close call it had been, and not just because he was acutely aware of Lloyd George's dereliction in denying soldiers to the Western Front at a crucial time the previous winter. In 1914 France 'was within an ace of being destroyed. A vy little more & the submarine warfare instead of bringing America to our aid, might have starved us all into absolute surrender . . . it was neck and neck to the very end.'[108] At Buckingham Palace the King carried out the plan he had devised for when he could consume alcohol again: he sent for a bottle of 1815 cognac that the Prince Regent had laid down to celebrate Wellington's victory at Waterloo. He found it 'very musty.'[109]

VI

Gwynne wrote to Esher on Armistice Day about the next challenge: Bolsheviks. 'The whole of the burden of their song is that England is corrupt, that the Government is corrupt, that Northcliffe is the real Prime Minister . . . They are just going along the right lines to create a revolution. The last man to stop a revolutionary feeling in this country is Lloyd George, for the simple reason that the Bolsheviks look upon him as the most corrupt man in the country . . .'[110] Haig, visiting soldiers in hospital in France, had overheard some of them asking why the British needed a king: it was not just those on the losing side who were taking the opportunity to question the prevailing social conditions.

Law was keen to maintain a strong coalition with Lloyd George, seeing it as the only way to keep Bolshevism down in Britain. However, some influential figures, notably the ever-pessimistic Northcliffe, were unsure it could be warded off: he felt the working class, especially that sizeable proportion who had been at the front, were ready for revolution on the European model if their wishes were unmet. To this end he had talks with Henderson and donated space in the *Daily Mail* to the Labour Party to express its views: he felt that accommodating the party and showing respect for its concerns was as good a way as any of calming potential revolutionaries. Luckily for him and for Britain, many in the Labour Party – not least Henderson, having been to Russia – were as keen to keep Bolshevism out of British politics as Northcliffe was. Nor was that his only concern: he had been anxious to go in an official capacity to the peace conference not solely out of megalomania, but because of a sincere fear that the Allied Powers would effectively let Germany off with a caution, and fail finally to destroy the Prussian militarism that he believed would remain a standing threat to British security.

With the announcement of the Armistice came an immediate end to recruitment and the easing of some war restrictions. Hotels and restaurants were allowed to open later; people could light bonfires and let off fireworks; bells could ring and public clocks could strike. For Armistice night only shops could light their windows, a concession withdrawn thereafter pending an improvement in the coal supply. It was announced that the Christmas meat ration would be doubled. Clothing manufacturers were told to stop making uniforms and start making civilian clothes. The resumption of association football was excitedly discussed, as was that of first-class cricket for the following summer. Within a fortnight most of the DORA restrictions – such as being forbidden to take photographs or make sketches of coastal areas, and the controversial Regulation 40D, which criminalised a woman with venereal disease copulating with a member of the Armed Forces – were lifted, as was most press censorship.

When a general election was finally called, there were also demands to end censorship completely, to allow freedom of speech during the campaign: this was especially potent in Ireland, where Sinn Féin, which would contest the election, remained a prohibited organisation. The government said some restrictions could go, but with peace not finally settled others had to remain. It was brave, in the circumstances, to give details – inaccurate and incomplete, but still awesome in the scale they suggested – of British war casualties sustained up to the day before the Armistice: an estimated 660,000 officers and men dead, 2.1 million wounded and 360,000 missing, including prisoners.[111] The gamble was that the perception of victory would cause calm acceptance of these figures. Had it failed, an already volatile society could have become unmanageable.

On 12 November Lloyd George addressed a Liberal Party meeting in which he promised social and economic reform: but his dependence on the Conservatives to remain prime minister tied his hands. The most memorable line from his address, often misquoted, was 'we must have habitations fit for the heroes who have won the war', and no repeat of the situation after 1815 when an opportunity for reform and progress had been passed up, causing years of discontent and unrest.[112] He refined his slogan at Wolverhampton on 23 November, in a speech in which he also advertised his desire to give grants of land to ex-soldiers to make them part of an agricultural revival, and to maintain the contribution of women to the economy, when he said: 'What is our task? To make Britain a fit country for heroes to live in.'[113]

Also on the day after the Armistice, Addison told the Commons that in accordance with a plan devised by a committee chaired by Montagu, 'industrial requirements' would govern the demobilisation of those heroes.[114] The Army had been divided into forty-two trade groups in order of importance to the civilian economy, and the most valuable would be released first. This would turn out not to be the brilliant idea the government thought, because of divided responsibilities: the War

Office dealt with a man until he left the colours, and the Ministry of Labour inherited the problem thereafter. It was up to firms to tell the Army of their needs: Addison said it was thought that 60 per cent of men had jobs awaiting them.

A pamphlet was being prepared to explain how demobilisation would work, and Addison set out the basic procedure for each individual:

> A man is sent primarily to a place that is called his dispersal station, which is near his home. There he receives a protection certificate, a railway warrant home, a cash payment of his war gratuity and an out-of-work donation policy, which lasts in the case of the soldiers twelve months and covers twenty-six weeks of unemployment, with benefit at the rate I have mentioned. He will receive the war gratuity. The precise method of the payment of that will be announced shortly. I believe it is likely that it will be paid in four weekly instalments. The man will receive twenty-eight days' furlough when he reaches his dispersal station, and will then receive pay and ration allowance during that time, and the separation allowance will also continue during that period.[115]

He added that any officer or suitably qualified man 'dislocated' from his normal employment as a result of the war would be able to secure a permanent career in the civil service, the offer to remain open for a year after demobilisation.[116] One disadvantaged group were former officers promoted from the ranks, who lacked the private means that before the war had usually gone with such status, and for many in this bracket the immediate post-war period of adjustment and resettlement would be a particular struggle.

There was some expertise in Whitehall at dealing with wounded officers who had been invalided out, for whom the Appointments Department at the Ministry of Labour had been set up. Contrary to the myth that psychological damage was disregarded, the department issued a pamphlet advising on how to handle the mental strain that followed an experience of trauma. It included advice 'that he should be encouraged to read – good novels, poetry, or whatever his taste leads him to. Afterwards he should have the opportunity of listening to lectures on natural history, poultry farming, travel, or anything that interests. By such means his brain would be kept going, and his idle hours safeguarded.'[117]

The department would, once the man had recovered sufficiently to contemplate a career, 'assume something like a parental control of him.' Using a nationwide network, it would then steer the man towards further education, training or a career. With the coming of peace the demands on such services would be enormous, and the system would not always cope. However, charities sprang up devoted to the rehabilitation of those maimed by war, with rural centres (including one on a 1, 000-acre estate near Andover) acting as what one charity called 'a bridge between the hospital and civil life', where men could be trained for a more active life under medical supervision; and a Ministry of Pensions Voluntary Fund was established to make grants and loans for those who wished to start their own businesses.[118]

The war had given birth to a cult of bureaucracy, which would flourish in the peace. The day after the Armistice a huge network of committees and advisory boards, composed of 'men and women of mature experience and distinction in affairs', was set up to advise the minister of reconstruction on all aspects of the procurement of raw materials and the rebuilding of Britain.[119] They would advise too on disposal of war surplus and on the stimulation of new trades, especially in engineering, to exploit technologies developed during the war to the service of the civilian population.

The immediate domestic difficulty – since it would take some time to demobilise soldiers – was what to do with 3 million munitions operatives whose services were no longer required, and who were working in between 40,000 and 50,000 firms that would need to find new customers. A week after the Armistice, Churchill told Lloyd George that 'although I am going very slow, and gaining time in every direction possible, I cannot help unloading from now onwards a continuous broadening stream of men and women workers. Others go on short time, & all lose their high wartime wages & fall to a mere pittance & consequent discontent.'[120] The workers were far from stupid. 'Workmen say freely that if the Government were ready to spend £8,000,000 a day for an indefinite period to win the war, they ought not to grudge a much smaller sum to carry the country over the transition period.'

A period of severe economic dislocation was beginning; the eventual return of fighting men would make it worse. Refashioning a peacetime economy was not the work of an afternoon, and both Liberals and Unionists saw the Labour Party ready to exploit the hardships many families would feel as former breadwinners searched for new work and returning soldiers hoped to resume their previous occupations. Some did: many did not. The government pinned its hopes of industrial and civil calm on its as yet vague plans for reconstruction, which would require an army of men to build new homes and commercial buildings, as well as for the new infrastructure of roads and renewed railways to support them. The forthcoming election campaign ought to have been the moment not just to spell these plans out in detail, but to outline how they would be accomplished. The question of execution of plans would come eventually and, in some cases, either incompletely or not at all.

It was confirmed on 14 November that the general election would be held exactly a month later. Labour, armed with a new constitution and a belief that the expanded electorate would supply it with an army of voters, had long contained a strong faction, based on its National Executive Committee, that wished to leave the coalition. The parliamentary party, who saw membership of the coalition as the best means of influencing the post-war settlement, wished to stay. An emergency conference was called, which featured a demand by George Bernard Shaw that his fellow socialists should tell Lloyd George 'nothing doing'. By a margin of almost three to one the party voted to fight the election as an opposition, leaving the coalition once Parliament was dissolved. Clynes, food controller since July when Rhondda had died of pneumonia brought on by overwork (and who had won some popularity by taking bacon and ham off the ration soon after his appointment, thanks to the success of the pig-breeding programme), resigned on 22 November to help lead his party. Henderson was optimistic about Labour's chances because, as he told Scott, 'they had existing trade union organisation in every town.'[121] Labour would field 361 candidates, 140 of whom were proposed by new local parties formed after the passing of the constitution; the others were union sponsored, the largest number – 51 – by the Miners' Federation of Great Britain.[122]

Many MPs, like their Sovereign, regarded the election as unpleasantly opportunist. Sir Leo Chiozza Money, a junior shipping minister, resigned because of the decision, stating his concerns about the ability of many men in uniform to vote. But it was also believed there was too much haste between the Armistice and the poll for the enormous considerations of the peace, and the challenges it offered, to be properly debated and considered by the electorate. Sir Leo – a gifted and influential economist who had been Lloyd George's parliamentary private secretary – believed the programme of reforms which the prime minister had outlined would not placate a population he believed more afflicted by unrest than the government realised.

Money deplored that a coalition party from which Labour had chosen to exclude itself would fight the election: 'Above all, I fear this: That the results of an election, such as this may be, will be to exclude from this House such a proper and full representation of Labour as to cause Labour to seek for other than Parliamentary means of expression. I say that that is a danger for the country which we have all got to face. The issue must be faced sooner or later. If we will not face it in this House, we may be quite sure it will be faced out of the House, and we shall have to face an extra-Parliamentary means of expression.'[123] Money argued that the working classes simply would not accept such conditions as they had lived and worked in before the war. He doubted the government's commitment to continue free trade; he believed it intended to postpone Home Rule for Ireland indefinitely. He saw both policies as against the will of the people, and he could not be a part of it.

Lloyd George made one last attempt to achieve Liberal unity, by inviting Asquith yet again to become Lord Chancellor; but he refused once more, and other Liberals declined to join the coalition. Asquith did tell Lloyd George, who asked to see him just before the election, that he would be happy to be a delegate to the peace conference; Lloyd George refused to give him an answer, and never did. The King, too, wrote to his prime minister to ask him to take Asquith with 'his worth as a lawyer, a statesman, and a man of clear dispassionate judgment' to Versailles, but his letter went unanswered.[124] In an audience of the King on 25 November Lloyd George prevaricated, saying nothing could be done until after the election – unless Asquith joined the ministry. After that, Lloyd George was predictably evasive. What he could not tell the King was about his loathing of the idea of sharing the limelight with his predecessor – for Lloyd George was being depicted in the campaign as the man who won the war – or to give him such standing in the Versailles process that it strengthened his credibility as an alternative prime minister. It was typical, though, that shortly after Asquith's death in 1928 he should claim, with breathtaking dishonesty but desperate to polish his reputation, that he had offered Asquith a place on the delegation.

The prime minister had told Hankey – who was much in favour of

Asquith – that he could not ask men such as 'Bonar Law, or Balfour, or Barnes, who had been loyal to him, to give place to Asquith.'[125] Hankey and the King conspired to have Lloyd George change his mind, but they failed: the King told Hankey that 'Lloyd George will say that the King wants Asquith to go to the peace conference, because he is his friend. But the truth is I want him to go for the good of the nation . . . and to make for unity.'[126] Hankey noted that the King 'hardly concealed his personal mistrust of Lloyd George . . . he thinks that if Ll G wins the election he will not last more than 15 months; that Labour is not ready to form a Govt; and that Asquith is certain to get back before long.' It would not quite happen that way.

Dropping in to debrief Stamfordham, Hankey endured another torrent of abuse of Lloyd George, this time for what the courtier regarded as his shocking breach of manners in absenting himself from the King's message to Parliament the previous Tuesday, to mark the Armistice. Hankey tried to convince Stamfordham that Lloyd George 'had really been seedy' with the flu – two months after he had had it in Manchester – but was told: 'well, I suppose one expects Lloyd George to cry off things that one would not expect in another man.' With judicious understatement Hankey observed that 'he clearly does not like or trust Ll G.' The next day he noted that 'the PM was very hostile about Asquith and annoyed with the King for wanting him to be at the peace conference.'[127]

Another factor in the electoral equation was the possibility of candidates representing ex-servicemen. The National Federation of Discharged and Demobilised Sailors and Soldiers, started in March 1917 during the row about recalling the medically unfit, had run a disabled ex-soldier in a by-election in Liverpool in June 1918 against Lord Stanley, heir to the Derby earldom, on a platform of better pensions, more rehabilitation for disabled ex-servicemen and a repeal of the Act reviewing exemptions. For a time Derby, who knew he was the target of the protest, thought of withdrawing his son from the field. He felt that 'the opposition of the discharged soldiers is much more serious' than was realised.[128] When it was feared a veteran would oppose Stanley, the War Cabinet decided to exempt wounded and discharged men who had served overseas, and further changes to the Act were announced before the poll: Stanley, who did not campaign as he was abroad on active service, won by 2,224 votes to 794. During the autumn the Directorate of

Intelligence in the Home Office detected a move by 'extremists' to take over the federation, but feared their populism would make them 'a very numerous and dangerous body'.[129]

Another veterans' group – the Silver Badge Party, named after the badge ex-servicemen could wear to show they had served, and thus avoid the obloquy of women armed with white feathers – ran on similar lines to the federation, but had policies such as equal pay for women and the deportation of enemy aliens that transcended veterans' demands. When nominations closed on 4 December there were thirty-one veterans' candidates, mostly federation men. Twenty had been wounded. As many candidates again withdrew before nominations closed; this was the first election at which a £150 deposit was required, forfeited if the candidate received less than an eighth of the vote, and it had a deterrent effect.

Many Liberals, like Money, regarded Lloyd George's desire to call an election immediately, and to issue what Asquith, in a speech at Huddersfield on 28 November, called a 'coupon' – a letter of endorsement signed by the prime minister and Law to candidates supporting their coalition – an outrageous act of exploitative cynicism.[130] Asquith had told Liberals on 18 November that he considered it 'a blunder and a calamity' to have the 'tumult and turmoil' of an election; he wanted the soldiers home first so their voices could be heard.[131] Auckland Geddes announced arrangements to ensure soldiers could vote by post; those not in France or Belgium could appoint proxies (though, as it turned out, few did). Samuel called the election timing 'indefensible': 'They allowed the people no interval for reflection, or for the consideration of policies for the future.'[132] The parties were in various states of disorganisation; the Unionists the least so, which boded well for the coalition's re-election. Indeed, it was mainly his awareness of the concerns of the Asquithians and of Henderson about their organisations' fitness for an election that impelled Lloyd George to want one so much.

The idea of the 'coupon' had come to him in the summer: as a way of ensuring that those Liberals who backed him, and Unionists who backed his administration, would be endorsed; and what was good for them was good for him. By denying so many Asquithian Liberals the coupon, and with Labour going its own way, the Unionists would have a substantial majority in the new House. Asquith still controlled the official Liberal Party, from which anyone seeking the coupon would be excommunicated; in any case, Lloyd George took the way men had voted in the Maurice debate as a key indicator of reliability, as he admitted in a speech at Wolverhampton on 23 November. Therefore he struggled to find credible candidates; which would leave him as prime minister but reliant on Unionists to keep him there.

He accused his opponents on the Maurice question of having run a 'parliamentary conspiracy to overthrow a Government that was in the midst of a crisis while wrestling for victory.'[133] That, at least, was his justification in isolating them. Asquith was appalled at yet another distortion of the truth, and in his Huddersfield speech said of his own role in the debate that 'there is no act in the whole of my parliamentary life . . . for which I am less repentant and ashamed.'[134] Eventually 541 coupons were issued for the 602 English, Scottish and Welsh constituencies; those who received them were 364 Conservatives, 159 Liberals and 18 National Democrats.[135] The latter were a working-class, anti-socialist party. In another respect it would be a quite different election from any held before. On 21 November the Royal Assent was given for the Parliament (Qualification of Women) Act 1918, settling that as well as being allowed to vote in the election, women could stand as candidates in it.

Lloyd George and Law's joint programme was published on 18 November, followed by various policy documents during the campaign. Asquith announced his the same day, claiming a direct political descent from Gladstone, and calling himself a 'liberal . . . without any prefix or suffix'.[136] He wanted to remove the state, which had taken over the lives of the people in the preceding four years, from those lives as swiftly as possible. Rothermere told Churchill the coalition programme was 'not sufficiently advanced'; he thought Lloyd George's natural radical instincts were 'being held back by reactionary Tories.'[137] Beaverbrook felt the apportionment of the coupon unduly sectarian, and used the *Express* to say so: he pledged to support candidates who had behaved well during the war, irrespective of whether the coalition endorsed them, despite his own recent service in that administration, and his close friendship with Law. Law seems to have taken a long view of his party's participation, seeing that its representation would be big enough to ensure its future independence of a coalition, when the time came. The Liberal Party would be permanently split, and incapable of governing.

Churchill was angry with Beaverbrook, scenting betrayal; Beaverbrook replied that 'it is unwise and wrong to ignore the public claims, based on service to the State, of many candidates who will not give all the Coalition pledges, and I claim the right to speak freely on this and other matters . . . where there is a good man outside those ranks, I intend to support him.'[138] On 31 October he had told Mrs Asquith that 'you really are mistaken in the view that I am strongly opposed to your husband in any inveterate manner. I have a great respect for Mr Asquith and there are few men in whom I would rather trust.'[139] He explained his support for Lloyd George in 1916 as having been provoked not by Asquith, but by 'the kind of barnacles, especially in the general staff, which had affixed themselves to his administration.' Beaverbrook claimed the outcome had justified Lloyd George's scepticism about Robertson and the War Office. 'I regretted the denouement as much as did the present prime minister; but we feel that we were battling for the National existence.' He hoped Asquith's advice 'will be taken on the conclusion of peace': hopes in which he, and Asquith too, would be disappointed. Mrs Asquith replied, with her customary disregard for whatever support her husband and his friends might have hoped for from the *Express*, that 'Sir H Wilson, Ll G, Northcliffe, you and your lot nearly landed us in the <u>greatest</u> military disaster that ever happened to English soldiers.'[140]

Even as signs of Germany's defeat multiplied – such as on 20 November, when the captured U-boat fleet assembled off Harwich to head for Scapa Flow – the British mood was ugly, and vindictive. That morning the press published the provisional casualty figures for the war. 'We must go back to Tamerlane, or Genghiz Khan, for slaughter to compare with that done by the disciples of *Kultur*,' *The Times* observed.[141] Demands to hang the Kaiser, and expropriate reparations from the Germans, were widespread, and irresistible for politicians to exploit. The cabinet decided on 28 November to try the Kaiser because, as Wilson (who was present) noted, 'the surest way to prevent a repetition of frightfulness was personal responsibility and punishment.' It would be easier said than done, now he was in neutral Holland. In Newcastle on 29 November Lloyd George said the law officers had agreed that by invading Belgium the Kaiser 'was guilty of an indictable offence for which he should be held responsible.'[142] It would come to nothing, but was a useful pose until the election was won; this was a moment when Lloyd George's lack of scruples and honesty could be given full rein. Keynes described his behaviour as 'a sad, dramatic history of the essential weakness of one who draws his chief inspiration not from his own true impulses, but from the grosser effluxions of the atmosphere which momentarily surround him.'[143] The thirst for vengeance – fed by tales from emaciated prisoners of war returning home after a long captivity – became stronger. Eric Geddes told an election meeting in December that 'we will get out of her all you can squeeze out of a lemon and a bit more . . . I will squeeze her until you can hear the pips squeak.'[144] Keynes described this as 'the grossest spectacle'.

Lloyd George sought to create an impression of dynamism during the campaign, especially in addressing social issues that, if left unattended, might harm his popularity. He put Geddes in charge of demobilisation, an operation whose scale the government was only just beginning to comprehend, with not just troops but also superfluous munitions workers to redeploy in civilian life. Lloyd George hoped to impress employers worried about getting back key workers as quickly as possible, to begin peacetime production. Meanwhile, Churchill arranged for railway companies to place orders for equipment and materials for the refurbishment of the permanent way, to use capacity in munitions factories. A fear of unemployment was worrying not just likely victims, but also politicians anxious to avoid discontent. However, the distraction of the election campaign removed any prospect of Lloyd George seriously addressing the problem.

The people were run-down, and not just those who had served, with their wounds, mutilations and shell shock. Auckland Geddes had compiled a report on the physical condition of the people, which had shown the dire effects of poverty and poor diet on the working classes, and why so many men had been passed unfit for military service, even with the bar set low. In districts with cotton mills men showed signs of decay at thirty that most would not exhibit until their fifties. 'I shall make it plain,' Lloyd George had told Riddell in August, 'that I shall not be party to the continuance of such a condition of affairs. It is useless to fight this war unless the condition of the poorer classes is to be improved.'[145] But Lloyd George's lack of focus showed how naturally he put his self-interest before the public interest. Amery told his wife on 26 November that 'the great British people are not the least interested in Social Reform or Reconstruction, but only in making the Germans pay for the war and punishing the Kaiser.'[146]

The election campaign required self-promotion, for which the end of the war provided spectacular opportunities, not all in ideal taste. Lloyd George decided there should be a ceremonial drive through London on 1 December that would include himself, Clemenceau and Orlando (the prime minister of Italy), and senior officers from those three nations. Haig was invited – Foch was taking part – but heard he would be riding in the fifth carriage 'along with General Henry Wilson. I felt this was more of an insult than I could put up with, even from the Prime Minister.' He ranted in his diary: 'For the past three years I have effaced myself . . . I have patiently submitted to Lloyd George's conceit and swagger, combined with much boasting as to "what *he* had accomplished, thanks to his *foresight*" . . . The real truth, which history will show, is that the British Army has won the war in France in spite of LG and I have no intention of taking part in any triumphal ride with Foch, or with any pack of foreigners . . . mainly in order to add to LG's importance and help him in his election campaign.'[147] The lack of self-knowledge this diary entry reveals is breathtaking. When Haig's diary and his other private papers were finally published in 1952 Beaverbrook described him as having 'committed suicide 25 years after his death.'[148]

Downing Street explained Haig's absence from this triumph by announcing that the King required his presence in France, where he was visiting the troops. The King, too, was appalled such an event should be held while he was abroad, and in an election campaign. Haig had his own official homecoming on 19 December. He was met at Charing Cross by the Duke of Connaught and Lloyd George with a guard of honour, and a band that played 'See, the Conquering Hero Comes', before being taken off in a royal carriage to lunch with the King at Buckingham Palace. Given Haig's largely deserved posthumous reputation as a butcher, it is worth noting that *The Times* felt there was a 'single and joyous' emotion on the streets of London at his return.[149]

The final statement of coalition policy appeared on 11 December, three days before the election. It had five points: 'Punish the Kaiser; Make Germany pay; Get the soldier home as quickly as possible; Fair treatment for the returning soldier and sailor; Better housing and better social conditions.'[150] Some candidates were more direct: Albert Martin, the Coalition Liberal candidate for Romford, put up posters that simply read: 'MAKE GERMANY PAY FOR THE WAR AND HANG THE

KAISER'.[151] Lloyd George reinforced the five points with a speech in Bristol, in which he confirmed an immediate end to conscription. A month of loud campaigning by Northcliffe in his newspapers had left its mark on him and his colleagues, who had become wary of departing too far from the line of the *Daily Mail* and, to a lesser extent, *The Times*. Keynes, who interpolated a sixth point – that of 'punishment of those responsible for atrocities' – dismissed the manifesto as 'food for the cynic'.[152] Northcliffe's approach angered Lloyd George, who sent him the rebuke: 'don't always be making mischief.'[153] However, the coalition's final words to the electorate, in this last general election before the advent of broadcasting, echoed Northcliffe's demands. Wilson's infatuation had worn off after witnessing the campaign. 'The bribing of [*sic*] Lloyd George at this election is simply disgusting,' he noted on 13 December. 'I won't vote tomorrow.'[154]

The results of the election were not published until 28 December. Of the 159 Liberals with the coupon 136 were returned: only 54 had voted for Asquith after the Maurice debate. Without the coupon, the Unionists would have crushed them. Just 29 un-couponed Liberals won, 8 unopposed by a couponed candidate. There were 333 Conservatives and 9 National Democrats. Only one candidate supporting veterans, James Hogge, who ran as an independent Liberal, was elected, the press having largely ignored their campaign. The plan for soldiers overseas to vote by post – which had delayed the results – had limited success, many spoiling their papers by writing across them: 'Send us home and we will vote', or 'Wait until we are demobilised.'[155] The lesson about the slowness of demobilisation was not quickly learned.

Asquith, who admitted that the possibility of defeat had hardly occurred to him, lost the seat in East Fife he had held since 1886; as he drove round on polling day he noted Conservative posters proclaiming: 'Asquith nearly lost you the War. Are you going to let him spoil the Peace?' McKenna, Samuel, Simon and Runciman all lost too. Labour ended up with sixty-one seats after some independents took their whip. Most of the party's leading figures, including Henderson, Snowden and MacDonald, also lost their seats after an election in which the largest-ever electorate – ten and a half million – had participated. Hankey noted that Lloyd George 'was almost stunned by his overwhelming victory and seemed really upset by Asquith's defeat' – the latter, though, being an inevitable consequence of his not having had the coupon, hence presumably Hankey's deployment of 'almost'.[156] He also recorded that Law 'admitted he was not elated, but greatly sobered'.

Lloyd George may have been prime minister, but he was now under the control of a Conservative majority, and living on borrowed time. Austen Chamberlain, who had been joined in the Commons by his half-brother Neville, voiced the views of many when he noted that 'the Govt would do better if it had a stronger Opposition in front of it.'[157] But that was never the point of the coupon system; electing Lloyd George was.

The outcome of the election in Ireland signalled a profound break with the past, and augured darkly for the future. The Irish Nationalists had tried to insist, in the last days of the war and of the 1910 Parliament, that no new settlement in Europe could be made unless the Irish were given Home Rule, which had to follow on rapidly from the Armistice. The government had refused to commit itself, relying still on the argument that the convention it had appointed to sort the matter out could not agree; and the argument returned to that of the pre-war stalemate, about whether Nationalist Ireland would be coerced, or Ulster. Shortt, six days before the Armistice, had stressed that the failure to agree to partition was paralysing any initiative; thus the way was opened to the two and a half years of bloodshed that followed the 1918 general election, and the extinction of the Irish Nationalists.[158]

The youngest MP in the House, Captain John Esmonde, who had succeeded his father as Member for North Tipperary on his death while serving with the Royal Army Medical Corps in 1915, had in a debate on the government of Ireland six days before the Armistice powerfully condemned this abandonment of what he regarded as an obligation consistent with Britain's war aims: 'I have seen myself buried in one grave 400 Irish Nationalist soldiers killed in one fight; I have seen the last resting place of a once distinguished Member of this House; and I ask you are all these lives, are all these Irishmen to lose their lives and shed their blood in order that every nation of Europe should be made free while Ireland is to be left under a system of coercion and oppression?'[159] His words had a massive impact on fellow MPs, of all parties, but not on the government.

The situation in Ireland now turned out to be as bad as the Nationalists had warned Lloyd George it would be. Dillon had told Scott in August that an election would lead to, at most, ten Nationalists being elected, while Sinn Féin swept the country and would refuse to take their seats in Parliament. In fact, after an election marked by a ruthless propaganda battle, in which exaggerated claims were made about the amount of money in taxes expropriated by Britain, and newly enfranchised women were urged to vote 'as Mrs Pearse will vote', Sinn Féin won 73 of the 105 Irish seats, including all but six previously held by Nationalists.[160] One of its victors was Countess Markievicz, the first woman elected to the United Kingdom Parliament; though like her comrades she did not take her seat. Dillon, standing in East Mayo, lost by 4,500 votes: de Valera beat him.

'The result,' Dillon told Scott, 'was brought about by a system of intimidation – the most ferocious and elaborately organised I have ever known of . . . Armed bands were brought from other counties – 400 or 500 from Clare – and the people were threatened with death if they voted for me.'[161] The story was repeated all over Ireland, with men in Volunteer uniform canvassing for Sinn Féin candidates. Intimidation was not entirely responsible for the Sinn Féin landslide, but Dillon was right to say it had played its part. Nationally, the party had 48 per cent of the vote, but outside the six counties of what would become Northern Ireland, it was 68 per cent.[162] Sinn Féin had been carried to victory by being the anti-British party rather than by having a coherent programme beyond demanding independence. Father Michael O'Flanagan, a priest from Roscommon who had, as a party vice president, been in charge of propaganda, allegedly said: 'The people have voted Sinn Féin. What we have to do now is explain to people what Sinn Féin is.'[163]

Dillon blamed Redmond for letting the party's machine lapse during the war; but even that would have been no match for armed groups threatening to kill anyone not voting the approved way. The Irish Nationalist Party had severed any connection it had with the young: Dillon believed that generation 'are ignorant of what our movement achieved for Ireland', but knew it was the party's fault for not having enlightened them.[164] The real culprits had been Asquith, for mishandling the Rising, and Lloyd George, for his absurd pursuit of Irish conscription. The government's position before the election was that there could be partition in Ireland once matters calmed down; but now the Nationalists were not the representatives of Ireland. Sinn Féin confirmed its policy of abstaining from Westminster, and – pending an appeal to President Wilson for support – proposed its own assembly in Dublin. Many who would sit in it were in prison or interned, and Ireland expected Britain to release them, given the election result.

French had proposed a formal veterans' organisation in Ireland to welcome back and support ex-soldiers, and land grants to recognise their service. It came to nothing. That it did not foretold the broken promises and unfulfilled rhetoric that would take the lustre off the peace for the men and women who had won it. Those broken promises would not be confined to Ireland.

G R
MINISTRY of LABOUR

DISCHARGED
SAILORS & SOLDIERS

GET THE JOB
THAT SUITS YOU
THROUGH THE NEAREST
EMPLOYMENT
EXCHANGE

The Exchange Manager will do his utmost for you — put you in touch with the right place and the right people —

Any Post Office can tell you where the nearest Exchange is.

CHAPTER 12

AFTERMATH

I

A paradox of the 1914–18 war was that its profound effects often became more apparent to the British people once it had ended. Hundreds of thousands of households had had one member or more who would never come home. In churchyards and cemeteries the volleys of firing parties rang out at the military funerals of those who had died of wounds after the Armistice. In the winter of 1919 the streets were filled with ex-soldiers, wrapped in the Army-issue greatcoats they had been allowed on demobilisation to keep against the cold, as they slowly returned home and went looking for work. A mentality of the war years had also taken root, of an unlimited reservoir of public money for any purpose enjoying popular support: this accounted for the high expectations of those who had fought and survived, and the families who had endured their absence. A doctrine of redistribution and state provision entered the national psyche after the Great War, not with its even more murderous second act, even though it would not be until the late 1940s that it was extensively acted upon. Public spending would, however, never be as low again as it was before 1914, partly because of the need to satisfy political expectations, but mostly because of the obligation to repay debts.

Bertrand Russell said that as a result of the war 'I changed my whole conception of human nature.'[1] So did others of less profound philosophical bent. The misery of the preceding years fed secularism; obedience to social superiors and institutions was questioned. The people's century had begun, not just in the revolutionised former empires and despotisms of Europe, but in a Britain of near-universal suffrage in which rulers had learned at close quarters that they held their places by popular consent and not by right of heredity or caste. The age of deference was not dead, but was dying. Among the poor bloody infantry returning home, there was much cynicism about the governing class, who had directed the slaughter they had survived; that, and the broken promises of the Lloyd George coalition, would be a great recruiting sergeant for the Labour Party. Class divisions, relatively rigid until 1914, had been profoundly undermined not in that the discrete classes ceased to exist – they palpably still did – but in the increasing failure to see that someone deserved respect simply because he or she occupied a superior social station. These were the greatest changes wrought by four years of war; and they were far from complete.

Nowhere was the unprecedented upheaval caused by the end of total war more apparent than in the position of women. With millions of men resuming work, and no further need for the army of females making munitions – there were 950,000 at the time of the Armistice – the country would have to be recalibrated. By the end of the war 46.7 per cent of the munitions workforce was female; in January 1918 women had made up 75.8 per cent of employees in the government's National Shell Factories. The total number of working women rose by 22.5 per cent during the war, to 7.3 million.[2] Within two months 750,000 had been made redundant.[3] Despite the numbers of women leaving factories there was a shortage of domestic servants; scores of thousands might no longer have jobs, but the war had hardened the attitudes of both sexes against taking a job that required subservience. Many who left domestic service in 1914 for the front or industry never returned below stairs; 13 per cent of women worked in service in 1914; by 1931 only 8 eight per cent did.[4] Middle-class families, used to having a housemaid or cook, had to learn that doing without was not just a wartime measure, but permanent.

One predominantly female vocation had risen further in status because of the war: that of nurse. To maintain the profession's high standards, to encourage more women to join it and to reflect the government's desire to improve public health, legislation was introduced in March 1919 to begin state registration of nurses. It would be a key underpinning of the welfare state whose creation had, almost by stealth, been begun. Politicians had to take careful account of the needs of women for the first time for the simple reason that those over thirty had the vote. After their contribution in factories and on the land, and in bearing the burden of rearing families without men, the place of women and the regard in which society held them was being transformed. Some would be happy to return to domesticity; many would not, but would compete with men for work in an age when women's pay was routinely less, and there was no legal redress for a woman denied work for no reason other than her gender. Enlightenment still had far to go, for all the progress of the preceding four years.

The social order had changed for men as well as for women. The rate of casualties had been three times as high among junior officers as among other ranks. The war had destroyed a slice of the old ruling class, which had absorbed a disproportionate blow: 18 per cent of public school-boys who had fought died, against 11 per cent of the total; and the generation that had left school between 1908 and 1915 – born between about 1890 and 1897 – had been especially badly hit.[5] Of all the public schools Eton had suffered the most deaths, with 1,157 old boys' names immortalised on a memorial occupying the length of an entire cloister. Many of the old officer class who had survived were returning to uncertainty and reduced private incomes. Great estates were broken up and great houses sold. Class barriers had been eroded or broken, not just because some NCOs became officers. Post-war reconstruction presented new opportunities for men and women to break out of their pre-war roles. Government grants would enable entrepreneurial ex-soldiers to start businesses, or to farm, and be their own masters.

The most significant factor with which the country had to deal was the aftermath of a terrible slaughter of its young men. In 1914 the British regular Army and its reserves had amounted to 733,514 soldiers. Over the next four years another 5.1 million had been recruited, so that by the Armistice 22.1 per cent of the UK male population was serving. Around 705,000 men from the British Isles had died: from the British Empire, another 250,000. Over 560,000 had fallen in Flanders: half had no known grave.[6] Given the controversy over Irish recruitment, and the consequences of its mishandling, one should note that 49,435 of the dead had been Irish. A disproportionate number were from what is now Northern Ireland.[7] Although a soldier had a higher chance of dying in the Crimean War (thanks to disease ravaging the Army there before Florence Nightingale fought the problem), Britain in November 1918 was, because of the sheer numbers who had fought, a land with a total of widows and orphans more historically disproportionate than at any time since the civil wars of the seventeenth century. It was overwhelmed with of mothers lacking sons to support them, and young women who would never find a husband. The proportion of women in the population had risen, especially in the younger age group. An estimated 340,000 children lost one or both parents.[8] 'Maybe the true misfortune of the war was that the older men remained obstinately alive,' A. J. P. Taylor reflected.[9] Influenza remained rampant, with a third wave (worse on mainland Europe than in Britain) taking hold by February 1919. Enemy action, for all the terror it wrought and the outrage it caused, had killed fewer than 1,500 civilians.

In the 1930s Arthur Mee, a popular topographer and journalist who wrote the county-by-county series *The King's England*, identified just thirty-two 'thankful villages' in England and Wales where no man had been killed in the war, and which therefore had no war memorial. It is now believed there are fifty-three, out of nearly 11,200 civil parishes in England and Wales; there is none in Scotland or Northern Ireland. Taylor wrote that in the British Isles the loss of men was actually lower than that caused by emigration before 1914, when many Irish went to America and many British to the 'white' parts of the Empire – Canada, Australia, New Zealand and, to a lesser extent, the recently formed Union of South Africa. Between 1903 and 1913 around 3.15 million Britons emigrated, around half of them to Canada, where another half million would follow them by the end of the Second World War.[10]

There was an understandable demand for formal means of remembering the dead. A temporary national cenotaph would appear in Whitehall in the summer of 1919, designed by Sir Edwin Lutyens after consultation with the government, and would the following year be replaced by a permanent stone structure. In the 1920s the poppy, symbol of the fields in Flanders where so much of the BEF's war had been fought, would become a ubiquitous symbol of remembrance in early November as the commemoration of the Armistice anniversary approached. But in the spring of 1919 one casualty of war above all others was lodged in the public's consciousness, as an example of the cost of the conflict and the values for which it had been fought. On 15 May Edith Cavell's funeral procession wound through London en route to Westminster Abbey. No aspect of pomp was left untouched to honour this most unpompous of women. When the ship bearing her remains arrived at Dover the bells of the town's church rang a solemn and lengthy peal. From Dover to London people lined the railway tracks to salute her train, which was met at Victoria by, among others, a phalanx of nurses. Her coffin, draped by a Union flag, was taken on a gun carriage along Victoria Street to the Abbey, the street lined with soldiers and the gun carriage escorted by men from the Coldstream Guards with arms reversed. 'Officers saluted,' *The Times* reported, 'and women and children stood in reverent quiet.'[11]

Flags flew at half-mast; the congregation in the Abbey included Queen Alexandra, ministers and ambassadors. The Asquiths were among the notables at the funeral, the ex-prime minister finding 'a crowded but most undistinguished and unrepresentative congregation' on reaching the Abbey.[12] After the service the procession continued through the City to Liverpool Street, and the coffin was placed in a railway carriage freshly painted and draped in purple, the colour of mourning, and white. Nurse Cavell's remains were taken by train to Norwich, where she was buried with full military honours in the precincts of the cathedral. The train was met in Norwich by a guard of honour of the Norfolk Regiment; the approach to the cathedral was thronged with people. 'Let us forgive, if we have the strength,' Rider Haggard, a Norfolk man, wrote, 'but forget – never!'[13]

The damaged living, as well as the dead, required society's attention. One and a half million men had been afflicted by gas or wounds, and shell shock was endemic. As long ago as August 1916 the question of how the nation should discharge its obligations towards those wounded too severely to work, and to their dependents and those of the Glorious Dead, had already started to vex MPs. In a long Commons debate it had been proposed that in addition to the statutory, state-funded benefits agreed by Parliament early in the war, the people of Britain should show their gratitude by contributing to voluntary funds, organised on a county-by-county basis, from which additional help could be given to families in special need. Yet not everyone felt the burden should fall on charity. William Rutherford, a Liverpool Unionist MP, had spoken for many when he said:

> Fourteen years ago I was Lord Mayor of Liverpool myself. In Liverpool in that year we had sixty veterans from the Crimean War and the Indian Mutiny, and three-quarters of those veterans who came to the little annual dinner that we gave them year by year had to be got out of the workhouse to attend, wearing their medals. It was a sight to impress anyone who had any respect or regard for their

own country to see these men, and to think that it was in the workhouses where they were driven to spend their days in order to get
the necessaries to eat and drink, and clothe. We believe, in making
this matter a question of principle, that in the midst of the splendid
sacrifices of this War—a sacrifice of lives, property, sons, limbs,
business and prospects—no man broken in this War, nor his wife,
his mother, nor his child, ought to suffer want or hardship, or to be
obliged to beg their bread. It is not charity to which these people
and these classes are entitled or for which they are asking; it is simple justice. Those who lose their lives for us in this War, we know
that God Almighty will look after them; but those whom they
leave behind are left as a legacy to the House of Commons, which
has charge of the funds of the country and ought to see that common justice is done, and to see that the bargain which was made
with these men is honourably carried out.[14]

Lady Haig investigated how best to care for men who through disability struggled to return to civilian life. Many wounded officers, who
unlike those of the old regular Army had no private incomes but had
risen from the ranks, faced penury. When a week after the Armistice
Haig heard from Lloyd George that the King, on his recommendation,
had wished to give his commander-in-chief a viscountcy, Haig asked for
any question of his rewards to 'stand over until the PM has fixed allowances for Disabled Officers and men', as well as gratuities 'for all ranks of
the Armies under my orders.'[15] Haig felt the war disabled had been 'disregarded', and explained to the King that he had refused a peerage to
bring greater pressure on the government to assist them.[16] For all his
faults, Haig was determined to do the right thing by those who had survived his tactical and strategic errors, and his concern led to the formation
in 1921 of the British Legion.

For some weeks, and despite questions in Parliament, Haig continued
to refuse a peerage. The Disabled Officers Fund was spending £5,000 a
month and had almost run out of money, and the number of 'very sad
cases' put before Haig distressed him.[17] The DOF money 'goes to help
(chiefly) Officers who have insufficient or no pensions at all and Doctors'
Certificates show many are unable to work and yet have no pensions or
subsistence. What is to be the future of these poor people? They have
given their all to the Country and without any bargaining.' It was a

powerful consideration for Haig that were he to relent and take the peerage offered him, it would give him a place in Parliament whence he could conduct his campaign far more formidably.

Lloyd George told Sir Philip Sassoon, Haig's private secretary, that the delay in looking after disabled ex-servicemen was the fault of John Hodge, pensions minister until the reconstruction in January 1919, who had caused 'lamentable chaos'. Given the political risks Hodge, originally a Labour MP, had taken during the war to stop strikes, this was unfortunate recompense, and another sight of the prime minister's familiar and unappealing trait of evading responsibility. He said Hodge's successor, Sir Laming Worthington-Evans, had promised the system would be working smoothly within two months.

Many old soldiers suffered from what was called 'shell shock'. This had been recognised from the beginning of the war, even if early treatment was not especially effective. At first the victims were called 'nerve-shaken soldiers' and the Lunacy Commission was responsible for their care. In 1916 the Hampshire County Lunatic Asylum was set aside for these soldiers, as was a part of Netley Hospital in the same county, and the Maudsley on Denmark Hill in south-east London; other such units soon proliferated, such as at Maghull on Merseyside, and the Springfield War Hospital at Wandsworth. Officers – most famously Siegfried Sassoon – were treated at Craiglockhart War Hospital in Scotland; Sassoon's doctor, and its medical officer, Captain William Halse Rivers, who in 1904 had co-founded the *British Journal of Psychology*, became the leading authority on shell shock.

Rivers, influenced by Sigmund Freud, thought the attempt by some of his colleagues to make the shell-shocked repress their memories was wrong. He believed that those who tried to bury them found them returning during sleep, and traumatising them, whereas learning to confront reality would help overcome the trauma: this would be achieved by what he called 'a process of prolonged re-education'.[18] Shell shock entirely misdescribed the mental damage done to soldiers by their experiences in the Great War; for all the efforts made by Rivers (who died in 1922) and his colleagues, some men's lives were blighted for decades, and some exhibited physical symptoms such as shaking. Afflicted men were an all too common sight in post-war Britain.

The government recognised the threat of returning soldiers creating an epidemic of venereal disease, unprecedented even by the standards of the war. Newspapers carried precautionary advertisements; and VD specialists were demobilised before the men, to ensure that treatment could be provided where it was needed. One in five demobilised men had VD: the government offered treatment free of charge to try to control it. The press, running articles about the dangers of syphilis, had lost much of its pre-war coyness, but still could not bring itself to describe the specific 'simple sanitary measures' – condoms – that would prevent VD spreading.[19] Men home on leave had been responsible for 55,000 new cases in 1918, with 16,000 – 10,000 men and 6,000 women – in the London district alone.[20] There were 140 treatment centres, but more were needed. While the government devoted more resources to clinics and education, Dr Randall Davidson, the Archbishop of Canterbury, whose understanding of the soldiery appeared limited, pronounced helpfully that 'I am sure it would not do good if we did not bear in mind that it is not only a medical question but a moral question too, and that we must look on the ethical aspects of it as well as upon those which deal simply with the physical results.'[21] What worried the government most was the infection of unborn children, and the consequent rise in stillbirths, infant mortality and disabled babies. Although VD had been rife in cities and around garrisons throughout the nineteenth century and until 1914, the way the problem was now admitted and openly discussed exemplified how the war had transformed society and its rules.

Official concern about the infection of unborn children was part of a broader concern about the declining birth rate that had accompanied the war; the population, too, required reconstruction. In June 1918 Sir Bernard Mallet, the Registrar General, lectured at the Royal Institute of Public Health about the decline of the birth rate: 881,890 children had been born in England and Wales in 1913, but only 668,346 in 1917.[22] A record number of marriages in 1915 had helped slow the fall, but Sir Bernard said he believed 650,000 lives had been 'lost' during the war because of failure to procreate. He was also concerned that with so many young men killed, and others badly maimed, the birth rate would take years to recover. He thought the equivalent of 7,000 lives were 'lost' each day to the nations of Europe, which he called 'race suicide . . . on the most colossal scale'.

Even more colourful language had been used by Hayes Fisher, when opening Baby Week in July 1918, a state-sponsored encouragement to procreate: 'We must take care that we were well supplied with a healthy population for the future,' *The Times* reported him as having said, 'and that the racial cradle gained a substantial victory over the racial coffin. Unless we did this the waste places of the earth would not be peopled by our race, but by another race with a different language and ideals, a people lower in the ranks of civilisation and Christianity.'[23] Such was the horror of the future felt after four years of the master race killing each other all over Europe. The Dowager Lady Londonderry had opened a Mothercraft Exhibition in London, to cater for 'girls' who had 'escaped from home quite early and did not know even how to hold a baby.' The desire to protect the well-being of mothers and babies drove the foundation of a ministry of health.

The range and scale of the challenges Britain faced required an unprecedented social and economic reconstruction. To dismantle a vast war machine and redeploy the people who had manned it, and to reconstruct a country after four years of privations, would require an unprecedented level of government intervention. As far as the public were concerned, reconstruction had to begin with Britain's fabric: except for accommodation for vital workers there had been little building during the war, and little refurbishment of crumbling properties. The people awaited the execution of election promises about housing. A conference on roads that reported in 1913–14 had had its findings put into abeyance, but with the war over and the restraints on motor traffic lifted along with petrol restrictions, the need to construct major highways became urgent. In greater London a programme of building arterial roads began, which would precipitate the spread of suburbs in the 1920s and 1930s.

The days of the minimal state and economic liberalism under Gladstone and Asquith were over. As soon as the War Cabinet met after the election it discussed what to do with the nationalised factories no longer required to make arms.[24] There were ideas – soon scotched – that they might manufacture goods and compete with the private sector; Lloyd George was enough of a Liberal to want them off the state's books, but finding buyers would be hard. Inflation had reduced the value of the allowances Parliament set in 1914: an urgent adjustment would be required if unease were not to become unrest. Asquith knew this. After the Easter Rising and the disaster of the Somme, when confidence in his rule was falling, he had made vague statements that things after the war could not be as before. This implied a more equitable distribution of wealth – perhaps even by the state – to ensure the poor were looked after. A Joint Labour Committee was established to ensure that, when the time came, demobilisation happened smoothly, and that men returning from the front and women whose working lives the conflict had transformed would have their needs accommodated. Now the time had come, Asquith was not even in Parliament, and his successor, with a fresh and hefty mandate, found it hard to apply himself to such inevitable but unglamorous consequences of peace, when for much of his time until June 1919 he would be at Versailles as an international statesman, seeking to conclude the peace treaty.

For the coalition to keep all the promises Lloyd George had made in the election campaign would require far more money than was available. Just to raise the revenues needed to meet essential challenges such as housing, health care and education would involve a fundamental economic reconstruction, as workers rejoined industries denuded of labour and capital. At the Armistice, Britain was spending almost half its gross domestic product in the public sector, four times the amount of 1914; and the gap between income and expenditure was £1.5 billion, eight times the 1913–14 figure. The national debt was fourteen times the level of 1914. When America entered the war, Law tried to persuade it to lend direct to Allied countries rather than via Britain: but it would not, thus saddling the Treasury and therefore the taxpayer with responsibility for the problem. Britain owed overseas creditors £1,365 million, £852 million to the United States: but was owed £1,741 million, £568 million of it by Russia. France owed Britain £508 million (mostly borrowed from America and lent on), Italy £467 million (ditto), Belgium £98 million, Serbia £20 million and others £79 million. Technically the American debt was no problem if Britain's debtors paid up; but the Russian loans had had no prospect of being repaid since the replacement of the Tsar by the Bolshevik government.[25]

Higher rates of taxes, and taxes paid by a larger proportion of workers, would become a permanent part of the economic landscape. This signalled not merely a determination to pay off the country's debts, but to finance what a political consensus now agreed and understood were its obligations for the future, if the expectations of those who had fought the war were to be met. Higher taxation helped Lloyd George convince the masses that the rich were surrendering their war profits for the national good. However, interest charges subsumed half of tax revenues. Labour suggested a capital levy, but Law rejected it. The war would cause little long-term financial damage: the collapse of free trade later on would do that. Yet there were immediate problems for British industry, which found it hard to compete internationally: for example, steel rails, which it made at £15 a ton, cost only £10 a ton in America. Other changes the country had to make, while not seismic, were symptomatic of the economic challenges it faced if it was to get back on its feet. The post-war world was different for everyone, from the top down. An early Act of the new Parliament repealed the law of Queen Anne, from 1707, requiring newly appointed cabinet ministers to offer themselves at a by-election to secure the approval of their electors; not just in the interests of efficiency, but to save unnecessary expense. Also, the people had become used to long summer evenings, and more daylight in working hours saved energy costs; so the government announced that the wartime innovation of British Summer Time would stay.

The precariousness of the international situation overhung even these serious domestic concerns. Too many politicians and military men believed the fight with Germany had been interrupted rather than ended, a view that would persist beyond the conclusion of the peace conference at Versailles. The defeated power was in ferment after the Kaiser's abdication, and in shock at its failure to triumph after the advances of March to July 1918 – although some realised it was the exhausting nature of that advance that, paradoxically, finished off Germany's chances. In the election campaign Lloyd George had been predictably upbeat, and publicly remained so. It was different in Paris. On Armistice Day Clemenceau's daughter had implored her father to tell her 'that you are happy'. He replied: 'I cannot say it because I am not. It will all be useless.'[26] For various reasons, starting with bereavement and privation, many British felt the same.

Curzon and Smith wanted Lloyd George to uphold the cabinet decision to try the Kaiser, because of concern about the effect on public opinion if he did not: the prime minister, despite his earlier, populist enthusiasm, knew that executing Wilhelm would be impossible. He also no longer needed the promise of it to impress an electorate. Labour and other politicians wanted reparations, which Lloyd George and Law saw would ruin Germany. Their wise view would not prevail at Versailles. The realities of the post-war world asserted themselves swiftly.

The election showed that the old Liberal Party was dead, with the Conservatives and Labour the main players. The war had effected a new polarisation in politics between hard-nosed conservatism and idealistic (but not, with the exception of odd pockets of militancy, revolutionary) socialism: which made Lloyd George's position, as a prime minister without roots in either movement, all the more peculiar. During the war the trades unions, strengthened during the Great Unrest before 1914, had grown from 4 million members to 6.5 million, forming the basis of Labour's support.[27] Ireland had been revolutionised, and worse would come. The new government did not lack potential opponents.

The new Parliament, whose members had been elected partly as a result of having fed those expectations, met in February. Stanley Baldwin, the financial secretary to the Treasury, famously told John Maynard Keynes that the new MPs were 'a lot of hard-faced men who look as if they had done well out of the war.'[28] Baldwin was an ironmaster whose business interests too had flourished, but who donated considerable sums to charity throughout the conflict partly, it seems, out of his sense of frustration at being too old to fight (he was forty-seven in 1914). He so lacked the hard face that in June, just before the peace treaty was concluded, he wrote anonymously to *The Times* to announce he had given a fifth of his fortune (£120,000) to the Treasury to contribute towards the alleviation of the financial crisis, and urging others like him to do the same.[29] The letter was published under the headline *'Richesse oblige'*. 'The whole country is exhausted,' he wrote. 'By a natural reaction . . . all classes are in danger of being submerged by a wave of extravagance and materialism. It is so easy to live on borrowed money; so difficult to realise that you are doing so.'[30] He called his gesture 'a thank offering'; *The Times* described his letter as 'nobly written'. J. C. C. Davidson, his confidant, used Baldwin's idiom when describing the new Tory MPs as containing a 'high percentage of hard-headed men, mostly on the make', who were 'to my mind unscrupulous.' Austen Chamberlain called his new colleagues 'a selfish, swollen lot.'[31] There were 260 new MPs; many were businessmen and a few were trades unionists. Yet Northcliffe, wedded to his progressive, anti-Bolshevism programme, worried that too many of the Tory 'Old Gang' (to use a phrase beloved by the *Daily Mail*) were not just in Parliament, but in power.

II

When Lloyd George reconstructed his administration on 10 January 1919 *The Times* pronounced that it would 'come as a deep disappointment to his gigantic following in the country' because of the failure to promote new blood, which it thought showed 'a hopeless want of imagination.'[32] It called Long's appointment as First Lord of the Admiralty 'frankly inexplicable', and said that Austen Chamberlain, the new chancellor, represented 'an obsolete tradition'; and noted that sending Churchill to the War Office put him in 'the one post where he is calculated to inspire the greatest distrust.' The paper could not bring itself to comment on Sir F. E. Smith's elevation to the Woolsack. The prime minister had, at least, had the inspired idea of appointing Sir S. P. Sinha, former president of the Indian National Congress, as an under-secretary at the India Office, with a peerage, the first Indian to sit in the government or in the Lords.

Lloyd George emphasised there would be no cabinet government on the old model, much to the annoyance of Chamberlain and others. It was argued that the main figures in the government would be at Versailles for the peace conference: cabinet government would be restored in October 1919. Chamberlain became chancellor despite, on 16 December, Hankey having witnessed 'Bonar Law urging Chamberlain's claim' to the job and 'Lloyd George absolutely refusing.'[33] His initial refusal was because he feared the press would attack him for the appointment, and it did. Chamberlain in turn was reluctant. First, he was offended by the brusque way in which Lloyd George, in the letter of 9 January offering him the Exchequer, said that because of the demands of reconstruction there would be 'great issues . . . when differences arise between the Treasury and other Departments', and that these should be dealt with not by the cabinet, but by a committee of Chamberlain, Lloyd George, Law (who remained Leader of the Commons) and one other minister.[34] Second, the usual proximity and access to a prime minister a chancellor had by living in 11 Downing Street would be denied him, as Lloyd George wanted Law to live there.

Third, Chamberlain learned that Lloyd George was considering a small wartime-style cabinet of which (unprecedentedly) he as chancellor would not be part. That was the last straw. Lloyd George tried flattery, arguing that in the circumstances of reconstruction a former chancellor such as Chamberlain (who had served under Balfour from 1903 to 1905) was exactly what was required. Chamberlain was less than impressed when he heard the list – including Churchill and Worthington-Evans – already considered but rejected on the advice of Lloyd George's financier friends. He told the prime minister: 'You will not be surprised that the office has no attractions for me. You offered it to me in what I must consider a very curt manner at the very last moment – very much as you would throw a bone to a dog. I must say I am not particularly flattered.'[35] His stiff reaction was again at odds with Smith's *bon mot* about playing the game, and always losing it.[36] Lloyd George eventually talked him round by promising him a War Cabinet place.

Churchill had wanted to return to the Admiralty (which Lloyd George offered him, but then withdrew) with responsibility also for Air, which he was now given at the War Office. Curzon, whom Lloyd George had grown to detest but whose experience and following in the Tory Party made him essential to the coalition, remained Leader of the Lords. Balfour kept the Foreign Office, Fisher stayed at Education and Montagu at the India Office. Shortt became home secretary and Milner succeeded Long at the Colonies. The most controversial appointment was of Smith, despite his having been Attorney General, as Lord Chancellor with the title of Lord Birkenhead. The King, who regarded him as vulgar and unreliable, was angry: 'His Majesty fears that the appointment will come as something of a surprise to the legal profession . . . His Majesty however only hopes he may be wrong in this forecast,' Stamfordham told Lloyd George.[37]

Birkenhead, risen from middle-class origins in the north-western town from which he took his title, having had a glittering career at Oxford and the Bar, chose as the motto on his coat of arms *faber meae fortunae* – 'Smith of my own fortune' – showing both the cleverness of which the King was suspicious and the flashiness and poor taste he deplored. Churchill, one of Birkenhead's closest friends, had urged the appointment because of his considerable constituency in the Conservative Party – Churchill called them 'Tory democrats' – that could be useful to Lloyd George.[38] For the *Morning Post*, however, 'it is carrying a joke beyond the limits of a pleasantry to make him Lord Chancellor. There are gradations in these matters.'[39] The bibulous Birkenhead could not resist, on his appointment, asking: 'Should I be drunk as a lord, or sober as a judge?'[40]

One of the most crucial appointments was of Addison as minister of local government. To an extent it was a continuation of his role at Reconstruction: but he would also oversee the distribution of state funds for council housing, to deliver Lloyd George's promise of homes fit for 'heroes'. This, like the other promises that had returned him to power, would be left to his ministerial colleagues to implement while Lloyd George spent most of the first half of 1919 posturing at Versailles.

Every statistic indicated a severe housing crisis. For the last two years of the war the Garden Cities and Town Planning Association regularly petitioned about the problem. A total of 1,103 local authorities in England and Wales had told the government during 1918 that they needed more housing for the working classes in their areas, with 510 of them needing more than 100 dwellings.[41] An estimated 610,000 houses were now needed, and that figure was quickly revised upwards after the Armistice. Political embarrassment was reinforced when some soldiers came home to find that for sanitary reasons their houses had been condemned and they were given immediate notice to quit. Moreover, the shortage of housing caused increases in rents, and there were many cases of landlords selling houses over the heads of their tenants.

The government had admitted as early as March 1917 that the provision of better working-class housing 'is the most pressing problem [it] would have to deal with after the war.'[42] Exactly a year later it had intimated it would seek to build 300,000 houses in the first year of peace.[43] During the winter of 1919 the War Cabinet discussed housing extensively, with H. A. L. Fisher telling it that, for example, in Sheffield there were 16,000 slum houses, yet plans to build only 500 new ones. Lloyd George concluded that central government would have to take control of the programme, as to rely on local authorities was 'useless'.[44] Councils were ordered to present plans within three months.

On 7 April Addison brought the Commons up to date. As well as five years of not building houses for the working class – which he estimated as meaning 350,000 houses unbuilt – he believed there were 370,000 that were either seriously defective or unfit for human habitation. He argued that such conditions had been a main cause of unrest in mining communities, and that nationally 3 million people lived in overcrowded conditions with more than two to a room, 750,000 of them in London alone.

He also cited a street in Shoreditch, east London, where 168 households lived in 129 houses, a total of 733 people. In many such streets there were numerous sufferers from tuberculosis, not only sharing a room with someone else, but quite often a bed. Addison argued that the cost of treating tuberculosis would equal the building of vast numbers of houses, so the cost to the country of not replacing poor living conditions was enormous. However, the 1,800 local authorities with the power to condemn a house were reluctant to do so until others were built to which they could move the inhabitants. It often required condemning whole areas, and the cost to the local authority of buying up large areas was prohibitive.

Addison offered various proposals to tackle the problem. He suggested that local authorities would be forced to make clearances, and owners would not be compensated for buildings that had become unfit for habitation, thus saving public money. New financial assistance would be offered to local authorities. Since January councils had applied to start 700 building programmes, using as labour men back from the war: Addison said these would provide 100,000 houses when completed: but that only represented about a seventh of the number needed in and around the capital. He also proposed improving the transport system out of London so that people could more easily live in houses further from the centre.

The government had an Acquisition of Land Bill designed to make it easier to buy plots of building land that were not occupied by defective housing; and Addison promised rents would be fixed at an economic level that would not suffocate private building, an assertion met with some scepticism from Tories. There was a sense that ministers were now so used to the state controlling all areas of life that it had insufficiently occurred to them that private enterprise might have a role to play in alleviating the housing problem. Addison reaffirmed his target of 3,000,000,000 bricks being made in 1919, and promised 5 million in 1920. On behalf of the government he put in an order for 300 million bricks in March 1919 alone, and said the demobilisation department had been ordered to get men out of uniform and into the brickyards as swiftly as possible. (Several MPs challenged his assertion that all brickyard workers had been demobilised, citing constituency cases to the contrary.)

There were fears of wholesale evictions in areas with the greatest demands for housing, and the government was urged to amend the Increase of Rents and Mortgage Interest Act of 1915 that had prevented such things happening for the duration; the lifting of controls that had come with the Armistice was the problem. Some ministers remained reluctant to interfere in the rights of landlords to treat or dispose of their property as they saw fit; but Addison, recognising that the difficulty could not be solved until more houses were built, promised the government would extend the Restriction of Rent Acts to alleviate the problem. In early March the government yielded to the inevitable, and introduced legislation extending rent restrictions for a further year.

In June 1919, after an Act of Parliament established it, Addison would run the Ministry of Health – appropriately, as he was a fellow of the Royal College of Surgeons – and would take responsibility for house building with him. This was a logical step. There was a connection back to the mid-nineteenth century between decent, or 'sanitary', housing and public health. This had been identified in slum-clearance legislation since the 1870s: but now the new ministry would announce that, to keep the prime minister's promise, another 500,000 houses would be required by the end of 1921: the rate of building before 1914 had been 80,000 a year, so to find the labour would require an enormous effort.[45] To make matters worse, there were acute shortages of bricks and timber.

In the event, only 213,000 houses would be built in the following two years, contributing to the coalition's downfall in 1922. Given the extent of the housing crisis, the government's fear about the development of Bolshevism in Britain, and the vulnerability of men with such genuine grievances to be recruited to leftist doctrines, the casualness with which Lloyd George in particular regarded the promises made during the election was remarkable.

The government's other main priority was to restore something resembling normality to the economy. Financial controls began to be loosened; Britain had never legally come off the Gold Standard, but the Bank of England had asked people to be 'patriotic' and not demand gold for their banknotes; there was no return to the Standard in 1919, even though the war was over: but this would come, with unfortunate results, in 1925. The pound fell to $3.50, which should, technically, have given an advantage to British exports, had manufacturing industry been in a position to capitalise upon it. Prices and wages both rose at the beginning of a post-war boom that would crash in 1920. This was driven not least by implementation of some campaign promises of the previous autumn; Eric Geddes announced an infrastructure programme to modernise road, rail, docks and canals, though overall government spending fell dramatically by 75 per cent in the two years from the Armistice, because of the end of wartime expenditure. To consolidate one of the necessities of a more modern future, the government also set about rationalising the electricity supply industry, and standardising the voltage of the grid.

With such a heavy workload for the government, this was a bad time for Lloyd George's methods to be put under continuing scrutiny. The election campaign, with its cynical promises of making a country fit for heroes and hanging the Kaiser, was already coming back to haunt him. Unlike, for example, Baldwin, too many of his associates did not meet pre-war standards of what it supposedly took to be in, or on the fringes of, public life. This last point was highlighted yet again because of suspected abuse of the honours system. A motion was debated in the Commons on 28 May, demanding transparency about the exchange of money for honours. It was seconded by, of all people, Horatio Bottomley, who had raised the £34,000 to have himself discharged from bankruptcy in time to stand in the general election. He would shortly preside over a massive swindle for 'Victory Bonds' that used the public's patriotism to part with huge sums of money that it thought would be invested in government stock, but in fact went into Bottomley's pocket: three years later he would go to jail.

The motion's proposer, Henry Page Croft – a brigadier general – said that 'the name "politician" has become one of opprobrium in every part of the country.'[46] The National Party – a group of Tories, of whom Croft was one, who had chosen not to enter the coalition – had stipulated that only British subjects could donate to its funds, and the names of those who did were available for inspection: but besides attracting money, the honours system was also being used to propitiate and cajole MPs and wreck their independence; it was changing the nature of politics and of the party system and therefore of the parliamentary democracy for which the war had just, in part, been fought.

Embarrassing facts were read into the parliamentary record: Croft said 290 members of the last Parliament had received either titles, or jobs, or preferment. From the day Lloyd George became prime minister until 29 April 1919, hereditary honours had been granted to 155 men, of whom 154 had been civilians. One was from the fighting services. Of the 154, many were MPs or peers; others were constituency chairmen or supporters, and people connected with no fewer than fourteen national or regional newspapers and one news agency had been beneficiaries. One hundred per cent of recipients of viscountcies were pressmen; as were 20 per cent of baronetcies. The distinction between, as Croft put it, those who had offered their lives and those who had offered only words was stark.

Echoing the Lords debate of the previous year, Croft gave no quarter about 'the character of the recipients of the honours.' He said:

> I am told, and I think it is generally recognised, that in the recent Honours List gentlemen received titles whom no decent man would allow to enter his house. According to a most distinguished journal, which I do not always fully agree with, several of them would have been blackballed by any respectable social London club. In this connection I heard an amazing story, probably not true, of the present Prime Minister. A friend of his said to him, 'Do not you think we have gone far enough in this direction?' The story is that the right hon. Gentleman responded, 'My dear fellow, I am not worse than Walpole.'[47]

Croft could not understand why, if a man thought a cause to which he was subscribing was just – be it a hospital or a political party – he should be ashamed of it being known he had done so.

Croft would pursue Lloyd George over the abuse of honours, and would play a part, eventually, in bringing him down. The lack of recognition of warriors, to which he referred, was, however, soon rectified. Days before the Versailles Treaty was signed Churchill made his recommendations for the rewards to those who had helped secure the victory. Haig had continued to stand out against his own peerage because of what he felt were the injustices towards the men he had commanded. Although he was unquestionably sincere in wanting his men taken care of before he was, the politician in him had ulterior motives in refusing the offer of a peerage, and not just because, as far as his former subordinates and their families were concerned, it was a superb public relations move. He could not resist recording that 'I also note that when FM French was *recalled* from the command of the Armies in France for *incompetence*, he was made a Viscount!' Stamfordham told Hankey that 'the people round the King are clamouring for a Dukedom on the precedent of the Duke of Wellington, whose army was not 1/10 the size of

Haig's.'[48] Apparently shocked by this ambition, Hankey replied 'that I was certain Lloyd George would never agree, and I suggested to work for an earldom.' He said that if Haig became a duke, Beatty would want a dukedom too: Stamfordham thought that unworkable, so the King was steered away from a confrontation with Lloyd George.

Haig at last agreed to have an earldom and £100,000; Generals Plumer and Allenby would be made field marshals and given baronies and £30,000; Wilson would be promoted to field marshal too, and Generals Byng and Rawlinson would have baronies and grants of £30,000. Other awards were made further down the scale, such as £50,000 to French, and a baronetcy and just £10,000 to the unfortunate Robertson: and, such was Lloyd George's grudge towards the former CIGS, that was largely only because of fear about the effect on Army morale if he were not rewarded. The other beneficiary was Hankey, awarded £25,000. According to the first edition of the *Dictionary of National Biography*: 'to his private secretary he gave a box of small cigars.'[49]

III

The question of smoothing the progress of soldiers back into civilian life had concerned government since early in the war. Thomas Jacobsen, an industrialist and Liberal MP, had asked Asquith in May 1916 whether he would appoint 'a commission to take into consideration the general position regarding employment that will arise upon the termination of hostilities, particularly for the purpose of making recommendations for dealing in a large and comprehensive manner with the question of ensuring that men returning from the forces to civil life obtain proper employment and that they do not suffer during any interval that may elapse before they are reabsorbed into our economic system?'[50] Asquith assured him the question was 'engaging the attention of the Government.'

It plainly did not engage its attention sufficiently, given the chaos of the winter of 1919. The first great scandal of the peace was the management of demobilisation, for which (despite Churchill's pleas) little had been done since the Armistice. Men still serving did so on one of two bases: either until the end of the war, which would come with the signing of a peace treaty; or six months after the cessation of hostilities, which meant 11 May 1919. At that point, without further legislation, most of the Army would vanish. Ministers, however, had privately admitted they were in no hurry to demobilise the Army. They had to work out what to do with the millions of armaments operatives and other war workers who would join them in a flooded labour market.[51] There were also the challenges of moving millions of men from a former theatre of war back home; and, at the same time, ensuring a sufficient force was left in France to enforce the terms of the Armistice and to be available, if necessary, should the Armistice collapse. And that army itself raised the question of who should serve in it and, if there were insufficient volunteers, whether an element of compulsion was still acceptable given the war was considered to be over. And even the men it was agreed could be demobilised posed a problem: was it first in, first out, or should the demands of the economy take precedence over all else? To establish a calm post-war society, it was perhaps better that the demands of men were attended to before those of the masters, even though the economy required industry to be 'restarted', a process in which the goodwill of the owners of capital would be essential. However, such was the political confusion (something Lloyd George, preoccupied first by the election and then by the Versailles peace conference, did little to resolve) that neither aim was properly pursued.

The Labour Party had discussed demobilisation at its conference in January 1917, and emphasised the importance of trades unions assisting the reabsorption of men into industry, and the creation of new labour exchanges: it had suggested 800 might be necessary. No Labour MP now sat in the cabinet to see that these intentions, or something approaching them, were carried out. Yet Addison, as the then minister of reconstruction, had announced on 24 January 1918 that the machinery of demobilisation was in place, with a plan for assigning men to essential post-war industries if they had no job to return to. So-called 'pivotal' men – those with skills essential to the reconstruction of Britain – would be released first.[52] It was a plan greatly found wanting in its execution.

Churchill urged Lloyd George to use government patronage to order metal goods from munitions factories, as he had with the railway companies, which needed a massive programme of investment to renew their long-neglected track and rolling stock. He felt the rapid implementation of the housing policy was essential, as was a plan to complete rural electrification. He had also implored the prime minister to make him responsible for demobilisation, given the importance to the process

of redeploying the massive, and potentially restive, civilian army working in the munitions industry; but at the War Cabinet on 19 December it
was agreed to give Eric Geddes the job, the duties of which he was supposed to discharge from the angle of 'restarting industry' rather than
getting men out of the Army.[53] Geddes had not wanted the post, but
changed his mind, Hankey imagining it was because Lloyd George had
'wangled' him.[54] Churchill was, according to Hankey, 'sulky and hostile'
at the decision.[55]

The public became increasingly angry with a system that appeared
slow and arbitrary, as did men who had volunteered, done their duty and
wished to return to their normal lives. Aside from the government's lack
of willingness to tackle the problem, the first obstacle to men's return
home was the shattered railway system of northern France, and the poor
repair into which the British system had fallen. It compounded the
absurdity that many soldiers who could be brought back were held in
camps on reaching Britain, rather than released from the Army. This
was because no final decisions had been taken about whether they would
again be needed for military purposes or, if not, the order in which they
could be released.

During the election campaign it had been promised – rashly, and despite the arbitrariness that would result – that men home on leave could be
immediately demobilised: now the Army Council issued an order that no
man would be demobilised while on leave. On 3 January 1919, the 12,000
men in 'rest camps' at Folkestone and Dover were asked to re-embark for
France to join an army of occupation. They refused, demanding an extension of their leave by a week. Wilson was livid: 'The whole of the
demobilisation has been completely boxed by Lloyd George, who, in his
anxiety to get votes at the recent election, kept adding every sort of
authority to help in demobilizing the army, a thing which we soldiers
could have done alone and without a hitch.'[56] The 2.25 million men waiting in France, as well as 200,000 horses and the stores for all of them,
presented a logistical problem not helped by the un cooperativeness of
the French army. The Quartermaster General's staff in London told
Churchill as he entered the War Office that 'both Marshal Foch and General Payot are inimical to the present Quartermaster General in France'
and were doing as little as they could to help.[57]

Soon Geddes was struggling. It was not entirely his fault: businesses
whose ex-workers were suddenly demobilised often lacked raw materials

to resume manufacturing, and a shortage of shipping to move any goods that were made, so were slow to rehire. On 29 December 1918 he wrote to Lloyd George that 'industry is not absorbing the worker turned over from war to peace work as rapidly as one might expect . . . trade is not showing enterprise and is inclined to lean on the government and submit to spoon-feeding'.[58] The process slowed, annoying men wanting to return to their families. In the first six weeks of peace only 42,000 were demobilised, less than 1 per cent of the Armed Forces. There were fourteen government departments involved in demobilisation, demonstrating the vastness of the bureaucratic state and what Geddes had to juggle.

Wilson implored Milner on 6 January 1919 to impress on Lloyd George that he must make a statement that the war was not over, and that soldiers must obey orders, or there would soon be no Army. Lloyd George was, however, less adept at dealing with reality than some around him: and refused to say the war was not over, not least because his election victory had in part been based on the absurd assertion that he had won it. Wilson had it out with him on 7 January and boasted: 'I frightened him.'[59] Still no announcement was made: Milner handed the War Office over to Churchill, who quickly grasped the point but encountered continued resistance from the prime minister. On 8 January 1919 a procession of 1,500 soldiers from a camp in north-west London arrived at Downing Street to ask Lloyd George what was happening; he was out at the time. Many soldiers believed they were being retained to fight the Bolsheviks in Russia, and few relished the prospect.

Geddes, whose reputation was on the line, wanted men out of uniform as swiftly as possible; and because of the inertia of business in telling the government the sort of men it most urgently needed to help complete its order-books began to make plans to demobilise by age and length of service rather than according to skill or vocation, or even simply by battalion. But before he could change anything – and any change required Haig's cooperation – grievances multiplied and the press joined in. Churchill, now he was Secretary of State for War, had the role in demobilisation he had wanted since the Armistice; but would have to cooperate with Geddes, who retained overall control of the task. On 15 January Geddes wrote to him suggesting it be decided how many men were needed for a 'transitional army' or army of occupation, and that they should be selected on a 'simple principle': the one he proposed was that 'all men now under 33 who joined the colours after 1ˢᵗ January 1916 . . . might be retained and all others be demobilized.' The cut-off date meant those men would have been conscripts under the Military Service Act and not volunteers.[60]

As was his habit, Churchill decided to take his own initiatives in this matter, even though the ultimate responsibility was not his. His first thought on assuming his new office was to stop demobilisation altogether, which showed little understanding of the restiveness of the men still in uniform, or their families. He warned Lloyd George on 19 January that Army discipline was being 'rotted' by 'the pulling out of people in ones and twos without any relation to what the ordinary man regards as fair play'.[61] By then 13,400 officers and 631,000 men had been released of the 3.67 million officers and men on the Army's payroll on Armistice Day.[62] Churchill believed that generals, all too used to the double-dealing of politicians in the preceding years, would not cooperate with demobilisation until given cast-iron assurances that the Army would not disappear, and could do the job the Armistice and the likely post-Versailles settlement would demand of it, in terms of occupying the Rhineland and dealing with the clear-up of the Western Front. He told Lloyd George by cable that 'briefly the scheme consists of releasing four men out of five and paying the fifth double to finish the job. I am extremely anxious about the present state of the Army and am serving you to the very best of my ability in preparing a comprehensive scheme for your approval.'[63]

Wilson admitted on 10 January, the day of Churchill's appointment, that he had received 'ominous letters' from commanders in France 'about the temper of the troops there.'[64] Haig issued a similar warning to Churchill about the effect of the delay on morale. These representations caused the war secretary to rethink, and delay demobilisation only for those in France for less than two years. A week after moving to the War Office Churchill further refined his ideas, and proposed releasing all men who had enlisted before 1 January 1916; the downside was that those called up last were those so highly skilled that they could least be spared. If industry were to be put on a peace footing again such workers should be recalled, rather than left hanging around in France.

It had been decided there would be an army of occupation in the Rhineland; it would be composed of five corps of two divisions each, plus a cavalry division. This gave a purpose to some of the men Churchill did not want to demobilise immediately, but the army of occupation rapidly decreased in size until by the summer of 1920 it was down to under 14,000 men. In any case, the numbers enlisted after 1 January 1916 and still serving were over 1.6 million, far in excess of what was required. It was agreed to demobilise at once men over forty and, with the cooperation of the Ministry of Labour, those essential to restarting British industry. No man wounded more than twice would be asked to stay, and only roughly two-thirds in those categories would in any case be needed. Men who wished to volunteer to stay on for a year could do so. However, he also proposed that any man who disobeyed military discipline and was found guilty of insubordination would go to the bottom of the list for discharge. The sweetener for those left behind was a substantial increase in pay and greater allowances of leave. There would be bonuses from 10s 6d a week for private soldiers to 42s a week for colonels and above. Churchill knew the old regular Army had to be remade, not so much for home defence as for overseas garrisons, and these bonuses were important in encouraging men to make a career out of the Army.

However, he, Sir Robert Horne (minister of labour) and the Geddes brothers had concocted this plan without consulting Lloyd George. Nor had they talked to the chancellor, despite the enormous financial considerations that would be entailed. The prime minister, in Paris, was furious when hearing it was proposed to keep a contingent of more than 1.6 million men in France, for the effect it might have on the Army itself, and because of the 'extravagant' nature of the plans.[65] He told Churchill: 'It is hardly treating the head of the government fairly. This is a question not of detail but of first class policy . . . I ought to have been consulted in the first instance.'[66]

In Lloyd George's absence the War Cabinet could discuss the plans but not make a decision. Churchill, reinforced by Wilson (who was invited to attend) said that unless a plan was settled at once there would soon be no army of occupation – he told Curzon on 16 January that the Army was 'liquefying fast and if we are not careful we shall find ourselves without the strong instrument on which our policy in Europe depends in the next few months.'[67] There would be no soldiers to try to keep the peace in Ireland, no imperial garrisons and no regular Army worth the name. Thus threatened, the War Cabinet gave Churchill and Wilson's proposals 'unwilling assent'.[68] Chamberlain was 'very frightened' of the cost; Law went to such lengths not to allow a decision to be taken that, in Hankey's absence in Paris, he did not ask for a secretary to take minutes.

The urge for demobilisation had other propellants. In mid-January 5,000 soldiers had been held at Southampton pending demobilisation, or so they were told. They then heard that they were being sent back to France for the army of occupation, and mutinied. They took over part of the docks, making their headquarters in a large customs shed, and refused to obey orders. Robertson, as head of the Home Forces, asked Trenchard, who had witnessed mutinies among French troops, to put down the attempted revolt, the officer notionally in charge of the men having proved incapable. Trenchard tried reason, summoning the men and telling them their grievances would be heard, but only once they accepted military discipline; they heckled and jostled him to the point where he was almost knocked down.

He retreated, and decided that only the threat of force would do. He asked for 250 soldiers and military policemen, which prompted the General Officer Commanding Southern Command to tell him he was not to shoot the mutineers. Trenchard replied that he was informing him of his intentions, not inviting his approval. The troops were issued with ammunition and surrounded the customs shed; Trenchard ordered them to load their weapons. He demanded that the mutineers surrender, prompting a sergeant to shout abuse at him; the military police arrested him and the other mutineers gave in. Some who would not surrender elsewhere in the docks did so after a dowsing with freezing water from a fire hose. Trenchard interviewed many men personally and gave a conditional discharge to any who expressed a willingness to return to France: but was horrified to learn that they had been lied to about the Army's intentions, a further sign of the incompetence with which the process was being handled.

Exercising his authority, Geddes started, with Milner's support, to release men *en bloc*, and by 28 January the rate of men being discharged was 35,000 a day – so fast that the government began to worry it would have too few troops for the 1.15-million-strong army it estimated would be needed until peace was settled. Churchill was angry that the statistics Geddes had given to the War Office were largely wrong, and sometimes enormously so: having been told there were 558,000 officers on the payroll at the Armistice the figure turned out to be 170,000, and there were in fact 3,350,000 NCOs and other ranks, not the 5,350,000 Geddes's office had claimed.[69] When Churchill realised the true figures he sought drastically to slow down demobilisation, careless of the effect it would have on morale. Haig too was concerned that the Army was 'disappearing' and there would soon be insufficient men for a proper army of occupation – which might mean 'the Germans would be in a position to negotiate another kind of peace'.[70] However, the government's election promise to end compulsory service meant men could not be pressed to join an army of occupation. Churchill's scheme to release only 'pivotal' men was also causing controversy, being deemed by many long-serving, non-pivotal men to be unfair.

Churchill and Wilson went to Paris and saw Lloyd George.[71] They convinced him to swallow their plan more or less whole. When Law learned this, he wrote to Lloyd George expressing concern about the timing of an announcement that so many men would be kept in the Army, which would entail a new Act of Parliament. Law believed the numbers needed might be raised from volunteers: Churchill doubted this, and wanted the government to be frank with Parliament, and the public, from the outset. Haig assured Wilson that any discipline problems among those retained would be solved by an announcement of greatly increased pay. Churchill urged Lloyd George not to allow Law's 'vague fears' to 'paralyse necessary action'.[72]

On 28 January Churchill, having at last received War Cabinet approval, and having carefully briefed Northcliffe – 'I ask you to do the utmost to further the measures that are necessary' – slowed down the rate of discharge, limiting it to men over thirty-seven and those in the rank of corporal or above; the rest were told they would be released as their skills were needed in industry.[73] Geddes, around whom by now Churchill was running rings, surrendered his responsibilities to his brother Auckland, taking instead a new commission to overhaul Britain's transport infrastructure, something to which he was by experience far more suited. Northcliffe instructed his editors to support Churchill's proposals, and 200,000 copies of the *Daily Mail* in which the plans were praised were handed out to soldiers in France.[74]

Those who had refused to become soldiers also impatiently awaited news of their fate. In late February 1919 there were still 1,500 conscientious objectors in prison, many serving consecutive sentences. The government had ignored a petition on 1 January by prominent public figures who had supported the war, arguing that the continued imprisonment of these men served no useful purpose. Among the signatories were three former Lord Chancellors – Loreburn, Haldane and Buckmaster – and other former ministers including Crewe, Morley and Bryce. Some MPs petitioned that those who had served their sentences be immediately discharged from any military obligation; but the government refused while men who had fought for King and country remained mobilised. Advocates for the imprisoned pacifists, such as Josiah Wedgwood, ridiculed this argument. 'I venture to say,' he told the Commons on 5 March, 'that it will not find support from any of the rank and file of the Army. To continue the imprisonment of people who have been in prison for two and a half years is not the sort of thing which the British Tommy would ask the Government to do for him.'[75] He said there could be no doubt of their sincerity as conscientious objectors, because they had been repeatedly sent to prison for refusing to fight, and many had been locked up for two and a half years. He was angry that some who had gone on hunger strike were being force-fed, and accused medical staff of being 'callous' and using 'the maximum amount of force and violence'.[76]

He claimed the new governor of Wandsworth prison had shouted out that 'I will not have these stinking COs mixed up with respectable men.'[77] A Quaker prisoner who had thanked the governor sarcastically had been clapped in irons; the governor had addressed others as 'bloody swine' and threatened them with a bread-and-water diet. Wedgwood claimed that 'many of the conscientious objectors have died already, and many more have gone insane, and are we in England in the twentieth century to tolerate a Home Secretary and a governor who torture men in prison and drive them insane?'[78] Sir Donald Maclean, the leader of the Asquithian Liberals, who blamed the government for not having arranged non-combatant National Service for such men – such as the spoilt types on Morrell's farm at Garsington had supposedly done – supported him. Conscientious objectors with connections had sometimes managed a rather cushy war; a far cry from the fates of those, often infinitely more sincere in their determination not to take life and endowed with far more courage, who ended up being repeatedly sentenced to terms in prison each time they refused to fight.

Shortt, the home secretary, said that if any man in jail would volunteer to do war work he could leave at once; but some had refused even to go to Belgium to help repair war damage. He said the behaviour of the governor of Wandsworth had been investigated, and he had denied everything; yet Shortt had to concede it had not been an independent inquiry, but one run by a Home Office official. He also denied that all the men concerned were religious, claiming that 'I myself have letters from conscientious objectors, men of the highest possible character, who repudiate any connection whatever with men in the same prison because of their conduct and the kind of men they are.'[79]

The Commons was against him, and Shortt was barracked: his defence that the men were subject to military discipline until demobilised, and could not be demobilised before those who had agreed to fight, did not impress. Lord Hugh Cecil demanded a change in the law so the men could be released, but Shortt refused to contemplate it; 'the absolute surrender of the government' was, he thought, all these men would accept. He claimed that even when conscientious objectors were released on health grounds – as some had been – it outraged men awaiting demobilisation, and their families. With the government seeking to avoid further provocation of a volatile citizenry, a policy of populism rather than common sense seemed likely. However, so embarrassed was the government that it announced an independent inquiry, under Sir Albion Richardson, a coalition Liberal MP and barrister who had chaired the conscientious objectors' appeal tribunal for the County of London.

On 3 April the Lords debated the subject. Whereas Liberal grandees had usually led demands for the release of pacifists, now Lansdowne added his voice. The government had run out of arguments, as the War Cabinet realised that morning when it discussed the matter: and so Viscount Peel, on its behalf, announced that 'the Government have decided that these men, who are looked upon as soldiers and who are in prison, shall be now discharged from the Army, and further, that those who have served, whether conscientious objectors or others, for two years or more in the aggregate in prison, shall be released from prison.'[80] Of the 'absolutists', seventy-one died in prison either from illness, the results of force-feeding or abusive treatment. When 'absolutists' were released, the War Cabinet agreed 'it was undesirable that men so discharged should receive unemployment benefit.'[81]

Soldiers, however, were not aggrieved only by sympathy for 'conchies'. At the end of January, at the time of the disturbances in Glasgow, a mutiny occurred at Calais among men angry at the slowness of their demobilisation, and at conditions in the camp; the last straw was the arrest of a private soldier for making a speech deemed to be seditious; his comrades rose up and got him out of jail. On 4–5 March Canadian troops at the Kinmel Park dispersal camp in North Wales rioted because of delays in their repatriation, due to a shortage of shipping; having been told they would be there for days they had stayed for weeks. Matters were aggravated by the sending home of men who had seen no fighting, while those who had were told to wait. The riot began at 9.30 p.m. on the evening of the 4th with, it was reported, a cry of 'Come on, Bolsheviks' shortly before the officers' quarters were looted in a search for drink.[82] The stores were then ransacked for cigarettes and cigars.

The men broke into quarters occupied by female canteen staff and stole their overalls, with the bizarre result that some rioters paraded around the camp next day dressed as women. They then looted a brewer's dray carrying four dozen barrels of beer, after which shooting broke out. With the fear that around 600 men (the riotous portion of the 17,000 in the camp) might go into nearby Rhyl to wreck the town, troops were sent in to put the mutiny down. It ended with five dead and twenty-eight injured, and twenty-five were subsequently convicted of mutiny. This did not deter the Canadians from further riots at Epsom on 17 June, after two compatriots were arrested for being drunk and disorderly. An estimated 400 to 500 men from a nearby convalescent camp marched on the town's police station, tore up iron railings outside, threw bricks through windows and smashed down doors. They released one prisoner and the police, fearing for their lives, released the other. Most policemen were injured and one, a sergeant named Green, died of his injuries. Having liberated their comrades, the soldiers returned to camp. The incident provoked outrage, and contrition from the Canadian high command: over 1,000 people attended Green's funeral, and a fund, led by Lord Rosebery, was set up to provide for his wife and children.

The government was not proving equal to its task of directing to useful work those men who had managed to get out of uniform. It claimed to be shocked in the winter of 1919 when it was reported that 57 per cent of the 3,887 men who had reported to the Holloway labour exchange a fortnight earlier had been ex-servicemen. Matters did not improve rapidly; in the last week of May a demonstration of between 10,000 and 15,000 discharged servicemen marched on Westminster to draw attention to the large numbers still unemployed, and especially to the numerous disabled ex-soldiers with no work. The government promised to set up factories where light manufacturing suitable for disabled men could be undertaken; but that, like promises to establish training schemes for soldiers, or to ensure that men who had been told their jobs would be kept open for them had the promise honoured, had yet to happen.

IV

The unrest among soldiers was mirrored in industry. With the war over and thus with accusations of lack of patriotism a thing of the past, trade after trade went on strike in the winter of 1919. George Lansbury, editor of the socialist *Daily Herald* and a future leader of the Labour Party, had used the *Herald* in 1917 to welcome the Russian revolution and would, in 1920, be an honoured guest of Lenin and other Bolshevik leaders in Russia. As the new government took office he wrote that:

> I see in every industrial centre of our country a growing mass of men and women becoming imbued with wrath and hatred, settling down to parasitical lives of indolence and ignorance, and I see the classes who wax richer and fatter each day by living on the labour of those workers who are permitted to toil. I see those rich and powerful ones engaged in the infamous business of driving those who work deeper and deeper into the bog of poverty – poverty that is of the mind as well as of body – and over it all is the spectre of another and early war which once again will call forth all the bitterness and hatred of which man is capable.[83]

He did not speak just for himself.

There was fear of a general strike, just as reconstruction became urgent, and calls to found a volunteer force to keep the country moving if it happened – as would occur in the General Strike of May 1926. The most disruptive dispute was of workers on the London Underground in early February, which paralysed the capital. But shipworkers on the Clyde, in London and in Belfast also came out, as did engineers and electricians, despite each trade's having set up its own Whitley Council; most disputes were over a reduction in working hours to forty a week. The government started to prepare for food shortages, as if the U-boat war were still on; and coal, in the depths of winter, was scarce even before a threat of strikes by rail and dockyard workers in South Wales, with whom miners came out in sympathy. Scottish miners went on strike separately, demanding a thirty-hour week and wages of £5. Even hotel workers came out, demanding an eight-hour day, and there was a threat to shut down London's power stations. That prompted the government to say it would be an offence under DORA, punishable by a £100 fine and six months in prison, for electricians to strike. Chamberlain, however, made the shrewd observation that 'unfortunately in recent years there had been an increasing reliance placed on the Government as the ultimate arbiter in Labour disputes'. He said this caused both sides to hold out in the expectation of that intervention: but it also dragged the government into a potentially damaging area.

By far the worst unrest was in Glasgow, caused by complaints over working hours – they too sought a forty-hour week – and also the level of rents. Behind this was an organisation of militant leftists deeply in sympathy with the Russian revolution, and seen by the Establishment as hell-bent on class war. Protests lasted several days, alerting the War Cabinet that firm action might be required. Churchill, usually belligerent, advised that 'we should wait until some glaring excess had been committed', but was ready to move in troops.[84] The *casus belli* occurred the next day, with what became known as the Battle of George Square on 31 January. A mass meeting in front of the City Chambers in the square was told the government had no intention of acceding to the strike committee's demands and intervening in the dispute between them and their employers. Strikers threw bottles at the police; the Sheriff Principal read the Riot Act, and was hit by flying glass as he did; the chief constable, standing next to him, was hit by a bottle; mounted police and constables on foot charged the mob.

Two strike leaders were arrested for incitement to riot. One was Willie Gallacher, who had led the shop stewards' movement on Clydeside during the war and served a jail sentence for violating DORA. Gallacher led the call for a forty-hour week, not least to help mitigate unemployment caused by men returning from the war; but he had wider and more strategic aims, as his membership of the Communist Party from 1921 showed. In the interests of restoring order he and his comrade David Kirkwood were allowed to address the crowd, and urged them to go to the city's traditional meeting place, Glasgow Green; they did, but more rioting broke out and trams were overturned, followed by police baton charges. Shops were smashed and looted, and gangs of youths roamed the streets as night fell. A third strikers' leader, Emmanuel Shinwell – who would sit in the Attlee cabinet and become notorious for his manipulation of policy to spite what he considered the ruling class – was also arrested. He ended up in the House of Lords, as did Kirkwood.

With Germany apparently on the verge of a Bolshevik takeover, the British authorities took nothing for granted. Thousands of soldiers in steel helmets filled Glasgow's streets the next day. Rising to this challenge the strikers, while not encouraging more rioting, promised to spread their action throughout Scotland. The strike committee claimed 100,000 men were out on the Clyde, but such was the force of intimidation and saturation picketing that there were doubts about how many were willingly on strike. In the succeeding days, according to *The Times*'s report, 'soldiers with fixed bayonets continue to guard the railway stations, the Post Office, the electric power station, and other vulnerable points, and platoons of kilted men, headed by pipers, who have paraded through the streets, serve to remind the malcontents that the authorities are prepared to deal with any attempts to provoke disturbances.'[85] Such was the fear of riots that five tanks arrived in Glasgow on 3 February. Speaking of the strikers, *The Times* said 'they did their best, but failed, to prevent us from winning the war. They are now scheming to prevent us from making a just and enduring peace.'[86] Kirkwood was acquitted; but Gallacher and Shinwell went to prison for five months.

It was considered that the more extreme Labour MPs had lost their seats at the election, but it worried the man who had become Leader of the Opposition in Asquith's absence, Sir Donald Maclean, that dissent would find a new home outside Parliament – as seemed to have happened in Glasgow. 'Anyone who reads the newspapers', he told the Commons on 17 February, 'knows what is going on outside, the dangerous spirit that is abroad—and the deliberate campaign against the authority of this House.'[87]

The King's Speech opening Parliament included pledges to raise the money for reconstruction and to pay down the debt resulting from the war. Then there came this key passage:

The aspirations for a better social order which have been quickened in the hearts of My people by the experience of the War must be encouraged by prompt and comprehensive action. Before the

War, poverty, unemployment, inadequate housing, and many remediable ills existed in our land, and these ills were aggravated by disunion. But since the outbreak of War every party and every class have worked and fought together for a great ideal. In the pursuit of this common aim they have shown a spirit of unity and self-sacrifice which has exalted the nation and has enabled it to play its full part in the winning of victory. The ravages of War and the wastage of War have not yet, however, been repaired. If we are to repair these losses and to build a better Britain, we must continue to manifest the same spirit. We must stop at no sacrifice of interest or prejudice to stamp out unmerited poverty, to diminish unemployment and mitigate its sufferings, to provide decent homes, to improve the nation's health, and to raise the standard of well-being throughout the community. We shall not achieve this end by undue tenderness towards acknowledged abuses, and it must necessarily be retarded by violence or even by disturbance. We shall succeed only by patient and untiring resolution in carrying through the legislation and the administrative action which are required. It is that resolute action which I now ask you to support.[88]

It was no wonder the government was pleading not just to stop violence, but to avoid even 'disturbance'. No sooner did the unrest in Glasgow end than a strike of gas and electricity workers paralysed Belfast, and the London Underground strike started. The War Cabinet's meetings became longer than in wartime, as it attempted to face the numerous threats to Britain's economy. It was not unrelated to this sense of crisis that, on 12 February, it decided it would be 'premature' to abolish censorship.[89] That month the railwaymen, miners and transport workers reaffirmed the Triple Alliance that between 1910 and 1913 had several times almost paralysed the country: it was a natural response to the poor parliamentary representation the working-class movement had secured at the election. The miners saw the post-war settlement, and the new mandate for the government, as an opportunity to establish themselves on a new footing; and they hoped to threaten a strike of the Triple Alliance to secure their aims.

J. H. Thomas, secretary of the National Union of Railwaymen, who was not keen on such action (though his union would strike in

September 1919), told Lloyd George that 'the trouble is they are trying to get the grievances of a century righted in five minutes, and they won't give you five an a 'arf.'[90] Before the war the wage bill for the railways had been £50 million a year; it had already risen to £110 million and if the new demands were met would be £151 million.[91] The railwaymen were determined to convert the extraordinary gains of the war years into a permanent wage, and the government was having none of it. Aware of the need to placate the miners, the government established a commission to discuss nationalising the collieries; it would take another war to achieve that, however.

In March, before the commission could report, a strike of miners and railwaymen broke out. As well as shorter hours, the miners also wanted highly preferential unemployment pay for demobilised colleagues struggling to find a job, and for men displaced by the return of former soldiers. The railwaymen wanted higher pay. Churchill told Wilson on 9 February that Lloyd George had expected this, and that it would lead to a 'trial of strength between the GOV & the Bolshevists.'[92] When the challenge came, Lloyd George told the War Cabinet that because wartime nationalisation was still in force, 'both miners and railwaymen are the servants not of employers, of the State . . . a strike would be against the State . . . the State must win and use all its power for that purpose, otherwise it would be the end of Government in this country.'[93] He remained prepared to use DORA against strike leaders if necessary. Despite all this rhetoric, and having had its fingers burned, the government strove to stay out of the arguments.

On 12 February the War Cabinet discussed a plan to distribute food in case of a general strike, sending the Army in to keep the ports open. This came against a background of discussing whether to reinforce the 14,000 British and Empire soldiers in northern Russia, sent by Milner the previous year, and wage an assault upon the Bolsheviks: something highly provocative to the British working-class movement. Churchill wanted all-out war; Lloyd George and the War Cabinet did not – not for logistical or manpower reasons, but through fear of inflaming organised labour.

With such considerations borne very much in mind, Lloyd George said in his remarks on the King's Speech that economic conditions in Britain in the preceding years had been better than anyone could remember: real wages had risen, there was no unemployment, no poverty on a pre-war scale and no distress. This was deeply disingenuous to say the least, and typical of his ability to bend the truth, something he did even more ruthlessly than usual in the immediate aftermath of his election landslide. He understood, however, that 'genuine fear' of unemployment now prevailed, and that 'the better educated the working classes become the deeper and stronger is their resentment at these social conditions' – by which he meant the notion of inequality, manifested in the overcrowded conditions in which many working people lived, that had fuelled unrest in defeated European countries, might not be impossible in one that had achieved victory.[94] Official figures on 16 January showed 537,000 men and 430,000 women drawing unemployed pay.[95] The jobless were sometimes offered work at less than their unemployed pay: if they refused it their benefit was cut off.

As spring approached there were no signs of improvement in the industrial situation. In mid-March around 50,000 miners went on strike in South Wales and Nottinghamshire, and the Triple Alliance was activated. Happily, the threat of a quasi-general strike receded without a confrontation. At so volatile a time it is hard to predict what its consequences might have been, not least because the police were also threatening to strike again: unrest was especially bad in Scotland, where officers had seen militant munitions workers bought off by the government, and expected something similar. That same month the War Cabinet refused to recognise a Metropolitan Police union, because the commissioner told them he could not administer a unionised force.[96] To make matters even more incendiary, the return of professional criminals from the forces precipitated a rise in crime, as did the presence in society of men with military training who had endured dangers and hardships for several years and saw little to lose by stealing to improve their lives. To cheer people up the War Cabinet sanctioned higher beer production, without either lowering its strength – indeed there was such discontent at beer quality that it proposed it should be stronger – or increasing its price; and directed additional supplies to areas where the population had increased because of returning soldiers.

Stepping up the brewing of beer was hardly an adequate answer to the problems facing the country because of workers' disquiet. Lloyd George knew that fears about industrial relations would hamper the commercial restart necessary to prevent unemployment, and that the building of confidence was essential. But he was aware that a rise in the costs of production – such as caused by excessive wage demands – would wreck competitiveness and put men out of work. Across the labour movement there were specific grievances that men felt were simply not being addressed. For example, the miners wanted a six-hour shift and not an eight-hour one, for humanitarian reasons; and they wanted the Minimum Wage Act, introduced in the teeth of his anti-interventionist beliefs by Asquith during the Great Unrest, amended to take more into account the average wages of each class of miner. The Labour Party's line was that stoppages were caused by a refusal of management to negotiate properly: and, speaking with the voice of the trades unions, it threatened that the 'down tools' policy would continue until reasonable demands were conceded.[97]

Labour also felt antagonised when the government set about doing what it could to rebuild private enterprise, selling shipyards and factories it had built or taken into ownership during the war. In the face of this capitalist gesture, Labour kept the causes of unrest before the government and the public. Announcements of increases in dividends inflamed workers' feelings; these caused labour unrest and class antagonism immediately after the Armistice. The Lancashire cotton trade was paying historically low real wages because of two years on short time, yet the return on capital to investors had risen by 45 per cent.[98] There were instances of profiteering that even the excess profits tax could not temper. Those that came to light were believed to be the tip of an iceberg, and the rumour took hold that the whole of the capitalist class was making excessive amounts while the workers struggled.

Labour sought the nationalisation of land, mines and railways 'not as any kind of Socialistic idea, but as a plain business proposition to business people', according to one of its longest-serving MPs, William Brace, who said such a policy would turn speculative industries into sound investments.[99] Brace conceded that the Bolshevik was an enemy of the state, but believed the profiteer was as dangerous. At a time of such volatility, he hardly exaggerated. 'I would say to employers,' he concluded, 'recognise the changed circumstances; recognise that the working classes are no longer going to be treated as "hewers of wood and drawers of water".'[100]

The readiness with which some rank-and-file trades unionists ignored their more moderate leaders, and embraced Bolshevik doctrine, caused great disquiet. Apparently fearing a revolution, Crewe, in the Lords on

4 March, sought to find common ground with the labouring classes: 'Do the workers seriously desire that all the elements of adventure and of good fortune should be eliminated from the prospect of the capitalist? Perhaps, to some extent, they may, and if they do one cannot be altogether surprised, because those elements, as industry is carried on in this country, are the exclusive property of the capitalists.' His idea that the fruits of capitalism should be shared more widely with the workers, instead of ending capitalism, was not far ahead of its time; profit-sharing firms had existed from the nineteenth century and started to proliferate before the war. Other such initiatives would grow up in the years of industrial strife that lay ahead, to the General Strike and beyond. Socialist policies lacked ministerial advocates, though Churchill, speaking in his constituency, Dundee, just before the election, had hinted that railway nationalisation would become government policy. This apparently throwaway remark caused great consternation to railway companies, and to the unions, none of whom realised such a thought had entered ministers' heads – and Churchill's own colleagues were appalled at the suggestion.

The unions wanted conciliation and negotiation; the government floated the idea of compulsory arbitration. However, it lacked confidence in the idea sufficient to include proposals for it in the King's Speech. Instead, Lloyd George appealed vaguely 'to the commonsense of all sections of the community, so that the victory won so largely by the heroism and the tenacity of this great nation in five years of sacrifice shall not be wantonly dissipated in a few weeks of frenzied strife.'[101]

It fell to the surviving Asquithian Liberals to apportion the real blame for the unrest: with Lloyd George, who, as Acland claimed in the same debate, had run an election campaign 'on stunts'; had, through the exercise of the coupon, done all he could to prevent the election of Labour MPs to give the working man and woman a voice in Parliament; and who on the eve of the election had made a 'tremendous onslaught' on Labour and its leaders.[102] Acland also attacked Lloyd George for operating a policy whereby there was restricted availability of shipping, which reduced imports and imposed a form of protectionism that kept prices – especially those of food – up at home; given that the prime minister had, in the debate on the King's Speech, demanded an export drive, this was grave hypocrisy. Another reason for the protectionist stance, Acland contended, was that the government had made

huge advance purchases of commodities in expectation of war, and did
not wish to make a loss – something it could prevent only by suffocating free trade. Despite the government's mismanagement of economic
and industrial affairs, and the high levels of agitation, Bolshevism would
not take hold in Britain.

By the time of the Versailles Treaty 80 per cent of soldiers were demobilised: and many went into work quickly, not least as women returned
to the home. The Discharged Soldiers' Association asked the government to initiate a 5 per cent quota in its workforce of men who had been
disabled, and to start a national scheme requiring private sector employers to do the same.[103] The DSA said it felt its 'extremist' members were
prepared to resort to violent protest unless something was done, which
worried Horne, the minister of labour. They also wanted women to be
replaced by ex-servicemen wherever practical, and for labour exchanges
to give ex-servicemen, especially those with a disability, preference over
others when offering jobs. The government, recognising the new order,
realised such a policy required union support, and was unlikely to get it:
the unions would not tolerate the dismissal of a fit man and his replacement by a disabled one. The DSA demanded to see the King; the King
was embarrassed, and intimated to Horne that he was minded to grant
Royal Warrants only to firms employing a 5 per cent quota of disabled
ex-servicemen.

The War Cabinet had few qualms about removing women from their
jobs: 'There were many women holding Government posts who did not
require this form of income at all and many of the women were married
and could be supported by their husbands,' Horne said. He was true to
his word. By 1921 there were fewer working women than in 1914. An
attempt was made, however, to allow women to obtain professional
qualifications and to serve in civil and judicial capacities, such as in the
civil service and the magistracy, on the same basis as men through a
Women's Emancipation Bill, introduced in the Commons in April. It
would also allow women to sit in the Lords as they now could in the
Commons – there were a handful of hereditary peeresses, and others
could be created. However, it would also enfranchise women at the age
of twenty-one, as it would men. The Bill was defeated, but most of its
provisions were brought in within a few years – although it took until
1958 for women to sit in the Lords. William Adamson, the Tory MP who
introduced it, said that 'during the great period of reconstruction in the

process of rebuilding the world, men and women must face the future together under more equal conditions than ever have obtained up to the present time. It is, therefore, in my opinion, the duty of this House to take the steps which are necessary for removing the barriers which still stand in the way of the womenfolk of the country.'[104] There was also a demand for the Commons to debate the need for the legal profession to admit women, as the medical profession had done in the late nineteenth century. The mood of the times was clear.

V

Just as one set of hostilities ceased, another reignited. On 19 December 1918 the Irish Republican Army had tried to assassinate French, the Viceroy; on 21 January the Sinn Féin MPs elected the previous month and who were at liberty – thirty-six were in prison – having refused to take their seats at Westminster as they abjured the authority of the Imperial Parliament over Ireland, convened the first Dáil Éireann at the Mansion House in Dublin. The building had just been used for a lunch to welcome home 400 repatriated prisoners of the Royal Dublin Fusiliers; the surrounding buildings were festooned with Union flags. With the weight of the vote behind them the MPs declared an Irish republic, and announced that a state of war existed between Ireland and England. Proving the point, that day Volunteers of the Tipperary Third Brigade killed two Royal Irish Constabulary officers guarding a consignment of gelignite at Soloheadbeg in Tipperary, an action unauthorised by the leadership of Sinn Féin, and initiating a spasm of worsening violence, destruction and bloodshed that would last more than three years.

Haldane had been in Ireland, being consulted by French about a way forward: Haldane's idea was to offer Dominion status to Ireland and with it a generous financial settlement. However, he had barely reached home when the Soloheadbeg murders happened, prompting French to write to him to say that 'it has been necessary to declare the whole county a military area . . . the Sinn Féin leaders cannot control their own people . . . circumstances have prevented any further progress being made in the direction we wished.'[105] Haldane thought French's response 'folly'. In the months ahead several Sinn Féin MPs would be arrested for sedition or unlawful assembly, either court-martialled or brought before resident magistrates, and sent to prison, usually for two or three years. The establishment of a coherent Irish policy seemed impossible; locking up republicans was about all the government could fathom to do, and each time opinion hardened further against Britain.

The response in Britain to the declaration of the republic was amazement and ridicule; but the republicans were not acting lightly. *The Times*'s reporter noted that the crowd that packed the Mansion House to watch the event included 'a considerable sprinkling of priests'; the Catholic Church was now strongly, if unofficially, behind Sinn Féin.[106] In the election campaign Sinn Féin's programme had not specified how Britain would be expelled from Ireland; the public response to these killings suggested they would not support violence. The two dead RIC men were both from local families and both popular, and the murders caused great dismay among the Irish.

For the moment the Volunteers – who from around this time came to be known by a new name, the Irish Republican Army – confined themselves to attacking RIC men: soon they would move on to British soldiers. The Mansion House meeting issued a call to the world's free nations to recognise the Irish republic and support it; and called for the 'foreign garrison' in Ireland to be evacuated. The new Dáil asserted that it alone had the right to make laws for Ireland and it alone was the just recipient of the allegiance of Irish people. A war of independence began that would last until July 1921.

On 4 February 1919 de Valera (described in his police 'wanted' poster as 'aged 35, a professor, standing 6ft 3in, and dressed in civilian clothes') and two others – John Milroy and John McGarry – escaped from Lincoln jail using a forged key smuggled in by a visitor. De Valera had made an impression of the jail's master key in candle wax from the chapel, having taken the key from the chaplain, and in the traditional manner the duplicate was brought into the prison in a cake.[107] He was spirited to Manchester and thence briefly to Ireland and the United States, before returning home in April to become president of the Dáil. Four comrades had escaped from the prison at Usk the week before; all had been incarcerated since French's round-up the previous May. To hit the Ascendancy where it hurt most Sinn Féin demanded a ban on fox-hunting in Ireland until the republican prisoners held in Britain since the round-up the previous July were released: this, however, backfired because so many of its supporters worked for hunts and bloodstock businesses. The Lord Mayor of Dublin appealed to Shortt, not just home secretary but also the last

Irish secretary, to release the prisoners because of the 'desperate' state of Ireland after the election landslide.[108] When he failed, the Lord Mayor pleaded directly to Lloyd George – 'no useful purpose can be served by still detaining them in prison', he said, and there would be 'deplorable results' from doing so.[109]

French too wanted the men released: he saw, shrewdly, that a moderate element in Sinn Féin was tussling with extremists, and he thought the moderates would obtain more traction if the government made a gesture. The schism he spotted would be played out in the civil war of 1921–22 that followed the formal partition of Ireland. The government was effectively leaderless on this question because of Lloyd George's absence in Paris: the War Cabinet decided on 4 March to release the prisoners 'gradually'.[110] Meanwhile, de Valera did a lap of honour around Irish America, raising money and gathering support.

When the King opened Parliament on 11 February he said, in the speech Lloyd George had had written for him, 'the position in Ireland causes Me great anxiety, but I earnestly hope that conditions may soon sufficiently improve to make it possible to provide a durable settlement of this difficult problem.'[111] There was no indication of how this nirvana would be achieved, though Sir Horace Plunkett suggested that 'Ireland must be given the status of a self-governing dominion' as the only means likely to avoid disaster.[112] Lord Hugh Cecil suggested a council should be formed in each of Ireland's four provinces and they should discuss among themselves how best to proceed while the Home Rule Act was suspended for five years. However, the old compromises were irrelevant to an Ireland dominated by republicans, as even the government could see; and time was running out. Britain was slow to denominate it thus, but the majority in Ireland had rejected constitutional change and was at the start of its war of independence.

Ireland was not the only British possession to be seeking self-determination in the aftermath of the Great War. India, too, was stepping up a campaign for independence, the impetus for which came not least from what the country felt Britain owed it after the sacrifices its people had made to support the mother country since 1914. A more direct cause of agitation was the passage in March 1919 of the Anarchical and Revolutionary Crimes Act (known as the Rowlatt Act, after the judge whose committee recommended it). This extended indefinitely provisions of the 1915 Defence of India Act that allowed detention without trial for up to two years for those engaged in terrorist or seditious behaviour. It provoked unrest on a scale unseen since the Mutiny of 1857.

A pivotal event in the history of British India occurred on 13 April 1919 in the Jallianwala Bagh, a garden in Amritsar, in the Punjab, when several parts of India were afflicted by famine. The Punjab had raised 360,000 men to fight in various theatres of the Great War, so its loyalty to the King–Emperor had been evident.[113] However, there had been days of unrest after the arrest and deportation of Dr Satya Pal and Dr Saifuddin Kitchlew, Indian nationalist leaders who had urged non-violent protests against the Rowlatt Act. Sir Michael O'Dwyer, the Punjab's Lieutenant Governor, and Acting Brigadier General Reginald Dyer, Indian-born and with over thirty years' experience in the Indian army, commanding the local garrison, feared a rerun of the Mutiny. Martial law was declared and a proclamation was made banning public meetings.

This was either ignored by, or did not reach, thousands of Indians who went to Jallianwala Bagh to mark the Punjabi festival of Baisakhi, and to hear speakers preaching passive resistance to British rule. Regarding this as a display of disobedience that threatened order, Dyer – with whom, under martial law, the initiative lay – took fifty men armed with rifles and, without warning those in the garden, ordered them to fire on the crowd; there were also forty Gurkhas armed with kukris. Once they opened fire from either side of the entrance to the garden the crowd panicked and a stampede began; the fusillade lasted for perhaps ten minutes.[114] An official report claimed the result was 379 dead and 1,000 wounded; local estimates put the number of dead at over 1,000. Indians and Britons alike execrated Dyer; though many Britons in India felt he had acted correctly, as did many at home, who received only partial and (to begin with) inaccurate reports in newspapers. The official line was that Dyer had avenged an assault on a British teacher, Marcella Sherwood, by an Indian mob: this assault had happened, but was used as an excuse to display exemplary force to cower militants. It was also said that in Amritsar three bank managers had been burned to death, one after being clubbed. *The Times*, on the basis of what the Viceroy's office chose to transmit back to Britain, berated the 'passive resistance' movement for lacking passivity, and (in drawing attention to his effect in leading the unrest), observed that 'Mr MK Gandhi . . . is a misguided and excitable person', a 'stalking horse' for 'dangerous' types fomenting revolution.[115]

In the immediate aftermath of the massacre, newspapers exuded indignation that British nationals had been killed, and shock at what Lord Chelmsford, the Viceroy, called 'open rebellion'. They demanded the immediate and severe punishment of the 'rebels'.[116] It was weeks before anything like the truth was revealed to the British public, and even when it was out those responsible retained their apologists. O'Dwyer, whom an Indian nationalist seeking revenge would murder in 1940 at a public meeting in London, was praised for running a tight ship. Dyer became known as 'the Butcher of Amritsar'; he expressed no regret, and Kipling, not only a major public figure but also one with a deep knowledge of India, praised him. A fund set up by the *Morning Post* raised £26,000 for him. It was a gesture reminiscent of Carlyle's in 1866 for another heavy-handed imperialist, Edward Eyre.[117] Montagu, the Secretary of State, called Dyer's actions 'a grave error in judgment'.

Dyer's defence was that, having noted disturbances in other cities, he had feared a conspiracy against British rule and believed it was his mission to prevent it, however ruthlessly: yet there was no conspiracy, and even had there been the lessons of the Easter Rising at least should have shown that bloodshed was not an ideal palliative. Politicians and the public writing to newspapers drew parallels between Ireland and India, with a common theme of the imperial power's mismanagement. Ireland would have a degree of resolution within three years: in India this would take three decades. However, the process of loosening imperial ties had begun. The massacre at Jallianwala Bagh became a defining moment for the nationalist movement; and whatever good the Montagu–Chelmsford reforms might have done was negated. Although some British politicians – notably Churchill – would continue to regard India as incapable of governing itself, the articulacy of India's advocacy in favour of self-determination, and the justice of its arguments, would in the years to come secure more and more supporters at Westminster.

VI

In the first two months of the peace conference, which began on 12 January, little progress was made. On 5 March Lloyd George went to Paris and over the next few weeks he, Clemenceau, Woodrow Wilson and Orlando started to thrash out the details. The principal problem the other leaders faced was Clemenceau's insistence on humiliating Germany to the benefit largely of France. Miss Stevenson noted that the French 'cannot believe that Germany is defeated, and feel that they cannot have enough guarantees for the future.'[118] The Americans irritated Lloyd George, planning, according to Wilson, to enlarge greatly the size of their army and navy, while holding up the conference by insisting on commitments to the League of Nations. At the request of the other leaders, Lloyd George agreed to stay in Paris until the preliminary terms were signed.

His absence abroad not only meant that the great reconstruction programme had to be set in motion without his constant oversight; the vacuum he left behind, and the removal of the unifying factor of war, encouraged sometimes unwelcome freelance operations by colleagues. It seemed at least one minister was already bored with the post-war world. The 'disloyal and ambitious' Churchill was giving Lloyd George 'great trouble,' Miss Stevenson recorded on 13 April. 'Being Secretary of State for War, he is anxious that the world should not be at peace, and is therefore planning a great war in Russia.'[119]

Lloyd George returned to London briefly on 16 April to advise the Commons on progress, not least about Russia, which (singing Churchill's tune) he absurdly said the Allies could conquer if they needed to; and then returned straight to Paris. In the course of his Commons speech, having claimed he did not want a 'vindictive peace' with Germany, he savaged Northcliffe – without naming him – for the way he was trying to orchestrate the approach taken to Germany at Versailles, and said: 'honestly, I would rather have a good peace than a good press.'[120] He continued:

When a man is labouring under a keen sense of disappointment, however unjustified and however ridiculous the expectations may have been, he is always apt to think the world is badly run. When a man has deluded himself, and all the people whom he ever permits to go near to him help him into the belief that he is the only man who can win the War, and he is waiting for the clamour of the multitude that is going to demand his presence there to direct the destinies of the world, and there is not a whisper, not a sound, it is rather disappointing; it is unnerving; it is upsetting.

Then the War is won without him. There must be something wrong. Of course it must be the Government! Then, at any rate, he is the only man to make peace. The only people who get near him tell him so, constantly tell him so. So he publishes the Peace Terms, and he waits for the 'call.' It does not come. He retreats to sunny climes, waiting, but not a sound reaches that far-distant shore to call him back to his great task of saving the world. What can you expect? He comes back, and he says, 'Well, I cannot see the disaster, but I am sure it is there. It is bound to come.' Under these conditions I am prepared to make allowances; but let me say this, that when that kind of diseased vanity is carried to the point of sowing dissension between great Allies, whose unity is essential to the peace and happiness of the world, and when an attempt is made to make France distrust Britain, to make France hate America, and America to dislike France, and Italy to quarrel with everybody, then I say that not even that kind of disease is a justification for so black a crime against humanity.[121]

When he uttered 'diseased vanity', Lloyd George tapped his head to indicate his belief that Northcliffe was mad. He had not quite finished; he wished to justify his assault on Northcliffe as essential to disabuse his Allied colleagues of certain notions. 'They still believe in France that *The Times* is a serious organ. They do not know that it is merely a threepenny edition of the *Daily Mail*. On the Continent of Europe they really have an idea that it is a semi-official organ of the Government.'

The lack of an opposition allowed the prime minister to launch this attack without anyone reminding him of his own earlier dependence on Northcliffe; the attack itself diverted attention from the peace settlement, which Lloyd George had no wish to discuss, given his difficulties on various matters with Wilson and Clemenceau. Northcliffe had just sacked Dawson, *The Times*'s editor (though he would be back eventually to fulfil his historical destiny as a leading appeaser of Hitler, along with Northcliffe's brother, Rothermere), and urged his replacement, Henry Wickham Steed, to attend the House to watch Lloyd George's report from Versailles. Steed noted that the House 'roared with delight' as it watched the prime minister's assault on his proprietor.[122] Northcliffe's retaliation included printing a black box in the *Mail* each day recording the numbers of killed, missing and wounded in the war, and elsewhere in the paper the prominent slogan 'Those Junkers will Cheat You Yet'.[123]

On 7 May German delegates at Versailles were presented with peace terms. The Allies had continued the blockade – and it would last until July – to ensure the Germans had to come to the table and agree terms. Clemenceau's determination for reparations was stimulated by the fact that in France more than half a million houses and 17,600 buildings had been either partly or completely ruined. Around 20,000 factories or workshops had been damaged or destroyed, with plant confiscated and taken to Germany. An estimated 860,400 acres of farmland were derelict, and a million head of cattle had been rounded up by the Germans and taken home. When the Germans retreated they had routinely laid waste the land they evacuated. The French estimated the damage, and the cost of fighting the war Germany had started against them, at between 35 billion and 55 billion pre-war gold francs.[124]

France was not, of course, alone in bearing that cost. Even if Britain had a substantial army to fight the Russians, whether it could afford to pay and supply it was another matter. On 30 April Chamberlain introduced his Budget; the problem of paying for the war continued, while that of paying for the peace began. With the 1918–19 deficit at £1,690,280,000 there would be no cut in taxation; even without a massive army to pay and equip, the projected deficit for 1919–20 was still £233,810,000. Beer and spirits duties rose, and death duties too, to the point where on the largest estates they were 40 per cent, leading to break-ups of more ancient landholdings. A new Victory Loan, in June 1919, raised £250,000,000, but matters remained parlous.

A week before the final act at Versailles, on 21 June, the German High Seas Fleet was scuttled at Scapa Flow on the orders of Rear Admiral Ludwig von Reuter, the officer in command of the captured ships. The sinking was in breach of the Armistice and therefore technically an act of war; it was announced that von Reuter would be court-martialled. The French were angry because they had wanted some of the ships; the British were relieved because they wished to avoid a row about how they would be parcelled out. Long told the Commons that as the ships were interned and not surrendered the Admiralty was unable to take precautions to prevent their sinking. Had guards been on the ships – more than seventy of which were either sunk or beached, Long reported – it would have breached the terms of the Armistice. The question of what their loss would add to the reparations bill was discussed at Versailles; it hardened the Allies' determination to enforce their terms without negotiation.

Mrs Webb, staying in the country with like-minded friends, all of them as with many on the Left still licking their wounds after Lloyd George's manipulation of the general election, wrote in her diary when hearing of the scuttling: 'We are all so disgusted with the Peace that we have ceased to discuss it – one tries to banish it from one's mind as an unclean thing that will be swept away by common consent when the world is once again sane.'[125] She added: 'The Germans will sink other things besides their fleet before the Allies repent of this victory: the capitalist system for instance. The Germans have a great game to play with Western civilisation if they choose to play it, if they have the originality and the collective determination to carry it through.'

On 28 June 1919, five years to the day after the assassinations in Sarajevo, Lloyd George convened a lunch in Paris before the signing of the peace treaty at Versailles. He assembled Law and Lord Robert Cecil, his main coalition partners; his closest confederates from Downing Street and the Garden Suburb, Frances Stevenson, Philip Kerr, Sir William Sutherland (as he had become), J. T. Davies and Law's right-hand man, Davidson; and his daughter Megan. After lunch, the party drove to Versailles, and Davidson recalled that 'the last quarter of a mile leading up to the Palace was lined on either side by French cavalry in steel helmets and blue field uniforms, knee to knee.'[126] A guard of honour presented arms as the dignitaries reached the entrance; they proceeded up a staircase lined by the Republican Guard in uniforms identical to those worn at Waterloo, 'of blue cloth with red facings, white buckskin breeches, and wonderful silver helmets with horsehair plumes, each man standing immobile with drawn sword held at the carrier. It was most artistic and very impressive, and must have made the Hun think when his turn came to ascend the stairs.'[127]

Other aspects of the spectacle were less impressive. Lloyd George and Law had to elbow their way through the crowd to reach the Hall of Mirrors. At three o'clock the Germans entered, bowed to Clemenceau, and after the French leader had spoken, signed the treaty. Lloyd George then wrote, in his own hand, a letter to the King. The news was telegraphed to London: crowds milled outside Buckingham Palace from late afternoon, and just after 6 p.m. the King and Queen and their children went out on to the central balcony and acknowledged 'a great demonstration of loyalty' for forty minutes while a hundred-and-one-gun salute was fired.[128]

Law and Davidson left for an aerodrome and flew to London; Davidson took the letter to the King at Buckingham Palace, which he entered 'through crowds of cheering people.'[129] It was 9.15, and the King had just finished dinner. He took the letter, which read:

> Mr Lloyd George with his humble duty to Your Majesty has the honour to announce that the long and terrible war in which the British Empire has been engaged with the German Empire for more than four years and which has caused such suffering to mankind has been brought to an end this afternoon by the Treaty of Peace just signed in this hall.
>
> He desires on behalf of all the Plenipotentiaries of Your Majesty's Empire to send their heartfelt congratulations to Your Majesty on the signature of a Treaty which marks the victorious end of the terrible struggle which has lasted so long and in which Your Majesty's subjects from all parts of the Empire have played so glorious a part.

The King, in the uniform of an Admiral of the Fleet, heard Davidson's impressions of the Versailles ceremony, and – with a crowd now estimated at 100,000 outside – returned to exchange salutes with his people from the balcony. 'Please God,' he wrote in his diary, 'this dear old country will soon settle down and march in unity.'[130]

BIBLIOGRAPHY

Primary Sources

Asquith Papers, Bodleian Library, Oxford
Balfour Papers, British Library
Beaverbrook Papers, Parliamentary Archives (PA)
Cabinet Papers, National Archives, Kew (NA)
Churchill Papers, Churchill College, Cambridge
Crewe Papers, Cambridge University Library
Esher Papers, Churchill College, Cambridge
George V Papers, Royal Archives, Windsor (RA)
Hankey Papers, Churchill College, Cambridge
Lansdowne Papers, British Library
Law Papers, Parliamentary Archives (PA)
Lloyd Papers, Churchill College, Cambridge
Lloyd George Papers, Parliamentary Archives (PA)
Northcliffe Papers, British Library
Parry Papers, Shulbrede Priory
Plunkett Papers, National Library of Ireland
Rayleigh Papers, owned privately by Lord Rayleigh
Stamfordham Papers, Royal Archives, Windsor (RA)

Secondary Sources

Adams I: *Arms and the Wizard: Lloyd George and the Ministry of Munitions, 1915–1916*, by R. J. Q. Adams (Cassell, 1978).
Adams II: *Bonar Law*, by R. J. Q. Adams (John Murray, 1999).
Adams III: *Balfour: The Last Grandee*, by R. J. Q. Adams (John Murray, 2007).
Amery: *The Leo Amery Diaries: Volume I: 1896–1929*, edited by John Barnes and David Nicholson (Hutchinson, 1980).

Andrew: *The Defence of the Realm: The Authorized History of MI5*, by Christopher Andrew (Allen Lane, 2009).

AP: *The Conscription Controversy in Great Britain, 1900–18*, by R. J. Q. Adams and Philip P. Poirier (Macmillan, 1987).

Asquith C.: *Diaries 1915–1918*, by Lady Cynthia Asquith (Hutchinson, 1968).

Asquith, Diary: *Margot Asquith's Great War Diary 1914–1916: The View from Downing Street*, edited by Michael and Eleanor Brock (Oxford University Press, 2014).

Asquith, MR: *Memories and Reflections, 1852–1927*, by the Earl of Oxford and Asquith KG (Cassell, 2 vols, 1928).

Asquith, VS: *HH Asquith: Letters to Venetia Stanley*, selected and edited by Michael and Eleanor Brock (Oxford University Press, 1982).

Barnett: *The Collapse of British Power*, by Correlli Barnett (Eyre Methuen, 1972).

Beaverbrook I: *Politicians and the War, 1914–1916*, by the Rt Hon. Lord Beaverbrook (Thornton Butterworth, 1928, vol. I; Lane Publications, 1932, vol. II).

Beaverbrook II: *Men and Power 1917–1918*, by Lord Beaverbrook (Hutchinson, 1956).

Bell: *Churchill and the Dardanelles*, by Christopher M. Bell (Oxford University Press, 2017).

Bell Q.: *Virginia Woolf: A Biography*, by Quentin Bell (Hogarth Press, 2 vols, 1972).

Bilton: *The Home Front in the Great War: Aspects of the Conflict 1914–1918*, by David Bilton (Pen & Sword, 2004).

Blake: *The Unknown Prime Minister: The Life and Times of Andrew Bonar Law, 1858–1923*, by Robert Blake (Eyre & Spottiswoode, 1955).

Boothby: *Recollections of a Rebel*, by Robert Boothby (Hutchinson, 1978).

Brandon: *The Spiritualists: The Passion for the Occult in the Nineteenth and Twentieth Centuries*, by Ruth Brandon (Alfred A. Knopf, 1983).

Brooke, 1914: *1914 & Other Poems*, by Rupert Brooke (Sidgwick & Jackson, 1915).

Brown: *Essays in Anti-Labour History: Responses to the Rise of Labour in Britain*, edited by Kenneth D. Brown (Macmillan, 1974).

Bullock: *The Life and Times of Ernest Bevin*, by Alan Bullock (Heinemann, 3 vols, 1960–83).

Callwell: *Field Marshal Sir Henry Wilson Bart, GCB, DSO: His Life and Diaries*, by Major General Sir C. E. Callwell KCB (Cassell, 2 vols, 1927).

Campbell: *F. E. Smith, First Earl of Birkenhead*, by John Campbell (Jonathan Cape, 1983).

Charman: *The First World War on the Home Front*, by Terry Charman (Andre Deutsch, 2014).

Chitty: *Playing the Game: A Biography of Sir Henry Newbolt*, by Susan Chitty (Quartet, 1997).

Churchill R.: *Lord Derby, King of Lancashire: The Official Life of Edward, Seventeenth Earl of Derby, 1865–1948*, by Randolph S. Churchill (Heinemann, 1959).

Churchill W.: *The World Crisis*, by Winston S. Churchill (Thornton Butterworth, 6 vols, 1923–29).

Clark: *The Sleepwalkers: How Europe went to War in 1914*, by Christopher Clark (Allen Lane, 2012).

Clark A.: *Echoes of the Great War: The Diary of the Reverend Andrew Clark 1914–1919*, edited by James Munson (Oxford, 1985).

Clarke: *The Locomotive of War: Money, Empire, Power and Guilt*, by Peter Clarke (Bloomsbury, 2017).

Cooper: *Old Men Forget*, by Duff Cooper (Rupert Hart-Davis, 1953).

Dangerfield: *The Damnable Question: A Study in Anglo-Irish Relations*, by George Dangerfield (Constable, 1977).

Darroch: *Ottoline: The Life of Lady Ottoline Morrell*, by Sandra Jobson Darroch (Chatto & Windus, 1976.)

Davidson: *Memoirs of a Conservative: J. C. C. Davidson's Memoirs and Papers*, edited by Robert Rhodes James (Weidenfeld & Nicolson, 1969).

DeGroot I: *Douglas Haig, 1861–1928*, by Gerard J. DeGroot (Unwin Hyman, 1988).

DeGroot II: *Back in Blighty: The British at Home in World War I*, by Gerard DeGroot (Vintage Books, 2014).

Dilks: *Neville Chamberlain: 1869–1929*, by David Dilks (Cambridge University Press, 1984).

DNB 1961–70: *The Dictionary of National Biography, 1961–70*, edited by E. T. Williams and C. S. Nicholls (Oxford University Press, 1981).

E&H: *All Quiet on the Home Front: An Oral History of Life in Britain during the First World War*, by Richard Van Emden and Steve Humphries (Headline, 2003).

Ensor: *England 1870–1914*, by R. C. K. Ensor (Oxford University Press, 1936).

Ferriter: *A Nation and not a Rabble: The Irish Revolution 1913–1923*, by Diarmaid Ferriter (Profile Books, 2015).

Fox: *British Art and the First World War, 1914–1924*, by James Fox (Cambridge University Press, 2015).

G&T: *British Documents on the Origins of the War 1898–1914*, Vol. XI, edited by G. P. Gooch and Harold Temperley (HMSO, 1926).

Gilbert, III: *Winston S. Churchill: Volume: III: 1914–1916*, by Martin Gilbert (Heinemann, 1971).

Gilbert, IV: *Winston S. Churchill: Volume: IV: 1916–1922*, by Martin Gilbert (Heinemann, 1975).

Gilbert, III(C): *Winston S. Churchill: Volume III Companion* (2 vols), by Martin Gilbert (Heinemann, 1972).

Gilbert, IV(C): *Winston S. Churchill: Volume IV Companion* (3 vols), by Martin Gilbert (Heinemann, 1977).

Gilmour: *Curzon*, by David Gilmour (John Murray, 1994).

Grey: *Twenty-Five Years, 1892–1916*, by Viscount Grey of Fallodon KG (Hodder & Stoughton, 2 vols, 1925).

Grigg I: *Lloyd George: From Peace to War 1912–1916*, by John Grigg (Methuen, 1985).

Grigg II: *Lloyd George: War Leader 1916–1922*, by John Grigg (Penguin Allen Lane, 2002).

Haig: *The Private Papers of Douglas Haig, 1914–1919*, edited by Robert Blake (Eyre & Spottiswoode, 1952).

Haldane: *Autobiography*, by Richard Burdon Haldane (Hodder & Stoughton, 1929).

Hamilton: *Listening for the Drums*, by General Sir Ian Hamilton (Faber & Faber, 1944).

Hammond: *C. P. Scott of the Manchester Guardian*, by J. L. Hammond (Bell, 1934).

Hankey: *The Supreme Command, 1914–1918*, by Lord Hankey (George Allen & Unwin, 2 vols, 1961).

Hardinge: *Royal Commission on the Rebellion in Ireland: Report of Commission* (HMSO, 1916).

Hart: *The Somme*, by Peter Hart (Weidenfeld & Nicolson, 2005).

Haste: *Keep the Home Fires Burning: Propaganda in the First World War*, by Cate Haste (Allen Lane, 1978).

Heffer, P&P: *Power and Place: The Political Consequences of King Edward VII*, by Simon Heffer (Weidenfeld & Nicolson, 1998).

Heffer, HM: *High Minds: The Victorians and the Birth of Modern Britain*, by Simon Heffer (Random House, 2013).

Heffer, AD: *The Age of Decadence: Britain 1880 to 1914*, by Simon Heffer (Random House, 2017).

Holmes: *The Little Field Marshal: A Life of Sir John French*, by Richard Holmes (Weidenfeld & Nicolson, 2nd edition, 2004).

Holroyd: *Bernard Shaw*, by Michael Holroyd (Chatto & Windus, 3 vols, 1988–91).

Hyman: *The Rise and Fall of Horatio Bottomley: The Biography of a Swindler*, by Alan Hyman (Cassell, 1972).

Hynes: *A War Imagined: The First World War and English Culture*, by Samuel Hynes (The Bodley Head, 1990).

Jeffery: *Ireland and the Great War*, by Keith Jeffery (Cambridge University Press, 2000).

Jellicoe: *Jutland: The Unfinished Battle*, by Nicholas Jellicoe (Seaforth Publishing, 2016).

Jolliffe: *Raymond Asquith: Life and Letters*, by John Jolliffe (Collins, 1980).

Judd: *Lord Reading: Rufus Isaacs, First Marquess of Reading, Lord Chief Justice and Viceroy of India, 1860–1935*, by Denis Judd (Weidenfeld & Nicolson, 1982).

Kerry: *Lansdowne: The Last Great Whig*, by Simon Kerry (Unicorn, 2017).

Keynes: *The Economic Consequences of the Peace*, by J. M. Keynes (Macmillan, 1920).

Kynaston: *Till Time's Last Stand: A History of the Bank of England 1694–2013*, by David Kynaston (Bloomsbury, 2017).

LG: *War Memoirs*, by David Lloyd George (Odhams, 2 vols, New Edition, 1938 (Vol. I) and 1936 (Vol. II)).

Lee: *A Good Innings: The Private Papers of Viscount Lee of Fareham PC, GCB, GSCI, GBE*, edited by Alan Clark (John Murray, 1974).

Lloyd I: *The Amritsar Massacre: The Untold Story of One Fateful Day*, by Nick Lloyd (IB Tauris, 2011).

Lloyd II: *Passchendaele: A New History*, by Nick Lloyd (Viking, 2017).

Lodge: *Raymond, or Life and Death: with Examples of the Evidence for Survival of Memory and Affection after Death*, by Sir Oliver J. Lodge (George H. Doran, 1916).

M&B: *Baldwin: A Biography*, by Keith Middlemas and John Barnes (Weidenfeld & Nicolson, 1969.

Martel: *The Month that Changed the World: July 1914*, by Gordon Martel (Oxford University Press, 2014).

Maurice: *The Maurice Case: from the Papers of Sir Frederick Maurice KCMG, CB*, edited by Nancy Maurice (Leo Cooper, 1972).

McKibbin: *The Evolution of the Labour Party 1910–1924*, by Ross McKibbin (Clarendon Press, 1974).

McKinstry: *Rosebery: Statesman in Turmoil*, by Leo McKinstry (John Murray, 2005).

Meleady: *John Redmond: The National Leader*, by Dermot Meleady (Merrion, 2014).

Midleton: *Records and Reactions 1856–1939*, by the Earl of Midleton, KP (John Murray, 1939).

Morley: *Memorandum on Resignation, August 1914,* by John, Viscount Morley (Macmillan, 1928).

Morley G.: *The Life of William Ewart Gladstone,* by John Morley (Macmillan, 2 vol. edition, 1905).

Morrell I: *Ottoline: The Early Memoirs of Ottoline Morrell,* edited by Robert Gathorne-Hardy (Faber & Faber, 1963).

Morrell II: *Ottoline at Garsington: Memoirs of Lady Ottoline Morrell,* edited by Robert Gathorne-Hardy (Faber & Faber, 1974).

Newton: *Lord Lansdowne: A Biography,* by Lord Newton (Macmillan, 1929).

Nicolson I: *Sir Arthur Nicolson, Bart, First Lord Carnock: A Study in the Old Diplomacy,* by Harold Nicolson (Constable, 1930).

Nicolson II: *King George V: His Life and Reign,* by Harold Nicolson (Constable, 1952).

O'Brien: *Milner: Viscount Milner of St James's and Cape Town, 1854–1925,* by Terence H. O'Brien (Constable, 1979).

OFMH: *Why We Are At War: Great Britain's Case,* by Members of the Oxford Faculty of Modern History (Clarendon Press, 3rd edition, 1914).

P&H: *Northcliffe,* by Reginald Pound and Geoffrey Harmsworth (Cassell, 1959).

Parker: *The Old Lie: The Great War and the Public School Ethos,* by Peter Parker (Hambledon Continuum, 2007).

Parry: *College Addresses, Delivered to Pupils of the Royal College of Music,* by Sir C. Hubert H. Parry, Bart, edited by H. C. Coles (Macmillan, 1920).

Petrie: *The Life and Letters of the Right Hon. Sir Austen Chamberlain KG, PC, MP,* by Sir Charles Petrie, Bt (Cassell, 2 vols, 1939–40).

Petrie, CT: *The Chamberlain Tradition,* by Sir Charles Petrie, Bt (Lovat Dickinson, 1938).

Pollock: *Kitchener,* by John Pollock (Constable, 2001).

Ponsonby: *Falsehood in War-Time: An amazing collection of carefully documented lies circulated in Great Britain, France, Germany, Italy and America during the Great War,* by Arthur Ponsonby MP (George Allen & Unwin, 1928).

Pope-Hennessy: *Queen Mary: 1867–1953,* by James Pope-Hennessy (George Allen & Unwin, 1959).

Postgate: *The Life of George Lansbury,* by Raymond Postgate (Longmans, Green & Company, 1951).

Repington: *The First World War 1914–1918: Personal Experiences of Lieut Col C. à Court Repington, CMG* (Constable, 2 vols, 1920).

Renwick: *Bread for All: The Origins of the Welfare State,* by Chris Renwick (Allen Lane, 2017).

Riddell: *Lord Riddell's War Diary 1914–1918*, by George Riddell (Ivor Nicholson & Watson, 1933).

Robertson: *Soldiers and Statesmen 1914–1918*, by Field Marshal Sir William Robertson, Bart (Cassell, 2 vols, 1926).

Ronaldshay: *The Life of Lord Curzon: Being the Authorized Biography of George Nathaniel, Marquess Curzon of Kedleston, KG*, by the Rt Hon. the Earl of Ronaldshay (Ernest Benn, 3 vols, 1928).

Rose I: *The Later Cecils*, by Kenneth Rose (Weidenfeld & Nicolson, 1975).

Rose II: *King George V*, by Kenneth Rose (Weidenfeld & Nicolson, 1983).

Roskill: *Hankey: Man of Secrets*, by Stephen Roskill (Collins, 3 vols, 1970–74).

RRJ: *Churchill: A Study in Failure 1900–1939*, by Robert Rhodes James (Weidenfeld & Nicolson, 1970).

Russell: *The Autobiography of Bertrand Russell* (George Allen & Unwin, 3 vols, 1967–69).

S&A: *Life of Herbert Henry Asquith, Lord Oxford and Asquith*, by J. A. Spender and Cyril Asquith (Hutchinson, 2 vols, 1932).

S&W: *Public Schools and the Great War: The Generation Lost*, by Anthony Seldon and David Walsh (Pen & Sword, 2013).

Samuel: *Memoirs*, by the Rt Hon. Viscount Samuel (The Cresset Press, 1945).

Scott: *The Political Diaries of C. P. Scott, 1911–1928*, edited by Trevor Wilson (Collins, 1970).

Searle: *Corruption in British Politics, 1895–1930*, by G. R. Searle (The Clarendon Press, 1987).

Simon: *Retrospect: The Memoirs of the Rt Hon. Viscount Simon GCSI, GCVO* (Hutchinson, 1952).

Sommer: *Haldane of Cloan: His Life and Times 1856–1928*, by Dudley Sommer (George Allen & Unwin, 1960).

Souhami: *Edith Cavell*, by Diana Souhami (Quercus, 2010).

Steed: *Through Thirty Years, 1892–1922: A Personal Narrative*, by Henry Wickham Steed (Heinemann, 2 vols, 1924).

Stevenson I: *With Our Backs to the Wall: Victory and Defeat in 1918*, by David Stevenson (Allen Lane, 2011).

Stevenson II: *1917: War, Peace and Revolution*, by David Stevenson (Oxford University Press, 2017).

Stevenson F.: *Lloyd George: A Diary*, by Frances Stevenson, edited by A. J. P. Taylor (Hutchinson, 1971).

Strachan: *The First World War: Volume I: To Arms*, by Hew Strachan (Oxford University Press, 2001).

Taylor I: *English History 1914–1945*, by A. J. P Taylor (Oxford University Press, 1965).

Taylor II: *Beaverbrook*, by A. J. P. Taylor (Hamish Hamilton, 1972).

Taylor F.: *The Downfall of Money: Germany's Hyperinflation and the Destruction of the Middle Class*, by Frederick Taylor (Bloomsbury, 2013).

Thompson I: *Northcliffe: Press Baron in Politics, 1865–1922*, by J. Lee Thompson (John Murray, 2000).

Thompson II: *Politicians, the Press and Propaganda: Lord Northcliffe and the Great War, 1914–1919*, by J. Lee Thompson (Kent State University Press, 1999).

Townshend I: *Easter 1916: The Irish Rebellion*, by Charles Townshend (Allen Lane, 2005).

Townshend II: *The Republic: The Fight for Irish Independence 1918–1923*, by Charles Townshend (Allen Lane, 2013).

Trevelyan: *Grey of Fallodon: Being the Life of Sir Edward Grey, Afterwards Viscount Grey of Fallodon*, by George Macaulay Trevelyan, OM (Longmans, Green & Co., 1937).

VBC: *Champion Redoubtable: The Diaries and Letters of Violet Bonham Carter, 1914–1945*, edited by Mark Pottle (Weidenfeld & Nicolson, 1998).

Webb: *The Diary of Beatrice Webb*, edited by Norman and Jean Mackenzie (Virago Press, 4 vols, 1982–85).

Wells, Britling: *Mr Britling Sees it Through*, by H. G. Wells (Uniform Edition, 1933).

Wells, JP: *Joan and Peter*, by H. G. Wells (Cassell, 1918).

Wilson: *The Rasp of War: The Letters of H. A. Gwynne to The Countess Bathurst, 1914–1918*, selected and edited by Keith Wilson (Sidgwick & Jackson, 1988).

Young: *Arthur James Balfour: The Happy Life of the Politician, Prime Minister, Statesman and Philosopher 1848–1930*, by Kenneth Young (G. Bell & Sons, 1963).

Periodicals

Daily Mail
The Daily Telegraph
Lancet
Manchester Guardian
Spectator
The Times
The Times Literary Supplement

Learned Journals

Biography
Britain and the World
The English Historical Review

The Historical Journal
Historical Reflections
Journal of British Studies
Journal of Contemporary History
Journal of Modern History
Social Service Review

Works of Reference

Hansard's Parliamentary Debates (Commons) Series 5, Volumes 64 to 117, (Lords)
    Series 5, Volumes 17 to 34.
The Dictionary of National Biography (Oxford University Press, 2nd edition).
Wisden's Cricketers' Almanack

NOTES

Chapter 1: Consequences

1. G&T, p. 12.
2. Ibid.
3. RA GV/PRIV/GVD/1914: 28 June.
4. G&T, p. 13.
5. *The Times*, 29 June 1914, p. 8.
6. G&T, p. 28.
7. Ibid.
8. See Heffer, *AD*, p. 768ff.
9. Hansard, Vol. 64 col. 214.
10. Ibid., col. 215
11. Ibid., col. 216.
12. G&T, p. 17.
13. Ibid., p. 15.
14. *The Times*, 1 July 1914, p. 11.
15. G&T, p. 18.
16. Ibid., p. 19.
17. Ibid.
18. Ibid., p. 28.
19. G&T, p. 21.
20. Ibid., p. 422.
21. Clark, p. 420.
22. Ibid., p. 24.
23. Ibid.
24. Ibid., p. 25.
25. Ibid., p. 27.
26. Ibid., p. 30.
27. Ibid., p. 32.
28. Ibid., p. 34.
29. *The Times*, 11 July 1914, p. 7.
30. G&T, p. 39.
31. Ibid., p. 40.
32. Ibid., p. 41.
33. *The Times*, 16 July 1914, p. 9.
34. Ibid., 13 July 1914, p. 5.
35. Ibid., 20 July 1914, p. 9.
36. G&T, p. 45.
37. *The Times*, 18 July 1914, p. 7.
38. G&T, p. 47.
39. Ibid., p. 49.
40. Ibid., p. 50.
41. *The Times*, 20 July 1914, p. 7.
42. G&T, p. xi.
43. Ibid., p. 54.
44. Ibid.
45. *The Times*, 21 July 1914, p. 7.
46. G&T, p. 63.
47. Ibid., p. 64.
48. *The Times*, 22 July 1914, p. 7.
49. Ibid., p. 8.
50. Ibid., p. 9.
51. G&T, p. 69.
52. Ibid., p. 70.
53. Ibid., p. 365.
54. Ibid., p. 72.
55. Ibid., p. 73.
56. Ibid., p. 73.
57. Clark, p. 456.
58. G&T, p. 74.
59. Asquith, II, p. 5.
60. Clark, p. 489.
61. Clarke, p. 117.
62. Beaverbrook I, I, p. 31.
63. G&T, p. 74.
64. Ibid., p. 75.
65. Ibid., p. 78.
66. Ibid., p. 79.
67. *The Times*, 25 July 1914, p. 10.
68. G&T, p. 80.
69. Ibid., p. 81.

70. Ibid.
71. Ibid., p. 82.
72. Grey, II, p. 63.
73. Ibid.
74. G&T, p. 83.
75. Ibid., pp. 83–84.
76. Ibid., p. 84.
77. Ibid., p. 85.
78. *The Times*, 25 July 1914, p. 9.
79. Ibid., p. 87.
80. G&T, p. 86.
81. Ibid.
82. Ibid, p. 88.
83. Ibid.
84. Ibid., p. 91.
85. Grey, I, p. 311.
86. G&T, p. 92.
87. Ibid., p. 93.
88. Grey, I, pp. 312–13.
89. See Heffer, *P&P*, pp. 155–66, pointing out how unwilling the Unionists at the time were to pursue the King's policy of an understanding with France.
90. G&T, p. 94.
91. Ibid., p. 96.
92. Ibid., p. 97.
93. Ibid., p. 99.
94. RA GV/PRIV/GVD/1914: 25 July.
95. G&T, p. 100.
96. Ibid., p. 102.
97. Martel, p. 280.
98. G&T, p. 102.
99. Ibid., p. 104.
100. Ensor, p. 488; G&T, p. 111.
101. Asquith, II, p. 5.
102. Ibid., p. 6.
103. G&T, p. 104.
104. Ibid., p. 107.
105. *The Times*, 27 July 1914, p. 7.
106. Hammond, p. 177.
107. Scott, p. 91.
108. Hansard, Vol. 65 col. 729.
109. Ibid., cols 727–28.
110. Hansard, Vol. 65 col. 937.
111. Ibid., col. 938.
112. Grey, I, p. 337.
113. Morley, p. 1.
114. Ibid., p. 2.
115. Ibid., p. 3.
116. Esher Papers: ESHR 2/13, diary entry for 17 January 1915.
117. Scott, p. 93.
118. Riddell, p. 1.
119. Ibid.
120. Ibid., p. 8.
121. Ibid., p. 7.
122. Ibid., p. 9.
123. G&T, p. 118.
124. Ibid., p. 121.
125. Ibid.
126. G&T, p. 123.
127. Ibid., p. 124.
128. Ibid.
129. Ibid., p. 127.
130. G&T, p. 130.
131. Ibid., p. 133.
132. Ibid., p. 134.
133. Trevelyan, p. 249.
134. Ibid.
135. G&T, p. 138.
136. Ibid., p. 139.
137. Ibid., pp. 140–41.
138. Martel, p. 281.
139. Hansard, Vol. 65 col. 1123.
140. Asquith, *VS*, p. 129.
141. G&T, p. 155.
142. Ibid., p. 157.
143. G&T, p. 162.
144. Ibid., p. 163.
145. Ibid., p. 164.
146. Ibid.
147. Grey, I, p. 321.
148. G&T, p. 169.
149. *The Times*, 29 July 1914, p. 9.
150. Haig, p. 67.
151. G&T, p. 160.
152. Morley, G, I, p. 976.
153. Repington, I, p. 8.
154. G&T, p. 170.
155. Ibid., p. 171.
156. Haldane, p. 270.
157. Grey, I, p. 339.
158. G&T, p. 180.

159. Hansard, Vol. 65 col. 1324.
160. *The Times*, 30 July 1914, p. 7.
161. Asquith, *VS*, p. 133.
162. *The Times*, 30 July 1914, p. 7.
163. Asquith, II, p. 6.
164. G&T, p. 185.
165. Ibid., p. 194.
166. Ibid., p. 186.
167. Grey, I, p. 326.
168. G&T, p. 186.
169. *The Times*, 30 July 1914, p. 9.
170. G&T, p. 193.
171. Ibid., p. 187.
172. Ibid., p. 198.
173. Ibid., p. 199.
174. Hansard, Vol. 65 col. 1574.
175. Asquith, II, p. 7.
176. G&T, p. 200.
177. Ibid., p. 201.
178. G&T, p. 202.
179. Kynaston, p. 267.
180. *The Times*, 1 August 1914, p. 8.
181. Kynaston, p. 269.
182. *The Times*, 31 July 1914, p. 9.
183. Ibid., p. 6.
184. Martel, p. 336.
185. Morley, p. 4. Asquith's catchphrase in the constitutional crisis of 1910–11 had been 'wait and see': see Heffer, *AD*, pp. 625–26.
186. Morley, p. 5.
187. Ibid., pp. 6–7.
188. G&T, p. 217.
189. Grey, I, p. 329.
190. G&T, p. 220.
191. Ensor, p. 493.
192. Hansard, Vol. 65 cols 1787–88; Asquith, *VS*, p. 138.
193. Grey, I, p. 332.
194. G&T, p. 222.
195. Ibid., p. 226.
196. Ibid., p. 227.
197. Asquith, *VS*, p. 139.
198. G&T, p. 230.
199. Asquith, II, p. 7.
200. G&T, p. 235.
201. Ibid.
202. Ibid., p. 236.
203. Ibid., p. 227.
204. Ibid., p. 228.
205. Ibid., p. 229.
206. Ibid., p. viii.
207. *The Times*, 1 August 1914, p. 6.
208. Ibid., p. 9.
209. RA GV/PRIV/GVD/1914: 1 August.
210. Asquith, II, p. 7.
211. Grey, I, p. 334.
212. Grey, II, p. 1.
213. Ibid., p. 10.
214. G&T, p. 241.
215. Ibid., p. 243.
216. Asquith, *VS*, p. 140.
217. Wilson, p. 19.
218. *The Times*, 4 August 1914, p. 2.
219. G&T, p. 253.
220. Ibid., p. 260.
221. Ibid., p. 252.
222. Ibid., p. 259.
223. Amery, p. 104.
224. Lloyd Papers: GLLD 28/6, diary entry for 1 August 1914.
225. Asquith, II, p. 7.
226. Kerry, p. 245.
227. PA: BL/34/3/3.
228. Crewe Papers: Letter from Asquith to Crewe, 11 August 1918. Aspasia was the mistress of Pericles and a friend of Socrates, and reputed to be a brothel-keeper.
229. *The Times*, 2 August 1914, p. 4.
230. Ibid., p. 6.
231. Quoted in *The Times*, ibid., p. 5.
232. Lloyd Papers: GLLD 28/6, diary entry for 2 August 1914.
233. Asquith, II, p. 8.
234. Ibid.
235. *The Times*, 3 August 1914, p. 8.
236. Asquith, II, p. 8.
237. Morley, p. 10.
238. Ibid., p. 12.
239. Ibid., p. 13.
240. Ibid.
241. G&T, p. 274.
242. Morley, p. 15.

243. Ibid., p. 18.
244. Samuel, p. 104.
245. *The Times*, 3 August 1914, p. 7.
246. Morley, pp. 22–23.
247. Esher Papers: ESHR 2/13, diary entry for 3 August 1914.
248. Heffer, *AD*, pp. 810–16.
249. Amery, p. 105.
250. Morley, p. 25.
251. Hankey, I, p. 162.
252. Asquith, II, p. 14.
253. Simon, p. 95.
254. G&T, p. 290.
255. Ibid., p. 294.
256. Asquith, II, p. 20.
257. *The Times*, 3 August 1914, p. 3.
258. Ibid., 4 August 1914, p. 2.
259. Grey, II, p. 14.
260. Hansard, Vol. 65 col. 1809.
261. Ibid., col. 1810.
262. Ibid., col. 1816.
263. Ibid., col. 1818.
264. Ibid., col. 1821.
265. Ibid., col. 1822.
266. Ibid., col. 1823.
267. Ibid., col. 1824.
268. Grey, II, p. 15.
269. Hansard, Vol. 65 col. 1825.
270. Ibid., col. 1826.
271. Ibid., col. 1827.
272. Trevelyan, p. 265.
273. Hansard, Vol. 65 col. 1828.
274. Ibid., col. 1829.
275. Ibid., col. 1831.
276. Riddell, p. 6.
277. Steed, II, p. 27.
278. G&T, p. 297.
279. Ibid., p. 302.
280. Asquith, *VS*, p. 148.
281. *The Times*, 4 August 1914, p. 4.
282. Hansard, Vol. 65 col. 1833.
283. RA GV/PRIV/GVD/1914: 3 August.
284. Hansard, Vol. 65 col. 1834.
285. Ibid., col. 1835.
286. Ibid., col. 1836.
287. Ibid., col. 1838.
288. Ibid., col. 1841.
289. Ibid., col. 1843.
290. Ibid., col. 1861.
291. Ibid., col. 1865.
292. Ibid., cols 1867–68.
293. Ibid., col. 1880.
294. Martel, p. 136.
295. Grey, II, p. 20.
296. Morley, p. 29.
297. Ibid., p. 30.
298. Ibid., p. 31.
299. G&T, p. 308.
300. Ibid.
301. Ibid., p. 311.
302. Ibid., p. 312.
303. Ibid., p. 314.
304. Ibid., p. 347.
305. Ibid., p. 351.
306. Hansard, Vol. 65 col. 1927.
307. Asquith, II, p. 21.
308. Scott, p. 99.
309. G&T, p. 318.
310. Ibid., p. 320.
311. Haig, p. 67.
312. G&T, p. 328.
313. Samuel, p. 105.
314. G&T, p. 330.
315. Ibid., p. 360.
316. Ibid., p. 355.
317. RA GV/PRIV/GVD/1914: 4 August.
318. Hankey, I, p. 165.
319. Strachan, p. 162.
320. *The Times*, 5 August 1914, p. 6.
321. Darroch, p. 141.
322. Russell, II, p. 15.
323. *The Times*, 5 August 1914, p. 9.

Chapter 2: War

1. *The Times*, 5 August 1914, p. 10.
2. Ibid., 10 August 1914, p. 9.
3. Keynes, p. 133.
4. *The Times*, 6 August 1914, p. 3.
5. G&T, p. 339.
6. Russell, II, p. 16.
7. Retrieved from http://www.nationalmuseum.af.mil/Visit/Museum-Exhibits/Fact-Sheets/Display/Article/579656/

neutrality-league-announcement-
no-2-1914/

8. *The Times*, 5 August 1914, p. 7.
9. Ibid, 6 August 1914, p. 3.
10. Ibid, 15 August 1914, p. 3.
11. Hyman, p. 149.
12. See Heffer, *AD*, pp. 337–57.
13. Hyman, p. 149.
14. Postgate, p. 152.
15. *The Times*, 5 August 1914, p. 8.
16. DeGroot II, p. 65.
17. Parker, p. 39.
18. Riddell, p. 13.
19. Russell, II, p. 17.
20. Parry, p. 216.
21. *The Times*, 7 August 1914, p. 1.
22. VBC, p. 7.
23. *The Times*, 12 August 1914, p. 7.
24. Webb, III, p. 218.
25. Hansard, Vol. 66 col. 38.
26. Scott, p. 101.
27. Hammond, p. 181.
28. *The Times*, 5 August 1914, p. 7.
29. Sommer, p. 307.
30. Heffer, *AD*, pp. 483–84.
31. Asquith, *Diary*, p. 24.
32. Asquith, *VS*, p. 153.
33. Ibid., pp. 39–40.
34. Lloyd Papers: GLLD 28/6, diary
    entry for 6 August 1914.
35. Asquith, *VS*, p. 157.
36. Adams I, p. 5.
37. Scott, p. 100.
38. Churchill R., p. 184.
39. Hansard, Vol. 66 col. 805.
40. Asquith, *VS*, p. 177.
41. Ibid., p. 241.
42. *The Times*, 15 August 1914, p. 3.
43. Hynes, p. 88.
44. Holroyd, II, p. 348.
45. Ibid., p. 349.
46. Ibid., p. 354.
47. Ibid., p. 355.
48. Hansard, Vol. 68 col. 305.
49. Ibid., col. 306.
50. Ibid., col. 307.
51. Ibid., col. 308.

52. Morrell I, p. 277.
53. *The Times*, 2 September 1914, p. 9.
54. Holroyd, II, p. 345.
55. Chitty, p. 220.
56. OFMH, p. 108.
57. Hynes, p. 36.
58. Hansard, Vol. 65, col. 2076.
59. Ibid., col. 2077.
60. Ibid., col. 2079.
61. Asquith, *VS*, p. 157.
62. Hansard, Vol. 65 col. 1986.
63. Andrew, p. 58.
64. See, for example, Hansard,
    Vol. 66 col. 267.
65. Hansard, Vol. 65 col. 1989.
66. Hansard (Lords), Vol. 18 col. 501.
67. *The Times*, 12 August 1914, p. 3.
68. Ibid., 15 August 1914, p. 3.
69. Ibid.
70. Fox, p. 47.
71. Stevenson F., p. 3.
72. *The Times*, 21 September 1914, p. 9.
73. Ibid., 23 October 1914, p. 4.
74. Ibid., 24 October 1914, p. 3.
75. Haste, p. 113.
76. Asquith, *VS*, p. 285.
77. Ibid., p. 286.
78. Searle, p. 245.
79. *The Times*, 30 October 1914, p. 10.
80. RA GV/PRIV/GVD/1914:
    29 October.
81. *The Times*, 30 October 1914, p. 9.
82. Gilbert III(C), I, p. 226.
83. *The Times*, 6 August 1914, p. 3.
84. Ibid., 15 August 1914, p. 3.
85. Andrew, p. 55.
86. *The Times*, 31 October 1914, p. 4.
87. Hansard, Vol. 68 col. 126.
88. Ibid., cols 134–35.
89. *The Times*, 11 November 1914, p. 9.
90. Hansard (Lords), Vol. 18 col. 72.
91. Andrew, p. 53.
92. Hansard (Lords), Vol. 18 col. 74.
93. Ibid., col. 83.
94. Hankey, I, p. 220.
95. Hansard (Lords), Vol. 18 col. 133.
96. Andrew, pp. 75–76.

97. *The Times*, 29 September 1914, p. 3.
98. Taylor I, p. 1.
99. Hankey, I, p. 4.
100. Asquith, *VS*, p. 326.
101. Hankey, I, p. 184.
102. Asquith, *VS*, p. 187.
103. Cooper, p. 52.
104. Hansard, Vol. 65, col. 2197.
105. Ibid., col. 2198.
106. *The Times*, 10 August 1914, p. 5.
107. Ibid., 11 August 1914, p. 2.
108. Hansard, Vol. 65 col. 2082.
109. Asquith, *Diary*, p. 15.
110. Repington, II, p. 198.
111. Hansard, Vol. 65 col. 2213.
112. Meleady, p. 301.
113. Ibid., Vol. 65 col. 2298.
114. Petrie, II, pp. 1–2.
115. PA: BL/34/5/2.
116. Blake, p. 229.
117. Petrie, II, p. 11.
118. *The Times*, 15 September 1914, p. 10.
119. Hansard, Vol. 66 col. 882.
120. Ibid., col. 893.
121. Ibid., col. 894.
122. *The Times*, 14 September 1914, p. 9.
123. Hansard, Vol. 66 col. 902.
124. Ibid., col. 905.
125. Asquith, *VS*, p. 240.
126. Hansard, Vol. 66 col. 905.
127. RA GV/PRIV/GVD/1914:
    17 September.
128. *The Times*, 17 September 1914, p. 10.
129. Haig, p. 69.
130. PA: BL/117/1/2.
131. Callwell, I, p. 159.
132. Robertson, I, pp. 56–57.
133. Haig, p. 70.
134. Asquith, *VS*, p. 164.
135. Holmes, p. 1.
136. Asquith, *VS*, p. 168.
137. Hansard (Lords), Vol. 66 col. 501.
138. Hankey, I, p. 187.
139. Asquith, *VS*, p. 190.
140. Ibid., p. 195.
141. Ibid., p. 197.
142. Ibid., p. 191.
143. Gilbert, III(C), I, p. 54.
144. Asquith, *Diary*, p. 23.
145. Hansard, Vol. 65 col. 2154.
146. Ibid., col. 2155.
147. Ibid., col. 2201.
148. Taylor II, p. 86.
149. Clark A., p. 3.
150. Wilson, p. 26.
151. Ibid., p. 27.
152. J. M. McEwen: 'Northcliffe and
    Lloyd George at War, 1914–1918', *The
    Historical Journal*, Vol. 24, No. 3, p. 651.
153. Hansard, Vol. 66 col. 373.
154. Ibid., col. 454.
155. Ibid., col. 455.
156. Ibid., col. 477.
157. Ibid., col. 481.
158. Esher Papers: ESHR 2/13, diary
    entry for 31 August 1914.
159. Campbell, p. 378.
160. *The Times*, 1 September 1914, p. 9.
161. Northcliffe papers: BL Add MS 65156.
162. Gilbert, III(C), I, p. 96.
163. Asquith, *VS*, p. 395.
164. *The Times*, 21 September 1914, p. 9.
165. Asquith, *VS*, p. 226. The French
    roughly translates as 'he who lives
    will see'.
166. E&H, p. 119.
167. *The Times*, 2 September 1914, p. 4;
    ibid., 3 September, p. 4.
168. From his Army Order of 19 August
    1914, retrieved from https://www.
    firstworldwar.com/source/
    kaisercontemptible.htm.
169. *The Times*, 3 September 1914, p. 4.
170. Hansard, Vol. 66 col. 607.
171. Ibid., col. 608.
172. Ibid., col. 610.
173. Ibid., col. 614.
174. Ibid., col. 664.
175. Ibid., col. 666.
176. Ibid., col. 667.
177. Asquith, *VS*, p. 234.
178. Ibid., p. 235.
179. Asquith, *Diary*, p. 34.
180. Webb, III, p. 217.

181. Bell, p. 22.
182. *The Times*, 5 September 1914, p. 9.
183. Asquith, *VS*, p. 246.
184. Churchill R., p. 193.
185. DeGroot II, p. 24.
186. *The Times*, 5 October 1914, p. 10.
187. Ibid., 28 September 1914, p. 4.
188. Asquith, *VS*, p. 260.
189. Bell, p. 28
190. Asquith, *VS*, p. 266.
191. Ibid., p. 275.
192. Ibid., p. 285.
193. Bell, p. 36.
194. Stevenson F., p. 6.
195. Asquith, *VS*, p. 221.
196. Ibid., p. 243.
197. Ibid., p. 225.
198. Ibid., p. 232.
199. RA GV/PRIV/GVD/1914: 29 October.
200. Asquith, *VS*, p. 298.
201. Ibid., p. 266.
202. Samuel, p. 107.
203. Hankey, I, p. 217.
204. *The Times*, 3 October 1914, p. 3.
205. Ibid., 7 August 1914, p. 2.
206. Retrieved from http://www.espncricinfo.com/magazine/content/story/763919.html.
207. *The Times*, 8 September 1914, p. 4.
208. Ibid., 4 March 1915, p 9.
209. Ibid., 5 March 1915, p. 9.
210. Ibid., p. 10.
211. Ibid., 6 March 1915, p. 9.
212. Ibid., 20 May 1915, p. 9.
213. Ibid., 22 May 1915, p. 5.
214. Asquith, *Diary*, p. 41. For a detailed account of these tribulations see Heffer, *AD*, Chapters 14 to 18 *passim*.

Chapter 3: Coalition

1. Hansard, Vol. 68 col. 4.
2. *The Times*, 12 November 1914, p. 9.
3. Hansard, Vol. col. 348.
4. Ibid., col. 349.
5. Ibid., col. 351.
6. Ibid., col. 354.
7. Ibid., col. 370.
8. Ibid., col. 376.
9. Hankey, I, p. 242.
10. Asquith, *VS*, p. 309.
11. Hankey, I, p. 239.
12. *The Times*, 17 December 1914, p. 8.
13. Asquith, *Diary*, p. 61.
14. *The Times*, 17 December 1914, p. 9.
15. Hansard (Lords), Vol. 18 col. 295.
16. Ibid., cols 300–01.
17. Ibid., col. 302.
18. *The Times*, 21 January 1915, p. 9.
19. Hansard, Vol. 69 col. 1111.
20. Ibid., Vol. 70 col. 402.
21. Ibid., Vol. 69 col. 1223.
22. *The Times*, 11 November 1914, p. 4.
23. Hansard, Vol. 70 col. 154.
24. *The Times*, 3 March 1915, p. 10.
25. Asquith, *VS*, p. 448.
26. *The Times*, 3 March 1915, p. 11.
27. Hansard (Lords), Vol. 18 col. 720.
28. Ibid., col. 721.
29. Ibid., col. 722.
30. *The Times*, 10 November 1914, p. 4.
31. LG, I, p. 194.
32. Asquith, *VS*, p. 520.
33. Rose II, p. 174.
34. RA GV/PRIV/GVD/1915: 29 March.
35. Marvin Rintala, 'Taking the Pledge: H. H. Asquith and Drink', *Biography*, Vol. 16 No. 2, p. 110.
36. Grigg I, p. 438.
37. Scott, p. 121.
38. Asquith, *Diary*, p. 92.
39. Asquith, *VS*, p. 525(n).
40. Asquith, *Diary*, p. 93.
41. Lee, p. 157.
42. Marvin Rintala, op. cit., p. 106.
43. Asquith, *VS*, p. 509.
44. Blake, p. 239.
45. Hansard, Vol. 71 col. 864.
46. Ibid., cols 872–73.
47. Ibid., col. 894.
48. Quoted in *The Times*, 1 May 1915, p. 10.
49. Ibid., 30 April 1915, p. 11.
50. Hansard, Vol. 71 col. 899.
51. *The Times*, 3 May 1915, p. 10.

52. Ibid.
53. *The Times*, 31 March 1915, p. 5.
54. Hansard, Vol. 71 col. 256.
55. *The Times*, 29 April 1915, p. 5.
56. Ibid., 1 April 1915, p. 5.
57. Ibid., 19 March 1915, p. 10.
58. Ibid., 19 April 1915, p. 5.
59. Stevenson F., p. 6.
60. Clark A., p. 57.
61. *The Times*, 23 April 1915, p. 5.
62. Ibid., 20 April 1915, p. 4.
63. Hansard, Vol. 71 col. 834.
64. Russell, II, p. 51.
65. Gilbert III(C), I, p. 107.
66. Riddell, p. 36.
67. Stevenson F., p. 3.
68. Asquith, *VS*, p. 298.
69. Asquith, *Diary*, p. 45.
70. Ibid., p. 311.
71. Ibid., p. 317.
72. Hankey, I, p. 238.
73. Asquith, *VS*, p. 184.
74. Asquith, *MR*, II, p. 43.
75. Asquith, *VS*, p. 327.
76. PRO CAB 42/1/11.
77. Asquith, *VS*, p. 331.
78. Esher Papers: ESHR 2/13, diary entry for 18 December 1914.
79. Grey, II, p. 69.
80. Asquith, *VS*, p. 345.
81. Ibid., p. 346.
82. Gilbert III(C), I, p. 347.
83. Asquith, *Diary*, p. 68.
84. Grigg I, pp. 192–93.
85. Asquith, *VS*, p. 356.
86. Ibid., p. 359.
87. Bell, p. 85.
88. Gilbert III(C), I, p. 380.
89. Ibid., p. 367.
90. *The Times*, 22 January 1915, p. 33.
91. Ibid.
92. Newton, p. 445.
93. Blake, p. 238.
94. Asquith, *VS*, p. 387.
95. Bell, p. 76.
96. Gilbert III(C), I, p. 433.
97. Esher Papers: ESHR 2/13, diary entry for 24 January 1915.
98. Gilbert III(C), I, p. 461.
99. Asquith, *VS*, p. 405.
100. Asquith, *MR*, II, p. 88.
101. Robertson, I, p. 147.
102. Rose II, p. 173.
103. Taylor F., p. 18.
104. *The Times*, 9 February 1915, p. 8.
105. Hansard, Vol. 69 col. 146.
106. Ibid., cols 220–22.
107. Ibid., col. 330.
108. Ibid., col. 332.
109. Ibid., col. 333.
110. *The Times*, 9 February 1915, p. 9.
111. Riddell, p. 62.
112. Ibid., p. 449.
113. Asquith, *VS*, p. 445.
114. Hansard, Vol. 70 col. 598.
115. Roskill, I, p. 168.
116. Gilbert III(C), I, p. 710.
117. Roskill, I, p. 168.
118. Barnett, p. 85.
119. Hansard, Vol. 70 col. 501.
120. Ibid., Vol. 71 col. 314.
121. Asquith, *Diary*, p. 73.
122. Ibid., pp. 88–89.
123. Newton, p. 445.
124. Asquith, *Diary*, p. 84.
125. Asquith, *VS*, p. 165.
126. Ibid., p. 423.
127. Hankey, I, p. 289.
128. Asquith, *VS*, p. 508.
129. Ibid., p. 484.
130. Ibid., p. 491.
131. See Asquith, *VS*, pp. 502–03.
132. Riddell, p. 65.
133. Wilson, p. 80.
134. Scott, p. 119.
135. Ibid., p. 120.
136. Riddell, p. 78.
137. Asquith, *VS*, p. 519.
138. Grigg I, p. 224.
139. Wilson, p. 75.
140. Asquith, *VS*, p. 514.
141. Ibid., p. 522.
142. Riddell, p. 98.

143. PRO CAB 42/2/17.
144. Asquith, *VS*, p. 520.
145. Wilson, p. 81.
146. Asquith, *VS*, p. 551.
147. Ibid., p. 553.
148. Hankey, I, p. 299.
149. *The Times*, 16 April 1915, p. 5.
150. VBC, p. 39.
151. Thompson II, p. 55.
152. *The Times*, 1 April 1915, p. 4.
153. Ibid., 19 April 1915, p. 4.
154. Ibid., 20 April 1915, p. 11.
155. Ibid., 21 April 1915, p. 9.
156. Ibid., p. 10.
157. Adams I, p. 15.
158. Asquith, *VS*, p. 560.
159. *The Times*, 21 April 1915, p. 9.
160. Asquith, *Diary*, p. 101.
161. Ibid., p. 103.
162. Asquith, *VS*, p. 557.
163. Ibid.
164. Ibid., p. 558.
165. Ibid., p. 562.
166. Ibid.
167. *The Times*, 22 April 1915, p. 11.
168. Ibid., 28 April 1915, p. 5.
169. Ibid., 22 April 1915, p. 11.
170. Asquith, *VS*, p. 564.
171. Hansard, Vol. 71 col. 313.
172. Ibid., col. 315.
173. *The Times*, 23 April 1915, p. 9.
174. Asquith, *VS*, p. 583.
175. Ibid., pp. 597 and 589.
176. Ibid., 6 May 1915, p. 9.
177. Wilson, p. 87.
178. *The Times*, 26 May 1915, p. 9.
179. Postgate, p. 157.
180. Hyman, p. 132.
181. Stevenson II, p. 15.
182. *The Times*, 10 May 1915, p. 9.
183. Ibid., 8 May 1915, p. 9.
184. *The Times*, 11 May 1915, p. 9.
185. Esher Papers: ESHR 2/14, diary entry for 9 May 1915.
186. Asquith, *VS*, p. 590.
187. Ibid., p. 593.
188. Ibid., p. 596.
189. Asquith Papers: MS.Eng. lett.c.542/1/6.
190. Asquith, *Diary*, p. 109.
191. Jolliffe, p. 202.
192. VBC, pp. 49–50.
193. *The Times*, 13 May 1915, p. 10.
194. Asquith, *Diary*, p. 112.
195. *The Times*, 15 May 1915, p. 9.
196. Ibid., p. 7.
197. Ibid., 13 May 1915, p. 9.
198. Hansard, Vol. 71 col. 1842.
199. Ibid., Vol. 83 col. 1071.
200. *The Times*, 13 May 1915, p. 9.
201. Ibid., 18 May 1915, p. 4.
202. For background details about Repington, see Heffer, *AD*, pp. 553–54.
203. *The Times*, 14 May 1915, p. 8.
204. P&H, p. 475.
205. Riddell, p. 87.
206. W. Michael Ryan, 'From "Shells Scandal" to Bow Street: The Denigration of Lieutenant-Colonel Charles à Court Repington', *The Journal of Modern History*, Vol. 50 No. 2, p. D1099.
207. *The Times*, 20 May 1915, p. 9.
208. Repington, I, p. 35.
209. *The Times*, 14 May 1915, p. 9.
210. Repington, I, p. 36.
211. *The Times*, 17 May 1915, pp. 9–10.
212. Gilbert III(C), II, p. 864.
213. Stevenson F., p. 49.
214. Petrie, II, p. 20.
215. Asquith, *Diary*, p. 110.
216. Ibid., p. 111.
217. Gilbert III(C), II, p. 887.
218. Stevenson F., p. 50.
219. Gilbert III(C), II, p. 888.
220. Ibid., p. 889.
221. Riddell, p. 93.
222. Esher Papers: ESHR 2/14, diary entry for 17 May 1915.
223. Asquith, *Diary*, p. 153.
224. Riddell, p. 94.
225. Hankey, I, p. 318.
226. VBC, p. 53.
227. Davidson, p. 25.

228. Hamilton, p. 253.
229. Asquith, *MR*, II, p. 95.
230. Esher Papers: ESHR 2/14, diary entry for 17 May 1915.
231. Beaverbrook I, I, p. 102.
232. Hankey, I, p. 315.
233. *The Times*, 18 May 1915, p. 9.
234. RRJ, p. 79.
235. DeGroot II, p. 120.
236. Petrie, II, p. 27.
237. Bell, p. 177.
238. Rose II, p. 189; RA GV/PRIV/GVD/1915: 22 May.
239. Gilbert III(C), I, p. 191.
240. RRJ, p. 77.
241. Esher Papers: ESHR 2/14, diary entry for 18 May 1915.
242. O'Brien, p. 262.
243. Asquith, *Diary*, p. 154.
244. *The Times*, 19 May 1915, p. 9.
245. Hankey, I, p. 316.
246. Asquith, *MR*, II, p. 93.
247. Roskill, I, p. 174.
248. Esher Papers: ESHR 2/14, diary entry for 19 May 1915.
249. Nicolson, p. 263.
250. Gilbert III(C), II, p. 911.
251. Asquith, *Diary*, p. 122.
252. Hansard, Vol. 71 col. 2392.
253. Ibid., col. 2393.
254. Asquith C., p. 25.
255. Asquith, *Diary*, p. 123.
256. *The Times*, 20 May 1915, p. 9.
257. Asquith, *Diary*, p. 124.
258. Gilbert, III(C), II, p. 919.
259. VBC, p. 53.
260. Gilbert, III(C), II, p. 921.
261. Asquith, *Diary*, p. 133.
262. VBC, p. 57.
263. Asquith, *Diary*, p. 107.
264. Stevenson F., p. 52.
265. Riddell, p. 89.
266. Gilbert, III(C), II, p. 924.
267. Asquith, *Diary*, p. 113.
268. Bell, p. 185.
269. Gilbert, III(C), II, p. 927.
270. Riddell, p. 90.
271. Scott, p. 244.
272. Davidson, p. 25.
273. LG, I, p. 147.
274. Adams I, p. 39.
275. Wells, *JP*, p. 579.
276. Searle, p. 275.
277. Haig, p. 125.
278. Hansard, Vol. 72 col. 162.
279. Asquith, *Diary*, p. 109.
280. Stevenson I, p. 382.
281. Haste, p. 157.
282. Asquith, *Diary*, p. 145.
283. Hankey, I, p. 319.
284. Wilson, p. 92.
285. Samuel, p. 109.
286. Asquith, *Diary*, p. 137.
287. Crewe Papers: Crewe to Asquith, 4 July 1915.
288. Haldane, p. 282.
289. Ibid., p. 283.
290. Grey, II, p. 237.
291. Ibid., p. 238.
292. Trevelyan, p. 278.
293. Hansard (Lords), Vol. 18 col. 1017.
294. Ibid., col. 1021.
295. Ibid., col. 1019.
296. *The Times*, 24 May 1915, p. 7.
297. Thompson I, p. 240.
298. Beaverbrook I, I, pp. 116–118.
299. *The Times*, 4 November 1915, p. 3.
300. Esher Papers: ESHR 2/14, diary entry for 21 May 1915.
301. Repington, I, p. 41.
302. Steed, II, p. 73.
303. Thompson I, p. 245.
304. Haig, p. 35.
305. *The Times*, 22 May 1915, p. 9.
306. Hankey Papers: HNKY 5/1/1.
307. Riddell, p. 84.
308. Taylor I, p. 27.
309. Hankey, I, p. 317.
310. *The Times*, 26 May 1915, p. 5.
311. RA PS/PSO/GV/C/R/225.
312. *The Times*, 27 May 1915, p. 9.
313. Hankey, I, p. 337.
314. Scott, p. 125.
315. Ibid., p. 126.

316. Hansard, Vol. 72 col. 557.
317. Ibid., col. 559.
318. Ibid., col. 560.
319. Asquith, *Diary*, p. 157.
320. Ibid., p. 158.
321. Asquith Papers: MS.Eng. lett.c.542/1/108.
322. Ibid.: MS.Eng.lett.c.542/1/118.
323. Ibid.: MS.Eng.lett.c.542/1/195.
324. Ibid.: MS.Eng.lett.c.542/1/198.
325. I am indebted to Hon. William Strutt for this information. Asquith's letters to Miss Strutt are in the Rayleigh Archive.
326. *The Times*, 18 June 1915, p. 5.
327. Grigg I, p. 264.
328. Barnett, p. 113.
329. *The Times*, 5 June 1915, p. 10.
330. Ibid., 9 June 1915, p. 8.
331. Ibid., 11 June 1915, p. 11.
332. Ibid., 14 June 1915, p. 8.
333. Webb, III, p. 235.
334. Adams I, p. 53.
335. *The Times*, 3 July 1915, p. 9.
336. Callwell, I, p. 236.
337. Asquith, *Diary*, p. 163.
338. Ibid, pp. 146–47.
339. *The Times*, 16 January 1915, p. 9.

Chapter 4: Conscription

1. *The Times*, 10 July 1915, p. 8.
2. Ibid., 7 July 1915, p. 3.
3. Ibid., 25 June 1915, p. 3.
4. Ibid., 15 February 1916, p. 8.
5. Boothby, p. 16.
6. *The Times*, 23 October 1915, p. 7.
7. Ibid., 18 October 1915, p. 5.
8. Haste, p. 90.
9. *The Times*, 23 October 1915, p. 7.
10. Ibid., 19 October 1915, p. 9.
11. Hansard (Lords), Vol. 19 col. 1103.
12. *The Times*, 22 October 1915, p. 9.
13. Ibid., 26 October 1915, p. 8.
14. Pope-Hennessy, p. 501.
15. Clark A., p. 90.
16. Asquith, *Diary*, p. 94.
17. Asquith, *VS*, p. 569.
18. *The Times*, 26 April 1915, p. 5.
19. Wells, *JP*, p. 582.
20. Brooke, *1914*, p. 11.
21. Ibid., p. 15.
22. Retrieved from https://www.poetryfoundation.org/poems/57324/i-saw-a-man-this-morning.
23. Hynes, p. 10.
24. *The Times*, 5 May 1916, p. 9.
25. D. H. Lawrence, *The Rainbow*, Chapter 12.
26. Morrell II, p. 74.
27. *The Times*, 23 May 1916, p. 5.
28. Parry Papers: Parry, diary entry for 10 March 1916.
29. Haste, p. 27.
30. For Mrs Fawcett see Heffer, *HM*, pp. 619–24, and Heffer, *AD*, pp. 709ff.
31. Riddell, p. 99.
32. Esher Papers: ESHR 2/14, diary entry for 24 June 1915.
33. *The Times*, 7 June 1915, p. 5.
34. Scott, p. 126.
35. *The Times*, 14 July 1915, p. 9.
36. Ibid., 16 July 1915, p. 10.
37. Ibid., 20 July 1915, p. 7.
38. Ibid., 22 July 1915, p. 7.
39. Ibid., 21 May 1915, p. 9.
40. Hansard, Vol. 72 cols 81–82.
41. Ibid., col. 349.
42. *The Times*, 7 June 1915, p. 9.
43. Crewe Papers: Asquith to Crewe, 4 July 1915.
44. Churchill R., p. 185.
45. Ibid., p. 186.
46. Adams I, p. 116.
47. *The Times*, 19 July 1915, p. 9.
48. Taylor I, p. 38.
49. *The Times*, 9 July 1915, p. 3.
50. Ibid., 3 August 1915, p. 2.
51. Clark A., p. 83.
52. *The Times*, 29 November 1915, p. 3.
53. Amery, p. 123.
54. Hansard, Vol. 73 col. 2395.
55. Ibid., col. 2397.
56. Ibid., col. 2398.
57. Ibid., col. 2425.

58. Ronaldshay, III, p. 135.
59. Amery, p. 124.
60. *The Times*, 18 August 1915, p. 7.
61. Gilbert III(C), II, p. 1139.
62. *The Times*, 25 August 1915, p. 7.
63. Asquith, *Diary*, p. 185.
64. Ibid., p. 187.
65. Wilson, p. 121 (n).
66. Riddell, p. 117.
67. Thompson II, p. 66.
68. Wilson, p. 119.
69. Scott, p. 132.
70. Ibid., p. 134.
71. Ibid., p. 135.
72. Esher Papers: ESHR 2/15, diary entry for 3 September 1915.
73. Gilbert III(C), II, p. 1170.
74. Webb, III, p. 238.
75. *The Times*, 10 September 1915, p. 9.
76. Grigg I, p. 291.
77. Bullock, I, p. 51.
78. Grigg I, p. 298.
79. Ibid.
80. Stevenson F., p. 87.
81. Grigg I, p. 300.
82. Hansard, Vol. 77 col. 802.
83. Ibid., col. 803.
84. *The Times*, 22 May 1916, p. 5.
85. Ibid., 2 November 1915, p. 5.
86. Taylor I, p. 41.
87. *The Times*, 30 September 1915, p. 7.
88. Ibid., 4 October 1915, p. 9.
89. Hansard, Vol. 74 col. 34.
90. Roskill, I, p. 217.
91. Stevenson F., p. 59.
92. Hansard, Vol. 74 cols 733–34.
93. Kerry, p. 254.
94. *The Times*, 4 October 1915, p. 5.
95. Ibid., 27 September 1915, p. 10.
96. Churchill R., p. 192.
97. Quoted in Martin Farr, 'Winter and Discontent: The December Crises of the Asquith Coalition, 1915–1916', *Britain and the World*, Vol. 4 No. 1, p. 118.
98. *The Times*, 6 October 1915, p. 4.
99. Thompson II, p. 78.
100. *The Times*, 11 October 1915, p. 9.
101. VBC, p. 81.
102. Ibid., p. 83.
103. Asquith, *Diary*, p. 198.
104. Scott, p. 144.
105. Riddell, p. 126.
106. Gilbert III(C), II, p. 1219.
107. Asquith, *Diary*, p. 199.
108. Roskill, I, p. 227.
109. Stevenson F., p. 70.
110. *The Times*, 20 October 1915, p. 8.
111. Repington, I, p. 53.
112. Thompson II, p. 77.
113. Hankey, I, p. 434.
114. Hankey, II, p. 444.
115. Lloyd Papers: GLLD 28/6, diary entry for 27 November 1915.
116. Hankey, II, p. 441.
117. Lloyd Papers: GLLD 28/6, diary entry for 27 November 1915.
118. Haig, p. 97.
119. Ibid., p. 109.
120. See Heffer, *AD*, pp. 811–16; and DeGroot I, pp. 144–45.
121. Esher Papers: ESHR 2/15, diary entry for 13 November 1915.
122. Haig, p. 109.
123. Esher Papers: ESHR 2/15, diary entry for 23 November 1915.
124. Ibid: ESHR 2/15, diary entry for 25 November 1915.
125. Holmes, p. 292.
126. Haig, p. 36.
127. See Heffer, *AD*, p. 258.
128. Asquith, *Diary*, p. 218.
129. DeGroot, p. 213.
130. Repington, I, p. 88.
131. DeGroot, p. 214.
132. Robertson, I, pp. 165–66.
133. Gilbert III(C), II, p. 1250.
134. Scott, p. 158.
135. Ibid., p. 165.
136. Grigg I, p. 321.
137. Hankey, I, p. 424; Wilson, p. 127.
138. Hansard, Vol. 75 col. 367.
139. Hankey, I, p. 426.
140. *The Times*, 19 October 1915, p. 5.

141. Ibid., 23 October 1915, p. 7.
142. Ibid., 19 October 1915, p. 9.
143. Ibid., 23 October 1915, p. 3.
144. Hankey, I, p. 427.
145. *The Times*, 3 November 1915, p. 14.
146. Ibid., p. 11.
147. Ibid., p. 12.
148. Ibid., p. 14.
149. Scott, p. 154.
150. AP, p. 128.
151. Ibid., p. 155.
152. Ibid.
153. Asquith, *Diary*, p. 180.
154. See Heffer, *AD*, pp. 483–84.
155. *The Times*, 25 November 1915, p. 9.
156. Ibid., 8 December 1915, p. 7.
157. Gilbert III(C), II, p. 1341.
158. *The Times*, 17 December 1915, p. 7.
159. Charman, p. 54.
160. Hansard, Vol. 77 col. 217.
161. AP, p. 134.
162. Ibid., p. 135.
163. *The Times*, 28 December 1915, p. 9.
164. RA PS/PSO/GV/C/R/260.
165. Stevenson F., p. 89.
166. Martin Farr, op. cit., p. 121.
167. Stevenson F., p. 90.
168. Trevelyan, p. 327.
169. Lloyd Papers: GLLD 28/6, diary entry for 3 December 1915.
170. VBC, p. 90.
171. Nicolson II, p. 271.
172. RA GV/PRIV/GVD/1915: 30 December.
173. Hammond, pp. 190–91.
174. Robertson, I, pp. 294–95.
175. Hansard, Vol. 77 col. 936.
176. Ibid., col. 950.
177. *The Times*, 5 January 1916, p. 4.
178. Hansard, Vol. 77 col. 951.
179. Ibid., Vol. 104 col. 1366.
180. Ibid., Vol. 77 col. 954.
181. Ibid., col. 957.
182. Ibid., col. 953.
183. Ibid., col. 963.
184. Ibid., col. 978.
185. Asquith, *Diary*, p. 236.
186. Scott, p. 172.
187. Ibid., p. 169.
188. Stevenson F., p. 96.
189. Ibid., p. 98.
190. Simon, p. 107.
191. Taylor I, p. 55.
192. AP, p. 148.
193. E&H, p. 251.
194. Wells, *JP*, p. 579.
195. Scott, p. 161.
196. Gilbert III(C), II, p. 751.
197. Sommer, p. 333.
198. *The Times*, 1 December 1915, p. 9.
199. Ibid., 21 December 1915, p. 11.
200. Hansard, Vol. 77 col. 96.
201. Ibid., col. 122.
202. Ibid., col. 117.
203. Ibid., col. 118.
204. Ibid., col. 121.
205. *The Times*, 21 December 1915, p. 11.
206. Ibid., 24 January 1916, p. 5.
207. Clark A., p. 106.
208. Thompson I, p. 251.
209. Hansard (Lords), Vol. 22 col. 107.
210. Ibid., col. 126.
211. *The Times*, 24 January 1916, p. 10.
212. Hansard (Lords), Vol. 21 col. 87.
213. Ibid., col. 90.
214. Scott, p. 182.
215. Haig, p. 129.
216. Hansard, Vol. 80 col. 1430.
217. Gilbert III(C), II, p. 1083.
218. Scott, p. 183.
219. Hammond, p. 193.
220. Hansard, Vol. 80 col. 1563.
221. Ibid., col. 1570.
222. Ibid., cols 1571–72.
223. Ibid., col. 1575.
224. Scott, p. 191.
225. Asquith, *Diary*, p. 243.
226. Heffer, *AD*, p. 316.
227. Scott, p. 193.
228. Gilbert III(C), II, p. 1450.
229. Stevenson F., p. 102.
230. Hankey, II, p. 481.
231. Roskill, I, p. 256.
232. *The Times*, 1 April 1916, p. 3.

233. Thompson I, p. 252.
234. *The Times*, 30 March 1916, p. 9.
235. Thompson I, p. 253.
236. *The Times*, 13 April 1916, p. 6.
237. Webb, III, p. 252.
238. Repington, I, p. 185.
239. Scott, p. 197.
240. Steed, II, p. 131.
241. Lee, p. 148.
242. Riddell, pp. 170–71.
243. Scott, p. 197.
244. Ibid., p. 198.
245. Stevenson F., p. 107.
246. Scott, p. 199.
247. Ibid., p. 200.
248. Stevenson F., p. 107.
249. RA PS/PSO/GV/C/R/285.
250. Hansard, Vol. 82 col. 44; Roskill, I, p. 266.
251. Hansard, Vol. 82 col. 181.
252. Churchill R., p. 207.
253. *The Times*, 26 May 1916, p. 9.
254. Ibid., 15 September 1916, p. 9.
255. Hansard, Vol. 82 cols 1853–55.
256. *The Times*, 12 February 1916, p. 3.
257. Hansard, Vol. 82 col. 1856.
258. *The Times*, 14 February 1916, p. 4.
259. Hankey, II, p. 477.
260. Morrell II, p. 104.
261. Hynes, p. 146.
262. Hansard, Vol. 82 col. 646.
263. Ibid., col. 647.
264. Ibid., col. 648.
265. Ibid., col. 650.
266. *The Times*, 11 April 1916, p. 5.
267. Hansard, Vol. 86 col. 1256.
268. Ibid., Vol. 83 col. 126.
269. *The Times*, 16 March 1916, p. 5; ibid., 17 March 1916, p. 5.
270. Russell, II, p. 24.
271. Charman, pp. 61–62.
272. Esher Papers: ESHR 2/15, letter to H. H. Asquith, 17 March 1916.
273. Repington, I, p. 333.
274. Grigg I, p. 338.
275. Wilson, p. 171.
276. Stevenson F., p. 105.
277. *The Times*, 29 March 1916, p. 10.
278. BL Add MS 62161 ff.100–101.
279. *The Times*, 24 May 1916, p. 5.

Chapter 5: Rising

1. Scott, p. 114.
2. Ibid.
3. Hardinge, p. 6.
4. *The Times*, 31 October 1914, p. 9.
5. Meleady, p. 314.
6. *The Times*, 31 October 1914, p. 9. For James Larkin and his followers, see Heffer, *AD*, pp. 794–98.
7. Wilson, p. 58.
8. Ibid., p. 59.
9. *The Times*, 31 October 1914, p. 9.
10. Townshend I, p. 71.
11. *The Times*, 21 January 1915, p. 6.
12. Retrieved from https://www.poetryfoundation.org/poems/57313/on-being-asked-for-a-war-poem
13. Meleady, p. 320.
14. *The Times*, 3 July 1915, p. 6.
15. Wilson, p. 59.
16. Retrieved from http://www.easter1916.net/oration.htm.
17. Townshend I, p. 115.
18. Ibid., pp. 83–84.
19. Dangerfield, p. 147.
20. Hardinge, p. 7.
21. Townshend I, p. 106.
22. Ibid., p. 78.
23. Ibid., p. 79.
24. *The Times*, 4 March 1916, p. 8.
25. Midleton, p. 229.
26. Townshend I, p. 124.
27. Hansard (Lords), Vol. 21 col. 964.
28. Hardinge, p. 11.
29. Andrew, p. 87.
30. Townshend I, p. 135.
31. Ibid., p. 138.
32. Asquith C., p. 128.
33. Ferriter, p. 154.
34. Dangerfield, p. 176.
35. See this point discussed at https://www.independent.ie/irish-news/

why-pearse-may-not-have-read-out-
the-1916-proclamation-at-gpo-after-
all-30589327.html.

36. Text taken from http://www.
firstdail.com/?page_id=75.
37. Townshend I, p. 108.
38. Hankey, II, p. 475.
39. Townshend I, p. 183.
40. Gilbert III(C), I, p. 268.
41. Asquith C., p. 163.
42. Ibid.
43. Esher Papers: ESHR 2/16, diary
entry 10 July 1916.
44. *The Times*, 29 April 1916, p. 9.
45. Hansard, Vol. 82 col. 675W.
46. Townshend I, p. 246.
47. Ferriter, p. 158.
48. Townshend I, p. 270.
49. *The Times*, 1 May 1916, p. 10.
50. Webb, III, p. 254.
51. Plunkett Papers: Diary, 4 May 1916.
52. Dangerfield, p. 216.
53. Samuel, p. 116.
54. Townshend I, p. 272.
55. Ibid., p. 274.
56. Grigg I, p. 347.
57. Townshend I, p. 279.
58. Holmes, p. 325.
59. Dangerfield, p. 210.
60. Townshend I, p. 280.
61. Meleady, p. 370.
62. Hansard, Vol. 82 col. 283.
63. Ibid., col. 284.
64. Ibid., col. 285.
65. *The Times*, 12 May 1916, p. 5.
66. Scott, p. 206.
67. Hansard, Vol. 82 col. 32.
68. Ibid., col. 33.
69. Ibid., col. 35.
70. Ibid., col. 35.
71. Ibid., col. 36.
72. Ibid., col. 37.
73. Ibid., col. 38.
74. Scott, p. 205.
75. Hansard, Vol. 82 col. 935.
76. Ibid., col. 937.
77. Ibid., col. 938.

78. Ibid., col. 940.
79. Ibid., col. 951.
80. Ibid., col. 953.
81. Ibid., col. 955.
82. Ibid., col. 956.
83. Ibid., col. 957.
84. Ibid., col. 959.
85. Crewe Papers: copy of letter from
Asquith to Samuel, 14 May 1916.
86. S&A, II, pp. 215–16.
87. Ibid., p. 216.
88. Ibid., p. 217.
89. Morrell II, p. 108.
90. *The Times*, 20 May 1916, p. 7.
91. Hansard, Vol. 82 cols 2075–76.
92. Scott, p. 207.
93. Hansard, Vol. 82 col. 2309.
94. Ibid., col. 2310.
95. Ibid., col. 2311.
96. Ibid., col. 2312.
97. Scott, p. 207.
98. Hansard, Vol. 82 col. 2535.
99. Meleady, p. 380.
100. Hansard, Vol. 82 col. 2958.
101. Scott, p. 217.
102. Riddell, p. 184.
103. Lloyd George papers: D 14/2/28.
104. Kerry, p. 259.
105. Ibid.
106. Adams III, p. 314.
107. RA PS/PSO/GV/C/R/291.
108. Hansard (Lords), Vol. 22 col. 388.
109. Ibid., col. 389.
110. *The Times*, 28 June 1916, p. 9.
111. Hansard (Lords), Vol. 22 col. 495.
112. Ibid., col. 496.
113. Ibid., col. 497.
114. Ibid., col. 498.
115. Ibid., col. 500.
116. Ibid., col. 501.
117. *The Times*, 30 June 1916, p. 6.
118. Hansard, Vol. 84 col. 57.
119. Ibid., col. 58.
120. Ibid., col. 59.
121. See Heffer, *AD*, pp. 820–21.
122. Hardinge, p. 6.
123. Ibid., p. 4.

124. Ibid., p. 7.
125. Ibid., p. 11.
126. Ibid., p. 12.
127. Ibid., p. 13.
128. Hansard, Vol. 84 col. 2126.
129. Hansard (Lords), Vol. 22 col. 615.
130. Ibid., col. 619.
131. Ibid., col. 616.
132. Ibid., col. 617.
133. Crewe Papers: Asquith to Crewe, 12 July 1916.
134. Riddell, p. 201.
135. Ibid., p. 205.
136. *The Times*, 21 July 1916, p. 9.
137. Hansard, Vol. 84 col. 1340.
138. Ibid., col. 1430.
139. Ibid., cols 1433–34.
140. Ibid., col. 1438.
141. Ibid., col. 1452.
142. Ibid., col. 1461.
143. Ibid., col. 2123.
144. Ibid., cols 2125–26.
145. Ibid., col. 2131.
146. Ibid., col. 2135.
147. *The Times*, 5 August 1916, p. 3.
148. Hansard, Vol. 84 col. 2153.
149. *The Times*, 1 August 1916, p. 9.
150. Ibid., 24 July 1916, p. 10.
151. Stevenson F., p. 109.
152. *The Times*, 9 August 1916, p. 3.
153. Scott, p. 222.
154. Darroch, p. 182.
155. *The Times*, 4 August 1916, p. 7.

Chapter 6: Slaughter
  1. Hankey, II, p. 479.
  2. Ibid., p. 480.
  3. Esher Papers: ESHR 2/16, letter to H. H. Asquith, 23 June 1916.
  4. Jellicoe, p. 136.
  5. Hankey, II, p. 491.
  6. Ibid., p. 492.
  7. Scott, p. 214.
  8. Riddell, p. 185.
  9. *The Times*, 5 June 1916, p. 9.
 10. Thompson II, p. 101.
 11. Beaverbrook I, I, p. 205.

12. Taylor, p. 58.
13. Esher Papers: ESHR 2/16, letter to Sir Douglas Haig, 9 June 1916.
14. Hansard, Vol. 83 col. 146.
15. Hankey, II, p. 508.
16. Churchill R., p. 210.
17. Scott, p. 215.
18. Hansard, Vol. 82 col. 1344.
19. Scott, p. 216.
20. Ibid., p. 217.
21. Ibid., p. 218.
22. Esher Papers: ESHR 2/16, letter to Sir Douglas Haig, 9 June 1916.
23. Rose II, p. 195.
24. *The Times*, 9 June 1916, p. 9.
25. Ibid., 21 June 1916, p. 9.
26. Scott, p. 219.
27. Ibid., p. 220.
28. Esher Papers: ESHR 2/16, diary entry for 15 June 1916.
29. Asquith, *Diary*, p. 267.
30. Ibid., p. 269.
31. Churchill R., p. 211.
32. Ibid., p. 268.
33. Petrie, II, p. 50.
34. Riddell, p. 207.
35. Scott, p. 224.
36. Roskill, I, p. 283; Haig, p. 135.
37. Haig, p. 139.
38. Hansard, Vol. 83 col. 1013.
39. Ibid., col. 1014.
40. Ibid., col. 1015.
41. *The Times*, 17 May 1916, p. 9.
42. Ibid., 6 June 1916, p. 5.
43. Brock Millman, 'HMG and the War against Dissent, 1914–18', *Journal of Contemporary History*, Vol. 40 No. 3, p. 424.
44. Morrell II, p. 111.
45. Hansard, Vol. 86 col. 826.
46. Morrell II, p. 124.
47. Ibid., p. 125.
48. Darroch, p. 219.
49. Ibid., p. 211(n).
50. Morrell, p. 126.
51. Hankey, II, p. 494.
52. Ibid., p. 495.

53. DeGroot I, p. 225.
54. Hankey, II, p. 495.
55. Ibid., p. 215.
56. Scott, p. 213.
57. Haig, p. 150.
58. Ibid., p. 153.
59. *The Times*, 4 July 1916, p. 9.
60. Haste, p. 68.
61. Retrieved from https://www.iwm.org.uk/history/what-happened-on-the-first-day-of-the-battle-of-the-somme.
62. Davidson, p. 39.
63. Haig, p. 154.
64. Esher Papers: ESHR 2/16, diary entry for 9 July 1916. *Degomméd* is Esher's Anglo-French bastardisation of *degommé*, to knock down or to fell with a shot or blow. Lawrence (*sic*) Burgis, as well as being a protégé of and former secretary to Esher, was also one of his crushes: Esher got him a job on Hankey's staff in London and Burgis had a long and distinguished career in the civil service.
65. Wells, *JP*, p. 585.
66. Roskill, I, p. 286.
67. DeGroot I, p. 256.
68. Riddell, p. 198.
69. *The Times*, 7 July 1916, p. 10.
70. Hart, p. 211.
71. Clark A., p. 165.
72. *The Times*, 29 May 1915, p. 9.
73. Hewett, p. 108.
74. Ibid., p. 109.
75. Ibid., p. 112.
76. Ibid., p. 113.
77. DeGroot II, p. 115.
78. *The Times*, 22 August 1916, p. 3.
79. Hynes, p. 122.
80. Ibid., p. 123.
81. Repington, I, p. 43.
82. Ibid., p. 44.
83. *The Times*, 13 July 1916, p. 5.
84. DeGroot I, p. 155.
85. Brandon, p. 220.
86. Ibid., p. 215.
87. Lodge, p. 197.
88. Wells, *Britling*, pp. 266–67.
89. Ibid., p. 269.
90. Riddell, p. 201.
91. Repington, I, p. 285.
92. Gilbert III(C), II, p. 1537.
93. Haig, p. 157.
94. Esher Papers: ESHR 2/16, diary entry 27 July 1916.
95. DeGroot I, p. 258.
96. Ibid., p. 256.
97. Ibid., p. 257.
98. Haig, p. 158.
99. Ibid., p. 159.
100. Esher Papers: ESHR 2/16, letter to Lt Col. M. Hankey, 3 August 1916.
101. Hansard, Vol. 85 col. 2298W.
102. Charman, p. 55.
103. Russell, II, p. 72.
104. *The Times*, 5 September 1916, p. 9.
105. Hansard, Vol. 86 col. 539.
106. Ibid., col. 827.
107. Ibid., col. 835.
108. *The Times*, 20 October 1916, p. 9.
109. Ibid., 12 September 1916, p. 5.
110. Ibid., p. 9.
111. Repington, I, p. 361.
112. *The Times*, 10 October 1916, p. 5.
113. Ibid., 26 October 1916, p. 9.
114. Ibid., 30 October 1916, p. 5.
115. Hansard, Vol. 86 col. 116.
116. Riddell, p. 215.
117. *The Times*, 7 October 1916, p. 10.
118. Ibid., 14 November 1916, p. 5.
119. Hansard, Vol. 86 col. 581.
120. Ibid., col. 583.
121. Ibid., col. 588.
122. Ibid., col. 652.
123. Ibid., col. 1483.
124. Ibid., col. 1485.
125. Ibid., col. 632.
126. Hansard, Vol. 85 col. 2508.
127. *The Times*, 9 August 1916, p. 3.
128. Ibid., 23 August 1916, p. 3.
129. Bilton, p. 127.
130. Haste, p. 32.

131. *The Times*, 25 September 1916, p. 10.
132. Wilson, p. 187.
133. Hansard, Vol. 85 col. 1451.
134. Ibid., cols 1451–2.
135. Wilson, p. 5.
136. Esher Papers: ESHR 2/16, diary
      entry 17 September 1916.
137. See Heffer, *AD*, pp. 573–94.
138. BL Add. MS49758 f.311.
139. Esher Papers: ESHR 2/17, diary
      entry 29 September 1916.
140. Grigg I, p. 425.
141. Ibid., p. 433.
142. PA: BBK/C/261.
143. Grigg I, p. 382.
144. Hansard, Vol. 86, col. 145.
145. Stevenson F., p. 115.
146. Esher Papers: ESHR 2/17, diary
      entry for 17 October 1916.
147. Repington, I, p. 351.
148. Stevenson F., p. 115.
149. Ibid., p. 117.
150. Ibid.
151. Grigg I, p. 384.
152. Robertson, I, p. 301.
153. Esher Papers: ESHR 2/17, diary
      entry for 26 October 1916.
154. Grigg I, p. 389.
155. Riddell, p. 219.
156. Hankey, II, p. 551.
157. Kerry, p. 264.
158. Asquith, *MR*, II, p. 142.

Chapter 7: Coup
  1. Riddell, p. 203.
  2. Hankey, II, p. 525.
  3. Bell, p. 236.
  4. Ibid., p. 246.
  5. Ibid., p. 247.
  6. Ibid., p. 205.
  7. Ibid., p. 206.
  8. See Heffer, *AD*, p. 497ff.
  9. Ibid., Ch. 18 passim.
 10. Gilbert, III(C), II, pp. 1542–43.
 11. Grey, II, p. 241.
 12. Cooper, p. 54.
 13. Haig, p. 183

 14. Ibid., p. 164.
 15. Hansard, Vol. 86 cols 101–2.
 16. Ibid., col. 103.
 17. Ibid., col. 106.
 18. Ibid., col. 108.
 19. Ibid., col. 111.
 20. Roskill, I, p. 311.
 21. Hankey, II, p. 556.
 22. Ibid., p. 557.
 23. Esher Papers: ESHR 2/17, letter to
      Sir Douglas Haig, 29 September 1916.
 24. Stevenson F., p. 121.
 25. Hansard, Vol. 86 col. 436.
 26. Ibid., col. 446.
 27. Ibid., col. 478.
 28. Ibid., col. 451.
 29. Hansard, Vol. 85 col. 2248.
 30. Ibid., Vol. 86 col. 1438.
 31. Ibid., Vol. 87 col. 827.
 32. Ibid., col. 828.
 33. Ibid., col. 832.
 34. Ibid., col. 837.
 35. Ibid., col. 845.
 36. Ibid., col. 853.
 37. Ibid., col. 861.
 38. Ibid., col. 863.
 39. *The Times*, 23 November 1916, p. 9.
 40. Ibid., 1 December 1916, p. 5.
 41. Grigg I, p. 438.
 42. Taylor, pp. 62–63; Hankey, II, p. 557.
 43. Hankey, II, p. 515.
 44. Stevenson F., p. 122.
 45. Davidson, p. 42.
 46. Blake, p. 301.
 47. Stevenson F., p. 123.
 48. Haig, p. 166.
 49. Beaverbrook I, II, p. 135; Stevenson
      F., p. 124.
 50. Beaverbrook I, II, pp. 127–28.
 51. Ibid., p. 138.
 52. Hankey, II, p. 564.
 53. Davidson, p. 42.
 54. Stevenson F., p. 127.
 55. Scott, p. 235.
 56. Ibid., p. 236.
 57. Stevenson F., p. 128.
 58. Lee, p. 159.

59. Blake, p. 307.
60. PA: BL 117/1/29.
61. Asquith, *MR*, II, p. 148.
62. Beaverbrook II, p. xvi.
63. Lee, p. 160.
64. *The Times*, 1 December 1916, p. 9.
65. Stevenson F., p. 129.
66. S&A, II, p. 252.
67. Asquith, *Diary*, p. 309.
68. Ibid., p. 254.
69. Blake, p. 310.
70. PA: BL/117/1/30.
71. Asquith Papers: MS.Eng.d.3216, diary entry for 8 February 1918.
72. PA: BBK/C/261.
73. *The Times*, 2 December 1916, p. 9.
74. Hankey, II, p. 565.
75. Wilson, p. 205.
76. Roskill, I, p. 323.
77. For the Marconi scandal see Heffer, *AD*, pp. 573–95.
78. Stevenson F., p. 130.
79. PA: BBK/C/220; Taylor II, p. 99; Beaverbrook I, I, p. 75.
80. Davidson, p. 43; Blake, p. 315.
81. Petrie, II, p. 57.
82. Hammond, p. 203.
83. Asquith, *Diary*, p. 307.
84. S&A, II, pp. 256–57.
85. Blake, p. 315.
86. Churchill R., p. 229.
87. Roskill, I, p. 326.
88. Asquith Papers: MS 31 f. 20.
89. Ibid., MS 32 f. 21.
90. Hankey, II, p. 568.
91. Beaverbrook I, II, p. 244.
92. See Martin Farr, 'Winter and Discontent: The December Crises of the Asquith Coalition 1915–1916,' *Britain and the World* Vol. 4 No. 1, p. 129.
93. S&A, II, p. 264.
94. Asquith, *MR*, II, p. 133.
95. RA GV/PRIV/GVD/1916: 4 December.
96. Sommer, p. 352.
97. Roskill, I, p. 327.
98. Samuel, p. 120.
99. S&A, II, p. 265.
100. Esher Papers: ESHR 2/17, letter to Sir Douglas Haig, 4 December 1916.
101. Scott, p. 248; S&A, II, pp. 266–67.
102. Blake, p. 332.
103. Gilmour, p. 457.
104. Grigg I, p. 466.
105. Young, p. 368.
106. Asquith Papers: MS Eng.d.3216, entry for 19 November 1917.
107. Asquith C., p. 241. Lady Cunard – known as 'Emerald' – was a leading society hostess.
108. Ibid., p. 242.
109. RA GV/PRIV/GVD/1916: 5 December.
110. Blake, p. 336.
111. RA PS/PSO/GV/C/K/1048A/1.
112. Ibid
113. PA: BL/81/1/1.
114. Martin Farr, op. cit., p. 137.
115. Ibid., p. 139.
116. Adams II, p. 239.
117. Lee, p. 162.
118. Grigg I, p. 475.
119. Thompson II, p. 115.
120. PA: BL 81/1/36.
121. McKinstry, p. 522.
122. Samuel, p. 124.
123. Gilbert, IV(C), I, p. 35.
124. Peter Fraser, 'Lord Beaverbrook's Fabrications in *Politicians and the War, 1914–1916*', *The Historical Journal*, Vol. 25 No. 1, pp. 151–52.
125. Riddell, p. 230.
126. Webb, III, p. 270.
127. Ibid., p. 271.
128. *The Times*, 7 December 1916, p. 9.
129. Ibid., 9 December 1916, p. 9.
130. Davidson, p. 45.
131. *The Times*, 9 December 1916, p. 6.
132. Stevenson F., p. 134.
133. Young, p. 372.
134. PA: BL 81/1/36.
135. Hankey, II, p. 570.
136. Keynes, p. 133.

137. Trevelyan, p. 333.
138. Riddell, p. 228.
139. S&A, II, p. 286.
140. Hankey, II, p. 573.
141. Ibid., p. 575.
142. Taylor I, p. 73.
143. BL Add MS 49831 f. 249.
144. *The Times*, 9 December 1916, p. 10.
145. Wilson, p. 206.
146. Ibid., p. 208.
147. Ibid., p. 212.
148. Thompson I, p. 263.
149. *Daily Mail*, 9 December 1916, p. 1.
150. Blake, p. 343.
151. Riddell, p. 213.
152. Ibid., p. 230.
153. Hansard (Lords), Vol. 23 col. 922.
154. Riddell, p. 243.
155. Grigg I, p. 484.
156. Hankey, II, p. 579.
157. S&A, II, p. 279.
158. Grigg II, p. 183.
159. Riddell, p. 231.
160. Hankey, II, p. 594.
161. Lloyd II, p. 22.
162. Robertson, I, p. 286
163. Ibid., p. 287.
164. Hankey, II, pp. 595–96.
165. See Heffer, *AD*, pp. 594–95 and 701–2.
166. Kerry, p. 269.
167. Newton, p. 455.
168. Boothby, p. 18.
169. Esher Papers: ESHR 2/17, diary entry for 1 January 1917.
170. PA: LG/F/29/1/2.
171. Repington, I, p. 412.
172. PA: LG/F/29/1/6.
173. PA: BL 81/1/67.
174. Hansard, Vol. 88 col. 796.
175. Retrieved from https://assets.publishing.service.gov.uk/government/uploads/system/uploads/attachment_data/file/733378/Civil-Service-Workforce-Headline-Statistics-March-2018.pdf.
176. Thompson II, p. 124.
177. Haig, p. 186.

178. Nicolson II, p. 294.
179. *The Times*, 13 December 1916, p. 11.
180. Hankey, II, p. 599.
181. Hansard, Vol. 88 col. 1333.
182. Ibid., col. 1338.
183. Ibid., cols 1340–41.
184. Ibid., col. 1341.
185. Ibid., col. 1342.
186. Ibid., col. 1343.
187. Ibid., col. 1346.
188. Ibid., col. 1347.
189. Ibid., col. 1348.
190. Ibid., col. 1350.
191. Ibid., col. 1352.
192. AP, p. 192. Wolfe would become a celebrated, if minor, poet of the inter-war years.
193. Hansard, Vol. 88 col. 1353.
194. Petrie, II, p. 65.
195. Hansard, Vol. 88 col. 1354.
196. Ibid., cols 1356–57.
197. Ibid., col. 1357.
198. Ibid., col. 1358.
199. Ibid., col. 1359.
200. Ibid., cols 1359–60.
201. *The Times*, 20 December 1916, p. 9.
202. Asquith Papers: MS Eng.d.3215, entry for 28 May 1917.

Chapter 8: Dictatorship

1. *The Times*, 7 March 1917, p. 17.
2. Hansard, Vol. 90 col. 38.
3. Ibid., col. 46.
4. PA: BBK/C/218a.
5. Hankey, II, p. 664.
6. NA: CAB 23/1: Minutes of meeting 20 of the War Cabinet, 27 December 1916.
7. Stevenson F., p. 138.
8. Haig, p. 192.
9. Esher Papers: ESHR 2/18, diary entry for 20 March 1917.
10. Haig, p. 200.
11. Ibid., p. 201.
12. Ibid., p. 204.
13. Ibid., p. 205.
14. RA GV/PRIV/GVD/1917: 1 March.

15. Haig, p. 126; Stevenson F., p. 147.
16. Haig, p. 203.
17. Robertson, II, p. 203.
18. Churchill R., p. 256.
19. Hansard, Vol. 91, col. 1755.
20. *The Times*, 9 March 1917, p. 9.
21. Hankey, II, p. 526.
22. Hansard, Vol. 91 col. 1754.
23. Ibid., cols 1758–59.
24. Ibid., col. 1760.
25. Ibid., col. 1764.
26. Ibid., col. 1765.
27. Ibid., col. 1798.
28. Ibid., col. 1803.
29. Ibid., col. 1807.
30. Brown, p. 84.
31. Thompson I, p. 273.
32. Hankey, II, p. 654.
33. Haig, p. 240.
34. Riddell, p. 249.
35. Gilbert, IV(C), I, p. 60.
36. Ibid., p. 59.
37. Stevenson F., p. 158.
38. Esher Papers: ESHR 2/19, letter to Sir Douglas Haig, 30 May 1917.
39. Gilbert, IV(C), I, p. 67; and see Heffer, *AD*, p. 808.
40. Gilbert, IV(C), I, p. 68.
41. Ibid., p. 69.
42. Ibid., p. 72.
43. Ibid., p. 74.
44. Ibid., p. 76.
45. Blake, p. 361.
46. Beaverbrook II, p. xiii.
47. Churchill R., p. 281.
48. Wilson, p. 220.
49. Grigg II, p. 193.
50. Beaverbrook II, p. 139.
51. Wilson, p. 221.
52. Gilbert, IV(C), I, p. 101.
53. Riddell, p. 257.
54. Renwick, p. 126.
55. Esher Papers: ESHR 2/20, letter to Lord Murray of Elibank, 28 July 1917.
56. Scott, p. 296.
57. Riddell, p. 291.
58. BL Add MS 62253 ff. 118–119.
59. Thompson I, p. 291.
60. Ibid., p. 293.
61. Esher Papers: ESHR 2/18, diary entry for 4 February 1917.
62. Searle, p. 310(n).
63. *The Times*, 4 June 1917, p. 9.
64. Ibid., 8 August 1917, p. 7.
65. Esher Papers: ESHR 2/19, diary entry for 9 June 1917.
66. NA: CAB 23/2: Minutes of meeting 122 of the War Cabinet, 18 April 1917, Appendix 3.
67. Davidson, p. 279.
68. Hansard (Lords), Vol. 26 col. 835.
69. Ibid., col. 837.
70. Ibid., col. 839.
71. Thompson II, p. 124.
72. Chitty, p. 240.
73. S&W, p. 101.
74. Ibid., p. 102.
75. *The Times*, 23 February 1917, p. 6.
76. NA: CAB 23/1: Minutes of meeting 71 of the War Cabinet, 17 February 1917.
77. Hansard, Vol. 90 col. 110.
78. See Heffer, *AD*, pp. 77-82.
79. Hansard, Vol. 92 col. 2455.
80. Ibid., col. 2252.
81. Ibid., col. 2456.
82. Stevenson I, p. 375.
83. PA: BBK/C/85.
84. Lee, p. 168.
85. Hankey, II, p. 643.
86. Hankey, II, pp. 639–40.
87. Stevenson II, p. 69.
88. E&H, p. 190.
89. Bilton, p. 92.
90. Riddell, p. 243.
91. For details of Devonport, see Heffer, *AD*, pp. 594–95 and 701–2.
92. *The Times*, 19 February 1917, p. 9.
93. Ibid., 19 April 1917, p. 3.
94. NA: CAB 23/1: Minutes of meeting 42 of the War Cabinet, 23 January 1917, Appendix 1.
95. *The Times*, 14 June 1918, p. 3.
96. Ibid., 31 March 1917, p. 3.

97. Ibid., 20 April 1917, p. 3.

98. Ibid., 26 April 1917, p. 9.

99. E&H, p. 194.

100. NA: CAB 23/2: Minutes of meeting 99 of the War Cabinet, 19 March 1917.

101. NA: CAB 23/2: Minutes of meeting 151 of the War Cabinet, 30 May 1917.

102. Stevenson F., p. 157.

103. Riddell, p. 253.

104. Ibid., p. 254.

105. *The Times*, 17 November 1916, p. 12.

106. Grigg II, p. 396.

107. *The Times*, 18 June 1917, p. 9.

108. Ibid., 6 August 1917, p. 4.

109. Ibid., 5 September 1917, p. 5.

110. Ibid., 3 October 1917, p. 3.

111. Ibid., 7 September 1917, p. 8.

112. Ibid., 8 September 1917, p. 8.

113. Ibid., 12 September 1917, p. 3.

114. Ibid., 5 December 1917, p. 5.

115. PA: LG/F/29/1/50.

116. PA: LG/F/29/1/51.

117. E&H, p. 217.

118. NA: CAB 23/4: Minutes of meeting 297 of the War Cabinet, 13 December 1917.

119. *The Times*, 19 December 1917, p. 7.

120. Ibid., 8 January 1918, p. 8.

121. Ibid., 4 January 1918, p. 7.

122. Stevenson I, p. 377.

123. Grigg II, p. 400.

124. Stevenson I, p. 377.

125. *The Times*, 14 January 1918, p. 3.

126. Retrieved from https://punch. photoshelter.com/image/ I0000TwvicTvztfo.

127. Hansard (Lords), Vol. 29 col. 143.

128. Ibid., col. 144.

129. Ibid., col. 147.

130. *The Times*, 8 December 1917, p. 5.

131. Ibid., 22 December 1916, p. 5.

132. Ibid., 30 March 1917, p. 7.

133. Ibid., 5 April 1917, p. 3.

134. Ibid., 23 April 1917, p. 5.

135. Ibid., 5 April 1917, p. 3.

136. Ibid., 13 April 1917, p. 3.

137. Ibid., 20 April 1917, p. 3.

138. Ibid., 25 April 1917, p. 9.

139. Ibid., 1 May 1917, p. 3.

140. Dilks, p. 210.

141. NA: CAB 23/1: Minutes of meeting 39 of the War Cabinet, 19 January 1917.

142. *The Times*, 7 February 1917, p. 9.

143. Riddell, p. 239.

144. Hansard, Vol. 90 col. 143.

145. Dilks, p. 230.

146. *The Times*, 27 August 1917, p. 6.

147. Hansard, Vol. 90 col. 917.

148. Ibid., col. 916.

149. *The Times*, 15 November 1917, p. 5.

150. Hansard, Vol. 90 col. 924.

151. Ibid.

152. Ibid., col. 1498.

153. Dilks, p. 237.

154. NA: CAB 23/3: Minutes of meeting 185 of the War Cabinet, 13 July 1917.

155. NA: CAB 23/4: Minutes of meeting 231 of the War Cabinet, 12 September 1917, Appendix 1.

156. *The Times*, 17 July 1917, p. 3.

157. Ibid., 3 May 1917, p. 9.

158. NA: CAB 23/1: Minutes of meeting 65 of the War Cabinet, 14 February 1917, Appendix 3.

159. *The Times*, 12 March 1917, p. 5.

160. Ibid., 22 January 1917, p. 9.

161. Ibid., 27 January 1917, p. 3.

162. Ibid., 22 January 1917, p. 10.

163. Webb, III, p. 279.

164. Woodward, p. 193.

165. Hankey, II, p. 678.

166. Stevenson II, p. 183.

167. Haig, p. 239.

168. Stevenson II, p. 187.

169. Haig, p. 240.

170. Stevenson II, p. 183.

171. Robertson, I, p. 184.

172. Ibid., II, p. 248.

173. Hankey, II, p. 684.

174. Riddell, p. 261.

175. Ibid., p. 273.

176. Lloyd II, p. 133.

177. *The Times*, 15 August 1917, p. 3.

178. Haig, p. 251.
179. Lloyd II, p. 134.
180. Haig, pp. 251–52.
181. Grigg II, p. 225.
182. Wilson, p. 232; Haig, p. 254.
183. Haig, p. 253.
184. Ibid., p. 254.
185. Hankey, II, p. 697.
186. Blake, p. 362.
187. Riddell, p. 273.
188. Lloyd II, p. 224.
189. Haig, p. 259.
190. Callwell, II, p. 18.
191. Hankey, II, p. 713.
192. Haig, p. 261; Stevenson II, p. 203.
193. DeGroot I, p. 346.
194. Haig, p. 263.
195. Esher Papers: ESHR 2/20, diary entry for 10 November 1917.
196. Amery, p. 179.
197. Esher Papers: ESHR 2/20, diary entry for 13 November 1917.
198. DeGroot I, p. 348.
199. Haig, p. 267.
200. DeGroot I, p. 349.
201. Hankey, II, p. 728.
202. Haig, p. 274.

Chapter 9: Attrition

1. NA: CAB 23/2: Minutes of meeting 130 of the War Cabinet, 2 May 1917.
2. Hynes, pp. 174–75.
3. Ibid., p. 175.
4. Hansard, Vol. 90 col. 340.
5. Ibid., col. 342.
6. Ibid., col. 344.
7. Ibid., col. 350.
8. Ibid., col. 698.
9. Postgate, p. 164.
10. Hansard, Vol. 90 col. 701.
11. Ibid., col. 702.
12. Ibid., col. 704.
13. *The Times*, 30 June 1917, p. 8.
14. Ibid., 2 July 1917, p. 6; 17 July 1917, p. 3.
15. NA: CAB 23/3: Minutes of meeting 201 of the War Cabinet, 1 August 1917.
16. *The Times*, 2 August 1917, p. 7.

17. Amery, p. 166.
18. *The Times*, 13 August 1917, p. 7.
19. NA: CAB 23/3: Minutes of meeting 211 of the War Cabinet, 10 August 1917.
20. *The Times*, 13 August 1917, p. 7.
21. Webb, III, p. 285.
22. Scott, p. 317; *The Times*, 11 February 1918, p. 3.
23. McKibbin, p. 96.
24. *The Times*, 19 October 1917, p. 7.
25. Russell, II, p. 17.
26. Ibid.
27. Ibid., p. 18.
28. Ibid., p. 19.
29. Morrell II, pp. 67–68.
30. Russell, II, p. 21.
31. Robertson, I, p. 313.
32. Ibid., p. 314.
33. Stevenson I, p. 464.
34. Kerry, p. 283.
35. Ibid., p. 284.
36. Ibid., p. 285.
37. Ibid., pp. 285–86.
38. Ibid., p. 288.
39. Ibid., p. 289.
40. Riddell, p. 296.
41. Ibid., p. 297; Thompson I, p. 294.
42. Haste, p. 174.
43. *The Times*, 30 November 1917, p. 9.
44. Riddell, p. 298.
45. Asquith Papers: MS.Eng.d.3216, diary entry for 29 November 1917.
46. Esher Papers: ESHR 2/20, diary entry for 29 November 1917.
47. Ibid.: ESHR 2/21, diary entry for 3 December 1917.
48. Newton, p. 472.
49. Ibid., pp. 472–73.
50. Kerry, p. 290.
51. Blake, p. 364.
52. *The Times*, 7 January 1918, p. 7.
53. Brock Millman, 'HMG and the War against Dissent, 1914–18', *Journal of Contemporary History*, Vol. 40 No. 3, p. 429.
54. Stevenson F., p. 159.

55. RA GV/PRIV/GVD/1917: 15 March.
56. RA PS/PSO/GV/C/1067/M/20.
57. RA PS/PSO/GV/C/1067/M/29.
58. Nicolson II, p. 301; *The Times*, 21 April 1917, p. 9.
59. RA PS/PSO/GV/C/1067/M/26.
60. RA PS/PSO/GV/C/1067/M/51.
61. RA PS/PSO/GV/C/1067/M/52.
62. RA PS/PSO/GV/C/O/1106/1. See also Heffer, *AD*, pp. 193–94.
63. RA PS/PSO/GV/C/1067/M/61.
64. Nicolson II, p. 302.
65. RA PS/PSO/GV/C/1067/M/61.
66. NA: CAB 23/2: Minutes of meeting 118 of the War Cabinet, 13 April 1917.
67. RA PS/PSO/GV/C/1067/M/65.
68. Hansard, Vol. 92 col. 2566.
69. RA PS/PSO/GV/C/1067/M/69.
70. RA GV/PRIV/GVD/1918: 25 July.
71. Asquith Papers: MS Eng.d.3215, entry for 16 July 1917.
72. Nicolson II, p. 308.
73. RA PS/PSO/GV/C/O/1153/320.
74. RA PS/PSO/GV/C/O/1153/346.
75. RA PS/PSO/GV/C/O/1153/251.
76. RA PS/PSO/GV/C/O/1153/252.
77. Nicolson II, p. 310.
78. RA PS/PSO/GV/C/O/1153/354.
79. RA GV/PRIV/GVD/1917: 17 July.
80. Asquith Papers: MS Eng.d.3215, entry for 21 July 1917.
81. Nicolson II, p. 310.
82. Charman, p. 90.
83. Churchill R., p. 273.
84. Esher Papers: ESHR 2/19, diary entry for 19 May 1917.
85. NA: CAB 23/2: Minutes of meeting 115 of the War Cabinet, 6 April 1917.
86. *The Times*, 4 April 1917, p. 6.
87. Ibid., 12 May 1917, p. 6.
88. Retrieved from https://www.ons.gov.uk/employmentandlabourmarket/peopleinwork/workplacedisputesandworkingconditions/articles/labourdisputes/2017#historical-context.
89. Grigg II, p. 112.
90. *The Times*, 2 June 1917, p. 3.
91. Ibid., 22 June 1917, p. 3.
92. Ibid.
93. *The Times*, 6 July 1917, p. 7.
94. Millman, op. cit., p. 436.
95. NA: CAB 23/3: Minutes of meeting 218 of the War Cabinet, 18 August 1917.
96. NA: CAB 23/4: Minutes of meeting 275 of the War Cabinet, 16 November 1917.
97. *The Times*, 25 September 1917, p. 9.
98. NA: CAB 23/4: Minutes of meeting 240 of the War Cabinet, 27 September 1917.
99. Stevenson I, p. 370, p. 372.
100. Hansard, Vol. 84 col. 190.
101. Adams II, p250.
102. Ibid., Vol. 95 cols 1493–94.
103. NA: CAB 23/2: Minutes of meeting 115 of the War Cabinet, 6 April 1917, Appendix 1.
104. *The Times*, 7 March 1917, p. 7.
105. Stevenson I, p. 371.
106. Hansard, Vol. 95 col. 1529.
107. Ibid., col. 1495.
108. Ibid., col. 1501.
109. Ibid., col. 1530.
110. *The Times*, 5 July 1917, p. 7.
111. Ibid., 23 May 1917, p. 7.
112. Repington, II, pp. 3–4.
113. Ibid., p. 5.
114. Hansard, Vol. 92 col. 2131.
115. Ibid., col. 2136.
116. Ibid., col. 2142.
117. Ibid., col. 2144.
118. Ibid., col. 2161.
119. Ibid., col. 2162.
120. Ibid., col. 2163.
121. NA: CAB 23/1: Minutes of meeting 59 of the War Cabinet, 8 February 1917, Appendix 2.
122. *The Times*, 30 July 1917, p. 3.
123. Ibid., 1 June 1917, p. 3.
124. NA: CAB 23/3: Minutes of meeting 154 of the War Cabinet, 5 June 1917.

125. *The Times*, 9 July 1917, p. 9.
126. NA: CAB 23/3: Minutes of meeting 180 of the War Cabinet, 10 July 1917.
127. Riddell, p. 254.
128. Robertson, II, p. 17.
129. Hansard, Vol. 95 col. 1703.
130. *The Times*, 23 July 1917, p. 3.
131. Stevenson II, p. 186.
132. *The Times*, 3 October 1917, p. 3.
133. NA: CAB 23/4: Minutes of meeting 262 of the War Cabinet, 1 November 1917.
134. Wilson, p. 239.
135. NA: CAB 23/5: Minutes of meeting 333 of the War Cabinet, 29 January 1918.
136. Hansard, Vol. 83 col. 301.
137. Ibid., Vol. 90 col. 446.
138. Ibid., col. 1103.
139. *The Times*, 8 July 1916, p. 5.
140. Bell Q., II, p. 36.
141. Hansard, Vol. 92 col. 2073.
142. Ibid., col. 2091.
143. *The Times*, 15 February 1917, p. 9; and see Heffer, *HM*, pp. 534–35.
144. *The Times*, 22 February 1917, p. 3.
145. Ibid., 28 February 1917, p. 3.
146. Ibid., 1 March 1917, p. 5.
147. Hansard, Vol. 92 col. 2075.
148. *The Times*, 19 August 1918, p. 9.
149. E&H, p. 268.
150. *The Times*, 28 June 1918, p. 4.
151. Ibid., 22 August 1918, p. 3.
152. Ibid., 3 February 1916, p. 5.
153. E&H, p. 242.
154. *The Times*, 13 March 1916, p. 5.
155. Hansard, Vol. 82 col. 132.
156. Ibid., Vol. 107 col. 726.
157. *The Times*, 18 October 1916, p. 5.
158. Ibid., 24 October 1916, p. 5.
159. Ibid., 26 January 1917, p. 11.
160. Ibid., 6 November 1916, p. 5.
161. Ibid., 5 December 1916, p. 5.
162. Hansard, Vol. 90 col. 963.
163. E&H, p. 241.
164. *The Times*, 6 February 1917, p. 5.
165. Edith Abbott, 'Juvenile Delinquency during the First World War: Notes on the British Experience, 1914–18', *Social Service Review*, Vol. 17 No. 2, p. 195.
166. *The Times*, 2 August 1917, p. 4.
167. NA: CAB 23/4: Minutes of meeting 252 of the War Cabinet, 18 October 1917.
168. *The Times*, 12 October 1917, p. 3.
169. NA: CAB 23/4: Minutes of meeting 115 of the War Cabinet, 6 April 1917, Appendix 1.
170. *The Times*, 17 January 1917, p. 9.
171. Hansard, Vol. 92 col. 463.
172. Ibid., col. 469.
173. Ibid., col. 470.
174. Ibid., col. 489.
175. Ibid., col. 493.
176. Ibid., col. 496.
177. See Heffer, *AD*, p. 707ff. Mrs Despard was Viscount French's sister.
178. *The Times*, 30 March 1917, p. 3.
179. Hansard, Vol. 92 col. 1549.
180. Ibid., Vol. 94 col. 1827.
181. Ibid., col. 1648.
182. NA: CAB 23/1: Minutes of meeting 73 of the War Cabinet, 19 February 1917.
183. Hansard, Vol. 91 col. 425.
184. Ibid., col. 455.
185. Ibid., col. 456.
186. Ibid., col. 458.
187. Ibid., col. 459.
188. Ibid., col. 461.
189. Ibid., col. 474.
190. Ibid., col. 476.
191. Ibid., col. 477.
192. Ibid., cols 478–79.
193. Ibid., Vol. 91 col. 481.
194. *The Times*, 9 March 1917, p. 6.
195. Judd, p. 134.
196. Ibid., p. 135.
197. Crewe Papers: Letter from Asquith to Crewe, 28 May 1917.
198. Stevenson F., p. 156.
199. Ibid., p. 155.

200. NA: CAB 23/2: Minutes of meeting
     120 of the War Cabinet, 16 April 1917.
201. *The Times*, 17 March 1917, p. 3.
202. RA PS/PSO/GV/C/O/1106/13.
203. Scott, p. 291.
204. *The Times*, 18 May 1917, p. 7.
205. Ibid., 19 May 1917, p. 7.
206. Midleton, p. 235.
207. Hansard, Vol. 94 col. 619.
208. Ibid., col. 1385.
209. Hansard, Vol. 94 col. 1608.
210. Townshend I, p. 331.
211. Midleton, p. 235.
212. Ibid., pp. 238–39.
213. Hankey, II, p. 692.
214. Hansard (Lords), Vol. 26 col. 1021.
215. Ibid., col. 1022.
216. NA: CAB 23/3: Minutes of meeting
     186 of the War Cabinet, 14 July 1917.
217. Townshend I, p. 333.
218. NA: CAB 23/4: Minutes of meeting
     249 of the War Cabinet, 15 October
     1917.
219. NA: CAB 23/4: Minutes of meeting
     242 of the War Cabinet, 1 October
     1917.
220. NA: CAB 23/4: Minutes of meeting
     245 of the War Cabinet, 4 October
     1917.

Chapter 10: Escape

  1. *The Times*, 28 July 1917, p. 3; 3 August
     1917, p. 3.
  2. Ibid., 15 September 1917, p. 5.
  3. Ibid.
  4. Ibid., 11 February 1918, p. 2.
  5. Russell, II, p. 34.
  6. Ibid., p. 35.
  7. Hankey, II, p. 740.
  8. Robertson, I, pp. 314–15.
  9. Gilbert, IV(C), I, p. 204.
 10. Callwell, II, p. 47.
 11. Haig, p. 271.
 12. Riddell, p. 299.
 13. Hansard, Vol. 101 col. 58.
 14. Ibid., col. 64.
 15. Ibid., col. 90.

 16. Ibid., col. 92.
 17. Ibid., col. 508W.
 18. *The Times*, 19 January 1918, p. 7.
 19. Hansard, Vol. 101 cols 62–63.
 20. Stevenson I, p. 39.
 21. Gilbert, IV(C), I, p. 233.
 22. Scott, p. 323.
 23. Esher Papers: ESHR 2/14, diary
     entry for 23 May 1915.
 24. Scott., pp. 324–25.
 25. Elizabeth Greenhalgh, 'David Lloyd
     George, Georges Clemenceau and
     the 1918 Manpower Crisis', *The
     Historical Journal*, Vol. 50 No. 2, p. 401.
 26. DeGroot I, p. 356.
 27. Maurice, p. 64.
 28. Amery, p. 199.
 29. Maurice, p. 66.
 30. Amery, p. 201.
 31. NA: CAB 23/5: Minutes of meeting
     340 of the War Cabinet, 7 February
     1918.
 32. *The Times*, 4 March 1918, p. 3.
 33. Ibid., 11 March 1918, p. 5.
 34. *The Times Literary Supplement*, 21
     June 1917, p. 299.
 35. *The Times*, 23 October 1917, p. 11.
 36. Short, p. 161.
 37. *The Times*, 6 March 1918, p. 7.
 38. Stevenson I, p. 467.
 39. Ibid., p. 386.
 40. Hansard, Vol. 105 col. 691.
 41. Ibid., col. 696.
 42. Ibid., col. 698.
 43. Ibid., col. 699.
 44. Ibid., col. 708.
 45. Ibid., col. 716.
 46. Repington, II, p. 149.
 47. Thompson I, p. 296.
 48. Ibid.
 49. NP: BL MS 62156.
 50. Repington, II, p. 187.
 51. *The Times*, 23 January 1918, p. 7.
 52. Esher Papers: ESHR 2/21, diary
     entry for 4 February 1918.
 53. Elizabeth Greenhalgh, op. cit., p.
     402; NA: CAB 23/5: Minutes of

meeting 342 of the War Cabinet, 11 February 1918.

54. *The Times*, 22 January 1918, p. 7.
55. Thompson II, p. 182.
56. PA: LG/F/29/2/6.
57. PA: LG/F/29/2/7.
58. Asquith Papers: MS.Eng.d.3216, entry for 7 February 1918.
59. Scott, p. 336.
60. Hansard (Lords), Vol. 29 col. 277.
61. Ibid., col. 34.
62. Hansard, Vol. 103 col. 655.
63. Ibid., col. 656.
64. Ibid., col. 657.
65. Ibid., col. 659.
66. Ibid., col. 671.
67. Amery, p. 208.
68. PA: BBK/C/79.
69. Searle, p. 322.
70. Petrie, II, p. 108.
71. Hansard, Vol. 104 col. 42.
72. Ibid., col. 83.
73. Ibid., col. 84.
74. Ibid., col. 87.
75. Ibid., col. 103.
76. Ibid., col. 124.
77. Fox, p. 88.
78. Thompson II, p. 180.
79. Repington, II, p. 197.
80. Ibid., p. 228.
81. Ibid., p. 231.
82. *The Times*, 31 July 1918, p. 3.
83. Hynes, p. 226.
84. *The Times*, 30 May 1918, p. 4.
85. NA: CAB 23/6: Minutes of meeting 425 of the War Cabinet, 4 June 1918.
86. PA: BL/83/4/19.
87. NA: CAB 23/7: Minutes of meeting 444 of the War Cabinet, 11 July 1918.
88. Ibid.
89. Repington, II, p. 193.
90. Haig, p. 282.
91. Maurice, p. 69.
92. Ibid., p. 52.
93. Ibid., p. 53.

94. Wilson, p. 254.
95. Ibid., p. 255.
96. Haig, p. 284.
97. Churchill R., p. 319.
98. Haig, p. 285.
99. Churchill R., pp. 323–24.
100. Nicolson II, p. 321.
101. RA GV/PRIV/GVD/1918: 13 February.
102. Robertson, I, p. 235.
103. Hansard, Vol. 103 col. 17.
104. Ibid., col. 19.
105. Ibid., col. 20.
106. Ibid., col. 26.
107. Ibid., col. 29.
108. Ibid., col. 30.
109. Ibid., col. 40.
110. Wilson, p. 256.
111. Stevenson I, p. 493.
112. Robertson, I, p. 237.
113. RA GV/PRIV/GVD/1918: 16 February.
114. Haig, p. 285.
115. Ibid., p. 286.
116. Ibid., p. 286.
117. Ibid., p. 287.
118. Taylor, p. 100.
119. Hansard, Vol. 103 col. 474.
120. Haig, p. 287.
121. PA: BL 84/7/3.
122. Hankey, II, p. 779.
123. Robertson, I, p. 237.
124. Maurice, p. 73.
125. Hansard, Vol. 104 col. 485.
126. Maurice, p. 74.
127. Ibid., p. 75
128. Haig, p. 292.
129. DeGroot I, p. 368.
130. Stevenson I, p. 55.
131. Repington, II, p. 254.
132. Maurice, p. 24.
133. Callwell, II, p. 73.
134. Hansard, Vol. 104 col. 1293.
135. Hankey, II, p. 785.
136. NA: CAB 23/5: Minutes of meeting 371 of the War Cabinet, 23 March 1918.

137. Riddell, p. 320.
138. Maurice, p. 25.
139. Robert K. Hanks, 'Georges Clemenceau and the English', *Historical Journal*, Vol. 45, p. 73.
140. Wells, *JP*, p. 694.
141. Maurice, p. 77.
142. Gilbert, IV(C), I, p. 273.
143. Ibid., p. 274.
144. Hankey, II, p. 786.
145. Riddell, p. 320.
146. *The Times*, 25 March 1918, p. 9.
147. NA: CAB 23/5: Minutes of meeting 374 of the War Cabinet, 27 March 1918.
148. NA: CAB 23/5: Minutes of meeting 375 of the War Cabinet, 27 March 1918.
149. *The Times*, 3 May 1918, p. 3.
150. Gilbert, IV(C), I, p. 277.
151. Stevenson I, p. 382.
152. Ibid., p. 383.
153. Hankey, II, p. 787.
154. AP, p. 231.
155. Sommer, pp. 356–57.
156. Alan J. Ward, 'Lloyd George and Irish Conscription', *The Historical Journal*, Vol. 17 No. 1, p. 109.
157. AP, p. 232; Alan J. Ward, op. cit., p. 110.
158. Plunkett Papers: Diary, 9 April 1918.
159. Midleton, p. 244.
160. NA: CAB 23/6: Minutes of meeting 388 of the War Cabinet, 10 April 1918.
161. NA: CAB 23/6: Minutes of meeting 389 of the War Cabinet, 11 April 1918.
162. Hansard, Vol. 104 col. 1357.
163. Ibid., col. 1358.
164. Ibid., cols 1361–62.
165. Roskill, I, p. 522.
166. Hansard, Vol. 104 col. 1367.
167. Ibid., col. 1378.
168. Ibid., cols 1378–79.
169. Ibid., col. 1405.
170. Ibid., col. 1406.
171. Ibid., col. 1407.
172. Ibid., col. 1528.
173. Ibid., col. 1527.
174. Ibid., col. 1538.
175. Ibid., col. 1541.
176. Repington, II, p. 272.
177. Plunkett Papers: Diary, 17 April 1918.
178. Alan J. Ward, op. cit., p. 117.
179. NA: CAB 23/6: Minutes of meeting 397 of the War Cabinet, 23 April 1918.
180. Riddell, p. 311.
181. Plunkett Papers: Diary, 11 January 1918.
182. Ibid., 15 February 1918.
183. *The Times*, 25 February 1918, p. 9; NA: CAB 23/5: Minutes of meeting 353 of the War Cabinet, 25 February 1918.
184. NA: CAB 23/5: Minutes of meeting 354 of the War Cabinet, 26 February 1918.
185. Hansard (Lords), Vol. 29 col. 369.
186. Ibid., col. 377.
187. Ibid., col. 378.
188. See Heffer, *AD*, p. 270ff.
189. Townshend II, p. 30.
190. Scott, p. 342.
191. Ibid., p. 344.
192. Riddell, p. 325.
193. Townshend II, p. 339.
194. Sir Horace Plunkett, by contrast, sought to persuade the Irish to join the American army: Plunkett Papers: Diary, 18 August 1918.
195. PA: BL 83/4/21.
196. Plunkett Papers: Diary, 23 August 1918.
197. Sommer, p. 358.
198. Midleton, p. 252.
199. Hammond, pp. 241–42.
200. Ibid., p. 240.
201. *The Times*, 25 May 1918, p. 7.
202. Hansard (Lords), Vol. 30 col. 329.
203. Esher Papers: ESHR 2/21, diary entry for 15 May 1918. Torres Vedras were the fortifications Wellington prepared in Portugal and that prevented the British Army from being defeated in the Peninsular War.
204. Hansard (Lords), Vol. 30 col. 297.
205. Hansard, Vol. 107 col. 906.
206. Ibid., col. 909.
207. Ibid., col. 911.

208. Ibid., col. 912.
209. Ibid., col. 913.
210. Ibid., col. 924.
211. *The Times*, 27 June 1918, p. 7, p. 10.
212. Hansard, Vol. 107 col. 934.
213. Ibid., col. 956.
214. Ibid., col. 960.
215. Ibid., col. 962.
216. Ibid., col. 1214.
217. Ibid., col. 606.
218. Ibid., Vol. 109 col. 94.
219. Ibid., col. 96.
220. Ibid., col. 103.
221. Ibid., col. 104.
222. Haig, p. 300.
223. Ibid., p. 301.
224. For background on Gough, see Heffer, *AD*, pp. 810–14.
225. Haig, p. 301.
226. Esher Papers: ESHR 2/21, diary entry for 11 April 1918.
227. RA GV/PRIV/GVD/1918: 13 April.
228. PA: BL 97/2/11.
229. Esher Papers: ESHR 2/21, diary entry for 12 April 1918.
230. *The Times*, 18 June 1918, p. 3.
231. David R. Woodward, 'Did Lloyd George Starve the British Army of Men Prior to the German Offensive of 21 March 1918?' *Historical Journal*, Vol. 27 No. 1, pp. 241–42.
232. Roskill, I, p. 522.
233. Hansard, Vol. 104 col. 1337.
234. Ibid., col. 1338.
235. Ibid., col. 1354.
236. Ibid., col. 1477.
237. Ibid., col. 1629.
238. AP, p. 237.
239. Wilson, p. 266.
240. Maurice, p. 31.
241. PA: LG/F/29/2/14.
242. Petrie, II, p. 118.
243. Ibid., p. 117.
244. Hansard, Vol. 105 cols 851–52.
245. Maurice, p. 36.
246. Ibid., p. 60.
247. Haig, p. 308.
248. Amery, p. 219.
249. Maurice, pp. 97–98.
250. Wilson, p. 276.
251. Maurice, p. 4.
252. Ibid., p. 5.
253. Ibid., p. 6.
254. Ibid., p. 9.
255. S&A, II, p. 303.
256. Hansard, Vol. 105 col. 1983.
257. Hankey, II, p. 798.
258. Maurice, p. 236.
259. Roskill, I, p. 541.
260. Asquith Papers: MS.Eng.d.3216, diary entry for 9 May 1918.
261. Hansard, Vol. 105 col. 2349.
262. Ibid., col. 2353.
263. Ibid., col. 2354.
264. Ibid., cols 2355–56.
265. Ibid., col. 2357.
266. Ibid., col. 2359.
267. Ibid., col. 2360.
268. Ibid., col. 2362.
269. Ibid., col. 2373.
270. Ibid., col. 2374.
271. Grigg II, p. 508.
272. Esher Papers: ESHR 2/21, diary entry for 13 May 1918.
273. *The Times*, 11 May 1918, p. 7.
274. Maurice, p. 107.
275. Ibid., p. 145.
276. Heffer, *AD*, p. 573ff.
277. Maurice, p. 111.
278. Ibid., p. 172.
279. Amery, p. 227.
280. Gilbert, IV(C), I, p. 361.
281. *The Times*, 27 July 1918, p. 7.
282. Ibid.
283. NA: CAB 23/7, Minutes of meeting 449 of the War Cabinet, 19 July 1918.
284. See Heffer, *AD*, p. 662ff.
285. NA: CAB 23/7: Minutes of meeting 460 of the War Cabinet, 16 August 1918.
286. Roskill, I, p. 595.
287. Hankey Papers: HNKY 1/5, entry for 30 August 1918.
288. *The Times*, 31 August 1918, p. 6.

289. Hansard, Vol. 107 cols 538–39.
290. Ibid., col. 539.
291. Ibid., col. 540.
292. Ibid., col. 541.
293. Ibid., col. 569.
294. Ibid., col. 576.

Chapter 11: Armistice

1. *The Times*, 5 August 1918, p. 4.
2. Ibid., 3 August 1918, p. 3.
3. Hansard, Vol. 109 col. 1412.
4. Ibid., col. 1429.
5. Ibid., col. 1430.
6. Ibid., col. 1431.
7. Ibid., col. 1456.
8. Samuel, p. 127.
9. Haig, p. 326.
10. Gilbert, IV(C), I, p. 367(n).
11. Hankey Papers: HNKY 1/5, entry for 23 July 1918.
12. Haig, p. 326.
13. Stevenson I, p. 245.
14. Taylor I, p. 110.
15. Hankey, II, p. 854.
16. Ibid., p. 856.
17. Ibid., p. 857.
18. Ibid., p. 862.
19. Haig, p. 338.
20. *The Times*, 9 November 1918, p. 6.
21. Haig, p. 339.
22. Ibid., p. 337.
23. Thompson II, p. 215.
24. *The Times*, 23 July 1918, p. 7.
25. Riddell, p. 349.
26. *The Times*, 20 August 1918, p. 7.
27. Hansard, Vol. 110 col. 814.
28. Ibid., col. 851.
29. *The Times*, 13 September 1918, p. 8.
30. Grigg II, p. 577.
31. Thompson II, pp. 208–9.
32. Riddell, p. 366.
33. Sommer, p. 352.
34. See Roy Douglas, 'The Background to the "Coupon" Election Arrangements', *English Historical Review*, Vol. 86 No. 339, p. 321.
35. Sommer, p. 330.

36. Riddell, p. 353.
37. Ibid., p. 365.
38. Hansard, Vol. 110 col. 80.
39. Ibid., col. 81.
40. Ibid., col. 82.
41. Ibid., col. 87.
42. Ibid., col. 91.
43. J. M. McEwen, 'Lloyd George's Acquisition of the *Daily Chronicle* in 1918', *Journal of British Studies*, Vol. 22 No. 1, p. 131.
44. Hansard, Vol. 110 col. 2350.
45. Ibid., col. 2351.
46. Ibid., col. 2352.
47. Ibid., col. 2364.
48. Hammond, p. 246.
49. RA GV/PRIV/GVD/1918: 5 November.
50. Hansard (Lords), Vol. 22 col. 655.
51. Ibid., col. 676.
52. Ibid., col. 657.
53. Ibid., col. 660.
54. Ibid., col. 671.
55. Hansard, Vol. 104 col. 388.
56. Ibid., cols 391–92.
57. Ibid., col. 396.
58. Ibid., cols 399–400.
59. Ibid., col. 339.
60. Ibid., col. 342.
61. Ibid., col. 347.
62. Wells, *JP*, p. 212.
63. Hansard, Vol. 110 col. 1119.
64. Ibid., col. 1140.
65. Ibid., col. 1156.
66. Ibid., col. 1167.
67. Ibid., col. 1169.
68. Ibid., col. 1174.
69. Postgate, p. 167.
70. *The Times*, 26 September 1918, p. 6.
71. NA: CAB 23/8: Minutes of meeting 490 of the War Cabinet, 24 October 1918.
72. *The Times*, 28 September 1918, p. 3.
73. Ibid., 27 June 1918, p. 7.
74. Ibid., 2 July 1918, p. 3.
75. Ibid., 15 July 1918, p. 9.
76. Hansard, Vol. 108 col. 1813.

77. *The Times*, 17 October 1918, p. 3.
78. Ibid., 19 October 1918, p. 3; 23 October 1918, p. 3.
79. Ibid., 22 October 1918, p. 3.
80. Ibid., 23 October 1918, p. 7.
81. Bilton, p. 108.
82. Hansard, Vol. 110 col. 1465.
83. Asquith C., p. 480.
84. Webb, III, p. 315.
85. Callwell, II, p. 148.
86. Amery, p. 243.
87. Hynes, p. 254.
88. Webb, III, p. 318.
89. Pope-Hennessy, p. 509.
90. Bilton, p. 111.
91. Chitty, p. 245.
92. Cooper, p. 92.
93. Asquith Papers: MS.Eng.d.3216, diary entry for 11 November 1918.
94. RA GV/PRIV/GVD/1918: 11 November.
95. Clark A., p. 258.
96. Esher Papers: ESHR 2/21, diary entry for 11 November 1918.
97. Plunkett Papers: Diary, 11 November 1918.
98. Russell, II, p. 37.
99. Bell Q., II, p. 62.
100. S&W, p. 186.
101. Hynes, p. 255.
102. Taylor I, p. 114.
103. NA: CAB 23/8: Minutes of meeting 502 of the War Cabinet, 14 November 1918.
104. Hankey Papers: HNKY 1/6, entry for 6–17 November 1918.
105. Hankey, II, p. 872.
106. Gilbert, IV(C), I, p. 410.
107. Callwell, II, p. 149.
108. Gilbert, IV(C), I, p. 421.
109. Charman, p. 301.
110. Wilson, p. 317.
111. Hansard, Vol. 110 col. 3347.
112. *The Times*, 13 November 1918, p. 9.
113. Ibid., 23 November 1918, p. 13.
114. Hansard, Vol. 110 col. 2596.
115. Ibid., col. 2598.
116. Ibid., col. 2599.
117. *The Times*, 29 June 1918, p. 3.
118. Ibid., 2 August 1918, p. 9.
119. Ibid., 13 November 1918, p. 12.
120. Gilbert, IV(C), I, p. 416.
121. Scott, p. 317.
122. McKibbin, p. 111.
123. Hansard, Vol. 110 col. 3201.
124. S&A, II, pp. 312–13.
125. Hankey Papers: HNKY 1/5, entry for 18 November 1918.
126. Ibid., entry for 23 November 1918.
127. Ibid., entry for 24 November 1918.
128. Stephen R. Ward, 'The British Veterans' Ticket of 1918', *Journal of British Studies*, Vol. 8 No. 1, p. 157.
129. Ibid., p. 159.
130. Asquith, *MR*, II, p. 170.
131. *The Times*, 19 November 1918, p. 8.
132. Samuel, p. 131.
133. Asquith, *MR*, II, p. 171.
134. S&A, II, p. 317.
135. Davidson, p. 87.
136. *The Times*, 19 November 1918, p. 8.
137. Gilbert, IV(C), I, p. 421.
138. PA: BBK/C/85.
139. PA: BBK/C/265.
140. PA: BBK/C/261.
141. *The Times*, 20 November 1918, p. 7.
142. Ibid., 30 November 1918, p. 6.
143. Keynes, pp. 127–28.
144. Ibid., p. 131.
145. Riddell, p. 349.
146. Amery, p. 246.
147. Haig, pp. 346–47.
148. Beaverbrook II, p. xviii.
149. *The Times*, 20 December 1918, p. 9.
150. Hammond, p. 247.
151. Retrieved from http://spartacus-educational.com/GE1918.htm.
152. Keynes, p. 131.
153. Lloyd George Papers: F/41/8/31.
154. Callwell, II, p. 155.
155. Stephen R. Ward, op. cit., p. 167.
156. Hankey Papers: HNKY 1/5, entry for 28 December 1918.
157. Petrie, II, p. 132.
158. Hansard, Vol. 110 col. 1988.

159. Ibid., col. 2000.
160. Ferriter, p. 181.
161. Scott, p. 362.
162. Townshend II, p. 61.
163. Ferriter, p. 184.
164. Ibid., p. 183.

Chapter 12: Aftermath
1. Russell, II, p. 39.
2. Stevenson I, pp. 447–48.
3. DeGroot II, p. 337.
4. Retrieved from http://www.bbc.co.uk/history/british/britain_wwone/women_employment_01.shtml.
5. S&W, p. 1.
6. Retrieved from http://www.longlongtrail.co.uk/army/some-british-army-statistics-of-the-great-war/.
7. Jeffery, p. 5.
8. E&H, p. 100.
9. Taylor I, p. 121.
10. Retrieved from englishemigrationtocanada.blogspot.com.
11. *The Times*, 16 May 1919, p. 13.
12. Asquith, *MR*, II, pp. 173–74.
13. *The Times*, 16 May 1919, p. 13.
14. Hansard, Vol. 85 cols 981–82.
15. Haig, p. 344.
16. Ibid., p. 345.
17. Ibid., p. 357.
18. *Lancet*, 2 February 1918.
19. *The Times*, 31 December 1918, p. 9.
20. Hansard (Lords), Vol. 34 col. 84.
21. Ibid., col. 76.
22. *The Times*, 13 June 1918, p. 3.
23. Ibid., 2 July 1918, p. 3.
24. NA: CAB 23/9: Minutes of meeting 514 of the War Cabinet, 8 January 1919.
25. Clarke, p. 187.
26. Stevenson I, p. 1.
27. Heffer, *AD*, p. 651ff; Stevenson I, p. 463.
28. Keynes, Ch. 5.

29. M&B, pp. 72–73.
30. *The Times*, 24 June 1919, p. 13.
31. Taylor I, p. 129.
32. *The Times*, 11 January 1919, p. 9.
33. Hankey Papers: HNKY 1/5, entry for 16 December 1918.
34. Petrie, II, p. 136.
35. Petrie, *CT*, p. 162.
36. Beaverbrook II, p. xiii.
37. PA: LG/F/29/3/1.
38. Gilbert, IV(C), I, p. 445.
39. Campbell, p. 460.
40. Ibid., p. 469 (n).
41. Hansard, Vol. 108 col. 1048.
42. Ibid., Vol. 92 col. 207.
43. *The Times*, 22 March 1918, p. 3.
44. NA: CAB 23/9: Minutes of meeting 541 of the War Cabinet, 4 March 1919.
45. Renwick, p. 139.
46. Hansard, Vol. 116 col. 1335.
47. Ibid., col. 1340.
48. Hankey Papers: HNKY 1/5, entry for 5 December 1918.
49. *DNB 1961–70*, p. 487.
50. Hansard, Vol. 82 col. 658.
51. Churchill puts this point to Lloyd George: see Gilbert, IV(C), I, p. 440.
52. *The Times*, 25 January 1918, p. 4.
53. Churchill W., VI, p. 52.
54. Hankey Papers: HNKY 1/5, entry for 18 December 1918.
55. Gilbert, IV(C), I, p. 443.
56. Callwell, II, p. 161.
57. Churchill Papers: CHAR 16/3/17.
58. Brown, p. 88.
59. Callwell, II, p. 161.
60. NA: CAB 23/8: Minutes of meeting 521 of the War Cabinet, 28 January 1918, Appendix.
61. Gilbert, IV(C), I, p. 462.
62. *The Times*, 22 January 1919, p. 10.
63. Churchill Papers: CHAR 16/3/39.
64. Gilbert, IV(C), I, p. 451.
65. Gilbert, IV(C), I, p. 474.
66. Churchill Papers: CHAR 16/3/30.
67. Ibid.: CHAR 16/3/18.
68. Gilbert, IV(C), I, p. 475.

69. Churchill Papers: CHAR 16/3/54–5.
70. Haig, p. 350.
71. Churchill Papers: CHAR 16/3/53.
72. Ibid.: CHAR 16/3/80.
73. Ibid.: CHAR 16/3/95.
74. Ibid.: CHAR 16/3/121.
75. Hansard, Vol. 113 col. 561.
76. Ibid., col. 562.
77. Ibid., col. 563.
78. Ibid., col. 564.
79. Ibid., col. 568.
80. Hansard (Lords), Vol. 34 col. 164.
81. NA: CAB 23/10: Minutes of meeting 555 of the War Cabinet, 10 April 1919.
82. *The Times*, 7 March 1919, p. 10.
83. Petrie, II, p. 140.
84. NA: CAB 23/9: Minutes of meeting 522 of the War Cabinet, 30 January 1918.
85. *The Times*, 4 February 1919, p. 9.
86. Ibid., 1 February 1919, p. 9.
87. Hansard, Vol. 112 col. 625.
88. Ibid., cols 49–50.
89. NA: CAB 23/9: Minutes of meeting 531 of the War Cabinet, 12 February 1919.
90. Stevenson F., p. 173.
91. NA: CAB 23/9, Minutes of meeting 547 of the War Cabinet, 19 March 1919.
92. Gilbert, IV(C), I, p. 520.
93. NA: CAB 23/9: Minutes of meeting 548 of the War Cabinet, 20 March 1919.
94. Hansard, Vol. 112 cols 72–73.
95. Ibid., col. 339.
96. NA: CAB 23/9: Minutes of meeting 544 of the War Cabinet, 13 March 1919.
97. Hansard, Vol. 112 col. 327.
98. Ibid., col. 340.
99. Ibid., col. 333.
100. Ibid., col. 345.
101. Ibid., col. 81.
102. Ibid., cols 352–53.
103. NA: CAB 23/10: Minutes of meeting 577 of the War Cabinet, 6 June 1919.
104. Hansard, Vol. 114 col. 1564.
105. Sommer, p. 363.
106. *The Times*, 21 January 1919, p. 9.
107. Ibid., 5 February 1919, p. 9.
108. Ibid., 7 February 1919, p. 9.
109. Ibid., 10 February 1919, p. 5.
110. NA: CAB 23/9: Minutes of meeting 541 of the War Cabinet, 4 March 1919.
111. Hansard, Vol. 112 col. 49.
112. *The Times*, 15 April 1919, p. 8.
113. Ibid., 17 April 1919, p. 12.
114. Lloyd I, p. xxii.
115. *The Times*, 15 April 1919, p. 13.
116. Ibid., 19 April 1919, p. 11.
117. See Heffer, *HM*, p. 579.
118. Stevenson F., p. 174.
119. Ibid., p. 179.
120. Hansard, Vol. 114 col. 2947.
121. Ibid., cols 2953–54.
122. Thompson I, p. 326.
123. Haste, p. 197.
124. Taylor F., pp. 21–22.
125. Webb, III, pp. 344–45.
126. Davidson, p. 91.
127. Ibid., p. 92.
128. RA GV/PRIV/GVD/1919: 28 June.
129. Davidson, p. 93.
130. RA GV/PRIV/GVD/1919: 28 June.

INDEX

PICTURE ACKNOWLEDGEMENTS

———————————⊂———————————

Images are reproduced by kind permission of: Mary Evans Picture Library: Thomas Cook Travel Company poster (© Thomas Cook Archive); advertisement for Milton (© Illustrated London News Ltd). © Imperial War Museum: 'Discharged Sailors and Soldiers' poster; recruits at the Whitehall Recruiting Office; the scene during the sitting of a tribunal for Conscientious Objectors; a cartoon depicting a lazy conscientious objector by Frank Holland; a female London General Omnibus Company bus conductor; women munitions workers' football team from the AEC Munitions Factory at Beckton; college girls collecting the pulled flax on a farm in Yeovil; Menu of No.74 Squadron R.F.C. dinner; female worker at a National Kitchen ticket office; C. R. W. Nevinson 'The Food Queue' (1918). Alamy: Armistice Day Celebrations (Chronicle); Kitchener and Haldane (Chronicle); advertisement for Oxo (Chronicle). Getty Images: meeting at the foreign office (Herbert Orth/The LIFE Images Collection); Herbert and Margot Asquith (© Hulton-Deutsch Collection/CORBIS); Admiral Jellicoe (Topical Press Agency); Scarborough Coast Guard Station (Popperfoto); Horatio Bottomley (Hulton Archive); Lord Northcliffe (Hulton Archive); shop window reading 'We are Russians' (Topical Press Agency); Edith Cavell (The Print Collector); common grave for *Lusitania* dead (Bettmann); Winston Churchill (Popperfoto via Getty Images); Sir Roger Casement (Culture Club); Easter Rebellion British troops with guns (Bettmann); policewomen being inspected (Museum of London/Heritage Images); miners leaving the pithead (Print Collector); Edith Cavell's funeral (Daily Mirror/Mirrorpix). © National Portrait Gallery, London: Edward Grey, 1st Viscount Grey of Fallodon; Bertrand Russell; Edward George Villiers Stanley, 17th Earl of Derby; David Lloyd George; Maurice Pascal Alers Hankey, 1st Baron Hankey; Bonar Law; George Nathaniel Curzon, Marquess Curzon of Kedleston; Alfred Milner, Viscount Milner; Sir Frederick Barton Maurice; Herbert Albert Laurens Fisher; David Alfred Thomas, 1st Viscount Rhondda; Lady Ottoline

Morrell and Julian Vinogradoff (née Morrell). © National Galleries of Scotland: George Allardice, 1st Baron Riddell of Walton Heath, 1865–1934 by Sir William Orpen. © National Library of Ireland: postcard of Éamon de Valera. Royal Collection Trust / © Her Majesty Queen Elizabeth II 2019: photograph of King George V in Buckingham Palace Gardens with Baron Stamfordham, June 1918. © Stirling Council Archives: front page of a National Ration Book. © King's Hall and College of Brasenose in Oxford: First Earl Haig, Field Marshal by Sir William Orpen. Warwick Modern Records Centre: circular regarding the organisation of a 'Labour, Socialist and Democratic Convention to hail the Russian Revolution', May 1917. Wikimedia Commons: Sir William Robertson, 1st Baronet; Arthur Henderson; John Redmond; 1917 cartoon of the Kaiser; Carl Hans Lody in the dock. All other images are the author's own or from the publisher's collection. Every effort has been made to trace copyright holders and to obtain their permission. The publisher apologises for any omissions and, if notified, will make suitable acknowledgment in future reprints or editions of the book.